Nineteenth-Century Literature Criticism

Guide to Gale Literary Criticism Series

When you need to review criticism of literary works, these are the Gale series to use:

If the author's death date is:

You should turn to:

After Dec. 31, 1959
(or author is still living)

CONTEMPORARY LITERARY CRITICISM

for example: Jorge Luis Borges, Anthony Burgess,
William Faulkner, Mary Gordon,
Ernest Hemingway, Iris Murdoch

1900 through 1959

TWENTIETH-CENTURY LITERARY CRITICISM

for example: Willa Cather, F. Scott Fitzgerald,
Henry James, Mark Twain, Virginia Woolf

1800 through 1899

NINETEENTH-CENTURY LITERATURE CRITICISM

for example: Fyodor Dostoevsky, Nathaniel Hawthorne,
George Sand, William Wordsworth

1400 through 1799

LITERATURE CRITICISM FROM 1400 TO 1800
(excluding Shakespeare)

for example: Anne Bradstreet, Daniel Defoe,
Alexander Pope, François Rabelais,
Jonathan Swift, Phillis Wheatley

SHAKESPEAREAN CRITICISM

Shakespeare's plays and poetry

Antiquity through 1399

CLASSICAL AND MEDIEVAL LITERATURE CRITICISM

for example: Dante, Homer, Plato, Sophocles, Vergil,
the Beowulf Poet

Gale also publishes related criticism series:

CHILDREN'S LITERATURE REVIEW

This series covers authors of all eras who have written for
the preschool through high school audience.

SHORT STORY CRITICISM

This series covers the major short fiction writers of all nationalities
and periods of literary history.

POETRY CRITICISM

This series covers poets of all nationalities, movements, and periods of
literary history.

ISSN 0732-1864

Volume 29

Nineteenth-Century Literature Criticism

Excerpts from Criticism of the
Works of Novelists, Poets, Playwrights,
Short Story Writers, Philosophers, and Other
Creative Writers Who Died between 1800
and 1899, from the First Published Critical
Appraisals to Current Evaluations

Laurie DiMauro
Editor

Michael W. Jones
David Kmenta
Marie Lazzari
Thomas Ligotti
Michelle L. McClellan
Joann Prosyniuk
Associate Editors

 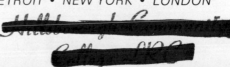 **Gale Research Inc.** · *DETROIT · NEW YORK · LONDON*

STAFF

Laurie DiMauro, *Editor*

Michael W. Jones, David Kmenta, Marie Lazzari, Thomas Ligotti,
Michelle L. McClellan, Joann Prosyniuk, *Associate Editors*

John P. Daniel, Ian A. Goodhall, Tina N. Grant, Alan Hedblad, Grace Jeromski,
Andrew Kalasky, James Poniewozik, Mark Swartz, Debra A. Wells, *Assistant Editors*

Jeanne A. Gough, *Permissions & Production Manager*
Linda M. Pugliese, *Production Supervisor*
Suzanne Powers, Maureen A. Puhl, Jennifer VanSickle, *Editorial Associates*
Donna Craft, Lorna Mabunda, James G. Wittenbach, *Editorial Assistants*

Victoria B. Cariappa, *Research Manager*
Paula Cutcher, H. Nelson Fields, Judy L. Gale, Maureen Richards, *Editorial Associates*
Jennifer Brostrom, Robin Lupa, *Editorial Assistants*

Sandra C. Davis, *Permissions Supervisor (Text)*
Josephine M. Keene, Kimberly F. Smilay, *Permissions Associates*
Maria L. Franklin, Michele M. Lonoconus, Shalice Shah,
Denise M. Singleton, Rebecca A. Stanko, *Permissions Assistants*

Patricia A. Seefelt, *Permissions Supervisor (Pictures)*
Margaret A. Chamberlain, *Permissions Associate*
Pamela A. Hayes, *Permissions Assistant*

Mary Beth Trimper, *Production Manager*
Mary Winterhalter, *External Production Assistant*

Arthur Chartow, *Art Director*
C. J. Jonik, *Keyliner*

Laura Bryant, *Production Supervisor*
Louise Gagné, *Internal Production Associate*
Yolanda Y. Latham, *Internal Production Assistant*

The paper used in this publication meets the minimum requirements
of American National Standard for Information Sciences—Permanence
Paper for Printed Library Materials, ANSI Z39.48-1984. ∞™

Copyright © 1991
Gale Research Inc.
835 Penobscot Bldg.
Detroit, MI 48226-4094

Library of Congress Catalog Card Number 84-643008
ISBN 0-8103-5829-8
ISSN 0732-1864

Printed in the United States of America

Published simultaneously in the United Kingdom
by Gale Research International Limited
(An affiliated company of Gale Research Inc.)

Contents

Preface

Since its inception in 1981, *Nineteenth-Century Literature Criticism* has been a valuable resource for students and librarians seeking critical commentary on writers of this transitional period in world history. Designated an "Outstanding Reference Source" by the American Library Association with the publication of its first volume, *NCLC* has since been purchased by over 6,000 school, public, and university libraries. With this edition, volume 29, the series has covered more than 300 authors representing 23 nationalities and over 15,000 titles. No other reference source has surveyed the critical reaction to nineteenth-century authors and literature as thoroughly as *NCLC*.

Scope of the Series

NCLC is designed to serve as an introduction for students and advanced readers to the authors of the nineteenth century, and to the most significant interpretations of these authors' works. The great poets, novelists, short story writers, dramatists, and philosophers of this period are frequently studied in high school and college literature courses. By organizing and reprinting the enormous amount of commentary written on these authors, *NCLC* helps students develop valuable insight into literary history, promotes a better understanding of the texts, and sparks ideas for papers and assignments. Each entry in *NCLC* presents a comprehensive survey of an author's career or an individual work of literature and provides the user with a multiplicity of interpretations and assessments. Such variety allows students to pursue their own interests; furthermore, it fosters an awareness that literature is dynamic and responsive to many different opinions.

NCLC continues the survey of criticism of world literature begun by Gale's *Contemporary Literary Criticism (CLC)* and *Twentieth-Century Literary Criticism (TCLC),* both of which excerpt and reprint commentary on authors of the twentieth century. For additional information about *TCLC, CLC,* and Gale's other criticism series, users should consult the Guide to Gale Literary Criticism Series preceding the title page in this volume.

Coverage

Each volume of *NCLC* is carefully compiled to present:

- criticism of authors who represent a variety of genres and nationalities

- both major and lesser-known writers of the period (including non-Western authors increasingly read by today's students)

- 8 - 12 authors per volume

- individual entries that survey the critical response to each author's works, including early criticism to reflect initial reactions, later criticism to represent any rise or decline in the author's reputation, and current retrospective analyses. The length of each author entry also indicates an author's importance, reflecting the amount of critical attention he or she has received from critics writing in English, and from foreign criticism in translation.

An author may appear more than once in the series because of the great quantity of critical material available or because of a resurgence of criticism generated by such events as an author's centennial or anniversary celebration, the republication or posthumous publication of an author's works, or the publication of a new translation. Usually, one or more author entries in each volume of *NCLC* are devoted to individual works or groups of works by major authors who have appeared previously in the series. Only those works that have been the subjects of extensive criticism and are widely studied in literature courses are selected for this in-depth treatment.

Organization of the Book

An author entry consists of the following elements: author heading, biographical and critical introduction, list of principal works, excerpts of criticism (each preceded by explanatory notes and followed by a bibliographic citation), and a bibliography of further reading.

- The **author heading** consists of the name under which the author most commonly wrote, followed by birth and death dates. When the name under which an author published is a pseudonym or a variation of his or her full name, the complete real name is given in parentheses on the first line of the biographical and critical introduction. Also located at the beginning of the introduction are any name variations under which an author wrote, including transliterated forms for authors whose languages use nonroman alphabets.

- A **portrait** of the author is included when available. Many entries also feature illustrations of materials pertinent to an author's career, including manuscript pages, letters, book illustrations, and representations of important people, places, and events in an author's life.

- The **biographical and critical introduction** contains background information that introduces the reader to an author and to the critical debate surrounding his or her work. When applicable, biographical and critical introductions are followed by references to additional entries on the author in other literary reference series published by Gale, including *Short Story Criticism, Dictionary of Literary Biography, Children's Literature Review,* and *Something about the Author.*

- The list of **principal works** is chronological by date of first book publication and identifies the genre of each work. In those instances where the first publication was in a language other than English, the title and date of the first English-language edition are given in brackets. Unless otherwise indicated, dramas are dated by the first performance, rather than first publication.

- **Criticism** is arranged chronologically in each author entry to provide a useful perspective on changes in critical evaluation over the years. All titles by the author featured in the critical entry are printed in boldface type to enable the user to ascertain without difficulty the works being discussed. Also for purposes of easier identification, the critic's name and the publication date of the essay are given at the beginning of each piece of criticism. Anonymous criticism is preceded by the title of the journal in which it appeared. Publication information (such as publisher names and book prices) and parenthetical numerical references (such as footnotes or page and line references to specific editions of works) have been deleted at the editors' discretion to provide smoother reading of the text.

- Critical excerpts are prefaced by **annotations** providing the reader with information about both the critic and the criticism that follows. Included are the critic's reputation, individual approach to literary criticism, and particular expertise in an author's works. Also noted are the relative importance of a work of criticism, the scope of the excerpt, and the growth of critical controversy or changes in critical trends regarding an author. In some cases, these notes include cross-references to excerpts by critics who discuss each other's commentary.

- A complete **bibliographic citation** designed to facilitate the location of the original essay or book follows each piece of criticism.

- An annotated bibliography of **further reading** appearing at the end of each author entry lists additional secondary sources on the author. In some cases it includes essays for which the editors could not obtain reprint rights.

Cumulative Indexes

Each volume of *NCLC* includes a cumulative index listing all authors who have appeared in Gale's Literary Criticism Series, along with cross-references to such biographical series as *Contemporary Authors* and *Dictionary of Literary Biography*. For readers' convenience, a complete list of Gale titles included appears on the first page of the author index. Useful for locating an author within the various series, this index is particularly valuable for those authors who are identified with a certain period but who, because of their death dates, are placed in another, or for those authors whose careers span two periods. For example, Fyodor Dostoevsky is found in *NCLC*, yet Leo Tolstoy, another major nineteenth-century Russian novelist, is found in *TCLC* because he died after 1899.

Each new volume in Gale's Literary Criticism Series includes a cumulative topic index, which lists all literary topics treated in *NCLC, TCLC, LC 1400-1800,* and the *CLC Yearbook*. In addition, each volume of *NCLC* contains a cumulative nationality index in which authors' names are arranged alphabetically under their respective nationalities.

Title Index

Beginning with volume 25, every fourth volume of *NCLC* contains a cumulative title index to all titles discussed in the series since its inception. This index is included in volume 29. Foreign-language titles that have been translated are followed by the titles of the translations—for example, *Notre-Dame de Paris (The Hunchback of Notre-Dame)*. Page numbers following these translated titles refer to all pages on which any form of the title, whether foreign-language or translated, appears. Titles of novels, dramas, nonfiction books, and poetry, short story, or essay collections are printed in italics, while individual poems, short stories, and essays are printed in roman type within quotation marks.

A Note to the Reader

When writing papers, students who quote directly from any volume in Gale's Literary Criticism Series may use the following general forms to footnote reprinted criticism. The first example pertains to material drawn from periodicals, the second to material reprinted from books.

> [1]T. S. Eliot, "John Donne," *The Nation and the Athenaeum,* 33 (9 June 1923), 321-32; excerpted and reprinted in *Literature Criticism from 1400 to 1800,* Vol. 10, ed. James E. Person, Jr. (Detroit: Gale Research, 1989), pp. 28-9.

> [1]Clara G. Stillman, *Samuel Butler: A Mid-Victorian Modern* (Viking Press, 1932); excerpted and reprinted in *Twentieth-Century Literary Criticism,* Vol. 33, ed. Paula Kepos (Detroit: Gale Research, 1989), pp. 43-5.

Suggestions Are Welcome

In response to suggestions, several features have been added to *NCLC* since the series began, including annotations to excerpted criticism, an index listing authors in all Gale literary criticism series, entries devoted to a single work by a major author, more extensive illustrations, and an index to titles. Readers who wish to suggest authors to appear in future volumes, or who have other comments regarding the series, are cordially invited to write the editors.

Authors to Be Featured in Forthcoming Volumes

Aloysius Bertrand (French poet)—Bertrand is acclaimed for his collection of prose poetry *Gaspard de la nuit*, which is credited with introducing the prose poem into French literature. His works, characterized by Gothic imagery and rich language, were virtually unknown during his lifetime, yet they have since gained recognition for significantly influencing the poetry of Charles Baudelaire and the French Symbolists during the late nineteenth century.

Nikolai Gogol (Russian novelist, short story writer, and dramatist)—One of the most brilliant and enigmatic figures of Russian literature, Gogol created multifaceted works that combine realism, romanticism, satire, fantasy, and farce. *NCLC* will devote an entry to *Myortvye dushi (Dead Souls)*, his most highly acclaimed novel.

Francis Jeffrey (Scottish journalist, critic, and essayist)—Jeffrey was an influential literary critic who was a founder and editor (1803–1829) of the prestigious *Edinburgh Review*. A liberal Whig, Jeffrey often allowed his political beliefs to color his critical opinions, and his commentary is judged the most characteristic example of "impressionistic" critical thought during the first half of the nineteenth century. Today he is best remembered for his brutal criticism of the early Romantic poets, exemplified by the first sentence of a review of William Wordsworth's *Excursion*: "This will never do."

Aleksis Kivi (Finnish novelist and dramatist)—One of Finland's most significant authors of the nineteenth century, Kivi was the first to use the Finnish language to write in modern literary forms. He is particularly praised for his novel *Seitsemän veljestä* (*Seven Brothers*), the tale of a peasant family's adventures in the wilderness.

José Joaquín Fernández de Lizardi (Mexican novelist, essayist, and pamphleteer)—A notorious political activist known to his contemporaries primarily through his essays and pamphlets, Lizardi has since gained recognition for his novel *El periquillo sarniento (The Itching Parrot)*. Written in the picaresque narrative tradition, *The Itching Parrot* displays Lizardi's concerns with the political and moral stability of Mexico, and the revealing portrayal of Mexican culture in the work marks it as a precursor of literary realism.

John Henry Newman (English theologian and writer)—An influential theologian, Newman was a key figure in the Oxford movement, whose adherents advocated the independence of the Church of England from the state and sought to establish a doctrinal basis for Anglicanism in the Church's evolution from Catholicism. Newman's subsequent conversion to Roman Catholicism inspired his best-known work, *Apologia pro vita sua*, an eloquent spiritual autobiography tracing the development of his beliefs.

Alexander Ostrovsky (Russian dramatist)—Ostrovsky is judged one of the most important Russian playwrights of the nineteenth century. Extremely popular during his time, Ostrovsky's best-known dramas meticulously portray Russian society of the era and are credited with bringing realism to the Russian stage.

Leopold Sacher-Masoch (Austrian novelist)—A prominent literary figure during his lifetime, Sacher-Masoch is today chiefly identified with the psychosexual condition of masochism, defined as a perverse pleasure at being cruelly treated. While contemporaries commended the presentation of history and folklore in his fiction, modern commentators debate whether Sacher-Masoch's works are best viewed as literature or as documents of a pathological obsession.

Friedrich Schelling (German philosopher)—A major figure of the German Idealist and Romantic movements, Schelling is noted for philosophical writings that encompass such diverse disciplines as art, science, and religion. Although some consider his philosophy evasive and uneven, his overall ideological scheme is esteemed for its poetic qualities and insight.

Alfred, Lord Tennyson (English poet and dramatist)—Often regarded as the poet whose work is most representative of the tastes and values of the Victorian era, Tennyson remains one of the most popular authors in the history of literature. The prosodic skills demonstrated in such memorable poems as "The Charge of the Light Brigade" and *In Memoriam* have especially contributed to his high standing among critics and readers.

Walt Whitman (American poet)—A preeminent American poet of the nineteenth century, Whitman introduced innovations in poetic content and form that have greatly influenced the development of modern free verse. *NCLC* will devote an entry to his masterpiece, *Leaves of Grass*, presenting recent criticism of the work that established Whitman as the definitive poet of democracy and the common man.

Acknowledgments

The editors wish to thank the copyright holders of the excerpted criticism included in this volume, the permissions managers of many book and magazine publishing companies for assisting us in securing reprint rights, and Anthony Bogucki for assistance with copyright research. We are also grateful to the staffs of the Detroit Public Library, the Library of Congress, the University of Detroit Library, the University of Michigan Library, and the Wayne State University Purdy/Kresge Library Complex for making their resources available to us. Following is a list of the copyright holders who have granted us permission to reprint material in this volume of *NCLC*. Every effort has been made to trace copyright, but if omissions have been made, please let us know.

COPYRIGHTED EXCERPTS IN *NCLC*, VOLUME 29, WERE REPRINTED FROM THE FOLLOWING PERIODICALS:

American Literature, v. 22, May, 1950. Copyright 1950, renewed 1977 by Duke University Press, Durham, NC. Reprinted with permission of the publisher.—*American Quarterly,* v. III, Summer, 1951 for "Billy Budd: 'The King's Yarn' " by Norman Holmes Pearson. Copyright 1951, American Studies Association. Reprinted by permission of the publisher.—*Eire-Ireland,* v. X, Autumn, 1975 for " 'Manor Sackville': Lady Morgan's Study of Ireland's Perilous Case" by James Newcomer; v. XV, Summer, 1980 for "Sydney Owenson, Lady Morgan: Irish Patriot and First Professional Woman Writer" by Colin B. Atkinson and Jo Atkinson. Copyright © 1975, 1980 Irish American Cultural Institute, 2115 Summit Ave., No. 5026, St. Paul, MN 55105. All reprinted by permission of the publisher and the respective authors.—*Modern Fiction Studies,* v. 23, Summer, 1977. Copyright © 1977 by Purdue Research Foundation, West Lafayette, IN 47907. All rights reserved. Reprinted with permission.—*The Nation,* New York, v. 186, June 7, 1958. Copyright 1958 *The Nation* magazine/The Nation Company, Inc. Reprinted by permission of the publisher.—*PMLA,* v. 91, March, 1976. Copyright © 1975 by the Modern Language Association of America. Reprinted by permission of the Modern Language Association of America.—*Studies in English Literature, 1500-1900,* v. XXI, Autumn, 1981 for "Hazlitt's Criticism in Retrospect" by Charles I. Patterson; v. XXIV, Autumn, 1984 for " 'The Soul Speaking in the Face': Hazlitt's Concept of Character" by Joel Haefner. © 1981, 1984 William Marsh Rice University. All reprinted by permission of the publisher and the respective authors.—*Studies in Short Fiction,* v. IV, Winter, 1967. Copyright 1967 by Newberry College. Reprinted by permission of the publisher.—*Victorian Poetry,* v. 26, Spring-Summer, 1988. Reprinted by permission of the publisher.

COPYRIGHTED EXCERPTS IN *NCLC*, VOLUME 29, WERE REPRINTED FROM THE FOLLOWING BOOKS:

Albrecht, W. P. From *Hazlitt and the Creative Imagination.* University of Kansas Press, 1965. © copyright 1965 by The University of Kansas Press. Reprinted by permission of the publisher.—Barricelli, Gian Piero. From *Alessandro Manzoni.* Twayne, 1976. Copyright 1976 by Twayne Publishers. All rights reserved. Reprinted with the permission of Twayne Publishers, a division of G. K. Hall & Co., Boston.—Bate, Walter Jackson. From "Romantic Individualism: The Imagination and Emotion," in *Criticism: The Major Texts.* Edited by Walter Jackson Bate. Harcourt Brace Jovanovich, 1952. Copyright 1952 by Harcourt Brace Jovanovich, Inc. Renewed 1980 by Walter Jackson Bate. Reprinted by permission of the author.—Baudelaire, Charles. From *Baudelaire as a Literary Critic.* Edited and translated by Lois Boe Hyslop and Francis E. Hyslop, Jr. The Pennsylvania State University Press, 1964. Copyright © 1964, The Pennsylvania State University Press, University Park, PA. All rights reserved. Reproduced by permission of the publisher.—Brereton, Geoffrey. From *An Introduction to the French Poets: Villon to the Present Day.* Methuen & Co., Ltd., 1973. © 1973 by Geoffrey Brereton. Reprinted by permission of the publisher.—Bromwich, David. From *Hazlitt: The Mind of a Critic.* Oxford University Press, 1983. Copyright © 1983 by Oxford University Press, Inc. Reprinted by permission of the publisher.—Buckler, William E. From *On the Poetry of Matthew Arnold: Essays in Critical Reconstruction.* New York University Press, 1982. Copyright © 1982 by New York University. Reprinted by permission of the publisher.—Chandler, S. B. From *Alessandro Manzoni: The Story of a Spiritual Quest.* Edinburgh University Press, 1974. © S. B. Chandler 1974. Reprinted by permission of the publisher.—Chase, Richard. From *Herman Melville: A Critical Study.* Macmillan, 1949. Copyright 1949 by Richard Chase. Renewed 1976 by Frances W. Chase. Reprinted with permission of Macmillan Publishing Company.—Coburn, Kathleen. From "Hazlitt on the Disinterested Imagination," in *Some British Romantics: A Collection of Essays.* James V. Logan, John E. Jordan, Northrop Frye, eds. Ohio State University Press, 1966. © 1966 by the Ohio State University Press. All rights reserved. Reprinted with permission of the publisher.—Collini, Stefan. From *Arnold.* Oxford University Press, Oxford, 1988. © Stefan Collini 1988. All rights reserved. Reprinted by permission of Oxford University Press.—Culler, A. Dwight. From *The Victorian Mirror of History.* Yale University Press, 1985. Copyright © 1985 by Yale University. All rights reserved. Reprinted by permission of the publisher.—de Jonge, Alex. From *Baudelaire, Prince of Clouds: A Biography.* The Paddington Press Limited, 1976. Copyright © 1976 Paddington Press Ltd. Reprinted by permission of the publisher and

1964, 1973. All rights reserved. Reprinted by permission of Woburn Books Ltd.—Wellek, René. From *A History of Modern Criticism: 1750-1950, The Romantic Age.* Yale University Press, 1955. Copyright 1955 by Yale University Press. Renewed 1983 by René Wellek. All rights reserved. Reprinted by permission of the publisher.—Woolf, Virginia. From *The Second Common Reader.* Harcourt Brace Jovanovich, 1932. Published in England as *The Common Reader.* Second series. L. & V. Woolf at the Hogarth Press, 1932. Copyright 1932 by Harcourt Brace Jovanovich, Inc. Renewed 1960 by Leonard Woolf. Reprinted by permission of Harcourt Brace Jovanovich, Inc. In Canada by the Literary Estate of Virginia Woolf and The Hogarth Press.—Woolford, John. From "The Sick King in Bokhara: Arnold and the Sublime of Suffering," in *Matthew Arnold: Between Two Worlds.* Edited by Robert Giddings. London: Vision Press, 1986. © 1986 by Vision Press Ltd. All rights reserved. Reprinted by permission of the publisher.

PHOTOGRAPHS AND ILLUSTRATIONS APPEARING IN *NCLC,* VOLUME 29, WERE RECEIVED FROM THE FOLLOWING SOURCES:

BBC Hulton Picture Library/The Bettmann Archive: **p. 1;** Culver Pictures: **p. 334.**

Matthew Arnold

1822-1888

English poet, critic, and essayist.

For further discussion of Arnold's career, see *NCLC,* Volume 6.

Arnold is considered one of the most significant writers of the late Victorian period in England. He initially established his reputation as a poet of elegiac verse, and such poems as "The Scholar-Gipsy" and "Dover Beach" are considered classics for their subtle, restrained style and compelling expression of spiritual malaise. However, Arnold asserted his greatest influence through his prose writings, in particular his literary criticism, which advances Arnold's classical ideals and advocates the adoption of universal aesthetic standards.

Arnold was the eldest son of Thomas Arnold, an influential educator who served as headmaster of Rugby School for a number of years. Arnold attended Rugby from 1837 to 1841, and while there he composed the prizewinning poem "Alaric at Rome," which was published in 1840. After graduating from Balliol College, Oxford, in 1844, he accepted a teaching post at the university and continued to write verse, publishing *The Strayed Reveller, and Other Poems* in 1849. Two years later he was appointed inspector of schools, a position he held until shortly before his death.

In 1852 Arnold released a collection entitled *Empedocles on Etna, and Other Poems.* The next year he reissued the volume without its title poem. Explaining his actions in his preface to the reissued collection, an essay that has become one of his most significant critical statements, Arnold denounced the emotional and stylistic excesses of late-Romantic poetry and outlined a poetic theory derived from Aristotelian principles of unity and decorum. He also stated that some of his own works, most notably the dramatic poem "Empedocles on Etna," were flawed by Romantic excess, and that he had therefore decided to suppress those most affected. Critics suggest that Arnold's recognition of the pervasive Romantic tendencies of his poetry, which conflicted dramatically with his classicist critical temperament, ultimately led him to abandon poetry as a form of self-expression.

Arnold's first major prose works, *On Translating Homer* and *The Popular Education of France, with Notices of That of Holland and Switzerland,* both published in 1861, inaugurated his career as a highly visible and sometimes controversial literary and social critic. With the appearance of *St. Paul and Protestantism, with an Essay on Puritanism and the Church of England* in 1870, Arnold's focus shifted to theological issues, particularly what he viewed as a crisis of religious faith in Victorian society. Arnold attributed this crisis to the conflict between the prevailing influence of scientific rationalism and the intransigence of conservative theology. His solution was a liberal, symbolic interpretation of biblical scripture, presented in *Literature and Dogma: An Essay towards a Better Apprehension of the Bible,* the publication of which caused an immediate up-

roar among conservative theologians. Two years later Arnold answered his critics in *God and the Bible: A Review of Objections to "Literature and Dogma,"* affirming his rejection of religious orthodoxy. During his final years, Arnold made two tours of the United States and recorded his overwhelmingly negative assessment of American culture in *Civilization in the United States: First and Last Impressions of America.* He died of heart failure on 15 April 1888.

Critics generally view Arnold's poetry as a reflection of the spiritual dilemma of the Victorian, who, in the words of Arnold's "Scholar-Gipsy," is caught between "two worlds, one dead / the other powerless to be born." The "dead" world is widely interpreted as a metaphoric evocation of the early Romantic period, during which Western culture was reinvigorated by newly developed humanist and democratic ideals, while the "unborn" world represents a not-yet-realized society in which the scientific materialism of industrialized nations would be tempered by a highly developed state of cultural enlightenment. Although Arnold strove to imitate classical models in his poetry, critics agree that his work manifests Romantic self-absorption rather than classical objectivity. Many of his poems assume the form of a soliloquy or confession in which the narrator communicates feelings of melancholy or regret. Critics note, however, that Arnold's essentially Romantic sentiments are expressed in a precisely wrought and measured fashion.

Arnold's prose writings articulate his desire to establish universal standards of taste and judgment based on classical models. In his highly regarded *Essays in Criticism,* he elaborated on this key principle, defining the role of critical inquiry as "a disinterested endeavor to learn and propagate the best that is known and thought in the world, and thus to establish a current of fresh and true ideas." For Arnold this endeavor should not be limited to literature, but should embrace theology, history, art history, science, sociology, and political theory, with pertinent standards drawn from all periods in world history. Arnold's approach was markedly eclectic, and in "The Literary Influence of the Academies," the second of the *Essays in Criticism,* he pointedly contrasted the isolation of English intellectuals with European urbanity, hoping to foster in his own country the sophisticated awareness enjoyed by writers and critics on the European continent. Similarly, *Culture and Anarchy: An Essay in Political and Social Criticism,* widely viewed as one of Arnold's most important writings, was motivated by his desire to redress what he saw as the smug provincialism and arrogance of English society. The essay is a sociopolitical critique of England's class structure in which Arnold identifies three major classes: Barbarians (the aristocracy), Philistines (the middle class), and the Populace (the lower class). While Arnold praised the aristocracy for their refined manners and social assurance, he also condemned them for their conservatism. "Philistines" Arnold considered hopelessly uncouth though innovative and energetic. The lower class he dismissed as an ineffectual, inchoate mass. Arnold argued that as the middle class gradually assumed control of English politics, they must be transformed from their unpolished state into a sensitive, sophisticated elite. The alternative, he contended, would be a dissolution of England's moral and cultural standards. Arnold also endorsed the eventual creation of a classless society in which every individual would subscribe to highly refined ideals based on the culture of ancient Greece.

Critics note Arnold's prescience in forecasting the problems that would arise with the transformation from an elite, aristocratic society to a democratic one. Nevertheless, his integration of social criticism and literary analysis is acknowledged as his most significant and lasting achievement, and Stefan Collini has written that Arnold "characterized in unforgettable ways the role that criticism—that kind of literary criticism that is also cultural criticism, and thus . . . a sort of informal political theory—can and must play in modern societies."

(See also *Dictionary of Literary Biography,* Vols. 32 and 57.)

PRINCIPAL WORKS

William E. Buckler   (essay date 1982)

[*In the following excerpt, Buckler defines the opposing Classicist and Romantic tendencies in Arnold's thought, noting in particular the theoretical ramifications of his Preface to the first edition of* Poems *and the Romanticism of "Empedocles on Etna."*]

That Matthew Arnold was a persistent critic of Romanticism is well recognized by students of his poetry, though there has been no comprehensive review of the way in which Arnold drew the English Romantics into the poetics of his prose by using them as metaphoric reference points throughout his critical writings, and there has been no consensus among the critics as to the exact character and justness of Arnold's evaluation of the Romantic experiment—its failures and, especially, its successes. Moreover, various broad results of Arnold's critical attentiveness to the Romantics have not been adequately examined and defined. For example, although his perception of Romanticism never lost its literary rootedness, it gradually underwent a process of expansion that enlarged it from a more or less specialized literary concern to an archetypal metaphor as large as one dominant aspect of life itself. In the Preface to *Merope* (1858), for example, he speaks of England as the "stronghold" of Romanticism and suggests thereby that the metaphor has assumed an encompassing psycho-cultural significance that, in the ensuing decade, must reconcile itself to that other dominant strain in the spirit of contemporary England, Philistinism. The idea of Romanticism gradually coalesces in Arnold's mind with the idea of Modernism; and because the archetypal contention between it and Classicism as an antiphonal metaphor necessarily persists, Arnold is gradually drawn into the larger arena where his critical consciousness can do battle with those general excesses of Romantic Modernism that have overwhelmed Classical correctives and induced a cultural crisis.

For further example, Arnold's relentless criticism of Romanticism was not just a matter of intellectual insight but gradually took control of his constructive imagination, of the way his whole mind worked—of how he thought poetically, how he adopted or created poetic subjects or actions, how he used language. This total integration of the critical consciousness with the creative imagination has not been adequately noted. There is also a corollary to this that requires more attention, or at least a different kind of attention, than it has received so far. Arnold carried his critical response to Romanticism beyond a poetry of statement to a poetry of experience. But being so thoroughgoing a critic, he apparently did not realize the degree to which he was himself susceptible to infiltration by the most massive spiritual tendency of his time. Especially during the period between his first and third volumes—say, from the end of 1849 to mid-1853—he underwent a subtle, unconscious, but profound absorption of Romantic influence. Then, like the Newman who had unconsciously drifted in the direction of Liberalism or who saw his own face in the Monophysite mirror, Arnold suddenly awakened to the climactic recognition that he, too, was a Romantic Modernist.

So the phrase "crisis of Classicism" has a double thrust, one personal, of the kind just described, and one psycho-cultural. On the psycho-cultural side, it points to the failures of imaginative insight, of wholeness and steadiness of view, that result from inadequately rooted enthusiasms or disproportionate glooms, even among supremely talented and impeccably intentioned persons, and, especially during periods of rapid shifts in power and allegiance, contribute to and compound the chaos of life in ignorance or neglect of or conscious contempt for such principles of an authentic renewal as are implicit in Goethe's statement, "From Homer and Polygnotus I every day learn more clearly . . . that in our life here above ground we have, properly speaking, to enact Hell. . . . " This is the kind of corrective insight that Classicism, rightly understood, offers to a Romantic Modernism that, despite the "great . . . sum of force . . . expended" upon it, has been so conspicuously inadequate to the needs of its times. It is to these defects and failures of imaginative insight, visible even in a Romanticism at the moment of its greatest glory but become systemic in a Romantic Modernism that, like Jude Fawley, is "in a chaos of principles," that the body of Arnold's poetry attends; it is the function of Arnold's criticism in both prose and verse. (pp. 180-82)

Every student of Arnold is aware not only of his profound veneration of and faith in the best literature but also of his general dissatisfaction with contemporary literature as an expression of a "deeply *unpoetical*" age and his oft-repeated unfavorable comparison of the greatest Romantic writers, despite full acknowledgment of their extraordinary achievement, with the greatest writers of Classical Greece. His was a failed age creatively, Arnold thought, and the second part of his career was largely devoted to

an explicit effort to establish the bases for a sound criticism that would enable the literature of the future to live fully up to such creative potential as it might have. But England had no exemplary creative writers (that is, no poets) during the 1840s, 1850s, and 1860s to whom the young writer of his generation could turn for guidance. There was more to be learned from Newman than from anyone else—habits of thought, style—but Newman was, by Arnold's terms, a supremely critical rather than a supremely creative writer.

In his prose criticism, Arnold would fault even the great Romantics for the inadequacy of their ideas (they did not know enough); for the negligent way in which they selected their poetic "actions" (their subjects or myths); and for their failure to give the action primary consideration in a poem's internal evolution, their disproportionate emphasis on phrase-making for its own sake, and their woeful inattention to the constructional or architectural aspect of poems. In his poetry, on the other hand, he sketched general patterns in the disheveled psychology of an age of Romantic Modernism to whose inadequacy an inadequate literature was contributive. Being an unheroic age, it had little capacity to recognize either human protagonists of truly heroic proportions or its own desperate need of them. Being blind to its own true character and yet fixated on itself, it lacked an understanding of the austere beauty and genuine poetic relationship between the Classical ideals of full self-knowledge and complete self-effacement; thus writers became its mentors in ignorance of the fact that they themselves were transparent products of the age and bore in their own persons its disqualifying faults. The growing tendency of contemporary writers to emphasize "psychology and the anatomy of sentiment" contradicted the Classical recognition that the "grand[est] moral effects" of literature are "produced by *style*"; thus literature's Classical capacity to treat the most complex moral themes was dissipated in formless ingenuity and capricious inflations of a poetic language whose salutary effects depend on simplicity, directness, and rapidity of movement. Moreover, its psychology of imaginative and moral development was grossly oversimplified, resulting in too great a dependence on "wonders," "rapture," and "Fancy's dispossession of reality" rather than on "stern resolve," "sterner will," sorrow, and terror, and a disposition to allow a "superfluity of joy," a "nectarous poppy," or stoical disdain to blind one to the deep revelation inherent in "Glooms that enhance and glorify the earth" and in the stark "majesty of grief." An age of Romantic Modernism needed, above all else, a strong current of critical thought, but instead there was a predominant allegiance to feeling, to sensuous delight in its most refined manifestations or to extremely volatile swings of passion, drawing man away from the austerer implications of thought and closer and closer to spiritual atrophy. As the craving for a life of sensation, whether of the gross or delicate sort, became systemic, as the age's demand for melodramatic fictions and apocalyptic themes became obsessive, its finer literary spirits almost despaired of establishing a cocreative relationship with their readers in which truly original and finely tuned aspects of poetry could continue to function processively. The therapeutic Classical process of myth-making, of creating effective fictions that enable a person to project outward the primary images of his own inner life and to discover satisfactory patterns of resolution to life's disappointments, ran the danger of being lost.

Arnold surveyed the field of letters in this era of Romantic Modernism and identified three barometric voices as representative of literature's position in relation to man's contemporary problems: the apocalyptic voice of an intense social conscientiousness, urgent, melodramatic; the aesthetic, pastoral voice piping reassurances about "breathless glades, cheered by shy Dian's horn, / Cold-babbling springs,—or caves"; and the grim, blunt, necessitarian voice dogmatically dismissing idealistic expectations of human redemption and renewal. Implicit in this literary construct was a thoroughly distressed attitude toward man's social situation insofar as it related to literature: when brought face to face through literature with a truly horrifying human evil, neither the most poetical voice of the age nor the least poetical touched the problem in any adequate way, each being enclosed in its own intellectual and literary system and in that sense imprisoned in irrelevance. Arnold certainly knew such conspicuous exceptions to this profile as Carlyle and Tennyson, but he was somewhat alienated from them both, and he was evaluating the literary situation in representative rather than exceptional terms.

He also judged as inadequate such archetypal attitudes toward poetry as that which makes the poet suffer the agonies of those whose actions he represents (sometimes called the Romantic or, after Schiller, the Sympathetic attitude) and that which invites the poet to emulate the gods, seeing and knowing all but remaining impervious, in their untroubled happiness, to the pain which they witness (sometimes called the Olympian attitude). As Arnold saw it, such essentially pre-Classical or primitive views, though ingratiatingly naive, ignored the moral imperative at the center of the age of the heroes, of *homo agonistes,* which simultaneously defines both literature and the human role in an entirely new way, lodging literature's function and man's identity, not in a sensual and riotous nature, but in moral values in which the gods themselves are complicit and in which empathetic understanding replaces the raw force of a soul-devouring identification through feeling.

Finally, there is the troublesome but indispensable question of literary models: to what predecessors could a young writer in such an age turn for guidance, what poets could he emulate? The question must be answered with a high degree of circumspection because, as some critics have failed to notice, nowhere in his poetry does Arnold answer it directly. Each speaker in his poetic canon is himself reacting to the pressures of Romantic Modernism, and it is not safe to assume that any two of them are the same except in poems designated by the poet as sequential, and even there the mood of the speaker and his assumption of a particular role in different but sequential poems can make a significant difference. Even the sonnet **"Shakespeare"** and the triple epicede **"Memorial Verses"** reflect very different moods of character that are explicitly generic ("We," "us") and therefore metaphoric rather than literally authorial. The result is that, however explicit the speaker's critical judgment may be, there is no firm implication of a crisp authorial judgment. Rather, criticism is angled into life, so to speak: what would a certain kind of temperament struggling with a personal, if representative, crisis of consciousness *feel* about Goethe or Wordsworth or Byron or Shelley or Senancour, for example? While the resultant evaluation is impressively implanted in the read-

er's awareness, the relative poetic circumstances are implanted too, and the reader-critic is invited to set aside for the moment so-called objective criticism and to judge, for example, the aptness of such critical metaphors as Shelley's "lovely wail," "The pageant of [Byron's] bleeding heart," and Senancour/Obermann's ostrich-like hidden head from inside the sensibility stresses of the speaker-protagonist of **"Stanzas from the Grande Chartreuse."**

In the prismatic view provided by Arnold's poetry as a whole, no nineteenth-century writer escapes qualification, and only Wordsworth emerges as a model, though a profoundly challenging model, for the young writer. Coleridge never attains a poetic presence; Shelley, though treated with a fair degree of tenderness, is indicted for an ineffectual eloquence rooted in doubtful motives and for a mournful birdsong having little or no significance; despite his formalistic usefulness to Arnold himself, Keats is associated with the "nectarous poppy" of **"To a Gipsy Child by the Sea-Shore"** and the withdrawn, inconsequential pastoral piper of **"To George Cruikshank . . . "**; Senancour, even for the speaker-protagonist of **"Stanzas in Memory of the Author of 'Obermann',"** gradually yields place to Wordsworth in the curve of the poem's narrative consciousness. Byron's Titanism and Goethe's Olympianism place them in very different positions on the spectrum of modern poetry, neither of which is in any sense negligible. But we watch their epic-like performances—Byron's "fiery . . . strife," Goethe's uncompromising seeing eye, looking undaunted upon the apocalyptic end of a dispensation—as we might watch quintessentially different heroes at the center of any cataclysmic world-rendering, affected even beyond our capacity to understand but unable to emulate either one. Wordsworth, on the other hand, performed the magical task, essential to all ages, of returning poetry to its earliest symbol, the lyre, to its earliest practiner, Orpheus, and to its earliest purpose, the redemption of Nature in the hearts of men—that is, the reconciliation of man to a universe that he can actually see, hear, touch, smell, taste, and love. Even in an age of Romantic Modernism, there will be embodiments of sagacity and force, if not quite Goethean sagacity or Byronic force, but these "dark days" make least likely the most essential functions of poetry—the centering of experience in the benign human emotions, the dissolution of the barriers between the harsh external appearance of things and their restorative inner reality, the attuning of the human ear to the eternal music of Nature's voice—and it is this that makes Wordsworth so incomparably important in this time of passionate grossness, myopic literalness, and spiritual deafness.

Titanism, Olympianism, Orpheanism—thus even Byron, Goethe, and Wordsworth have their analogues in Classical myth and poetry. But more explicitly, Homer, Sophocles, and Epictetus are offered as Classical correctives to Romantic Modernism. Homer is there because of the clarity of his spiritual insight, a clarity that, working through inherited myth or human "history," enabled him, though blind, to see the physiognomy of the world with such wholly dependable imaginative truth that even his physical blindness did not lead him into fancifulness and caprice. The authority of the spiritual eye is also Sophocles' chief credential: his sight/insight was so "whole" and "steady" and "even-balanced" that he never fell into the inadequacies of dullness or the misleading volatilities of passion; despite the penetration of his tragic vision, he remained "mellow" and "sweet," never falling into the de-animating, eclipsing mournfulness of a Byronic Manfred. Between these two strands Epictetus, and such company justifies our seeing his insight into the truth of the human prospect as his singular merit too. He was the philosophical spokesman for the detached, self-effacing attitude toward human experience and conduct that, in their individual fashions, Homer and Sophocles absorbed into their epics and tragedies. He was the great corrector of disproportionate human expectation, not a de-spiritualizer of man but his great equalizer, postulating a philosophy of human attitudes that would enable man, at the most dependable level, to be reconciled to the truth of his situation in his universe. Seeing "things as they in fact are," then, seeing the truth without attitudinal extravagance or rebellion, is what the mind "in these bad days" most needs, and one has to overleap, not just the greater part of Romanticism, but much of the Christian tradition in literature, to find firm foundations upon which to build mental attitudes adequate to the present and the future.

Arnold's subtle, unconscious, but profound absorption of the influence of Romantic Modernism and the close correlation between his recognition and rejection of that influence and the virtual end of his career as a poet at the age, say, of thirty-five is a tantalizing subject that defies conclusive resolution. Even if one had full and relevant external data on Arnold's thoughts and motives, a detailed account in his own hand of his recognitions and resolutions in this matter, it would still generate enough theoretical questions to keep the issue forever in solution. As it is, we have very little specific guidance for dealing with a literary event that is not only the chief critical turning in Arnold's own literary life but also the prototype of one of the major critical dilemmas of modern poetry, the difference between Arnold and his successors being that he faced it first and with incomparable *éclat.* The two fundamental questions at the heart of the event are these: what is the purpose of poetry, especially though not exclusively poetry in a modern context, and how imperative for my own poetic practice, indeed for my very continuation as a poet, is a deep and conscientious sense of poetry's purpose? Inherent therein is one of the most relentless of moral questions—*am* I what I *believe?*—and an understanding of the true dimensions of Arnold's essentially aesthetic "action" requires a moral context.

The two documents that Arnold himself placed at the center of the issue are **"Empedocles on Etna"** and the critical **"Preface"** of 1853, the one "A DRAMATIC POEM" Classically monitored and Romantically faulted, the other a poetic manifesto subscribing unequivocally to the dramatic principles of Classical theory and practice and faulting Romanticism for its deviations from those principles. Such central placement is perfectly apt—these are the crucial exemplary documents—but something more than a literal view of them, in fact a metaphoric or symbolic view, must be taken in order to appreciate fully their subtle, oblique significance. **"Empedocles on Etna"** was Arnold's Iphigenia, the symbolic sacrifice that he made to appease the wrath of the goddess of pure poetry for an offense that, though innocently committed, had become systemic in his practice of her art. The **"Preface"** of 1853, besides being an explicit declaration of full faith in the simple, austere, unimpeachable poetic rules of the Classical goddess, is an

implicit confession of personal culpability, a plea of "guilty, with an explanation."

The issue is not whether or not Arnold was right in thus indicting the major tendency of his poetic art: that is a legitimate but different issue upon which much critical impressionism has been expended. Here our concern is simply with how he saw the matter, and since the **"Preface"** is the chief summary of evidence external to the poetry, the **"Preface"** is the place to begin.

Throughout Arnold's **"Preface,"** aesthetics is rooted in ethics: that is good poetry which increases the world's pleasure, that is bad poetry which increases the world's pain is how the **"Preface"** begins. It ends with a fingering of culture's amoralists, poetry's *dilettanti,* and a solemn moral charge to its writer-audience: "Let us not bewilder our successors: let us transmit to them the practice of poetry, with its boundaries and wholesome regulative laws, under which excellent works may again, perhaps, at some future time, be produced, not yet fallen into oblivion through our neglect, not yet condemned and cancelled by the influence of their eternal enemy, caprice." Thus it is an action preface, a call to self-recognition and self-renewal or self-restraint, in the light of a refreshed view of the highest kind of moral seriousness involved in the practice of poetry, and a challenge even to accept what for the writer is the ultimate self-sacrificial insight, namely, that an age of no poetry is better than an age of bad poetry. That "human actions" are the "eternal objects" of poetry makes it axiomatic that aesthetic considerations, however indispensable, are secondary to the moral imperative; even the selection of "an excellent action"—one which "belong[s] to the domain of our permanent passions"—invokes, in the first place, a high degree of moral sophistication, though it is at this point that ethics and aesthetics merge and become inseparable as poetic functions, moral affect being thereafter dependent on style. But even such stylistic matters as construction and diction are dealt with in the language of morality, the rhetoric of conscience: the "severe and scrupulous self-restraint of the ancients" in these matters has, for those who have commerce with them, "a steadying and composing effect upon their judgment, not of literary works only, but of men and events in general."

So pervasive in the **"Preface"** that it determines its structure is the contrast between the ancients and the moderns, between the Classical Greeks and Romantic Modernist Englishmen. Against the illusion exuded by "the great monuments of early Greek genius"—"the calm, the cheerfulness, the disinterested objectivity"—is set the frenzied chaos of contemporary English poetic practice, with its fragmentariness of view and of performance, its preference for the rhetorical over the genuinely poetical, for the novel and curious part over the impressive and salutary whole, its subjectivity, its inflated contemporaneity, its overabundance of critical counselors, its spiritual confusion, incoherence, and discomfort inducing feelings of contradiction, irritation, and impatience, its lack of moral grandeur, its excessive self-congratulation, its "bewildering confusion" and uncertainty in all respects, the imperious demands it makes for devotion to such provincially topical subjects as theories of progress, industrial development, and social amelioration, its blind expectation that a poetry can be true to the best poetic principles and at the same time faithfully represent so fundamentally unpoetical an age.

And here is where we identify the implicit confession of personal culpability: although Arnold acknowledged at the time of writing the **"Preface"** that a poetry that took as its essential object the representation of such an age as that described above could hardly be anything but poetically inadequate because its subject was woefully inadequate and no craftsmanship, however expert, could make adequate poetry out of an inadequate subject, he had largely done just that. It is true that he had consistently represented the age in order to subject it and the Romantic writers who had fathered it to relentless criticism; one may easily yield him credit for having done something far more poetically imaginative than simply creating verse structures through which his persistent critical consciousness could function at a subtle and highly stimulating level. But on the whole and despite notable exceptions, the dominant impression that Arnold's poetry gives to one who knows something of his age is of a representation of that age.

Arnold rooted the feeling of his poems and the rhetoric expressive of that feeling in the Classical tradition of mimetic, representational art, his lyrical as well as his dramatic and narrative poems having, despite their confessional mode, the essential objectivity of action-centered poetry that is "in a large degree dramatic or personative in conception." That he lacked the "discipline" to do it plainly and simply and thoroughly, he confesses, and he admits that therefore his poems do not "breathe its spirit"; but he still claims, even in the face of confessed failure, that throughout his career as a young poet he had, in an immature, undisciplined, unsuccessful way, aspired to the goal of the ancients—"not to praise their age, but to afford to the men who live in it the highest pleasure which they are capable of feeling." Judged by the severe standards of the **"Preface,"** he had been prone to three basic types of error: of allowing too many relatively inconsequential pieces a place among his published works; not only of critically interpreting his age, but of interpreting it in such a way as to make too many of his poems time-dependent; of grossly miscalculating what gives readers of poetry "the highest pleasure which they are capable of feeling." He had succeeded in catching "the main movement of mind of the last quarter of a century," "the main line of modern development"; he had been more attentive than any of his contemporaries before Swinburne to the relevance of Classical style to a modern outlook, to the wholesome persistence in an unpoetical age of a supremely poetical tradition. He had put in place, however unsatisfactorily from his own point of view, a canon of poetry that, though it is the least revolutionary in appearance, has had a profound relevance for modern poetry. As Arnold was both the most Wordsworthian and Classical of Victorian poets, so Hardy and Eliot have been the most Arnoldian and Classical of twentieth-century poets.

Clearly, then, Arnold did not need to go on simply doing more of the same, especially in the face of the firmest possible declaration of the purpose and guiding principles of poetry that was at the same time an implicit confession of the inadequacy of his own poetic practice. He was not a dilettante according to Goethe's strict definitions cited in the final paragraph of the **"Preface,"** but it would have been dilettantish to go on producing confessedly inade-

quate poems. There is an unmistakable and decisive self-reference in the following perorative sentence: "If we must be *dilettanti*: if it is impossible for us, under the circumstances amidst which we live, to think clearly, to feel nobly, and to delineate firmly: if we cannot attain to the mastery of the great artists—let us, at least, have so much respect for our art to prefer it to ourselves." It is a moral principle leading, for a thoroughly honest man, to a moral decision: better no poetry at all than more of the same inadequate poetry.

Arnold had specifically claimed for **"Empedocles on Etna"** the literary virtue of firm delineation, and it is perhaps easiest to credit Arnold's poems generally with that quality, including the poems or conceptions of poems that Arnold would have had to fault by other standards. So it seems most profitable to look elsewhere for *the reason for the fault* of **"Empedocles on Etna"** and the other poems for which it was a symbolic sacrificial stand-in, such poems, for example, as **"Stanzas in Memory of the Author of 'Obermann',"** **"Tristram and Iseult,"** **"The Scholar-Gipsy,"** and **"Stanzas from the Grande Chartreuse."** Arnold designates the fault quite explicitly—a spiritually devastating pathos rather than a tragedy that becomes spiritually restorative through the credible conversion of human catastrophe into human admiration and delight. But the really teasing question is how a poet so Classically oriented as Arnold and so persistently critical of Romantic Modernism as we have seen him to be could have fallen or drifted into a position so untenable for one like him—in short, *the reason for the fault.*

In the first place, we should note that the fault was not poetically inherent in the "historical" account of Empedocles—historically inherent, perhaps, but not poetically inherent. Arnold specifically says that the error was a liter-

Tristram and Iseult.

ary one—"as I have endeavoured to represent him." This points to one reason for an error in judgment: Arnold was so fascinated by the historical Empedocles that he very carefully portrayed the historical Empedocles, unmindful for the moment of something that he knew very well, namely, Aristotle's distinction between historical responsibility and a higher poetic responsibility: "The true difference is that one relates what has happened, the other what may happen. Poetry, therefore, is more philosophical and a higher thing than history: for poetry tends to express the universal, history the particular." Further, Arnold describes his discovery of Empedocles in terms that suggest why he was led into a disproportionate emphasis on history: "Into the feelings of a man so situated there entered much that we are accustomed to consider as exclusively modern. . . ." That was itself a lesson that might be well taught to his chauvinistic contemporaries; and, along with certain other tendencies of his overtly pedagogical temperament, this led Arnold to teach a truth somewhat lower than the highest poetical truth to which his subject was susceptible.

This failure of the poet to interfere with history in the name of poetry's higher purpose is also characteristic of the other poems cited above: relentless fidelity to character and imagined circumstance brings them to the end of a linear progression for which there is no compensatory reversal and recognition, no establishment of a sternly reassuring alternative possibility (the "what may happen" of poetry versus the "what has happened" of history). No imaginative salvation is made available to any of the protagonists. The chilling last line of **"Tristram and Iseult"** suffuses the whole literary experience with a hint of spiritual bitterness; the coda of **"The Scholar-Gipsy"** darkens the future prospect into a suggestion of futility and ultimate failure; the speaker-protagonists of **"Stanzas in Memory of the Author of 'Obermann'"** and **"Stanzas from the Grande Chartreuse"** are victims of a temperamental malaise, the one engaged in an endless search for the very "dreams" that his sceptical nature rejects, the other in a myth of no return.

Why? Because Arnold the poet, despite his persistent critical insights, had become to a significant degree the victim of the very modern history, the Romantic Modernism, that he delineated so firmly and so well. That there should be this discrepancy between his principles and his practice shows that, "under the circumstances in which [he] live[d]," he could not "think clearly" at that imaginative level of thinking that holds poetry true to the poet's principles. Though he could articulate a resounding defense of the modern hero—an Odysseus-like figure who accepts the "general law" of the universe as it in fact is, sees "one clue to life, and follow[s] it," and, "Laborious, persevering, serious, firm," pursues his "track, across the fretful foam / Of vehement actions without scope or term, / Called history . . . "—he so suffered from his era's despair of modern heroism that he devoted his poetic talent and energy to the creation of human types who had ceased to "feel nobly" except in vastly diminished remnant terms and declined the responsibility of the poet-in-charge to give their myths an ennobling turn. Thus the critic of Romantic Modernism had himself become a Romantic Modernist. When Arnold recognized this, he made the most critical decision a poet who venerates his art can make—to correct it even at the cost of ceasing to be a poet altogether.

Despite an essentially detached and good-humored record, it is difficult to imagine that Arnold underwent this crisis in his literary life without some degree of *Sturm und Drang*. It may not have been an event as traumatizing as Carlyle's detection and defiance of the Devil or Mill's irrepressible "No!" to happiness or Newman's discovery of the face of a heretic in his Monophysite mirror or Tennyson's sudden loss of the chief support of his imaginative and emotional life, but it is reminiscent of them all. It was certainly more severe an act of moral/aesthetic self-measuring than most gifted young poets ever subject themselves to, and the results were about as far-reaching as possible, altering the whole course of Arnold's literary life. But Arnold kept his own counsel with Classical aplomb. He was not himself subject to the demonic self-consciousness that possessed some of his contemporaries and some of his own imaginary characters, and even his most confessional moments show an admirable restraint. Modern life was a most serious business, and modern poetry was modern man's chief instrument of articulation and reconciliation. He had, for a substantial period of time, offered it his dedicated service, but as the task became more and more demanding, the need more and more urgent, he recognized with exemplary honesty and without the least suggestion of false modesty his own poetic limitations. His contribution had been substantial, and though he had a genuine if limited faith in its ultimate serviceability, he saw no need to go on replicating it. Instead, he undertook the difficult and delicate task of writing a brief but full-bodied declaration of poetic faith and an oblique confession of poetic inadequacy. It was a very courageous and forthright action for a young man who had thus far appeared before the reading public only as "A." As literary history would have it, both the difficulty and the delicacy were richly rewarded: in the whole century, Arnold's **"Preface"** of 1853 is surpassed in importance only by Wordsworth's Preface to the Second Edition of *Lyrical Ballads*. With it, Arnold launched the most spectacular critical career in the history of English letters. (pp. 188-201)

> *William E. Buckler, in his* On the Poetry of Matthew Arnold: Essays in Critical Reconstruction, *New York University Press, 1982, 206 p.*

A. Dwight Culler   (essay date 1985)

[*In the following excerpt, Culler delineates Arnold's theory of history, accentuating its importance for his thoughts on political systems, literary culture, and religious history.*]

Arnold seems to have begun thinking seriously about history in the mid-1840s, when he subjected himself to an intensive course of reading in the Romantic German philosophers and historians. He was particularly impressed by the idea of the Zeitgeist. The concept of the Spirit of the Age had been introduced into England from French sources about the time of the Revolution of 1830, but now, in the time of the Revolution of 1848, Arnold reintroduced it from German sources. He probably first encountered it in Carlyle, who uses it in "Characteristics" and *Sartor Resartus*, but he seems always to have associated it with Goethe. His first use of it was in a letter to Clough on July 20, 1848: "Goethe says somewhere that the Zeitgeist when he was young caused everyone to adopt the Wolfian theories about Homer, himself included: and that when he was in middle age the same Zeitgeist caused them to leave these theories for the hypothesis of one poem and one author: inferring that in these matters there is no certainty, but alternating dispositions." Fifteen years later he alluded to the same passage in Goethe's *Schriften zur Literatur* (the section entitled "Homer noch einmal (1827)") and went on to say, "Intellectual ideas, which the majority of men take from the age in which they live, are the dominion of this Time-Spirit; not moral and spiritual life, which is original in each individual." Style is also original with the individual. "In a *man*," Arnold wrote to Clough, "style is the saying in the best way *what you have to say.* The *what you have to say* depends on your age." Style he evidently thought of as subjective; the moral and spiritual life, though also unique to the individual, is surely in some degree objective. It is the area in between the subjective and objective—the vast area of human culture—that depends upon the age. The phrase "alternating dispositions" indicates that Arnold was thinking in terms of critical and creative or organic and mechanical periods.

The phrase "Zeitgeist" differs from the "Spirit of the Age" in its greater emphasis on Time and therefore change. It notes that the Spirit of the Age changes continuously with the passage of time, although it may be only at moments of revolutionary change, as in 1830 and 1848, that people become conscious of the fact and comment upon it. As to why change occurs, Arnold does not say. There is a large fatalistic element in his thought, and the image of the River of Life or Time, which is as pervasive in his prose as in his poetry, suggests that change is simply a cosmic process. It is an aspect of Time. Without change, external or internal, there would be no Time. In the area of knowledge, though not in that of the arts, Arnold believes in progress, though perhaps only *en ligne spirale,* as Goethe did. But in other areas he suggests a law of action and reaction, possibly because life, as he sees it, is a harmonious balance of opposing qualities. Hence, whenever one element, such as Hebraism, becomes dominant there is a natural reaction in favor of its opposite, Hellenism. This law is thus a self-protective device on the part of life itself to preserve the good health of the organism. It is a kind of spiritual sensor which detects in advance changes which need to be made by the body politic if it is to be in harmony with its own inward life. For Arnold agrees with Carlyle that changes are initially spiritual and that the forms of society (Carlyle's "clothes") are continually lagging behind. He does not frequently use his father's analogy between the life of the individual and the history of the world, but he certainly thinks of society as alive and as changing because it is alive.

The changes society undergoes are both positive and negative, for the Time-Spirit is both a Creator and a Destroyer. Fraser Neiman, who has studied this matter in detail, says that Arnold had two widely differing conceptions of the Zeitgeist, in the forties thinking of it as "the temper of the times, with the additional idea that time is a local, changeable phenomenon opposing eternal values;" in the seventies, when he was writing on the Church and the Bible, thinking of it as "an aspect of the eternal, promoting change as a manifestation of its own being." It may be, however, that it was not Arnold's conception of the Zeit-

geist that changed but rather the position from which he viewed it. When Arnold felt himself on the burning plain, he necessarily found the Zeitgeist inimical and attempted to refuge himself from it; but when he felt he was approaching the wide-glimmering sea, then the Zeitgeist was working in his favor and he naturally elevated it to a cosmic process. It was the same power in both cases, but in the one operating as the destroyer of the old world, in the other as the creator of the new.

Throughout his life Arnold varied in his view of the Time-Spirit, sometimes regarding it as a mere metaphor for collective shifts in human opinion and sometimes hypostatizing it as a real entity that produced those shifts. He tells his sister, for example, "It is only in the best poetical epochs (such as the Elizabethan) that you can descend into yourself and produce the best of your thought and feeling naturally . . . ; for then all the people around you are more or less doing the same thing. It is natural, it is the bent of the time to do it; its being the bent of the time, indeed, is what makes the time a *poetical* one." The Elizabethan age is poetical *because* many people were then writing and reading poetry. On the other hand, in ***St. Paul and Protestantism*** Arnold makes the Zeitgeist independent of individual human actions, identifying it with the logic or life in ideas themselves. He associates it with the power which Newman made responsible for the development of Christian doctrine and with St. Paul's "divine power *revealing* additions to what we possess already." The ambiguity of Arnold's feeling is apparent in the fact that he sometimes uses the phrase Zeitgeist along with another phrase—"the 'Zeit-Geist' and the general movement of men's religious ideas" or "the 'Zeit-Geist' and the mere spread of what is called *enlightenment*"—where one cannot tell whether the second phrase is in addition to or in explanation of the first. Generally speaking, in view of Arnold's (along with Goethe's) "imperturbable naturalism" one is inclined to think that the reification of the Time-Spirit is less a matter of real belief on Arnold's part than of rhetorical strategy. Just as he will personify Culture or Criticism in order to give authority to his own ideas and will chastise the provinciality of the English by telling them what "Europe" thinks of them, so here he undertakes to speak for "History." The Time-Spirit is a device whereby Arnold can project his own sense of change onto a persona that is simply irresistible. The change is coming whether people like it or not. On the other hand, when Arnold defines God as "the stream of tendency by which all things seek to fulfill the law of their being," one does not feel that this is a mere rhetorical strategy. There is a distinct element in Arnold that reaches forward to a Bergsonian Life Force, and the only Absolute he really believes in is placed within the evolving forms of life itself. He may mythologize the Time-Spirit for rhetorical purposes, but when he divinizes it, he is probably being serious.

The Time-Spirit embodies itself in external institutions and then, moving on, creates a sense of discordancy between these institutions and its own inner life. This discordancy grows until at last the institutions break up, either rapidly by revolution or more slowly by gradual change, and at such times we feel we are at the end of an era. Thus, the periodization of history is created by the breakup of systems rather than by the more or less constant movement of the Zeitgeist itself.

It is sufficiently obvious that this view of history derives from the Philosophy of Clothes in Carlyle's *Sartor Resartus* and from his German and French sources. Some scholars have perceived in Arnold's work the influence of Vico, but Arnold never quotes Vico, and although the *Scienza nuova* appears in his reading lists for 1876, there is no evidence he read it. He of course knew his father's "Essay on the Social Progress of States," but his father had so far modified Vico, reducing his Ages of Gods, Heroes, and Men to periods dominated by the aristocracy, the middle class, and the populace, that there was little left peculiar to the Italian. Both father and son did, of course, hold that every society, at least ideally, goes through a threefold evolution and therefore that modern societies tend to repeat the development of those in antiquity. To that extent they are Viconian. But Arnold could have gotten this scheme more easily from Goethe and Carlyle.

Like his predecessors, he does not apply the scheme rigorously or systematically. The alternating epochs tend to fall into a threefold dialectical pattern, but this is not always the case. Moreover, the pattern may be on a very extended time-scale, as with the great divisions of the Middle Ages, the Renaissance, and modern times, or it may be so reduced that epochs of concentration and expansion come and go with bewildering rapidity. In all likelihood Arnold believed that there are cycles within the great cycles of human history, even down to the cycles of individual human life. Thus, though the Middle Ages is a kind of childhood of the world, followed by a harsh maturity from the Elizabethan age on, Romanticism is certainly a miniature childhood within that larger cycle. Moreover, it should be understood that individual nations do not necessarily move in phase. England in 1848 was "*far behind* the Continent," according to Arnold, and the French Revolution, which produced an epoch of expansion in the country in which it occurred, provoked in England an epoch of concentration. Even within a country the various aspects of national life were not always in phase, and it goes without saying that Arnold held different views of different periods at different times. He had a particularly hard time making up his mind about the Elizabethan period, whether it was, as he said in his letter to Tom, a "second-class epoch" with an occasional genius like Shakespeare or one of the great synthetic periods of world history like its counterpart in Italy. Arnold read much history and thought deeply about it, but he was neither an accurate historian of the past nor a systematic philosopher of history. His aim was to draw from the past a paradigm of the stages through which nations and individuals ideally would pass in realizing their full potential.

Arnold applied his philosophy of history in three main areas, the evolution of political society, the course of literary culture, and the history of religion. As might be expected, his terminology and concepts vary from one field to another. In the area of politics Arnold believed, along with his father, that society was moving inevitably towards a greater degree of democracy. Thus, it would evolve through periods dominated by the aristocracy, the middle class, and the populace. But whereas his father believed that in 1830 England was at the crisis point between the second phase and the third, Arnold regarded the process as much less advanced and likely to be less catastrophic. He acknowledged that 1688 was an important date but held that the aristocracy was still well in charge

Portrait of Arnold by H. Weigall.

through 1815 and that even after the first Reform Bill the actual reins of government were in their hands. The problem now was to persuade them to relinquish their power, for as Arnold looked back through history he thought he saw that the Roman aristocracy had fallen because it was unable to deal with the ideas of the mature period of Roman history after the Punic Wars, and that the Venetian and French aristocracies had fallen because they were unable to deal with the ideas of modern Europe. An aristocracy is naturally unsympathetic to ideas, which it regards as visionary and even dangerous, and thus, as the old order ceases to satisfy, there is a need for a new class to come into power that will be sympathetic to ideas. This will be the middle class, and despite Arnold's recognition of the narrowness and lack of intelligence of this group, he believes that it does have the capacity for that role. The "master-thought" of his political writings is the need to educate the middle class so that it can properly perform its role in history. As for the ultimate transfer of power to the people, that is a more distant event which Arnold regards with some unease but as in itself desirable.

In his literary essays Arnold initially used the Goethean-Carlylean terminology of critical and creative periods, saying, in **On Translating Homer** and **"The Function of Criticism at the Present Time,"** that the main effort of the intellect of Europe, for now many years, has been a critical effort, and that the exercise of the creative power in the production of great works of literature is, in the present epoch, simply impossible. But then, a little way into the essay, Arnold shifts to "epochs of concentration" and "epochs of expansion," doubtless because these have a broader cultural application. The two sets of terms are not identical. An epoch of concentration is that great centripetal movement in society whereby a culture draws in upon itself, orders and consolidates its world-view, and defends that view against external enemies long after it has ceased to be alive. It is the epoch of aristocracies, and although it presupposes an earlier act of creation, it really comprehends only the last phase of that act and the first, destructive phase of criticism. An epoch of expansion, on the other hand, is the great centrifugal movement whereby a culture creates, initially through criticism, a new worldview which it then enhances and brings into relation with the lives of men through artistic creation. Arnold differs from Carlyle primarily in his insistence that criticism is creative too and, living as he did a generation later than Carlyle, in his emphasis on its creative rather than its destructive aspect. His terms focus on the systole and diastole of human society rather than on the moment of stasis when either criticism or creation is at its height.

It is not difficult to relate these terms to Arnold's political thought. The epoch of concentration is that of the fading of the aristocracy and the epoch of expansion that of the rise of the middle class, but presumably at some time in the future there will be a new epoch of concentration as the middle class attempts to hold on to its power against the new expansive movement of the populace. There is a certain sense in which the three social classes correspond to the three regions of Arnold's imaginative world, for the aristocracy is the childhood of the world, the middle class is transitional, and democracy is the period in which joy will be "in widest commonalty spread." But Arnold's experience of history is limited to the first two classes, and so he tends to see the new expansive movement of the middle class (it is not irrelevant that it is his own class) as the "wide-glimmering sea." He records its coming very precisely in his essays. In the *Essays in Criticism* (1864-65) he is living in "an epoch of dissolution and transformation"—the last phase of an epoch of concentration—and the promised land is far in the distance. "But epochs of concentration cannot well endure for ever; epochs of expansion, in the due course of things, follow them. Such an epoch of expansion seems to be opening in this country." Five years later it apparently had opened, for in *Culture and Anarchy* (1869) Arnold asks, "Is not the close and bounded intellectual horizon within which we have long lived and moved now lifting up, and are not new lights finding free passage to shine in upon us? For a long time there was no passage for them. . . . But now the iron force of adhesion to the old routine . . . has wonderfully yielded." And a few pages later he speaks of "epochs of expansion . . . , such as that in which we now live." In 1880 he reiterated his entire doctrine in a letter to M. Fontanes, the French critic, and in 1886 declared, "The epoch of concentration has ended for us, the ice has broken up." "We are living in an epoch of expansion."

Arnold seems never to have applied the terms *epoch of concentration* and *epoch of expansion* to any except the modern period, but in *Culture and Anarchy* he devised another set of terms which he could use of the entire course of civilization. Hebraism and Hellenism originally denote two constituent elements in human nature: on the one hand, the impulse to right conduct, obedience to God, and

strictness of conscience; on the other, the impulse toward intelligence, seeing the object as it really is, and spontaneity of consciousness. But because these two elements are embodied, the one in the Judaeo-Christian, the other in the Graeco-Roman tradition, they may also be observed in human history. They have but one aim, human perfection, but they pursue this aim by different means and each is disposed to regard itself not as a contribution to the whole but as the *unum necessarium,* the one thing needful. Therefore history has proceeded by alternating epochs, in which an exclusive pursuit of one quality has led to a practical neglect of the other and so produced a reaction into the opposite error, which had to be corrected in turn. The bright promise of Hellenic culture, for example, was ultimately found to be unsound simply because it had not provided the indispensable basis of conduct and self-control. It led into the moral enervation and self-disgust of late paganism. In that context Christianity, a more inward and spiritual form of Hebraism, came as a rebirth of the human spirit, but it led, through the austerities of St. Paul, into medieval asceticism and so provoked the Renaissance, a second phase of Hellenism. Arnold pondered deeply about the Renaissance and its relation to the Reformation. He sharply disagreed with Froude that "the Reformation caused the Elizabethan literature." It was rather that "both sprang out of the active animated condition of the human spirit in Europe at that time. After the fall of the Roman Empire the barbarians powerfully turned up the soil of Europe—and after a little time when the violent ploughing was over and things had settled a little, a vigorous crop of new ideas was the result." The Reformation was the "subordinate and secondary side" of the Renaissance, and though it was a Hebraising revival within the church, it was so infused with the subtle Hellenic spirit that "the exact respective parts, in the Reformation, of Hebraism and of Hellenism, are not easy to separate." This great hybrid movement, in other words, which initiated the modern world, was in some degree a synthesis of antiquity and the Middle Ages. Nonetheless, even with the Reformation, the Renaissance had its side of moral weakness, just as later paganism had, and in England Puritanism came as the reaction of Hebraism against this weakness precisely as primitive Christianity had at the time of St. Paul.

> Yet there is a very important difference between the defeat inflicted on Hellenism by Christianity eighteen hundred years ago, and the check given to the Renascence by Puritanism. . . . Eighteen hundred years ago it was altogether the hour of Hebraism. Primitive Christianity was legitimately and truly the ascendant force in the world at that time, and the way of mankind's progress lay through its full development. Another hour in man's development began in the fifteenth century, and the main road of his progress then lay for a time through Hellenism. Puritanism was no longer the central current of the world's progress, it was a side stream crossing the central current and checking it.

If one asks how Arnold knows that it is a side stream, his reply is that it is only in England that this happened. On the continent Hellenism remained the dominant movement from the Renaissance to the present time, but in England, in the seventeenth century, the middle class "entered the prison of Puritanism, and had the key turned upon its spirit there for two hundred years." If Arnold were speaking to the French, he would doubtless recommend some additional Hebraism, but speaking to the English, he recommends their peculiar deficiency, Hellenism.

Though both Hebraism and Hellenism have both critical and creative phases, Hebraism, as Arnold views it, is often simply the moral and religious aspect of an epoch of concentration and Hellenism the cultural aspect of an epoch of expansion. The new terms have the virtue, however, of denoting the powers which produce this systole and diastole of human history and so are more useful for tracing the development of civilization. But Arnold also needs to analyze a development within the Hebraic tradition, and for this he turns, in *Literature and Dogma,* to another set of terms, verifiable religious experience *vs. Aberglaube.*

The Bible, in Arnold's view, is not a theological work which sets forth in precise, scientific terms the dogmas of the Christian religion, but is simply the literature of the Hebrew people. Like any literature it is couched in the language of metaphor and symbol, for these alone could shadow forth the profound spiritual experiences of the Old Testament prophets. At least in the early golden years the people had no difficulty interpreting it. Gradually, however, as they suffered misfortunes and weakened in faith, they began to interpret these insights literally, to look for a miraculous change that would restore their fallen fortunes—to expect a Messiah. These new beliefs were not such as could be verified by experience. They were "extra-beliefs"—*Aberglaube*—not exactly superstitions but beliefs *in addition* to what they knew by their own experience of the moral law to be true. When the Messiah did come, then, his function was not to fulfill this mechanical religion but to renew and deepen the experience on which true religion was based—to renew it by the method of inwardness, the secret of renunciation, and the mildness of his own temper. Unfortunately, his followers were once again prone to take literally what he meant only spiritually, and so once again a new Aberglaube, that of Christian theology, grew up. By Arnold's day it had become so entangled in metaphysics and the supernatural that the masses of men were ready to reject the Bible altogether rather than believe what they were told it meant. And so Arnold, who believed the Bible was the greatest repository of spiritual wisdom the world possessed, broke through this web of musty theology to re-present the Bible, as Coleridge and his father had before him, as the religious experience of the Hebrew people. So viewed, the joy announced by Christ would become a "joy whose grounds are true" and so would once again be accepted by the masses, as a "joy in widest commonalty spread." Far more truly than by the advent of democracy or of a new Hellenism, this would bring about the New Heavens and the New Earth that Arnold desired.

The period that Arnold found most analogous to his own was the period of late paganism immediately before the birth of Christ. For twenty years Arnold tried to write a tragedy on Lucretius, for he found the passage at the end of the third book where Lucretius depicts the tedium and ennui of the Roman noble, driving furiously abroad in order to escape from himself and then driving furiously home again, one of the most powerful and solemn in all literature. He quoted it in his lecture **"On the Modern Element in Literature"** and used it again in **"Obermann Once More."** To Clough he wrote in 1835, "We deteriorate in spite of our struggle—like a gifted Roman falling on the uninvigorating atmosphere of the decline of the Empire." The later period covered by Gibbon he was not so interested in, but when he was passing through Arles in the south of France, he wrote to his sister,

> I cannot express to you the effect which this Roman south of France has upon me—the astonishing greatness of the ancient world, of which the provincial corners were so noble—its immense superiority to the Teutonic middle age—its gradual return, as civilization advances, to the command of the world—all this, which its literature made me believe in beforehand, impresses itself upon my senses when I see these Gallo Roman towns. I like to trace a certain affinity in the spirit of these buildings between the Romans and the English; "you and the Romans," Guizot said to me the other day, "are the only two governing nations of the world.

This was in 1859; a dozen years earlier he had written in his notebook:

> The Roman world perished for having disobeyed reason and nature.
>
> The infancy of the world was renewed with all its sweet illusions.
>
> but infancy and its illusions must for ever be transitory, and we are again in the place of the Roman world, our illusions past, debtors to the service of reason & nature.
>
> O let us beware how we again are false to them: we shall perish, and the world will be renewed: but we shall leave the same questions to be solved by a future age.

In **"Obermann Once More,"** alluding to the birth-time of Christianity, he said,

> Oh, had I lived in that great day,
> How had its glory new
> Fill'd earth and heaven, and caught away
> My ravish'd spirit too!

But he added that in the modern rebirth of Christianity one must remain "unduped of fancy," lest one be doomed to repeat the Middle Ages all over again.

Of the Middle Ages Arnold wrote to his sister, "I have a strong sense of the irrationality of that period, and of the utter folly of those who take it seriously, and play at restoring it; still, it has poetically the greatest charm and refreshment possible for me. The fault I find with Tennyson in his *Idylls of the King* is that the peculiar charm and aroma of the Middle Ages he does not give in them. There is something magical about it, and I will do something with it before I have done." Oxford, "steeped in sentiment as she lies, spreading her gardens to the moonlight, and whispering from her towers the last enchantments of the Middle Ages," was for Arnold the very symbol of that magic, but it was also the "home of lost causes, and forsaken beliefs, and unpopular names, and impossible loyalties"—in particular, of Newman, who had vainly attempted to revive there the dream of the Catholic Church. Of the Celtic people, whom Arnold treated in his lectures *On the Study of Celtic Literature,* the bard had said, "They went forth to the war, *but they always fell.*" They were characterized by sentiment, the willful rebellion against the despotism of fact, and though they contributed to English poetry its element of "natural magic," they contributed nothing more. The Middle Ages was the childhood of the modern world, and though one might yearn for the beauty and charm of one's childhood, it was impossible to return. It was impossible to return to the monastery of the Grande Chartreuse, whose religion offered a refuge, but the refuge of the tomb. One of Arnold's sharpest criticisms of the Romantic poets was that they did seek to return. When he wished to say that Wordsworth "voluntarily cut himself off from the modern spirit," he said that he "retired (in Middle-Age phrase) into a monastery." At the same time "Scott became the historiographer-royal of feudalism," and Coleridge took to opium. The same was true of the German Romantics. Carlyle had declared that Tieck, Novalis, Richter, and others were the chief inheritors and continuators of Goethe's work, but Arnold declared that they were a minor current; the main current flowed from Goethe to Heine.

> The mystic and romantic school of Germany lost itself in the Middle Ages, was overpowered by their influence, came to ruin by its vain dreams of renewing them. Heine, with a far profounder sense of the mystic and romantic charm of the Middle Age than Görres, or Brentano, or Arnim, Heine the chief romantic poet of Germany, is yet also much more than a romantic poet: he is a great modern poet, he is not conquered by the Middle Age, he has a talisman by which he can feel,—along with but above the power of the fascinating Middle Age itself,— the power of modern ideas.

To Arnold the Renaissance put European civilization back upon the right road after the long detour of the Middle Ages. . . . Uniting as it did Hebraism and Hellenism, the senses and understanding of late antiquity with the heart and imagination of the Middle Ages, it was one of the great epochs of the "imaginative reason," the beginning of the modern world. Moreover, Arnold had somehow persuaded himself that the high culture of the Renaissance pervaded a large body of the community, creating a current of fresh ideas, and that it is this broad basis of culture that is "the secret of rich and beautiful epochs in national life; the epoch of Pericles in Greece, the epoch of Michael Angelo in Italy, the epoch of Shakespeare in England." It created a "national glow of life and thought" that made for a great creative and expansive epoch. Raphael, Arnold thought, was probably the ideal representative of this age, but unfortunately Arnold knew little about Raphael or Michelangelo, and so he had to confine himself to his own country. There he was less enthusiastic. Though he never said publicly what he said in a private letter to Tom, that the Elizabethan Age was a "second-class epoch" (indeed, he always acknowledged that it was England's greatest), he did not consider it really modern. It retained too much of the Middle Ages upon it, had not really entered into the classical decorum. Or rather, having been so long repressed by the Middle Ages, it burgeoned forth into a fantasticality and playfulness that was simply extravagant. It did so partly because it did not have a complex body of thought and feeling to wrestle with and so could devote itself to curious and exquisite expression. For this reason Arnold did not think it provided a good model for the modern poet. "More and more I feel that the difference between a mature and a youthful age of the world compels the poetry of the former to use great plain-

ness of speech as compared with that of the latter: and that Keats and Shelley were on a false track when they set themselves to reproduce the exuberance of expression, the charm, the richness of images, and the felicity of the Elizabethan poets." Indeed, the literature of the eighteenth century was simply "a long reaction against this eccentricity," and ultimately it perished through its own provinciality. On the continent, however, Goethe and Voltaire had created a great critical effort which, in the completeness of its culture, was almost the equivalent of a true creative age. It only lacked the "national glow of life and thought" which one finds when ideas are widely diffused among the people and not derived from books. Moreover, it was in the eighteenth century that Hellenism, checked by the Puritan reaction, achieved its full development, and Arnold was strangely drawn to the period. "I am glad you like Gray," he wrote to his wife; "that century is very interesting, though I should not like to have lived in it; but the people were just like ourselves, whilst the Elizabethans are not."

The truly great synthetic epoch in the past is the Periclean Age in Athens. "There is a century in Greek life," wrote Arnold, "the century preceding the Peloponnesian war, from about the year 530 to the year 430 B.C.,—in which poetry made, it seems to me, the noblest, the most successful effort she has ever made as the priestess of the imaginative reason, of the element by which the modern spirit, if it would live right, has chiefly to live. Of this effort . . . the four great names are Simonides, Pindar, Æschylus, Sophocles." Arnold does not claim that these poets are perfect, but no other poets have so well balanced the thinking power by the religious sense. As he contemplates their work, he is impressed by their objective excellence and solidity: they are like a group of statuary seen at the end of a long dark vista. "I know not how it is," he says in the Preface to *Poems* (1853),

> but their commerce with the ancients appears to me to produce, in those who constantly practise it, a steadying and composing effect upon their judgment, not of literary works only, but of men and events in general. They are like persons who have had a very weighty and impressive experience: they are more truly than others under the empire of facts, and more independent of the language current among those with whom they live.

The Periclean Age is modern in the sense that it has a deep, inward affinity with contemporary life, but it rises so far above the level of that life that it is an ideal rather than an analogy.

In his later years Arnold turned more and more from the Greeks to the Hebrew scriptures. Indeed, he had no sooner recommended an increase of Hellenism to the English people than he began to think that an increase of Hebraism was what they needed. "If I was to think only of the Dissenters," he wrote to Kingsley in 1870, "or if I were in your position, I should press incessantly for more Hellenism; but, as it is, seeing the tendency of our *young* poetical litterateur (Swinburne), and on the other hand, seeing much of Huxley . . . , I lean towards Hebraism, and try to prevent the balance from on this side flying up out of sight." It was, of course, balance that Arnold was trying to maintain. He was in no sense a relativist, saying that whatever the Zeitgeist brought was to be accounted a blessing. It was rather that the whole course of history presented an ideal of totality or comprehensiveness, the harmonious development of one's powers that was lacking in any particular age. It was also lacking in any particular nation. Just as Newman sought the note of Catholicity by looking to Rome and the note of Apostolicity by looking to Jerusalem, so Arnold also sought these values by looking, on the one hand, to the modern civilizations of France and Germany and, on the other, to the Graeco-Roman tradition. But after the Franco-Prussian War of 1870 he became increasingly disgusted with the modern French. *Madame Bovary* was not to be recommended, and Balzac, unlike Arnold's beloved George Sand, was to be deplored. Whereas previously the French had been characterized by their widespread intelligence, they were now a nation of *hommes sensuels moyens* who worshipped the goddess Lubricity, and their downfall was only a matter of time. "[It] is mainly due" wrote Arnold to his mother, "to that want of a serious conception of righteousness and the need of it, the consequences of which so often show themselves in the world's history, and in regard to the Graeco-Latin nations more particularly. The fall of Greece, the fall of Rome, the fall of the brilliant Italy of the fifteenth century, and now the fall of France, are all examples." Earlier it was the inability to cope with modern ideas that had produced these downfalls.

As Arnold swung back from the Latin to the Saxon races and from Hellene to Hebrew, he turned increasingly to the Old Testament. In 1872 he published an edition of the Second Isaiah for school use and declared in the Introduction that the work provided a key to "universal history."

> Many of us have a kind of centre-point in the far past to which we make things converge, from which our thoughts of history instinctively start and to which they return; it may be the Persian War, or the Peloponnesian War, or Alexander, or the Licinian Laws, or Caesar. Our education is such that we are strongly led to take this centre-point in the history of Greece or Rome; but it may be doubted whether one who took the conquest of Babylon [538 B.C.] and the restoration of the Jewish exiles would not have a better. Whoever began with laying hold on this series of chapters [40-66] as a whole, would have a starting-point and lights of unsurpassed value for getting a conception of the course of man's history and development as a whole.

Here, then, is an alternative to the Age of Pericles, the slightly earlier age of the Second Isaiah. One reason that Arnold so prized it was that the majority of people require joy in their literature, "and if ever that 'good time coming,' for which we all of us long, was presented with energy and magnificence, it is in these chapters" of the Second Isaiah. Hence, in the lecture "Numbers," which Arnold delivered on his tour of America, he contrasted Plato's conception of the "remnant," the small band of honest followers who, in the madness of the multitude, seek shelter under a wall till the storm is over and then depart in mild and gracious mood, with Isaiah's "remnant" (in this case the first Isaiah's), who will actually restore the state. Isaiah's hope is foolish, says Arnold, for the numbers, either in Athens or in Israel, are far too small. But Arnold's father had told him that numbers were the characteristic of democracy, and so in America's fifty millions there will perhaps be found a remnant of sufficient magnitude to accomplish the task.

Arnold's conception of the remnant seems overstrained and dubious, but it is not unrelated to a conception much more fundamental to his thought, that of the lonely individual who carries on, in a climate uncongenial to his genius, to transmit to the future the values of civilization. Such a man was Marcus Aurelius, a "truly modern striver and thinker" who nonetheless had "a sense of constraint and melancholy" upon him because he longed for something more than his age could provide. Such a man was Falkland, a martyr of moderation and tolerance amid the violence of the English civil war. "Shall we blame him for his lucidity of mind and largeness of temper?" By no means. "They are what make him ours; what link him with the nineteenth century. He and his friends, by their heroic and hopeless stand against the inadequate ideals dominant in their time, kept open their communications with the future, lived with the future." Such a person was Gray, a born poet who fell upon an age of prose and so "never spoke out." "Coming when he did, and endowed as he was, he was a man . . . whose spiritual flowering was impossible. The same thing is to be said of his great contemporary, Butler." It may be said too of Joubert, who, though passing with scant notice through his own generation, was singled out by the light-armed troops of the next as a person to be preserved and, like the lamp of life itself, handed on to the next generation. It is as one of these that Arnold saw himself, not as a great poet but as one who, living in the days of the Philistines, yet kept his gift pure and so was a forerunner, a preparer, an initiator of the age to come.

"I think," Arnold wrote to his sister in 1863, "in this concluding half of the century the English spirit is destined to undergo a great transformation; or rather, perhaps I should say, to perform a great evolution." He never ceased to think so or to aid in that evolution. Unlike some of his contemporaries he did not settle down into a fixed position as old age came upon him. By looking to the past he kept himself oriented towards the future. He had in his mind's eye the image of a society in which the whole body of men should come to live with a life worthy to be called *human.* "This, the humanisation of man in society, is civilisation." He knew, however, that this ideal was simply to be sought; it would never be reached once and for all.

> Undoubtedly we are drawing on towards great changes; and for every nation the thing most needful is to discern clearly its own condition, in order to know in what particular way it may best meet them. Openness and flexibility of mind are at such a time the first of virtues. *Be ye perfect,* said the Founder of Christianity. . . . Perfection will never be reached; but to recognise a period of transformation when it comes, and to adapt themselves honestly and rationally to its laws, is perhaps the nearest approach to perfection of which men and nations are capable.
>
> (pp. 136-51)

A. Dwight Culler, "Matthew Arnold and the Zeitgeist," in his The Victorian Mirror of History, *Yale University Press, 1985, pp. 122-51.*

James C. Livingston   (essay date 1986)

[*In the following excerpt from his full-length study of Arnold's theory of religion, Livingston reviews Arnold's attempts at a liberal nineteenth-century "reinterpretation" of Christian theology.*]

The two movements of mind that best characterize English thought in the second half of the nineteenth century are evolution and agnosticism concerning man's knowledge of the ultimate objects of metaphysical and theological belief. Arnold's intellectual development reveals the deep impress of these ideas on his mind and on his understanding of the directions that any religious reconstruction must take. The two movements are, of course, but the reverse sides of the same intellectual phenomenon. The profound sense of change, movement, and development as constitutive of reality implied that the forms and words men use to apprehend and speak of what is "real" or "ultimate" or "true" are themselves fluid, partial, symbolic.

The intellectual question that troubled the age was: Does the fact that the means which we use to shape and communicate our experience of the world are ever changing imply that *what* we experience is relative? For some, such as Pater, the answer was affirmative; for others, and Arnold was one of them, the answer remained negative. And yet, for those who wished to maintain both the fact of historical change and relativity as well as the enduring truth of certain religious or metaphysical beliefs, the challenge was very great indeed. The problem obviously is much with us still.

Arnold possessed a deep-rooted historical consciousness, a sense of the relativistic spirit of the age and the workings of the *Zeitgeist.* Yet by the time he reached his middle years his historicism was accommodated to a distinctly progressive view of historical development. Three particularly important influences were determinative in Arnold's developing theory of history: Goethe and Carlyle, Thomas Arnold and the liberal Anglican philosophy of history, and Newman.

Carlyle was one of the four "voices" that most impressed Arnold while at Oxford. Doubtless it was Carlyle's use of the term *Zeitgeist,* both in "Characteristics" (1831) and in *Sartor Resartus* (1833-34) that, with Goethe, influenced Arnold's use of the term. In a letter to Arthur Clough in July 1848, Arnold refers to Goethe's saying "that the *Zeitgeist* when he was young caused everyone to adopt the Wolfian theories about Homer, himself included: and that when he was in middle age the same *Zeitgeist* caused them to leave these theories for the hypothesis of one poem and one author: inferring that in these matters there is no certainty, but alternating dispositions." Arnold tells Clough that he finds this relativity of intellectual judgment "congenial" and applies it to the reception of Clough's poem "Adam and Eve," which had not suited Arnold but which, he is confident, is "calculated to suit others." Arnold thus sees the time-spirit as productive of an inescapable temper of mind which informs an age. It is a force that cannot be ignored and that can, therefore, pose a severe challenge to beliefs and values which have their source in other times and cultural settings.

The *Zeitgeist* of his own present age, Arnold believed, signaled a movement of mind and a new sensibility which demanded that the ancient beliefs and values be apprehended in a new key if they were to endure. Here Matthew was very much his father's son, for Thomas Arnold also believed that to attempt to preserve the old state of things

in their ancient forms was to court disaster. He maintained that the natural law of history is what he called the principle of accommodation, providence's adjustment of society and religion to the state of knowledge and moral conduct reached in the course of historical development. For example, Thomas Arnold was convinced that as men grow in moral and intellectual stature, the need for miracles as religious sanction and explanation recedes. It is the ability of religion to adapt itself, to follow the principle of accommodation, that is a sign of its strength and truth. In the words of Thomas Arnold's disciple, Arthur Stanley, "The everlasting mountains are everlasting not because they are unchanged but because they go on changing their form, their substance with the wear and tear of years. 'The Everlasting Gospel' is everlasting not because it remains stationary, but because, being the same, it can adapt itself to the constant change of society, of civilization, of humanity itself." Thomas Arnold wrote that "It is worse than kicking against the pricks to oppose our vain efforts to an eternal and universal law of God's Providence."

Matthew Arnold shared this Liberal Anglican philosophy of history. He believed that the *forms* in which doctrines come to us are under the dominion of the time-spirit; men cannot help taking them as self-evident, yet they are also liable to significant historical development and change. In the essay **"Dr. Stanley's Lectures on the Jewish Church"** (1863), Arnold writes: "Intellectual ideas are not the essence of the religious life; still the religious life connects itself . . . with certain intellectual ideas, and all intellectual ideas follow a development independent of the religious life." Thus it is that the Articles of the Church of England are intellectual ideas with which the church, at the time of the Reformation, connected itself. But as ideas of the English Reformers they are ideas *of their time,* requiring development and adaptation. The time-spirit makes their inadequacy plain, but "as this consciousness becomes more and more distinct, it becomes more and more irksome." The moment arrives when the religious man finds himself in a false position, and "it is natural that he should try to defend his position, that he should long prefer defending his position to confessing it untenable, and demanding to have it changed." But reconstruction becomes inevitable, difficult as is the challenge, and the times when these changes are wrought are the epochal movements of religious history, and the agents of these intellectual revolutions are the great religious reformers. For Arnold, the importance of these men is not to be found "in their having these new ideas, in their originating them. The ideas are in the world. . . . They are put into circulation by the spirit of the time. The greatness of a religious reformer consists in his reconciling them with the religious life, in starting this life upon a fresh period in company with them."

Arnold's profound sense of the work of the *Zeitgeist* has been viewed as a weakness, an excessive present-mindedness. It was, and perhaps still is, fashionable to associate Arnold's recognition of the *Zeitgeist* with Dean Inge's damning quip: "He who marries the spirit of the age will soon find himself a widower." Yet for Arnold the *Zeitgeist* does not involve being carried away by every wind of doctrine. Rather, the time-spirit brings with it those emergent models or paradigms which, as T. E. Hulme pointed out, an entire culture assumes as foundational:

There are certain doctrines which for a particular
period seem not doctrines, but inevitable categories
of the human mind. Men do not look at them merely as correct opinion, for they have become so much
a part of the mind, and lie so far back, that they are
never really conscious of them at all. They do not
see them, but other things through them. . . .
There are in each period certain doctrines, a denial
of which is looked on by the men of that period just
as we might look on the assertion that two and two
make five.

For Arnold the *Zeitgeist* presents us with those beliefs that
Hulme refers to as "*doctrines* felt as facts." (pp. 47-50)

According to Arnold, the *Zeitgeist* frames not only the
questions but the paradigms or forms in which the answers are given. And Arnold perceived that the form in
which Christianity had been taught and defended was unintelligible in terms of those categories of understanding
current in his time. He recognized that most clergymen
were in a false position when they attempted to speak
forthrightly because Anglican theology was tied to an outmoded world view and psychology. In a letter written to
his mother in 1862 he points out how troubled his father
would be had he been living then as a young man. "His
attention," writes Arnold,

would have been painfully awake to the truth that
to profess to see Christianity through the spectacles
of a number of second or third-rate men who lived
in Queen Elizabeth's time—men whose works one
never dreams of reading for the purpose of enlight-
ening and edifying oneself—is an intolerable absurdity, and that it is time to put the formularies of the
Church of England on a solider basis.

Arnold was fond of referring to Goethe's epigram: "Religion itself, like time, like life and knowledge, is engaged
in a constant process of advance and evolution." It was the
failure of the Dissenting churches to grasp this fact that
served as motivation for the writing of **St. Paul and Protestantism.** Arnold believed that the Dissenters, as well as
many orthodox churchmen, were simply riveted to their
opinions, "opposed to that development and gradual exhibiting of the full sense of the Bible and Christianity,
which is essential to religious progress." They exhibit their
religious doctrines "as a sort of cast-iron product, rigid,
definite, and complete, which they have got once and for
all, and which can no longer have anything added to it or
anything withdrawn from it."

On the contrary, Arnold contends that time and experience, the movement of mind, has shown that the theological formularies of the sixteenth century have "given way
and cannot be restored," any more than the Ptolemaic or
the feudal systems or belief in magic can be restored. Arnold's understanding of the working of the time-spirit on
the older theology—namely, on the proofs from prophecy,
miracles, and on the inerrancy of Scripture, as well as the
claims of natural theology—takes up much of **Literature
and Dogma** and **God and the Bible** and need not be discussed here in detail. One striking illustration with regard
to miracle will characterize his approach. He rejects the
insistent demand of his critics that he engage in a "proof"
that miracles do not happen: "To engage in an *a priori* argument to prove that miracles are impossible, against an
adversary who argues *a priori* that they are possible, is the
vainest labour in the world. . . . The time for it is now

past, because the human mind, whatever may be said for
or against miracles *a priori,* is now in fact losing its reliance upon them." Arnold is arguing that the belief in miracle has given way not because of devastating logical arguments but because miracle is no longer part of that set of
concepts regarded as necessary to those modes of description used in our actual everyday thought and life. (pp.
51-2)

Arnold's awareness of the inevitable effect of the *Zeitgeist*
on the forms of Christian apologetic was prescient. However, there remains the repeated charge that he looked
upon the workings of the *Zeitgeist* as necessarily progressive, that for him there appears to be no intellectual back-
sliding, no retrogression in the ever-progressive movements of history. Like Hegel, Arnold did envision the ongoing funding of historical experience as essentially a progressive deepening of reality and truth, and this is because
the historical process is the outworking of divine reason.
He writes, for example, that

thought and science follow their own law of development, they are slowly elaborated in the growth
and forward pressure of humanity . . . and their
ripeness and unripeness, as Dr. Newman most truly
says, are not an effect of our wishing or resolving.
Rather do they seem brought about by a power
such as Goethe figures by the *Zeitgeist* or Time-
Spirit, and St. Paul describes as a divine power *revealing* additions to what we possess already.

The charge against Arnold of an uncritical progressivism
is, in my opinion, substantially just; and in this respect, as
in others, Arnold was very much a man of the mid-
nineteenth century and the Liberal Anglican philosophy
of history. It is a serious charge, nevertheless, because it
would seem to reveal his failure to recognize the profound
ironies and ambiguities of history, as well as the relativistic character of *any and all* cultural revolutions or new intellectual paradigm changes. The first charge will hold, I
believe, but the second will not. For while Arnold assumes
that the movement of history is progressive, he explicitly
acknowledges—unlike Hegel in this regard—that while
his conceptions are "new and true and a genuine product
of the *Zeitgeist*," as historical forms of reconceiving the
tradition they are also partial and limited and will inevitably be superseded. This is evident in his defense of his
reading of St. Paul's doctrine against his critics. While he
argues that his interpretation of Paul is but the giving of
a plain, popular exposition of what "belongs to the *Zeitgeist*," that is, what is in the air, anticipated and prepared
for by others, nevertheless he wishes to make clear that

we by no means put forth our version of St. Paul's
line of thought as true, in the same fashion as Puritanism puts forth its *Scriptural Protestantism,* or
gospel as true. . . . Our rendering of St. Paul's
thought we conceive rather as a product of nature,
which has grown to be what it is and which will
grow more; which will not stand just as we now exhibit it, but which will gain some aspects which we
now fail to show in it, and will drop some which we
now give to it. . . . Thus we present our conceptions neither as something quite new nor as something quite true.

To appreciate his sense of the *Zeitgeist* and its hermeneutical significance for religion, one needs to grasp not only

Arnold's understanding of the limits of language but also his theory of the development of doctrine. (pp. 53-4)

Arnold had read Newman's *Essay on the Development of Christian Doctrine* prior to writing the essays that comprise **St. Paul and Protestantism,** and the impress of Newman's essay is evident in Arnold's argument. In November 1869 Arnold had written to his mother about the church "resting on Catholic antiquity, historic Christianity, development, and so on, which open to it an escape from all single doctrines as they are outgrown." He acknowledged that it was Newman who "has set forth, both persuasively and truly," a theory of development which no reading of church history could but convey. Arnold's choice of citations from Newman's *Essay* is instructive. They clearly reflect his own views and give important clues to the ideas that represent the ground principles of his hermeneutical program. Newman writes:

> We have to account for that apparent variation and growth of doctrine which embarrasses us when we would consult history for the true idea of Christianity. The increase and expansion of the Christian creed and ritual, and all the variations which have attended the process in the case of individual writers and churches, are the necessary attendants on any philosophy or polity which takes possession of the intellect and heart, and has any wide or extended dominion. From the nature of the human mind, time is necessary for the full comprehension and perfection of great ideas. The highest and most wonderful truths, though communicated to the world once for all by inspired teachers, could not be comprehended all at once by the recipients; but, as admitted and transmitted by minds not inspired, and through media which were human, have required only the longer time and deeper thought for their full elucidation. . . .

> Ideas may remain when the expression of them is indefinitely varied. Nay, one cause of corruption in religion is the refusal to follow the course of doctrine as it moves on, and an obstinacy in the notions of the past. So our Lord found his people precisians in their obedience to the letter, he condemned them for not being led on to its spirit—that is, its development. . . .

> It may be objected that inspired documents, such as the Holy Scriptures, at once determine doctrine without further trouble. But they were intended to create *an idea,* and that idea is not in the sacred text, but in the mind of the reader; and the question is, whether that idea is communicated to him in its completeness and minute accuracy on its first apprehension, or expands in his heart and intellect, and comes to perfection in the course of time.

In these citations one can see *in nuce* several of the ideas that are formative in Arnold's working out of his own very different religious apologetic: that time is necessary for the full comprehension and perfection of ideas; that doctrines may be expressed with infinite variation, and therefore it is false to "rivet" doctrines to past formulations; and that in Newman's notion of the "idea" of Christianity one discerns the abiding truth within the flux of history. According to Newman, the development of Christian doctrine moves, in the first instance, from implicit, nonreflexive beliefs to the explicit articulation in doctrine. However, there remains the further historical stage of doctrinal ex-

pansion and elaboration, and, for Newman, in this process there is never a complete delineation of the idea of Christianity. Doctrinal development never reaches some exact linguistic completion; and yet, through the shifting historical process, the essential identity and continuity of the Christian idea remains.

Arnold had a far more radical sense than did Newman of the historical contingency of all dogma and was more sensitive to what he considered false developments. Nevertheless, he believed in the continuity of the Christian idea through the relativities of historical process and change. (pp. 54-6)

Arnold was confirmed in the belief that time and historical experience are the friends, not the enemies, of the spiritual life, and that this implies that the full elucidation and truth of religious doctrines cannot be contained within any particular formulation of the past. Religious doctrines must remain open to further adaptation required by time's ever-variable course, open to what [Alfred] Loisy called "the constantly changing condition of human life and intelligence." The fact that Arnold acted on his belief in doctrinal adaptation has caused critics to assert that he abandoned *historical* Christianity. Often associated with this charge is the further claim that in Arnold's symbolic reinterpretation of key Christian doctrines the words are stretched to the point that any common signification between the traditional words and their new use no longer obtains. These are important charges which demand attention.

First, can Arnold's symbolic reinterpretation lay claim to represent *historical* Christianity? Leslie Stephen, among others, asserted that it could not. If Arnold wished to gain for the Church of England the place in English national life that he desired, Stephen maintained he must "restore the feeling and the beliefs which were current two centuries ago"—"a task of some little difficulty," Stephen acknowledged. For those who hold the position here represented by Stephen, there can be no development; Anglican Christianity must literally subscribe to the verbal formularies as commonly understood by the seventeenth-century divines. Surprisingly, this static, unhistorical form of criticism is even today frequently directed at Arnold. It appears to be implied, for example, in A. O. J. Cockshut's comment that, while Arnold's system is profoundly religious, it is "not in any acceptable historical sense, Christian." But what notion of "historical sense" is at work here?

The issue can perhaps best be focused by posing the following question: Can Christian belief and practice be identified with any particular past age of the Christian church—e.g., with primitive Christianity (whatever that was), with the fifth century, the thirteenth or sixteenth centuries, with the formularies of the seventeenth-century Anglican divines? Arnold's answer is *no.* It is the answer of every Alfred Loisy, of Adolf von Harnack, of Ernst Troeltsch; it is the answer of every historian of Christian origins and doctrine trained in and committed to modern historiographical work. For to refuse to answer no is to be required to select some period of the past as *the* primitive or *the* classical expression of *historical* Christianity. To do so is to "rivet" Christian belief and practice to a particular linguistic and cultural formulation expressive of a distinctive anthropology, cosmology, or world view. It is to fail to take seriously the historicity of conceptual forms or to acknowledge the fundamental hermeneutical significance of the modern revolutions in epistemology and historical consciousness. It is to fail to take seriously A. N. Whitehead's insight that one cannot claim absolute finality for a dogma without claiming commensurate finality for the sphere of thought within which it arose. (pp. 59-60)

Christianity is not, as Whitehead wisely remarked, a metaphysics; it is rather a community of faith and a way of life in search of a metaphysics or a coherent set of doctrines that by their nature involve ever new reconceptions.

This raises, however, another related question that is a more difficult matter. Assuming recognition of the fact of a development of doctrine and practice, what about the continuity of language and meaning between past and present formulations of belief? What, if any, are the acceptable limits of the use and reconception of Christian language in the evolution of belief? The issue is well stated by Renford Bambrough in a discussion of Arnold and reinterpretation:

> It seems at least at first sight that there is an important parallel between what is done by Arnold . . . and what is done by Euripides, and there is room for the same doubt in the case of . . . Arnold as there is in the case of Euripides: a doubt as to whether what is now being affirmed is what it purports to be; a suspicion that the use of traditional words has now been carried so far away from the original and basic use that an element of deception or at least self-deception is involved in the use of old words for the expression of the new belief.

Arnold played a key role in provoking this suspicion and in setting the terms of the debate over the symbolic interpretation of the Bible and the creeds that was to occupy theologians and ecclesiastics in England for decades after 1870. He was to exert a personal influence on a number of the English Modernists writing between 1880 and 1920 on the question of symbolism in doctrinal formulation and on the function of creeds.

The Church of England reached something of an official consensus on the question of symbolic interpretation with the appearance of the Report of the Commission on Doctrine in the Church of England (1938). The commission had been appointed by Archbishop Davidson in 1922 and included many eminent theologians, representing all schools of thought in the church. The Report proposed the following hermeneutical rule:

> Statements affirming particular facts may be found to have value as pictorial expressions of spiritual truths, even though the supposed facts did not actually happen. . . . It does not appear possible to delimit with finality or precision the extent to which symbolic elements of this . . . kind may enter into the historic tradition of the Christian faith. The possibility cannot be excluded that in this sense also a symbolic character may attach to the truth of articles in the Creeds. It is not therefore of necessity illegitimate to accept and affirm particular clauses of the Creeds while understanding them in this symbolic sense.

What is implied in the church's position is the recognition that the ethical question of the veracity of belief is dependent on the theological interpretation of the particular belief, which in turn is subject to the judgment of criticism that frequently demands to be open-ended. Symbolic interpretation reflects the recognition of that fact. Does this mean that there are no limits, that the future development of belief is radically open-ended? The Report attempted to answer this by establishing a new interpretive fence: "In some cases the use of traditional phrases is censured as dishonest. This charge could only be sustained if the traditional phrase is being used in a sense wholly different from that originally conveyed by it. The reason for the continued use of such phrases is that *there is a core of identical meaning.*"

Arnold would have approved the commission's insistence on a core of identical meaning. There is ample evidence that his own reinterpretation of Christianity involved symbolic interpretations of doctrines such as the virgin birth, the resurrection, and the last judgment—in a number of instances strikingly similar to those proposed by the Anglican and Catholic Modernists. However, Arnold would have wished to go beyond the commission's Report. Many of the Anglican Modernists insisted on maintaining the formularies and creeds of the Church as long as their use was accompanied by a relaxing of subscription and a wide latitude of interpretation. In this respect Arnold's position is more radical, for, while advocating symbolic interpretation, he also calls for setting aside the creeds as liturgically *essential* and theologically *normative.* Here his position is more akin to that of the English liberals and Modernists influenced by the German historians Adolf von Harnack and Ernst Troeltsch.

Arnold believed that for the true elucidation of certain questions involving philosophic or scientific-historical criticism "time and favorable developing conditions are confessedly necessary." "Surely," he insists, "historic criticism, criticism of style, criticism of nature, no one would go to the early or middle ages of the Church for illumination on these matters." Of a true criticism of nature or history the early

> Church had no means of solving either the one problem or the other. And this from no fault at all of the Church, but for the same reason that she was unfitted to solve a difficulty in Aristotle's "Physics" or Plato's "Timaeus," and to determine the historical value of Herodotus or Livy; simply from the natural operation of the law of development, which for success in philosophy and criticism requires certain conditions, that in the early and medieval Church were not to be found.

Arnold would have agreed with Harnack's judgment that "the gospel did not enter the world as a statutory religion and can therefore have no classical and permanent manifestation in any form of intellectual or social expression, not even in the first one." Harnack wrote his learned and massive 12-volume *Dogmengeschichte* to demonstrate that "the history of dogma furnishes the most suitable means for the liberation of the church from dogmatic Christianity." For Harnack believed, as did Arnold, that the essence of Christianity is not coincident with either the apostolic witness or with those doctrines later hammered out in church councils. These are forms which, needless to say, have played their role in protecting and transmitting the Christian gospel, but they are not that gospel. Of these various historical forms Harnack wrote:

Either Christianity is . . . identical with its first form (in this case, one is forced to conclude that it came and went at a certain time) or *it contains something which remains valid in historically changing forms.* Starting with the beginnings, church history shows that it was necessary for "early Christianity" to perish in order that "Christianity" might remain. So, too, there *followed,* later on, one metamorphosis upon another.

Harnack concluded that a historical understanding of Christianity requires that one make an effort to separate the distinctive essence or continuum of this great historical phenomenon from the doctrinal forms in which it has been variously clothed. This he attempted in *Wesen des Christentums,* as did Arnold a quarter century earlier in **Literature and Dogma.** Both books were bold attempts at reconstruction or, better, at historical development by pruning. Both were efforts at criticism as a historical responsibility.

What sets apart the approach of Arnold, Harnack, or Troeltsch from that of either traditional Protestantism or Catholicism is the fact that for them modern experience and knowledge enter into the consideration of the development of doctrine as genuine coefficients. That is, certain presuppositions with regard to the warrants of critical judgment enter *materially* into any theological reconstruction. Hermeneutically it implies acceptance of the modern cognitional revolution in historical consciousness, Foucault's *mutation epistemologique.* Historical consciousness denies any classical normative form or doctrine for articulating the nature or essence of Christianity, namely, the gospel. Rather, it affirms that the expression of that essence always appears in forms shaped by the historical *Zeitgeist.*

Are there, then, no theological norms? If not, would it not imply such a radical accommodation to modernity that the ever-changing *Zeitgeist* (i.e., culture) becomes, in fact, the substantive norm? The worry is expressed in David De Laura's judgment about Arnold's hermeneutic: "The churches, quite literally, have no mind of their own. . . . Christianity must submit and adapt itself to the 'developing' and (presumably) changing standards of the 'philosophy and criticism' of each age for any metaphysical description of the reality that Christianity admittedly speaks to."

Some clarifications are here in order. For Arnold, as for Harnack and Troeltsch, Christianity must indeed adapt in view of changes that take place in philosophy and criticism. But this, of course, is what it has done throughout its history; for, as Harnack demonstrated, early Christianity had to perish, as did the substance philosophy of the Church Fathers of Nicaea and Chalcedon and the Aristotelian categories of the Scholastics, in order that Christianity might live during new epistemic mutations. Here culture is a formative factor, but it is not the substantive norm.

Arnold recognized a tension and discontinuity that exist between culture and that continuum or essence of Christianity which remains valid in historically changing forms. The continuum or essence was what he sought to bring out in **Literature and Dogma,** although, as with Harnack, the articulation of such an essence meant the historical risk of "assuming the royal function of a judge." It involved an

act of deconstruction in which the literal antique reading is seen as a debasement of the essential spiritual or metaphoric meaning. Arnold recognized that the transformations which Christianity has undergone, and will undergo in the future, may efface any obvious or homogeneous continuity with the antique doctrinal formulations; on the other hand, these transformations may make the real continuity transparent. In any case, the essence or continuum is not coextensive with or reducible to any single historical formulation. In his important essay "What Does 'Essence of Christianity' Mean?" Troeltsch speaks of the normative essence of Christianity in terms that illuminate Arnold's position:

> One of the main difficulties is the definition of this continuum itself, the connecting unity in this multiplicity of formations developing out of the original form. This continuum can of course neither simply be taken from the preaching of Jesus as being that major part of it which persists through all times, nor can it be in the generic character of that which all the formulations of Christianity have in common. Then again this continuum by no means consists in an idea which can be briefly formulated in a simple main idea, but in a spiritual power. . . . The essence has to be an entity with an inner, living flexibility, and a productive power for new creation and assimilation. It cannot be characterized at all by one word or one doctrine, but only by a concept which includes from the start both flexibility and richness; *it must be a developing spiritual principle,* a germinative idea . . . not a metaphysical or dogmatic idea, but a driving spiritual force.

Arnold saw the essence of Christianity as such a source and such a power, a source and power capable of adapting and assimilating themselves to continuous historical change. To return to the original worry, expressed by Bambrough, Arnold would reply that in the case of symbolic interpretation it is, of course, possible to stretch words beyond their ancient use so as to court both deception and self-deception. But such reinterpretation does not, as such, involve dissembling. Arnold would argue that only if the metaphysical conceptions or historical forms of the ancient creedal statements are accepted as normative does a problem arise. The future may, however—on the grounds of historical-critical research or religious experience—controvert any notion of homogeneous continuity with these past conceptions since the substantive norm, the continuum of belief, the essence of Christianity, is not synonymous with these ancient doctrinal conceptions. On the other hand, a truly imaginative act of interpretation may disclose the original meaning of Jesus' logia, lost on the literalizing reporters and redactors.

A further consideration, nevertheless, remains. If Arnold believed that modern critical judgment is necessary and formative, was he not guilty or at least susceptible of subsuming religion, in this case Christianity, within culture or the *Zeitgeist*? Arnold's understanding of the relations between religion and culture needs to be examined to see if this sheds additional light on these questions.

Critics from J. C. Shairp to T. S. Eliot have asserted that Arnold does subsume religion within culture—i.e., that "literature, or Culture, tended with Arnold to usurp the place of Religion." I believe that a careful reading of Arnold's developing idea of culture and its relation to religion will demonstrate the fundamental error of these

Arnold about 1860.

race has manifested its impulse to perfect itself," nevertheless "religion comes to a conclusion identical with that which culture—culture seeking the determination of this question through *all* the voices of human experience . . . —likewise reaches." Here the ideal of religion coincides with that of culture. They both perceive the character of perfection as "not a having and a resting, but a growing and a becoming." Arnold goes further and predicts that "the idea of a human nature perfect on all sides, which is the dominant idea of poetry . . . is destined, adding to itself the religious idea of a devout energy, to transform *and govern* the other."

Between the delivery of this, his final lecture as Professor of Poetry, and the commencement of the decade devoted to the writing of his four books on religion, several events had joined to give Arnold pause in commending his Hellenic ideal. Thus while he found many of the replies to **"Culture and Its Enemies"** off the mark and even amusing, some of them cut to the quick and forced him to clarify his definition of culture and its perfection. With Kierkegaardian sarcasm Frederic Harrison had mocked Arnold's culture, which "sits high aloft with pouncet-box to spare her senses ought unpleasant" while "death, sin, cruelty stalk amongst us." Henry Sidgwick was even more severe. He charged Arnold with a refined and supercilious eudaemonism. Life confronts us with a fundamental conflict. "On the one hand," wrote Sidgwick, "are the claims of harmonious self-development, on the other are the cries of struggling humanity." The former, he observed, does not crush our sympathies; no, far worse, it only represses them, keeps them safely at arm's length. But what the nation requires, Sidgwick angrily admonished, is a work that "must be done as self-sacrifice, not as self-development."

It was impossible, Arnold responded, "that all these remonstrances and reproofs should not affect me." In fact, they gave him the golden opportunity "to profit by the objections" and to expand—to five succeeding articles—and to revise and clarify what he had said in **"Culture and Its Enemies."** The result was ***Culture and Anarchy,*** published in 1869.

In this book Arnold takes pains to clarify that his ideal of culture, of perfection, has nothing to do with an aloof, Paterian aestheticism or with the suppression of the social sympathies. "Perfection, as culture conceives it," he writes,

> is not possible while the individual remains isolated. The individual is required, under pain of being stunted and enfeebled in his own development if he disobeys, to carry others along with him in his march towards perfection. . . . The idea of perfection as a *general* expansion of the human family is at variance with our strong individualism . . . [with] our maxim "every man for himself."

The effort which Arnold makes to bring home this point accentuates the perversity of T. S. Eliot's criticism that the "thinness which Arnold's 'culture' conveys to a modern reader is partly due to the absence of social background to his picture." To claim that Arnold's culture recommends a selfish personal cultivation or that society must wait upon the process of the individual's self-perfection only can be, as Raymond Williams has remarked, "a deliberate misunderstanding" if, indeed, Arnold has been read. Williams rightly places Arnold's discussion of cul-

charges and will clarify his position with regard to Christianity's real autonomy and the place of theological norms.

The careless and partisan allegations of Eliot and others have done much mischief. They have focused on passages in the essays of the 1860s in which Arnold appears to be saying that religion simply subserves culture. However, as David DeLaura has shown, from 1867 onward Arnold draws back from any notion of religion as simply ministering to other more important ends. The writings reveal a growing awareness of the tension and dialectic between religion and culture. Finally, in Arnold's mature writings on religion culture clearly becomes ancillary to religion, although the agency of imagination and criticism remains indispensable for the hermeneutical task of religious understanding and reconstruction.

In January 1865 Arnold wrote to his mother expressing what was by then his often-voiced dislike of "all overpreponderance of single elements," and avowing that his efforts now "are directed to enlarge and complete us." This pledge was central to his purpose in the farewell lecture delivered at Oxford in June 1867, namely, to declare "culture as having its origin in the love of perfection." In this address, entitled **"Culture and Its Enemies,"** later revised and published as the first chapter of ***Culture and Anarchy,*** Arnold asserts that while religion is "the greatest and most important of the efforts by which the human

ture in the wider context of his life: "Those who accuse him of a policy of 'cultivated inaction' forget not only his arguments but his life. . . . *Culture and Anarchy* needs to be read alongside the reports, minutes, evidence to commissions, and specifically educational essays which made up so large a part of Arnold's working life."

In *Culture and Anarchy* Arnold specifically takes care to address the charges of aestheticism and a self-indulgent individualism that had been made against **"Culture and Its Enemies."** The book also displays a greater balance and sense of tension in Arnold's perception of the relations between culture and religion. Hellenism is now clearly balanced by Hebraism, or what Arnold calls "self-conquest, self-devotion, the following not our own individual will, but the will of God, obedience"—in other words, Sidgwick's work of self-sacrifice. Moreover, Arnold's Hellenic ideal, sweetness and light, becomes more dominantly the intellectual standard of light: "Sweetness and light evidently have to do with the bent or side of humanity which we call Hellenic. Greek intelligence has obviously for its essence the instinct for what Plato calls the true, firm intelligible law of things; the law of light, of seeing things as they are." For even Greek art, "Greek beauty, have their root in the same impulse to see things as they really are, inasmuch as Greek art and beauty rest on fidelity to nature."

Throughout *Culture and Anarchy* the tension and balance between "the scientific passion as well as the passion for doing good," between Bishop Wilson's dual reason and the will of God are essentially sustained. "Hebraism and Hellenism are, neither of them, *the* law of human development, as their admirers are prone to make them; they are, each of them, *contributions* to human development." Different times and circumstances will, of course, mean that one ideal will become preponderant over the other and, inevitably, presume itself to be *the* law of human perfection.

> But sooner or later it becomes manifest that when the two sides of humanity proceed in this fashion of alternative preponderance, and not of mutual understanding and balance, the side which is uppermost does not really provide in a satisfactory manner for the needs of the side which is undermost. . . . The true and smooth order of humanity's development is not reached in either way. And therefore, while we willingly admit with the Christian apostle that the world by wisdom,—that is by the isolated preponderance of its intellectual impulses—knew not God, or the true order of things, it is yet necessary, also, to set up a sort of converse to this proposition, and to say likewise (what is equally true) that the world by Puritanism knew not God. And it is on this converse of the apostles' proposition that is particularly needful to insist in our own country just at present.

Sidgwick's demand for fire and strength rather than sweetness and light only proves to Arnold that Sidgwick has forgotten "that the world is not all of one piece, and every piece with the same needs at the same time." The Roman world in the infancy of the Christian church or French society in the eighteenth century may have needed fire and strength. "But can it be said," asks Arnold, "that the Barbarians who overran the empire needed fire and strength even more than sweetness and light; or that the Puritans needed them more; or that Mr. Murphy, the Birmingham

lecturer, and his friends, need them more?" While it is true that there is no *unum necessarium,* no one thing needful, which can free human nature, still what Sidgwick overlooks and what Arnold wished to bring home is that while Hellenism is not "always for everybody more wanted than Hebraism . . . for Mr. Murphy at this particular moment, and for the great majority of us his fellow-countrymen, it is more wanted!"

In the years between the completion of *Culture and Anarchy* and the writing of *Literature and Dogma,* Arnold remained a believer in culture but, as in the case of his liberalism, one "tempered by experience, reflection, and renouncement." Religion and conduct now begin to emerge as the larger and more important part of life. While Hellenism remains indispensable to the flowering of whatever is to be genuinely human, the emphasis now begins to shift to its special function in the service of religion. First, it serves as the instrument of intellectual discrimination: "Culture or 'letters' is again a form of 'criticism' exhibited in 'justness of perception,' 'tact' and a 'sense' of history—in short the right method or instrument for reading religious documents." Furthermore, culture serves, in the form of imagination, poetry, and emotion, as a means of "lighting up morality," of supplying the mythopoetic language, imagery, and feeling by means of which certain great religious ideas alone can properly be grasped and expressed.

The hermeneutical role of culture, in terms of both intellectual discrimination and imagination, became *the* pressing matter for Arnold in his effort after 1868 to sustain the Bible and Christian belief in an age of the apotheosis of science. In November 1870 he writes to his mother lamenting how little the English Bible-reading public derived from their study, and "how much more profit they would get from this Bible reading if they combined it with other things, and other things with it." Arnold's challenge to the Dissenters in *St. Paul and Protestantism* diverts attention from his chief concern, which was to show how their cultural provinciality and their false reading of St. Paul and the Bible were inextricably connected. The relationship is fully elaborated in the preface to *Literature and Dogma.*

There he shows that the received theology had failed in its efforts to bring the Bible to the people because the construction which it placed on the Scriptures was "rigid, fixed, and scientific." It was a false construction that could not be put right without the aid of culture, for it was this very absence of culture—i.e., criticism and imagination—which disposed men "to conclude at once, from any imperfection or fallibility in the Bible, that it was a priestly imposture."

By culture Arnold here means intellectual breadth, "the acquainting ourselves with the best that has been known and said in the world, and thus with the history of the human spirit." Such an acquaintance involves, of course, knowledge of how men have thought and expressed themselves, but it includes also "not only knowledge but right tact and justness of judgment," which turns out to be "in relation to the Bible, getting the power, through reading, to estimate the proportion and relation in what we read." For "if we read but a very little, we naturally want to press it all; if we read a great deal, we will be willing not to press the whole of what we read, and we learn what ought to be pressed and what not."

It is not, then, simply reading a great deal that Arnold counsels and that ensures a just criticism, for culture implies breadth of learning and experience. A specialist such as D. F. Strauss may skillfully apply negative criticism to the Bible, but, Arnold insists, the reality of the Bible requires a richer, deeper, more imaginative mind. It requires the quality of mind that Arnold calls "justness of perception" and for the possession of which no mere specialist training is a guarantee. Arnold insists that true culture and a genuine criticism include both a knowledge of the facts and a justness of perception that come only from wide and sympathetic experience.

Literature and Dogma is witness to the fact that for Arnold religion in no sense merely subserves culture. What Arnold is insistent to maintain is that any sane and true reading of the Bible, and thus any authentic as well as relevant religious interpretation, requires the hermeneutical interdependence of religious text and "critical tact" and that the latter can come only from a wide experience of how men have thought and expressed themselves. (pp. 61-71)

Matthew Arnold insisted that putting a right construction on the Bible, like the development of human perfection, requires culture. The key to his understanding of the interdependence of religion and culture is therefore to be found in the tension, counterpoise, and harmony of "all the voices of human experience" which can save us from that narrow, rigid, and, finally, false understanding that comes from imagining that we are in possession of the "one thing needful."

Attention to this point will result in a more accurate reading of that *locus classicus* referred to so often by critics who insist that Arnold's culture usurps the place of religion. This passage in **"Culture and Its Enemies,"** which has already been referred to, speaks of perfection as "the harmonious expansion of *all* the powers which make the beauty and worth of human nature," an expansion "not consistent with the overdevelopment of any one power at the expense of the rest." Arnold concludes that "here culture goes beyond religion, as religion is generally conceived by us." If read with due attention to the two critical qualifiers, even this seemingly damning passage cannot be interpreted as proposing culture's usurpation of religion. Arnold is saying that the overdevelopment of any one power is not consistent with culture's love of perfection only when it is accomplished *at the expense of the rest.* Hebraism may well have been in need of overdevelopment in Leo X's court at the time of the Reformation; but this is certainly not the case in Edward Miall's editorial room in the Dissenting Midlands of Victorian England. In the case of Miall, such an overdevelopment is at the expense of beauty and a sense of history. The religion, then, that culture—as the harmonious expansion of all our powers—"goes beyond" is the religion "as *is generally conceived by us,*" that is to say, the religion of the Dissenters, the religion that crushes or denies the operation of historical knowledge, imagination, or beauty in the religious life.

True religion, which, Arnold maintains, is "the greater part of life," will always remain dependent on these Hellenic ideals. In *Literature and Dogma,* for instance, Arnold claims much more for religion—"six-eighths of life, while art and science are only two-eighths." And yet, he adds, "the world cannot do without art and science." Ar-

nold did not believe that culture would or should usurp the place of religion or that religion simply subserves culture. Their true relationship and interdependence is indicated in his preface to **Last Essays on Church and Religion:**

> Christianity will find the ways for its own future. What is certain is that it will not disappear. Whatever progress may be made in science, art, and literary culture—however much higher, more general, and more effective than at present the value for them may become—Christianity will still be there as what these rest against and imply; as the indispensable background, the *three-fourths of life.* It is true, while the remaining fourth is ill-cared for, the three-fourths themselves must also suffer with it. But this does but bring us to the old and true Socratic thesis of the interdependence of virtue and knowledge.

(pp. 71-2)

If Arnold were to be placed in a comparative typology of positions regarding the relations between Christianity and culture—for example, as delineated in the work of Ernst Troeltsch and H. R. Niebuhr—he would stand with those mediating thinkers who reject both the positions of those who see Christianity in sharp antithesis to culture and those who call for a radical accommodation of Christianity to culture. Like Arnold, the mediating thinkers recognize both the incommensurability of Christianity and culture and, at the same time, their critical interdependence. They see Christ as "the fulfillment of cultural aspirations and the restorer of the institutions of a true society. Yet there is in him something that neither arises out of culture nor contributes directly to it. He is discontinuous as well as continuous with social life and its culture."

It is in this tradition, which recognizes the unique and inescapable authority of both religion and culture and yet their essential interdependence, that Arnold must be placed. Modern critical judgment must be engaged in the interpretive task, but that is not to confuse it with the substantive norm, the essence of Christianity. (p. 73)

> *James C. Livingston, " 'To Make Reason and the Will of God Prevail': Arnold on Religion and Culture," in his* Matthew Arnold and Christianity: His Religious Prose Writings, *University of South Carolina Press, 1986, pp. 47-74.*

John Woolford   (essay date 1986)

[*In the following essay, Woolford evaluates the relation of Arnold's poetic discourse to the Romantic conception of the sublime, asserting that Arnold's poetry displays an inversion of the Romantic notion of the sublime suffering experienced by the creative genius.*]

> Years went on, and his friends became conspicuous authors or statesmen; but Joubert remained in the shade. His constitution was of such fragility that how he lived so long, or accomplished so much as he did, is a wonder: his soul had, for its basis of operations, hardly any body at all: both from his stomach and from his chest he seems to have had constant suffering, though he lived by rule, and was as abstemious as a Hindoo. Often, after overwork in thinking, reading, or talking, he remained for

days together in a state of utter prostration,—condemned to absolute silence and inaction; too happy if the agitation of his mind would become quiet also, and let him have the repose in which he stood in so much need. With this weakness of health, these repeated suspensions of energy, he was incapable of the prolonged contention of spirit necessary for the creation of great works.

This description of Joubert seems to typify certain recurring features of Arnold's perception of other writers of his own period. He favoured shy and reclusive merit. Like Joubert, Maurice de Guerin 'remained in the shade', and 'died in the year 1839, at the age of 28 without having published anything'; Etienne de Senancour earned 'little celebrity in France, his own country; and out of France . . . is almost unknown'; Edward Quinillan evoked the comment:

> I saw him sensitive in frame,
>   I knew his spirits low;
> And wished him health, success and fame—
>   I do not wish it now.

The third line indicates how closely, for Arnold, obscurity, as the obverse of 'success and fame', was tied to illness, the obverse of 'health'; and the other figures I have mentioned were also diseased. Illness was the cause of early death for Guerin and Quinillan, and the constant affliction of the longer lives of Joubert, Senancour, and Heine, the subject of one of Arnold's most moving descriptions:

> In 1847 his health, which till then had always been perfectly good, gave way. He had a kind of paralytic stroke. His malady proved to be a softening of the spinal marrow: it was incurable; it made rapid progress. In May 1848, not a year after his first attack, he went out of doors for the last time; but his disease took more than eight years to kill him. For nearly eight years he lay helpless on a couch, with the use of his limbs gone, wasted almost to the proportions of a child, wasted so that a woman could carry him about; the sight of one eye lost, that of the other greatly dimmed, and requiring, that it might be exercised, to have the palsied eyelid lifted and held up by the finger; all this, and, besides this, suffering, at short intervals; paroxysms of nervous agony. I have said he was not pre-eminently brave; but in the astonishing force of spirit with which he retained his activity of mind, even his gaiety, amid all his suffering, and went on composing with undiminished fire to the last, he was truly brave.

The controlled crescendo of this passage, moving from the staccato opening sentences into longer ones, haunted by the stabbing repetitions of 'eight years' and 'wasted', and the carefully placed 'palsied', and the false pause before 'all this', and the subsequent addition of anguish to anguish, marks an unusual intensity of feeling, or at least an unusual rhetorical interest in incurable disease.

Of course, Heine was not, like the others, a little-known writer; yet in Arnold's sense he ought to have been. In calling him 'not pre-eminently brave', Arnold recalls the qualification with which he began the essay, and which, though never fully explicated, colours it throughout: that Heine lacked *courage,* the 'natural force', the 'inborn force and fire' pre-eminent in Byron; and that, lacking these qualities, he appears by comparison the diminutive figure which his illness actually made of him. This sense of being

crushed by a prestigious predecessor applies to other cases as well. Guerin comes under the malign and blighting influence of his Jesuit teacher Lammenais, who

> never appreciated Guerin; his combative, rigid, despotic nature, of which the characteristic was energy, had no affinity with Guerin's elusive, undulating, impalpable nature, of which the characteristic was delicacy.

These words might with equal aptness be applied to the relation between Quinillan, the minor poet, and his father-in-law Wordsworth, at whose contribution to Quinillan's decline Arnold glances in his **'Stanzas'.** In an obliquer fashion, Arnold regards Senancour too as threatened by the proximity of the mighty dyad of Wordsworth and Goethe, who, in company with Byron, are wheeled on time and again in Arnold's work to represent the giants before the flood, by comparison to whom modern writers appear paltry, shrill and insincere.

Various possible explanations of this complex of preoccupations in Arnold's work seem possible; here, I shall consider three. Figures like Guerin, Heine, Joubert, Senancour, Quinillan—at this point, Arnold's friend Clough might be added to the list—may be seen as representative fragments of Arnold's diagnosis of his own culture as diseased and deficient; as portraits, or even occult self-portraits, of the writer struggling to create in the wake of the giant flood of Romanticism; or as modifications of the Romantic sublime of suffering. Needless to say, these possibilities are intimately interconnected and in no way mutually exclusive.

> . . . this strange disease of modern life
> With its sick hurry, its divided aims. . . .

Arnold's diagnosis of his culture as inherently *ill* is famous, though hardly original. Elizabethan concepts of the 'body politic' mediated by, among others, Shakespeare in his history plays, had grounded the political process in metaphors of bodily health and sickness. Carlyle, following Hegel, expanded the metaphor within the context of a historical story built in phases or periods, an idea which his essay, 'Characteristics' definitively characterized for his Victorian disciples, including Arnold. Arnold's social polemic, as it developed during and after the 1860s, was based, indeed, upon criteria not very similar to Carlyle's, but relied on Carlyle's argument that English society of the nineteenth century was diseased and in need of cure. Like Carlyle, Arnold casts Goethe in the rôle of the physician who

> took the suffering human race,
> And read each wound, each weakness clear;
> And struck his finger on the place,
> And said: *Thou ailest here, and here!*

Wordsworth he saw as a 'healing power', the medicine, so to speak, prescribed by Goethe, Byron as a Titanic transformation of disease, the 'bleeding heart', into a 'pageant', a gigantic, near-tragic exhibition of power. But these various triumphs all depend upon living at the right time. Arnold qualifies his praise of Goethe in **'In Memory of the Author of "Obermann" '** with the comment,

> For though his manhood bore the blast
> Of a tremendous time,
> Yet in a tranquil world was passed

His tenderer youthful prime.

But we, brought forth and reared in hours
Of change, alarm, surprise—
What shelter to grow ripe is ours?
What leisure to grow wise?

Wordsworth's 'sweet calm', similarly, results from his cultivation of an artificial 'shelter' and 'leisure': sequestered in Nature, his 'eyes avert their ken / From half of human fate'. Senancour, who serves for Arnold as the Romantic who anticipates the central character of Arnold's own period, appears by comparison gripped by a disease he can neither escape, diagnose nor cure:

A fever in these pages burns
Beneath the calm they feign;
A wounded human spirit turns,
Here on its bed of pain.

In **'Obermann'**, Arnold is prepared to rank Senancour with Goethe and Wordsworth; his more usual response, however, is to superimpose a moral indictment of his age upon his Hegelian sense of it *as* an age, with a distinctive 'spirit'. Byron, the Romantic poet he felt closest to his own period's anguish (hence his omission from **'Obermann'**, where Senancour is credited with some of his characteristics), provokes the most agonizing contrasts:

And Byron! let us dare admire,
If not thy fierce and turbid song,
Yet that, in anguish, doubt, desire,
Thy fiery courage still was strong.

The sun that on thy tossing pain
Did with such cold derision shine,
He crushed thee not with his disdain—
He had his glow, and thou hadst thine.

Our bane, disguise it as we may,
Is weakness, is a faltering course.
Oh that past times could give our day,
Joined to its clearness, of their force!

'Courage', the title of this poem, will recall Arnold's critique of Heine; the elder Romantics epitomize 'courage', the will and power to be great; their successors evince 'weakness', they fold under the strain and exhibit pathos where only heroic strength will serve. As Arnold remarked in an MS note to **'Tristram and Iseult'**,

> The misery of the present age is not in the intensity of men's suffering—but in their incapacity to suffer, enjoy, feel at all, wholly and profoundly; in having their susceptibility eternally agacee by a continual dance of ever-changing objects.

Here the 'sick hurry' repeats itself within the individual mind as a shallowness which corresponds to and promotes the 'weakness' afflicting Victorian man.

Such comparisons—and they are very widespread in Arnold's work—lead naturally to my second hypothesis: that the 'illness' of Arnold's period is directly *caused* by the elder Romantics, whose greatness inflicts an irreparable 'anxiety of influence' upon their successors. It is certainly not difficult to rephrase Arnold's statements about Wordsworth, Byron and Goethe into confessions of such anxiety, or to interpret his own stylistic irresoluteness, his proclivity for pastiche of Romantic modes, as consequential evidence. The Freudian raw material which, for Bloom,

would underlie and promote influence-anxiety is richly prominent in Arnold's life, overwhelmed as he was, like his partial surrogate Clough, by Thomas Arnold's cult of conscience and duty. The **'Sohrab-Rustum'** story, with its father-son conflict and ironic victory to the father, or **'A Picture at Newstead'**, where the father stands mourning the idiocy he has himself inflicted on his son, are only the most obvious dramatizations of Arnold's sense of filial bondage. An even more extraordinary portrait of the resulting neurosis of inadequacy is found in his poem upon the death of an even closer surrogate than Clough, his brother Tom. Like so many of Arnold's figures, Tom died young, and died of a painful illness. Arnold waxes peevish on the feebleness of Tom and his wife, 'two jaded English', who, like the rest, 'never once possess [their] soul / Before [they] die'. It is an affront to their burial-places, India and the Mediterranean, that representatives of such an inadequate culture should usurp the place which rightfully belongs to 'Some sage to whom the world was dead', or 'Some grey crusading knight austere', or

Some youthful troubadour, whose tongue
Filled Europe once with his love-pain,
Who here outworn had sunk, and sung
His dying strain;

Some girl, who here from castle-bower,
With furtive step and cheeks of flame,
'Twixt myrtle-hedges all in flower
By moonlight came

To meet her private-lover's ship;
And from the wave-kissed marble stair
Beckoned him on, with quivering lip
And floating hair.

Allot complains that 'the Byronic romanticism of this [the last] vignette was outmoded even in 1859', but that seems to me to be the point: Arnold's list of heroic types is a sequence of Romantic vignettes whose very simplicity, crudity even, evinces a strength uncompromised by doubt or irony. The 'floating hair' of Arnold's girl adds to this strength the nuance that it might include that of the inspired poet of 'Kubla Khan', whose power has leaked away in the ignominious time to which Tom and his wife belong, rendering them unworthy tenants of the ground their bodies usurp:

But you—a grave for knight and sage,
Romantic, solitary, still,
O spent ones of a work-day age!
Befits you ill.

The only thing that saves this distinctly unamiable passage is its evident applicability to Arnold himself, its illustration of his own panic before the formidable adequacy of the 'Romantic' and 'solitary'.

But if, as I argue, Arnold's anxiety arises from the contrast between his own writing and that of the Romantics, what of his own contrast, most famously drawn in the 1853 **'Preface,'** between the writing of his own period and that of *classical* times? If there is a contradiction here, it arises from the very intensity of Arnold's anxiety about the Romantics, resulting in their displacement by the safer, less adjacent authority of the classics. But even in Arnold's own thought there is no necessity to suppose a real contradiction. As he makes clear in *On the Modern Spirit in Literature,* and, indeed, though obscurely, in [the critical preface of 1853], the characteristics of 'modernity' can be found flourishing in all historical epochs, including superficially 'classical' ones; conversely, the 'classical' virtues may and do appear in so-called 'Romantic' writers. So much (with reservations) Arnold himself concedes. What he is less ready to concede is that the quality for which he admires both Sophocles and Wordsworth, the quality which he christened with the ambiguous name 'the grand style', is not 'the calm, the cheerfulness, the disinterested objectivity', but an 'action' which is 'greater', 'personages' who are 'nobler', 'situations' which are 'more intense': in other words, the *sublime*, whether of classical or Romantic art. His uppermost sense is of the contrast between weakness and strength, and strength, the Longinian or Burkean Sublime, belongs—in different ways and degrees—to Sophocles, to Dante, to Shakespeare, to Milton, to Wordsworth, Byron and Goethe. It does not belong to any Victorian writer, and that, for Arnold, is the real contrast: between an enfeebled and emaciated present, a Heine, a Guerin, a Thyrsis writhing on his 'bed of pain', and the loftier anguish of their predecessors.

The third possibility I wish to consider is that the very 'weakness' of which Arnold complains, and the illness and obscurity which result from it, are precisely extensions of the sublimity which they appear, and appear to him, to compromise. In order to explain what I mean by this, I must describe what I call 'the sublime of suffering' in Romantic art.

Burke's theory of the sublime joins together the ideas of suffering, solitude and infinity with that of power. Having argued that negative experiences like *'pain, sickness,* and *death'*, and the so-called negative emotions, such as grief, are sources of pleasure to the mind contemplating or experiencing them, he introduces his principal subject in these terms:

> Whatever is fitted in any sort to excite the ideas of pain, and danger, that is to say, whatever is in any sort terrible, or is conversant about terrible objects, or operates in a manner analogous to terror, is a source of the *sublime*.

He explains that the reason behind this apparently perverse delight in suffering is its proximity to an idea of *power*:

> I know of nothing sublime which is not some modification of power. . . . pain is always inflicted by a power in some way superior, because we never submit to pain willingly. So that strength, violence, pain and terror, are ideas that rush in upon the mind together.

The pleasure derives, however, not from submission to power, but from identification with it:

> Now whatever either on good or upon bad grounds tends to raise a man in his own opinion, produces a sort of swelling and triumph that is extremely grateful to the human mind; and this swelling is never more perceived, nor operates with more force, than when without danger we are conversant with terrible objects, the mind always claiming to itself some part of the dignity and importance of the things which it contemplates.

Logically, this 'swelling' becomes greatest when the object contemplated is omnipotence, or 'infinity': 'hardly any thing can strike the mind with its greatness, which does not make some sort of approach towards infinity.' And this is not only because infinity is the most gigantic thing we can conceive, but also because it is the *obscurest,* the most intellectually inaccessible. Burke remarks, 'To make any thing very terrible, obscurity seems in general to be necessary.' Therefore it is precisely the fact that 'there is nothing of which we really understand so little' which makes 'The ideas of eternity, and infinity, . . . among the most affecting we have'.

Commentators have not failed to note the importance of the Burkean sublime in Romantic thought, yet I am not sure it has been given its full weight. It figures, for Wordsworth, Coleridge, Byron, Shelley, and De Quincey, less as a repertoire of effects than as a definition of the poetic imagination itself as a dark, demonic power born of pain. Such a definition emerges plainly from two passages, one by Wordsworth, the other by Byron (for Arnold, the two greatest, and, more importantly, the definitive English Romantics). The first is a speech from *The Borderers,* Wordsworth's abortive early drama, a speech which reappears as the epigraph to a crucial poem in his development, 'The White Doe of Rylstone':

> Action is transitory—a step, a blow,
> The motion of a muscle—this way or that—
> 'Tis done; and in the after-vacancy
> We wonder at ourselves like men betrayed:
> Suffering is permanent, obscure and dark,
> And has the nature of infinity.

This passage gathers together most of Burke's criteria for the sublime. Suffering is 'dark', it is 'obscure'; most importantly, and also, in a sense, consequently, it 'has the nature of infinity'. Only the antithesis to 'action' is not directly borrowed from Burke, but that too is implicit in Burke's distinction between the *solitude* necessary for the sublime, and the essentially *social* character which the 'beautiful' derives from its basis in sexual attraction. Action is social; suffering, as it is inherently internal, isolates the sufferer and may end by denying the social altogether.

The latter point is reinforced in another major statement of the sublime, the final speech in Byron's *Manfred.* Manfred addresses it to the spirits who have arrived to conduct him to Hell:

> Thou hast no power upon me, *that* I feel;
> Thou never shalt possess me, *that* I know:
> What I have done is done; I bear within
> A torture which could nothing gain from thine.
> The mind which is immortal makes itself
> Requital for its good and evil thoughts,
> Is its own origin of ill and end,
> And its own place and time.

Manfred states here what is in effect an absolute independence of what he calls 'the fleeting things without', an absolute solitude, a solitude produced by 'torture' and productive of an entire self-creation. The cause of Manfred's suffering is never made explicit, remaining, as Wordsworth would say, 'obscure', and that obscurity both prevents it from competing with the sublime mind's self-origination and adds a dimension to the 'immortal' stature of that mind by equating it, in Burke's terms, with the mystery of infinitude.

Only suffering, then, brings about 'the repetition in the finite mind of the infinite I AM', as the human mind produces what Burke calls 'the artificial infinite' by 'claiming to itself some part of the dignity and importance of the things'—Burke calls them 'terrible objects'—'which it contemplates'. Hence, for example, the Romantic fascination with storm and tempest; agents of destruction, they become, in the mind's identification with them, premises of creation. Shelley's west wind is 'destroyer and preserver both' not because its ferocity prefaces spring as well as concluding summer, but because its power stings the contemplating mind into a rivalry—'Be thou me, impetuous one'—which is the precondition of creative effort. Burke argues that 'a state of rest or inaction' will produce 'melancholy, dejection, despair, and often self-murder' unless counterbalanced by 'exercise or labour'; but 'labour' is not the antithesis of suffering, but a creative form of it: 'labour is a surmounting of difficulties, an exertion of the contracting power of the muscles; and as such resembles pain.' It is creative labour, as a counterpart to suffering rather than its anodyne, that involves the Romantic imagination in the toil of poetic creation.

Arnold's relation to the Romantic sublime of suffering is a highly complex one. In **'A Summer Night',** he presents a portrait of what Allott calls 'the Romantic poet-outlaw' in a spectacular apotheosis of storm, suffering and effort:

> And then the tempest strikes him; and between
> The lightning-bursts is seen
> Only a driving wreck,
> And the pale master on his spar-strewn deck
> With anguished face and flying hair
> Grasping the rudder hard,
> Still bent to some port he knows not where,
> Still standing for some false impossible shore.

Allott is right to note the debt to *Adonais,* but in the 'pale master' Arnold has added to Shelley's picture a purely Byronic image of resistance and defiance. There is an even more striking resemblance to a passage Arnold probably never read, the 'analogy' sequence in the 1804 *Prelude,* where Wordsworth, to illustrate the nature of the poetic imagination, adduces a series of calamitous images of storm and shipwreck: of Dampier, confronted by

> the sea
> Roaring and whitening at the night's approach,
> And danger coming on

—danger, which for 'Sir Humphrey Gilbert, that bold voyager', takes the similar shape of a 'furious storm' in which 'The ship and he a moment afterwards' were 'Engulphed and seen no more'. Wordsworth comments that

> Kindred power
> Was present for the suffering and distress
> In those who read the story at their ease,

and his phrasing links writer, reader and subject in a common apothesis of the sublime of suffering in calamitous death. But Wordsworth broke off and abandoned this draft, perhaps in alarm at the demonic character imputed to the imagination by such analogies; Arnold's revulsion, despite what Allott calls 'some involuntary admiration', arises from embarrassment at the ritual strength evinced by his Romantic mariner, whom he calls a 'madman'. The alternative is to abandon resistance, and adopt what Wordsworth himself calls a 'wise passiveness'. But in the 1853 **'Preface'** Arnold rejects this in turn:

What then are the situations, from the representation of which, though accurate, no poetical enjoyment can be derived? They are those in which the suffering finds no vent in action; in which a continuous state of mental distress is prolonged, unrelieved by incident, hope, or resistance; in which there is everything to be endured, and nothing to be done. In such situations there is inevitably something morbid, in the description of them something monotonous.

The echo of Wordsworth's terms, with their echo, in turn, of Burke's, indicates that this statement repudiates the sublime of suffering, despite the apparent contrast between the convulsed effort of Arnold's 'poet-outlaw' and the absence of 'incident, hope, or resistance' which he cites in the **'Preface.'** But the contrast is more apparent than real. In **'A Summer Night'** the 'morbid' and 'monotonous' suffering mentioned in the **'Preface'** appears as the dreary tribulations of ordinary Victorian men, living 'in the sun's hot eye' 'in a brazen prison', who 'languidly / Their lives to some unmeaning taskwork give'. As this state protracts itself 'year after year',

> Gloom settles slowly down over their breast;
> And while they try to stem
> The waves of mournful thought by which they are pressed,
> Death in their prison reaches them.

A comparison of the language of this passage with that describing the shipwreck of the 'poet-outlaw' shows that the two conditions are tied more closely together than they seem; both suffer 'gloom' and experience the oppression of 'waves'; the difference is merely that for the Romantic 'madman' these are externalized into spectacular and sublime apparitions, while for the wretched 'slave' they are purely internal. This covert bond specifies the real nature of the relation between the Romantic and the modern for Arnold. Both suffer, and suffer analogous anguish. But the Romantic experiences, or transforms his suffering into an encounter with the spectacular in nature and an emulation of the infinite in metaphysics. The modern has not the comfort of this extravagance. A world deserted by visible or metaphysical grandeur turns his suffering into a Carlylean dyspepsia or an Arnoldian depression: into *illness,* considered as an internalization of external meaninglessness and frustration. Burke mentions 'sickness' as one manifestation of sublime pain, but the idea is undeveloped, preference being given to 'pain' and 'death'; Arnold, after his cameo of the 'poet-outlaw' in **'A Summer Night',** turns to the present as a spectacle of imprisonment, gloom, and triviality which contrasts with, but also continues, sublime pain. The covert kinship of the two conditions is what causes Empedocles to reject not simply the 'hot prison of the present' but also its apparent obverse, the solitude of sublime creativity:

> And lie thou there,
> My laurel bough!
> I am weary of thee.
> I am weary of the solitude
> Where he who bears thee must abide.

'The Strayed Reveller' indicates the indissoluble link between such solitude, sublime pain, and the diurnal ennui of 'most men'. The gods do not suffer. They

> are happy.
> They turn on all sides

Their shining eyes,
And see below them
The earth and men.

. . . . .

These things, Ulysses,
The wise bards also
Behold and sing.
But oh, what labour!
O prince, what pain!

Sharing the infinite perspective of the gods, poets participate, as the gods do not, in the sufferings they perceive:

> such a price
> The Gods exact for song:
> To become what we sing.

When, therefore, in **'A Summer Night'** or **'A Southern Night'**, Arnold directly contemplates the 'brazen prison', he too suffers the pain of 'sick hurry' without the marginal solace of companionship with those who suffer.

This leads me to a curious feature of the poem which lent me the title of this essay, **'The Sick King in Bokhara'**, which is that in it everyone *but* the poet appears sick. The poem's first sickness is that of the 'Moollah' who, in a fever, curses the friends and relatives who have drunk the water he was saving for himself. For him, such an act represents the greater sickness of mortal sin, and he demands that the king ordain his trial and punishment, death by stoning. Twice the king refuses him; the third time he allows punishment, but orders that the man should be allowed to escape if he wishes; he does not, dies; the king falls sick. The poem opens at this point, with the Vizier, who has missed the story through being 'sick / These many days', hearing it in the king's presence from the poet Hussein, after which the king, despite the Vizier's objections, gives the Moollah a splendid burial.

The varieties of sickness here reflect Arnold's reading of his time and of himself. The Moollah is a glorious anachronism, sublimely sick of a moral disease which however he himself, like Manfred, can cure by willing his own destruction. His sickness reveals, and is a mode of, power, not its negative; the king's sickness reflects his discovery of his own weakness: wishing to pardon the Moollah, and thus enforce his own clemency, he finds himself conquered by the Moollah's will to self-punishment, and encounters the boundaries, the finitude of his power. His sickness, then, reflects his weakness, and his posthumous glorification of the Moollah is a forlorn tribute to sublimity he cannot emulate. The fact that he buries the Moollah *in his own grave* completes the portrait of usurpation. The Vizier's sickness is more straightforwardly a mechanism to get the story told, but it also spreads the sickness of the two central figures into a more widespread social malaise, and proleptically punishes / expresses his flinty refusal of charity to the man he calls a 'dead dog'.

The only person in the poem who is not literally ill is the poet Hussein, yet he, as the thoroughfare through which the story proceeds, is, in the terms of **'The Strayed Reveller'**, the greatest, and perhaps the only true sufferer. The poet is isolated from his kind and apparently shielded from their diurnal anguish, but in reality perceives and feels the entire panorama of human suffering. Empedocles' rejection of his solitude presages Arnold's rejection of **'Empedocles on Etna'**, which in turn represents the rejection of poetry itself, since Arnold could neither free

himself from the Romantic conception of poetry as the product of the sublime of suffering, nor reconcile himself to paying the price exacted.

But Arnold's attitude was hardly as simple, and his gesture hardly as complete, as such an account implies. His interest in illness sees him bring the sublime of suffering from the mountain-tops to the sickbed, and reduce it to the merely painful and ignominious; yet that reduction simultaneously retrieves an occult reaffirmation of that sublime, and allowed Arnold to continue, for a while, to create.

'Men spent by sickness, or obscure decay'. Considering the case of Maurice de Guerin, Arnold glimpses the possibility of reading illness as a privilege, not a privation:

> In him, as in Keats, . . . the temperament, the talent itself, is deeply influenced by their mysterious malady; the temperament is *devouring*; it uses vital power too hard and too fast, paying the penalty in long hours of unutterable exhaustion and in premature death.

The argument is very close to that of **'Early Death and Fame'**, the short poem which was all that remained in [*New Poems,* 1867] of a long poem published in *Fraser's Magazine* in 1855, **'Haworth Churchyard'**. **'Haworth Churchyard'** was Arnold's elegy for Charlotte Brontë, recently dead of consumption, and for Harriet Martineau, apparently on the point of death when the poem appeared (it was her recovery which presumably caused Arnold to withhold the poem from all collections until after her death in 1876). As in the case of Guerin, Arnold was clearly fascinated by the conjunction of early death and literary talent in the Brontë family (all four siblings are mentioned), and **'Early Death and Fame'** suggests in general terms the ferocious appetite for life which the premature approach of its end engenders:

> Fuller for him be the hours!
> Give him emotion, though pain!
> Let him live, let him feel: *I have lived.*
> Heap up his moments with life!
> Triple his pulses with pain!

Charlotte Brontë's celebrity causes him to add 'fame' to the heap of benefits which the early-dying can accumulate; in the case of Guerin, a more characteristic Arnold alterego, this is lacking, but its absence is seen as an occult benefit rather than—or as well as—a privation.

> So he lived like a man possessed; with his eye not on his own career, not on the public, not on fame, but on the Isis whose veil he had uplifted. He published nothing: 'There is more power and beauty,' he writes, 'in the well-kept secret of one's self and one's thoughts, than in the display of a whole heaven that one may have inside one.

Here the illness which threatens the life with closure gives rise, within the logic of Arnold's reasoning, to *secrecy,* a voluntary rather than enforced obscurity which contributes directly to the 'power and beauty' (note the Burkean resonance of the terms) of the abbreviated life. Arnold's admiration for the heroic effort of secret creation shades off, however, into an interest in the weakness it accompanies and expresses. He concludes his translation of a particularly weary and dispirited passage from Guerin with the remark: 'Such is this temperament in the frequent hours when the sense of its own weakness and isolation crushes it to the ground.' The phrase 'weakness and isolation' distinguishes Guerin's state from the sublime of suffering, in which isolation produces and is produced by *power*; the contrast with a more directly Romantic contemporary, Browning, reinforces the point:

> VALENS.   *(Advancing)*   The lady is alone!
> BERTHOLD.   Alone, and thus? So weak and yet so bold?
> VALENS.   I said she was alone—
> BERTHOLD.   —and weak, I said.
> VALENS.   When is man strong until he feels alone?

Weakness, in wholesale contrast to the 'courage' of Byron, is linked to obscurity in Arnold's thought, and that even in the case of Arnold's strongest modern, Senancour. His work, in contrast to Byron's, is pervaded by 'languor', he has surrendered to 'despair', and the result is a work which is 'fraught too deep with pain' to attract 'the world around'. But that very despair, the weakness it expresses, and the obscurity it engenders, are themselves manifestations of the sublime of suffering. Arnold refuses, in retrospect, to demand 'health, success and fame' for Quinillan not for the reasons he gives—that fame as a poet would have made him less amiable as a man—but because the Arnoldian sublime adopts and transforms qualities which seem the reverse of sublime, qualities such as weakness, obscurity, illness, and even mediocrity. Hence in the palinode to **'A Southern Night'** Arnold praises his brother and sister-in-law for qualities—gentleness, grace, charm—which are the direct product of the ordinariness which the main body of the poem mocks and deplores; as in the Guerin essay, such qualities are the cherished and fragile obverse of a ruder Romantic strength.

But the logic of Arnold's position goes beyond the discovery and praise of a Burkean 'beauty' in the lives of the obscure. It involves a kind of self-annihilation, the cultivation of weakness and obscurity *in his own work*. Arnold hears Senancour call out *'Strive not! Die also thou!'*, and the fact that these words are in turn not Senancour's but Homer's diagnoses the weakness of the modern as a capitulation to predecessors, a collapse before the illustrious forefathers. In the Preface [of 1854] Arnold remarks that one reason for choosing great—i.e., classical—subjects is that they possess 'an immortal strength':

> the most gifted poet, then, may well be glad to supplement with it that mortal weakness, which, in presence of the vast spectacle of life and the world, he must forever feel to be his individual portion.

To confess such 'weakness' while bowing down to the superior power of earlier writers is what Arnold seems here to advocate, but there is another answer. A *refusal to write*—literary death, to which Arnold's [critical writings of 1853 and 1854] visibly sentenced him—can, in its very feebleness and inadequacy, represent a decisive innovation and an exhibition of paradoxical strength.

It will be sufficiently obvious that I have it in mind to argue that Arnold stopped writing poetry in obedience to the logic of his reversed sublime. As Gottfried notes, it is a cliché of Arnold criticism to note 'Arnold's failure as a poet to satisfy his own classical standards' and to suggest that he frustrated his own talent with his theories; I add that the process was in some sense a deliberate achievement, a dismantling of talent as the ultimate display of talent. And I think that Arnold's work, and his treatment of his work, evidences this. I will not enlarge here on the stylistic features that might be adduced: the halting, stark-naked diction, the sparse and banal metaphors, the coat-of-many-Romantic-colours bleached out by enervated pessimism. I am interested in the drift towards *fragmentation* that besets his works both initially and through the process of revision. The parts of Arnold's poems split apart and drift away not only in the part-metaphorical sense that he 'cannot make it cohere', but in the literal sense that the revisionary process often takes, in his case, the form of a series of predatory raids upon the body of the finished work, in the course of which it is mutilated, if not slain outright.

Everything about the story of **'Empedocles on Etna'** is significant, and nothing more so than its dismemberment, in 1853 and 1855, into a few brief passages—mainly the lyrics of Callicles—after the suppression of the whole poem in 1853 on a policy explained in the famous **'Preface'**. Those lyrics were always, in some sense, disjoined, and the poem actually thematizes the disjunction, as Empedocles, hearing the songs, comments on his own mental alienation from 'the freshness of the early world' they represent. The one passage in 1855 in which Empedocles speaks—ll. 276-300, renamed 'The Philosopher and the Stars'—adheres to the same pattern: Empedocles is momentarily seduced into mythologizing the stars into a history of disillusionment like his own. In **'Empedocles'**, Empedocles goes on to deny the identification; without that palinode, 'The Philosopher and the Stars', like the lyrics of Callicles without Empedocles' commentary, settles into a simpler and less demanding shape. Taken together, then, these passages 'complete' the poem by obeying its logic of separation; they also, like the **'Preface,'** *dramatize* Arnold's self-extinction by refusing to allow it to become complete or remain private. A similar pattern arises in the case of **'The Youth of Man'**, another victim of the surgery of 1853. Of the 118 lines of the 1852 poem only two short fragments, one of nine lines entitled **'Richmond Hill'**, the other of seven lines entitled **'Power of Youth'**, survived in 1853 (though the whole poem was restored in 1855; here again, the result is that a poem which the 1853 Arnold presumably thought morbid is replaced by two of its own lyric passages which, out of context, suggest a more hopeful outlook. (The other more mournful and discouraged poems of [*Empedocles on Etna, and Other Poems*], such as **'Despondency'**, **'The Buried Life'** and **'Youth's Agitations'**, were simply suppressed, **'Despondency'** never to be reprinted.)

Arnold's stated policy was to banish the morbid and ineffectual, but the resulting simplifications produce more album-leaves than epic actions, and the overall effect of the omission or fragmentation of all the serious poems of [*Poems,* 1853] was of Arnold *turning himself into a minor poet.* **'Courage'**, significant both in title and in content to Arnold's sense of the drama of the sublime, disappeared as well, as though to suggest that for Arnold that drama was at an end. His devastation of his own work points, however, not to the inception of a heroic future but an aftermath of poetic silence, which in turn, advertised and even flaunted as it is in [*Poems,* 1853], becomes the gesture of the reversed sublime. In [*Poems,* 1853] Arnold turned his contention with the Romantics into a psychomachia, a self-inflation which the simultaneous part-extinction of his own talent only threw into sharper relief.

This gesture was repeated in the case of **'Haworth Churchyard'** which, though suppressed, as I noted above, between 1855 and 1877, contributed a fragment of itself under the title **'Early Death and Fame'** to the intervening collections. In this case, the body was never reassembled, since **'Early Death and Fame'** was kept separate from **'Haworth Churchyard'** in 1877, and this fact itself has significance, both in that the mutilation is, as it were, preserved by it, and in that the fragment's demand for 'life' and 'fame' for the early-dying is kept away from Charlotte Brontë, modulating her into something close to the obscured strength, the reversed-sublime, of Arnold's other 'heroes'. Arnold simultaneously stripped from the poem other passages affirming the vigour and achievement of Brontë and Martineau, and one which contrasts them with himself: 'I beheld; the obscure / Saw the famous.' The removal of these lines seems to me almost whimsically double. For Arnold, famous in 1877, to paint out the original picture of his 'obscure' self at once denies and enhances the 'obscurity', as his deletions elsewhere had brought the Brontës closer to the counter-sublime of 'obscure decay'. In his revision and finally his cancellation of his own poetry, Arnold accuses it of the sickness of modernity and punishes it by mutilation and terminal illness, surrendering himself, as in another way Tennyson did, to the anonymity and mediocrity of the times; yet these gestures amount to and anticipate Beckett's plenary negation of creativity. 'Helpless to write' because 'there is nothing to write and nothing to write about', the Beckett who 'exits weeping' from his dialogues with Georges Duthuit extracts never-diminishing returns from failure and silence, as Arnold did. (pp. 100-19)

> John Woolford, "The Sick King in Bokhara: Arnold and the Sublime of Suffering," in Matthew Arnold: Between Two Worlds, *edited by* Robert Giddings, London: Vision Press, 1986, pp. 100-20.

Virginia Carmichael (essay date 1988)

[*In the following essay, Carmichael explores the meaning and function of lyrical episodes in Arnold's poetry, focusing on the conflict between his Romantic impulse toward the lyrical and his classical intellectual standards.*]

Although his poetry has long been faulted for reiterating in melancholy and "unpoetic" ways a thoroughly Victorian argument, Matthew Arnold remains, in T. S. Eliot's words, "a poet to whom one readily returns." Contemporary readers who readily return to Arnold do so with a literary tradition enlarged by the powerful lyric mediations of high modernism, and Arnold's poems represent, not so much a flawed recapitulation of Victorian concern with design as a troubled and equally flawed engagement with what we now understand as modernist and postmodernist formal and thematic preoccupations. For these readers for whom Arnold's poetry resists facile cultural-historical categorization, David J. DeLaura's statement of 1969 is to the point: "We still do not know how to 'read' Arnold and *why* we should read him, especially the poetry."

The challenge for historical, biographical, and New Criti-

cal readings has continually been that of accommodating, into some sort of coherence or narrative, the radical discontinuity and vexed multiple voicings of Arnold's poems. But what Arnold gives us is a body of fractured poetry, dispersing, blocking or repudiating the "momentary brightenings" of lyric mediation, and giving voice instead to non-identity and confusion, or philosophical rationality. By attending specifically to these voices that do not cohere, and to what is being interrupted, and how it is being interrupted, one discerns an anguished and unresolved meditation on the paradox of lyric itself: the paradox that a manner of writing intended to redeem the alienation between self and world is also, always and inevitably, an expression of the limits, momentariness, and loss of any such constructed or felt interaction.

Arnold's poems in no way constitute a body of lyric poetry; they are too often something other than lyric; long philosophical and dramatic poems predominate. But these same poems often contain insets of lyric, what Arnold himself calls "momentary brightenings," and even the philosophical and dramatic passages are continuations, in another register, of the ongoing problem he has with lyric. In order to examine these lyric passages and what Arnold does with them, it seems necessary to attempt a provisional means of distinguishing between that which is lyric in the poems and that which is not. Many would argue—and persuasively—that all poetry, if not all writing, can be shown to be voiced and troped, and that voicing is itself a linguistic construction, or a trope; so notions of expressed subjectivity, overheard utterance, and lyric figuration, even though often invoked as critical aspects of lyric, are not necessarily its distinguishing qualities. While the relative subjectivity or objectivity of any lyric utterance varies historically, as does its temporal orientation, the only constant throughout its history is that lyric, as distinguished from drama or narrative, is melody: an agreeable part of a not necessarily determinate larger something, the agreeableness of which depends upon an articulated coherence, be it tonal/formal or verbal/intellectual. So for our purposes here let us define Arnold's lyric passages as short, voiced, and troped meditations on the relation of self to world that announce themselves formally as melodic insets in a larger discourse.

These passages break down or abruptly end in various and specific ways. Inscribed by classical, medieval, neoclassical, and romantic precursors, they are fractured and interrupted by desire-become-fear, distanced and repudiated by rational and theological voices, fractured by a return to the world's commerce, and transformed by various aesthetic strategies into the formal fixations of symbol or myth. These gestures of fending off and distancing of lyric may be interpreted as defenses against subjectivity, against that which "make[s] us feel." But the dilemma for Arnold is more complicated than that. The speaker of these poems is afraid of the costs of writing lyric because it somehow leads to an encounter with the "unmating reality" that the lyric mediation is intended to exclude. He sees lyric, as Theodor Adorno does, as a testing of the philosophical proposition "that subject and object are no rigid, isolated poles, but can only be identified within the process in which they interact," but it is this interaction that gives Arnold difficulty. As so often, he tells us explicitly what the problem is: he is "wandering between two worlds" (**"Stanzas from the Grande Chartreuse"**). Ostensibly the two worlds are historical epochs, "one dead / The other powerless to be born"; but they also suggest an inner-outer dichotomy, a familiar but rationalized opposition that produces for Arnold a state of paralysis. In wandering between these two "spaces," Arnold continually expresses a desire for and an inability to achieve, as well as a resistance to making, any sort of connection between this individual self and that historical world. The lyric mediation must be protected from the world in order for it to exist at all, but rejected as soon as it comes into existence because it either implicates its speaker in a painful relation to that same world, or establishes an illusory relationship that is no connection at all. Lyric, as Arnold responds to it, is either a kind of lost and unavailable experience, or an implication of self in a world that is too costly to mortal beings, or a lie or dream to be resisted as having nothing to do with lived experience. His poetry's reactions to its own lyric moments express simultaneously nostalgic longing, fearful distancing, and tense ethical refusal.

One of the earliest and clearest poetic expressions of the dilemma for Arnold comes in **"The Strayed Reveller."** A dramatic poem in free verse, with lyric passages of colorful local description, it depicts the world as the gods see it, and then the same world as seen by the poet. Here we already have Arnold's "two worlds," and the difference is revealing. The gods see, in a long passage threaded by "and," the pagan world, the Indian in harmony with nature, the pastoral shepherd, the merchants beside their riches, and the heroes of history:

> They see the Scythian
> On the wide steppe, unharnessing
> His wheeled house at noon.
> He tethers his beast down, and makes his meal—
> Mares' milk, and bread
> Baked on the embers; all around
> The boundless, waving grass-plains stretch, thick-starred
> With saffron and the yellow hollyhock
> And flag-leaved iris-flowers.

As soon as the Gods glance into the historical world, however, a troubled note enters, signaled by "but":

> but astern
> The cowering merchants, in long robes,
> Sit pale beside their wealth.

Then, in a sequence of passages negating the lyric vision of the gods, in verses fractured by the repeated "but," the reveller tells Ulysses what the poets see when they contemplate the same world: they see with despair; the pagan pleasures burst their veins and cause them "wild pain"; the Indian's nature is hostile to them, stormy, and worm-eaten "to the heart"; the pastoral shepherd's environment parches and freezes them; and they must share the merchants' worries about property and financial politics and disease, as well as the heroes' life of war and strife: "but care / Must visit first them too, and make them pale." In a final gesture of distancing repudiation, the reveller announces his position to Ulysses:

> But I, Ulysses,
> Sitting on the warm steps,
> Looking over the valley,
> All day long, have seen,
> Without pain, without labor

This untroubled and lyric vision is possible to him, only

"for a moment," by means of Circe's cup. But in choosing to stay above in order to escape the pain, in refusing "To become what we sing," he gives up the very possibility of singing.

In Arnold's most powerful poems we will often find the one who cannot sing enclosed and abandoned, formally and semantically, by the words of one who can; such are the poet figure and the speaker in **"Resignation."** As a revision of Wordsworth's "Tintern Abbey," the poem's voice is not that of the poet, but of one who, hemmed in by life's *"iron round,"* is observing the poet observe. The poet figure might be the mature strayed reveller, for even though the speaker is developing what is structured as a logical argument for the poet's being "more than man" and thus feeling more deeply, at no point does this poet *sing*. His "dumb wish is not missed"; he only "gazes" with "His sad lucidity of soul," because he, like the reveller, "From some high station . . . looks down." The singing that does occur is in the narrator's pastoral description of what the poet sees, a nature appropriated not only by rich particularity of naming, with echoes of "Lycidas" and "L'Allegro," but also by anthropomorphized language:

> The cuckoo, loud on some high lawn,
> Is answered from the depth of dawn;
> In the hedge straggling to the stream,
> Pale, dew-drenched, half-shut roses gleam;
> But, where the farther side slopes down,
> He sees the drowsy new-waked clown
> In his white quaint-embroidered frock
> Make, whistling, tow'rd his mist-wreathed flock—
> Slowly, behind his heavy tread,
> The wet, flowered grass heaves up its head.

As soon as the speaker begins analyzing the poet figure's response to this scene, however, that which was lyrical becomes syntactically fractured with "but," multiple "if 's," and dashes; deprived of particularity and organic vitality; and metaphysically abstracted:

> Before him he sees life unroll,
> A placid and continuous whole—
> That general life, which does not cease,
> Whose secret is not joy, but peace;
> That life, whose dumb wish is not missed
> If birth proceeds, if things subsist;
> The life of plants, and stones, and rain,
> The life he craves—if not in vain
> Fate gave, what chance shall not control,
> His sad lucidity of soul.

The shift to the abstractions of the lucid soul occurs through a turn away from the evocation of sensual nature to the questionable "life" of "plants, and stones, and rain"; it is also an interruption of lyric by rational, argumentative voices from Arnold's external world: it is a revision of Schiller (peace, not joy we gain from this poet's vision), and an expression of the renunciative stances of Marcus Aurelius, Goethe, and Senancour, all of whom were frequent contributors to Arnold's "dialogue of the mind with itself."

In what is probably the most familiar example of the interrupted lyric in the poetry, Callicles in **"Empedocles on Etna"** offers his Pindaric-styled songs as reminders of the healing possibilities of music and a previous harmony with nature, and as a soothing but nostalgic alternative to the distress of Empedocles' lonely mind. Callicles has been

Illustration of the school inspector by Charles Keene, 1860s.

singing a description of the natural beauty of his surroundings in "the last / Of all the woody, high, well-watered dells / On Etna," and with the enjambment at "last" we know that something having to do with water and trees is or is about to be lost. He then interrupts his lyric outpouring with the retrospective cancellation of "but," to tell us harshly that the landscape he is celebrating ends here, "but glade, / And stream, and sward, and chestnut-trees, / End *here*" (italics mine). The "but" has signaled the negation of something and the "here" locates the spatial boundary on the actual mountainside between the water and trees, and the bare, unshaded peaks of Etna. Callicles continues, in lines linked by the repetition of "and," with a nostalgic description of the pagan imaginative exploration that *used* to occur "in such a glen," when Chiron taught Achilles "all the wisdom of his race." Retrospectively, then, "here" has in addition marked both an historical and a metaphoric boundary between the work of the imagination and the arid, barren activity of abstracted mind. Lyric activity "end[s] here" for us also, as though its momentum is self-consciously stopped by "here" announcing itself as *here*. The music ceases, and Empedocles begins his long train of philosophical stanzas ending with the imperative that man "must not dream"; repeatedly in Arnold's poetry, "dream" figures lyric. Throughout the poem the syntactic negation of "but," or the formal rupture of disjunction marks a similar turn from lyric to its philosophical renunciation. After Empedocles has dissolved himself in the elements by leaping into

the crater, Callicles, in a final disjunctive lyric, urges that Apollo and his muses

> Not *here*. . .
>   . . . . .
> But, where Helicon breaks down
> In cliff to the sea,
>   . . . . .
> O speed, and rejoice! (italics mine)

Another stridently ethical and at the same time more nostalgic repudiation of lyric occurs in a dense passage uttered by Empedocles in which he laments the lost time of his "power to feel," when

> The smallest thing could give us pleasure *then*—
> The sports of the country-people,
> A flute-note from the woods,
> Sunset over the sea. (italics mine)

That was a time of "pure natural joy," when "the brow [was] unbound," and "the thoughts flow[ed] free"; he and Parmenides were not yet "Thought's slaves," and "The smallest thing could give us pleasure then." Empedocles then elaborates and justifies—in a hypotactic passage marked by the repeated disjunctive "but," multiple negations, fractured syntax, and constraining imperatives—his turn away from a time of power, ease, flow, and joy, and from a space of lyric expression, to the enclosed, unyielding world of isolated mind:

> *But* he. . .

But he. . .

. . . . .

Whose habit of thought is fixed, who will *not* change,
But, in a world he loves *not, must subsist*
In ceaseless opposition, be the guard
Of his own breast, fettered to what he guards,
That the world win *no* mastery over him—
Who has *no* friend, *no* fellow left, *not* one;
Who has *no* minute's breathing space allow'd
To nurse his dwindling faculty of joy—
Joy and the outward world *must die* to him,
As they are dead to me. (italics mine)

The abstractions, denials, negations, and negative imperatives not only describe a rupture with the world for Empedocles, but also produce a break-down and stoppage of the mediated relationship and melodic articulation necessary to lyric expression.

The relegation of the lyric impulse to an inaccessible and inadmissable realm is a recurrent phenomenon in Arnold's poetry: lyric is defined as abandoned to the time of Wordsworth and the romantics, as in **"Memorial Verses"** and **"Stanzas in Memory of the Author of 'Obermann,'"** lost to the time of childhood, as in **"Youth and Calm"** and **"Empedocles on Etna,"** or confined to the realm of the dream, as in **"Isolation: to Marguerite."** Such a structure of renunciation encloses the extended and sensuously particular sleeping children passage in **"Tristram and Iseult."** The narrative voice finds it necessary to introduce such a passage with a disjunctive "but," as well as a contrary-to-fact conditional clause, for a double enclosure of this lyric moment:

—Ah, tired madcaps! you lie still;
But were you at the window now,
To look forth on the fairy sight
Of your illumined haunts by night,
To see the park-glades where you play
Far lovelier than they are by day,
To see the sparkle on the eaves,
And upon every giant-bough
Of those old oaks, whose wet red leaves
Are jewelled with bright drops of rain—
How would your voices run again!
And far beyond the sparkling trees
Of the castle-park one sees
The bare heaths spreading, clear as day,
Moor behind moor, far, far away,
Into the heart of Brittany.
And here and there, locked by the land,
Long inlets of smooth glittering sea,
And many a stretch of watery sand
All shining in the white moon-beams—

As we reach the end of this imaginative space, which leads, as it often does for Arnold, to the sea, we are distanced by the dash and then brought up short by a final enclosing and negating "but" that devalues and cancels what we have just experienced poetically: "But you see fairer in your dreams!" A similar negation occurs at the end of the lyric passage celebrating the healing beauty of Senancour's poetry in **"Stanzas in Memory of the Author of 'Obermann.'"** There is an especially anguished and desperate tone in the speaker's renunciation of this lyric vision:

. . .—Away!
Away the dreams that but deceive
And thou, sad guide, adieu!

I go, fate drives me; but I leave
Half my life with you.

A different sort of devaluation occurs at the end of **"The Buried Life,"** after the recounting of a rare moment of human connection. In typical fashion, the speaker begins the lyric expression by fracturing it with a qualification introduced by "but": "Only—but this is rare— / When a beloved hand is laid in ours." And then he ends what is one of Arnold's more felicitous blendings of rhythm, rhyme, figure, and diction with a metaphysical statement that—even though hesitantly stated—overburdens the lyric moment just experienced: "And then he thinks he knows / The hills where his life rose, / And the sea where it goes." The metrical continuity with what has come before carries one through this ending with a soothing sense of the self-awareness, rest, and calm experienced through contact with a loved person; but the movement at the end is also away from the imaged immediacy of the lyric to a metaphysical "knowledge" and imagined certainty of origins and endings. This shift is not offensive or jarring; it is actually a poignant reflection of human experience. But it suggests something about the momentariness of lyric—and of the connection with another person—especially when an overburdening demand is imposed on it, or unpoetic certainty is required of it. And once again, the psychological distancing produced by this tonal shift simultaneously gives voice to an external and rational, if not metaphysical, authority; these last lines echo an unpublished poem by Arnold's father.

The most radical rejection of lyric in Arnold's poems is a deliberate and disjunctive turning away from it, without dialectical tension or transition of any kind. While there are disjunctions between Empedocles' speeches and Callicles' songs in **"Empedocles on Etna,"** they work as a kind of formally contained argument/counter-argument: the subject of the argument can be construed as the very possibility of lyric sensibility, the possibility of a dialectical relationship of self to world that, avoiding the deadly isolation of "a naked, eternally restless mind," can also resist the fragmentation of external demands. And although the dramatic protagonist has cancelled the dilemma with his death, in this poem Callicles' songs poetically and formally carry the day.

In other poems, however, a moment of lyric is followed by a passage of abstracted philosophical assertions, and the effect of this obtrusive shift is a devaluation or cancellation or outright repudiation of what has just been experienced in the poetry. In **"A Summer Night,"** in a long and sustained metaphor, the speaker gives us a description of the wretched life of that rare person who, achieving freedom from the world, can follow his heart's lead: lost in a storm, making for an unknown port, "he too disappears, and comes no more." Then the poet makes a leap to the untroubled divine clearness of the gods, in order to assert their transcendent mind as the model for the madman or slave who would escape bondage from heart or world. With its failure to achieve a formal or intellectual tension between these discontinuous fragments of world, heart, and mind, the poem breaks down, enacting the impossibility of even a lyric mediation between human experience and the "world above man's head." The poet once again has stopped lyric expression in a double move—first by the loss of the subject, followed by an assertion of metaphysical abstraction: "How vast, yet of what clear transparency!"

Almost all of Arnold's strategies for fracturing, stopping, enclosing, or refusing lyric occur in **"The Scholar Gipsy,"** a microcosm, not only of the phenomenal world of the poetry, but also of its rhetorical and formal strategies for containment. In Keatsian stanzas of abundant particularity, filled with echoes of Milton, Johnson, Gray, Shelley, and Tennyson, the speaker situates the Scholar Gipsy in a timeless rural life. Only rarely does he show him entering the margins of the social world: "The blackbird, picking food, / Sees thee, nor stops his meal, nor fears at all." Shepherds, Oxford rowers, maidens, reapers, housewives, and children are all familiar with him as a natural, if momentary, observer in their world. When there is potential interaction between the world and the Scholar Gipsy, it is averted with the usual "but": "But none hath words she can report of thee," and "But, when they came from bathing, thou wast gone!" And then this imagined private world of self in nature closes abruptly when the speaker remembers time and relegates the lyric to the status of dream: "But what—I dream! Two hundred years are flown / Since first thy story ran through Oxford halls." Not surprisingly, another disjunctive "but" and a relegation of the lyric vision to the devalued world of dream, a familiar double move in Arnold's poetry, have signaled a turning away from lyric toward the diseased world.

The troubled speaker leaves the Scholar Gipsy "exempt from age" and "with powers / Fresh, undiverted to the world without," with his *"one* aim, *one* business, *one* desire." While he laments his own fluctuation in the world's multitudinousness, he cautions the Scholar Gipsy to turn away from him and his world, to "Fly hence, our contact fear!", just as Dido in Hades shunned the approach of her "false friend." This image figuring safety for lyric, as so often in the poems, is a problematic haven. For Dido in the underworld, as the analogue to the Scholar Gipsy, represents poetry not only as feminized, victimized, and betrayed, but also as mythic, aestheticist, and dead.

Then, in the speaker's desire to resurrect from the grave his master figure, he abruptly places him once again within a space of pastoral lyric: "where none pursue, / On some mild pastoral slope / Emerge." With the Scholar Gipsy's escape from the fragmentation of worldly involvement, and emergence from a death of mythic figuration, the speaker attempts a final and more satisfying transformation. The extended image of the disjunctive coda of the poem transforms the vulnerable Scholar Gipsy into the complicated figure of a Tyrian trader, fleeing Greek ships to "un[do] his corded bales," *"There,* where . . . / Shy traffickers, the dark Iberians come" (italics mine). There, not here, is where he has to be to escape the intrusive sensuality and commerce of the Greek traders, and to practice his special gift. Whatever it is that requires such safety and protection, it is no longer the Scholar Gipsy's capacity for momentary presence in the world, nor is it the unity of single purpose; it has been shaped instead into something carried in "corded bales" which must be opened up for "Shy traffickers." Lyric has given way to the secure structure of symbolic configuration.

The **"Scholar Gipsy"** is a catalogue of the anomalies of Arnold's poetry: denial and negation of the lyric mediation through disjunction, qualifications, or relegation to an irretrievable, lost time or dream; the turn from lyric particularity and organic vitality to an abstract or oppositional discourse that refuses the dialectic tension of lyric; interruptions by rational and theological voices offering disappointing or unacceptable alternatives to the implication of self and world; and passages, sometimes also disjunctive, that assert resolution or freedom while figuring death. In this poem it is the symbolic which survives the "strange disease of modern life" that threatens lyric mediation. But it is problematic for poetry intended to serve as healer of the self and transformer of the world that survival for **"The Scholar Gipsy"** is accomplished by a transition from lyric to an isolated symbolic fixation, while the speaker remains in the historical world without hope, joy, power, or poetry.

Arnold's ending passages, often called codas, achieve a sense of resolution of the division voiced by the poems. They are almost always disjunctive, and they generally qualify as lyric moments, but they neither resolve the divisions established by the poem, nor hold open and contain the lyric tension or dialectic. Reading them evokes a feeling not just that the poem "end[s] here," but that human existence and meaning in effect "end here"; in that sense, these endings tend to negate the human struggle that precedes them. "The murmur of the moving Nile" at the end of **"Mycerinus"** functions in that way, although not in a disjunctive fashion: this imaged temporality has been the ground of Mycerinus' dilemma, but it also functions as a dispersal of his experience into the general and endless time of nature. In the River Oxus passage at the end of **"Sohrab and Rustum,"** the soldiers are passing back over the River into life, leaving "Rustum and his son . . . alone" in the place of death. The ending lines begin with the usual disjunctive "but": "But the majestic river floated on, / . . . / rejoicing" in "his watery march" until he is "shorn and paralleled" by the sands, "A foiled circuitous wanderer." Personification and repeated images of division and limitation establish metaphoric identity between the river and Sohrab and Rustum, but the river's "longed-for" emergence into the Aral Sea affirms not the tragic recognition between father and son before death, but rather the luminous, tranquil home of death figured by the sea.

The migrating storks at the end of **"Balder Dead,"** the children around the Abbey in **"Stanzas from the Grande Chartreuse,"** and the Epilogue to **"Haworth Churchyard"** work in a darker and more complicated way. **"Balder Dead"** is a paradoxical allegory, in which Balder prefers his life in Hell to a strife-filled life with the Gods in Heaven. In the meantime, while he awaits the realization of his millennial vision, he intends to remain in the gloom of the "joyless kingdom," resisting any of Hermod's efforts to return him to the "vineyards, and crofts, and pastures, bright with sun." As Balder and Nanna turn back toward the realm of death, though, a simile introduced by "but" suddenly reverses the previously established values of life's bright warmth and death's cold gloom. As Hermod stands "beside his drooping horse, / Mute, gazing after them in tears," he discovers that he longs to follow them, "Though they to death were bound, and he to Heaven."

> And as a stork which idle boys have trapped,
> And tied him in a yard, at autumn sees
> Flocks of his kind pass flying o'er his head
> To warmer lands, and coasts that keep the sun;
> He strains to join their flight, and from his shed

Follows them with a long complaining cry—

This kind of reversal—death figured as warmth and light and community—is of course the program of elegy. And the ending line, "At last he sighed, and set forth back to Heaven," is not unlike "At last he rose, and twitched his mantle blue: / Tomorrow to fresh woods, and pastures new" ("Lycidas"). But Balder is in Hell, preferring the "life" of death, and Hermod's attraction to Balder's death is more an echo of the problematic ending of "Adonais." In some ways the poem's paradoxical meditation on life and death is richly compelling, but it also enacts a familiar turn in Arnold's poetry toward unmediated or non-contingent life, a resolution that forestalls life, as well as the possibility for lyric. In other codas we find, in diction and tone promising peace and respite, human life figured by and fixed in death. In **"Stanzas from the Grande Chartreuse,"** the "children reared in shade / Beneath some old-world abbey wall" and "its close of graves" shun active life for "Emblems of hope over the grave," and prefer to "leave our desert to its peace!" In the Epilogue to **"Haworth Churchyard,"** the Muse interrupts the poet's song of a springtime resurrection, leaving him only to assert paradoxically to Charlotte Brontë and Harriet Martineau that they will find themselves "In the dark fermentation of earth"; this is of course the Empedoclean "solution," which, as Arnold acknowledged, is hardly to be recommended.

The disjunctive ending of **"Tristram and Iseult"** also fixes life in death and seems unrelated to the preceding drama. But what at first appears to be one of Arnold's darkest and most puzzling endings may be rather a rare example of wit and affirmation—accomplished not by means of the mythic security of a Dido figure, but through the imaginative freedom of an Iseult. Iseult of Brittany chooses to tell her children the tale of Vivien's freeing herself from a constraining passion by fixing Merlin in a magic circle, leaving herself free "whither she will [to] rove / . . . For she was passing weary of his love." Tristram is similarly enclosed, in the stone tableau of his death scene, in an eternal and harmless impotence. And Iseult, freed by Tristram's death from the tragic role she played as the unloved but loving woman, is not only content, but also able to "rove" as she will, experiencing and expressing the "momentary brightenings" in life with her children, in nature, playing games and telling stories. By transforming herself from victim of betraying passion to narrator of her own life, she is able to accomplish what the poem's intrusive narrator—and Arnold the poet—is apparently powerless to effect: an imaginative easing of the "tyrannous single thought"—"ambition, remorse, or love"—which renders life joyless and meaningless. Survival of the subject in a tragic world is achieved in this poem, not by a shift from lyric to symbol, as in **"Scholar Gipsy,"** but by a shift from lyric to narrative; the result is not a sense of resolution in imaged death, or the finality of symbolic closure, but a sense of the life-enhancing and on-going function of narrative as that which somehow protects and enables the momentary brightenings of life and art. For a moment, in the throes of personal feeling that comprehended the ambivalence and simultaneity of love and loss, Arnold wrote in **"Tristram and Iseult"** a poem which could achieve and allow the momentary brightenings of lyric. And for another moment, in **"Dover Beach,"** he perfected this kind of writing.

Ending this examination of Arnold's poetic treatment of lyric with **"Tristram and Iseult,"** one of the earlier poems, written between 1849 and 1852 following his interlude with the mysterious Marguerite, is to counter any notion of "development" in Arnold's use of lyric; his argument continues throughout the poetry as he alternately evokes moments of mediation and then repudiates them in the various ways elaborated here. His ongoing struggle to achieve lyric mediation gives voice to and articulates not contingent, fragile, and ambivalent moments of harmony between self and world, but instead defiant and complicated refusals of the consolation, pain, or evasion of such moments; and he constructs formal endings that figure not momentary life, peace, and harmony, but isolation, fragmentation, and death. The aesthetic strategies he attempted—symbolism, myth, irony, tragedy, discontinuous verse, or narrative—were finally unacceptable to him, given his program for poetry. It was left for modernism to carry out and "complete" them, as it were. If we return to the suggestion that Arnold's poetry represents a moment in the history of subjectivity and lyric, we can see the various strategies of the modernist poets as *formally* more satisfying responses to and defenses against the dilemma so thoroughly elaborated by Arnold. As is well known, Arnold ultimately resolved his own difficulty with lyric by ceasing to write poetry altogether.

Arnold's painful elaboration of the paradox of any lyric affirmation makes it difficult now to read the various modernist resolutions without also recognizing the evasions and foreclosures upon which such moments are based. But it is equally difficult after Arnold to read postmodernist anti-lyric programs urging the "return [of] the material so rigidly excluded—political, ethical, historical, philosophical—to the domain of poetry," in the interest of having poetry that makes "contact with the *world,*" without reading the impulse or need to reject lyric as an aspect of the problematical history of lyric itself. Arnold's experience would suggest that a programmatic collapsing of the categories means the end of poetry as we know it, but it is hardly conceivable that any such program or desire could actually stop the lyric impulse. For readers who wish to find in poetry also an expression of the historical world and its social contradictions, rejecting lyric is not the task; "thinking it through" is what is required. Matthew Arnold's poetry is the occasion of such a thinking through of lyric, and perhaps that is how and why we would want to read it in its fullest offering. (pp. 61-73)

Virginia Carmichael, "The Moment of Lyric in Matthew Arnold's Poetry," in Victorian Poetry, *Vol. 26, Nos. 1-2, Spring-Summer, 1988, pp. 61-74.*

Clyde de L. Ryals (essay date 1988)

[*In the following essay, Ryals discusses the ironic perspective of Arnold's poetry as the key to understanding the complex and ambiguous levels of meaning in his poetic works.*]

Irony is a term not often associated with the poetry of Matthew Arnold. Instead critics like Lionel Trilling more often speak of Arnold's "sincerity"; and even when they perceive a certain irony in his work, it is to his prose and not to his poetry that they look. Douglas Bush, for example, in his [*Matthew Arnold: A Survey of His Poetry and Prose* (1971)], allows that "although he was to become a master of irony in prose, he rarely approached it in verse." Yet almost every contemporary account that we have about the man, from early youth to the time of his death, testifies to his playfulness, his posturings, his poses. Many of his friends and family were surprised that he was even capable of the seriousness that they discovered in his first published volume of poems. And later, when his seriousness was no longer to be questioned, his readers were often amazed by the frivolity that frequently seemed to invade his work. In his autobiography the philologist Max Mueller noted that Arnold "trusts . . . to *persiflage,* and the result was that when he tried to be serious, people could not forget that he might at any time turn round and smile, and decline to be *au grand serieux.*" Jest and seriousness, artless openness and dissimulation—these seem to have been the characteristics of Arnold the man. The same qualities define his poetry, which is to say, the poet is an ironist.

In Arnold's world all is in a state of change. Characterized by an endless process of creation and decreation, nature in its plentitude is always in a state of becoming, everything being both itself and something else. In this world the individual, seeing that A is both A and A > B, faces contradictions on all sides; and this perception engenders the most contradictory impulses within himself, the desire for, simultaneously, both fixity and fluidity, involvement and detachment, subjectivity and objectivity, bondage and freedom. Further, the self recognizes its own instability, its essential nothingness. "I am nothing," Arnold wrote to his friend Arthur Clough, "and very probably never shall be anything—but there are characters which are truest to themselves by never being anything, when circumstances do not suit." And speaking of his poems to his sister Jane, Arnold urged: "Fret not yourself to make my poems square in all their parts. . . . The true reason why parts suit you while others do not is that my poems are fragments—i.e. that I am fragments . . .; the whole effect of my poems is quite vague & indeterminate . . .; & do not plague yourself to find a consistent meaning." His was, he confessed to Clough, a chameleon personality: "I can go thro: the imaginary process of mastering myself and see the whole affair as it would then stand, but at the critical point I am too apt to hoist up the mainsail to the wind and let her drive." For like Goethe, he was quite willing to believe that in most matters "there is no certainty, but alternating dispositions." Yes, "this little which we are / Swims on an obscure much we might have been." One cannot "talk of *the* absolutely right but of *a* promising method with ourselves." " 'Hide thy life,' said Epicurus, and the exquisite zest there is in doing so can only be appreciated by those who, desiring to introduce some method into their lives, have suffered from the malicious pleasure the world takes in trying to distract them till they are as shatter-brained and empty-hearted as the world itself." Years later Arnold was to claim the chameleon personality as the ideal critic: "The critic of poetry should have the finest tact, the nicest moderation, the most free, flexible, and elastic spirit imaginable; he should be indeed the 'ondoyant et divers,' the *undulating and diverse* being of Montaigne."

An undulating and diverse being—such a one is, in Arnold's view, an ironist, not a traditional ironist of local, verbal, and corrective ironies but a Romantic Ironist, whose way of regarding the world requires an artistic mode correspondent to his world-view. A literary work in this mode avoids closure and determinate meanings; deconstructs the invented fictional world that it pretends to offer; mirrors its author and itself to the end that it represents only itself and its maker; is permeated by a sense of play; and permits transcendence to the creative self of its own image and representational system, thereby allowing the self to hover above the work and glorify in its own self-activity. In brief, works of Romantic Irony forego meaning for metaphysical and aesthetic play.

In his poetry Arnold presents a number of varying positions all of which are deemed of equal value. Let us consider the matter of fate, for example, in *The Strayed Reveller and Other Poems* (1849). Poem after poem deals with characters as victims of fate, yet in almost every case the working of fate is called into question. **"Mycerinus"** considers whether there is a "Force" that makes all "slaves of a tyrannous necessity," or whether the gods are "mere phantoms of man's self-tormenting heart." The chorus in the **"Fragment of an 'Antigone' "** praises both those who flee from fate and those who observe its dictates. The eager response of **"To a Republican Friend"** is mitigated in **"Continued"** by the "Uno'erleaped Mountains of Necessity, / Sparing us narrower margin than we deem." The laborer in **"The World and the Quietist"** is granted a sense of omnipotence although his and others' actions are limited by how "Fate decreed." The speaker in **"Written in Emerson's Essays"** contends that "the will is free" so "Gods are we, bards, saints, heroes, if we will"; but the last line of the poem asks whether this be "truth or mockery" (the manuscript reading being the more decisive "O barren boast, O joyless Mockery"). The colloquist in **"Resignation"** staunchly maintains that persons "who await / No gifts from chance, have conquered fate," while also freely admitting that fate thwarts our expectations of life.

This same ambivalence about fate marks the poems of Arnold's later volumes as well. The initial lyrics of the **"Switzerland"** series assume that the relationship with Marguerite is doomed to fail, and subsequent ones impute the lovers' parting to "a God [who] their severance ruled" (**"To Marguerite—Continued"**) because for "durability . . . they were not meant" (**"The Terrace at Berne"**). The workings of fate are inexorable: "I knew it when my life was young; / I feel it still, now youth is o'er." Communication on the deeper levels of sensibility is impossible because that which seals the lips "hath been deep-ordained," yet occasionally there come moments when we talk openly and sincerely (**"The Buried Life"**). Arnold's speakers are forever questioning whether they are free or determined, and they conclude, hopefully but questioningly, with the possibility that they are both: "Ah, *some* power exists there, which is ours?" (**"Self-Deception"**).

Arnold's views of nature are likewise contradictory. In **"Quiet Work," "Lines Written in Kensington Gardens," "A Summer Night,"** and **"The Youth of Man"** nature is the great moral exemplar, teaching "toil unsevered from tranquility" (**"Quiet Work"**). In **"In Harmony with Nature," "The Youth of Nature," "Self-Dependence,"** and **"A Wish,"** on the other hand, nature is shown to be a distinct realm of being that mankind cannot possibly emulate and would not wish to if it could: "Nature and man can never be fast friends" (**"In Harmony with Nature"**). No attempt is made to come down on either side of the question, as Arnold presents not certainties but possibilities. Here it is not a matter of either / or but of both / and.

We may say the same of Arnold's many verses dealing with love. In poems like **"Dover Beach"** and **"The Buried Life"** love is regarded as redemptive, whereas in the Marguerite poems and **"Tristram and Iseult"** it is shown to be a snare and delusion. While love alone appears able to fill the void in which "we mortal millions live alone" (**"To Marguerite—Cont."**), passion, or the love that engenders it, is too unstable, too transient to provide a firm basis for life.

Arnold favors situations that are intrinsically ironic. Mycerinus, the good king, is condemned to an early death while his father, who spurned justice, lived long and happily. Homer, though blind, saw much (**"To a Friend"**). Shakespeare, the greatest of poets, "didst tread on earth unguessed at" (**"Shakespeare"**). The Duke of Wellington, the leader of conservative forces, sponsored revolution but in accordance with law (**"To the Duke of Wellington"**). The strayed reveller "enswines" himself in Circe's palace, the enchantress having "lured him not hither."

From basically ironic situations Arnold develops, even in his earliest poems, narratives of more complex irony. In **"A Memory Picture"** lovers' promises are made to be broken and "new made—to break again." The Modern Sappho waits for her lover whose attention is now focused on another but who, "as he drifts to fatigue, discontent, and dejection / Will be brought, thou poor heart, how much nearer to thee!" The New Sirens argue that, "only, what we feel, we know." Yet since feeling is evanescent and ignorance the way of life, the speaker, eschewing roses and lilies for cypress and yew, approaches love from a new point of view: "Shall I seek, that I may scorn her / Her I loved at eventide?" In similar fashion the speaker of **"The Voice"** hears a compelling voice that issues "a thrilling summons to my will" and makes "my tossed heart its life-blood spill" yet to which his will ultimately remains unshaken and his heart unbroken. On the other hand, the speaker of **"To Fausta,"** in full realization that joys flee when sought and that dreams are false and hollow, nevertheless may go in pursuit of them. The gipsy child has "foreknown the vanity of hope, / Foreseen [his] harvest—yet proceed[s] to live" (**"To a Gipsy Child by the Sea-Shore."** The busy world is made aware of its power only when reminded of the vanity of its busyness, just as Darius was most mindful of his power when made aware of the one check to it (**"The World and the Quietist"**).

A number of the early poems dramatize Arnold's perception that each moment is a watershed "whence, equally, the seas of life and death are fed" (**"Resignation"**). This is particularly true of the verses dealing with moral problems, the point of which is that the arguments are about as good on one side as another. In the **"Fragment of an 'Antigone' "** the chorus is right in its praise of Antigone, who in respect for universal law buried her brother in violation of the civil law and with disregard to her lover; but Haemon is also right in his claim that Antigone preferred a corpse to her lover. No wonder then that the chorus is forced to conclude that praise is due both him who "makes his own welfare his unswerved-from law" and him who "dares / To self-selected good / Prefer obedience to the primal law." In **"The Sick King in Bokhara"** the vizier is

right in his respect for the law and its demand that the individual follow it unswervingly, yet the king is surely not wrong to heed the claims of conscience and seek to mitigate the punishment of the moolah. In **"The Forsaken Merman"** Arnold shows Margaret as both right and wrong in her return to land: a wife and mother, she has obligations in the sea-world to her family, which she leaves desolate; but a human, she also has responsibilities in the land-world, where she must fulfil her religious duties among her kind.

Such poems, which are dramatizations of irony, reflect the young poet's embrace of irony as a cosmic view. In the modern world certainty is rarely if ever possible. What is required in confronting such a world, Arnold evidently believes, is an ironic posture that permits toleration of indeterminacy. Thus whether the poet sees deeply or widely—possibilities entertained in, respectively, **"The Strayed Reveller"** and **"Resignation"**—is not easily determined and both alternatives should be entertained. Thus whether the universe is of divine or purely physical origin one should be prepared (**"In Utrumque Paratus"**) or, to use a favorite term of Arnold's, resigned.

Critics have frequently elaborated on Arnold's stoic resignation and his supposedly bleak view of life. But as his Empedocles says, one need not despair if one cannot dream. Life is still worth living even though one has "foreknown the vanity of hope" (**"To a Gipsy Child"**). Often the poet's stoic attitude seems no more than that, an attitude, a posture, a pose. Where Mycerinus was a stoic posing as a reveller, Arnold not infrequently appears to be a reveller posing as a stoic. As a poet he is always exploring possibilities with a tentativeness, a drawing back that does not permit conclusiveness. In his work as in his letters there are constant oscillations as he explores options that receive, even at the moment he seems to embrace them, only provisional assent. The narrator's "It may be" in his examination of Mycerinus' inner self well expresses the poet's own qualified positions; and his explorations are not experiments in despair but, frequently, playful exercises "not of mere resigned acquiescence, not of melancholy quietism, but of joyful activity." As he told Clough, "composition seems to keep alive in me a *cheerfulness*—a sort of Tüchtigkeit, or natural soundness and valiancy." Even in his apparently darkest poems there is something of Mycerinus' "clear laughter . . . ringing through the gloom," issuing from the poet's playful acceptance of the ironic fact that man is born with desires that cannot be fulfilled:

> Why each is striving, from of old,
> To love more deeply than he can?
> Still would be true, yet still grows cold?
> —Ask of the Powers that sport with man!
>
> They yoked in him, for endless strife,
> A heart of ice, a soul of fire;
> And hurled him on the Field of Life,
> An aimless unallayed Desire. (**"Destiny"**)

The "sport" of the gods can be the poet's, and the poet's serious play is illustrative of the belief Arnold shared with Schiller that "lofty thought lies oft in childish play" (**"Thekla's Answer"**).

The poems of *Empedocles on Etna, and Other Poems* (1852) portray characters playing out their roles in complex dramas of undefined irony. Let us look, for example, at **"The Church of Brou."** To memoralize her dead husband and their love for each other the duchess erects a church and inside it an ornate tomb on the top of which are effigies of the pair lying side by side and in which she too is eventually buried. Centuries pass as the dead lovers are left alone in their church undisturbed except for Sunday services. The meaning of their memorial is now forgotten as people after mass visit the tomb "and marvel at the Forms of stone, / And praise the chiselled broideries rare" until they part and "the princely Pair are left alone / In the Church of Brou." Here in this lonely sepulchre there is no life, only the silent art of glass and stone. Wishing them well the narrator apostrophizes: "So sleep, for ever sleep, O marble Pair!" And then momentarily indulging in the dream of eternal love that might have been theirs or what at the instant might be his, he considers two possibilities of their awaking: first, when the western sun shines through the stained glass and throws a dazzling array of colors throughout the church and they will say, *"What is this? we are in bliss—forgiven— / Behold the pavement of the courts of Heaven!"*; or second, when the autumn rains come and the moon occasionally shines out and through the windows of the clerestory illuminates the "foliaged marble forest" and they will say, *This is the glimmering verge of Heaven, and these / The columns of the heavenly palaces!"* This is of course but a fancy, and even in the fancy the lovers would be deluded because it is not in heaven but in the church of Brou wherein the putatively awakened pair find themselves. The fact is that they continue to lie under "the lichen-crusted leads above" on which there is but the dream of listening to "the rustle of the eternal rain of love." In the long run, art serves as neither a memorial nor a transformation; it remains but beautiful forms at which to marvel.

In poem after poem Arnold recalls us to the fact that what we witness in his verse is not life but art. The action of **"Empedocles on Etna"** centers on the Sicilian philosopher, but the last word is given to Callicles, who undercuts the poem by stating explicitly that what we have just witnessed is not the proper subject matter for poetry—"Not here, O Apollo! / Are haunts meet for thee"—and in effect saying pretty much what Arnold himself said in his **"Preface to the 1853 *Poems*"** when he explained why he was not reprinting the poem. The poet is likewise separated from the poem in the **"Stanza in Memory of the Author of 'Obermann',"** wherein after praising the author and his book the poet bids farewell to both, although leaving "half of my life with you." In such verses the poet, like God, is both in and out of his creation, subjective and objective, immanent and transcendent. He "moves, but never moveth on" (**"The Hayswater Boat"**).

Although doubleness and dividedness are commonplace of Victorian literature, the degree of self-reflexivity in Arnold is uncommon. Arnold is always splitting himself up into various "selves"—the best self and the ordinary self, the buried self and the masked self. On the one hand modern life, with its constant claims and banalities calling us out of ourselves, necessitate this. On the other hand the ennui of solitude and the fear that there is no real self at all compel such a separation. "Two desires" toss the poet about: "One drives him to the world without / And one to solitude" (**"Stanzas in Memory of the Author of 'Obermann'"**). "And I," puzzles the speaker of **"A Summer Night,"**

I know not if to pray
Still to be what I am, or yield and be
Like the other men I see.

The answer is clearly that he will have to be both.

The inadequacy of language, its inability to permit one to delve into oneself and express what is there or what is lacking, in part mandates the answer. Arnold perhaps best explores the deficiences of language in **"The Buried Life,"** in which the speaker and his beloved, though engaging in a "war of mocking words," cannot communicate openly. Love is apparently too weak to open the heart and let it speak, yet the desire remains to apprehend the buried life and to share it with another. After investigating the impossibility of such communication the speaker, seemingly unmindful of the presence of his beloved, then says that it is possible:

When a belovéd hand is laid in ours,
. . . . .
The eye sinks inward, and the heart lies plain
And what we mean, we say, and what we would, we know

This seems to be but hypothetical, however, since the nature and destiny of the buried self are not revealed. Further, in looking into his beloved's eyes he sees himself mirrored there: his eye sinks inward and he becomes aware of the flow of his life and thinks he knows where his life rose and where it goes.

What the speaker discovers about the buried life is that which in fact cannot be said. Silence is all that is possible in consideration of the great questions of life. Thus the models Arnold held up for emulation can be both superhuman—like Shakespeare and the poet of **"Resignation"**—or subhuman—like the gipsies of **"Resignation"** and the gipsy child—but they have one trait in common: they do not or cannot break their silence to offer any counsel. It is each person's own impossible struggle to find the right words. Man has the letters God has given him to "make with them what word he could." Different civilizations have combined them in different ways and "somewhat was made." But man knows that "he has not yet found the word God would," and if only he could achieve the right words in the right order, then he would be relieved of a terrible oppression and at long last breathe free (**"Revolutions"**). But this will never happen: human language belongs to the phenomenal world and it can never encompass the noumenal world to speak God's word. The poet, Arnold knows, can never fully replicate or re-present anything. That is why it must always be admitted "that the singer was less than his themes." No, even the best of poets—"who have read / Most in themselves—have beheld / Less than they left unrevealed" (**"The Youth of Nature"**). The truth is that the buried self cannot be expressed because without the proper words it cannot be apprehended.

To attempt to view their inner being from various perspectives Arnold's heroes don masks and play roles, just as Arnold did when he assumed the role of dandy in the late 1840s. And with their roles and masks they not only view themselves but also become spectators watching others watching themselves watch others. To refuse to engage in this kind of dramatic play is, in the mid-nineteenth century at any rate, to admit to inelasticity, to be spiritually moribund: "only death / Can cut his oscillations short, and so / Bring him to poise" (**"Empedocles"**). Poise, peace, rest, calm—those qualities which speaker after speaker claims to desire—are, Arnold knows, the attributes of death:

> 'Tis death! and peace, indeed, is here
>
> . . . . . .
>
> But is a calm like this, in truth,
> The crowning end of life and youth,
> And when this boon rewards the dead,
> Are all debts paid, has all been said?
> ("Youth and Calm")

The answer is a ringing no:

> *Calm's not life's crown, though calm is well.*
> 'Tis all perhaps which man acquires,
> But 'tis not what our youth desires.

In Arnold's world there is always more to say; there are always visions to be revised.

After 1852 most of Arnold's better poems were written in the elegiac mode. Elegy was a congenial mode for him because it allowed for the irony of reversal: Lycidas is dead and we lament his loss as we celebrate his talents; but Lycidas is not dead, he lives on in another state. As Arnold employed it, his poems in this mode call into question the meaning of their opening parts. We see this clearly in **"The Scholar-Gipsy."** The poem begins by building up the myth of the scholar-gipsy to the point where the narrator himself asserts the living reality of the young Oxonian of two hundred years ago: "Have I not passed thee?" But then this assertion in the form of a question is almost immediately denied: "But what—I dream / . . . / thou from earth art gone / Long since, and in some quiet churchyard laid." The scholar is indeed dead, and the verbs associated with him change to the past tense. This is however but momentary, for while talking of how the scholar fled with his powers unsullied and undiverted to the world, the speaker again resurrects him and speaks of him in the present tense: "Thou waitest for the spark from heaven." It is an imaginative recovery as the speaker grants him "an immortal lot" because he "imagine[s] thee exempt from age." But immortal lot or not, the scholar is still apparently subject to the ills which afflict mortals living nowadays. And so if he is ever to encounter the divine spark, the scholar must flee the infection of modern life to which present-day mortals are subject and like the Tyrian trader establish his enterprise elsewhere.

The poem complicates itself still further by purportedly dealing with two quests—the speaker's for the scholar-gipsy and the scholar's for some kind of revelation—that are in fact one and the same. Although the scholar quests for the secret knowledge of nature which can be gained only by nonrational means, he himself is already the embodiment of that knowledge, as the poet makes him a kind of nature-spirit who in the first part of the poem can be perceived only by the simple and untutored or those, like poets, who live imaginatively, and who near the end of the poem is granted life "On some mild pastoral slope" listening "with enchanted ears" to nightingales. In sum, the scholar is the object of his own quest. And the speaker, questing for the scholar and the secret possessed by him, locates within himself the imaginative insight that the scholar embodies, which is to say that the speaker is the object of his own quest.

If all the elements seem to cancel each other out, what finally are we left with? In the end we are left with the poet himself who, in the elaborate simile concluding the poem, reminds us that this is not a transcription of life with its sick hurry or of nature with its pale pink convolvulus but art—a poem, a making, over which looms the figure of the poet himself. In the end we see that the imaginative donnée of the poem is not the scholar-gipsy and his quest or modern life with its ills or meaning of any kind; rather, its imaginative donnée is Romantic Irony, which permits the poet to rise above his finite subject matter to a realm of aesthetic consciousness.

The coda of **"Sohrab and Rustum"** serves also to recall the reader from the poem to the poet. In this narrative of ironic situations in which two persons longing for union are frustrated in that desire and come together only through conflict, when one slays the other, the dead son is transformed into art: first when he makes himself known by the vermilion seal, which is compared to "some clear porcelain vase" painstakingly made by a Chinese workman for the emperor, and second when there is erected over his grave a giant pillar which also serves as a seal not only of the son but of the father too in that those who see it say, *"Sohrab, the mighty Rustum's son, lies there, / Whom his great father did in ignorance kill."* In the end Arnold makes of the concluding symbol of the Oxus the same use as Rustum made of the tomb erected for his son. It "seals" the narrative into art and reminds the reader of its maker, saying in effect: " **'Sohrab and Rustum,'** poema, Matthew Arnold fecit." Its composition was an exercise in the development of aesthetic consciousness and as a result the consciousness of the poet, like the winding River Oxus, spirals toward its "luminous home."

Arnold's twistings and turnings in his memorial poems are remarkable in the **"Stanzas in Memory of Edward Quillinan."** While his friend was alive, the speaker wished him health, success, and fame—qualities that are their own reward, "leave no good behind," and "oftenest make us hard, / Less modest, pure, and kind." But the dead man did not receive them and thus he was "a man unspoiled." Implicit in the tribute is the notion that Quillinan is therefore better dead than alive: "Alive, we would have changed his lot, / We would not change it now."

In **"Haworth Churchyard,"** the elegy for Charlotte Brontë and prematurely for Harriet Martineau, Arnold followed the usual elegiac reversal of awakening when the poem was first published in 1855:

> Sleep, O cluster of friends,
> Sleep!—or only when May,
> Brought by the west-wind, returns
> Back to your native heaths,
> And the plover is heard on the moors,
> Yearly to behold
> The opening summer, the sky,
> The shining moorland—to hear
> The drowsy bee, as of old,
> Hum o'er the thyme, the grouse
> Call from the heather in bloom!
> Sleep, or only for this
> Break your united repose.

When the poem appeared in revised form in 1877, Arnold added an Epilogue, which is nothing less than a palinode. Denying the possibility of a May awakening, the Muse angrily shakes her head and says that this shall not be: these "unquiet souls" will not awaken but will remain "in the dark fermentation of earth," "the never idle workshop of nature," "the eternal movement" of the universe of becoming, and there "ye shall find yourselves again!"

With even less cordiality Arnold elegizes Heinrich Heine in **"Heine's Grave."** Heine too was an ironist but he lacked love and charm, and his irony was in consequence bitter. Properly situated in Montmartre Cemetery in Paris and not in Naples' bay or among Ravenna's pines or by the Avon's side, where poets like Virgil, Dante, and Shakespeare belong, Heine's grave reeks of a kind of poison distilled from the harshness and malignity of his life. Once the poet had admired the dead man, but it was necessary that he part from Heine lest he be infected by his mocking laughter. Obviously Arnold has come to re-bury Heine and not to praise him. Yet near the end of his elegy, after 198 lines of mocking derision of the German writer, the poet decides not thus to take leave of him but "with awe / Hail, as it passes from earth / Scattering lightnings, that soul!" At the very end however the poet returns to himself as he asks "the Spirit of the world" to grant that "a life / Other and milder be mine" and that his work be made "a beat of thy joy!" Evidently what Arnold repudiates in Heine is not his irony but his lack of playfulness and joy, characteristic of a higher irony.

In **"Thyrsis"** Arnold is again critical of the subject to be elegized. Clough-Thyrsis was a "too quick despairer" who deserted the landscape of the scholar-gipsy's haunts by his own will, and because of the storms of which "he could not wait their passing, he is dead." Seemingly Thyrsis, out of silly impatience, had willed his own death, leaving the speaker here alone in these fields that "our Gipsy-Scholar haunts, outliving thee." Yes, the scholar-gipsy remains "a wanderer still; then why not me?" Why not indeed? And so the speaker and the scholar go off, as fellow questers, seeking for the light of the truth and apparently putting Thyrsis, the deserter, out of mind. This is, however, an elegy in memory of his friend, and Arnold cannot afford to leave the matter at this point. Adding three final stanzas to the poem, he allows that Thyrsis too was bound on a like quest though in foreign territory. Further, he gives Thyrsis the last word. But addressed to the poet, it urges him to wander on in his quest, thereby in the end returning the focus of the poem to the poet himself who hovers above the work.

From this hasty survey of Arnold's poetry we see many of the conflicts that the poet faced and found unresolvable. He was well aware of "wandering between two worlds" (**"Stanzas from the Grande Chartreuse"**) and being caught between at least "two desires" (**"Stanzas in Memory of the Author of 'Obermann' "**) and that it was impossible for him to take either side or bring them into accord. So much about Arnold has long been clear. But what has not been clear is the degree to which Arnold exhibits his conflicts ironically—so as to transcend them. Far from being the poet of "sincerity" Arnold is self-conscious, playful, problematic, and equivocal. His is, in sum, the art of the Romantic Ironist that presents a self always in process and always relishing and extolling its own self-activity. (pp. 91-101)

Clyde de L. Ryals, "Romantic Irony in Ar-
nold's Poetry," in Victorian Poetry, *Vol. 26, Nos. 1-2, Spring-Summer, 1988, pp. 91-102.*

Wendell Harris   (essay date 1988)

[*In the following essay, Harris discusses varying interpretations of Arnold's "The Function of Criticism at the Present Time" from Victorian England to late twentieth-century postmodernism, emphasizing the essay's enormous influence on the development of the modern critical tradition.*]

From the time it was first delivered in 1864 as one of Arnold's lectures as Professor of Poetry, **"The Function of Criticism at the Present Time"** has been a text in the special, pulpit sense: selected portions have been made the point of departure for disquisitions by major critics in every decade and representing virtually every theoretical persuasion. Arnold is indeed, as Eugene Goodheart phrases it, "an abiding presence in literary studies," but also a plastic presence, remolded by critic after critic for polemical purposes. While Arnoldian banners have floated over the academic profession of English for over a hundred years now, Arnold's shade must often have yearned to put new essays in criticism through the press, correcting with sprightly irony the ever-lengthening series of misunderstandings of his critical program together with our discipline's ever-changing budget of excesses and deficiencies.

. . . . .

To begin with, the long campaign for the inclusion of English literature at Oxford and Cambridge rings with Arnoldian arguments and slogans. That the phrase "the best known and thought" is so well known, and until recently at least, retained so much of its authority, results largely from the central role it played in the long and sometimes bitter struggle over the place of vernacular literature in the university. Though the University College and King's College professorships in English literature date from 1828 and 1835 respectively and the Scottish universities had established chairs of English literature even earlier, so radical a curricular addition was still well in the future at Oxford and Cambridge at the time Arnold accepted the Oxford Chair of poetry. Vigorous debate over formal provisions for the study of English literature at Oxford and Cambridge began in the 1880s, the most dogged extra-mural agitator for formal provision for the study of English literature being John Churton Collins. No one who had read Arnold could have failed to hear his echo in such a passage as this from Collins' *The Study of English Literature* (1891):

> Making due allowance for the distinction which must be drawn between the world for which Pericles legislated, and the world in which our busy millions are striving, it still remains that there exists no essential distinction between what men needed then and what men need now. They needed then and they need now to be taught how to live. They need aesthetic culture, that life may not only be brightened, but refined and elevated by sympathetic communion with what is truly beautiful in Art and literature; they need moral culture, and that on broader lines than when it ran wholly in theological and conventional grooves; they need

Balliol College in Arnold's time.

political culture, instruction, that is to say, in what pertains to their relation to the State.

Thanks to the wide currency of Arnoldian arguments most fully developed in **"The Function of Criticism at the Present Time,"** readers found nothing strained in Collins' assumption that these several goals were to be achieved through the study of English literature.

The fact is, however, that Arnold's own attitude toward the inclusion of English literature was ambivalent. In developing his campaign for a School of English Literature, Collins sent in 1886 a set of leading questions to a number of prominent people, including Arnold. Arnold's initial reply was brief and guarded, but after further exchanges Collins succeeded in eliciting the following letter:

> My Dear Sir,
> I have no difficulty in saying that I should like to see standard English Authors joined to the standard Authors of Greek and Latin literature, who have to be taken up for a pass, or for honours, at the Universities.
>
> I should be sorry to see a separate School, with degrees and honours, for the modern languages as such, although it is desirable that the professors and teachers of those languages should give certificates of fitness to teach them.
>
> I would add no literature except that of our own country to the classical literature taken up for the degree, whether with or without honours, in Arts.
>
> These seem to me to be elementary propositions, when one is laying down what is desirable in respect to the University degree in Arts. The omission of the mother tongue and its literature in school and University instruction is peculiar, so far as I know, to England. You do a good work in urging us to repair the omission.
>
> But I will not conceal from you that I have no confidence in those who at the Universities regulate studies, degrees, and honours. To regulate these

matters great experience of the world, steadiness, simplicity, breadth of view are desirable. I do not see how those who actually regulate them can well have these qualifications; I am sure that in what they have done in the last forty years they have not shewn them. Restlessness, a disposition to try experiments and to multiply studies and schools, are what they have shewn, and what they will probably continue to shew—and this though personally many of them may be very able and distinguished men. I fear, therefore, that while you are seeking an object altogether good—the completing of the old and great degree in Arts—you may obtain something which will not only not be that, but will be a positive hindrance to it.

> I am, my dear Sir,
>
> > Your faithful servant,
> > Matthew Arnold

Evidently Arnold was more troubled by the likely deficiencies of implementation than optimistic about the powers of literature.

Collins chose to cite only those portions of Arnold's letter that supported his cause, passing over the reservations, but even had the total letter been made public, Arnold had long before forged the weapons necessary to win the battle for an Oxford School of English literature. The proponents of such a School had to meet two major objections. First, it was feared that the School might become too philological, giving too much attention to what Henry Craik called "the imported legend of *Beowulf* and other "obscure and dreary fragments" of early English literature. Collins wrote of philology:

> Instead of encouraging communion with the nobler manifestations of human energy, with the great deeds of history, or with the masterpieces of art and letters, it tends, as Bacon remarks, to create unintelligent curiosity about trifles. It too often resembles that rustic who, after listening for several hours to Cicero's most brilliant conversation, no-

ticed nothing but the wart on the great orator's nose.

Or the study of literature might degenerate into literary gossip, for instance what Edward A. Freeman notoriously referred to as "chatter about Shelley." As Freeman later explained:

> I mentioned that I had lately read a review of a book about Shelley in which the critic, in the gravest way in the world, praised or blamed the author—I forget which, and it does not matter—for his "treatment of the Harriet problem." I added that I thought we at Oxford hardly needed to add the "Harriet problem" to our studies, that we had enough to do with the problems of Helen, Theodora, and Mary Stewart, without going into the problem of a Harriet in our own century. . . . Now surely this is a fair specimen of a kind of thing which is not necessarily involved in the kind of study of "literature" which is proposed, but which that kind of study is almost certain to bring with it as its shadow.

Arnold's formula "the best known and thought" could be quoted against either, for it identified the study of literature with criticism rather than philology and further identified criticism with enlightened judgments about and participation in the total culture—aesthetic, social, political—rather than biographical detail.

Collins' use of Arnold's concept of the power of literary (and, of course, other) culture was only the first of many influential co-optations. Versions of the Arnoldian vision reverberated through the developing English literature curriculum. Walter Raleigh expressed his concern with how to fit an Arnoldian program into the academy at his Inaugural Lecture at Glasgow in 1899 before taking charge of the English School at Oxford in 1904. "Literature is the expression in words of all the best that man has thought and felt: how are we to catch it and subdue it to the purposes of the classroom?" Quiller-Couch, attempting to establish the Cambridge English Tripos, urged an Arnoldian model in contrast to that of the founders of the Modern Language Trips: "Criticism, as Sainte Beuve, Matthew Arnold, or Pater understood and practiced it, they merely misprized." Raleigh's and Quiller-Couch's misgivings confirmed Arnold's doubts: assigning students good literature, literature that presumably makes up the best known and thought, is not enough to bring them—or their teachers—to the proper practice of criticism. The crux is the sort of understanding of that literature that is expected, and the use made of that understanding.

Present-day detractors have more conspicuously distorted Arnold's program. The best-known recent use of **"The Function of Criticism at the Present Time"** as a text to preach upon is perhaps that by Geoffrey Hartman in *Criticism in the Wilderness* (1980). Now, Hartman's somewhat scornful dismissal of what he calls "The Arnoldian Concordat," that is, the sundering of creativity and criticism and consequent assignment of a distinctly lower mission to criticism, is an egregious misreading of Arnold. One would feel it unnecessary to rehearse the evidence that Arnold neither sharply divided criticism from creativity nor conceived criticism to be simply a commentary on literature if such skewed readings of Arnold by eminent critics were not so prevalent. The fact is, of course, that in assigning criticism a central role in the improvement of culture

and the quality of life, Arnold gave it a higher value than it had traditionally been accorded.

If Arnold does not make criticism autotelic, neither does he make literature autonomous—each has as its ultimate end the improvement of the total culture. And one surely ought not to forget that the first sentence of the penultimate paragraph of **"The Function of Criticism"** is "I conclude with what I said in the beginning: to have the sense of creative activity is the great happiness and the great proof of being alive and it is not denied to criticism to have it." Indeed, one can argue, as has Eugene Goodheart, "that for Arnold criticism as a speculative function is not a dependent activity. On the contrary, it is imaginative literature that depends on the prior activity of criticism for its full success." Nor should one forget in reading Arnold's plaint from which Hartman takes the title of his book, "That promised land it will not be ours to enter, and we shall die in the wilderness," that ironic mock modesty prevails in all of Arnold's prose. Most important, Arnold's own criticism has long since been accorded that status of literature to which Hartman believes criticism has the right to aspire. That it has would gratify but not surprise Arnold—he intended that it should.

However, the point, again, is not so much that Hartman has misrepresented Arnold but that practically everyone who has chosen him as a text has to some extent done so. One could regard this as one more evidence that "all readings are misreadings" and simply take Arnold's text as the occasion for the spinning of airy eristic and witty commentary. One could equally tease out its inadequacies and contradictions as exemplifications of the necessarily self-conflicting nature of all rhetoric. However, I am interested in the intent of Arnold's efforts and the actual nature of his influence rather than the reduction of his writing to grist for the post-structuralist, or, Hartman would say, "revisionist," mill.

Once one begins to trace the form of the argument, **"The Function of Criticism at the Present Time"** turns out to be quite a strange essay. Let us briefly recall it. In one sense the essay is exactly what the opening paragraph implies that it will be, a defense of Arnold's now all-too-familiar remark in an earlier essay that "Of the literature of France and Germany, as of the intellect of Europe in general, the main effort, for now many years, has been a critical effort, the endeavour in all branches of knowledge, theology, philosophy, history, art, and science, to see the object as in itself it really is." Recognizing objections to the importance he has given to criticism, he asks, "But is it true that criticism is really, in itself, a baneful and injurious employment; is it true that all time given to writing critiques of others would be much better employed if it were given to original composition, of whatever kind this may be?" Not only is that question tactically understated, the answer is an excellent example of what Burke called "strategies for dealing with situations." The function of the answer is to expand the boundaries of the argument, vastly extending the original topic.

First, literature is the source of criticism, then criticism becomes a "line" of literature, shortly to be magnified to a "power" acting on all branches of knowledge. Criticism then appears as the foundation for creative literature, expands to become the foundation of culture, and is subsequently narrowed back to commentary on literature. Then criticism again becomes a product of literature before a final return to it as a comment on literature, this time in the form of a succession of communications of fresh knowledge. Such a summary of the protean properties of criticism in Arnold's handling of course distorts the emphasis: the turnings and twistings occur primarily in the opening and closing sections; the central two-thirds of the essay concentrates on the larger criticism which is the preserver and purifier of culture, not its subcategory which directly treats literature. The original title of the essay pluralized "function"; the most accurate title would pluralize "criticism." Arnold profits in various ways from the ambiguity, not least in making seeing the object as it is and knowing the best known and thought seem interchangeable: as everyone knows, this allows him to seem to make synonymous culture, criticism, and literature. At the same time, they cannot be actually synonymous, for each corrects the errors of the others. By the point toward the close of the essay where Arnold restates his definition of criticism as "a disinterested endeavour to learn and propagate the best that is known and thought in the world," that endeavor seems to encompass the whole duty of the responsible intellect.

. . . . .

A basic procedure of deconstruction is explained by Gayatri Spivak in a brief passage in the introduction to her translation of [Jacques Derrida's] *Grammatology* that is the unacknowledged source of more than one American critic's summary:

> If in the process of deciphering a text in the traditional way we come across a word that seems to harbor an unresolvable contradiction, and by virtue of being *one* word is made sometimes to work in one way and sometimes in another and thus is made to point away from the absence of unified meaning, we shall catch at that word.

Arnold has offered any number of hostages to denizens of the deconstructive abyss. If we wish to demonstrate that the significant words in any discourse appeal to a hierarchy that might be reversed in another discourse, or are employed in several senses, or necessarily imply the existence of their opposites, or are indeterminate in meaning outside the context of each use, Arnold has almost done the work for us. To which a de Mannian answer would be that that is why his criticism is literature.

But even if one abjures Derrida and all his works and seeks simply to read Arnold in an old-fashioned critically analytical way, logical and metaphysical weaknesses are visible enough. To begin with, the object as it is and the best known do not actually reduce to the same thing, and we note that the first is the object of criticism in a wider sense than that criticism responsible for the second. Difficulties surround Arnold's "object as in itself it really is." First advanced as the goal of criticism in the second of the lectures *On Translating Homer,* the "object as in itself it really is" may have seemed to Arnold perfectly self-defining. Or it may be that with his distaste for metaphysics, he felt that anyone who insisted on trying to look behind it deserved to disappear in whatever ontological quicksand might be found there. One would hardly expect Arnold to interest himself in disputations on the existence of primary and secondary qualities or objective and subjective attributions. Nevertheless, as I have argued elsewhere, even with-

in the context of the lectures on translating Homer, where it originated, the formula "the object as in itself it really is" is of doubtful meaning. There the "object" in question is Homer, but the validity of an English translation is to be determined by comparing the effect of the translation with the effect of the original on competent readers. Not only is that effect at some distance from the work itself, but Arnold's argument also admits that the effect on the modern reader may well be different from that on the original Greek auditors. The *Iliad* is thus transformed into the effect it creates, and the effect it creates disintegrates into different effects in different ages.

In essence, though Arnold would wish criticism, and as a corollary, major literary works, to reveal a permanent (if not noumenal) reality, he is unable to deny that differences in historical and intellectual vantage points will determine the objects the author sees embodied in the text and the text as object which the reader finds. Unfortunately there were no practitioners of *rezeptionästhetik* around to point out to Arnold that readers of different periods bring different horizons to the same text. That is why Arnold's goal of "the object as in itself it really is," despite its fame, has never been effectively incorporated into literary theory. Its major importance lies in its transmogrifications by Pater and Wilde.

But as everyone knows, there are three central slogans in **"The Function of Criticism at the Present Time,"** and the other two are, fortunately, independent of the idea of "the object as in itself it really is." The second, "the best known and thought," has had a much more visibly prosperous career. This singularly happy phrase has been widely appropriated—and at times hammered into shapes that Arnold would hardly have recognized. The obvious question nevertheless remains: how are we to know the best known and thought, especially if it cannot be judged against things as in themselves they are. If Arnold had admitted the existence of a set of values revealed through dogmatic religion or mystic transcendence, the best known and thought would presumably be judged against these. But as we know, Arnold's realm of the "best" was intended precisely as a substitute for such a transcendent realm. The best known and thought, one assumes from Arnold's abhorrence of metaphysics, exists only insofar as it has actually been known and thought. Whatever is to be judged is to be looked at in the light of, or measured against, the best available ideas. But the best ideas can hardly form a static or eternal order, for out of the contemplation of the best knowledge and thought flows a current of "true and fresh ideas"—perhaps through the very process of judging the existing order of things against the sphere of ideas. The "best known" must somehow be known to be best without comparing it either with an eternal order of reality or with an eternal set of values.

That is precisely what the phrase "the best known" implies—not the best in a transcendental sense, but the best that is known to fallible human beings. We will hardly reach agreement on "the best," though that does not vitiate the value of the concept. For a) human kind has often been able to agree about, to rule out, what is *not* best; b) few would claim that their own unaided thought is necessarily "the best"; c) the more one knows of what others have thought to be the best, the less likely one is to settle for the clearly not-best; d) the critic is called upon simply to be acquainted with as much as possible of what others have cogently argued to be the best and to try to propagate what he/she believes to be the best of that. Moreover, the "best" any critic should urge depends on the circumstances of the time: Arnold thus admits in *Culture and Anarchy* that he is so much the champion of sweetness and light because "the ruling force is now, and has long been, a Puritan force—the care for fire and strength."

Arnold never assumes that the best known is simply an achieved body of thought to be acquired. His third slogan, "the free play of the mind," assures us that this is not the case. To "create a current of true and fresh ideas," to experience the "free play of the mind on all subjects it touches"—if these are the business of criticism, then it is not called upon to state apodictic truths, nor eternal, irrefutable propositions. That adjective "true" is worth pondering. Arnold does *not* say that the critic discovers or pronounces "truths": rather he/she *creates* true and fresh ideas, where "true" would seem to mean "worthy of consideration and applicable to the existing situation." Those of Arnold's demi-disciples who created the concept of the creative critic were not wholly apostate: they may indeed be said to have created a (not *the*) true and fresh idea of the critical function.

Arnold, of course, is partly responsible for the contracted understanding of the best known and thought which identifies it primarily with poetry. **"The Study of Poetry,"** amplifying his prediction that "the future of poetry is immense, because in our poetry, where it is worthy of its high destinies, our race, as time goes on, will find an ever surer and surer stay," would have seemed to countenance such an understanding even if it had not included the definition of poetry as "a criticism of life." The epigram is so neat and striking that the modifying phrase "under the conditions fixed for such a criticism by the laws of poetic truth and poetic beauty," is all too easily overlooked. In any case, Arnold does not say that poetry is *the* criticism of life. What he is saying is that it is one of the judgments of criticism that poetry is one of the sources of the best upon which a comprehensive criticism rests.

. . . . .

Looking back at **"The Function of Criticism at the Present Time"** from this, *our* present time, we understand that Arnold offered a rich range of perspectives that finally refuse to coalesce. That they were not a full and final summation of the methods, powers, and goals of the critical endeavor ought to surprise no one—it would not have surprised Arnold, who knew that the social structure, cultural assumptions, knowledge, and functions of criticism all change. Nor would it have prostrated him that readers have difficulty accepting the total set of arguments. The success of the essay is that so many readers have been intrigued by one or more portions; its weakness is that Arnold's manifest failure to bring his major arguments into a convincing unity—not a unity to defy the deconstructionist, but simply one to satisfy our ordinary practical sense of coherence—has seemed to authorize readers to detach whatever single slogan especially appeals to them and develop it for their own purposes. No wonder the essay has been so continuously plundered—and that the plunderings have been so partial and selective. But, finally, that Arnold was attempting to respond to the central issues is evidenced by a kind of centripetal force that

causes perceptive partial followers to acknowledge that whatever portion of Arnold's argument they have especially singled out is not in itself adequate.

We know that simply by translating "effect" into "impression," Pater was able to place in the foreground the element of subjectivity, and thus creativity, already lurking in Arnold's use of the formula. Both artist and critic become merchants in impressions. But, Pater could not, we also know, be entirely content to argue that art is of value only for the impressions it produces, however intense. In addition to the famously inconsistent concession in the essay "Style" that great art requires devotion "to the increase of men's happiness, to the redemption of the oppressed, or enlargement of our sympathies," one discovers the less well-known but more consistent comment at the conclusion to the essay on *Measure for Measure*:

> It is not always that poetry can be the exponent of morality; but it is this aspect of morals [human sympathy] which it represents most naturally, for this true justice is dependent on just those finer appreciations which poetry cultivates in us the power of making, those peculiar valuations of action and its effect which poetry actually requires.

Pater could have said that whereas the critic deals in impressions of impressions, he might just as well be creative in the expression of his impressions. He did not, but of course Wilde did, giving a new salience to the concept of the free play of the mind. "Who cares whether Mr. Ruskin's views on Turner are sound or not? What does it matter?" "Who, again, cares whether Mr. Pater has put into the portrait of Mona Lisa something that Leonardo never dreamed of?" Criticism thus read for its own aesthetic qualities, vying to become itself part of the best known and thought (best because most aesthetically interesting) rather than merely to transmit it, seems to have turned 180 degrees from the position that Arnold assigned it. But even a path that starts off in the opposite direction may arrive at something like Arnold's destination. In the midst of the joyous assertions that all art is immoral and all criticism dangerous to society, we find many of Arnold's conclusions emerging from Wilde's paradoxes: the dangers of identifying virtue with action, the need for the critical spirit, the duty of the critic to wake the age into consciousness, "lending it his larger vision and his nobler moods," the necessity of a criticism which "creates the intellectual atmosphere of the age."

The Wildean combination of a hyperbolic transformation of Arnold's assertion of the creativity of criticism with his insistence on the larger purpose of criticism is found in less florid form in critics like John Middleton Murry. Criticism as much as poetry is required to give delight: "If it gives this delight criticism is creative," writes Murry. "Critical articles and essays are read for themselves; at their best they are perfectly self-contained; they do not demand that the reader should dash out and purchase the books which they discuss." The function of criticism is "to provide self-expression for the critic." But like others, Murry is able to pronounce a relaxed view of the function of the critic in one place only through drawing on Arnold's immense fund of seriousness elsewhere. His "Reason and Criticism," for instance, not only reproduces much of Arnold's argument about the alternation of creative and critical periods, the difficulties for the artist in a critical period when he must work out his own synthesis as well as express it ("build his loom and spin his thread"), and the creativeness of criticism, but urges that the function of criticism is "to justify literature." Literature brings to birth the Reason which is "the understanding of life." The critic thus has a high duty: "We have been granted a moment of the pure life of Reason; it is our duty not to degrade it into a function of our ordinary consciousness, but to seek a way to lift our ordinary consciousness to the condition we have been privileged to share."

The American Humanists Paul Elmer More and Irving Babbitt, while taking as their text the second of the chief Arnoldian slogans, "the best known and thought," gave no less importance to the creativity of criticism. The importance of Arnold for More is placarded in the essay "Criticism" (1910). Looking perhaps to the touchstone methodology of **"The Study of Poetry"** as well as to **"The Function of Criticism,"** More felt that Arnold had made culture/criticism seem too much a judge and not enough a creator, that is, that Arnold had not developed the consequences of the creativity he allowed to criticism. More amplifies this aspect of Arnold through his concept of the "critical memory" that actively selects those elements of thought and experience which bear upon the present; the result is the "conscious creation of the field of the present out of the past." Similarly, More took greater pains than Arnold to distinguish his own position from absolutism. The trick is best carried off in one of More's brightest essays, "The Demon of the Absolute" (1917), where he turns relativism against itself by playing upon the apparent absurdity of an "absolute relativism." If there are neither absolute standards nor an absolute relativism, culture becomes the one reasonable source of standards. Standards are not simply "there"; they must be created by the intelligent juxtaposition of the present with the comprehended past that culture makes available.

Perhaps the most striking measure of the power of Arnold's continuing influence in the twentieth century is the improbable amount of effort T. S. Eliot devoted to trying to put it behind him. The influences and parallels, many and grudging, are notorious. To say, as does Eliot in his first important essay, "The poet must be very conscious of the main current. . . . He must be aware that the mind of Europe—the mind of his own country . . . is a mind which changes, and that this change is a development which abandons nothing *en route*" is to produce a version of Arnold's insistence that the literary genius must somehow "find itself amidst the order of ideas." The novelty of "Tradition and the Individual Talent" is of course the concept that the existing order of literature is modified by the truly new work. But though Arnold never worked out so explicit and arresting a statement of the matter, he could hardly have placed so high a value on a "current of fresh and true ideas" somehow interacting with the best of what had been known and thought if he had not understood what Eliot later meant in saying that "the past is and should be altered by the present as much as the present is directed by the past."

After issuing challenges to the Arnoldian view in *The Sacred Wood,* "The Function of Criticism," and the essays on Bradley, Eliot steadied his lance and tried to unhorse Arnold decisively in "The Place of Pater." In that celebrated essay, looking more to **"The Study of Poetry"** and

Arnold's excursions into the meaning of religious belief than to **"The Function of Criticism,"** Eliot unequivocally locates Arnold's error in his allowing culture to assume the place of religion, thus begetting two groups of erring disciples, Humanists who try to replace religion with a culture conceived essentially as morals, and Aesthetes who try to replace religion with a culture conceived essentially as art. Nevertheless in Eliot's final return to the question of the relationship of criticism to culture, "The Aims of Education," we find an intriguing return to Arnold. Though education may not be able to improve or even maintain the health of culture in Eliot's larger sense of the word, "It should be an aim of education to maintain the continuity of our culture." The program for that is, despite its Eliotian elitism, unexpectedly Arnoldian:

> What I wish to maintain is a point of view from which it appears more important—if we have to choose, and perhaps we do have to choose—that a small number of people should be educated well, and others left with only a rudimentary education, than that everybody should receive a share of an inferior quality of education. . . . And what I plead for is what Matthew Arnold spoke of as "the knowledge of the best that has been thought and said in the world."

Eliot's tradition remains Arnold's culture.

I. A. Richards' relation to Arnold is the most interesting, and most misunderstood, of all. Richards evidently began with a conviction that poetry must have enormous value: Arnold's belief in the saving virtues of poetry operates like a hidden axiom in *Principles of Literary Criticism* (1924). Explicit acknowledgment of the importance and source of the axiom awaited the publication of *Science and Poetry* two years later, which builds on the four sentences that open Arnold's **"The Study of Poetry,"** beginning "The future of poetry is immense." It is easy to see how the strategy underlying the attempt of the early Richards to justify the Arnoldian faith required dichotomizing "scientific" and "emotive" language. If good literature leads to the experiencing of valuably complex attitudes, demonstrating the possibility of and preparing the mind for finer adjustments of manifold impulses, it would seem to provide just that disinterested "touchstone" with which Arnold's culture shows up the unsatisfactoriness of the crude, tawdry, and incomplete. However, as Richards himself soon realized, the distinction between emotive and referential language divorced literature from the human experience Arnold believed it illuminated. Therefore while the New Critical orthodoxy busied itself in finding ways to smuggle the Arnoldian values back in, Richards rethought his position while writing *Practical Criticism* and *Coleridge on the Imagination.*

The result was *The Philosophy of Rhetoric* (1936) which, without anywhere announcing it, reverses the position Richards took in *Principles of Literary Criticism. The Philosophy of Rhetoric* practices an Arnoldian criticism on language itself, a topic Arnold had slighted. Since the meanings of words shift as they are brought into relation with other words and since poetry provides the most complex and creative context, it is the poetic use of language that can most nearly refer to the world as it actually is. Literature, in an ultimate sense, is the most referential use of language, while scientific uses are limited, special, and ultimately misleading. They are misleading, paradoxically, precisely because they are conventional. "We rediscover that the world—so far from being a solid matter of fact—is rather a fabric of conventions, which for obscure reasons it has suited us in the past to manufacture and support." Arnold's belief that literature presents us with a comprehensive view is given a new basis.

Perhaps the most striking evidence of Arnold's continuous prominence is the succession of influential critics—those I have mentioned and others as different as Saintsbury, Stuart Sherman, and Leavis—who have felt it necessary to seriously modify, if not directly challenge, his conceptions of literature and criticism. The old king has to be defeated in the sacred wood if the crown is to descend. However, each new aspirant finds that the king to be slain remains Arnold, not the preceeding challenger.

I have tried to suggest through this quick survey of a variety of ways in which Arnold's influence appears in the brief history of literary criticism since **"The Function of Criticism"** that while the "object as in itself it really is" gave way to "the best known and thought," neither formulation could be held without recognizing the creativity of criticism. That creativity would seem, in fact, best expressed in the third slogan, "the free play of the mind," the formulation that ought indeed today to seem most sympathetic to us. It is just that free play which poststructuralists of many hues most desiderate. Hartman, advocate of the playfully serious critical performance, could as easily have used Arnold for his model as for his antagonist. However, if we accept Arnold's explicit principle of the need for balance, decades like ours in which the exuberant, hyperbolic, and ingenious draw the most sustained applause require to give at least as much attention to the *function* of the best known and thought as to the creativity of the criticism grounded in it. As Pater and Wilde earlier recognized, the best cannot be made up solely of the most aesthetically intriguing.

To say that the function of criticism is to create fresh currents of thought is of course equally too vague and too bland. When Arnold himself came to apply instances of what he regarded as the wisdom of great men of the past, they became touchstones for the judging of current situations. (Arnold's poetic touchstones were perhaps finally less important to him than his practical, ethical, rational ones.) It is well to remember that for Arnold "culture" is not a state but a source of criteria and the motivation to apply them. The improvement of both the individual and society, theory driving at practice, was Arnold's goal. That is the element of which the New Critical program lost sight. Those who think that recognition of the practical and psychological, social and economic consequences of canons of "the best" is the contribution of Marxist or feminist criticism, or perhaps of sociolinguistics, ought to look at Arnold once again. In place of narrowly focused theories, each with its own end in view, Arnold offers the possibility of total engagement—the entire circumambient society potentially to be judged, corrected, and creatively rethought against the "best," that is, the most interesting, relevant, stimulating, experientially validated thought available from human history. Neither the best that the critic propagates nor the objects to which it is relevant are narrowly literary.

Arnoldian critics have one function—criticism that encourages the intellectual ventilation of an institution or issue—and politicians another. Chris Baldick [in *The Social Mission of English Criticism, 1848-1932* (1983)] makes a cogent point in noting that Arnold's pursuit of an "innocent language" led toward practical activity being "successively substituted, postponed, concealed, and quarantined." But though Arnold may too often have hesitated to be explicit about the ultimate implications of his thought on social and political questions (he can hardly be accused of timidity in following out implications when writing on religious beliefs), he saw the critic's role as raising the intellectual temper of the nation as the means of improving its political, social, and economic structure.

The Arnoldian program decrees that no one ideology, no one scheme of social reformation, can be exempt from continual comparative evaluation. Nor can any one critical evaluator—Arnold included—be presumed infallible. One can, then, understand the motivation, if not condone the errancy of interpretation when a Marxist critic like Terry Eagleton [in *Literary Theory, An Introduction*] writes sneeringly of the Arnoldian endeavor.

> Since literature, as we know, deals in universal human values rather than in such historical trivia as civil war, the oppression of women, or the dispossession of the English peasantry, it could serve to place in cosmic perspective the petty demands of working people for decent living conditions or greater control over their own lives, and might even with luck render them oblivious of such issues in their high-minded contemplation of eternal truths and beauties.

Rather it is just such issues that criticism is fitted to address, better fitted than any single socioeconomic ideology. Precisely because all values and beliefs are ideological, no single mode of thought can replace the free play of mind. Nor should we confuse the value of Arnold's particular judgments with the value of the process he advocated. He hardly thought that the pursuit of the best thought should cease when he laid down his pen.

One frequently enough now encounters among avant-garde critics of various theoretical allegiances the desire to root out the last of Arnoldism in literary study. However, Arnold's notions of the functions of the study of literature and practice of criticism not only ushered these into the academy but have been their constant guarantors of value. It may be that Arnold was wholly in error; perhaps he will yet be consigned to the crowded shelves of historical curiosities. But if so, faculties of literature can hardly be surprised if they are in turn perceived as amusing curiosities, a group of intellectual jesters licensed to entertain a somewhat precious coterie with their ingenious wit and clever eristic. Alternatively, to recognize that the function of criticism is the creative application to present circumstances of the most stimulating of past formulations is simply to remember that Arnold urged and exemplified an ever applicable method of critical thought, not a set of timeless judgments.

In an essay that deserves to be far better known than it is ["The Decline of the Humanities; or, Where's the Bloody Horse?" *New Directions* 17 (1961)], Georg Mann, without ever mentioning Arnold, offered one of the most accurate translations of the argument of **"The Function of Criticism"** into more contemporary phrasing:

In spite of limiting themselves to the pursuit of a hobby, in spite of their attempt to make transcontinental highways out of blind alleys, in spite of panic-stricken professional hedging, the humanists are, whether they like it or not, still the masters of the big choice. If the men who were once committed to know why cheerfully assume a seat next to the aurochs and the whooping crane, they leave the world committed to the dangerous mercies of the men who merely know how.

(pp. 117-30)

Wendell Harris, "The Continuously Creative Function of Arnoldian Criticism," in Victorian Poetry, *Vol. 26, Nos. 1-2, Spring-Summer, 1988, pp. 117-33.*

George Levine   (essay date 1988)

[*In the following essay, Levine explains the interdependence of Arnold's intellectual position on critical theory, literature, and religion, and his awareness of the importance of modern science, asserting that Arnold ultimately affirms his flexible critical style as superior to empirical scientific procedures.*]

"Do you ask of culture what are its principles and ideas? The *best* principles, the *best* ideas, the *best* knowledge; the perfect! the ideal! the complete!"

"But how does it recognise these," he asked helplessly, evidently now striking at random, "if it has neither system, method, nor logic?"

"By Insight," I replied triumphantly; "by its own inborn sensibility to beauty, truth and life."

"But if a man is born without it?" he asked.

"God help him then," I rejoined, "for I cannot."
(Frederic Harrison, "Culture: A Dialogue")

Harrison's attack on Arnold reflects the unease of a developing scientific and even positivistic culture with the casually unsystematic nature of Arnold's prose. We, like Harrison, will "seek vainly in Mr. A." for "a system of philosophy with principles coherent, interdependent, subordinate, and derivative." Much of the important criticism of Arnold through a century has focussed on this absence either as a failure of intellectual seriousness, or as a virtue of humane flexibility. We remember T. S. Eliot's remarks in his well-known essay on Arnold and Pater: "Arnold had little gift for consistency of definition, . . . and what Culture and Conduct are, I feel that I know less well on every reading." There have, of course, been formidable defenses, but the majority position, even from among Arnold's greatest admirers, consents to the view that precision of definition and intellectual clarity—as opposed to rhetorical force—are not his special strengths.

I want to argue here that the problem of Arnold's evasive manner can be approached fruitfully through a consideration of his attitudes toward science, and with special attention to his own efforts to *be* "scientific." Curiously, as Fred Dudley has pointed out [in "Matthew Arnold and Science" *PMLA* 57 (1942)], "in spite of a certain distrust of and distaste for science and a fairly comprehensive ignorance of its details, [Arnold] believed he was following

in important ways the lead of the scientific spirit." Dudley was certainly correct, but I want to take his arguments further. Arnold's "ignorance" of science had to do not only with the "details," as Dudley put it, but with the whole enterprise—its methods and principles, and the programmatic vulnerability of its conclusions. Yet Arnold believed in science with a very Victorian faith, and his strategies of argument, as well as many of his major ideas, may be understood as responses, often defensive, to the authority of science. His ideas often reflect attitudes either distinctly homologous with that of scientific theory or even more "scientific" than science itself would allow.

Contrary to the notion propagated because of his notorious debate with Huxley, Arnold has much to say in essays, letters, and school reports in favor of science. For true education in "perception," he writes to Mrs. Foster, she must train her niece in "science." He believed that science should be a component in every student's education, and that as science becomes "more of a power in the world, the weight of the nations and men who have carried the intellectual life farthest will be more and more felt." Even in **Culture and Anarchy,** Arnold identifies the "scientific passion," by which he means the pursuit of knowledge for its own sake, as one of the essential elements of culture."

Arnold's deference to the authority of science suggests an innocent awe of the facts it generates. The third sentence of **"The Study of Poetry"** is a famous instance of such deference: "Our religion has materialised itself in the fact, in the supposed fact; it has attached its emotion to the fact, and now the fact is failing it." Fact is the province of science: the geological, philological, archaeological fact demonstrates the falsity of religious doctrine. Arnold's commitment to science becomes most explicit when he discusses religion, which, ironically, he always addresses from a thoroughly secular position. As Joseph Carroll points out [in *The Cultural Theory of Matthew Arnold* (1982)], Arnold felt that "the growth of the scientific mentality has not only altered the substance of belief but also rendered more complex and rigorous the means by which conviction might be attained." Moreover, even when Arnold defines religion, he affirms positions to which, as Ruth apRoberts puts it [in *Arnold and God* (1983)], "a man of science can subscribe, and [he] says they are all in literal fact the religious man need subscribe to." Science, then, emerges in Arnold's religious writings in a way that should throw light on his entire enterprise as writer and critic. I will want consequently to consider, towards the end of this essay, Arnold's specific arguments about religion, particularly in **Literature and Dogma.**

Of course, Arnold does not participate in the occasional Victorian jingoistic pride in the empire of science, and he insists strenuously on the separation of the language of science from the language of literature. The authority of science is in the world of "facts," but it has nothing directly to say about culture, society, religion. The facts it accumulates may become matters of interpretation in considerations of these institutions, but the scientist cannot as scientist discuss them:

There is truth of science and truth of religion; truth of science does not become truth of religion till it is made religious. . . . Let us have all the science there is from the men of science; from the men of religion let us have religion.

In the interests of poetry and religion he cedes the field of knowledge to science, and only wrests authority away by imagining another *kind* of knowledge, which can find no expression in the rigorously systematic and logical language that science requires.

That other kind of knowledge is to be located in the language of poetry. Not surprisingly, the status of this knowledge is a little obscure. In a certain sense it does not displace scientific knowledge, but supplements it. In another, it is a superior replacement. Science gives us facts; it means a "true knowledge of things." It makes its progress, Arnold says, "not merely by close reasoning and deduction, but also, and much more, by the close scrutiny and correction of the present commonly received data." But for poetry, "the idea *is* the fact," the transformation and interpretation of the knowledge science gives, and thus the humanizing of it. Religion and its modern surrogate, poetry, attain to truths fuller than those of science, not only because they appeal to the "three fourths of life" that is conduct, and to that other fragment of life, the sense of beauty, but because poetry looks at objects differently. "The interpretations of science," Arnold says,

> do not give us this intimate sense of objects as the interpretations of poetry give it; they appeal to a limited faculty, and not to the whole man. It is not Linnaeus or Cavendish or Cuvier who gives us the true sense of animals, or water, or plants, who seizes their secret for us, who makes us participate in their life.

The poet, then, gives us a "true sense of things," but the scientist gives us the truth.

For the most part, therefore, all Arnold can do against the authority of the scientific fact, as he does implicitly in the opening passage of **"The Study of Poetry,"** is evade what he regards as undeniable: let us attach our emotion to the "idea." Let the idea become the fact. Science then becomes—in Arnold's way of thinking—irrelevant. For science only appeals to a "limited faculty," the intellect; and the intellect, Arnold argues, is valuable only as it in turn appeals to the human need for beauty, for conduct, for manners. He invokes from science "facts," those elements that are least constrained by disciplined thought, even while he often uses the word "science" to mean systematic knowledge.

The locus classicus for Arnold's confrontation with science as enemy is **"Literature and Science."** There, in the midst of a brilliant dramatic performance, much of his ambivalence and much of the weakness of his use of science are manifest. Arnold claims to adopt what he describes, amusingly, as a tone of "tentative inquiry, which befits a being of dim faculties and bounded knowledge." Thus, disguised as the ordinary man, not bright enough to write systematically or to contend with such a brilliant opponent as Huxley, he still somehow manages to argue for the superior value of the humanities. Professing not to know much about the sciences, he drops a great many "scientific" facts—as, for example, "the pulmonary artery carries dark blood and the pulmonary vein carries bright blood, departing in this respect from the common rule for the division of labour between the veins and the arteries."

Unfortunately, Arnold seems to have been as little knowledgeable about science as his mask professes to be. The very "facts" he gives in surreptitiously showing off about how much he really does know about science confirm the literal assertion that he knows little. As we shall see, for the scientific education against which Arnold contended, facts are nothing unless they can be generalized and seen as part of a system revealing the laws of nature. The rhetoric of humility rings false, though funny, since the pretense of ignorance implies a shrewdness that transcends ignorance—and Arnold's caricature of science fails to achieve that transcendence. In dropping facts about the artery, or telling us that "when a taper burns the wax is converted into carbonic acid and water," the rhetoric backfires. He simply never troubled to think deeply about the question of scientific knowledge. As Dudley points out, "except for a certain interest in botanical handbooks, he seldom read any scientist later than Bacon."

Science produces knowledge that, for Arnold, brings light without sweetness. The idea with firm outlines, expressed in language "rigid, fixed, and scientific" has no relation to our distinctively human needs. He concedes in **"Literature and Science,"** for example, that Darwin's "proposition that 'our ancestor was a hairy quadruped furnished with a tail and pointed ears, probably arboreal in his habits'," is "interesting." But then, with that characteristic irony that disguises laughter and made him irresistible as a speaker, Arnold elevates his diction and tells us that once we have noted the idea

> there will be found to arise an invincible desire to relate this proposition to the sense in us for conduct, and to the sense in us for beauty. But this the men of science will not do for us.

This has it both ways, allowing for the possibility of the truth of Darwin's proposition, but dismissing its form. The truth Arnold seeks will have no such sharp outlines, and the language he finds to express it will be emotion-laden. In other words, Arnold seeks a way to avoid the implications of what science is telling him (and requiring him to believe); the "way" he finds is in a language that will not be pinned down to an idea or to a fact. That is, the language of poetry.

Attractive as is Arnold's refusal of positivist demands for strictly empirical and rational modes of truth, there is a deep contradiction in his thought. He resists the rigid and fixed language of science, but seeks precisely analogous authority. "The sense in us for conduct, the sense in us for beauty," for example—these are undebatable givens in Arnold's argument. Of course we have these "senses"; and of course Darwin makes no appeal to them. Everywhere, he points and asserts that we have here an irrefutable, one might almost say, scientific, fact: Chaucer is less serious than Dante; this passage is absurd; this is provincial; this is mature. How do we know? Arnold rarely explains "the ground and authority" of his assertions.

In the Huxley debate, he concedes the usefulness of knowing "the great results of the scientific investigation of nature." But he refuses to believe that we should know, as Huxley demands, "the processes by which those results are reached." The processes are precisely what Arnold does not understand about science, and what he refuses to make clear to himself or his readers about his own different kind of knowledge.

Notoriously, he cloaks his own partiality in the verbal play

Matthew Arnold, 1883.

rebuke innovation in the name of painfully acquired wisdom, to check fanaticism and blind materialism by reminders of the spiritual needs of man, to help us live by that happy fusion of powers he calls "the imaginative reason." He offers, not a rounded and coherent philosophy, but rather a set of humanistic ideals which stress the need for balance and a sane perspective.

But Arnold's charming strategies of common sense and moderation are not always adequate to the issues. Surely some of those issues—the place of poetry in culture, the nature of criticism, the rights of traditional political authority, the structure of the academic curriculum, the survival of traditional religion, the validity of German higher criticism of the Bible—depend on a precision Arnold never wished to achieve. Where we look for clarity we find amusing "counters," racial or national stereotypes, catchphrases—the Celtic, the Germanic, the Barbarian, the Philistine, the Populace, Hebraism, sweetness, light, and, of course, culture.

Studied imprecision is pervasive through all of Arnold's prose, which is often characterized by intellectual opacity, a point always teasingly, temptingly deferred, the intimation that if we were to read only one more sentence, hear one more iteration, we would finally get it clear. The delightful seductiveness of Arnold's prose stems from its simplicity, vivacity, and (apparent) clarity. Exploiting (despite some extraordinary rhetorical contortions) the rhythms of speech, it stylishly, sometimes playfully, often combatively, appeals to the interests and needs of its audience. The apostle of high seriousness is captured well in Beerbohm's cartoon, in which Arnold's niece cries out, "Why, Uncle Matthew, oh why, will not you be always wholly serious?"

Surely Arnold was smiling at some of his own evasions: at his rhetorical hits; at his "vivacity," for which he vivaciously and perhaps mockingly apologizes; and, in particular, at his remarkably artful and memorable phrasemaking.

We remember those phrases because Arnold relentlessly reiterates them, in dozens of contexts, until they begin to feel comfortably familiar and clear. Inevitable as the phrases have become, their very familiarity cloaks the imprecision of meaning that gives them the flexibility and authority Arnold wants. Consider, for a moment, what exactly is denoted by such phrases as: "a disinterested endeavour to propagate the best that is known and thought in the world"; "to make reason and the will of God prevail"; "Conduct is three fourths of life"; "to know the object as in itself it truly is"; "a current of true and fresh ideas"; "Hebraism and Hellenism"; "the eternal power not ourselves that makes for righteousness"; "sweetness and light"—and so on. It may be that these survive *because* nobody knows exactly what they mean.

Yet obviously Arnold valued clarity and intelligence. Indeed, along with the contemporary criticism that he lacked seriousness, there was the charge that he was too much concerned with the intellect. As Frederic Faverty noted [in *Matthew Arnold the Ethnologist* (1951)], he was often accused of " 'deficiency in sympathies lying beyond the intellectual sphere'." His almost lifelong pursuit of the Philistines and of what he thought of as the Teutonic element in English life is sufficient evidence that the life of

of catchphrases. He creates new categories (often out of science, particularly ethnology), and plays them against each other. But such categories, aping contemporary scientific interest in taxonomy, grow from intuitions untested or literature unsystematically read, and disguise from Arnold and his readers that they participate in the values of science without exploiting its methods. At least theoretically, science opened the possibility of falsification; Arnold is a controversialist, but his appeal to authority is so splendidly cloaked that he alone, as Harrison is suggesting, has access to it.

His verbal playfulness has always attracted attention, but favorable critics normally assume that the playfulness is an aspect of his method and of the objectives they are ready to concede him: the concern to avoid narrow or extreme, *merely* rational, or abstract judgments in order to respond fully to the wisdom of large human experience and the appeals of common sense. The case for Arnold's method is an important one, and I do not want to dismiss it. It is perhaps most convincingly put by William Robbins. "Arnold's function," Robbins says [in *The Ethical Idealism of Matthew Arnold* (1959)],

> is to remind enthusiasts and extremists of the Aristotelian golden mean, to reject obscurantism on behalf of man's instinct for expansion and change, to

the mind mattered deeply to him and that his evasions of intellectual precision and coherence were not a rejection of the value of reason. The Hellenism he espoused in the first phase of his critical career led him notoriously to blame poor Wordsworth because he "did not read more books." The greatest poetry is informed by ideas. Certainly, in **"The Function of Criticism at the Present Time,"** Arnold is emphasizing "pure reason," important for a world in which "so little of mind, or anything so worthy and quickening as mind, comes into the motives . . . of men."

Nevertheless, in Arnold's hierarchy of values, precision of thought and argument is secondary to feeling. Even his affirmation of the importance of ideas transforms them into objects governed not by reason but by nonintellectual forces. Burke, he says, is great because "he *saturates* politics with thought." "Ideas" in Arnold's dramatization of them, seem to be valuable for their own sake. Burke "lived by ideas"; Shakespeare lived "in a *current* of ideas"; Arnold seeks "a *free play* of mind on all subjects" (my italics throughout this paragraph). Criticism should lead towards "perfection by making the mind *dwell* upon what is excellent in itself, and the absolute beauty and fitness of things." Putting aside for the moment the extraordinary uncertainty of what constitutes "perfection," the complexities of determining what is "excellent in itself," the audacity in the affirmation of "the absolute beauty and fitness of things," we see that Arnold describes the activity of mind in language that allows the strongest implication of the objectivity of his own values, and that resists system, definition, precision. The mind "plays," or "dwells," or in Burke's case it "turns" upon itself, and "saturates" its subject with ideas.

We must, urges Arnold, "think of quietly enlarging our stock of true and fresh ideas." Here ideas are separate items to be stockpiled, moved about, laid on. They are different from, although they can be used by feeling; they have their own solidity and authority apart from any interpretation or theory. The value of true ideas is that they are based in experience, in the reality, as Arnold would have it, of human experience. Despite his own penchant for generalizing, Arnold rejects reason, theory, the "abstract" in his determination to avoid extremes and to affirm the moderating value of large human experience.

Arnold's evasive relation to the intellect is conditioned by his ambivalence toward science. Many of his key ideas—like the commitment to experience as authority—are closely akin to those of science. In what follows, I will be making frequent reference to John Herschel's *Preliminary Discourse on the Study of Natural Philosophy* (1831), a classic consideration of the aims and methods of science that helped inspire Darwin to choose a scientific career. Arnold probably did not read this splendid little book, but whether he did or not does not matter. Herschel's ideas were well known; Mill's *System of Logic* owes much to it; and it represents a central position of pre-Darwinian science. Much of what Herschel expects from science, Arnold asks of criticism. Yet Herschel seems more aware than Arnold of the limitations of science, and he raises questions about method that might have strengthened Arnold's arguments.

Arnold's epistemology (a word, I am sure, he would not have wanted connected with his name) was empiricist. As we shall see, his attempt to reconceive the role of religion in modern society is based initially on an appeal to experience, as against the abstractions and dogmatisms of theology. Experience is the best teacher, or at least the necessary preliminary one. In his critique of Bishop Butler's moral science, he appeals beyond Butler's premature attempt to catalogue and discriminate moral faculties. In an explanation of the relation of conscience to experience—"the real experience of the race"—Arnold argues that we know it to be a fact that the instinct to live is served by loving one's neighbor; and we know it by "experience." A peculiar experience this may be, but Arnold precisely needs experience as opposed to abstract speculation in order to provide an equivalent of scientific ground for morality.

That appeal to experience is the appeal of Baconian science itself. Herschel puts his emphasis there: "The great, and indeed only ultimate source of our knowledge of nature and its law is EXPERIENCE." But notice Herschel's succeeding Arnoldian qualification. By "experience" Herschel means "not the experience of one man only, or of one generation, but the accumulated experience of all mankind in all ages, registered in books or recorded by tradition." Science, that is, never depends on a single observer's perceptions. Every scientist reaches beyond personal knowledge to test it against the larger experience of what Arnold might have called "the race."

The scientist, like Arnold's critic, must know the best that has been thought and said. Pure "experience" is always inadequate, even for a good empiricist, because it cannot be disproved: one cannot deny the reality of anyone's personal experience. The stick is *experienced* as crooked in the water. Thus, empiricism compromises the ideal of objective authority. So Arnold's "criticism" may be taken as an attempt to validate experience without compromising authority, and he announces that the instinct of criticism "[prompts] it to try to know the best that is known and thought in the world." How does one avoid the distortions of special interest, of individual desire, of the tendency to use knowledge for some end beyond itself?

In Arnold and in Herschel, the prerequisite for valid thought is disinterest and objectivity. Against the intensifying subjectivity of some Romantic epistemologies, the impending solipsism of Paterian thought, and the political celebration of partisan debate, Arnold affirmed the primary importance of "a free disinterested play of mind." In a secularized world, authority depends on transcending the limits of personal interest. Thus, only through a "best self" can the critic achieve objectivity and trustworthy judgment. Rather than require such moral transcendence, Herschel carefully considers the nature of prejudice and possible ways to circumvent it. "It is unfortunately," he concedes, "the nature of prejudices of opinion to adhere, in a certain degree, to every mind." The scientist must try to hold prejudices "without bigotry, retain them till he shall see reason to question them, and be ready to resign them when fairly proved untenable." Such a scientist would be able to "turn," like Arnold's Burke, when the evidence accumulates against a former belief. (Arnold does not tend to attribute this kind of flexibility to science or the scientific processes he will not examine.)

Herschel recognizes a second kind of prejudice, "prejudice of sense," besides that of "opinion" and points to some obvious ways in which seeing is deceptive—the apparent size of the moon at rising, the distortions of feeling when we are very hot or very cold. In forming judgments on what we see, "we must of necessity take into account . . . modifying or accompanying circumstances, whatever they may be." We must notice everything, measure where possible, employ the same standards of measurement as are used generally. While Arnold is concerned with the powers of self-interest to distort judgment, he rarely questions the conditions of his own judgment, and allows for a much less total and complex influence of prejudice than Herschel. He thus ends with far more confidence in scientific "fact."

Closely related to the idea of disinterest is that of objectivity, the possibility of knowing what is not-self in all its fullness of being. Arnold repeatedly contends that the critic must try to "know the object as in itself it really is," showing no unease at all about the perilous condition of the ding an sich in the nineteenth century. That it is not problematic for Arnold partly reflects his overestimation of science. Herschel may be optimistic about the possible reach of scientific knowledge, but he does not believe that we will "ever be enabled to attain a knowledge of the ultimate and inward processes of nature in the production of phenomena." "We know nothing of the objects themselves which compose the universe," he claims, "except through the medium of the impressions they excite in us." Like Arnold, Herschel seeks the universal—that is, general laws. Like the Newtonian physics of his time, Arnold's theory of criticism and culture assumes a timeless standard. But science does *not* tell us what the thing in itself is. (And while Herschel did assume "timeless" laws, in Arnold's own time W. K. Clifford was arguing, not against "laws" but against the idea that any axiom held true universally, regardless of conditions. The Newtonian timelessness of Arnold's world was being undermined by the science Arnold did not know.)

When Arnold regards science as a producer of facts, he arrives at a major point of difference with Herschel. Herschel consistently argues that science is not particularly interested in the sort of facts Arnold so cutely cites for us in **"Literature and Science."** "The only facts" science cares for, says Herschel, "are those which happen uniformly and invariably under the same circumstances." Near the end of his first chapter, he is already telling us that "we must never forget that it is principles, not phenomena,—laws, not insulated independent facts,—which are the objects of inquiry to the natural philosopher." Thus, part of Arnold's implicit critique of scientific knowledge, that it presents us with insulated independent facts, breaks down; and the distinction he wishes to give the humanities turns out to be a distinction of science as well. Scientific method tells sharply against Arnold's refusal of method. The Arnoldian ideals of disinterest, selflessness, flexibility, and grounding in the natural and observable are the ideals of Herschelian science. Herschel's alertness to the obstacles to these ideals would have stood Arnold in good stead.

But Arnold's strongest case against science is that it provides knowledge without feeling and thus without human appeal. One might expect that an ideal of selflessness would lead to feelingless knowledge, but Arnold argues that through poetry the ideals of selflessness and human

appeal can be conjoined. Obviously, he is right about science insofar as it makes its formal cases with an appeal to method rather than to feeling. But when Arnold tells us that Darwin's theory does not appeal to the sense in us for conduct, the sense in us for beauty, he is covertly defining those senses in quite a narrow way. We need not claim that Darwin was *attempting* to appeal to those "senses," but *The Descent of Man* is very much about whether we have them, and if so, how we got them. The notion that we are descended from "hairy quadrupeds" did have an enormous impact on the culture's sense both of conduct and of beauty and was even inspiring to some—for better or worse—as it helped to naturalize morality and aesthetics. To be sure, those were extra- or quasi-scientific developments, but they were nonetheless integral to the Darwinian project. We might prefer Milton's creation myth to Darwin's; but Darwin's also had the force of myth.

Beyond this unselfconscious acceptance of the reality and authority of his own personal (or, better, class-defined) experiences, Arnold had little sense of the strong imaginative and emotional appeal of science. He argues that a passion for science like Darwin's belongs only to the "born naturalist," and the very "zeal" of such a scientist "marks him off from the bulk of mankind." In his introductory chapter on "the advantages of the study of the physical sciences," Herschel describes man's increasing knowledge of nature and increasing sense of "a Power and Intelligence" that shape nature. He can see no limit to their extent, and

> the farther he inquires, and the wider his sphere of observation extends, they continually open upon him in increasing abundance; and that as the study of one prepares him to understand and appreciate another, refinement follows on refinement, wonder on wonder, till his faculties become bewildered in admiration, and his intellect falls back on itself in utter hopelessness of arriving at an end.

Herschel talks of the experience of science as the Romantic poet would talk of the sublime. Unlike the later scientific naturalists Herschel wants to reaffirm that science and religion are compatible. But not only does his Romantic and religious science reflect the dominant view of science in England through the first half of the century, it carries over in many respects even into the anti-religious discourse of the scientific naturalists.

The rhetoric of late-century arguments for science is often more austere, but it too seeks to appeal to the full range of human needs. Take Huxley, for example. He claims, in his essay "On the Educational Value of the Natural History Sciences," that the study of animal life has a direct bearing on human life. Replacing Herschel's Designer with a less splendid but equally careful Governor, he expects

> that all will admit there is definite Government of this universe—that its pleasures and pains are not scattered at random, but are distributed in accordance with orderly and fixed laws. . . . I cannot but think that he who finds a certain proportion of pain and evil inseparably woven up in the life of the very worms, will bear his own share with more courage and submissions.

If we were Arnoldian, we might find it in ourselves to mock this. What matters here, however, is that this expresses a characteristic concern to see science within the full spectrum of human activity.

Such concern particularly marks the activities of the scientific naturalists in the last third of the century. Their prose often attains the vivacity of Arnold's and employs a religious rhetoric. Note here W. K. Clifford's upbeat definition of the scientist's activity:

> That the scientific thinker may consider his business in relation to the great life of mankind; that the noble army of practical workers may recognise their fellowship with the outer world, and the spirit which must guide both; that this so-called outer world may see in the work of science only the putting in evidence of all that is excellent in its own work—may feel that the kingdom of science is within it: these are the objects of the present discourse.

The kingdom of science rhetorically replaces the kingdom of God. This kind of effort disturbed Arnold but it precisely parallels his own replacement with "the kingdom of poetry." Arnold's unease at this sort of move surely implies a fear that science had achieved the authority and the range of religion. In any case, Clifford refuses to allow that his work does not appeal to the sense in us for conduct, the sense in us for beauty.

The appeal, for Huxley, also extends to "the sense in us for beauty." He does *not* claim that as such "natural history knowledge can increase our sense of the beautiful in natural objects." And he even uses scientific terminology satirically, much as Arnold himself might do, to suggest how emotionally arid it can be. Yet he goes on to say, in a rather nice extended metaphor,

> To a person uninstructed in natural history, his country or seaside stroll is a walk through a gallery filled with wonderful works of art, nine-tenths of which have their faces to the wall. Teach him something of natural history, and you place in his hands a catalogue of those which are worth turning round.

There is a large literature of this kind, and an at least equally extensive one, more or less serious, claiming that the practice of science entails intense use of the imagination—Tyndall, Clifford, Lewes, among others, see science as opening new worlds, transcending the visible. Arnold will not attend to such claims and does not believe in an interconnection between scientific activity and human feeling except as, in the notorious case of Darwin, science appears to have numbed feeling.

Arnold's conception of science tended to be more positivistic, more dualistic, more mechanistic, than the scientists', and he was unable to see the remarkable flexibility of science. Science, he argued, has to do with things, not words; it produces facts, and the processes by which it does so are not important to most people; it is concerned entirely with the intellect, which is entirely divorced from feeling. No wonder, then, that Arnold turned to poetry to fill the breach created by his own absolute categorization of the faculty of thought, and of the separate faculty of feeling.

I want to turn, at last, to some of Arnold's writing on religion. Here, particularly in **Literature and Dogma,** we find most overtly his ambivalence toward science; and here we can detect the ways he both invoked and misused science, and was forced to retreat to a kind of argument that, in the name of science and intelligence, submits intelligence to the power of feeling. In the religious books, a fundamentally secular intellectual position becomes the foundation for a new reading of the Bible; Arnold faces the scientific "fact" that has failed religion, while he tries to save the Christianity of the Bible. His major point, frequently repeated, is that fact has nothing to do with the primary needs of human feeling. "The best scientific specialists are forward to confess, what is evident enough, both that religion must and will have its claims attended to, and that physics and religion have, as Joubert says, absolutely nothing to do with one another." In these works, where Arnold most frequently invokes natural science, he is ostensibly rejecting science because he associates it with a theology that builds abstract systems on already controverted facts, or on facts too obscure to define precisely. He directs his arguments towards those like himself, who have in accepting the facts of the new science lost the power to believe in dogmatic Christianity.

Yet his method will be outspokenly "scientific," not in the sense of systematic and logical, but in the sense of "experimental." Much of the discontent with Arnold's arguments had to do with the way they assumed the authority of science without earning it. An impressive critique of *Literature and Dogma* by Edward Dowden locates Arnold in the world of Victorian scientism with painful acuity:

> Breathing the atmosphere of our time, he has come to attach a measureless importance to the words "verified," "scientific," "experience"; but Mr. Arnold ordinarily gets his "science," his "verification," by the facile literary method of assuming them. We must believe that his results are scientific, as we are bound to believe the heroes of second-rate novels are persons of extraordinary genius, because we are told that they are such.

The spuriousness of Arnold's science is not simply a consequence of rhetorical game-playing (although that is always a possibility with Arnold) but of a genuine misunderstanding of the nature of natural science.

His appeal is always to ways of feeling rather than to ideas. His handling, in *God and the Bible,* of scientific discourse and of W. K. Clifford's direct attacks on Christianity, should suggest what I mean. With his wonderful easy command he sounds like the voice of common sense urging that what really matters is not the elaboration of thought but the direct human appeal. So at the start of Chapter V, he "explains" his "disrespect towards metaphysics," not by analysis but by his "impulse" to tell complaining youthful philosophers that they "had much better have been reading Homer." In his characteristically playful way he invokes a saying, "not at all a grand one," of Homer's; "we are almost ashamed," he says,

> to quote it to readers who may have come fresh from the last number of the *North American Review,* and from the great sentence there quoted as summing up Mr. Herbert Spencer's theory of evolution:—"Evolution is an integration of matter and concomitant dissipation of motion during which the matter passes from an indefinite incoherent homogeneity to a definite coherent heterogeneity, and during which the retained motion undergoes a parallel transformation." Homer's poor little saying

comes not in such formidable shape. It is only this:—*Wide is the range of words! words may make this way or that way.*

This barely pretends to be an argument. It is rather an invocation of Arnold's method of cultural criticism, teasingly juxtaposing Spencer's ponderous and self-important prose to Homer's Arnoldian simplicity and flexibility. What choice can there be? (One might ask, further, what have they to do with one another?) Where Spencer provides an elaborately abstract theory of the way all things evolve, Homer simply warns us that words do a lot of different things. He speaks humanly and implies that interpretations insinuate themselves into facts, and that Spencer may be giving us metaphysics rather than physics. In any case, Spencer's kind of language has nothing human about it. Note, however, that Arnold does not dismiss the possibility that Spencer's statement is true; he offers another truth, the superior truth of poetry.

Religion is the tying together of knowledge and feeling; so too is poetry. The Bible is poetry; it cannot be dismissed simply because it is neither literally true nor composed by God. It remains great poetry, and thus performs the function of religion: it ties imagination and conduct together; it lays upon fact that warmth of feeling that humanizes it and, therefore, gives it moral force. The conception is, despite the invocation of Wordsworth even in the formulation of the ideas, almost mechanistic. Science gives us fact without feeling. Poetry gives us imagination with feeling, which is a kind of fact.

The opening chapters of **Literature and Dogma** lay out Arnold's method and expose clearly the impact of the strategies I have been discussing on his major thought and arguments. The religious books, as apRoberts has argued, are logically continuous with the earlier work, and in its unusual explicitness about method, **Literature and Dogma** helps explain why Arnold so persistently defers meaning, avoids definition, makes his points by iteration rather than analytic clarification. His project is to save Biblical religion from false science by grounding it in true: the Bible offers not metaphysical systems and myths that we must believe, but a reality confirmed by universal experience. Arnold argues that it makes no claims to literal truth, and he selects from its poetry what requires to be saved, just as in his later criticism he defines what matters about Wordsworth and Byron by making selections from their writings.

He begins by rejecting the "axiomatic basis" of contemporary Christianity: "Whatever is to stand," he says, "must rest upon something which is verifiable, not unverifiable." And **Literature and Dogma** in the tradition of Baconian science that has challenged axioms, attempts to establish a "verifiable" basis for religion. The language becomes explicitly scientific shortly after, when Arnold audaciously asserts that he will "give to the Bible a real experimental basis, and keep on this basis throughout." Breathtakingly, he then goes on to find that basis, or at least what might be thought of as a uniform standard of measurement, in "*culture,* the acquainting ourselves with the best that has been known and said in the world, and thus with the history of human spirit."

The clue to much of Arnold's writing, it seems to me, is in the well-known explanation of how "culture" can help

to establish the proper basis for Biblical religion. The student of culture will understand that "the language of the Bible is fluid, passing, and literary, not rigid, fixed, and scientific." The true student of the Bible, not narrowly educated like "the people," knows that it is inappropriate to ask of Biblical language that it be literally true. Scientific education, Arnold announces unhappily, teaches the people to ask "the ground and authority" for all they hear and read. Literary education teaches, rather, how to respond flexibly. Culture turns out to be "*getting the power, through reading, to estimate the proportion and relation in what we read.*" Here again, in another form, is the Arnoldian distinction between fact and feeling. He cannot tell us *how* to estimate the proportion and relation in what we read, but only tells us to read—and then we will see. Strategically, this keeps us from asking, as he proceeds, where he finds the ground and authority for his quite peculiar interpretation of the Bible. And yet these strategies of literature and culture are in the service of "experimental" and "verifiable" knowledge!

Against the fixed, rigid language of science Arnold opposes a literary language that is vaguely "thrown out" at its object. He is not made uneasy by imprecision (as he was, in **"The Function of Criticism,"** by "anomalies"), but accepts them as a condition of the subject. Imprecision leaves him free to avoid the extremes and rigidities he despises, to argue for some elements of Biblical doctrine and dismiss others. Alarmingly for an intellectual, Arnold affirms the value of vagueness in coming at truth, and develops a distinction between knowledge and wisdom to give wisdom all to literature:

> The good of letters may be had without skill in arguing, or that formidable logical apparatus, not unlike a guillotine, which Professor Huxley speaks of somewhere as a young man's best companion;— and so it *would* be his best companion, no doubt, if all wisdom were come at by hard reasoning.

But it is precisely hard reasoning Arnold wants to avoid, or at least the kind of hard reasoning he associates with science.

In distinguishing letters from science, Arnold is particularly eager to show that one need not be a specialist to attain wisdom. The process of acquiring wisdom is *easy.* Disarmingly, like a regular fellow (in a passage that accounts, I believe, for the strategy of the dim-witted persona in many of Arnold's essays), Arnold claims that no special training is required, no detailed consideration of method. Verifiability is built into culture.

> But the valuable thing in letters,—that is, in the acquainting oneself with the best which has been thought and said in the world,—is, as we have often remarked, the judgment which forms itself insensibly in a fair mind along with fresh knowledge; and this judgment almost anyone with a fair mind, who will but trouble himself to try and make acquaintance with the best which has been thought and uttered in the world, may, if he is lucky, hope to attain to. For this judgment comes almost of itself; and what it displaces it displaces easily and naturally and without any turmoil of controversial reasonings. The thing comes to look different to us, as we look at it by the light of fresh knowledge. We are not beaten from our old opinion by logic, we are not

driven off our ground;—our ground itself changes with us.

Where in this world of easy and "natural" judgments are we to find a way to determine whether, in fact, everyone with a fair mind will agree? And, of course, how do we know whose mind is "fair" in the first place? And what is it that constitutes the "best" that everyone must read? What if, in fact, everyone does not agree?

Yet Arnold sticks to his language of verifiability and remains steadfastly secular. Eschewing metaphysics (which he takes as a version of scientific thought), he returns to common experience. And he makes the radical move that has kept traditional religion hostile to these books from their first publication: "The object of religion," he says, "is *conduct.*" Conduct, like everything else of consequence, is the "simplest thing in the world." (It is also, of course, three-fourths of life!) The Bible, Arnold claims, is based in this universal experience—the sense in man for conduct. Religion differs from ethics only in that religion "is ethics heightened, enkindled, lit up by feeling"; it is "morality touched by emotion."

The Old Testament is preoccupied, Arnold says, with righteousness. And "God" in the Old Testament is the manifestation of that feeling, universally shared, that there is something in our sense of conduct and morality, its intensity, its tendency to make us feel that we know better than to do what we want to do, our feeling at the recognition of the right, that seems outside ourselves. We *experience* this otherness. Thus Arnold argues, of course with an authority he does not document, that

> at the time they produced those documents which give to the Old Testament its power and its true character, the *not ourselves* which weighed upon the mind of Israel and engaged its awe, was the *not ourselves* by which we get the sense for *righteousness,* and whence we find the help to *do right.* This conception was indubitably what lay at the bottom of that remarkable change which under Moses, at a certain stage of their religious history, befell the Hebrew people's mode of naming God. This was what they intended in that name, which we wrongly convey, either without translation, by *Jehovah,* which gives us the notion of a mere mythological deity, or by a wrong translation, *Lord,* which gives us the notion of a magnified and non-natural man. The name they used was: *The Eternal.*

The next step inevitably follows. "God" is "the eternal not ourselves which makes for righteousness."

There is no need to follow in detail beyond these moves the nature of Arnold's "verifiable" and "experimental" arguments. That he manages to treat as *Aberglaube*—a secondary after-belief to the primary natural truth of conduct—the rest of what has been derived from or placed in the Bible is merely part of the method he adopted. He accepts only what is "natural" in Christian tradition (the problem being that he is also defining "natural"). Yet he wants to accept the Bible—the morality it inspires, the literature that has become part of Western History, the civilizing force it continues to exercise.

Aware that he will be accused of affirming a merely natural religion, with no personal God, no spiritual realities beyond the human, Arnold sets up his defense:

> Let us anticipate the objection that the religion here spoken of is but natural religion, by pointing out the falseness of the common antithesis, also between *natural* and *revealed.* For that in us which is really natural is, in truth, *revealed.* We awake to the consciousness of it, we are aware of it coming forth in our mind; but we feel that we did not make it, that it is discovered to us, that it is what it is whether we will or not. If we are little concerned about it, we say it is *natural;* if much, we say it is *revealed.*

The blurring of the distinction nevertheless serves the "natural." We may call it revealed, but that is merely because we feel it more intensely, just as we feel religion more intensely than morality. Call it revealed, if you like, but recognize that it is based not in the spirit world but in common experience.

Against alternative interpretations, which he knows are inevitable since the Bible will not tell us what the correct interpretation of itself is, Arnold returns to the grounds of science and of common sense: "Our appeal is to . . . the test of reason and experience." Experience, he argues, "constantly confirms" his interpretation, and though "it cannot *command* assent, it will be found to *win* assent."

I have been emphasizing the logical weaknesses in Arnold's arguments, weaknesses he himself would probably have conceded, because they do not affect his argument against the power of logic. Certainly, **Literature and Dogma** is a remarkable rhetorical performance and a humane and touching attempt to translate Christianity into terms that his contemporary science might find acceptable. But I want to emphasize here how much science looms as a presence in the shaping of its arguments and rhetorical strategies. Arnold accepts both the conclusions of science and its secular implication, surrendering a personal God and all conscious metaphysical system. But he cannot let himself surrender the Bible itself, with its traditional power to restrain by virtue of its remarkable force of feeling; nor is he willing to cede the authority that religion had seemed to offer, and that he thought science had in fact taken. So he claims for his literary method a scientific authority and grounds religion in "experience," avoiding the confrontation with the intellectual complications of his argument or the need to demonstrate its "ground and authority." He seeks a language that will not be strenuous, and turns from what he was to call "the vigour and rigour" of higher Biblical criticism to the strategies and evasions of rhetoric, which he defends in **God and the Bible** as the "loose and wavering" movement that characterizes "the growth of human things." At last, he is claiming defensively, with scant knowledge of the science he rejects and emulates, although with broad and humane ambitions, that his fuzzy science is the better one, that truth belongs not to the specialists who know how to work up facts, but to those of us who, like good scientists, trust in experience, but who also happen to have read a lot. (pp. 143-60)

George Levine, "Matthew Arnold's Science of Religion: The Uses of Imprecision," in Victorian Poetry, Vol. 26, Nos. 1-2, Spring-Summer, 1988, pp. 143-62.

Stefan Collini (essay date 1988)

[*In the following excerpt from his full-length study of Arnold's literary and critical achievement, Collini traces the development of Arnold's critical method from his early theory of poetry to his mature literary and cultural criticism of the 1860s, arguing that Arnold's clear understanding of the critic's role in modern life and his timeless phrasing rank him among the great critics of the Western tradition.*]

It is his work as a critic, more than anything else, that has earned Arnold his pedestal among the immortals. Naturally, there has been a good deal of wailing and lamenting that his emergence as a critic should have been accompanied by—whether as cause or consequence has teased biographers ever since—the drying up of his poetic gift; but he would, without question, cut a smaller figure today had he never turned to criticism, and through his precept and his example he has exercised an enduring and unrivalled influence over the place of criticism in our culture. T. S. Eliot's famous observation that Arnold was 'rather a propagandist for criticism than a critic' was ungenerous on several counts, not least because Eliot's cultural criticism owed much to Arnold: the implied judgement is too dismissive of Arnold's actual criticism, while 'propagandist' is too redolent of a loudspeakerly dogmatism to do justice to the sinuous suggestiveness of Arnold's essays. There was tendentiousness of a different kind in the remark by F. R. Leavis, another critic to feel the length of Arnold's shadow, that Arnold's 'best work is that of a literary critic even when it is not literary criticism'. But we do not have to accede to the restrictive notion of 'literary criticism' underlying Leavis's comment any more than we have to endorse the terms of Eliot's judgement to recognize that, taken together, these two remarks provide a helpful orientation to the true nature of Arnold's achievement. It is on account of what he did *for* criticism as much as what he did *in* it that we value him, while, conversely, we are aware that the qualities he brought to the wide range of subjects he treated were pre-eminently the qualities of an outstanding literary critic.

Every poet is a critic of poetry. The practice of the craft impels an awareness of the possible uses of the resources of form and language, and where this is combined with an intelligent interest in the work of one's predecessors and contemporaries, there is criticism going on though a line of prose never be written. In this sense, Arnold was a critic from the start. His letters to Clough in the late 1840s constitute a playful, informal seminar on poetic theory. He stands out, with self-conscious sternness, against the Keatsian tradition in early Victorian verse, with its rich abundance of imagery and lush word-pictures but also its lack of large controlling ideas or proper elevation of tone. By way of a corrective, he turns to his favourite classical authors and their English descendants. 'There are', he responds to Clough in a letter of 1849,

> two offices of Poetry—one to add to one's store of thoughts and feelings—another to compose and elevate the mind by a sustained tone, numerous allusions, and a grand style. What other process is Milton's than this last, in Comus for instance? . . . Nay in Sophocles what is valuable is not so much his contributions to psychology and the anatomy of sentiment, as the grand moral effects produced by *style*. For the style is the expression of the nobility of the poet's character, as the matter is the expression of the richness of his mind: but on men character produces as great an effect as mind.

These precociously grave observations (Arnold was 26) contain the germ of much of his later criticism.

The severe reaction against what he took to be the inhibiting reflectiveness of some of his earlier poetry—the reaction that led him to omit **'Empedocles on Etna'** from his *Poems* of 1853—also provoked his first statement of poetical principles in the **'Preface'** to that volume. The somewhat mannered, exaggeratedly olympian tone of the piece was a further expression of that wilful serenity which had already irritated some of his contemporaries. . . . The **'Preface'** calls for a return to the themes of the Ancients: the great primary affections and their expression in noble actions. A young writer's attention (the author of this greybeard advice was now 30) 'should be fixed on excellent models that he may reproduce, at any rate, something of their excellence, by penetrating himself with their works and by catching their spirit. . . .' Their great quality, he ruled, is 'sanity', and therefore (as he restated his point the following year) 'it is impossible to read carefully the great Ancients, without losing something of our caprice and eccentricity'. The central insistence of his mature criticism on the need for 'centrality' as a corrective to the provincial and the eccentric is already evident here. He adumbrates another theme of his later criticism, as well as revealing an abiding reservation about Shakespeare, when he remarked that the latter 'has not the severe and scrupulous self-restraint of the Ancients, partly, no doubt, because he had a far less cultivated and exacting audience'.

The 1853 **'Preface'** has a particular biographical interest, both as a repudiation of aspects of a former poetic self, and as Arnold's first public engagement in those critical controversies that were to be the stimulus to his best work. Implicitly, it was a lofty dismissal of those Keatsian epigoni slightly referred to as the 'Spasmodic' school of lyric poets. But, as with his own experiments with classical poetic forms and subjects in the 1850s, his prose writings of this decade reveal him trying on certain doctrines and tones, searching for a voice in which to express his prematurely Stoic withdrawal from the empty bustle of modern society.

His inaugural lecture as Professor of Poetry at Oxford, **'On the Modern Element in Literature'** (which he delivered in 1857 but did not publish until 1869, and which, significantly, he never republished), saw him adopting a more historical approach. At least, it was ostensibly historical, with much talk of the development of society in different periods, yet in fact the argument of the lecture rests on a historical typology and deliberate anachronism. That argument, which perhaps owed something to his father's cyclical view of history, was that the present age needed to be brought to recognize its special affinity with the literature of those other ages which could also be characterized as 'modern', that is, ages which were 'culminating epochs', which exhibited a 'significant spectacle' in themselves and which sought for an 'adequate' literature as a means of comprehending that spectacle. Predictably, especially at this point in Arnold's development, the two candidates for this status which he considers are Greece and Rome. The latter, however, though a 'highly modern' and 'deeply significant' epoch, did not produce an 'adequate' literature, and so the resounding conclusion of the inaugural lecture by the first holder of the Chair to break with tradition and deliver his lecture in English (rather than in Latin) was to 'establish the absolute, the enduring interest of Greek literature, and, above all, of Greek poetry'.

This lecture and the Preface to his verse-drama **Merope,** published in the following year, represent the classicizing tendency in Arnold's aesthetic at its highest pitch. Their cultivated remoteness from the concerns of his own society was regarded as affected antiquarianism, though it in fact expressed, albeit in a displaced form, an absorbing antagonism to some of the features of that society's sensibility. In retrospect, we may discern a close connection between the facts that Arnold had yet to find his own prose voice and that he had still to engage more directly with the cultural preoccupations of his contemporaries. Ironically, he was to do both these things by turning to the most distant point in the Western tradition, the poetry of Homer.

Although the three lectures that Arnold published in 1861 under the title **On Translating Homer** are festooned with allusions to long-forgotten controversies about an already arcane subject, this slim volume, together with its pamphlet sequel **Last Words,** remains an impressive and surprisingly accessible statement of the indispensable role of critical judgement and tact even, perhaps especially, in matters where technical scholarship may seem to exercise unchallengeable authority. The middle of the nineteenth century saw an unusual concentration of attempts at that perennially fascinating task of rendering Homer into English. The greatest claim on posterity's attention now exercised by either Ichabod Charles Wright or F. W. Newman (brother of the theologian) is as authors of the translations that furnished the chief butts for Arnold's witty criticisms. Indeed, some readers, both then and since, have judged Arnold too funny by half, and have regretted that his statement of critical principles should have appeared in this polemical form. But it is arguable that this misconstrues Arnold's purpose, as well as perhaps failing to recognize the role of such controversy in setting his mind in motion. No writer can be entirely indifferent to the anticipated verdict of posterity, but the cultural critic, to take only the most relevant category, necessarily has a more immediate audience primarily in mind. Arnold well knew that his 'vivacities' were a calculated risk, but he was convinced that his was a more effective way of gaining the ear and winning the heart of his contemporary English readers than through more solemn and systematic statement. Moreover, the movement of his own mind was—to call upon a still useful sense of an over-used word—dialectical. He needed to have a one-sided or exaggerated view to correct in order to be stirred to articulate his own more complex sense of a truth.

There is far more in these lectures than destructive criticism, but they undeniably contain some destructive criticism of a very high order. He was unsparing on the failings of translators who are deaf to the subtler literary qualities of the original, and he was brilliantly effective in showing how preconceptions derived from historical learning produced misapprehensions of rhythm and poetic effect. High among Arnold's targets was what might be called the pedantry of authenticity, those various ways in which a misplaced fidelity to the assumed conditions of an earlier period can hamstring creative interpretation in the present.

For example, he observed of Newman's theory that, because the dialect of Homer was itself archaic, the translator should confine his vocabulary as far as possible to the elements in the language of Anglo-Saxon origin:

> Such a theory seems to me both dangerous for a translator and false in itself. Dangerous for a translator, because wherever one finds such a theory announced . . . it is generally followed by an explosion of pedantry, and pedantry is of all things in the world the most un-Homeric. False in itself, because, in fact, we owe to the Latin element in our language most of that very rapidity and clear decisiveness by which it is contradistinguished from the German, and in sympathy with the languages of Greece and Rome; so that to limit an English translator of Homer to words of Saxon origin is to deprive him of one of his special advantages for translating Homer.

There was a similar realism and good sense in his response to the proposal that the familiar, and for Arnold and his readers deeply resonant, forms of Greek names should be changed to correspond with a more 'correct' transliteration in the hope that this would come to seem natural to the next generation:

> For my part, I feel no disposition to pass all my own life in the wilderness of pedantry, in order that a posterity which I shall never see may one day enter an orthographical Canaan; and, after all, the real question is this: whether our living apprehension of the Greek world is more checked by meeting in an English book about the Greeks, names not spelt letter for letter as in the original Greek, or by meeting names which make us rub our eyes and call out, 'How exceedingly odd!'

More importantly, Newman and his fellow-offenders were for Arnold symptomatic of something much deeper. 'The eccentricity, . . . the arbitrariness of which Mr Newman's conception of Homer offers so signal an example, are not a peculiar failing of Mr Newman's own; in varying degrees they are the great defect of English intellect, the great blemish of English literature'. Whereas in Europe 'the main effort, for now many years, has been a *critical* effort; the endeavour, in all branches of knowledge— theology, philosophy, history, art, science—to see the object as in itself it really is', the play of criticism, in this wide sense, has been, he alleged, notably lacking in England. **On Translating Homer** was the first instalment of Arnold's emerging programme to bring some of this critical light to bear on the benighted attitudes of his countrymen. Actually, some of the most telling points were made in the pamphlet which he published in response to Newman's reply to his original criticisms. Newman lodged numerous complaints against both the tone and substance of Arnold's lectures, not all of them unjustified. But his final accusation allowed Arnold a reply in his most provoking manner, in the course of which he gave a marvellously perceptive account of the perennial obstacles to good criticism:

> And he ends by saying that my ignorance is great. Alas! that is very true. Much as Mr Newman was mistaken when he talked of my rancour, he is entirely right when he talks of my ignorance. And yet, perverse as it seems to say so, I sometimes find myself wishing, when dealing with these matters of poetical criticism, that my ignorance were even great-

er than it is. To handle these matters properly there is needed a poise so perfect that the least over-weight in any direction tends to destroy the balance. Temper destroys it, a crotchet destroys it, even erudition may destroy it. To press to the sense of the thing itself with which one is dealing, not to go off on some collateral issue about the thing, is the hardest matter in the world. The 'thing itself' with which one is here dealing, the critical perception of poetic truth—is of all things the most volatile, elusive, and evanescent; by even pressing too impetuously after it, one runs the risk of losing it. The critic of poetry should have the finest tact, the nicest moderation, the most free, flexible, and elastic spirit imaginable.

This passage is a good example of the way Arnold's mind moves from an intuitive perception of the lack of balance in an apparently unexceptionable thought to a widely-ramifying articulation of the basis of that intuition. His tone is initially ironic and personal, but the weight of the argument itself pulls it into a more serious and impersonal register. The unfolding of the implications of that quint-essentially Arnoldian term 'poise' has a persuasive momentum. Temper destroys the crucial balance because through the fumes of his own emotion the critic can see nothing as in itself it really is; a crotchet—that is, a pet theory or idiosyncratic preoccupation—destroys it because the critic is inevitably looking for evidence of what he wants to see, he is obsessed with his theory rather than responding to the object of critical attention; then that splendid culminating clause, 'even erudition may destroy it', that is, that the critic may become so absorbed in points of historical or philological detail, that he loses all sense of proportion, and his learning, instead of serving as a helpful auxiliary, obstructs his appreciation of the poem as a whole. And finally the insight, itself an expression of poise, that the 'critical perception of poetic truth' is so 'volatile, elusive, and evanescent' that 'by even pressing too impetuously after it, one runs the risk of losing it'. This surely catches very well that sense, itself elusive and evanescent, that when we press to try to grasp the nature of some complex literary experience, we run the risk of somehow driving it away, or prematurely fixing on a description which is, in fact, inadequate and hence distorting. He is pointing to the way that we have, in some sense, to let the experience come to us a little more, and then to enter and explore its dimensions in a meditative, noticing sort of way, rather than rushing to try to pin it down. And here again we should feel the force of that deceptively simple Arnoldian injunction to try to see the object as in *itself* it *really* is.

The fact that *Essays in Criticism* (1865) now seems such a coherent book, despite its origin as a collection of lectures and periodical pieces from the preceding two or three years, is testimony to, among other things, the constancy of polemical purpose that animated Arnold in these years. Actually, coherence is not what first strikes the reader on looking at the contents page. The first edition of the book contained nine essays and a specially-written preface: two of the essays are the subsequently famous general statements **'The Function of Criticism at the Present Time'** and **'The Literary Influence of Academies'**; of the remaining seven, three deal with relatively minor French authors (Maurice de Guérin, Eugénie de Guérin, Joubert) and there is one each on Heine, Spinoza, Marcus

Illustration of "The Scholar-Gipsy" from a 1900 edition of Arnold's poems.

Aurelius, and **'Pagan and Mediaeval Religious Sentiment'**. In other words, one of the most famous works of literary criticism in the English language appears to contain much that would not now be regarded as 'literature', very little on indisputably significant authors, and nothing at all on any literature in English. But there is a unity to it, and as so often with Arnold one can best grasp this by looking at the way the essays developed in response to the controversies he was engaged in.

The starting-point is an essay that did not appear in this form in the book at all. In 1862, the Anglican Bishop of Natal, J. W. Colenso, published the first instalment of his *The Pentateuch and Book of Joshua Critically Examined*, a work which sparked off one of those now-forgotten storms that shook the Victorian church. Colenso questioned the plausibility of certain passages of the Bible if interpreted literally, as for many their faith still obliged them to do. Arnold might have been sympathetic to this enterprise had it been carried out with more finesse and tact, but these were hardly Colenso's distinguishing qualities. To make the point, Arnold conceived the plan of contrasting Colenso's 'jejune and technical manner of dealing with Biblical controversy with that of Spinoza in his famous treatise on the *Interpretation of Scripture*'. (Spinoza had long been one of Arnold's favourite authors; some passages from this initial article were to be reused in the one that eventually appeared in *Essays in Criticism* under the title **'Spinoza and the Bible'**. What it was about Colenso's absurdly reductionist calculations that so irked Arnold is easily gleaned from the following specimens of the Higher Knockabout: Colenso's mathematical demonstrations are, as Arnold described them,

> a series of problems, the solution of each of which is meant to be the *reductio ad absurdum* of that Book of the Pentateuch which supplied its terms. . . . For example, . . . as to the account in Leviticus of the provision made for the priests: *"If three priests have to eat 264 pigeons a day, how many must each priest eat?"* That disposes of Leviticus. . . . For Deuteronomy, take the number of lambs slain at the Sanctuary, as compared with the space for slaying them: *"In an area of 1692 square yards, how many lambs per minute can 150,000 persons kill in two hours?"* Certainly not 1250, the number required, and the Book of Deuteronomy, therefore, shares the fate of its predecessors.

But what really disturbed Arnold and prompted him to ridicule the already ridiculous was the extent to which Colenso was taken seriously by large sections of educated opinion in England. This demonstrated yet again the parochialism of English intellectual life, the want of those standards of critical judgement by which such an eccentric performance could be properly judged. And this meant, Arnold insisted, pursuing his larger purpose, being judged not simply from a theological point of view, but 'before another tribunal', that of what he called 'literary criticism'. But what business, he asks rhetorically, has literary criticism with books on religious matters? His answer is worth quoting *in extenso,* because though he was to refine his statement of the tasks of criticism, no other passage reveals so clearly the ideal animating his larger critical campaigns.

> Literary criticism's most important function is to try books as to the influence which they are calculated to have upon the general culture of single nations or of the world at large. Of this culture literary criticism is the appointed guardian, and on this culture all literary works may be conceived as in some way or other operating. All these works have a special professional criticism to undergo: theological works that of theologians, historical works that of historians, philosophical works that of philosophers, and in this case each kind of work is tried by a separate standard. But they have also a general literary criticism to undergo, and this tries them all, as I have said, by one standard—their effect upon general culture. Everyone is not a theologian, a historian, or a philosopher, but everyone is interested in the advance in the general culture of his nation or of mankind. A criticism, therefore, which, abandoning a thousand special questions which may be raised about any book, tries it solely in respect of its influence upon this culture, brings it thereby within the sphere of everyone's interest.

At first sight, this may appear to be another of those pieces of intellectual imperialism whereby the proponent of one discipline attempts to assert its sovereignty over neighbouring intellectual territories. But it should be clear that Arnold was not writing on behalf of the academic practice we have come to know as 'literary criticism'. He was, to begin with, using 'literary' in a very wide sense: works of theology, history, or philosophy are, in this now somewhat archaic sense, all branches of 'literature'. But an ambitious sense of 'criticism' is involved, too. He does not, after all, say that literary criticism is qualified to discriminate or assess some purely *literary* qualities of these works; he says the 'most important function' of criticism is to 'try books as to the influence which they are calculated to have upon the general culture'. No small task: above all, not a task for the specialist, or even a team of specialists. It requires the exercise of cultivated judgement, formed by responsive engagement with work of the highest standard. 'Literary criticism' is the name Arnold was here giving to this task of general judgement.

These large claims predictably provoked indignation and hostility from several quarters, which may have hardened Arnold in his already exaggerated conviction that genuine criticism was unknown and unwelcome in England. The essays which he wrote between 1862 and 1864, and which were then collected in *Essays in Criticism,* were intended both as a direct response to these objections and as a demonstration of the role of criticism in practice, while the choice of subject-matter was meant to supply another lack by encouraging a more discriminating appreciation of just those writers and cultural traditions likely to be scorned or undervalued in mid-Victorian England.

Arnold generalized his case in the two essays he placed at the head of his collection, which have become two of the most frequently cited pieces he ever wrote. It is in the first, **'The Function of Criticism at the Present Time'**, that we meet his famous definition of criticism as 'the disinterested endeavour to learn and propagate the best that is known and thought in the world'. His explanation of that crucial Arnoldian word 'disinterested' is worth pondering for a moment, especially since it has come in for more than its share of misunderstanding.

> And how is criticism to show disinterestedness? By keeping aloof from what is called 'the practical view of things'; by resolutely following the law of its own nature, which is to be a free play of the mind on all subjects which it touches. By steadily refusing to lend itself to any of those ulterior, political, practical considerations about ideas, which plenty of people will be sure to attach to them, which in this country at any rate are certain to be attached to them quite sufficiently, but which criticism really has nothing to do with.

It is true that this is one of those passages that collaborate in their own misinterpretation, but in the context of the essay as a whole it should be clear that Arnold is *not* claiming that criticism exists in some transcendental sphere, unconnected with the social and political realities of the world; if he were, his whole programme for the impact of criticism upon that world would be absurd. Nor is he claiming that the critic has no political, religious, or moral values, or that he is uninterested in the relation of the objects of his criticism to those values—'disinterested' does not, it ought to be unnecessary to say, mean 'uninterested'.

What Arnold is attacking here is any attempt to subordinate criticism to some other purpose. The aim of criticism, as he had already insisted more than once, is 'to see the object as in itself it really is', and that means not immediately and primarily responding to a book or idea in terms of whether its consequences may be acceptable by the criteria of some moral or religious or political view which we are already committed to, but trying first to let it register on our minds and sensibilities in the fullest ways possible, trying to let its own nature manifest itself to us without prematurely foreclosing on whether it is or is not acceptable in terms of a standard imported from some other sphere. Arnold's reference in that passage to the situation in England gives the clue to what he was trying to avoid. Those 'ulterior, political, practical considerations about ideas' that he is urging criticism to keep aloof from were precisely the kinds of habits that, in his view, narrowed and stultified the intellectual life of Victorian England. Books and ideas were judged, he was complaining, by whether they were consistent with the true tenets of the Protestant religion, or by whether they supported a Whig or Tory view of the English constitution, or by whether they had an immediate bearing upon the great policy issues of the moment. By urging the critic to practise a kind of 'disinterestedness', he was not encouraging a posture of withdrawal from the world, but rather that kind of openness that is not so blinded by partisan preconceptions that it cannot recognize a new idea or appreciate a new form when it meets it.

It is certainly arguable that Arnold himself did not always live up to this ideal in practice, so committed was he to promoting a particular set of changes in English sensibilities; he could be unfair and tendentious in his own ways, and he sometimes takes that kind of self-conscious pleasure in his own verbal felicity that is itself an obstacle to the truly disinterested treatment of a subject. But to an impressive extent Arnold *did* successfully embody this quality; certainly by the standards of the literary journalism of his day (as exhibited in, for example, the political propagandizing and hanging-judge severity of the *Edinburgh* and *Quarterly* reviews), his criticism was remarkably free from partisan spirit, and it can still communicate a sense of spaciousness and long perspectives. And, of course, some of his choices revealed that kind of disinterestedness which is akin to courage, especially when his subjects challenged some of the entrenched prejudices of his society, as, for example, in elevating Marcus Aurelius over his Christian detractors as a model of 'spiritual refinement', or in writing such an enthusiastic appreciation of Joubert, whom he called 'the French Coleridge', when he knew that Joubert, as an enlightened Frenchman, would probably be suspected by the English public of atheism, materialism, levity, and syphilis.

The second essay, **'The Literary Influence of Academies',** has also come in for its share of misinterpretation. It is often described as a lament about the absence in England of an authoritative institution comparable to the French *Académie française.* But this way of putting it then seems to bring us up against the following paradox in Arnold's views about criticism. As we have seen, one of the general terms he uses most frequently to characterize the distinctive qualities of criticism in his sense is 'flexibility'. But it is the essence of the idea of an Academy that it should be authoritative, and indeed, where its pronouncements are made *ex cathedra,* that it should be somewhat authoritarian. 'Rigidity' rather than 'flexibility' might seem to be the quality an Academy would be most likely to foster. How, therefore, was Arnold able to recommend both these things simultaneously?

Although this question does point to an enduring tension in Arnold's mind between two not entirely compatible inclinations, the tension falls some way short of a genuine contradiction in this case. To begin with, we have to recognize that Arnold was *not* in fact recommending the establishment of an Academy in England. Rather, he was trying to highlight the weaknesses of English intellectual life and literature by contrasting them with the qualities encouraged by, and in fact expressed in, the existence of an authoritative institution like an Academy. The very existence of an Academy along the lines of the *Académie française* expresses a public recognition of the importance of maintaining the highest standards in any sphere of intellectual activity. As Arnold makes clear, he is not talking about works of genius: the English were, he argued, already too prone to compliment themselves on having Shakespeare, Milton, and a string of great poets, and so complacently to conclude that the conditions for literary and intellectual achievement in their country must be in pretty good order. But that is not the point; individuals of genius, especially in a genre like poetry, may appear from time to time, without the general culture of the society being in good order at all. What about what Arnold calls the 'journey-man work of literature' (in the wide sense of that latter term), that is, the work of reviewing and journalism, of translation, reference, and biography? He gives some telling examples of how poorly this was done in England, and then observes:

> Ignorance and charlatanism in work of this kind are always trying to pass off their wares as excellent, and to cry down criticism as the voice of an insignificant, over-fastidious minority; they easily persuade the multitude that this is so when the minority is scattered about as it is here; not so easily when it is banded together as it is in the French Academy.

Again, we see his concern to make criticism effective and to combat that ethos of lax relativism which allows every opinion, no matter how eccentric or ill-grounded, to pass itself off as the equal of any other. Notice, too, his reference to the opposition between the minority and the multitude, in fact the assumption of an antagonistic relation between them. This raises the interesting question . . . of how Arnold squares his recognition of the fact that the business of culture will in the first instance be carried on by a minority, or as he calls them elsewhere, adopting a biblical phrase, 'the saving remnant', with his claim that disinterested judgement can only proceed from a position of cultural centrality. Can a 'remnant' be 'central'?

In fact, this very notion of 'cultural centrality' itself points toward a deeper resolution of our initial paradox about the conflict between flexibility and authoritativeness. The opposite of an open and flexible mind is, of course, a closed and rigid one, but there are many ways of being closed and rigid. The particular way that Arnold intends is where one is a prisoner of a narrow, partisan, obsessive point of view, where one is confined within the limits of a parochial preoccupation, a provincial standard of judgement, a purely personal range of reference. In this sense, to be brought to participate in the mainstream of European culture is to be emancipated from the constraints of provincial narrowness, and to have access to the highest standards is to be liberated from the despotism of the mediocre and secondrate. In contrasting the eccentric, wayward, opinionated quality of much English prose with the classical lucidity and restraint of the best French writers, Arnold cites a passage from the French writer Bossuet and says: 'There we have prose without the note of provinciality—classical prose, prose of the centre'. That reference to prose of 'the centre' is crucial, and very revealing of the shape of Arnold's concerns in this essay. To be central in this sense is, if you like, to operate within the largest space; the contrast is the way in which one is cramped if confined just to the margin or periphery. Arnold, then, is not recommending the establishment of an Academy in England: he is trying to bring out how the strengths of a culture that can create and sustain an Academy are precisely the kinds of qualities most lacking in England. He is not so much saying that English intellectual life exhibits such a low level and a lack of standards because it does not have an Academy, but rather that, because of the qualities manifested in its low level and its lack of standards, it could never understand the virtues of having an Academy in the first place.

In 1865 Arnold prefaced his collection with a high-spirited response to some of the criticisms that had accumulated over the previous three or four years. Actually, the Preface which now (since the second edition of 1869) stands at the front of the volume is a considerably toned-down version of the original. In the first edition, he indulged his taste for making his critics look ridiculous while artfully retaining the reader's sympathy for himself. 'It will make you laugh', he told his mother, but it didn't, and he had sadly to recognize that 'from their training and habits of thinking and feeling' his family were unlikely to appreciate some of his immoderate sallies. Nor were many of his other readers very appreciative of the facetious mockery of Arnold's minor Dunciad. *The North British Review* was typical in objecting to what, in a term that was to stick, it called Arnold's 'vivacities' ('but then', as he explained to his mother, 'it is a Scotchman who writes'). For all his confident swagger, Arnold soon realized that the tone of his raillery could be counter-productive, and thereafter omitted some of the offending passages. Still, it remains one of the least dull Prefaces to a work of criticism ever written, and as a counterpoint to the coarse practicality of some of his Benthamite critics, it concludes with his famous aria to the charms of Oxford, 'steeped in sentiment as she lies, spreading her gardens to the moonlight, and whispering from her towers the last enchantments of the Middle Age'.

Although, as I have suggested, it was controversy that brought Arnold's mind to life at this period, the volume we hold in our hands today as *Essays in Criticism, First Series* (the suffix was added by the publishers after Arnold's death in 1888 when they collected some of his later pieces, as he had been planning to do, under the title *Essays in Criticism, Second Series*) is remarkably free from disfiguring birth-scars. The volume has idiosyncrasies of its own, to be sure. Arnold's typically nineteenth-century method of reproducing very long extracts from his authors without much comment is apt to seem tiresome (and to raise ungenerous thoughts about reviewers who are paid by length). In fact, this practice makes us aware how little there is in the book of what we now generally regard as the distinctive activity of the literary critic, the close attention to the way in which the language of particular passages works; Arnold, here true to his late-Romantic pedigree, was always better at characterizing *what* effect a

work has upon the reader than he was at analysing *how* that effect is achieved. As a result, we are sometimes left wondering why what may seem to us a rather laboured passage is being held up for our admiration: Arnold's method is very vulnerable to changes of taste in this respect. Certainly, the de Guérins, for example, now seem inadequate vehicles for the case he wants to make. This owed something to following the taste of his admired Sainte-Beuve too closely, perhaps, but it also brings out how some of the writing in these essays is less a response to the authors in question, and more a matter of using those authors to illustrate an argument about the nature of criticism.

At times, too, the essays seem to be marked by thumpingly dogmatic judgements (for example, this piece of unfairness to Jeffrey, first editor of *The Edinburgh Review:* 'All his vivacity and accomplishments avail him nothing; of the true critic he had in an eminent degree no quality, except one—curiosity'). But these dicta are almost invariably a way of establishing a larger, comparative point. In order to show up and correct the eccentricity of English taste, Arnold constantly invokes the wider frame of judgement provided by comparison: his preoccupation with 'ranking' authors, with assigning them their proper place in the league tables of literary greatness, which was later to become a disfiguring tic, here simply takes its place as part of his overall strategy. That strategy, as we have seen, was not a modest one: in Arnold's sense of the term, criticism took all human knowledge as its province, where 'its best spiritual work', as he put it, was 'to keep man from a self-satisfaction which is retarding and vulgarising'. In the end, what gives *Essays in Criticism* a surprising unity and coherence is the presence in each essay of the idea of criticism itself, embodied in that distinctive Arnoldian voice. 'The great art of criticism is to get oneself out of the way and to let humanity decide'. Arnold could hardly be said always to have lived up to this injunction, so recognizable, so much a personality of its own, was that voice. But it accompanied rather than drowned its subject-matter. Here, he admirably embodied his own ideal: the critic, he observed in a passage which catches the spirit of the book very sweetly, should not always be delivering judgements, but should endeavour rather to be communicating what he sees to the reader 'and letting his own judgment pass along with it—but insensibly, and in the second place not the first, as a sort of companion and clue, not as an abstract lawgiver'.

Apart from the curious little book of lectures *On the Study of Celtic Literature,* published in 1867, which was more an essay in the comparative analysis of national character than about Celtic literature as such, Arnold published little of note on literary matters for twelve years after *Essays in Criticism.* During that time he was largely absorbed in . . . social and religious criticism. . . . When in the last decade of his life he did again return to literary topics, his sense both of the task and the audience had changed somewhat. In the early 1860s he had, with pardonable exaggeration, felt himself to be struggling to obtain for criticism any kind of hearing at all; by the late 1870s he felt the need to distance himself from the 'historical' and 'aesthetic' schools of criticism then growing up. Again, in his earlier criticism he had dealt almost exclusively with classical and European literature, calling the narrowness of English taste before the bar of the highest cosmopolitan standards; in the essays of his last decade he returned more and more to establishing the canon of English classics, self-consciously revising and completing the work of Dr Johnson, impelled above all by the urge to settle accounts with the great masters of English Romanticism whose literary stepchild he was. And finally, his sense of the relevant audience had changed too: in his earlier work he had been addressing that minority which shared a classical education and read the quarterly and monthly periodicals, whereas from the late 1870s he was aware that the changed educational and social circumstances of Britain in the last quarter of the nineteenth century were creating a far wider market for a certain sort of instruction and moral sustenance.

These changes, acting in conjunction with the darker colours assumed by Arnold's own sorrow-shadowed sensibilities, gave his later work a more didactic and moralistic tone. The easy, conversational intimacy of the earlier work became less marked, though it never entirely disappeared; instead, the greater distance and inequality between author and implied reader produced a more insistent and preachy literary manner. As Arnold himself increasingly required his reading to console rather than to animate, he entrusted literature with the heavy duty of making the truths of religion and morality effective. The essays on Wordsworth, Byron, Keats, and Gray, which all originated as introductions to popular editions of selections of their poetry, still contain some interesting criticism (especially that on Wordsworth), but they are not his best work. It is particularly unfortunate that the most widely anthologized of all of Arnold's prose writings should have been the programmatic essay on **'The Study of Poetry'**, written as a general introduction to T. H. Ward's popular compilation *The English Poets* (and hence addressed to a relatively unsophisticated audience), since it displays these characteristics of his last period in their most marked form.

It is in this essay that he expounds his famous doctrine of the 'touchstones', those lines of indisputably great poetry (from Homer or Dante, Shakespeare or Milton) that we should bring to the task of helping us discriminate between good and bad poetry, and indeed between great and merely good poetry. This approach has come in for severe, and largely justified, criticism: abstracting single lines from complex poetic wholes is an exercise fraught with pitfalls, just as there are obvious difficulties about comparing these lines with poetry of different genres or written in different languages, and so on. But Arnold was not in fact proposing this as a complete scholarly method (he was not writing at that level), and his own account of the value of this approach is more modest:

> Indeed, there can be no more useful help for discovering what poetry belongs to the class of the truly excellent, and can therefore do us most good, than to have always in one's mind lines and expressions of the great masters, and to apply them as a touchstone to other poetry. Of course we are not to require this other poetry to resemble them; it may be very dissimilar. But if we have any tact we shall find them, when we have lodged them well in our minds, an infallible touchstone for detecting the presence or absence of high poetic quality, and also the degree of this quality, in all other poetry which we may place beside them.

Once again, 'critical tact' is indispensable; the touchstones can, of course, be applied clumsily and mechanically, but any critical approach can be travestied when it falls into clumsy and mechanical hands. The touchstones are, as this passage says, only a 'help' for discovering the quality of a given piece of poetry, not a sufficient recipe in themselves. But they have the effect of disciplining our taste: in their presence it becomes impossible to be taken in by the fraudulent and second-rate; the contrast jars our sensibilities too much. Arnold had himself deployed essentially this approach at various times in his Homer lectures, as well as in ***Essays in Criticism:*** in this essay, the touchstones are simply being proffered as the handy pocket-version of the Arnoldian conception of criticism.

But in that passage about the touchstones there was a single word which encapsulated the later Arnold's argument about the high function to be assigned to literature. 'There can be no more useful help for discovering what poetry belongs to the class of the truly excellent, and can *therefore* [my emphasis] do us most good . . . '. This raises several questions—what kind of 'good' does poetry do us? why does the best poetry do us the most good?—but at the heart of the connection Arnold is asserting lies the question of arousing the feelings or sentiments. He is, that is to say, not so much concerned with questions about how we *decide* what is right and wrong—like so many of his contemporaries, he thought the answers to those questions were for the most part not obscure or in doubt—but rather with how we are to become the kind of person who habitually and spontaneously *does* what is right, how we discipline our will, how we overcome selfishness, laziness, doubt, and despair. In Arnold's view, it is precisely the opposite of these negative states that poetry, above all other agencies, fosters in us. Put very briefly, his view is that poetry (by which he means literature in general, though he always gives pride of place to poetry in the narrow sense) can not only express these convictions, but can give them such beauty or power that they act on our emotions and thus arouse or console us in a way that mere philosophical statement of them cannot do. The better the poetry, the more effectively it engages our emotions and stirs us to action, and the more, therefore, we become the *kinds* of people that it is morally desirable we should become. And a crucial part of this, especially in Arnold's later writings, is the way the most noble or elevated poetry *reconciles* us to the universe, gives us that kind of consolation that can make existence seem bearable.

This is the thought that informs the famous opening sentence of the essay: 'The future of poetry is immense, because in poetry, where it is worthy of its high destinies, our race, as time goes on, will find an ever surer and surer stay'. 'Stay' aptly suggests the propping-up of something otherwise doomed to crumble (and thus also calls up the opening line of his early sonnet 'Who prop, thou ask'st, in these bad days, my mind?', which famously assigns Sophocles this role). Literature is to console and sustain us in hard times, with the strong implication that life is mostly hard times. . . . Thus alerted, we notice how the touchstones themselves are nearly all lines that express a melancholy or stoic mood, a certain noble resignation in the face of the universe; and this is the dominant note of his late essays.

Arnold had his limitations as a critic; so many, in fact, especially in his later work, that his inclusion in the pantheon of criticism can sometimes seem puzzling. To begin with, his tastes were severely traditional and in some ways surprisingly narrow. The classics cast too long a shadow: no subsequent literature could match them, and this can sometimes give a note of slightly chilly disdain to his judgements of recent authors, certainly a lack of enthusiasm. He was not above treating experiment and innovation as wilful neglect of 'the best that has been thought and said'; and with the best always in the past, and a pretty distant past at that, he could seem to be inflexibly judging later literature by (as it has nicely been put) 'doomsday standards'. Further, he consistently underappreciated all the lighter genres. He lauded tragedy, but never did justice to comedy—indeed, scarcely paid attention to it in his major critical manifestos. He prized the epic above all forms of poetry, but undervalued wit and satire. In not regarding the Metaphysical Poets of the seventeenth century as a major moment of English poetry he was, of course, only sharing the received Victorian view, but share it he did; a greater critic might have revised it (as T. S. Eliot was to do). Similarly, he had a late-Romantic aversion to what he regarded as the mere polish and artificiality of the Augustans; he dismissively (but memorably) declared of Dryden and Pope that they 'are not classics of our poetry; they are classics of our prose'. He disparaged Chaucer; and has any English critic of standing written so little or so poorly about Shakespeare?

Then, apart from one very late essay on Tolstoy (which was chiefly an exposition of *Anna Karenina* and an assessment of his moral teaching), Arnold almost entirely neglected prose fiction; writing in one of the most abundantly creative ages of the English novel, he never turned his critical attentions to Dickens, Thackeray, the Brontës, George Eliot, Meredith, or the earlier works of Hardy or James. His letters reveal that in the latter part of his life, at least, he read several of these authors with admiration; but his taste was not formed on them, and he never incorporated any recognition of their achievements into his critical pronouncements. For Arnold, it would seem, poetry still outranked prose, Europe largely outranked England, the past always outranked the present.

Moreover, as with so many critics, his sympathies were most limited with those qualities he least shared. He penned several good lines about Macaulay ('a born rhetorician . . . a perpetual semblance of hitting the right nail on the head without the reality'), but his considered conclusion was 'Macaulay is to me uninteresting, mainly, I think, from a dash of intellectual vulgarity which I find in all his performance'. The 'intellectual vulgarity' all readers of Macaulay will recognize, but it is surely a limitation of Arnold's own to find him *therefore* 'uninteresting'. The charge of over-fastidiousness has some bite here. Again, his judgement of Charlotte Brontë (admittedly only in an early letter) indicates the limits of his range in another direction. 'Why is *Villette* disagreeable? Because the writer's mind contains nothing but hunger, rebellion, and rage, and therefore that is all she can, in fact, put into her book'. Even if one allowed that there was a grain of truth in this observation (though by the exaggeration of the 'all' it forfeits much respect), it is still a reminder that those who are themselves culturally 'central' can too easily take offence at the tone of such protests and extend too little imaginative sympathy to their sources. And one might

extend the list of his defects by including some of the tics I have already mentioned in passing, such as his obsession with 'ranking' authors in the timeless canon, or his increasing tendency to over-value weighty moral utterance.

But despite all this, his most recent biographer is right to declare that Arnold 'is a very great critic: *every* English and American critic since his time has felt his impact'. This is partly because he has characterized in unforgettable ways the role that criticism—that kind of literary criticism which is also cultural criticism, and thus . . . a sort of informal political theory—can and must play in modern societies. He introduced a level of self-consciousness about the critic's activities which will never go away. But he also earns the tribute because at his best, as in the last of his Homer lectures or several of the essays in *Essays in Criticism,* he could combine the fine discrimination, the just appraisal, and the telling phrase in a way that has few equals. He could be economical yet devastating: he pounced on F. W. Newman's description of Homer's style as 'quaint, garrulous, prosaic, low': 'Search the English language for a word which does not apply to Homer, and you could not fix on a better than *quaint,* unless perhaps you fixed on one of the other three'. He could be mercilessly perceptive: Kinglake's style, he damningly pointed out, was that of 'the good editorial': 'it has glitter without warmth, rapidity without ease, effectiveness without charm. Its characteristic is, that it has no *soul;* all it exists for, is to get its ends, to make its points, to damage its adversaries, to be admired, to triumph'. He could be discerning and exact: 'the emotion of Marcus Aurelius does not quite light up his morality, but it suffuses it; it has not power to melt the clouds of effort and austerity quite away, but it shines through them and glorifies them; it is a spirit, not so much of gladness and elation, as of gentleness and sweetness; a delicate and tender sentiment, which is less than joy and more than resignation'. And he could be shrewdly realistic: Joubert may have had 'less power and richness than his English parallel, [but] he had more tact and penetration. He was more *possible* than Coleridge; his doctrine was more intelligible than Coleridge's, more receivable'. When these elements combine, as they do in Arnold's best work, we get that sense of the irresistible rightness of the judgements that only comes when we are reading one of the great critics. (pp. 46-68)

Stefan Collini, in his Arnold, *Oxford University Press, Oxford, 1988, pp. 46-68.*

FURTHER READING

Allott, Miriam. " 'Both/And' or 'Either/Or'?: Arnold's Mind in Dialogue with Itself." *The Arnoldian* 15, No. 1 (Winter 1987-88): 1-16.

     Assesses the formal and aesthetic implications of the "habitual juxtaposition of differing or opposing ideas which shapes so much of Arnold's work, whether as a poet or prose writer."

apRoberts, Ruth. *Arnold and God.* Berkeley and Los Angeles: University of California Press, 1983, 299 p.

Study of Arnold's writings on religion and the Bible, emphasizing their integral relation with his poetry and critical essays.

Armstrong, Isobel, ed. *The Major Victorian Poets: Reconsiderations.* Lincoln: University of Nebraska Press, 1969, 323 p.
Includes "Matthew Arnold and the Passage of Time: A Study of *The Scholar-Gipsy* and *Thyrsis*" by Philip Drew and "The Importance of Arnold's *Merope*" by Gabriel Pearson.

Bright, Michael. "*Merope* and the Poetics of Literary Revivalism." *The Arnoldian* 15, No. 1 (Winter 1987-88): 49-58.
Discusses Arnold's approach to composing *Merope* with regard to the Victorian controversy concerning the imitation of historic literary models.

Buckler, William E. *Matthew Arnold's Prose: Three Essays in Literary Enlargement.* New York: AMS Press, 1983, 116 p.
Three essays on Arnold's literary criticism that "seek to enlarge the reader's understanding of Matthew Arnold's essential literariness, to show how basically dependent his critical effectiveness is upon his literary art."

Burnham, R. Peter. "Arnold and the Verifying Check of Experience." *The Arnoldian* 14, No. 2 (Summer 1987): 1-16.
Argues that "a correct reading of [Arnold's] religious works will show Arnold to be thoroughly idealistic in his assumptions and methodology" and that his "empirical pose . . . masks a transcendental absolutism that, ironically, relies on the verifying check of experience for its acceptance."

Bush, Douglas. *Matthew Arnold: A Survey of His Poetry and Prose.* New York: The Macmillan Co., 1971, 202 p.
Survey of Arnold's career tracing the "main lines and attitudes" reflected in his works.

Carroll, Joseph. *The Cultural Theory of Matthew Arnold.* Berkeley and Los Angeles: University of California Press, 1982, 275 p.
Analysis of Arnold's theories on culture and religion, asserting that "the fundamental source of Arnold's critical importance is his own sense that literary theory must not be isolated from other types of knowledge, that it must take its place within a comprehensive vision of man's place in nature and in history."

Coulling, Sidney. "The Gospel of Culture and Its Critics." *The Arnoldian* 15, No. 1 (Winter 1987-88): 27-35.
Discusses critical responses to *Culture and Anarchy* since the late nineteenth century, arguing that the intelligence of the ideas expressed in the essay transcends its apparent flaws and contradictions.

Frykman, Erik. *"Bitter Knowledge" and "Unconquerable Hope": A Thematic Study of Attitudes Towards Life in Matthew Arnold's Poetry, 1849-1853.* Göteborg, Sweden: Acta Universitatis Gothoburgensis, 1966, 75 p.
Assesses the principal themes of Arnold's early poetry, presenting "a concentrated examination of the expressions which Arnold gave to his conflicting attitudes towards life and the human situation in his verse from *The Strayed Reveller, and Other Poems* up to and including the edition of 1853."

Fulweiler, Howard W. "Literature or Dogma: Matthew Arnold as Demythologizer." *The Arnoldian* 15, No. 1 (Winter 1987-88): 37-47.

Considers Arnold's thoughts on the relative importance of literature and dogma in modern society.

Grob, Alan. "The Poetry of Pessimism: Arnold's 'Resignation'." *Victorian Poetry* 26, Nos. 1-2 (Spring/Summer 1988): 25-44.
Argues that Arnold's poem "Resignation" "is certainly the first and perhaps the fullest exposition of metaphysical pessimism in nineteenth-century English poetry."

Honan, Park. *Matthew Arnold: A Life.* Cambridge, Mass.: Harvard University Press, 1983, 496 p.
Definitive biography aimed at "the Arnold specialist and general reader alike."

Neiman, Fraser. *Matthew Arnold.* New York: Twayne Publishers, 1968, 190 p.
Study of Arnold's life and literary achievements.

Riede, David G. "The Function of Arnold's Criticism at the Present Time." *The Arnoldian* 15, No. 1 (Winter 1987-88): 17-26.
Reviews the historiography of Arnold's critical *ouevre,* concluding that "his function at present *is* to remain at the center of critical debate, not to provide answers to our questions, but to remind us of the continuing urgency and difficulty of problems that Arnold was among the first to feel."

———. *Matthew Arnold and the Betrayal of Language.* Charlottesville: University Press of Virginia, 1988, 239 p.
Textual analysis of Arnold's poetry. The author argues that "the best in Arnold's poetry results from a tension between his poetic ambition and his doubts about his medium."

Robbins, William. *The Arnoldian Principle of Flexibility.* Victoria, B.C.: University of Victoria, 1979, 85 p.
Probes the thematic development of Arnold's critical writings.

———. "A Centenary View of Arnold's Culture: An Essay." *English Studies in Canada* XIII, No. 3 (September 1987): 315-22.
Positive assessment of Arnold's contribution to a theory of modern culture, suggesting that "in Arnold's humanistic philosophy the poet and critic, the idealist and realist, the man of studious retreat and the man of the active world, maintain a self-correcting if often uneven balance."

Rowse, A. L. *Matthew Arnold: Poet and Prophet.* London: Thames and Hudson, 1976, 208 p.
Comprehensive biography.

Schneider, Mary W. *Poetry in the Age of Democracy: The Literary Criticism of Matthew Arnold.* Lawrence: University Press of Kansas, 1989, 228 p.
Analytical and contextual study of Arnold's literary criticism.

Simpson, James. *Matthew Arnold and Goethe.* London: Modern Humanities Research Association, 1979, 197 p.
Assesses the nature and extent of the influence of Johann Wolfgang von Goethe's writings on Arnold's poetry and criticism.

Stange, G. Robert. *Matthew Arnold: The Poet as Humanist.* Princeton, N. J.: Princeton University Press, 1967, 300 p.
Thematic discussion of Arnold's poetry. Stange suggests

that "the main bearing of [Arnold's] poems was to offer a positive alternative to Romantic theories of life and literature."

Super, R. H. *The Time-Spirit of Matthew Arnold.* Ann Arbor: University of Michigan Press, 1970, 118 p.
> Transcripts of lectures on Arnold fusing psychological and textual analysis.

Thorpe, Michael. *Matthew Arnold.* London: Evans Brothers, 1969, 176 p.
> Biographical and critical overview of Arnold's literary career that aims "to introduce and suggest how we may appreciate the main body of his work in relation to his life and times—and *our* life and times."

Tollers, Vincent L., ed. *A Bibliography of Matthew Arnold, 1932-1970.* University Park: Pennsylvania State University Press, 1974, 172 p.
> Compiles primary and secondary sources, the latter limited to the period 1932-1970.

Watson, George. "Matthew Arnold." In his *The Literary Critics: A Study of English Descriptive Criticism,* rev. ed., pp. 131-47. London: Hogarth Press, 1986.
> Concise critical and historical summary of Arnold's writings.

Charles Baudelaire

1821-1867

French poet, critic, translator, essayist, novelist, diarist, and dramatist.

For further information on Baudelaire's career, see *NCLC*, Volume 6.

Regarded among the world's greatest lyric poets, Baudelaire is the author of *Les fleurs du mal* (*The Flowers of Evil*), one of the most influential works in French literature. Considered shocking at the time of its publication for its depictions of sexual perversion, physical and psychological morbidity, and moral corruption, the book was a critical and popular failure during Baudelaire's lifetime. Today, *The Flowers of Evil* is esteemed both for its technical artistry and as the first collection of poems to depict human life from a distinctly modern perspective.

Baudelaire was born in Paris to financially secure parents. His father, who was thirty-four years older than his mother, died when Baudelaire was six years old. Afterward Baudelaire grew very close to his mother, and he later remembered their relationship as "ideal, romantic . . . as if I were courting her." When Madame Baudelaire married Jacques Aupick, a military officer, in 1828, Baudelaire became deeply resentful. Initially he had excelled in school, but as he grew older he increasingly neglected his studies in favor of a dissipated, rebellious life-style. In 1841 the Aupicks sent him on a trip to India in hopes that his experiences abroad would reform him. During his travels he began writing poetry and composed the first poems that would be included in *The Flowers of Evil*. When Baudelaire returned to Paris in 1842, he received a large inheritance and began to live as a highly self-conscious dandy. In Baudelaire's view, the dandy was one who glorified the ego as the ultimate spiritual and creative power—a heroic individualist revolting against society. At this time, Baudelaire fell in love with Jeanne Duval, a French woman of African descent who inspired the verse that formed Baudelaire's "Black Venus" cycle of love poems in *The Flowers of Evil*. He also began to experiment with opium and hashish, documenting his drug usage in *Les paradis artificiels: Opium et haschisch (Artificial Paradises: On Hashish and Wine as a Means of Expanding Individuality)*, a volume which also contains his translation of Thomas De Quincey's *Confessions of an English Opium Eater* and his own "Poème du haschisch" ("Hashish Poem").

In 1844 Baudelaire's mother obtained a court order blocking his inheritance, and thereafter he supported himself by his writing, much of it art criticism. During this time, he established friendships with such painters as Eugène Delacroix and Gustave Courbet. In 1846 he first read the works of Edgar Allan Poe, whose critical writings stressed technical perfection and the creation of an absolute beauty. Baudelaire found confirmation of his own artistic philosophy in the works of Poe, whom he regarded as his "twin soul." Determined to gain recognition for Poe in Europe, Baudelaire devoted several years to translating his works. These translations were widely acclaimed and are considered among the finest in French literature. In 1855 Baudelaire published several poems in the journal *Revue des deux mondes;* two years later his collected poems were published as *The Flowers of Evil*. Upon publication of this volume, Baudelaire was denounced by critics as immoral, and even Charles Sainte-Beuve, a close friend of Baudelaire, refused to praise the book. Subsequently, Baudelaire and his publisher were prosecuted and convicted of offenses against religion and public morality. Six poems deemed obscene were published later the same year in Belgium as *Les épaves*. These poems had scandalized Paris with their detailed eroticism and graphic depiction of lesbianism and vampirism. *The Flowers of Evil* was reissued in 1861 and 1868 with some poems added and others reworked, but the ban on the suppressed poems was not lifted in France until 1949. After the publication of the 1861 edition, Baudelaire's publisher went bankrupt, and in an attempt to regain both his reputation and his financial solvency, Baudelaire traveled to Belgium on a lecture tour. The tour was unsuccessful, however, and in 1866 Baudelaire returned to Paris, where he suffered a debilitating stroke. Having recently reconciled with his mother, he remained in her care until his death in 1867.

In *The Flowers of Evil*, Baudelaire analyzed—in candid

terms—erotic love, the underclasses and lowlife of Paris, and, above all, his own moral, psychological, and spiritual conflicts. His exploration of spiritual issues and concern for salvation have prompted some critics to label him a religious writer, while others deny that any definite belief can be perceived in his works. Most agree, however, that Baudelaire firmly believed that individuals are inherently evil and that a type of salvation can be found in the creation and contemplation of art. For Baudelaire the function of poetry was to create beauty from even the most unpleasant aspects of human existence. According to Geoffrey Brereton, the reader of *The Flowers of Evil* "must pass through eye-splitting perspectives of pink and black, rooms of incredible dilapidation tenented by moustached harpies, fungous alleys haunted by cats, boudoirs rancid with rotting flowers, the whole evening tour of tawdry vice." Baudelaire, in his own words, sought to depict "the horror and ecstasy of life." He found beauty in the horrific, particularly exploring the perplexities of a soul both sinful and repentant. Organized in six sections—"Spleen and Ideal," "Parisian Scenes," "Wine," "Flowers of Evil," "Revolt," and "Death"—*The Flowers of Evil* juxtaposes an ideal of perfect beauty with the knowledge of the futility of such an ideal.

Critics note that Baudelaire expressed a profound sense of both good and evil. Satanic imagery pervades *The Flowers of Evil,* effectively evincing the conflict between sensual pleasure and spiritual redemption. This conflict is most clearly exemplified by the three cycles of love poems included in *The Flowers of Evil.* In addition to the "Black Venus" cycle, Baudelaire included poetry written for his two other mistresses, Apollonie Sabatier and Marie Daubrun. Sabatier, the "White Venus," inspired a cycle of reverent, celestial poetry reminiscent of his early adoration of his mother. The "Green Venus" poems depict Baudelaire's unrestrained passion for Daubrun. Evoking a sensuality similar to the "Black Venus" cycle, these pieces are more sexually explicit and display elements of sadism. Collectively, the love poems provide an important and, to some, disturbing commentary on Baudelaire's conflicting feelings about women. Contrary to the moral objections once expressed against these and other poems comprising *The Flowers of Evil,* Baudelaire has long been recognized as a poet whose works testify to an agonizingly acute sense of morality. His perceptiveness and candor in writing of both his personal misery and that of the world around him have exerted a profound influence on every generation of poets to succeed him, leading many critics to observe that the grim vision of life proffered by much of modern literature is a tradition that began with Baudelaire.

(See also *Poetry Criticism,* Vol. 1.)

PRINCIPAL WORKS

La fanfarlo (novel) 1847
  [*La fanfarlo,* 1986]
Histoires extraordinaires [translator; from the short stories of Edgar Allan Poe] (short stories) 1856
Les épaves (poetry) 1857
Les fleurs du mal (poetry) 1857; also published as *Les fleurs du mal* [revised editions], 1861 and 1868
  [*The Flowers of Evil,* 1909]
Nouvelles histoires extraordinaires [translator; from the

short stories of Edgar Allan Poe] (short stories) 1857
Aventures d'Arthur Pym [translator; from the novel *The Narrative of Arthur Gordon Pym* by Edgar Allan Poe] (novel) 1858
*Les paradis artificiels: Opium et haschisch (autobiography and poetry) 1860
  [*Artificial Paradises: On Hashish and Wine as a Means of Expanding Individuality,* 1971]
Curiosités esthétiques (criticism) 1868
L'art romantique (criticism) 1869
Petits poèmes en prose: Le spleen de Paris (poetry) 1869
  [*Poems in Prose from Charles Baudelaire,* 1905; also published as *Paris Spleen,* 1947 and *The Parisian Prowler,* 1989]
**Journaux intimes (diaries) 1887
  [*Intimate Journals,* 1930]
Lettres: 1841-1866 (letters) 1905
Oeuvres complètes de Charles Baudelaire. 19 vols. (poetry, criticism, essays, novel, letters, journals, autobiography, and translations) 1922-63
The Letters of Charles Baudelaire (letters) 1927
Baudelaire on Poe (criticism) 1952
The Mirror of Art: Critical Studies (criticism) 1955
Baudelaire as a Literary Critic (criticism) 1964
Art in Paris, 1845-1862: Salons and Other Exhibitions Reviewed by Charles Baudelaire (criticism) 1965
Selected Writings on Art and Artists (criticism) 1986

*This work includes Baudelaire's translation of Thomas De Quincey's *Confessions of an English Opium Eater.*

**This work includes the diaries "Fusées" ("Skyrockets") and "Mon coeur mis á nu" ("My Heart Laid Bare").

André Gide   (essay date 1917)

[*Gide is regarded as one of France's most influential thinkers and writers of the twentieth century. In his fiction, as well as his criticism, he stressed autobiographical honesty, unity of subject and style, modern experimental techniques, and sincere confrontation of moral issues. The following essay originally appeared as a preface to a 1917 edition of* The Flowers of Evil.]

One suspects that one of Baudelaire's most ingenious paradoxes was to have dedicated his *Fleurs du mal* to Théophile Gautier, to offer this cup, all overflowing with emotion, music, and thought, to the most dry, least musical, least meditative artisan that our literature has ever produced. Was he deluding himself? He was a critic with too lucid a vision not to be sensitive to the poverty of those *Emaux et camées,* which owed their reputation not to what they are but to what they claim to be. The *Fleurs du mal* are dedicated to what Gautier claimed to be: magician of French letters, pure artist, impeccable writer—and this was a way of saying: Do not be deceived: what I venerate is the art and not the thought, my poems will have merit not because of their movement, passion, or thought, but because of their form.

Form, that justification for the work of art, is what the public never perceives until later. Form is the secret of the work. Baudelaire never takes for granted that harmony of contours and sounds in which the art of the poet is displayed; he achieves it through sincerity; he conquers it; he imposes it. Like every unaccustomed harmony, it was shocking at first. For many long years, and I would be tempted to say: even until now, certain misleading appearances of this book have hidden its most radiant treasures, while, at the same time, it protected them. Certain gestures, certain harsh tones, certain subjects of the poems, and, as I think, some affectation, an amused satisfaction in being misunderstood, deluded his contemporaries and many of those who came later. Without doubt, Baudelaire is the artist about whom the most nonsense has been written, who has been ignored the most unjustly. I know of certain manuals of French literature of the nineteenth century in which he is not even mentioned.

The fact that in the eyes of certain persons the figure of Gautier has long appeared and still appears more important than that of Baudelaire is explained by the very simple attitude (oversimple or simplified) of Gautier, from which he did not for a moment swerve, thanks to which he held on to that place in the limelight which he had acquired right at the very first; it is also explained by the cordial banality of his face, which suddenly opens up when we encounter it and never means anything more than what it first promised. Whereas we glimpsed a disconcerting complexity in Baudelaire, a cabal of strange contradictions, antagonisms almost absurd, which could be taken for pretense, the more easily because he was capable of pretense as well.

I should not swear that Baudelaire, elsewhere so perspicacious, was not somewhat mistaken about his own merit, about what constituted his value. He worked, not always consciously, at that misunderstanding which isolated him from his period; he worked at it all the more because this misunderstanding was already taking shape in him. His private notes, published posthumously, are painfully revealing in this respect; to be sure, Baudelaire felt his essential originality, but he did not succeed in defining it clearly to himself. As soon as this artist of incomparable ability speaks of himself, he is astonishingly awkward. Irreparably he lacks pride to the point where he reckons incessantly with fools, either to astonish them, to shock them, or after all to inform them that he absolutely does not reckon with them.

"This book has not been written for my wives, my daughters, or my sisters," he says, speaking of the *Fleurs du mal*. Why warn us? Why this sentence? Oh, simply for the pleasure of affronting bourgeois morals with these words "my wives" slipped in, as if carelessly; he values them, however, since we find in his private journal: "This cannot shock my wives, my daughters, nor my sisters."

This ostentatious pretense, which came to shelter Baudelaire's fervor, antagonized certain readers, the more violently because some of his early admirers were most enthusiastic about this very pretense. He especially felt the need of taking cover from his admirers.

People thought they were completely rid of him when they buried these feints along with the romantic devices. He reappears, stripped of disguise, rejuvenated. He went about it in such a way that we understand him much better today than they did in his day. Now he quietly converses with

each one of us. Certainly he begs and obtains from each reader a sort of connivance, almost a collaboration; in this way his power is proved.

"He was the first," says Laforgue, "to recount himself in the restrained mode of the confessional, without assuming an inspired air" [see *NCLC*, Vol. 6, p. 88]. In this respect he calls to mind Racine; Baudelaire's choice of words is perhaps more disquieting and of more subtle pretension; I claim that the sound of his voice is the same; instead of giving the greatest possible sonority to their inspiration, in the manner of Corneille or Hugo, each of them speaks in a whisper, with the result that we listen to them at length.

What a disquieting sincerity the kindred spirit, attentive to this discreet song, soon discovers! With Baudelaire, antithesis, born from personal contradictions, is no longer merely exterior and verbal, a technique as it is in Hugo; rather it is honest. It blossoms spontaneously in this catholic heart, which experiences no emotion without having the contours fade immediately, without having its opposite reflected like a shadow, or better, like a reflection in the duality of this heart. Thus everywhere in his verses, there is sorrow mingled with joy, confidence with doubt, gaiety with melancholy, and he seeks uneasily a measure of love in the horrible.

However, the anguish of Baudelaire is of a still more secret nature. At this point I seem to lose sight of his poetry: but where does one find the source and the prompting of so faithful a melody, if not in the soul of the poet?

We are often told that there is nothing new in man. Perhaps; but all that is in man has probably not been discovered. Yes, trembling, I convince myself that many discoveries are still to be made, and that the outlines of the psychology of the past, according to which we judge, think, and even act, have acted up to now, will soon appear more artificial and out of date than do the outlines of the chemistry of the past, now that radium has been discovered. If chemists have now come to the point of speaking to us of the decomposition of simple bodies, why should "we psychologists" not be tempted to envisage the decomposition of simple feelings? A simple way of considering feelings is what allows anyone to believe in simple feelings.

I shall not go so far as to say that Baudelaire felt as clearly as did Dostoevsky, for example, the existence—opposite to that force of cohesion which keeps the individual consistent with himself, through which, as Spinoza said, "the individual tends to persist in his being"—the existence of another force, centrifugal and disintegrating, through which the individual tends to be divided, dissociated, through which he tends to risk, gamble, and lose himself. But it is not without a shiver of recognition and terror that I read these several sentences from his private journal: "In a mature man, the impulse toward productive concentration must replace that toward wasting his forces." Or again: "Concerning the vaporization and the centralization of the self. Everything lies in this." Or: "In every man there are always two *simultaneous* [the whole interest of the sentence lies in this word] postulations: one toward God and the other toward Satan." Are these not traces of that infinitely precious radium in contact with which the old theories, laws, conventions, and the pretensions of the soul are all volatilized?

I shall not affirm that these fragments which I have just isolated are the only ones in his prose work; at least, it can be said that they have left a perceptible imprint on his entire poetic work.

And none of all this is sufficient to make of Baudelaire that incomparable artist whom we praise. Quite to the contrary, the admirable fact is, that in spite of all this, he has remained that artist. As Barbey d'Aurevilly said magnificently in that fine article which consoles us for the silence of Sainte-Beuve: "The artist has not been too defeated." (pp. 256-60)

> *André Gide, in a preface to "Fleurs du Mal,"*
> *translated by Blanche A. Price, in his* Pretexts:
> Reflections on Literature and Morality, *edited*
> *by Justin O'Brien, Meridian Books, Inc., 1959,*
> *pp. 256-60.*

W. T. Bandy   (essay date 1933)

[*Bandy is an American critic and translator who has written extensively on the works of Charles Baudelaire. In the following excerpt, Bandy outlines Baudelaire's reputation among French critics during his lifetime.*]

[What] is actually known of the reception of Baudelaire's works by his contemporaries? It may safely be asserted that the opinion of most present-day readers is based upon the factual evidence of his ignominious trial and upon the articles which have appeared for the past sixty years in the Lévy edition of the works. Few writers have done more than point out the great change that has taken place in the public's attitude regarding Baudelaire without taking the trouble to verify their statements and seek underlying causes. (p. viii)

Before the year 1855, Baudelaire's name was barely known outside the small group of writers and artists with whom he came into frequent contact. These he alternately charmed and exasperated by his brilliant conversation, filled with original or profound ideas upon questions of aesthetics, and by his propensity for mystification. Although he passed as a continuator of the bourgeois-baiting tradition begun by the minor Romanticists, his talent as a poet and art-critic was undisputed by the few who had been privileged to examine samples of his work. The two *salons* with which he inaugurated his literary career were spoken of in glowing terms by his friends Champfleury, Vitu and Fournier, who compared them with the most noted criticism from the pens of Diderot and Stendhal, predicting for the young critic a future of much promise.

Baudelaire did not follow up these modest but real successes which, however much they owed to personal friendship, were unquestionably merited. He well knew that his surest bid for fame was his poetry and he employed most of his time polishing and enlarging the volume of verse, begun in 1842, that was later to bear the successively abandoned titles of *Les lesbiennes* and *Les limbes,* finally appearing as **Les fleurs du mal.** [Charles] Asselineau stated that most of the poems were completed before 1846 but the collection remained unpublished for over ten years, with the exception of a dozen poems which appeared in various ephemeral and obscure periodicals. Most of them were well known in Baudelaire's circle, however, from his own readings and from manuscript copies that were passed from hand to hand. That the poet had his admirers and even his fanatics cannot be doubted; even his enemies later acknowledged that "for a small group of individuals who salute him as their god", Baudelaire was an immense figure. But his votaries were few in number and their enthusiasm was unfortunately limited to oral applause.

It is obvious that the public at large could be pardoned its ignorance of the very existence of this young writer whose works were dispersed in unimportant periodicals and consisted of only two *nouvelles,* several poems and a handful of short articles. An indication of the inaccessibility of Baudelaire's writings is the fact that diligent research has never succeeded in unearthing a copy of the review that published his first translation from Poe. In 1848, Baudelaire and two of his acquaintances amassed sufficient capital to found a revolutionary newspaper, but the enterprise failed after two issues when their news-boys forgot to return with the receipts. The poem **"Lesbos,"** later condemned with five others of the **Fleurs du mal,** appeared with impunity and attracted no attention whatever when it was included in an anthology of *Poètes de l'amour* printed in 1850. Even his excellent article on Poe seems to have passed unnoticed in the *Revue de Paris,* although it was showered with praise when Baudelaire used it as the introduction to his first volume of translations. It is not surprising that Baudelaire, discouraged at the reception given his writings, thought seriously of renouncing the career of letters.

In June, 1855, however, he took new heart as the potent *Revue des deux mondes* opened its portals,—with a word of counsel and admonition,—to eighteen of his most remarkable poems. This was a genuine opportunity to enlarge the circle of his readers, since that august publication was almost a literary dictator and the honor of appearing in its pages was usually reserved for contributors of distinction. The publicity won by this stroke of fortune was augmented by an uncompromising attack upon the poems, published soon afterwards in the *Figaro,* a paper catering to a public less serious but equally as numerous as that of the *Revue.* Thus a magazine in which Baudelaire has subsequently been treated most disdainfully and a furious diatribe in a popular gazette were largely responsible for the spread of his literary reputation beyond the boundaries of personal acquaintance. The importance of these two events cannot easily be over-emphasized: they mark the first appearance of the famous title, **Les fleurs du mal,** and if there were neither cheers nor invectives to greet the daring of these acrid verses, the public had at least a taste of their unforgettable strangeness.

When his translation of Poe's **Histoires extraordinaires** appeared the following year, Baudelaire stood in no need of an introduction to many readers. The tales had filled the *feuilleton* of the *Pays* for the previous six months but it was the published volume that rekindled the curiosity aroused by the poems revealed to the public by the *Revue des deux mondes.* It is no exaggeration to say that this translation created an *événement littéraire;* its reception by the critics was no less immediate and favorable than its adoption by the public. Even those most hostile to Baudelaire, including the same *Figaro* that had denounced the poet, admitted the power of the translator and were impressed by the book's commercial success. Certainly no other of Baudelaire's works before or afterwards, including the **Fleurs du** *mal,* was so widely read and reviewed. Adverse criticism was not lacking, to be sure; some critics accused Baudelaire of seeking to conceal his own imperfections under the cloak of his *protégé,* others decried his over-literal translation and frequent use of neologisms. The majority paid tribute to the faithfulness and stylistic perfection of the translation, however, while commending Baudelaire for the excellence of his introduction.

We are convinced, after careful comparison of the reviews of both books, that the *Fleurs du mal* were something of an anticlimax after the popular success of the *Histoires extraordinaires.* The stage had been set for their triumphant entry: first the extract printed in the *Revue des deux mondes,* followed by a second extract of nine poems in the *Revue française* only a few weeks before the volume left the press increased the interest of many persons, who had been hearing Baudelaire's friends sing his praises for more than ten years, in the long-promised volume that had never seemed to materialize. But when their expectancy was finally rewarded, the response was rather disappointing. Critics did not rise in a body to revile or defend the poet for his immorality or his artistry. Only the *Figaro,* already committed to a hostile position, took the pains to launch an organized attack,—and it is probable that its policy was dictated by the ministry of justice, piqued at the recent acquittal of *Madame Bovary,* rather than by personal conviction. No doubt many articles were held in abeyance after news of the book's seizure was received; this is known to be true of a particularly vituperative review by Paulin Limayrac, who considerately suppressed it on learning of police intervention. Rigid censorship by the authorities is the only possible explanation for the singular apathy of most critics toward a work that was calculated to stir up violent polemics; this censorship was responsible for the suppression of the articles of d'Aurevilly and Asselineau, the former intended for the *Pays* (where it was refused), the latter held back by the *Revue française* until after the trial, when it was published with certain revisions. An article favorable to Baudelaire, which appeared in the state-controlled *Moniteur universel,* drew fire from official quarters after it was too late to have it withdrawn. *Le présent,* a weak but determined champion of Baudelaire, published an ardent and intelligent review of his book, signed, however, with the obscure name of F. Dulamon, and consequently possessing little weight. The four articles may have been based, in part, upon Baudelaire's own suggestions; at any rate, he printed them together, in a small brochure intended to strengthen his case with the judges. Although unimpressive, either for or against Baudelaire, this handful of articles cannot suffice to substantiate the assertions of many recent biographers who attribute Baudelaire's fame or notoriety to a *succès de scandale* originating with the condemnation of six poems of his *Fleurs du mal.* There were few allusions to the outcome of the trial in the press and such as there were could only be termed sympathetic. It is easy to conceive that the public as a whole never had an inkling of what had taken place,—it is certainly a fact that there was no general hue and cry over either the book or its misfortune.

After the disappointing reception given his cherished poems, Baudelaire turned his hand to other forms of literature,—but with even less success. The appearance of the *Nouvelles histoires extraordinaires* had confirmed but not equalled the ovation given its predecessor, and a third volume in 1858, *Les aventures d'Arthur Gordon Pym,* was doomed to meet with complete failure. The slim brochure on Gautier, reprinted from *L'artiste,* shed no added luster on the name of Baudelaire, despite friendly puffing in papers sympathetic to him.

Realizing he was losing the slight prestige he had already won, Baudelaire made haste to publish his *Paradis artificiels,* upon which he counted "to put him back into circulation." Simultaneously, he prepared a revised and augmented edition of his poems, which were out of print. The spirited discussion centering about Wagner's personally directed Parisian opening of his opera, *Tannhäuser,* inspired Baudelaire to defend the master in the face of almost the entire body of music critics of the capital; his impassioned article, which may still be read today with pleasure, had a moderate amount of success while the Wagnerian quarrel was raging.

When the *Paradis artificiels* finally appeared, it was apparent that Baudelaire's dream of striking the public's fancy with De Quincey as he had with Poe was impossible of realization. Some critics were gracious enough to mention the volume, but the public refused to read it. Two years later, it was listed as a "publisher's remainder", at one-third its original price.

The second edition of his *Fleurs du mal* fared little or no better than the first. It is true that it was hailed as a "petit événement littéraire" in the *Revue anecdotique,* but that organ was hardly more than the trade journal of Baudelaire's publisher. The lone article that stands out (if we except the splendid tribute of Swinburne in the *Spectator* for September, 1862 . . .), the only mention made of this new edition by an important writer, is a review by Leconte de Lisle, who made an effort to be kind in spite of his inability to understand anything whatever of Baudelaire's genius except the vague similarity between his own studied form and the chiseled perfection of the *Fleurs du mal.*

It was not his translations, his criticism or even his poetry that was to place Baudelaire's name before the public in large letters. True to its love of paradox, the Parisian press welcomed the poet's decision to become a candidate to the Academy with unconcealed delight as an excellent target for the lampoons of its popular columnists. The scandal of this unexpected candidature surpassed immeasurably that of the *Fleurs du mal,* for until his desistance, the presumptuous aspirant to the chair of Scribe was a leading subject of gossip and laughter in the cafés where journalists congregated.

Ostensibly to increase his meager income by delivering a series of lectures, but probably to escape the inanities and rebuffs of Paris, the poet set out for Brussels. His experiences there being even more humiliating than those to which he was accustomed, he conceived a violent dislike for the country and its people and even planned to depict their Boeotian character in a book entitled, *Poor Belgium!* A sudden attack in the spring of 1866 presaged the malady that was to cause his death and necessitated his giving up all thoughts of further work. News reached Paris that he had passed away in an humble hôtel room, abandoned by his friends, and before a denial was received, several death notices appeared in the newspapers. Far from deserting him, Baudelaire's friends brought him back to Paris and did all that was possible to brighten the last terrible days of his struggle against death and paralysis. As welcome surcease to his long suffering, death finally came on the last day of August, 1867.

The number of articles inspired by the event will no doubt surprise many persons who, upon the authority of most biographers, have believed that Baudelaire's death, like his words, was shunned by the press. It was remarked at the time that many readers must have been puzzled at the amount of attention paid this author, of whom they had never even heard, while he was alive. Baudelaire's funeral was indeed a very modest affair, with hardly sixty persons present at the church services and even less at the cemetery; his newspaper burial, however, was gaudy, if not imposing.

The necrological articles fall into three principal groups, corresponding to the motives that inspired their authors. The first and largest of these groups is made up of notices depending upon apocryphal anecdotes, bizarre *mots* and sensational details to intrigue the casual reader, bored at the death of political news and by the sluggish autumn season. These may be termed, with entire justice, products of yellow journalism, no more and no less malicious than usual when the important thing is to produce a good "story". It must also be confessed that the legend of eccentricity and diabolism Baudelaire left behind was irresistible material for the exaggerations of this type of reporter. Victor Noir, whose death at the hands of Prince Bonaparte was soon to make of him the sacred martyr of the opposition movement, concocted a fantastic masterpiece of the *genre,* from which his less inventive fellows borrowed freely. Needless to say, his account of Baudelaire's life is partly pure fiction, partly literal interpretation of the poet's own words, as Baudelaire's self-stultification was often accepted for gospel truth by his over-credulous listeners. A typical example of Noir's method is his adaptation of one of Baudelaire's prose poems to form an anecdote which he offers as a chapter from real life. In the prose poem, Baudelaire describes a depraved individual who takes pleasure in destroying the entire stock in trade of a poor glazier by dropping a flower-pot from his lofty window upon the back of his victim. In Noir's anecdote, Baudelaire soaps the stairs to his apartment and allows the unfortunate glazier to break his neck upon them. These anecdotes abound in all the articles of this group, and although it cannot be denied that their authorship must often be attributed to Baudelaire himself, their authenticity is invariably doubtful. Authentic or not, they served the purpose of the writers, desirous solely of amusing a jaded public at any cost.

A second group comprises the articles inspired by dislike or jealousy. Basing their disapproval upon moral or religious grounds, the writers condemn the spirit and subjects of Baudelaire's work, while grudgingly conceding the stylistic perfection of its form. The most excessively brutal of these obituaries is that of Jules Vallès, printed not once, but twice within a week after Baudelaire's burial. Vallès, who was one of the leading firebrands of the *Commune* and who contended that the future of humanity rested upon the total destruction of all museums and libraries, forgot even the common respect due the family of any dead man in his unbelievably ferocious attack, directed more at the artist than at his work. While unqualified assault of this degree was not typical, yet petty hatred rears its ugly head in many of the articles, where an attempt is made to conceal the real motivation behind a thin veneer of outraged righteousness.

It must be said, to the credit of Baudelaire as well as that of his friends, that those who had known him best and longest were quick to avenge the slurs and mockery cast upon his memory. Anticipating the reaction that was sure to set in, Banville and Asselineau defended, the former Baudelaire the artist, the latter Baudelaire the man, in their fervent and highly emotional addresses over his open grave. Even an impartial outsider was moved by the ignominious accusations of Vallés to write an article wittily turning them back upon their originator. The faithful Nadar, whose aeronautical exploits made him one of the best-known and most popular figures of Paris, threw the full weight of his influence to the support of his old friend, answering, if not silencing the calumny of those who had never seen beneath the surface of the man whom they reviled.

One scarcely expects to find impartial objectivity in the necrological comment upon an author, particularly when the issue is obscured by a veil of legend such as that which blinded Baudelaire's contemporaries. The verdict of posterity differs enormously from that of 1867, but it is not true that Baudelaire's merit was totally unrecognized by his contemporaries, for we find in their criticism many observations upon the value of the *Fleurs du mal* or the translation of Poe that would appear just and acute, even in the light of modern opinion. Many writers made the assertion, daring for the time, that Baudelaire's work would live, that his one book of poems would stand out as a great event in the literary history of the nineteenth century. None, of course, even among the most sanguine of his friends, ventured to imagine that his fame would attain the eminence it now occupies, but nearly all esteemed his work a valuable and original contribution to French literature. There was some doubt, also, concerning which of his productions would bear most weight in the judgment of the future, some considering him solely as a poet, others pointing out the superiority of his prose, of his art-criticism and of his *Spleen de Paris.* Surprisingly enough, one critic affirmed that if the *Fleurs du mal* should not survive, the translation of De Quincey would remain to assure his fame. A small minority were of the opinion that his reputation would probably endure for a tiny group of bibliophiles and collectors of erotica, but that it probably would not outlast the fortnight of obituary comment. (pp. 1-12)

> W. T. Bandy, in his Baudelaire Judged by His Contemporaries (1845-1867), *Columbia University, 1933, 188 p.*

Michael Hamburger   (essay date 1951)

[*Hamburger is a German-born English poet, translator, and critic. An accomplished lyric poet in his own right, he has been widely praised for his translations from the works of several German poets previously unfamiliar to English readers, notably Friedrich Hölderlin, Georg Trakl, and Hugo von Hofmannsthal. He has also written extensively on modern German literature. In the following excerpt, he surveys the diverse critical views of*

Baudelaire's works and examines his contradictory attitudes and ideas.]

It would be interesting to collect all the statements which distinguished writers and critics have made about Baudelaire. The reader of such a collection would be confronted with dozens of different Baudelaires; but, though he might well fail to discover the authentic one, he would learn a great deal about the nature and the limitations of criticism. Indirectly, he might even arrive at a better understanding of the nature of poetry.

I shall begin by recalling a few of these opinions. Victor Hugo, in a letter to Baudelaire, praised him for creating a *frisson nouveau,* and proceeded: "I have never said: Art for Art's sake. I have always said: Art for the sake of Progress. Basically, that is the same thing, and your mind is too penetrating not to perceive it. . . . What are you doing? You are going ahead. You are moving forward." Our first Baudelaire, then, is a progressive one, marching forward; it is not surprising that he bears a certain resemblance to Victor Hugo.

Sainte-Beuve, who wrote to Baudelaire in 1857, soon after the publication of the *Fleurs du mal,* was sympathetic and patronizing: "You must have suffered deeply, my dear child," he observed; and he went on to implore Baudelaire to "cultivate his angel," to "let himself go," "not to be afraid of being too common," to be more spontaneous and more passionate and to forsake his morbid preoccupations. In other words, he was asking Baudelaire to renounce his originality, to become respectable. This was an attitude which Baudelaire could understand; but if he had adopted it, his renunciation would have been a complete one: he would have given up poetry. "What is art?", Baudelaire asked himself in "Fusées," and replied: "Prostitution." He was capable of jumping from one extreme to the other, but never of compromise; the kind of cant by which Sainte-Beuve attempted to justify himself in *Volupté* was the very thing which Baudelaire abominated and felt called upon to expose.

A very different Baudelaire emerges from an article written in the same year by Barbey d'Aurevilly: "The poet, terrible and terrified, has wanted us to inhale the abomination of that gruesome basket which, a pale canephorus, he carries on his head bristling with horror." Apart from the exotic analogies and a vocabulary worthy of a specialist in horror and heresy, this article was the first to state a point of view which many later critics have taken up: "These are not the *Flowers of Evil,* these poems of M. Baudelaire. They are the most powerful essence that has ever been extracted from those accursed flowers. The torment, then, which such a poison must produce saves us from the danger of being intoxicated by it." The conclusion of Barbey's article is the one which Huysmans paraphrased at the end of his preface to *A rebours:* "After the *Flowers of Evil* there are only two courses open to the poet who made them unfurl: either to blow his brains out . . . or to become a Christian." E. Thierry had already compared Baudelaire to Dante; but Barbey was the first to draw attention to the Christian aspect of the *Fleurs du mal.* His opinion was that Baudelaire's "Satanism" was a conscious attitude, an artifice, and that such an attitude implies its opposite. He quotes the lines:

Ah! Seigneur! donnez-moi la force et le courage

De contempler mon cœur et mon corps sans dégoût!

[Lord, give me the strength and courage
To contemplate my heart and my body without disgust!]

as an example of inconsequence, of an involuntary lapse into Christian piety. Baudelaire's greatest achievement, he suggests, was that he was guilty of few such lapses and succeeded in imposing his will on the refractory medium of verse. He calls Baudelaire "one of those sophisticated and ambitious materialists who can hardly conceive of more than one kind of perfection—material perfection," and, elsewhere, praises him in these terms: "The artist, vigilant and incredibly persistent in the fixed contemplation of his idea, has not been too badly defeated." We can hardly fail to notice that even within the confines of Barbey's article there is a major contradiction. Granted that Baudelaire was a Christian in disguise, how could he be a materialist? This contradiction is at the root of most of the controversies for which Baudelaire has provided the pretext.

Baudelaire's own critical writings will shed some light on the contradiction; but before considering his works I should like to summarize the opinions of some of his later critics. Gautier's long essay, which serves as an introduction to many editions of the *Fleurs du mal,* was written in 1868, soon after Baudelaire's death. In his own way—that of an intimate friend rather than that of a critic—Gautier tried to destroy the legendary Baudelaire, the Satanist, the *poseur,* the decadent who had set out to emulate the involuntary eccentricities of Gérard de Nerval and made a science of shocking the *bourgeoisie.* While many of his judgments of the works were commonplace, Gautier contributed more than anyone else to our knowledge of the man; the Baudelaire of his essay had at least become humanly plausible. The Journal of the brothers Goncourt contains other first-hand impressions of the poet.

In his *Histoire du Romantisme,* written in 1874, Gautier added another sketch of Baudelaire:

> Besides, the poet has no indulgence for the vices, the depravities, and the monstrosities which he records with the coolness of a painter employed in a museum of anatomy. He repudiates them as offences against the rhythm of the universe; for, in spite of his eccentricities, he loves order and the 'Norm.' Pitiless towards others, he judges himself no less severely; with virile courage he tells of his errors, his aberrations, his frenzies, his perversities, without sparing the hypocrisy of the reader afflicted in secret with similar vices.

It should be noted that, though Gautier turns Baudelaire into a moralist, he does not attempt to turn him into an impersonal and intransigent spectator; Baudelaire remains the victim, as well as the analyst, of his own vices.

Henry James, like such professional critics as Brunetière and Faguet, continued to regard Baudelaire either as an impostor or as a poet of the second order. In 1884 James wrote: "*Les fleurs du mal* is evidently a sincere book—so far as anything for a man of Baudelaire's temper and culture could be sincere. Sincerity seems to us to belong to a range of qualities with which Baudelaire and his friends were but scantily conversant" [see *NCLC,* Vol. 6, p. 85]. Who, one wonders, are the friends referred to by James?

A poet more solitary than Baudelaire can scarcely have existed. Either the friends in question were a mere rhetorical device or James was misled by the dedication of the *Fleurs du mal* into thinking that Baudelaire was a disciple of Gautier. James continues: "Our impatience is of the same order as that which we should feel if a poet, pretending to pluck the *Flowers of Good,* should come and present us, as specimens, a rhapsody on plumcake and *eau de Cologne.*" According to Brunetière, Baudelaire "was the dupe of his own mystifications" and a poet who used rhetoric to cover up his banality. Faguet thought that "Baudelaire est souvent très mauvais écrivain" ["Baudelaire is often a very bad writer"].

On the other hand, Baudelaire had already acquired a large posthumous following, especially among the poets; Verlaine, Rimbaud, Laforgue, and Mallarmé praised him in the most fervent terms. Swinburne in England, Stefan George in Germany—to name only major poets—added their tribute. Verlaine recognized in Baudelaire the poet of modern life: "He was profoundly original in this respect: powerfully and essentially, he represents modern man as he has become as the result of the refinements of excessive civilization; modern man with his senses sharpened and vibrant, his mind painfully subtle, his brain saturated with tobacco, his blood boiling with alcohol." Rimbaud called him "the first seer, king of poets," but censured him for failing to express his new vision in new forms. Remy de Gourmont drew attention to Baudelaire's indebtedness to Racine. Anatole France pointed out that "his moral attitude does not differ much from that of the theologians."

In more recent years, Paul Valéry has written: "With Baudelaire, French poetry has at last transcended national frontiers. It has found readers everywhere; it has imposed itself as the very poetry of modern times." His argument is that French poetry rarely appeals to foreigners; Baudelaire, he claims, combined the intelligence of a critic with the poetic impulse and, by reacting against the vagueness, the egocentricity and the vulgarity of the Romantic poets, created a modern classicism which can be appreciated by those whose knowledge of French is imperfect.

Mr. Aldous Huxley called Baudelaire "a Christian inside out," ridiculed his pretensions and accused him of bigotry: "Baudelaire was a puritan inside out. Instead of asceticism and respectability he practised debauchery." Mr. T. S. Eliot's judgment, at first sight, resembles Mr. Huxley's: "The important fact about Baudelaire is that he was essentially a Christian born out of his due time and a classicist born out of his due time." But a "Christian inside out" is a very different person from a "Christian born out of his due time"; Mr. Eliot's Baudelaire is a Christian whose faith has been weakened by the ideas current in his age; Mr. Huxley's is a fanatic in pursuit of the "absolute of evil."

Here I must end my survey of Baudelaire's critics; though both arbitrary and incomplete, it will serve to convey some of the outlines. . . . Already our Baudelaire is progressive and traditional, original and banal, classical and modern, a Christian, a Satanist and a materialist, a visionary, a consummate craftsman and a bad writer, a moralist and a man incapable of sincerity. (pp. 24-8)

It would be easy enough to exorcise almost every one of these Baudelaires by quoting passages from his own works; it would be just as easy to select other passages which confirm the opinion of almost every one of the critics. At the present moment Hugo's conception of a democratic, if not a revolutionary, Baudelaire seems the most extravagant of all; in order to prove it so, we need only refer to one of many statements contained in his *Journaux intimes:* "What can be more absurd than Progress, since man, as the event of each day proves, is always like and equal to himself—that is to say, always in a state of primitive savagery." We could also quote the following comment on Hugo made by Baudelaire towards the end of his life, in a letter from Brussels: "I should accept neither his glory nor his fortune if, at the same time, I were obliged to take over his vast absurdities." Even Hugo's assertion, however, is not wholly unfounded; not only did Baudelaire appear at the barricades in 1848, but he contributed to two revolutionary manifestos published in that year. His essay on Dupont, the revolutionary poet, was written four years later; there can be no doubt that this essay expressed an admiration not confined to the artistic merits of Dupont. As for Victor Hugo, no eulogy could be more enthusiastic than Baudelaire's essay on him, published in 1861; evidently Baudelaire made ample use of "the right to contradict oneself." In **"Mon cœur mis à nu,"** he noted: "*Politics.* I have no convictions, as men of my century understand the word, because I have no ambition," and interpreted his conduct in 1848 as "desire for revenge. Natural delight in demolition. Literary drunkenness, reminiscences of books read."

Baudelaire's *L'art romantique* abounds in pronouncements on aesthetics; the problem which preoccupied Baudelaire as a critic is the relationship between art and morality. In his essay on **"L'ecole païenne"** (1852) he concluded: "The time is not distant when it will be understood that all literature which refuses to march fraternally between science and philosophy is a homicidal and suicidal literature." Seven years later, in **"Théophile Gautier,"** he wrote: "Poetry cannot become assimilated to science or morality without dying or decaying; the object of poetry is not Truth, the object of poetry is Itself." We can hardly blame Baudelaire's critics for contradicting one another; Baudelaire himself, one of the most penetrating and brilliant critics of all times, was extraordinarily inconsistent. In **"Pierre Dupont"** (1852), he condemned the doctrine of "art for art's sake": "The puerile utopia of the school of Art for Art's sake, by excluding morality and often even passion, was inevitably sterile"; a later essay, **"Barbier"** (1861) contains the aphorism: "Poetry is sufficient unto itself."

Inconsistency is often mistaken for insincerity; "his criticism was truly creative," M. Soupault wrote of Baudelaire, and it is characteristic of the creative process that opposites must be clearly perceived before they can be reconciled. In a late essay, that on **"Guys"** (1863), Baudelaire was able to combine the conflicting opinions expressed in earlier essays: "Beauty consists of an eternal and invariable element, the quality of which is extremely difficult to determine, and of a relative, incidental element which, if you like, will be the period, the fashion, morality or passion, each in turn or all at the same time." In the same year Baudelaire wrote a letter to Swinburne, who had published a defence of the *Fleurs du mal* in the *Spectator;* it is fortunate that this letter, which never reached Swinburne, has been recovered, for it contains an important comment on the moral intentions attributed to Baudelaire:

> However, forgive me for telling you that you have gone a little too far in defending me. I am not as much of a *moralist* as you so obligingly pretend to believe. I simply believe 'like you, no doubt' that every poem, every work of art that is *well made* naturally and necessarily suggests *moral conclusions.* That is the reader's business. I even feel a very decided hatred for any exclusively moral *intention* in a poem.

Much of Baudelaire's originality is due to the violence of his thought; his mind was attracted to antithetical extremes, juggled with them, compared them and only rarely abandoned them in favour of a moderate solution. In this respect he resembles Nietzsche, another master (and victim) of antitheses. Baudelaire's attitude to religious matters was no more fixed than his attitude to politics, aesthetics or morality. Not only the Catholic orthodoxy which has been claimed for him, but his adherence to any faith which can be called Christian, is questionable. What, for instance, are we to make of this aphorism in **"Fusées"**: "God is the sole being who does not even need to exist in order to reign." In 1861 Baudelaire wrote to his mother: "And God? you will say. With all my heart (with how great a sincerity no one can know except myself) I wish to believe that an external and invisible being is interested in my destiny, but how can I succeed in believing it?" Even in **"Mon coeur mis à nu,"** the journal of his last years, we find a note which, though tentative, is characteristic of Baudelaire's mind: "*Theology.* What is the Fall? If it is unity become duality, it is God who has fallen. In other words, would not the creation be the fall of God?"

These examples could be multiplied, supported by argument or neutralized by other quotations; but it is not my object to add another Baudelaire to the collection, far less to discredit his critics or himself. What I wish to do is to make clear that most of those critics who have attempted to judge Baudelaire's opinions have selected only such evidence as fitted their respective themes. Antitheses, contradiction and paradox were the chief processes of Baudelaire's thought; it was from the conflict of opposites that he derived creative energy. I have confined my attention to those works of Baudelaire in which the views expressed may reasonably be considered his own. *Les fleurs du mal,* the prose poems and *Les paradis artificiels* are even less accessible to interpretation in terms of ideas, beliefs and principles. The aesthetic value of these works will not be discussed; the opinions of Brunetière and Faguet on the subject no longer need to be refuted. If Baudelaire had been a poor, or an unequal craftsman, his achievement would be an even greater one. In order to win the admiration of Mallarmé and Valéry, a poor craftsman would have needed qualities unique even in the domain of the inexplicable.

Critics are too apt to resolve contradictions on the wrong level; if a different Baudelaire is conjured up in these pages, he should be, not a new one, but one who, reconstituted, has been permitted to retain some of the untidiness of the living.

It is not the business of lyrical poets to think methodically—or to think at all, in the accepted sense of the word; poetic thought is intuitive and *emotional,* closer to that of a mystic than to that of a philosopher. Baudelaire thought not consistently but experimentally; *fusées* (rockets) was the name he gave to the aphorisms recorded in his journal—and the function of such fireworks is to amuse, to amaze, to inspire awe, if not fear. Those who are accustomed to a different kind of thought—the kind which takes off at a certain point and rises only in order to land at another point already determined—are likely to accuse Baudelaire of insincerity, frivolity or even charlatanism. In order to be wholly sincere, Baudelaire needed more than one identity; his *personae* included the dandy (and *dandyisme,* to Baudelaire, meant a whole creed centering around the *culte de soi-même*), the gentleman, the bohemian, the pariah, the clown, the criminal and the superman. He differed from other poets in his awareness of being all these and none of them. Every poet is full of contradictions; but Baudelaire was the first to subject himself to merciless criticism, to create and, at the same time, to observe the processes of creation:

> Je suis la plaie et le couteau!
> Je suis le soufflet et la joue!
> Je suis les membres et la roue,
> Et la victime et le bourreau!
>
> [I am the wound and the knife!
> I am the blow and the cheek!
> I am the limbs and the wheel,
> I am the victim and executioner!]

This heightened consciousness of his own duality, or rather multiplicity, is what makes Baudelaire so disturbing, so complex and so *modern* a writer. The aberrations described in **Les fleurs du mal** were anything but new; they had been implicit both in life and literature, but they had never been incorporated in the work of a writer who combined the flexibility of a poet with the strictness of a judge. (Since Baudelaire's time, the critical faculty has tended more and more to develop at the expense of the creative impulse, or vice versa; even Baudelaire, who maintained a precarious and admirable balance, was not a prolific writer. Minor poets nowadays seem to invite classification into those whose poems are treatises or critical essays put into verse and those who, in self-defense, endeavour to let their poetry flow like lava out of the unconscious.) While a part of him remained detached, Baudelaire never ceased to be capable of the self-abandonment required for creation. When he wrote that "art is prostitution"—and thereby likened it to love, which he defined in almost identical terms—he meant that the artist, at the moment of creation, is not a responsible being, but the instrument of whatever power may be possessing him. These, according to Baudelaire, are more likely to be evil than good: "Evil is done without effort, *naturally* by fatality; goodness is always the product of an art."

The statement that "all books are immoral" is only another comment on the dilemma with which Baudelaire's critical writings are so deeply concerned: where is the link between beauty and goodness? How, if there is no such link, can the artist serve both? And how can these two be reconciled with yet another of the artist's obligations, that to be truthful—neither to suppress nor to falsify his own experience of life for the sake of beauty or goodness?

Baudelaire made countless attempts to resolve this dilemma; no critic incapable of doing so will ever be able to judge more than the surface and accessories of his art. His own critical works, journals and correspondence are the only reliable means of approaching the problems relevant to his poetry; the contradictions contained in both prove that he attacked the same problems constantly and from all sides and that he never succeeded in wholly solving them.

Baudelaire had the courage to expose his own weaknesses and the honesty to reveal the limitations of his art; more he could not do, short of renouncing poetry. "Every lyrical poet, by virtue of his nature, is fated to work for a return to the lost Eden," he remarked in his essay on Banville; in other words, the imagination of a lyrical poet moves in a realm which is beyond morality; every poet contains a pagan. (pp. 28-33)

Poets who live in an age of disruption cannot, as more fortunate poets can, employ that part of them which is pagan only in elaborating and embellishing a single message. As a moralist, Baudelaire did his best to stand apart from his age; but he could not sever himself from his own experience or wholly resist the influence which had formed his mind and nourished his imagination. The writers of the eighteenth century had made him sceptical; the Romantics—and especially Chateaubriand—had suggested tortuous possibilities to his imagination, as well as introducing him to the cult of Nature and impulse. Finally, Edgar Allan Poe and Paris—the two decisive influences—had educated his ingenuity and given him a taste for the latest refinements of depravity. Inasmuch as he set out to *interpret* his age, he had to know it, know it with his senses, as well as his brain; inasmuch as his purpose was poetic effect, he was what Barbey called him, a materialist. The imagination is omnivorous; to place it on too strict a diet, is to starve it.

In the same essay on Banville, Baudelaire wrote of the lyrical poet: "Out of ugliness and stupidity he will create a new kind of enchantment." If we apply this dictum to the *Fleurs du mal,* we must conclude that, whatever his intentions may have been, his function, as a poet, was to enchant the reader. While it is possible that, at a single moment, a reader may experience both aesthetic pleasure and moral disgust, one of the two sensations must outweigh the other; and even if we agree with Baudelaire that beauty is twofold, the fundamental contradiction remains unresolved. "I pity those poets who are guided only by instinct; I consider them incomplete." Baudelaire noted and, elsewhere, expressed contempt for those poets who look upon themselves as mere instruments; yet, better than anyone else, he knew that a poet's imagination—his power to recreate myth, discover new symbols and translate his own experience into significance—can be guided, but not commanded, by the intellect and the will. (pp. 33-4)

> *Michael Hamburger, "Baudelaire: A Study in Contradiction," in* The Month, *n.s. Vol. 5, No. 1, January, 1951, pp. 24-34.*

Anna Balakian   (essay date 1958)

[*Balakian is a critic of French literature who has concentrated on the writers of the Symbolist, Surrealist, and Dadaist movements. In the following excerpt, she considers Baudelaire's banned love poems, focusing on his treatment of lesbianism.*]

The centenary of *Les fleurs du mal* throws the spotlight once more on that handful of poems which a French tribunal found offensive to the public taste. The poems, deleted by judicial order, have been subsequently restored to their rightful place in the book and have lived down their initial notoriety. The censorship, instigated by two *Figaro* critics who had found the entire bouquet of *Les fleurs du mal* odious and ignoble, has been discussed too vividly and too often in Baudelaire biographies to need repetition here. The point of interest today is not the scandal but its effect on critical judgments and attitudes as they pertained to the intrinsic qualities of the poems. A return to the texts, now freed of publicity and prejudice, reveals the poems in a new perspective to the nonindignant reader, a hundred years removed from the need of defending a poet against bourgeois morality.

Although in the course of the trial many of Baudelaire's subjects of poetic interest were found questionable, including his cavalier treatment of religion, why did the brunt of the tribunal's condemnation fall upon his love poetry, principally on six poems, one of which, **"Lesbos,"** had been published previously without having aroused any particular admiration or alarm? The question involves Baudelaire's concept of love and its relation to the taste and mores of his time. The poems must be re-examined not individually but as part of a pattern which contains the various facets of Baudelaire's representation of love.

Portrait of Apollonie Sabatier in 1853.

Three types of women appear in Baudelaire's poetry. Two of these were interpretations of his own personal relationships: his mistress, the voluptuous Jeanne Duval, and his friend, Mme Sabatier, whose love had remained for a time on a platonic level. The femininity of Jeanne evoked powerful sensuous imagery of form, scent, and texture in his poems; the other became—until she succumbed to temptation—the symbol of an ideal, less concretely represented but suggesting harmony of beauty and virtue, and variability of emotional appeal. These two prototypes created a duality in his love poetry. Passionately possessive, as in **"La chevelure"** or **"Le balcon,"** Baudelaire reached in the condemned **"Léthé,"** **"Les bijoux,"** and **"Les métamorphoses du vampire"** a state of unrestrained fascination for the animality of love and its almost chemical enticement as experienced with Jeanne. Although in the poems making allusion to Mme Sabatier the point of departure was the spiritual side of love, the unrequited character of the passion was expressed in even more intimate and indiscreet terms. In the condemned **"A celle qui est trop gaie,"** the poet resorted to a form of verbal sadism as if to punish the loved one for her elusiveness and inaccessibility.

Certainly in 1857 when the cult of feminine beauty was as much of an obsession as it is today, and when the poets vied with the artists in the stark vividness of their representations, the erotic imagery of Baudelaire could not in itself have caused astonishment. It is not their lack of moral tone that made these poems objectionable. If they shock it is because in them Baudelaire equates his two essentially different concepts of love and reduces them to the same basic carnal level. While in terms of Jeanne, the feminine soul is entirely circumscribed within physical proportions and made an object of play or a form of narcotic for the male, Baudelaire's ideal love fares no better, the poet *verbally* humiliates and violates it for its inability to provide physical satisfaction.

With the perspective of a hundred years, and mindful of the aesthetic taste of the readers of the Second Empire, whose ideal was the nude Venus, the sculptures of Pradier and Clésinger, and the paintings of the Pagan School, one is inclined to conclude that what proved revolting or immoral in these four poems was *not* his representations of love but the utter joylessness of his approach to beauty whether on a physical or spiritual plane. In defending his poems against the accusation, Baudelaire contended that his saving grace was the attitude of horror he conveyed in all his interpretations of evil. But evil is a deed more than a state. In these poems there is no actual action that might induce horror or even pity. There is, however, perverse intent: the poet's inclination to debase the object of his attraction. It is this will to defile beauty which proved distasteful in these poems despite his careful artistry of words.

There is still a third love expressed in Baudelaire's poetry: the equivocal love traditionally attributed to Sappho and her women disciples. This love, as evidenced in the other two condemned poems, created the most controversy, and, curiously, it has thereafter remained the least discussed and analyzed aspect of Baudelaire's poetry.

It is a strange phenomenon that Sappho has come to symbolize in poetry the peak of eroticism, exhausting the normal and overflowing into the abnormal. Poets since the time of Ovid and Catullus, all the way to Baudelaire,

Swinburne and Tennyson, have let fall on Sappho the full impact of the love expressed in her poems. Her ability to write of love has been identified with her personal capacity for love, making it a tall order when one considers that the fragments handed down to us include the loves of impatient maidens, frightened brides, dreamy youths, and passionate bridegrooms. With feminine flexibility of emotion—sometimes incomprehensible to men—Sappho was able to personify each of her characters as they sang of love. But they were roles which she played, transforming her from woman to man, from virgin to youth, as the circumstances of her love song suggest. In each instance her writing has a tone of authenticity but is never lascivious. Since the poetic object of masculine love is more apt to offer aesthetic variations than that of woman, Sappho aimed at this broader scope by shifting at times her point of perspective. She adroitly conjured up images of limbs on soft cushions, tender feet, rosy arms, soft hands, lovely hair, etc. However, this dramatic technique, so subtly inherent in her lyricism, seems to have been overlooked by the Greek comic writers as well as by most of her modern European readers, who have taken her poetic transfigurations literally and interpreted them as masculinity of taste or inclination. The basic reason for this ambiguity, no doubt, is that love poets rarely dissociate the real from the impersonal, and traditionally their lyricism has a strong autobiographical character. It is their love life, the lips they have known or desired, the heart they have sought or possessed, and no other. Ovid, alone, suggested the blamelessness of Sappho's hypothetical loves. Not so Baudelaire, nor any of the other artists of his time who were interested in Sappho. For them she was not so much a poet as an unorthodox prototype of love. The author of **"Lesbos"** did not reflect on the imprecise and tender purity of expression in poems of Sappho such as her "Hymn" to Venus and the shorter fragments; like his contemporaries he went to legend and not to the text for his inspiration.

In Baudelaire's **"Lesbos"** Sappho is two things: lover and poet. As lover she lures her disciples into dangerous erotic paths and remains the patron saint of unconventional love; but paradoxically—although he does not sense this incongruity in his poem—Baudelaire reminds us that she fell victim to the natural love of woman for man and, despairing of the indifference of her lover, threw herself into the sea. As poet, she gives fame and enchantment to the island of her birth and leaves it a symbol of the full gamut of sensuality. The poem with its haunting refrains has the hypnotic effect of a love elixir and is prohibitive of logical explanation. But if we were to set aside Baudelaire's elegiac empathy with the island of Lesbos and its heroine in order to look at the poem with a dispassionate eye, we might find in it a curious confusion about Sappho and the nature of her love. Sappho is pictured as "mâle," yet gives proof of extreme femininity in committing suicide for love of a man. Under these dramatic circumstances, the word "mâle" appears incongruous if taken literally as it was by the tribunal which condemned the poem. But we come much closer to the true sense of the word if we consider Baudelaire's use of it in reference to Sappho as a typically masculine reaction to extraordinary intellectual capabilities in a woman. Judging by the personality of the poet and the nature of his associations with women, he comprehended the physical and spiritual attributes of a woman but did not appreciate the intellectually creative. The attitude which he reveals in calling Sappho "mâle" is also evidenced in his derogatory remarks about George Sand and is confirmed by a generalized statement elsewhere that in his opinion an intellectual woman is "un homme manqué" who could be loved only by a pervert.

The two poems about **"Femmes damnées,"** one of which was included among the condemned, give no more evidence than **"Lesbos"** that Baudelaire was particularly destined by nature to write of Lesbian loves. His language is suggestive and tantalizing, but suggestive of what? A close scrutiny of the two poems reveals that Baudelaire's "poor sisters" were actually suffering from narcissism and fear of sex. These delicate, alluring creatures cling to each other because they are wary of the realities of love and prefer to them the transparent pleasures of the illusion. They sense the touch of man to be brutal and satisfy themselves with the lighter touch of woman. Their wrong is that they thus deviate from nature—which implies that they are basically normal. Theirs is the song of regret, apprehension and frustration—a far cry from both nineteenth-century literary comprehension of Lesbianism and twentieth-century physiological explanations of inversion. In the works of many of the artists of the nineteenth century Lesbianism served to represent heightened sensuality in woman. In Théophile Gautier's *Mlle de Maupin* the heroine's apparently perverted tendencies are eventually explained as sexual impatience, and her erotic imagination, nostalgia and romantic ardor are at the end requited through normal channels of love. In contrast, Baudelaire's erotics anticipate no ultimate joy in regularized relationships. On the other hand, in representing their love attitude Baudelaire did not intend to accept it within the bounds of nature's normal patterns as Gide has done in *Corydon.*

In a conversation between Gide and Proust as reported in Gide's *Journal,* Proust expressed the belief that Baudelaire was an invert. Gide answered that he would like nothing better than to be able to receive Baudelaire into the fold but was skeptical of Proust's contention. Indeed, Baudelaire's portrait of his frightened maidens gives little intimation of being a reflection of the poet's own experience. If his women are "damned" it is because they are not following the true dictates of their nature. It is their common inhibitions that attract them to each other and make them flee conventional love. Baudelaire's verbal composition contains neither the self-conscious manner of Proust nor Gide's evangelistic convictions on the subject. If Baudelaire wrote of Lesbianism at all he had a practical reason and at the same time a less perceptible psychological one. In the first instance, judging from his contemporaries' as well as his own testimony, he was enough of a journalist to recognize a subject (or a certain type of imagery) that might make his book salable, and the Sappho theme was a fad of the moment. But the eye that was sensitive to publicity had a strange contingency with the poet's vision of his inner self. The role of dandy, which in his self-search he had found most comfortable to assume, was to be best represented in the characters of Delphine and Hippolyte. Baudelaire was able to project himself into these half-frightened, half-daring, self-adoring, and self-pitying fabrications of his imagination, whom he categorized as Lesbians for lack of a better word, but who were as far removed from the common notion of the Sappho image pictorially and verbally prevalent in mid-nineteenth century as they are from our own understanding of the term today.

Sketch of Jeanne Duval by Baudelaire.

"Femmes damnées"—both the condemned poem and the supposedly more innocuous piece—are for Baudelaire a triumph of originality such as he has not attained even in his famous **"Correspondances"** or **"Le voyage."** They contain images of love unique and independent of contemporary models and of personal experiences. He owes these creations to no one. His technique in conjuring them bypasses both the Parnassians' objective realism and the overplay of idealized autobiography so dear to the Romanticists who were still active at the time. Baudelaire achieves in these two poems an intermingling of the sensuous with the ideal as nowhere else in his love imagery. He translates his innate delicacy, his unconscious narcissism, his fear of love's accepted rules and social consequences into these ethereal subjects, prey to frenzied but uncertain desires. He offers his own limitless pity to their furtive aspirations and to their fear of passion. Love is not debased here, nor the ideal of beauty reduced to ludicrous materialism, as in the four condemned poems in which there were allusions to real persons.

Indeed, if an injustice was done to Baudelaire it was not in fining him three hundred francs but in associating through this unfortunate condemnation four poems of uneven value with three of his most original and aesthetically unusual masterpieces. For it is in **"Lesbos"** and the two poems of **"Femmes damnées"** that Baudelaire reached the apex of his love poetry.

In liberating love from good and evil, and in detaching it

from social implications and real life models, he seems to metamorphose his own complicated human entanglements and triumph over the particular. In so doing, he transcends the irritating and sometimes monotonous duality of his love. Instead, the physical and the spiritual are molded into each other to create a single melancholy pattern as sensuality proves unsatisfying and the ideal assumes the illusiveness of the dream. The poetic synthesis thereby achieved, ironically, purges his work of whatever ugliness there could be found elsewhere to serve as a target for censorship. (pp. 273-77)

Anna Balakian, "Those Stigmatized Poems of Baudelaire," in The French Review, *Vol. XXXI, No. 4, February, 1958, pp. 273-77.*

Alain Bosquet   (essay date 1958)

[*A Russian-born American poet, novelist, translator, and critic writing in French, Bosquet is among the most prominent figures in modern French literature. In the following excerpt, he contends that Baudelaire was less a poet than he was a thinker who propounded new perspectives on poetry.*]

Baudelaire, because of the notorious trial in 1857 following the publication of **Les fleurs du mal,** became a famous poet, but famous for the wrong reasons. In a France that was settling into a bourgeois way of life and addicted to parliamentarism, it was up to the official critics to make Baudelaire pass for a monster. They succeeded so well that even as late as 1914 a number of sixteen-year-old students were expelled from school for the sole crime of reading **Les fleurs du mal.** The French Republic, like the early Second Empire, was prudish, to a degree that would have frightened Voltaire and even Louis XV. The conviction of Baudelaire on moral grounds established the principle that all poetry must be moral. The formalities were, of course, observed and circumstances extenuating to Baudelaire were found: he was a sick man, prematurely old, not well-balanced; he lived with a Negress, he detested his stepfather, and lacked all sense of dignity. Still more serious, however, is the fact that the legend emphasized these accusations, and it is paradoxical that it should have been Paul Verlaine, a highly talented poet, who made acceptable the ridiculous and pejorative notion of *"le poète maudit."* Poets were thus by definition damned; and therefore the official critics, whenever they found themselves confronted with a work they could not understand, placed the blame on the physical and mental defects of the poet, just as the well-meaning Zola explained his time in terms of alcoholism.

The twentieth century—doubtless because it is itself a little mad, a little hysterical—diverges more and more from the concept of the *maudit* that is so easily confused with the concept of profound poetry. The twentieth century also put aside any idea of the monstrous or the freakish as applied to poetry after Rimbaud (who remains beyond question for Americans the most undeniable poetic genius in the last hundred years, and who for the French is one of the two most revered saints in their history, the other being Jeanne d'Arc). We now prefer to regard the poet not as a lunatic, not as a sick man, not as a "seer" who has something of the prophet and something of the astrologer, but rather as a man of extraordinary mental balance (ex-

ceptions like Antonin Artaud merely prove the rule), a man who knows how to exploit with perfect lucidity whatever it is that chance (i.e., inspiration) may bring him. In short, for us a poet is a man who should be able to provide his readers with a certain amount of instinctive knowledge, rather than a magician who rules by terror, seductive as that terror may be.

If we are willing to reread Baudelaire in the light of these few simple principles, we see that he is in no way the unbalanced creature he has been made out to be. Even if his body was subject to atrocious suffering, even if his flesh was most spectacularly accursed, his mind remained to the end remarkably rigorous and lucid. He was the embodiment of intelligence, one of those tempered, farseeing intellects that resemble a Montaigne or a Bossuet. All things considered, his intelligence is his major virtue, for in spite of what has been claimed, he is not a great creator. He lacks *élan,* and indeed he is singularly lacking in madness. He never lets himself go to the point of euphoria, and he believes more in the need for self-analysis than in the endless need to translate feelings into works of art. It is enough to read his letters to see that his most insistent purpose is to *understand,* that emotion occupies only a secondary place.

This implacable analyst decided, therefore (his was a calculated decision, no mere surrender to some obscure, postromantic urge), that *understanding* was not enough for an intelligent man, that self-analysis and the analysis of others are not enough to fill a man's life. Deliberately, calmly, with great effort, he made himself a creator. Natural aptitudes he certainly had, but fewer gifts, perhaps, and certainly less spontaneity than a Hugo, a Browning, a Vigny. He forced his intelligence to grow as he played this magnificent game; nevertheless it always remained a game— the incarnation of himself in a splendid work of art. For it was difficult for him truly to create; he wrote little, and he was comfortable only in those pages where his analytic faculty retained its control over the rest. This is true of **Le spleen de Paris;** it is especially true of his writings on art. For let us make no mistake, Baudelaire's most enduring claim to fame is in never having been wrong about his contemporaries, whether poets or painters, novelists or sculptors. He is fundamentally the only Sainte-Beuve France has had, without Sainte-Beuve's monumental errors, without his shabby injustices.

What is important . . . is not that Baudelaire wrote some very beautiful poems (on the whole, Villon, Nerval, Rimbaud, Mallarmé, Corbière, Apollinaire and Saint-John Perse are either more perfect or closer to what we call inspiration); it is that Baudelaire determined in a sure and definitive way the role of the poet and of poetry, both in society and in the entire realm of human activity, intellectual and emotional. No one has said *truer* things about poetry and the poet than he or, if one prefers, no one has explained more clearly or in simpler terms what had been basically obscure, equivocal and approximate in the state of poetry. He took the naïveté out of poetry; he even took out the poetics so as to give it a meaning in which instinct and knowledge, the unexpected and the known, balance each other at all times, although, by definition, this balance must always remain hazardous. He has said, "The poet rejoices in that incomparable privilege of being himself or another person as he pleases. Like those wandering souls in search of a body, he enters, when he likes, into everyone's personality. For him alone everything is open; and if certain places seem closed to him it is because in his eyes they are not worth the trouble of exploring." Elsewhere he also says: "I find it futile and dull to picture what exists because nothing in existence satisfies me. Nature is ugly, and I prefer the monster of my imagination to the triviality of the actual. . . . Imagination is the queen of truth, and the *possible* is one of the provinces of truth. Imagination is related to the infinite in a positive way."

Passages like these still serve us as a breviary, for it is only thanks to his having written them that we have renounced the real crime of Greco-Latin civilization: the determination to reduce art, and particularly poetry, to a single, rational explanation. Since Baudelaire, we have known that poetry cannot be explained or, rather, that it can always be explained in six, ten or thirty different ways, and that all these ways are contradictory. Indeed, in this same period, and using the same word *possible,* didn't Emily Dickinson say, "I dwell in Possibility, / A fairer house than prose"?

Thanks to the luminous intelligence and the exceptional intellectual mastery of Baudelaire we know the extent to which poetry must be a mystery—something to be approached, encircled, besieged, but remaining forever a mystery. Thanks to him, too, poetry seems to us rich only according to the number of disagreements it engenders, whereas formerly we believed in it only if a definite agreement about its meaning had been reached. Since Baudelaire, only one other poet has helped persuade us that poetry is "irreducible"—a poet who, like Baudelaire, was an *amateur* of thought and philosophy: Paul Valéry.

We must see in Baudelaire a man who freed poetry from the lies and the fogs that true poets like Rimbaud made all the denser. This means that in his soul Baudelaire was not a true poet; like Valéry he was a complete man who trained his sensibility by means of poetry. He succeeded as a poet only insofar as he tricked his own lucidity; he succeeded as a poet only by exaggerating his morbid side and by carrying a purely verbal cruelty to the point of utter darkness. (pp. 517-18)

> *Alain Bosquet, "Baudelaire Reconsidered," in* The Nation, *New York, Vol. 186, No. 23, June 7, 1958, pp. 517-18.*

A. E. Carter (essay date 1959)

[*Carter is a Canadian educator, translator, and critic whose works include* The Idea of Decadence in French Literature: 1830-1900 *(1958) and* Charles Baudelaire *(1977). In the following excerpt, Carter elaborates on the modern qualities of Baudelaire's poetry.*]

[Baudelaire's] life, 1821-67, spans what is in many ways the nineteenth century's core, the years when it evolved, dropped the dead limbs of the past, and became that historical entity we call "Nineteenth Century." Baudelaire was born in the reign of Louis XVIII, when the *ancien régime* and the Revolution were still potent memories, and lived to within three years of the Third Republic. His contemporaries were President Lincoln and Mr. Disraeli, Louis Philippe, Florence Nightingale, and Napoleon III; he grew to maturity under the July Monarchy and wrote

and died during the Second Empire; he wore the stovepipe hat and frock coat of the period, dressed his mistresses in crinolines, and watched them waltzing to the music of Strauss and Offenbach. It is all a dead world now, much further from us in spirit than the mere distance in time would seem to indicate. . . . And the fact that Baudelaire's work is now so relished—the fact that poetry which is still not merely read but extravagantly praised could have been written by this child of an age that seems more remote from us than the boudoirs of La Dubarry—is one of the curiosities of literary history. For while many writers have been neglected by their contemporaries and appreciated later on, very few have been appreciated as we now appreciate Baudelaire. We call him a "modern" poet, sometimes even *"the* modern poet"; and the definition, given the circumstances, certainly has few parallels. No volume of verse published in 1757 would have been called "modern" a century later, or indeed a good many years before.

The reasons for some of this posthumous glory are obvious enough. Baudelaire had, of course, great talent in the technical sense, the ability to write mere "poetry." But it would be rash to maintain that he was more endowed in this respect than his contemporaries—when they were Hugo, Musset, Vigny, and Leconte de Lisle. He differed from them, and that is all. Since many of us prefer his poetry to theirs, it is interesting to know how he differed. If we read criticism of his work produced at any time within the last sixty or seventy years, we find that, along with his modernism, it was especially his novelty which struck his admirers: he was hailed as a "poète nouveau" who had produced a "poésie nouvelle." What was this "new" poetry? The subject is odiously hackneyed: Baudelaire introduced the theory of *correspondances* into poetry and with it new techniques employing verbal harmonies, colours, perfumes; and thus he was the founder of the Symbolist school. None of this seems very thrilling nowadays, partly because later poets (Verlaine, Mallarmé, Laforgue, Rimbaud) carried the new technique further than did Baudelaire, partly because, despite this great "reform," French verse at the end of the century was no better than it was at the beginning, in fact, rarely as good. To found a school of poetry is no sound claim to glory—Marino also founded a school. And anyone who has had to read systematically the works of Baudelaire's minor disciples, such as Samain, Ghil, and Kahn, where the Baudelairean paraphernalia is used and re-used to the point of nausea, finds himself regretting that Baudelaire ever invented this particular kind of novelty. The truth of the matter is that Baudelaire's theories, like all poetic theories, are unimportant; their value lies solely in the way he used them to produce verse which we like better than poetry written at the same time, even when it was composed by men whose talents certainly equalled his.

Baudelaire had a keen ear for the musical possibilities of French, the keenest since Racine's, perhaps; and this influenced his writing in a number of ways. There is first a marked drop in key. Much of his poetry is almost conversational, spoken rather than declaimed:

> Si, par une nuit bleue et froide de décembre,
> Je la trouvais tapie en un coin de ma chambre,
> Grave, et venant du fond de son lit éternel
> Couver l'enfant grandi de son oeil maternel,
> Que pourrais-je répondre à cette âme pieuse,

Voyant tomber les pleurs de sa paupière creuse?

Is it possible to imagine that written in the Romantic style of Baudelaire's day? Owing to its Latin origins, French verse, both classical and Romantic, has always been rhetorical; the poet is on a platform, addressing an audience, whether he slanders Napoléon le Petit or describes a broken heart. Baudelaire is an exception. While there is some rhetoric in **Les fleurs du mal,** it is very low-pitched, so low-pitched that we can scarcely hear it. And we find this very much to our taste. Our modern sensibility does not take kindly to the grand manner; our blood and nerves are not rich enough for declamation: it wearies us, and makes us self-conscious. We prefer Baudelaire because he seldom raises his voice. As Gide said, it is because he speaks in a low tone that we listen to him longest [see essay dated 1917]. It might even be said that his style is the best of nineteenth-century French poetry—a perfect equilibrium between Romantic exuberance and Symbolist refinement. If Hugo now seems bombastic, there are times when Verlaine is too plaintive and attenuated, and Mallarmé too hermetic and sterile.

Baudelaire's interest in musical effects goes much deeper than a skillful juggling with verbal harmonies. His best poems in this style (**"Le jet d'eau," "Le balcon," "Harmonie du soir"**) are, like music itself, more suggestive than definite. Their meaning is not confined within the limitations of idea and expression; behind the precision of the form there is a wide region hinted at rather than described, a whole universe of associations in which a reader can lose himself indefinitely. Like Chopin's nocturnes, such poems are evocations rather than statements, and in this field Baudelaire is pretty well unrivalled. This evocativeness is the source of the curiously obsessive quality of his verse, which makes short poems (and all his poems are short) seem long. Before Baudelaire's time nobody made an attempt at this effect, or made it less successfully, and afterwards, as in Verlaine and Samain, the verbal side of the matter is carried to such a point as to give harmony and little else.

The mystic tone of **Les fleurs du mal** is another point that has been much stressed; so much, in fact, that, with the aid of the **Journaux intimes,** it is frequently the only side of Baudelaire that is discussed at all. The whole question, I think, should be treated very cautiously. Mysticism, when Baudelaire began to write, had been a standard literary ingredient for over forty years. Ever since its beginnings in Chateaubriand, Romanticism had a mystic tinge, a tendency to trifle about in churches and dabble with holy water. There was much talk about confessionals, Madonnas, God, and the Devil long before Baudelaire was born. Yet his religiosity has been seized upon as though it were unique, seized upon and exaggerated until we have had Catholic and even Jansenist Baudelaires these past twenty-five years. It is becoming fashionable to write about him as though he were one of the Fathers of the Church. This type of criticism seems to me quite absurd. It could end by making Baudelaire as conventionally dull as Jean-Baptiste Rousseau, and fossilizing one of the least static writers who ever existed.

Fortunately for Baudelaire's future popularity it will always be difficult to present him in an orthodox light—at least as long as sexual promiscuity, various perversions, and overindulgence in drugs and alcohol are considered undesirable amusements. Baudelaire was haunted all his life by the forbidden, and so much the better for him! He was one of those unquiet spirits who are always straying from the highway of convention. He never could conform—either to the official rationalism of his time or to the official orthodoxy demanded by the Church. This obsession is one of the reasons why we still read him, and it is probably one of the reasons why he will always be read. His poetry was written "in the midst of life"; he was fascinated by the brilliant and appalling spectacle of the world, and fascinated not as a detached and Olympian judge, like Hugo and Vigny, but as an actor, a victim, a hero of the drama. His poetry springs from direct experience; and for all his erudition, which was considerable, he is one of the least bookish of poets. It is amusing to find M. Sartre attacking him for his moral paralysis and his weakness. Of course he was weak, when confronted with his stepfather's military arrogance and Jeanne Duval's squalid lies. And then? His failure as a man had a great deal to do with his success as a poet. If he had been able to regulate his finances profitably and drop a worthless mistress back into the gutter where he found her, he would not have been Baudelaire, and he would not have written **Les fleurs du mal.** He might instead have written something like M. Sartre's *Chemins de la liberté,* in which case his work would now be slumbering undisturbed in the stacks of the Bibliothèque Nationale, where that immense stodge will undoubtedly be reposing a half-century hence.

Baudelaire's very lack of fixed ideas and settled convictions, his tendency to lose himself in inextricable situations until he had sucked the last drop of bitterness from them, explains his attraction. One's own despair will always find an echo in Baudelaire; he will sympathize, but will not judge. He does not force one to accept a complicated apparatus of beliefs and prejudices before one can understand him. Had he been either a thorough-going agnostic or a convinced Catholic he would be infinitely less moving; but he was equally distant from both skepticism and Revelation. He was not a Voltairean, but he was far, very far, from being a good son of the Church. His life and works are there to prove it.

To see how ill he fits the Catholic pattern we need merely imagine him in an orthodox age, such as the seventeenth century. He would have been a Théophile de Viau, in constant danger of excommunication or the stake; he would have written fewer poems like **"Bénédiction"** and many more like **"Les promesses d'un visage"** and **"Le rêve d'un curieux."** He had a wide knowledge of erotica (Diderot, Nerciat, Laclos, De Sade)—he enjoyed reading it; and he was well acquainted with some of the shadiest dives of Paris. He sought much more in the big city than vice, but he sought vice too; and whatever quotations of a "moral" nature may be found in his diaries and letters, **Les fleurs du mal** will always smack of forbidden fruit. They would not be **Les fleurs du mal** else. Artist as he was, he was quite capable of using Christian symbolism to throw vice and crime into higher relief. His religious convictions were uncertain and fluctuating, like those of his age. At times he was a complete unbeliever, and he never frequented churches with any assiduity, except to admire the architecture. It would be interesting to know how many times during his adult life he took Communion and went to confession. I make the suggestion simply because, if we believed a lot of modern writing on the subject, we should see him as a kind of lay monk, with his nose in a volume of Eusebius and his fingers in the holy water soup. His knowledge of doctrine was no greater than what might be derived from an ordinary Catholic upbringing, extended in later years by readings of a mystical cast such as the works of Swedenborg, Tertullian, and Edgar Allan Poe—none of them very sound from the point of view of doctrine.

As for the Jansenist tone one finds here and there in Baudelaire's work, and about which so much nonsense has been written, its source is easier found in the tradition of French literature itself than in what has been called his "Jansenist childhood." Nobody who studies French literature, particularly the great seventeenth-century school, can avoid admiring the austere heroes of Port Royal, especially when their ideas are presented in such masterpieces as *Phèdre* and *Les pensées*. And Baudelaire found this intransient theology particularly seductive for another reason: it corresponded admirably to the disgust his penetrating mind felt when confronted with the humanitarian drivel and wishful thinking of so much nineteenth-century utopianism and progressive theory. He believed because his age disbelieved; his faith was a negative reaction, the result of a dilemma. The period was officially rationalist; religion was a matter of good works or a comfortable panacea to justify self-indulgence. The idea of good had obscured the idea of evil. Baudelaire saw quite clearly the results of this—a wishy-washy sentimentality which was the worst possible atmosphere for poetry. He realized that most great verse is religious, not in a narrow doctrinal sense, but inasmuch as it views man in a metaphysical light and attempts to fix his relationship to good and evil. It must have drama, and evil is the greatest drama of all.

Here, however, Baudelaire came up against a difficulty; he was never quite sure that he believed in evil, much as he wanted to. There is a certain amount of pose in his attitude; he often uses metaphysics indiscriminately. Woman as a Temptress may be a striking figure; but when she is always a Temptress—or what is a variation of the same thing, an immaculate Madonna—she begins to look like a piece of highly coloured stage scenery. There is too much of this kind of painted cardboard in *Les fleurs du mal.* Baudelaire threw away the conventional symbols of nineteenth-century progress, and quite rightly, since most of them were shams. But unfortunately he lacked the ability to invent something convincing to put in their place. He went back to the no less conventional symbols of early Romanticism—devils, succubi, Fatal Women—in which, for all his determination, he was much too intelligent to really believe. The results are not always satisfactory. There is often a startling discrepancy between the profound significance of his poems and the technique (ideas and imagery) he uses to express it, and some of his finest work is irreparably damaged as a result. This is true of **"Le voyage."** It is one of the best poems in *Les fleurs du mal,* symphonic in conception, and filled with splendid lines. . . . Baudelaire seldom wrote better. Yet the poem leaves, somehow, a disappointing impression, falls short of what it promised. This failure, I believe, results directly from Baudelaire's rather artificial metaphysics. He tells us that the main thing one discovers during life's voyage is "le spectacle ennuyeux de l'immortel péché" ["the boring spectacle of ever-lasting sin"], and further narrows it down to mere sexual sin. In the splendid context of marine horizons and

sumptuous adventure, this conclusion is almost ludicrously weak, dragged in peevishly, at all costs, for no other purpose than to scandalize the nineteenth-century believers in progress, and, what is much more serious, without any real conviction on Baudelaire's part. For how can he, with his penetrating intelligence and his profound knowledge of the human heart, have seriously held to such a simplified morality? We need merely look through the rest of his work to see that he found much more during his life's voyage than "sin." Had he not, we should scarcely be reading him today. Moreover, after taking up this rigorous Augustinian stand, he is unable to sustain it. It bores him, and he shrugs off the whole matter in the final lines by demanding not absolution, but "something new," even if he has to die to get it. To believe in sin and then ask nothing from Death but novelty is worse than inconsistent, it is flippant. There is a smart touch about **"Le voyage"** which, while it certainly avoids the pomposity of other writing of the period (and that is something) weakens an otherwise admirable poem. Of the same order are the "shocking" passages which occur here and there in *Les fleurs du mal:*

> Les yeux étaient deux trous, et du ventre effondré
> Les intestins pesants lui coulaient sur les cuisses, .
> Et ses bourreaux, gorgés de hideuses délices,
> L'avaient à coups de bec absolument chatré

> [The eyes were holes, and from the ruined belly
> The heavy entrails spilled over the thighs,
> And his butchers, gorged on hideous delicacies,
> Had castrated him with their pecking beaks.]

Such lines no longer appear atrocious, merely dull. We have had so much worse since! Nothing dates faster than the horrible. Balzac says somewhere that bread and water are the only two things we never tire of because they are tasteless; and while some spice is frequently indispensable in literary cookery, it must be admitted that Baudelaire often used it very clumsily. Of course we excuse his mistakes, but mistakes they remain.

Fortunately, if the "shocking" Baudelaire must be dismissed as an authentic child of late Romanticism, in the line of the Borels and O'Neddys, the metaphysical Baudelaire, despite occasional lapses, managed to turn his interest in evil to good poetic account. Evil, besides providing him with drama, defended him from the contagion of nineteenth-century optimism. It was a sort of spiritual prophylactic, a means of rediscovering the tragic point of view. Tragedy can exist only when vice becomes sin; and when Baudelaire talks about sin he has this necessity in mind. A man with vices is a nuisance doomed to the Small Debts Courts and the disapproval of his relatives. Considered as vice, Macbeth's murder of Duncan does not go beyond the limits of any other squalid crime. It is murder for profit, and nothing else. But considered as sin (which it is to Shakespeare) it at once becomes fit material for poetry. The haunting introspection, Banquo's ghost, the Weird Sisters, follow as matters of course. Lady Macbeth can go mad with no impropriety; the squalor and confusion become significant and tragic. Baudelaire was born too late to write tragedies; the *genre* was dead over a century before his time. But his verse is the nearest thing to tragic verse the nineteenth century has left us.

This was perhaps Baudelaire's greatest triumph: he succeeded in making the nineteenth century tragic. Other poets of the time, such as Tennyson and Hugo, felt the need; but with less judgment than Baudelaire they found no better means of satisfying it than by turning out conventional tragedies, only slightly rejuvenated by Romantic methods, about Bloody Mary and the Borgias. Perhaps if Baudelaire had lived twenty years earlier he might have done the same, although this is doubtful. His critical sense was too keen; it would have saved him from any sterile attempt to beat the great classical dramatists on their own ground. He seems to have understood that poetry, to be truly valid, must be contemporary, must deal with and interpret its own age, must be, in other words, "modern," even when (as in *Paradise Lost*) it chooses settings which are not immediately familiar.

For a number of reasons it had become very difficult to write poetry of this kind by the middle of the nineteenth century. The industrial revolution had transformed civilization to such an extent that poetry was at a loss. What "poetry" could be made of the modern city—factory chimneys, railroads, stench of chemicals? None, apparently, if we are to judge by most of the verse which appeared at the time. It is usually escapist, infected with a particularly virulent species of exoticism, both of space and time. Nearly all the French poets lived in Paris, but they avoided the city as subject-matter. Hence Bloody Mary and the Borgias. If the poets remained modern, they went to the tropics for their subject matter, or toyed with mantillas and roses in Andalusia. The cult of Nature itself became exotic, as escapist as the rest. The city was left to the prose writers like Balzac; poetry dealt in distant landscapes and civilizations, or in lush evocations of the vegetable universe.

Baudelaire turned his back on this convention. He chose modern life as his subject, or, as he called it in **"Le salon de 1845,"** one of his earliest works, "l'héroisme de la vie moderne" ["the heroism of modern life"]. He developed the idea in subsequent essays, such as **"Le salon de 1859"** and the studies of Méryon and Guys; and to find this modern heroism he sought it where it might best be seen, in the great city. This was certainly original. Poems like Wordsworth's sonnet on London are rare in all literatures; yet poems of this kind form a large proportion of *Les fleurs du mal.* Baudelaire is the least exotic of nineteenth-century French poets. There is no exoticism of time in his poetry, no search for glamorous epochs; he remained in the nineteenth century. What exoticism of space occurs (based on memories of his trip to Mauritius) is usually employed to throw into high relief what he called "la noire majesté de la plus inquiétante des capitales" ["the black majesty of the most disquieting of capitals"].

The proceeding was no accident; it was quite deliberate; and it preoccupied Baudelaire more and more as time passed. He found the initial idea for his prose poems in Aloysius Bertrand's little work *Gaspard de la nuit,* a typical Romantic evocation of Renaissance Paris. But, he says, "ce qu'il [Bertrand] avait fait pour la vie ancienne et pittoresque, je voulais le faire pour la vie moderne et abstraite" ["what he (Bertrand) did for an old and picturesque way of life, I would like to do for abstract modern life"]. Most of the prose-poems, like most of the *Fleurs du mal,* are set in Paris or imply an urban background—as the title Baudelaire chose for the volume (*Le spleen de Paris*) implies. The section of the *Fleurs du mal* subtitled

"Tableaux parisiens" was added to the second edition in 1861, and only a few of its poems had appeared in the first edition four years before. Among Baudelaire's papers was found an unfinished **"Epilogue à la ville de Paris,"** in which . . . the capital was represented as the inspiration and source of the whole book. Paris was in many ways the most significant world of its time, and the world Baudelaire knew best. He sought his material there just as Dante looked for his in the scandals and intrigues of fourteenth-century Italy. In other words, Baudelaire was simply returning to a great tradition, to poetic sources of much greater authenticity than the oriental bric-à-brac and exotic scenery which pleased so many of his contemporaries. "N'est-il pas l'habit nécessaire à notre époque," he says of modern dress, "souffrant et portant sur les épaules noires et maigres le symbole d'un deuil perpétuel?" ["Isn't it the garb necessary for our suffering epoch which wears upon its black and narrow shoulders the symbol of perpetual mourning?"] For the first time modern man, recognizably such, and not rigged out in a breastplate or trunk-hose, became a subject for poetry, as authentic and tragic on his streets and boulevards, in his boudoirs, brothels, workhouses and gambling dens as the heroes of Shakespeare or Racine.

> Fourmillante cité, cité pleine de rêves,
> Où le spectre, en plein jour, raccroche le passant! . . .
>
> [Swarming city, city full of dreams,
> Where the specter, in broad daylight, accosts the passerby! . . .]

This spectre, the genius and spirit of the city, presides over all Baudelaire's work, from *Les fleurs du mal* to the tortured jottings of his diaries. It accompanied him on his solitary walks; it was always at his elbow, now ironic, now pathetic, suggesting the hidden drama of things, glimmering like a will-o'-the-wisp on the stone coping of a bridge and the long perspectives of quays and boulevards. It permeates the atmosphere with its uneasy voice, brooding in the green and pink silence of dawn along the river . . . or stirring restlessly in the sinister golden hush of evening. . . . Sometimes it lights up an interior with sudden brilliance—a café, a music-hall—or throws into high relief some human specimen, **"Mlle Bistouri,"** a drunken *clochard,* a widow in black listening to a band-concert in the Luxembourg. These evocations of the city are not just a picturesque backdrop of streets and lamp-standards (as they become in the work of some of Baudelaire's disciples); they are significant in the highest degree; they are "le douloureux et glorieux décor de la civilisation" ["the dolorous and glorious decor of civilization"], a revelation of man, his greatness and his squalor, his passions, his perversities, his "goût de l'infini." ["appetite for the infinite"].

Now this sort of thing, despite Baudelaire's apparent ease, was extremely difficult to handle. Not only had it never been used before, but the very spirit of the time was against it. The exoticism of contemporary literature was something more than a craze for the picturesque or a dislike of the new industrialized landscapes. It had a long tradition behind it, summed up in the idea that civilization is somehow artificial and corrupt, decadent in short—the word will out. Popularized by Rousseau and Chateaubriand, the theory had become one of the planks of the Romantic platform, and we find it both before and after Baudelaire, not merely in the *avant garde* and the lunatic fringe of contemporary letters, but in serious philosophers like Taine and in a whole school of psychopathologists—Morel, Moreau de Tours, Richet, Nordau. The modern was equated with the decadent, and if one wrote about the modern, one's work was decadent. Civilization thus being identified with degeneracy, primitivism was identified with health. The idea is by no means dead in our time, and presumably has a long life before it. When Baudelaire chose the city as his theme, he was going against the grain of his age with a vengeance. Most of the outcry raised against his book in his own time and after his death was due to his subject-matter and (the admission must be made) to the way he presented it.

For of course Baudelaire did not entirely escape the influence of his age—*à rebours.* Throughout his essays on the modern one finds a paradoxical tone, a desire to shock and astonish. He likes to stress all the most scabrous modern details (in **Le salon de 1845,** for example, where he chooses "criminels, filles entretenues et les faits-divers du *Moniteur* et de la *Gazettee des tribunaux"* ["criminals, show girls, and news items in the *Moniteur* and the *Gazettee des tribunaux"*] as examples of modern heroism), a habit which is nothing more than a drift towards agreement with the naturists, an admission that the modern is both sickly and depraved. There are times when Baudelaire's modernism, like his mysticism, seems merely perverse, as it is in the poems and novels of such writers as Huysmans, Mendès, Rachilde, and Jean Lorrain. Much of the literature of the century's end is based on the very easy paradox that since civilization is corrupt one can be evilly glamorous in writing about its corruptions. The authors who dealt in this kind of tainted material liked to claim Baudelaire as their predecessor, and they had some justification. Another form of the same thing, considerably dehydrated, however, occurs in our own time in the Waste Land, that languid cocktail party where our dying occidental culture is supposed to be waiting for the regenerating Barbarians. Baudelaire, as Dr. Clark has pointed out, is the first and greatest poet of the Waste Land. He too was frequently exhausted, sterile, and oppressed by his sterility; he too found the modern world played out and decadent. But this is not the dominant theme of his work—however much it may have been relished by the *fin de siècle.* A morbid satisfaction in decadence was not all he found in the modern, much less all he was looking for. In fact, it occurs in only one poem, **"J'aime le souvenir de ces époques nues."** Baudelaire wanted modern heroism, which is something quite different. In **Les fleurs du mal** and the prose works there is a sincere pity for human suffering which makes Baudelaire one of the most touching and human of poets. **"La mort des pauvres," "Le rebelle," "Les petites vieilles,"** and **"La servante au grand cœur"** are among the best verse of this kind that has ever been written. (pp. 61-71)

Baudelaire's religious bias was of great value: his sense of evil kept his pity from degenerating into sentimentality. It is the sentimentality of so much nineteenth-century writing of the same kind, even when produced by the greatest poets, which makes it seem false and dated. Evil lifted Baudelaire's view of man onto an eternal plane. He was never in danger of supposing that human defects were temporary, and that the men of his time could be transformed into virtuous demi-gods by social reform and scientific progress. This is another reason for his twentieth-century popularity. The twentieth century may not write tragedies, but it has certainly recovered the tragic sense; it is insecure.

Insecurity was the one thing the nineteenth century lacked. Its sneaking distrust of its own civilization was confined to a small group of thinkers, and was, at bottom, nothing more than an urge towards the vigorous life. The age was fundamentally self-confident—in all its undertakings, from the conquest of Africa to the design of a whatnot. . . . Other centuries designed their vases to hold flowers and used bronze and silver as part of a logical pattern. Not so the nineteenth. Not one of its enormous urns would hold so much as a rose. As for ornament, it was employed for display, with a magnificent disregard of both utility and aesthetics. Form disappeared, and form, in its profoundest sense, is man's effort to shape and tame the chaotic forces of his nature, or, if they prove too strong for that, to placate them. Man is a monstrous creature, and during most of his history he has been quite conscious of the fact. Hence his hieratic, propitiatory faiths, with their Molochs and their *autos-da-fé,* his tragic poetry and his symphonies, his self-immolation to impossible ideals. But during the prodigious years between 1814 and 1914 his whole nature seemed to undergo a change. He cut himself off from his past, became a creature of free will. Like some fabulous crayfish he built himself a shell so massive and all-embracing that he could not imagine himself without it. His civilization no longer appeared the fragile thing civilization always is—a complex of tastes and habits suspended on a delicate web of neurosis and passion. It became an economic phenomenon, as solid as the new railways and the new iron ships. To see that the old absolutes were still operating behind the massive façade of power and success required an uncommon intuition. Baudelaire had it; and for this reason the catastrophes of our time which have discredited so much of the nineteenth century, have not discredited him. His work does not date in the lurid atmosphere of the present because, while it is much slighter than the verse of Dante or Milton or Aeschylus, it is of the same kind, based on the same problems of good and evil. "La vraie civilization," he wrote in a well-known passage in his diary, "n'est pas dans le gaz, ni dans la vapeur . . . elle est dans la diminution des traces du péché originel" ["True civilization is not in gas or steam . . . it is in the diminution of the traces of original sin"]. From Baudelaire's point of view (and here it is quite orthodox), man is always responsible for his actions. His misery excites pity, not just a subscription for housing and soup-kitchens.

This attitude, of course, is not without its dangers. A hatred of "progress" usually leads to some variety or other of obscurantism; the victim becomes reactionary, over-religious, takes up Fascism or Communism. More than one writer has gone this way in recent years. For some time literature has shown an increasing tendency to welcome this or that ideology, and the more ferocious and absolute the ideology, the better. The results have been uniformly deplorable, as we can see from what Fascist and Communist writing we have had; and it must be admitted that this bent, which is based on a disavowal of logic and which leads to a disavowal of reason, exists in Baudelaire. It probably has something to do with his present-day popularity, at least in certain circles. Several things saved him from its worst consequences. He was, after all, the child of an age which was largely Voltairean. He hated Voltaire, but chiefly because Voltaire's ideas had been vulgarized into platitudes. At bottom both men were in agreement on a number of essential points—such as the superiority of the civilized to the primitive: they both had a great admiration for human achievement. This view comes out again and again in Baudelaire's **"Salons,"** with their splendid passages on painting, sculpture, literature, and science, and it is one of the themes of *Les fleurs du mal.* It is another reason why he chose the city for his subject: if the metropolis displays best the *héroisme de la vie moderne,* it does so because it contains within its limits the most convincing proofs of man's greatness—both material and moral.

All of this is well illustrated by the "Tableaux parisiens." Two examples will suffice. **"Le jeu"** begins with a description of a gambling den of the Second Empire. The worn armchairs, the gas-jets, the green baize, the old strumpets and toothless gamesters who watch the cards—we might be looking at an etching by Daumier. Baudelaire is describing something he has seen himself; and at first glance, it does not seem promising. These lurid décors have been the ruin of more than one poet; their evil glamor is so fascinating that he often forgets to tell us why he is describing them. But there was no danger of this with Baudelaire: his pity for human suffering and his admiration for human greatness saved him from the contrary extremes of superiority and sentimental gush. His initial idea enlarges itself: the gaming table becomes not merely a symbol of man's life (the metaphor is common enough), but of his very nature which, however guilty, depraved, and desperate it may be, and whatever the hopeless odds against it, is somehow admirable in its very excess and its refusal to lapse into inaction and sterility:

> Moi-même, dans un coin de l'antre taciturne,
> Je me vis accoudé, froid, muet, enviant,
>
> Enviant de ces gens la passion tenace,
> De ces vieilles putains la funèbre gaieté. . . .
> Et mon cœur s'effraya d'envier maint pauvre homme
> Courant avec ferveur à l'abime béant,
> Et qui, soûl de son sang, préférerait en somme
> La douleur à la mort et l'enfer au néant.
>
> [I saw myself leaning in a corner of that hushed lair, cold, mute, and envious of the tenacious passion of such men, the funereal gaiety of those old sluts. . . . And my heart feared to envy these wretches careering toward the gaping abyss, and each, drunk on his own blood, preferring grief to death and hell to nothingness.]

It is the old Prometheus legend; and to have evoked Prometheus successfully among the crinolines and the gas-jets of the 1860's was an achievement of no small order.

"Le cygne" grows out of another incident—a swan Baudelaire had noticed wandering on the pavements of the Place du Carrousel, seeking the waters of its native lake. The theme is thus exile, and in developing it, Baudelaire has used several poetic techniques of great interest. The poem, like Racine's tragedies, has a classical lower story. The swan recalls that most famous of exiles, Andromache, and with her the antique legend of Euripides and Virgil. A historical and emotional link is established between past and present which enables the contemporary incident:

> Andromaque, je pense à vous! Ce petit fleuve
> Pauvre et triste miroir où jadis resplendit
> L'immense majesté de vos douleurs de veuve,
> Ce Simois menteur qui par vos pleurs grandit
>
> A fécondé soudain ma mémoire fertile
> Comme je traversais le nouveau Carrousel. . . .
>
> [Andromache, I think of you! This little river,
> Poor unhappy mirror in which once shone
> The immense majesty of your widow's sorrow,
> This deceptive Simois, swollen by your tears,
>
> Has suddenly aroused my fertile memory
> As I wandered the new Carrousel. . . .]

All men are exiles, whether in ancient Epirus or modern Paris; all have lost "ce qui ne se retrouve jamais" ["what is never recaptured"]; and in the concluding lines Baudelaire opens an epic perspective where his personal experience embraces all experience:

> Ainsi dans la forêt où mon esprit s'exile
> Un vieux Souvenir sonne à plein souffle du cor! . . .
> Je pense aux matelots oubliés dans une île,
> Aux captifs, aux vaincus . . . A bien d'autres encor!
>
> [Thus in the forest where my spirit is exiled
> An old Memory blasts like a hunting horn! . . .
> I think about sailors forgotten on an island,
> Of the captured, the vanquished . . . and of many others too!]

Such verse has none of the defects which damaged the productions of Baudelaire's contemporaries—Romantic prose and bombast, Parnassian sclerosis; nor does it suggest the glamorous corruptions of the *fin de siècle* and the morbid self-consciousness of the Symbolists which drove them to tie up their meaning in verbal knots whose unravelling too often leaves one with a sense of dupery. Nor is there any of the squeamish erudition of the Waste Landers, whose poems smell already of the dust of the archives. Baudelaire was attempting something else; and the basis of his poetry, after a hundred years, is surely clear: he wanted to give modern life the vehemence which only poetry can give, and which Antiquity and the Renaissance had both received from their poets. In a sense, every civilization is like his Andromache, "Auprès d'un tombeau vide en extase courbée" ["Bending enraptured beside an empty tomb"]. Each one must have its legend, and at the bottom of every legend there is a tomb—to remind man of the physical and moral realities of his condition, which, however he may complicate and embellish it, still rises, like the great Roman basilica, over a grave. The nineteenth century is the only age without a legend. It was too busy on its frantic career of conquest, in an uproar of railroads, steam, and gas, to bother about such things. One cannot be both an annexer of continents and a fallen Prometheus. The miracle of Baudelaire is that he should have sprung from such a period. In the midst of his century . . . Baudelaire was able to see man, modern man, unobscured by the prodigious apparatus of his success.

The success has long since disappeared. The jungle has reabsorbed the railways, and the deserts are drifting quietly across the great highways; the crinolines and the diamond collars, the gasoliers and the pintrays and the flowered bedroom porcelain, have vanished with the snows of yesteryear. . . . Nobody unscrews the silver-stoppered scent-bottles, ladies no longer have "days," and when the police want a confession they have it whipped out of the culprit—all signs, symptoms, and results of the prodigious changes of the last forty years. Baudelaire's popularity is in part due to these changes. Failure produces a morbid state of soul; like our own age he had failed—failed to pay his debts, failed in his contests with his mother and General Aupick, failed to achieve any sort of tranquillity with Jeanne Duval, though he transferred her from lodging to lodging, clinic to clinic, and ended by becoming so exasperated that he beat her with a candlestick. He was frustrated and depressed; he sat for long hours nourishing his spleen in cafés or watching the rain fall outside his windows; he tried to make capital of his frustration, and, indeed, frequently succeeded, thanks to his genius. All of this flatters our own tastes, corresponds to our own sense of disaster. So much so that certain clairvoyant spirits, examining Baudelaire's present vogue, have wondered how long it can continue, and have warned us that his verse, with its themes of sterility, decay, sin, and death is a little too modern to be permanent. The criticism is very just—up to a point. Baudelaire, like most nineteenth-century poets, is extremely uneven; a good deal of his poetry is bad, and will seem worse as time passes. But a large proportion of it is quite otherwise. He handled some of literature's greatest themes, and, by giving them contemporary expression, brought them home to us as no poet of the last hundred years has done. If the day ever comes when nobody reads that side of his work—well, the possibility need not worry us much. For in that day nobody will be reading poetry of any kind, anywhere. (pp. 71-6)

A. E. Carter, "Baudelaire," in University of Toronto Quarterly, Vol. XXIX, No. 1, October, 1959, pp. 59-76.

Henri Peyre　(essay date 1960)

[*Peyre is a French-born critic who has lived and taught in the United States for most of his career. One of the foremost American critics of French literature, he has written extensively on modern French literature in works that blend superb scholarship with a clear style accessible to the nonspecialist reader, most notably in* French Novelists of Today *(rev. ed. 1967). Peyre is a staunch defender of traditional forms of literature that examine the meaning of life in modern society and the role of individual destiny in an indifferent universe; he dislikes experimentalism for its own sake, noting that "many experimenters are the martyrs of a lost cause." Peyre particularly disagrees with critical trends that attempt to subsume literary analysis under the doctrines of restrictive theories, such as those of structuralism. Regarding his critical stance, Peyre has written that "there is no single approach that is infallible or systematically to be preferred when dealing with literature. Pluralism seems to me to be a far more fruitful attitude. . . . Any dogmatism, while it may provide the lover of systems with a cheaply acquired consistency and unity of point of view, soon proves detrimental to the most varied of human pursuits—the pursuit of beauty, truth, and 'greatness' in works of art. In the following essays, Peyre provides literal translations and line-by-line analyses of two of Baudelaire's most important poems, "Correspondences" and "Spleen."*]*

"Correspondances"

La nature est un temple où de vivants piliers
Laissent parfois sortir de confuses paroles;
L'homme y passe à travers des forêts de symboles
Qui l'observent avec des regards familiers.

Comme de longs échos qui de loin se confondent
Dans une ténébreuse et profonde unité,
Vaste comme la nuit et comme la clarté,
Les parfums, les couleurs et les sons se répondent.

Il est des parfums frais comme des chairs d'enfants,
Doux comme les hautbois, verts comme les prairies,
—Et d'autres, corrompus, riches et triomphants,

Ayant l'expansion des choses infinies,
Comme l'ambre, le musc, le benjoin et l'encens,
Qui chantent les transports de l'esprit et des sens.

No other poem by Baudelaire has had the impact of **"Correspondances"** upon modern literature. Yet at first it aroused little attention. There is no "Baudelairianism" here, no obsession with death or with ugliness, and the form has majestic gravity. The poet, after being portrayed in the first three *Fleurs du mal* as an accursed creature, an albatross ludicrous when forced to tread on the ground, is in this fourth poem hailed as the decipherer of correspondences: it is he who translates the secrets of the world and fuses sensations into one another. He creates the world anew.

The title recalls the Swedish mystic, Swedenborg, to whom Baudelaire had been drawn (probably through Balzac) as early as 1845. Mysterious voices respond to each other in nature; they announce a correspondence between the visible and the invisible, between matter and spirit. The title, the plural form of an abstract word (*Correspondances*) suggests the multiplicity of those correspondences, philosophical or sensuous, that conceal an underlying unity. The tone is that of a geometric theorem, formulated with prophetic assurance.

The two quatrains have the solemnity of a lofty cathedral; their sounds unroll slowly, with deep pauses at the caesura of line 1 and after the third syllable of line 4. The second quatrain introduces the notion of the senses, hence of the arts, as parallel translations of the deeper identity of essential nature.

(1) *Nature is a temple where living columns* (2) *Sometimes murmur indistinct words (allow confused words to escape);* (3) *There man passes through forests of symbols* (4) *That watch him with familiar glances.* (5) *Like prolonged echoes that mingle in the distance,* (6) *In a shadowy and profound unity,* (7) *Vast as night and as the light of day,* (8) *Perfumes, colors, and sounds respond to (answer to) one another.*

The more solemn assertion rises from the first quatrain. Nature is a vast ancient temple, its pillars covered with hieroglyphics. They are familiar and benevolent signs, but they are unnoticed by most passers-by and scrutinized only by the poet, whom Baudelaire characterized elsewhere as "a decipherer of analogies." The key phrase set off at the rime in line 3 (*forêts de symboles:* "forests of symbols") was to enjoy an astonishing fortune, at first to deride and later to laud the Symbolist poets. The Greek verb from which "symbol" stems means to throw, or fuse, together the sign and the object denoted by the sign. (Parable [that which has another side meaning], hyperbole [an exaggeration, thrown above], problem [thrown in front of us to be solved] are coined from the same word.) The word "symbol" has a long history; many thinkers, from Plato and St. Paul down to the moderns, have called the visible world the other face of the invisible one. This sonnet claimed for the poet the privilege of translating into evocative concrete terms the ultimate secret of things: he ceased to be a narrator or a describer; he tore off the veil that covers the true nature of objects thus to reveal the identity behind the illusory appearances, the One behind the Many, as Plato and Shelley had put it.

There is no virtuoso musical effect in the quatrains, no attempt at surprising the reader, no metaphor that fuses discordant elements. The lines have a classical beauty, their sweep is majestically and deliberately slow. An ample comparison in line 5 is prolonged further through four nasal sounds; two long abstract adjectives in line 6 delay the essential noun, *unité* ("unity"); again, a double comparison exalts, in line 7, the correspondences of the senses by linking them to the alternation of darkness and light; three nasal sounds in *um* and *on* (line 8) lengthen the distant echoes conjured up in line 5.

The grave density of the quatrains gives way to a lighter tone in the tercets. Baudelaire no longer stresses the vertical correspondences. Plunging deep into the unknown, even into the morbid, and pointing toward the realm of the spirit, he illustrates the horizontal correspondences, or synesthesia. Our senses—and, by extension, the several arts—perceive the central mystery of nature differently and render it into parallel languages, which are convertible into one another. (9) *There are perfumes, fresh as the flesh of children,* (10) *Sweet as oboe music, green as meadows,* (11) *—Others [are] corrupt, rich, and triumphant,* (12) *Having the expansion of things infinite,* (13) *Like amber, musk, benzoin, and frankincense,* (14) *Which sing the raptures of spirit and of sense.*

The last lines stress the olfactory sensations, the richest of all for so sensuous a poet as Baudelaire, the richer for some trace of corruption in them, and, as Proust was later to insist, the ones most likely to carry a whole train of associations in their wake. The end of the sonnet links—as in Baudelaire's renowned poem **"Une charogne"** (**"A Carrion"**)—the ecstasy of the senses and that of the spirit, both closely corresponding, the former being but the reflection of the latter. In one of Baudelaire's essays, the Poet proudly declares: "I wish to illuminate things with my spirit and to project that reflection onto other spirits." (pp. 8-9)

. . . . .

"Spleen"

Quand le ciel bas et lourd pèse comme un couvercle
Sur l'esprit gémissant en proie aux longs ennuis,
Et que de l'horizon embrassant tout le cercle
Il nous verse un jour noir plus triste que les nuits;

Quand la terre est changée en un cachot humide,
Où l'Espérance, comme une chauve-souris,
S'en va battant les murs de son aile timide
Et se cognant la tête à des plafonds pourris;

Quand la pluie étalant ses immenses traînées
D'une vaste prison imite les barreaux,

Et qu'un peuple muet d'infâmes araignées
Vient tendre ses filets au fond de nos cerveaux,

Des cloches tout à coup sautent avec furie
Et lancent vers le ciel un affreux hurlement,
Ainsi que des esprits errants et sans patrie
Qui se mettent à geindre opiniâtrement.

—Et de longs corbillards, sans tambours ni musique,
Défilent lentement dans mon âme; l'Espoir,
Vaincu, pleure, et l'Angoisse atroce, despotique,
Sur mon crâne incliné plante son drapeau noir.

Charles Baudelaire, in whom his contemporaries saw a sensuous and morbid poet, appears to our century as a classic, a profound psychologist, a master of evocative imagery and of rich music. As a poet and also as an esthetician, he stands at all the crossroads of modern poetic achievement.

The longest section of **Les fleurs du mal,** entitled "Spleen et Idéal", contrasts the poet's aspiration after the beauty through which he hopes to transfigure life's sorrows with his temptation to despair. **"Spleen"** denotes a physical and nervous affliction far more intense and corrosive than the declamatory *mal du siècle* ("sickness of the age") of Baudelaire's Romantic predecessors. It is described graphically in this stark poem as a weight pressing down upon the poet's skull; elsewhere Baudelaire called it his hysteria and we know that he had tried to soothe it by the use of laudanum and other "artificial paradises." Into this intense pain there also entered a sense of the tragedy of life, of cosmic anguish with all that is wrong in the world, an insidious urge toward self-disintegration. The poet confessed repeatedly to being torn between two opposite "postulations," to being driven toward the divine and also the diabolical. Despair has seldom if ever been portrayed more memorably than in these twenty lines:

(1) *When the low and heavy sky weighs like a lid* (2) *On the groaning spirit, a prey to long tedium,* (3) *When, embracing all the horizon,* (4) *It pours upon us black day, far gloomier than nights;* (5) *When earth is changed into a humid dungeon,* (6) *In which Hope, like a bat,* (7) *Flits to and fro, beating the walls with its timid wing* (8) *And knocking its head against the rotted beams;* (9) *When the rain deploying its immense shafts* (10) *Mimics [imitates, has the look of] the bars of a vast prison,* (11) *While a silent race of loathsome (heinous) spiders* (12) *Comes and stretches their meshes into the depths of our brains,* (13) *Bells suddenly leap in frenzy* (14) *And hurl a ghastly howl toward the sky,* (15) *As would [a host of] wandering homeless spirits* (16) *Who stubbornly start their wailing.* (17) *—And long hearses, without drums or music,* (18) *Slowly file through my soul; Hope,* (19) *Vanquished, weeps, and fierce, despotic Anguish* (20) *Plants his black banner upon my drooping skull.*

The forcefulness of **"Spleen"** is due in large part to its inexorable, slow-moving tension and its masterful rhythm and sound. The central image is that of the poet's skull oppressed by the pain of his spleen, while correspondingly the lid of the low, heavy sky presses down upon the earth. The word "lid" (*couvercle*) occurs at the rime in line 1, the word "skull" (*crâne*) appears only in line 20.

One feels a certain majesty in the structural control. The sky, then the earth, then the rain linking the two fill, respectively, the first, second, and third stanzas, each beginning with *quand* and making use of repeated, haunting nasal sounds: *gémissant, long, embrassant,* etc. Present participles, usually avoided in French poetry as being heavy, crowd the lines, as do repetitions of harsh sounds such as *quand, que, qu'un* and alliterations of *s* (2, 3) and of *f* (11, 12, 14). Occasionally, the pause fails to coincide with the sixth syllable, as in line 6, where the limping renders the blind fluttering of the black bat Hope in the cell.

The punctuation of **"Spleen"** is noteworthy. Except for line 6, all the commas in the first four stanzas come at the end of the lines and these four stanzas make up one endless sentence. In the fifth stanza, on the contrary, the pauses marked by commas are multiplied. The alternate rimes in the *abab* pattern make for an effect of cumulative and imprisoning tension that enmeshes the splenetic sufferer.

A suggestion of madness runs through the poem: the *ennui* (from Latin *odium,* hàtred and disgust of life) is close to the morbid dread of nothingness, alluded to elsewhere in *Les fleurs du mal.* The spider crawling in the brain of the prisoner is a symbol of mad desperation; the bells themselves seem to howl, like mad dogs, to a listless heaven. The poet's skull has sheltered lugubrious visions of funerals beneath its *couvercle,* which is also the scene of a dual between Hope and Anguish. Anguish has triumphed and in submission the victim bends his head on which the flag of bitter victory will be nailed. (pp. 18-19)

> Henri Peyre, *"Correspondances" and "Spleen," in* The Poem Itself, *edited by Stanley Burnshaw, Holt, Rinehart and Winston, 1960, pp. 8-9, 18-19.*

Joseph Chiari (essay date 1960)

[*Chiari is a French poet, playwright, and critic. In the following excerpt, he provides a Christian reading of* The Flowers of Evil.]

The *taedium vitae,* the horror of the abyss are the dominant elements of Baudelaire's sensibility, which correspond with the emerging sensibility of the time. A few years later, the rest of Europe, with Swinburne, the Pre-Raphaelites, Wilde, d'Annunzio, Stefan George and Rilke, was to echo this sensibility and confirm Baudelaire in the position which Byron occupied a few years before him, as the perfect representative of the European sensibility of his time.

The so-called satanism of Baudelaire is a very complex problem. For him, as for Pascal, 'l'homme est un ange déchu qui se souvient des cieux' ['man is a fallen angel who remembers heaven']. Creation is God's word or speech, and man, informed with essence, can, when in a state of grace, read the great Book of God and live through instants when Time fades into Eternity. Torn between the horror and the ecstasy of life, Baudelaire sought in vain to forget through 'les paradis artificiels' of a woman's love, of drunkenness or drugs, the gaping abyss at the foot of which lurk death and eternal hell. While the ecstasy lasted, the stained past—his own and that of man stained by original sin, recedes and dissolves into the magic of dreams and a partial state of innocence. Each return to time and to reality, however, becomes more and more terrifying for it brings back with it the awareness that the preceding temporary stupor has only been attained through

corrupt matter and by means which carried the stigma of a guilt that nothing human could wash away. The agony of hell, for Baudelaire, Villon or for any Christian alienated from God through weak will, lack of Divine Grace or attempted distortions of God's will, lay in the awareness of separation in the knowledge that nothing could stifle the voice which reminded him of what he had lost, or abolish the vision which, though it receded with the deepening fall into the abyss, remained as vivid as ever and was the very source of his terror. Satan himself, the most beautiful of the angels, the nearest to God with the exception of Christ, knows what he has lost, and seeks in vain to abolish, through denial or destruction, the source of his duality and separation in order to return to oneness and bliss. (pp. 165-66)

[Villon] was undeniably much more profound, and a greater poet than Baudelaire. Within the narrow scope of his work, his vision was Dantesque; he had the genius to see things in their true nakedness, and he recorded them in images which conveyed emotions in their absolute purity and reality without the slightest trace of rhetoric, personal interference or commentary.

Baudelaire's realism is never of that purity, and one has only to read **"La ballade des pendus"** and **"La charogne"** or **"Le voyage à Cythère"** to realize at once the difference. The maladive scent, the sadistic strains which went to Swinburne's head, are hardly ever absent from *Les fleurs du mal,* and neither is the poet's presence which relates or comments. The simile 'comme une femme lubrique' ['like a lubricious woman'] of **"Une charogne"** introduces at once all sorts of elements extraneous to the exact description and which can only refer back to the author's obsessions; then, after 'la carcasse superbe', comes the rhapsodizing and the violent contrasts *à la Delacroix,* to end with the *recherché* and artifice of the final commentary which shows that the author enjoyed this composition rather more for its effect than because it was deeply felt. Similar flaws mar the end of **"Le voyage à Cythère."**

The dandyism and self-consciousness about the macabre and the gruesome in order to shake the bourgeois are part of the artistic attitude of his age. Flaubert and Hugo revelled in this kind of attitude, and ruin and decay were part of the properties of nineteenth-century art, or, to be precise, of Romanticism. But the slight affectation of certain attitudes, the use of certain properties and conventions common to an age do not affect the artist's sincerity and the genuineness of his experiences. In France, the ballad was certainly hackneyed and lifeless when Villon came to use it, but his genius transformed it and left its unforgettable imprint on it.

The fact that the Faustian hero was as much in rebellion against conventions and society as Milton's Satan was in rebellion against the heavenly hierarchy must not be confused with the obsession with Satan and evil of the true Christian, who is aware of his own weight of matter and of his remoteness from salvation without Divine Grace.

Baudelaire did not transform suffering 'en un instrument diabolique' ['into a diabolic instrument'] as some critics have suggested; he knew all too well why his behaviour 'change l'or en fer et le paradis en enfer' ['exchanges gold for iron and paradise for hell'] for he knew . . . that creation and matter were what men made of them. Therefore the poem **"Horreur sympathique"** is not 'une correspondance infernale', for that would mean granting evil a positiveness that it does not have, but simply a straight piece of Berkeleyan or Humean thinking: things are what the subject perceives that they are—and the subject in this case is 'un libertin', that is to say a wilfully irreverent atheist who, unable to resist his sensuousness, restlessness and urge to grasp the immediacy of spirit, has chosen himself against the rest of the world and, wallowing in his fall, despair and pride, walks on the edge of the abyss, hurling defiance at the One whose attention he desperately wishes to attract. Baudelaire was that libertine, he was both Don Juan and Faust; he had the daemonic urge to explore the flesh and to know, irrespective of the silt or stench which such explorations may raise, and he retained throughout 'la conscience dans le mal'—the harrowing awareness that he was doing something evil and forbidden, something which must not be confused with 'l'inévitabilité du mal' or with the doom which befalls anything or anybody connected with the typically romantic or Byronic hero.

The sin of sensuousness can only exist within the context of Christianity, which rests above all on the primacy of the spirit. Buddhism posits spirituality as a fundamental principle, but in its context life and matter are merely transient stages towards final refinement and pure spirituality. In Christianity, time and existence are part of Eternity; they

Self-portrait of Baudelaire.

share in the immanence and, through Divine Grace, in the transcendence of God; therefore their existential manifestations determine their essential status, and the fear of being damned or alienated from God for Eternity is no mean fear for anyone who holds such beliefs. 'The opposite of sin,' Kierkegaard said, 'is not virtue but faith', for within Christianity there cannot be any virtue without faith. Baudelaire's faith, like that of countless Christians, was not strong enough to protect him from sin, yet with the consciousness of his fallen state and the agony of his separation from Eden, he had greater possibilities of being touched by Divine Grace and saved than the self-satisfied negatively virtuous men who have never known the lure of sin.

Satan is only conceivable as the opposite of God whose positive reality he postulates, just as hell postulates Eden as a memory of harmony and order glimpsed from chaos, and with the awareness that such a memory—the fading light of a fast-receding star—can never be recaptured. In the Christian world every action is irrevocable, and evil cannot be washed away or forgotten, except through Divine mediation operating first and foremost through Christ and also through actual grace. Hegelians, whatever their various guises, can deal with individual failures through the dictates of the State or through immanent reason which can absolve individual responsibility. Baudelaire failed to understand Christ's historical mission on earth, and as an anarchist, a rebel against society, he could not trust the State or society with his redemption, nor could he abolish his sense of selfhood; therefore he was alone, 'la plaie et le couteau' ['the wound and the knife'], like Satan and with Satan. The only means he had of creating a new world was through replacing the lost Eden by artistic creation, and that was obviously a satanic gesture, a replacement of the true reality by a graven image. Art has always been daemonic; that is why it was forbidden by God's second commandment. The world of art is not Eden, for it is transient and it is only a vision or image of the supernal world, yet it transcends hell and it is the only consolation that wounded, fallen man, deprived of Divine Grace, can offer himself, and that is why Baudelaire addressed Satan as the protector of the artists and of all those who have lost Eden. . . . (pp. 166-69)

Baudelaire's self-loathing and disgust at his abject submission to flesh and to his mistress, together with his outbursts of rebellion and attempts to hide his fears through boasts or glorifications of Satan, have nothing to do with Swinburne's 'acid relish of suffering felt or inflicted'; they are part of the road which led Job to the understanding of his sores and to his humble acceptance of God's hidden ways, an attitude which is summed up in the words:

> O Seigneur, donnez-moi la force et le courage
> De contempler mon cœur et mon corps sans dégoût.

> [Lord, give me the strength and the courage to contemplate my heart and my body without disgust.]

(p. 170)

Joseph Chiari, "Realism and 'Satanism' in Baudelaire," in his Realism and Imagination, *Barrie and Rockliff, 1960, pp. 164-170.*

Hugo Friedrich   (essay date 1967)

[*Friedrich is a German educator and author of several critical studies of modern European poetry. In the following excerpt, he details Baudelaire's contribution to the development of modern poetry and poetic theory.*]

With Baudelaire, French poetry became a matter of concern for all Europe, as can be seen by the effect it had in Germany, England, Italy, and Spain. In France, as well, it soon became obvious that the influence exerted by Baudelaire, reaching Rimbaud, Verlaine, and Mallarmé, was different from, and more exciting than, anything from the romantics. Mallarmé admitted that he had begun where Baudelaire had had to leave off. Valéry, nearing the end of his life, traced a direct line of communication from Baudelaire to himself. T. S. Eliot called Baudelaire's work "the greatest example of modern poetry in any language." In 1945, Jean Cocteau wrote: "From behind his grimaces, his gaze slowly wanders over to us, like light from the stars."

Many such statements speak of the poet of "modernity." This is a perfectly justifiable designation, since Baudelaire was one of the first to use this word. Employing it in 1859, he apologized for the neologism, explaining that he needed it to express the modern artist's special ability to look at the desert of a metropolis and not merely see the decline of mankind but also sense a mysterious beauty hitherto undiscovered. This was Baudelaire's own problem: how is poetry possible in our commercialized and technologized civilization? His verse points out the way, and his prose makes an exhaustive study of it. The road leads as far as possible from the banality of real life to a zone of mystery, but in such a way that the subject matter found in civilized reality is brought into this zone and thus becomes poetically viable. This new outlook touched off modern poetry, creating its corrosive but magical substance.

Basic characteristics of Baudelaire are his intellectual discipline and the lucidity of his artistic consciousness. He united poetic genius and critical intelligence. His insights into verse-making are, as with Novalis, even superior to his own poetry. Indeed, Baudelaire's critical insights had a stronger effect on later times than did his verse. His ideas are set down in his essay collections *Curiosités esthétiques* (1865) and *L'art romantique* (1868), which contain interpretations and programs developed from an observation of contemporary painting and music as well as literature. As in Diderot, but on a higher level and with new goals, his ideas on poetry draw upon the other arts. The essays constantly expand into analyses of contemporary sensibilities, of modernity in general, because Baudelaire conceived of poetry and art as converting the fate of an era into form. He thus anticipated Mallarmé's contribution: ontological poetry and an ontological theory of poetry.

Scholars have made great headway in revealing Baudelaire's connections with the romantics. But here we want to discuss his uniqueness and what it was that enabled him to transmute the romantic legacy into verse and thought, which in turn evoked later poetry.

Les fleurs du mal (1857) is neither confessional poetry nor a diary of private states and circumstances, no matter how much it may contain of the suffering of a sick, lonely, unhappy man. Unlike Victor Hugo, Baudelaire never dated any of his poems. None of them can be thematically elucidated by biographical data. Baudelaire sparked off the depersonalization of modern poetry, at least in the sense that the lyrical word no longer derives from a fusion of the poetic persona and the empirical person, which fusion had been a goal of the romantics, as opposed to many of the poets of earlier centuries. We cannot overestimate the importance of Baudelaire's comments on this subject. Nor are they weakened by their indebtedness to similar statements by Edgar Allan Poe. On the contrary, this fact merely puts them in the proper context.

Outside of France, it was Poe who most decisively separated poetry and the heart. He wanted the subject of poetry to be an enthusiastic excitement that had no connection with personal passion or the "intoxication of the heart." What he meant was a comprehensive mood which, for want of a better name, he called "soul," but always added, "not heart." Baudelaire repeats such statements faithfully, varying them in his own words. "The sensitivity of the heart"—as opposed to "the sensitivity of the imagination"—"is not beneficial to the poetic process." Here we must take into account that Baudelaire considers the imagination an intellectually guided operation (as remains to be shown). This conception sheds the necessary light on the above-quoted words, which demand a rejection of any personal sentimentality in favor of a lucid imagination far more capable of solving difficult problems. Baudelaire provides the poet with a motto: "My task is extrahuman." In a letter, he talks about the "deliberate impersonality of my poetry," by which he means that his poetry can express any human sensibility, preferably the most extreme. Tears? By all means, but only those which "do not come from the heart." Baudelaire justifies poetry for being able to neutralize the personal heart. He gropes along; his ideas are often clouded by older ones. And yet we can recognize the historical necessity of the future development, from the neutralization of the person to the dehumanization of the lyrical persona (the "I"). Baudelaire introduced the depersonalization which T. S. Eliot and other poets later viewed as a requirement for the precision and validity of versecraft.

In almost all the poems in *Les fleurs du mal,* it is the "I," the poetic voice, that is speaking. Baudelaire is totally wrapped up in himself. But, egocentric as he may be, the poet pays scant heed to his empirical ego when he writes his verses. He writes out of himself only insofar as he considers himself a sufferer of modernity, which is cast over him like a spell. He explained often enough that his own suffering was not peculiar. Characteristically, any vestiges of his personal life to appear in his poems are expressed hazily. He would never have written anything like Victor Hugo's poem on the death of a child. With a dogged, methodical thoroughness, he subjectively goes through all the phases growing out of modernism: anxiety, inescapableness, the collapse of ardently desired, but Void-bound, ideality. Baudelaire talks of his obsessive wish to make that destiny his own. *Obsession* and *destiny* are two of his key words. Others are *concentration* and *centralization of the ego.* He adopts Emerson's dictum: "He who is immovably centered is a hero." Its antithetical concepts are "dissolution" and "prostitution." The latter term, derived from the French illuminati of the eighteenth century, means abandonment, an illegitimate remission from one's intellectual fate, flight to others, betrayal through dissipation. These are the symptoms of modern civilization, as

Baudelaire points out, dangers even he must beware of—he, "the master by virtue of the fate of his faculties," by virtue of the concentration on a self that has canceled out the aleatoriness of the individual person.

Les fleurs du mal, permeated with a network of themes, is a concentrated organism. One might even speak of a system, especially since Baudelaire's essays, journals, and even some of his letters provide for this carefully thought-out network. There are not many themes. And they crop up astonishingly early—in the 1840s. From the publication of *Les fleurs du mal* up to his death, Baudelaire scarcely went beyond them. He preferred revising an early draft to writing a new poem. Although some critics have viewed him as unproductive, his was the productivity of intensity, which, having attained a breach, increases in depth and strength. His was a productivity activating artistic perfectionism, because the suprapersonal validity of the contents is assured only in the maturity of the form. Baudelaire's themes, few in number, are to be seen as a set of conveyers, variations, metamorphoses, of a basic tension which we can characterize as a struggle between satanism and ideality. The tension is never resolved. But, as a whole, it has the same order and logic as every individual poem.

Two possibilities of future poetry are united here. In Rimbaud, the unresolved tension will increase into an absolute dissonance, destroying all order and coherence. Mallarmé, too, will intensify the conflict, but will shift it to other themes, creating a Baudelaire-like order only to mask it in a new obscure language.

With the concentration of themes in his verse, Baudelaire was abiding by the decree of not surrendering to "intoxication of the heart." This state may occur in poetry but is not poetry per se; it is only material. The act leading to pure poetry is labor, systematic construction of an architecture, manipulation of the impulses of language. Baudelaire often pointed out that *Les fleurs du mal* was not meant to be an album, but a whole, with a beginning, an articulate development, and an end. His indication is valid. The poems embrace despair, paralysis, feverish soaring into the unreal, a death wish, a morbid playing with sensation. But all these negative themes can be encompassed by a methodical composition. Next to Petrarch's *Canzoniere,* Goethe's *Westöstlicher Divan,* and Guillén's *Cántico, Les fleurs du mal* exhibits the most rigorous architecture of any book of European poetry. Everything Baudelaire added to the initial publication was planned in such a way (according to his letters) as to fit into the framework he had laid out in 1845 and completed in the first edition. Here, even the old custom of numerical composition played a part. The original edition contained one hundred poems divided into five groups—a further sign of the poet's formal intention, definitely corresponding to a general romantic striving for form. Moreover, the obvious vestiges of Christian ideas suggest that the conspicuously precise formal structure is an echo of high medieval symbolism, which reflected cosmic order in compositional forms.

In subsequent editions, Baudelaire gave up the numerical system but strengthened the internal order. This can easily be discerned. After the introductory poem, which anticipates the entirety, the first group (**"Spleen et idéal"**) offers a contrast between elevation and downfall. The next group ("Tableaux parisiens") shows an abortive escape into the external world of a metropolis; the third set ("Le vin"), the attempt to flee into an artificial paradise. This flight, too, fails to bring peace. Hence, there is a surrender to the fascination of the destructive: this makes up the contents of the fourth group, which bears the same name as the whole book ("Fleurs du mal"). The result is the scornful rebellion against God in the fifth group ("Revolte"). The final endeavor, in the sixth and last group ("La mort"), is the search for peace in death, in the absolute unknown. The architectural plan is also evident within the individual groups as a kind of dialectical reasoning in the poems. A demonstration is unnecessary, since the essential form can be seen in the book as a whole. It is an agitated order whose lines change in themselves, an order that forms an over-all downward curve. The lowest point is the end, the "abyss," because only the abyss offers a hope of seeing the "new." What "new"? The hope in the abyss has no word for it.

Baudelaire's architectural construction of *Les fleurs du mal* proves his renunciation of romanticism, whose books of poems are mere collections, their haphazard arrangement a formal echo of the chance inspiration. His methodical architecture also bears witness to the role of formal energy in his verse. These forces mean more than simple decoration or proper form. They are means of salvation, sought after to the utmost in an extremely unsettling intellectual situation. Poets have always known that grief dissolves in song, that suffering is purged and purified by being transmuted into sublimely formed words. But it was only in the nineteenth century, when purposeful suffering turned into purposeless suffering, desolation, and ultimately nihilism, that forms became so crucial to salvation, although their rigidity and calmness were a dissonant contrast to restless contents. Once again we encounter a basic dissonance of modern poetry. Just as the poem has separated from the heart, so the form has separated from the content. Language is rescued by the salvation of form, while the content is left unresolved.

Baudelaire often spoke of salvation through form. An example is the following, whose meaning is more provocative than the conventional wording would make it seem: "It is a wonderful privilege of art that if something terrible is expressed artistically it becomes beautiful, and that pain, rhythmically arranged and articulate, fills the mind with a calm joy." This sentence veils something that has already occurred in Baudelaire's work: the ascendancy of the desire for form over the desire for mere expression. Yet these words reveal the extent to which he longed for security through form—the "life preserver of form," as Guillén put it. Elsewhere Baudelaire writes: "Obviously, metrical laws are not arbitrarily invented tyrannies. They are rules demanded by the organism of the mind itself. They have never prevented originality from manifesting itself. The very opposite is infinitely closer to the truth: they have always helped originality to mature." Stravinsky will refer to this passage in his *Poetics of Music.* The idea will be reiterated by Mallarmé and Valéry—not only because it confirms the old romantic sense of form but also because it supports a practice favored by many of the moderns: i.e., handling the conventions of rhyme, metrics, and stanza like instruments that cut into the language and provoke reactions which would never have emanated from the thematic plan of the poem.

Baudelaire extols Daumier's ability to depict with precision and clarity the base, the trivial, the degenerate. He could have similarly praised his own poems. They unite deadliness and precision and are thus a prelude to future verse. Novalis and Poe introduced the concept of calculation into poetics, and Baudelaire followed suit. "Beauty is the product of reason and reckoning," he writes in a highly characteristic discussion of the superiority of the artificial (that is, the artistic) over mere nature. He even considers inspiration to be mere nature, impure subjectivity. As the poet's only impulse, it leads to lack of precision, as does intoxication of the heart. But it is welcome as a reward for the artistic labor which precedes it and which has the status of an exercise; in this case inspiration assumes grace, akin to a dancer who "has broken his bones a thousand times in private before exhibiting himself to an audience." The high quota of intellectual and voluntative factors that Baudelaire assigns to the poetic act is not to be overlooked. Like Novalis, he draws the concept of mathematics into such reflections. Thus, in characterizing the accuracy of style, Baudelaire compares it to the "wonders of mathematics." The metaphor is given the value of "mathematical precision." All these ideas go back to Poe, who spoke of the relationship between poetic tasks and "the strict logic of a mathematical problem." The effects are apparent in Mallarmé as well as in the poetics of our time.

Even in Baudelaire's themes we can discern his withdrawal from romanticism. Everything he inherited from that period—and the legacy is great—he turned into such a difficult experience that, by comparison, the romantics look like dilettantes. They had taken the eschatological interpretation of history—which, Greco-Roman and Christian in origin, had been gaining ground since the late Enlightenment—and had developed it further, defining their own era as a terminal one. Yet this was primarily a mood, rendered harmless by the lovely hues that they managed to capture from the cultural sunset. Baudelaire, too, placed himself and his time in this terminal era; but he did so with different images and emotions. The eschatological consciousness permeating Europe since the eighteenth century and reaching into our own time went through a phase of terrified and terrifying sagacity with Baudelaire. In 1862 he wrote the poem **"Le coucher du soleil romantique" ("Romantic Sunset"),** which contains a series of lessening degrees of light and joy, descending to cold night and a horror of swamps and repulsive beasts. The symbolism leaves no doubt as to its meaning. It alludes to ultimate darkening, to a loss of the soul's self-intimacy, which can survive even in decline. Baudelaire knew that a poetry suitable to his time could be achieved only by seizing the nocturnal and the abnormal: they constitute the only place where the self-estranged soul can produce poetry and escape the triviality of "progress," the disguise of the terminal era. Accordingly, he called his *Fleurs du mal* a "dissonant product of the muses of the terminal era."

Baudelaire's exhaustive pondering of the concept of modernity was very different from that of the romantics. It is a highly complex notion. Negatively, it signifies the world of big cities, devoid of vegetation, with their ugliness, their asphalt, their artificial lighting, their stone canyons, their sins, their lonely crowds. Furthermore, it refers to the technological era of steampower, electricity, and progress. Baudelaire defined progress as "the progressive

decay of the soul and the progressive domination of matter," and then again as "atrophy of the mind." We hear of his "utter disgust" at advertising posters, newspapers, and the "rising tide of all-leveling democracy." The same was said by Stendhal and Tocqueville and, a bit later, by Flaubert. However, Baudelaire's concept of modernity goes further. It is dissonant and turns the negative into something fascinating. Poverty, decay, evil, the nocturnal, and the artificial exert an attraction that has to be perceived poetically. They contain secrets that guide poetry on to new paths. In the refuse of urban centers, Baudelaire smells a mystery, which his poetry depicts as a phosphorescent shimmer. In addition, he approves of anything that banishes nature in order to establish the absolute realm of the artificial. Since the cubic stone masses of cities are unnatural, and since, although constituting the place of evil, they belong to the freedom of the mind, they are inorganic landscapes of the pure intellect. Only vestiges of this rationale will appear among later poets. But even twentieth-century poetry will bathe the metropolis in the mysterious phosphorescence that Baudelaire discovered.

In his lyrics, the dissonant images of the big city are extremely intense. They join gaslight and evening sky, the fragrance of flowers and the reek of tar; they are filled with desire and lament, and they contrast with the sweeping oscillation of the verses. Extracted from banality, like drugs from toxic plants, the images are poetically transmuted into antidotes for "the vice of banality." The repulsive is joined to the nobility of sound, acquiring the "galvanic shudder" (*frisson galvanique*) that Baudelaire praises in Poe. Dusty windows with traces of rain; gray, washed-out façades; the venomous green of metals; dawn as a dirty splotch; the animal sleep of prostitutes; the roar of busses; faces without lips; old hags; brass bands; eyeballs soaked in gall; stale perfumes: these are some of the contents of the "galvanized" modernity in Baudelaire's poetry. And they survive in Eliot.

Baudelaire frequently speaks of beauty; yet, in his lyrics, beauty is confined to the metrics and vibration of language. The subject matter no longer fits in with older ideas of beauty. He uses complements that are paradoxical and reinterprets the "splice of amazement" in order to lend beauty an aggressive attraction. To shield itself against the banal and to provoke banal taste, beauty must be bizarre. "Pure and bizarre" is one of his definitions of the beautiful. But he frankly desires ugliness as the equivalent of the secret that must be fathomed anew, as the possible beginning for an ascent to ideality. "From ugliness, the poet evokes new enchantment." The deformed creates surprise, which in turn causes the "unexpected assault." More violently than ever before, abnormality becomes a goal of modern verse-making, as does one of the reasons for abnormality—irritation at the banal and conventional, which, in Baudelaire's eyes, exist even in the beauty of older style. The new "beauty," which can coincide with ugliness, acquires its restlessness by both assimilating the banal and being deformed into something bizarre, and through the "union of the terrifying with the foolish."

These are intensifications of ideas that were current since Friedrich Schlegel's "transcendental buffoonery" and Victor Hugo's theory of the grotesque. Baudelaire expressed his approval of Poe's title *Tales of the Grotesque and Arabesque* (1840) "because the Grotesque and the Arabesque are offensive to human sight." For Baudelaire, the grotesque has nothing to do with the comical. Intolerant of "simple comedy," he welcomes the "gory fool's-play" in Daumier's caricatures, develops a "metaphysics of the absolute comical," views the grotesque as a clash of ideality with the devil, and adds to it a concept that is to make a mark for itself: the absurd. His own experiences, as well as those of man, who is torn between ecstasy and collapse, are derived from "the law of the absurd." It is the law that compels man to "express suffering through laughter." Baudelaire speaks of the "justification of the absurd," and lauds dreams because things impossible in reality are endowed by them "with the terrible logic of the absurd." The absurd becomes a view of unreality, which Baudelaire and later poets want to penetrate in order to flee the constriction of reality.

A poetry requiring concepts like the above for its justification will either annoy the reader or elude him. Rousseau's chasm between the author and the audience had led to the notion of the lonely poet, a favorite theme of the romantics, who treated it with some degree of melodiousness. Baudelaire took up the theme, but his tone was sharper. He added the aggressive dramatics that henceforth were to characterize European art and literature—even when the intention to shock, though not proclaimed as a principle, was sufficiently obvious in the work itself. Baudelaire still had such principles. He spoke of "the aristocratic pleasure of displeasing," called *Les fleurs du mal* "the passionate joy of resistance" and "a product of hate"; he was glad that poetry caused a "nervous shock" and prided himself on irritating the reader and no longer being understood by him. "Poetic consciousness, once an endless source of delight, has now turned into an inexhaustible arsenal of instruments of torture." All this is more than an imitation of romantic ways. The internal dissonances of poetry have logically become dissonances between the work and the reader. (pp. 19-27)

"To fathom a poet's soul, one must look for those words which occur most often in his works. The word reveals his obsession." These lines of Baudelaire's contain an excellent principle of interpretation, one that can be applied to Baudelaire himself. The rigor of his intellectual world, the persistence of its few but intense themes, allows us to find its focal points in the words occurring most frequently. They are key words and can easily be arranged in two polar groups: on the one side, *darkness, abyss, fear, desolation, desert, prison, cold, black, rotting;* on the other, *elevation, azure, heaven, ideal, light, purity.* The elaborate antithesis runs through almost every poem. Often compressed in a minimal space, the antithesis becomes a lexical dissonance, as in "dirty greatness," "decaying and enchanting," "beguiling horror," "dark and light." Such a union of normally incompatible things is known as an oxymoron—an old artistic figure of poetic diction, designed to articulate complicated psychological situations. In Baudelaire, the oxymoron is used to a conspicuous degree. It is the key figure of his fundamental dissonance. And it was a good idea on the part of Baudelaire's friend H. Babou to employ an oxymoron in the title *Les fleurs du mal.*

These word groups conceal traces of Christianity. Baudelaire's work is inconceivable without the Christian religion. But he is no longer a Christian. This fact is not refuted by his frequently discussed "satanism." The man who knows himself to be possessed by Satan may bear Christian stigmata; but this is quite different from Christian belief in salvation. As far as it may be stated succinctly, Baudelaire's satanism is the victory of the evil devised by the intelligence over the merely animal evil (and thereby, the banal), with the goal of gaining in an acme of evil some entry into ideality: hence, the cruelties and perversities in *Les fleurs du mal.* Out of "thirst for infinity," they degrade nature, laughter, and love into the satanic in order to find the point at which to escape into the "new." According to another key word, man is "hyperbolic," always straining upward in his intellectual fever. Yet, essentially torn asunder, he is a *homo duplex* who must satisfy his satanic pole in order to understand his heavenly one. Manichaean and Gnostic forms of early Christianity return in this schema via the illuminati of the eighteenth century and Joseph de Maistre. However, the recurrence cannot be attributed solely to outside influences. This schema voices a need of Baudelaire's. Symptomatically, and not just for him, the modern intellect falls back upon ancient ways of thinking that correspond to its inner dissension.

Nor do the many quotations culled from Baudelaire as proof of his Christianity alter the picture. Baudelaire manifested a will to pray, spoke in all earnestness about sin, and was deeply permeated with a sense of human sinfulness—so much so that he would have smiled at the clever psychologists of our day who diagnose his illness as a "repressed mother-fixation." He himself could not find a road. His praying languished into impotence and finally ceased to exist. He wrote of suffering, viewed it as the insignia of man, and knew damnations that hint at the existence of an isolated Jansenism within him. Yet there was no other determination than to exacerbate his dissension, which grew more and more excessive. One can see it in his attitude toward women. His malediction misses the more human intermediary position. His "hyperbolic" tension would be Christian only within the context of faith in the mystery of salvation. But this very belief is lacking. Christ occurs in Baudelaire's poems only as a fleeting metaphor or as he whom God abandoned. Behind the awareness of being damned, there is a desire "to enjoy damnation intensely." Naturally, all this is inconceivable without a Christian legacy. But what remains is a ruinous Christianity. In the Thomistic conception of creation, evil has only accidental significance. But, like the ancient Manichaeans, Baudelaire isolates it as an essential force. In the depth and the paradoxical complexities of this force, his poetry develops the courage of abnormality. Later poets, except for Rimbaud, forget that abnormality grew out of the purulence of moribund Christianity. But abnormality itself has remained. Even poets who are more rigorously Christian cannot or will not escape it. T. S. Eliot is a prime example.

This ruinous Christianity explains another peculiarity of Baudelaire's poetry, and one of great consequence for later times, a peculiarity attached to concepts like "ardent spirituality," "ideal," "elevation." But elevation to where? Occasionally God is named as an end, but more often the names are indefinite. What is it? The answer is supplied in the poem **"Elévation."** Its content and tone are lofty. Three stanzas appeal to the *esprit* ("spirit," "mind") to soar above the ponds, valleys, mountains, forests, clouds, seas, sun, ether, and stars into the fiery sphere beyond, which purges of the miasmas of earthliness. The apostrophe ends. A more general statement follows: Happy is the man who can ascend to these heights and learn to grasp the language of "flowers and mute things."

The poem moves within a familiar schema of Platonic and Christian-mystical origin. According to this schema, the spirit rises to a transcendence which so alters it that, upon looking back, it can see through the outer covering of the earthly and perceive the true essence. It is the schema known in Christian terms as *ascensio* or *elevatio*. The latter designation gave the poem its title. Further congruities can be observed. In both ancient and Christian doctrines, the highest heaven is true transcendence, the heaven of fire, the empyrean. Baudelaire calls it "clear fire." And the imperative, "Purge thyself," recalls the well-known mystical act of *purificatio*. Finally, mysticism tended to divide elevation into nine levels; the substance of each level was not always consistent, the sacred number nine being the important thing. And the same number occurs in our poem. There are exactly nine realms that the spirit is to transcend. A striking feature! Was this compelled by the mystical tradition? Perhaps. It would be akin to the compulsion that the Christian heritage exercised on Baudelaire. No decisive answer can be given, especially since possible influences of Swedenborg and other modern mystics must be taken into account. But we are concerned with something more important. For the very reason that the poem corresponds to so great an extent to the mystical schema, it becomes apparent that something is lacking to make them *fully* congruent: the arrival at the elevation, the very will to arrive. The Spanish mystic St. John of the Cross once wrote: "I flew so high, so high, that my hunt reached its goal." In **"Elévation"**, the possibility of arrival is known, and yet it is not granted to Baudelaire, as the closing stanzas explain. They speak vaguely of "divine beverage," of "profound immensity," "limpid space." There is no mention of God. Nor do we learn what the newly understood language of flowers and mute objects is. Not only is the goal of transcendence far; it is empty as well, an ideality devoid of content, a mere pole of tension, hyperbolically striven for but never reached.

This process is ubiquitous in Baudelaire's works. Empty ideality has a romantic source. But Baudelaire dynamically transforms it into a force of attraction that arouses an excessive upward tension and simultaneously repulses a downward tension. Like evil, it is a compulsion that must be obeyed, although obedience will bring no relief of tension: hence the equation of "ideal" and "abyss"; hence expressions like "gnawing ideal," "I am shackled to the pit of the ideal," "inaccessible azure." Such phrases are familiar to us from the classical mystics, for whom they connoted the painfully pleasurable compulsion of divine grace, the first step toward bliss. In Baudelaire, the two poles of satanic evil and empty ideality are meant to sustain the excitement made possible by escape from the banal world. Yet such flight is directionless, never exceeding dissonant excitement.

"Le voyage", the final poem in **Les fleurs du mal,** scrutinizing all attempts at escape, ends with a decision to die. The poem does not know what death will bring; yet death is enticing, for it constitutes an opportunity leading into the "new." And what is the "new"? The indefinable, the empty antithesis to the desolation of reality. At the peak of Baudelaire's ideality we find the completely negative and new meaningless concept of death.

The chaos of such modernity resides in its being both tormented to the point of neurosis by an intense craving for escape from reality, and powerless to believe in or create a substantially precise, meaningfully structured transcendence. This chaos brings the poets of modernity to a dynamic of tension devoid of release and to secrecy and mysteriousness for their own sake. Baudelaire often speaks of the supernatural and of mystery. What he means can be comprehended only by refusing, as he does, to fill these words with any meaning other than absolute mysteriousness itself. The empty ideality, the vague "otherness"— even vaguer in Rimbaud, and turning into nothingness in Mallarmé—and the involuted mysteriousness of modern poetry correspond to one another.

Les fleurs du mal is not obscure poetry. It frames its abnormal consciousness, its mysteries and dissonances, in comprehensible verse. And Baudelaire's theory of poetry, too, is entirely lucid. Yet he developed judgments and programs which, although not carried out in his own poems (or, at best, to a rudimentary degree), paved the way for the obscure poetry that followed. The two main points were the theories of language magic and imagination.

Poetry, especially in Latin and the Romance languages, had always known moments in which the verse achieved an absolute sonority more compelling than the semantic content. Acoustic figures of harmonious vowels and consonants or of rhythmic parallels enchanted the ear. Yet older poetry never abandoned the content at such moments; instead, it strove to intensify the meaning through the sound. Examples can be easily culled from Vergil, Dante, Calderón, Racine. Ever since European romanticism, different circumstances have prevailed. There are verses that sound rather than say. The acoustic material acquires suggestive force. In conjunction with words full of associative overtones, it discloses a dreamy infinity. A case in point is Brentano's poem that begins, "Wenn der lahme Weber träumt, er webe (When the lame weaver dreams, he's weaving)." Such lines are not meant to be understood but are to be taken as sonorous suggestiveness. Language experiences a stronger division than ever between its function to communicate and its function as an independent organism of musical fields of energy. But language also determines the poetic process itself, which surrenders to the impulses residing in language. Poets realize the possibility of creating a poem with the aid of mathematical combinations that handle the acoustic and rhythmic elements of language like magic formulas. It is those elements, rather than the thematic planning, that produce the meaning—a vague, gliding meaning whose enigmatic quality is embodied not so much in the essential denotation of the words as in their sonorous forces and semantic peripheries. This possibility became the dominant practice in modern verse. The poet became a wizard of sound.

The knowledge that poetry and magic are related is as old as time but had to be reacquired after being discarded by humanism and trans-Alpine classicism. This reacquisition began at the end of the eighteenth century and led to the theories of Edgar Allan Poe. His ideas met the growing, specifically modern need to join poetry to archaic practices and to intellectualize it. Novalis' juxtaposition of concepts like mathematics and magic in his discussions of poetry is characteristic of such modernity. Both (or similar) concepts may be found, from Baudelaire right down to the present, whenever poets think about their art.

Baudelaire translated Poe, thereby precipitating his influence in France, even in the twentieth century—to the great astonishment of Anglo-Saxon writers (most recently, T. S. Eliot). The works of Poe to be taken into account are his essays *A Philosophy of Composition* (1846) and *The Poetic Principle* (1848). Monuments to an artistic intelligence, they arrive at their conclusions by an observation of Poe's own verse. They embody that marriage of poetry and equally great (in this case even greater) reflections on poetry which constitutes another essential feature of modernity. Baudelaire translated the first essay and part of the second, and explicitly adopted their theories. They can therefore be regarded as his own.

It was Poe's idea to reverse the order of poetic acts as stated in earlier poetics. What seems to be the result, the "form," is actually the origin of the poem; what seems to be the origin, the "meaning," is actually the result. The beginning of the poetic process is the "tone," an insistent tone that precedes meaningful language, a shapeless mood. To give it shape, the author seeks in language the acoustic material that comes closest to such a tone. The sounds are attached to words, which are then grouped into themes, which are ultimately joined into a cohesive context of meaning. Novalis' adumbration has thus become a consistent theory: poetry is born of the impulse of language which, obeying the prelinguistic "tone," points the way for the content. The content is no longer the true substance of the poem; content conveys the tonal powers and overtones of the poem, which are superior to the meaning. Poe shows, for example, that the word *Pallas* in a poem of his owes its existence to a free association in the preceding lines and to its sonorous attraction as well. A bit further on, he describes the (incidental) train of thought as a mere suggestivity of vagueness, since in this way the tonal dominant is kept and does not lose its effect because of the semantic dominant. Such versification is understood as a surrender to the magic forces of language. The poet, in attributing a subsequent meaning to the primary tone, must be "mathematically precise." The poem per se is complete in itself. It does not communicate truth, "intoxication of the heart," or anything else, it *is:* the poem per se. These ideas of Poe's establish the modern theory of poetry that will gravitate around the concept of *poésie pure.*

Novalis and Poe probably were familiar with the teachings of the French illuminati; and Baudelaire certainly was. These teachings (which contain many roots of symbolism) include a speculative theory of language: A word is not a chance human product; it proceeds from the cosmic Primal One; to speak it is to establish a magic contact between the speaker and the source; the poetic word reimmerses trivial things in the mystery of their metaphysical origin and illuminates hidden analogies between parts of being. Since Baudelaire was conversant with these ideas, it was natural that he borrow Poe's thoughts on poetry, which probably were inspired by the same source. The French poet, too, spoke of the necessity of the word, in a sentence that Mallarmé was to quote later. "There resides in the Word, the *logos,* something sacred that prohibits our turning it into a game of chance. Handling a language skillfully is tantamount to practicing a kind of evocative

sorcery." The formula *sorcellerie évocatoire* recurs often, even being applied to the fine arts. It expresses a thinking that belongs to the realm of magic and secondary (occult) mysticism. Phrases such as "magic formulas" or "magic operation" are no less frequent. And, finally, we have another key word, *suggestion,* which we shall presently discuss.

It makes no difference that such pure linguistic magic obtains at only a few points in *Les fleurs du mal*—in the form of unusual rhyme clusters, distant assonances, tonal curves, vowel series guiding, rather than guided by, the senses. Baudelaire's theoretical discussions go a good deal further. They anticipate a poetry which, for the sake of magical sound forces, will more and more do away with thematic, logical, emotional, and even grammatical order, and will acquire its content from verbal impulses, a content which would never have been found by methodical reflection. The meaning is abnormal; it exists on the periphery, or beyond the pale, of understanding. Here the circle closes; here we see a further logical consistency in the structure of modern poetry. A poetry whose ideality is empty escapes reality by creating an incomprehensible mysteriousness. Thus it can be supported all the more by language magic. For, by operating in the acoustic and associative possibilities of the word, the poet releases further obscure contents, as well as mysterious magical powers of pure sound.

Baudelaire frequently speaks of his "disgust with reality." This applies to any part of reality that is banal or merely natural—both of which are, for him, synonymous with the unspiritual and the material. Characteristically, the thing that most upset him in the legal judgement against *Les fleurs du mal* was the charge of realism. Who can blame

Baudelaire in his early twenties.

him, especially since, in those days, the term referred to a literature that depicted the morally and aesthetically repugnant dregs of reality simply for the sake of depicting them? Baudelaire's poetry does not aspire to copy, but to transform. It dynamically changes instinctive evil into the satanic, ignites images of misery into "galvanic shudders," treats more neutral phenomena in such a way that they symbolize inner states of being or that vague world of mystery which (for him) fills empty ideality. Labeling Baudelaire a realist or a naturalist is nonsense. His harshest and most shocking themes are violently ablaze with his "ardent spirituality," which tends to recede from all reality. Furthermore, this tendency can be observed in many details of his poetic technique. The precision of the objective statement grasps mainly a reality that is driven to a downward extreme, i.e., one that is already transformed, while otherwise there is a conspicuous lack of fixed location in the imagery; there is a tendency to use emotional adjectives instead of objectively accurate ones; there is a synesthesia that removes the borders between different sensory areas; and so forth.

Baudelaire applies various names to this ability to transform reality and make it unreal, and two of these names recur persistently: *dream* and *imagination.* He is more decisive than Rousseau or Diderot about raising the same thing that they meant to a level of superior "creative" power. The Romance word *creative* is more precise in this case than the German *schöpferisch.* The latter has certain associations that could divert attention from the intellectual and voluntary forces so crucial in Baudelaire: these forces are found in his concepts of dream and imagination, which include references to mathematics and abstraction.

This is not to say that Baudelaire does not use the concept of dream in its older sense—for example, when he applies it to the various forms of subjectivity, inner time, yearning for faraway places. But here, too, the superiority over concrete proximity, the qualitative contrast between the distance of dreams and the confinement of the world, is apparent. The term must be taken in its highest and hardest sense: there where the dream is expressly distinguished from "mellow melancholy," from mere "outpouring," from the "heart." In the preface to his *Nouvelles histoires,* a translation of Poe's tales, he calls the dream "sparkling, mysterious, perfect as crystal." It is a productive rather than a perceptive power, one that works in an exact and systematic rather than a chaotic and haphazard fashion. No matter what this power may focus on, the crucial factor is the production of unreal contents. The dream may be a natural poetic talent, but it can also be fueled by narcotics or result from a psychopathic state. All such impulses are suitable to the "magic operation" with which the dream puts created unreality above reality.

In calling the dream "perfect as crystal," Baudelaire was not making use of a random simile. This expression guarantees the position of the dream by assimilating it to inorganic material. It was Novalis who wrote: "Stones and matter are supreme; man is the true chaos." This reversal of the hierarchy (going back to alchemistic sources) recurs regularly in Baudelaire, whenever he touches on the dream. He adds to it by degrading nature to chaos and impurity. This attitude may come as no surprise in a romantic author, yet it cannot be explained in terms of romantic thinking alone. For Baudelaire, "nature" means not only

the vegetative, but also the banal lowness of man. Together with inorganic formations, the symbol of the absolute intellect is placed so high that once again a dissonant tension issues forth. This still occurs among painters of the twentieth century. In line with their cubic pictures and their unreal colors, they (Marc, Beckmann, et al.) speak of nature as something impure and chaotic: structural compulsion and not influence. In Baudelaire's eyes, the inorganic achieves its supreme significance when it is used as artistic material: a statue is worth more than a living body; the sylvan backdrop on a stage, more than a natural forest. This is certainly romantic thinking; but the extreme application is modern. Such a strong equation of art and the inorganic, such a categorical banishment of reality from literature, can, at best, be found in the literature of earlier ages from which secret trails lead to modern poetry: baroque literature in Spain and Italy.

But even that era could never have produced a poem like Baudelaire's **"Rêve parisien"**, the chief text of his spiritualization of the artificial and the inorganic. Not a real metropolis, but a dream city, deliberately artificial; cubic forms from which all vegetation has been banished; gigantic arcades surrounding water, the one element that—although dead—moves; diamond abysses, tunnels of precious stones; no sun, no stars, a blackness that shines out of itself; a whole city devoid of human beings, devoid of place, time, and sound. We can see what the title word *rêve* ("dream") signifies: a constructive intellectuality has become an image, an intellectuality that pronounces its victory over nature and man in symbols of mineral and metal, one that projects its constructed images into empty ideality, from which they shine back, glittering to the eye and uncanny to the soul.

Baudelaire's discussions of imagination are probably his most significant contribution to the genesis of modern poetry and art. For him, imagination—which he equated with dreaming—meant the creative faculty itself, "the queen of human faculties." How does it operate? In 1859 he wrote: "Imagination decomposes all creation; according to laws that emerge from the depths of the soul, it gathers and coordinates the parts and creates a whole new world." Prefigured in theories since the sixteenth century, this idea has become a tenet of modern aesthetics. Its modernity consists in its placing at the beginning of the artistic act an analysis, a decomposition, a destructive process; Baudelaire emphasizes this in a similar passage in which he supplements "decompose" with "separate." Analyzing, decomposing, separating reality (i.e., what can be perceived by the senses) into its parts means deforming it. The concept of deformation is frequent in Baudelaire and is always meant positively. The act of deforming evinces the power of the intellect, whose product has a higher rank than the thing deformed. The "new world" resulting from such destruction can no longer be a world structured by reality. It is an unreal formation that cannot be measured by normal standards of reality.

For Baudelaire, these ideas remain theoretical sketches. His poems rarely correspond to them. One example might be the passage in which "clouds jostle the moon." But viewed retrospectively—and it suffices to think of Rimbaud—the boldness of those lines concerning the imagination and their meaning for the future become clear. We should not, however, lose sight of the main direction: a striving away from confining reality. The true subtlety of the concept of imagination becomes comprehensible when imagination is contrasted with a process of mere copying: hence Baudelaire's protest against the recent invention of photography—a protest that can be found near the above-quoted sentence. The working of the imagination is called "forced idealization." Idealization no longer means what it did in older aesthetics: embellishment. It now refers to the process of depriving something of its reality; it signifies a dictatorial act. It seems that at the very point at which the modern world applied its technological skill and knowledge to a mirroring of reality (in the form of photography), this positive, limited reality wore out all the more quickly, and artistic energy turned all the more vigorously to the nonobjective world of the imagination. This situation is analogous to the reaction sparked by scientific positivism. Baudelaire's condemnation of photography is on the same level as his condemnation of the natural sciences. Such artistic sensibilities experience the scientific fathoming of the world as a narrowing of the world and a loss of mystery, and therefore respond with an extreme increase in the power of the imagination. Two decades after Baudelaire's death, the same answer to the loss of mystery will be labeled "symbolism."

The process that took place in Baudelaire has had an incalculable significance right up to the present. Baudelaire once said, "I would like fields dyed red, flowers dyed blue." Rimbaud was to write of such fields, and artists of the twentieth century were to paint them. Baudelaire's term for an art arising from the creative imagination was *surnaturalisme.* He meant an art which deobjectifies objects into lines, colors, movements, autonomous accidentals, and which bathes them in the "magic light" that annihilates their reality in mystery. In 1917, Apollinaire was to transform the word *surnaturalisme* into *surréalisme*—and rightfully so, for this new term signified a continuation of Baudelaire's aims.

Another statement of Baudelaire's unites imagination and intelligence: in 1856 he wrote, "The poet is the highest intelligence, and the imagination is the most scientific of all faculties." The paradox in this line sounds no less paradoxical today: poetry which escapes from a scientifically deciphered and technologized world and flees into unreality claims, in its creation of the unreal, the very same precision and intelligence that have made the world confining and banal. . . . [Baudelaire's train of thought] leads logically to a new concept of this kind: abstraction. Friedrich Schlegel and Novalis had already used abstraction as an essential characteristic of the imagination. This is understandable, since imagination is construed as the faculty of creating the unreal. Baudelaire employs abstract mainly in the sense of "intellectual, spiritual," i.e., "not natural." Further beginnings of abstract poetry and art become visible here, acquired from the concept of an unlimited imagination whose equivalents are nonobjective lines and motion. Baudelaire calls them "arabesques"—and this concept, too, will have a future. "The arabesque is the most spiritual of all designs." The rapprochement of the grotesque and the arabesque goes back to Novalis, Gautier, and Poe. And Baudelaire brought the two concepts even closer together. In his aesthetic system, the grotesque, the arabesque, and the imagination all belong together: the imagination is the power of the free spirit to perform abstract (i.e., nonobjective) motion; the grotesque and the arabesque are products of this power.

The prose poems contain a short piece on the Bacchic thyrsus. The creative imagination transmutes it into a formation of dancing lines and colors, for which, as the poem puts it, the staff is merely a pretext—a pretext, as well, for the "curving motion of words." This phrase indicates a connection with linguistic magic. The concept of the arabesque, the meaningless linear pattern, fits in with the concept of the "poetic sentence." The latter, as Baudelaire writes in a draft of the foreword to *Les fleurs du mal,* is a sequence of pure sound and motion; it can form a horizontal, a rising, or a falling line, a spiral, a zigzag of superposed angles. And for this very reason, poetry borders on music and mathematics.

Dissonant beauty, the removal of the heart from the "I" of poetry, abnormal consciousness, empty ideality, deobjectification, mysteriousness, all of which were produced from the magic powers inherent in language and from the absolute imagination, and were brought close to the abstractions of mathematics and the curving motion of music, were used by Baudelaire to prepare possibilities that were to be realized in future poetry.

The way was paved by a poet who bore the stigmata of romanticism. He turned romantic play into unromantic seriousness, and, with peripheral ideas of his mentors, he erected an intellectual system that had its back toward them. We can therefore call the poetry of his heirs deromanticized romanticism. (pp. 27-38)

> *Hugo Friedrich, "Baudelaire," in his* The Structure of Modern Poetry: From the Mid-Nineteenth to the Mid-Twentieth Century, *translated by Joachim Neugroschel, Northwestern University Press, 1974, pp. 19-38.*

Kenneth Rexroth   (essay date 1968)

[*Rexroth gained prominence in American letters as a critic and translator. As a critic, his acute intelligence and wide sympathy allowed him to examine such varied subjects as jazz, Greek mythology, the works of D. H. Lawrence, and the cabala. As a translator, he was largely responsible for introducing the West to both Chinese and Japanese classics. In the following excerpt, he comments on Baudelaire's life and works.*]

"Baudelaire is the greatest poet of the capitalist epoch." True or not, this statement, with its Marxist implications, is appropriate, because he is specially the poet of the society analyzed in *Capital* or described in *The Condition of the English Working-Class.* His subject was the world of primitive accumulation, of the ruthless destruction of all values but the cash nexus by the new industrial and financial system—of bankers and their mistresses in sultry boudoirs; of the craze for diabolism, drugs, flagellation, barbarism; of gin-soaked poor dying in gutters, prostitutes dying under bridges, tubercular and syphilitic intellectuals; of the immense, incurable loneliness of the metropolis; of the birth of human self-alienation, as Marx called it—Baudelaire called it vaporization of the Ego—of the Communist Manifesto; and of revolution and revolution betrayed.

Baudelaire's Catholic apologists deny that he had an Oedipus complex. He is the archetype, a far more extreme example than Rousseau or Stendhal. Yet neither Marx nor Freud is an adequate guide to Baudelaire. They diagnose the illness of the nineteenth century in its own materialistic terms. Far more afflicted than they, Baudelaire transcends his century. His ultimate meanings are emerging only in the decline of the twentieth. He is the founder of the modern sensibility—not just of that of its first century, but of a special character that will, as far as we can see ahead, endure throughout the age of the breakdown of our civilization. Some learn to cope with this sensibility. He was at its mercy, because he embodied it totally. He lived in a permanent crisis of the moral nervous system. His conviction that social relationships were one immense lie was physiological.

The Romantics had a rhetoric of secession; Baudelaire had a life commitment, an organic divorce. Further, he was literally outcast—expelled from his caste. Few men have ever had a stronger conviction of their clerisy, of their belonging to the clerkly caste of the responsibles. Yet because of the terms of his wardship, he was continually dispossessed, forced to recognize his loss and shame every time he had to beg from his mother or his guardian. His writing, which he looked on as prophetic utterance, he was forced to sell as a cheap commodity. At the end of his life he told a friend he had received a total of about three thousand dollars from all the writing he had ever done.

He spent his life in a state of demoralization, and his work is a relentless attack on that demoralization. Much of his life and most of his poetry are tortured by a consciousness of sin. He thought of sin as the corruption of the will to vision. Only very rarely does he ever seem to realize that it is the corruption of the organ of reciprocity. His human relationships are all charades.

It has been said that Baudelaire chose the life he lived, that nobody has to live like that. True, but what did he choose? He did not choose his degrading trust fund, his Hamletic relation with his mother, his obsessive ritualized oral sex and masochism, or his syphilis, all of which worked together to multiply his guilt, to close to him person-to-person relations with women, and to turn women into melodramatic actresses in his own internal theater of frustration. Nor did he choose a debilitating oral opium addiction; in youth he chose the ecstasies of drugs before he realized the consequences—not just painful addiction, but destruction of the will, and a *vaporisation de Moi* worse than that caused by the dehumanizations of a commercial society.

He chose to place himself at the disposal of experience, and he chose to place his experience at the mercy of a conscience conceived as an instrument of mystery and a key to the enigma of being. Transports, ecstasies, orgies— what is the *secret?* The poet, says Baudelaire, is a decipherer, a Kabbalist of reality, a decoder. Ordinary life, if it is not a message in code, a system of symbols for something else, is unacceptable. It must be a cryptogram; it can't be what it seems. The poet's task is to decode the incomprehensible obvious. His life becomes a deliberately constructed paranoia, as Rimbaud, Breton, Artaud were to say generations later.

As we read him we discover that Baudelaire believes in the charm, the incantation, the cryptogram, but he ceases to believe in the *secret.* The spirits have not risen. The code says nothing. This is the mystery concealed by the disorder of the world. The visionary experience ends in itself; the light of the illuminated comes only from and falls only on himself. This is not unlike Buddhism in its starkest form, the end result of a rigorous religious empiricism— which is why similar minds find him so congenial today.

Baudelaire liked to call his verse Classical, and gullible modern critics echo him. It is not, although it is so Latinate as to begin the corruption of logical syntax that reaches its culmination in Mallarmé and Reverdy. It is ritualistic; the tonic patterns of French verse are flattened out, and a reverberating sonority of vowel music as in English or Medieval Latin takes their place. A poem like **"La cloche fêlée"** is written Gregorian chant—*"media vitae,* in the midst of life we are in death."

Nor is Baudelaire the poet of the modern megalopolis in any realistic sense. Corpses spilling worms in the ditch, ancient courtesans cackling over gaming tables in the dawn, boulevards lit with prostitutes, Negresses lost in the winter fog, sweaty lesbians in beds dizzy with perfume, a wounded soldier dying under a heap of dead—is this everyday life in the modern city? It is the city as the mother of hallucinations of the alienated. He presents it with the utmost tension of abstract and concrete, "in a noble, distant, superior manner," said Laforgue—a hieratic manner, the manner of a priest. He claimed the power of transubstantiation—"Paris, you gave me mud, and I turned it to gold and gave it back to you."

It has been said that Baudelaire, like Blake, had no philosophy, or had to make one up out of himself. Like Blake, he states his philosophy clearly enough. It is the orthodoxy of the heterodox, older far than Aquinas or even Plato. Correspondences, the doubled world, the doctrine of signatures, the ambivalence of microcosm and macrocosm—he found all these notions in Swedenborg; some in Coleridge; some in Poe; all in Blake, whom he may have read; and all worked out in vulgarized detail by his friend Eliphas Lévi, the founder of modern occultism.

More sophisticated, more desperate than his masters, Baudelaire uses his gnosticism in an anti-gnostic sense, to contradict itself. Man is not saved by knowledge; *gnosis* does not produce *ecstasis,* but vice versa. Vision produces the knowledge of the irrelevance of knowledge, a state of being beyond the vaporized ego, beyond the temporal order, an end in itself. This is the secret of clerisy, of the *sanior pars,* the saving remnant of doom. It is the substance of a new ordination.

In youth he called the disengaged man of conscience the Dandy. As he grew older, the Dandy merged with a new kind of priest or shaman. His clerkly role explains his distinctive dress, his strange caste standards, far more strict than those prevailing amongst *les autres,* peculiar to the clergy—"benefit of clergy"—a people set apart.

He chose the life that enabled him to do what he did. Above all other writers, poetry was to him a vocation, a calling to a new kind of holy orders. So to the degree to which he could manage it, his life was monastic—like the celibacy of the brothel: an almost complete sacrifice of domesticity and the amenities of secular man to the liberation and refinement of a sensibility and a conscience that he considered synonymous. He insists on the poet and artist as *vates;* as the visionary eye of the body politic, as he says explicitly; as the priest who sacrifices himself and atones vicariously for The Others. (pp. 173-76)

Kenneth Rexroth, *"Baudelaire: Poems,"* in his Classics Revisited, *New Directions, 1986, pp. 173-76.*

Alfred Garvin Engstrom   (lecture date 1975)

[*In the following excerpt, Engstrom provides an overview of the poems in* The Flowers of Evil.]

Les fleurs du mal! Even today, after long acquaintance with the poetry of Baudelaire, when I see the famous title I am puzzled as to how it can be adequately rendered into English. *Flowers of Evil* once seemed a simple and clear and precise translation; but I find these words now so lacking in the rich semantic echoes and interplays to be found in the French and so misleading in their single emphasis that they no longer seem to me valid equivalents.

There has, in fact, been a long controversy over Baudelaire's title, and I suspect that this, too, has arisen in part from a failure to recognize the richness and irony and humanity in his use of the words *Fleurs du mal.* Thibaudet, a fine and sensitive critic, once wrote that surely the most fanatical champion of Baudelaire would hardly defend what Thibaudet called his "ridiculous and rococo title." Other critics have cited the statement by one of Baudelaire's friends that the title was not even his creation, but was suggested by Hippolyte Babou. Yet, whatever its origin, Baudelaire chose *Les fleurs du mal* as the title for his masterpiece; and its pertinence to his poems can, in my judgment, not only be demonstrated, but can serve to show that the whole volume deserves to be considered from a more diversified viewpoint than that entailed in seeing the poems under the unique focus of *Flowers of Evil.*

We shall see hereafter examples of flowers in Baudelaire's verses; but it is worth noting that overt and implied flower imagery is evident in a remarkable number of the poems, that there is in the volume a continuing sense of natural ripening, flowering and fading of flowers and other vegetation, and that Baudelaire on a number of occasions specifically refers to poems as flowers. It was the ironic combination of such a word as *Fleurs* (with its connotations of beauty and purity and innocence, as well as of quintessence) with the word *Mal,* taken in the sense of *Evil,* that furnished much of the provocative shock in the title *Les fleurs du mal,* conceived precisely even by the French as *Flowers of Evil.*

But the word *mal* does not mean only *evil* in the moral and theological sense, as it seems most often to have been uniquely understood and translated in Baudelaire's title. The first definition of *le mal* in Littré's great dictionary in 1873 is "ce qui nuit, ce qui blesse; le contraire du bien" ("what harms or hurts; the opposite of *le bien*"); and thereafter, along with the sense of moral and metaphysical *evil,* the word is given the definition of "les souffrances, les maladies, la mort" ("sufferings, diseases, death"). So there is a richer sense to *Les fleurs du mal* than merely *Flowers of Evil,* however pertinent this title may be to a pervading atmosphere in the book and to many of its poems. The

word *mal* must be seen here to include the sense of *suffering* of all kinds and *misfortune* and *death,* along with the sense of moral and metaphysical *evil*—and *Les fleurs du mal* thus becomes, in addition to *Flowers of Evil,* Flowers of any of the myriad forms of human Suffering (that is, Flowers of *Boredom* and *Illness* and *Despair* and *Loneliness* and *Humiliation* and *Degradation* and *Remorse* and *Regret* and the *Fear of Passing Time* and the like) and Flowers of *Death*—a long trail of Baudelaire's major themes in *Les fleurs du mal.* All this seems to me to entail a broader sense of humanity than that implied in restricting the sense of *mal* to *evil* in the title of the poems.

According to Baudelaire, *Les fleurs du mal* "must be judged as a whole, and then there emerges from it a terrible morality." Later, after his trial, he wrote of the volume: " . . . into this *atrocious* book I have put *my whole heart, all my love, all my religion* (disguised), *all my hatred.*" Beyond all else it seems to have been through *Les fleurs du mal* that Baudelaire gave meaning to his life, and in turning now to the collection itself we shall try to show something of the poet's thought and the alchemy of his art in the poems of his masterpiece.

The dedication of *Les fleurs du mal* to Théophile Gautier is of unusual interest, not only for its homage to a gifted poet and friend, but for certain revelations as to Baudelaire's own conception of the poet's art. The dedication is phrased as follows:

> To the impeccable poet
> To the perfect magician in French letters
> To my very dear and very revered
> Master and friend
> Théophile Gautier
> with feelings
> of the most profound humility
> I dedicate
> these sickly flowers.
> C. B.

In the phrase "impeccable poet" Baudelaire pays homage to exquisite form—to the poet as artist and craftsman; and Baudelaire's own influence continues this tradition of the poet, which he drew in part from Gautier and, in a somewhat different sense, from Poe and passed on to Mallarmé and Valéry. The phrase "perfect magician," on the other hand, implies a very different conception of poetry; and here we sense the idea of the poet as mage or seer that Baudelaire was to transmit to Rimbaud and his followers. Finally, in the phrase "sickly flowers" for his poems we see clear evidence in the very dedication to his work that the *Fleurs du mal* were not seen by the poet only as flowers of moral and theological evil.

Of even greater interest than the dedication is the introductory poem, **"Au lecteur" ("To the Reader")**, which serves as a preface to the whole collection. This is a scathing denunciation of the age in which it was written, but it shows at the same time the poet's own harrowing metaphysical and religious preoccupations and his despair at the hopelessness of the human situation. The brilliant and unexpected imagery in the poem's forty verses creates an unforgettable atmosphere of evil and human degradation and provides a strange and terrible entry into the remarkable world of Baudelaire's poetry.

The first word in **"Au lecteur"** (and thus the first word in

Les fleurs du mal) is *sottise* ("stupidity"), a quality that Baudelaire loathed as deeply as Flaubert; and the poem's last verse is one of the most famous satiric lines in modern literature: "—Hypocrite lecteur,—mon semblable,—mon frère!" ("Hypocritical reader,—my fellowman,—my brother!") Here Baudelaire was not flattering the "gentle reader" of polite society. He was flaying his age. Perhaps not since Dante created his Vestibule for the trimmers, who were not even worthy of Hell, has there been so cruel a representation of mediocrity as in this prefatory poem.

Like Dante, Baudelaire uses vulgar imagery for vulgar characterizations; but his art, like Dante's, transforms the vulgar into powerful, imaginative creation. He describes contemporary man's mind and body as occupied and shaped by "stupidity, error, sin, and stinginess" (this last a base fault, lacking the intensity and magnitude of avarice); and he adds:

> Et nous alimentons nos aimables remords
> Comme les mendiants nourissent leur vermine.

> (And we nourish our charming remorse
> As beggars nourish their vermine.)

Here the brilliance of the language centers on the word *remords* (in the plural) and its etymology and its relationship with other words in the poem, so that unless one thinks of the root meaning of *remorse* the power of the imagery is lost.

In its true sense, *remorse* is a "biting back"—a cruel self-devouring. Remorse is so fearful a state that we have, in warning against it, a famous Greek adage attributed to Pythagoras: "Eat not the heart." But in Baudelaire's indictment of his age *remorse* is attractive and man is seen nourishing his remorse "as beggars nourish their vermine." Thus the deep bite of true remorse has given way to something that can be equated with the vulgar and superficial irritations of a beggar's lice; and the beggar imagery itself suggests a further degradation in man's superficially begging forgiveness for his sins. Baudelaire continues his indictment with cruel insistence:

> Nos péchés sont têtus, nos repentirs sont lâches;
> Nous nous faisons payer grassement nos aveux,
> Et nous rentrons gaiement dans le chemin bourbeux,
> Croyant par de vils pleurs laver toutes nos taches.

> (Our sins are headstrong, our repentances base;
> We arrange to be well paid for our confessions,
> And we return gaily into the muddy way,
> Thinking by vile tears to wash clean all our stains.)

Here the poet introduces the first of his great images of Satan, whom he calls Satan Trismégiste (Satan Trismegistus—Thrice-Powerful Satan) and thus establishes a relation with Hermes Trismegistus, the supposed author of esoteric books on magic and alchemy. This is one of the most dramatic appearances of Satan in all the writings of Baudelaire, where his presence is so often felt.

> Sur l'oreiller du mal c'est Satan Trismégiste
> Qui berce longuement notre esprit enchanté,
> Et le riche métal de notre volonté
> Est tout vaporisé par ce savant chimiste.

> (On the pillow of evil [i. e., Sloth, one of the Seven Deadly Sins] it is Satan Trismegistus
> Who lulls for a long while our enchanted spirit,
> And the rich metal of our will

Is all vaporized by this learned chemist.)

In his book on opium and hashish called *The Artificial Paradises,* Baudelaire refers to the will as "the most precious of all the faculties" and as "cette précieuse *substance*" ("this precious *substance*"). Thus Satan is seen as a diabolical alchemist who, instead of transforming the baser metals into gold, vaporizes the most precious gold of the will as man lies enthralled to Sloth.

Once his will is dissolved, man is an easy prey; and the next stanza of the poem introduces the Devil as the great puppet-master, pulling the threads that govern human actions, until man without horror goes down each day one further step towards Hell, while demons carouse in his brain and Death descends into his lungs like an invisible stream. In this weird puppet-show, if man is not guilty of rape and poisoning and stabbing and setting fire to things around him, it is not from his native virtue—"It is because our soul, alas! is not bold enough."

Baudelaire writes in a letter of 1856 that he has often thought that this world's maleficent and disgusting animals "were perhaps only the vivification, the corporification, the flowering, in material life, of man's evil thoughts." And he adds: "Thus all *nature* participates in original sin." And so in **"Au lecteur"** he imagines seven yelping, howling, crawling monsters in what he calls "the infamous menagerie of our vices"—and he adds an eighth that will make its presence felt thereafter as one of the most terrible forces in *Les fleurs du mal.* In addition to the seven monsters, then . . .

> Il en est un plus laid, plus méchant, plus immonde!
> Quoiqu'il ne pousse ni grands gestes ni grands cris,
> Il ferait volontiers de la terre un débris
> Et dans un bâillement avalerait le monde;

> C'est l'Ennui!—l'œil chargé d'un pleur involontaire,
> Il rêve d'échafauds en fumant son houka.
> Tu le connais, lecteur, ce monstre délicat,
> —Hypocrite lecteur,—mon semblable,—mon frère!

> (There is one more ugly, more wicked, more foul!
> Although he makes no great motions or cries,
> He would willingly reduce the earth to ruin
> And in one yawn swallow all the world.

> He is ENNUI!—His eye laden with an involuntary tear,
> He dreams of scaffolds as he smokes his houka.
> You know him, reader, this delicate monster,
> —Hypocritical reader,—my fellowman,—my brother!)

Ennui, the "delicate monster," a nineteenth-century equivalent of the deadly sin of Sloth or Tristitia or *taedium vitae* or *acedia,* which he called "the malady of monks," will pursue Baudelaire all the rest of his life.

Apart from the verses **"To the Reader,"** the 1861 edition of *Les fleurs du mal* has 126 poems grouped in six unequal divisions called in turn "Spleen and Ideal," "Parisian Scenes," "Wine," "Fleurs du Mal," "Revolt," and "Death." For our purposes . . . , however, I have decided to consider Baudelaire's poems under certain selected headings that seem to afford especially pertinent insights into his art. We shall thus examine first of all in some detail Baudelaire's rather complex and perverse aesthetic ideas as shown in certain of his poems on beauty. Thereafter we shall consider briefly in turn his treatment of sin and love and woman; of spleen or ennui; of the sea and voyages; and of Death. Finally, at the last, in order to see something of the poet's own ordering and imaginative creation and shaping of materials on a concentrated subject, we shall consider the poems in the division of *Les fleurs du mal* called "Tableaux parisiens" ("Parisian Scenes"), Baudelaire's remarkable evocation of the human dramas and the spiritual and moral forces at work in one of the great capitals of modern Europe—what he himself called, as we shall see hereafter, "the heroism of modern life."

Baudelaire writes in the part of his *Intimate Journals* called **"My Heart Laid Bare"** that even in childhood he had felt "two contradictory sentiments, the horror of life and the ecstasy of life"; and he notes that "there are in every man, at every hour, two simultaneous postulations, one towards God and the other towards Satan" . . . the spiritual and the animal. In the representations of Beauty in *Les fleurs du mal* we find interplay of comparable dualities, as is evident from an examination of such poems in "Spleen and Ideal" as **"Correspondences," "The Lighthouses," "Beauty," "The Ideal,"** and **"Hymn to Beauty"**—five poems that deserve special consideration for their summary of much of Baudelaire's aesthetics and for the rich insights they give us into the imagination of a great poet who defined the study of the beautiful as "a duel in which the artist cries out in terror before being conquered" (**"Le confiteor de l'artiste"**).

In **"Correspondences,"** the first of these poems, Baudelaire sees Nature as a temple with living pillars from which confused words come forth. Man passes there through "forests of symbols" that look upon him as if there were some intimate relation between him and them. This conception of correspondence between material objects in nature and spiritual, human realities is apparently drawn from Swedenborg. Here Baudelaire develops a second kind of correspondence in his description of the interrelation of sense-perceptions, or what is known as synaesthesia—the metaphor of the senses. This is a phenomenon recurrent in western literature from the *Iliad* to the present day; but it was so consciously employed as a part of late nineteenth-century aesthetics in France that Baudelaire's proclamation of it is of special interest when he writes:

> Comme de longs échos qui de loin se confondent
> Dans une ténébreuse et profonde unité,
> Vaste comme la nuit et comme la clarté,
> Les parfums, les couleurs et les sons se répondent.
> Il est des parfums frais comme des chairs d'enfants,
> Doux comme les hautbois, verts comme les prairies,
> —Et d'autres, corrompus, riches et triomphants,
> Ayant l'expansion des choses infinies,
> Comme l'ambre, le musc, le benjoin et l'encens,
> Qui chantent les transports de l'esprit et des sens.

> (Like long echoes which from far away are fused
> In a shadowy and deep oneness,
> Vast as night and as light,
> Perfumes, colors and sounds correspond.
> There are fragrances cool as children's flesh,
> Sweet as oboes, green as prairies,
> —And others, tainted, rich and triumphant,
> Having the expansiveness of infinite things,
> Like ambergris, musk, benzoin and incense
> That sing the ecstasies of the spirit and the senses.)

Here we have not only a complex and fascinating relationship between physical objects and spiritual realities, and between the different senses, but also a subtle relationship

between these two different kinds of correspondences arranged in a recurrent chiastic pattern that seems to me of special interest.

Critics have suggested that the Swedenborgian correspondences in the poem are "vertical" and that the correspondences between the senses are "horizontal"; and I take this to imply that there is a loftier value given to the first than to the second kind of correspondences. But the chiastic patterns in syntax here suggest that the two different sorts of correspondence combine in a transcendent relationship for the creation of beauty.

Baudelaire cites, for example, as we have seen, fragrances "having the expansiveness of infinite things"—and these are identified as being "like ambergris, musk, benzoin and incense," of which the first two are animal secretions used as a base in sensual perfumes, and the last two are aromatic resins, gums or spices employed in church ritual. But the next verse says that these four fragrances "sing the ecstasy of the spirit and the senses"—and here the pattern of the sensual and the spiritual is reversed so that (in the chiastic relationship) ambergris and musk are counterbalanced by the spirit, and benzoin and incense by the senses. This is a recurrent kind of pattern in Baudelaire, and it seems to me here to imply his belief that interplay with the senses is essential in poetry for the representation of the spiritual. The fact that the perfumes "having the expansiveness of infinite things" are called *corrompus* ("tainted") is a jarring note; but, as will be more evident hereafter, Baudelaire includes elements of this sort in his conception of ideal beauty. For Baudelaire, the shadow of original sin apparently falls as darkly over the aesthetic world as over the moral and spiritual worlds.

In a second poem, **"The Lighthouses,"** great works of art are seen as "maledictions, blasphemies, and complaints"—but also as "ecstasies, cries, tears and Te Deums." They are lighthouses "lighted on a thousand citadels," the best witness that man can give of his worth—"[a] burning sob that rolls from age to age and comes to die at the edge of [God's] eternity." Thus Baudelaire recognizes the ephemeral quality of even the greatest art and, though he sees it as witness of what is best in man, he does not confuse art with religion in the dimension of eternity.

The poem called **"Beauty"** has been interpreted in Thomistic terms, as if it were written under the influence of St. Thomas's statement that, "since God (the noblest of beings) is motionless, in the absolute, immobility is nobler than motion." This sonnet is so memorable a statement of one aspect of Baudelaire's aesthetics that it deserves to be cited as nearly as it can be translated for our purposes. Here Beauty speaks in her own voice:

> I am fair, O mortals! as a dream in stone,
> And my breast, where each one is bruised in turn,
> Is made to inspire in the poet a love
> Eternal and mute as matter.

> I am throned in the azure like an uncomprehended sphinx;
> I unite a heart of snow with the whiteness of swans;
> I hate motion that displaces lines,
> And I never weep and I never laugh.

> The poets, before my grand attitudes,
> That I seem to borrow from the proudest monuments,
> Will consume their days in austere studies;

For, to fascinate these docile lovers, I have
Pure mirrors that make all things more fair;
My eyes, my wide eyes with their eternal lights!

The eyes of *Les fleurs du mal* are unforgettable reflectors of human moods and sorrows and despairs; but here the wide eyes of Beauty open suddenly to show us lights that are eternal.

In the poem called **"The Ideal"** a more perverse conception of beauty is presented—and it is clearly related to Baudelaire's discussion of his ideal beauty in the **"Skyrockets"** of his *Intimate Journals,* where he writes:

> I have found the definition of the Beautiful,—of what is for me the Beautiful. It is something ardent and sad, something a little vague, leaving room for conjecture.

Applying these ideas to a woman's beautiful and seductive head, Baudelaire describes it as

> a head that makes one dream at the same time— though confusedly—of voluptuous happiness and of sadness; that admits of an idea of melancholy, of lassitude, even of satiety,—or a contrary idea, that is, an ardor, a desire to be alive, associated with a countercurrent of bitterness, as if coming from deprivation or despair. Mystery and regret are also characteristics of the Beautiful.

As for masculine beauty, Baudelaire would find it hard not to conclude "that the most perfect type of virile Beauty is *Satan,*—as Milton saw him."

Thus, in the poem called **"The Ideal,"** when Baudelaire discusses the ideal woman who would satisfy a heart like his, he finds little charm in what he calls the "hospital beauties" of the women in Gavarni's drawings, and he adds (with remarkable imagery):

> For I cannot find among these pale roses
> One flower that resembles my red ideal.

The first stanza in the sestet of the sonnet is of special interest here:

> What this heart, deep as an abyss, needs
> Is you, Lady Macbeth, soul powerful in crime,
> Dream of Aeschylus that has opened [like a flower] in a region of storms.

Here the contrast between the flower of his "red ideal" and the "pale roses" of Gavarni's sickly women is heightened when the poet cites his ideal as Lady Macbeth, a "dream of Aeschylus." This clearly links Lady Macbeth with Clytemnestra, and the two murderesses serve to identify the red in the flower of the Ideal as the color of blood.

In **"Hymn to Beauty,"** Baudelaire develops similar ideas in his conception of Beauty as having a glance both infernal and divine, as being comparable to wine in her good and bad effects, and as being omnipotent and responsible to nothing. Does Beauty come down from deep heaven or up from the abyss? Baudelaire pretends not to care, and notes that Horror is not the least charming of her jewels and that Murder, among her most precious trinkets, dances amorously on her proud belly. The concluding stanzas of the poem sum up a despairing aspect of the function of Beauty in this world:

> Que tu viennes du ciel ou de l'enfer, qu'importe,

> O Beauté, monstre énorme, effrayant, ingénu!
> Si ton œil, ton souris, ton pied, m'ouvrent la porte
> D'un Infini que j'aime et n'ai jamais connu?

> De Satan ou de Dieu, qu'importe? Ange ou Sirène,
> Qu'importe, si tu rends,—fée aux yeux de velours,
> Rhythme, parfum, lueur, ô mon unique reine!—
> L'univers moins hideux et les instants moins lourds?

> (What matter whether you come from heaven or hell,—
> O Beauty! enormous, terrifying, ingenuous monster!
> If your eye, your smile, your foot, open for me the door
> Of an Infinite I love and have never known?

> From Satan or from God, what matter? Angel or Siren,
> What matter—fay with the velvet eyes,
> Rhythm, perfume, light, O my only queen!—
> If you make the universe less hideous and the moments less dull?)

The poet seems here at the last to define the ultimate function of beauty as being merely to help make endurable the terrible boredom of human life. But he suggests that this may be accomplished by her opening a door on the Infinite.

In the consideration of five poems from "Spleen and Ideal" we have thus seen how Baudelaire, in his search for beauty, urged the use of correspondences in both the Swedenborgian and synaesthetic senses—the concept of art as proof of man's essential worth—the idea of the remoteness and austerity of Beauty—the recognition that in human beauty there can be sinister qualities like those in Lady Macbeth and Clytemnestra, and in Satan as Milton saw him—and a belief that such elements as horror and murder can be adornments of Beauty when man seeks it to relieve the boredom of existence and to open a door on the infinite. Here, amidst the strange and perverse elements in Baudelaire's aesthetics, there is still the notion of eternity (Beauty's eyes with their eternal lights, and "an Infinite I love and have never known"); but it may be seen, as we have suggested earlier, as an aesthetics darkened in Baudelaire's terms by the grim shadow of original sin.

In *Les fleurs du mal* sin itself is Baudelaire's most terrible subject, for his Catholic background had left in his thought a peculiarly acute and hopeless sense of the evil in man. Thus his ideas of love and woman were inseparably related to the idea of sin; and the unnatural violence of his thought in this regard is all too clear when, in the *Intimate Journals,* he remarks that "woman is natural, that is to say abominable," refers to "the natural ferocity of love," likens the act of love itself to a torture or a surgical operation, notes that in love the one who loves the less of two lovers or who is the more self-possessed will be the executioner or the surgeon and the other the victim, and observes finally that "the unique and supreme voluptuous pleasure of love lies in the certainty of doing evil."

One is hardly surprised, then, to find love treated most often by Baudelaire from the viewpoint of despair. He seems driven by an agonizing nostalgia of the flesh, but has no hope for consolation or enduring satisfaction. And so it is that he writes in the cycle of poems to his mulatto mistress, Jeanne Duval:

> tu me parais, ornement de mes nuits,
> Plus ironiquement accumuler les lieues
> Qui séparent mes bras des immensités bleues.

(you seem to me, ornament of my nights,
More ironically to increase the leagues
That separate my arms from the blue immensities.)

The harshest epithets in the love poems to his various mistresses show Baudelaire's recurrent misery in sensuality: "impure woman" . . . "drinker of the world's blood" . . . "blind, deaf machine, rich in cruelties" . . . "queen of sins" . . . "vile animal" . . . "vessel of sorrow" . . . "implacable and cruel beast" . . . "pitiless demon."

Yet Baudelaire wrote in a famous letter that "woman is the being who projects the greatest shadow or the greatest light into our dreams. Woman is fatally suggestive; she lives with another life than her own; she lives spiritually in the imaginations that she haunts and enriches." Some of his poems to Marie Daubrun and to Mme Sabatier are Platonic idealizations of woman; and, for Jeanne Duval (along with such bitter and cruel erotic poems as **"Sed non satiata," "The Vampire,"** and **"Duellum"**), we find the voluptuous and tender verses of **"The Balcony."** For all the agony that they experienced together, Jeanne Duval was undoubtedly the person, along with his mother, whom Baudelaire loved most in his life. And so he can write, in the four poems called **"Un fantôme" ("A Ghost"),** long after Jeanne has lost her health and her youth and her beauty, that in the shadows of his unfathomable sorrow a spectral figure takes shape—graceful and shining. When it attains its full form he recognizes Jeanne: "It is She! dark and yet luminous." The perfume of her pure youth seems a magic charm like the scent of incense in a church, and he recalls how jewels and furniture and the materials of her dress all served to set off her voluptuous beauty. Then he remembers her as she is now in reality, ravaged by disease:

> La Maladie et la Mort font des cendres
> De tout le feu qui pour nous flamboya.
> De ces grands yeux si fervents et si tendres,
> De cette bouche où mon cœur se noya,
>
> . . . . .
> Que reste-t-il? . . .
> . . . . .
>
> Noir assassin de la Vie et de l'Art,
> Tu ne tueras jamais dans ma mémoire
> Celle qui fut mon plaisir et ma gloire!

(Illness and Death turn to ashes
All the fire that blazed for us.
What is left now of those great eyes so glowing and tender,
And of that mouth where my heart was drowned. . . .

[O Time!] dark murderer of Life and of Art,
You will never kill in my memory
The woman who was once my pleasure and my glory!)

Baudelaire sees voluptuous enjoyment on the whole as leading to remorse, and he refers to "the whip of Pleasure, that merciless executioner." In a powerful poem called **"Femmes damnées" ("Damned Women"),** one of the six poems condemned by the court, he describes the hellish descent of two Lesbians into a Dantesque Inferno. The rhythms of the original verses are an important part of the hypnotic horror of the poem:

> —Descendez, descendez, lamentables victimes,
> Descendez le chemin de l'enfer éternel!
> Plongez au plus profond du gouffre, où tous les crimes,

> Flagellés par un vent qui ne vient pas du ciel,
> Bouillonnent pêle-mêle avec un bruit d'orage.

(—Descend, descend, lamentable victims,
Descend the road of eternal Hell!
Plunge to the depths of the gulf where all crimes,
Whipped by a wind that is not from the sky,
Come billowing pell-mell with the sound of a storm.)

These are clearly Dante's storm-winds blowing the carnal sinners as they were blown in life by the dark winds of their passions. And so it is, ultimately, always with the sensual pleasures in the thought of Baudelaire.

We have seen earlier, in the verses **"To the Reader,"** the terrible role of Ennui or Spleen in Baudelaire's poems. The "delicate monster's" presence is usually attended by despairful imagery: deserts, frozen suns, green waters of Lethe, spiders and their webs, long funeral processions, lowering skies, sheets of rain that resemble prison bars, the tolling of a cracked bell, the dull sound of falling logs as firewood is unloaded in courtyards at the end of autumn.

One of Baudelaire's most remarkable symbols of boredom—as memorable in its way as Eliot's coffee-spoons—is an old deck of playing-cards, whose Jack of Hearts and Queen of Spades "talk in sinister fashion of their dead loves." But above all in Baudelaire's depiction of boredom there is the image of the slow, inexorable passing of time, which envelops the poet like an immense snowfall or ticks away in a clock's remorseless warnings 3600 times an hour. The supreme horror, amidst the boredom, is that, while to man the taedium of life seems endless, when his time on this earth finally runs out it is too late for repentance. And so the poet writes in his terror at the passing hours:

> The day declines; night comes on; *remember!*
> The abyss is always thirsty; the water-clock runs dry.

Man's dignity for Baudelaire was related to the boundless nature of his longing. In contrast with his friend Gautier who called himself primarily "a man for whom the visible world exists," Baudelaire wrote that through every window he saw only the infinite, and it was this unappeased longing that made him love the sea and that made the idea of the voyage so vital a part of his imagination. He discovered in what he called "the immense, tumultuous, green sea" an image of man and "the humors, the agonies and the ecstasies of all souls who have lived, are living, and will live hereafter!" Yet the sea is not so vast as human longing, and in **"The Voyage,"** his major poem on death, Baudelaire describes how we set out on the rhythm of the wave,

> Berçant notre infini sur le fini des mers. . . .

"cradling the infinite within us on the finite of the seas." The poem is the last of *Les fleurs du mal* and brings to a rather ambiguous conclusion the volume's numerous and varied references to death. The final verses have a strange power, but they leave us still in doubt as to what Baudelaire's ultimate word might be:

> O Mort, vieux capitaine, il est temps! levons l'ancre!
> Ce pays nous ennuie, ô Mort! Appareillons!
> Si le ciel et la mer sont noirs comme de l'encre,
> Nos cœurs que tu connais sont remplis de rayons!
>
> Verse-nous ton poison pour qu'il nous réconforte!
> Nous voulons, tant ce feu nous brûle le cerveau,

Plonger au fond du gouffre, Enfer ou Ciel, qu'importe?
Au fond de l'Inconnu pour trouver du *nouveau!*

(O Death, old Captain, it is time! let us weigh anchor!
This world bores us, O Death! Let us get under way!
If sky and sea are black as ink,
Our hearts that you know are filled with rays of light!

Pour out your poison to comfort us!
We desire, so fiercely this fire burns our brain,
To plunge to the depths of the abyss, what matter whether
    it be Heaven or Hell?
To the depths of the Unknown to find something *new!*)

Now, by way of ending, we come to the part of *Les fleurs du mal* called "Tableaux parisiens" ("Parisian Scenes"), that marvellous division of the poems in which Baudelaire transmits to us over the years his imaginative evocation of the teeming life of the great French capital in the mid-nineteenth century. Paris has changed since then, just as the poet himself wrote of its changing a hundred years ago:

—Le vieux Paris n'est plus (la forme d'une ville
Change plus vite, hélas! que le cœur d'un mortel). . . .

(Old Paris is no more [the form of a city
Changes more swiftly, alas! than a mortal heart]. . . .)

But one has only to recall the first verses of **"Les petites vieilles" ("The Little Old Women")** in the "Tableaux parisiens" to have the wonder and mystery of Baudelaire's Paris rise up before his eyes:

Dans les plis sinueux des vieilles capitales,
Où tout, même l'horreur, tourne aux enchantements. . . .

(In the sinuous folds of old capitals,
Where everything, even horror, turns to enchant-
    ments. . . .)

As I read these lines I see again the Paris of the Latin Quarter as I knew it thirty years ago.

And so it is that Baudelaire's evocation of the Paris of his day in *Les fleurs du mal* survives for us with a strangeness and mystery and beauty unique in literature. Only Villon and Balzac are comparable with him here, and in neither of these great writers is there so brooding and concentrated a spiritual quality as in Baudelaire. The moral and spiritual malaise of an age is in these pages; and it is an uneasiness of the spirit that remains with us, intensified and unrelieved, in our time.

In his *Salon of 1846,* Baudelaire comments on what he calls "a new and special beauty, which is not that of either Achilles or Agamemnon." He found this in Paris, and he wrote of it: "Parisian life is rich in poetic and marvellous subjects. The marvellous envelops us and permeates us like the atmosphere; but we do not see it." Baudelaire identifies here "a new element," which he calls *la beauté moderne* (modern beauty); and in Balzac and his heroes he finds something (greater than in the heroes of the *Iliad*) which he designates under the complex and rather ironic term, "l'héroïsme de la vie moderne" ("the heroism of modern life")—a phrase peculiarly pertinent, in Baudelaire's terms, for our own uneasy age.

In the first of the "Tableaux parisiens" **("Paysages" ["Landscapes"])**, Baudelaire says that he intends to compose his "eclogues" in a garret high above Paris, where he can see the tall church steeples "and the vast skies that make one dream of eternity." Here he can watch the seasonal changes in the great city and see the Parisian mists and the evening star rising and lamps at windows and "the moon pouring out its pale enchantment." In the following poems we have what may be said to constitute a day and a night of Parisian life, a period from sunrise to dawn of the following day (roughly the time-limit of ancient tragedy); and we shall trace briefly here some of its details from the verses of Baudelaire.

In **"Le soleil"** the sun enters, like a kindly father, a poet and a king, to reanimate nature and bring joy and nobility to mankind. Then a red-haired beggar-girl appears ("A une mendiante rousse"), so beautiful, in spite of her rags, that she would have stirred desires in the Valois kings and inspired sonnets in Remy Belleau. But she goes along the street begging, and the poet cannot even afford the cheap trinkets that attract her glance as she passes by.

Baudelaire crosses the street near the Louvre and notices how the Paris he knows is changing **("Le cygne").** Suddenly he thinks of Andromache and of a great white swan he once saw that had escaped from its cage and was dragging its magnificent plumage along the dusty Parisian street. The two beautiful figures, the swan and the lonely, captive widow of Hector—both separated forever from what they love—combine in the poet's mind to form an allegory of exile. He thinks of other lonely figures in the great capital—of a consumptive Negress, walking through the mud and seeking beyond the immense wall of Parisian mist "the absent coconut palms of proud Africa"—of orphaned children who are withering away like flowers—of whoever has lost what can never be found again. And the poem closes on this note of loneliness:

Thus in the forest where my mind is exiled
An old Memory sounds a full blast on the horn!
I think of the sailors forgotten on an island,
Of the captives and the conquered! . . . Of many others,
    besides!

Then, from the mysterious channels of the great city, out of the filthy, yellow mist, a hideous old man appears, bent over at right angles and leaning on a cane **("Les sept vieillards").** He has a beard stiff as a sword-blade, and his eyes are as malignant as if they had been steeped in gall. He is followed by another figure just like him . . . and another . . . and another, until seven sinister old men, all in the same hideous image, walk by with the same step towards an unknown destination. The hallucinative vision leaves the poet close to madness, and he flees to his room and locks himself in, terrified at the possibility of seeing an eighth old man emerge from the Parisian mists.

Sometimes, though, Baudelaire watches the old women of the city **("Les petites vieilles")** with a sympathy that recalls Villon's for La Belle Heaulmière in the shadows of mediaeval Paris so long before. These were the young Parisian women of yesterday. They move now like marionettes, their bodies broken, misshapen, and shrunken by the years. Baudelaire writes, "Let us love them. They are still souls." Their eyes are young like those of little girls full of wonder at everything that shines; but yet they are "wells made of a million tears." These are the beautiful actresses, the faithful and faithless wives, the martyred mothers of other days. Children and drunk men make fun of them, and no one greets them kindly as they suffer in their strange destinies. They are human wreckage, "ripe for eternity." The poet follows them very tenderly in his thought, for they seem to be his family; and he bids them each evening a solemn farewell, thinking it may indeed be the last. And so he wonders in the final verses of the poem:

> Where will you be tomorrow, octogenarian Eves,
> Upon whom weighs the awful claw of God?

Next some of the blind people of Paris pass by (**"Les aveugles"**) with their faces turned forever upward toward the heavens—"terrible, strange, like sleepwalkers" as they go through their "unbounded darkness, that brother of eternal silence." But, for all their suffering, Baudelaire finds himself even more lost than they; and, amidst the wild uproar of Paris trying to amuse itself, he wonders what it is that all those blind people seek in the sky.

Suddenly, a beautiful woman appears in the crowd (**"A une passante"**) and disappears like a lightning-flash, leaving behind awakened and unfulfilled longings. Then, in the bookstalls along the quays, the poet discovers an anatomy chart with skeletons digging in the earth (**"Le squelette laboureux"**), and he wonders grimly whether there is, after all, any rest for mankind even in death.

At last twilight comes over Paris (**"Le crépuscule du soir"**), bringing solace to suffering and rest to the weary scholars and working men. But it is the hour also that awakens unhealthy demons in the great city. Prostitution lights up in the streets and is busy in its mysterious ways. Kitchens hiss with evening meals, and one hears the sounds of the theatres and orchestras. Gambling halls are filled with swindlers and courtesans, and merciless thieves set about breaking into houses and strong-boxes to gain their livelihood and buy their women clothes. But the poet summons his soul to turn inward upon itself in this darkening hour. Night is coming on, and in the hospitals some will never again be home with those they love; but most of them have never had a home and never really been alive.

The scene shifts to a gambling hall (**"Le jeu"**) where dishonored men and women watch feverishly the fate of their games; and, in spite of their degradation, the poet envies them their preference for suffering to death and hell to nothingness.

Then comes a "Danse Macabre" drawn from a figurine by the sculptor Ernest Christophe. Here a coquettish female skeleton, whose deep eyes are "made of emptiness and shadows," weaves flowers about her skull as she prepares for "the universal swing of the dance of death."

An indolent beauty passes by (**"L'amour du mensonge"**), and her ripe loveliness reminds the poet that melancholy eyes often conceal a nullity deeper and more empty than the heavens. But he worships her beauty, however stupid or indifferent she may be.

He recalls the small white house where he lived as a child and the late sunlight falling over the long, silent dinners there; and he remembers a serving-woman who loved him long ago in his childhood. She is dead now, and he thinks how lonely the dead must be when October winds blow over the Parisian cemeteries and when the winter snows begin to melt away. He wonders what he could say to the dead woman if some cold, blue December night he should find her in a chair by the fire with tears falling from her empty eyes.

When the mists and rains of late autumn come (**"Brumes et pluies"**) and one hears the rusty weathercocks turning in the long nights, Baudelaire imagines the pleasures of love lulling his grief in the moonless dark. Then he has a strange vision (**"Rêve parisien"**) that seems to come from an opium dream. The whole countryside is without vegetation, and one sees monotonously only metal, marble and water. There are stairways and arcades, pools and waterfalls. Space is limitless, and one comes upon unheard-of precious stones and magic flowers, vast rivers, and gulfs of diamonds. All things seem crystal-clear, and over the whole vision there hovers "(Everything for the eye, nothing for the ears) A silence of eternity." But when he awakens it is the horrible present in his wretched room, and his clock is striking the hour.

The last poem of the series is called **"Le crépuscule du matin" ("Morning Twilight")**. Reveille sounds in the barracks, and the morning wind blows on the lanterns. This is the hour when the brown adolescents toss on their pillows because of their dreams. The first lamps are lighted. The air is full of the sound of things fleeing away, "and man is weary of writing and woman of love." Smoke comes from chimneys, and the women of pleasure sleep stupidly with open mouths. The poor stir up their fires and blow on their cold fingers, and women in childbirth have the added sufferings of cold and nagging want. A cockcrow in the distance sounds like a sob cut off by blood. Mist rises like a sea around the buildings. People are dying in the hospitals. The roués return home, broken by their search for pleasure; and, as the rose and green dawn comes shivering up the deserted Seine, sombre Paris rubs its eyes and, like a hard-working old man, picks up its tools for the new day's toil.

In *Les fleurs du mal* Baudelaire affords us an unforgettable representation of the beauty and sadness and confusion and suffering of what he called "the heroism of modern life." His dark view of man and the human situation and his own spiritual, moral and physical anguish clearly lie behind the poems, whose strange and at times perverse beauty we have considered in some detail. . . . Yet beyond the sufferings and despair and boredom in *Les fleurs du mal* we find still an ardent spirituality and a consciousness, however dim and wavering, of eternal values. If we see the poems as Flowers of Evil and Flowers of Suffering we must recall that Baudelaire still recognized in man's nature the mark of the infinite and that he did not see human suffering merely in terms of sterile misery.

Evelyn Underhill, in her beautiful book on *Mysticism*, refers to suffering as "the 'gymnastic of Eternity,' the 'terrible initiative caress of God,' " and notes that "the highest types have accepted it eagerly and willingly, have found in Pain the grave but kindly teacher of immortal secrets, the conferer of liberty, even the initiator into amazing joys." Baudelaire did not attain completely to such mystical understanding; but he realized, as a great poet must, the relationship between suffering and the creation of beauty, and he wrote of it that "it is one of the prodigious privileges of Art that . . . *suffering* (*"la douleur"*) put to rhythm and cadence may fill the mind with a calm *joy.*" It is significant here that Baudelaire underlines both *joy* and *suffering* as if to further emphasize their inter-relationship.

For Baudelaire there was a dignity and even a purifying grace in human suffering, and he depicts it on occasion, as we have seen, with a profound understanding and sympathy that seem to me unique in the literature of his age and perhaps, apart from Villon, unique in the whole of French letters. He proclaims suffering the only nobility that earth and hell cannot erode; and he writes of it in the poem called **"Benediction"**:

> —Soyez béni, mon Dieu, qui donnez la souffrance
> Comme un divin remède à nos impuretés
> Et comme la meilleure et la plus pure essence
> Qui prépare les forts aux saintes voluptés!
>
> (Praised may you be, my God, who give suffering
> As a divine remedy for our impurities
> And as the best and purest essence
> That prepares those who are strong for holy joys!)

In incomplete verses intended as an epilogue for the second edition of his poems Baudelaire tells of his love for the city of Paris and of its "taste for the infinite"; and he calls upon its angels, dressed in purple, hyacinth and gold, to

> . . . be witnesses that I have done my duty
> like a perfect chemist and like a holy soul.

Then he turns to the city itself for the last two lines:

> Car j'ai de chaque chose extrait la quintessence,
> Tu m'as donné ta boue et j'en ai fait de l'or.
>
> (For I have from each thing extracted its quintessence,
> You gave me your mire and I changed it to gold.)

(pp. 13-34)

> *Alfred Garvin Engstrom, "Charles Baudelaire (1821-1867) and the Alchemy of 'Les fleurs du mal',"* in his *Darkness and Light: Lectures on Baudelaire, Flaubert, Nerval, Huysmans, Racine, and Time and Its Images in Literature, Romance Monographs, Inc., 1975, pp. 11-34.*

Alex de Jonge   (essay date 1976)

[*De Jonge is an English biographer and critic. In the following excerpt from his critical biography of Baudelaire, de Jonge examines* The Flowers of Evil *as a collection of poems with a unifying narrative framework.*]

In the first edition of **Les fleurs du mal,** Baudelaire was still uncertain of the book's focus. Although it would not take final shape until 1861, it is appropriate to consider it in its revised, and final, form. The book is much more than a collection of poems, as Baudelaire very clearly pointed out in a letter to Alfred de Vigny. He wrote that the only praise he wanted for his work was the recognition that it was not an anthology, but a coherent work with a beginning and an end. Indeed, the work tells a story. Although it consists of poems written at various times and for various reasons, Baudelaire had rearranged them to make a kind of narrative. The restriction of his medium prevents him from achieving the kind of continuity and development we expect from prose fiction. At times the story line is very clear, at others the focus softens and the narrative element remains in the background. Moreover, the attempt to tell a kind of story through a series of individual poems makes for a certain jerkiness of narrative rhythm. It is as if we were seeing not a film, with smooth linking passages, but a series of still photographs flashed on a screen in a set order. Each picture can stand alone, but the spectator is also free to associate them and make a story out of their arrangement.

Les fleurs du mal is the story of a life, but not necessarily of Baudelaire's life. Baudelaire believed that art must be much more than self-expression. The artist must use his experience to pass beyond it, to try to capture the quintessence of his age through his art. It is only when poetry goes beyond the personal to achieve universality that it aspires to greatness.

Baudelaire composed many of the poems of **Les fleurs** in response to his own experiences—his love of Jeanne, his reaction to Marie Daubrun's betrayal. But this is by no means true of all the poems. There is no reason to believe that he was ever a Satanist or that he frequently associated with lesbians. Many of the pieces were written to fit the narrative framework of the book. Even those that were initially more personal take on a new function when fitted into **Les fleurs du mal.** They develop the narrative, rather than act as a medium for self-expression. Although Baudelaire has integrated his most intimate and painful experiences, the book goes beyond these to become a poetic allegory. It is a *Pilgrim's Progress* in reverse, but Baudelaire is no more its hero than Bunyan was Mister Christian.

The book tells the story of its protagonist from birth to just before death. It is the story of his self-destruction and of the reasons for it. The protagonist, like Baudelaire, seeks to fulfill his craving for idealism the lazy way—through sensation. He learns, to his cost, that such intensity of sensation is subject to the law of diminishing returns—an ever-increasing dose is needed to provoke an ever-fainter response. By the time he has learned that harsh lesson he is doomed. There is nothing left for him but to try to exult in the inevitability of his own complete destruction.

The introduction reminds us that we are reading our own life story. The protagonist is not any one individual, he is modern man. Baudelaire saw the craving for sensation as the supreme characteristic of his age. Hence his freaks' gallery of lesbians, drunkards, and sex criminals all striving desperately for a fulfillment they cannot find. In short, Baudelaire has composed the first handbook on the psychology—and the poetry—of absolute addiction, "the habit." He does not tie himself down to any particular opiate; he spells out, in general and poetic terms, the anatomy of addiction of any and every kind.

The book is also a study in evil. Evil for Baudelaire was rarely so obviously the devil's work that it smelled of sulfur. Satanism as such plays a modest part in **Les fleurs du mal.** Satan prefers to remain behind the scenes, yet it is he who encourages our readiness to indulge our sloth, indolence, and thirst for sensation—at the expense of our spirituality and concentration. Baudelaire believed man to be a divided creature; set halfway between heaven and hell, man combines characteristics of them both:

> In all men, at all times, there are two simultaneous postulations, one towards God, the other towards Satan. The Invocation to God, or spirituality, is a

desire to elevate oneself; that to Satan, or animality, a delight in descent.

Baudelaire believed in the devil as he believed in his *guignon* ["bad luck"], and in the likelihood of his own damnation for absolute gracelessness and spiritual disorder:

> I have always been obsessed by the impossibility of accounting for certain sudden thoughts and actions in man, without the hypothesis of the intervention of an evil force external to him. There is a great confession which the entire nineteenth century conspiring against me will not make me ashamed of!

Indeed, it was history's refusal to recognize the intervention of the devil that made the composition of *Les fleurs du mal* necessary. A note he wrote for the preface reads:

> The Devil. Original sin. Man good. . . . It is harder to love God than to believe in Him. On the contrary, it is harder for the people of this age to believe in the devil than to love him. Everybody feels him and no one believes in him. Sublime subtlety of the devil.

Moreover, modern man was quite capable of sinning anew, after a moment's tearful repentance, with the reassuring conviction that he was in a state of grace; believing in good, he cheerfully did evil.

Les fleurs du mal was divided into six sections of varying length: "Spleen et idéal," "Tableaux parisiens," "Le vin," "Les fleurs du mal," "Révolte," and "La mort."

"Spleen et idéal" opens with a birth. In a parody of the Annunciation a mother curses her son and God for having chosen her of all women to give birth to a monster. However the monster, or poet, grows up under the tutelage of a guardian angel. He knows he will have to suffer, but as a poet he will achieve nobility and spirituality through suffering.

The earliest poems of the section deal with the young poet, who is only at home when soaring above base reality. He understands the secret doctrine of correspondences, and can see the world in terms of harmony and meaning. He has a sense of idealism and spirituality.

Almost at once, however, he begins to lose a grip on spiritual truths. His imagination dwells increasingly on grotesque and violent images. He still believes in the high spirituality of art, but that art has become the art of decadence.

Degeneration goes a stage further with a series of poems, among them **"Le guignon,"** which describes the failure of his own art. Inspiration, high seriousness, spirituality have all left him, he can no longer sustain his efforts. But even though he can no longer create it himself, he still retains a love of beauty. Beauty, however, has grown fatally ambiguous: it could be a promise of hell or of heaven, divine or infernal. He elects, in a fatal decision, to disregard that ambiguity. Any beauty will do provided that it supplies sensations strong enough to relieve his boredom. The choice is made: he has committed himself to the dark side of beauty and henceforward his life will consist of a perpetual search for satisfaction, through sensations which can only aggravate, never satisfy, his need.

Next comes the Black Venus cycle, the poems written to Jeanne Duval, in which the protagonist has turned from beauty to sex. Their tone varies from languid sensual evocations of sexual fulfillment in pieces such as **"Parfum exotique"** or **"La chevelure"** (**"Hair"**) to violent attacks upon the sexual cruelty of his woman, as in **"Tu mettrais l'univers entier dans tu ruelle"** (**"You Would Place the Whole Universe in Your Alley"**). **"Une charogne"** (**"A Rotting Corpse"**), perhaps the most remarkable piece of the cycle, reconciles the two main strains of adoration and disgust. The poet evokes a rotting carcass, legs in the air, and describes its malodorous maggot-ridden appearance in strangely gentle detail. He then turns to his woman in a blend of savagery and confidence, telling her that one day she too will rot; and yet—through the medium of his poetry—he will have preserved the form and divine essence of his decomposing lover. It is a violent and, at first sight, shocking poem, but also a superb example of what Baudelaire means by drawing beauty from horror. Its theme is the poet's ability to transcend the pathetically short life of the flesh and create immortality through great art. Its music, its texture are extraordinarily beautiful. The very savagery of the description of the corpse is mitigated by the control of artistic form. Baudelaire could create horror through his art, but he did so only to take his readers beyond that horror.

Next comes the White Venus cycle, the poems dedicated to Mme Sabatier, followed by those to his Green-eyed Venus, Marie Daubrun. The tone of individual poems oscillates: moments of ecstasy are qualified by poems which bring the protagonist down to flat and stale reality; longings for peace are qualified by professions of irrefutable sinfulness; moments of calm, by sadistic fantasies.

The focus then softens, and it is here that we find some of the poet's greatest and most melancholy poems. The protagonist is now so dulled by sensation that he can no longer either enjoy or provoke it. He is left alone with the dreadful consciousness of time's passing. He longs for death and oblivion, yet succumbs to fits of helpless rage. Overwhelmed by a thirst for vengeance, he has no victim on whom to wreak his revenge. He can only get drunk on dreams of hate and violence, but hate can never procure oblivion.

These savage pictures of spiritual and emotional devastation are succeeded by four poems with the same leaden title—**"Spleen."** They depict a terrible emptiness, as the clock ticks on, rain falls and a smoky log fire burns in the hearth. The protagonist is "king of a rainy country." Young, yet dreadfully old, nothing amuses him anymore—neither women, nor his jester, nor the hunt, nor even his people dying at his feet. What is the reason for his terrible condition? It is that instead of blood, the waters of forgetfulness run through his veins.

This is an important comment on the quest for fulfillment through sensation. Since the addict cannot maintain a state of perpetual physical excitement, he becomes dependent on his memory, upon the ability to recreate excitement in the mind. As long as he can do so, he can, to some extent, leave his perpetual search for new stimuli by escaping into memory. Some of the finest poems in *Les fleurs du mal* describe peace and serenity achieved through remembrance—but now even memory has failed him. Unlike the artist, the pure sensation seeker, be he pervert, alcoholic, drug addict, or gambler, has no memory. If he could recreate in his mind the texture of past experiences he would not always be obliged to renew experience. But he can do nothing of the sort, and is doomed to take another little drink as soon as he comes round from the last bout.

The last poems of "Spleen et idéal" portray the protagonist's realization of what he has done. He has so abused his responses that he has destroyed his capacity to feel or remember. He can only long for oblivion, cultivate self-destruction to escape from the remorseless passage of time. Accordingly he wallows in sado-masochistic fantasy. He looks to pain for stimulus and is indifferent to whether he receives or inflicts it. The section culminates in the full recognition of his own damnation, a black picture with only a single point of illumination—the ironic, infernal lantern of "consciousness in evil." The last poem, **"L'horloge" ("The Clock")**, is a final reminder that time is passing and life wasted. At any moment it may be too late to repent for it will be time to die.

"Spleen et idéal" is a remorseless study in the destruction of an individual through his quest for fulfillment in the world of sensation. He abuses his spirituality, commits sins, destroys his capacity to feel and to remember what he has felt, and is left a wasted, burned-out hulk waiting for death.

With the next section, "Tableaux parisiens," the focus softens. This series of poems, loosely based on the theme of the modern city, provide a backdrop to the drama just enacted. *Les fleurs du mal* is not the story of Everyman; it is the story of modern man living in the infernal world of the big city, a place of exile and of loss. Drawing inspiration from city life, the poems paint pictures of loneliness, loss, and hallucination. In **"Les sept vieillards" ("The Seven Old Men")**, the poet, wandering through the narrow twisting streets of old Paris in the fog, sees a succession of identical, grotesque old men, which brings him to the verge of insanity. He then evokes a chance encounter with a woman whose eyes he catches in the crowd; he knows that he could have loved her, but she is swept away before they can meet. Elsewhere he portrays a gambling den, prostitutes, grotesque statues, even an evocation of a drug-induced vision of Paris as a Piranesi-like confusion of elaborate architectural shapes with still-frozen fountains.

"Le vin" is a short section reflecting the poet's belief that drunkenness was a characteristic phenomenon of the age—and one of his own weaknesses. It opens with a favorable view of wine: wine as the working man's solace, a source of consoling illusions to the ragpicker who would be king. But wine too turns sour. **"Le vin de l'assassin" ("The Wine of the Assassin")** describes an exultant drunken murderer; the assassin is free and happy at last. Having just pushed his nagging wife down a well, he breathes deeply the air of his release and drinks to celebrate it. That night he will drink himself into oblivion and lie down in the road, only to have a cart come along and crush the life out of him. The last poem of the section, **"Le vin des amants" ("Lovers' Wine")**, is the most subtle. It is apparently a splendid celebration of drunken lovers, yet they are less fulfilled than they seem. Although they believe they are in harmony, each lover pursues a parallel course.

"Les fleurs du mal" describes the desperate measures to

which sensation seeking drives the addict. Its tone is perverse and sadistic—a love of pain and destruction of the self and others dominates. **"Une martyre" ("A Martyr")** is the strongest of all Baudelaire's evocations of secret and perverse eroticism, with its boudoir of heady perfumes, its headless, bleeding corpse, the legs spread wide, and its killer who even then could not satisfy the immensity of his desire. This note of perversion is continued with the lesbian poems, the lesbians representing aggravated and frustrated appetite.

Baudelaire takes his view of the essential hollowness of sexual pleasure a stage further with **"Un voyage à Cythère,"** a poem based partly on Watteau's *Embarquement pour Cythère* and the expectations those ladies and gentlemen entertain as they set off, and partly upon Gérard de Nerval's account of an imaginary voyage to the island of love, and what he found there—a three-branched gibbet. The emblem is enough to spark off Baudelaire's enduring disgust at the animality of sex and the banal fantasies of sexual expectation. His character has the highest hopes of the island of Venus, only to find it a sad, dark place—"the banal Eldorado of old bachelors"—in no way does it live up to its Watteauesque promise. A corpse hangs from the gibbet, eaten by dogs, pecked by birds. As the protagonist observes the wretched carcass he realizes that his own body is ravaged by no less painful forces; he ends the piece with a prayer to God, begging for the strength and the courage to contemplate his own heart and body without disgust.

The next section, "Révolte," earned Baudelaire the reputation of a Satanist, and procured such unwelcome admirers as the Great Beast, Aleister Crowley. Baudelaire was nothing of the sort. "Révolte," although blasphemous, is a phase in the development not of Baudelaire, but of his protagonist. After exhausting all other modes of perversion, only to recognize the futility of sexual experience, and having damned himself in the process, the protagonist has little left. Accordingly he turns to metaphysical perversion, and adores the evil principle that has engineered his destruction. If he is irredeemably damned he may as well get what he can from that damnation. It must be said that the three poems that make up this section are not among his most successful. They are shot through with a note of hysterical strain that makes them monotonously unmodulated. One, however, **"Le reniement de Saint-Pierre" ("The Abjuration of St. Peter")**, contains a line that explains the mood of frustration and dissatisfaction that runs right through *Les fleurs du mal.* The protagonist declares himself all too happy to leave "un monde où l'action n'est pas la soeur du rêve." "A world in which action is not sister to the dream" is the perfect description of Baudelaire's sense of the reality in which he had his being. Now he understood that that reality—the crass reality of nineteenth-century France—could never match his expectations. Hence his striving for escape and fulfillment out of this world, a striving that could only lead to self-destruction.

The final poem of "Révolte" is a prayer to Satan. It is the only piece of actual devil worship in the entire book, but it is the piece which has consolidated Baudelaire's enduring reputation as a Satanist. It is simply the poem of a loser, with nothing left but to adore the cause of his own loss. At least that can give the derisory illusion that he retains some control, some responsibility for his plight. Rather than reeking of evil and the black masses it is a pathetic poem, the work of someone with nothing else left to turn to. Satan is the only game in town.

"Révolte" was the ultimate surge towards destruction, the attempt to collaborate in the damnation of an immortal soul. Yet it is not the end. The final section, "La mort" ("Death"), is marked by a new calm and serenity. The first piece, **"La mort des amants" ("Lovers' Death"),** is a reply to **"Le vin des amants,"** in which death brings the couple a genuine harmony. No longer in pursuit of parallel fantasies, their two hearts beat as one; in a languorous death they find serenity and the promise of salvation. Death is also the consolation of the poor; it keeps them alive, enables them to get through their day. For artists it is the final hope. They exhaust their lives in clowning and histrionics in the pathetic attempt to capture beauty. Their one hope is that death itself may provide inspiration where life has failed them. The penultimate poem, **"Le rêve d'un curieux,"** reveals a last flicker of anxiety. The protagonist dreams that he dies—but death, far from providing the revelation he longs for, is yet another disappointment. Death is nothing, and he is waiting still.

The last poem, **"Le voyage,"** is also Baudelaire's greatest. Written while he was staying with his mother in Honfleur, and a reflection of the peace and clarity of vision he achieved there, it crystalizes the movement of the entire book, giving it that precision of focus which it lacked in its original form. Travelers set off into a world that seems great with promise, only to make the bitter discovery that it is not. They are disappointed, finding nothing to assuage their curiosity; some settle for intoxication, but the real searchers travel on, for traveling's sake. Nothing can match their restlessness because they crave for an experience out of this world, and their dissatisfaction is heroic. All they find is violent and futile appetite; delusion after delusion and never any rest. In its despair, the poetry has the tonality of Wagner's *Flying Dutchman*. Imagination makes every landfall an Eldorado in anticipation, but in reality the landfall is only a barren reef. The most glorious sunsets, the richest cities offer no contentment. The travelers see nothing but the unchanging spectacle of immortal sin: mankind living stupidly through sensation, and damning itself in the process.

Yet the traveler does achieve something—the something the protagonist has achieved in the course of *Les fleurs du mal.* He has learned not to be taken in by promises of satisfaction in this world. Such promises can only deceive. He will henceforward turn his back on hope and lotus eating. The lesson has been a costly one. The protagonist has been to the extremes of self-destruction, and come back. He has learned to abandon hope of fulfillment and achieved the only serenity possible, a serenity born of despair. He is now ready to greet death:

> Death, old captain, it is time! Let's hoist the anchor!
> This country bores us, Death! Let us set sail!
> If sky and sea may be as black as ink
> Our hearts, as you know, are filled with light!
>
> Pour us your poison that it may comfort us!
> We wish, so fiercely does that fire burn our brain,
> To plunge to the depths of the gulf, Heaven or Hell, what matter,
> To the depths of the Unknown to find something *new!*

> O Mort, vieux capitaine, il est temps! levons l'ancre!
> Ce pays nous ennuie, ô Mort! Appareillons!
> Si le ciel et la mer sont noirs comme de l'encre,
> Nos coeurs que tu connais sont remplis de rayons!
>
> Verse-nous ton poison pour qu'il nous reconforte!
> Nous voulons, tant ce feu nous brûle le cerveau,
> Plonger au fond du gouffre, Enfer ou Ciel, qu'importe?
> A fond de l'Inconnu pour trouver du nouveau!

This, the ending of *Les fleurs du mal,* is profoundly ambiguous. Baudelaire was reluctant to examine his truths too closely. On the one hand it suggests that the protagonist has learned nothing. Like Baudelaire himself, he remains to the end a perverse victim, indifferent to the alternatives of damnation and salvation. He simply looks forward to death as to the "big one," the definitive sensation which cannot disappoint. Yet there is another, optimistic interpretation. The protagonist has reached serenity. Free of the treadmill of sensation he has learned that life cannot satisfy his craving. In that escape from striving he has achieved release from sin itself to achieve otherworldliness. His inner being is purified and ablaze with light. Heaven and hell are simply earthly concepts, and through death he will achieve a new life which will transcend such distinctions. It is an interpretation in tune with Baudelaire's own desperate optimism, the optimism which made him attempt suicide because he had an immortal soul and "he hoped." It is not possible to make a clear choice between the two readings. Baudelaire himself is hesitant, unable to reconcile the optimism and the despair which struck such a strange balance in his being. At all events his was not the kind of ruthless personality which would destroy optimism if it threatened clarity of thought and feeling. He would rather retain ambiguity than destroy hope.

It should be remembered that the poem deals not with Baudelaire but with his protagonist. The point is important. Very early on the latter turned his back on poetry. Baudelaire has given the protagonist some but not all the aspects of his own self. He has kept back the lion's share—the ability to turn his own hopeless sinfulness and self-destruction into some of the most beautiful and spiritual poems in the language. The poet believed in all sincerity that in the writing of poetry lay his own salvation. By a typically Baudelairian paradox he tells the story of the steady self-destruction of his protagonist, and ensures his own salvation by using the fate of his protagonist to inspire a string of beautiful poems. The protagonist, or Baudelaire the man, may go under, but Baudelaire the poet is saved, redeemed by his own artistic achievement.

The secret of Baudelaire's art, and indeed of his otherwise utterly miserable life, lies in this conception of poetry. It was for him a kind of alchemy, a spiritualizing process. By dint of intense concentration of all that was good and noble in him, he believed he could convert the squalor and ugliness of his world, his circumstances, and his inner self into the spiritual perfection of art. God kept a place for poets, and as long as Baudelaire believed in poetry, the author of this "atrocious book" and the subject of this atrocious life could never be damned. This is what Baudelaire means when he calls beauty a religion. When he composed *Les fleurs du mal* he believed passionately in the power of art to transmute evil into good. He makes this abundantly clear in one of his projected prefaces. Addressing Paris, the infernal city and his great inspiration, he writes a ringing phrase which is also, with a little luck, his own epitaph:

> You gave me your mud
> And I made it into gold.
>
> (pp. 159-68)

Alex de Jonge, in his Baudelaire, Prince of Clouds: A Biography, *The Paddington Press Limited, 1976, 240 p.*

Reinhard Kuhn   (essay date 1976)

[*Kuhn is a German-born American critic and translator. In the following excerpt from his* Demon of Noontide: Ennui in Western Literature, *he examines Baudelaire's perception of ennui as reflected in* La fanfarlo *and* The Flowers of Evil.]

The triumph of the artist over ennui is not an easy one. In his early short story, *La fanfarlo* (1847), Baudelaire analyzed the difficulties involved by depicting an artist who failed to overcome them. His Samuel Cramer, an ironic autoportrait, had passed through what Baudelaire dismisses as "the good old days of romanticism," during which he had composed his one volume of poetry, *The Ospreys.* To justify himself and his contemporaries for writing such melancholy verses instead of celebrating "the health and joys of the honest man," Cramer invokes a fatal and hereditary predestination: "Woe, three times woe upon the infirm fathers who made us ill-shaped and misbegotten, predestined as we are to give birth only to the still-born." It is the fault of the sickly children of the century that the new poets are stunted and incapable of producing life. These tainted forefathers are to blame that, after the initial publication of his abortions, Cramer succumbs to ennui and ceases to write. At best his interlocutor, blinded by the dazzling light of the fire, can momentarily envision him as the god of sterility:

> The sun of sloth that ceaselessly shone within him, vaporized and corroded that part of genius with which heaven had endowed him. . . . Samuel was a sickly and fantastic creature . . . who, around one o'clock in the morning between the bedazzlement of a pit-coal fire and the tick-tock of a clock, always appeared to me like the god of impotence—a modern hermaphroditic god—an impotence so colossal that in its enormity it is epic.

Like Lazare, Cramer is capable only of unexecuted projects; even his attempt to make of his own life a work of art is doomed to failure. This modern hermaphrodite is not the god of sterility Baudelaire was to celebrate in his works of maturity nor is his impotence really of superhuman proportions. He is incapable of such negative grandeur. Baudelaire sardonically informs us at the end of the novella that Samuel Cramer has settled down with his mistress, La Fanfarlo, engendered a set of twins, composed useful studies on such topics as a new system of advertisement, and become involved in politics. . . . Unable to live with metaphysical ennui, he has become a part of a utilitarian society that functions within ennui.

In the prelude to *The Flowers of Evil* (1857) and in its opening section, "Spleen and Ideal," Baudelaire elevates ennui to the epic stature that Samuel Cramer had been unable to attain. In these poems the delicate monster of spleen becomes capable of reducing the world to a rubble heap, of swallowing the entire earth in an immense yawn, and finally of rivaling immortality:

> Nothing equals in length the lamed days,
> When under the heavy flakes of snow-bound years,
> Ennui, fruit of bleak incuriosity,
> Takes on the proportions of immortality.

The tone of the "spleen" poems, dominated by the spirit of the impotent colossus, is as uniformly somber as that of the verses of Leopardi. The burden of the past is an intolerable one, and the poet's brain is nothing but a vast mausoleum: "It is a pyramid, an immense cellar, / that contains more corpses than the potter's field." Time is as fleeting as the past is cumbersome, and the inexorable frost of ennui is upon the poet:

> Soon we shall plunge into the chilly shadows,
> Farewell, bright clarity of our summers too brief!
> Already I hear the funereal thuds of the wood
> Falling, resounding on the pavement of the courtyards.

The familiar and normally reassuring sound of wood being piled up in provision for winter, transformed into the funereal thuds of a scaffold being constructed and a coffin being nailed together, becomes menacing and ominous. In another poem from this series the spirit, "moaning and prey to long ennui," is imprisoned in the "humid dungeon" of the world. Ennui and despair become universal phenomena transcending the individual sufferer:

> —And long trains of hearses, without drums or music,
> Slowly march past in my soul; Hope,
> Conquered weeps, while atrocious despotic Anguish
> Plants on my bowed skull its black flag.

The despair of the mind in agony becomes the despair of the cosmos. Baudelaire is preparing the way for the funeral dirges that Jules Laforgue will compose in honor of the death of the world.

In "Spleen and Ideal" Baudelaire simultaneously evokes the monster of ennui and explores the various means of combating it. There is love in its various forms, mystic and angelic, perverse and bestial, culminating in the fury of sadomasochism in which the Baudelairian *homo duplex,* the remorseful executioner and the impassive juggler, can find momentary relief. The mistress whose "mysterious rage" inspires her to grant him both "the bite and the kiss" can apparently cure him:

> My soul cured by you,
> By you, light and color!
> Explosion of warmth
> In my black Siberia!

This eruption of warmth capable of illuminating the somber land of exile is only a momentary palliative; love, even in its extreme forms, cannot permanently melt the Siberian ice. It does, however, lead to another solution, very similar to the one proposed by Stendhal, namely, salvation through art. Not just idealized love, but even the most sordid passion, can lead to reverie, and any woman can serve as the catalyst for a creative imagination capable of transforming mud into gold. In the alembic of the dreamer the body is sublimated, and the repulsive physical form of a decaying prostitute can become the springboard for dreams. In the same fashion, the poet can find in the blue-black tresses of Jeanne Duval an entire poetic universe, "A whole world, distant, absent, almost defunct." The work of art, the product of transmutation that can find its matter as easily in the putrefying carcass of a horse as in the body of a woman, represents salvation. It becomes an illuminated lighthouse "casting light over a thousand citadels." Baudelaire considers the work of art as a beacon that can guide man, lost in the night of ennui, between the shoals. Such creation, however, requires an extraordinary effort of the will, which is itself constantly menaced by ennui. The "I" is always in danger of being vaporized and thus dispersed; it becomes subject to an enervating lethargy that makes the slightest effort impossible. It is this disintegration of the will, the cracking of the soul, that renders the poet incapable of curing himself through art and casts doubt upon the efficacy of the aesthetic solution. Baudelaire compares himself unfavorably with "the bell with the vigorous voice," which despite its age is alert and healthy and stands guard faithfully:

> As for me, my soul is cracked, and when in its ennui,
> It wants to people the cold night air with its songs,
> It often happens that its enfeebled voice
>
> Resembles the thick death rattle of a forgotten invalid,
> At the edge of a lake of blood, under a great pile of dead,
> Who dies without moving, with immense efforts.

The discouragement inspired by spleen leads to the bleak ending of "Spleen and Ideal," to the irremediable ticking of a clock that is a "sinister, frightful, and impassive god." The beacon of art is extinguished and replaced by the satanic light that is consciousness in evil. The opposition between ennui and a higher reality, which forms the substance of "Spleen and Ideal," ends with the draining of the clepsydra, with the running dry of the water clock that occurs simultaneously with the realization that it is forever too late.

In the finale of this chapter the epic god of impotence triumphs over love and art, and the vigorous bell is silenced. The artificial paradises of aesthetic intoxication and amorous warmth are but the antechambers of hell. Despite the crushing weight of discouragement, the poet is not yet vanquished; in the later poems of *The Flowers of Evil,* he proposes no less than three efficacious arms against ennui. The first of these is evoked in **"The Swan,"** in which a higher form of love enables the poet to transcend himself. The opening words, "Andromaque, I think of you!", indicate that the poet has turned from the narcissistic contemplation of the self toward the other. This self-oblivion is sufficient to restore his failing creative powers. The meditation upon the factitious stream, swollen by the widow's tears, "suddenly fecundated my fertile memory." The Andromaque of the past and the captured swan of the present become for him tragic symbols of exile, and through a natural association of ideas evoke all those others who dream with nostalgia of what they have forever lost. The poet opens his heart to all those who have been banished:

> Thus in the forest of my spirit's exile
> An old memory sounds ringing the horn!
> I think of sailors forgotten on an island,
> Of the captives, of the vanquished, . . . and of many others.

The poet's carnal love for the mulatto Jeanne Duval has been transformed into an immense and disinterested passion for "the emaciated, phthisical negress." By turning outward, Baudelaire has been able to overcome his own misery through the compassion that he feels for the sufferings of others. Memory is no longer an intolerable burden but a clarion call that can rally fellow sufferers. The pity in which the poet embraces mankind excludes no one.

By turning away from himself, Baudelaire also becomes sensitive to the reality of the external world and to the beauty of being, which he celebrates in the "Parisian Tableaux." His description of a Parisian dawn opens with the dramatic joyfulness of a flourish of trumpets ringing in the courtyards and with the refreshing morning breeze extinguishing the lanterns of the night: "Reveille was singing in the barracks courtyards, / And the matinal wind was blowing against the lanterns." The vision that follows is an all-inclusive one of prematinal activities, centered around the critical struggle between life and death. The joyous note prevails, for dawn is the moment of renewal, the moment when the fresh air effaces all traces of suffering: "Like a tear-stained face dried by the breezes, / The air is suffused with the shiver of fleeting things." This is also a moment of the highest gravity when women in labor give birth and moribund patients die. In the midst of the multitudinous activities, which, whether trivial or weighty, all assume a momentous significance, there is heard the crowing of a cock, which provides the central image for the poem. The song of the rooster rends the fog in which the city lies enveloped, making possible the emergence of the sun and the return to work; in similar fashion, the poet's hymn to existence, tearing apart the shroud of ennui, makes a resurrection possible.

Even the marvels of reality pale, but the poet goes on to discover the marvels of the transmundane. The last verses of **"The Voyage,"** the closing poem of *The Flowers of Evil,* are radiant with the joy of expectancy: "We shall embark on the sea of Shadows / With the joyful heart of a young voyager." The world that the weary traveler has explored is a flat one whose delights have been exhausted by ennui, but a greater voyage lies ahead:

> Oh death! This country bores us! Let us weigh anchor!
> While the sky and the sea are black as ink,
> Our hearts, which you know, are filled with rays!

Even the somberness of the external world cannot extinguish the joy that, in anticipation of the otherworldly, the poet expresses.

In one of his prose poems, **"The Double Chamber,"** Baudelaire describes his room as a narrow world suffused with disgust, in which he inhales the fetid stench of stale tobacco and the nauseating rot that is the rancid odor of desolation. The embers of the fire have been extinguished, and the hearth is soiled with spittle. With despair the poet realizes that this is indeed his abode: "Horror! I remember! I remember! Yes, this hovel, this abode of eternal ennui is really mine." Because of works like this, Baudelaire is often considered the poet of pessimism, a French successor of Leopardi, who founders in the hopelessness of spleen. But Baudelaire succeeds in breaking out of the double chamber of spleen and ideal, just as he escapes from the "profound and deserted plains of ennui" where the demon had led him "far from the countenance of God." Although it is the title of one of his poems, Baudelaire did not have "the taste for nothingness" of the later symbolist poets. Much of his verse is suffused with compassion and sings of the beauties of modern reality. Certainly *The Flowers of Evil* ends with the triumphant exaltation of one who has conquered ennui. This jubilation is attenuated in one of Baudelaire's last poems, **"Meditation" ("Recueillement"),** and becomes the resignation of one standing above the battle. In the opening verses the poet, like a mother with her child, gives solace to suffering. The time of tranquility sought for in the past has arrived, and the poet can finally turn inward to find true peace. Like Pascal, Baudelaire had to discover that happiness cannot be found in either the external or the internal world before achieving that extraordinary synthesis from which ennui is excluded and in which happiness is found within both the internal and the external world. (pp. 309-14)

> *Reinhard Kuhn, "The Draining of the Clepsydra," in his* The Demon of Noontide: Ennui in Western Literature, *Princeton University Press, 1976, pp. 279-329.*

F. W. J. Hemmings   (essay date 1982)

[*Hemmings is an English biographer and critic who has written extensively on French literature and culture. In the following excerpt from his critical biography of Baudelaire, he discusses Baudelaire's prose poems, providing social, biographical, and literary background for these works and comparing them to the poems in* The Flowers of Evil.]

Over the last six years of Baudelaire's life, between 1861 and 1867, the Second Empire reached a zenith of prosperity and self-confidence. The Treaty of Villafranca (1859) had marked the conclusion of Napoleon III's successful campaign against Austria, in which France reasserted herself as the dominant military power in Europe, for the time being at any rate. There followed a period of peace on the Continent and of economic expansion inside France, powerfully assisted by a free trade treaty with Great Britain and by the completion of the internal railway network. The new era was symbolized by a surprising transformation of the external appearance of the capital, achieved within the space of a very few years thanks to the vision and energy of Baron Haussmann and the exertions of his hundreds of demolition and construction crews, working with pick, shovel, and wheelbarrow. Old slums disappeared, new squares and boulevards were laid out, and on all sides arose glittering restaurants, cafés, department stores and apartment houses, while below ground miles of sewers were tunnelled, helping to make the fearsome cholera outbreaks of earlier times nothing but a bad memory. All these extensive public works provided something like full employment in building and allied trades, which in that age were far more labour-intensive than today. The amusement industry—show-business—flourished too as never before; the old theatres of the Boulevard du Crime were pulled down and huge new ones, the Châtelet, the Vaudeville, the Gaîté, were erected in their place but in more convenient locations. This was the period when Offenbach popularized the *opéra-bouffe* and when the *café-concert* came into its own; while horse-racing, a sport imported from England, attracted crowds of onlookers and punters to Longchamp, the Paris equivalent of Epsom Downs, on the edge of the Bois de Boulogne. Everywhere there was bustle, noise, activity and gaiety, as the well-sprung carriages swept down the streets and the gold napoleons chinked on marble counters.

Although the term had not yet been invented, it was already a consumer society ruled by the values appropriate to such a society. Baudelaire stood aloof from it, partly because he remained as poor as a church-mouse, partly because he judged these values to be immoral in any case or, as he would have put it, satanic; did they not depend on the exploitation of instincts rooted in at least four of the seven deadly sins: avarice, envy, lust and greed? If an eighth were to be added, it would be insensitivity, that amalgam of egoism and callousness which he saw as peculiar to his age and native country and which he denounced in a fable short enough to be quoted here in full.

> The New Year had exploded in a chaos of snow and slush, everyone's carriage on the street, toys and confectionery glittering in the shops, greed and despair rampant everywhere; the licensed delirium to which the city had succumbed was of a kind to turn the brain of the most strong-minded solitary.
>
> In the midst of this hubbub and hurly-burly, a donkey was trotting along briskly, harassed by a great brute armed with a whip.
>
> As the donkey was rounding a corner near the footpath, a fine gentleman wearing gloves and patent leather shoes, his throat cruelly constricted in a tightly knotted cravat and his body squeezed into a suit of clothes straight from the tailor, swept off his hat and executed a courtly blow in front of the lowly animal, exclaiming as he did so: 'A happy and prosperous New Year to you!' Then he turned around to the rest of the party accompanying him, grinning fatuously as if to invite them to add their applause to his self-satisfaction.
>
> The donkey, not seeing this elegant humorist, continued to trot zealously to where his duty called him.
>
> As for me, I was left grinding my teeth in a towering rage against this witless exquisite, who seemed to me to embody the very quintessence of our sense of humour in France.

This text is one out of twenty similar pieces published in *La presse,* at that time edited by Arsène Houssaye, between August 26th and September 24th, 1862, under the general heading *Petits poèmes en prose.* The words designated the form rather than the content of this new kind of literature; at a later stage Baudelaire tried out an alternative title, *Le spleen de Paris,* using it for a collection of six prose poems published in *Le figaro* on February 7th, 1864. In the same issue of this newspaper Gustave Bourdin—the very man who had written the unfortunate review of *Les fleurs du mal* which had precipitated the prosecution of the book—offered an explanation of the title, an explanation almost certainly furnished by the author himself.

> *Le spleen de Paris* is the title adopted by M. Charles Baudelaire for a book he is engaged on writing and which he hopes will prove a worthy complement to *Les fleurs du mal.* All the specificities of ordinary life which by their nature are impossible, or at least difficult, to express in verse have

their place in a prose work in which the ideal and the trivial are fused in an inseparable amalgam.

As for the significance of the title, Bourdin goes on,

> there are those who believe that Londoners alone enjoy the aristocratic privilege of suffering from spleen and that Paris, gay Paris, has never been subject to that grievous affliction. But it may be that, as the author claims, there exists a special kind of Parisian spleen, known, as he argues, to many people who will recognize what he is talking about.

The prose poem was to all intents and purposes a literary form of Baudelaire's own invention. He himself suggested he had a forerunner in the minor romantic Aloysius Bertrand, whose *Gaspard de la nuit* (published posthumously in 1842) can, however, at most have provided him with a starting-point. Bertrand's pseudo-medieval fantasies are poles apart from Baudelaire's rigorously modern and realistic street scenes; and his archaic vocabulary and contorted syntax have nothing in common with Baudelaire's limpid, contemporary style. He appreciated Bertrand's book, which is not without its special charm to which Debussy in his turn proved susceptible, but soon dismissed the idea of imitating him, if that idea ever really crossed his mind. At the most, *Gaspard de la nuit* may have suggested the title 'Poèmes nocturnes' under which the first specimens of his prose poetry appeared in the press in 1857.

This was only two months after the publication of the original edition of **Les fleurs du mal** and long before the appearance of the second edition with its numerous new poems. There was in fact a period of five years or so during which Baudelaire appeared to be hesitating between prose and poetry as his proper medium for creative writing in the future. Among the first prose poems to be published are several which are simply prose versions of what had previously been written as verse. Such doublets are sometimes even given identical titles; thus, we have two versions, the earlier in verse, the later in prose, of **'L'invitation au voyage'** and of **'La chevelure'**. It sometimes happens, however, that the same title was used for two compositions, one in verse and one in prose, of which the actual contents bear little resemblance to one another. Thus, **'Crépuscule du soir'** was the title used for an ode written towards the end of 1851 and included in the first edition of **Les fleurs du mal;** it was also the title given to a prose poem which exists in various versions, though the oldest certainly postdates the ode. In spite of the identical title, suggesting an identity of themes, the two works are very dissimilar in mood and content. The poem stresses the sinister aspects of the coming of dusk; under its cover the criminal will go about his business and the prostitute will steal forth to hunt for clients. The prose poem begins, it is true, in a similarly sombre tone by discussing how nightfall tends to darken still further the minds of those unfortunates who are subject to attacks of mania; but it finishes with a couple of paragraphs describing how very differently the crepuscular hour can affect a man of poetic disposition.

> Twilight, soft and gentle hour! The pale red streaks that glimmer still above the horizon like the day's death-wound delivered by night's victorious scimitar—the glow of street-lamps crimsoning dully against the ultimate incandescent glory of the sunset—the heavy hangings drawn from the abyssal

east by an unseen hand—what are all these but a visible projection of the warring emotions in man's heart at the gravest hours of his life?

> Yet again the beholder will be put in mind of certain fantastic dresses worn by ballet-girls, whereon through a dark, transparent gauze shine the dimmed splendours of a skirt of brilliant colours, even as past joys shimmer through the sombre veil of the present; and the gold and silver spangles with which it is stitched, and which dance as the dancer moves, figure those lights of fantasy which never glint so brightly as under the funereal canopy of Night.

In the first section of this prose poem, to illustrate his contention that those whose minds are unhinged grow more frenzied as the night approaches, Baudelaire relates two brief but striking anecdotes. In **Les fleurs du mal,** narrative passages are rarely found, whereas in the prose poems they are a fairly constant feature, and it is indeed likely that Baudelaire, in switching to prose poetry, was at least partly impelled by the desire to appear in a new guise, as story-teller. Sometimes the story encapsulated in the prose poem is manifestly of his own invention, at other times it can be shown to have been borrowed from some earlier author, and occasionally it derives from an incident he witnessed or heard about. In this last category falls **'La corde'** (**'The Rope'**), one of the few prose poems which bears a dedication: 'To Edouard Manet'. In Antonin Proust's reminiscences of Manet one may read how 'while living in the Rue de la Victoire, he completed *The Child with the Cherries,* using as his model a little boy employed to wash his brushes and clean his palette. This poor lad, temperamentally very unstable, hanged himself; Manet was greatly upset by the tragic end of the little fellow to whom he was deeply attached.' The story, which Baudelaire must have had from Manet's own lips, is related in very much greater detail in **'La corde'**. We are told how the painter came to take the urchin under his roof, how his presence in the studio enlivened Manet's lonely and laborious life, and how he used him as the model for several pictures. We also learn how Manet gave him a severe scolding after discovering he had been raiding the larder—his great weakness being 'an unreasonable craving for sweetmeats and liqueurs'—and how, returning later in the day to the house, he found the boy had hanged himself from a nail driven into the same cupboard where Manet kept his provisions.

Up to this point the story sounds exactly as Manet might have told it to Baudelaire; but the sequel may as easily have been the poet's invention, though it gives point to what would otherwise be no more than a horrifying news-item. We are told how Manet had to cut down the corpse, face an embarrassing police inquiry, and finally break the news to the dead child's parents, who were poor, uneducated folk living in the neighbourhood. The mother appeared quite stunned and lost in thought; she asked only one thing of Manet, to be allowed into the studio, ostensibly to view the corpse; once admitted, she begged him with a kind of morbid insistence to let her carry away the rope with which her little son had hanged himself. The reason why she was so intent on gaining possession of this grisly relic became apparent the following day, when the bemused painter received a stack of letters from his neighbours on other floors of the house, all requesting a snippet of the fatal rope. It was only then that it dawned on him

Baudelaire when living in Brussels.

other person or fact as it exists objectively, we experience a strange feeling, compounded in equal measure of regret for the phantom that is no more, and pleasurable astonishment at the novelty, the reality. If there is one universal, unmistakable, and unchanging phenomenon, of a nature that can mislead no one, it is surely maternal love. It is as hard to imagine a mother without maternal love, as it is to imagine a source of light that is not also a source of heat; is it not therefore very understandable that we should attribute to maternal love everything a mother does, everything she says, where her child is concerned?'

After which the story is related, its unexpected purpose being to demonstrate how unwise we are to make any assumptions whatsoever about human nature, or perhaps to illustrate how events continually upset our preconceived view of reality.

(Of course, with the knowledge we now possess, but which was not available to his first readers, of Baudelaire's warped relations with his own mother, it would be perfectly possible to interpret **'La corde'** in terms of a private allegory in which he is obliquely denouncing Mme Aupick's scale of values where maternal affection took second place, in his judgement at least, to money and possessions.)

Dearly as Baudelaire would have liked to follow in Poe's footsteps and adopt the lucrative profession of short-story writer, he was never able to convince himself that an intelligent reader's interest could be sustained by nothing more than the dramatic tension generated by the narrative itself; the fiction had to point to some specific, if ambiguous, philosophical conclusion predetermined by the story-teller. This was never Poe's practice in the best of his works. What morals are implicit in 'The Black Cat' or 'The Pit and the Pendulum'? In the absence of any direction by the author, the reader could only reach some such banal conclusion as that 'murder must out' or that the instinct for self-preservation will survive everything. It is certainly not for such bits of humdrum wisdom that one reads the *Tales of Mystery and Imagination.*

Anecdotes play a part in perhaps thirty of the fifty prose poems that make up *Le spleen de Paris* as we have it. Not all of them are 'realistic' in the way **'The Rope'** is; a few are pure fables, like **'Which is the True One?'**; others, like **'The Port'**, are non-narrative descriptive pieces, but still mingled with moralistic reflections. But a sufficient number are infused with the authentic flavour of contemporary life to demonstrate that, having by the 1860s reached some kind of resigned accommodation with his private predicaments, Baudelaire was ready to turn his vision outwards and interest himself in the humble dramas of ordinary life and in the sad, unassuming, sometimes pitiable lives of lowly folk. In **'Les fenêtres'** he describes himself looking out at night from his balcony into the uncurtained windows of other houses in the crowded, working-class district where he had his lodgings.

> Beyond a tossing sea of roofs I descry a woman advanced in years, her face already lined, poor, always bent over something, never leaving the room. Guided by what I can see of her face and her garb, by the movements of her hands, by the slightest hint or nothing at all, I have reconstructed this woman's history, or rather her legend, and now and again I weep to retell it to myself.

why the mother had been so intent on making off with it; he remembered the old superstition that a piece of the rope that has served a suicide brings good luck. She had lost her son, but had gained something she perhaps valued more: a highly marketable piece of merchandise.

As it stands, this gruesome little episode might have furnished Maupassant with the subject for one of his *contes;* it has everything that master of the short story required, even down to the 'whiplash ending'. But Maupassant would have been content to let the story stand for itself; not so Baudelaire, for whom the whole point of an anecdote was that it should serve as peg for some moral reflection, which sometimes frames it, sometimes concludes it, or else, as in **'La corde'**, precedes it. However, since Baudelaire's moral outlook was original to the point of perversity, the lessons he draws from the stories he tells in his prose poems are invariably unexpected and usually disconcerting. A more commonplace moralist might have used the tale of the rope as pretext for denouncing the prevalence of idle superstition among the lower classes. Baudelaire has something much more profound in mind. This is how he introduces his idea, in the first paragraph of **'La corde'.**

> 'It may well be,' my friend said to me, 'that illusion is present in all the dealings men have with one another or with the world of natural objects; and when the illusion ceases, that is, when we see the

Had it been a poor old man, I should have reconstructed his with as little trouble.

And so I retire to bed, proud to have lived and suffered in others beside myself.

You may ask: 'Are you sure this legend is the truth?' But what do I care for the facts, if this reality which is outside me has helped me to live, to know I exist, to understand the kind of man I am?

The subjective imagination still counts for more than fact-finding inquiry, and Baudelaire is still as much concerned with his own self as he always was and always would be; but the poetic gift is now allowed a wider sphere of operation.

Possibly De Quincey helped to point the way here, in those passages of his *Confessions* where he describes himself wandering, homeless and short of food, through the modern Babylon of broad streets and narrow passageways, splendid palaces and rat-infested hovels that made up the London of his youth. In his analysis of the book Baudelaire comments, concerning these chapters:

> Even if he had not naturally been, as the reader must have noticed, gentle, sensitive, and affectionate, one might readily suppose him to have learned, in the course of those long days spent wandering hither and thither and of the even longer nights passed in anguish of spirit, to love and pity the poor. The erstwhile scholar now desires to make fresh acquaintance with the lives of the humble; he wishes to plunge into the midst of the throng of the disinherited and, as the swimmer opens his arms to the sea and so embraces nature directly, so he too longs to bathe, as it were, in the multitudinous sea of men.

This last phrase (in the original, *prendre un bain de multitude*), is found textually repeated at the beginning of another of the pieces in **Le spleen de Paris**, entitled simply **'Les foules' ('Crowds')**. Baudelaire here speaks of the poet as a man peculiarly adapted to participate in the lives of others and thus, while retaining his singularity, to embrace thanks to his imaginative gift and powers of empathy, a plurality of existences.

> The poet enjoys an incomparable privilege: he has the right, when he so desires, to be himself or someone other. Like those spirits that drift through the world seeking to be made flesh, he can enter into what soul he will. For him alone, there are no bolts nor bars; and if certain habitations seem closed to him, it is simply that in his eyes they are not worth his while to visit.

> The solitary, pensive wanderer will derive a singular delight from this universal communion. He who finds no impediment in wedding the crowd makes himself familiar with such heady ecstasies as are for ever denied to the egoist padlocked like a strong-box, to the indolent loafer shut up like a shellfish. He adopts as his own all professions, and has his part in every joy and every sorrow that circumstance reveals to him.

> What men call love is a pitifully mean, pinched, anaemic thing compared with this ineffable orgy, this temple prostitution of the soul which in poetic

charity embraces whole-heartedly every unexpected appearance, every unknown passer-by.

(pp. 186-93)

F. W. J. Hemmings, in his Baudelaire the Damned: A Biography, *Charles Scribner's Sons, 1982, 251 p.*

John H. Johnston   (essay date 1984)

[*Johnston is an American critic and educator. In the following excerpt, he discusses the poems in the "Parisian Sketches" section of* The Flowers of Evil *as unprecedented in the way they depict city life and as central works in the expression of Baudelaire's worldview.*]

In one of the crucial descriptive passages of *Coopers Hill,* John Denham visualizes, synoptically, the streets of seventeenth-century London: he sees the citizens of that great city locked in a feverish competitive struggle in which the strong (those who "undo") triumph over the weak (those who are "undone"). But of the English poets who write of the city before the twentieth century, only Blake seems to have grasped—in terms which appeal much more directly to the modern imagination—the full symbolic import of the commercial-industrial city as a concentration of evil forces productive of vice, crime, war, disease, sorrow, fear, suffering, and death. In "London" Blake dramatizes the plight of the "undone" as symptomatic of a "charter'd" urban society; his people are not ruthlessly engaged competitors but disabled victims, and the midnight streets of the city are, inevitably, the only appropriate setting for their misery. After Blake, Baudelaire is the first poet of genius to enlarge this special sense of evil and suffering and to give it a memorable imaginative expression.

With Baudelaire, however, the image and essence of the city seem to change. All of Baudelaire's city people are in one way or another victims of forces that operate within urban society, but the state of being helplessly "undone" has suddenly and for the first time become a matter of spiritual or metaphysical complexity. When Blake portrays the evils of London he implies that some sterile or restrictive human agency is responsible: Church, or State, or the exploitative structures of eighteenth-century commercial enterprise. But for Baudelaire, evil seems to exist in the very nature of things. Being "undone" is not merely the state of being defeated or deprived in the economic sense; it is the essential fact of the human condition. We see Baudelaire's perception of this fact brought to an extraordinary focus in the two dozen or so poems of **Les fleurs du mal** which evoke the realities of nineteenth-century Paris.

Unlike the English topographical poets of the eighteenth century, who feel compelled to deal rather directly with the visible effects of the Industrial Revolution, Baudelaire only occasionally takes into account the specific consequences of the industrial and commercial progress that began to alter the national character of France during the 1830s and 1840s. Though he draws, necessarily, upon the living substance of Paris—a Paris dominated by the acquisitive and materialistic temper of Napoleon III's Second Empire—the author of **Les fleurs du mal** is neither a moralist nor a satirist: he presents the city as an illustration and a symbol of man's inherent imperfection and his obscure but painful consciousness of spiritual loss or betrayal. Behind the impressive neoclassical facades that line Haussmann's splendid new boulevards lurks the squalor that reveals the truth of the human condition. Industrial and commercial progress had of course given man's imperfect nature its contemporary form and hue, but Baudelaire's spiritual sensibilities as well as his deepest poetic inclinations impel him to visualize the plight of modern man as a question related not to the fluctuations of historical time but to eternity itself. (pp. 125-26)

Baudelaire goes directly to the heart of the city and finds in it a gritty, unmistakable essence; aside from one youthful poem, his work manifests from first to last a single, unchanging conception which may admit ambivalence and varying degrees of emphasis but which excludes illusion, doubt, perplexity, retreat, and self-contradiction. . . . Baudelaire does not need to reason or grope his way to any tentative ideas about the city: he knows intuitively what constitutes the real character of modern life and he knows exactly what the role of the poet should be as he moves through the streets of the metropolis and contemplates the mystery of its living, breathing presence. (p. 126)

The group of poems entitled "Tableaux parisiens" appeared not in the first (1857) but in the revised second edition (1861) of *Les fleurs du mal.* Eight of the poems in this new section had been printed in the first edition; to these, ten new ones were added in 1861 for a total of eighteen "Tableaux" (in a collection that totaled 127 poems). Of the eighteen, perhaps five may not be regarded as city poems at all because they lack explicit reference to urban materials, whereas at least ten poems not included by Baudelaire in "Tableaux parisiens" are among his best evocations of metropolitan life. Even though Baudelaire carefully arranged both editions of *Les fleurs du mal* on a topical or thematic basis, the evidence shows that as a topic the city was by no means as logically binding as, for example, "La mort," a section wherein all six poems deal with death. However, the effort to establish some kind of order among the poems of *Les fleurs du mal* (as well as the author's apparent willingness to violate that order) would seem to support one's larger sense of Baudelaire's artistic commitment to a special image of man: the poet's vision of the city is part of an extended vision of life itself and not the product of a separable category of experience with its own distinctive subject matter and established formulas of response. . . . [The] modern city may be many diverse things—place, spirit, fact, dream, symbol, image, event, process, nightmare, myth—and it is clearly with Baudelaire that this harrowing sense of complexity and multiplicity begins. (p. 127)

Just as there are episodes in Dante's *Inferno* which remain fixed in the memory because of their special poignancy or horror, so there are parts of *Les fleurs du mal* which embody a central essence which tends to dissolve all polarities in an apparently untransformable vision of evil, suffering, and death. In writing of the city, topographical poets such as Virgil and Sir John Denham actualize the subject . . . by establishing a basic moral and imaginative relationship between the city and its encompassing physical totality. Baudelaire, however, is the first great poet to describe the city without the aid of such topographical reference. Paris is not a place defined by its existence in a natural or a human context; it is *the* place, the unique, ultimate human reality, where age, deformity, decrepitude,

blindness, poverty, vice, and crime constitute the central experience of life. Hence these realities are presented not in mere realistic or satiric terms as obvious departures from the human norm; what we see of Paris is created mainly in terms of the poet's singular power of moral and imaginative intensification. Though he does not approach Baudelaire by the route we have followed, T. S. Eliot was referring to one aspect of this power when he wrote that Baudelaire excelled "not merely in the use of imagery of common life, not merely in the use of imagery of the sordid life of a great metropolis, but in the elevation of such imagery to the *first intensity*—presenting it as it is, and yet making it represent something more than itself. . . . " This intensification—which I see as more than a matter of imagery alone—is of course visible in **"Le vin des chiffonniers"** and in other poems . . . but only when it appears as an effect of the poet's dramatized, simultaneous awareness of the city "as it is" and the city as "something more than itself " do we begin to understand the major informing insight—not always developed or made explicit—to which Baudelaire's city poems make their cumulative contributions.

Perhaps the only way to describe the essential Baudelairean city "as it is" would be to say that it is a place close to the fact and form of death itself. In **"Le spleen"**, the corpses in the municipal cemeteries and the living or partly living inhabitants of the metropolis seem to share the same numb vulnerability to the elements:

> Pluviôse, irrité contre la ville entiére,
> De son urne à grands flots verse un froid ténébreux
> Aux pâles habitants du voisin cimetière
> Et la mortalité sur les faubourgs brumeux.

> (The god of rain, irked by the whole city, is pouring
> great dark waves of cold upon the pale occupants
> of the nearby cemetery and immersing the fog-
> bound suburbs in the very essence of death.)

In other poems keyed to this macabre extremity we are drawn into previously undelineated depths of suffering and despair, where those who live in the shadow of moral and physical disintegration enact the unwholesome drama of life in the streets. Yet, as Eliot says, Baudelaire always makes the city "represent something more than itself " because even in the darkest poems of *Les fleurs du mal* there is a sense of a heritage lost, an expectation defeated, a fulfillment denied. If Whitman (in "Starting from Paumanok") off-handedly concedes that evil is as important "as any thing else" in life, the existence of evil is such an overwhelming certainty for Baudelaire that he cannot fully deal with human experience without suggesting that the spiritual privation of evil is equivalent, poetically, to the physical privation of death. In *Les fleurs du mal,* man is a creature who knows, senses, and obscurely suffers that double privation.

If in **"Le vin des chiffonniers"** sleep and wine are only temporary measures of relief from the pain of living, death—and the certainty of a change for the better—provides the ultimate consolation in **"La mort des pauvres"** (**"The Death of the Poor"**):

> C'est la Mort qui console, hélas! et qui fait vivre;
> C'est le but de la vie, et c'est le seul espoir
> Qui, comme un élixir, nous monte et nous enivre,
> Et nous donne le coeur de marcher jusqu'au soir.

(It is death, alas, which comforts us and keeps us going. Death is the aim of life; it is the only hope which, like some magic potion, enlivens and intoxicates us and gives us courage to trudge on till evening.)

Baudelaire goes on to speculate about the rewards of the afterlife as mildly ironic departures from the traditional promises of Christianity. Evil is so pervasive, so universal, however, that death ("the poor man's purse") may really conceal an almost unimaginable eternity of horror. In **"Le squelette laboureur" ("The Laboring Skeleton")**, Baudelaire, viewing grotesque bone-and-muscle anatomical illustrations of men "digging like farm-hands," contemplates the frightening possibility that all of life's toil is a mere prologue to the eternal drudgery of the laboring skeleton, a "shocking emblem" that mocks the comforting Christian *requiescat in pace.* "Do you wish to show," he asks the poor "flayed ones,"

> Que tout, même la Mort, nous ment,
> Et que sempiternellement,
> Hélas! il nous faudra peut-être
>
> Dans quelque pays inconnu
> Ecorcher la terre revêche
> Et pousser une lourde bêche
> Sous notre pied sanglant et nu?
>
> (That everything, even death, deceives us, and that for ever and ever, alas, in some unknown land we will have to scrape the rough earth and push a heavy spade beneath our bleeding, naked foot?)

It is ironic that this appalling image of agricultural labor prolonged *ad infinitum* is an unconscious but telling reversal of Virgil's *labor improbus*—that unremitting toil which, though harsh, is essential to man's life and his productive relationship with the earth. Though it does not seem to take its meaning directly from city experience, **"Le squelette laboureur"** nevertheless appears among the eighteen "Tableaux parisiens" poems. In more than one sense, Baudelaire's classification is appropriate. The vision of the skeleton laborers comes to the poet as he leafs through medical texts in a bookstall by the Seine. That vision, in effect, is a product of the attitudes and feelings that have developed exclusively within the realm of urban squalor and hopelessness, and of course within the context of **Les fleurs du mal** itself. For Baudelaire, the negative biblical and archetypal associations of elemental earth labor are obviously much more powerful and dramatically revealing than any reference to the pointlessly repeated rounds of urban existence, overwhelmingly familiar and almost totally lacking in poetic or symbolic resonance. The laboring skeleton is an ironic symbol of man's fate, and man's fate—as Baudelaire implies again and again—is inevitably shaped by conditions of life in the modern city. Here, unhappy multitudes—trudging, stumbling, plodding, and groping—undergo their own apparently endless struggle to exist. In **"La mort des pauvres"** Baudelaire, with tender irony, extends to these multitudes the consolation of death; in **"Le squelette laboureur"** he shows that death is not a consolation but—possibly—a nightmare that embodies more than the worst that can be imagined of life.

The transitional poise of night and day at evening and at dawn is the subject of the two "Crépuscule" poems: **"Le crépuscule du soir" ("Evening Twilight")** and **"Le crépus-cule du matin" ("Morning Twilight")**. Wordsworth was susceptible to such moments; in "Westminister Bridge" time seems to be suspended, and early-morning London is revealed "All bright and glittering in the smokeless air." But in both "Crépuscule" poems Baudelaire describes the secret world of darkness rather than the more aesthetically entrancing phenomena of receding or growing light. In **"Le crépuscule du soir"** twilight simply indicates the boundaries of the compact, enclosed darkness of a cage or a trap: "le ciel / Se ferme lentement comme une grande alcôve, / Et l'homme impatient se change en bête fauve." ("The sky shuts slowly like a great alcove, and feverish man changes into a wild beast.") Evening, "ami du criminel," breeds not only wild beasts but malignant demons as well: the turbid night throngs with evil spirits as whores, gamblers, and thieves vigorously ply their trades (the *labor improbus* of the city); and we ask ourselves, is Baudelaire suggesting that darkness paradoxically reveals and makes more prominent the common human occupations of daylight hours? The accompanying din of Parisian nightlife is overpowering: the sizzling sounds from restaurant kitchens, the raucous shouts from theater audiences, and the blaring of maddened orchestras; these sounds, associated with hectic self-indulgence, make more lonely and more pitiful the sighs of the sick and the dying, whom "dismal Night seizes by the throat." If the endless work of the laboring skeleton is a vision of eternity, then the strident, sleazy, and ephemeral night world of **"Le crépuscule du soir"** is its appropriate prelude.

Dealing with the remnants rather than with the beginnings of darkness, **"Le crépuscule du matin"** shows both sleepers and wakers: the ennervated whores "sleep their stupid sleep," while "Les pauvresses, traînant leurs seins maigres et froids, / Soufflaient sur leurs tisons et soufflaient sur leurs doigts." ("Poor old women, trailing their skinny, frozen breasts, blew now upon their embers, now upon their fingers.") Other women, passing along the burdens of life to another generation, sob in the pangs of childbirth, and again, as in **"Le crépuscule du soir,"** we hear the last groans and gasps of the dying. The final stanza presents two images that summarize this effect of sorrowful continuity; we see both frightened, apprehensive youth, and helpless, acquiescent old age:

> L'aurore grelottante en robe rose et verte
> S'avançait lentement sur la Seine déserte,
> Et le sombre Paris, en se frottant les yeux,
> Empoignait ses outils, vieillard laborieux.
>
> (The shuddering dawn, in her pink and green dress, moved slowly along the deserted Seine; and morose Paris, rubbing his eyes, laid hold of his tools, an old man doomed to toil.)

Darkness—the "boundless dark" of the blind—is also the theme of **"Les aveugles" ["The Blind"]**. In *The Prelude . . .* Wordsworth devotes a dozen or so lines to the blind beggar, who wears an identification paper upon his chest. Wordsworth's mind is "caught by the spectacle": the bit of paper "seemed of the utmost we can know, / Both of ourselves and of the universe." The poet is humbled by this reminder of human limitations and gazes at the blind man "as if admonished from another world." Baudelaire's blind men, however, are the source of a much more complex response: they are both frightful and vaguely ridiculous. They move like mannequins or sleepwalkers;

yet their sightless eyeballs, "from which the divine spark has departed," dart back and forth grotesquely. Wordsworth's blind beggar has an "upright," "steadfast" face—implying no more than a certain dignity and courage in the acceptance of his misfortune. But as they walk the streets of Paris, Baudelaire's blind men have their eyes perpetually lifted toward the sky: "on ne les voit jamais vers les pavés / Pencher rêveusement leur tête appesantie." ("You never see them dreamily bow their heavy heads toward the streets.") Here, of course, the unbowed head does not suggest a moral quality, as in Wordsworth; for in their "boundless dark," amid the noisy commotion of the streets, the blind men are searching. The poet, instead of receiving moral "admonishment" from another world, is conscious of something more nearly related to the condition of humanity in the strange and terrible (and yet realistically depicted) posture of the blind:

> O cité!
> Pendant qu'autour de nous tu chantes, ris et beugles,
>
> Eprise du plaisir jusqu'à l'atrocité,
> Vois! je me traîne aussi! mais, plus qu'eux hébété,
> Je dis: Que cherchent-ils au Ciel, tous ces aveugles?

> (O city, while you sing, laugh, and bellow all around us, outrageously smitten by the desire for pleasure, see, I myself trudge along; but even more dazed than they, I ask myself: What are they looking for in the sky, all those blind men?)

While Wordsworth preserves a comparatively detached, speculative attitude, Baudelaire closely identifies himself with the blind men in terms of their weariness; at the same time he dissociates himself—as one who can "see" very well in the ordinary sense—from the mystery of their extraordinary search. Presenting himself as dazed or stupefied by the gross preoccupations of the pleasure-seeking city, the poet appears, at the end, as one who cannot understand the very symbol on which his poem turns. Baudelaire thus utilizes an ironic drama of imperception as yet another measure of what the city does to the entrapped soul, dimly conscious of a lost heritage but powerless to find and claim it, or even to understand the purpose of those who, despite a "boundless dark," obsessively continue to seek it.

Is Paris real? Is it a dream, a haunted place, an empty revel, a workhouse, a labyrinth, a living symbol of the human condition? If blind men search for the light that will make them free, age also has its symbolic suggestivity in this strange city where anything is possible. The opening stanza of **"Les sept vieillards" ("The Seven Old Men")** might serve as an epigraph for all of Baudelaire's city poetry, which so persistently refuses to yield to the tyranny of the real:

> Fourmillante cité, cité pleine de rêves,
> Où le spectre, en plein jour, raccroche le passant!
> Les mystères partout coulent comme des sèves
> Dans les canaux étroits du colosse puissant.

> (Swarming city, city full of dreams, where the ghost accosts the passer-by in broad daylight! Mysteries flow everywhere like sap in the narrow veins of this powerful giant.)

Baudelaire then describes the first of what prove to be seven identical old men, tramping through the "dirty yellow fog" of a Paris morning with their malevolent eyes,

stiff "Judas" beards, bent backs, and beggarly rags. To the terrified poet, whose nerves are already strained by the noise and ugliness of the streets, these hideous old men (the seven deadly sins?) seem wickedness incarnate, an embodiment of the eternal nature of evil, and the poet himself (perhaps man in the state of innocence) the frightened victim of an "infamous conspiracy." Turning away from that "satanical procession," he seeks the safety of his room. Behind his locked door, "terrified, nauseated, and depressed," he tries to cope with the meaning of this "enigma," this "absurdity." Though his faculties are deranged and he is in a state of emotional shock, the poet knows very well that he has experienced a seven-fold diabolical epiphany: not in the secret depths of the night, but in the midst of the banal and commonplace, in the wan light of ordinary day, evil itself—an aspect of eternity tricked out as an impudent and sinister masquerade—stalks the public streets. Baudelaire is the first city poet whose imagination is equipped to dramatize the impact of what he means us to accept in **"Les sept vieillards"** as the true efflorescence of evil. Going far beyond the sense-preoccupations of the simple realist and the shibboleths of the conventional moralist, he insists that in the city one is never more than a step away from the inconceivable; beyond this point, he tells us, reason fails, and the forsaken soul finds itself rocked "like some old mastless ship on a monstrous, shoreless sea." Thus the experience which begins in the constricted streets of the great temporal city concludes with a suddenly expanded image of infinite spiritual desolation.

Age is the subject of another, longer poem, **"Les petites vieilles" ("Little Old Women")**. But this time the old people are harmless wrecks ("Débris d'humanité"): little old women who, weak and decrepit, inevitably attract the poet's sympathetic eye. These "charming" creatures—the irony has a Baudelairean tenderness—creep or trot along the city streets clutching their queer handbags and trembling at the thunderous noise around them. Insulted, mocked, or more often totally ignored, they display to the poet the innocence and wonder of a second childhood that is really only a tottering step away from death. "—Avez-vous observé que maints cercueils de vieilles / Sont presque aussi petits que celui d'un enfant?" ("Have you noticed that many old women's coffins are almost as small as those of little children?") asks Baudelaire, once more striking that complex note of mingled horror, tenderness, and pity which seems to be the only appropriate response to certain kinds of urban experience. Although age, infirmity, neglect, and immanent death are the themes of **"Les petites vieilles,"** the tone of the poem is far from somber. Sometimes the little old women, retaining somehow a stoic pride and dignity, prove to be unexpected exemplars of that "heroism of modern life" which Baudelaire perceived and sought to define. Usually, however, these broken-down creatures—mothers, courtesans, and saints—are so much like helpless children that they arouse the poet's anxious, almost paternal solicitude as his "uneasy eye" follows their "wavering steps." The final stanza of **"Les petites vieilles"** is one of Baudelaire's most eloquent personal statements about life in the modern city. All of the feelings expressed earlier—curiosity, fascination, and warm solicitude—are subordinated to a remarkably heightened and purified range of emotion that includes love, regret, fear, sorrow, pity, and protest. All of these feelings coalesce and are in turn suffused by that generous, self-forgetful identification with suffering that marks the most intense city poetry of *Les fleurs du mal:*

> Ruines! ma famille! ô cerveaux congénères!
> Je vous fais chaque soir un solennel adieu!
> Où serez-vous demain, Eves octogénaires,
> Sur qui pèse la griffe effroyable de Dieu?
>
> (O ruins, O my family, O you of like minds, every evening I bid you a sad farewell! Where will you be tomorrow, octogenarian Eves, upon whom God's dreadful claw is ready to fall?)

Children, and at the same time primordial mother figures, these old women are embraced by a son who is also an adoptive father; the family of man, fragmented by "the chaos of our living cities," is thus recreated in the warmth of a human love that contrasts almost unbearably with the terrible final image of brutal and even bestial Power. (pp. 139-46)

[A] brief passage from **"Le cygne" ("The Swan")** . . . deals with the consumptive black woman who trudges through the mud and fog of the great industrial city, a permanent exile from her "superbe Afrique." . . . **"Le cygne"** is Baudelaire's most elaborate and most successful effort to broaden his treatment of the city: the black woman is only one of a number of images and symbols which enlarge the central theme of a heritage lost or betrayed. These images and symbols revolve around a poignant myth from the classical past: that of the widowed Andromache after the fall of Troy, when she is living as a captive in the kingdom of Pyrrhus and grieving over the deaths of her husband and son. The story of Andromache comes to Baudelaire's mind because as he describes a rebuilt section of Paris through which he happens to be passing, he recalls the sight of an escaped swan whose flutterings in the dusty street had seemed to signify the pathos of captivity in an alien, hostile environment:

> . . . de ses pieds palmés frottant le pavé sec,
> Sur le sol raboteux traînait son blanc plumage.
> Près d'un ruisseau sans eau le bête ouvrant le bec
>
> Baignait nerveusement ses ailes dans la poudre,
> Et disait, le coeur plein de son beau lac natal:
> "Eau, quand donc pleuvras-tu? quand tonneras-tu, foudre?"
>
> (. . . his webbed feet vainly stroking the arid roadway, he trailed his white plumes on the rough ground. Beside a parched gutter the poor animal, with gaping beak, was frantically bathing his wings in the dust and, with his heart full of longing for his native element, cried out: "O water, when will you rain down? O thunder, when will you sound out?")

Ancient myth and modern image thus meet and rise above temporal, changing Paris, and the mood of the poet is deepened by his recognition of the essential, eternal sadness of things: Haussmann's Paris may change, with new bridges and new buildings, but "rien dans ma mélancolie / N'a bougé!" ("Nothing in my melancholy has changed.") But as the poet moves on toward the Louvre, myth and image gain an emotional, visionary power in terms of their momentary relationship, and temporal Paris is suddenly revealed as the home of exiles, the home of "all those who have lost what they can never, never find again." In the final stanza of **"Le cygne"** we turn from the distant classical archetype of Andromache to the personal consciousness of the poet, whose memory is haunted with images of those who have been cast off or forgotten or downtrodden:

> Ainsi dans la forêt où mon esprit s'exile
> Un vieux Souvenir sonne à plein souffle du cor!
> Je pense aux matelots oubliés dans une île,
> Aux captifs, aux vaincus! . . . à bien d'autres encor!
>
> (Thus in the forest where my mind is exiled, an old memory sounds its horn! I think of sailors forgotten on an island, of those who are captive, of those who are defeated! . . . and of many another!)

Like the bedraggled swan, these neglected spirits are both "ridiculous and sublime"—and therefore tragically memorable—in their varied states of unhappy isolation. Baudelaire's attitude toward them is neither sentimental on the one hand nor politically conceived on the other: the types of symbolic alienation glimpsed here are beyond mere sympathy and certainly beyond the corrective measures of social or economic reform. The final, suspended phrase of **"Le cygne"** suggests the mood of the poet as he gazes pensively about, conscious of the anonymous multitudes who have suffered a spiritual deprivation they hardly know how to define.

Although references to myth and mythological figures are fairly common in eighteenth-century English topographical poetry, these references are decorative rather than functional; certainly they are never symbolic in the modern sense. Thus, early in *Windsor-Forest* Pope has occasion to speak of Pan, Pomona, Flora, and Ceres. More distinctly functional, among the later topographical poets of the eighteenth century, is the use of figures such as Tubal and Vulcan in descriptions of the crude, smoky labor of primitive industrial production, but again the device is casual and without true symbolic import. Even Baudelaire uses the myth of the golden age rather conventionally in **"J'aime le souvenir de ces époques nues."** But his employment of the Andromache myth in **"Le cygne"** is something entirely new in the poetry of the modern city: the essence of Andromache's fate is imaginatively and emotionally linked to that of the swan, and both become symbolically expressive of the fate of those imprisoned in the metropolis, where walls of brick and fog enclose the "labyrinthe fangeux" from which there is no escape. In **"Le cygne"** we see an early example of the idea advanced by Paul Ginestier [in his *The Poet and the Machine*]: poetry of the modern technological era tends, paradoxically, to actualize or revive the basic archetypes of the human imagination. This process is a response to the negative qualities of a mechanized civilization and its sterile, repressive effects; overwhelmed by his experience of complexity, isolation, loneliness, alienation, and unfulfillment, the modern city poet instinctively seeks meaningful parallels in the classic, concentrated purity of archetypal myth. As city poets, neither Wordsworth nor Whitman attempt to extend their imaginative efforts in this fashion. Wordsworth is too much intent upon the fluctuations of his own moods and attitudes; Whitman is too busily engaged in fashioning the dynamic new myth of American progress. In this particular aspect of modern urban verse, as in so many other aspects, Baudelaire leads the way. (pp. 146-48)

John H. Johnston, "Baudelaire," in his The Poet and the City: A Study in Urban Perspectives, *The University of Georgia Press,* 1984, pp. 125-52.

FURTHER READING

Austin, Lloyd. "Baudelaire: Poet or Prophet?" In his *Poetic Principles and Practice: Occasional Papers on Baudelaire, Mallarmé and Valéry,* pp. 1-18. Cambridge: Cambridge University Press, 1987.
Compares the short prose text "The End of the World" and the poem "The Voyage," two works with a similar theme, in order to distinguish Baudelaire the prophet from Baudelaire the poet.

Aynesworth, Donald. "Humanity and Monstrosity in *Le spleen de Paris:* A Reading of 'Mademoiselle Bistouri'." *Romanic Review* LXXIII, No. 2 (March 1982): 209-21.
Maintains that Baudelaire's "prose poems appear as a kind of esthetic monstrosity, fragmented, never finished, designed solely to entertain or distract."

Benjamin, Walter. "On Some Motifs in Baudelaire." In his *Illuminations,* edited by Hannah Arendt, translated by Harry Zohn, pp. 155-200. New York: Schocken Books, 1969.
Considers *The Flowers of Evil* as an indictment against modern society.

Bloom, Harold, ed. *Charles Baudelaire.* New York: Chelsea House Publishers, 1987, 168 p.
Collection of reprinted essays on various aspects of Baudelaire's work.

Bowie, Malcolm; Fairlie, Alison; and Finch, Alison, eds. *Baudelaire, Mallarmé, Valéry: New Essays in Honour of Lloyd Austin.* Cambridge: Cambridge University Press, 1982, 456 p.
Includes essays on various aspects of Baudelaire's poetry and prose poems.

Boyd, Greg. Introduction to *La fanfarlo,* by Charles Baudelaire, edited by Kendall E. Lappin, translated by Greg Boyd, pp. 7-22. Berkeley: Donald S. Ellis / Creative Arts Book Co., 1986.
Examines *La fanfarlo.* According to Boyd, "The years during which [Baudelaire] wrote *La fanfarlo* were years of growth, conflict, and transition—transition from youth to maturity, from literary apprentice to poet."

Brombert, Victor. "Baudelaire: City Images and the 'Dream of Stone'." *Yale French Studies,* No. 32 (1964): 99-105.
Discusses the urban imagery of Paris in Baudelaire's poetry.

Burton, Richard D. E. *Baudelaire in 1859: A Study in the Sources of Poetic Creativity.* Cambridge: Cambridge University Press, 1988, 213 p.
Devoted to an analysis of works Baudelaire wrote in 1859, which the critic isolates as the most important and productive year of his literary career.

Cargo, Robert T. *Baudelaire Criticism, 1950-1967: A Bibliography with Critical Commentary* University, Ala.: University of Alabama Press, 1968, 171 p.

Includes a bibliography of works by Baudelaire.

Carter, A. E. *Charles Baudelaire.* Boston: Twayne Publishers, 1977, 139 p.
Biographical and critical study.

Chadwick, Charles. "Baudelaire's 'Correspondences'." In his *Symbolism,* pp. 8-16. New York: Methuen, 1971.
Discusses Baudelaire as an influence on the French Symbolist movement.

Chesters, Graham. *Baudelaire and the Poetics of Craft.* Cambridge: Cambridge University Press, 1988, 184 p.
Study designed "to bring to awareness the principles underlying the skill with which Baudelaire satisfies and manipulates the demands of French versification and the skill with which he orchestrates the raw material of the French language within a formal framework."

Clements, Patricia. *Baudelaire & the English Tradition.* Princeton: Princeton University Press, 1985, 442 p.
Traces the influence of Baudelaire and the diverse readings of his work among English poets and critics.

Cohn, Robert Greer. "Baudelaire's Beleaguered Prose Poems." In *Textual Analysis: Some Readers Reading,* edited by Mary Ann Caws, pp. 112-20. New York: Modern Language Association of America, 1986.
Refutes late twentieth-century deconstructionist criticisms of Baudelaire's *Poems in Prose.*

Ellis, Havelock. "The Human Baudelaire." *The Living Age* IX, No. 460 (9 March 1918): 624-29.
Psychological profile of Baudelaire and three persons central to his life: his mother, Maitre Ancelle, and Jeanne Duval.

Emmanuel, Pierre. *Baudelaire: The Paradox of Redemptive Satanism.* Translated by Robert T. Cargo. University, Ala.: University of Alabama Press, 1970, 189 p.
Study "that looks at Baudelaire in the broad pattern of Christian tradition but with careful attention being paid to the poet's spiritual aspirations as seen in terms of aesthetics and artistic creation."

Fairlie, Alison. "Some Remarks on Baudelaire's 'Poème du haschisch'. In *The French Mind: Studies in Honour of Gustave Rudler,* edited by Will Moore, Rhoda Sutherland, and Enid Starkie, pp. 291-317. Oxford: Oxford University Press, 1952.
Argues that the thematic progression of Baudelaire's "Poème du haschisch" mirrors the arrangement of the poems in *The Flowers of Evil.*

Fowlie, Wallace. "Baudelaire and Eliot: Interpreters of Their Age." *The Sewanee Review* LXXIV, No. 1 (January-March 1966): 293-309.
Demonstrates Baudelaire's influence on T. S. Eliot.

Gilman, Margaret. *Baudelaire the Critic.* New York: Columbia University Press, 1943, 264 p.
The foremost study of Baudelaire's critical writings. Analyzes the roots of Baudelaire's critical theory, stressing the importance of his criticism to the creation of *The Flowers of Evil.*

Gilson, Etienne. "Baudelaire and the Muse." In his *Choir of Muses,* translated by Maisie Ward, pp. 56-80. London: Sheed and Ward, 1953.
Expounds on the women who provided the impetus be-

hind Baudelaire's creativity, particularly Marie Daubrun and Apollonie Sabatier.

Hearn, Lafcadio. "Baudelaire." In his *Talks to Writers,* edited by John Erskine, pp. 120-29. New York: Dodd, Mead and Co., 1920.
    Compares the style of Baudelaire's *Poems in Prose* with the style of Rudyard Kipling's prose writings.

————. "The Idol of a Great Eccentric (Baudelaire)." In his *Essays in European and Oriental Literature,* edited by Albert Mordell, pp. 55-64. New York: Dodd, Mead and Co., 1923.
    Highlights the Oriental and tropical influences evident in Baudelaire's poetry, especially in the "Black Venus" cycle.

Heck, Francis S. "The Evolution in Baudelaire's Later Poetry from Eternal Beauty to the goût de l'infini." *Nottingham French Studies* 20, No. 2 (1981): 1-8.
    Argues that Baudelaire's later conception of beauty became "concomitant with suffering."

————. "The Illusion of Beauty and Volupté in the Works of Baudelaire." *Renascence* XXXV, No. 1 (Autumn 1982): 39-48.
    Demonstrates how Baudelaire's poetic style transforms and sublimates sensual pleasure into "a spiritual emotion."

Hiddleston, J. A. *Baudelaire and "Le spleen de Paris."* Oxford: Clarendon Press, 1987, 124 p.
    Designed to clarify some of the obscurities surrounding the composition and intentions of Baudelaire's prose poems by "examining the position of the artist and his attitude towards his art, the complex and often ambiguous moral message the poems suggest, and above all the relationship between prose and poetry."

Houston, John Porter. "Baudelaire: Innovation and Archaism." In his *The Demonic Imagination: Style and Theme in French Romantic Poetry,* pp. 85-124. Baton Rouge: Louisiana State University Press, 1969.
    Analysis of Baudelaire's poetry.

Howells, Bernard. "On the Meaning of Great Men: Baudelaire and Emerson Revisited." *Romantic Review* LXXVIII, No. 4 (November 1987): 471-489.
    Suggests that Baudelaire's aesthetic and ethical values resemble those of Ralph Waldo Emerson, particularly in Baudelaire's pre-1852 writings.

Hubert, Judd D. "Baudelaire's Revolutionary Poetics." *Romanic Review* XLVI, No. 3 (October 1955): 164-77.
    Identifies Symbolist and modern features in Baudelaire's poetry, asserting that with Baudelaire "poetry, for the first time, becomes conscious of itself."

Hyslop, Lois Boe. *Baudelaire: Man of His Time.* New Haven: Yale University Press, 1980, 207 p.
    Considers Baudelaire's personal and professional relationship with artists, musicians, politicians, and writers of his era.

Leakey, F. W. "Baudelaire: The Poet as Moralist." In *Studies in Modern French Literature,* edited by L. J. Austin, Garnet Rees, and Eugène Vinaver, pp. 196-219. Manchester, England: Manchester University Press, 1961.
    Traces the evolution of moral themes in Baudelaire's poetry.

Lloyd, Rosemary. *Baudelaire's Literary Criticism.* Cambridge, England: Cambridge University Press, 1981, 338 p.
    Argues that Baudelaire's critical writings served as the inspiration for his creative writings.

Marriage, Anthony X. "Whitman's 'This Compost,' Baudelaire's 'A Carrion': Out of Decay Comes an Awful Beauty." *Walt Whitman Review* 27, No. 4 (December 1981): 143-49.
    Focuses on images of mortification and decay utilized by both poets in their respective poems.

Monroe, Jonathan. "Baudelaire's Poor: The *Petits poèmes en prose* and the Social Inscription of the Lyric." *Stanford French Review* IX, No. 2 (Summer 1985): 169-88.
    Argues that Baudelaire's prose poems illustrate the "self-alienation of the human subject, the perception that the self is an object existing for others than the self."

Peyre, Henri, ed. *Baudelaire: A Collection of Critical Essays.* Englewood Cliffs, N.J.: Prentice-Hall, Inc., 1962, 184 p.
    Collection of essays by various commentators on Baudelaire.

————. "Baudelaire as a Love Poet." In *Baudelaire as a Love Poet, and Other Essays,* edited by Lois Boe Hyslop, pp. 3-39. University Park: Pennsylvania State University Press, 1969.
    Examines the "sensual, the sentimental, and the cerebral" aspects of Baudelaire's love poetry.

Poulet, Georges. "Baudelaire." In his *Studies in Human Time,* translated by Elliott Coleman, pp. 263-79. Baltimore: The Johns Hopkins Press, 1956.
    Discourses on the nature of original sin as revealed in Baudelaire's lyrics.

Raser, Timothy. "Language and the Erotic in Two Poems by Baudelaire." *Romanic Review* LXXIX, No. 3 (May 1988): 443-51.
    Posits that language and eroticism are intimately fused in Baudelaire's poetry, focusing on the poems "Les bijoux" and "A une passante."

————. *A Poetics of Art Criticism: The Case of Baudelaire.* Chapel Hill: The University of North Carolina at Chapel Hill, Department of Romance Languages, 1989, 197 p.
    Attempts to relate systematically "the elements of judgement, explanation, and description in Baudelaire's art criticism."

Sieburth, Richard. "Poetry and Obscenity: Baudelaire and Swinburne." *Comparative Literature* 36, No. 4 (Fall 1984): 343-53.
    Examines the critical outcry of Second Empire France and Victorian England against the "obscenity" of Baudelaire's *Flowers of Evil* and Algernon Swinburne's *Poems and Ballads.*

Starkie, Enid. *Baudelaire.* London: Faber and Faber, 1957, 622 p.
    The definitive biography in English. According to Starkie, Baudelaire's writing indicates his desire to rid himself of vice and to reflect "the beauty of God's creation."

Turnell, Martin. *Baudelaire: A Study of His Poetry.* Norfolk, Conn.: New Direction Books, 1953, 328 p.
    Examines the meaning and artistic value of *The Flowers of Evil* and appraises Baudelaire's impact on French poetry.

Wilson, Edmund. "The Sanctity of Baudelaire." In his *Clas-*

sics and Commercials: A Literary Chronicle of the Forties, pp.
419-22. New York: Farrar, Straus and Co., 1950.

    Challenges Christian readings of Baudelaire's work.

Toru Dutt

1856-1877

Indian poet, translator, and novelist.

Dutt is ranked among the most important Indian poets writing in English during the nineteenth century. One of India's first prominent women writers, she is best known for her English translations of French poetry and her original English poems adapted from Hindu epics.

Dutt was born in Calcutta into a socially distinguished and cultured Hindu family. Her father was a poet and linguist, and her mother was a gifted storyteller and a translator of English prose. At the insistence of her father, Dutt and her family were converted to Christianity, and in 1869 they left the Hindu community in Calcutta to live in Europe. Dutt attended schools in Nice, London, and Cambridge, quickly becoming proficient in French and English, but due to chronic health problems she received most of her instruction from her parents and private tutors. During her years in Europe, Dutt became fascinated with French history and culture. Her enthusiasm for French society led her to produce *Le journal de Mademoiselle d'Arvers,* a novel written in French. Dutt began, but never finished, a novel in English entitled *Bianca; or The Young Spanish Maiden;* parts of this work that were serialized in an Indian periodical attracted little notice. While in England, Dutt began to translate French poetry into English, and she continued this practice after she and her family returned to Calcutta in 1873. Some of these translations were published in Indian periodicals, and a volume of her translations, *A Sheaf Gleaned in French Fields,* was published in 1876. This collection, which included translations of works by such poets as Victor Hugo, Charles Augustin Sainte-Beuve, and Charles Baudelaire, met with mixed critical reaction. While critics found that some of her translations were technically imperfect as English verse, they regarded the general accuracy and ambition of this work as indicative of a promising career. Dutt's intense study and mastery of Sanskrit prompted her to adapt the classic Indian legends contained in the *Mahabharata,* the *Ramyana,* and the *Vishnu Purana* for an English-speaking audience. This original English poetry was collected in *Ancient Ballads and Legends of Hindustan,* a posthumously published volume that was well received by critics. Dutt died in 1877 of tuberculosis.

Ancient Ballads and Legends of Hindustan is considered Dutt's best work. The collection begins with nine ballads based on didactic legends of gods, goddesses, monsters, and heroes. Critics regard the writing of *Ancient Ballads* as an exercise that enabled Dutt, after her years in Europe, to rediscover and appreciate her Hindu heritage. The respect and sympathy with which Dutt presents her subjects in these ballads suggests to some critics that she felt innately at ease in employing themes of Hindu thought and tradition, regardless of her own Christian faith. "Savitri," the tale of a widow who bargains with Death so that her husband might be restored to her, is the most popular of the ballads. It is cited for its striking descriptive passages, its lyrical merit, and the haunting quality of the scene between Savitri and Death. The second section of *Ancient Ballads* contains seven "miscellaneous" poems based on Dutt's personal experiences. Of these poems, "Our Casuarina Tree," which explores Dutt's nostalgia for her childhood, is often included in anthologies of Indian literature. Critics praise the poem as emotionally engaging and comparable in style to John Keats's odes. Critical reaction to most of the "miscellaneous" poems has been similarly favorable. More generally, commentators have focused on Dutt's role as a poet instrumental to the development of Indian literature written in English.

PRINCIPAL WORKS

A Sheaf Gleaned in French Fields [translator] (poetry) 1876
Le journal de Mademoiselle d'Arvers (novel) 1879
Ancient Ballads and Legends of Hindustan (poetry) 1882
A Slender Sheaf Gleaned in French and Indian Fields (poetry) (1978)

The Saturday Review, London   (essay date 1879)

[*In the following excerpt from a review of* Le journal de Mademoiselle d'Arvers, *the critic praises the novel but suggests that Dutt might have written more effectively about Indian rather than French culture.*]

It is not too much to say that in [Toru Dutt] passed away the only writer of Indian birth who has yet shown any prospect of enriching English literature. The writings of other Hindoos in our language have been creditable, and even clever, experiments; Toru Dutt alone seems to have possessed the combination of original genius and absolute knowledge which would have enabled her to succeed. From the ruins of her career have been collected the translation of the *Vishnu Purana* and some original poems in English, neither yet published, and a novel in French which has been presented to the public by Mlle. Clarisse Bader, the author of *La femme dans l'Inde antique,* with the assistance of M. Garcin de Tassy. After reading this romance, we are inclined to think that Toru Dutt wrote French with more perfect fluency than English, but that she preserved in the latter language more poetic sentiment of style. Mlle. Bader pledges herself for the textual integrity of the book; she has very properly not attempted to remove the minute errors likely to be made by the most gifted writer who composes in a foreign language.

The ambition of Toru Dutt unfortunately induced her not merely to write her novel in French, but to lay the scene of it in French society. Marguerite d'Arvers commences the journal on her fifteenth birthday; but, though a Breton by birth, and educated in a convent, she has nothing of a child about her but an innocent *naïveté.* Toru Dutt has drawn her heroine in the colours of the land familiar to her. Mlle. d'Arvers is a slender creature, languid by turns and wild with energy; her masses of hair and her large eyes are brilliantly black; and she is quiet and childish only because no breath of disturbance has ever crossed her life . . . . We have a marvellous picture given us of the inexperienced and innocent girl thrown into the society of [a] strange family,—the excitable Countess, who showers affection on her, and the two sons—Dunois, morbid and eccentric, subject to long paroxysms of torpor, followed by violent accessions of excitement, and Gaston, with a strange jubilant look always on his face, avoiding the others as much as possible. . . .

Le journal de Mlle. d'Arvers is a very melancholy and tragic novel, but it is one of great power and beauty.

Every reader, however, will regret that Toru Dutt's ambition led her to imagine life in Europe instead of describing what lay around her. A novel of Hindoo manners by a Hindoo of such genius and insight would have been, not a mere curiosity, as *Mlle. d'Arvers* must always remain, but an invaluable addition to our knowledge of the East. There is every reason to believe that in intellectual power Toru Dutt was one of the most remarkable women that have lived. Had George Sand or George Eliot died at the age of twenty-one, they would certainly not have left behind them any proof either of application or of originality superior to those bequeathed to us by Toru Dutt; and we discover little of merely ephemeral precocity in the attainments of this singular girl. Mr. Carlyle's definition of genius as the ability to take infinite pains is exemplified in what we know of Toru Dutt's untiring energy and literary

pertinacity. We have left her story, like that of Cambuscan, half told; but the reader will not be inclined to quit *Mlle. d'Arvers* till her history is closed, and will be ready to admit that, however little real knowledge of France and French society the story shows, it displays great truth and force in the delineation of character, and a surprising command over pathos and passion.

> *"A Hindoo Poetess," in* The Saturday Review, *London, Vol. 48, No. 1243, August 23, 1879, pp. 241-42.*

Edmund W. Gosse   (essay date 1882)

[*Gosse was a prominent English man of letters during the late nineteenth century. A prolific literary historian, biographer, and critic, he is most esteemed today for a single and atypical work,* Father and Son: A Study of Two Temperaments *(1907), an account of his childhood that is considered among the most distinguished examples of Victorian spiritual autobiography. In the following excerpt, he offers an overview of Dutt's principal works.*]

The *Sheaf Gleaned in French Fields* is certainly the most imperfect of Toru's writings, but it is not the least interesting. It is a wonderful mixture of strength and weakness, of genius overriding great obstacles and of talent succumbing to ignorance and inexperience. That it should have been performed at all is so extraordinary that we forget to be surprised at its inequality. The English verse is sometimes exquisite; at other times the rules of our prosody are absolutely ignored, and it is obvious that the Hindu poetess was chanting to herself a music that is discord in an English ear. The notes are no less curious, and to a stranger no less bewildering. Nothing could be more naïve than the writer's ignorance at some points, or more startling than her learning at others. On the whole, the attainment of the book was simply astounding. (pp. xv-xvi)

As a literary composition *Mlle. d'Arvers* deserves high commendation. It deals with the ungovernable passion of two brothers for one placid and beautiful girl, a passion which leads to fratricide and madness. That it is a very melancholy and tragical story is obvious from this brief sketch of its contents, but it is remarkable for coherence and self-restraint no less than for vigour of treatment. Toru Dutt never sinks to melodrama in the course of her extraordinary tale, and the wonder is that she is not more often fantastic and unreal.

But we believe that the original English poems . . . will be ultimately found to constitute Toru's chief legacy to posterity. . . . No modern Oriental has given us so strange an insight into the conscience of the Asiatic as is presented in the stories of **"Prahlad"** and of **"Savitri,"** or so quaint a piece of religious fancy as the ballad of **"Jogadhya Uma."** The poetess seems in these verses to be chanting to herself those songs of her mother's race to which she always turned with tears of pleasure. They breathe a Vedic solemnity and simplicity of temper, and are singularly devoid of that littleness and frivolity which seem, if we may judge by a slight experience, to be the bane of modern India.

As to the merely technical character of these poems, it may be suggested that in spite of much in them that is rough and inchoate, they show that Toru was advancing in her mastery of English verse. Such a stanza as this, selected out of many no less skilful, could hardly be recognized as the work of one by whom the language was a late acquirement:—

What glorious trees! The sombre saul,
  On which the eye delights to rest,—
The betel-nut, a pillar tall,
  With feathery branches for a crest,—
The light-leaved tamarind spreading wide,—
  The pale faint-scented bitter neem,
The seemul, gorgeous as a bride,
  With flowers that have the ruby's gleam.

In other passages, of course, the text reads like a translation from some stirring ballad, and we feel that it gives but a faint and discordant echo of the music welling in Toru's brain. For it must frankly be confessed that in the brief May-day of her existence she had not time to master our language as Blanco White did, or as Chamisso mastered German. To the end of her days, fluent and graceful as she was, she was not entirely conversant with English, especially with the colloquial turns of modern speech. Often a very fine thought is spoiled for hypercritical ears by the queer turn of expression which she has innocently given to it. These faults are found to a much smaller degree in her miscellaneous poems. Her sonnets . . . seem to me to be of great beauty, and her longer piece entitled **"Our Casuarina Tree,"** needs no apology for its rich and mellifluous numbers.

It is difficult to exaggerate when we try to estimate what we have lost in the premature death of Toru Dutt. . . . When the history of the literature of our country comes to be written, there is sure to be a page in it dedicated to this fragile exotic blossom of song. (pp. xxii-xxvii)

> *Edmund W. Gosse, "Toru Dutt: Introductory Memoir," in* Ancient Ballads and Legends of Hindustan *by Toru Dutt, Kegan Paul, Trench & Co., 1882, pp. vii-xxvii.*

Edward J. Thompson   (essay date 1919)

[*In the following excerpt, Thompson challenges the popular opinion that the ballads in* Ancient Ballads and Legends of Hindustan *are Dutt's best work and contends that the individual poems that follow them in the collection are superior. For a rebuttal, see the excerpt by Padmini Sen Gupta dated 1968.*]

The fact of Toru Dutt's achievement may be quite simply stated. So far as actual performance goes, her fame rests on two books, neither of any great size, and one published posthumously. Each of these, judged by any fair standard, represents, in differing ways, a really astonishing measure of actual, undeniable success. But, further, both are affected by the number of indications they contain of possibilities of development, often in directions where the poet's real achievement was slight. There are outcroppings of veins that were never, during her brief day of work, touched to any considerable extent. It is the knowledge of this that compels diffidence and hesitation in criticism of her verse. It is easy to feel that in the work done, she never escaped from the influence of her favourite English poets, such writers as Mrs. Browning, whose work did not fur-

nish satisfactory prosodic models. The metres used by Toru Dutt are nearly always of the simplest, and her use of them is marred by much crudity. Against this must be set the many signs of haste and lack of opportunity to finish. The punctuation of the ballads, for example, is chaotic. She heard, as Lowell surmises that Keats did, a voice urging: 'What thou doest, do quickly.'. . . Yet, even amid the many marks of immaturity and haste, there are signs that she would have escaped before long from many of her prosodic limitations. **'Our Casuarina Tree,'** surely the most remarkable poem ever written in English by a foreigner, shows her already possessed of mastery over a more elaborate and architectural form of verse. In any case, there is enough to show that experience and practice would have brought release from the cramping and elementary forms that she used. . . . (pp. 195-96)

And, with regard to shortcomings far more serious, there is, again, evidence that a few more years would have brought emancipation. Her work, as it stands, is not deeply rooted. It is usual to say that her Indian ballads are that portion of her poetry which has most chance or permanence, for its own sake. This, I am convinced, is an error. I am not blind to their scattered beauties, the noble picture of Savitri in her following of Death, the touches of Indian scenery which spread a kind of woodland shade over **'Buttoo'**; nor can the most casual reader fail to feel the presence of power, careless and diffused, yet binding the whole into unity. But the facts remain, of carelessness, and, what is more serious, lack of sympathy in the author. She stands outside her themes, and does not enter deeply into them. Nor can I consider these themes as of anything like first-class value. Some have a rustic charm which strikes the mind pleasantly enough, but not deeply; others had been handled, ages before Toru took them up, by writers whose minds were primitive, as hers emphatically was not, and in sympathy, as hers, again, was not. These ballads do not adequately reveal her poetic gift. Yet, since Mr. Gosse and practically every one who has written on Toru's work has rested her fame chiefly on these, we must notice them. In the very first of them, **'Savitri,'** we open upon a beautiful image:

Savitri was the only child
Of Madra's wise and mighty king;
Stern warriors, when they saw her, smiled,
As mountains smile to see the Spring.

But such verbal felicities are few. 'Savitri' is diffuse; but it is a lovely story, beautifully told. Through all the shortcomings of the poem, as of those that follow it, is apparent a very remarkable narrative gift. Death is finely put before us, and the picture of Savitri following him is a haunting one. Part III, the description of Death in his court, is the most condensed and best-wrought part of the poem.

'Jogadhya Uma' is a version of a popular Hindu myth, connected with many places, and Toru's excuse for writing it is a sufficient one:

Absurd may be the tale I tell,
  Ill-suited to the marching times.
I loved the lips from which it fell,
  So let it stand among my rhymes.

Even in these fragments, the reader cannot fail to notice the neat turn of the octosyllabics, and wonder at this Indian girl's easy command of our tongue.

'Buttoo' is a story of heroic selflessness, with some fresh scenes of Indian jungle:

> The Indian fig's pavilion-tent
>   In which whole armies might repose,
> With here and there a little rent,
>   The sunset's beauty to disclose,
> The bamboo-boughs that sway and swing
> 'Neath bulbuls, as the south wind blows,
> The mango-tope, a close, dark ring,
>   Home of the rooks and clamorous crows.

It would be ungracious to dwell upon such slips as the occasional introduction of references distinctively Western—such as, for instance, in the lines just quoted, the quite unnecessary and untruthful 'rooks'—even though, with one who knew as well as Toru did, these are not slips but carelessness; ungracious, too, to stress the occurrence of such a line as:

> Worried, and almost in a rage.

At any rate, what other Indian has used our language so freely and so colloquially? And all these poems are experimental.

Of far higher value, and deserving of much more attention than they have received, are the half-dozen intensely personal poems which follow the ballads. I have spoken of **'Our Casuarina Tree.'** One of the stanzas drops into conventionality, and uses adjectives and thought that are secondhand and otiose. But the poem's strength is independent of this. The dying girl turns to the memories of her childhood, memories now shared with the dead, and sees them symbolized in the tree. The blending of pathos and dignity of spirit, the stretching out of ghostly hands to those other haunted trees of Wordsworth's in Borrowdale, the conclusion—so recalling the last work of another poet, far inferior in genius but dying equally young, Kirke White, in the touching close of his 'Christiad,'—all this forms a whole of remarkable strength and beauty, and should achieve her hope of placing the tree of her childhood's memories among those immortalized by

> Mighty poets in their misery dead.

'Near Hastings' is a lyric which brings a lump to the throat, and should convince the most careless and supercilious of the grace and wisdom, the political expediency even, of receiving with kindness these strangers with whom God has so strongly linked us, and who so often find our manners, like our northern climate, cold.

These last poems have a boldness and imaginative vigour which had not appeared before in Toru's work. Nothing could be finer or more vivid than the line on the simuls in blossom, in the **'Baugmaree'** sonnet:

> Red, red, and startling like a trumpet's sound.

The whole sonnet is beautiful, and should be in every sonnet anthology. Her poems on France and French affairs misread the political situation, but are a most interesting personal revelation. Her love for France leads her to scorn for 'Levite England,' who stood aside in the 1870 agony. But no one to-day is likely to quarrel with her enthusiasm for the generous nation that has so long and so signally served civilization. Her letters show how the Franco-Prussian War stirred her sympathies; no Frenchwoman could have felt more poignantly for her bleeding country.

It is interesting to compare Toru's verses with those written by her contemporary, Christina Rossetti:

> She sitteth still, who used to dance.

But the verses grip most for their pictorial power, especially the lines beginning:

> Wavered the foremost soldiers—then fell back,

and for the vehement soul that they reveal, a soul which has had few fellows throughout time. Toru Dutt remains one of the most astonishing women that ever lived, a woman whose place is with Sappho and Emily Brontë, fiery and unconquerable as they; and few statements, one feels, can more triumphantly sustain fair examination. The remarkable verses, **'The Tree of Life,'** of deep pathos and beauty, though their meaning is obscure, chronicling the dream which foreran death, strengthen this same conviction of power and fire. These verses, intensely personal all, and by that intensity breaking loose from convention and fetters, show her feeling her way to freer rhythms, and even handling blank verse—of which no Englishwoman has given a satisfactory example—in a way that promised ultimate mastery, or at least a very great degree of strength and adequacy. These poems are sufficient to place Toru Dutt in the small class of women who have written English verse that can stand. (pp. 196-200)

> *Edward J. Thompson, "Toru Dutt," in* The London Quarterly Review, *Vol. CXXXII, October, 1919, pp. 194-204.*

Harihar Das   (essay date 1931)

[*In the following excerpt, Das comments on each section of* Ancient Ballads and Legends of Hindustan, *identifying those poems adapted from the Sanskrit as Dutt's most effective.*]

It is impossible to read [**Ancient Ballads and Legends of Hindustan**] without visualizing the affinity, discovered and established long ago, between the two great classical languages of Europe, the parents of many of its modern languages, and the great classical language of India, to which many of [Toru Dutt's] modern vernaculars owe their origin. With the passage of time proceeded the gradual unfolding of the affinity between the classical literatures of ancient Europe and those of ancient India. Both the ancient Epics of Hindustan, like the ancient Epics of Europe, contained many episodes in Song and Legend that gave birth to the lyrical literatures of those two continents. In both, these episodes preserved in writing what had, before the epic ages, been handed down orally by successive generations of bards and minstrels. It is from these writings that lyrical poets, in both East and West, have found the sources of their inspiration, and have given it expression in language of delicate sentiment and fervid emotion. One of these later poets was Toru Dutt in India.

Ancient Ballads and Legends of Hindustan, in the judgment of competent critics, is her best work in English. It shows how Toru's intellect, while thoroughly assimilating the spirit of French and English literature, found eventually its truest expression in Sanskrit literature: and this was the final phase in the evolution of the mind of this sensitive, intensely Indian poetess. (pp. 695-96)

As a distinguished Indian educationist, Principal Seshadri, remarks [in his brochure on Toru Dutt]: "In her *Ballads and Legends of Hindustan* she has successfully striven to interpret the spirit of the East to the West. . . . The lays are steeped in Hindu sentiments, and breathe throughout the spirit of Hindu tradition, and Hindu thought. Her poetry is essentially of her race and her country." Possibly such a verdict, coming, as it does, from one of her own race, may be held to counterbalance the opinion of the English critic [R. W. Frazer], who says:

> The poems, often faultless as they are in technical execution, sometimes the verse, as Mr. Gosse truly says, being exquisite to a hypercritical ear, can never take an abiding place in the history of English or Indian literature. The old ballads and legends have lost all their plaintive cadence, all the natural charm they bore when wrapped round with the full sounding music of the Sanskrit, or, in what lay ready to the hands of the poetess, her own classical Bengali.
>
> The imagery, the scenery has even lost its own Oriental colour and profusion of ornamentation. The warmth of expression and sentiment has of necessity been toned down by the very use of a language which, even had it been plastic in the hands of Toru Dutt, could never have afforded her the delicate touch and colour which she found in the French. [*Literary History of India*]

Doctors, we see, disagree, and we leave the reader to form his own opinion as to the justice of their verdicts, when he has followed the detailed examination of each poem. In the meantime, we quote another critic, whose name is well known in India for his sympathetic attitude towards all that is best in Indian life and thought, Mr. C. F. Andrews, who wrote [in his *Renaissance in India*]:

> Just as Greek and Roman poetry have become the classics of Christian Europe, and have not been put under a ban because pagan mythology is mingled with them, so the ancient Sanskrit literature of India will always remain the classics of the land, and its stories will be cherished in future ages by Christians. To Toru Dutt such an assimilation of the best life of India to Christianity came as a natural instinct. Her passionate love for the traditions of her country, inherited from her mother, in no way militated against her Christian faith. . . .
>
> At a time when the name of Bengal was held in low esteem in Europe, Toru Dutt raised it high among the nations of the West. In days when Bengalis were losing heart and despairing of themselves and their country, she turned deliberately from the paths of foreign song to write of the glories of her own dear motherland.

We will now consider the two earliest poems in the book, entitled **"The Legend of Dhruva"** and **"The Royal Ascetic and the Hind."** . . . (pp. 696-97)

Both these earlier poems are written in blank verse, and it is unfortunate that Toru Dutt should have chosen this as her medium for her first translations into English verse. It was a natural choice, however, and one not without precedents in English. Blank verse in the hands of a master such as Shakespeare, or Milton, is at once the most splendid and flexible of instruments. Novices are tempted to handle it because of its apparent freedom from restraint,

in that it dispenses with rhyme. Nevertheless, in the hands of the unskilled, blank verse can develop a monotony and colourlessness beyond that of almost any other metre. Considering how little practice Toru Dutt had had in English versifying, her handling of blank verse in these two poems is remarkable. The verse runs as a rule fluently and gracefully, though the reader is sometimes pulled up before a line rebellious as the following, which refuses absolutely to come under the discipline of scansion:

> My resolve unchangeable. I shall try.

It is, however, not merely in the form, but in the spirit of these early poems that Toru Dutt fails. **"The Legend of Dhruva"** fails because of the way in which it is represented to us. The impression left on our minds should be one of admiration for a boy, who, wise beyond his years, saw that the only thing that really counted was not place or power, but holiness of life. Instead, we are left in a state of moral perplexity, because the child's determination to avenge the slight from which he suffered by gaining a higher place in the world's esteem than was occupied by either his father or his brother, is to be carried out "by prayer and penance." Strange means these for so worldly an ambition as revenge! The poem, in fact, is a failure because the authoress has failed to keep in line with both the present and the past, but, apparently, has isolated the past, and thereby induced a wrong impression in the minds of her readers.

Strange to say, the fault in **"The Royal Ascetic and the Hind"** arises from the very opposite attitude. In this the authoress is altogether modern, and out of line with the past. So far is she carried away by her own views that she forgets altogether that she is ostensibly relating an old legend, and that is her main purpose, and, instead, she uses it (and, we cannot help feeling, she does it with great relish) as the text for her sermon. The old pandit's story, meant, as it was, to instil into a disciple's mind the pathos and the tragedy of failure in the narrow, difficult road to self-conquest, is disapproved of and reinterpreted out of all recognition.

The dialogue form of the original has been maintained to very little purpose, and adds still further confusion, artistically, to the poem.

We pass on now to a consideration of the story of Savitri, which never fails in its appeal to the heart of India. The constancy of the heroine, her purity, and her extraordinary devotion to her husband Satyavan are still considered as the highest standard of conjugal love today. It is one of the most beautiful legends in the *Mahabharata*, for it describes in moving and impassioned language the persistence with which Savitri pleads with Death to restore her husband's life, and her unfailing love is sufficient to overcome all obstacles. Throughout the poem one is conscious of the deep enthusiasm for the subject in the mind of Toru Dutt, and it is with breathless anxiety that the reader anticipates the final victory of Savitri. (pp. 699-700)

Poetically, the poem is a great advance on its predecessors. Savitri's speeches abound in fine, dignified passages which seem to augur great future possibilities in the development of Toru Dutt's genius. Quotation is difficult where the average is so high, and we must content ourselves with one such specimen. This is Savitri's reply to her father, when he tried to dissuade her from persisting in her choice of Satyavan:

Once, and once only, so 'tis writ,
　Shall woman pledge her faith and hand;
Once, and once only, can a sire
　Unto his well-loved daughter say,
In presence of the witness fire,
　I give thee to this man away.
Once, and once only, have I given
　My heart and faith—'tis past recall;
With conscience none have ever striven,
　And none may strive, without a fall.
Not the less solemn was my vow
　Because unheard, and oh! the sin
Will not be less, if I should now
　Deny the feeling felt within.

Toru Dutt's phrase that Satyavan's soul was "no bigger than the human thumb," though a common one in Sanskrit, is a crude expression in English. The tendencies of English literature are all towards vagueness in description of what is greater than the mere human. Milton's description of the size of Satan in *Paradise Lost,* and the famous

What seem'd his head
The likeness of a Kingly Crown had on,

are classical instances of this. To the English reader, then, these minute descriptions of the size of the soul, and the idea, too, of Death's drawing it out with a noose of string, convey an impression of incongruity if not actually of the ludicrous.

The nature descriptions are often beautiful, although maybe a little artificial. The most ambitious description perhaps, and one which is typical of Toru Dutt's delicate touch, is the following:

Oh, lovely are the woods at dawn,
　And lovely in the sultry noon,
But loveliest, when the sun withdrawn,
　The twilight and a crescent moon
Change all asperities of shape,
　And tone all colours softly down,
With a blue veil of silvered crape.

The poem is not without its faults, beautiful as is the general effect. Some of these arise from the authoress's youth and inexperience. Although perfectly correct in the original, it is a mistake in English, for instance, to institute so close a connection between Brahmins and birds as is done in the following lines:

Savritri, who with fervid zeal
Had said her orisons sublime,
And fed the *Bramins and the birds.*

Toru Dutt is occasionally guilty of mannerisms, in the repetition of a word to fill up the requisite number of syllables in a line. The following are instances:

It was that *fatal, fatal* speech.
A gleam of *faint, faint* hope is born.
Pale, pale the stars above them burned.
The day *long, long* will not appear.

On the whole, however, it must be confessed that Toru Dutt has chosen her metre (the octo-syllabic rhyming quatrain) well, and has managed it with great ability. **"Savitri"** is a long poem, but it is free from monotony, which is a remarkable achievement. (pp. 703-04)

Toru Dutt's originality has fullest play in ["**Jogadhya**

Uma"]. Her own comment upon the story is found among its closing lines:

Absurd may be the tale I tell,
Ill-suited to the marching times.

And there is, indeed, an antique flavour about it. Yet we think no other among the stories is so admirably suited as this to Toru Dutt's translucent simplicity of touch. From first to last, in spite of rare lapses into classical allusion to "the goddess of the chase on Latmos hill," and to Echo "sleeping within her cell," there is a delicate, old-world, essentially Indian flavour about the poem.

"Buttoo," or **"Ekalavya,"** again, is a poem essentially Indian in its appeal. It is a popular version of one of the stories of the *Mahabharata,* and has for its hero a low-caste hunter's son. (p. 708)

From the point of view of technique, **"Buttoo"** is an advance on any other of the poems considered up to now. Weak lines are few and far between, and when they *do* occur are guilty of mannerism, not of jingle, as, for instance, in the familiar repetition of a word:

And lo—a *single, single* tear.

The comparatively long and not too truthful description of the forest scenes through which Buttoo passed is rather unnecessary, if not altogether out of place. Its object is to drive home to the reader, the beauty and strength of inspiration which come to a man from contact with Nature. The necessary impression, however, is given far more forcibly later on in the poem, by the description of the fawn's unconscious sympathy, and the renewal of courage which came to Buttoo as a result.

All through the poem we have been carefully prepared for Buttoo's reverent devotion to Dronacharjya, who had aroused in the boy an instinct almost of worship. Under the circumstances, the reader is a little jarred by the unexpectedness of the description of Buttoo's attitude at the crucial moment of his test for obedience:

There was no tear in Buttoo's eye,
He left the matter with his God.

From the ideal disciple, we pass in **"Sindhu"** to the story of an ideal son. (p. 710)

There are no data to go upon to show when this poem was composed. It seems unfortunate that doggerel intrudes at those crises in the poem where it is most intolerable. As Sindhu is struck down, we read:

Ah me! what means this?—Hark a cry,
　A feeble human wail,
"Oh God!"—it said—"I die—I die,
　Who'll carry home the pail?"

(pp. 711-12)

[When] relating the story of his shooting of the dove, Sindhu describes it thus:

And killed one bird—it was the male,
　Oh, cruel deed and base!
*The female gave a plaintive wail
And looked me in the face!*

It is true that simplicity, at times, is characteristic of good poetry, as in the classic instance of Wordsworth's "Lucy Poems," but such passages as the above turn pathos into bathos. That Toru Dutt was capable of better verse is shown in the description of the hunt, which, in spite of its classical allusions to "Echo waking from the bed," and the "Argus wings" of the peacock, is quite a good, spirited description of a royal hunt in an Indian jungle. The description of the closing in of darkness upon the river scene is also good, though marred by an inconsistency, for darkness is said to settle,

> Like a pall
> The eye would pierce in vain. . . .

On the whole, however, the standard of poetry in **"Sindhu"** sinks to a low level. (p. 712)

As far as technique goes, **"Prahlad"** (which is written in eight-lined stanzas, the lines consisting of eight syllables, and rhyming alternately) is far in advance of that of the earlier poems. Very rarely do we meet a false rhyme (as in "heart" and "thwart") or a line which mars effects by its colloquialism (*e.g.,* "Or there will come a fearful crash"). The poem reveals, too, a growing skill in selection on the authoress's part. For instance, the original story dwells at great length on the various means employed to kill Prahlad, after the failure of the first attempts, and luxuriates in details of each. Toru Dutt dismisses them in one stanza, and then attributes them to "vague rumours," which is a great gain from an English reader's point of view.

The phraseology used by Prahlad in his defence has at times too distinctively Biblical a flavour, or is reminiscent of English hymns, but, on the whole, his speeches form the best work in the poem. (p. 714)

There are seven miscellaneous poems contained in the second part of the volume which are more or less autobiographical. . . . [We] are tempted to recall what has been considered one of the most successful experiments of a foreigner in the field of English poetry, the little piece written to **"Our Casuarina Tree."** This particular tree was one bound up with many recollections of her childhood and had been sanctified by memories of a dead brother and sister who long before had played with her beneath its shade. The poem is rich in imagery and musical cadences, and it seems reminiscent of Keats' "Ode to a Nightingale" as well as of Wordsworth's "Yew Trees." (p. 715)

> *Harihar Das, "The Classical Tradition in Toru Dutt's Poetry," in* The Asiatic Review, *Vol. XXVII, No. 92, October, 1931, pp. 695-715.*

Padmini Sen Gupta (essay date 1968)

[*In the following excerpt, Sen Gupta addresses Edward J. Thompson's comments on Dutt's lack of sympathy and depth in her rendering of ancient Indian legends (see excerpt dated 1919).*]

However much Toru loved England and France, she was subconsciously never at home in writing about these countries or in translating their literature, and it was only when she gathered a Sheaf in Sanskrit fields that her real poetic worth awoke. (p. 80)

The *Ballads* brought Toru home to rest in a world of her own.

E. J. Thompson comments that, as in the case of Keats, a persistent voice kept sounding in her ears admonishing her with the words: 'What thou doest, do quickly,' and that after Aru's death she was even more in a hurry. 'Yet, even amid the many marks of immaturity and haste, there are signs that she would have escaped before long from many of her prosodic limitations.' Her greater faults would have been removed by experience, for they were not too deeply rooted. Mr. Thompson continues: 'The *Ballads* are that portion of her work which has most chance of some sort of permanence for its own sake.' They were 'careless and diffused, yet binding the whole into unity.' 'But the fact remains, of carelessness, and, what is more serious, lack of sympathy in the author. She stands outside her themes and does not enter deeply into them.' Thompson may be judging Toru in this instance too much as a foreigner, and does not seem to quite understand that, despite Toru being a Christian, she was certainly able thoroughly to become a part of the Hindu themes of which she wrote. Neither could the ancient Indian myths ever be old and primitive or lacking in 'first-class value.' The stories Toru chose were quite well-known and spoke of an ancient culture and heritage, as traditional as the Greek legends. Toru herself commented: 'The Sanskrit is as old and as grand a language as the Greek.' Toru also had the advantage over the writers of today in being among the first to be able to present Sanskrit themes to a foreign world. (pp. 80-1)

Toru's interpretations of Hindu ethics are entirely sympathetic, except in one instance in **'The Royal Ascetic'** when she feels that the Royal sage should not give up his love for things of this world completely:

> but we, who happier, live
> Under the holiest dispensation, know
> That God is Love, and not to be adored
> By devotion born of stoic pride,
> Or with ascetic rites, or penance hard,
> But with a love, in character akin
> To His unselfish, all-including love.

Toru insisted that little sympathy could be offered to the Brahman who implied that King Bharat had committed a sin because he loved his pet deer too much. There is not a sign otherwise of Toru not being entirely in sympathy with the ancient world of India.

Thompson commented, justifiably one feels, that Toru's adjectives and thought 'are second-hand and otiose.' Certainly she was in the unfortunate habit of using redundant adjectives, often to make up the rhythm. Her punctuation, too, abounds in commas, dashes and semi-colons. But her *Ballads* run much more smoothly and do not 'limp' as much as her French translations and are at the same time almost inspired. Toru gazes at the sea of rich Sanskrit literature before her like Cortez in Keats' sonnet:

> . . .When with eagle eyes
> He stared at the Pacific—and all his men
> Looked at each other with a wild surmise—
> Silent, upon a peak in Darien.

It is again the case of what might have been when Toru was denied the life span to study deeper the treasures of her own classical language.

[Original manuscript of Dutt's translation of de Lamartine's The Cedars of Lebanon. *The handwritten text reads:]*

> He saw the tribes as captives led,
> He saw them back return anon;
> As rafters have our branches dead
> Covered the porch of Solomon.
> And later, when the Word made Man
> Came down in God's salvation-plan
> To pay for sin the ransom price,
> The beams that formed the Cross we gave,
> These, red in blood of power to save,
> Were altars of the Sacrifice
>
> In memory of such great events,
> Men come to worship our remains,
> Kneel down in prayer within our tents,
> And kiss our old trunks' weather-stains
> The saint, the poet and the sage
> Hear, and shall hear from age to age
> Sounds in our foliage like the voice
> Of many waters In these shades
> Their burning words are forged like blades,
> While their uplifted souls rejoice
>
>   Toru Dutt.
>
> 1st November 1876.   Calcutta.

Original manuscript of Dutt's translation of de Lamartine's The Cedars of Lebanon.

In spite of her many faults, mostly due to her immaturity, Toru's poems are strong. Here, for instance, are two of the many beautiful stanzas from the **Ballads:**

> Oh, lovely are the woods at dawn,
>   And lovely in the sultry noon,
> But loveliest, when the sun withdrawn
>   The twilight and the crescent moon
> Change all asperities of shape,
>   And tone all colours softly down,
> With a blue veil of silvered crape!
>   Lo! By that hill which palm-trees crown,
> Down the deep glade with perfume rife
>   From buds that to the dews expand,
> The husband and the faithful wife
>   Pass to dense jungle,—hand in hand.
>
> I know in such a world as this
>   No one can gain his heart's desire,
> Or pass the year in perfect bliss;
>   Like gold we must be tried by fire;
> And each shall suffer as he acts
>   And thinks,—his own sad burden bear!
> No friends can help,—his sins are facts
>   That nothing can annul or square,
> And he must bear their consequence.
>   Can I my husband save by rites?
> Ah, no,—that were a vain pretence,
> Justice eternal strict requites.

But though the beginning of both the above quoted verses are very lovely, Toru seems to be unable to sustain the beauty and richness of the lines for long. By the end of the stanza, the words definitely 'limp' and the music of the lines is spoilt in order somehow to proceed with the narrative.

Toru respected the gods of ancient India, and her praise of Yama and other deities is everywhere evident. There is deep reverence for an old faith and Toru's Christianity does not in anyway clash with it. She was the true Christian in that she did not look on other religions with narrow eyes. She was the genuine daughter of Hinduism in that she was not dogmatic, but broad-minded and tolerant.

Though Toru's 'lays' are 'steeped in Hindu sentiment and tradition' and 'though her poetry is essentially of her race and her country' [Principal Seshadri, brochure on Toru Dutt], some critics feel that Toru was not able to reproduce the rich Sanskrit language in English. (pp. 81-3)

On reading Kalidasa, Bana or any of the Sanskrit writers, there is a flowery phraseology, an excess of praise of the hero and heroine, a magnificence in the descriptions of the grandeur of the gods and kings, a profusion and splendour of nature which Toru has not been able accurately to reproduce, for she has modernised and shortened her translations to suit a foreign audience. But she will nevertheless be termed a classical writer, because the legends themselves are classical and epic. . . .

Considering the stories as they appear in the fifth edition of *Ancient Ballads and Legends of Hindustan,* 'Savitri' is the longest and the most popular. The verses are dignified and to the point. Nature is described in all its grandeur and the octo-syllabic quartets are not monotonous. There is epic grandeur and sublimity, but at the same time the verses are also lyrical and romantic.

The choice of Toru's other poems from the Puranas and epics are individual episodes which are well chosen.

Toru's sympathies were with the humble and the insignificant, and the happy culling of these stories adds to their moral strain. In 'Savitri' she brings out her great admiration for the true Indian wife and heroine as she does in 'Sita.' Their steadfastness greatly impressed Toru. (p. 84)

'The Royal Ascetic and the Hind' and **'Dhruva'** both first appeared in the *Bengal Magazine.* Both the poems are in blank verse, unlike the others, a medium Toru certainly wielded well. Both are from the *Vishnu Purana.* The first is the story of King Bharat becoming an ascetic and saving a new-born hind from drowning. It becomes his only companion in his lonely life, and he loves it to such a degree that his human weakness tends to hamper his religious austerities. But Toru upholds the right to love, and questions the ethics of abandoning the world entirely, as the sages of India were wont to do.

The legend of Dhruva is well-known. Toru tells it simply and ends:

> By prayer and penance Dhruva gained at last
> The highest heavens, and there he shines a star!
> Nightly men see him in the firmament.   (p. 85)

Thus perhaps has Toru herself earned a name which has lived a hundred years and will continue to be renowned for many more years to come. In her 'pride in her country's great inheritance, she was Indian to the core.' And she herself has become a heritage of India, bringing renown to her motherland through the arches of the years—a name ever to be remembered. Toru, a frail and exotic blossom which bloomed but for a short while, has left a fragrance which will never die.

Among her 'Miscellaneous Poems' published at the end of the ***Ballads, 'Our Casuarina Tree'*** has proved its own last line, 'May love defend thee from Oblivion's curse.' The poem is ever remembered and often quoted, and as E. J. Thompson remarked, it is 'surely the most remarkable poem ever written in English by a foreigner.' It is the most revealing of Toru's verses, with its nostalgia for the past and an 'inner vision' of sublime beauty. This poem alone can number her with the deathless English poets of her age. (p. 86)

> *Padmini Sen Gupta, in his* Toru Dutt, *Sahitya Akademi, 1968, 94 p.*

A. N. Dwivedi (essay date 1977)

[*In the following excerpt, Dwivedi discusses various features of Dutt's poetry and prose.*]

As a poetess, Toru "compels attention" [K. R. S. Iyengar, see Further Reading]. The most striking feature of her poetry is its lyricism. Some of her renderings in the ***Sheaf*** and most of the poems in ***Ancient Ballads*** are marked by lyrical fire. One may take up the following from the ***Sheaf*** as an illustration:

> Love cheered for a while
>   My morn with his ray,
> But like a ripple or smile
>   My youth passed away.
> Now near Beauty I sigh,
>   But fled is the spring!
> Sing—said God in reply,
>   Chant poor little thing.
>
> All men have a task,
>   And to sing is my lot—
> No meed from men I ask
>   But one kindly thought.
> My vocation is high—
>   'Mid the glasses that ring,
> Still—still comes that reply,
>   Chant poor little thing.
>
> ("My Vocation")

There is a sweep in these lines. A soft music rings in our ears while we are reading them. The following extract taken from ***Ancient Ballads*** presents a fine example of soothing rhythm in Toru's verse:

> Past all the houses, past the wall,
>   Past gardens gay, and hedgerows trim,
> Past fields, where sinuous brooklets small
>   With molten silver to the brim
> Glance in the sun's expiring light,
>   Past frowning hills, past pastures wild,
> At last arises on the sight,
>   Foliage on foliage densely piled. . . .
>
> ("Savitri")

The poetess grows rapturous here in describing the joyous marriage procession marching along the streets of Madra. This is very clear in the repetitive device adopted in the use of words by her. The occasion of description is such as renders the poetess lyrical and effusive in the expression of her soft, secret feelings. The simplicity of her verse reminds one of Keats and Shelley.

In describing natural scenes and sights, Toru was an expert. The *champak* and the lotus and the *kokila* ever inspired her to sing melodious songs. In the face of a natural beauty, she was deeply moved. It made her heart leap up with an unspeakable delight, and her lips, like Keats's, quiver in a state of ecstasy. Here is a wonderful description of the sunset on an Indian lake:

> Upon the glassy surface fell
>   The last beams of the day,
> Like fiery darts, that lengthening swell
>   As breezes wake and play.
> Osiers and willows on the edge
>   And purple buds and red,
> Leant down,—and 'mid the pale green's edge
>   The lotus raised its head
> And softly, softly, hour by hour
>   Light faded and a veil
> Fell over tree, and wave, and flower,
>   On came the twilight pale.
>
> ("Sindhu")

Toru was keenly sensitive to Nature, especially to sound and colour. Her poems like **"Baugmaree," "The Lotus,"** and **"Our Casuarina Tree"** bear it out.

Toru had a remarkable faculty of observation. It is this that led her to comment on men, women and their manners. She sometimes presented sketches of Indian social life and reflections on social problems. The following passage highlights the sorrows of a Hindu widow:

> And think upon the dreadful curse
>   Of widowhood; the vigils, fasts,
> And penances; no life is worse
>   Than hopeless life,—the while it lasts.
> Day follows day in one long round
>   Monotonous and blank and drear;
> Less painful were it to be bound
>   On some bleak rock, for aye to hear—
> Without one chance of getting free—
>   The ocean's melancholy voice!
> Mine be the sin,—if sin there be,
>   But thou must make a different choice.
>
> ("Savitri")

On the conditions of Indian womanhood in the glorious past, Toru's comments are:

> In those far-off primeval days
>   Fair India's daughters were not pent
> In closed zenanas.
>
> ("Savitri")

The impact of some such lines is the change in outlook that we witness today in our country.

Toru's poetry is essentially of her race and her land. She was fully soaked in Hindu myths and legends; her mother was greatly instrumental in it. She aptly interpreted the culture of her country to foreign lands. Many Hindu ideals find room in her poetry. As a young girl of open heart and broad mind, Toru definitely gave utterance to her soft feelings about France and England; she was a connoisseur of the rich languages of these countries. But she remained an Indian at heart, and her poetry, especially *Ancient Ballads,* is steeped in Hindu thought and tradition. Though a converted Christian, she had a deep respect for Hindu gods and goddesses, heroes and heroines; she never felt, as Sir Gosse supposes, that Vishnu and Shiva were 'childish things.' Sir Gosse himself in the latter part of his "Introductory Memoir" remarks that Toru's ballads "breathe a Vedic solemnity and simplicity of temper, and are singularly devoid of . . . littleness and frivolity. . . ." The ancient Vedic gods surely fascinated her. She uttered aloud the fatalistic doctrine of popular philosophy of her nation in the following lines:

> Death comes to all or soon or late
> And peace is but a wandering fire;
>
> ("Savitri")

There is another passage typically Indian, bearing the unmistakable stamp of *Vedanta* and expressing a philosophy which she had inherited and a creed which she had naturally imbibed. This passage is:

> I know that in this transient world
>   All is delusion,—nothing true;
> I know its shows are mists unfurled
>   To please and vanish. To renew
> Its bubble joys, be magic bound
>   In *Maya's* network frail and fair,
> Is not my aim!
>
> ("Savitri")
> (pp. 141-45)

It is not that Toru is simply primitive and naive, and nothing more. On the contrary, she gave a modern twist to some of her lays, and this adds a flavour to them. The story of Prahlad, thus, suggests a political moral which might well have served as a motto for a Parisian mob during the French Revolution:

> The echoes rang from hill to hill,
> "Kings rule for us and in our name."
>
> Tyrants of every age and clime
> Remember this,—that awful shape
> Shall startle you when comes the time,
> And send its voice from cape to cape
> As human peoples suffer pain,
> But oh, the lion strength is theirs,
> Woe to the king when galls the chain!
> Woe, woe, their fury when he dares!

In the rebellious spirit of a Burns, she delivered a message of Democracy:

> . . . what is rank or caste?
> In us is honour, or disgrace,
> Not out of us. . . .
>
> ("Buttoo")

She was also familiar with varied characters in political and public life. She spoke with accuracy of the timeserving politician:

>   A man
> Among the flatterers in the court
> Was found, well-suited to the plan
> The tyrant had devised. Report
> Gave him a wisdom owned by few,
> And certainly to trim his sail,
> And veer his bark, none better knew,

> Before a changing adverse gale.
>
> ("Prahlad")

She cherished a passionate love of liberty that prompted her to write in **"France"** as under:

> Head of the human column, thus
>   Ever in swoon wilt thou remain?
> Thought, Freedom, Truth, quenched ominous,
>   Whence then shall Hope arise for us,
> Plunged in the darkness all again?

The poetess had certainly anticipated the sneers of the sceptic, proud of his modernism, when she remarked in **"Jogadhya Uma"** thus:

> Absurd may be the tale I tell,
>   Ill-suited to the marching times,
> I loved the lips from which it fell,
>   So let it stand among my rhymes.

In choosing the legends of the past, she was simply feeding, as the modern poet-critic T. S. Eliot believes, the present, for anything creative can be built only on the edifice of tradition. So we can say, in a way, that Toru was one of the 'modern' poets drawing for her sources upon the popular tales of the past.

It may be reasonably said that Toru had a rare gift of story-telling, of arousing interest and curiosity, of creating suspense, and of delineating memorable characters (as one finds in *Ancient Ballads*). She did attain some distinction in narrative poetry and, according to Jha, her descriptive poetry is of a superior order. She described the death of Satyavan with a masterly skill.

One may easily mark Toru's scholarly taste as reflected in her poetry. If *Ancient Ballads* indicates her background of Sanskrit, the *Sheaf* shows her sound knowledge of French. She also knew Bengali to some extent. The two volumes of her poetry reveal her vast readings in English literature too. She showed discrimination in selecting the French poets for her renderings. Even as a translator, Toru earned tributes from her own land and from abroad. It is in her translations that the germ of her future poetry lies. It is in them that her scholarship is quite evident. Critics have invariably praised her notes appended to the *Sheaf.* She had the real worth, as Gosse holds, of a literary critic.

Toru's imagery is often drawn with a masculine vigour and fearlessness. Though a frail woman herself, she exhibited a wonderful power in grappling with the sublime and the terrible. In her **"Savitri,"** we have:

> night with ebon wing / Hovers above.

and in **"Prahlad":**

> A terror both of gods and men
> Was Heerun Kasyapu, the king:
> No bear more sullen in its den,
> No tiger quicker at the spring.

and again:

> He spurned the pillar with his foot,
> Down, down it tumbled, like a tree
> Severed by axes from the root,
> And from within, with horrid clang
> That froze the blood in every vein,
> A stately sable warrior sprang,

Like some phantasma of the brain.

She could describe a gallant party with the zeal and gusto of a Sir Walter Scott:

Oh gallant was the long array!
   Pennons and plumes were seen,
And swords that mirrored back the day,
   And spears and axes keen.

Rang trump, and conch, and piercing fife,
   Woke Echo from her bed!
The solemn woods with sounds were rife
   As on the pageant sped.

                   ("Sindhu")

Toru's images are usually bold and startling, yet pertinent and revealing.

Toru's poetic diction is mostly simple and clear. Occasionally, there is archaism in it. Sometimes we come across twisted phrases and expressions. But on the whole, her diction is often in accord with the theme and context. In short, it beguiles her years, and the reader is left winking at the rich resourcefulness of her vocabulary. Toru did not hesitate to use even French words and expressions when the need arose.

The metrical skill of Toru Dutt is no less admirable. Although her metre, as pointed out by her critics, limps at times, it is often powerful enough to meet the occasion. She used blank verse in both poetical works, but it tended to be wooden and monotonous sometimes. Had she lived longer, let us so hope, she might have attained some distinction in it. (pp. 145-49)

Finally, Toru Dutt occupies a prominent place, perhaps next to none, in Indo-Anglian poetry. (pp. 149-50)

There can be no two opinions about the fact that Toru Dutt is a greater poet than a prose writer. She is remembered today for her poetry more than for her prose. As in case of her poetry, her prose is small in output but significant in marking yet another milestone in Toru's artistic development. (p. 150)

In the two novels [*Le journal de Mademoiselle d'Arvers* and *Bianca; or, The Young Spanish Maiden*], Toru displayed her rare ability as a novelist. In weaving a tragic plot, in drawing subtle characters, in creating suspense, and in describing a person, place or thing, Toru shows a remarkable inventiveness and vigour. Of the two novels, *Bianca* is incomplete and ends abruptly, while *Le journal* grows to a moderate proportion and ends somewhat convincingly. Both the novels are dominated by female characters. Bianca dominates the action in the first novel and Marguerite in the second.

Toru's art of characterization is full of economy and suggestiveness. She excels in portraying female characters and their inner secrets and longings. She reveals her characters not very quickly but in a gradual process, holding the reader's attention to the last. Her character-portrayal is usually performed with a few masterly strokes. Her characters are both types and individuals, flat and round. The heroines—Bianca and Marguerite, mostly the latter—are the examples of the first category, and Lord Moore, Lady Moore, Gaston, and the Countess of the second. Both the novels present a set of characters who are partly lovable and partly not.

The *motif* of the novels is love. The plot moves through tragedy and suffering. In *Bianca,* Lord Moore is despatched to the battlefield; in *Le journal,* Count Dunois commits suicide, clearing the deck for the heroine's marriage with Louis Lefevre. (pp. 150-51)

Like her poetry, Toru's prose is sweet and simple. It may be appropriately called 'poetic prose,' marked by eloquence and lucidity. It is not only sparkling in style, but natural and intimate in content. In her prose, Toru's expressions are usually direct and undistorted, and shows her remarkable command of English and French. Wit, humour, and pathos generally enliven her prose. (p. 152)

       A. N. Dwivedi, in his Toru Dutt, *Arnold-Heinemann, 1977, 168 p.*

K. R. Ramachandran Nair   (essay date 1987)

[*In the following excerpt, Ramachandran Nair examines the literary and historical significance of* Ancient Ballads and Legends of Hindustan.]

Though Toru Dutt's developing personality and genius were being moulded by western influence, she never lost touch with India and Indian traditions. The study of Sanskrit stimulated her innate Hindu impulses and drew her close to the essentially poetic and mystic side of the religion of her ancestors. . . . The Sanskrit saga was most certainly a vicarious attempt to establish an identity of her own and to discover her roots. (p. 60)

Ancient Ballads and Legends of Hindustan has been the most popular of Toru's work and her reputation as a pioneer in Indo-Anglian poetry rests mainly on the nine ballads and legends and the single non-mythological poem, **"Our Casuarina Tree."** They are the most personal of Toru's poems, her "chief legacy to posterity" [see Gosse excerpt dated 1882]. The legends were chosen at random from the immortal classics like the *Ramyana*, the *Mahabharata* and the *Vishnu Purana*. Despite being a Christian, Toru was moved by the beauty and sanctity of these age old legends and interpreted them with insight and sympathy. They are also stories recollected in the tranquillity of personal agony from early childhood memories. Thus an aura of nostalgia surrounds these narrations, a feeling too deep for any other kind of expression. The legends had been a part of India's racial consciousness for centuries and it was Toru Dutt who first presented and interpreted them to the English-speaking world. "From the nursery the children live with these heroes and heroines, and neither maturity nor sophistication does much to lessen the hold of these tales on our imaginations. It was thus with a sure instinct that Toru sought in these deathless stories the right material for the expression of her own maturing poetic powers" [see Iyengar entry in Further Reading]. By the vigorous and pleasing narration of these ancient legends of Hindustan Toru Dutt struck a genuinely Indian note and conveyed to the West the intellectual and philosophical traditions of this ancient land. For the first time the splendrous soul of India was revealed to the West. Though Toru's range of selection was limited, her poetic vision encompassed the whole of medieval religious culture of India. Each legend exemplified a few of the immortal values and verities of life as conceived by our rishis and savants. Toru had accepted soul and God as the main themes in her poetry and the retold legends were a repeated quest after the ultimate truth that lurks behind the *maya* of man's relationship with man, nature and God. (pp. 61-2)

Toru Dutt's **Ancient Ballads** was the outcome of a year's study of Sanskrit. The memory of the stories she had heard in childhood from her mother was stirred by this new learning. The ballads mark a new phase in the development of Toru's poetic personality. Four years sojourn in Europe and the involvement in the study of French and English had alienated her from the literary and cultural milieu of her own land. In **Ancient Ballads** she rediscovered her roots. All the ballads except **"Jogadhya Uma"** were based on legends drawn from India's imperishable classics . . . Thus Toru was the first among Indian poets to present these Sanskrit themes to the West in a language it understood. All the legends were essentially Hindu stories, steeped in the age-old values of Hindu culture. Toru herself was a product of these values. So she could not be totally free from didacticism. However, her propensity for didacticism is perceptible only in patches (except in **"Royal Ascetic and the Hind"**) because of the lyrical excellence of her verse, the rhythmic and syntactic discipline of her versification and her genius to arouse our curiosity and suspense.

There are some beautiful descriptions of nature and Indian life in these ballads. Toru was keenly sensitive to sights and sound of nature and she had a remarkable eye for colours. The lotus and the champak, the kokil and the bulbul, trees of all shades, herds of animals and combination of colours always kindled her sensibility. The description of the forest in **"Buttoo"** is remarkable for its detailed mention of trees, plants, flowers, birds and colours. The description of the gently spreading dusk in the forest where Satyavan goes to collect fuel is another instance of sensitive observation of nature. Immediately after the restoration of soul to Satyavan, the whole forest assumes a new colour and a new light as if to share the joy and triumph of Savitri.

> Under the faint beams of the stars
> How beautiful appeared the flowers,
> Light scarlet, flecked with golden bars
> Of the palasas, in the bowers
> That nature there herself had made
> Without the aid of man. At times
> Trees on their path cast densest shade,
> And nightingales sang mystic rhymes
> Their fears and sorrows to assuage.
>   **"Savitri"**

Toru's descriptions of persons and scenes are picturesque and evocative. There is hardly any conflict between the nuances of narration and the demands of description. The picture of Yama, the god of Death, is a combination of two concepts—Dharma and Death. Yama is at once "irradiate" and "severe."

> She saw a stranger slowly glide
> Beneath the boughs that shrunk aghast
> Upon his head he wore a crown
> That shimmered in the doubtful light;
> His vestment scarlet reached low down,
> His waist, a golden girdle dight.
> His skin was dark as bronze; his face
> Irradiate, and yet severe;
> His eyes had much of love and grace,

> But glowed so bright, they filled with fear.
> A string was in the stranger's hand
> Noosed at its end.
>   **"Savitri"**

The juxtaposition of words with opposite connotations— "shimmered" and "doubtful light," "scarlet" and "golden," "dark" and "irradiate," "love" and "fear"— imaginatively suggests the combination of the two concepts of Dharma and Death. Toru's attempt to give a word-picture of the God of Death is characterised as "artistic immaturity" by a critic [M. K. Naik, *A History of Indian English Literature*]. Such criticism ignores the inherent dual character of the god and the symbolic significance of the words describing him.

Another memorable picture Toru presents is that of the lovely maiden in Jogadhya Uma. The hunting scene in **"Sindhu,"** the court scene in **"Prahlad"** and the marriage procession in **"Savitri"** are some of the other charming descriptions Toru has given in the **Ancient Ballads.**

Though the ballads are based on classical Hindu legends, Toru has lent them a universality by giving a modern turn to their presentation. In **"The Royal Ascetic and the Hind"** she goes to the extent of rebuking the author of the *Vishnu Purana* from which the story is taken, for having implied that the hermit-king had sinned in loving the fawn at the cost of his own ascetic practices. She declares that asceticism without compassion is futile.

> Know
> That God is love, and not to be adored
> By a devotion born of stoic pride
> Or with ascetic rites, or penance hard,
> But with a love in character akin
> To His unselfish, all including love.
>   **"The Royal Ascetic and the Hind"**

The legend of **"Prahlad"** focuses the attention on the problem of tyranny. Tyranny demoralises not only the tyrant but also those who are subjected to it. It paralyses the human will and the only hope is an abiding faith in a power beyond us, a vision still unrealised. Prahlad has that vision which inspires him to challenge the tyranny of his father. Heerun Kasyapu's tyranny consists in regimenting individual faith and brutalising knowledge. Tyranny contains the seeds of its own destruction. So when the king falls dead, the sovereignty of the people asserts itself and proclaims:

> Kings rule for us and in our name.
>   **"Prahlad"**

Toru closes the ballad with a warning to the "tyrants of every age and clime" that the fury of suffering humanity will overthrow them one day or the other. In the character of Sonda Marco, the teacher, Toru presents a self-seeking lackey of the man in power. He is a man among the flatterers in the court and is ready to surrender his intellect to the demands of the tyrant.

Toru's awareness of the social inequalities and iniquities of the time is reflected in her frequent references to widowhood, caste, religious superstition and class distinctions. Savitri is warned about the possibility of widowhood:

> And think upon the dreadful curse
> Of widowhood; the vigils, fasts
> And penances, no life is worse

Than hopeless life.

                                             "Savitri"

However, Toru refers to the freedom women enjoyed in those days citing the example of Savitri who "at her pleasure went whither she chose." Toru bitterly contrasts the contemporary condition of women with that of the bygone days.

> In those far off primeval days
> Fair India's daughters were not pent
> In closed zenanas.

                                             "Savitri"

"Jogadhya Uma" is an ironic comment on the futility of observing rituals and fasts without simplicity of heart; **"Sindhu,"** a gentle censure of royal over-indulgence and **"Buttoo"** an exposition of the arrogance of caste and the severity of class distinctions. Buttoo lashes out at caste in explicit terms:

>   what is rank or caste?
> In us is honour, or disgrace
> Not out of us.

                                             "Buttoo"

This is the earliest voice of the resurgence of human dignity in Indo-Anglian poetry and it foreshadows the expansive and jingling protest against social evils by Sarojini Naidu three decades later.

It was the stirrings of a profound Hindu humanistic idealism that prompted Toru to narrate these legends. Her narration is alive with sympathy, enthusiasm and objectivity. Among the idealistic characters presented Savitri is the most fascinating and real. Her determination, courage and sacrifice are rarely matched in the annals of Indian legends. (pp. 78-81)

> *K. R. Ramachandran Nair, "Toru Dutt," in his* Three Indo-Anglian Poets (Henry Derozio, Toru Dutt and Sarojini Naidu), *Sterling Publishers Private Limited, 1987, pp. 51-87.*

FURTHER READING

Bose, Amalendu. "Evaluation of Toru Dutt: A Starting Point." *Commonwealth Quarterly* 3, No. 12 (September 1979): 4-17.

   Suggests that the study of Dutt's poetry might be enhanced by the discovery of more biographical material and speculation on Dutt's personal life.

"Toru Dutt." *The Century Magazine* XXVII, No. 3 (January 1884): 372-74.

   Favorably reviews Dutt's literary accomplishments.

Das, Harihar. *Life and Letters of Toru Dutt.* London: Oxford University Press, 1921, 364 p.

   Biography of Dutt, including her extensive correspondence with Mary E. R. Martin, several illustrations and photographs, and a foreword by H. A. L. Fisher.

Dwivedi, A. N. "Toru Dutt and Her Poetry." *World Literature Written in English* 14, No. 2 (November 1975): 278-90.

   Appreciation of Dutt's translations and poetic renderings of Indian legends and myths.

———. "Toru Dutt and Sarojini Naidu." *Commonwealth Quarterly* 3, No. 9 (December 1978): 82-94.

   Compares Dutt's literary practices and ideals to those of her contemporary Sarojini Naidu.

Frazer, R. W. "A Fusing Point of Old and New." In his *A Literary History of India,* pp. 431-34. London: T. Fisher Unwin, 1898.

   Claims the tales in *Ancient Ballads and Legends of Hindustan* have lost "all the natural charm they bore when wrapped round with the full-sounding music of the Sanskrit."

Gowda, H. H. Anniah. "Homage to Toru Dutt." *The Indian P.E.N.* 43, No. 9-10 (September-October 1977): 6-10.

   Discusses Dutt as a modern poet.

Guptara, Praphu S. "Toru Dutt: Lover of France." *The Literary Half-Yearly* XX, No. 1 (January 1979): 49-61.

   Suggests that Dutt's poetry was influenced more by her admiration for and knowledge of French culture than by her Hindu heritage.

Iyengar, K. R. Srinivasa. "Toru Dutt." In his *Indian Writing in English,* pp. 55-73. New York: Asia Publishing House, 1973.

   Survey of Dutt's literary career.

Jha, Amaranatha. Introduction to *Ancient Ballads and Legends of Hindustan,* by Toru Dutt, pp. 7-36. Allahabad, India: Kitabistan, 1969.

   Describes Dutt as having "a rare gift of story-telling, of arousing interest and curiosity, of creating suspense, and of drawing character."

Mitra, Dipendranath. "The Writings of Toru Dutt." *Indian Literature* IX, No. 2 (1966): 33-8.

   Overview of Dutt's life and literary career.

"Minor Notices." *The Saturday Review,* London 53, No. 1,380 (8 April 1882): 441-43.

   Favorable review of *Ancient Ballads and Legends of Hindustan.*

Stokes, Eric. "Closing the Gulf." *Times Literary Supplement,* No. 3976 (14 April 1978): 411.

   Review of *A Slender Sheaf Gleaned in French and Indian Fields,* a selection of Dutt's poetry reprinted in commemoration of the centenary of her death.

William Hazlitt

1778-1830

English essayist, critic, and biographer.

Hazlitt was one of the leading essayists of the early nineteenth century. Influenced by the concise social commentary in Joseph Addison's eighteenth-century magazine the *Spectator,* and by the personal tone of the sixteenth-century creator of the essay form, Michel de Montaigne, Hazlitt developed his "familiar" essay. Characterized by conversational diction and personal opinion on topics ranging from English poets to washerwomen, his familiar style is best represented by the essays in *The Round Table, Table-Talk,* and *The Plain Speaker.* While he also produced an important body of critical works, Hazlitt's familiar essays are the most esteemed and successful of his writings.

Hazlitt was born in Wem, Shropshire, and educated by his father, a Unitarian minister whose radical political convictions influenced the reformist principles that Hazlitt maintained throughout his life in opposition to England's antireform majority. In 1793 Hazlitt entered Hackney Theological College, a Unitarian seminary. There his studies included philosophy and rhetoric, and he started writing the treatise on personal identity that would later be published as *An Essay on the Principles of Human Action.* During this time he also began to question his Christian faith, and, considering himself unsuited to the ministry, withdrew from the College and returned to Wem. In 1798 Hazlitt was introduced to the poet and philosopher Samuel Taylor Coleridge, whose eloquence and intellect inspired him to develop his own talents for artistic and intellectual expression.

In 1800 Hazlitt followed the example of his older brother John in pursuing a career as a painter. Hazlitt lived in Paris and studied the masterpieces exhibited in the Louvre, particularly portraits painted by such Italian masters as Raphael and Leonardo, whose technique he adopted. Commissioned by Coleridge and William Wordsworth to paint their portraits, Hazlitt spent the summer of 1803 at their homes in the Lake District. His political views and quarrelsome nature, however, offended Coleridge and Wordsworth. Moreover, his moral conduct was suspect, and his friendship with the poets ended when he was forced to leave the Lake District in fear of reprisals for his assault on a woman who rejected his sexual advances. As a painter, Hazlitt had achieved little success; moving to London in 1804, he directed his energies toward writing.

In London Hazlitt became a close friend of Charles and Mary Lamb, at whose weekly social gatherings he became acquainted with literary society. Through the Lambs he also met Sarah Stoddart, whom he married in 1808. During this time Hazlitt's writings consisted of philosophical works which were criticized for their dense prose style. In 1811 Hazlitt began working as a journalist. He held the positions of parliamentary correspondent for the *Morning Chronicle* and drama critic and political essayist for Leigh Hunt's *Examiner* and was a frequent contributor to the

Edinburgh Review. The liberal political views expressed in Hazlitt's writing incurred resentment from the editors of and contributors to Tory journals such as *Blackwood's Magazine* and the *Quarterly Review.* These magazines published articles that attacked both Hazlitt's works and his character. In 1818 Hazlitt published a collection of his lectures on English literature, and in 1822 John Scott of the *London Magazine* invited him to contribute essays to a feature entitled "Table-Talk." The reflective pieces he wrote were largely well received and are now among Hazlitt's most acclaimed works. During this successful time in his career, however, Hazlitt's marriage was failing, and he became involved in an unfortunate affair with the daughter of an innkeeper. He chronicled his obsession with this young woman in *Liber Amoris; or, the New Pygmalion.* After a divorce from his wife, Hazlitt entered into a second marriage with a rich widow, a union which was also unsuccessful. He continued to write until his death in 1830, producing numerous essays, a series of sketches on the leading men of letters of the early nineteenth century entitled *The Spirit of the Age,* and a biography of Napoleon Bonaparte.

Hazlitt's most important works are often divided into two categories: literary criticism and familiar essays. Of his literary criticism, Hazlitt wrote: "I say what I think: I think what I feel. I cannot help receiving certain impressions from things; and I have sufficient courage to declare (somewhat abruptly) what they are." Representative of his critical style is *Characters of Shakespeare's Plays,* which contains subjective, often panegyrical commentary on such individual characters as Macbeth, Othello, and Hamlet. This work introduces Hazlitt's concept of "gusto," a term he used to refer to those qualities of passion and energy that he considered necessary to great art. In accord with his impressionistic approach to literature, Hazlitt's concept of gusto also suggests that a passionate and energetic response is the principal criterion for gauging whether or not a work achieves greatness. Characteristic of his independent mind as a critic, Hazlitt felt that Shakespeare's sonnets lacked gusto, judging them as passionless and unengaging despite the "desperate cant of modern criticism." Hazlitt was no less opinionated on the works of his contemporaries, and in the final section of *Lectures on the English Poets* he criticized Coleridge and Wordsworth, whose emphasis on nature and the common aspects of life acknowledged, in his view, "no excellence but that which supports its own pretensions." In addition to literature, Hazlitt also focused on art and drama in his critical essays, many of which are collected in *A View of the English Stage* and *Sketches of the Principal Picture-Galleries in England.*

The many and varied familiar essays that Hazlitt wrote for magazine publication and collected in the volumes of *The Round Table, Table-Talk,* and *The Plain Speaker* are considered his finest work. Critics differentiate between the essays of *The Round Table* and those in *Table-Talk* and *The Plain Speaker:* the former contain observations on "Literature, Men, and Manners" in a style that tends to imitate the essays of Addison and Montaigne, while the latter focus on Hazlitt's personal experiences in a more original and conversational style. Often beginning with an aphorism, such as, "Those people who are uncomfortable in themselves are disagreeable to others," Hazlitt's familiar essays contain the informal diction and emotional tone of such statements as, "There is nothing I hate more than I do this exclusive, upstart spirit." This informal style, in Hazlitt's words, "promises a greater variety and richness, and perhaps a greater sincerity, than could be attained by a more precise and scholastic method." Hazlitt described the method of his essays as "experimental" rather than "dogmatical," in that in writing he preferred to use the model of common conversation to discuss ordinary human experiences rather than to write in what he believed was the abstract and artificial style of conventional nonfiction prose. Hazlitt's essays express discomfort with his reputation as irascible ("On Good Nature"), question his abilities as a writer ("The Indian Juggler"), extol the benefits of common sense which, he felt, comprises "true knowledge" ("On the Ignorance of the Learned"), and otherwise express and defend his character. Many critics suggest that the lack of affectation with which Hazlitt recorded his opinions not only represents Hazlitt's belief, as R. L. Brett noted, that "ideas are best seen as an expression of personality," but also contributes to the permanent relevance of the essays.

PRINCIPAL WORKS

An Essay on the Principles of Human Action (essay) 1805

A Reply to the "Essay on Population," by the Rev. T. R. Malthus (essay) 1807

Characters of Shakespeare's Plays (criticism) 1817

The Round Table: A Collection of Essays on Literature, Men, and Manners. 2 vols. [with Leigh Hunt] (essays) 1817

Lectures on the English Poets (criticism) 1818

A View of the English Stage (criticism) 1818

Lectures on the English Comic Writers (criticism) 1819

Letter to William Gifford, Esq. (letter) 1819

Political Essays, with Sketches of Public Characters (essays) 1819

Lectures Chiefly on the Dramatic Literature of the Age of Elizabeth (criticism) 1820

Table-Talk. 2 vols. (essays) 1821-22

Characteristics: In the Manner of Rochefoucauld's Maxims (aphorisms) 1823

Liber Amoris; or, the New Pygmalion (dialogues and letters) 1823

Sketches on the Principal Picture Galleries in England (essays) 1824

The Spirit of the Age (essays) 1825

Notes of a Journey through France and Italy (travel essays) 1826

The Plain Speaker: Opinions on Books, Men, and Things. 2 vols. (essays) 1826

The Life of Napoleon Bonaparte. 4 vols. (biography) 1826-30

Conversations of James Northcote, Esq., R.A. (dialogues) 1830

Literary Remains of the Late William Hazlitt. 2 vols. (essays) 1836

Sketches and Essays (essays) 1839; also published as *Men and Manners,* 1852

Winterslow: Essays and Characters Written There (essays) 1850

The Complete Works of William Hazlitt. 21 vols. (essays, criticism, letters, dialogues, and biography) 1930-34

The Letters of William Hazlitt (letters) 1978

The Anti-Jacobin Review and Magazine (essay date 1807)

[*In the following excerpt, the reviewer unfavorably assesses* An Essay on the Principles of Human Action.]

We are truly at a loss what to say of [***An Essay on the Principles of Human Action***]. An attentive and repeated perusal of it has not enabled us to guess with what intention it was written. We are, however, disposed to think, that the object of it is very different from what it is professed to be. Under the title of a Philosophical Essay it bears the characteristical marks of a highly finished burlesque. Perhaps the author, teased and out of patience with the extravagancies of metaphysical writers, has resolved to avenge himself upon that vexatious tribe, by holding up to the world an overcharged picture of their absurdities. This view of the performance is certainly more friendly than any other to the reputation of its author; for the merit it certainly possesses, as a vehicle of ridicule must necessarily vanish when we regard it as a serious attempt to develope the principles of human action. (pp. 17-18)

A review of "An Essay on the Principles of Human Action," in The Anti-Jacobin Review and Magazine, *Vol. XXVI, January, 1807, pp. 17-22.*

The Edinburgh Review   (essay date 1817)

[*In the following excerpt, the reviewer of* Characters of Shakespeare's Plays *praises Hazlitt's explication and commentary.*]

[*Characters of Shakespeare's Plays*] is not a book of black-letter learning, or historical elucidation;—neither is it a metaphysical dissertation, full of wise perplexities and elaborate reconcilements. It is, in truth, rather an encomium on Shakespeare, than a commentary or critique on him—and is written, more to show extraordinary love, than extraordinary knowledge of his productions. Nevertheless, it is a very pleasing book—and, we do not hesitate to say, a book of very considerable originality and genius. The author is not merely an admirer of our great dramatist, but an idolater of him; and openly professes his idolatry. We have ourselves too great a leaning to the same sentiment, to blame him very much for his enthusiasm: and though we think, of course, that our own admiration is, on the whole, more discriminating and judicious, there are not many points on which, especially after reading his eloquent exposition of them, we should be much inclined to disagree with him. (p. 472)

When we have said that his observations are generally right, we have said, in substance, that they are not generally original; for the beauties of Shakespeare are not of so dim or equivocal a nature as to be visible only to learned eyes—and undoubtedly his finest passages are those which please all classes of readers, and are admired for the same qualities by judges from every school of criticism. Even with regard to these passages, however, a skilful commentator will find something worth hearing to tell. Many persons are very sensible of the effect of fine poetry on their feelings, who do not well know how to refer these feelings to their causes; and it is always a delightful thing to be made to see clearly the sources from which our delight has proceeded—and to trace back the mingled stream that has flowed upon our hearts, to the remoter fountains from which it has been gathered; and when this is done with warmth as well as precision, and embodied in an eloquent description of the beauty which is explained, it forms one of the most attractive, and not the least instructive, of literary exercises. (pp. 472-73)

"Hazlitt on Shakespeare," in The Edinburgh Review, *Vol. 28, No. LVI, August, 1817, pp. 472-88.*

The New Monthly Magazine   (essay date 1817)

[*In the following excerpt, the reviewer deprecates Hazlitt's commentary* Characters of Shakespeare's Plays.]

We have long since been disgusted with the commentators and illustrators of Shakspeare, who continue, however, to swarm in abundance every season, as if there was something new to be said upon the genius of that immortal bard. [*Characters of Shakespeare's Plays*] is a fresh offspring of vanity, and exhibits no other novelty than profaneness, of which we shall give an instance in what this critic says of the wit of Falstaff:—"He carves out his jokes as he would a capon or a haunch of venison, where there is *cut and come again;* and pours out upon them the oil of gladness. His tongue drops fatness, and in the chambers of his brain 'it snows of meat and drink.' He keeps up perpetual holiday, and open house, and we live with him in a round of invitations to a rump and dozen."

Poor Shakspeare! when will thy spirit be suffered to rest from the exorcising torture of criticism! To our readers, however, we owe perhaps an apology for this extract, in which it would be difficult to shew whether the blasphemy or the stupidity be most prevalent. In his preface the author abuses Dr. Johnson as an ignoramus, who had neither genius nor taste; but who measured every subject by a two foot rule, or counted it upon ten fingers. From the passage we have selected, and many others, we might with more reason infer, that the calumniator of the great moralist has no higher sense than that which is attracted by the charms of a full flask, or a rump and dozen!

A review of "Characters of Shakespeare's Plays," in The New Monthly Magazine, *Vol. VIII, No. 43, August 1, 1817, p. 51.*

William Gifford   (essay date 1818)

[*Gifford was one of the most controversial English literary critics of his age. As the editor of the Tory journal the* Quarterly Review, *he maintained an intolerance of Whigs and liberal politics that is prominently displayed in his criticism. Claiming that his duty was "to brand obtrusive ignorance with scorn," he frequently made Percy Bysshe Shelley, John Keats, Leigh Hunt, Hazlitt, and others the subjects of his hostile reviews. In the following excerpt, Gifford reviews Hazlitt's* Lectures on the English Poets. *For Hazlitt's response to Gifford, see excerpt dated 1819.*]

[Though Mr. Hazlitt's *Lectures on the English Poets*] is dull, his theme is pleasing, and interests in spite of the author. As we read we forget Mr. Hazlitt, to think of those concerning whom he writes. In fact, few works of poetical criticism are so deplorably bad, as not to be perused with some degree of pleasure. The remarks may be trite, or paradoxical, or unintelligible; they may be expressed in a vague and inanimate style: but the mind is occasionally awakened and relieved by the recurrence of extracts, in which the powers of taste and genius are displayed.

This is the case with Mr. Hazlitt's book. We are not aware that it contains a single just observation, which has not been expressed by other writers more briefly, more perspicuously, and more elegantly. The passages which he has quoted are, with one or two exceptions, familiar to all who have the slightest acquaintance with English literature. His remarks on particular quotations are often injudicious; his general reasonings, for the most part, unintelligible. Indeed he seems to think that meaning is a superfluous quality in writing, and that the task of composition is merely an exercise in varying the arrangement of words. In the lately invented optical toy we have a few bits of coloured glass, the images of which are made to present themselves in an endless variety of forms. Mr. Hazlitt's mind appears to be furnished in a similar manner, and to act in a similar way; for its most vigorous operations are limited to throwing a number of pretty picturesque phrases into senseless and fantastic combinations.

Mr. Hazlitt's work may be regarded as consisting of two parts; first, of general reasonings on poetry, under which we include his remarks on the characters of particular poets; secondly, of minute remarks upon the passages which he has quoted. The greater part of the volume belongs to the first of these classes; for though many fine extracts are given, little pains have been employed to bring their latent beauties into view. Looking upon such a task as too humble for his genius, Mr. Hazlitt prefers appearing chiefly in the character of a philosophical reasoner. In this choice he is unfortunate; for his mode of thinking, or rather of using words, is most singularly unphilosophical. Some vague half-formed notion seems to be floating before his mind; instead of seizing the notion itself, he lays hold of a metaphor, or of an idea connected with it by slight associations: this he expresses; but after he has expressed it, he finds that he has not conveyed his meaning; another metaphor is therefore thrown out, the same course is trodden over and over again, and half a dozen combinations of phrases are used in vague endeavours to express what ought to have been said directly and concisely in one. The mischief, thus originating in indistinctness of conception, is increased by the ambition of the writer. Mr. Hazlitt wishes to dazzle: but with no new matter to communicate, without an imagination capable of lending new force to old observations, and without skill to array them in appropriate language, he can only succeed (as Harlequin does with children) by surprizing us with the rapid succession of antic forms in which the same, or nearly the same thought is exhibited. He is ever hovering on the limits between sense and nonsense, and he trusts to the dimness of the twilight which reigns in that region, for concealing the defects of his arguments and increasing the power of his imagery. There is no subject on which it is of more importance that those terms only should be used whose meaning is well fixed, than in treating of the emotions and operations of the mind; but Mr. Hazlitt indulges himself in a rambling inaccuracy of expression, which would not be tolerated even in inquiries, where there was little hazard of error from the vague use of words.

Next to want of precision, the most striking peculiarity of his style is the odd expressions with which it is diversified, from popular poets, especially from Shakspeare. If a trifling thing is to be told, he will not mention it in common language: he must give it, if possible, in words which the bard of Avon has somewhere used. Were the beauty of the applications conspicuous, we might forget, or at least forgive, the deformity produced by the constant stitching in of these patches; unfortunately, however, the phrases thus obtruded upon us seem to be selected, not on account of any intrinsic beauty, but merely because they are fantastic and unlike what would naturally occur to an ordinary writer.

The most important of Mr. Hazlitt's general reasonings are contained in the first lecture. As a specimen of the work we shall extract the commencement, which bears evident marks of elaborate composition, and in which the intellect of the writer, fresh and unfatigued, may be expected to put forth its utmost vigour. He sets out with a definition of poetry.

> 'The best general notion,' he says, 'which I can give of poetry, is that it is the natural impression of any object or circumstance, by its vividness exciting an involuntary movement of imagination and passion, and producing, by sympathy, a certain modulation of the voice, or sounds, expressing it.'

This is not a definition of poetry—it neither is nor can be a definition of any thing, because it is completely unintelligible. The impression, of which Mr. Hazlitt talks, is an impression producing by sympathy a certain modulation of sounds. The term sympathy has two significations. In a physiological sense it is used to denote the fact, that the disorder of one organ produces disorder in the functions of certain other parts of the system. Does Mr. Hazlitt mean, that the impression produces the modulation of sound essential to poetry, in a mode analogous to that in which diseases of the brain affect the digestive powers? Sympathy, again, in its application to the moral part of our constitution, denotes that law of our nature by which we share in the feelings that agitate the bosom of our fellow creatures. This signification obviously will not suit Mr. Hazlitt's purpose. His meaning therefore must be left to himself to divine. One thing is clear, that the modulation of verse is the result of great labour, consummate art, and long practice; and that his words, therefore, can admit no interpretation, conformable to truth, till sympathy becomes synonimous with skill and labour.

The passage which immediately follows the definition, and is devoted to the illustration of it, can scarcely be equalled, in the whole compass of English prose, for rapid transitions from idea to idea, while not one gleam of light is thrown upon the subject; for the accumulation of incoherent notions; and for the extravagance of the sentiments, or rather of the combinations of words. (pp. 424-27)

> Man is a poetical animal: and those of us who do not study the principles of poetry, act upon them all our lives, like Molière's *Bourgeois Gentilhomme,* who had always spoken prose without knowing it. The child is a poet, in fact, when he first plays at hide-and-seek, or repeats the story of Jack the Giant-killer; the shepherd-boy is a poet when he first crowns his mistress with a garland of flowers; the countryman, when he stops to look at the rainbow; the city-apprentice, when he gazes after the Lord-Mayor's show; the miser, when he hugs his gold; the courtier, who builds his hopes upon a smile; the savage, who paints his idol with blood; the slave, who worships a tyrant, or the tyrant, who fancies himself a god.'

(p. 427)

[Hazlitt] says, that all that is worth remembering in life is the poetry of it; that fear is poetry, that hope is poetry, that love is poetry; and in the very same sense he might assert that fear is sculpture and painting and music, that the crimes of Verres are the eloquence of Cicero, and the poetry of Milton the criticism of Mr. Hazlitt. When he tells us, that though we have never studied the principles of poetry, we have acted upon them all our lives, like the man who talked prose without knowing it, we suspect that the common-place allusion at the end of the sentence has tempted him into nonsense at the beginning. The principles of poetry a reader would naturally imagine to be the chief rules of the art; but by that phrase Mr. Hazlitt means the principal subjects of which poetry treats. These are the passions and affections of mankind; we are all under the influence of our passions and affections; that is, in Mr. Hazlitt's new language, we all act on the principles of poetry, and are, in truth, poets. We all exert our muscles and limbs, therefore we are anatomists and surgeons; we have teeth which we employ in chewing, therefore we are dentists; we use our eyes to look at objects, therefore we are oculists; we eat beef and mutton, therefore we are all deeply versed in the sciences of breeding and fattening sheep and oxen. Mr. Hazlitt will forgive us for anticipating these brilliant conclusions, which he no doubt intends to promulgate in a course of lectures at some future day; we claim no merit for announcing them; the praise, we admit, is exclusively his own, for they are merely legitimate inferences from his peculiar mode of abusing English.

As another specimen of his definitions we may take the following. 'Poetry does not define the limits of sense, or analyse the distinctions of the understanding, but signifies the excess of the imagination beyond the actual or ordinary impression of any object or feeling.' Poetry was at the beginning of the book asserted to be an impression; it is now the excess of the imagination beyond an impression: what this excess is we cannot tell, but at least it must be something very unlike an impression. Though the total want of meaning is the weightiest objection to such writing; yet the abuse which it involves of particular words is very remarkable, and will not be overlooked by those who are aware of the inseparable connection between justness of thought and precision of language. What, in strict reasoning, can be meant by the impression of a feeling? How can *actual* and *ordinary* be used as synonymous? Every impression must be an actual impression; and the use of that epithet annihilates the limitations, with which Mr. Hazlitt meant to guard his proposition. In another part of his work he asserts, that 'words are the *voluntary* signs of certain ideas.' By *voluntary* we suppose he means that there is no natural connection between the sign and the thing signified, though this is an acceptation which the term never bore before. . . . [He] says that 'wherever there is a sense of beauty, or power, or harmony, as in the motion of a wave of the sea, or in the growth of a flower, there is poetry in its birth.' Can the motion of a wave, or the growth of a flower have any sense of beauty, or power, or harmony; or can either form a convenient cradle for newly born poetry? If he meant to place the beauty, and not the sense of beauty, in the wave and the flower, he ought to have expressed himself very differently.

One of the secrets of Mr. Hazlitt's composition is to introduce as many words as possible, which he has at any time seen or heard used in connection with that term which makes, for the moment, the principal figure before his imagination. Is he speaking, for instance, of the heavenly bodies—He recollects that the phrase *square of the distance* often recurs in astronomy, and that in Dr. Chalmers's Discourses a great deal is said about the sun and stars. Dr. Chalmers's Discourses, and the square of the distance, must, therefore, be impressed into his service, without caring whether they are or are not likely to be of

the least use. 'There can never be another Jacob's dream. Since that time the heavens have gone farther off and grown astronomical. They have become averse to the imagination; nor will they return to us on the squares of the distances, or in Dr. Chalmers's Discourses.' We really have not a variety of language adequate to do justice to the variety of shapes, in which unmeaning jargon is perpetually coming upon us in this performance. We can therefore only say, what we have said of so many other passages, that we have not the faintest conception of what is meant by *the heavenly bodies returning on the squares of the distances, or in Dr. Chalmers's Discourses*. As to the assertion that there can never be another Jacob's dream, we see no reason why dreams should be scientific; particularly as Mr. Hazlitt's work is a convincing proof, that even the waking thoughts of some men are safe from the encroachments of reason and philosophy.

The passages, which we have quoted hitherto, are all taken from the Lecture on Poetry. But Mr. Hazlitt is a metaphysician; and in his criticisms upon individual poets, loves to soar into general remarks. Thus he tells us, that when a person walks from Oxford Street to Temple Bar, 'every man he meets is a blow to his personal identity.' Much puzzling matter has been written concerning personal identity, but nothing that surpasses this. 'There is nothing more likely to drive a man mad, than the being unable to get rid of the idea of the distinction between right and wrong, and an obstinate constitutional preference of the true to the agreeable.' The loss of all idea of the distinction between right and wrong is the very essence of madness, and not to prefer the true to the agreeable, where they are inconsistent, is folly. Mr. Hazlitt's doctrine therefore is, that the inability to become mad is very likely to drive a man mad.

Mr. Hazlitt is fond of running parallels between great poets; and his parallels have only two faults—the first, that it is generally impossible to comprehend them—the second, that they are in no degree characteristical of the poets to whom they are applied. 'In Homer the principle of action or life is predominant; in the Bible, the principle of faith and the idea of providence; Dante is a personification of blind will; and in Ossian we see the decay of life, and the lag end of the world.'

The following extract is still more exquisite. 'Chaucer excels as the poet of manners or of real life; Spenser as the poet of romance; Shakespeare as the poet of nature (in the largest use of the term); and Milton, as the poet of morality. Chaucer most frequently describes things as they are; Spenser as we wish them to be; Shakspeare as they would be; and Milton as they ought to be. The characteristic of Chaucer is intensity; of Spenser, remoteness; of Milton, elevation; of Shakspeare, everything.' The whole passage is characteristical of nothing but Mr. Hazlitt.

We occasionally discover a faint semblance of connected thinking in Mr. Hazlitt's pages; but wherever this is the case, his reasoning is for the most part incorrect. (pp. 428-30)

The pleasure derived from tragedy has puzzled the most ingenious critics and metaphysicians to explain. Du Bos, Fontenelle, Hume, Campbell, have all endeavoured to account for it; and none of them perhaps with complete success. The question, which perplexed these men, occasions no perplexity to Mr. Hazlitt: from the peremptoriness of his decision, we are almost tempted to suppose that he was not aware of the existence of any difficulty. 'The pleasure,' he asserts, 'derived from tragic poetry, is not any thing peculiar to it as poetry, as a fictitious and fanciful thing. It is not an anomaly of the imagination. It has its source and groundwork in the common love of strong excitement. As Mr. Burke observes, people flock to see a tragedy, but if there were a public execution in the next street, the theatre would soon be empty.' We doubt this; at all events, those who flocked to the execution would not be the persons who derived the greatest pleasure from the tragedy. Mr. Hazlitt's explanation is in truth nothing more than a misstatement of the fact. The point to be solved is this:—What is the cause of the pleasure which we receive from the exhibition in poetry of objects and events which would in themselves be painful? Mr. Hazlitt replies,—that the poetical exhibition of them pleases, because the objects and events would please in real life by being the cause of strong excitement. If this were true, racks and tortures and stage-executions would be the height of dramatic poetry.

The account which we have given of the general reasonings contained in Mr. Hazlitt's book, renders it less necessary to enter into a minute examination of his criticisms on particular poets, or particular passages. He gives many beautiful extracts, but his remarks will not guide the reader to a livelier sense of their beauties. Thus, when Iachimo says of Imogen, that the flame of the taper

> ———would underpeep her lids,
> To see the enclosed lights—

Mr. Hazlitt admires the quaint and quaintly-expressed conceit, and calls it a passionate interpretation of the motion of the flame! The following lines from Chaucer are very pleasing:—

> ———Emelie that fayrer was to sene
> Then is the lilie upon his stalke grene,
> And fresher than the May with flowres newe,
> For with the rose-colour strove hire hewe;
> I n'ot which was the finer of hem two.

But surely the beauty does not lie in the last line, though it is with this that Mr. Hazlitt is chiefly struck. 'This scrupulousness,' he observes, 'about the literal preference, as if some question of matter of fact were at issue, is remarkable.' (pp. 431-32)

Mr. Hazlitt's criticism affords some strange instances of presumptuous assertion. 'Longinus,' says he, 'preferred the *Iliad* to the *Odyssey* on account of the greater number of battles it contains.' We wish he had told us where Longinus says so; for we can recollect no such passage. If he alludes to the eloquent eulogy upon Homer in the ninth section of the Treatise on the Sublime, he has totally mistaken the meaning of Longinus. The remark of the Greek critic is, 'that the Iliad was written in the prime of life and genius, so that the whole body of the poem is dramatic and vehemently energetic; but that, according to the usual peculiarity of old age, the greater part of the Odyssey is devoted to narrative.' This criticism has no reference to the multitude of battles; it relates merely to the dramatic character which pervades the Iliad, as contrasted with the narrative, highly poetical indeed, which occupies a great part of the Odyssey. If it were worth while to account for Mr.

Hazlitt's mistake, we might perhaps find the source of it in the Latin translation of Longinus. Εναγωνιον is there translated, absurdly enough, *pugnax;* and pugnax, either directly or through the medium of a French version, (for we believe Mr. Hazlitt to be completely ignorant of the learned languages,) has led to this misrepresentation of Longinus and of Homer. (p. 433)

Mr. Hazlitt asserts that Dr. Johnson condemns the versification of *Paradise Lost* as harsh and unequal. Johnson has devoted three papers of the *Rambler* to the examination of the structure of Milton's verse, and in these has given us a most profound and elegant specimen of English metrical criticism. Let us hear his opinion out of his own mouth. 'If the poetry of Milton be examined with regard to the pauses and flow of his verses into each other, it will appear that he has performed all that our language would admit; and the comparison of his numbers with those who have cultivated the same manner of writing will show, that he excelled as much in the lower as in the higher parts of his art, and that his skill in harmony was not less than his invention and learning.' These surely are not words of condemnation.

Upon the whole, the greater part of Mr. Hazlitt's book is either completely unintelligible, or exhibits only faint and dubious glimpses of meaning; and the little portion of it that may be understood is not of so much value, as to excite regret on account of the vacancy of thought which pervades the rest. One advantage of this style of writing is, that Mr. Hazlitt's lectures will always be new to his hearers, whether delivered at the Surrey Institution or elsewhere. They may have been read or they may have been heard before; but they are of that happy texture that leaves not a trace in the mind of either reader or hearer. Connected thought may be retained, but no effort of recollection has any power over an incoherent jumble of gaudy words. (pp. 433-34)

> *William Gifford, "Hazlitt's 'Lectures on the English Poets'," in* The Quarterly Review, *Vol. XIX, No. XXXVIII, December, 1818, pp. 424-34.*

William Hazlitt   (letter date 1819)

[*Hazlitt's anger over the critical attacks of William Gifford inspired him to publish a counterattack. In the following excerpt, he responds in an open letter to Gifford's criticism of* Lectures on the English Poets *(see excerpt dated 1818).*]

SIR,—You have an ugly trick of saying what is not true of any one you do not like; and it will be the object of this letter to cure you of it. You say what you please of others: it is time you were told what you are. In doing this, give me leave to borrow the familiarity of your style:—for the fidelity of the picture I shall be answerable.

You are a little person, but a considerable cat's-paw; and so far worthy of notice. Your clandestine connexion with persons high in office constantly influences your opinions, and alone gives importance to them. You are the *Government Critic,* a character nicely differing from that of a government spy—the invisible link, that connects literature with the police. It is your business to keep a strict eye over all writers who differ in opinion with his Majesty's Ministers, and to measure their talents and attainments by the standard of their servility and meanness. For this office you are well qualified. (p. 13)

There is something in your nature and habits that fits you for the situation into which your good fortune has thrown you. In the first place, you are in no danger of exciting the jealousy of your patrons by a mortifying display of extraordinary talents, while your sordid devotion to their will and to your own interest at once ensures their gratitude and contempt. To crawl and lick the dust is all they expect of you, and all you can do. Otherwise they might fear your power, for they could have no dependence on your fidelity: but they take you with safety and fondness to their bosoms; for they know that if you cease to be a tool, you cease to be anything. If you had an exuberance of wit, the unguarded use of it might sometimes glance at your employers; if you were sincere yourself, you might respect the motives of others; if you had sufficient understanding, you might attempt an argument, and fail in it. But luckily for yourself and your admirers, you are but the dull echo, 'the tenth transmitter' of some hackneyed jest: the want of all manly and candid feeling in yourself only excites your suspicion and antipathy to it in others, as something at which your nature recoils: your slowness to understand makes you quick to misrepresent; and you infallibly make nonsense of what you cannot possibly conceive. What seem your wilful blunders are often the felicity of natural parts, and your want of penetration has all the appearance of an affected petulance! (p. 15)

There cannot be a greater nuisance than a dull, envious, pragmatical, low-bred man, who is placed as you are in the situation of the Editor of such a work as the *Quarterly Review*. Conscious that his reputation stands on very slender and narrow grounds, he is naturally jealous of that of others. He insults over unsuccessful authors; he hates successful ones. He is angry at the faults of a work; more angry at its excellences. If an opinion is old, he treats it with supercilious indifference; if it is new, it provokes his rage. Everything beyond his limited range of inquiry, appears to him a paradox and an absurdity: and he resents every suggestion of the kind as an imposition on the public, and an imputation on his own sagacity. He cavils at what he does not comprehend, and misrepresents what he knows to be true. Bound to go through the nauseous task of abusing all those who are not like himself the abject tools of power, his irritation increases with the number of obstacles he encounters, and the number of sacrifices he is obliged to make of common sense and decency to his interest and self-conceit. Every instance of prevarication he wilfully commits makes him more in love with hypocrisy, and every indulgence of his hired malignity makes him more disposed to repeat the insult and the injury. His understanding becomes daily more distorted, and his feelings more and more callous. Grown old in the service of corruption, he drivels on to the last with prostituted impotence and shameless effrontery; salves a meagre reputation for wit, by venting the driblets of his spleen and impertinence on others; answers their arguments by confuting himself; mistakes habitual obtuseness of intellect for a particular acuteness, not to be imposed upon by shallow appearances; unprincipled rancour for zealous loyalty; and the irritable, discontented, vindictive, peevish effusions of bodily pain and mental imbecility for proofs of refinement of taste and strength of understanding.

Such, Sir, is the picture of which you have sat for the outline:—all that remains is to fill up the little, mean, crooked, dirty details. (p. 17)

The article in the last *Review* on my **Lectures on English Poetry,** requires a very short notice.—You would gladly retract what you have said, but you dare not. You are a coward to public opinion and to your own. . . . You were 'principally excited to notice' the **Round Table** by some political heresies which had crept into it: you 'condescended to notice' the **Characters of Shakespear's Plays,** 'to shew how small a portion of talent and literature was necessary to carry on the trade of sedition.' You have been tempted to watch my movements in the present work to shew how little talent and literature is necessary to write a popular work on poetry. 'But though his book is dull, his theme is pleasing, and interests in spite of the author. As we read, we forget Mr. Hazlitt, to think of those concerning whom he writes.' Do you think, Sir, that a higher compliment could come from you?

It would neither be for my credit nor your own, that I should follow you in detail through your abortive attempts to deny me exactly those qualifications which you feel conscious that I possess, or afraid that others will ascribe to me. You are already bankrupt of your word, nor can I be admitted as an evidence in my own case. You say that I am utterly without originality, without a power of illustration, or language to make myself understood!—I shall leave it to the public to judge between us. There is one objection however which you make to me which is singular enough: viz. that I quote Shakespear. I can only answer, that 'I would not change that vice for your best virtue.' (p. 43)

You quote my definition of poetry, and say that it is not a definition of anything, because it is completely unintelligible. To prove this, you take one word which occurs in it, and is no way important, the word *sympathy,* which you tell us has two significations, one anatomical, and the other moral; and poetry, according to you, 'has no skill in surgery or ethics.' I do not think this shews a want of clearness in my definition, but a want of good faith or understanding in you.

You say that I get at a number of extravagant conclusions 'by means sufficiently simple and common. He employs the term poetry in three distinct meanings, and his legerdemain consists in substituting one of these for the other.' . . . It is true I have used the word poetry in the three senses . . . imputed to me, and I have done so, because the word has these three *distinct* meanings in the English language, that is, it signifies the composition produced, the state of mind or faculty producing it, and, in certain cases, the subject-matter proper to call forth that state of mind. Your objection amounts to this, that in reasoning on a difficult question I write common English, and this is the whole secret of may extravagance and obscurity.—Do you mean that the distinguishing between the compositions of poetry, the talent for poetry, or the subject-matter of poetry, would have told us what *poetry* is? This is what you would say, or you have no meaning at all. I have expressly treated the subject according to this very division, and I have endeavoured to define that common something which belongs to these several views of it, and determines us in the application of the same common name, viz. an unusual vividness in external objects or in our immediate impressions, exciting a movement of imagination in the mind, and leading by natural association or *sympathy* to harmony of sound and the modulation of verse in expressing it. This is what you, Sir, cannot understand. I could not 'assert in the same sense that fear is sculpture and painting, &c.' because this would be an abuse of the English language: we talk of the *poetry of painting, &c.* which could not be, if poetry was confined to the technical sense of 'lines in ten syllables.' The crimes of Verres, I also grant, were not the same thing as the eloquence of Cicero, though I suspect you confound the crimes of revolutionary France with Mr. Pitt's speeches; and as to Milton's poetry and my criticisms, there is almost as much difference between them as between Milton's poetry and your verses. . . . [We] are all poets, inasmuch as we are under the influence of the passions and imagination, that is, as we have certain common feelings, and undergo the same process of mind with the poet, who only expresses in a particular manner what he and all feel alike; but in exerting our muscles, we do not dissect them; in chewing with our teeth, we do not perform the part of dentists, &c. There is nothing parallel in the two cases. 'You anticipate,' you say, 'these brilliant conclusions for me'; and do not perceive the difference between the extension of a logical principle, and an abuse of common language. . . . Poetry at the beginning of the book was asserted to be not simply an impression, 'but an impression *by its vividness exciting an involuntary movement of the imagination*': now, you say it is *the excess of the imagination beyond an impression;* and you bring this as a proof of a contradiction in terms. An impression, by its vividness exciting a movement of the imagination, you discover, must be something very unlike an impression, and as to the imagination itself, you cannot tell what it is; it is an unknown power in your poetical creed. What is most extraordinary is, that you had quoted the very passage which you here represent as a total contradiction to the latter, only two pages before. What, Sir, do you think of your readers? What must they think of you!—'Though the *total want of meaning,*' you add, 'is the weightiest objection to such writing, yet *the abuse* which it involves of *particular words and phrases*' (in addition to a total want of meaning) 'is very remarkable,' (it must be so,) 'and will not be overlooked by those who are aware of the inseparable connexion between justness of thought and precision of language.' (You are not aware that there is no precise measure of thought or expression.) 'What, in strict reasoning, can be meant by the impression of a feeling?' (The impression which it makes on the mind, as distinct from some other to which it gives birth, is what I meant.) 'How can *actual* and *ordinary* be used as synonymous?' (They are not.) 'Every impression must be an actual impression'; (there is then no such thing as an imaginary impression;) 'and the use of that epithet annihilates the limitations which Mr. Hazlitt meant' (in the total want of all meaning,) 'to guard his proposition.' *We must speak by the card, or equivocation will undo us.* You say, 'you have not the faintest conception of what I mean by the heavenly bodies returning on the squares of the distances or on Dr. Chalmers's Discourses.' Nor will I tell you what I meant. *A knavish speech sleeps in a fool's ear.* 'As to the assertion that there can never be another Jacob's dream, we see no reason why dreams should be scientific.' Shakespear says, that dreams *'denote a foregone conclusion.'* You quote what I say of Swift, and misrepresent it. 'Mr. Hazlitt's

doctrine, therefore, is, that the inability to become mad, is very likely to drive a man mad.' My doctrine is, that the inability to get rid of a favourite idea, when constantly thwarted, or of the impression of any object, however painful, merely because it is true, is likely to drive a man mad. It is this tenaciousness on a particular point that almost always destroys the general coherence of the understanding. I do not say that the inability to get rid of the distinction between right and wrong continued in Swift's mind after he was mad—I say it contributed to drive him mad. I mean that a sense of great injustice often produces madness in individual cases, and that a strong sense of general injustice, and an abstracted view of human nature such as it is, compared with what it ought to be, is likely to produce the same effect in a mind like that of the author of *Gulliver's Travels.* Do you understand yet? (pp. 44-6)

You next run foul of my account of the pleasure derived from tragedy. You are afraid to understand what I say on any subject, and it is not therefore likely you should ever detect what is erroneous in it. I have shewn by a reference to facts, and to the authority of Mr. Burke (whom you would rather contradict than believe me) that the objects which are supposed to please only in fiction, please in reality; that 'if there were known to be a public execution of some state criminal in the next street, the theatre would soon be empty'—that therefore the pleasure derived from tragedy is not anything peculiar to it, as poetry or fiction; but has its ground in the common love of strong excitement. You say, I have misstated the fact, to give a false view of the question, which, according to you, is 'why that which is painful in itself, pleases in works of fiction.' I answer, I have shewn that this is not a fair statement of the question, by stating the fact, that what is painful in itself, pleases not the sufferer indeed, but the spectator, in reality as well as in works of fiction. The common proverb proves it—'What is sport to one, is death to another.' (p. 48)

You charge me with misrepresenting Longinus, and prove that I have not. The word ἐναγώνιον signifies not as you are pleased to paraphrase it 'vehemently energetic,' but simply 'full of contests.' Must the Greek language be new-fangled, to prove that I am ignorant of it?

The only mistake you are able to point out, is a slip of the pen, which you will find to have been corrected long ago in the second edition.—Your pretending to say that Dr. Johnson was an admirer of Milton's blank verse, is not a slip of the pen—you know he was not. There is as little sincerity in your concluding paragraph. You would ascribe what little appearance of thought there is in my writings to a confusion of images, and what appearance there is of imagination to a gaudy phraseology. If I had neither words nor ideas, I should be a profound philosopher and critic. How fond you are of reducing every one else to your own standard of excellence!

I have done what I promised. You complain of the difficulty of remembering what I write; possibly this Letter will prove an exception. There is a train of thought in your own mind, which will connect the links together: and before you again undertake to run down a writer for no other reason, than that he is of an opposite party to yourself, you will perhaps recollect that your wilful artifices and shallow cunning, though they pass undetected, will hardly screen you from your own contempt, nor, when once exposed, will the gratitude of your employers save you from public scorn. (p. 49)

I have some love of fame, of the fame of a Pascal, a Leibnitz, or a Berkeley (none at all of popularity) and would rather that a single inquirer after truth should pronounce my name, after I am dead, with the same feelings that I have thought of theirs, than be puffed in all the newspapers, and praised in all the reviews, while I am living. I myself have been a thinker; and I cannot but believe that there are and will be others, like me. If the few and scattered sparks of truth, which I have been at so much pains to collect, should still be kept alive in the minds of such persons, and not entirely die with me, I shall be satisfied. (pp. 58-9)

> *William Hazlitt, in a letter to William Gifford in February, 1819, in* The Complete Works of William Hazlitt, Vol. 9, *J. M. Dent and Sons, Ltd., 1932, pp. 11-59.*

Charles Lamb   (essay date 1821)

[*Along with William Hazlitt, Lamb developed the personal essay into an important literary form in English literature. Written under the pseudonym "Elia," his essays are considered by many critics to epitomize the "familiar" style. This style is also apparent in Lamb's critical writings, in which his self-professed method was to point out fine passages in particular works and convey his enthusiasm to his readers. The following excerpt is from Lamb's review of* Table Talk. *Written in 1821, this review remained unpublished until 1980.*]

A series of Miscellaneous Essays, however well executed in the parts, if it have not some pervading character to give a unity to it, is ordinarily as tormenting to get through as a set of aphorisms, or a jest-book.—The fathers of Essay writing in ancient and modern times—Plutarch in a measure, and Montaigne without mercy or measure—imparted their own personal peculiarities to their themes. By this balm are they preserved. The Author of the *Rambler* [Samuel Johnson] in a less direct way has attained the same effect. Without professing egotism, his work is as essentially egotistical as theirs. He deals out opinion, which he would have you take for argument; and is perpetually obtruding his own particular views of life for universal truths. This is the charm which binds us to his writings, and not any steady conviction we have of the solidity of his thinking. Possibly some of those Papers, which are generally understood to be failures in the *Rambler*—its ponderous levities for instance, and unwieldy efforts at being sprightly—may detract less from the general effect, than if something better in kind, but less in keeping, had been substituted in place of them. If the author had taken his friend Goldsmith into partnership, and they had furnished their quotas for alternate days, the world had been gainer by the arrangement, but what a heterogeneous mass the work itself would have presented!

Another class of Essayists, equally impressed with the advantages of this sort of appeal to the reader, but more dextrous at shifting off the invidiousness of a perpetual self-reference, substituted for themselves an *ideal character;* which left them a still fuller licence in the delivery of their peculiar humours and opinions, under the masqued battery of a fictitious appellation. Truths, which the world would have startled at from the lips of the gay Captain Steele, it readily accepted from the pen of old Isaac Bickerstaff. But the breed of the Bickerstaffs, as it began, so alas! it expired with him. It shewed indeed a few feeble sparks of revival in Nestor Ironside, but soon went out. Addison had stepped in with his wit, his criticism, his morality—the cold generalities which extinguish humour—and the *Spectator,* and its Successor, were little more than bundles of Essays (valuable indeed, and elegant reading above our praise) but hanging together with very slender principles of bond or union. In fact we use the word *Spectator,* and mean a Book. (pp. 300-01)

Since the days of the *Spectator* and *Guardian,* Essayists, who have appeared under a fictitious appellation, have for the most part contented themselves with a brief description of their character and story in the opening Paper; after which they dismiss the Phantom of an Editor, and let the work shift for itself, as wisely and wittily as it is able, unsupported by any characteristic pretences, or individual colouring.—In one particular indeed the followers of Addison were long and grievously misled. For many years after the publication of his celebrated "Vision of Mirza," no book of Essays was thought complete without a Vision. It set the world dreaming. Take up any one of the volumes of this description, published in the last century;—you will possibly alight upon two or three successive papers, depicting, with more or less gravity, sober views of life *as it is*—when—pop—you come upon a Vision, which you trembled at beforehand from a glimpse you caught at certain abstractions in Capitals, Fame, Riches, Long Life, Loss of Friends, Punishment by Exile—a set of denominations part simple, part compounded—existing in single, double, and triple hypostases.—You cannot think on their fantastic essences without giddiness, or describe them short of a solecism.—These authors seem not to have been content to entertain you with their day-light fancies, but you *must* share their vacant slumbers & common-place reveries. The humour, thank Heaven, is pretty well past. These Visions, any thing but visionary—(for who ever dreamt of Fame, but by metaphor, some mad Orientalist perhaps excepted?)—so tamely extravagant, so gothically classical—these inspirations by downright malice aforethought—these heartless, bloodless literalities—these "thin consistencies", dependent for their personality upon Great Letters—for write them small, and the tender essences fade into abstractions—have at length happily melted away before the progress of good sense; or the absurdity has worn itself out. We might else have still to lament, that the purer taste of their inventor should have so often wandered aside into these caprices; or to wish, if he had chosen to indulge in an imitation of Eastern extravagance, that he had confined himself to that least obnoxious specimen of his skill, the Allegory of Mirza.—

The Author before us is, in this respect at least, no visionary. He talks to you in broad day-light. He comes in no imaginary character. He is of the class of Essayists first mentioned. He attracts, or repels, by strong realitites of individual observation, humour, and feeling.

The title, which Mr Hazlitt has chosen, is characteristic enough of his Essays. The tone of them is uniformly conversational; and they are not the less entertaining, that they resemble occasionally the *talk* of a very clever person, when he begins to be animated in a convivial party. You fancy that a disputant is always present, and feel a disposition to take up the cudgels yourself [o]n behalf of the other side of the question. *Table-Talk* is not calculated for cold or squeamish readers. The average thinker will find his common notions a little too roughly disturbed. He must brace up his ears to the reception of some novelties. Strong traits of character stand out in the work; and it is not so much a series of well argued treatises, as a bold confession, or exposition, of Mr Hazlitt's own ways of feeling upon the subjects treated of. It is in fact a piece of Autobiography; and, in our minds, a vigorous & well-executed one. The Writer almost every where adopts the style of a discontented man. This assumption of a character, if it be not truly (as we are inclined to believe) his own, is that which gives force & life to his writing. He murmers most musically through fourteen ample Essays. He quarrels with People that have but one idea, and with the Learned that are oppressed with many; with the man of Paradox, and the man of Common-Place; with the Fashionable, and with the Vulgar; with Dying Men that make a Will, and those who die & leave none behind them; with Sir Joshua Reynolds for setting up study above genius, and with the same person for disparaging study in respect of genius; lastly, he quarrels with himself, with book-making, with his friends, with the present time, and future—(the last he has an especial grudge to, and strives hard to prove that it has no existence)—in short, with every thing in the world, *except what he likes*—his past recollections which he describes in a way to make every one else like them too; the Indian Jugglers; Cavanagh, the Fives-Player; the noble

Portrait of Charles Lamb by William Hazlitt.

art and practice of Painting, which he contends will make men both healthy and wise; and the Old Masters.

He thus describes (*con amore*) his first visit to the Louvre, at its golden period before Taste had cause to lament the interposition of ruthless Destiny. (pp. 301-03)

With all [Hazlitt's] enthusiasm for the Art, and the intense application which at one time he seems to have been disposed to give to it, the wonder is, that Mr. Hazlitt did not turn out a fine painter, rather than writer. Did he lack encouragement? or did his powers of application fail him from some doubt of ultimate success?

One of my first attempts was a picture of my father, who was then in a green old age, with strong-marked features, and scarred with the small-pox. I drew it with a broad light crossing the face, looking down, with spectacles on, reading. The book was Shaftesbury's *Characteristics,* in a fine old binding, with Gribelin's etchings. My father would as lieve it had been any other book; but for him to read was to be content, was "riches fineless." The sketch promised well; and I set to work to finish it, determined to spare no time nor pains. My father was willing to sit as long as I pleased; for there is a natural desire in the mind of man to sit for one's picture, to be the object of continued attention, to have one's likeness multiplied; and besides his satisfaction in the picture, he had some pride in the artist, though he would rather I should have written a sermon than painted like Rembrandt or like Raphael. Those winter days, with the gleams of sunshine coming through the chapel-windows, and cheered by the notes of the robin-red-breast in our garden (that "ever in the haunch of winter sings")—as my afternoon's work drew to a close,—were among the happiest of my life. When I gave the effect I intended to any part of the picture for which I had prepared my colours, when I imitated the roughness of the skin by a lucky stroke of the pencil, when I hit the clear pearly tone of a vein, when I gave the ruddy complexion of health, the blood circulating under the broad shadows of one side of the face, I thought my fortune made; or rather it was already more than made, in my fancying that I might one day be able to say with Correggio, "*I also am a painter!*" It was an idle thought, a boy's conceit; but it did not make me less happy at the time. I used regularly to set my work in the chair to look at it through the long evenings; and many a time did I return to take leave of it before I could go to bed at night. I remember sending it with a throbbing heart to the Exhibition, and seeing it hung up there by the side of one of the Honourable Mr. Skeffington (now Sir George). There was nothing in common between them, but that they were the portraits of two very good-natured men. I think, but am not sure, that I finished this portrait (or another afterwards) on the same day that the news of the battle of Austerlitz came; I walked out in the afternoon, and, as I returned, saw the evening star set over a poor man's cottage with other thoughts and feelings than I shall ever have again. Oh for the revolution of the great Platonic year, that those times might come over again! I could sleep out the three hundred and sixty-five thousand intervening years very contentedly!—The picture is left: the table, the chair, the window where I learned to construe Livy, the chapel where my father preached, remain where they were; but he himself is gone to rest, full of years, of faith, of hope, and charity!

There is a *naivete* commingled with pathos in this little scene, which cannot be enough admired. The old dissenting clergyman's pride at his son's getting on in his profession as an artist, still with a wish rather that he had taken to his own calling; and then an under-vanity of his own in "having his picture drawn" coming in to comfort him; the preference he would have given to some more orthodox book, with some sort of satisfaction still that he was drawn with a book—above all, the tenderness in the close—make us almost think we are perusing some strain of Mackenzie; or some of the better (because the more pathetic) parts of the *Tatler*. Indeed such passages are not unfrequent in this writer; and break in upon us, amidst the spleen and severity of his commoner tone, like springs bursting out in the desert. The author's wayward humour, turning inwards from the contemplation of real or imagined grievances—or exhausting itself in gall and bitterness at the things *that be*—reverts for its solace, with a mournfully contrasting spirit of satisfaction, to the past. The corruption of Hope quickens into life again the perishing flowers of the Memory.—In this spirit, in the third, and the most valuable of his Essays, that **"On the Past and Future"**,—in which he maintains the reality of the former as a possession in hand, against those who pretend that the future is every thing and the past nothing—after some reasoning, rather too subtle and metaphysical for the general reader—he exclaims with an eloquence that approximates to the finest poetry. . . .

(pp. 303-04)

The Tenth Essay, **"On Living to One's-Self,"** has this singular passage.

> Even in the common affairs of life, in love, friendship, and marriage, how little security have we when we trust our happiness in the hands of others! Most of the friends I have seen have turned out the bitterest enemies, or cold, uncomfortable acquaintance. Old companions are like meats served up too often, that lose their relish and their wholesomeness.

We hope that this is more dramatically than truly written. We recognise nothing like it in our own circle. We had always thought that Old Friends, and Old Wine were the best.—We should conjecture that Mr Hazlitt has been singularly unfortunate, or injudicious, in the choice of his acquaintance, did not one phenomenon stagger us. We every now & then encounter in his Essays with a *character*, apparently from the life, too mildly drawn for an enemy, too sharply for a friend. We suspect that Mr Hazlitt does not always play quite fairly with his associates. There is a class of critics—and he may be of them—who pry into men with "too respective eyes." They will "anatomize Regan", when Cordelia would hardly bear such dissection. We are not acquainted with Mr Hazlitt's "familiar faces", but when we see certain Characters exposed & hung up, not in Satire—for the exaggerations of *that* cure themselves by their excess, as we make allowance for the over-charged features in a caricature—but certain poor whole-length figures dangling with all the *best & worst* of humanity about them displayed with cool and unsparing impartiality—Mr Hazlitt must excuse us if we cannot help suspecting some of them to be the shadows of defunct Friendships.—This would be a recipe indeed, a pretty sure one, for converting friends "into bitterest enemies or cold, uncomfortable acquaintance".—The most expert at drawing Characters, are the very persons most likely to be deceived in individual & home instances. They will seize an infirmity, which irritates them deservedly in a companion, and go on piling up every kindred weakness they have found by experience apt to coalesce with that failing (gathered from a thousand instances) till they have built up in their fancies an *Abstract,* widely differing indeed from their poor *concrete friend!* What blunders Steele, or Sterne, may not in this way have made *at home!*—But we forget. Our business is with books. We profess not, with Mr Hazlitt, to be Reviewers of Men. (pp. 304-05)

We cannot take leave of this agreeable and spirited volume without bearing our decided testimony to Mr Hazlitt's general merits as a writer. He is (we have no hesitation in saying) one of the ablest prose-writers of the age. To an extraordinary power of original observation he adds an equal power of familiar and striking expression. There is a ground-work of patient and curious thinking in almost every one of these Essays, while the execution is in a high degree brilliant and animated. The train of reasoning or line of distinction on which he insists is often so fine as to escape common observation; at the same time that the quantity of picturesque and novel illustration is such as to dazzle and overpower common attention. He is however a writer perfectly free from affectation, and never rises into that tone of rapid and glowing eloquence of which he is a master, but when the occasion warrants it. Hence there is nothing more directly opposite to his usual style than what is understood by *poetical prose.*—If we were to hazard an analytical conjecture on this point, we should incline to think that Mr H. as a critic and an Essayist has blended two very different and opposite lines of study and pursuit, a life of internal reflection, and a life of external observation, together; or has, in other words, engrafted the Painter on the Metaphysician; and in our minds, the union, if not complete or in all respects harmonious, presents a result not less singular than delightful. If Mr H. criticises an author, he paints him. If he draws a character, he dissects it; and some of his characters "look a little the worse" (as Swift says) "for having the skin taken off". If he describes a feeling, he is not satisfied till he embodies it as a real sensation in all its individuality and with all the circumstances that give it interest. If he enters upon some distinction too subtle and recondite to be immediately understood, he relieves it by some palpable and popular illustration. In fact, he all along acts as his own interpreter, and is continually translating his thoughts out of their original metaphysical obscurity into the language of the senses and of common observation. This appears to us to constitute the excellence and to account for the defects of his writings. There is a display (to profusion) of various and striking powers; but they do not tend to the same object. The thought and the illustration do not always hang well together: the one puzzles, and the other startles. From this circumstance it is that to many people Mr Hazlitt appears an obscure and unconnected and to others a forced and extravagant writer. He may be said to paint caricatures on gauze or cobwebs; to explain the mysteries of the Cabbala by Egyptian hieroglyphics. Another fault is that he draws too entirely on his own resources. He never refers to the opinions of other authors (ancient or modern) or to the common opinions afloat on any subject, or if he does, it is to treat them with summary or elaborate contempt. Neither does he consider a subject in all its possible or most prominent bearings, but merely in those points (sometimes minute and extraneous, at other times more broad and general) in which it happens to have pressed close on his own mind or to have suggested some ingenious solution. He follows out his own view of a question, however, fearlessly and patiently; and puts the reader in possession without reserve of all he has thought upon it. There is no writer who seems to pay less attention to the common prejudices of the vulgar; or the common-places of the learned; and who has consequently given greater offence to the bigotted, the self-sufficient, and the dull. We have nothing to do with Mr Hazlitt as a controversial writer; and even as a critic, he is perhaps too much of a partisan, he is too eager and exclusive in his panegyrics or invectives; but as an Essayist, his writings can hardly fail to be read with general satisfaction and with the greatest by those who are most able to appreciate characteristic thought and felicitous expression. (pp. 306-07)

> *Charles Lamb, "Hazlitt," in his* Lamb as Critic, *edited by Roy Park, University of Nebraska Press, 1980, pp. 299-307.*

The Edinburgh Review   (essay date 1837)

[*In the following excerpt, the reviewer of* Literary Remains *assesses the strengths and weaknesses of Hazlitt's writings in an attempt to achieve a balance of opinion between Hazlitt's detractors and his admirers.*]

When the reputation of an author is vehemently cried down by a party of detractors, his friends are tempted to overstep the limits of sober approbation, in their zeal for his defence; and those who join with more of reserve and hesitation in his cause, are suspected of acting an ungenerous part, and lending a covert support to his enemies. But, believing as we do, that Hazlitt had merits able to speak eloquently enough for themselves, when he shall no longer be judged with the obliquity of party criticism, we shall not hesitate to glance at a few of those essential qualities in which both his merits and his defects had their origin. (p. 398)

In Hazlitt's best criticisms on art and poetry, the reader cannot fail to observe the repeated recurrence to his own feelings and sentiments as criteria;—how the impression produced on himself is accurately reproduced and analyzed, and general canons laid down, as if by induction, from his own particular experience. Hence those passages and those characters always call forth his highest admiration, and his most searching commentary, which seem to strike on some favourite chord of his own reflections. Every one is apt, in his reveries, to identify himself with some familiar imaginary personage—with Hamlet, for example, in his melancholy and philosophic moods. (p. 402)

In all the range of subjects of which he treats, including even metaphysical discussion, the same tendency prevails; and it is singular how personal he has contrived to render the most abstruse topics. All his philosophy is controversial. He opposes some established system, and the opposition is immediately converted into a species of duel between himself and an imaginary supporter of it; in which all his reasoning seems drawn from the incompatibility of his own feelings and experience with the principles laid down by his adversary. . . . He seems frequently to misunderstand the author whom he would confute, and to

waste his copious energy in fighting shadows. The reason is obvious—he is always rather following out a parallel train of thought, conceived in his own individual mind, than closely pursuing the argument of his antagonist; and his reasonings, moreover, are almost always *ab homine* and *ad hominem.* And when he approaches the confines of political and social science, within which his enthusiasm is more easily warmed into action, all his theories are fought with the earnestness of personal quarrels; and from the Bourbons on their throne, down to the Quarterly Reviewer at his desk, all of the opposite array seem challenged into the field as the individual foes of William Hazlitt.

But there is another and very comprehensive class of Hazlitt's Essays which turn wholly or chiefly on subjects of more homely interest—on the working-day philosophy of actual life. Less abstruse in subject, they are both truer and more profound in sentiment, than his more laboured compositions. They furnish a more appropriate field for that discursive egotism which characterised him; and, consequently, they are the most popular, and, to our minds, incomparably the most genuine offspring of his genius. How acute is the repeated, but scarcely conscious analysis of self—by what subtle self-deceit are his own conclusions, modified by his own habits of mind, and drawn from his own experience, laid down as general principles of human action—how singular the unintentional artifice by which the writer's own microcosm is made to stand in the place of this greater world, and reflection clad in the mask of observation! These Essays are all coloured with the passing as well as the abiding sensations of the writer. They represent not only his deliberate convictions, but his most fleeting notions and fancies. They are full of rapid transitions from melancholy to gaiety; yet there is a fixed sense of disappointment, producing, under all these changeable tints, a permanent hue,—sickly, but not unpleasing,—in certain states of the reader's mind. There is much real independence of spirit; but sometimes it is paraded after too vapouring a fashion. But in all of them it is easy to perceive that the writer's power lay in himself; and that when taken out of his own experience his strength failed him. (pp. 403-04)

> *"Hazlitt's 'Literary Remains'," in* The Edinburgh Review, *Vol. 64, No. CXXX, January, 1837, pp. 395-411.*

Edmund Gosse   (essay date 1894)

[*Gosse was a prominent English man of letters during the late nineteenth century. A prolific literary historian, biographer, and critic, he remains most esteemed for a single and atypical work:* Father and Son: A Study of Two Temperaments *(1907), an account of his childhood that is considered among the most distinguished examples of Victorian spiritual autobiography. Gosse was also a prominent translator and critic of Scandinavian literature, and his importance as a critic is due primarily to his introduction of Henrik Ibsen to an English-speaking audience. In the following excerpt, he discusses Hazlitt's art criticism.*]

The contributions of William Hazlitt to literary criticism were so numerous and prominent, and were, moreover, so characteristic of the central instincts of his nature, that they have obscured his essays in the criticism of fine art. The latter were, by their very essence, of less durable interest; they soon were superseded in their authority, and neglected as guides to taste. They were comparatively few in number, and were scattered through the series of his miscellaneous writings. They discussed modern paintings which are now of little importance to us, or else ancient paintings about which we have become far more exactly informed than Hazlitt was.

Yet if the art-criticisms of this brilliant writer are no longer of eminent value as instructors or guides to art, their function in illustrating a side of Hazlitt's own genius is not easily to be overrated. (p. ix)

In the first place, Hazlitt as an art-critic was boldly nonacademic. Among his earliest papers are two, contributed in 1814 to the *Champion,* called **"An Inquiry Whether the Fine Arts Are Promoted by Academies."** Here his language was temperate if stringent, but things went from bad to worse, and, two years later, he published that essay on **"The Catalogue Raisonné of the British Institution"** which produced so wide a sensation and created for him so many enemies. Here he lifts the lash high in air, and brings it down with a will on the shoulders of official art. He returned to the same favourite theme in his graver monograph on **"The Fine Arts,"** in 1824, still doubting, though no longer strenuously denying, the service done to art by corporate institutions of any kind. The English painting of that day was a poor affair, bolstered into prominence by prejudice and flattery. The bolts of Hazlitt seem, at this distance of time, almost ludicrously heavy. Why, we may ask ourselves, expend powder and shot on people like Beechey, and Westall, and Dance? It must not be forgotten, however, that to their own generation these seemed very great men. The arrogance of Beechey, for instance, knew no bounds; and it showed real courage in Hazlitt, and coolness of perception too, to strike at these Court favourites of Somerset House.

Hazlitt was no less courageous in defending unpopular merit. . . . He was not lavish in his allusions to particular artists. He was more interested in the principles of his contemporaries than in their practice, but it will be difficult to point to a single instance, in the most ephemeral of his essays, where he has praised any painter because he was a public favourite, or neglected one because he was out of critical favour with the age.

The style of Hazlitt as an art-critic is of two kinds. When he deals with the theory of art, he is strenuous, close, and sententious. We observe him here to be still a little under the influence of the eighteenth-century theorists. He does not quite, like Burke, tell us that sub-fusc hues are indispensable from the sublime, but we find ourselves regretting that he had not read Lessing more or to better purpose. Hazlitt seems to have been conscious of the shortcomings of Reynolds's *Discourses,* but his own theoretical essays on the same subject are no infinitely less technical authority.

The student of to-day, desirous of examining this department of Hazlitt's work, can do no better than to read the sensible and elegant essay **"On the Judging of Pictures."** It contains some reflections on "the exclusiveness of the initiated" which may be wholesomely contrasted with certain recent utterances. Hazlitt's elaborate excursus upon

"The Fine Arts," published in 1824, is, on the other hand, only to be skimmed through or dipped into. It is ill constructed, and, what is worse, it is dull. But the least effective of his theoretical essays, and that in which the limitations of his judgment are most clearly seen, is the review of *Flaxman's Lectures.* It is true that Flaxman was a very poor critic, and Hazlitt has no difficulty in effectively pulling to pieces his flashy truistic philosophy. But when he leaves Flaxman the professor to deal with Flaxman the sculptor, Hazlitt becomes insufferable. His training had been limited; of sculpture he knew less than the least of Academy students; and his views about modern statuary, in spite of his enthusiasm for the Elgin Marbles, are practically worthless.

But when we turn from Hazlitt on the principles of art, to Hazlitt on particular pictures, the change is extraordinary. We pass into a different order of style. Here, so far from being abstruse or dry, he errs a little in the other direction. His notices of pictures are, indeed, wonderfully free from mere artistic jargon. A reader of to-day may smile, it is true, at a few such words as "gusto" and "vertù," but they belonged to the age. For the rest, what Hazlitt aims at, is nothing more nor less than a spiritual reproduction of a physical impression. He describes, but with the design of producing, on the mental retina, an image which shall create a like enthusiasm on the mind as the sight of the picture does when the physical eye regards it. This is not quite the same thing as repeating the impression made on the physical eye, because the critic endeavours, by subtly heightening his effects, to compensate for the necessary absence of colour and form. Hazlitt writes, to be short, not so much for those who are about to see the picture, as for those who will never have the chance of seeing it, and his object is to give these latter as much pleasure as the former will presently enjoy. Hence his rich and sometimes over-luscious descriptions can hardly be read side by side with the paintings they deal with.

The most perfect type of this class of Hazlitt's criticism is his **"Portrait by Vandyck."** This is no photographer's or auctioneer's catalogue of features, and still less a technical examination of methods of work, of *facture;* it rather is an involved, amorous, highly-coloured rhapsody, a communicated rapture. Hazlitt thought it interesting to read of pictures he himself would never see; and in those days, when facilities were rarer and public galleries fewer, he believed that it would stimulate a great number of sequestered lovers of the beautiful, to be supplied with these materials for dream-compositions.

Sometimes Hazlitt's epithets were too much loaded with sweetness; this error is exemplified in his essay on **"William's Views."** But the higher his theme, the more noble and appropriate were his flights of ecstasy, the more completely did he fulfil his purpose of stimulating the imagination. The process of his analysis was always literary, and his trust in his optical memory too confiding, so that sometimes, between poetry and a confused recollection, we get a description of an ancient master, which fits no recognised example. Yet it is always true to the master. Hazlitt, so fiery and fitful in real life, has no prejudices in art, unless, indeed, it be against Poelemberg and against the modern French.

In **"Pictures at Wilton"** Hazlitt says, "No one ever felt a longing, a sickness of the heart, to see a Dutch landscape twice; but those of Claude, after an absence of years, have this effect, and produce a kind of calenture." This is a remark which is highly characteristic of its author. Although Hazlitt had been, to some imperfect extent, trained in the technical practice of a painter, the fragments of his art-criticism do not show any great appreciation of the niceties of execution. He is always led away from the mode in which a picture is painted, to the subject and the exposition. It is by no means certain, indeed it is rather improbable, that a work of art, very splendidly performed, but of no sentimental interest, would attract his attention; on the other hand, a heroic or romantic theme, inadequately treated, was only too likely to impose upon his fancy. In other words, Hazlitt, the art-critic, wandering through a gallery of pictures, was always Hazlitt the man of letters, steeped in poetical association, and principally charmed with Titian because he reminded him of Spenser and of Ariosto. (pp. xxi-xxvii)

If it be true that to look for "literature" in a picture be the worst of faults in an art-critic, then, indeed, little can be said to palliate the errors of Hazlitt. His system, we must allow, was primitive, and his range of knowledge narrow. But, in his own time and way, he also was a transmitter of the sacred fire. He possessed, what so many of our modern quidnuncs have absolutely lost the idea of, the passion of beauty. His eye, as he finely says in speaking of Titian, had gazed on lovely pigments till it was "saturated" with their loveliness.

Hazlitt's criticism is transitional between the dry and formal philosophy of the eighteenth century, and the many-coloured enthusiasm of Mr. Ruskin. At a time when little real attention was paid to art-criticism, when in England at least it was bound up with an empty connoisseurship, and lost in the jargon of the dilettanti, it is the glory of William Hazlitt that he claimed for it the dignity of a branch of literature, and expended on it the wealth of his own fervid and impassioned imagination. (p. xxvii)

> *Edmund Gosse, "An Essay on Hazlitt as an Art-Critic," in* Conversations of James Northcote, R. A. *by William Hazlitt, Richard Bentley & Son, 1894, pp. ix-xxvii.*

George Saintsbury (essay date 1904)

[*Saintsbury was an English literary historian and critic of the late nineteenth and early twentieth centuries. A prolific writer, he composed several histories of English and European literature as well as numerous critical works on individual authors, styles, and periods. Saintsbury's critical qualities have been praised by René Wellek, who commended his "enormous reading, the almost universal scope of his subject matter, the zest and zeal of his exposition," and "the audacity with which he handles the most ambitious and unattempted arguments." In the following excerpt, he surveys Hazlitt's critical writings.*]

Hazlitt is not, like Coleridge, remarkable for the discovery and enunciation of any one great critical principle, or for the emission (*obiter* or otherwise) of remarkable mediate *dicta,* or for *marginalia* on individual passages or lines, though sometimes he can do the last and sometimes also

the second of these things. What he is remarkable for is his extraordinary fertility and felicity, as regards English literature, in judgments, more or less "grasped," of individual authors, books, or pieces. As, by preference, he stops at the passage, and does not descend to the individual line or phrase, so, by preference also, he stops at the individual example of the Kind, and does not ascend to the Kind itself, or at least is not usually very happy in his ascension. But within these limits (and they are wide enough), the fertility and the felicity of his criticism are things which strike one almost dumb with admiration; and this in spite of certain obvious and in their way extremely grave faults.

The most obvious, though by far the least, of these,—indeed one which is displayed with such frankness and in a way so little delusive as to be hardly a fault at all, though it is certainly a drawback,—is a sort of audacious sciolism—acquiescence in ignorance, indifference about "satisfying the examiners"—for half a dozen different names would be required to bring out all the sides of it.

His almost entire ignorance of all literatures but his own gives him no trouble, though it cannot be said that it does him no harm. In treating of comic writers, not in English only but generally, he says (with perfect truth) that Aristophanes and Lucian are two of the four chief names for comic humour, but that he shall say little of them, for he knows little. Would all men were as honest! but one cannot say, "Would all critics were as ignorant!" In his *Lectures on the English Poets* he is transparently, and again quite honestly, ignorant of mostly all the earlier minorities, with some not so minor. He almost prided himself upon not reading anything in the writing period of his life; and he seems to have carried out his principles so conscientiously that, if anything occurred in the course of a lecture which was unknown to him, he never made the slightest effort to supply the gap. His insouciance in method was equal to that in regard to material; and when we find Godwin and Mrs Radcliffe included, with no satiric purpose, among *The English Comic Writers,* they are introduced so naturally that the absurdity hardly strikes us till some accident wakes us up to it. If inaccuracies in matters of fact are not very common in him, it is because, like a true critic, he pays very little attention to such matters, and is wholly in opinion and appreciation and judgment, and other things where the free spirit is kept straight, if at all, by its own instinct. But he does commit such inaccuracies, and would evidently commit many more if he ran the risk of them oftener.

The last and gravest of his drawbacks has to be mentioned, and though it may be slurred over by political partianship, those who admire and exalt him in spite of and not because of his politics, are well entitled to call attention to it. To the unpleasantness of Hazlitt's personal temper we have the unchallengeable testimony of his friends Lamb, who was the most charitable, and Hunt, who with all his faults was one of the most good-natured, of mortals. But what we may call his political temper, especially when it was further exasperated by his personal, is something of the equal of which no time leaves record. Whenever this east wind blows, the true but reasonable Hazlittian had better, speaking figuratively, "go to bed till it is over," as John Hall Stevenson is said to have done literally in the case of the literal Eurus. Not only does Hazlitt then cease to be a critic,—he ceases to be a rational being. Sidney and Scott are the main instances of its effect, because Sidney could not have annoyed, and Scott we know did not in any way annoy, Hazlitt personally. Gifford is not in this case, and he was himself so fond of playing at the roughest of bowls that nobody need pity him for the rubbers he met. But Hazlitt's famous letter to him [see excerpt dated 1819], which some admire, always, I confess, makes me think of the Doll's-dressmaker's father's last fit of the horrors in *Our Mutual Friend,* and of the way in which the luckless "man talent" fought with the police and "laid about him hopelessly, fiercely, staringly, convulsively, foamingly." Fortunately the effect was not so fatal, and I know no other instance in which Hazlitt actually required the strait waistcoat. But he certainly did here: and in a considerable number of instances his prejudices have made him, if not exactly *non compos mentis,* yet certainly *non compos judicii.*

Fortunately, however, the wind does not always blow from this quarter with him, and when it does the symptoms are so unmistakable that nobody can be deceived unless he chooses to be, or is so stupid that it really does not matter whether he is deceived or not. Far more usually it is set in a bracing North or fertilising West, not seldom even in the "summer South" itself. And then you get such appreciations, in the best, the most thorough, the most delightful, the most *valuable* sense, as had been seldom seen since Dryden, never before, and in him not frequently. I do not know in what language to look for a parallel wealth. Systematic Hazlitt's criticism very seldom is, and, as hinted above, still seldomer at its best when it attempts system. But then system was not wanted; it had been overdone; the patient required a copious alternative. He received it from Hazlitt as he has—virtue and quantity combined—received it from no one else since: it is a "patent medicine" in everything but the presence of quackery. Roughly speaking, Hazlitt's criticism is of two kinds. The first is very stimulating, very interesting, but, I venture to think, the less valuable of the two. In it Hazlitt at least endeavours to be general, and takes a lesson from Burke in "prodigious variation" on his subject. The most famous, the most laboured, and perhaps the best example is the exordium of the *Lectures on the English Poets,* with its astonishing "amplification" on what poetry in general is and what it is not. A good deal of this is directly Coleridgean. I forget whether this is the lecture which Coleridge himself, when he read it, thought that he remembered "talking at Lamb's"; but we may be quite sure that he had talked things very like it. Much in the **"Shakespeare and Milton"** has the same quality, and may have been partly derived from the same source: the critical character of Pope is another instance, and probably more original. For Hazlitt had not merely learnt the trick from his master but had himself a genius for it; and he adorned these disquisitions with more *phrase* than Coleridge's recalcitrant pen usually allowed him, though there seems to have been plenty in his speech.

The Pope passage is specially interesting, because it leads us to the second and, as it seems to me, the chief and principal class of Hazlitt's critical deliverances—those in which, without *epideictic* intention, without, or with but a moderate portion of, rhetoric and amplification and phrasemaking, he handles separate authors and works and pieces. I have said that I think him here unsurpassed, and

perhaps unrivalled, in the quantity and number of his deliverances, and only surpassed, *if so,* in their quality, by the greatest things of the greatest persons. These deliverances are to be found everywhere in his extensive critical work, and it is of a survey of some of them, conditioned in the manner outlined above, that the main body of any useful historical account of his criticism must consist. The four main places are the *Lectures on the English Poets* (1818), on *The English Comic Writers* (1819), on *Elizabethan Literature* (1820), and the book on *Characters of Shakespeare* (1817). We may take them in the order mentioned, though it is not quite chronological, because the chronological dislocation, in the case of the second pair, is logically and methodically unavoidable.

How thoroughly this examination of the greater particulars (as we may call it) was the work which he was born to do is illustrated by the sketches (at the end of the first lecture on the English poets) of *The Pilgrim's Progress, Robinson Crusoe,* the *Decameron,* Homer, the Bible, Dante, and (O Groves of Blarney!) *Ossian.* Hazlitt's faults (except prejudice, which is here fortunately silent) are by no means hidden in them—irrelevance, defect of knowledge, "casualness," and other not so good things. But the *gusto,* the spirit, the inspiriting quality, are present in tenfold measure. Here is a man to whom literature is a real and live thing, and who can make it real and alive to his readers—a man who does not love it or its individual examples "by allowance," but who loves it "with personal love." Even his Richardsonian digression—horrible to the stop-watch man—is alive and real and stimulating with the rest. The Dante passage is a little false perhaps in parts, inadequate, prejudiced, what you will in others. But it is criticism—an act of literary faith and hope and charity too—a substance; something added to, and new-born in, the literary cosmos. He is better (indeed he is here almost at his very best) on Spenser than on Chaucer, but why? Because he *knew* more about Spenser, because he was plentifully read in sixteenth- and hardly read at all in fourteenth-century literature. And so always: the very plethora of one's notes for comment warning the commentator that he is lost if he indulges rashly. Where Hazlitt is inadequate (as for instance on Dryden) he is more instructive than many men's adequacy could be, and where he is not—on Collins, on the Ballads, and elsewhere—he prepares us for that ineffable and half-reluctant outburst—a very Balaam's blessing—on Coleridge, which stands not higher than this, not lower than that, but as an *A-per-se,* consummate and unique.

In a sense the *Comic Writers* are even better. The general exordium on Wit and Humour belongs to the first class of Hazlitt's critical performances as defined above, and is one of the cleverest of them; though it may perhaps have the faults of its class, and some of those of its author. That on Comedy—the general part of it—incurs this sentence in a heavier degree; for Aristotle or somebody else seems to have impressed Hazlitt too strongly with the necessary *shadiness* of Comedy, and it is quite clear that of the Romantic variety (which to be sure hardly anybody but Shakespeare has ever hit off) he had an insufficient idea. He is again inadequate on Jonson; it is indeed in his criticism, because of its very excellence, that we see—more than anywhere else, though we see it everywhere—the truth of his master's denunciation of the "criticism which denies." But his lecture or essay on the capital examples of the comedy which he really liked—that of the Restoration—is again an apex: and, as it happens, it is grouped for English students with others—the morally excellent and intellectually vigorous but rather purblind onslaught of Collier, the again vigorous but somewhat Philistine following thereof by Macaulay, the practical confession of Lamb's fantastic and delightful apology, Leigh Hunt's rather feeble compromise—after a fashion which shows it off to a marvel. While as to the chapter on the Eighteenth-century Novel it has, with a worthier subject, an equal supremacy of treatment. You may differ with much of it, but always agree to differ: except in that estimate of Lovelace which unfortunately shows us Hazlitt's inability to recognise a *cad* in the dress and with the manners of a fine gentleman.

The *Lectures on the Age of Elizabeth* (which succeeded the *Comic Writers,* as these had succeeded the *Poets*) maintain, if they do not even raise, the standard. Perhaps there is nothing so fine as the Coleridge passage in individual and concentrated expression; nor any piece of connected criticism so masterly as the chapter on the Novel. But the level is higher: and nowhere do we find better expression of that *gusto*—that amorous quest of literary beauty and rapturous enjoyment of it—which has been noted as Hazlitt's great merit. His faults are here, as always, with him and with us. Even the faithful Lamb was driven to expostulate with the wanton and, as it happens, most uncritical belittlement of Sidney, and (though he himself was probably less influenced by political partisanship or political feeling of any kind than almost any great writer of whom we know) to assign this to its true cause. It is odd that a critic, and a great critic, should contrive to be inadequate both on Browne and on Dryden: and again one cannot but suspect the combination to be due to the fact that both were Royalists. But the King's Head does not always come in: and it is only fair to Hazlitt to say that he is less biassed than Coleridge by the ultra-royalism of Beaumont and Fletcher, and the supposed republicanism of Massinger. And in by far the greater part of the book—nearly the whole of that part of it which deals with the dramatists—there is no disturbance of this kind. The opening, if somewhat discursive, is masterly, and with very few exceptions the lecturer or essayist carries out the admirable motto—in fact and in deed the motto of all real critics—"I have endeavoured to feel what was good, and to give a reason for the faith that was in me when necessary and when in my power." Two of his sentences, in dealing with Beaumont and Fletcher, not merely set the key-note of all good criticism but should open the stop thereof in all fit readers. "It is something worth living for to write or even read such poetry as this, or to know that it has been written." Again, "And so it is something, as our poets themselves wrote, 'far above singing.'"

The *Characters of Shakespeare's Plays* is perhaps not as good as any of these three courses of Lectures; but it should be remembered that it came earlier in time, and that the critic had not "got his hand in." The notes are as a rule nearly as desultory as Coleridge's, with less suggestiveness; there is at least one outburst, in the case of *Henry V.*, of the usual disturbing influence; there is very much more quotation than there need be from Schlegel; and there are other signs of the novitiate. Yet the book contains admirable things, as in the early comparison of Chaucer and Shakespeare, where, though Hazlitt's defec-

tive knowledge of Chaucer again appears, there is much else good. Among the *apices* of Shakespearian criticism is the statement that the poet "has no prejudice for or against his characters," that he makes "no attempt to force an interest: everything is left for time and circumstance to unfold." There is perhaps something inconsistent with this as well as with truth in the observation on *Lear,* that "He is here fairly caught in the web of his own imagination"; but, like most of the greater critics, Hazlitt cares very little for superficial consistency. The characters of Falstaff and Shylock are masterpieces in his *bravura* style, and one need perhaps nowhere seriously quarrel with any critical statement of his except the astonishing one, that *All's Well that Ends Well* is "one of the most *pleasing*" of the plays.

In the remaining volumes the literary articles or passages are only occasional, and are often considerably adulterated with non-literary matter. In *The Plain Speaker,* for instance, the opening paper on **"The Prose Style of Poets"** holds out almost the highest promise, and gives almost the lowest performance. Hazlitt, as is not so very uncommon with him, seems to have deliberately set himself to take the other side from Coleridge's. That it happens also to be the wrong side matters very little. But even his attack on Coleridge's own prose style (open enough to objection) has nothing very happy in it except the comparison, "To read one of his disquisitions is like hearing the variations to a piece of music without the score." So, too, **"On the Conversation of Authors,"** though intensely interesting, has no critical interest or very little—the chief exception being the passage on Burke's style. Far more important is the glance at the theory of the single word in **"On Application to Study,"** and in that in **"On Envy"** on the taste of the Lake School.

Much of *The Plain Speaker* is injured as a treasury of criticism, though improved as a provision of amusement, by Hazlitt's personal revelations, complaints, agonies; but the critical *ethos* of the man was so irrepressible that it will not be refused. There is a curious little piece of critical blasphemy, or at least "dis-*gusto*" (the word is wanted and is fairly choice Italian), in **"On the Pleasure of Hating,"** and, almost throughout the series, the sharp flux and reflux of literary admiration and political rage in respect of Scott is most noteworthy. **"On the Qualifications Necessary to Success in Life"** contains yet another of those passages on Coleridge which are like nothing so much as the half-fond, half-furious, retrospects of a discarded lover on his mistress—which are certainly like nothing else in literature. But **"On Reading Old Books"** does not belie the promise of its title, and is a complete and satisfactory palinode to the fit of critical headache noted just now. One must not venture to cite from it; it is to be read and reread, and hardly any single piece, except the immortal **"Farewell to Essay-Writing,"** gives us so much insight into Hazlitt's critical temperament as this. (pp. 251-60)

Table-Talk, one of the greenest pastures of the Hazlittian champaign generally, is among the least literary of the books, and yet so literary enough. **"On Genius and Common Sense"** contributes its Character of Wordsworth, on whom Hazlitt is always interesting, because of the extraordinary opposition between the men's temperaments. The companion on Shelley, which is supplied by **"On Paradox and Commonplace,"** is hardly less interesting, though, for the reasons above indicated, much less valuable. **"On Milton's Sonnets,"** however, is, as it ought to be, a pure study and an admirable one. **"The Aristocracy of Letters"** carries its hay high on the horn, yet it is not negligible: and **"On Criticism,"** which follows, really deserves the title, despite its frequent and inevitable flings and runnings-amuck. The good-humoured, though rather "home" description of "The Occult School" (*v. supra* on Lamb) is perfectly just. **"On Familiar Style"** is also no false promiser, and yet another passage on Coleridge meets us in the paper **"On Effeminacy of Character."**

Nor is the interesting "omnibus" volume, which takes its general title from *The Round Table,* of the most fertile. The collection of short papers, properly so called, was written earlier (1817) than most of the books hitherto discussed, and therefore has some first drafts or variants of not a little that is in them. In a note of it occurs the passage on Burke, which, with that on Scott in the *Spirit of the Age,* is Hazlitt's nearest approach to the sheer *delirium tremens* of the Gifford Letter: but he is not often thus. **"The Character of Milton's Eve"** is a fine critical paper of its kind, and "takes the taste out" well after the passage on Burke. The long handling of *The Excursion* is very interesting to compare with that in the *English Poets,* as is the earlier "Midsummer Night's Dream" with similar things elsewhere. **"Pedantry"** and others give something: and though no human being (especially no human being who knows both books) has ever discovered what made Hazlitt call *John Buncle* "the English Rabelais," the paper on Amory's queer novel is a very charming one. **"On the Literary Character"** does somewhat deceive us: **"Commonplace Critics"** less so: but to **"Poetical Versatility"** we must return. Of the remaining contents of the volume, the well-known *Conversations with Northcote* (where the painter plays Hazlitt's idea of an Advocatus Diaboli on Hazlitt) gives less still. But there is a striking passage on Wordsworth, a paradox (surely?) on Tom Paine as "a fine writer" (you might as well call a good getter of coal at the face "a fine sculptor"), an interesting episode on early American nineteenth-century literature; and not a few others, especially the profound self-criticism (for no doubt Northcote had nothing to do with it) on Hazlitt's abstinence from society. (pp. 261-62)

On the other hand, *The Spirit of the Age* (with the exception of some political and philosophical matter) is wholly literary; and may rank with the three sets of *Lectures* and the *Characters of Shakespeare* as the main storehouse of Hazlitt's criticism. Here, too, there is much repetition, and here, at the end of the Scott article, is the almost insane outburst more than once referred to. But the bulk of the book is at Hazlitt's very best pitch of appreciative grasp. If he is anywhere out of focus, it is in reference to Godwin's novels—the setting of which in any kind of comparison with Scott's (though Hazlitt was critic enough from the first to see that Godwin could by no possibility be the "Author of *Waverley*") is a remarkable instance of the disadvantage of the contemporary, and, to some extent, the sympathiser. But the book certainly goes far to bear out the magnificent eulogy of Hazlitt for which Thackeray took it as text, quite early in his career.

The *Sketches and Essays* are again very rich, where they are rich; and advertise the absence of riches most frankly where they are not. **"On Reading New Books"**; not a little

of **"Merry England"**; the whole of **"On Taste"** and **"Why the Heroes of Romances Are Insipid"** speak for themselves, and do not bewray their claim. **"Taste,"** especially, contains one of Hazlitt's own titles to critical supremacy in his fixing on Perdita's primrose description as itself supreme, when "the scale of fancy, passion, and observation of nature is raised" high enough. And as for *Winterslow,* its first and its last papers are "things enskied" in criticism, for the one is **"My First Acquaintance with Poets,"** and the last **"The Farewell to Essay Writing."**

These two last, the sentence on

> That come before the swallow dares, and take
> The winds of March with beauty;

and (say) the paper referred to a little above on **"Poetical Versatility,"** will serve as texts for some more general remarks on Hazlitt's critical character. We have said at the beginning of this notice everything that need be said by way of deduction or allowance; we have only hinted at the clear critical "balance to credit" which remains; and these essays and passages will help to bring this out.

To take the **"Poetical Versatility"** first, it is an interesting paper, and with the aid of those "characters" of poets, &c., which have been indicated in the survey just completed, gives the best possible idea of one (and perhaps the most popular) of Hazlitt's forms of critical achievement and influence. In it he eddies round his subject—completing his picture of it by strokes apparently promiscuous in selection, but always tending to body forth the image that presents itself to him, and that he wishes to present to his readers. "Poetry dwells in a perpetual Utopia of its own." It "does not create difficulties where they do not exist, but contrives to get rid of them whether they exist or not." "Its strength is in its wings; its element the air." We "may leave it to Time to take out the stains, seeing it is a thing immortal as itself." Poets "either find things delightful or make them so," &c. &c., some of the etceteras drawing away from the everlasting, and condescending rather lamentably to the particular.

Now there is no need to tell the reader—even the reader of this book, I hope—that this, of these utterances, is a reproduction of Longinus (whom Hazlitt most probably had not read), or that of Coleridge, whom most certainly he had both read and heard. "The man who plants cabbages imitates too": and it is only the foolishest folk of rather foolish times who endeavour to be original, though the wisest of all times always succeed in being so. The point with Hazlitt is that in these circlings round his subject—these puttings of every possible way in which, with or without the help of others, it strikes him—he gives the greatest possible help to others in being struck. One of the blows will almost certainly hit the nail on the head and drive it home into any tolerably susceptible mind: many may, and the others after the first will help to fix it. Of method there may not be very much—there is rather more here than in most cases; but whether there is method or not, "everything," in the old military phrase, "goes in"; the subject and the reader are carried by assault, mass, variety, repetition of argument, imagery, phrase. Hazlitt will not be refused; he takes towns at a hand-gallop, like Condé at Lerida—and he does not often lose them afterwards.

In this phase of his genius, however, there is perhaps, for some tastes at any rate, a little too much of what has been called *bravura*—too much of the merely epideictic. It is not so in the other. Appreciate the appreciation of the *Winter's Tale* passage; still more take to heart (they will go to it without much taking where there is one) the **"First Acquaintance with Poets,"** or still better the marvellous critical swan-song of the **"Farewell,"** and there can be no more doubt about Hazlitt. *Quia multum amavit* is at once his best description and his greatest glory. In all the range of criticism which I have read I can hardly think of any one except Longinus who displays the same faculty of not unreasonable or unreasoned passion for literature; and Longinus, alas! has, as an opportunity for showing this to us, scarcely more than the bulk of one of Hazlitt's longest Essays, of which, long and short, Hazlitt himself has given us, I suppose, a hundred. Nor, as in some others (many, if not most of whom, if I named them, I should name for the sake of honour), is a genuine passion made the mere theme of elaborate and deliberate literary variations. As we have seen, Hazlitt will often leave it expressed in one sentence of ejaculatory and convincing fervour; it seldom appears at greater length than that of a passage, while a whole lecture or essay in the key of rapture is exceedingly rare. Hazlitt is desultory, irrelevant, splenetic, moody, self-contradictory; but he is never merely pleonastic,—there is no mere verbiage, no mere virtuosity, in him.

And the consequence is that this enthusiastic appreciation of letters, which I have, however heretically, taken throughout this book to be really the highest function of criticism, *catches:* that the critical yeast (to plagiarise from ourselves) never fails to work. The order of history, as always, should probably be repeated, and the influence of Coleridge should be felt, as Hazlitt himself felt it, first: it is well to fortify also with Longinus himself, and with Aristotle, and with as many others of the great ones as the student can manage to master. But there is at least a danger, with some perhaps of not the worst minds, of all this remaining cold as the bonfire before the torch is applied. The *silex scintillans* of Hazlitt's rugged heart will seldom fail to give the vivifying spark from its own inward and immortal fire. (pp. 262-66)

> *George Saintsbury, "Wordsworth and Coleridge: Their Companions and Adversaries," in his* A History of Criticism and Literary Taste in Europe from the Earliest Texts to the Present Day: Modern Criticism, Vol. III, *William Blackwood & Sons Ltd., 1904, pp. 200-98.*

Paul Elmer More (essay date 1905)

[*More was an American critic who, along with Irving Babbitt, formulated the doctrines of New Humanism in early twentieth-century American thought. The New Humanists were strict moralists who adhered to traditional conservative values in reaction to an age of scientific innovation and artistic experimentalism. In regard to literature, they believed a work's support for the classic ethical norms to be as important as its aesthetic qualities. More was particularly opposed to Naturalism, which he believed accentuated the animal nature of humans, and to any literature, such as Romanticism, that broke with established classical tradition. His importance as a critic derives from the rigid coherence of his ideology, which polarized American critics into hostile opponents (Van Wyck Brooks, Edmund Wilson, H. L. Mencken) or devoted supporters (Norman Foerster, Stuart Sherman, and, to a lesser degree, T. S. Eliot). He is especially esteemed for the philosophical and literary erudition of his multivolume* Shelburne Essays *(1904-21). In the following excerpt, he finds Hazlitt's impassioned sensibility to be the defining quality of his work.*]

If one should turn to William Hazlitt expecting to find critical essays like those we connect with writers of more recent days, he would be sadly disappointed. There is in Hazlitt's work little—were it not for a few exceptional passages that occur to memory, I should say nothing—of that looking before and after, that linking of literary movements with the great currents of human activity, which has become a part of criticism along with the growth of the historical method. He is not concerned with the searching out of larger cause and effect, but is intensely occupied with the individual man, and studies to deduce the peculiar style of each writer from his character and temperament. Nor can we hope to find in him—I say "hope" from the common point of view to-day—any trace of that scientific method which would analyse the products of the human brain as a chemist deals with "vitriol and sugar." He wrote before these things were known. He was, quite as much as Byron or Wordsworth, a child of the revolution, and his blood tingled with the new romanticism. Yet even here certain distinctions must be drawn. When we speak to-day of the romantic critic, we think of one who has joined the sensibility and fluency of the revolutionary temperament to the sympathies of the later historic method, and has taught his soul to transform itself cunningly into the various types that it chooses to study. We associate the word with that kind of fluctuating egotism which makes of the critic one "qui raconte les aventures de son âme au milieu des chefs-d'œuvre" ["who recounts the adventures of his soul in the presence of masterpieces"]. Hazlitt was an egotist in all conscience, but of this particular form of the disease we can hardly hold him guilty. His was one of the rarest, yet most characteristic, traits of the revolutionary spirit—*gusto* he himself would call it. But a still stronger term than gusto is needed, I think, to describe the swift qualities of Hazlitt's mind; he is the writer, to a supreme degree, of *passion*.

What he loved—the few great books, the one great man, the chosen scenes of nature, his youthful scheme of philosophy—he laid to his heart with passionate zest and clung to with desperate tenacity; what was hateful to him he spurned with equal vehemence. Byron speaks of his own mind as having the motion of a tiger; if he missed his leap there was no retrieving the error. That is true of Byron, who almost alone shares with Hazlitt the untamed passion of the revolutionary spirit; but it is still more true of Hazlitt, and, apart from the stress of journalism, accounts for the singular unevenness of his work. There is something even in the keen sinewy language of Hazlitt that suggests the tiger's spring. His sentences succeed one another like the rapid bounds of such an animal, and at the last comes one straight unerring leap and the prey is fixed, bleeding, you might almost say, in his grasp. There is nothing just like it among English authors. Genuine passion, indeed, if one considers it, is a rare, almost the rarest, trait in literature. Certainly in English it would not be easy to find another author whose work is so dominated by this quality as Hazlitt's. It gives the tone to his critical writing; it explains the keenness and the limitations of his psychological insight; it causes the innumerable contradictions that occur in his views; it gives rapidity to his style; it imparts a peculiar zest to his very manner of quoting; it lends exhilarating interest to his pages, yet in the long run, if we read him too continuously, it wearies us a little, for not many of us are keyed up to his high pitch. We go to him for superb rhetoric, for emotions in literary experience that stir the languid blood, but we hardly look to him for judgment. There is much in English that assumes the passionate tone; place it beside Hazlitt and for the most part it appears tame or false. (pp. 73-6)

> *Paul Elmer More, "The First Complete Edition of Hazlitt," in his* Shelburne Essays, *second series, Houghton Mifflin Company, 1905, pp. 73-86.*

Jacob Zeitlin   (essay date 1913)

[*Zeitlin was a Russian-born American critic. In the following excerpt, he discusses the display of both analytical power and emotion in Hazlitt's essays.*]

The rare union in [Hazlitt's] nature of the analytic and the emotional gave to his writings the very qualities which he enumerated as characteristic of the age, and his consistent sincerity made his voice distinct above many others of his generation. (pp. xi-xii)

The analytical gift manifested itself in Hazlitt precociously in the study of human nature. He characterized some of his schoolmates disdainfully as "fit only for fighting like stupid dogs and cats," and at the age of twelve, while on a visit, he communicated to his father a caustic sketch of some English ladies who "require an Horace or a Shakespeare to describe them," and whose "ceremonial unsociality" made him wish he were back in America. His metaphysical studies determined the direction which his observation of life should take. He became a remarkable anatomist of the constitution of human nature in the abstract, viewing the motives of men's actions from a speculative plane. He excels in sharp etchings which bring the outline of a character into bold prominence. He is happy in defining isolated traits and in throwing a new light on much used words. "Cleverness," he writes, "is a certain *knack* or aptitude at doing certain things, which depend more on a particular adroitness and off-hand readiness than on force or perseverance, such as making puns, making epigrams, making extempore verses, mimicking the company, mimicking a style, etc. . . . Accomplishments are certain external graces, which are to be learnt from others, and which are easily displayed to the admiration of the beholder, *viz.* dancing, riding, fencing, music, and so on. . . . Talent is the capacity of doing anything that depends on application and industry, such as writing a criticism, making a speech, studying the law." These innocent looking definitions are probably not without an ironic sting. It requires no great stretch of the imagination, for example, to catch in Hazlitt's eye a sly wink at Lamb or a disdainful glance toward Leigh Hunt as he gives the reader his idea of cleverness or accomplishment.

Hazlitt's definitions often startle and give a vigorous buffet to our preconceptions. He is likely to open an essay on **"Good-Nature"** by declaring that a good-natured man is "one who does not like to be put out of his way. . . . Good-nature is humanity that costs nothing;" and he may describe a respectable man as "a person whom there is no reason for respecting, or none that we choose to name." . . . Though the opening of an essay may appear perverse, he is sure to enforce his point before proceeding very far. He accumulates familiar instances in such abundance as to render obvious what at first seemed paradoxical. He writes **"On the Ignorance of the Learned"** and makes it perfectly clear that no person knows less of the actual life of the world than he whose experience is confined to books. On the other hand he has a whole-hearted appreciation of pedantry: "The power of attaching an interest to the most trifling or painful pursuits, in which our whole attention and faculties are engaged, is one of the greatest happinesses of our nature. . . . He who is not in some measure a pedant, though he may be a wise, cannot be a very happy man." These two examples illustrate Hazlitt's manner of presenting both views of a subject by concentrating his attention on each separately and examining it without regard to the other. On one occasion he anatomizes the faults of the dissenters, and on another he extols their virtues. "I have inveighed all my life against the insolence of the Tories, and for this I have the authority both of Whigs and Reformers; but then I have occasionally spoken against the imbecility of the Whigs, and the extravagance of the Reformers, and thus have brought all three on my back, though two out of the three regularly agree with all I say of the third party." The strange thing is not that he should have incurred the wrath of all parties, but that he should show surprise at the result.

Very often Hazlitt's reflections are the generalization of his personal experience. The essay **"On the Disadvantages of Intellectual Superiority"** is but a record of the trials to which he was exposed by his morbid sensitiveness and want of social tact, and amid much excellent advice **"On the Conduct of Life,"** there are passages which merely reflect his own marital misfortunes. It is not so much that he is a dupe of his emotions, but in his view of life he attaches a higher importance to feeling than to reason, and so provides a philosophic basis for his strongest prejudices. "Custom, passion, imagination," he declares, "insinuate themselves into and influence almost every judgment we pass or sentiment we indulge, and are a necessary help (as well as hindrance) to the human understanding; to attempt to refer every question to abstract truth and precise definition, without allowing for the frailty of prejudice, which is the unavoidable consequence of the frailty and imperfection of reason, would be to unravel the whole web and texture of human understanding and society."

It is this infusion of passion and sentiment, the addition of the warm breath of his personal experience, that gives the motion of life to his analytic essays, and a deep and solemn humanity to his abstract speculations. (pp. xvi-xx)

Hazlitt gave himself freely and without reserve to his reader. By his side Leigh Hunt appears affected, De Quincey theatrical, Lamb—let us say discreet. Affectation and discretion were equally alien to Hazlitt's nature, as they concerned either his personal conduct or his literary exercises. In regard to every impression, every prejudice, every stray thought that struggled into consciousness, his practice was, to use his own favorite quotation,

> To pour out all as plain

As downright Shippen or as old Montaigne.

He has drifted far from the tradition of Addison and Steele with which his contemporaries sought to associate him. . . . In Hazlitt's hands the essay was an instrument for the expression of serious thought and virile passion. He lacked indeed the temperamental balance of Lamb. His insight into human nature was intellectual rather than sympathetic. Though as a philosopher he understood that the web of life is of a mingled yarn, he has given us none of those rare glimpses of laughter ending in tears or of tears subsiding in a tender smile which are the sources of Lamb's depth and his charm. The same thing is true of his humor. He relished heartily its appearance in others and had a most wholesome laugh; but in himself there is no real merriment, only an ironic realization of the contrasts of life. When he writes, the smile which sometimes seeks to overpower the grim fixity of his features, is frozen before it can emerge to the surface. He lacks all the ingratiating arts which make a writer beloved. But if one enjoys a keen student of the intricacies of character, a bold and candid critic of human imperfections, a stimulating companion full of original ideas and deep feelings, he will find in Hazlitt an inexhaustible source of instruction and delight. (pp. xxxii-xxxiii)

> *Jacob Zeitlin, in his* Hazlitt on English Literature: An Introduction to the Appreciation of Literature, *Oxford University Press, Inc., 1913, 441 p.*

Oliver Elton   (essay date 1920)

[*Elton was an English critic who is best known for his six-volume study* Survey of English Literature: 1730-1880 *(1912-28). In the following excerpt from that work, he evaluates Hazlitt's familiar essays.*]

Hazlitt lived by making articles, like De Quincey and Leigh Hunt and the young Carlyle. In the essay form, none of them wrote so much that wears so well. He is the essayist, as Shelley is the lyrist, *par excellence*. He has left more than a hundred compositions of this sort, and that apart from his lectures; it is doubtful if Addison has left so many that can be read with pleasure as Hazlitt. No one approaches him in the kind of work that allies him with Fielding or Borrow, such as **'The Fight'** or 'John Cavanagh the Fives-Player.' In the splendours and exaltations of elaborate prose, and in finesse of style, others of his tribe excel him; but he bears them all down if range, and mass, and vitality are reckoned together. He was brought up on the eighteenth-century essay, of which the big quarterly review-notice is a scion. The essence of a paper by Steele or Goldsmith was to take a single text, or theme, of a sort neither too commonplace nor too remote, and work it out on a moderate scale. Hazlitt is much lengthier, but he often begins in the same way. His discourse buds out of an aphorism; and he will face the hazard of a dull-sounding topic. He must have been the last good writer who sat down to pen a sheet on Envy, or Fame, or Depth and Superficiality. The tendency of such an essay is to fall into separate atoms of crystal. In his *Characteristics of Rochefoucauld's Maxims,* where he not immodestly challenges the ghost of La Rochefoucauld, he shows the integer of his style in all its bareness. The book is a series of detached maxims, numbered. Butler, Halifax,

and Swift found this kind of thing hard enough to do well. Hazlitt comes not ill out of the trial; but such imitations of proverbial or popular wisdom are risky. Truth, in English, seldom boils down to a dozen words. But out of Hazlitt's five hundred examples it is easy to pick some that betoken no common mind:

> 'We as often repent the good we have done as the ill.'—'It has been observed that the proudest people are not nice in love. In fact, they think they raise the object of their choice above every one else.'—'It is better to desire than to enjoy—to love than to be loved.'—'To marry an actress for the admiration she excites on the stage, is to imitate the man who bought Punch.'—'If the world is good for nothing else, it is a fine subject for speculation.'

De Quincey reproaches Hazlitt for a certain choppiness in his mode of composition—so different from his own complex reticulation and embroidery of his themes. The curt, pellet-like, uncompounded sentences grate on the ear of that master of harmonies. It is true that Hazlitt thinks in such sentences. But Bacon's method of hiving pros and cons in a notebook is abhorrent to him. He gives, on the contrary, the effect of living if abrupt speech. Each sentence smoulders like touchwood, and the next catches fire by attrition. A little wind of passion comes, and the whole is ablaze. Such a habit of mind and style, grafted on the approved manner of the *Tatler* or the *Bee,* will explain some of the phenomena of Hazlitt's writing.

He does not think much of his own work, this late and bold survivor of the classical age, with his new rebel temper bursting through the ancient moulds. He is essentially modest about his handicraft, though his modesty is dissembled by pride and emphasis. He feels himself the inferior of the Indian jugglers who can keep four brass balls in the air at once; he envies their professional skill:

> What abortions are these Essays! What errors, what ill-pieced transitions, what crooked reasons, what lame conclusions! How little is made out, and that little how ill! Yet they are the best I can do. I endeavour to recollect all I have ever observed or thought upon a subject, and to express it as nearly as I can. Instead of writing on four subjects at a time, it is as much as I can manage to keep the thread of one discourse clear and unentangled.

Such self-distrust is often rewarded and refuted in the issue. Hazlitt is in the ranks of the classic English writers whom he knows so well. He has read Bacon, and Dryden, and Earle, and Addison, and Swift, and has got something from most of them; for one thing, his manly strength and remarkably undefiled purity of diction; which cannot well be described, for it is not strange or mannered, and for this reason defies parody. It is good to go to school to him for vocabulary and idiom; the great distillers of language, the Elizabethans re-incarnate, like Charles Lamb, may produce something more rare and wonderful, but they are not such good models. Hazlitt simply uses right English, and the only way to profit by him is to do the same.

Certain of his habits of speech, or rather of method, it is easy to notice. He has his favourite overture, which is of a traditional kind. Like Bacon, he is fond of starting with an epigram, of ringing down a solid gold coin upon the marble, to arrest or startle us; and this he does because he knows it will make us go on:

'No young man believes he shall ever die.'—'Life is the art of being well deceived.'—'Food, warmth, sleep, and a book; these are all I at present ask; the Ultima Thule of my wandering desires.'—'People have about as substantial an idea of Cobbett as they have of Cribb. His blows are as hard, and he himself is as impenetrable.'—'Footmen are no part of Christianity.'

Hazlitt sees to it that he does not lose the advantage which these openings afford. As he proceeds, his phrases sometimes fall, especially in his early essays, into the patterns set by the old Character-books, and practised by Butler and Steele and many others. Save in the best hands, this is the most monotonous and nauseating form in the world. It is a catalogue of traits and tricks; the mere raw material for the dramatist or analyst. The order of the sentences is accidental or indifferent, and their syntax of the baldest. When the Character is taken up by a master like Clarendon, it acquires shading, and variety, and life; but then it loses, while so justifying, its existence. This is said without disesteem to the witty authors of *Microcosmographie,* or of *A Duke of Bucks,* or to Hazlitt himself; but he broke away from the habit, though pleasant traces of it can be found in abundance in his *Spirit of the Age.* The more formal species, well managed, can be seen in the essay **'On the Clerical Character'**:

> The Priest is not a negative character; he is something positive and disagreeable. . . . He thinks more of external appearances than of his internal convictions. He is tied down to the prejudices and opinions of the world in every way. The motives of the heart are clogged and censured at the outset, by the fear of idle censure; his understanding is the slave of established creeds and formulas of faith, etc.

This, however, is but the lusty shout of a Jacobin. But we have also the character of **'A Jacobin,' 'A Reformer,' 'A Government-Man,'** and the like. Hazlitt does better when he comes to real persons like Fox or Godwin; and here he often deals in that excellent if old-fashioned form, descended from antiquity, and practised by Johnson, of the Contrast. Feature is paired off against feature, and if the effect is too like that of a row of handcuffs interlinked, it is definite enough. His comparison of Burke and Chatham shows what can be done with this figure, which has gone out of vogue, perhaps because no one can use it so well. Johnson's comparison of Dryden and Pope is in the same fashion, but its antitheses are much more mechanical; Hazlitt's, though formal, sound more like real speech:

> Chatham's eloquence was popular; his wisdom was altogether plain and practical. Burke's eloquence was that of the poet; of the man of high and unbounded fancy; his wisdom was profound and contemplative. Chatham's eloquence was calculated to make men *act;* Burke's was calculated to make them *think.* Chatham could have roused the fury of a multitude, and wielded their physical energy as he pleased; Burke's eloquence carried conviction into the mind of the retired and lonely student, opened the recesses of the human heart, and lighted up the face of nature around him. . . . The power which governed Burke's mind was his Imagination; that which gave its impetus to Chatham's was Will (1807).

Such a style leads at once to the habit, as native to Hazlitt

as to Burke himself, though he practises it differently—the habit of dilating. . . . Hear him **'On the Pleasure of Hating,'** where he takes a neglected half-truth—he has a passion for the racy and unnoticed sides of familiar truth—and persuades himself more and more of it as he kindles, and never has enough of it:

> Pure good soon grows insipid, wants variety and spirit. Pain is a bitter-sweet, which never surfeits. Love turns, with a little indulgence, to indifference or disgust; hatred alone is immortal. Do we not see this principle at work everywhere? Animals torment and worry one another without mercy; children kill flies for sport; every one reads the accidents and offences in a newspaper, as the cream of the sport; a whole town runs to be present at a fire, and the spectator by no means exults to see it extinguished. It is better to have it so, but it diminishes the interest; and our feelings take part with our passions rather than with our understandings.

This is in the good Montaignesque tradition of watching humanity in undress and telling the facts. Hazlitt has not Montaigne's flexibility, or his wise readiness to return upon and contradict himself; there is something of a *parti pris* about it all. Still we feel that he is speaking faithfully as an onlooker, a connoisseur in spectacles and sensations, and that he enjoys the burning town like a play. The effect is higher when he expands upon memories, and sorrows, and his imagination is freely at work. 'It is *we,*' he says somewhere, 'who are Hamlet'; and a passage in his noble piece **'On the Feeling of Immortality in Youth'** bears out the saying. This is an unequalled utterance of the heartache which stamps Hazlitt as a tragic and not merely a poetic soul. The same amplifying, dilating method is here applied to matter which will bear it well:

> As we grow old, our sense of the value of time becomes vivid. Nothing else, indeed, seems of any consequence. We can never cease wondering that that which has ever been has ceased to be. We find many things remain the same: why, then, should there be a change in us? This adds a convulsive grasp of whatever is, a sense of a fallacious hollowness in all we see. Instead of the full, pulpy feeling of youth tasting existence and every object in it, all is flat and vapid—a whited sepulchre, fair without, but full of ravening and all uncleanness within. The world is a witch that puts us off with false shows and appearances. The simplicity of youth, the confiding expectation, the boundless raptures, are gone; we only think of getting out of it as well as we can, and without any great mischance or annoyance.

In all this there is no monotony, but neither is there much progression. At the end of the essay he is much where he started; he has been his journey, in a circle, and said all there is to say. As to the thought, we can but protest that such a man can never be old. If the memory of youthful zest is so sharp, however qualified with sour, then youth itself is not gone. This, at least, is not the state lamented by the poet:

> When we are frozen up within, and quite
> The phantom of ourselves.

The same mode of descant is found in the best of Hazlitt's meditative papers, like those **'On the Fear of Death'** and

'On Going a Journey,' though the shade of feeling is different.

One feature of Hazlitt's writing, namely his use of quotations, which are often given at length, and still oftener glimmer like burnished threads in the texture of his prose, might have been dangerous but for its naturalness and spontaneity. The passages are frequently familiar, and yet verbally incorrect; they are given from memory. Yet they do not sound dragged-in or hackneyed, but rather, in Dante's words, *venusti et sapidi,* gracious and racy, because they are as much a part of the writer's mental furniture as his own diction. Quotation forms no small part, we may say, of Hazlitt's relish in life; literature gives him perhaps the least alloyed element of his happiness, and good words are like a glass of wine to him. This we feel when he describes Coleridge reading 'with a sonorous and musical voice the ballad of "Betty Foy",' and other things, in the year 1798:

> In the 'Thorn,' the 'Mad Mother,'
> and the 'Complaint of a Poor [sic]
> Indian Woman,' I felt that deeper
> power and pathos which have been
> since acknowledged,
>
> In spite of pride, in erring reason's spite,
>
> as the characteristics of this author;
> and the sense of a new style and a new
> spirit in poetry came over me. It had to
> me something of the effect that arises
> from the turning up of the fresh soil, or
> of the first welcome breath of Spring,
>
> While yet the trembling year is unconfirmed.
>
> Coleridge and myself walked back to Stowey that
> evening, and his voice sounded high
>
> Of Providence, foreknowledge, will, and fate,
> Fix'd fate, free-will, foreknowledge absolute,
>
> as we passed through echoing grove, by fairy
> stream or waterfall, gleaming in the summer moonlight!

This is what is meant by a new birth, a new date, in literature; and it was almost worth while having been through the dry years and long dearth of poetry, that such sensations might be possible. The passages cited come into the middle of the sentences, and are not intrusive; they chequer the prose like Bible phrases well woven into some lofty thanksgiving. Hazlitt draws impartially on all sorts of authors; Dryden and Pope and the prose comic dramatists provide him with what he wants, as well as the inspired poets.

He goes to work differently when he has something to describe. He revolves less than in his passages of *morale observatrice* or reflection. The incidents carry him on, and he keeps pace with things seen and heard. He steps lightly and athletically, and does not stop and tease language, like the precious writers; indeed he likes just the scenes that they avoid as carefully as a cat avoids dashing into fresh water. **'The Fight'** (between Bill Neate and 'the Gasman') will occur to every reader. Byron and Meredith would have rejoiced to report such a heroic event; but Hazlitt's simplicity and keeping, and the perfection of his literary-colloquial English, they might not have attained. The

magazine articles of John Hamilton Reynolds are nearest in spirit to his. We only wish that Hazlitt had written oftener on such occurrences, which show us mankind stripped and in a state of brisk competition. He reflects rather too inveterately, and runs off into too many 'middle axioms,' as Bacon called them, on life and conduct. But his descriptions of pictures, or of play-acting, or of landscape, or of 'still life' are equally full of vitality. The ***Notes of a Journey through France and Italy*** are motley, pleasant reading; happily innocent, as he says, 'of history or antiquities or statistic.' He seems more at home in the Louvre or the Pitti than even on the road; or in describing, with a British bias that he comically disclaims and reveals at every change of horses, the weaknesses of the French national character. His praises of our neighbours have the value of reluctance, and his remarks, in contradiction to the vulgar view, on the gravity, solidity, and taciturnity of that race are true and happy. He often shows a bad, John-Bull-on-his-travels disposition, that reminds us of Smollett's:

> The women in Italy (so far as I have seen hitherto)
> are detestably ugly. They are not even dark and
> swarthy, but a mixture of brown and red, coarse,
> marked with the small-pox, with pug-features,
> awkward, ill-made, fierce, dirty, lazy, neither attempting nor hoping to please.

But when he is alone with art or scenery he recovers his temper. He is not exactly a mystic in the presence of nature, but he has been touched by the spirit of Wordsworth. Like Gray and Matthew Arnold, he feels the peace of the Grande Chartreuse; it is in contrast with the fierce vexation of his own fate. 'Life must there seem a noiseless dream; Death a near translation to the skies!' It is a 'country full of wild grandeurs and shadowy fears.' The Apennines, and Parma, and Siena, and Perugia tempt him out of himself, and some of their beauty gets into his rhythm. This was in 1824-5; the voice of Ruskin was to be heard in the following decades, and has inevitably drowned that of earlier travellers. But Hazlitt has still the virgin brain, the freshness of sensation that meets us in the diaries of Gray and Beckford,—the note of the man who is the first to see, or to note, wonderful things. These emotions had not yet become obligatory, like going to church; and the feeling for natural beauty was still forcing its way under difficulties into the educated mind. But Hazlitt is more at home in England, and apprehends many of her beauties and humours just as well as Cobbett. His papers on **'The Letter-Bell'** or on **'Merry England'** are pieces of pure enjoyment and rumination, and his genius is at work untroubled by bad dreams or didactics. In these essays, as in poetry, there is no argument, and there is nothing concluded, or which can be contested. (pp. 361-68)

Oliver Elton, "William Hazlitt," in his A Survey of English Literature: 1780-1880, Vol. II, *The Macmillan Company, 1920, pp. 357-77.*

H. W. Garrod   (lecture date 1925)

[Garrod was an English critic. In the following excerpt, he examines Hazlitt's literary criticism.]

Whether Hazlitt is the greatest of the English literary critics must depend upon the view you take of what literary criticism is or should be. If it is the business of literary criticism to criticize itself, to be chastened before it chastens, Hazlitt has no pretension to do this. He has many prejudices, and few reserves; he is sometimes mean, more often generous, rarely or never merely just. If it is the duty of the critic to separate the accidents of a literary work from its permanent effects, to isolate it, in analysing, from all possible contamination with interests and passions not completely relevant, to work upon it with no instruments of judgement not properly sterilized,—this, and the like, lies outside Hazlitt's scope and care. Again, if the best criticism rests upon the best information, upon a wide acquaintance with literatures ancient and modern, upon scholarship and the comparative method, here too Hazlitt is defective—his reading is deep and not wide. Indeed, he is bold to affirm that 'our love for foreign literature is an acquired or rather an assumed taste . . . like a foreign religion adopted for the moment to answer a purpose or to please an idle humour'. If it is a part of criticism, once more, to formulate laws, to reach inductively general principles of literature, and to bring particular examples of prose or poetry before this court of principles, then the talent of Hazlitt is not more than a brilliant empiricism. Nor, where he can find no law, has he that instinct for adjournment which serves lesser men; he never wants to wait for posterity; of that higher court he entertains no apprehensions; he must get on with his business—a part of which is writing for his living and living by his writing. In a word, if the essential qualities of criticism are knowledge, patience, impartiality, analytic industry, stay of judgement—these are not Hazlitt's characteristic virtues; and in some of them he is more wanting than is proper either to genius or good sense. On the other hand, the defects which come from the excess of some of them it is a principal merit in him that he escapes. He is never, like Macaulay, a prig, nor a posterity-server. He does not, as Matthew Arnold does, just miss being a study of criticism; and he never, like Bagehot, commits the fault of philosophizing beyond what he can carry—of being deeper than he was dug.

His positive merits are numerous and palpable; indeed, I know no writer of such open excellencies, of excellencies so readily seizable and so delightfully handle-able. First among them I should put, what seems not so much a talent of literature, as an accidental grace of nature, his astounding *memory*. That sounds nothing much; but it all depends on what you remember, and how it is done. Of Hazlitt's memory, the principle is, not mental accuracy, but sentiment. No man ever quoted so much, and in no writer, I am afraid, will you find the same quantity of misquotation; as an advertisement for the Pelman Company, Hazlitt is no good at all. But it makes no difference—none, that is, if you take a free spirit freely. Macaulay draws upon a memory extraordinarily apt and accurate; he draws upon it—very impressively and deliberately. What is so delightful in Hazlitt is that he never *draws* upon memory at all. It all gushes, the spontaneity of it is never suspect; of themselves the springs of memory well up in inexhaustible freshness. Very often, as I say, the quotations are inaccurate; and very often they emerge, less their inverted commas, their patent marks effaced—just Hazlitt himself, the swift flash of his own prose. You must have plenty of the pedant in you to mind this. But it is easier to be a pedant than the unlearned believe; and there are not wanting people to tell you that this element in the style of Hazlitt bores them. Only bores are bored; and the truth

is that this is neither an artifice nor an artlessness in Hazlitt's style, but the native resonance of his temperament. The great phrases of the great masters of speech were a part of his life, perhaps the part most real and effective; it was as natural for him to express himself in these as it is hard for other men to express themselves in any other terms than the meagre symbols of their individual crafts. (pp. 98-100)

I do not feel that Hazlitt is properly to be thought of as a deep, or profound, writer. Yet upon the whole I conceive him to have a flair for truth in which no English critic rivals him; to have a quicker sense than any other for the difference between good and bad, between the genuine and tinsel. This he owes partly to the fact that his mind is *steeped* in good literature; and still more, I am inclined to think, to a fundamental genuineness in himself—a genuineness that all his faults are not enough to overlay. He really is disinterested—and not merely morally, but (what matters almost as much) intellectually—that is to say, he is unpedantic, for pedantry is only a want of intellectual disinterestedness, it is an interest in something other than the direct object of criticism. Hazlitt's flair for the truth is especially illustrated in his judgement of contemporaries. I know no critic who has placed so well the great writers of his own time. It is usually esteemed a difficult and delicate business; and perhaps Hazlitt is successful in it because he thought it neither. All his judgements are direct, unhesitating, unembarrassed; and most of them are right. At least they are right on the broad issues. Upon points of detail he is sometimes perverse; as when he prefers Byron's *Heaven and Earth,* of which the whole is rubbish, to *Don Juan,* of which the best is better than anything else in Byron. Yet he always knows who is who, even if he cannot always say unerringly what is what. He is better in genial outline than in minute study. (pp. 103-04)

'We are mighty fine fellows,' said [Robert Louis] Stevenson, 'but we cannot write like William Hazlitt.' The grand style Hazlitt has not; but of the *telling* style he is the consummate master. The method of his style is sweeping and hurried. He paints a broad slashes, caring little for subtlety in detail or for harmonization of effects. He is wrongly spoken of as an impressionist. There is a definiteness in the effects of his style, a certainty of outline, which is in no way impressionistic. His style has no mysteries, no seclusions of depth, no faint horizons: it never runs into distance. It is written in paragraphs but thought in sentences. It holds together, not by any natural unity of the thoughts, but by the astonishing swiftness of their succession. Telling stroke follows telling stroke so rapidly that there is no time to ask questions. Between the individual deliverances there is no bond of unity save that all are telling. I suppose that he should be called an epigrammatic writer. I suppose that it is an epigram when, for example, of the Rev. Mr. Irving—who took advantage of being a big man to pose as a great one—he says, 'Take a cubit from his stature, and his whole manner resolves itself into an impertinence'; or when he says of Mr. Gifford that 'he is admirably qualified for the situation which he has held for some years by a happy combination of defects, natural and acquired'; or even when he says of Sir Francis Burdett that 'he could not have uttered what he often did (in the House of Commons) if, besides his general respectability, he had not been a very honest, a very good-tempered, and a very good-looking, man'. For epigram, however, as a study in perfect expression, or as the art of saying what you think so concisely as to suggest that you do not think it, Hazlitt has no real aptitude. He has no real aptitude for it, firstly, because he is an honest man in a hurry; and secondly, because, as I have said, more than most men he hated coxcombry and pedantry.

Will you bear with me still if I try to sum in half a dozen sentences some of the merits in critical writing which I suppose myself to discover in Hazlitt? First, I would say, it is a good thing *not to be a dull writer;* I care little how it is managed, it is a good thing in itself. Secondly, it is a good thing to write about books as though they really meant something to you. It is a good thing, again, if you write about books, to be somebody—not to be somebody else, but to be individual, to make criticism reflect personality. It is a good thing, once more, even if you pay for it in prejudice, to know what you like and don't like. It is a still better thing—though this, again, is not a complete insurance against prejudice—to be disinterested. Best of all is it to have a natural flair for the truth, an eye for what is vital and vivifying. The first book to kindle Hazlitt's interest in literature was Burke's *Letter to a Noble Lord.* There, said Hazlitt, you have 'a man pouring out his mind on paper'. Just that praise is Hazlitt's own everywhere. To that praise you may add something further. For his writings as a whole Hazlitt made in his last years the claim that, whatever their general merits, at least he had 'written no commonplace, and no line that licks the dust'. That is a high claim for a man to make for himself who wrote always for his living. But it is, I think, a just claim; and because it is so, I should think Hazlitt, of all men who, in this kind, have written for their living, the most likely to live long. (pp. 107-09)

> *H. W. Garrod, "The Place of Hazlitt in English Criticism," in his* The Profession of Poetry and Other Lectures, *Oxford at the Clarendon Press, 1929, pp. 93-109.*

Virginia Woolf   (essay date 1932)

[*An English novelist, essayist, and critic, Woolf is one of the most prominent figures of twentieth-century literature. Like her contemporary James Joyce, with whom she is often compared, Woolf employed the stream-of-consciousness technique in her novels. Concerned primarily with depicting the life of the mind, she rebelled against traditional narrative techniques and developed a highly individualized style. Woolf's works, noted for their subjective explorations of characters' inner lives and their delicate poetic quality, have had a lasting effect on the art of the novel. Her critical essays, which cover almost the entire range of English literature, contain some of her finest prose and are praised for their insight. Along with Lytton Strachey, Roger Fry, Clive Bell, and others, Woolf and her husband, Leonard, formed the literary coterie known as the "Bloomsbury Group." In the following excerpt, she delineates some idiosyncrasies of Hazlitt's style.*]

The essays of Montaigne, Lamb, even Addison, have the reticence which springs from composure, for with all their familiarity they never tell us what they wish to keep hidden. But with Hazlitt it is different. There is always something divided and discordant even in his finest essays, as if two minds were at work who never succeed save for a few moments in making a match of it. In the first place there is the mind of the inquiring boy who wishes to be satisfied of the reason of things—the mind of the thinker. It is the thinker for the most part who is allowed the choice of the subject. He chooses some abstract idea, like Envy, or Egotism, or Reason and Imagination. He treats it with energy and independence. He explores its ramifications and scales its narrow paths as if it were a mountain road and the ascent both difficult and inspiring. Compared with this athletic progress, Lamb's seems the flight of a butterfly cruising capriciously among the flowers and perching for a second incongruously here upon a barn, there upon a wheelbarrow. But every sentence in Hazlitt carries us forward. He has his end in view and, unless some accident intervenes, he strides towards it in that "pure conversational prose style" which, as he points out, is so much more difficult to practise than fine writing.

There can be no question that Hazlitt the thinker is an admirable companion. He is strong and fearless; he knows his mind and he speaks his mind forcibly yet brilliantly too, for the readers of newspapers are a dull-eyed race who must be dazzled in order to make them see. But besides Hazlitt the thinker there is Hazlitt the artist. There is the sensuous and emotional man, with his feeling for colour and touch, with his passion for prize-fighting and Sarah Walker, with his sensibility to all those emotions which disturb the reason and make it often seem futile enough to spend one's time slicing things up finer and finer with the intellect when the body of the world is so firm and so warm and demands so imperatively to be pressed to the heart. To know the reason of things is a poor substitute for being able to feel them. And Hazlitt felt with the intensity of a poet. The most abstract of his essays will suddenly glow red-hot or white-hot if something reminds him of his past. He will drop his fine analytic pen and paint a phrase or two with a full brush brilliantly and beautifully if some landscape stirs his imagination or some book brings back the hour when he first read it. The famous passages about reading *Love for Love* and drinking coffee from a silver pot, and reading *La nouvelle Héloïse* and eating a cold chicken are known to all, and yet how oddly they often break into the context, how violently we are switched from reason to rhapsody—how embarrassingly our austere thinker falls upon our shoulders and demands our sympathy! It is this disparity and the sense of two forces in conflict that trouble the serenity and cause the inconclusiveness of some of Hazlitt's finest essays. They set out to give us a proof and they end by giving us a picture. We are about to plant our feet upon the solid rock of Q.E.D., and behold the rock turns to quagmire and we are knee-deep in mud and water and flowers. "Faces pale as the primrose with hyacinthine locks" are in our eyes; the woods of Tuderly breathe their mystic voices in our ears. Then suddenly we are recalled, and the thinker, austere, muscular, and sardonic, leads us on to analyse, to dissect, and to condemn.

Thus if we compare Hazlitt with the other great masters in his line it is easy to see where his limitations lie. His range is narrow and his sympathies few if intense. He does not open the doors wide upon all experience like Montaigne, rejecting nothing, tolerating everything, and watching the play of the soul with irony and detachment. On the contrary, his mind shut hard with egotistic tenacity upon his first impressions and froze them to unalterable convictions. Nor was it for him to make play, like Lamb, with the figures of his friends, creating them afresh in fantastic flights of imagination and reverie. His characters are seen with the same quick sidelong glance full of shrewdness and suspicion which he darted upon people in the flesh. He does not use the essayist's licence to circle and meander. He is tethered by his egotism and by his convictions to one time and one place and one being. We never forget that this is England in the early days of the nineteenth century; indeed, we feel ourselves in the Southampton Buildings or in the inn parlour that looks over the downs and on to the high road at Winterslow. He has an extraordinary power of making us contemporary with himself. But as we read on through the many volumes which he filled with so much energy and yet with so little love of his task, the comparison with the other essayists drops from us. These are not essays, it seems, independent and self-sufficient, but fragments broken off from some larger book—some searching enquiry into the reason for human actions or into the nature of human institutions. It is only accident that has cut them short, and only deference to the public taste that has decked them out with gaudy images and bright colours. The phrase which occurs in one form or another so frequently and indicates the structure which if he were free he would follow—"I will here try to go more at large into the subject and then give such instances and illustrations of it as occur to me"—could by no possibility occur in the *Essays of Elia* or *Sir Roger de Coverley*. He loves to grope among the curious depths of human psychology and to track down the reason of things. He excels in hunting out the obscure causes that lie behind some common saying or sensation, and the drawers of his mind are well stocked with illustrations and arguments. We can believe him when he says that for twenty years he had thought hard and suffered acutely. He is speaking of what he knows from experience when he exclaims, "How many ideas and trains of sentiment, long and deep and intense, often pass through the mind in only one day's thinking or reading!" Convictions are his lifeblood; ideas have formed in him like stalactites, drop by drop, year by year. He has sharpened them in a thousand solitary walks; he has tested them in argument after argument, sitting in his corner, sardonically observant, over a late supper at the Southampton Inn. But he has not changed them. His mind is his own and it is made up.

Thus however threadbare the abstraction—**"Hot and Cold,"** or **Envy,"** or **"The Conduct of Life,"** or **"The Picturesque and the Ideal"**—he has something solid to write about. He never lets his brain slacken or trusts to his great gift of picturesque phrasing to float him over a stretch of shallow thought. Even when it is plain from the savagery and contempt with which he attacks his task that he is out of the mood and only keeps his mind to the grindstone by strong tea and sheer force of will we still find him mordant and searching and acute. There is a stir and trouble, a vivacity and conflict in his essays as if the very contrariety of his gifts kept him on the stretch. He is always hating, loving, thinking, and suffering. He could never come to terms with authority or doff his own idiosyncrasy in deference to opinion. Thus chafed and goaded the level of his essays is extraordinarily high. Often dry, garish in their bright imagery, monotonous in the undeviating energy of their rhythm—for Hazlitt believed too implicitly in his own saying, "mediocrity, insipidity, want of character, is

the great fault", to be an easy writer to read for long at a stretch—there is scarcely an essay without its stress of thought, its thrust of insight, its moment of penetration. His pages are full of fine sayings and unexpected turns and independence and originality. "All that is worth remembering of life is the poetry of it." "If the truth were known, the most disagreeable people are the most amiable." "You will hear more good things on the outside of a stage-coach from London to Oxford, than if you were to pass a twelvemonth with the undergraduates or heads of colleges of that famous University." We are constantly plucked at by sayings that we would like to put by to examine later.

But besides the volumes of Hazlitt's essays there are the volumes of Hazlitt's criticism. In one way or another, either as lecturer or reviewer, Hazlitt strode through the greater part of English literature and delivered his opinion of the majority of famous books. His criticism has the rapidity and the daring, if it has also the looseness and the roughness, which arise from the circumstances in which it was written. He must cover a great deal of ground, make his points clear to an audience not of readers but of listeners, and has time only to point to the tallest towers and the brightest pinnacles in the landscape. But even in his most perfunctory criticism of books we feel that faculty for seizing on the important and indicating the main outline which learned critics often lose and timid critics never acquire. He is one of those rare critics who have thought so much that they can dispense with reading. It matters very little that Hazlitt had read only one poem by Donne; that he found Shakespeare's sonnets unintelligible; that he never read a book through after he was thirty; that he came indeed to dislike reading altogether. What he had read he had read with fervour. And since in his view it was the duty of a critic to "reflect the colours, the light and shade, the soul and body of a work", appetite, gusto, enjoyment were far more important than analytic subtlety or prolonged and extensive study. To communicate his own fervour was his aim. Thus he first cuts out with vigorous and direct strokes the figure of one author and contrasts it with another, and next builds up with the freest use of imagery and colour the brilliant ghost that the book has left glimmering in his mind. The poem is re-created in glowing phrases—"A rich distilled perfume emanates from it like the breath of genius; a golden cloud envelops it; a honeyed paste of poetic diction encrusts it, like the candied coat of the auricula". But since the analyst in Hazlitt is never far from the surface, this painter's imagery is kept in check by a nervous sense of the hard and lasting in literature, of what a book means and where it should be placed, which models his enthusiasm and gives it angle and outline. He singles out the peculiar quality of his author and stamps it vigorously. There is the "deep, internal, sustained sentiment" of Chaucer; "Crabbe is the only poet who has attempted and succeeded in the *still life* of tragedy". There is nothing flabby, weak, or merely ornamental in his criticism of Scott—sense and enthusiasm run hand in hand. And if such criticism is the reverse of final, if it is initiatory and inspiring rather than conclusive and complete, there is something to be said for the critic who starts the reader on a journey and fires him with a phrase to shoot off on adventures of his own. If one needs an incentive to read Burke, what is better than "Burke's style was forked and playful like the lightning, crested like the serpent"? Or again, should one be trembling on the brink of a dusty folio, the following passage is enough to plunge one in midstream:

> It is delightful to repose on the wisdom of the ancients; to have some great name at hand, besides one's own initials always staring one in the face; to travel out of one's self into the Chaldee, Hebrew, and Egyptian characters; to have the palm-trees waving mystically in the margin of the page, and the camels moving slowly on in the distance of three thousand years. In that dry desert of learning, we gather strength and patience, and a strange and insatiable thirst of knowledge. The ruined monuments of antiquity are also there, and the fragments of buried cities (under which the adder lurks) and cool springs, and green sunny spots, and the whirlwind and the lion's roar, and the shadow of angelic wings.

Needless to say that is not criticism. It is sitting in an armchair and gazing into the fire, and building up image after image of what one has seen in a book. It is loving and taking the liberties of a lover. It is being Hazlitt. (pp. 191-98)

Virginia Woolf, "William Hazlitt," in her The Common Reader, First and Second Series, *Harcourt Brace Jovanovich, 1948, pp. 186-99.*

Charles Morgan   (essay date 1948)

[*Morgan was an English novelist, playwright, and critic. In the following excerpt, he reappraises* Liber Amoris *as a work deserving of more critical attention.*]

[A re-assessment of **Liber Amoris**] is overdue. In spite of persistent attack, the **Liber Amoris** has stubbornly survived. It was called "disgusting" by Crabb Robinson, using the word, not in its earlier sense of "distasteful," but as we use it, violently, to mean "revolting" or "repulsive." Le Gallienne called it "silly," and, even as late as 1947, so wise and humane a critic as Mr. Frank Swinnerton, spoke of it as "that tragic piece of futility." And yet it lives with its own life, and not merely because the great essayist wrote it. No one who reads ever forgets it.

One reason is that it constitutes what a lawyer might call a leading case in the psychology of love. It said on the subject something that had not been said before in English prose, and has not been said since with the same directness and candour. What it said, and the value of the evidence it gave, we, in the midst of the Twentieth Century, are better able to discern than were those Victorians and pre-Victorians to whom its truth was unfamiliar and disturbing. Either they had not read Stendhal or they discounted him as French. (p. 10)

The whole story of the **Liber Amoris** is a flawless example of Stendhal's theory of crystallization, the more valuable because it was almost certainly written without knowledge of that theory. . . . In Paris [Hazlitt] met Stendhal for the first time, and Howe tells us, "Stendhal's *De l' amour* formed Hazlitt's travelling companion during his tour. . . ." With thoughts of Miss Walker in his mind, he must have read it with deep attention, for he himself, in the heat of blood, had set down his experience, asking again and again: "What does it mean? Why am I, who see so clearly, yet so bewitched?" and here was Stendhal telling him precisely why.

Almost too precisely. *De l' amour* was brilliant analysis. It isolated, and held up for intellectual observation, a truth about love which, though others had expressed it often enough—Shakespeare in his *Sonnets,* for example, and Montaigne in his *Essays*—had never been so isolated before. We know more of ourselves (when we have leisure to examine ourselves) because Stendhal wrote, but we have not, in time of trouble, the mental detachment and coolness necessary to be his pupils. Hazlitt's book, without so well understanding what it says, says the same thing in such a way that passionate youth, or passionate middle-age for that matter, may see, reflected in its pages, an aspect of love which the aloof world calls "disgusting" or "silly" or "futile" and which the passion-stricken one half-knows to be so in himself. Yet he may find, in these same pages, that assuagement which is given by imagination shared, and is, to the tormented and enraptured, more precious than counsel.

What is this truth that Montaigne knew, and Stendhal reiterated, and Hazlitt exemplified? That we project our own imagining of Love on to her whom we say we love. We re-create her in an ideal shape—Hazlitt called Miss Walker "the statue"—and worship her in that shape, and struggle to bring the statue to life. "Like the passion of Love," said Montaigne, "that lends Beauties and Graces to the person it does embrace; and that makes those who are caught with it, with a depraved and corrupt Judgment, consider the thing they love other and more perfect than it is."

Hazlitt goes further than this, further than Montaigne, further even than Stendhal, in his laying bare of the process of crystallization. He shows, because he is a supreme realist and is unafraid to give himself away, that the crystallizing lover is by no means the blind fool that he is traditionally supposed to be. He thus deprives himself of the only romantic defence with which an aloof and self-righteous world might be disposed contemptuously to cover him. The lover, Hazlitt says in effect, is not even a dupe; he is worse, he is a half-dupe, and yet persists; his desire is, as Shakespeare has said, "*past reason hunted*" . . .

> All this the world well knows, yet none knows well
> To shun the heaven that leads men to this hell.

Hazlitt made no attempt to dignify his obsession. His division of mind between knowledge of Miss Walker's inadequacy and passionate exaltation of the ideal she represented is made plain in his terrible alternation of blame and praise, of angry distrust and wild confidence, of sickening triviality and high romance. (pp. 13-16)

[**Liber Amoris**] is not, to use *Blackwood's* word, "manly." The letters, even as they were published, expose their writer to all the shafts of ridicule and contempt. But they are an invaluable document because they are not dressed-up, because they are fearless of being laughed at, because they pour out the vast and the petty inconsistencies of the truth. If they are read contemptuously or in moral indignation, they will yield nothing. If they are read pitifully, they will yield not much more. But if they are read compassionately, in a spirit of "feeling with," they respond with compassion. That is why no lover who opens the **Liber Amoris** puts it down easily, and why no one who reads—though he resist and hate—ever forgets it.

It is an extreme book. For that reason, and because its extremism is sexual, and because it was written by genius and, therefore, not palely but with blood, it has hitherto been a cause either of rage or of bridling and embarrassment in many readers. Even to-day, after the lapse of a century and a quarter, it will not be received dispassionately; nor should it be; it is not a dispassionate book: you pick up what might, after so many years, be a spent ember, and it burns.

Nevertheless, we may hope, as our predecessors could not, to see the *Liber Amoris* as it is in itself and to judge it by its faults and virtues in its own kind. Our intolerances, even when political, are not those of Hazlitt's age, and, even when sexual, are no longer of the sort that made Crabb Robinson cry out, after reading the book, that "it ought to exclude the author from all decent society." (pp. 16-17)

The *Liber Amoris* is a vulnerable book. Nothing is easier than to quote from it derisively. Even to the point of self-humiliation in the little shames, Hazlitt, following Rousseau, had not hesitated to give himself away, and the reviewer did only what was to be expected of him. There is, moreover, a sense in which it is true to say that the *Liber Amoris* is a failure. It is not, even within its own intention, the great book it might have been; it does not take rank—and no one can have been more bitterly aware of this than its author—with or near the *Confessions* of Rousseau or *La nouvelle Heloise*. It was written too close in time to the experience from which it sprang. The period of distillation was too short, and its shortness prevented Hazlitt from entering imaginatively into Sarah Walker's mind. (p. 18)

The simple and probably inadequate explanation of Miss Walker is that she was an early nineteenth century equivalent of what is nowadays called a "good-timer"—a girl, that is to say, with no rule except her own pleasure but without the capacity or courage to drink pleasure deep; a weak creature seeking always the petty re-assurances of vanity; anaemically indifferent rather than callous; desiring change not for adventure's sake but to cheat the natural emptiness of her mind; conventional, defensive, always afraid of missing something, an intuitive hater of distinction, vulgarly refined. Miss Walker had some of these qualities, but the character does not fit her. It does not fit her because it is a mass-product, and she, whatever her faults, was not mass-produced.

It seems by no means improbable that, before she met Hazlitt, she had loved in her fashion a man who had vanished from her life. She said so; she gave it as her reason for holding Hazlitt back; and the man is more likely to have existed than to have been invented by her. That he was altogether a fiction, it is hard to believe, and, if he existed, she may well have crystallized in him her idea of love, and so have become, as it were, chilled against all but the minor sensualities in which she indulged with Hazlitt and Mr. C. All that we are told of her suggests that she was in some sense numb rather than naturally cold or deliberately cruel.

[Benjamin Robert] Haydon says that the dialogues given in the *Liber Amoris* were "literal." They bear the stamp of truth. Consider then, these passages:

> H. Tell me why you have deceived me, and singled me out as your victim?
> S. I never have, Sir. I always said I could not

love. . . . I have always been consistent from the first.

Hazlitt demands why, then, she had kissed him at first asking. She had seemed "so reserved and modest" that "whatever favours you granted must proceed from pure regard." To a long tirade, she answers only: "I am no prude, Sir." Then, later:

> S. I'll stay and hear this no longer.
> H. Yes, one word more. Did you not love another?
> S. Yes, and ever shall most sincerely.

Hazlitt himself believed it at the time, for he replied: "Then, *that* is my only hope." Sarah never swerved from it.

Hazlitt came afterwards to believe that she had lied. It was an explanation supplied by rage and disappointment. If he had waited until he was able to recollect his emotion in tranquillity and had then re-imagined Miss Walker, he might have seen himself as she, perhaps, saw him: a man different from any she had formerly known, belonging to a world she had never guessed at, having powers she had never felt. His imagination, the force of crystallization that drove him mad, could not be without its effect on her. She was, or thought of herself as being, ordinary; but imagination has creative power, and this extraordinary man was imagining her as an extraordinary girl. (pp. 20-2)

Whether, if he had given himself time, Hazlitt would have interpreted her in this way or another, he would certainly, being an artist, have interpreted her from the inside. That he did not do so unbalances his book if we consider it as we might consider a novel. From that point of view, it is incomplete. But this very one-sidedness, this extreme subjectivity, gives it rare value as a document written at white-heat by a man of genius at the height of passionate obsession. At the time, Hazlitt was afflicted by the terrible loquaciousness which is often a consequence of spiritual loneliness and despair. (p. 23)

The *Liber Amoris* was his relief. It has the defect of being unbalanced in its treatment, or in its failure to treat with interior sympathy the other protagonist of the tale. But balance, except in very dull leading articles and very pedestrian men, is not all. Pressure is one of the evidences of genius, and another, when you can write Hazlitt's prose, is a complete carelessness for the moderate and unsentimental sneer that will greet the end of your sentence. Hazlitt wrote this:

> . . . I am now inclosed in a dungeon of despair. The sky is marble to my thoughts; nature is dead around me, as hope is within me; no object can give me one gleam of satisfaction now, nor the prospect of it in time to come. I wander by the sea-side; and the eternal ocean and lasting despair and her face are before me. Slighted by her, on whom my heart by its last fibre hung, where shall I turn? I wake with her by my side, not as my sweet bed-fellow, but as the corpse of my love, without a heart in her bosom, cold, insensible, or struggling from me; and the worm gnaws me, and the sting of unrequited love, and the canker of a hopeless, endless sorrow. I have lost the taste of my food by feverish anxiety; and my favourite beverage, which used to refresh me when I got up, has no moisture in it. Oh! cold, solitary, sepulchral breakfasts . . .

Who will may smile at that. It is extreme, unbalanced, and, fortunately, without a sense of humour. But it is true with a truth that a regulated and discreet sanity could not have communicated. "The sky is marble to my thoughts," wrote Hazlitt, and the saying is of Shakespeare's breed. It has the terrible flash of *Troilus and Cressida.* (pp. 23-4)

[The] value of the *Liber Amoris* is that it expresses a kind of love—no less love for being also a kind of madness—which a great part of Victorian opinion persisted in regarding as inhuman baseness, so vile and so exceptional that it was not a fit subject for literature or even for thought. From this point of view, passion—of which the existence could scarcely be denied by readers of *Romeo and Juliet*—was seen as a lamentable intrusion upon the ordered decencies of society. It was, therefore, carefully distinguished, as an aberration, from that love which conformed to the social rule. When it appeared in the very young, it was treated, unless it led to extra-matrimonial disaster, as a naïveté to be wryly smiled at, and, if it could not be suppressed, to be tolerated under the name of calf-love. In all other circumstances, it was ruthlessly hunted, as it was in Parnell; and, in order that it might be hunted, it had first to be outlawed—that is to say, it had to be proclaimed as something freakish and unnatural, abnormal as crime is abnormal. This attitude towards passion, and a corresponding attitude towards crystallization, were expressed by Richard Le Gallienne with the ingenuous candour of the period.

> Though, as we have seen, the illusion did credit to Hazlitt's heart, it is impossible not to feel that no man of forty should be able to mistake a woman for a goddess or an angel . . . It is unnatural, uncanny, in the bearded man. Naïveté is charming up to twenty, but the naïveté of middle-age is unattractive, and the *Liber Amoris* is full of that unattractive quality—much like the naïveté we sometimes find in the poetical effusions of criminals.

It is an adroit piece of special pleading. To mistake a woman for a goddess would indeed be naïve, but this precisely is what Hazlitt did not do. He saw the woman and the goddess at the same time; was agonizingly aware both of the distinction between them on one plane of his consciousness and of their identity on another plane; was unceasingly observant of his self-division; was the sane, unsparing analyst of his own madness, and, therefore, racked. (pp. 25-6)

Charles Morgan, in an introduction to Liber Amoris and Dramatic Criticisms *by William Hazlitt, Peter Nevill Limited, 1958, pp. 7-28.*

Walter Jackson Bate   (essay date 1952)

[*Bate is an American critic and biographer who has written what is considered the definitive study of the life and works of John Keats as well as several surveys of literary criticism. He is particularly interested in late eighteenth-century literature, which he considers a watershed in the history of ideas, marking the transition from classical to romantic influences. In the following excerpt, he describes how Hazlitt's literary criticism typifies the aesthetic tenets of English Romanticism.*]

Because of his comparative diffuseness, Hazlitt's virtues as a critic are not quickly grasped from reading a few essays; he has therefore been less read since his death than more condensed but less significant critics, and his importance has thus tended to be underrated. Yet Hazlitt is easily the most representative critic in English romanticism, and this representativeness is shown in several ways. (1) Like the majority of romantic critics, he was strongly interested in the way in which the human mind and emotions react in creating or responding to art. (2) Like Wordsworth and Coleridge, he was much concerned with moral theory and its relation to psychology. (3) More than any other major English critic of any period, Hazlitt dwelt upon and accepted the romantic values of "gusto" and emotional excitement in art. Yet (4) he also saw, with perhaps a clearer eye than his contemporaries, the dangers of emotional subjectivism, and the degree to which his own age was moving toward it in literature and the other arts. Hence the moderation of English thought, in all periods, is typified by Hazlitt. The extreme romantic was as rare in England as the extreme neoclassicist had been.

Hazlitt's criticism moved in and around subjects other than those concerned with abstract esthetic theory. When he turned, for example, to such problems as the nature of the comic, he wrote with more practical understanding than the seriously speculative Coleridge, not to mention Continental critics of the time. The result is a less rarified, a more ample and empirical approach, which never loses its grasp on specific works of literature and art. With the exception of Wordsworth and Keats—neither of whom is essentially a critic—Hazlitt, in his moral, critical, and psychological premises, represents more than any other writer of his time a union of eighteenth-century English empiricism and emotional intuitionalism, a combination which—with its distrust of abstraction, its confidence in concrete nature, its values of sympathy and emotional immediacy—had encouraged the disintegration of classical rationalism and sustained the development of European romanticism as a whole. In Hazlitt, as in English romanticism generally, these attitudes center in a conception of the imagination.

The various principles and assumptions that run through Hazlitt's criticism were nowhere collected by him in one place and then unified by any one comprehensive but specific standpoint. But there is one point of view which permeates and colors many of his other principles, and gives a certain unity to his criticism: that is, his conception of the sympathetic character of the imagination, and his belief in the absolute dependence of great art upon it. . . . In art, an intense awareness of the object, an absorption in it, arises from sympathetic identification. Not only human characters, as in a drama, but imagery vividly presented, line and color in a painting, the rhythmic flow of music, all arouse an identification that lifts the reader, observer, or hearer beyond himself. Hazlitt carried the conception of the sympathetic imagination further than any other critic. His first work, written when he was quite young—an *Essay on the Principles of Human Action* (1805)—tries to establish sympathy as the basis of all moral action. It is an answer to the belief of Thomas Hobbes and his followers that all men are basically selfish, that self-love is the mainspring of human action: if we act generously, for example, it is because we wish to be praised, we wish to get along with people, we wish to think well of ourselves, etc. Hazlitt's answer is that we have no innately implanted love of ourselves—or of others, for that matter. Suppose that I love myself, that I want to do something to help myself or avoid pain in the future. How can I know and "love" my own identity? I know my past and present identity through memory and sensation. If a child burns his finger, he knows only through *sensation* that it is he and not someone else who feels the pain. In a similar way, he knows only through *memory* that it was he, and not someone else, who felt pain in the past. If our identities until now depend on sensation and memory, what can give me an interest in my future sensations? Sensation and memory are not enough; I can picture my future identity only in my *imagination.* The child who has been burned will recoil from the fire, with its prospect of future pain, only because, through his imagination, he "projects himself forward into the future, and identifies himself with his future being."

Now this sympathetic, identifying ability is able to turn in any direction. It does not *have* to turn in one way—toward oneself, for example—more than another. The same ability that enables a person to "throw himself into the future," and anticipate events that do not yet exist, also enables him to enter into the feelings of others. I therefore "could not love myself, if I were not capable of loving others." If stronger ideas than those of one's own identity are present in the mind, the identifying imagination can as easily turn to them. Knowledge may broaden and direct sympathy, and habituate it to ideas other than that of our own identity. The more we know of what another is undergoing, the more we sympathize; and long acquaintance increases sympathy—if certain qualities in the other person, or monotony, have not weighed against it. If the child is insensible to the good of others, it is not from self-love, but from lack of knowing any better. Self-centeredness in an adult results from a long, habitual narrowing of the mind to one's own feelings and interests. Greatness in art, philosophy, or moral action—the "heroic" in any sense—all involve losing the sense "of our personal identity in some object dearer to us than ourselves."

Hazlitt's small book on the *Principles of Human Action* is a more ingenious argument than this summary would indicate, and the critical principles in his later writing emanate from the problem of sympathetic identification. (pp. 282-84)

Hazlitt's conception of the sympathetic imagination interweaves with his other critical attitudes at almost every point. For example, it underlies his conception of the drama as the most objective and therefore the highest form of poetry. As contrasted with lyric verse, the aim of the drama can never be to express the subjective feelings of the poet, but rather to represent human life. Hazlitt's position led him to feel, at times, that the French mind often fails to "identify itself with anything, but always has its own consciousness." This premise also underlies the harsher criticism of his own contemporaries, especially Wordsworth, Byron, and Shelley. He sensed an increasing obtrusion of the poet's own personal feelings and interests, and a tendency to lose the "chameleon" form of genius.

The sympathetic identification he believed so essential in art especially underlies his stress on what he called "gusto." As generally used by Hazlitt, "gusto" seems to imply a strong excitement of the imagination by which, geared to its highest activity, it seizes and draws out the dynamic and living character of its object into telling expression. This emphasis on strong emotion in art is, of course, characteristically romantic. But the stress is on emotion turned *outward* toward its object, to the external world, not on subjective emotion directed inward. Strong emotion, for Hazlitt, is necessary if there is to be sympathetic identification, and hence the understanding which that identification brings. In a state of strong excitement, the imagination so grasps its object that the various elements and qualities of that object become animated into a living unity. "Gusto," in other words, is the state in which the imagination's fusing power comes into play through a strong sympathetic excitement. In doing so, it brings into focus and unifies, for example, all the senses. This is not "synesthesia" in the ordinary sense, but it is so living a grasp of the separate sense impressions by the imagination that all the senses are brought into focus, interpreting and substantiating each other. Hence Hazlitt's remark that Claude Lorrain's landscapes lack gusto because "they do not interpret one sense by another . . . his eye wanted imagination. . . . He saw the atmosphere but did not feel it." Chaucer's descriptions of natural scenery have gusto, and give "the very feeling of the air, the coolness or moisture of the ground."

This conception of "gusto" should be taken into consideration in approaching Hazlitt's essay **"On Poetry in General,"** where he says, for example, that "Poetry is only the highest eloquence of passion, the most vivid form of expression that can be given to our conception of anything, whether pleasurable or painful, mean or dignified, delightful or distressing." This does not, we repeat, imply the extreme romantic contention that "feeling is all"—that the end of poetry is self-expression, or the boiling over of one's inner lava. . . . In stating that poetry is the "highest eloquence of passion," Hazlitt is maintaining something very different. He is stressing a passionate and objective understanding of what is beyond the personal and subjective. In those who lack sufficient imagination, feeling is localized largely in self. But in those who possess it, the imagination can broaden and direct feeling, lifting it beyond self, and riveting it to other objects. Hence he took issue with Mme. de Staël's remark that imagination was the dominant faculty of Rousseau's mind; Rousseau had only an "extreme sensibility," and that was centered almost exclusively in his own impressions.

Hazlitt, in fact, seemed to find a marked absence of objective imagination in the English poetry of his own day. In reviewing Wordsworth's *Excursion,* he divided poetry roughly into two classes: the poetry of imagination, and that of sentiment. Poetry should ideally combine the two. He cites Chaucer, Shakespeare, and Milton as examples of such a combination. Cowley and Young show a certain kind of imaginative activity divorced from feeling; while Wordsworth has the feeling without a corresponding strength of imagination. The point seems a suggestive anticipation of T. S. Eliot's remarks on the "dissociation of sensibility" that took place after the mid-seventeenth century. Combining much feeling and little objective imagination, said Hazlitt, Wordsworth's *Excursion* "is less a poem on the country than on the love of the country." It describes the feelings associated with objects rather than portraying the objects themselves. (pp. 285-86)

Hazlitt, then, despite his stress on emotional "gusto,"

stood opposed to the extreme offshoots of the doctrine of "original genius" and self-expression in art. No critic has urged originality more fervently. On the other hand, the mere expression of subjective feeling is very easy, and what is really rare and original is the ability to uncover and express the living reality of nature and human nature. The writings of Hazlitt probably contain the most consistent onslaught, since the broad neoclassicism of Johnson and Reynolds, on the belief in art as self-expression. In modern poetry, as he states in his lecture **"On Shakespeare and Milton,"** there seems to be a widespread "experiment to reduce poetry to a mere effusion of natural sensibility," or surround "the meanest objects with the . . . devouring egotism of the writers' own minds." Milton and Shakespeare "owe their power over the human mind to their having had a deeper sense than others of what was grand in the objects of nature, or affecting in the events of human life. But to the men I speak of there is nothing interesting . . . but themselves." Hazlitt, it should be noted, is here opposing the occasional romantic belief that any subject will serve equally well in art if the artist is sufficiently affected by it and treats it with enough technical skill. This belief was to develop throughout the nineteenth century, and be encouraged by critics at the beginning of the twentieth century. To Hazlitt, this was essentially a form of subjectivism. As he stated in his lecture **"On the Living Poets,"** "A thorough adept in this school of poetry and philanthropy is jealous of all excellence but his own. He does not even like to share his reputation with his subject . . . he sympathizes only with what can enter into no competition with him . . . "

Hence art is not an expression of the artist himself. Its aim is to express a heightened and perceptive grasp of objective reality. To Hazlitt, who is very English in being empirically minded, this reality is to be found in the concrete, particularized world about us. . . . In Hazlitt's words the arts "resemble Antaeus in his struggle with Hercules, who was strangled when he was raised above the ground, and only revived and recovered his strength when he touched his mother earth." When art, in any way, departs from concrete reality, it loses truth and force. (pp. 286-87)

Similarly, the diction of poetry must evolve from the concrete image. One of Hazlitt's reasons for preferring English poetry to French was his feeling that the French poetry up to his own day often lacked the necessary ballast of concrete imagery—that it lacked "natural bones or substance. Ours constantly clings to the concrete, and has a *purchase* upon matter." English thought and writing in the late Renaissance, particularly during the early seventeenth century, has this "clinging to the concrete" to a marked degree. The minds of these thinkers and writers, as Hazlitt stated in an essay called the **"British Senate"** . . . were stored with facts and images almost to excess; there was a tenacity and firmness in them that kept fast hold of the impressions of things. . . . Facts and feelings went hand in hand . . . " Ideas were not yet "squeezed" out of the concrete to fly like ghosts through a "vacuum of abstract reasoning, and sentimental refinement."

The arts, then, rest on concrete nature. But Hazlitt would insist that actual concreteness is never static. Static or fixed objects, qualities, or generalizations are simply the artificial creation of our categorizing faculty, reason. Nature, in its actuality, is characterized by flux, by the interweaving of relationships, by elements mutually modifying each other. Art tries to arrest and express this evolving concreteness, and give it qualitative value. It does this by going beyond the separate sense impressions, and by evoking a sympathetic gusto or intensity that centralizes the various isolated impressions of the senses into a unified and living conception. Hence, as Hazlitt says in **"On Poetry in General,"** "Poetry puts a spirit of life and motion into the universe. It describes the flowing, not the fixed." In doing so, art does not declare and stamp a form upon the mind so much as it tries, by *suggestion,* to encourage the mind, through its *own* imaginative activity, to fill out nuances and relations, and thus realize them more vividly. This is the value of suggestive "imitation" in art. It stimulates the mind to greater activity by encouraging it to compare the imitation with the original object, and thus "excites a more intense perception of truth." The principles of connection and interrelation between the various elements of nature—the relation between the parts of an object as they combine to make up the identity and totality of that object; the connection between various objects and forms as they make up larger patterns of meaning or form; the mutual interaction of various passions, feelings, and thoughts in the human character, and their modifying of each other—constitute a primary aspect of concrete truth. Art, in its highest function, tries to lay bare and communicate the value and meaning of this interrelation as it evolves in its concrete setting. To seize suggestively upon it in what Hazlitt calls an "excess of power," and communicate it with intense gusto and force, constitutes "sublimity." "Beauty," on the other hand, is the harmonizing of different objects and qualities. Moreover, "truth," grasped in a vivid way, may justly be called beautiful or sublime "since all things are connected, and all things modify one another in nature." In other words, beauty, to Hazlitt, may be described as the truthful blending and harmonizing of elements and qualities into a vital significance, and the sublime may be described as their truthful heightening. It might be added that the comic, in one of its aspects, consists in the knocking out of interconnection.

Hazlitt's critical writing, then, supports one of the most characteristic of the romantic esthetic values: the conception of art as intense naturalistic expression—that is, the sympathetic and objective expression of the particular and concrete. (pp. 288-89)

The sympathetic grasp of concrete reality, and the transmitting of it through a given medium of art, is the product not of rules and logical reason but of the imagination. Hazlitt admitted that certain broad rules naturally have a place in all art. But these are not so much rules deliberately and consciously followed as they are injunctions learned by experience and good sense, and as such are automatically *felt* in the actual process of creating or responding to art. What is needed, then, is the ability to absorb knowledge and experience, and the ability to apply them automatically, with instinctive immediacy. The logical reason is not a direct realizing of the concrete. In fact, it abstracts *from* the concrete. It categorizes; somewhat like a minting machine, it stamps out and coins static and definite concepts; and with these as its counters—in place of the fluid, living process of actual nature—it proceeds piecemeal, step by step, instead of with a total and immediate comprehension. Hazlitt's standpoint may be called characteristically romantic. His point, in effect, is similar to that of the late Professor Whitehead in his remarks on the "fallacy of misplaced concreteness." Abstraction, says Whitehead, fails by its very nature to conceive the whole truth. It is an act of mind which draws out or abstracts from reality only certain elements, and then combines them for special purposes of thought. The danger of "misplaced concreteness" is that one may mistakenly regard an abstraction as equivalent to the concrete truth. Hazlitt discusses this in an early philosophical essay, and describes abstraction as a kind of "short-cut" in thinking—a trick to supply our lack of complete comprehension. Abstractions are necessary; thinking is impossible without them. What is needed is to anchor them as much as possible in the concrete reality.

The ability to absorb experience and apply it immediately and relevantly to concrete objects and circumstances is the principal characteristic of what Hazlitt calls the imagination. Sympathetic identification is its most successful form of applying knowledge and experience, and of attaining a strongly felt understanding. Sir Joshua Reynolds stated that the ability needed in art was not so much "reason" in the ordinary sense, with its confidence in rules, but—as in life itself—a "sagacity" that supersedes "the slow progress of deduction," and "goes at once, by what appears a kind of intuition, to the conclusion": a sagacity drawing upon "the accumulated experience of our whole life." In his essay **"On Genius and Common Sense,"** Hazlitt repeated and expanded what Reynolds said,

> In art, in taste, in life, in speech, you decide from feeling, and not from reason; that is, from the impression of a number of things on the mind, which impression is true and well-founded, though you may not be able to analyse or account for it in the several particulars. In a gesture you use, in a look you see, in a tone you hear, you judge of the expression, propriety, and meaning from habit, from innumerable instances of like gestures, looks, and tones, in innumerable other circumstances, variously modified, which are too many and too refined to be all distinctly recollected, but which do not therefore operate the less powerfully. . . .

The imagination acts, then, not by retaining in memory all the separate particles of our knowledge, employing them one by one, but by having transformed them all into what might be called a *readiness of response.* To discover this ability, to describe its working, to justify confidence in it, had been the unique achievement of English psychological criticism during the eighteenth century, particularly the latter half of that century. Where it is most successful and informative, the romantic conception of the imagination simply assumes and expands the theory of mind that was developed during the eighteenth century by English empirical psychology—a theory of mind that had supported and had developed along with the empirical emphasis on concrete, particularized nature. Of its application to romantic values in literary criticism, Hazlitt is the most notable example. (pp. 290-92)

> *Walter Jackson Bate, "Romantic Individualism: The Imagination and Emotion," in* Criticism: The Major Texts, *edited by Walter Jackson Bate, Harcourt Brace Jovanovich, Inc., 1952, pp. 281-92.*

G. D. Klingopulos (essay date 1956)

[*In the following excerpt, Klingopulos proposes a re-evaluation of Hazlitt's reputation as a literary critic.*]

Hazlitt's reputation at the present time is not too securely based on his essays and his literary criticism. He is quoted, but much as Crabb Robinson is quoted. In both capacities he has been much criticized in our time, but more objectively and therefore more absolutely than in the days of the great reviews. (p. 386)

Essays, when they are not discussions of books, pictures or persons, survive because they contain useful reflections on life, or because they have a period charm, of the kind to be found as much in Pepys as in Addison. It is at least doubtful whether Hazlitt's essays in *The Round Table, Table-Talk* and *The Plain Speaker,* can give much satisfaction to a reader who expects to be interested in either of these ways. If we remove from a representative collection such as *The Round Table* the two essays on Wordsworth's *The Excursion,* we are left with matter which is always readable but scarcely memorable. Assertions are made with too little persuasiveness. Hazlitt's remarks on Methodism—'religion with its slobbering-bib and go-cart. It is a bastard kind of Popery, stripped of its painted pomp and outward ornaments, and reduced to a state of pauperism'—remind us, despite a certain penetration, of the eighteenth-century prejudice in some of his judgments. It was not Hazlitt's gift to see provincial religion as the author of *Adam Bede* saw it. The last epithet in Stendhal's description of Hazlitt, 'homme d'esprit, Anglais, et misanthrope', seems for once appropriate, after a reading of **'The Causes of Methodism'**. The Burke-like emphasis of style—one essay is entitled **'On Gusto'**—appropriate enough when Hazlitt is laying down the law, as in **'The Progress of Art'**, can also remind us disagreeably of Swift:

> Life is the art of being well deceived; and in order that the deception may succeed, it must be habitual and uninterrupted. A constant examination of the value of our opinions and enjoyments, compared with those of others, may lessen our prejudices, but will leave nothing for our affections to rest upon.

It is part of the definition of a Romantic writer that he lacks but seeks serenity. Each reports on his own kind of unhappiness and the difficulty of transcending it. The two sentences of the last quotation suggest the tension of attitudes which accounts in part for Hazlitt's temperament, 'brow-hanging, shoe-contemplative, *strange*', as Coleridge described him in 1803. Hazlitt loved to philosophize but his temper was active, sympathetic and *engagé,* rather than philosophical. His scepticism was not a lazy habit; his long-meditated and earnest *Essay on the Principles of Human Action,* in which he affirms, against Hobbes, Hartley and Helvetius, the natural unselfishness of the human mind, its capacity for altruism, does represent a good deal of strenuous thinking.

> I naturally desire and pursue my own good (in whatever this consists) simply from my having an idea of it sufficiently warm and vivid to excite in me an emotion of interest, or passion; and I love and pursue the good of others, of a relative, of a friend, of a family, a community, or of mankind for just the same reason.

Hazlitt dislikes but does not underestimate or rail at

Hobbes. In his lectures on *The History of English Philosophy* he stresses Hobbes's importance as the founder of the 'material or *modern* philosophy'. . . . Yet Hazlitt was an individualist and a radical who never tired of refuting, in and out of season, minimal accounts of human nature, and of attempting to steer a middle course between the Jacobins and Romantic Tories. This mediating attitude was not the result of moral timidity but of a strong grasp of actualities, and considerable self-knowledge.

Hazlitt's standing as a literary critic at the present time is not much more definite or secure than his standing as an 'essayist'. He has incurred one of Mr. [T. S.] Eliot's disparaging mentions, tellingly supported with chapter and verse. 'Hazlitt, who had perhaps the most uninteresting mind of all our distinguished critics, says: "Dryden and Pope are the great masters of the artificial style of poetry in our language, as the poets of whom I have already treated, Chaucer, Spenser, Shakespeare, and Milton, were of the natural." ' After pulling this remark to pieces, Mr. Eliot classes Hazlitt with those nineteenth-century critics, including of course Arnold, who felt 'a repugnance for the material out of which Dryden's poetry is built'. No doubt Hazlitt's dictum is indefensible: it is the sort of opening sentence we should expect from a harassed lecturer surveying the whole of English poetry in eight public lectures before the days of systematic literary history. But it is not possible to read the whole lecture on Dryden and Pope, from which the quotation is taken, and still maintain that Hazlitt felt 'a repugnance for the material out of which Dryden's poetry is built'. Hazlitt was not Johnson but he still felt at home with eighteenth-century poetry, and even with Restoration comedy. The impression he gives is not of a meaningless catholicity of taste. The judgment that 'Dryden was a better prose-writer and a bolder and more varied versifier than Pope. He was a more vigorous thinker, a more correct and logical declaimer, and had more of what may be called strength of mind than Pope: but he had not the same refinement and delicacy of feeling' seems to come from a genuine responsiveness to the work of both poets, despite its imprecision. (pp. 387-90)

To demur at a too ready 'placing' of Hazlitt as a literary critic is not, however, to argue that the question of his relative importance is as wide open as H. W. Garrod implied in his essay on 'The Place of Hazlitt in English Criticism' where he wrote: 'Whether Hazlitt is the greatest of the English literary critics must depend upon the view you take of what literary criticism is or should be' [see excerpt dated 1929]. By the standard of Hazlitt's best work, much of his criticism is without distinction. He is too often content, especially in his lecture courses, to survey a large number of writers, novelists, playwrights or poets, commenting superficially. As with Coleridge, the public lecture did not make for concentration, but encouraged a certain obviousness, and even a topicality like the Rev. Mr. Irving's. That Hazlitt knew what standards of criticism were, and that he did not overrate his own performance is made plain by his letter to Macvey Napier (August 26th, 1818), regretting his inability to accept the latter's invitation to write the article on Drama for the Supplement of the *Encyclopaedia Britannica:* he had written, two years earlier, the article on the Fine Arts. He explains that he has to write 'between this and the end of October', the series of lectures on English Comic Writers, and goes on to say, with what seems excessive modesty, that 'to get up an

article in a Review on any subject of general literature is quite as much as I can do without exposing myself'. An authoritative summary of the Drama would be beyond his powers. 'I know something about Congreve, but nothing at all of Aristophanes, and yet I conceive that the writer of an article on the Drama ought to be as well acquainted with the one as the other. If you should see Mr. Constable, [the proprietor of the *Edinburgh Magazine* and of the *Encyclopaedia Britannica*] will you tell him I am writing *nonsense* for him as fast as I can?'

None of the three lecture courses, *On the English Poets* (1818), *On English Comic Writers* (1819), *On the Dramatic Literature of the Reign of Queen Elizabeth* (1821), is of course entirely dull. The third is less useful than the other two, in which redeeming passages, the result of a better familiarity with their subjects, occur rather more frequently. There are some good perceptions in the lecture on eighteenth-century novelists (*Comic Writers,* Lecture Six) where he writes of Richardson that he 'seemed to spin his materials entirely out of his own brain, as if there had been nothing existing in the world beyond the little room in which he sat writing. There is an artificial reality about his works, which is nowhere else to be met with. They have the romantic air of pure fiction, with the literal minuteness of a common diary'.

Although, in the previous course, Hazlitt had claimed little knowledge of Donne's poetry ('Of Donne I know nothing but some beautiful verses to his wife, dissuading her from accompanying him on his travels abroad, and some quaint riddles in verse, which the Sphinx could not unravel'), he shows himself, in the third lecture on Comic Writers, not at all prone, as Johnson had been, to depreciate on principle. He quotes the first lines of *The Blossom* and comments: 'This simple and delicate description is only introduced as a foundation for an elaborate metaphysical conceit as a parallel to it in the next stanza'; which he gives, and then remarks: 'This is but a lame and impotent conclusion from so delightful a beginning.' There is something to be said for this snap judgment, uncorrupted with modern literary prejudices. (pp. 390-92)

Much of the interest of the *Lectures on the English Poets* lies in the freshness of Hazlitt's impressions even when they seem wrong or limited, like those on Crabbe. He is at his weakest when discussing critical theory; the first lecture, 'on poetry in general', in which he attempts a definition of poetry, is repetitive and inadequate. Nor is he an analytical critic. His comments are his conclusions, vigorously and variously stated; in his best passages they form a structure of perceptions with considerable persuasive power. No literary taste was ever corrupted or misdirected by Hazlitt's genuine 'enthusiasm' for poetry. (pp. 393-94)

A good deal of adverse criticism of Hazlitt has been concerned with the limitations and bad influence of one of the best known of his works, *The Characters of Shakespeare's Plays,* which was not a collection of lectures. The risks of misunderstanding in the 'character approach' to a Shakespeare play are real, but it is inappropriate to regard Hazlitt as a disseminator of limited conceptions of the plays, or his book as a mere instance of such limited conceptions. A different sense of cultural history developed slowly in the course of the nineteenth century; it was the necessary preliminary to an alteration, in the twentieth century, in our attitude to language and communication. . . . Hazlitt's book is still a useful primer. He does not, like Dr. Johnson, prefer the comedies to the tragedies; among the tragedies *Lear* is the standard of meaning. Not all the plays have been transformed by modern criticism. Hazlitt's *Othello* is not rendered worthless by the more extensive analyses of our time. 'The movement of the passion in *Othello* is exceedingly different from that of *Macbeth*. In *Macbeth* there is a violent struggle between opposite feelings, between ambition and the stings of conscience, almost from first to last: in *Othello,* the doubtful conflict between contrary passions, though dreadful, continues only for a short time, and the chief interest is excited by the alternate ascendancy of different passions, by the entire and unforeseen change from the fondest love and most unbounded confidence to the tortures of jealousy and the madness of hatred.' This suggests an adequate grasp of the play and does not sentimentalize Othello's character. Hazlitt is not in difficulties over the 'motiveless malignity' of Iago. 'Some persons, more nice than wise, have thought this whole character unnatural, because his villainy is *without a sufficient motive.* Shakespeare, who was as good a philosopher as he was a poet, thought otherwise. He knew that the love of power, which is another name for the love of mischief, is natural to man . . . Iago in fact belongs to a class of character, common to Shakespeare and at the same time peculiar to him; whose heads are as acute and active as their hearts are hard and callous. Iago is to be sure an extreme instance of the kind; that is to say, of diseased intellectual activity, with the most perfect indifference to moral good or evil, or rather with a decided preference of the latter, because it falls more readily in with his favourite propensity, gives greater zest to his thoughts and scope to his actions.' After that, a discussion of Iago in terms of 'conventions' would be a step away from, not towards, the direct impact of the play. Hazlitt is morally engaged by the play; the Hobbist flavour of some of his remarks is not inappropriate. (pp. 394-95)

The limitations of such a survey of Shakespeare are obvious. It is not sufficiently recognized that they reveal a grasp of the plays that is commendable, and that some of Hazlitt's comments have worn at least as well as Johnson's or Coleridge's. Even on the evidence adduced so far, it may be claimed that Hazlitt's influence was beneficial. His example made for clarity, firm judgment and catholicity. We should, however, expect an important critic to show his real quality when dealing with the literature of his own day. (pp. 396-97)

Hazlitt's essays on nineteenth-century writers, especially those in *Lectures on the English Poets, The Spirit of the Age* and *The Round Table,* and those contributed to the *Edinburgh Review,* seem the work of a man who was writing at the point of concentration of the intellectual stresses of his time. This concentration gives his critical masterpiece *The Spirit of the Age* all the force of original creation. (p. 397)

In its success in justifying an ambitious title *The Spirit of the Age* is an impressive achievement. It must be one of the most sustained and even exciting evaluations of contemporaries in the language. The active prejudices of the author cannot greatly diminish the persuasiveness of these mature appreciations, their sense of fact; indeed they enhance this impression of actuality. Hazlitt is not vindictive; all his characters are recognizably human.

> Mr. Bentham relieves his mind sometimes, after the fatigue of study, by playing on a fine old organ, and has a relish for Hogarth's prints. He turns wooden utensils in a lathe for exercise, and fancies he can turn men in the same manner. He has no great fondness for poetry, and can hardly extract a moral out of Shakespeare.

> Mr. Wilberforce is far from being a hypocrite; but he is, we think, as fine a specimen of *moral equivocation* as can well be conceived.

> He [Southey] writes a fair hand, without blots, sitting upright in his chair, leaves off when he comes to the bottom of the page, and changes the subject for another, as opposite as the Antipodes.

Hazlitt's treatment of the minor and less difficult authors would make an excellent starting point for a study of critical method. . . . (p. 398)

The section on Southey is interesting for, among other things, its modulation of tone which enables Hazlitt to give in a few pages a three-dimensional portrait of an associate of the greater Romantics, and to make it clear why he is no more than an associate. 'His passions do not amount to more than irritability.' The remarks on the political tendencies of Scott's novels are very perceptive though they do not upset Hazlitt's judgment. 'Sir Walter may, indeed, surfeit us: his imitators make us sick!' He is as firm and friendly about Landor as about Lamb, and his account of Cobbett is indispensable because it is without the modern tendency to idealize the peasantry. The tone of critical admiration is conveyed in the two sentences: 'His egotism is delightful, for there is no affectation in it. He does not talk of himself for lack of something to write about, but because some circumstance that has happened to himself is the best possible illustration of the subject, and he is not the man to shrink from giving the best possible illustration of the subject from a squeamish delicacy.'

The major figures lend themselves to many different assessments and interpretations. Hazlitt's critiques, though brief and incomplete, remain intrinsically interesting. Even when the impression of bias is strong, the modern reader cannot lightly assume that his own understanding of the writers discussed is sounder or better informed. Many of Hazlitt's remarks, such as that 'Mr. Wordsworth's mind is obtuse', plainly come from long and affectionate study; all the critiques have an attractive intimacy and inwardness. . . . The review of Shelley which Hazlitt contributed to the *Edinburgh Review* (July 1824) deserves to be much better known than it is. Shelley's style is described as 'a straining after impossibilities, a record of fond conjectures, a confused embodying of vague abstractions—a fever of the soul, thirsting and craving after what it cannot have . . . In him, fancy, will, caprice, predominated over and absorbed the natural influences of things'. Hazlitt comments interestingly on 'Julian and Maddalo', 'The Witch of Atlas' and 'The Triumph of Life'. 'It is curious to remark everywhere the proneness to the marvellous and the supernatural in one who so resolutely set his face against every received mystery, and all traditional faith.' As always in Hazlitt, there is a credit side.

> Yet Mr. Shelley, with all his faults, was a man of genius, and we lament that uncontrollable violence of temperament which gave it a forced and false direction . . . There was neither selfishness nor

malice at the bottom of his illusions. He was sincere in all his professions; and he practised what he preached—to his own sufficient cost . . . His fault was, that he had no deference for the opinions of others, too little sympathy with their feelings (which he thought he had a right to sacrifice, as well as his own, to a grand ethical experiment)— and trusted too implicitly to the light of his own mind, and to the warmth of his own impulses.

In comparison with this review, Arnold's essay seems to be less clear in its judgments, more ponderous in tone—it is one of Arnold's points against Shelley that he shows an 'utter deficiency in humour'—and more sentimental about the 'ineffectual angel'. Hazlitt's estimate of Byron also compares well with Arnold's attempt to define Byron's achievement in relation to Wordsworth and Leopardi. (pp. 399-400)

The claim I would make for Hazlitt is that as a literary critic he is at least as interesting, as useful and as important as Matthew Arnold; and that as a social critic he reveals, not fanaticism or misanthropy but responsible intelligence, and so represents an important link in the continuities of English life. His attitudes to most of the questions of his day are perennially interesting, for most of the questions are permanent ones. (p. 403)

> G. D. Klingopulos, "Hazlitt as Critic," in Essays in Criticism, *Vol. VI, No. 4, October, 1956, pp. 386-403.*

Bonamy Dobrée   (essay date 1961)

[*A highly regarded English historian and critic, Dobrée distinguished himself both as a leading authority of Restoration drama and as a creator of biographical studies which seek, through vivid depiction and captivating style, to establish biography as a legitimate creative form. Dobrée is also known for his skillful editing of* The Oxford History of English Literature *and* Writers and Their Work *series. In all his writings, Dobrée's foremost concern was that of effectively communicating to the reader his aesthetic response to the work under discussion. In the following excerpt, he defines Hazlitt's essays as "commentary" rather than "criticism."*]

One can see why [Hazlitt] was unpopular. However much he might like or admire a man, when he discussed him he was not content to tell the truth and nothing but the truth about him, he would always tell the whole truth. That is why, more than from any other writer of his day, we get the sense of the time as a whole, and not from some theoretical point of view. Reading, say, '**My First Acquaintance with Poets**' or '**On the Conversation of Poets**', we get a vivid sense of the people as such, of how they moved and talked. Independent though he is, he is not at all egotistical, nor puffed up about his unique merits; he is content to live to himself.

> What I mean by living to one's-self is living in the world, as in it, not of it: it is as if no one knew there was such a person, and you wished no one to know it: it is to be a spectator of the mighty scene of things . . . to take a thoughtful, anxious interest in what is passing in the world, but not to feel the slightest inclination to make or meddle with it.

('**On Living to One's-Self** '.*Table Talk.*)

It was this attitude that enabled him to achieve that centrality of mind that makes him so useful, so sane, so discriminating a commentator upon literature.

A commentator rather than what we nowadays call a critic; and a brilliant one, for:

> He was, in the truest sense, a man of original mind; that is, he had the power of looking at things for himself, or as they really were, instead of blindly trusting to, and fondly repeating what others told him what they were. He got rid of the go-cart of prejudice and affectation, with the learned lumber that follows at their heels, because he could do without them. . . . He was neither a pedant nor a bigot. . . . In treating of men and manners, he spoke of them as he found them, not according to preconceived notions and abstract dogmas. . . . In criticising books he did not compare them with rules and systems, but told us what he saw to like or dislike in them.

That extract is not from an essay on Hazlitt, as it might fittingly be, but part of what he himself wrote about Montaigne ('**The Periodical Essayists**', *The English Comic Writers*). For he was no theorist, no elaborator of systems; he had 'no fangs for recondite research'. In considering any work, whether of literature or painting, he asked, 'What does this mean for me, do for me?': for though he paid tribute to Schlegel for his work on Shakespeare, he was free of the Teutonic disease of distorting everything through transcendental or categorical lenses. He lived the literature that he read, tasting it fully, relating it to his experience as the whole man that he was. Take the opening lecture *On the English Poets,* '**On Poetry in General**', an essay at once brilliant and solid:

> Impassioned poetry is an emanation of the total and intellectual part of our nature, as well as of the sensitive—of the desire to know, the will to act, and the power to feel; and ought to appeal to those different parts of our constitution, in order to be perfect.

Or, a little later, where he touches on what we have come to call 'the objective co-relative':

> Poetry is the highest eloquence of passion, the most vivid form of expression that can be given to our conception of any thing, whether pleasurable or painful, mean or dignified, delightful or distressing. It is the perfect coincidence of the image and the words with the feeling we have, which we cannot get rid of in any other way, that gives an instant 'satisfaction to the thought'.

This is all an appeal to experience, to the sense common to all of us: there are no Sidneyan showers of sweet discourse, no pretence that the poet is the unacknowledged legislator of the world, not even the more modest claims of the Preface to *Lyrical Ballads*. What he looks for are words and sentiments that 'come home to the bosoms and businesses of men' (he was as fond of using that tag from Bacon as Bagehot—who in many way resembles him— was to be); and he does not mind where, or in what form he finds it. He is no fastidious excluder, thinking that because one thing is good another must be bad. In '**A Farewell to Essay-Writing**' he tells of how, after a walk in his beloved country, something having reminded him of Dryden's *Theodore and Honoria:*

> I return home resolved to read the entire poem through, and, after dinner, drawing my chair to the fire, and holding a small print close to my eyes, launch into the full tide of Dryden's couplets (a stream of sound), comparing his didactic and descriptive pomp with the simple pathos and picturesque truth of Boccaccio's story, . . .

Hazlitt could taste both dishes with equal relish.

That is why he is so sound a guide as an appreciator, if you wish to deny the name of critic to a man who can respond to so many imaginative delights, knowing what he likes, and, more importantly, why. Take some of the lectures on poetry, where he preferred to pair poets, so as to contrast their flavours, though he does not deny himself discursive comments on other poets of the same time. A good example is his lecture on **'Dryden and Pope'**, in which, incidentally there is very little on Dryden to whom he refers mainly to show—and how well he does it!—in what way he differs from Pope. Pope he places in the front rank of the poets of art rather than of nature, and therefore deserving of a place above the second-raters in the latter class. 'Young . . . Gray, or Akenside, only follow in the train of Milton and Shakespeare: Pope and Dryden walk by their side, though of an unequal stature, and are entitled to a first place in the lists of fame'. He is acutely aware of Pope's limitations, but can thoroughly enter into a delighted appraisal of his qualities, as he felt them. After quoting the end of the 'Epistle to Jervas', he bursts out: 'And shall we cut ourselves off from beauties like these with a theory?' Similarly, in discussing **'Thomson and Cowper'**—a lecture which, it might be remarked, should, if read, dispel the silly theory one still hears bleated at intervals, that Wordsworth discovered nature—he beautifully distinguishes their qualities, and the way they feel nature. There are some remarks, too, on Crabbe, who 'describes the interior of a cottage like a person sent there to distrain for rent'. The lecture closes with some quotations from Wordsworth. Or, to take another kind of instance, though as a painter what he most admired about Spenser was his pictorial quality, he does not ignore other aspects. 'People', he says, 'are afraid of the allegory, as if they thought it would bite them.'

It was this even temper that enabled Hazlitt to welcome the work of his contemporaries, whether or no he admired them personally. He was the first popular writer to do justice to Wordsworth. Though he disliked him intensely, repelled by his monstrous egotism (as comes out again and again), he praised him highly, both in these lectures and in **The Spirit of the Age,** as 'the most original poet now living'. In the earlier essay he says:

> Of many of the Lyrical Ballads it is impossible to speak in terms of too high praise, such as [he names a few] and a hundred others of inconceivable beauty, of perfect originality and pathos. They open a finer and deeper vein of feeling than any poet in modern times has done or attempted.

The later one contains as much praise, but is tempered by severe criticism of Wordsworth's narrowness of sympathy; he remarks *en passant:*

> We do not think our author has any very cordial

sympathy with Shakespear. How should he? Shakespear was the least of an egotist of any body in the world.

It was, in part, this capacity for detachment that lost him his friends—except for Lamb—and this capacity may in some degree have been a result of lost illusions, a refusal to compromise. He would not steal a march upon public opinion in any way, nor upon private. His greatest disappointment was Coleridge, leaving aside the blighting of revolutionary hopes. One thinks of his superb description of Coleridge in **'My First Acquaintance with Poets'**, or of a passage in **'On Going a Journey'**, the recognition of real genius coming in his lecture on **'The Living Poets'**:

> . . . I may say of him here, that he is the only person I ever knew who answered to the idea of a man of genius. He is the only person from whom I ever learnt anything. . . . His genius at that time had angelic wings, and fed on manna. He talked on for ever; and you wished him to talk on for ever. . . .

And so on. But then we come to *The Spirit of the Age,* and Hazlitt sums up the waste of this genius, in talk rather than in writing; how Coleridge busied himself with 'vibrations and vibratiuncules', how he 'lost himself in the labyrinths of the Hartz Forest and the Kantean philosophy, and amongst the cabalistic names of Fichte and Schelling and Lessing and God knows who'. There follows the cry of pain:

> Alas! 'Frailty, thy name is *Genius!'*—What is become of all this mighty heap of hope, of thought, of learning and humanity? It has ended in swallowing doses of oblivion and in writing paragraphs in the *Courier.* Such and so little is the mind of man!

Yet if Coleridge, abandoning 'Liberty (the philosopher's and the poet's bride) had fallen a victim . . . to the murderous practices of the hag Legitimacy,' at least he had not, like Southey, allowed himself to be trammelled into a poet laureate, or, like Wordsworth, into a stamp-distributor. How the old dream, including the fantasy of Pantisocracy, had vanished!

Luckily, with men of long ago, such considerations are out: Shakespeare is removed from all these battles. And how wholesome to go back to Hazlitt on Shakespeare after reading the erudite wisdom of modern commentators, each determined to make Shakespeare the prophet of what he will, each striving to discover what, more likely than not, was never there. Shakespeare, for Hazlitt, was not a man of genius to be pondered in the study, but to be encountered on the stage. (One suggests, hesitantly, that Shakespeare might rather have liked that.) He takes it that Shakespeare meant his people to mean what a spectator of his plays might suppose them to mean; Troilus is a lover, not a kind of F. H. Bradley worrying about the nature of reality. For him Shakespeare was above all a man who loved human beings for what they were, not as pegs upon which to hang some morality or other. So in the essay on *Measure for Measure,* 'a play as full of genius as it is of wisdom', we read:

> Shakespeare was in one sense the least moral of writers; for morality (commonly so called) is made up of antipathies; and his talent consisted in sympathy with human nature, in all its shapes, degrees, depressions and elevations. . . . In one sense he was no moralist at all; in another he was the great-

est of all moralists. He was a moralist in the sense that nature is one.

Here De Quincey is in line with him, saying in his essay on Pope: 'Poetry . . . can teach only as nature teaches, as forests teach, as the sea teaches, viz., by deep impulse, by hieroglyphic suggestion'.

And as we read Hazlitt on Shakespeare we may feel how refreshing it is to escape from the fascinating webs woven round him for us by modern commentators, as Hazlitt escaped from those of his day.

Maybe Mr. J. B. Priestley [see Further Reading] is right when in his recent finely appreciative pamphlet (in the Writers and their Work Series), he prefers to call Hazlitt an essayist rather than a critic. You may, it is true, not go very deep with him as a critic, but you cannot go wrong. Certainly as an essayist he is invigorating to read, if only for the vitality of the language which so well expresses the virility of his being. And again, when writing of Montaigne, the words are applicable to him—'no juggling tricks or solemn mouthing, no laboured attempts at proving himself always in the right, and everybody else in the wrong', except, so far as the last statement goes, when he is furiously fighting his attackers, as in the splendid invective of *A Letter to William Gifford, Esq.* . . . It is concise without being terse, save when he wants it to be so; a great admirer of Burke's writings, he had no objection to eloquence. He achieved this, however, by the use of the right word, not by being inflated. 'I hate to see a load of bandboxes go along the street, and I hate to see a parcel of big words without anything in them.'

Thus he can be dexterously incisive, as when he tells Gifford: 'But you are a nuisance, and ought to be abated.' Or in that splendidly modulated passage on Bentham in *The Spirit of the Age,* when he says: 'He turns wooden utensils in a lathe for exercise, and fancies he can turn men in the same manner.' That he thought about prose a good deal is plain from the admirable criticisms of Addison in **'On the Prose Style of Poets'**, of Johnson in **'The Periodical Essayists'** (*The English Comic Writers*), apart from the disquisition **'On Familiar Style'** (*Table Talk*). He abominated jargon of any kind, or any pretentiousness. He is infinitely readable. True, he sometimes goes on too long, makes his point too often; he quotes too much. But he is full of delightful surprises. Who would expect to find in the description of Cavanagh, the fives-player, such a delightful jump as 'His blows were not undecided and ineffectual—lumbering like Mr. Wordsworth's epic poetry, nor wavering like Mr. Coleridge's lyric prose, nor short of the mark like Mr. Brougham's speeches, nor wide of it like Mr. Canning's wit, nor foul like the *Quarterly,* nor *let* balls like the *Edinburgh Review*' (**'The Indian Jugglers'**, *Table Talk*). He is enormously varied in his subjects; he can be brilliantly descriptive as in his account of a boxing match (**'The Fight'**); he is full of common sense and citizen-like acumen in his essays on public affairs, he is penetrating in his character studies, revealing of ourselves in the essays that deal with what we might call general psychology. And for those of us who pretend to be critics, the chapter **'On Criticism'** should be a stimulating as well as a salutary discipline. (pp. 141-48)

Bonamy Dobrée, "William Hazlitt," in his

Milton to Ouida: A Collection of Essays, *Frank Cass and Co., Ltd., 1970, pp. 140-48.*

W. P. Albrecht (essay date 1965)

[*Albrecht is an American critic and Hazlitt scholar. In the following excerpt, he analyzes the style and structure of Hazlitt's works.*]

Hazlitt's familiar essays are not . . . distinguished from his earlier work by any clear change in subject matter. In them we still find his long-standing ideas on literature and art, on politics, and on the workings of the human mind, but these ideas tend to be more completely assimilated to "the world of men and women, . . . their actions, . . . motives, . . . whims, . . . pursuits, . . . absurdities, [and] inconsistencies." There are further differences. Although Hazlitt never achieved a high degree of negative capability, much less the dramatic form that marks its culmination, he made an approach to both. In the essays after 1820, Hazlitt is less aggressive in asserting his convictions; his tone is less strident, more tolerant, more aphoristic. His "dark and doubtful views" are less immediately provoked by the political situation. His style, now completely his own, has become a flexible instrument for his thought and feeling. As his mood requires, his style is simple or elaborate, dryly colloquial or richly figurative. Ideas that once resisted statement attain clarity and precision. In his earlier work, Hazlitt's efforts to clarify abstract propositions often drove him into desperate convolutions, but in the rich essays of his last decade, where he is not so much concerned with consequitive reasoning, he puts his turns of thought and feeling to good use. Although Hazlitt's basic ideas remain the same, he has gradually learned to express them—as he thought all ideas should be expressed—imaginatively. (pp. 149-50)

His prose is frequently rich with *imagery* in his own sense of the word—that is, with concrete particulars which have expressive associations. Hazlitt also wrote a dry style, relatively bare of images, crisply idiomatic and sometimes ironical. Although this style may occasionally dominate a paragraph or even an essay, it is usually not prolonged. Hazlitt's feelings were too strong, and the resulting associations too abundant, for him to sustain a style either concise or detached. In many of his best essays his crisp style is interwoven with his more imaginative style into an intricate design of varying moods. Hazlitt says that his essays are poorly constructed, but his best ones testify to the power of emotion to channel associations into a unified pattern. His structures—syntactic and larger—are not the result of formal planning but are what Hazlitt would call "discursive" as opposed to "consecutive." They frequently employ symmetrical elements, but these are likely to merge into a larger asymmetrical design. To use the inevitable Romantic figure, they are not mechanically contrived but have grown organically. They are the product of a free but disciplined imagination.

The prose essay, as Hazlitt defines it, is a work of the imagination. In applying Hazlitt's own criteria to his own work, we should begin with his critical statements about the kind of writing that he himself attempted. His comments on prose style are numerous, the longest and most systematic being one of his *Table-Talk* essays, **"On Familiar Style."** To write the familiar style, says Hazlitt, is "not to take the first word that offers, but the best word in common use; it is not to throw words together in any combinations we please, but to follow and avail ourselves of the true idiom of the language." This is not a "random" style or one that is "easy to write." It demands rigorous precision in selecting and combining words free from eccentric or jarring tones and appropriate to the writer's total meaning. The familiar style gains "universal force" by eschewing the pedantic, the pompous, the disgusting, the obsolete or archaic, the hyperbolic, the commonplace, the merely technical or professional, the cant or slang phrase, the newly coined word, and the "*slipshod* allusion." In order to "clench a writer's meaning," moreover, each word must be "fitted . . . to its place" in the whole structure of a work. This selection and arrangement cannot be achieved according to any "mechanical rule or theory": it is an act of the imagination requiring a "fine tact"—a practiced ear and an identifying sympathy. Hazlitt offers the analogy of reading aloud. One's ability "to give the true accent and inflection to the words" is determined by "the habitual associations between sense and sound, and . . . by entering into the author's meaning." Similarly a habitual sensitivity to language and a continual awareness of the total effect must guide a writer to a "spontaneous" choice and arrangement of words. Although it seems that Hazlitt himself did little revising, he explains the apparently conflicting demands of spontaneity and careful revision. He does not agree with Cobbett "that the first word that occurs is always the best," but he insists that if a better word is to be found, as it often may be, "it should be suggested naturally . . . and spontaneously, from a fresh and lively conception of the subject." During revision the imaginative process must be allowed to start up again "by touching some link in the chain of previous association" and reach a point where the pattern of the whole work is clearly grasped. The universality of the imaginative style is a matter not only of language charged with thought and feeling but of words linked to each other by associations based on much experience and consequently reflecting the order of human life. In imaginative writing the words "not only excite feelings, but they point to the *why* and *wherefore*. Causes march before them, and consequences follow after them." They are not Hobbesian abstractions but "links in the chain of the universe, and the grappling-irons that bind us to it."

Although the style of both poetry and prose makes similar demands on the imagination, there is an essential difference, which may be traced to the differences in purpose and subject matter. Hazlitt, of course, is thinking of the essay rather than prose fiction when he says that the prose writer aims at "truth, not beauty—not pleasure, but power." More specifically, he continues, "the man of genius" writing or speaking prose "can have but one of these two objects; . . . to furnish us with new ideas, . . . or . . . to rivet our old impressions more deeply. . . . " In either case, the subject matter, however "remote or obscure, . . . must be rendered plain and palpable" in concrete terms. In requiring palpable detail, poetry and prose are alike, but "abstract truths or profound observations" resist concrete illustration more than "natural objects and mere matters of fact" do. In his search for truthful and convincing expression, the prose writer is both freer and more restricted than the poet. He is free from having to observe the "decorum" of poetry and "all such idle respect to appearances." Specifically Hazlitt applies the word "deco-

rum" to the "balance" he finds lacking in Burke's Windsor Castle metaphor, but judging from his own as well as Burke's practice, he would also allow the prose writer the kind of non-elevating comparisons that he objects to in the metaphysical poets or even the low materials he criticizes in Wordsworth. On the other hand, the prose writer is not as free as the poet to select his own subjects (especially if he is a political writer or a journalist) or to mold his materials into imaginative creations which, although perhaps true to general nature, would not illuminate the specific situation or problem he must deal with. "Invention, not upon an imaginary subject, is a lie. . . . " The prose writer may not allow one "pleasing or striking image" to suggest another, for each image must bear directly on the subject. " . . . nothing can be admitted by way of ornament or relief, that does not add new force or clearness to the original conception."

Burke was the most successful prose writer that Hazlitt knew of. "It has always appeared to me that the most perfect prose-style, the most powerful, the most dazzling, the most daring, that which went the nearest to the verge of poetry, and yet never fell over, was Burke's." In a passage which suggests Burke's own coalescing dilation, Hazlitt compares Burke's style to a chamois rather than an eagle: "it climbs to an almost equal height, touches upon a cloud, overlooks a precipice, is picturesque, sublime—but all the while, instead of soaring through the air, it stands upon a rocky cliff, clambers up by abrupt and intricate ways, and browses on the roughest bark, or crops the tender flower." Burke's style is "airy, flighty, adventurous," yet it retains its "solidity," never out of sight of its subject, "ris[ing] with the lofty, descend[ing] with the mean, luxuriat[ing] in beauty, gloat[ing] over deformity"— precluded by his materials from "continual beauty" but not from continual "ingenuity, force, originality." Nor from sublimity. Burke achieves—notably in such passages as his comparison of the English Constitution to Windsor Castle—the kind of imaginative aggregation that Hazlitt attributes elsewhere, in almost the same phrasing, to Shakespeare. "Burke most frequently produced an effect by the remoteness and novelty of his combinations, . . . by the striking manner in which the most opposite and unpromising materials were harmoniously blended together. . . . " Despite its elaborateness, Burke's style remains organic. He avoids both the trite affectation of the "florid style" and the set formality of the "*artificial*" style. His thought and feeling determine diction and structure, and are never dissipated by merely "dignified and eloquent" language or by the demands of balance or antithesis. He does not multiply words "for want of ideas, but because there are no words that fully express his ideas, and he tries to do it as well as he can by different ones."

What Hazlitt says of the familiar style in general—and of Burke's style in particular—applies to his own style at its best. He did not, however, learn immediately to render "remote and obscure" ideas "plain and palpable" in concrete language, or to keep his sentences firm with meaning. In the *Essay on the Principles of Human Action* and in his lectures on philosophy his diction is often abstract and bookish, and his sentences do not sustain their length. In his metaphysical arguments, he becomes verbose, repetitious, and tedious, as in an effort to make himself clear he goes over the same ground time and again. In his early political writings, however, he saw the need to become more "impressive and vigorous" to combat the "cold, philosophic indifference" of his time. As a result there are passages, standing out from labored exposition reminiscent of the ***Essay,*** that are rhetorically elaborate and others that are incisively simple. Some of his sentences exfoliate with picturesque images and melodramatic metaphor, along with emphatic rhythms, elaborate parallelism, and occasional alliteration. One of the opening sentences of ***Free Thoughts on Public Affairs*** pounds home Hazlitt's idea of patriotism.

> It has been called patriotism, to flatter those in power at the expence of the people; to sail with the stream; to make a popular prejudice the stalking-horse of ambition, to mislead first and then betray; to enrich yourself out of the public treasure; to strengthen your influence by pursuing such measures as give to the richest members of the community an opportunity of becoming richer, and to laugh at the waste of blood and the general misery which they occasion; to defend every act of a party, and to treat all those as enemies of their country who do not think the pride of a minister and the avarice of a few of his creatures of more consequence than the safety and happiness of a free, brave, industrious, and honest people; to strike at the liberty of other countries, and through them at your own; to change the maxims of a state, to degrade its spirit, to insult its feelings, and tear from it its well-earned and proudest distinctions; to soothe the follies of a multitude, to lull them in their sleep, to goad them on in their madness, and, under the terror of imaginary evils, to cheat them of their best privileges; to blow the blast of war for a livelihood in journals and pamphlets, and by spreading abroad incessantly a spirit of defiance, animosity, suspicion, distrust, and the most galling contempt, to make it impossible that we should ever remain at peace or in safety, while insults and general obloquy have a tendency to provoke those passions in others which they are intended to excite.

Hazlitt's polemical "impressiveness," in a fashion of the day in which Hazlitt soon excelled, also led to personal abuse and ridicule. He would have preferred to attack Malthus' theories "without attacking the author. . . . But the thing was impossible." *The Essay on Population,* therefore, becomes "a miserable reptile performance" disguising "the little, low, rankling malice of a parish-beadle, or the overseer of a workhouse . . . in the garb of philosophy." Malthus seems never to have heard of other passions that disturb society. "But the women are *the devil.*" In his satirical passages, Hazlitt's language becomes plain, and the rhythm conversational. " . . . he must be a strange sawney who could turn back at the church-door after bringing a pretty rosy girl to hear a lecture on the principle of population. . . ." Thus in the midst of tortuous and wearisome restatements of Hazlitt's "refutation" of Malthus, there are swift passages that look forward to the ***Letter to William Gifford*** and *A Reply to 'Z'.*

As Hazlitt learned to write more imaginatively, the labored exposition of abstract ideas disappeared from his work and he brought all his "impressive" devices under control. As might be expected of someone devoted to the drama, Hazlitt also learned to make good use of narration and dialog. He is capable of short passages of swift and economical narrative, but, as in **"The Fight,"** such passages are interrupted with "reflections" in the manner of

his ***Table-Talk.*** In his later metaphysical essays—such as **"Self-Love and Benevolence"**—he uses dialog to attain an economy and precision lacking in his earlier discussions of these matters. This dialog, which is weighted with some pretty long speeches, is only superficially dramatic; and its success, as intended, is as a means of communicating ideas and not of illuminating character or advancing action. However, Hazlitt frequently assimilates dialog as well as narrative into the structure of his more imaginative essays. He uses these devices, along with others, to convey the intricate pattern of moods and thoughts that his imagination leads him into.

Hazlitt describes his method as the opposite of "systematic and scientific. . . . Supposing the reader in possession of what is already known, [an author] supplies deficiencies, fills up certain blanks, and quits the beaten road in search of new tracts of observation or sources of feeling." It is a method—unsustained by narrative or logical progression—that puts a great demand on the emotional resources of language to keep the parts in tension. Hazlitt, of course, has abundant resources of this kind. What he says of Burke applies equally well to his own style: he "makes use of the most common or scientific terms, of the longest or shortest sentences, of the plainest and most downright, or of the most figurative modes of speech. He gives for the most part loose reins to his imagination, and

Manuscript page from "The Fight."

169

follows it as far as the language will carry him." Hazlitt's essays are rich with images, metaphors, and—less often—similes. Unhampered by the decorous restrictions that he placed on the poets of paradox, Hazlitt ranges widely for sense impressions to mold into a reflection of his thought and feeling. Hazlitt's images and figures bear directly on his subject; they are integral with thought and feeling. As Hazlitt and Coleridge walk back to Shrewsbury, the Welsh mountains in the distance are charged with Hazlitt's delight: "As . . . I eyed their blue tops seen through the wintry branches, or the red rustling leaves of the sturdy oak-trees by the road-side, a sound was in my ears as of a Siren's song. . . . " Sometimes, as often noted, an image recreates Hazlitt's experience with a poem or a painting; or it may illustrate his own technique as a painter: "Beneath the shrivelled yellow parchment look of the skin, there was here and there a streak of blood-colour tinging the face; this I made a point of conveying. . . . "

Hazlitt's aggregated images and metaphors frequently attain the diversity and topographical sweep that he considered essential to sublimity. Hazlitt is fond of using a metaphor or pair of metaphors to characterize a person or thing and then elaborating each metaphor, sometimes in literal language but more often in a complex of additional metaphors or similes. Irish eloquence is "all fire"; Scotch eloquence is "all ice." Byron's verse "glows like a flame"; Scott's "glides like a river." The elaborating figures usually burst impatiently through the confines of the original comparison. The chamois figure used to describe Burke's style is an exception. More typical is Hazlitt's description of Byron: "He is like a solitary peak, all access to which is cut off not more by elevation than distance. He is seated on a lofty eminence, 'cloud-capt,' or reflecting the last rays of setting suns; and in his poetical moods, reminds us of the fabled Titans, retired to a ridgy steep, playing on their Pan's-pipes, and taking up ordinary men and things in their hands with haughty indifference. He raises his subject to himself, or tramples on it; he neither stoops to, nor loses himself in it. . . . Nature must come to him to sit for her picture. . . . " The power of Hazlitt's metaphors most often resides in their pungency, their individual force, in their swift abundance and variety, rather than in a close texture of association either between the things compared in each metaphor or in a series of metaphors. Partly because of the rapid shifting from image to image in a long series and partly because of the diversity of the images themselves, they often do not attain that "indissoluble coalescence" through mutual modification that Hazlitt praises in the great poets and in Burke. The images are charged with enough feeling but not always with highly congruent associations. Sir Walter Scott "strewed the slime of rankling malice and mercenary scorn over the bud and promise of genius, because it was not fostered in the hot-bed of corruption, or warped by the trammels of servility" and so on, for a closely printed page. It would be difficult to supply the equivalent of Antony's "black vesper's pageants" to reduce all this multeity to unity. But in prose, Hazlitt would have said, it is more important to "lay open the naked truth" by making every image bear on the subject. At other times, in the best Romantic tradition of the imagination, an image will reduce a whole essay to concrete oneness. ". . . Milton's *Eve* is all of ivory and gold," says Hazlitt, epitomizing not only his idea of Eve but his analysis of epic poetry. More elaborately, a central image unifies **"On the Fear of Death."** Looking at a dead child, the writer "could not bear the coffin-lid to be closed—it almost stifled me; and still as the nettles wave in a corner of the churchyard over his little grave, the welcome breeze helps to refresh me and ease the tightness at my breast!" The stifling identification with the dead is dispelled by waving nettles and their suggestion of life's "just value."

Hazlitt also wrote a dry, plain style which gets its effects not from image or metaphor but from terseness or irony, with or without the support of syntactic balance. In the opening sentence of his *Letter to William Gifford* (1819), the direct conversational tone enforces Hazlitt's scorn: "Sir,—You have an ugly trick of saying what is not true of any one you do not like; and it will be the object of this letter to cure you of it." Burke could also flay an opponent, but here the direct insult, the casual despising tone, the easy but malignant assumption of superiority, are more in the manner of Junius. Hazlitt concludes his portrait of Gifford in *The Spirit of the Age* with a double antithesis that once again recalls Junius: "But as Mr. Gifford assumes a right to say what he pleases of others—they may be allowed to speak the truth of him!"

Another clear influence on Hazlitt's curt style, after 1823, is La Rochefoucauld. "I was so struck," Hazlitt writes in his *Characteristics: In the Manner of Rochefoucault's Maxims* (1823), "with the force and beauty of the style and manner, that I felt an earnest ambition to embody some occasional thoughts of my own in the same form. This was much easier than to retain an equal degree of spirit." Hazlitt had difficulty in retaining "an equal degree of spirit" because his imagination frequently got the better of his wit. The aphorism, as La Rochefoucauld uses it, exploits some sort of paradox—not the extreme sort of illogicality or idiosyncrasy that Hazlitt usually calls by that name, but an apparent contradiction which nevertheless strikes the reader as true to much of his experience. It is this contradiction, pointed up by repetition and parallelism, which holds the parts of the aphorism in tension and gives it solidity. Hazlitt sometimes achieves in La Rochefoucauld's manner—"He will never have true friends who is afraid of making enemies"—as well as his cynicism—"We as often repent the good we have done as the ill"—but Hazlitt's aphorisms lack the sustained detachment, as well as the polish, of his models. The differences from La Rochefoucauld are in keeping with what we know of Hazlitt's habit of writing with little polishing or revision, and also with his play of imagination. In La Rochefoucauld the contradiction that binds together the parts of an aphorism usually lies between a commonplace, bland assumption of human virtue and the corrosive evidence of self-love. This loosening of the affections is the method of wit, which Hazlitt admired for its truth (of a sort) and texture, but which he himself could not often sustain. Hazlitt occasionally lets his associations carry him into long aphorisms with specific details. At times the allusions are clearly autobiographical. Numbers 248, 249, 251, 254 ("The contempt of a wanton for a man who is determined to think her virtuous, is perhaps the strongest of all others") remind us that *Characteristics* and *Liber Amoris* were published the same year. Hazlitt, it has been said apropos of his aphorisms, was "bitter and sardonic; and he hated rather than loved his fellow human beings" [Logan Pearsall Smith, *A Treasury of English Aphorisms*]. This statement is not supported either by the *Characteristics* or by

Hazlitt's other essays. Many of Hazlitt's aphorisms level their accusations at only part of mankind or suggest at least as much good in human nature as bad. Whereas La Rochefoucauld's aphorisms, in general, are short, detached, cynical, and abstract, Hazlitt's more frequently incline to length, involvement, sympathy, and particulars. His most effective use of the aphorism is probably in combination with his richer style, as in the *Table-Talk* essays, where his occasional short, pointed utterances provide force, variety, unity, and conclusiveness. (pp. 150-61)

As a prose writer Hazlitt may have been guided by the principle of "truth, not beauty—not pleasure, but power"; but when he is at his best—which is often—he attains not only power but a kind of form which gives pleasure. . . . Hazlitt does not make a sharp distinction between truth and beauty (in poetry, they are apparently the same thing) or between poetry and prose. In poetry truth and beauty result from revealing essential (general) qualities in the subject, from discovering order in a variety of objects or events, and from exciting and extending, thereby, the reader's powers of association. Prose does the same thing, but in view of its "practical purpose," the prose writer is less free to use his imagination. His, and the readers', flow of associations must be continually checked by returning to the actual subject. As Hazlitt freed himself, to some extent at least, from the pressure of political writing and dramatic criticism, he freed his imagination at the same time; and in many of his familiar essays it would be difficult to say wherein his subject imposed imaginative limitations different from those of poetry or to say how the pleasure provided thereby differs from the pleasure of what Hazlitt calls truth and beauty.

Hazlitt's essays illustrate the operation of the human mind which Hazlitt explained in his philosophical works and on which he based his political ideas as well as his critical criteria. The mind, he says, is not simply a machine informed and activated by the phenomena of sensation; nor can truth be encompassed in the abstract propositions of Hobbes' kind of reason. The perception of truth and the expression of moral values is, on the contrary, an imaginative and therefore creative process integrating sensation with thought and feeling. Ideas do not have an a priori existence but are formed by the creative mind operating on the data of sensation. As a man's experience accumulates—especially through sympathetic identification with others—he becomes aware of what is generally true in human life; and when in a state of association-stimulating emotion, if he is creative enough, he finds particular means of embodying these general truths. A work of art or a democratic state thereby becomes an expression of general truth, but more immediately it is a reflection of its creator or creators, whereby he or they bring various powers—sensation, thought, feeling, and moral judgment—into dynamic harmony. Man is naturally free to engage in this creative process, but its consummation may be hindered in various ways: especially by preconceived ideas (often imposed by political institutions) or by selfish preoccupation. The self-fulfillment that is one result of the process is important to both good citizenship and artistic creation, leading in each case to organic form.

Hazlitt's later essays show this creative process at work. As he molds his materials to reflect his thoughts and feelings, his structures show the balance of organic growth rather than formal planning. He also approaches a kind of negative capability as he becomes less dogmatic in asserting his political views and less shrill in voicing his resentments. He does not exclude the "dark and doubtful views" of life; in fact, his essays are sometimes a record of their gradual exploration in varied imagery, as in **"On the Fear of Death."** He does not, of course, achieve the loss of self that results in dramatic form propulsive through a strong unifying action; but he did not pretend to write anything but what he defined as prose. His chief character, like Wordsworth's, remains himself. In his latter essays, however, we have a kind of more generalized Hazlitt, whom, despite the pervasive "I," we are ready to accept as a spokesman for more general nature. In fact, the "I" is not invariably easy to identify with the actual Hazlitt and perhaps we should not always try. At times there is still the old anger, of course, and we should not want it lost; if this later Hazlitt has become sympathetic in his treatment of his old enemies, he is no more tolerant of the evils which he thought they represented. He remains as uncompromising as ever in his hatred of fraud, selfish ambition, and tyrannical power.

These essays approach the kind of unity that Hazlitt expected in works of the imagination. As the parts fall into patterns of association, thought and emotion fuse with imagery and rhythm. The essays do not advance like soldiers in close-order drill (which Hazlitt would have detested) but move along like a man out for a walk, who occasionally hurries but who has time to circle through some interesting by-paths. The images emerge crisp and bright or dark and night-blooming. The sentences often strike like bullets or, to use one of Hazlitt's own figures, coil and thrust like a crested serpent. Hazlitt has charged his materials so highly that, long after he expected his essays to be forgotten, they have not dwindled away to paradox, "common places," or mere fancy. They still engage the reader's imagination in the creation of truth and beauty. (pp. 169-71)

> *W. P. Albrecht, in his* Hazlitt and the Creative Imagination, *The University of Kansas Press, 1965, 203 p.*

Kathleen Coburn   (essay date 1966)

[Coburn is a Canadian critic. In the following excerpt, she traces the development of Hazlitt's critical sensibility by examining his first and last published works.]

By a paradox, two of the works by which Hazlitt set most store are perhaps among the most completely forgotten in his twenty volumes; certainly they are not referred to either for authority on their subjects or in corroboration of Hazlitt's high standing as literary critic and supreme prose stylist in his kind. *On the Principles of Human Action* was his first completed work, published in 1805; the third and fourth volumes of his life of Napoleon Bonaparte appeared a few months before his death in December, 1830. The "metaphysician" he thought himself to be, the passionate social critic and moralist in him, the strenuous thinker, the close reasoner wearing himself and his friends out with arguments and anger, endearing though he may be for his idealism, is less to us now than the ardent playgoer, the reviewer, the journalist, the table-talker, the conversationist, the familiar essayist.

Yet can such a man, especially the critic, be so altogether wrong about his own work? Was it merely a wrong guess about the tastes of posterity? No work from such a mind can be valueless, and works such as these should reveal some of the mainsprings of his writing. A sympathetic look at them should discover at the very least some of the sources of that intensity and conflict which subsist in all our impressions of his temperament and interests, and in any survey of his work as a whole. (p. 169)

The Essay on the Principles of Human Action now reads as rather less a work of "originality" than it did to Coleridge, who so described it in a footnote to his second *Lay Sermon* (1817). In defense of the "Natural Disinterestedness of the Human Mind," Hazlitt attacks the doctrines of self-love, enlightened or otherwise. In the background are Rousseau, the Bishop Butler of the *Sermons,* the Hume of the *Treatise,* Shaftesbury, Berkeley's *Essay on Vision,* and James Ussher's *Theory of the Human Mind,* not to mention Hartley and Helvetius.

The argument itself is trite, circular, ill-defined in its terms, wholly on a rationalist level, and without the psychological awarenesses already developing in the nineteenth century and, contrary to Coleridge, to deepen later in Hazlitt's own writings. The essay shows, however, that his first interest was ethical rather than psychological, and that he had not read much, if any, Kant. Broadly the argument is:

> If we admit that there is something in the very idea of good and evil, which naturally excites desire or aversion, which is in itself the proper motive of action, which compels the mind to pursue the one and to avoid the other by a true moral necessity, then it cannot be indifferent to me whether I believe that any being will be made happy or miserable in consequence of my actions, whether this be myself or another. I naturally desire & pursue my own good, in whatever this consists, simply from my having an idea of it sufficiently warm and vivid to excite in me an emotion of interest, or passion; and I love and pursue the good of others, of a relative, of a friend, of a family, a community, or of mankind for just the same reason.
>
> . . . In this sense self-love is in its origin a perfectly disinterested, or if I may say so, *impersonal* feeling. The reason why a child first distinctly wills or pursues his own good is not because it is *his,* but because it is *good.*

Or again:

> I can only abstract myself from my present being and take an interest in my future being in the same sense and manner, in which I can *go out of myself* entirely and enter into the minds and feelings of others.

Clearly the whole question of what "moral necessity" is, what is "natural" and what acquired, abnormal, individual, irrational, or in some sense *non*-necessary, is here begged. And to boot, as he says with youthful disingenuousness, "There is nothing in the foregoing theory which has any tendency to overturn the fundamental distinctions between truth and falsehood, or the common methods of determining what these are: all old boundaries and landmarks remain just where they were." Philosophically speaking, this is our difficulty; they are just where they were. There is here indeed no new method for determining truth and falsehood, for distinguishing true benevolence and concealed self-interest. What he himself described as his "incorrigible attachment to a general proposition" had landed him in a position that could be used by the most ardent royalist defender of Louis XVI; he had described "a system which founds [he said in a letter to his father in 1796] the propriety of virtue in its coincidence with the pursuit of private interest," yet all the while he hopes for and trusts to its general application by the forces sympathetic to the French Revolution.

When in 1807 he abridged Abraham Tucker's *Light of Nature* and wrote his Preface to the *Abridgement,* the theme of disinterestedness versus self-love was still pre-occupying him and he was eager to improve some statements in the *Principles,* and especially to gainsay the notion that our motives are "blind mechanical impulses" derived only from associated feelings. He comes close to saying—but does not quite say it—that our motives are not all subconscious, but that a distinction can be made between involuntary (subconscious) and voluntary (conscious) ones. He singles out Tucker's essay on consciousness for special praise, and is enthusiastic about the chapters on morality, vanity, education, and death. He signs the *Abridgement* as by "The Author of *An Essay on the Principles of Human Action,"* clearly the work by which he hopes and expects to be known.

That the subject was an enduring (and sometimes scarcely a not lightly endured) one all his life can be seen throughout the twenty volumes of his works, peppering with asides the literary criticism, or, for better and for worse, driving him to large moralistic themes.

It comes out with significant vividness in a late essay on **"Self-Love and Benevolence,"** first printed in the *New Monthly Magazine for 1828.* That essay, like the state of Hazlitt's mind, is in the form of a debate, though the more it changes the more we have the same thing. "The imagination or understanding is no less the enemy of our pleasure than of our interest. It will not let us be at ease till we have accomplished certain objects with which we ourselves have no concern but as melancholy truths." The negative aspects of his equation of self-interest and disinterestedness are more apparent, plainly, than they were twenty-five years before. But the same arguments about the nature of personal identity, the possibilities of awareness of the self in the future, and of other selves, goes on. And *imagination* has now in the discussion become a more important word.

> A. . . . The imagination on which you lay so much stress is a part of one's-self.
>
> H. I grant it: and for that very reason, self-love, or a principle tending exclusively to our own immediate gratification or future advantage, neither is nor can be the sole spring of action in the human mind. . . . Imagination is another name for an interest in things out of ourselves, which must naturally run counter to our own.

The capacity for imagination depends entirely for Hazlitt on feeling. It is not "the whole soul" called "into activity," "a synthesizing and magical power," though it does discover "the hitherto unapprehended relation of things." "Those who have the largest hearts have the soundest understandings," he maintains in another late essay (**"Belief, whether Voluntary?"**); "and he is the truest philosopher who can forget himself."

The most remarkable and unexpected defense of the equation of self-interest and public devotion, illustrating the hold the belief had on Hazlitt's faith and his need to preach it, occurs in his ***Buonaparte.*** Hazlitt's Preface, suppressed in the original edition by his publishers, and later concealed by Hazlitt in the first chapter of his third volume, was, in 1828-30, naturally a defense for writing a biography of Bonaparte at all. He admires the man, whose first virtue was that as the "child and champion of the Revolution" he was a "thorn in the side of Kings." He was also a glorious figure, and succeeded by what Hazlitt valued above all things, "personal merit." And not least among his merits was the disinterested conception, in contrast with the Bourbon view that "millions were made for one," of one having been made for the millions—namely himself, saviour of liberty for the many. He was, Hazlitt argues, not entirely a free agent; "there was but one alternative between him and that slavery, which kills both the bodies and souls of men." France "required a military dictator to repress internal treachery and headstrong factions, and repel external force." It was George III and English interference with French liberty, "the pressure from without that caused the irregularities and conflicts within." The horrors of the revolution arose out of the Coalition of Allied Powers against France, not the Coalition out of the horrors; and similarly, the rupture of the Peace of Amiens was owing to English snobbery and George III's insane refusal to treat with an "upstart." He argues that the French would never have prepared for invasion of England if England had minded her own business. Had she not seized French shipping in English ports, British subjects would not have been detained in France; and so on through the whole dire calendar of events. The initiative in wrongs is English, from motives of self-aggrandizement in the court and the ruling class.

More interesting than the interpretations of episodes, undocumented as they are, the asides of a political and moral sort convey Hazlitt in his passionate quiddity. To choose but two: In the account of Corsica as Napoleon's background, in Chapter II, there is a diversionary attack on Malthusianism as "a paradox founded neither on facts, nor reasoning, but which has gained converts because it serves as a screen for the abuses of power and to shift the responsibility for a number of evils existing in the world from the shoulders of individuals on the order of Providence or on the mass of the people"; or in Chapter III, there is a five-page digression on a subject of early interest to Coleridge as well as Hazlitt, "the relative social efficacy of printing and organized religion." "The French Revolution might be described as a remote but inevitable result of the invention of the art of printing."

The incorrigible tendency he noticed in himself to generalize on the human situation often proceeds less out of social observation or abstract theorizing than out of immediate personal feeling. To quote the first chapter, "Friendship and good will are often neither conciliated by benefits nor effaced by injuries, but seem to depend on a certain congeniality of temper or original predilection of mind." And there is something touching in the identification with his hero shown in his account of Napoleon's destruction of a

youthful essay on "What are the sentiments most proper to be cultivated, in order to render men happy," because, says Hazlitt, "the style of the work was highly romantic and extravagant, abounding in sentiments of liberty suggested by the warmth of a fervid imagination, at a moment when youth and the rage of the times had inflamed his mind, but too exalted (according to his own account of the matter) ever to be put into practice." So his hero had a smack of the writer about him, at least in youth. But it is the man of action who exemplifies the possibility of disinterestedness on a grand scale; not a man of letters, not an artist, qualifies for such a biography. With Bonaparte, private ambition and public beneficence, both written large, were the same thing, in spite of admitted personal weaknesses. And it is in the various subtle analyses of Bonaparte's weaknesses, for all his power, that Hazlitt shows himself at his paradoxical best.

> Excess of strength always inclines to a degree of weakness. . . . He sometimes seemed disposed to mistake the number and extent of the means that he called into existence and the clearness and comprehension with which he arranged them . . . for the final success of his measure. . . . The very boldness and strength of will which are necessary to great actions must often defeat them; for a high spirit does not easily bend to circumstances or stoop to prudence. Whatever were his own resources, he could not always command the co-operation of others; yet his plans were on too large a scale not to require it. . . .

> Neither can I think so poorly of my countrymen (with all my dissatisfaction with them) as to suppose that even if Buonaparte had made good his landing, it would have been all over with us. He might have levelled London with the dust, but he must have covered the face of the country with heaps and *tumuli* of the slain, before this mixed breed of Norman and Saxon blood would have submitted to a second Norman Conquest. Whatever may be my opinion of the wisdom of the people, or the honesty of their rulers, I never denied their courage or obstinacy. They do not give in the sooner in a contest for having provoked it.

It is for such aphoristic pronouncements we can still extract pleasure from a work no longer read for its main contention, or its recounting of events. Hazlitt's passionate belief in Napoleon's disinterestedness scarcely concerns us now; his arrows in his asides sometimes, as Coleridge noticed, unerringly find their mark in the wider panorama of the human condition and its hidden pulsations.

The older the nineteenth century got, and the more he talked with Lamb and Coleridge, the more Hazlitt must have recognized—and did recognize as his lectures on the Elizabethans show—the importance of imagination. In the essay already referred to on **"Self-Love and Benevolence,"** the imagination "or understanding" [*pace* Coleridge!] "is no less enemy of our pleasures than of our interest." It will not let us be at ease till we have accomplished certain objects with which we ourselves have no concern but as melancholy truths.

The ability to sublimate the self, go out of oneself, became, perhaps was from first to last, for Hazlitt a kind of touchstone. (pp. 173-82)

[Hazlitt] reports himself as saying to Northcote, in 1830,

the last year of his life, "the hardest lesson seems to be to look beyond ourselves." The double irony is that he whose lifelong desire it was to believe in that possibility did not really manage to find it in the best imaginations of his own age, and did not achieve it himself, though he struggled with the conflict between the appearance and the reality with a candor that must move all who recognize it. There is a sense in which he did not need to achieve it. For by another irony, what we most value in Hazlitt are those inward recognitions by which he illuminates those experiences of literature and art that engage his real, and not an outward or theoretical, interest. Yet there is a continuity in his views, if only of irritation and conflict. The moralistic Puritan background of his idealism was inadequate, in any systematic sense, to the magnitude of the reconciliations demanded of the men of his age. Nor had Hazlitt the scientific knowledge—or even, perhaps it is not too much to say, the scientific curiosity—nor the philosophic range and training, to build a system. Theology had early been rejected. There remained the literary and moral engagement, dependent on a capacity for independent literary pleasure, and on an integrity unsurpassed for candor and rashness. When he is free to exercise and expand in his incomparable love and understanding for literature, and to unleash his wit, whether enthusiastic or malicious, he discharges the first and highest duties of a critic. He enhances our enjoyment of literature, and in the very act of so doing, creates a critical literature difficult to overestimate. When the gospel of disinterestedness becomes the whip for his prejudices and private conflicts, this youthful admonition to himself can reduce his work to a series of brilliant aphorisms or digressions, sometimes perverse or extreme, lacking largeness—lacking, in fact, disinterestedness. The question is, is it really any the worse for that, or is not its very absence sometimes the source of his critical strength? (pp. 187-88)

> Kathleen Coburn, "Hazlitt on the Disinterested Imagination," in Some British Romantics: A Collection of Essays, *James V. Logan, John E. Jordan, Northrop Frye, eds., Ohio State University Press, 1966, pp. 169-88.*

George Watson   (essay date 1973)

[*In the following excerpt, Watson contends that Hazlitt's criticism is insubstantial.*]

[Hazlitt's] criticism is purely descriptive, with no motive beyond analysis and judgement: or rather judgement and then analysis, for he understood perfectly what some later critics have laboured to deny, that evaluation is rather the starting-point of criticism than its aim and object. If you are any sort of reader (let alone a professional critic) you begin with an opinion—it is nonsense to talk of 'arriving at' one: 'to feel what is good, and give reasons for the faith that is in me', as Hazlitt defined his task. He was, at any rate, good at getting his priorities right.

To feel well, however, implies a wide and delicate sensitivity, and to give reasons that matter calls for analytic gifts. Hazlitt's criticism has enjoyed a sizeable reputation for more than a century, but it is doubtful if it will bear examination on either of these counts. For sensitivity, he possesses only a familiar clutch of *a priori* notions of a romantic radical born a little too late; and since he never pursues

analysis beyond a few phrases, it is in no way certain that he was capable of it.

The range of his interests is at first sight impressive. At the age of thirty-eight he turned to criticism with a study entitled **Characters of Shakespear's Plays** (1817), in which he attempted to 'vindicate the characters of Shakespeare's plays from the stigma of French criticism', allowing some credit to August Wilhelm Schlegel as a precursor. But Hazlitt's account of Shakespeare is as simple as his title suggests, and he commits the elementary offence of detaching figures from their dramatic contexts, as Schlegel and Coleridge rarely do. In the same year appeared a collection of essays entitled **The Round Table,** including his review of Wordsworth's *Excursion,* and in 1818 a collection of his dramatic reviews, **A View of the English Stage,** and the eight **Lectures on the English Poets,** a synoptic view of the major poets from Chaucer to the contemporary scene. In 1819 the **Lectures on the English Comic Writers** were published, mainly on eighteenth-century literature, and in 1820 the **Lectures on the Dramatic Literature of the Age of Elizabeth;** and finally, after the period of his marital crisis of 1823-4, **The Spirit of the Age,** or essays on writers of the previous half century, which appeared anonymously in 1825. The achievement is no doubt deliberately comprehensive; so far as verse and drama are concerned, little or nothing that he valued highly in modern English escapes this battery of essays and lectures, all composed in the last fifteen years of his life.

And yet, when all is said, what are the merits of it all, beyond a few telling phrases? Hazlitt's language has at times a certain splendour, but a splendour flyblown and empty of significance, like a schoolboy in a hurry with his homework anxious to impress a master with a taste for rhetoric. His language abuses meaning: look, for instance, at the famous 'general notion' of poetry in the introductory lecture of 1818, **'On Poetry in General':** 'the natural impression of any object or event, by its vividness exciting an involuntary movement of imagination and passion and producing, by sympathy, a certain modulation of the voice, or sounds, expressing it'. There are grave confusions here—whose impression (poet's or reader's?); and how does anyone's impression 'produce' modulations? Or consider the pompous claims for poetry in the paragraphs that follow, father to so many confusions; 'wherever there is a sense of beauty, or power, or harmony, as in a motion of a wave of the sea . . . Fear is poetry, hope is poetry . . .' Does 'is' mean 'equals', or 'is the subject of '? But no use the machinery of siege—there is nothing in all this to be taken. Hazlitt, in such instances, is not saying anything: he is simply making a noise to suggest that he is, or has been, excited about something. He is eminently the kind of descriptive critic who flaunts his own personality at the expense of his subject, and finds in poetry an admirable and infinitely various excuse for a favourite exercise of self-exposure. He is the father of our Sunday journalism. It is a pursuit of nothing to ask for evidence and elucidation of his impression of Chaucer, which (as it happens) looks just enough—'his poetry reads like history. Everything has a downright reality'—or of Spenser, which is riotous nonsense—'In reading the *Faery Queen,* you see a little withered old man by a woodside opening a wicket, a giant, and a dwarf lagging far behind, a damsel in a boat upon an enchanted lake, wood-nymphs, and satyrs . . .' His quotations, which (as in many of our early critics) are nearly all misquotations, do not illustrate passages before or after, and De Quincey was surely justified in condemning as 'indolent' and 'dishonest' his habit of using quotations and misquotations in irrelevant abundance to advance his own argument. His criticism is void of scholarship even in the most elementary sense, and he commits, as a professional critic, elementary errors (such as attributing the Spenserian stanza to the Italians) which we should hesitate to forgive in the hurried work of such good poets as Dryden and Coleridge. It is easy to guess what the biographers' evidence confirms to the hilt: that Hazlitt's criticism is not about the English poets, but about Hazlitt's memory—years, sometimes decades, old—of the English poets as he first knew them. A friend reports that 'unless what he was employed on was a review, he never had a book or paper of any kind about him when he wrote' [see Howe in Further Reading], and his confessions in **The Plain Speaker** that 'I hate to read new books', and that 'books have in a great measure lost their power over me' is one of the frankest statements of incompetence in the record of literary journalism. 'I know how I should have felt at one time', was his sad comment on Keats's 'Eve of St Agnes'. And at no time did he have patience for difficulties. 'Of Donne,' he wrote in the fourth lecture of 1818, 'I know nothing but some beautiful verses to his wife, dissuading her from accompanying him on his travels abroad, and some quaint riddles in verse which the Sphinx could not unravel.' This suggests a mind already closed to critical endeavour. The contrast with Coleridge's sensitive, compassionate regard for what is strange, as in his hesitating but just recommendation of Herbert's *Temple* in the nineteenth chapter of the *Biographia Literaria,* seems unchallengeable. Unless one looks to criticism for a few portable phrases—such phrases as Dryden's 'magnanimity of abuse', or Scott's 'pleasing superficiality' as a poet—Hazlitt is not useful as a critic of English. His gustiness and vigour may, as rhetoric, approach the virtues; but they also serve to mask a coarseness of apprehension and a conservative hatred of ideas which the nineteenth-century reader tolerated with alarming readiness. (pp. 126-30)

George Watson, "Lamb, Hazlitt, DeQuincey," in his The Literary Critics: A Study of English Descriptive Criticism, *second edition, The Woburn Press, 1973, pp. 122-33.*

Charles I. Patterson, Jr. (essay date 1981)

[*In the following excerpt, Patterson finds that a lack of formal method and thorough analysis detracts from Hazlitt's literary criticism.*]

One of the great English critics—some tend to think him the greatest—was a man who wanted to be a portrait painter, who boasted that critical writing required no effort or revision, who expressed aversion to theories of literature, and who abhorred the transcendental philosophy, the philosophy which chiefly underlies the literature of his time. Although designating Coleridge the only man of genius he had ever known, Hazlitt could see nothing in "Kubla Khan" or "Christabel," which he undoubtedly heard Coleridge recite, nor in "Dejection: An Ode," nor in *Biographia Literaria* or *The Friend* or any other of Coleridge's prose works. He considered Coleridge a "has been" and said that William Godwin's name would live longer.

He considered Shelley's poems complete failures and said almost nothing about Blake. Hazlitt never mentioned Jane Austen, even though he wrote extensively on prose fiction. He saw very little in Byron, even in *Don Juan* and *Childe Harold's Pilgrimage,* not understanding at all what kind of poems they were. Hazlitt included Keats's "Ode to a Nightingale" in an anthology, *Select British Poets* (1824), but he never mentioned Keats's odes individually or as a group elsewhere, or "La Belle Dame Sans Merci," *Lamia,* or *Hyperion,* even though he knew Keats personally and said that Keats had the greatest promise of all the poets of the age. Leigh Hunt, Richard Woodhouse, and Charles Brown discerned the worth of these poems; and Byron was lavish in praise of *Hyperion.* But their beauties, that have now captivated the world, meant almost nothing to William Hazlitt at the height of his career as a critic.

The truth is, Hazlitt would not examine a writer's whole canon developmentally and organically, taking account of all his works in interrelationship. Similarly, he seldom examined an individual piece of literature in a systematic, methodical, or inclusive way. In his determination to be free of the trammels of literary theories, systems, and "schools" he emphatically refused to do formal analysis. By this term I do not mean discussion in a stiff and formal manner; I mean examination of the *form* of the work— that is, the taking into account of all its major elements: plot, characterization, style, and theme in drama and narrative; diction, imagery, rhythm, theme, and especially *structure* in lyrical poetry. He gave entirely too little attention to plot and to structure, but was frankly impressionistic, centering on the one element that interested him most, usually characterization. Although emphasis on character study is understandable in light of the Romantic fascination with the individual and with the world within, still the resulting fragmentary quality and incompleteness in Hazlitt's work is frequently a real blemish. His best-known book, **Characters of Shakespeare's Plays,** is marred by it and by statements about characterization that contradict each other and that do not square with the plot. The "beauties" tradition, in which a critic was expected simply to point out the finer passages, was still much in vogue; but, aside from the obvious fact that the real beauties of a work are more clearly apparent from the perspective of the whole, Hazlitt should have gained from various predecessors a sense of the importance of the whole. In spite of his steady disparagement of literary theory, he thought highly of Aristotle's *Poetics* and could hardly have missed Aristotle's emphasis on the importance of the total effect of a work. The medieval tradition of *explication de texte* had for centuries stressed the importance of the whole. John Dryden had maintained that the plot of a play is the base on which the total structure rests and therefore must be taken into account along with characterization, theme, style, and other elements. Even Alexander Pope in his *Essay on Criticism* emphatically admonishes "Survey the whole," and states that otherwise a critic usually sacrifices "all to one lov'd folly." Also, A. W. Schlegel, whom we know Hazlitt read, stressed the importance of the whole, but Hazlitt seems to have been perversely opposed to learning from predecessors and contemporaries. Thus I am not censuring him for not writing like a twentieth-century "new critic."

I am not objecting to his repudiating narrow systems and allegiances, his refusal to follow precisely in the track of

Dryden or Dr. Johnson, or to be like Coleridge. I am objecting only to his unwillingness to attempt inclusiveness of some kind, for the lack of it often impaired his judgment. Evidently, he never understood the full import of organic unity. He believed with Aristotle that literature is an imitation of life—mimesis—and he understood that an imitation did not mean a copy, but meant the fundamental elements of life worked up into new and probable combinations. Hazlitt even talked volubly of the creative mind's ability to add to the imitation a crucial element that comes only from *that mind itself,* which is an aspect of transcendentalism. Yet Hazlitt, who consistently scoffed at transcendentalism, continually assumed that this transforming power in creativity was fully explainable in terms of the basically empirical epistemologies of Thomas Hobbes, John Locke, and David Hartley. Hence Hazlitt seems never to have understood that mimesis—the imitation of life—could be carried considerably beyond representation into analogy, *and* even farther than analogy into mythical and symbolical rendering. In his antipathy to the philosophy underlying the transforming, remolding, reshaping, restructuring transcendental power in creativity, he was almost blind to this germinal contribution of his age to literary practice as well as to literary theory. Hence his complete obliviousness to Blake and thoroughly negative response to Shelley.

In addition to brief discussions of mimesis and the ideal, Hazlitt makes his chief attempt at literary theory in **"On Poetry in General,"** the initial chapter of *Lectures on the English Poets* (1818), where he tries to lay out his criteria and define his critical method. But nearly all he says redounds into an imprecise and repetitive assertion that feeling is the prime requisite for both the creative work of the poet and the evaluative work of the critic. Statements like these abound: "Poetry is only the highest eloquence of passion, the most vivid form of expression that can be given to our expression of anything, whether pleasurable or painful. . . . It is the perfect coincidence of the image and the words with the feeling we have." "Poetry in its matter and form is natural imagery or feeling, combined with passion and fancy." "Wherever any object takes such a hold of the mind as to make us dwell upon it, and brood over it, melting the heart in tenderness, or kindling it to a sentiment of enthusiasm;—wherever a movement of imagination or passion is impressed on the mind, by which it seeks to prolong and repeat the emotion, to bring all other objects into accord with it, . . .—this is poetry." . . . These fuzzy statements are variations on the widespread Romantic idea that feeling, by initiating the process of empathy, sets in motion the intuitive powers of mind that lead to the direct apprehension of imaginative truth. Hazlitt defines imagination here as "not only a direct but also a reflected light, that while it shows us the object, throws a sparkling radiance on all around it: the flame of the passions, communicated to the imagination, reveals to us . . . the inmost recesses of thought, and penetrates our whole being. . . . Imagination is that faculty which represents objects not as they are in themselves, but as they are molded by other thoughts and feelings, into an infinite variety of shapes and combinations of power." Though in line with Romantic ideas of creativity, all this seems much too vague and imprecise to comprise very helpful criteria for the analysis and evaluation of specific works. (pp. 647-50)

Yet Hazlitt still had very considerable powers which enabled him to write of literature interestingly, vigorously, and commandingly *without* inclusiveness. To his credit, he wrote of literature as an object of delight and contemplation. He deliberately sacrificed *structural* analysis for the *psychological* analysis of a work's effects, much in vogue at the time. He possessed a remarkably sympathetic and empathetic imagination, which enabled him to empathize and identify with the characters in dramatic and narrative fiction. They seemed to stir archetypal patterns of response in Hazlitt, allowing him intuitively to penetrate into their character and consciousness beyond what many readers could discern but in accord with what most of them could grasp when it was pointed out, so that they could readily add Hazlitt's perceptions to their own. Hence he usually appealed to a wide range of readers. Further he could express these perceptions with verve, zest, and vigor—with something of what in a great writer or painter he called *Gusto.* . . . He could write tremendously effective sentences one after another, all tracking perfectly and smoothly as they carried forth the gushing tirade of his thoughts and feelings. And these sentences are notably varied in length and type; he had an almost limitless range of styles. Very much because of this gift, what he says is usually interesting one way or another; he is seldom dull. His enthusiasm tends to mesmerize the reader and carry conviction by its own power. He liked all genres, provided excellence was present, but he was vexed with what was tawdry and cheap and was quick to censure it severely. Most of the time he exhibited good taste, which Keats admired strongly.

But these capabilities are just the sort that can largely cover up the effects of his lack of structural analysis and lack of inclusiveness. These were his cardinal defects as a critic. They remain beneath the vibrant surface of his critical writing, and they may yet deny him lasting fame in spite of his enthusiastic admirers in our day. A few judicious voices are raising questions about his high place. (pp. 651-52)

In his handling of specific works within various genres, I shall point out the results of his lack of inclusiveness, as well as the benefits of an occasional effort at it, when structural analysis does enter briefly. (p. 652)

Hazlitt brought forth his book, *Characters of Shakespeare's Plays,* in 1817. . . . No single book had included a treatment of all the plays, and Hazlitt thought that to produce one might be an easy task, for he had done some work on the characters of Shakespeare earlier and had closely observed character portrayals by leading actors on the stage. . . . Hazlitt's book follows no consistent pattern or plan; the "gusto" at the beginning dies out before the end; and the total effect is anticlimactic. But the book did explore psychological subtleties in the characters, in spite of carelessness, superficiality, and inaccuracies. (pp. 652-53)

In the essay on *Hamlet* Hazlitt mentions the universality in Hamlet's character and proclaims him "as real as our own thoughts. . . . It is *we* who are Hamlet." Hamlet is filled not with "strength or passion, but with refinement of thought and sentiment . . . high enthusiasm and quick sensibility." Hazlitt thinks that most actors take too much of the flexibility out of Hamlet; there should be no sullen gloom, no harshness in him, but melancholy and sadness.

Hamlet is wrapped up in his reflections and thinks aloud. His moral quality is questioned only by those who misunderstand him. However, Hazlitt's inveterate refusal to check his assertions about character against the action in the plot results in his contending that Hamlet is incapable of deliberate action and is continually hurried into extremes on the spur of the moment, as when he kills Polonius. But this assertion is contradicted by most of the earlier incidents in the plot: Hamlet's command of himself and his friends during the visit of the ghost; his handling of Polonius, his mother, Rosencrantz and Guildenstern; and his command of the players and rigging of the play within the play to catch the conscience of Claudius. Further, Hazlitt's failure to take account of these incidents in the first half of the plot facilitated his voicing the stock view that Hamlet's ruling passion is *to think, not to act.* But shortly afterward he contradicts this statement, I think, by saying that Hamlet's "habitual principles of action are unhinged by the events," a view more in accord with the plot. Here Hazlitt is actually on the threshold of putting the two views together in proper relationship: that is, Hamlet's paralysis of will is a *result* of the tragedy he is undergoing, not *the cause* of it; for he is vigorous and commanding in action at first, before the burden of the tragic events destroys his healthy mental balance. But Hazlitt does not pursue the implications of the statement this far and does not really add appreciably to our knowledge of the character of Hamlet. Like Coleridge, Lamb, and A. W. Schlegel, Hazlitt says that the full richness of Shakespeare, especially of *Hamlet* and *Lear,* cannot be obtained from the stage and that we must read the plays to penetrate their depths. Hazlitt has thus helped to bring about the predominant study of Shakespeare as poetry rather than drama, which some critics and scholars deplore.

His treatment of Falstaff is one of his best and most nearly faultless discussions. Hazlitt sees in him an exuberance of good humor and good nature, love of laughter and good fellowship, contentment with others and with himself. Hence his fatness is in keeping: the pampered luxury of his physical appetites parallels the "boundless luxury of his imagination." He deliberately exaggerates his own vices to amuse others. He is "an actor in his life as well as on the stage." "The disparity between his inclinations and his capacity for enjoyment (since he is old) helps to mellow his assumed vices into the ludicrous." Best of all, Hazlitt proclaims, "the secret of his wit is a masterly presence of mind, an absolute self possession which nothing can disturb." Falstaff has a kind of effrontery that wards off all that would "interrupt the career of his triumphant jollity." Here again his size helps to float him out of difficulties "in a sea of rich conceits," and his exaggerations are "open, palpable, monstrous as the father than begets them."

The discussion of *King Lear* is probably the very best in the book, the one in which Hazlitt's sympathetic imagination probes most fruitfully. He calls it the play in which Shakespeare is most in earnest, where he strikes deepest in the heart. Lear's passion, Hazlitt says, stems from the wrenching apart of the strongest human ties, filial piety and family love, and therefore brings the greatest tumult of the emotions, a "tug and war of the elements of our being" torn from their "accustomed holds and resting-places in the soul." Shakespeare presents "the mind of Lear staggering between the weight of attachment" to his children "and the hurried movements of passion," "like a tall ship" struggling in a gale, "having its anchor fixed in the bottom of the sea," that is, in the unalterable claims of paternal love. Hazlitt says that the finely conceived character of Lear is the only ground on which such a story could be built with greatest truth and effect. Here he is turning upside down Dryden's dictum that the plot is the base on which all rests. But Hazlitt does discuss the relation of plot to character in this play. He praises the handling of the subplot in relation to the main plot and the interaction of characters with each other; the more than comic function of the Fool in carrying pathos to the highest by pointing up the consequences of Lear's actions; and the expressive power of the storm on the heath in its similarity to the storm within the breast of Lear. This discussion thus takes account of structural matters and shows that Hazlitt *could* be inclusive and analytical when he wished to be, and with better results, for here we find no assertions about character which the plot will not support, and no glaring contradictions.

The quality of the whole book is very uneven, however. Sometimes he only summarizes the story of a play without comment, or gives quotations. At the end the book simply peters out, with his stating that he does not admire Shakespeare's poems as much as the plays and that he does not know what to say about the sonnets except that some are "highly beautiful in themselves," of which four are given in full.

In fact, Hazlitt is a poor critic of lyrical poetry generally. Since there are no characters to discuss and no story to follow, and since he would not analyze structure, he found little to say when dealing with lyrical poems. In this genre he is most vague and impressionistic. He often quotes, but nowhere enters and traces out meaning or development, never explicates or interprets. Consequently, he never sees a lyric in its fullness and richness, and therefore often equates the poorest with the best, as when he indicates the same high level of excellence for Wordsworth's "Tintern Abbey" (which he calls "The Banks of the Wye"), "Hart-Leap Well," "Reverie of Poor Susan," "To the Cuckoo," "To the Daisy," and "Complaint of an Indian Woman." (pp. 653-55)

In narrative poetry he is somewhat better, and he deals with poets from Chaucer through Burns in **Lectures on the English Poets** (1818). But his unwillingness to notice structure and his belief that the character of Satan is the base of the piece inevitably led him to proclaim Satan the protagonist of *Paradise Lost,* as have Blake, Shelley, and others. Admittedly, Milton did not succeed in making the Father and Son vivid and striking; but a critic should know that a heroic antagonist is a necessity in the structure of an epic and that he must be of comparable stature to the protagonist if the latter's deeds and accomplishments are to be considered in any sense heroic. (pp. 656-57)

In the criticism of the novel, however, Hazlitt is probably of some historical significance, for he was the first critic of high repute to devote much time or space to the genre and he said things concerning it that others had not said. He was the first to consider the novel unequivocally one of the great genres, generally on the same plane as drama and epic. He applied the same aesthetic theory to prose fiction that he applied to the drama—Aristotle's theories of imitation and the ideal—which underpinned his ranking of novelists over a wide scale. The representation of actual life is at the bottom, and Hazlitt excoriates what he called "The Dandy School," which included the novels of Theodore Hook and the young Disraeli's *Vivian Grey*. Fanny Burney, Le Sage, and even Smollett fared but little better; Burney was a mere observer of external behavior, Le Sage a describer of manners, not character, and Smollett a portrayer of "the ridiculous accidents and reverses" of life who excelled most in caricature. . . . The greatest novel in Hazlitt's eyes was Cervantes's *Don Quixote*. He thought that it combined the actual and the ideal and turned them into the universal. Its hero is "more stately, more romantic, and at the same time more real to the imagination than any other hero upon record." The other characters in the story, he continued, "are strictly individuals. . . . They are unlike anything we have seen before—may be said to be purely ideal; and yet identify themselves more readily with our imagination." The merits of the work, he thought, had not been sufficiently understood: "There cannot be a greater mistake than to consider *Don Quixote* as a merely satirical work. . . . Through the crazed and battered figure of the knight, the spirit of chivalry shines out with undiminished lustre." Hazlitt's balance between the actual and the ideal, his insistence that the actual should condition the conceptual, possibly helped to strengthen the relationship between literature and reality at a crucial time and to encourage in the genre "that awakening of the soul and imagination" which was "the very essence" of romanticism [E. A. Baker, *History of the English Novel*]. In addition, his interest in novels possibly enhanced the respectability of the genre at a time when great fiction was not being produced and when the single best novelist of the age—Jane Austen—was hardly recognized critically. (pp. 658-59)

In the re-ranking of genres, [Hazlitt] can hardly be said to have brought about any real change, although his proclaiming that the novel is worthy of serious critical attention is an indication that this genre was forging its way into something like parity with epic and drama. His four volumes as a critic of painting did much to establish criticism of painting as a branch of literature and led on to Ruskin. Hazlitt's experience as painter and critic of art made him vivid and graphic in literary criticism, and he sometimes compared a painting with a poem or a story; but he did not adhere exclusively to the current doctrine of *ut pictura poesis:* as picture, so poem. What he said about drama he said excitingly and provocatively, and his discussions of *King Lear* and of Falstaff are noteworthy and useful even now.

All things considered, however, I cannot believe that as a critic Hazlitt deserves to rank with Dryden, Coleridge, Arnold, and T. S. Eliot. He was not as responsible as they were, would not grapple with totalities, seldom analyzed, and was too impressionistic. But removed from the group of top-ranking critics and considered as a commentator on literature, he deserves high place. His best will long be read; for, where he is not corruptingly wrong (as he is with Spenser and Milton, I think), he helps readers to develop taste and discernment. As personal and familiar essayist he may justly rank only a little below Lamb, but the need for thorough reappraisal of his criticism and his present high standing as critic seems evident. (pp. 662-63)

Charles I. Patterson, Jr., "Hazlitt's Criticism in Retrospect," in Studies in English Literature, 1500-1900, *Vol. XXI, No. 4, Autumn, 1981, pp. 647-63.*

John L. Mahoney   (essay date 1981)

[*Mahoney is an American educator and critic. In the following excerpt, he examines the concept of "gusto" as it is developed in Hazlitt's literary, drama, and art criticism.*]

Hazlitt's strong emphasis on the centrality of nature in the artistic process is certainly not unique. Such a criterion is basic to a number of theories of art from the mimetic to the pragmatic to the "slice of life." What is distinctive is his special concern with the degree of engagement between the artist and nature and, subsequently, between the critic and the work of art. His are new questions and concerns: What is the posture of the artist vis-à-vis nature? What is the nature of the involvement? What does he bring to nature and what does nature bring to him, and what is the specific character of the new reality created by this interaction? What is the peculiar quality of the pleasure communicated by the poem, or play, or novel, or painting? Questions like these are persistently raised by Hazlitt, and the answers generally revolve in one way or another around the familiar, although much popularized and much misunderstood, concept of gusto.

This concern with gusto or emotional strength in a work of art is [a] . . . cardinal tenet in Hazlitt's critical *modus operandi*. It is a highly psychological concern which once again suggests his debt to eighteenth-century aesthetic theory and distinguishes him from the more abstract and more philosophically minded Coleridge. He seems more interested in how art affects and less in how it is created; more interested in recording the quality of emotional excitement evoked, less in abstract theories of creativity.

As one moves through the great variety of his more general observations on literature, to say nothing of his practical criticism, it is remarkable to note the consistency with which the standard of gusto was utilized. He described the phenomenon in many colorful ways and in many different contexts, but there was one recurring emphasis. Gusto is "power or passion defining any object." It is "the conveying to the eye the impressions of the soul, or the other senses connected with the sense of sight, such as the different passions visible in the countenance, the romantic interest connected with scenes of nature, the character and feelings associated with different objects." Hardly an object lacks expression, a special and quite essential character, a close association with pleasure or pain, and "it is in giving this truth of character from the truth of feeling, whether in the highest or the lowest degree, but always in the highest degree of which the subject is capable, that gusto consists." In the fine art of painting gusto is "where the impression made on one sense excites by affinity those of another," the term here suggesting a totality of response involving the full range of human potential. It is, then, a strong emotional response triggered by the object in nature and brought to that object. W. J. Bate's description, "a strong excitement of the imagination by which, geared to its highest activity, it seizes and drains out the dynamic and living character of its object into telling expression," is perhaps the most perceptive attempt to come to terms with the entire process.

Gusto is absolutely central to the experience of art and criticism; it is ultimately what distinguishes art from a mere representation of reality, from what Hazlitt regarded as mere "objects of sight." Only when these objects become the objects of taste and imagination, when they penetrate to the sense of beauty and pleasure in the human heart and are revealed to the view in their inner core and structure, does great art begin. One of his most famous definitions of poetry underlines his overriding preoccupation with emotional immediacy in his practical criticism. It is, he said, "the language of the imagination and the passions. It relates to whatever gives immediate pleasure or pain to the human mind. It comes home to the bosoms and businesses of men; for nothing but what so comes home to them in the most general and intelligible shape, can be a subject for poetry. Poetry is the universal language which the heart holds with nature and itself."

Singularly absent in the definition just cited, as well as in his general association of gusto with great art, is the more classical ideal of decorum, of suitable subjects for the arts. As noted earlier, Hazlitt saw a fundamental rightness in nature and in the response to her workings, and he had little patience with the kind of moralism which views the artist and the critic as creators of moral patterns or as defenders of the sacred ground of an ideal nature against the incursions of the vicious and the ugly. The essential thing is that the artist be true to his response to nature and that the critic be true to his response to art. If nature is allowed to speak for herself, there is no need for a religious or moral arbiter to defend the cause of values. Nature is true, and art which records honestly our response to her presence is moral in the highest and fullest sense. In his important essay **"On Poetry in General,"** he states quite categorically that poetry is "the most vivid form of expression that can be given to our conception of any thing, whether pleasurable or painful, mean or dignified, delightful or distressing. It is the perfect coincidence of the image and the words with the feeling we have, and of which we cannot get rid in any other way, that gives an instant 'satisfaction to the thought'."

Hazlitt is extremely illuminating in his analyses of the place of emotion in human experience, and specifically in the formation of critical judgments. Here also is the strong psychological orientation, the preoccupation with human motivation, the suspicion of abstract theorizing. His credo is aptly summarized in his statement in **"On Genius and Common Sense"**: "In art, in taste, in life, in speech, you decide from feeling, and not from reason; that is, from the impression of a number of things on the mind, which impression is true and well-founded, though you may not be able to analyse or account for it in the several particulars." To rob a man of strong feeling, he contended, is to rob him of all that transcends the immediate objects of experience and the artificial ways in which men deal with them and to reduce him to an automaton. As already suggested, association is a vital part of the process, not the merely mechanical, automatic variety which he came to deplore in Hartley, but a much more subjective and emotional activity. For Hazlitt, nature does not operate in accordance with some preconceived rule of association; indeed, the

workings of nature and of human response determine the rule.

> In a gesture you use, in a look you see, in a tone you hear, you judge of the expression, propriety, and meaning from habit, not from reason or rules; that is to say, from innumerable instances of like gestures, looks, and tones, in innumerable other circumstances, variously modified, which are too many and too refined to be all distinctly recollected, but which do not therefore operate the less powerfully upon the mind and eye of taste.

The genre of tragedy was frequently cited in Hazlitt's discussions of gusto. Once more he probed human motivation, and built a premiss which he confidently called "the common love of strong excitement." People are fascinated by and drawn to tragedy not simply out of a sense of escape or a preoccupation with the grotesque or abnormal. The explanation is quite the contrary: man's fascination with the tragic, his continuing desire to view the spectacles of Oedipus, Medea, Othello, Lear, and others is tied intimately to his basic humanity. Citing Burke's famous observation that although people flock to see a tragedy on stage, they would quickly leave the theater to view a public execution in the next street, Hazlitt went on to develop his own analysis. The explanation lies not simply in the differences between art and reality. Children still like ghost stories in journalistic form, and there are large audiences for the familiar, full, and true accounts of murder and robberies. The clergyman paints his dark and frightening canvas of hell much more often than he sketches an idyllic heaven. When we seek to discover why we would indulge our violent passions as soon as we read a description of those of others, Hazlitt pleaded succinctly that "we cannot help it. The sense of power is as strong a principle in the mind as the love of pleasure."

Human beings yearn for excitement and love all those aspects of life and art which convey a rich sense of living things. And such exercise of the emotions is not necessarily harmful. Quite the contrary. If the vision of the artist is such that our sympathies are drawn to all the forms of imagination, good and evil, beauty and ugliness, hope and despair, exaltation and debasement, the effect is in the highest sense educative, formative, moral. Our experience is enriched and broadened, and much of the potential which is our heritage as human beings is tapped and realized. Strong passion represented dramatically in this fashion "lays bare and shews us the rich depths of the human soul: the whole of our existence, the sum total of our passions and pursuits, of that which we desire and that which we dread, is brought before us by contrast."

Hazlitt was generally unhappy about post-Elizabethan tragedy, largely on the grounds discussed above. The plays of Moore and Lillo are morbid and melodramatic; they "oppress and lie like a dead weight upon the mind, a load of misery which it is unable to throw off." Dryden's plays, characterized by extravagant images, bombastic language, and a general exaggeration of the commonplace, are failures as tragedies. Addison's Cato is more a lifeless statue than a living man. As a matter of fact, Otway is the only Restoration writer who has produced a successful example of the genre, an example which rises above the ordinary to touch the human heart with its emotional strength. Contemporary German tragedy seems chiefly concerned with effect. Byron, a frequent *bête noire,* has turned tragedy into a vehicle for self-dramatization, a high-flown rhetorical drama in which the poet-hero pours forth his personal anguish for all to behold. Great tragedy, argued Hazlitt in the metaphorical manner which is such a hallmark of his critical writing, is "like a vessel making the voyage of life, and tossed about by the winds and waves of passion" while contemporary dramatists have converted it into "a handsomely-constructed steam-boat, that is moved by the sole expansive power of words." Instead of to a number of characters affected by particular and concrete incidents and speaking directly in response to them, audiences are treated to the spectacle of poet-heroes mounting a pulpit and delivering high-flown declamations on life, death, fate, and other great themes, all the while smothering nature with the virtuosity of their own rhetoric. What such drama offers are "the subtleties of the head, instead of the workings of the heart, and possible justifications instead of the actual motives of conduct." Rising to the level of principle, Hazlitt articulated the premiss which underlies such practical judgments. The trouble with such failures in the tragic genre is their intense and almost perverse preoccupation with the ego of the artist, and their consequent appeal to only one side of man's complex nature. More fundamentally, such plays manifest that ignorance of and indifference to that great cornerstone of gusto, its roots in the great world beyond the self and its magic ability to communicate strength of feeling as it is evoked by worthy and grand objects beyond the individual.

Shakespeare is the tragedian of gusto, and here Hazlitt challenges the Johnsonian notion that Shakespeare is more successful as a writer of comedy. His concern is not the analysis of some predominant or all-consuming passion; "it is passion modified by passion, by all the other feelings to which the individual is liable, and to which others are liable with him." Again taking issue with Johnson's argument concerning the superiority of Shakespeare's comic genius, he contends that Shakespeare is the only tragic poet in the world in the highest sense, that Molière was a greater writer of comedy, that both Rabelais and Cervantes excel in such qualities as ludicrous description and the invention of comic character. Shakespeare, however, controls "the stronger passions," and the stronger the passions, the greater the work of art. His tragedies are "on a par with, and the same as Nature, in her greatest heights and depths of action and suffering. There is but one who durst walk within that mighty circle, treading the utmost bound of nature and passion, shewing us the dread abyss of woe in all its ghastly shapes and colours, and laying open all the faculties of the human soul to act, to think, and suffer, in direct extremities." The third act of *Othello* and the first three acts of *King Lear* are great exemplars of what Hazlitt regarded as the logic of passion. They

contain the highest examples not only of the force of individual passion, but of its dramatic vicissitudes and striking effects arising from the different circumstances and characters of the person speaking. We see the ebb and flow of the feeling, its pauses and feverish starts, its impatience of opposition, its accumulating force when it has time to recollect itself, the manner in which it avails itself of every passing word or gesture, its haste to repel insinuation, the alternate contraction and dilatation of the soul, and all "the dazzling fence of controver-

sy" in this mortal combat with poisoned weapons, aimed at the heart, where each wound is fatal.

A problem play like *Measure for Measure* lacks gusto; the emotions seem at a standstill, and all our sympathies seem repulsed. *Macbeth* is a play in which lofty imagination triggers a tumultuously violent action, an action brought home to us with the vividness of our own experience. As in so many of Shakespeare's plays, the opening, with its wildness of setting, growing suspense, quick shifting of characters and actions, conveys a sense of absolute truth. The incredible designs of Iago, the dialogues in *King Lear* and *Macbeth*, the exchanges of Brutus and Cassius in *Julius Caesar*—these are still further examples of the dramatic fluctuation of passion which Hazlitt associated with gusto at its best. Marlowe, although a dramatist of great power, reveals "a lust of power in his writings, a hunger and thirst after unrighteousness, a glow of the imagination, unhallowed by any thing but its own energies." Beaumont and Fletcher begin the departure from the genuine tragedy of Shakespeare, thinking less of their subject and more of themselves. They lack gusto, for they lack that firm control of their subject and, consequently, are too often given to gimmickry and display.

It may be that for Hazlitt drama was the supreme exemplar of gusto and Shakespeare the practitioner *par excellence* of that genre, but his utilization of gusto was by no means limited to drama and dramatists. Gusto must be a vital effect of any successful work of art, the effect which must be experienced by critic and audience before any other criteria are brought to bear. It may reveal itself in the command of subject or grasp of character or intensity of expression, but its absence cannot be compensated for by mere form or moral or style. The poem, painting, or novel, like the drama, must engage its audience almost at once, must draw them into a vital relationship, must touch off a kind of emotional electricity. Milton, for example, "had as much of what is meant by *gusto* as any poet. He forms the most intense conceptions of things, and then embodies them by a single stroke of his pen." Although a more serious and sublime poet than Shakespeare or Chaucer, an artist whose essential genius was undramatic, he nevertheless possessed that strength of mind and vividness of conception which is at the root of gusto. His imagination "has the force of nature." Satan is his great masterpiece whose "love of power and contempt for suffering are never once relaxed from the highest pitch of intensity," whose "thoughts burn like a hell within him." It is in Satan and in the majestic account of the Edenic happiness and then the loss of it by Adam and Eve that *Paradise Lost* finds its greatest strength, and not in the battle of the angels or the rather stodgy dialogues in heaven. Milton takes his Biblical source and proceeds to describe its persons and objects with "the vividness of actual observation." Not so *Comus*, which is without strong interest and passion. The great sonnet "On His Deceased Wife" reveals how the poet's mind elevated his thoughts through brilliant classical allusions and then enriched the allusions by the passionate involvement of actual thoughts and feelings.

Chaucer's gusto is different but no less effective. His descriptions of nature are pure examples of gusto, with "a local truth and freshness, which gives the very feeling of the air, the coolness or moisture of the ground. Inanimate objects are thus made to have a fellow-feeling in the interest of the story; and render back the sentiment of the speaker's mind." More so than almost any other poet, he describes, not what his characters might be like, but what they actually felt, with all their impulses and prejudices. There is an absolute directness in his communication of the unique dimensions of his characters. "In depth of simple pathos, and intensity of conception," Hazlitt contends, "never swerving from his subject, I think no other writer comes near him, not even the Greek tragedians." Compared with him, Spenser seems more remote from the vitality of life, interested more in beauty than in truth; consequently, his poetry lacks immediacy of feeling. His are the emotions of romance, "all that belongs to distant objects of terror, and uncertain, imaginary distress." The inventiveness of his allegory is remarkable, but he has little comic talent and little subtlety of characterization.

Hazlitt had extraordinary praise for Edmund Burke among prose writers, a statesman who charges essentially non-poetical material with imaginative power and emotional intensity. In "Thoughts on the Present Discontents," "Reflections on the French Revolution," the "Regicide Peace," and other works, the full force of his genius is revealed. "He was completely carried away by his subject. He had no other object but to produce the strongest impression on his reader, by giving the truest, the most characteristic, the fullest, and most forcible descriptions of things, trusting to the power of his own mind to mould them into grace and beauty." His is not the set or formal style of Johnson, which

> selects a certain set of words to represent all ideas whatever, as the most dignified and elegant, and excludes all others as low and vulgar. The words are not fitted to the things, but the things to the words. Every thing is seen through a false medium. It is putting a mask on the face of nature, which may indeed hide some specks and blemishes, but takes away all beauty, delicacy, and variety.

Hazlitt's observations on gusto in painting are both instructive and exciting. He praises highly the Italian masters, especially Raphael and Correggio, as "conveying to the eye the impressions of the soul." Titian's coloring is superb; his heads seem to think and his bodies feel. His flesh-color conveys the feeling of life, while Van Dyke's "wants gusto," since it has no "internal character," no "living principle in it." Rembrandt is a master; "everything in his pictures has a tangible character." Rubens is less successful, having "a great deal of gusto in his Fauns and Satyrs, and in all that expresses motion, but in nothing else." Raphael's "gusto was only in expression; he had no idea of the character of anything but the human form. . . . His trees are like sprigs of grass stuck in a book of botanical specimens." The landscapes of Claude Lorrain, "perfect as they are, want gusto. . . . They are perfect abstractions of the visible images of things; they speak the visible language of nature truly. . . . He saw the atmosphere, but he did not feel it." The kind of total absorption effected by works of great gusto is dramatically exemplified by the Greek statues where the "sense of perfect form nearly occupies the whole mind, and hardly suffers it to dwell on any other feeling." While Michaelangelo's forms are full of gusto and "everywhere obtrude the sense of power upon the eye," Benjamin West, in his picture of *Christ Rejected*, "sees and feels nothing in the human face

but bones and cartilages: or if he does avail himself of this flexible machinery, it is only by rule and method."

Gusto, then, a strong and passionate excitement in the artist which communicates itself to whatever object in nature it turns to, an emotional immediacy which pervades artistic subject and manner, form and expression, a psychological power which communicates the variety and complexity of human response, was a singular emphasis in the criticism of Hazlitt. (pp. 61-71)

> *John L. Mahoney, in his* The Logic of Passion: The Literary Criticism of William Hazlitt, *revised edition, Fordham University Press, 1981, 125 p.*

David Bromwich   (essay date 1983)

[*In the following excerpt, Bromwich examines Hazlitt's critical theories and practices.*]

Hazlitt's reputation today is puzzling. He is cherished as an essayist, and honored as a name even by those who have scarcely read him. Yet writers can be lost track of by thoughtless selection as well as complete omission, and Hazlitt has suffered both sorts of neglect at different times. The result has been a refinement and a diminishment of our idea of him. Three or four specimens of his writing, repeated in as many generations of anthologies, have sketched a figure in the minds of most readers—sprightly, debonair, essentially worldly—that blends into the atmosphere of Robert Louis Stevenson's hearty compliment: "though we are mighty fine fellows nowadays, we cannot write like Hazlitt." The figure we have come to know is indeed something like Stevenson. And once we have him before us, we can think of celebrated lines that confirm his reality. "Reader, have you ever seen a fight?" "This is that Hamlet the Dane, whom we read of in our youth." "To be young is to be as one of the Immortal Gods." His ease is admirable, and it makes admiration easy. Even in a melancholy fit he stays on the best terms with everything. "This," he seems to say, "is how we wrote once, when all topics were grateful to the pen; this is how the world stood with us, when even our self-knowledge kept us warm." The Hazlitt who speaks these lines has held the stage for almost a century, and made us cosy in our seats; but, reader, I never cared for him much. . . . (p. 3)

The Hazlitt I care for is fiercer and less reconciled. Once discovered he is hard to forget, and some dubious critical tactics have been required to suppress him. Early in this century, for example, a scholar undertook to characterize Hazlitt's style by listing a few words. They were: "brilliance, buckle, lake, lamp, library, lustre, mariner, masquerade-dress, bosom, brow, dew-drops, garden, glass, spring, sun, pale, paste, cottage, glittering, smooth, soft, stamped, stripped, trembles, laugh, wandered, winged" [see Chandler entry in Further Reading]. The list would please the compiler only if it seemed all of a piece. From its consistency he could infer that the tact and particularity which made these words "modern" had come at the expense of a certain weight, a dignity of abstract statement: with a minimum of effort he could then gratify the common wisdom about style, which holds that the virtues of sensory vividness and discursive generality are seldom found together. This is not too much to surmise from a single list, if the list is representative. But it happens that the page in question belongs to Hazlitt's lecture on Pope. He is in fact describing the qualities that he regards as distinctively Popean, to explain his judgment that "within this retired and narrow circle how much, and that how exquisite, was contained. . . . It is like looking at the world through a microscope." Hence the remarkable unity of the list, the charm and even daintiness of the prose one imagines it fairly to represent. A great many estimates of Hazlitt's achievement are founded on this sort of evidence. Nevertheless any reader will follow a received view until he discovers a sufficiently imposing obstacle in its way.

Mine was a paragraph on *The Merchant of Venice.*

> Shylock is *a good hater;* "a man no less sinned against than sinning." If he carries his revenge too far, yet he has strong grounds for "the lodged hate he bears Anthonio," which he explains with equal force of eloquence and reason. He seems the depositary of the vengeance of his race; and though the long habit of brooding over daily insults and injuries has crusted over his temper with inveterate misanthropy, and hardened him against the contempt of mankind, this adds but little to the triumphant pretensions of his enemies. There is a strong, quick, and deep sense of justice mixed up with the gall and bitterness of his resentment. The constant apprehension of being burnt alive, plundered, banished, reviled, and trampled on, might be supposed to sour the most forbearing nature, and to take something from that "milk of human kindness," with which his persecutors contemplated his indignities. The desire of revenge is almost inseparable from the sense of wrong; and we can hardly help sympathising with the proud spirit, hid beneath his "Jewish gaberdine," stung to madness by repeated undeserved provocations, and labouring to throw off the load of obloquy and oppression heaped upon him and all his tribe by one desperate act of "lawful" revenge, till the ferociousness of the means by which he is to execute his purpose, and the pertinacity with which he adheres to it, turn us against him; but even at last, when disappointed of the sanguinary revenge with which he had glutted his hopes, and exposed to beggary and contempt by the letter of the law on which he had insisted with so little remorse, we pity him, and think him hardly dealt with by his judges.

Such a passage of course says nothing final about the play. The man who wrote it appears as a skeptic for whom skepticism is not a disease to be cured. He seeks no unity, offers no "resolution of tensions."

Trampled, brooding, and *indignities* had replaced *trembles, glittering,* and *dew-drops.* This gave me a jolt. . . . I have listened to the author who "can hardly help sympathising," to whom sympathy means anger at an injustice and scorn for its apologists; who wonders, "Why should one not make a sentence of a page long, out of the feelings of one's whole life?"; who says of a "person" obviously himself, that he is "the last to quit his seat in your company, grapples with a subject in conversation right earnestly, and is, I take it, backward to give up a cause or a friend." He is the most restless of the English romantics, the most dangerous to his enemies, and in one sense the most shocking, since his familiarity of manner recommends him to those who would not knowingly welcome the products of a new school. That he is also shockable gives his work its

delicacy and its depth. In English there is no one even roughly comparable to him: in French there is Stendhal. The Hazlitt of the Victorians, however, and of their followers almost to our own day, I neither wish nor expect to supplant. He is another character with the same name, who multiplies the lights and shadows that hold our interest in any given essay, whether it is called **"On the Pleasure of Painting"** or **"On the Pleasure of Hating."**

By his earliest writings Hazlitt came to be known above all as a champion of embattled causes: republicanism, democracy, and the freedoms of conscience and the imagination for which he sometimes reserved a single word, *expression.* To this role he was fitted equally by precept and conviction. (pp. 3-5)

He wrote for those who could understand him as he was; he had many shared aims but, it must be admitted, few shared words with working-class revolutionaries—he was poor at "accommodation"; in this sense alone it is fair to consider him a middle-class Radical. (p. 8)

Hazlitt wrote with such continuous and unexampled vehemence, fires stoked and ablaze for the strictest of deadlines, that his legend has joined and helped to keep alive the journalist's romance, from which the novice at the worst of times gets some encouragement. What makes for the romance? In part an ideal of independence, which is never altogether marred by the realities of shifting employment; and the sense that writing has its place in a larger cultural conversation, where the merits of everything are to be warmly debated, where indeed a thing's value lies partly in the discussion it provokes. The unhappier features of the romance were sketched by Virginia Woolf in an essay on Lockhart's criticism. Posterity may have gibbeted Lockhart for his ridicule of Keats, and yet "No one who sees him swinging in the wind can help a shudder and a sigh lest the same fate may one of these days be his. After all, new books of poems still appear." But even for what we may consider his mistakes, Hazlitt cannot serve as a salutary warning, because he never tries to close off part of the conversation. He conveys, better than any other writer of any age, the charge and retreat of its battles, the skirmishes and stray shots, and trials of valor. Desertions are reported with unmerciful accuracy, and when the reporter cannot give his own name, he writes a letter with the signature SEMPER EGO AUDITOR. All this is carried off in a style that cannot be parodied, the style of a man who has listened to those whom he regards as his equals. It makes the great difference between Hazlitt and sages like Carlyle and Ruskin, whose every word carries the injunction, "Now, attend!" but whom we can hardly picture in the attitude of attending to someone else. And there is another difference: Hazlitt is angry without being a scold. Often, in the daily round of talk, he won arguments without wishing to reform his opponents altogether, or to make them over as disciples. Why should he put on a different face in his prose? (pp. 8-9)

In criticism, where Hazlitt would seem to have made his largest claim on us, he has come to be regarded impatiently. He is found wanting in theory, though prolific of "impressions"; welcomed into our reading lists, and read for the analogies he provides to critics of a more imposing dignity. We live at a time of immense sophistication in criticism, yet the state of our dealings with Hazlitt might suggest other thoughts than the consoling one that we have advanced beyond him. We operate on a narrower basis, with better-defined targets, perhaps. Yet Hazlitt's decline and our progress did not take place overnight. A. C. Bradley's *Oxford Lectures on Poetry* (1909) mention him frequently in company with the romantic poets, as a critic who made his share of mistakes, but still a writer of genius with whom it was dangerous to disagree. A few years later, T. S. Eliot receives him with some show of embarrassment, as a poor relation of the responsible critic, guilty of "crimes against taste," and worth the trouble of decapitating only because there is still a price on his head. Once he had been disposed of Hazlitt could be treated generously, and in *Literary Criticism: A Short History* W. K. Wimsatt describes him as "a kind of Addisonian spokesman for the romantic age, a very knowledgeable educator who blurted out secret meanings in quite plain prose." This is a compliment, though a strange one, given Hazlitt's low opinion of Addison. In any case Hazlitt, the spokesman and educator, has been deprived of the name of critic. What had happened, between 1909 and 1957, to make that possible, was the rise of academic criticism. (p. 13)

When Keats attended Hazlitt's lectures on poetry at the Surrey Institution, he went to hear not criticism but Hazlitt. Yet as he listened—as he revolved in his mind, along with certain phrases and ideas, some conception of the energies which the speaker himself appeared to exemplify—he began to think in a new way about poetry. His letters bear witness to his sense of the change; again and again they associate it with Hazlitt. Yet this is a sort of occurrence about which we have everything to learn. Keats praised a sentence of Hazlitt's as "a Whale's back in the Sea of Prose." We have lost the tact for such appreciation. Criticism now warns us against reducing poetry to statement, or against elevating it into statement, but we are baffled by the suggestion that critical prose be read as anything but statement. The audiences of Emerson, Ruskin, and Pater, like that of Hazlitt, went to criticism for something more than durable precepts; they searched out the intensities of the critic, his "sensations." Reading could lead to further sensations; it did not end in a "view." Compared with other masters of critical prose, Hazlitt seems at once stronger and subtler, infinitely finer in his modulations, and more stark in his shadings. We do not say of his description of a thing, "He has taken it up, and submerged it in his medium, and converted it into a Hazlitt-thing." Poetic statements, William Empson has said, "differ . . . from prosaic ones in imposing the system of habits they imply more firmly or more quickly." More firmly or more quickly; not more subtly or more completely. Prose too has its way with us in the end, and the better we come to know its by-roads and clearings, the longer we want to pause at the intervals it affords, and the less paradoxical it appears that the difference between poetry and prose should be a difference only of degree.

But Hazlitt's style is familiar to us in a way we feel almost too closely to understand. For it is still modern. The fact may be concealed through whole passages which seem to exist for the sake of a clenching epigram in Bacon's style: "Prosperity is a great teacher; adversity is a greater. Possession pampers the mind; privation trains and strengthens it." Yet a look at the context of such sayings generally reveals what different and unsententious motives underlie the conduct of Hazlitt's prose. In the foregoing sentences, from an essay **"On the Want of Money,"** he had been imagining the easy freedoms of "a man of rank and fortune" in letters, who is not obliged to pursue anything to the point of pedantry, or sink his pretensions deeply in the subject he writes on. The epigram occurs inconspicuously, in mid-paragraph, and is meant not to close the argument in favor of the imagined noble writer (someone like Byron), but to open it to the claims of a writer who has nothing to recommend him but his work (someone like Hazlitt). The argumentative valor and surprise of gestures like this prepare us for those aphorisms—chiefly collected in ***Characteristics,*** though a good anthology might be made from his earlier books—in which Hazlitt seems a precursor of Nietzsche, condensing into three lines the sort of psychological observation that issues in entire novels: "When the imagination is continually led to the brink of vice by a system of terror and denunciations, people fling themselves over the precipice from the mere dread of falling."

His prose is extraordinarily varied. It is also extraordinarily responsive, and he knew that he owed something of that quality to the luck of his birth. A writer who came of age as Hazlitt did, about 1800, found himself at a confluence of the Augustan and romantic idioms: Hazlitt was only more resourceful than others in feeling what this could mean. He could *choose* to retain the eighteenth-century pattern of balance and antithesis. In fact, Hazlitt carries on the inherited mode wherever it suits him, comfortably for any stretch of sentences, though as a rule he breaks it up before a paragraph is done. He also strives to create effects of an oratorical grandeur, like Burke's, with a fierceness that once it comes into his tone will have come to stay. He can be grave and clever, irritable and above dispute in the quick succession of his moods as his sentences move straight to the mark. The pace and consistency, the head-on stubbornness and willing imperfection of a man talking to you about what concerns him most are his constant strengths, and I know of no other writer in English who combines them. (pp. 14-16)

Readers of Hazlitt may seem peculiarly drawn to questions about influence and originality. The truth is that he never lets one forget them for long. Apart from the fragment on progress in the arts—an essay which he took the trouble to revise, reprint, and even quote approvingly but without attribution as the opinion of "a contemporary critic"—his further speculations on the subject have a way of surfacing at apparently unapt moments and usurping the privilege of other topics. A list of such moments would cover half of his writings on art; none is more striking than the sudden descent with which he brings to a close his ***Lectures on the English Poets:*** "I have felt my subject gradually sinking from under me as I advanced, and have been afraid of ending in nothing. The interest has unavoidably decreased at almost every successive step of the progress, like a play that has its catastrophe in the first or second act." The first act had been Shakespeare, the second Milton; after them, the flood: this is the lament of a baffled survivor.

Originality, as Hazlitt uses the word, is inseparable from such other words as *imagination, power,* and *sublimity.* In his first book, ***An Essay on the Principles of Human Action,*** Hazlitt proposed that the imagination, naturally outgoing, and so not naturally selfish, was the governing faculty of the mind. Being disinterested, however, it was not *a priori* good or evil; and its distinctive activity, the projection of a possible future, could lead with equal plausibility to sympathy or self-sympathy, to the sort of action we call altruistic or egoistic. There is thus a moral ambiguity implicit in every exertion of power to which the imagination moves us. The power of poetry which Hazlitt loved, and the power of tyranny which he hated, were not easy for him to confine within discrete categories, and he sometimes resigned himself to supposing that they were the same power. . . . A name that does not mislead us for the single aspect under which all power was comprehended by Hazlitt is the sublime. It was indeed the Burkean sublime of terror, of astonishment, and of privation—but still an experience as properly identified with the witness as with the participant. This conclusion is only a beginning; but it does show why Hazlitt's love of power was acceptable to himself.

By the strength of his speculations Hazlitt was equipped to be the most complex romantic exponent of an expressive poetics. The metaphysical sanction he required for this came from Hume's *Treatise of Human Nature:* "the memory, senses, and understanding [are] all of them founded on the imagination, or the vivacity of our ideas." What Hazlitt learned from that sentence and others, might be summed up in the phrase, *ideas travel.* Hence, the expressive and affective moments of art could be interpreted as a single extended movement of sympathetic imagining—the listener is moved as the speaker was himself moved. This was an empiricist's, not a pantheist's, community of feeling. Nevertheless it is commonly assumed that Hazlitt took his critical preconceptions from Coleridge. The honor of having been the first to say so goes to Coleridge himself: the person best situated to judge the truth of his claims was Charles Lamb, who regarded them as important chiefly to the history of spleen. Reason enough for doubting them can be found in the works of Hazlitt and Coleridge; and one ought in any case to be wary of confusing personal gratitude with intellectual debt. Coleridge begins as an enthusiastic associationist, names his son after the founder, then makes significant rumblings at so "necessitarian" a doctrine, and imagines he has disproved it. Hazlitt reads Hartley once, advances his objections, and keeps to them: he argues as a thinking disciple of Hume. (pp. 17-18)

Hazlitt's politics were in accord with his criticism. They are not, however, the self-conscious, the refined or anxious, politics of a literary man. For all his confessed hates, and his relish in saying that hatred with him was a more rooted passion than love, he speaks less against kings and aristocrats than on behalf of those whom they traduce. If an essay like **"What Is the People?"** moves with a high disdain far beyond the apprehension of the people themselves, he is capable of a humbler and not less persuasive eloquence. Reading in *The Statesman's Manual* of the dangers of nurturing a "Reading Public," he remembers how a friend once observed, "on seeing a little shabby volume of *Thomson's Seasons* lying in the window of a solitary ale-house, at the top of a rock hanging over the British Channel—*'That is true fame!'* If [Coleridge] were to write fifty Lay-Sermons, he could not answer the inference from this one sentence, which is, that there are books that make their way wherever there are readers, and that there ought every where to be readers for such books." (p. 19)

[Hazlitt] could not belong wholeheartedly to any one age however all-disposing its spirit. The critic of an intellectual movement who was himself, in his practice, committed to the premises of that movement, he had the faculty of holding two opposed ideas in his mind at the same time. And that is the stumbling-block he puts in the way of all who take satisfaction in knowing a critic's "stance": for, though never an obscure writer, he is often an ambivalent one. Some of his essays are deliberately constructed as arguments with himself; but even when they are not, turning at random to a page in his own voice, we are likely to find him arguing with propulsive force one side of a question against which he is happy to argue somewhere else. It is not skittishness, or mere versatility, but the unpredictable outcome of sympathy, of what he was content to call "a certain morbid interest in things." In this light the steadiness of principle of which he was justly proud looks like an effort to unite his warring impulses, and his assurance at the end—in the last words, "Well, I've had a happy life"—may have been in proportion to his initial despair at the undertaking. But if Hazlitt could not have predicted the extent of his struggle, and the toll it would exact, his idea of the imagination took exhaustive account of its necessity. This idea, propounded lucidly, after long reflection, and in the spirit of disinterested action that he never tired of praising in others, is what we ought most to honor in reading him. For it freed him to imagine other things. (pp. 22-3)

David Bromwich, in his Hazlitt: The Mind of a Critic, *Oxford University Press, 1983, 450 p.*

Joel Haefner   (essay date 1984)

[*In the following excerpt, Haefner explores Hazlitt's understanding of human character as it is conceptualized in his works.*]

"On the Pleasure of Painting" . . . is Hazlitt's prose portrait of portraiture: it is an attempt to re-create, in the reader, the texture of character which the viewer of art perceives. Hazlitt, re-enacting his role as a spectator in the Louvre, asks his readers to play their own parts as viewers of his work, and the truth so staged is the variety of human nature. The representation of character is the means by which artist and audience, essayist and reader, make most intimate contact. The word, like many of the critical terms in Hazlitt's lexicon, undergoes a number of transformations. In all its mutations, however, character refers to the unique qualities each individual possesses and, even more importantly, to the motives and springs of his or her actions. Such an essential nature, embodied in particularities, Hazlitt often called the "soul" of a person. Hazlitt wrote in **"On Personal Character"** that "the character, the internal, original bias, remains always the same, true to itself to the very last."

Character, this "internal, original bias," remained a constant factor in Hazlitt's thinking and writing throughout his career as an essayist. It played such a central role in Hazlitt's opus because he believed that the representation of human character imaginatively aroused his readers. . . . Hazlitt was in the mainstream of Romantic thought in his philosophical meditations on character; he was in the vanguard of Romantic artists in using character to shape and vitalize his periodical essays. (pp. 655-56)

Hazlitt laid the philosophical foundation for his notion of character in his 1805 "metaphysical discovery," *An Essay on the Principles of Human Action,* the fruition of Hazlitt's efforts "To anatomise the frame of social life," as Wordsworth called his own inquiry into "moral questions." Hazlitt divides the human mind into memory, appetite, and imagination, corresponding to the past, present, and future. The mind is self-reflexive; and furthermore each person is unique, because unique past experiences, linked peculiarly by association in the mind, are the constant objects of human thought. Individuals "differ in size, in complexion, in features, in the expression of their countenances, in age, in the events and actions of their lives, in situation, in knowledge, in temper, in power." As this last passage suggests, the nature of the human mind is loosely analogous to the singularities of the human face—an idea, though not new with Hazlitt, which nevertheless has pervasive importance for his aesthetics and his essayistic craft. The essence of human character is engraved on the face, Hazlitt believed; the modes of art which best capture character—portraiture and biography—are aesthetically and morally paramount precisely because they can re-create character and hence get to the roots of the human mind.

Given the essential uniqueness of human beings, how can we ever understand others and penetrate into their inner character, Hazlitt asks. The answer lies in the imagination. Unlike memory and self-consciousness, imagination is not self-centered; it deals with the future, not the past or present.

> The imagination, by means of which alone I can anticipate future objects, or be interested in them, must carry me out of myself into the feelings of others by one and the same process by which I am thrown forward as it were into my future being, and interested in it.

This power of imagination is the key to Hazlitt's model of human action and human relations. Not only is imagination a faculty shared by all human beings, but more importantly it is the means by which we penetrate into the character of others—it is the power that allows us to hear and record the soul speaking behind the masks of the crowds around us. . . . This power, the "natural benevolence" of the human mind, becomes a kind of benign demonic possession, a power which inflames the poet, the critic, *and* the reader—a point which has too often been overlooked.

In fact, by the logic of Hazlitt's moral argument, the true critic and the true reader must possess sympathetic imagination equally with the artist, or the basis of communication, and even the bonds of society, are lost. . . . Hazlitt's central statement about the imagination in his later writings falls at the end of **"On Reason and Imagination,"** an essay from *The Plain Speaker* (1826):

> Our feeling of general humanity is at once an aggregate of a thousand different truths, and it is also the same truth a thousand times told. As is our perception of this original truth, the root of our imagination, so will the force and richness of the general impression proceeding from it be. The boundary of our sympathy is a circle which enlarges itself according to its propulsion from the centre—the heart.

The sympathetic imagination is the faculty that allows us to experience our human diversity—that we all have unique pasts but we all share common modes of feeling and knowing.

Morally and ethically, Hazlitt's idea of sympathetic imagination, and his concomitant notion of the diversity of human character, explains how society can be rich in variety and still homogenous. Imagination, "our feeling of general humanity," is the realization that we are all different yet all alike. The consciousness of character, that humanity is creator, spectator, and object, underpins Hazlitt's prosaic apostrophe to Imagination. Since it was Hazlitt's belief that passionate imagination, not just pure reason, leads to truth, character and the nature of the human mind constitute an important feature of Hazlitt's ideas about writing. The essay cited above, **"On Reason and Imagination,"** opens with an attack on bloodless logicians, those

> who, deeming that all truth is contained within certain outlines and common topics, if you proceed to add colour or relief from individuality, protest against the use of rhetoric as an illogical thing; and if you drop a hint of pleasure or pain as ever entering into "this breathing world," raise a prodigious outcry against all appeals to the passions. . . . They stick to the table of contents, and never open the volume of the mind.

In Hazlitt's schema, writing has everything to do with human passions and the depiction of human character. The purpose of the writer *is* exactly to arouse passions, to call feeling to duty in the cause of speculation: "Those evils that inflame the imagination and make the heart sick, ought not to leave the head cool," Hazlitt wrote. Prose, real prose that matters, is "the glowing language of justifiable passion" which should not be attenuated into "cold indifference, . . . self-complacent sceptical reasoning," which takes "out the sting of indignation from the mind of the spectator." Logic is not to be abandoned, but enriched and invigorated through imagination.

Imaginatively arousing his readers was one of Hazlitt's primary aims. When he turns to criticizing and analyzing painting and painters, it is clear that he is as much concerned with the spectator's role in perceiving the work of art as he is in the artist's hand in creating it. At the Louvre, it was the revelations *he* felt when viewing art, not the artists' creative processes, which Hazlitt recorded and which he sought to convey to his readers. Particularly in painting, it is not the physical perception of art, but its inner impact on the viewer, on his or her sense, memory, and especially imagination, that is crucial to Hazlitt the critic. Hence the tangible artifact—the painting—is significant chiefly as the point at which artist and audience meet, as an act between two human beings. "In a word," Hazlitt wrote,

> the objects of fine art are not the objects of sight but as these last are the objects of taste and imagination, that is, as they appeal to the sense of beauty, of pleasure, and of power in the human breast, and are explained by that finer sense, and revealed in their inner structure to the eye in return.

For Hazlitt, the light of sense must go out before the full, imaginative meaning of art can be experienced. Significantly, Hazlitt is speaking here of the audience's imaginative, creative role, not the artist's function, as Wordsworth does when he conveys a similar idea in *The Prelude*. This is not an idea Hazlitt applies only to painting; it applies equally to poetry and all art. The object of art is not external reality but the universe within: "The arts of painting and poetry are conversant with the world of thought within us, and with the world of sense without us—with what we know, and see, and feel intimately."

Hence portraiture, which Hazlitt labeled "the biography of the pencil," is the apogee of art in Hazlitt's aesthetics; it is "the prototypical model for all expression in art" because it is *"a relation of self to self,"* as Kinnaird put it [see Further Reading]. "The more there is of character and feeling in any object" in art, Hazlitt wrote, "the closer will be the affinity between the imitation and the thing imitated."

The "affinity" between art and reality occurs through the "character and feeling" which both viewer and artist bring to the work of art. Such affinity, Hazlitt believed, must be conveyed through particular detail, through contrast and uniqueness. Titian's portraits (Hazlitt's favorites) display "the living principle": "the blood circulates here and there, the blue veins just appear." Hazlitt claims, with Boswell, that the finest biography catches the life of its subject through minute detail. "That is the best portrait," Hazlitt wrote, "which contains the fullest representation of the individual nature." Hazlitt opens his essay **"On the Knowledge of Character"** by declaring that a great portraitist can intuitively penetrate the deceptive masks of a man and "stamp his true character on the canvas, and betray the secret to posterity."

The noblest subject for a painter is, in Hazlitt's critical terminology, "character." . . . Portraiture ranks high in Hazlitt's canon because it does focus minutely on human character; and character is a keystone of his aesthetics because it is the means by which artist, writer, and audience are bound together.

Art, then, is as much a matter of seeing as vision, as much the altered viewpoint of the audience as the new world seen by the artist. The Great Masters of the Louvre were great because they cleansed the viewer's doors of perception. Rembrandt, Hazlitt declared,

> lived in and revealed to others a world of his own, and might be said to have invented a new view of nature. He did not discover things *out of* nature, . . . but saw things *in* nature that every one had missed before him, and gave others eyes to see them with.

For Hazlitt, Schneider notes [see Further Reading], "The greatness of Raphael and Titian consists . . . largely in their power to represent what is 'internal' in thought and feeling" and, in a different realm of art, "Shakespeare 'imitates that within which passeth shew.' "

The importance of character as a depiction of the internal nature of humanity, and as a conjunction of the artist's and readers' sympathetic imaginations, is a constant factor in Hazlitt's aesthetics and is not, as Schneider's analysis suggests, limited to painting. Besides portraiture, the fullest expression of character comes in drama, and more particularly in Shakespearean drama. Shakespeare was "like the genius of humanity," Hazlitt proclaimed, "changing places with all of us at pleasure, and playing

with our purposes as with his own." The quality Hazlitt most admired and revered in Shakespeare was his "generic quality," or, as Keats styled it, his "negative capability." Shakespeare's greatest triumph as a dramatist was his imaginative penetration of the diversity of human character, its uniqueness, and its uniformity.

Some of Hazlitt's ideas about Shakespeare may well have been borrowed from Wilhelm von Schlegel. Hazlitt quoted Schlegel's *Lectures on Dramatic Art* (translated by John Black in 1815) extensively and admiringly in the Preface to his ***Characters of Shakespear's Plays,*** and in fact Hazlitt reviewed Schlegel's *Lectures* for the *Edinburgh Review* in February 1816. . . . The features of Shakespeare's characters that Schlegel praises—and that Hazlitt repeats—are familiar from Hazlitt's earlier writings, especially his ***Principles of Human Action.*** Above all, it is the particularity, social diversity, passion, and imagination of Shakespeare's characters that most please Schlegel and Hazlitt. (pp. 656-62)

It is important to remember, Hazlitt says, that the greatest writers do not simply impose their personalities on their characters (as the French or Wordsworth would) in a kind of "egotistical sublime," but actually become—and allow their audience to become—those characters. "The true poet," Hazlitt wrote in the Preface to his ***Characters,*** "identifies the reader with the characters he represents; the French poet only identifies him with himself." The distinctive quality of modern literature is that it is "the poetry of effect," that it is affective at base. And modern tragedy in particular succeeds in affecting the viewer by "represent[ing] the soul utterly subdued. . . , or at least convulsed and overthrown by passion or misfortune."

Thus great drama, like all forms of great art, must display the soul speaking forth and must charge the reader with passionate participation. The means of doing so is, in Hazlitt's view, through character. The Romantic conception of character, which Hazlitt shared with Madame de Stäel, the Schlegel brothers, and Schelling, received its most philosophical formulation in Hegel's *Philosophy of Fine Art* where Hegel defines the Romantic idea of character as particular, self-subsistent (unique), and inward (an expression of "the *innermost* of soul-life"). Such an idea of character, which Hazlitt clearly shared, may have destroyed drama in the nineteenth century, as Robert Langbaum suggests [in his *The Poetry of Experience*], but if it did so, it created new forms, like the dramatic monologue, in its stead. One of the forms this Romantic notion of character reshaped was the periodical essay, particularly as Hazlitt crafted it.

Hazlitt has a humble estimation of his own place as an essayist. Essay-writing is far inferior to painting because it is worldly and contentious. Painting and poetry both aim at grandeur or beauty, while prose aims "to impart conviction," to "lay open the naked truth;" and truth-saying, as all academicians know, leads to the vicious arena of opinion. While the essayist/critic must not shrink from the truth, at the same time he must remain "disinterested," selfless:

> I would rather be a man of disinterested taste and liberal feeling, to see and acknowledge truth and beauty wherever I found it, than a man of greater and more original genius, to hate, envy, and deny all excellence but my own.

The good writer does not sacrifice taste to "egotism and vanity"; he feels as humanity does, as Isaac Bickerstaff and Montaigne did, and participates in that most human of activities, the workings of the sympathetic imagination. Since imagination is the link between writer and reader, then, in Hazlitt's aesthetic of the essay, the *ethos* of the narrator is significant. Hazlitt consciously adopted Montaigne's conversational and autobiographical qualities in his *Table-Talk* pieces, as he noted in the Advertisement to the Paris edition.

But the central task of the critic/essayist is not to convey a picture of himself—such would be an exercise in egotism—but to sympathetically "reflect the colours, the light and shade, the soul and body of a work." It is the *effect* of art on the reader's mind, how well the critic can convey the essence, the passion, and the tone of the work of art to the viewer that is the chief critical task. (pp. 662-64)

The essay can only achieve such power over its readers if it depicts detail. It is, like a true mirror or scrupulous minutes, uncompromisingly particular. Hazlitt here clearly says that the essay tears the mask away from humanity, penetrates to its inner nature, its character, and, just as importantly, performs the moral function of driving us into, and making us play out, the varieties of human experience. If Hazlitt praises detail and the exact word, and condemns "sounding generalities" and "tinkling phrases," it is because vacuity in prose tells us nothing about human nature and character. For Hazlitt the essayist, the sympathetic portrayal of others lies at the heart of the craft of essay-writing. Kinnaird remarks that

> Hazlitt continually sought, even in the familiar essays, to "go out of" himself . . . into the "character" of others, whether living, historical, or imaginary—to go from self-consciousness to "disinterested" sympathy or contemplation, where he could project and master his own conflicts in their generic form, as "contradiction and anomaly in the mind and heart of man" [see Further Reading].

Whether self-mastery was Hazlitt's motive is open to question; but he did clearly project himself into the characters of others, and, more importantly, sought to carry his readers with him. The drama of human character is not just Hazlitt's story; it is the story of all of us, "the same truth a thousand times told."

Such projection was central to Hazlitt's ethics and aesthetics, and pivotal to his craft as a journalist and persuasive critic. Nowhere can Hazlitt's preoccupation with character and its power to move the viewer be more clearly seen than in his comments on Edmund Kean's performances, particularly in the title role of *Othello.* Certainly it was Hazlitt's favorite, one which "may be reckoned among the consolations of the human mind."

Hazlitt was not content merely to describe the role of Othello or to recount Kean's acting. He also had to explain his own fascination with the character and arouse curiosity and excitement in the reader as well, charting his own imaginative involvement in the role so his readers could join the "game of human life" as well as the play. In a passage strikingly reminiscent of his comments on the English essay, Hazlitt, at the opening of his chapter on *Othello* in his *Characters of Shakespear's Plays,* tells us that tragedy

opens the chambers of the human heart. . . . It excites our sensibility by exhibiting the passions wound up to the utmost pitch by the power of imagination or the temptation of circumstances; and corrects their fatal excesses in ourselves by pointing to the greater extent of sufferings and of crimes to which they have led others. Tragedy creates a balance of the affections. It makes us thoughtful spectators in the lists of life.

Hazlitt, we recall, saw himself performing the same functions as an essayist that the dramatist does—to teach and forearm readers by letting them feel with and for others.

Hazlitt strove to draw his readers into the spirit of his characters by a number of means. In the sentence that follows, we are invited to join Hazlitt's passionate discourse by the use of second-person plural possessive pronouns; by the variety of "active" verbs; by the serial construction which culminates literally in a flood; and by the carefully modulated antitheses within that catalogue driving us deeper and deeper into the secret motivations of men.

> It is in working his [Othello's] noble nature up to this extremity through rapid but gradual transitions, in raising passion to its height from the smallest beginnings and in spite of all obstacles, in painting the expiring conflict between love and hatred, tenderness and resentment, jealousy and remorse, in unfolding the strength and weakness of our nature, in uniting sublimity of thought with the anguish of the keenest woe, in putting in motion the various impulses that agitate this our mortal being, and at last blending them in that noble tide of deep and sustained passion, impetuous but majestic, that "flows on to the Propontic, and knows no ebb," that Shakespear has shown the mastery of his genius and of his power over the human heart.

For Hazlitt, Shakespeare's pre-eminence as an artist resides in his affective impact on his audience, an impact effected through the depiction of a single human character that, in its broad outlines, is universal to all humans.

Shakespeare's artistic mastery of the diversity of human nature is accomplished through the powers of the sympathetic imagination. Hazlitt's conviction that Shakespeare's "generic quality," his ability to "throw his imagination out of himself " sets his drama above all others, has already been discussed; just as important for Hazlitt's criticism, however, is the realization that the critic and reader must throw themselves into Shakespeare's characters as well. It is a real test of imagination, for the critic must not only project himself into the characters as *written,* but into the characters as *played;* and he must try to carry his readers along on the current of his imagination. As a theater critic, Hazlitt had to present a portrait of the mind of the critic at work. Through that portrait, his readers could imaginatively experience the truth of universal human character which the actor on the boards was striving to deliver. Such a great performance on the part of the critic and the reader demands an equally rich performance from the actor; and so Hazlitt wrote with the greatest enthusiasm about the mercurial roles of Kean.

No one, in Hazlitt's eyes, filled Shakespeare's great roles as well as Edmund Kean, except perhaps Mrs. Siddons. Kean "exhibited all that energy and discrimination, that faculty of identifying himself with the character he represents," Hazlitt wrote. Hazlitt admits in the Preface to his

A View of the English Stage (1817), a collection of his dramatic essays from London newspapers, that Kean often disappointed him, because no actor could ever completely satisfy the critic's ideal of these Shakespearean characters; yet Kean came the closest because he conveyed the passion of the roles so powerfully. For Hazlitt, Othello was Kean's masterpiece. "Into the bursts, and starts, and torrents of the passion in Othello, this excellent actor appeared to have flung himself completely: there was all the fitful fever of the blood, the jealous madness of the brain: his heart seemed to bleed with anguish, while his tongue dropped broken, imperfect accents of woe." Kean's complete possession of the part appealed powerfully to Hazlitt. (pp. 664-67)

The stage "gives at once a body to our thoughts, and refinement and expansion to our sensible impressions," Hazlitt declared. In Hazlitt's view of the English stage, its undisputed master was Kean because he could so effectively embody that within which passeth shew. One of the critic's last tributes to the actor is among his finest and his most illuminating distillations of his affective aesthetics.

> To see him in this character [Othello] at his best, may be reckoned among the consolations of the human mind. It is to feel our hearts bleed by sympathy with another; it is to vent a world of sighs for another's sorrows; to have the loaded bosom "cleansed of that perilous stuff that weighs upon the soul," by witnessing the struggles and the mortal strokes that "flesh is heir to."

The great problem for the critic, as well as the actor, is how to deliver such experience to the reader. Hazlitt at several points complains of the impossibility of adequately describing a performance, especially one of Kean's: "the player's art is one that perishes with him, and leaves no trace of itself, but in the faint descriptions of the pen or pencil." Nevertheless, it is the only task of which he feels worthy and capable. Certainly Hazlitt felt keenly—and wants us to realize—the frustrations of authorship. At times, too, his irritation with the stupidity and insensitivity of his readers breaks through. But such complaints, we should recognize, are again attempts to make us join Hazlitt in his probings of human character. The difficulty of the task, and our obtuseness as readers, are challenges Hazlitt the critic sets us; if we take up the gauntlet, we are bound to be taunted and lured into that imaginative participation Hazlitt admired, aimed at, and achieved.

In some ways, Hazlitt's accounts of Kean playing Othello are an apotheosis of his ideas of character and of his efforts to take his readers into the labyrinth of real human nature. But we can see Hazlitt's concept of character coming into play in his criticism of painting, his biographical sketches, and his familiar essays. The Romantic idea of character, with its elements of particularity, diversity, passion, and imagination, is integral to Hazlitt's brand of writing, and while the concept was not Hazlitt's alone, he perhaps was one of its finest theorists and practitioners. Character, because it is at once unique to each person, yet universal in its contours, became the common denominator between writer and reader. The depiction of character was, for Hazlitt, the real stuff of the imagination; and hence the idea of character was important not only in Hazlitt's aesthetic but in his daily writing as well. The powerful portrayal of human character can win the hearts of readers,

and so "impart conviction" and "lay open the naked truth."

It is a mode of writing that has had a vast impact on the history of criticism and essay-writing after Hazlitt. . . . When he set out to catch the *Spirit of the Age,* Hazlitt chose a series of short, acutely probing biographies to do so. The former portraitist could have found no more congenial way to let his readers relive the tumult of his times than through portrayals of the human face divine. We are mistaken if we think that Hazlitt's character sketches are simply mirror images of the critic himself. He strove, above all else, to preserve the mortal, to let us hear the soul speaking in the face. (pp. 668-70)

> *Joel Haefner, " 'The Soul Speaking in the Face': Hazlitt's Concept of Character," in* Studies in English Literature, 1500-1900, *Vol. 24, No. 4, Autumn, 1984, pp. 655-70.*

FURTHER READING

Albrecht, W. P. "Liberalism and Hazlitt's Tragic View." *College English* 23, No. 2 (November 1961): 112-18.
  Concludes that although Hazlitt largely subscribed to the social and political principles of liberalism, he rejected the "non-tragic" worldview derived from the liberal doctrine of progress.

————. "Hazlitt on Wordsworth; or, The Poetry of Paradox." In *Six Studies in Nineteenth-Century English Literature and Thought,* edited by Harold Orel and George J. Worth, pp. 1-21. Lawrence: University of Kansas Publications, 1962.
  Focuses on Hazlitt's view of Wordsworth's poetry as "poetry of paradox," which Hazlitt defined as having "its origins in the French Revolution, or rather in those sentiments and opinions which produced that revolution" and being founded "on a principle of sheer humanity, on pure nature void of art."

Archer, William. Introduction to *Hazlitt on Theater,* edited by William Archer and Robert Lowe, pp. vii-xxx. New York: Hill and Wang, 1957.
  Account of Hazlitt as a playgoer and admirer of the theater.

Baker, Herschel. *William Hazlitt.* Cambridge: Harvard University Press, 1962, 530 p.
  Critical biography that places Hazlitt "in his literary, political, and philosophical milieu," and traces "the development and expression of his main ideas, relating them to the facts of his career in so far as these are known or can be ascertained."

Birrell, Augustine. *William Hazlitt.* London: MacMillan and Co., Limited, 1926, 230 p.
  Biography concluding with an evaluation of Hazlitt's character and genius.

Bloom, Harold, ed. *William Hazlitt.* New York: Chelsea House Publishers, 1986, 184 p.

Collection of critical essays by prominent Hazlitt scholars, including David Bromwich, John Kinnaird, and John L. Mahoney.

Review of *The Round Table: A Collection of Essays on Literature, Men, and Manners,* by William Hazlitt and Leigh Hunt. *The British Critic* VII (June 1817): 554-69.
Attacks the essays for their lack of moral instruction, declaring "supreme contempt for the talents, and pity for the bad principle displayed by" Hazlitt and Leigh Hunt.

Bromwich, David. "The Originality of Hazlitt's Essays." *The Yale Review* 72, No. 3 (Spring 1983): 366-84.
Discusses Hazlitt as "the first writer in English to have understood his task as the sort of trial that the word 'essay' by its etymology implies."

Bullitt, John M. "Hazlitt and the Romantic Conception of the Imagination." *Philological Quarterly* XXIV, No. 4 (October 1945): 343-61.
Cites Hazlitt's works as among the most explicit, consistent, and detailed explorations of the concept of the imagination in English romantic criticism.

Cecil, Lord David. "Hazlitt's Occasional Essays." In his *The Fine Art of Reading, and Other Literary Studies,* pp. 243-56. Indianapolis: Bobbs-Merrill Co., 1957.
Comments on Hazlitt's characteristics as a prose writer.

Chandler, Zilpha E. *An Analysis of the Technique of Addison, Johnson, Hazlitt, and Pater.* Iowa City: University of Iowa Press, 1928, 110 p.
Includes a technical, stylistic analysis of Hazlitt's "On Dryden and Pope."

Coleridge, S. T. *Biographia Literaria,* Vol. II., edited by J. Shawcross, pp. 311-314. Oxford: Clarendon Press, 1907.
Coleridge's response to an anonymous, unfavorable review of "Christabel" believed to have been written by Hazlitt.

Howe, P. P. *The Life of William Hazlitt.* London: Martin Secker, 1928, 484 p.
Sympathetic biography which extensively quotes from Hazlitt's writings and letters.

Ireland, Alexander. *William Hazlitt: Essayist and Critic.* London: Frederick Warne and Co., 1889, 510 p.
Selections of Hazlitt's writings with a biographical and critical memoir proclaiming Hazlitt one of the finest English men of letters "in instruction and delight."

Jones, Stanley. *Hazlitt: A Life from Winterslow to Frith Street.* Oxford: Clarendon Press, 1989, 397 p.
Examines the areas of Hazlitt's life that previous biographies have left obscure, such as the details of his disputes with his family and colleagues.

Ker, W. P. "Hazlitt." In *Collected Essays of W. P. Ker, Vol. 1,* edited by Charles Whibley, pp. 242-57. London: MacMillan, 1925.
Rambling appreciation of Hazlitt's works.

Kinnaird, John. *William Hazlitt: Critic of Power.* New York: Columbia University Press, 1978, 429 p.
Examines the life of Hazlitt as "the journey of a self-exploring mind revealed only through his works," characterizing Hazlitt as a "critic of power" whose criticism is informed by his "vision of the continuity of 'power' and its motives."

Lahey, Gerald. Introduction to *Liber Amoris: or, The New Pygmalion,* by William Hazlitt, pp. 1-48. New York: New York University Press, 1980.
Discusses the *Liber Amoris* as a "specifically 'Romantic' narrative expressing a notable phase of the temperament or imaginative sensibility of its period."

Law, Marie Hamilton. *The English Familiar Essay in the Early Nineteenth Century.* New York: Russell & Russell, 1965, 238 p.
Includes discussion of Hazlitt's contribution to the development of the familiar essay.

MacLean, Catherine MacDonald. *Born Under Saturn.* New York: MacMillan Co., 1944, 632 p.
Explores Hazlitt's life in relation to political struggles in France and England during the early nineteenth century.

Nabholtz, John R. "Modes of Discourse in Hazlitt's Prose." *The Wordsworth Circle* X, No. 1 (Winter 1979): 97-106.
Explores the many stylistic and tonal "controls, orders, and movements employed in [Hazlitt's] works."

Noxon, James. "Hazlitt as Moral Philosopher." *Ethics* LXXIII, No. 4 (July 1963): 279-83.
Discusses Hazlitt's theory of morality in *An Essay on the Principles of Human Action.*

Park, Roy. *Hazlitt and the Spirit of the Age.* Oxford: Clarendon Press, 1971, 259 p.
Examines Hazlitt's role in nineteenth-century scholarship concerning the nature of poetry and function of the artist, focusing on Hazlitt's objections to abstract thought.

Patterson, Charles I. "William Hazlitt as a Critic of Prose Fiction." *PMLA* LXVIII, No. 5 (December 1953): 1001-16.
Discusses Hazlitt's criticism of fiction and his influence on the development of the novel.

Pearson, Hesketh. *The Fool of Love.* New York: Harper & Brothers, 1934, 285 p.
Popular biography.

Praz, Mario. "Is Hazlitt a Great Essayist?" *English Studies* XIII, No. 1 (February 1931): 1-6.
Concludes that Hazlitt was a mediocre writer and thinker.

Priestley, J. B. *William Hazlitt.* London: Longmans, Green & Co., 1960, 38 p.
General essay on Hazlitt's life and work.

Ready, Robert. *Hazlitt at Table.* London: Associated University Presses, 1981, 126 p.
In-depth analysis of the unifying elements of the essays collected in *Table Talk.*

Sallé, J. C. "Hazlitt the Associationist." *The Review of English Studies* n.s. 15, No. 57 (1964): 38-51.
Argues that "the concept of a network of relations uniting the mind with nature occupies a central position in Hazlitt's thought."

Schneider, Elisabeth. *The Aesthetics of William Hazlitt.* 1933. Reprint. New York: Octagon, 1952, 205 p.
Places Hazlitt's aesthetic theories in the history of aesthetic thought.

Stapleton, Laurence. "William Hazlitt: The Essayist and the Moods of the Mind." In his *The Elected Circle: Studies in the Art of Prose,* pp. 93-118. New Jersey: Princeton University Press, 1973.

Offers an overview and analysis of Hazlitt's principal works.

Stephen, Leslie. "William Hazlitt." In his *Hours in a Library,* pp. 235-86. New York: G. P. Putnam's Sons, 1904.

General discussion of Hazlitt's character and works, concluding that if Hazlitt was "not a great rhetorician . . . [he] has yet an eloquence of his own."

Story, Patrick. "Hazlitt's Definition of the Spirit of the Age." *The Wordsworth Circle* VI, No. 2 (Spring 1975): 97-108.

Analyzes the meanings Hazlitt attached to the phrase "the spirit of the age" in his book of that title.

[Talfourd, T. N.]. Review of *Lectures on the Dramatic Literature of the Age of Elizabeth,* by William Hazlitt. *The Edinburgh Review* 34, No. LXVIII (November 1820): 438-49.

Favorable review of the lectures and a survey of their contents.

Uphaus, Robert W. *William Hazlitt.* Boston: Twayne, 1985, 119 p.

Biographical and critical study. Includes insightful discussion of Hazlitt's conception of "the moral, political, and literary uses of the imagination."

Wardle, Ralph M. *Hazlitt.* Lincoln: University of Nebraska Press, 1971, 530 p.

Critical biography.

Wellek, René. "Hazlitt, Lamb, and Keats." In his *A History of Modern Criticism: 1750-1950,* pp. 188-215. New Haven: Yale University Press, 1955.

Contends that the prefaces to the *Lyrical Ballads* by William Wordsworth and S. T. Coleridge "are clearly basic texts from which much of Hazlitt's own theory is derived."

Felicia Hemans

1793-1835

(Born Felicia Dorothea Browne) English poet and dramatist.

Hemans was one of the most popular and prolific poets of the early nineteenth century. Her works include long narrative poems and verse dramas, as well as such short lyric poems as "Casabianca" and "The Graves of a Household." Focusing on religious, patriotic, and domestic subjects, Hemans's verse was widely published throughout the nineteenth century.

Born into the family of a Liverpool merchant, Hemans spent her childhood in the Welsh countryside, an environment that fostered the love of natural beauty evident in much of her poetry. She was educated at home by her mother, who taught her German, French, Italian, Spanish, and Portuguese. In addition, she studied Latin and wrote verse. Two volumes of poetry, *Poems* and *England and Spain,* published in 1808 when she was fourteen, displayed her wide reading, technical facility, and a propensity for natural description and historical subjects. While they attracted little critical attention, they established Hemans's reputation as a poet of promise. These were followed in 1812 by *The Domestic Affections, and Other Poems,* a collection of poems about family life; it was also during this year that Hemans married. Despite the demands of a growing family, she continued to write, producing such well-received works as *The Restoration of the Works of Art to Italy* in 1816 and *Modern Greece* in 1817. For undocumented reasons, she and her husband separated in 1819. While Hemans never referred to her failed marriage, biographers speculate that her husband might not have been sympathetic to her literary pursuits, and some commentators have attributed the pathos in many of Hemans's poems after this date to the breakup of her family. During the next decade, Hemans supported her five sons by publishing numerous volumes of verse, including *Tales and Historic Scenes in Verse, The Sceptic, The Forest Sanctuary, and Other Poems,* and the verse drama *The Siege of Valencia.* By 1826, her popular and critical reputation prompted a complete edition of her works in the United States, and her poems became widely imitated. Hemans continued to write throughout the last years of her life; she died in Dublin in 1835.

As a poet, Hemans is noted for her emphasis on such Romantic subjects as the beauty of nature, poetic inspiration, and freedom. While Romantic in subject, Hemans's works generally emulate eighteenth-century Neoclassical poetic forms and ideology. For example, *The Sceptic* supports the eighteenth-century religious principles of deism, and *Modern Greece* decries the passing of the civilization of Classical antiquity. These works are also cited as examples of Hemans's adherence to Neoclassical poetic conventions in meter, rhyme, and diction. Hemans's poetry is further distinguished by religious, patriotic, and historical subjects, as illustrated by *The Sceptic, National Lyrics and Songs for Music,* and *Tales and Historic Scenes in Verse.* Other typical aspects of her works are exotic locales and the evocation of a sentimental mood. During the nineteenth century, Hemans was much admired for what were termed the moral and feminine qualities of her works, and her verse influenced popular taste in poetry long after her death. More illustrious writers, including Lord Byron, William Wordsworth, and Sir Walter Scott, admired selected works of Hemans, although their reaction, summarized by Scott's remarks that Hemans's poetry was "too poetical," bearing "too many flowers . . . too little fruit," was less enthusiastic than that of the public. Modern critical consensus holds that most of Hemans's works lack depth and do not translate well from her age to the present. Nonetheless, a number of her poems continue to be anthologized, and her works retain importance as indicators of the values and sensibility of the reading audience of the nineteenth century.

PRINCIPAL WORKS

England and Spain (poetry) 1808
Poems (poetry) 1808
The Domestic Affections, and Other Poems (poetry) 1812

The Restoration of the Works of Art to Italy (poetry) 1816

Modern Greece (poetry) 1817

Translations from Camoens and Other Poets, with Original Poetry (translations and poetry) 1818

Tales and Historic Scenes in Verse (poetry) 1819

The Sceptic (poetry) 1820

Stanzas to the Memory of the Late King (poetry) 1820

Dartmoor (poetry) 1821

The Siege of Valencia. The Last Constantine, with Other Poems (poetry) 1823

The Vespers of Palermo (drama) 1823

The Forest Sanctuary, and Other Poems (poetry) 1825

Records of Woman, with Other Poems (poetry) 1828

Songs of the Affections, with Other Poems (poetry) 1830

Hymns for Childhood (poetry) 1833

National Lyrics and Songs for Music (poetry) 1834

Scenes and Hymns of Life, with Other Religious Poems (poetry) 1834

The Works of Mrs. Hemans. 7 vols. (poetry and verse dramas) 1839

The Quarterly Review (essay date 1820)

[*In the following excerpt, the critic appraises several of Hemans's works.*]

This certainly is not the age in which those who speak slightingly of female talent should expect to be listened to with much attention. In almost every department of literature, and in many of art and science, some one or other of our own contemporaries and countrywomen will be found, in spite of all the disadvantages of an imperfect education, occupying a respectable, at least, if not a prominent situation. And this remark, if true any where, is undoubtedly so when applied to poetry: no judicious critic will speak without respect of the tragedies of Miss Baillie, or the *Psyche* of Mrs. Tighe; and, unless we deceive ourselves greatly, the author of [*The Restoration of the Works of Art to Italy; Tales and Historic Scenes in Verse; Translations from Camoens and Other Poets, with Original Poems; The Sceptic, a Poem;* and *Stanzas to the Memory of the Late King*] . . . requires only to be more generally known and read to have her place assigned at no great distance from that of the two distinguished individuals just mentioned. Mrs. Hemans indeed, if we may judge from her writings, is not merely a clever woman, but a woman of very general reading, and of a mind improved by reflection and study. There is another circumstance about these poems in which we cannot well be deceived, and which demands notice, the progressive and rapid improvement of them; not five years have elapsed from the appearance of the first to that of the last, and the difference of the two is very surprising; the merits of the one are little more than correct language, smooth versification, and chaste ideas; the last, written on a difficult subject, is one of the most able productions of the present day. The facility given by practice may have done much towards this; but when the improvement is principally in the richness and novelty of thought, careful study and diligent training of the reason must have borne a much larger share. If we

may judge too of her, in another point, from her writings, Mrs. Hemans is a woman in whom talent and learning have not produced the ill effects so often attributed to them; her faculties seem to sit meekly on her, at least we can trace no ill humour or affectation, no misanthropic gloom, no querulous discontent; she is always pure in thought and expression, cheerful, affectionate, and pious. It is something at least to know, that whether the emotions she excites be always those of powerful delight or not, they will be at least harmless, and leave no sting behind: if our fancies are not always transported, our hearts at least will never be corrupted: we have not found a line which a delicate woman might blush to have written. When speaking of an English lady this ought to be no more than common praise, for delicacy of feeling has long been, and long may it be, the fair and valued boast of our countrywomen; but we have had too frequent reason of late to lament, both in female readers and writers, the display of qualities very opposite in their nature. Their tastes, at least, have not escaped the infection of that pretended liberality, but real licentiousness of thought, the plague and the fearful sign of the times. Under its influence they lose their relish for what is simple and sober, gentle or dignified, and require the stimulus of excessive or bitter passion, of sedition, of audacious profaneness. Certain we are, that the most dangerous writer of the present day finds his most numerous and most enthusiastic admirers among the fair sex; and we have many times seen very eloquent eyes kindle in vehement praise of the poems, which no woman should have read, and which it would have been far better for the world if the author had never written. This is a melancholy subject on which we have much to say at a fit opportunity, but which it would not satisfy us to treat so cursorily as our present limits would render necessary:—with Mrs. Hemans, at least, such thoughts as it suggests have no connection, and we will not, therefore, any longer detain our readers with general remarks, but give them a brief account of her several poems, with such extracts and observations as may serve to justify what we have before advanced respecting the author. The earliest on the list is a Poem on *The Restoration of the Works of Art to Italy,* and, as we have intimated above, is decidedly inferior to all that follow it. We do not think the subject, indeed, very happily chosen, except for a very short and spirited sketch: when treated of at so much length as by Mrs. Hemans, it was sure to lose all unity, and be broken up into a number of separate descriptions, which, even if very truly drawn and striking, when severally examined, can never form a complete whole. The versification, however, is always flowing, though the style wants clearness and compression.

The next volume, the *Tales and Historic Scenes,* is a collection, as the title imports, of Narrative Poems. (pp. 130-31)

The principal poem in this volume is the **'Abencerrage'**; it commemorates the capture of Granada by Ferdinand and Isabella, and attributes it in great measure to the revenge of Hamet, chief of the Abencerrages, who had been induced to turn his arms against his countrymen, the Moors, in order to procure the ruin of their king, the murderer of his father and brothers. During the siege he makes his way by night to the bower of Zayda his beloved, the daughter of a rival and hated family; her character is very finely drawn, and she repels with firmness all the solicitations and prayers of the traitor to his country. The following lines form part of their dialogue;—they are spirited and pathetic, but perfectly free from exaggeration.

> Oh wert thou still what once I fondly deem'd,
> All that thy mien express'd, thy spirit seem'd,
> My love had been devotion—till in death
> Thy name had trembled on my latest breath.
> But not the chief, who leads a lawless band
> To crush the altars of his native land;
> The apostate son of heroes, whose disgrace
> Hath stain'd the trophies of a glorious race;
> Not *him* I lov'd—but one whose youthful name
> Was pure and radiant in unsullied fame.
> Hadst thou but died ere yet dishonour's cloud
> O'er that young name had gather'd as a shroud,
> I then had mourn'd thee proudly—and my grief
> In its own loftiness had found relief,
> A noble sorrow, cherish'd to the last,
> When every meaner woe had long been past.
> Yes, let affection weep—no common tear
> She sheds when bending o'er a hero's bier;
> Let nature mourn the dead—a grief like this,
> To pangs that rend *my* bosom, had been bliss.

The next volume in order consists principally of translations. It will give our readers some idea of Mrs. Hemans's acquaintance with books, to enumerate the authors from whom she has chosen her subjects; they are Camoens, Metastasio, Filicaja, Pastorini, Lope de Vega, Franciso Manuel, Della Casa, Cornelio Bentivoglio, Quevedo, Juan de Tarsis, Torquato and Bernardo Tasso, Petrarca, Pietro Bembo, Lorenzini, Gessner, Chaulieu, Garcilaso de Vega; names embracing almost every language in which the Muse has found a tongue in Europe. Many of these translations are very pretty, but it would be less interesting to select any of them for citation, as our readers might not be possessed of, or acquainted with the originals. We will pass on, therefore, to the latter part of the volume, which contains much that is very pleasing and beautiful. The poem which we are about to transcribe is on a subject often treated; and no wonder:—it would be hard to find another which embraces so many of the elements of poetic feeling; so soothing a mixture of pleasing melancholy and pensive hope; such an assemblage of the ideas of tender beauty, of artless playfulness, of spotless purity, of transient yet imperishable brightness, of affections wounded, but not in bitterness, of sorrows gently subdued, of eternal and undoubted happiness. We know so little of the heart of man, that when we stand by the grave of him whom we deem most excellent, the thought of death will be mingled with some awe and uncertainty; but the gracious promises of Scripture leave no doubt as to the blessedness of departed infants, and when we think what they now are, and what they might have been; what they now enjoy, and what they might have suffered; what they have now gained, and what they might have lost; we may, indeed, yearn to follow them; but we must be selfish indeed to wish them again 'constrained' to dwell in these tenements of pain and sorrow. The dirge of a child, which follows, embodies these thoughts and feelings, but in more beautiful order and language.

> No bitter tears for thee be shed,
> Blossom of being! seen and gone!
> With flowers alone we strew thy bed,
>   O blest departed one!
> Whose all of life, a rosy ray,
> Blushed into dawn, and passed away.

> Yes, thou art gone, ere guilt had power
> To stain thy cherub soul and form!
> Clos'd is the soft ephemeral flower
>   That never felt a storm!
> The sunbeam's smile, the zephyr's breath,
> All that it knew from birth to death.

> Thou wert so like a form of light,
> That heaven benignly called thee hence,
> Ere yet the world could breathe one blight
>   O'er thy sweet innocence:
> And thou that brighter home to bless
> Art passed with all thy loveliness.

> Oh hadst thou still on earth remain'd,
> Vision of beauty, fair as brief,
> How soon thy brightness had been stain'd
>   With passion, or with grief!
> Now not a sullying breath can rise
> To dim thy glory in the skies.

> We rear no marble o'er thy tomb,
> No sculptured image there shall mourn,
> Ah! fitter far the vernal bloom
>   Such dwelling to adorn.
> Fragrance and flowers and dews must be
> The only emblems meet for thee.

> Thy grave shall be a blessed shrine,
> Adorn'd with nature's brightest wreath,
> Each glowing season shall combine
>   Its incense there to breathe;
> And oft upon the midnight air
> Shall viewless harps be murmuring there.

> And oh! sometimes in visions blest,
> Sweet spirit, visit our repose,
> And bear from thine own world of rest
>   Some balm for human woes.
> What form more lovely could be given
> Than thine to messenger of heaven?

Had Mrs. Hemans stopped here, she might have claimed a considerable share of praise for elegant composition; but her last two publications are works of a higher stamp—works, indeed, of which no living poet need to be ashamed. The first of them is entitled *The Sceptic,* and is devoted, as our readers will easily anticipate, to advocating the cause of religion. Undoubtedly the poem must have owed its being to the circumstances of the times, to a laudable indignation at the course which literature in many departments seemed lately to be taking in this country, and at the doctrines disseminated with industry, principally (but by no means exclusively, as has been falsely supposed), among the lower orders. Mrs. Hemans, however, does not attempt to reason learnedly or laboriously in verse; few poems, ostensibly philosophical, or didactic, have ever been of use, except to display the ingenuity and talent of the writers; people are not often taught a science or an art in poetry, and much less will an infidel be converted by a theological treatise in verse. But the argument of *The Sceptic* is one of irresistible force to confirm a wavering mind; it is simply resting the truth of religion on the necessity of it, on the utter misery and helplessness of man without it. This argument is in itself available for all the purposes of poetry; it appeals to the imagination and passions of man, it is capable of interesting all our affectionate hopes and charities, of acting upon all our natural fears. Mrs. Hemans has gone through this range with great feeling and ability, and when she comes to the mind that has clothed itself in its own strength, and relying proudly on that alone in the hour of affliction, has sunk into distraction in the contest, she rises into a strain of moral poetry not often surpassed.

> Oh what is nature's strength? the vacant eye
> By mind deserted hath a dread reply,
> The wild delirious laughter of despair,
> The mirth of phrenzy—seek an answer there!
> Turn not away, though pity's cheek grow pale,
> Close not thine ear against their awful tale.
> They tell thee, reason wandering from the ray
> Of faith, the blazing pillar of her way,
> In the mid-darkness of the stormy wave
> Forsook the struggling soul she could not save.
> Weep not, sad moralist, o'er desert plains
> Strew'd with the wrecks of grandeur—mouldering fanes
> Arches of triumph, long with weeds o'ergrown—
> And regal cities, now the serpent's own:
> Earth has more awful ruins—one lost mind
> Whose star is quench'd, hath lessons for mankind
> Of deeper import, than each prostrate dome
> Mingling its marble with the dust of Rome.
>
> (pp. 132-35)

The last poem is to the memory of his late Majesty: unlike courtly themes in general, this is one of the deepest, and most lasting interest. Buried as the King had long been in mental and visual darkness, and dead to the common joys of the world, his death, perhaps, did not occasion the shock, or the piercing sorrow which we have felt on some other public losses; but the heart must be cold indeed, that could, on reflection, regard the whole fortune and fate of that venerable, gallant, tender-hearted and pious man, without a more than common sympathy. There was something in his character so truly national; his very errors were of so amiable a kind, his excellencies bore so high a stamp, his nature was so genuine and unsophisticated, he stood in his splendid court amidst his large and fine family, so true a husband, so good a father, so safe an example; he so thoroughly understood the feelings, and so duly appreciated the virtues, even the uncourtly virtues of his subjects; and, with all this, the sorrows from heaven rained down upon his head in so 'pitiless and pelting a storm',—all these—his high qualities and unparalleled sufferings form such a subject for poetry, as nothing, we should imagine, but its difficulty and the expectation attending it, would prevent from being seized upon by the greatest poets of the day. We will not say that Mrs. Hemans has filled the whole canvass as it might have been filled, but unquestionably her poem is beyond all comparison with any which we have seen on the subject; it is full of fine and pathetic passages, and it leads us up through all the dismal colourings of the fore-ground to that bright and consoling prospect, which should close every Christian's reflections on such a matter. (p. 137)

Our readers will have seen, and we do not deny, that we have been much interested by our subject: who or what Mrs. Hemans is, we know not; we have been told that, like a poet of antiquity,

> ———Tristia vitæ
> Solatur cantu———

if it be so (and the most sensible breasts are not uncommonly nor unnaturally the most bitterly wounded), she seems from the tenor of her writings to bear about her a higher and a surer balsam than the praises of men, or even the 'sacred muse' herself can impart. Still there is a plea-

sure, an innocent and an honest pleasure, even to a wounded spirit, in fame fairly earned; and such fame as may wait upon our decision, we freely and conscientiously bestow:—in our opinion all her poems are elegant and pure in thought and language; her later poems are of higher promise, they are vigorous, picturesque, and pathetic. (p. 139)

> *A review of "The Restoration of the Works of Art to Italy" and Others, in* The Quarterly Review, *Vol. XXIV, No. XLVII, October, 1820, pp. 103-39.*

George Bancroft   (essay date 1827)

[*Bancroft was an American poet, diplomat, and historian most often remembered for his well-documented, multivolume* History of the United States from the Discovery of the American Continent *(1834-74). In the following excerpt, Bancroft praises the moral, religious, and feminine aspects of Hemans's poems and plays.*]

Had [Mrs. Hemans's] writings been merely harmless, we should not have entered into an analysis of them; but the moral charm, which is spread over them, is so peculiar, so full of nature and truth and deep feeling, that her productions claim at once the praise of exquisite purity and poetic excellence. She adds the dignity of her sex to a high sense of the duties of a poet; she writes with buoyancy, yet with earnestness; her poems bear the impress of a character worthy of admiration. In the pursuit of literary renown she never forgets what is due to feminine reserve. We perceive a mind, endowed with powers to aspire; and are still further pleased to find no unsatisfied cravings, no passionate pursuit of remote objects, but high endowments, graced by contentment. There is plainly the consciousness of the various sorrows to which life is exposed, and with it the spirit of resignation. She sets before herself a clear and exalted idea of what a female writer should be, and is on the way to realize her own idea of excellence. Living in domestic retirement in a beautiful part of Wales, it is her own feelings and her own experience, which she communicates to us. We cannot illustrate our meaning better than by introducing our readers at once to Mrs Hemans herself, as she describes to us the occupations of a day.

> **"An Hour of Romance"**
> There were thick leaves above me and around,
> And low sweet sighs, like those of childhood's sleep,
> Amidst their dimness, and a fitful sound
> As of soft showers on water—dark and deep
> Lay the oak shadows o'er the turf, so still,
> They seem'd but pictur'd glooms—a hidden rill
> Made music, such as haunts us in a dream,
> Under the fern tufts; and a tender gleam
> Of soft green light, as by the glowworm shed,
> Came pouring through the woven beech boughs down,
> And steep'd the magic page wherein I read
> Of royal chivalry and old renown,
> A tale of Palestine.—Meanwhile the bee
> Swept past me with a tone of summer hours,
> A drowsy bugle, wafting thoughts of flowers,
> Blue skies, and amber sunshine—brightly free,
> On filmy wings the purple dragonfly
> Shot glancing like a fairy javelin by;
> And a sweet voice of sorrow told the dell
> Where sat the lone wood-pigeon.

But ere long,
All sense of these things faded, as the spell,
Breathing from that high gorgeous tale, grew strong
On my chain'd soul—'twas not the leaves I heard;
—A Syrian wind the lion-banner stirr'd,
Through its proud floating folds—'twas not the brook,
Singing in secret through its grassy glen—
A wild shrill trumpet of the Saracen
Peal'd from the desert's lonely heart, and shook
The burning air.—Like clouds when winds are high,
O'er glittering sands flew steeds of Araby,
And tents rose up, and sudden lance and spear
Flash'd where a fountain's diamond wave lay clear,
Shadow'd by graceful palm-trees.—Then the shout
Of merry England's joy swell'd freely out,
Sent through an Eastern heaven, whose glorious hue
Made shields dark mirrors to its depths of blue;
And harps were there—I heard their sounding strings,
As the waste echoed to the mirth of kings.

The bright masque faded—unto life's worn track
What call'd me, from its flood of glory, back?
—A voice of happy childhood!—and they pass'd,
Banner, and harp, and Paynim trumpet's blast—
Yet might I scarce bewail the vision gone,
My heart so leapt to that sweet laughter's tone.

The poetry is here as beautiful as the scene described is quiet and pleasing. It forms an amiable picture of the occupations of a contemplative mind. The language, versification, and imagery are of great merit, the beauties of nature described by a careful observer; the English scene is placed in happy contrast with the Eastern, and the dream of romance pleasantly disturbed by the cheerfulness of life. But we make but sorry work at commenting on what the reader must feel. (pp. 449-50)

In 1820 Mrs Hemans published *The Sceptic*, a poem of great merit for its style and its sentiments, of which we shall give a rapid sketch. She considers the influence of unbelief on the affections and gentler part of our nature, and, after pursuing the picture of the misery consequent on doubt, shows the relief that may be found in the thoughts that have their source in immortality. Glancing at pleasure as the only resort of the skeptic, she turns to the sterner tasks of life.

E'en youth's brief hours,
Survive the beauty of their loveliest flowers. . . .
The soul's pure flame the breath of storms must fan,
And pain and sorrow claim their nursling—Man.

But then the skeptic has no relief in memory, for memory recalls no joys, but such as were transitory, and known to be such; and as for Hope,

She, who like Heaven's own sunbeam smiles for all,
Will *she* speak comfort? Thou hast shorn her plume,
That might have raised thee far above the tomb,
And hush'd the only voice whose angel tone
Sooths, when all melodies of joy are flown.

The poet then asks, if an infidel dare love; and, having no home for his thoughts in a better world, nurse such feelings as delight to enshrine themselves in the breast of a parent. She addresses him on the insecurity of an attachment to a vain idol, from which death may at any time divide him *'forever.'*

If there be sorrow in a parting tear,
Still let *'forever'* vibrate on thine ear.
. . . . . .

It is not thine to raise
To you pure heaven, thy calm confiding gaze,
No gleam reflected from that realm of rest,
Steals on the darkness of thy troubled breast;
Not for thine eye shall Faith divinely shed
Her glory round the image of the dead;
And if, when slumber's lonely couch is prest,
The form departed be thy spirit's guest,
It bears no light from purer worlds to this;
Thy future lends not e'en a dream of bliss.

For relief the infidel is referred to the Christian religion, in a strain, which unites the fervor of devotion with poetic sensibility.

But perhaps the skeptic scorns the advice, and like the heathen who was chained to a rock to be the constant prey of the vulture, for whom he himself produced sustenance, the pride of reason may support the infidel principles which gnaw at his heart. To him the mirth of frenzy, the laughter of delirious despair must read a lesson.

They tell thee, reason, wandering from the ray
Of Faith, the blazing pillar of her way,
In the mid darkness of the stormy wave,
Forsook the struggling soul she could not save.
Weep not, sad moralist! o'er desert plains,
Strew'd with the wrecks of grandeur—mouldering fanes,
Arches of triumph, long with weeds o'ergrown,
And regal cities, now the serpent's own;
Earth has more awful ruins—one lost mind,
Whose star is quench'd, hath lessons for mankind
Of deeper import than each prostrate dome,
Mingling its marble with the dust of Rome.

The poem proceeds to depict in a forcible manner, the unfortunate state of a mind, which acquires every kind of knowledge but that which gives salvation, and, having gained possession of the secrets of all ages, and communed with the majestic minds that shine along the pathway of time, neglects nothing but eternity. Such an one, in the season of suffering, finds relief in suicide, and escapes to death as to an eternal rest. The thought of death recurs to the mind of the poet, and calls forth a fervent prayer for the divine presence and support in the hour of dissolution; for the hour, when the soul is brought to the mysterious verge of another life, is an 'awful one.'

In the pride
Of youth and health, by sufferings yet untried,
We talk of death, as something, which 't were sweet
In Glory's arms exultingly to meet,
A closing triumph, a majestic scene,
Where gazing nations watch the hero's mien,
As undismay'd amidst the tears of all,
He folds his mantle regally to fall!
    Hush, fond enthusiast! still obscure and lone,
Yet not less terrible because unknown,
Is the last hour of thousands;—they retire
From life's throng'd path, unnoticed to expire,
As the light leaf, whose fall to ruin bears
Some trembling insect's little world of cares,
Descends in silence—while around waves on
The mighty forest, reckless what is gone!
Such is man's doom—and, ere an hour be flown,
—Start not, thou trifler!—such may be thine own.

This is followed by an allusion to the strong love of life which belongs to human nature, and the instinctive apprehension with which the parting mind, musing on its future condition, asks of itself mystic questions, that it cannot solve. But through the influence of religion,

> He, whom the busy world shall miss no more
> Than morn one dewdrop from her countless store,
> Earth's most neglected child, with trusting heart,
> Call'd to the hope of glory, shall depart.

After some lines expressing the spirit of English patriotism, in a manner with which foreigners can only be pleased, the poem closes with the picture of a mother, teaching her child the first lessons of religion by holding up the divine example of the Savior.

We have been led into a longer notice of this poem, for it illustrates the character of Mrs Hemans's manner. We perceive in it a loftiness of purpose, an earnestness of thought, sometimes made more interesting by a tinge of melancholy, a depth of religious feeling, a mind alive to all the interests, gratifications, and sorrows of social life. (pp. 451-53)

The *Vespers of Palermo* was the earliest of the dramatic productions of our author. The period in which the scene is laid, is sufficiently known from the title of the play. The whole is full of life and action. The same high strain of moral propriety marks this piece, as all others of her writings. The hero is an enthusiast for glory, for liberty, and for virtue; and on his courage, his forbearance, the integrity of his love, making the firmness of his patriotism appear doubtful, rests the interest of the plot. It is worthy of remark, that some of its best parts have already found their way into an excellent selection of pieces for schools, and thus contribute to give lessons of morality to those who are most susceptible of the interest of tragedy. (p. 454)

The *Siege of Valencia* is a dramatic poem, but not intended for representation. The story is extremely simple. The Moors, who besiege Valencia, take the two sons of the governor, Gonzalez, captive, as they came to visit their father; and now the ransom demanded for them is the surrender of the city; they are to die, if the place is not yielded up. Elmina, the mother of the boys, and Ximena, their sister, are the remaining members of a family, to which so dreadful an option is submitted. The poem is one of the highest merit. The subject is of great dignity, being connected with the defence of Spain against the Moors, and at the same time it is of the greatest tenderness, offering a succession of the most moving scenes that can be imagined to occur in the bosom of a family. The father is firm; the daughter is heroic; the mother falters. She finds her way to the Moorish camp, sees her children, forms a plan for betraying the town, and then is not able to conceal her grief and her design from her husband. He immediately sends a defiance to the Moors; his children are brought out and beheaded; a *sortie* is made from the besieged city; finally the king of Spain arrives to the rescue, the wrongs of Gonzalez are avenged; he himself dies in victory, and the poem closes with a picture of his wife, moved by the strongest grief, of which she is yet able to restrain the expression. The great excellence of the poem lies in the delineation of the struggle between the consciousness of duty and maternal fondness. We believe none but a mother could have written it. (pp. 454-55)

We will now say a few words of *The Forest Sanctuary.* But it so abounds with beauty, is so highly finished, and animated by so generous a spirit of moral heroism, that we can do no justice to our views of it in the narrow space, which our limits allow us. A Spanish Protestant flies from persecution at home to religious liberty in America. He has imbibed the spirit of our own fathers, and his mental struggles are described in verses, with which the descendants of the pilgrims must know how to sympathize. We dare not enter on an analysis. (p. 457)

It has been said, that religion can never be made a subject of interest in poetry. The position is a false one, refuted by the close alliance between poetic inspiration and sacred enthusiasm. Irreligion has certainly no place in poetry. There may have been atheist philosophers; an atheist poet is an impossibility. The poet may doubt and reason like Hamlet, but the moment he acquiesces in unbelief, there is an end to the magic of poetry. Imagination can no longer throw lively hues over the creation; the forests cease to be haunted; the sea, and the air, and the heavens to teem with life. The highest interest, we think, attaches to Mrs Hemans's writings, from the spirit of Christianity which pervades them.

The poetry of our author is tranquillizing in its character, calm and serene. We beg pardon of the lovers of excitement, but we are seriously led to take notice of this quality as of a high merit. A great deal has been said of the sublimity of directing the passions; we hold it a much more difficult, and a much more elevated task, to restrain them; it may be sublime to ride on the whirlwind, and direct the storm; but it seems to us still more sublime to appease the storm, and still the whirlwind. (pp. 459-60)

It is the high praise of Mrs Hemans's poetry, that it is feminine. The sex may well be pleased with her productions, for they could hardly have a better representative in the career of letters. All her works seem to come from the heart, to be natural and true. The poet can give us nothing but the form under which the objects he describes present themselves to his own mind. That form must be noble, or it is not worthy of our consideration; it must be consistent, or it will fail to be true. Now in the writings of Mrs Hemans we are shown, how life and its concerns appear to woman; and hear a mother entrusting to verse her experience and observation. So in 'The Hebrew Mother,' 'the spring tide of nature' swells high as she parts from her son, on devoting him to the service of the temple.

> Alas! my boy, thy gentle grasp is on me,
> The bright tears quiver in thy pleading eyes,
>   And now fond thoughts arise.
> And silver cords again to earth have won me;
> And like a vine thou claspest my full heart—
>   How shall I hence depart?
>
> And oh! the home whence thy bright smile hath parted,
> Will it not seem as if the sunny day
>   Turn'd from its door away?
> While through its chambers wandering, wearyhearted,
> I languish for thy voice, which past me still
>   Went like a singing rill?
>
> I give thee to thy God—the God that gave thee,
> A wellspring of deep gladness to my heart!
>   And precious as thou art,
> And pure as dew of Hermon, He shall have thee,
> My own, my beautiful, my undefil'd!
>   And thou shalt be His child.
>
> Therefore, farewell!—I go, my soul may fail me,
> As the hart panteth for the water brooks,

Yearning for thy sweet looks—
But thou, my firstborn, droop not, nor bewail me;
Thou in the Shadow of the Rock shalt dwell,
The Rock of Strength.—Farewell!

(pp. 460-61)

Of other spirited, and lively, and pathetic short poems of Mrs Hemans, which form some of the brightest ornaments of the lyric poetry of the language, we take no particular notice, for in what part of the United States are they not known? So general has been the attention to those of her pieces adapted to the purposes of a newspaper, we hardly fear to assert, that throughout a great part of this country there is not a family of the middling class, in which some of them have not been read. The praise which was not sparingly bestowed upon her, when her shorter productions first became generally known among us, has been often repeated on a careful examination of her works; and could we hope that our remarks might one day fall under her eye, we should hope she would not be indifferent to the good wishes which are offered her from America, but feel herself cheered and encouraged in her efforts by the prospect of an enlarged and almost unlimited field of useful influence, opened to her among the descendants of her country in an independent land. The ocean divides us from the fashions as well as the commotions of Europe. The voice of America, deciding on the literature of England, resembles the voice of posterity more nearly than anything else, that is contemporaneous, can do. We believe that the general attention which has been given to Mrs Hemans's works among us, may be regarded as a pledge that they will not be received with indifference by posterity. (p. 463)

George Bancroft, "Mrs. Hemans's Poems," in The North American Review, *Vol. XXIV, No. LV, April, 1827, pp. 443-63.*

Francis Jeffrey   (essay date 1829)

[*Jeffrey was a founder and editor (1803-1829) of the* Edinburgh Review, *one of the most influential periodicals in early nineteenth-century England. His literary criticism has been characterized as impressionistic and subjective, reflecting his liberal political principles and his personal standard of beauty in literature, which he judged according to the power of a work to evoke sensations of tenderness or pity. Seeking a universal standard of beauty and taste, Jeffrey exhorted artists to "employ only such subjects as are the natural signs, or the inseparable concomitants of emotions, of which the greater part of mankind are susceptible." In addition, he wanted literature both to be realistic and to observe standards of social propriety. He became famous for his harsh criticism of the Romantic poets, particularly William Wordsworth. In the following excerpt, Jeffrey praises Hemans's poetic imagery and evaluates her contribution to English literature.*]

We think the poetry of Mrs Hemans a fine exemplification of Female Poetry. . . . (p. 34)

It may not be the best imaginable poetry, and may not indicate the very highest or most commanding genius; but it embraces a great deal of that which gives the very best poetry its chief power of pleasing; and would strike us, perhaps, as more impassioned and exalted, if it were not regulated and harmonized by the most beautiful taste. It is infinitely sweet, elegant, and tender—touching, perhaps, and contemplative, rather than vehement and overpowering; and not only finished throughout with an exquisite delicacy, and even serenity of execution, but informed with a purity and loftiness of feeling, and a certain sober and humble tone of indulgence and piety, which must satisfy all judgments, and allay the apprehensions of those who are most afraid of the passionate exaggerations of poetry. The diction is always beautiful, harmonious, and free—and the themes, though of infinite variety, uniformly treated with a grace, originality and judgment, which mark the same master hand. These themes she has borrowed, with the peculiar interest and imagery that belong to them, from the legends of different nations, and the most opposite states of society; and has contrived to retain much of what is interesting and peculiar in each of them, without adopting, along with it, any of the revolting or extravagant excesses which may characterise the taste or manners of the people or the age from which it has been derived. She has thus transfused into her German or Scandinavian legends the imaginative and daring tone of the originals, without the mystical exaggerations of the one, or the painful fierceness and coarseness of the other—she has preserved the clearness and elegance of the French, without their coldness or affectation—and the tenderness and simplicity of the early Italians, without their diffuseness or languor. Though occasionally expatiating, somewhat fondly and at large, amongst the sweets of her own planting, there is, on the whole, a great condensation and brevity in most of her pieces, and, almost without exception, a most judicious and vigorous conclusion. The great merit, however, of her poetry, is undoubtedly in its tenderness and its beautiful imagery. The first requires no explanation; but we must be allowed to add a word as to the peculiar charm and character of the latter. (pp. 34-5)

[It] was solely for the purpose of illustrating this great charm and excellence in her imagery, that we have ventured upon this little dissertation. Almost all her poems are rich with fine descriptions, and studded over with images of visible beauty. But these are never idle ornaments: All her pomps have a meaning; and her flowers and her gems are arranged, as they are said to be among Eastern lovers, so as to speak the language of truth and of passion. This is peculiarly remarkable in some little pieces, which seem at first sight to be purely descriptive—but are soon found to tell upon the heart, with a deep moral and pathetic impression. But it is a truth nearly as conspicuous in the greater part of her productions; where we scarcely meet with any striking sentiment that is not ushered in by some such symphony of external nature—and scarcely a lovely picture that does not serve as a foreground to some deep or lofty emotion. We may illustrate this proposition, we think, by opening either [**Records of Woman, with Other Poems** or **The Forest Sanctuary, and Other Poems**] at random, and taking what they first present to us.—The following exquisite lines, for example, on a Palm-tree in an English garden:

It waved not thro' an Eastern sky,
Beside a fount of Araby,
It was not fann'd by southern breeze
In some green isle of Indian seas,
Nor did its graceful shadow sleep
O'er stream of Afric, lone and deep.

But far the exiled Palm-tree grew
'Midst foliage of no kindred hue;
Thro' the laburnum's dropping gold
Rose the light shaft of orient mould,
And Europe's violets, faintly sweet,
Purpled the moss-beds at its feet.

Strange look'd it there!—the willow stream'd
Where silvery waters near it gleam'd;
The lime-bough lured the honey-bee
To murmur by the Desert's Tree,
And showers of snowy roses made
A lustre in its fan-like shade.

(p. 37)

The following, which the author has named, **'Graves of a Household,'** has rather less of external scenery, but serves, like the others, to show how well the graphic and pathetic may be made to set off each other:

They grew in beauty, side by side,
  They fill'd one home with glee;—
Their graves are sever'd, far and wide,
  By mount, and stream, and sea.

The same fond mother bent at night
  O'er each fair sleeping brow;
She had each folded flower in sight,—
  Where are those dreamers now?

One, midst the forests of the West,
  By a dark stream is laid,—
The Indian knows his place of rest,
  Far in the cedar shade.

The sea, the blue lone sea, hath one,
  He lies where pearls lie deep:
He was the loved of all, yet none
  O'er his low bed may weep.

One sleeps where southern vines are drest
  Above the noble slain:
He wrapt his colours round his breast,
  On a blood-red field of Spain.

And one—o'er *her* the myrtle showers
  Its leaves, by soft winds fann'd;
She faded 'midst Italian flowers,—
  The last of that bright band.

And parted thus they rest, who play'd
  Beneath the same green tree;
Whose voices mingled as they pray'd
  Around one parent knee!

They that with smiles lit up the hall,
  And cheer'd with song the hearth,—
Alas! for love, if *thou* wert all,
  And nought beyond, oh earth!

We have taken these pieces chiefly on account of their shortness: But it would not be fair to Mrs Hemans not to present our readers with one longer specimen—and to give a portion of her graceful narrative along with her pathetic descriptions. This story, of **'The Lady of the Castle,'** is told, we think, with great force and sweetness:

Thou seest her pictured with her shining hair,
  (Famed were those tresses in Provençal song,)
Half braided, half o'er cheek and bosom fair
  Let loose, and pouring sunny waves along
Her gorgeous vest. A child's right hand is roving
'Midst the rich curls, and, oh! how meekly loving
Its earnest looks are lifted to the face,

Which bends to meet its lip in laughing grace!
Yet that bright lady's eye methinks hath less
Of deep, and still, and pensive tenderness,
Than might beseem a mother's—on her brow
  Something too much there sits of native scorn,
And her smile kindles with a conscious glow.
—These may be dreams—but how shall woman tell
Of woman's shame, and not with tears?—She fell!
That mother left that child!—went hurrying by
Its cradle—haply, not without a sigh;
Haply one moment o'er its rest serene
She hung—but no! it could not thus have been,
For *she went on!* —forsook her home, her hearth,
All pure affection, all sweet household mirth,
To live a gaudy and dishonour'd thing,
Sharing in guilt the splendours of a king.

  Her lord, in very weariness of life,
Girt on his sword for scenes of distant strife;
He reck'd no more of glory:—grief and shame
Crush'd out his fiery nature, and his name
Died silently. A shadow o'er his halls
Crept year by year; the minstrel pass'd their walls;
The warder's horn hung mute:—meantime the child,
On whose first flowering thoughts no parent smiled,
A gentle girl, and yet deep-hearted, grew
Into sad youth; for well, too well, she knew
Her mother's tale! Its memory made the sky
Seem all too joyous for her shrinking eye;
Check'd on her lip the flow of song, which fain
Would there have linger'd; flush'd her cheek to pain,
If met by sudden glance; and gave a tone
Of sorrow, as for something lovely gone,
Even to the spring's glad voice. Her own was low
And plaintive!—Oh! there lie such depths of woe
In a *young* blighted spirit! Manhood rears
A haughty brow, and age has done with tears;
But youth bows down to misery, in amaze
At the dark cloud o'ermantling its fresh days,—
And thus it was with her. A mournful sight
  In one so fair—for she indeed was fair—
Not with her mother's dazzling eyes of light.
  Hers were more shadowy, full of thought and prayer;
And with long lashes o'er a white-rose cheek,
Drooping in gloom, yet tender still and meek,
Still that fond child's—and, oh! the brow above,
So pale and pure! so form'd for holy love
To gaze upon in silence!—But she felt
That love was not for her, though hearts would melt
Where'er she moved, and reverence mutely given
Went with her; and low prayers, that call'd on Heaven
To bless the young Isaure.

            One sunny morn,
  With alms before her castle gate she stood,
'Midst peasant-groups; when, breathless and o'erworn,
  And shrouded in long robes of widowhood,
A stranger through them broke:—the orphan maid
With her sweet voice, and proffer'd hand of aid,
Turn'd to give welcome; but a wild sad look
Met hers; a gaze that all her spirit shook;
And that pale woman, suddenly subdued
By some strong passion in its gushing mood,
Knelt at her feet, and bathed them with such tears
As rain the hoarded agonies of years
From the heart's urn; and with her white lips press'd
The ground they trode; then, burying in her vest
Her brow's deep flush, sobb'd out—'Oh! undefiled!
I am thy mother—spurn me not, my child!'

  Isaure had pray'd for that lost mother; wept
O'er her stain'd memory, while the happy slept
In the hush'd midnight; stood with mournful gaze

Before yon picture's smile of other days,
But never breathed in human ear the name
Which weigh'd her being to the earth with shame.
What marvel if the anguish, the surprise,
The dark remembrances, the alter'd guise,
Awhile o'erpower'd her?—from the weeper's touch
She shrank—twas but a moment—yet too much
For that all-humbled one; its mortal stroke
Came down like lightning, and her full heart broke
At once in silence. Heavily and prone
She sank, while, o'er her castle's threshold-stone,
Those long fair tresses—*they* still brightly wore
Their early pride, though bound with pearls no more—
Bursting their fillet, in sad beauty roll'd,
And swept the dust with coils of wavy gold.

    Her child bent o'er her—call'd her—'twas too late—
Dead lay the wanderer at her own proud gate!
The joy of courts, the star of knight and bard,—
How didst thou fall, O bright-hair'd Ermengarde!

(pp. 38-41)

But we must stop here. There would be no end of our extracts, if we were to yield to the temptation of noting down every beautiful passage which arrests us in turning over the leaves of the volumes before us. We ought to recollect, too, that there are few to whom our pages are likely to come, who are not already familiar with their beauties; and, in fact, we have made these extracts, less with the presumptuous belief that we are introducing Mrs Hemans for the first time to the knowledge or admiration of our readers, than from a desire of illustrating, by means of them, the singular felicity in the choice and employment of her imagery. . . . (pp. 46-7)

We have seen too much of the perishable nature of modern literary fame, to venture to predict to Mrs Hemans that hers will be immortal, or even of very long duration. . . .

If taste and elegance, however, be titles to enduring fame, we might venture securely to promise that rich boon to the author before us; who adds to those great merits a tenderness and loftiness of feeling, and an ethereal purity of sentiment, which could only emanate from the soul of a woman. She must beware of becoming too voluminous; and must not venture again on any thing so long as the *Forest Sanctuary.* But, if the next generation inherits our taste for short poems, we are persuaded it will not readily allow her to be forgotten. For we do not hesitate to say, that she is, beyond all comparison, the most touching and accomplished writer of occasional verses that our literature has yet to boast of. (p. 47)

> *Francis Jeffrey, "Felicia Hemans," in* The Edinburgh Review, *Vol. L, No. XCIX, October, 1829, pp. 32-47.*

Letitia E. Landon   (essay date 1835)

[*Landon was an English poet, novelist, journalist, dramatist, and editor who achieved widespread popularity during the early nineteenth century. Her poetry, with its exotic settings and effusive, passionate style, strongly appealed to readers of the Romantic age. In the following excerpt from a review of Hemans's poetry, Landon identifies what she considers four principal elements of the poet's works: a longing for ideal affection, picturesque*

settings, a musical poetic style, and a strong moral sense.]

No emotion is more truly, or more often pictured in [Mrs. Hemans's] song, than that craving for affection which answers not unto the call. The very power that she possesses, and which, in early youth, she perhaps deemed would both attract and keep, is, in reality, a drawback. Nothing can stand its test. The love which the spirit hath painted has too much of its native heaven for earth. In how many and exquisite shapes is this vain longing introduced on her page. Some slight incident gives the framework, but she casts her own colour upon the picture. In this consists the difference between painting and poetry: the painter reproduces others,—the poet reproduces himself. We would draw attention especially to one or two poems in which the sentiment is too true for Mrs. Hemans not to have been her own inspiration. Is it not the heart's long-suppressed bitterness that exclaims—

    Tell me no more—no more
Of my soul's lofty gifts! are they not vain
To quench its panting thirst for happiness?
Have I not tried, and striven, and failed to bind
One true heart unto me, whereon my own
Might find a resting-place—a home for all
Its burden of affections? I depart
Unknown, though fame goes with me; I must leave
The earth unknown. Yet it may be that death
Shall give my name a power to win such tears
As might have made life precious.

How exquisitely is the doom of a woman, in whose being pride, genius, and tenderness contend for mastery, shadowed in the lines that succeed! The pride bows to the very dust; for genius is like an astrologer whose power fails when the mighty spell is tried for himself; and the tenderness turns away with a crushed heart to perish in neglect. We proceed to mark what appears to bear the deep impress of individual suffering:—

One dream of passion and of beauty more:
And in its bright fulfilment let me pour
My soul away! Let earth retain a trace
Of that which lit my being, though its race
Might have been loftier far. . . . .
. . . . . . For thee alone, for thee!
May this last work, this farewell triumph be—
Thou loved so vainly! I would leave enshrined
Something immortal of my heart and mind,
That yet may speak to thee when I am gone,
Shaking thine inmost bosom with a tone
Of best affection—something that may prove
What she hath been, whose melancholy love
On thee was lavished; silent love and tear,
And fervent song that gushed when none were near,
And dream by night, and weary thought by day,
Stealing the brightness from her life away.

And thou, oh! thou on whom my spirit cast
Unvalued wealth—who knew not what was given
In that devotedness, the sad and deep
And unrepaid farewell! If I could weep
Once, only once, beloved one! on thy breast,
Pouring my heart forth ere I sink to rest!
But that were happiness, and unto me
Earth's gift is fame.

    I have been
Too much alone.

(pp. 428-29)

We have noticed this yearning for affection—unsatisfied, but still unsubdued—as one characteristic of Mrs. Hemans's poetry: the rich picturesque was another. Highly accomplished, the varied stores that she possessed were all subservient to one master science. Mistress both of German and Spanish, the latter country appears to have peculiarly captivated her imagination. At that period when the fancy is peculiarly alive to impression—when girlhood is so new, that the eagerness of childhood is still in its delights—Spain was, of all others, the country on which public attention was fixed: victory after victory carried the British flag from the ocean to the Pyrenees; but, with that craving for the ideal which is so great a feature in her writings, the present was insufficient, and she went back upon the past;—the romantic history of the Moors was like a storehouse, with treasures gorgeous like those of its own Alhambra. (p. 429)

Besides the ideal and the picturesque, Mrs. Hemans is distinguished by her harmony. I use the word harmony advisedly, in contradistinction to melody. Melody implies something more careless, more simple, than belongs to her style: it is song by snatches; our English ballads are remarkable for it. To quote an instance or two. There is a verse in that of "Yarrow Water":—

> O wind that wandereth from the south,
>   Seek where my love repaireth,
> And blow a kiss to his dear mouth,
>   And tell me how he fareth.

Nothing can exceed the tender sweetness of these lines; but there is no skill. Again, in "Faire Rosamonde," the verse that describes the cruelty of Eleanor,—

> With that she struck her on the mouth,
>   So dyed double red;
> Hard was the heart that gave the blow,
>   Soft were the lips that bled.

How musical is the alliteration; but it is music which, like that of the singing brook, has sprung up of itself. Now, Mrs. Hemans has the most perfect skill in her science; nothing can be more polished than her versification. Every poem is like a piece of music, with its eloquent pauses, its rich combinations, and its swelling chords. Who that has ever heard can forget the exquisite flow of **"The Voice of Spring?"**—

> I come! I come!—ye have call'd me long;
> I come o'er the mountains with light and song!
> Ye may trace my step o'er the wakening earth,
> By the winds that tell of the violet's birth,
> By the primrose stars in the shadowy grass,
> By the green leaves opening as I pass.

It is like the finest order of Italian singing—pure, high, and scientific. (p. 430)

To the three characteristics of Mrs. Hemans's poetry which have already been mentioned—viz., the ideal, the picturesque, and the harmonious—a fourth must be added,—the moral. Nothing can be more pure, more feminine and exalted, than the spirit which pervades the whole: it is the intuitive sense of right, elevated and strengthened into a principle. It is a glorious and a beautiful memory to bequeath; but she who left it is little to be envied. (p. 431)

What is poetry, and what is a poetical career? The first is

to have an organization of extreme sensibility, which the second exposes bareheaded to the rudest weather. The original impulse is irresistible—all professions are engrossing when once begun; and acting with perpetual stimulus, nothing takes more complete possession of its follower than literature. But never can success repay its cost. The work appears—it lives in the light of popular applause; but truly might the writer exclaim—

> It is my youth—it is my bloom—it is my glad free heart
> I cast away for thee—for thee—ill fated as thou art.

If this be true even of one sex, how much more true of the other. Ah! Fame to a woman is indeed but a royal mourning in purple for happiness. (pp. 431-32)

> *Letitia E. Landon, "On the Character of Mrs. Hemans's Writings," in* The New Monthly Magazine, *Vol. XLIV, No. CLXXVI, August, 1835, pp. 425-33.*

William Henry Smith and D. M. Moir   (essay date 1848)

[*In the following excerpt, Smith and Moir discuss* The Vespers of Palermo, De Chatillon, The Forest Sanctu-

Bust of Mrs. Hemans.

ary, *and other of Hemans's poems and plays and consider her place among contemporary English poets.*]

The Vespers of Palermo is not perhaps the most popular, even of [Mrs Hemans'] longer productions—it is certainly written in what is just now the most unpopular form—yet it appears to us one of the most vigorous efforts of her genius. (p. 648)

It was not the natural bent of genius which led her to the selection of the dramatic form; and when we become thoroughly acquainted with her temperament, and the feelings she loved to indulge, we are rather surprised that she performed the task she undertook with so much spirit, and so large a measure of success, than that she falls short in some parts of her performance. Nothing can be better conceived, or more admirably sustained, than the character of Raimond de Procida. The elder Procida, and the dark revengeful Montalba, are not so successfully treated. We feel that she has designed these figures with sufficient propriety, but she has not animated them; she could not draw from within those fierce emotions which were to infuse life into them. The effort to sympathise, even in imagination, with such characters, was a violence to her nature. The noble and virtuous heroism of the younger Procida was, on the contrary, no other than the overflow of her own genuine feeling. Few modern dramas present more spirit-stirring scenes, than those in which Raimond takes the leading part. Two of those we would particularly mention—one when, on joining the patriot-conspirators, and learning the mode in which they intended to free their country, he refuses, even for so great an object, to stain his soul with assassination and murder; and the other, where, towards the close of the piece, he is imprisoned by the more successful conspirators—is condemned to die for imputed treachery to their cause, and hears that the *battle* for his country, for which his spirit had so longed, is going forward. (p. 649)

The failure of the play at Covent Garden theatre was attributed, amongst the friends of the authoress, to the indifferent acting of the lady who performed the part of Constance. In justice to the actress, we must confess she had a most difficult part to deal with. There is not a single speech set down for Constance which, we think, the most skilful recitation could make effective. The failure of Mrs Hemans, in this part of the drama, is not very easily accounted for. Constance is a gentle, affectionate spirit, in love with the younger Procida, and the unfortunate cause of the suspicion that falls upon him of being a traitor. It is a character which, in her lyrical effusions, she would have beautifully portrayed. But we suppose that the exclusion from her favourite haunts of nature—the inability of investing the grief of her heroine in her accustomed associations of woods, and fields, and flowers—the confinement of her imagination to what would be suitable to the *boards* of a theatre—embarrassed and cramped her powers. Certain it is, she seems quite at a loss here to express a strain of feeling which, on other occasions, she has poured out with singular fluency and force. Constance has no other manner of exhibiting her distress but by swooning or dreaming, or thinking she must have been dreaming, and recovering herself to the remembrance of what no mortal so situated could ever have forgotten—the most common, and, to our taste, one of the most unfortunate expedients that dramatists and novelists have recourse to. (pp. 650-51)

It ought to be borne in remembrance, however, that the *Vespers of Palermo,* although not the "first" with respect to publication, was the first written of Mrs Hemans' dramatic works. It was produced in solitude, and away from the bustle of theatres, and, be it also confessed, probably with a very scanty knowledge of what stage-representation required. Indeed, the result proved this to be the case. The *Siege of Valencia,* written on a different principle, although probably even less adapted for stage representation, possesses loftier claims as a composition, and, as a poem, is decidedly superior. Its pervading fault consists in its being pitched on too high a key. All the characters talk in heroics—every sentiment is strained to the utmost; and the prevailing tone of the author's mind characterises the whole. We do not say that it is deficient in nature—it overflows alike with power and tenderness; but its nature is too high for the common purposes of humanity. The wild, stern enthusiasm of the priest—the inflexibility of the father—the wavering of the mother between duty and affection—the heroic devotion of the gentle Ximena, are all well brought out; but there is a want of individuality—the want of that, without which elaboration for the theatre is vain, and with which, compositions of very inferior merit often attract attention, and secure it.

Passing over *Sebastian of Portugal,* and the two or three sketches in the *Scenes and Hymns of Life,* as of minor importance, *De Chatillon* is the only other regular drama that Mrs Hemans subsequently attempted. Unfortunately for her, the *Vespers,* although long prior in point of composition, had not been brought out when the *Siege of Valencia* was written; and, consequently, she could not benefit by the fate and failure which was destined for that drama. This is much to be lamented, for *De Chatillon,* as a play, far exceeds either in power and interest. The redundancies in imagery and description, the painting instead of acting, which were the weaker side of its precursors, were here corrected. It is unfortunate that it wanted the benefit of her last corrections, as it was not published till some years after her death, and from the first rough draft—the amended one, which had been made from it, having been unfortunately lost. But, imperfect in many respects as it may be found to be, it is beyond compare the best and most successful composition of the author in this department. Without stripping her language of that richness and poetic grace which characterises her genius, or condescending to a single passage of mean baldness, so commonly mistaken by many modern dramatists as essentially necessary to the truth of dialogue, she has in this attempt preserved adherence to reality, amid scenes allied to romance; brevity and effect, in situations strongly alluring to amplification; and, in her delineation of some of the strongest as well as the finest emotions of the heart, she has exhibited a knowledge of nature's workings, remarkable alike for minuteness and truth.

When we consider the doubtful success which attended the only drama of Mrs Hemans which was brought out, we cannot wonder that she latterly abandoned this species of writing, and confined herself to what she must have felt as much more accordant with her own impulses. The most laboured of all her writings was *The Forest Sanctuary,* and it would appear that, in her own estimation, it was considered her best. Not so we. It has many passages of exquisite description, and it breathes throughout an exalted spirit; but withal it is monotonous in sentiment, and possesses not the human interest which ought to have attached to it, as a tale of suffering. To us *The Last Constantine,* which appears to have attracted much less attention, is in many respects a finer and better poem. Few things, indeed, in our literature, can be quoted as more perfect than the picture of heroic and Christian courage, which, amid the ruins of his empire, sustained the last of the Cæsars. The weight of the argument is sustained throughout. The reader feels as if breathing a finer and purer atmosphere, above the low mists and vapours of common humanity; and he rises from the perusal of the poem alike with an admiration of its hero and its author.

The Last Constantine may be considered as the concluding great effort of Mrs Hemans, in what of her writings may be said to belong to the classical school. She seems here first to have felt her own power, and, leaving precept and example, and the leading-strings of her predecessors, to have allowed her muse to soar adventurously forth. The *Tales and Historic Scenes,* the *Sceptic, Dartmoor,* and *Modern Greece,* are all shaped according to the same model—the classical. The study of modern German poetry, and of Wordsworth, changed, while it expanded, her views; and *The Forest Sanctuary* seems to have been composed with great elaboration, doubtless, while in this transition state. In matter it is too flimsy and etherial for a tale of life; it has too much sentiment and too little action. But some things in it it would be difficult to rival. The scenery of Southern America is painted with a gorgeousness which reminds us of the Isle of Palms and its fairy bowers; and the death and burial at sea is imbued with a serene and soul-subduing beauty. (pp. 651-52)

Of [Mrs Hemans' lyrics and shorter pieces] we prefer such as are apparently the expressions of spontaneous feelings of her own to those which are built upon some tale or legend. It happens too, unfortunately, that in the latter case we have first to read the legend or fable in prose, and then to read it again in verse. This gives something of weariness to the *Lays of Many Lands.* Still less fortunate, we think, is the practice Mrs Hemans indulges in of ushering in a poem of her own by a long quotation—a favourite stanza, perhaps—of some celebrated poet. We may possibly read the favourite stanza twice, and feel reluctant to proceed further. For instance, she quotes the beautiful and well-known passage from *Childe Harold* upon the spring, ending with—

> I turned from all she brought to all she could not bring;

and on another occasion, that general favourite, beginning—

> And slight, withal, may be the things which bring;

and then proceeds to enlarge upon the same sentiments. Her own strain that follows is good—but not *so* good. Is it wise to provoke the comparison?—and does it not give a certain frivolity, and the air of a mere exercise, to the verse which only repeats, and modifies, and *varies,* so to speak, the melody that has been already given? Or if the quotation set out with is looked on as a mere prelude, is it good policy to run the risk of the prelude being more interesting than the strain itself? The beautiful passage from Southey—

> They sin who tell us love can die, &c.,

is too long to be quoted as merely a key-note to what is to follow, and is too good to be easily surpassed. (pp. 652-53)

In any notice of Mrs Hemans' works, not to mention *The Records of Woman* would seem an unaccountable omission. Both the subject, and the manner in which it is treated especially characterise our poetess. Of all these *Records* there is not one where the picture is not more or less pleasing, or drawn with more or less power and fidelity. Estimated according to sheer literary merit, it would perhaps be impossible to give the preference to any one of them. (p. 653)

An eminent critic in the *Edinburgh Review* has spoken of the neatness and perfect finish which characterise female writers in general, and Mrs Hemans in particular. Now, these qualities imply a certain terseness and concentration of style, which is no more a peculiarity of all authoresses than of all authors, and which we should not pronounce to be peculiarly characteristic of Mrs Hemans' poetry. To us it often appears wanting in this very conciseness; we occasionally wish that some lines and verses were excluded—not because they are faulty in themselves, but because they weaken the effect, and detract from the vigour of the whole: we wish the verses, in short, were more closely packed together, so that the commencement and the close, which are generally both good, could be brought a little nearer to each other. It is not so much a redundancy of expression, as of images and illustrations, that we have sometimes to complain of in Mrs Hemans. She uses two of these where one would not only suffice, but do the work much better. . . . The verses beginning "I dream of all things free" might . . . be cited as an instance of this tendency to overamplify—a tendency which seems the result of a great affluence of poetical imagery. This would be a more powerful poem merely by being made shorter. We wait too long, and the imagination roves too far, before we arrive at the concluding lines, which contain all the point and significance of the piece:—

> My heart *in chains* is bleeding,
> And I dream of all things free.

Of the measures and the melody of a lyrical poet something is expected to be said. But what we feel we have chiefly to thank Mrs Hemans for here is, that, in the search after novelty and variety of metre, she has made so few experiments upon our ear, and that she has not disdained to write with correctness and regularity. She has not apparently laboured after novelties of this kind, but has adopted that verse into which her thoughts spontaneously ran. An author who does this is not very likely to select a rhythm, or measure, which is incongruous with the subject-matter of his poem; nor, do we think, could many instances of such a fault be detected in Mrs Hemans. (pp. 655-56)

We must now draw to a conclusion. One great and pervading excellence of Mrs Hemans, as a writer, is her entire dedication of her genius and talents to the cause of healthy morality and sound religion. The sentiment may be, on occasion, somewhat refined; it may be too delicate, in some instances, for the common taste, but never is it mawkish or morbid. Never can it be construed into a palliative of vice—never, when followed out to its limits, will it be found to have led from the paths of virtue. For practical purposes, we admit that her exemplars are not seldom too ideal and picturesque. The general fault of her poetry consists in its being rather, if we may use the term, too *romantical*. We have a little too much of banners in churches, and flowers on graves,—of self-immolated youths, and broken-hearted damsels;—too frequent a reference to the Syrian plains, and knights in panoply, and vigils of arms, as mere illustrations of the noble in character, or the heroic in devotion. Situations are adduced as applicable to general conduct, which have only occurred, or could only have occurred, in particular states of society, and are never likely, from existing circumstances, to occur again. Far better this, however, than a contrary fault; for it is the purpose of poetry to elevate, and not to repress. Admitting that the effervescence is adventitious, still it is of virtuous growth, and proceeds from no distortion of principle. If not the reflection of human nature as it actually is, it is the delineation of the *fata morgana* of a noble mind—of something that occurs to us "in musings high," and which we sigh to think of as of something loftier and better, to which that nature would willingly aspire. We can readily conceive, that to a woman of the exquisite taste possessed by Mrs Hemans, any attempt at the startling or *bizarre*, either in conception or subject, was a thing especially to be avoided. We do not mean to imply by this, that, as every true poet must have, she had not a manner of her own. To this honour, no author of our day has higher or less equivocal claims. She knew what to admire in others, but she felt that she had a mission of her own. To substantiate this, we have only to suppose her productions blotted out from our literature, and then remark whether or not any blank be left; for, wherever we have originality, we have accession. We admit that originality is of all shades and grades, from a Burns to a Bloomfield, from a Crabbe to a Clare— still the names of the second and the fourth are those of true poets, as well as those of the authors of "The Cotter's Saturday Night," and "Sir Eustace Gray,"—Parnassus, as Dr Johnson observes, having its "flowers of transient fragrance, as well as its cedars of perennial growth, and its laurels of eternal verdure." In the case of Mrs Hemans, this question is set at rest, from her having become the founder of a school, and that only eclipsed in the number of its adherents and imitators by those of Scott, Byron, and Wordsworth. In America especially has this been the case; a great part of the recent poetry in that country— more particularly that of its female writers—has been little more than an echo of her *Records of Woman,* and *Lays of Many Lands,* and lyrical strains; and, from Mrs Sigourney—"the American Mrs Hemans"—downwards, there are only corroborative proofs of a Cisatlantic fact, that no copyist, however acute and faithful, has ever yet succeeded in treading on the kibes of his master, far less of outstripping him in the struggle for excellence.

Like all original writers, Mrs Hemans has her own mode and her own province. In reading the poetry of Wordsworth, we feel as if transferred to the mountainous solitudes, broken only by the scream of the eagle and the dash of the cataract, where human life is indicated but by the shieling in the sheltered holm, and the shepherd boy, lying wrapt up in his plaid by the furze-bush, with his "little flock at feed beside him." By Scott we are placed amid the men and things of departed ages. The bannered castle looms in the distance, and around it are the tented plain— the baron and his vassals—all that pertains to "ladye-love and war, renown and knightly worth." We have the cathe-dral-pomp, and the dark superstition, and the might that stands in the place of right,—all the fire and air, with little of the earth and water of our elemental nature. The lays of Wilson reflect the patriarchal calm of life in its best, and purest, and happiest aspects—or, indeed, of something better than mere human life, as the image of the islet in the sunset mirror of the lake is finer and fairer than the reality. Coleridge's inspiration is emblemed by ruins in the silver and shadow of moonlight,—quaint, and queer, and fantastic, haunted by the whooping owl, and screamed over by the invisible nighthawk. Campbell reminds of the Portland vase, exquisite in taste and materials, but recalling always the conventionalities of art.

When placed beside, and contrasted with her great contemporaries, the excellences of Mrs Hemans are sufficiently distinct and characteristic. There can be no doubt of this, more especially in her later and best writings, in which she makes incidents elucidate feelings. In this magic circle—limited it may be—she has no rival. Hence, from the picturesqueness, the harmony, the delicacy and grace, which her compositions display, she is peculiarly the poet of her own sex. Her pictures are not more distinguished for accuracy of touch than for elegance of finish. Every thing is clear, and defined, and palpable; nothing is enveloped in accommodating haze; and she never leaves us, as is the trick of some late aspiring and mystical versifiers, to believe that she must be profound because she is unintelligible. She is ever alive to the dignity of her calling, and the purity of her sex. Aware of the difficulties of her art, she aspired towards excellence with untiring perseverance, and improved herself by the study of the best models, well knowing that few things easy of attainment can be worth much. Her taste thus directed her to appropriate and happy subjects; and hence it has been, as with all things of sterling value, that her writings have not been deteriorated by time. They were not, like the ice-palace of the Empress Catherine, thrown up to suit the whim of the season, or directed to subjects of mere occasional interest, to catch the gale of a passing popularity. Mrs Hemans built on surer foundations, and with less perishable materials. The consequence is, that her reputation has been steadily on the increase. Of no one modern writer can it be affirmed with less hesitation, that she has become an English classic; nor, until human nature becomes very different from what it now is, can we imagine the least probability that the music of her lays will cease to soothe the ear, or the beauty of her sentiment to charm the gentle heart. (pp. 656-58)

> *William Henry Smith and D. M. Moir, "Mrs. Hemans," in* Blackwood's Edinburgh Magazine, *Vol. LXIV, No. CCCXCVIII, December, 1848, pp. 641-58.*

William Michael Rossetti   (essay date 1873)

[*Rossetti was an English critic, essayist, and biographer who, early in his career, edited* The Germ, *a literary periodical designed to advance the artistic doctrines of the Pre-Raphaelite Brotherhood, a group of artists who, in defiance of conventional theory, advocated a return to the ideals of fifteenth-century Italian painting. Rossetti later wrote for the* Spectator, *published a collection of biographies entitled* Lives of Some Famous . Poets

(1878) and a Life of John Keats *(1887), and edited the works and memoirs of his siblings, Dante Gabriel and Christina Rossetti. In the following excerpt from his 1873 edition of Hemans's works, Rossetti provides a mixed assessment of Hemans's poetic talents.*]

In Mrs. Hemans' poetry there is . . . a large measure of beauty, and, along with this, very considerable skill. Aptitude and delicacy in versification, and a harmonious balance in the treatment of the subject, are very generally apparent: if we accept the key-note as right, we may with little misgiving acquiesce in what follows on to the close. Her skill, however, hardly rises into the loftier region of art: there is a gift, and culture added to the gift, but not a great native faculty working in splendid independence, or yet more splendid self-discipline. Her sources of inspiration being genuine, and the tone of her mind feminine in an intense degree, the product has no lack of sincerity: and yet it leaves a certain artificial impression, rather perhaps through a cloying flow of "right-minded" perceptions of moral and material beauty than through any other defect. "Balmy" it may be: but the atmosphere of her verse is by no means bracing. One might sum up the weak points in Mrs. Hemans' poetry by saying that it is not only "feminine" poetry (which under the circumstances can be no imputation, rather an encomium) but also "female" poetry: besides exhibiting the fineness and charm of womanhood, it has the monotone of mere sex. Mrs. Hemans has that love of good and horror of evil which characterize a scrupulous female mind; and which we may most rightly praise without concluding that they favour poetical robustness, or even perfection in literary form. She is a leader in that very modern phalanx of poets who persistently co-ordinate the impulse of sentiment with the guiding power of morals or religion. Everything must convey its "lesson," and is indeed set forth for the sake of its lesson: but must at the same time have the emotional gush of a spontaneous sentiment. The poet must not write because he has something of his own to say, but because he has something *right* to feel and say. Lamartine was a prophet in this line. After allowing all proper deductions, however, it may be gratefully acknowledged that Mrs. Hemans takes a very honourable rank among poetesses; and that there is in her writings much which both appeals, and deserves to appeal, to many gentle, sweet, pious, and refined souls, in virtue of its thorough possession of the same excellent gifts. According to the spiritual or emotional condition of her readers, it would be found that a poem by this authoress which to one reader would be graceful and tender would to another be touching, and to a third poignantly pathetic. The first we can suppose to be a man, and the third a woman; or the first a critic, the second a "poetical reader," and the third a sensitive nature, attuned to sympathy by suffering. (p. xiv)

> *William Michael Rossetti, in an introduction to* The Poetical Works of Felicia Hemans *by Felicia Hemans, edited by William Michael Rossetti, 1873. Reprint by Ward, Lock & Co., Limited, 1879, pp. v-xiv.*

Arthur Symons   (essay date 1909)

[*An English critic, poet, dramatist, short story writer, and editor, Symons gained initial notoriety during the 1890s as one of the leading figures of the Decadent movement in England, eventually establishing himself an important critic of the modern era. His sensitive translations from the works of Paul Verlaine and Stéphane Mallarmé offered English poets an introduction to the poetry of the French Symbolists. Though he was a gifted translator and linguist, it was as a critic that Symons made his most important contribution to literature. His* The Symbolist Movement in Literature *provided his English contemporaries with an appropriate vocabulary with which to define their new aesthetic—one that communicated their concern with dreamlike states, imagination, and a reality that exists beyond the boundaries of the senses. Symons also discerned that the concept of the symbol as a vehicle by which a "hitherto unknown reality was suddenly revealed" could become the basis for an entire modern aesthetic, and he thereby laid the foundation for much of modern poetic theory. In the following excerpt, Symons assesses Hemans's poetry.*]

It was said at the time of Mrs. Hemans' death that she had 'founded a school of imitators in England, and a yet larger one in America.' 'So general has been the attention,' it was said in America, 'to those of her pieces adapted to the purposes of a newspaper, we hardly fear to assert that throughout a great part of this country there is not a family of the middling class in which some of them have not been read' [see excerpt dated 1827]. And the same writer assures us that 'the voice of America, deciding on the literature of England, resembles the voice of posterity more nearly than anything else that is contemporaneous can do.' Has the voice of posterity, in this instance, corroborated the voice of America?

Out of the seven volumes of her collected works, not seven poems are still remembered, and these chiefly because they were taught, and probably still are, to children. There are **'Casabianca,' 'The Graves of a Household,'** *The Homes of England,* **'The Fall of d'Assas,'** with a few others; these are not fundamentally different from the hundreds of poems which have been forgotten, or which seem to us now little more than the liltings of a kind of female Moore. But they have the merit of being not only very sincere and very straightforward, but of concentrating into themselves a more definite parcel of the floating sensibility of a woman who was tremulously awake to every appeal of beauty or nobility. 'The highest degree of beauty in art,' she wrote, 'certainly always excites, if not tears, at least the inward feeling of tears.' She has 'a pure passion for flowers,' and suffers from the intense delight of music, without which she feels that she would die; the sight and society of Scott or Wordsworth fill her with an ecstasy hardly to be borne; she discovers Carlyle writing anonymously on Burns in the *Edinburgh Review* and she notes: 'I wonder who the writer is; he certainly gives us a great deal of what Boswell, I think, calls bark and steel for the mind.' She had all the feminine accomplishments of her time, and they meant to her, especially her harp, some form of personal expression. She wrote from genuine feeling and with easy spontaneity, and it may still be said of her verse, as Lord Jeffrey said of it: 'It may not be the best imaginable poetry, and may not indicate the highest or most commanding genius, but it embraces a great deal of that which gives the very best poetry its chief power of pleasing,' [see excerpt dated 1829].

Its chief power, that is, of pleasing the majority. In spite of an origin partly Irish, partly German, blended with an Italian strain, there was no rarity in her nature, or if it was there, it found no expression in her poems. She said of Irish tunes that there was in them 'something unconquerable yet sorrowful'; but that something, though she compared herself to an Irish tune, she never got. Living much of her life in Wales, and caring greatly for its ancient literature, she loses, in the improvisations of the *Welsh Melodies,* whatever is finest and most elemental in her Celtic originals. It is sufficient criticism to set side by side the first stanza of **'The Hall of Cynddylan'** and the opening of the poem of Llwarch Hen. Mrs. Hemans says, lightly:—

> The Hall of Cynddylan is gloomy to-night;
> I weep, for the grave has extinguished its light;
> The beam of the lamp from its summit is o'er,
> The blaze of its hearth shall give welcome no more.

But what Llwarch Hen has said is this: 'The Hall of Cynddylan is gloomy this night, without fire, without bed: I must weep awhile, and then be silent.'

That is poetry, but the other is a kind of prattle. It is difficult to say of Mrs. Hemans that her poems are not womanly, and yet it would be more natural to say that they are feminine. The art of verse to her was like her harp and her sketch-book, not an accomplishment indeed, but an instrument on which to improvise. One of her disciples, Letitia Landon, imagined that she was only speaking in her favour when she said: 'One single emotion is never the original subject' of her poems. 'Some graceful or touching anecdote or situation catches her attention, and its poetry is developed in a strain of mourning melody and a vein of gentle moralising.' Her poems are for the most part touching anecdotes; they are never without some gentle moralising. If poetry were really what the average person thinks it to be, an idealisation of the feelings, at those moments when the mind is open to every passing impression, ready to catch at similitudes and call up associations, but not in the grip of a strong thought or vital passion, then the verse of Felicia Hemans would be, as people once thought it was, the ideal poetry. It would, however, be necessary to go on from that conclusion to another, which indeed we find in the surprising American Professor, who, 'after reading such works as she had written,' could not but perceive, on turning over 'the volumes of a collection of English poetry, like that of Chalmers,' that 'the greater part of it appears more worthless and distasteful than before.' (pp. 293-95)

> *Arthur Symons, "Felicia Dorothea Hemans (1793-1835)" in his* The Romantic Movement in English Poetry, *Archibald Constable & Co. Ltd., 1909, pp. 293-95.*

Janet E. Courtney   (essay date 1933)

[*Courtney compares Hemans's poetry with that of a number of her predecessors and contemporaries and evaluates her works.*]

Among the many feminine verse-writers of the post-Byronic period, there are two who stand out from the rest as possessing the true poet's sensibility. Felicia Hemans and Caroline Bowles at their best deserve a place in any anthology of English poetry. But, like their lesser contemporaries—'L. E. L.', Caroline Norton, Lady Emmeline and the rest—they lacked the critical spirit. They were at no trouble to select. Once recognized as professional poets, they seem to have felt bound to be always committing effusions to paper. They could let no event occur, and no guest arrive or depart, without addressing to it, him or her, the appropriate copy of verses.

This is true even of Mrs. Hemans, whose forty years of life yielded poetic material to fill seven volumes, most of it justly forgotten, though a few of her ballads and lyrics show what she might have done, had she ever developed the selective instinct of the true artist. To do her justice, she knew this, and late in life she regretted the facility, 'amounting almost to improvisation', which poured out those *Songs of the Domestic Affections,* as well as the domestic necessities which impelled her to publish them. But if only she had known the difference between, say, the opening of the *Pilgrim Fathers:*

> The breaking waves dashed high
> On a stern and rock-bound coast
> And the woods against a stormy sky
> Their giant branches tossed.

and the beginning of **'The Land of Dreams'**:

> O spirit-land! thou land of dreams!
> A world thou art of mysterious gleams.

she had been a truer poet. (pp. 19-20)

Mrs. Hemans immediately preceded [Longfellow], . . . with whom she has much in common. Compare, for instance, her **'Casabianca'** with his 'Wreck of the Hesperus,' and then both of them with Browning's 'Incident of the French Camp' to see how modern poetry has gained in directness of expression. Or again compare her *Forest Sanctuary* with his *Evangeline*. In narrative poetry the advantage is with Longfellow; but in sound, if not in sentiment, his 'Psalm of Life' is commonplace compared with her **'Hour of Death'**:

> Leaves have their time to fall,
> And flowers to wither at the north wind's breath,
>   And stars to set—but all,
> Thou hast *all* seasons for thine own, O Death!

This has the true note of a dirge, just as the last stanza of her **'Invocation'** breathes the spirit of silence:

> No voice is on the air of night,
> Through folded leaves no murmurs creep,
> Nor star nor moonbeam's trembling light
> Falls on the placid brow of sleep.
> Descend, bright visions! from your airy bower:
> Dark, silent, solemn, is your favourite hour.

Not very profound, perhaps; but we do not go to Mrs. Hemans, or to Longfellow for that matter, for profundity of thought. We go to her for sensitive femininity, for perception of natural beauty, for heroic sentiment, for graceful and tender tributes to 'the domestic affections'. And at her best, we do not go to her in vain. She loved, as Chorley says, the pathetic side of life and 'was never more happily employed than in lamenting the beloved and early called'. She wrote a great deal too much, but so did Wordsworth. Like him she has her *longueurs;* there are pages and pages which we can spare. Sometimes the domestic affections descend to mere banality as in *The Homes of England;* but sometimes they sound a note of true tenderness as in **'The Graves of a Household.'** And to appraise her at her true worth, we have to look back to the poetic tradition which nurtured her, and to compare her with contemporary poets both of her own sex and of the other.

To begin with, she was a contemporary of Byron, but also of Southey, Coleridge and Wordsworth—in other words in between the romantic and the natural schools of poetry. She was clearly influenced by Cowper—her **'Charmed Picture'** was definitely occasioned by reading his lines to his Mother's picture, and many of her 'occasional' verses have something of his felicity. She had been bred in the traditions of classical elegance, illustrated by such contemporary poets as Samuel Rogers and Thomas Campbell. She has a good deal of affinity with Campbell both in treatment and choice of subjects. She touched Byron only in so far as she shares with him the idea that there are subjects in themselves poetical, instead of thinking with Wordsworth and Coleridge that poetry resides in the treatment, not the subject. Consequently she is sometimes too ambitious. She is less concerned with what she has to say than with what, given the subject chosen, ought to be said. And in a sense she was too cultivated. The result, to borrow a phrase of Mr. Courthope's originally applied to Rogers, was that she brought 'a tasteful mind cultivated by reading and devoid of inspiration' to bear upon subjects, such as Belshazzar's Feast, which, if dealt with at all by a modern poet, should be dealt with greatly. She could only deal with them adequately, sometimes scarcely that. But when she was taking herself less seriously, she could achieve a simple directness worthy of Wordsworth. **'Christ Stilling the Tempest'** is a good example:

> Fear was within the tossing bark
> When stormy winds grew loud
> And waves came rolling high and dark
> And the tall mast was bowed.
> And men stood breathless in their dread
> And baffled in their skill;
> But One was there, who rose and said
> To the wild sea—*Be still!*

For that one may forgive such obvious straining after missed effect as

> And He who sleeps not heard the elated throng
> In mirth that plays with thunderbolts, defy
> The Rock of Zion.

And one can understand why 'L. E. L.', hearing of her death, claimed for her that she would be held 'in lasting remembrance'. (pp. 30-3)

> *Janet E. Courtney, "The Poets," in her* The Adventurous Thirties: A Chapter in the Women's Movement, *Oxford University Press, London, 1933, pp. 19-43.*

Donald H. Reiman   (essay date 1978)

[*Reiman focuses on the nature and value of Hemans's poetry.*]

I suggest two elements to be included in [the final evaluation of Mrs. Hemans' poetry]: First, Hemans will be found, in spite of her admiration of Wordsworth, Byron, and other Romantic poets, to exhibit in her own themes

and ideals a substantial case of cultural lag, drawing most of her inspiration from the Enlightenment and remaining closer to Pope and Cowper than to her greater contemporaries. Second, the very neatness and polish of versification and the clarity of the syntax and diction of Hemans' poetry will be seen as attributes of this cultural lag. Repeating the truisms of her upbringing, Hemans never evidences the struggle toward self-discovery that characterizes such poems of growth as *Religious Musings,* "Tintern Abbey," *Childe Harold, Alastor,* or *Endymion.* For her, the thinking process and the moral conclusions are prior to, not inherent in, the poetic act.

Hemans won two fine poetic tributes, but it is noteworthy that they were written late in the careers of poets who had been fixed in their thinking for many years. Walter Savage Landor placed her high among his dead contemporaries in "Epistle LXII: On the Classick and Romantick" in *The Last Fruit Off an Old Tree* (1853); he identifies her as the author of that perennial anthology-piece **"Casabianca"** ("The boy stood on the burning deck"). . . . Wordsworth wrote of her in his "Extempore Effusion upon the Death of James Hogg" (1835),

> Mourn rather for that holy Spirit,
> Sweet as the spring, as ocean deep;
> For Her who, ere her summer faded,
> Has sunk into a breathless sleep.

A similar fate has now befallen the bulk of Felicia Hemans' poetry, perhaps because she spoke only from the past to her age and not, as well, from her age to the next. (pp. x-xi)

> *Donald H. Reiman, in an introduction to* Records of Woman *by Felicia Dorothea Hemans, Garland Publishing, Inc., 1978, pp. v-xi.*

Peter W. Trinder   (essay date 1984)

[*Trinder considers Hemans's literary influences, her poetic techniques, and the lasting value of her works.*]

[Mrs. Hemans' poetry] falls naturally into three kinds according to ambition or length: there are the three dramatic performances including the only finished regular drama *The Vespers of Palermo* the longer narrative or lyrical poems; and the short lyrics which contain those poems by which, if at all, Mrs Hemans is still known, such as **'The Hour of Death,'** which begins:

> Leaves have their time to fall,
> And flowers to wither at the north-wind's breath
> And stars to set—but all,
> Thou hast *all* seasons for thine own, O Death.

If the fashion for reading poetry aloud in an intimate family group, or for the more public recitation, should ever return then she will come into her own again, for most of her work has that quality of immediate accessibility which characterizes the hymn or lyric for music. There is enough intellectual content in much of it to satisfy the curiosity without puzzling the reason; there is much to please the ear and generally an underlying structure to present the feeling of achievement, of time well spent in the hearing. It is strange that with all these positive if modest qualities she does not appear in any of the standard hymnaries. The truth is that her religious convictions, though no doubt strongly held, were not deep in her nature as it appears in her work. The figure of Christ stilling the tempest comes often to her mind as an image of calm assurance, but she does not draw on the more recondite regions of scripture. (pp. 56-7)

Mrs Hemans was comparatively little influenced by any individual in the English literary scene, though her most obvious model was Byron, and in the literary histories she is generally classed with the school of Scott and Campbell; most of her works appeared while they held sway. Her debt to Wordsworth is more subtle since she does not appear to have paid attention to *Lyrical Ballads* apart from 'Tintern Abbey' and of course she cannot have known the *Prelude,* though perhaps it is likely that when she stayed at Rydal Mount the ageing poet who clearly took her under his wing and enjoyed her company in spite of some trepidation before her arrival, might well have shown her his work in progress which always included *The Prelude.* The clearest influence on her career as a writer conscious of her femininity was Mme de Stael. She refers often to *Corinne* and that extraordinary book, with its picture of the elevation of a poetess to Olympian heights, had wide influence among the London 'blue-stockings,' Lady Bessborough and her circle—to which Mrs Hemans was never attached, except indirectly through Jeffrey and through Campbell who published her work in the *New Monthly* magazine. Perhaps her independence alarmed the ladies of Rydal Mount and Abbotsford, certainly her presence intimidated them. She was classical among the romantics, being most impressed by "Laodamia" and the severer side of Wordsworth. Strangely she was hardly touched by Shelley or Keats and her reaction to Jane Austen is nowhere on record.

Perhaps it would be fairer to call her sense of form a methodical instinct. At times one feels that it is a kind of artistic extension of the efficient housewife's urge to see everything put in its proper place. Many of the structurally organized poems do carry this sense of near contrivance, a domestic tidiness about them. Take **'The Festal Hour,'** for example: there is the rhetorical opening, a moral question posed, and in the second stanza we sense immediately that there is to be a multiple answer whose parts will form the structure of the whole poem. Such a sense of form so often repeated and apparently so effortlessly reproduced comes to be felt as mechanical contrivance—the art that does not conceal art; indeed the characteristic that vitiates so much of her work is precisely this air of contrivance. She wrote so easily when there should have been more effort and further consideration. She has a string of metaphors and basic images to hand; the same adjectives are assorted with the same features of nature in slightly adjusted combinations so regularly, in poems whose subjects and themes fall within a narrow range of stock situations or emotions so often, that to close the book after a session on the lyrics is to have the distinct sense of looking into a child's kaleidoscope. You take the toy and shake it, and the same glitter appears in a pretty, new arrangement. The prettiness, too, is evident in the poems; their pleasing value as entertainment has often endured; many of the lyrics sparkle yet, but seldom does the verse move the modern sophisticated reader to recognize it as poetry.

Yet this should not be the final judgement on Mrs Hemans. In the first place she made her living and that of her boys by her writing. . . . In the second place, the honour paid to her by critics and poets of her own day must be remembered together with her great contemporary popularity in America. Professor Norton of Harvard admired her work greatly and corresponded with her; she was strongly pressed to take over the editorship of a literary magazine in America. And in the third place her contribution in helping to create the popular literary taste of the next hundred years cannot properly be ignored, however vitiated it is now fashionable to regard that taste. (pp. 57-60)

The truth is that Mrs Hemans was a genuinely popular poet, much read and admired by those who aspired to be cultivated in an age just later than her own. In this age of Tennyson and the parlour piano, the popular taste for poetry was hardly to be distinguished from the religious cultivation of fashion. The ladies were her most devoted readers, of course: Florence Nightingale copied out **'The Better Land'** for her cousin in a letter; George Eliot wrote to a friend: *I am reading eclectically Mrs Hemans' poems, and venture to recommend to your perusal, if unknown to you, one of the longest ones—***The Forest Sanctuary.*** I can give it my pet adjective—exquisite!* A lady wrote home from India, *Dear Mrs Hemans, I dote on that book. She just said the things I was thinking.*

She is a social as well as a literary phenomenon and as such, as an indicator of changing literary fashion, she claims attention. Whether she does so in her own right as a poet is, of course, a matter of taste. In all but the most strictly intellectual part of that which we can ask of poetry she claims attention, but that intellectual part has become too much the touchstone of poetry, and the qualities for which she was distinguished are those now at a discount. Her poetry is everywhere heavily charged with the patriotism and the domestic affections which are dismissed as narrow, bourgeois or self-indulgent today. The moral framework of society, the background against which a poet writes, the assumptions and social values have changed to such an extent that the undoubted charm of many of her best poems remains only a charm. Where there were tears there is often a faint smile of disdain in the modern reader. In short, she remains frozen within her own period and seldom speaks to the sophisticated poetry-reader of our day. And yet if we can pierce the surface jingoism of Kipling we should be able to penetrate the lace trimmings of Mrs Hemans. But when all is said she seldom perceives those trimmings for what they are, and only for brief passages in her more personal poems, when something deep in her nature is engaged, does she sustain a universality that transcends the differences which separate her period from our own. (pp. 62-3)

Peter W. Trinder, in his Mrs Hemans, *University of Wales Press, 1984, 75 p.*

FURTHER READING

"A Literary Progenitress of Rudyard Kipling." *The Academy and Literature* LXV, No. 1642 (24 October 1903): 444-45.

Discerns a patriotic strain in Hemans's poetry that foreshadows the themes of Rudyard Kipling.

Review of *Modern Greece,* by Felicia Hemans. *Blackwood's Edinburgh Magazine* I, No. V (August 1817): 515-18.
Favorable critical notice of *Modern Greece.*

Chorley, H. F. *Memorials of Mrs. Hemans, with Illustrations of Her Literary Character from Her Private Correspondence.* 2 vols. Philadelphia: Carey, Lea & Blanchard, 1836, 272 p.
Account of Mrs. Hemans's literary development including excerpts from her letters.

Review of *Memorials of Mrs. Hemans,* by H. F. Chorley and *The Poetical Works of Mrs. Felicia Hemans. The Christian Review* 2, No. VII (September 1837): 356-72.
Discusses Chorley's biography of Hemans and an 1836 edition of her works.

"Mrs. Hemans and the Picturesque School." *Fraser's Magazine for Town and Country* XXI, No. CXXII (February 1840): 127-46.
Biographical and critical essay that also relates Mrs. Hemans's powers of picturesque description to those of Homer, Virgil, Thomas Gray, and others.

[Hughes, Harriet]. *The Works of Mrs. Hemans with a Memoir of Her Life,* Vol. 1. Edinburgh: William Blackwood and Sons, 1857, 352 p.
Biography of Hemans by her sister.

[Park, L. J.]. Review of *The Forest Sanctuary and Other Poems,* by Felicia Hemans. *The Christian Examiner and Theological Review* III, No. V (September and October 1826): 403-18.
Praises Hemans's *Forest Sanctuary.*

———. Review of *Mrs. Hemans's Earlier Poems* and *Records of Woman with Other Poems,* by Felicia Hemans. *The Christian Examiner* XXXI, No. 1 (March 1829): 35-52.
Positive review of *Mrs. Hemans's Earlier Poems* and *Records of Woman.*

Ritchie, Lady. "Felicia Felix." In her *Blackstick Papers,* pp. 16-30. New York: G. P. Putnam's Sons, the Knickerbocker Press, 1908.
Biographical portrait of Mrs. Hemans including quotations and correspondence from literary friends.

Tuckerman, H. T. "Essay," In *Poems by Felicia Hemans with an Essay on Her Genius,* edited by Rufus W. Griswold, pp. v-xvi. New York: Leavitt & Allen, n.d.
Evaluative essay on Hemans's poetry in which the critic concludes: "[Mrs. Hemans's] strength lay in earnestness of soul. Her best verses glow with emotion. When once truly interested in a subject, she cast over it such an air of feeling that our sympathies are won at once. We cannot but catch the same vivid impression; and if we draw from her pages no great number of definite images, we cannot but imbibe what is more valuable—the warmth and the life of pure, lofty, and earnest sentiment."

Williams, I. A. "Wordsworth, Mrs. Hemans, and Robert Perceval Graves." *The London Mercury* VI, No. 34 (August 1922): 395-401.
A collection of William Wordsworth's letters to Mrs. Hemans and her protégé Robert Graves on a variety of subjects.

Charles-Marie-René Leconte de Lisle

1818-1894

French poet, translator, historian, and dramatist.

Leconte de Lisle was the leading figure of the Parnassian movement in French poetry during the mid and late nineteenth century. His works exemplify the primary stylistic tenets of the Parnassians, who rejected the Romantic emphasis on subjective expression and unrestricted imagination and practiced rigid formalism, semantic precision, and pictorial imagery. Thematically Leconte de Lisle's poetry reflects his own literary and philosophic interests in its use of ancient myths and folklore and in its distinctly pessimistic metaphysical perspective.

The son of a Breton sugar-planter, Leconte de Lisle was born in Saint-Paul on the island of Bourbon, now Réunion, in the Indian Ocean. He spent much of his youth on the island, but lived in France from 1821 to 1828 and from 1837 to 1843; during the latter period he studied law at the University of Rennes. While at the university, Leconte de Lisle began to write poetry, and he gradually abandoned his legal studies in favor of a literary career. In 1845 Leconte de Lisle moved to Paris where he worked as a journalist, tutor, and translator. During this time he contributed poetry to and worked on the staff of several periodicals associated with Fourierism, a political philosophy named for French social scientist François-Marie-Charles Fourier which advocated communal living and republican government. In Paris Leconte de Lisle also met the noted Hellenist scholar Louis Ménard, who encouraged his developing interest in classical antiquity.

As a proponent of republicanism, Leconte de Lisle supported the revolution in France in 1848. He became discontented with the oligarchical leanings of the newly formed government, however, and had distanced himself from politics by the time the monarchical empire was reestablished in 1852. Published during that year, Leconte de Lisle's first poetry collection, *Poèmes antiques,* expresses his disillusionment with the modern world. The volume received slight attention, yet with the appearance of his *Poèmes barbares* in 1862, Leconte de Lisle was recognized as a notable opponent of Romanticism, and his contributions to the Parnassian journal *Le parnasse contemporain* during the 1860s and 1870s established him as the movement's leader. Throughout these decades Leconte de Lisle also published esteemed French translations of classical works, and in 1872 he was appointed a Senate librarian. He continued to write poetry and translate during the 1880s, publishing *Poèmes tragiques* in 1884 and earning the critical recognition that led to his election to the French Academy in 1886 as the successor of Victor Hugo. Leconte de Lisle died in 1894 at Louveciennes.

Critics consider *Poèmes antiques* and *Poèmes barbares* Leconte de Lisle's most significant works. In the former volume, he addresses subjects from Greek and Eastern mythology. Commentators observe that in spite of his attempts to adhere to the objective facts of his source materials, Leconte de Lisle poetically idealizes past civilizations in *Poèmes antiques,* finding them more conducive to artistic beauty than his own era. The poems in the collection also reflect Leconte de Lisle's worldview in their depictions of the conflict between earthly struggle and a transcendent existence that resembles the Buddhist concept of nirvana. Poems such as "Midi" and "Dies Irae" particularly portray a universe indifferent to humanity and are representative of the cosmic despair expressed throughout Leconte de Lisle's work.

Poèmes barbares treats a number of historical cultures, termed "barbaric" in that they stand apart from the Greco-Latin tradition. Included in the volume are works that adapt the legends and folklore of Egyptian, Scandinavian, Celtic, and Polynesian societies, among others, as well as poems derived from biblical stories. As with *Poèmes antiques,* the works in the collection glorify past civilizations, often those on the verge of historical transition, and espouse the "art for art's sake" ideal that characterized the Parnassians. Poems such as "Qaïn" exemplify Leconte de Lisle's philosophical pessimism and skepticism toward religion. Other works in the volume depict exotic natural settings or animals and are praised for their vivid description and precise imagery. Leconte de Lisle's later work largely reiterates the themes of his early poetry, and subsequent collections such as *Poèmes tragiques* are considered inferior to *Poèmes antiques* and *Poèmes barbares.*

Leconte de Lisle also wrote verse dramas, the most notable being *Les Errinyes,* and historical treatises that address religion and politics, typically voicing support for republican government and criticizing religious clericalism. However, he is chiefly remembered for the philosophical and metaphysical insights of his poetry, which critics deem an important artistic reflection of the intellectual currents of his time. Although English-language criticism and translations of his works remain limited, within France Leconte de Lisle is acknowledged as one of the most influential poets of the later half of the nineteenth century.

PRINCIPAL WORKS

Poèmes antiques (poetry) 1852; also published as *Poèmes antiques* [enlarged edition], 1872
Poèmes et poésies (poetry) 1855
Poésies de Leconte de Lisle (poetry) 1858
Poésies barbares (poetry) 1862; also published as *Poèmes barbares* [enlarged edition], 1874
Catéchisme populaire républicain (dialogue) 1871
Histoire populaire de la Révolution française (history) 1871
Histoire populaire du Christianisme (history) 1871
Les Errinyes (drama) [first publication] 1873 [*Orestes* (adapted by André Tridon and Arthur Guiterman), 1909]
Œuvres de Leconte de Lisle. 4 vols. (poetry) 1881-1899
Poèmes tragiques (poetry) 1884

L'Apollonide (drama) [first publication] 1888
Derniers poèmes (poetry, drama, and essay) 1895
Première poésies et lettres intimes (poetry and letters) 1902
Poésies completes. 4 vols. (poetry) 1927-28
Seven Poems (poetry) 1963

Charles Baudelaire (essay date 1861)

[*Baudelaire is considered one of the world's greatest lyric poets, and his masterpiece,* Les fleurs du mal (*1857; The Flowers of Evil*), *is ranked among the most influential volumes of French poetry. In* The Flowers of Evil, *Baudelaire analyzes, often in shocking terms, his urban surroundings, erotic love, and the conflicts within himself. Informing his treatment of these topics is his belief that human beings are inherently evil; only that which is artificial can be construed as absolutely good. Poetry, according to Baudelaire, should serve only to inspire and express beauty. This doctrine forms the basis of both his poetry and his equally esteemed criticism. In the following excerpt, he praises Leconte de Lisle's poetic craftsmanship and the depiction of nature in his works.*]

The distinctive character of [Leconte de Lisle's] poetry is a feeling of intellectual aristocracy, which would be sufficient in itself to explain the unpopularity of the author, if, on the other hand, we didn't know that in France unpopularity attends everything that approaches any kind of perfection. Through his innate taste for philosophy and through his power of picturesque description he rises far above those melancholy drawing-room poets, those makers of albums and keepsakes where everything, philosophy and poetry, is adapted to the emotions of young girls. . . . The only poet to whom Leconte de Lisle could be compared, without absurdity, is Théophile Gautier. These two minds take equal delight in travel; these two imaginations are naturally cosmopolitan. Both like a change of scene and both like to dress their thought in the variable fashions that time scatters through eternity. But Théophile Gautier gives detail sharper relief and heightened color, while Leconte de Lisle is more concerned with the philosophic armature. Both love the Orient and the desert; both admire repose as a principle of beauty. Both flood their poetry with a warm light, more sparkling in Théophile Gautier, more restful in Leconte de Lisle. Both are equally indifferent to all human deceits and succeed, without effort, in never being dupes. There is still another man, though in a different category, with whom Leconte de Lisle may be compared, and that is Ernest Renan. In spite of the differences separating the two, all discerning minds will detect a similarity. In the poet, as in the philosopher, I find that lively yet objective interest in religions and that same spirit of universal love, not for humanity taken in itself but for the various forms, depending on the era and the climate, with which man has clothed beauty and truth. In neither one is there ever any absurd impiety. To paint in beautiful verse, luminous and serene in nature, the various ways in which man, until now, has worshipped God and sought the beautiful, such has been, as far as one can judge from his most complete collection, the goal which Leconte de Lisle has assigned to his poetry.

His first pilgrimage was to Greece; and from the very first his poems, with their echo of classic beauty, were singled out by connoisseurs. Later, he did a series of imitations of Latin poems, which I for my part value infinitely more. But to be entirely fair, I must confess that my liking for the subject may well influence my judgment in this case, and that my natural predilection for Rome prevents me from feeling all the enjoyment that I should in the reading of his Greek poems.

Little by little his taste for travel drew him towards worlds of more mysterious beauty. The role that he has given to Asiatic religions is enormous, and it is there that he has poured out in majestic torrents his natural dislike for transitory things, for the frivolous things of life, and his infinite love for the immutable, for the eternal, for *divine nothingness.* At other times, with what seems capricious suddenness, he turned to the snows of Scandinavia and told us of the Northern gods, overthrown and dispelled, like the mist, by the radiant child of Judea. But whatever the majesty of manner and the soundness of reason displayed by Leconte de Lisle in these varied subjects, what I prefer in his works is a certain vein that is completely new, which belongs to him and to him alone. The poems of this type are few, and it may be that he neglected this genre the most, because it was the most natural to him. I am referring to the poems where, without preoccupation with religion and the successive forms of human thought, the poet described beauty as it appeared to his original and individual eye—the powerful, crushing forces of nature, the majesty of animals in movement or in repose, the charm of woman in sunny regions, and lastly the sublime calm of the desert or the fearful magnificence of the ocean. Here, Leconte de Lisle is a master and a great master. Here, triumphant poetry has no goal other than itself. True lovers of poetry know that I am referring to such poems as **"Les hurleurs," "Les eléphants," "Le sommeil du condor,"** etc., and above all to **"Le manchy"** which is an incomparable masterpiece, a true evocation, where glisten with all their mysterious charm the beauty and magic of the tropics, which no beauty, Southern, Greek, Italian, or Spanish can equal.

I have little to add. Leconte de Lisle has the ability to control his ideas; but that would mean almost nothing if he didn't also have the ability to handle his tools. His language is always noble, firm, strong, without shrill notes, without false modesty; his vocabulary vast; his linking of words is always distinguished and conforms perfectly with the nature of his mind. He employs rhythm with breadth and sureness, and his instrument has the mellow but full and deep tone of the viola. His rhymes, always exact without being too finical, fulfill the conditions that beauty requires and always comply with that contradictory and mysterious love of the human mind for surprise and symmetry.

As for that unpopularity which I mentioned at the beginning, I think I am echoing the poet's own thought when I say that it causes him no sadness and that the contrary would add nothing to his satisfaction. It is enough for him to be popular among those who are themselves worthy of pleasing him. Furthermore, he belongs to that family of minds which has for all that which is not superior a scorn so quiet that it doesn't even deign to express itself. (pp. 277-79)

Charles Baudelaire, "Leconte de Lisle," in
Baudelaire as a Literary Critic, edited and
translated by Lois Boe Hyslop and Francis E.
Hyslop, Jr., The Pennsylvania State University
Press, 1964, pp. 275-79.

Edward Dowden   (essay date 1889)

[An Irish educator and man of letters, Dowden was primarily a Shakespearean scholar, editing many of the
dramatist's plays and numbering among his several critical studies Shakespeare, His Mind and Art (1875).
Also a biographer of some note, Dowden believed that
criticism of a literary work must be allied with an understanding of the personality and circumstances of the author. In the following excerpt, he examines the themes
and aesthetic creed of Leconte de Lisle's poetry.]

To associate poetry fraternally with the higher thought of
our own day has been part of the work of M. Leconte de
Lisle. The effort of criticism in our time has been before
all else to see things as they are, without partiality, without
obtrusion of personal liking or disliking, without the impertinence of blame or of applause. To see things as they
are is the effort of Leconte de Lisle's poetry. Critical curiosity gratifies itself by the accurate perception of facts, and
of their relations one to another. In like manner the imagination delights to comprehend after its own fashion the
chief attitudes which the spirit of man has assumed in
presence of external nature, of God, of life and death, to
enter into the faiths of past ages and races while yet holding essentially aloof from them, to distinguish the main
features of former societies of men, and to illuminate these
without permitting our passions to disturb their calm.
Baudelaire [see excerpt dated 1861] happily compared Leconte de Lisle to his distinguished contemporary Ernest
Renan.

> Notwithstanding the difference between their re-
> spective provinces, every person of clear-sighted in-
> telligence will feel that the comparison is just. In
> the poet, as in the philosopher, I find the same ar-
> dent yet impartial curiosity with reference to reli-
> gions, and the same spirit of universal love, not for
> humanity in itself, but for the various forms in
> which man in every age and clime has incarnated
> beauty and truth. Neither the one nor the other
> ever offends by absurd impiety. To portray in beau-
> tiful verses, of a luminous and tranquil kind, the
> different modes in which man, up to the present
> time, has adored God, and sought the beautiful,
> such has been the object . . . which Leconte de
> Lisle has assigned to his poetry.

Such poetry, it will be perceived, has close affinities with
science, and yet it is in its essence the work of the skilled
imagination. It possesses the ardour and the calm of science. One cannot look at the remarkable portrait of the
poet by Rajon without recognising the aspiring intellect,
the robust enthusiasm, the capacity for sustained effort, of
Leconte de Lisle. The lifted head, with eyes which gaze
steadfastly forward, might well be that of a sculptor contemplating the block in which he sees the enthralled form
of beauty whose deliverance he is presently to effect. The
products of this enthusiasm possess a marmoreal calm;
and it is the union of the highest energy with a lofty tranquillity which distinguishes the method of this artist. To

persons who expect from poetry a shallow excitement, to
persons whose imagination has not yet been nourished by
the intellect, it is possible that Leconte de Lisle's chief
poems may seem masterpieces of the genre ennuyant
["tiresome kind"]. It calls for some disengagement from
self, and from the common preoccupations of our lives, to
be able to transfer our total being into a world of thoughts
and things remote and alien. The imaginative Pantheon of
the average reader contains the familiar figures of the gods
of Greece and Rome; it is embarrassing when house-room
and welcome are required all at once for a throng of
strangers of appalling aspect and names gathered from
India, from Egypt, from Scandinavia, even from the Polynesian islands, and still more embarrassing to find among
the antique gods certain well-known shapes arrived from
Palestine which seek admission on equal terms with the
rest. And it must be admitted that, after a trial of one's
powers of sustained receptiveness by Leconte de Lisle, a
trial which cannot be carried through without some fortitude of the imagination, we turn with a peculiar sense of
relief to such lyrical sprightliness as that of Théodore de
Banville, and find no small recreation for the eye in his
mirthful antics upon the tight rope.

Yet Leconte de Lisle's poems are no mere works of erudite
archæology. He too, although possessed of a social faith,
is, like Baudelaire, ill at ease in the present time. At first
upon making his acquaintance we say, Here at least is a
man who has escaped the sorrow of our age, who has not
known "the something that infects the world;" and we
surmise that perhaps it is his Creole blood, perhaps the un-
vitiated air of his native Isle of Bourbon, which has left
him sane and sound. But presently we perceive that this
is not so. The stoicism, the impassiveness, the enforced serenity, the strict self-suppression, the resolved impersonality of his writings reveal the fact that he too has been a sufferer. These constitute the regimen by which he would
gain sanity and strength. Are you unhappy? Then utter no
cry, suppress the idle tear, forbear to turn the tender emotion upon yourself, place yourself under the influence of
things beautiful, calm, and remote, resign your imagination in absolute obedience to the object. And if, after prac-
tising such discipline, your unhappiness still survive, the
physician adds, Accept the inevitable. Is it so strange and
bitter to be defeated? Or does not every law of nature fulfil
its course indifferent to our joy or suffering? Bear your sorrow as you would bear the shining of the stars or the falling of the rain.

Thus, while Baudelaire studied with curious attention the
evils of his time, and tasked his imagination to render an
account of what was abnormal and diseased in the world
around him, Leconte de Lisle turns away to seek for calm
in the contemplation of nature in her virgin grace or her
teeming maternal forces, and of man in states of society
and under religious beliefs which possess for us an imaginative and scientific interest rather than the more pressing
and painful interest of actuality. To Greece he is attracted
as to the immortal patron of beauty; to the primitive peoples of the North, because among them he finds a massive
force of passion and of muscle which contrasts happily
with the trivialities of the boulevard; to India, because her
sages had learned the secret that this turmoil of life is
Mâyâ (the divine illusion), and that behind Mâyâ lies the
silence and calm of "le divin Néant" ["the divine Nothingness"]. We may prepare ourselves for a fashion of pessi-

mism among our small poets of culture at an early date, and doubtless "le divin Néant" will be celebrated by many self-complacent prophets of despair. Leconte de Lisle is not a pessimist; for the race of men he sees a far-off light towards which it advances, and for his own part life is to be endured and rendered as beautiful and grand as may be with noble forms and the light of large ideas.

Among the poems of Leconte de Lisle his studies of external nature take a high place. When he sets himself down before an object resolved to make it his own by complete imaginative possession, he is not a mere descriptive poet. The great animal painter is not he who can most dexterously imitate wools and furs, but he who can pluck out the heart of the mystery of each form of animal life; and a like remark holds true of the painter of mountain or of sea. That which he seeks to discover is the ideal—that is to say, that part of the real which is the most essential as distinguished from the accidental, the permanent as distinguished from the temporary, the dominant as distinguished from the subordinate. He who by penetrative vision can discover the ideal in each thing, or, in plain words, its essential characteristics, may fearlessly go on to paint furs and wools to perfection. And such is the method of Leconte de Lisle. In his choice of subjects (for the poet chooses rather than is chosen by them) he is attracted by the beauty and the wonder of strange exotic things and places. Two moments of the day in the tropics seem to contain for his imagination the highest poetry of the four-and-twenty hours—the dawn, with its solitude, its freshness in the heavens, and light odours rising from the earth, its tender stirring in the foliage and the flowers; and then mid-noon, with the torrent of light, the oppression of loaded heat, the moveless air, and the languor of all living things. Life in the jungle at midday is the subject of a remarkable study familiar to all readers of Leconte de Lisle. The huge panther lies asleep, his belly to the air, his claws dilating unconsciously, his burning breath escaping as from a furnace, his rosy tongue lolling; around him perfect silence, only the gliding python advancing his head, and the cantharides vibrating in the transparent air. . . . (pp. 413-18)

In contrast with ["Les jungles"], and others of the torrid atmosphere, we find all that is delicious in shadowy repose, in dewy freshness, in the light singing of streams, in the flowers of wan green places, present with us while we read **"La fontaine aux lianes"** and **"La ravine Saint-Gilles."** **"Le manchy"** ("manchy," the palanquin of the Isle Bourbon), so softly breathed upon by the sea-wind and impregnated with exquisite odours of the East, moves delicately forward like the rhythmical stepping of the Hindoo bearers. But of higher imaginative power than any of these is the short piece entitled **"Le sommeil du condor."** No study of the poetry of animal life is of more exciting strangeness and at the same time of more mysterious solemnity than this. (pp. 418-19)

None of the most characteristic poems of Leconte de Lisle treat of social subjects which lie near to us in time and place. His poetry selects as its organs certain of his faculties, and rejects others. To express his political creed he would require to formulate it in prose. Christian and mediæval subjects are treated with the same aloofness, the same *hauteur,* and the same sympathy of intellect as those belonging to ancient Greece and Rome, or to the "barbar-

ian" nations of Judea, of Egypt, of pagan Europe. But under this impartiality as an artist lie strenuous convictions both with respect to the régime of feudalism and the dogma of the age of faith, and, indeed, the impartiality at times impresses the reader who compares the poems with the author's prose confessions of belief as partaking somewhat of the nature of an imperturbable artistic irony. The commoner, more superficial irony is excluded from Leconte de Lisle's work as an artist, but it is made ample use of in the volume *Histoire populaire du Christianisme,* a little treatise which, professing to represent Christian history as told by Christian historians, is certainly not distinguished by the judicial spirit or even by common historical accuracy.

It is not to be wondered at that Leconte de Lisle should be regarded as a master by younger poets who aspire to be something more than mere singers of love and wine. He represents intellect, he represents science in connection with art; he has more of mass than Gautier, more of sanity, or at least serenity, than Baudelaire; he is distinguished by a rare self-regulating energy of the imagination; he owns a sovereign command over form, a severity and breadth of poetical style which is not to be found in the *Émaux et camées,* nor even in the *Fleurs du mal.* But it is true that his subjects of predilection are too much subjects from the museum. He is not a mere antiquary; in his manner of aloofness and of intellectual sympathy he is essentially modern, and in the museum he remains a poet. Still we should like to know of love which was other than that possessed by a mummy; we should like to know of a religion which is not on show as a curiosity in a glass-case; outside we hear the throng in the streets of a great city, and wonder what the lives of our fellow-men are like, and what they signify to them; we think of the fields in which we ourselves were children, and which we did not study curiously, but so tenderly loved. (pp. 419-21)

> *Edward Dowden, "On Some French Writers of Verse, 1830-1877," in his* Studies in Literature: 1789-1877, *fifth edition, Kegan Paul, Trench & Co., 1889, pp. 392-427.*

Ferdinand Brunetière   (essay date 1894)

[*Brunetière was an influential French critic of the latter part of the nineteenth century, who, for many years, taught at the prestigious Ecole Normale Superieure and edited and contributed frequently to the journal* Revue des deux mondes. *Conservative and Neoclassical in his tastes, Brunetière opposed the aesthetics of Romanticism, Realism, and Naturalism. His most important contribution to literary criticism is his Darwinian-based theory of the evolution of genres, which he explicated in his* L'évolution de la critique *(1890). In the following excerpt, Brunetière describes Leconte de Lisle's divergence from nineteenth-century French Romanticism in his poetry. Translations from the French originally appeared in the essay in footnote form.*]

In order to form a correct idea of the work of Leconte de Lisle, and to fix the relative importance of his *Poèmes antiques* and *Poèmes barbares* in the history of contemporary poetry, it is above all necessary to see therein, as in the writings of Flaubert to whom I shall more than once compare him, especially the *Tentation de Saint-Antoine* and *Salammbô,* a protest against the Romantic school. I do not mean to say that both Flaubert and Leconte de Lisle did not largely benefit by the revolution brought about by Hugo. The solidarity uniting the generations of man never permits us to get entirely free from the influence of those who preceded us, and it would be as impossible to explain Leconte de Lisle without Hugo as it would have been to explain Racine without Corneille, or Malherbe without Ronsard. (p. 891)

[While] the Romantic School, sprung partly from the revolt against the "Greeks and Romans," remained faithful in [Hugo's poetry collection] *Légende des siècles* to its origin, the mere title, **Poèmes antiques,** is both eloquent and significant. I say nothing of the preface, to be found in the early editions, and since the poet thought well to suppress it, I will not quote from it. But some lines taken from the beautiful poem, **"Hypatie,"** the virgin of Alexandria and Cyril's victim, are not less characteristic:

> O vierge, qui, d'un pan de ta robe pieuse,
> Couvris la tombe auguste où s'endormaient tes
>   Dieux,
> De leur culte éclipsé prêtresse harmonieuse,
> Chaste et dernier rayon détaché de leurs cieux!
>
> Je t'aime et te salue, ô vierge magnanime!
> Quand l'orage ébranla le monde paternel,
> Tu suivis dans l'exil cet Œdipe sublime,
> Et tu l'enveloppas d'un amour éternel.

> ["O virgin, who, with a fold of thy pious robe,
> Didst cover the august tomb wherein thy gods
>   slumbered,
> Musical priestess of their extinguished worship,
> Chaste and last ray fallen from their heavens!
>
> I love thee and greet thee, O great-hearted maiden!
> When the tempest shattered the world of thy fa-
>   thers,
> Thou didst follow that sublime Œdipus into exile,
> And thou didst enfold him with an eternal love."]

This is a real profession of faith. With a touch of impiousness, the poet goes back beyond those Middle Ages—of which the Romanticists, while exploiting them for their picturesque odds and ends, formed, nevertheless, so false an idea—to Grecian sources, to draw thence together with the favourite subjects of his Muse, the long-lost feeling for plastic art.

> Marbre sacré, vêtu de force et de génie

> ["Hallowed marble, clothed with power and with
>   genius"]

he cries, addressing himself to the Venus of Milo,

> Déesse irrésistible au port victorieux,
> Pure comme un éclair, et comme une harmonie,
> O Vénus, ô beauté, blanche mère des Dieux.

> ["Irresistible goddess, of victorious mien,
> Pure as the lightning, and like a harmony,
> O Venus, O beauty, white mother of the gods."]
>
> (p. 892)

It would not be possible to declare war more openly against the Romantic School, or to go over more resolutely to the side of those "classics" whose altars the Hugos, the Dumas, and the Mussets imagined themselves to have completely overthrown; it would not be possible more frankly to write oneself down an enemy to the "Génie du Christianisme," or to renew more deliberately the tradition of Chénier, Racine, and Ronsard.

The truth is, as to-day we see clearly, that that for which the Romantic School had the least perception was the Beautiful; in the preface to [Hugo's drama] *Cromwell* it had actually been denied as a legitimate end or aim of art, and in its place was substituted the representation of what was called "character," although it would have been more candid to have named it the "ugly" outright. Of all the heroes of Homer's epic, Hugo cared for none but Thersites, the "Ursus," or "Quasimodo" of the Trojan war; and of all the Greek plays, I doubt whether he understood much else than the low jesting in the *Frogs.* But the Beautiful, merely a word for the Romanticists, and a word which they misunderstood, was a reality for the author of the **Poèmes antiques**; indeed, the only reality. Though the ideal model perhaps nowhere existed, it is the glory of art to have created it. Something of it was to be found in the Parthenon and the Venus of Milo; something in those legends which alone consoled him for the spectacle of contemporary ugliness and mediocrity; and an idyll of Theocritus, or an ode of Anacreon, appeared to him as much superior through the correctness of sentiment, the perfection of execution, and the depth of æsthetic emotion to Musset's "Nuits," for instance, or Hugo's *Orientales,* as a statue of the already decadent school of Pergamus, the Farnesian Bull, the Laocoon, or a Praxitelean Venus to the declamatory style of sculpture of David of Angers. I do not say he was altogether in the right. Were I here to discuss his opinions, I might reproach him with some little injustice towards the Romantic School, some little weakness for the antique. Twenty centuries can scarcely have gone by without profit for Humanity, and therefore for Art. But what is for the moment of more importance, is to follow out through the poet's works his development of these premisses, and to observe, as we proceed, how his teaching combats point by point that of the Romanticists.

What his example teaches first of all is the cult of Art, and rigid respect for Form. No lesson was at that time, about the year 1852, more necessary than this one, when in the silence maintained by Hugo for over a dozen years, Lamartine's easy grace and Musset's literary dandyism had begun to found a school of their own; unless indeed it were to re-learn how to write verse which was genuine verse. There is none more beautiful in the French language than Leconte de Lisle's, and his **"Midi"** is invariably quoted in proof.

> Midi, roi des étés, épandu sur la plaine,
> Tombe en nappes d'argent des hauteurs du ciel
>   bleu.

> ["Noon, the king of summer seasons, showered
>   upon the plain,
> Falls in sheets of silver from the heights of the blue
>   heaven."]

Now that the poet is dead, I venture to quote these lines in my turn, for I may remark, he did not much care to hear them quoted, and to find that his name invariably recalled them to mind; it had on him the same sort of effect which Flaubert experienced, on always hearing himself spoken of as the author of *Madame Bovary.* But one may quote at hazard from the **Poèmes antiques**:

O jeune Thyoné, vierge au regard vainqueur,
Aphrodite jamais n'a fait battre ton cœur;
Ah! si les Dieux jaloux, vierge, n'ont pas formé
La neige de ton corps d'un marbre inanimé,
Viens au fond des grands bois, sous les larges ramures,
Pleines de frais silence et d'amoureux murmures.
L'oiseau rit dans les bois, au bord des nids mousseux.
O belle chasseresse, et le vent paresseux
Berce du mol effort de son aile éthérée
Les larmes de la nuit sur la feuille dorée.

["O young Thyoné, virgin with the conquering glance,
Never has Aphrodite made thy heart beat;
Ah, if the jealous gods, virgin, have not formed
Thy snowy body from inanimate marble,
Come to the depths of the vast woods, under the great
   branches,
Full of cool silence and amorous murmurs.
The bird laughs in the woods, on the edge of his mossy
   nest,
O beautiful huntress! and the lazy wind
Softly sways with its ethereal wing
The tears of the night on gilded leaves."]

(pp. 893-94)

If ever one has painted, or, better, carved in verse, it is in such lines as these, which, naturally, I have selected with the intention of thereby showing how care for form is united to the study of the antique. Gautier, who was no great scholar, and assuredly no "great Greek," had also had a glimmering of the same idea. But he was too devoted to Spain; and besides, how could he possibly free himself from his early Romanticism? The **Poèmes antiques** did that which neither the "Psyche" of Victor de Laprade (for which the honour has sometimes been claimed, although this poem is but Lamartine over again, and a more hazy and obscure Lamartine) nor even the too few poems in [Gautier's] *Émaux et camées* could do. Leconte de Lisle won no fame thereby, above all, no popularity; but the Antique was vindicated from the stupid contempt it had been the fashion to affect for it during the last quarter of a century, the classic tradition was again taken up where Romanticism had broken it, and Romanticism itself was stricken, in the breed of spurious Elegiacs who fancied they represented it.

And in fact, these did represent it; for should one inquire what in France was the essential character of the Romantic movement, it would be found, . . . to be neither broader nor deeper than the personal exaltation or hypertrophy of the poet himself. Under the specious name—freedom in art—the Romanticists in general sought merely to emancipate themselves from social usages, literary traditions, and the conditions of Art herself. In consequence, they succeeded only in the Ode and in the Elegy, and perhaps in lyrical satire. But even here, and in a style which may be properly termed personal, we know to what—with their talent for exaggeration, or rather licence in all things, which is not the least interesting or displeasing trait in their physiognomy—they eventually fell; to what depths of imbecile self-analysis and self-exposure. Did a mistress deceive them? Instantly they must inform the whole universe of the fact. Had not Lamartine, Hugo, Musset, and Sainte-Beuve already set them the example?—and even the further one of "confessing" in public; very little to the advantage of God and morality, still less to that of poetry.

Nothing could be more opposed to the genius of Leconte de Lisle, and here again one cannot imagine a greater con-

trast than that between the **Poèmes antiques** or the *Feuilles d'automne* [by Hugo], for instance, and Musset's "Nuits."

Tel qu'un morne animal, meurtri, plein de pous-
   sière,
La chaîne au cou, hurlant au chaud soleil d'été,
Promène qui voudra son cœur ensanglanté
Sur ton pavé cynique, ô plèbe carnassière!

Pour mettre un feu stérile en ton œil hébété,
Pour mendier ton rire ou ta pitié grossière,
Déchire qui voudra la robe de lumière
De la pudeur divine et de la volupté.

Dans mon orgueil muet, dans ma tombe sans
   gloire,
Dussé-je m'engloutir pour l'éternité noire,
Je ne te vendrai pas mon ivresse ou mon mal,

Je ne livrerai pas ma vie à tes huées,
Je ne danserai pas sur ton tréteau banal,
Avec tes histrions et tes prostituées.

["Like a poor beast, wounded, covered with dust,
A chain round its neck, moaning to the hot sum-
   mer's sun,
Let who will drag his bleeding heart
Through thy cynical streets, O bloodthirsty rabble!

To bring a barren gleam to thy dull eye,
To beg thy laughter, or thy coarse pity,
Let who will rend the luminous robe
Of heavenly modesty and of passionate joy.

In my dumb pride, in my inglorious tomb,
Even though I must remain buried through black
   eternity,
Yet will I not sell thee my ecstacy or my pain.

I will not deliver up my life to thy shouts,
I will not dance on thy vulgar stage,
   with thy mummers and harlots."]

Those who knew the poet know how faithfully these well-known lines express the depths of his feelings. Unexpansive in character, infusing usually a shade of irony into manners of exquisite courtesy, he held himself always in perfect self-command; but did you desire to draw him out of his habitual reserve, you had but to get him on this subject to see that he would never forgive the Romanticists their prostitution of Art to base uses. *"Les montreurs"* is the title he himself gave to that sonnet, the rough energy of which testifies to the strength of his indignation. After this I have no need to add that, faithful to the first article of his Æsthetics, he but once or twice makes allusion in his writings to the history of his personal feelings: in the **"Manchy,"** one of his best known poems, and in **"Illusion suprême"**:

Celui qui va goûter le sommeil sans aurore
Dont l'homme ni le Dieu n'ont pu rompre le sceau,
Chair qui va disparaître, âme qui s'évapore,
S'emplit des visions qui hantaient son berceau.

Rien du passé perdu qui soudain ne renaisse:
La montagne natale et les vieux tamarins,
Les chers morts qui l'aimaient au temps de sa jeu-
   nesse
Et qui dorment là-bas dans les sables marins. . . . .

["He who is to taste the sleep that has no morrow,

> Whereof neither Man nor God has been able to
>   break the seal,
> Vanishing flesh, soul melting into air,
> He is filled with the visions that haunted his cradle.
>
> Nought of the lost past but is suddenly born anew:
> His native mountain, and the old tamarind-trees;
> The dear ones dead who loved him in the time of
>   his youth,
> And who sleep, away yonder, in the sands of the
>   shore."]

And this is but a sigh, at once repressed, from the poet's overcharged heart; and the involuntary confidence promptly fades away into a description of the splendours of the scene:

> Sous les lilas géants où vibrent les abeilles,
> Voici le vert coteau, la tranquille maison,
> Les grappes de Letchis et les mangues vermeilles
> Et l'oiseau bleu dans le maïs en floraison.
>
> ["Under giant lilacs, where bees are humming,
> There is the green hillside, there the quiet house,
> There are the clusters of letchis, and the scarlet
>   mangoes,
> And the blue bird in the flowering maize."]

But Leconte de Lisle disliked the Romanticists no less on account of their perpetual self-absorption than for what was the natural consequence of this, the enormity of their ignorance. And although some few among them have figured in politics, it must be admitted that save there and in poetry, they were indeed ignorant. Put aside some two or three, with Sainte-Beuve at their head; it would be impossible to imagine an indifference more complete than Musset's, unless, indeed, it were Hugo's, for the great historical, philosophical, and scientific movement with which they were contemporary. Such indifference exasperated Leconte de Lisle, who held that "science and art, too long divided as the result of diverging efforts, should be linked by the intellect in intimate union, if not totally merged one in the other." He wrote again:

> Art is the primitive revelation of the Ideal in Nature, Science its reasoned and enlightened exposition. But Art has lost its intuitive spontaneity, or rather has exhausted it. It is for Science to recall the meaning of its forgotten traditions, and infuse them with a new life under suitable characteristic forms.

And thus, having made himself master of these "forms" before composing the *Poèmes antiques,* he found himself led to the expression of nothing but what was "objective" or impersonal as the forms themselves; while in the *Poèmes barbares* he was brought to realise in an unexpected manner, through the alliance of Science and Art, a more contemporary ideal, if I may so describe it, than that of the most determined partisans of "modernity in Art." Let me try to define this, and make clearer the difference between it and the ideal of the Romantic School.

"On the monuments of Persepolis," says Ernest Renan,

> you may see the various nations, tributary to the King of Persia, represented by an individual clothed in the fashion of his own country, and bearing in his hands specimens of its produce, to offer in homage to his suzerain. Such is Humanity; every nation, every intellectual, religious, or moral movement leaves behind it a brief formula, which is, as

the abridged type, surviving to represent those forgotten millions who once lived and died grouped around it.

It is this representation of the "abridged type" of the race which Leconte de Lisle sought first of all to immortalise in his work; in **"Qaïn,"** in the **"Vigne de Naboth,"** in **"Néférou-Ra,"** the **"Vérandah,"** the **"Mort de Valmiki,"** the **"Epée d'Angantyr,"** and in other poems which differ from the apparently analogous poems of the *Légende des siècles,* exactly in so far as the erudition of truth differs from the caprices of the imagination.

> Ils s'en venaient de la montagne et de la plaine,
> Du fond des sombres bois et du désert sans fin,
> Plus massifs que le cèdre et plus hauts que le pin,
> Suants, échevelés, soufflant leur rude haleine
> Avec leur bouche épaisse et rouge, et pleins de faim.
>
> . . . . .
>
> C'est ainsi qu'ils rentraient, l'ours velu des cavernes
> À l'épaule, ou le cerf, ou le lion sanglant
> Et les femmes marchaient, géantes, d'un pas lent
> Sous les vases d'airain qu'emplit l'eau des citernes.
> Graves, et les bras nus, et les mains sur le flanc.
>
> Les ânes de Khamos, les vaches aux mamelles
> Pesantes, les boucs noirs, les taureaux vagabonds
> Se hâtaient, sous l'épieu, par files et par bonds,
> Et de grands chiens mordaient le jarret des chamelles;
> Et les portes criaient en tournant sur leurs gonds.
>
> ["They came from the mountain and from the
>   plain,
> From the depth of dark woods, and from the limitless desert,
> More massive than the cedar, and taller than the
>   pine,
> Sweating, dishevelled, breathing in harsh gasps,
> With their thick red mouths, and full of hunger.
>
> . . . . .
>
> It was thus that they came home; the shaggy cavebear
> Slung from their shoulders, or the deer, or the
>   bleeding lion.
> And the women, giantesses, marched with slow
>   steps,
> Bearing brazen urns filled with the water of the cisterns,
> Grave, their arms bare, their hands on their hips.
>
> Asses of Khamos, cows with heavy udders,
> Black rams, wild bulls,
> Hastened under the goad, in leaping ranks,
> And great dogs worried the heels of the she-camels;
> And the gates screamed as they turned on their
>   hinges."]

In these fine lines there is not a word, not a detail, which does not serve to paint some prehistoric trait; not one which is the mere invention of the poet. The exact contrary may be asserted of Hugo's sense of conscientiousness, and of his **"Qaïn."** The *Poèmes barbares* are to the *Légende des siècles* what Flaubert's *Madame Bovary* is to the *Indiana* or *Valentine* of George Sand; or in another line, what Taine's *Origines de la France contemporaine* is to Lamartine's *Girondins,* or Michelet's *Révolution.* As with the historian and the novelist, the poet, abdicating his own personality, has set himself to get at the truth of things, and taking advantage of all the information afforded him by the erudition of the age, was the first to turn out really critical and naturalistic work. His conception of Egypt was obtained through the younger Champollion; and though ignorance of the language prevented him from reading the *Baghavata-Purana,* or the *Lalita-Vistara,* in the vernacular, he has nevertheless written of India and of Buddhism, on the authority of Lassen and Burnouf. To put it again in another way, Leconte de Lisle did not see in history or tradition a personal pretext for the composition of sonorous verse, but he consecrated his Muse to the utterance of truths acquired by means of tradition and history. His attitude was not that of the mere scholar, but actually that of the zoologist or botanist, towards his own special subject; and it was thus that he first realised in a truly novel manner, and in one that completely satisfied his ambition, the alliance or union of Science and Poetry.

For this reason, too, while his conception of history differs fundamentally from that of the Romanticists, his conception of nature is no less divergent from theirs. . . . [The Romanticists] belittled it to man's measure, and, while never tired of chanting its praises, cut down the whole universe to their own field of vision. Going further still, they held that man had been given the world in fief, and that the birds of the air, no less than the fishes of the sea, had been in a manner created for his benefit. But it is precisely now, when we most wish for such a belief, that we can no longer hold it; and the author of *Poèmes antiques* and *Poèmes barbares* never held it. He knew that we, like the beasts of the field, are but tenants of a day on the earth's surface, and if, on the infinite ladder of life, we stand perchance on the topmost rung, nevertheless we are yet a part of the whole; hence, in his works, the characteristics of so many of his descriptions, which are no less antithetical to those of Lamartine and Hugo than to those even of Lemercier and the Abbé Delille—see, for instance, the **"Eléphants,"** the **"Hurleurs,"** the **"Sommeil du condor,"** the **"Rêve du jaguar,"** the **"Panthère noire,"** or the **"Chasse de l'aigle"**. . . . (pp. 895-900)

Then read **"Le Bernica,"** the **"Ravine Saint-Gilles,"** the **"Forêt vierge,"** a **"Coucher de soleil,"** each matchless for truth, without analogy in the history of French poetry—like Barye's animals in the history of sculpture—and notice the philosophic sense and tendency of all these descriptions. In the instincts and desires of the brute world, the poet unveils for us the far-off origins, the obscure genesis of our own, and, indeed, we recognise ourselves therein. In the bosom of nature we constitute no empire in an empire, and there is no such thing as a reign of humanity. Here lies the novelty, here, the originality of these "pictures," which might each be taken straight out from Humboldt's *Cosmos.* The elephants that roam over the desert, the dogs that howl upon the water's edge—these, too, have souls, though it may be but rudimentary ones:

> Devant la lune errante aux livides clartés,
> Quelle angoisse inconnue, au bord des noires ondes,
> Faisait pleurer une âme en vos formes immondes?
> Pourquoi gémissiez-vous, spectres épouvantés?

> ["Beneath the wandering moon, with its livid light,
> Beside the dark waters, what unknown anguish
> Made a soul weep in your unclean forms?
> Why did you moan, terrified spectres?"]

The answer is simple: something is taking place in them, analogous to that which takes place in us; for they, like us,

are but the mobile and ever-changing expression of nature's manifestations within them. The whole of nature is One, always the same groundwork beneath a multiplicity of forms; a truth which the ancient wisdom of India and mythology in general understood well. When the albatross, king of space and of the "shoreless seas"

> Vole contre l'assaut des rafales sauvages,

> ["Flies against the assault of savage blasts,"]

though he cannot speak of it, the pride of combat, and the joy of victory display themselves in every beat of his wings. And when the eagle carries off from the valley prey for his young he is neither cruel, rapacious, nor sanguinary, as we in our narrowness are wont to describe him, but is simply acting according to his nature, just as we act according to ours; and his so-called ferocity is but the manifestation of his paternal love. He works for his own preservation, and for that of his species. Here are sentiments which are not, I think, common; and if these are the soul of Leconte de Lisle's descriptions, it is that, as I said just now, which makes them above all things scientific and philosophic.

By a natural consequence—a necessary one even, as could be proved—his well-defined preoccupation with nature led him to study in a special manner the various religious systems, religion being in reality nothing but the expression of man's relations with the world around him. Ernest Renan, about the same time, was saying, in his own fashion, the same thing when he announced his celebrated paradox, "the desert is monotheistic." With Renan, therefore, and I am not the first to remark upon it, the author of *Poèmes antiques* and *Poèmes barbares* sought the abridged type, the ethnical formula which the vanished races bequeath as memorials to those which come after them in religious symbols. (pp. 900-01)

If this is the real metaphysical direction of his writings, I have no need to point out that nothing differentiates it more completely from those of the Romantic school. I know no more determined optimists than Lamartine and Alfred de Musset; and though Victor Hugo, and George Sand have sometimes appeared to believe in the existence of evil, on the other hand, they have always believed—the *Misérables* and the *Compagnon du tour de France* had no other end but to prove it—and they have died believing that just a little good-will was all that was necessary to drive poverty, suffering, injustice, crime and vice from off the surface of the globe. Leconte de Lisle held, on the contrary, that a man's greatest happiness was never to have been born; the next best was his death; which is the very formula of both Schopenhauer's and Sakya-Mouni's pessimism. Having discovered in nature and in history, and above all in the religions of the world, nothing but reasons for despairing of God, the author of the *Poèmes antiques* and *Poèmes barbares* went to the root of the doctrine. Nothing is less Romantic, we must confess. For Romanticism means hope, is the chimera or hippogriff that one spurs across the impossible; it is faith also, and the heart's reasoning, which one sets up triumphantly against the "reasoning of the intellect." And doubtless, here is one form of poetry, but the **"Dies Iræ"** . . . shows that another kind also exists; nor is it the less elevated, or the less noble for having preserved, even in negation, that sereneness which perhaps belongs to the definition of Art. I

Portrait of Leconte de Lisle in 1841 by Jean-François Millet.

would here remind my readers that want of "sentimentality" in nowise implies "impassibility."

In truth, we must not confound two very different things; the natural facility we all possess for eloquent complaints respecting our own sufferings; and the difficulty we experience even in understanding those of our neighbour. I will not again quote from **"L'illusion suprême,"** or **"Le manchy,"** but assuredly the poet who wrote **"La fontaine aux lianes,"** was neither "impassive" nor "insensitive." . . . (p. 903)

[Although] Leconte de Lisle made a religion to himself of art for art's sake, he nevertheless forgot occasionally its rigorous and narrow application, and his writings, as I have endeavoured to show, are more interpenetrated with humanity that he himself perhaps knew.

> O nuit! Déchirements enflammés de la nue,
> Cèdres déracinés, torrents, souffles hurleurs,
> O lamentations de mon père, ô douleurs,
> O remords, vous avez accueilli ma venue,
> Et ma mère a brûlé ma lèvres de ses pleurs.
>
> Buvant avec son lait la terreur qui l'enivre,
> A son côté gisant livide et sans abri,
> La foudre a répondu seule à mon premier cri:
> Celui qui m'engendra m'a reproché de vivre,
> Celle qui m'a conçu ne m'a jamais souri!

["O night! Fiery rendings of the cloud,
Uprooted cedars, torrents, howling blasts,
O lamentations of my father! O sorrows!
O remorse! You welcomed my coming;
And my mother scalded my lips with her tears.

Drinking in with her milk the terror that filled her,
Lying at her side, livid and unsheltered,
The thunder alone answered my first cry.
He who begot me reproached me for living.
She who conceived me never smiled upon me."]

The cry of Cain will doubtless last as long as the French language; and may we not ask of what eloquence consists, if not in the memory of Adam's sin, which still, after so many centuries, lies heavy upon his sons? or what is there more human?

It is time to conclude. Tendencies pass, but great works endure; and in the history of literature and of art, those are the real masters whose productions outlive the tendency. Leconte de Lisle is such a one. Marked out for immortality from the instant of their first appearance, the *Poèmes antiques* and *Poèmes barbares* remain unmarred by time.

> Les ans n'ont pas pesés sur leur grâce immortelle;
>
> ["The years have not weighed on their immortal grace";]

or, not to sacrifice the exactness of the phrase to the pleasure of quoting a last line from the poet, it were better said that time has neither tarnished their lustre nor diminished their solid worth. No doubt all are not of equal value, and the future will make its choice. But what may be asserted to-day is, that no one has given us in French, neither Ronsard in his *Odes,* nor, above all, in his *Hymnes,* nor Chénier in his *Idylles,* a more vivid and accurate picture of Grecian beauty than has the author of the **"Plainte du cyclope"** or **"Hèraklès au Taureau."** Should, however, the hypercritical, deeming this merit as one belonging rather to the archæologist than to the poet, acknowledge it but from the lips only, I will not insist upon it, nor point out to them that 'tis precisely this they praise most in Theocritus and Virgil. But I will remind them that no one has drawn with greater truthfulness and grandeur than Leconte de Lisle those nature-pictures of which the **"Panthère noire"** and the **"Sommeil du condor,"** the **"Eléphants"** and the **"Hurleurs,"** the **"Jungles"** and the **"Forêt vierge,"** are perhaps the masterpieces. And since one must seek to be armed at all points, should it be denied that in giving it an enumerative picturesqueness and a truly lyrical didactiveness, he has added to the art of poetical description a value hitherto unknown in our tongue, we may at any rate honour in the author of **"Qaïn"** and of the **"Fin de l'homme"** one of the poets who has sung the most eloquently all that is most painful, most tragic, and most universal in pessimism. (pp. 907-08)

> *Ferdinand Brunetière, "Leconte de Lisle," in* Contemporary Review, *Vol. LXVI, December, 1894, pp. 890-908.*

Irving Brown (essay date 1924)

[*In the following excerpt from his* Leconte de Lisle: A Study on the Man and His Poetry, *Brown examines the poet's portrayal of love and passion in several representative poems.*]

In his later years, protesting to Jules Huret against the oft-repeated criticism of the younger Dumas that he had "sacrificed his personal emotions, overcome passion, annihilated sensation, strangled sentiments," Leconte de Lisle exclaimed familiarly: "Will they ever get through talking such stuff and nonsense? Impassive poet! Just as long as one doesn't tell how he buttons his trousers, and how his flirtations are going, he is an impassive poet! It's stupid!" It is not surprising however that Dumas *fils* should have failed to see in the poet the very thing that was so evidently lacking in himself. Must we think the same of most of his brother critics?

"**Le manchy**" is the incarnation of the "eternal first love" that makes poets of us all. It is a vision, evanescent yet exact, beautified by the illusions of youth and rendered clear and indelible by the freshness of the young imagination. The fleeting moment, so precious to the poet in his later years and to those who have felt the same sweet thrill, has been preserved forever, with simple, plastic clarity. It is in a mood of worship that the poet sees the charming object of his first dreams descend from the heights, in the quiet early morning, to commune with God. The sun is sparkling along the green of the meadows that reach out into the infinite sea; while the clear, winged sound of the bells rises into space like the long flight of birds, visible far off above the gleaming waves. The loved one is not walking on the dusty road; instead she seems to float along in a sort of light sedan chair called a *manchy,* made of rattan and bamboo, and borne by supple Hindus, accompanying their rhythmic step with singing. Through the transparent curtain of the *manchy,* she appears in a cool cloud of filmy white. White, too, are the tunics of the Hindu bearers.

There is another mood. She is the diaphanous phantom of his youthful worship; but she is also the vision of a living body, the phantom of youthful desire. The languid air is fragrant from tamarind trees, and purple fruits. Groups of joyous negroes are responding to the animation of their own music. Languorously the young creole reclines in her *manchy,* at the edge of which one sees a rosy foot and an ankle encircled by an anklet. Her golden hair falls sinuously across a pillow, and her eyes, the color of deep amethyst, are almost closed. A butterfly settles for an instant on her soft skin. Its flower-like wings are tinged with the azure of youthful spirituality and the scarlet of budding desire. Her image was as young and fresh in the heart of the poet as the day he first beheld her, although for many years her body had lain in one of the little cemeteries that the creoles of Bourbon set apart in the sands beside the ever murmuring sea. Such is the force of his boyhood love that the years can not blot it out, and all who read the poem must likewise feel, as vividly as he, the youthful delicacy and force of that love.

More has been written about "**Le manchy**" than any of his other poems. It was one of the first to be translated into English. Most interesting of all is the light which Leconte de Lisle himself has thrown upon the poem, in a note to Jean Dornis, in which he says:

> This might be called: "How Poetry was Awakened in the Heart of a Boy of Fifteen." In the first place it is thanks to the good fortune of being born in a land that is marvelously beautiful and half wild, rich in strange vegetation, beneath a dazzling sky. Above all, it is thanks to the eternal "first love," a mingling of vague desires and delightful timidity: the budding impressionability of a virgin heart and soul, stirred with an innate feeling for nature. . . .

Already we have an intimation of the method of expression most often associated with the Parnassians. We are made to feel the emotion indirectly, through a description of surroundings that are completely expressive.

We find the vision of this maid who charmed his earliest dreams, recurring in his later poems like the prolongation of an echo. Gradually the image grows less voluptuous, until in "**Epiphany**" it is wholly etherealized, much as the little Bice of Dante's "New Life" becomes the radiant Beatrice of the *Paradise*. (pp. 85-7)

In the "**Illusion suprême**," we behold again the same diaphanous phantom, like a soft and melancholy emanation of the dawn, in the midst of sorrow and disillusion. Her grace and beauty transcend death and time. She smiles to him now from an enchanted world, with eyes that are divine.

In "**Epiphany**" the spiritualization is complete. We are no longer in the real world of the Tropics, with its languor and voluptuousness. We are in a dream world of the far North. It is still dawn. The dazzling sea has given place to the pale azure of a cool and limpid lake. Instead of the purple fruits and odorous tamarind trees, there is the silvery birch. Desire has given way completely to a mood of serene worship, of mysticism. In "**L'illusion suprême**," her immortality was still worldly, albeit enchanted, as she smiled to the poet. In "**Epiphany**" she passes into the presence of Divinity, in a world of celestial love. The *ideal* alone remains.

The poem is unique in modern French literature, although the process of idealization which produced it is inherent in each one of us. For a parallel one must go to Plato, to the poets of chivalry, and to Dante, or to a modern disciple of Dante, the author of the "Blessed Damozel."

In "**Le parfum impérissable**" we feel again the beautifying force of memory. Like Musset in the poem entitled "Souvenir," the poet recalls a love that was unhappy, but recalls it with joy. With the passing of time, all the bitterness and sorrow has been transformed by "the good fairy," Memory. Sorrow and pain have an intensity more acute than joy or pleasure, as Schopenhauer has ably pointed out. What he fails to point out is that the normal individual banishes the memory of pain into the depths of the subconscious, while the memory of the experience, and any joy associated with it, remains. Musset, simply describing the memory of his unhappy love for George Sand as recalled some years later by a visit to the scene of their love, has produced one of the most beautiful poems in the French language. "**Le parfum impérissable**" is less definitely autobiographical, and far more condensed. It is a not unworthy companion-piece however to "Souvenir."

Musset uses a landscape revisited to evoke the memory of an old love. Other poets have employed familiar sounds, but Leconte de Lisle has used the nostalgic power of perfume; and nothing brings up the past with all its fringe of feeling, more swiftly, more hauntingly, than odors laden with association. Furthermore there is something physical yet secret, invisible, and mysterious—one might almost say spiritual—which establishes a natural association between perfume and love, especially the perfume of the rose and love. One might write a volume on the use of the rose as a symbol of love in poetry, from the earliest verse of the Persians, to that of the Pléiade, in whatever lands the rose is cultivated. The persistency of certain perfumes is truly amazing. The crystal vial that holds the essence of the rose may break, the sea may flood it with its countless waves, and yet the broken bits retain the fragrance. It is this subtle persistence that Leconte de Lisle has seized upon, with originality and striking fitness, to express the undying joy of a love preserved and beautified by memory. . . . It is one of the greatest blessings of human nature that even our deepest sorrows may be transformed by time and may even come to be a source of pleasure. (pp. 87-90)

"Thestylis" is one of the poems most universally admired by Anglo-Saxon readers, though usually omitted from the anthologies because of its length. The landscape is that of Sicily, and the manner much like that of Theocritus. There is a period in the life of nearly every human being when one is more in love with love than with any particular person. It is a semi-religious sentiment, a tranquil exaltation tinged with sadness. It is this transitory feeling that Leconte de Lisle has so adequately expressed in these verses. The poem is so simple and clear, and yet so fragile and ethereal withal, that one hesitates to burden it with comments.

It opens with the tranquil evening, bearer of mysteries. The maiden is standing on a mountain above the sea, which gives her a feeling of infinite elation. The twilight, the distant lowing of oxen, and the far-off murmur of the sea add a touch of melancholy. She is alone and waiting for the unseen lover, the young Immortal, on whose altar she has poured all the perfumes of her heart, whose lovely music she imagines she has heard in the thickets leading the chorus of the Muses. Her lover does not appear; but such is her beauty, and above all her confidence in the power of beauty over gods as well as men, that her sadness is only momentary. It is this accent of pure love exalted by a mystic cult of the beautiful which gives the poem its seal of originality.

It never could have been written by any one save Leconte de Lisle. (pp. 90-1)

Leconte de Lisle's most original contribution to literature lies in his marvelous understanding and interpretation of the literature of a country which esthetically and metaphysically long ago had reached an extraordinary state of refinement—India. In "Çunacépa" he has taken an episodic legend from the *Ramayana*, and with different heroes and different incidents, he has given the spirit of the great epic, and some of the chief elements of interest. In doing so he has given added life to the original, without violating the character of the epic as a whole. For those who prefer their literature with a label, one might call it a narrative epic lyric. It is a story, in which the gods appear; but every part tends to make us share the love of Çunacépa and Çanta. (pp. 91-2)

Perhaps nowhere in the ancient world has love been expressed with as much directness and naturalness as in the sacred writings of the Hindus. In Greece its highest expression was inclined to be mystical, often between persons of the same sex. In Rome it was more sensual and often attended by a touch of cruelty. The tendency of Christianity was to stamp it as a sin, or as a handmaiden to duty or pride. Perhaps our conception is more moral, and the source of great beauty, but theirs too is full of poetry.

Fully to realize Leconte de Lisle's creative power, one has only to compare this poem with its source, as Taine compared La Fontaine's fables with their sources. This shows us graphically and in as concrete a manner as possible the greatness of the French poet. The comparison has been made in an admirable scholarly fashion by Joseph Vianey in *Les sources de Leconte de Lisle*.

The Master has not only condensed much of the spirit of the *Ramayana,* a poem which has proved its greatness by age-long survival in the hearts of cultivated readers, but has added to its beauty. The original episode expresses love of life struggling against filial duty, when the young man is sold by his father. In the version by Leconte de Lisle this love of life gains force through the addition of the love element (borrowed from other portions of the Hindu epic), through the heightening of the ascetic background, and through the mood expressed by the landscape. The essence of the original remains, but in a form that is more colorful, stronger, and more delicate.

[In "Le baiser suprême," it] would seem impossible that so much feeling could be crowded into five lines. Perhaps it could not be, were it not for the statue by Christophe on which it is carved, and which is to be seen in the Luxembourg in Paris. The work of the poet and that of the sculptor complete each other. "Çunacépa" also helps us to feel the force of this poem. The means of expression are similar. Compare the lines:

> And yet what tears, what evil can destroy
> The lasting sweetness of thy briefest joy!

In a sense Leconte de Lisle is a pessimist. His life was a series of disappointments, yet he does not negate life and beauty. He is not an ascetic. He merely realizes that life is fundamentally a tragedy, in the sense that for one good thing that we obtain, we must sacrifice a hundred others, and the greater the good that we obtain, the greater usually are the sacrifices that we must make. He who hitches his wagon to a star must be prepared to be hurled through space!

There are two possible interpretations. The poem may express *"la soif de l'idéal,"* love of the impossible, or it may be interpreted simply as a sex symbol, as revealed by the Freudian psychology. As such, it touches on a universal human complex. It is a vision such as everyone has dreamed, but it is more complete, more intense: the sex dream of a race, or of a genius. The chimera, half human, half beast, is the expression of a universal sex association. (pp. 95-7)

Greece and Rome were familiar ground for the French public and critics. Lack of familiarity with Leconte de Lisle's Hindu material caused even as sympathetic a person as Daudet to laugh instead of trying to understand. Similarly his Northern poems are the object of derision on the part of a critic as intelligent as Maurice Spronck, who claims that there is, in Leconte de Lisle, a "tearful versifier, who—when the man of genius sleeps—is fond of pseudo-German ballads like 'The Elfs' and 'Christine.' "

In the first place they are not pseudo-German, but authentically Scandinavian, except for the changes and additions made by the poet in the spirit of the original literatures, to heighten them, and give them unity. In these poems, as in 'Çunacépa,' the improvements reveal the touch of genius. In reworking the folk-lore of the North he followed in the footsteps of Heine and Goethe with the same deftness and insight, bringing us the mystery and profound sadness that hovers over the poetry of the North like a mist above a great pine forest. Sunlight is beautiful, but darkness too casts a spell.

Love and death, are they not the two great springs of feeling revealed in the poetry of the people? The Swedish folk-song from which **"Christine"** is taken expresses the pathos of two lovers separated by death, but ends on a note which tends to negate the pathos, although in itself it carries a beautiful thought.

> Each time you let a tear fall, my coffin is filled with blood.
> Each time your heart is gay, my coffin is filled with rose
> petals.

The thought that the dead would not wish us to grieve is one which makes us bear our grief with lighter heart. It has occurred to everyone. Christine returns consoled from the tryst with her dead lover.

In Leconte de Lisle's poem it is an emotion, love, which we find expressed. Christine does not heed his plea to return. . . . (pp. 99-100)

Quite in keeping with the supernatural atmosphere of the source, this dénouement, in which the maiden offers to share his "icy tomb . . . when the winter wind sighs in the forest, and the cold rain drips upon the graves," brings out the strength of her affection. (p. 100)

The folk-song from which **"Les elfes"** was taken was extremely popular. No less than fifteen different versions had been collected in Sweden. The one used by Leconte de Lisle was published by Heine, and forms an excellent poem in itself. Leconte de Lisle kept all the finest touches and has rendered it more powerfully poetic, until it is a worthy companion piece to Goethe's "Erlking." In the original we miss the suggested loveliness of the elves; and their queen is more prosaic:

> Listen, Lord Oluf, come and dance with me:
> I will give you two ram-hide boots.

Also the introduction of the knight's mother, who shares in the final tragedy, divides the interest and lessens the effect.

The poem of **"The Elves"** is highly appreciated. . . . It is very musical. There is something haunting about the refrain; which is not only repeated after each verse, but appears also at the beginning.

> Couronnés de thym et de marjolaine,
> Les Elfes joyeux dansent sur la plaine.
>
> ["With thyme and marjoram all sweetly crowned
> The merry elves are dancing in a round." (Translation by
> Brown)]

Primitive songs, especially the old ballads of the North,

owe half their charm to the refrain. Here it is used as a foil, a gay lilting note of mockery, against the somber tragedy of the verses suggested in the opening by the mass of dark shadows, pierced by a single ray of light. The description is intentionally vague. It is with the eyes of our imagination that we see the young queen and her whirling band, and seem to hear the magic strains of the Berlioz *Ballet des Sylphes*. But as the vision of his bride, with her clear, sweet eyes, is ever before the knight, all the enchantments of the fairy queen fail. He not only does not yield to her offers of magic gifts, but braves her terrible powers, of which he is well aware; for although he repulses her unhesitatingly, the warrior trembles, brave man though he is, when she touches his heart with her white finger. After thus building up the strength of the knight's love, what could be more dramatic than the dénouement? Her fatal touch, instead of killing him, takes from him what is far more precious than his own life—the life of his bride, whom he does not recognize at first in the white phantom that lifts its arms to him. Thus we are prepared gradually for the final tragedy, which gathers increasing momentum, until, as in *Romeo and Juliet,* we feel the supreme force of love that manifests itself in the death of both lovers. (pp. 101-02)

> *Irving Brown, in his* Leconte de Lisle: A Study
> on the Man and His Poetry, *1924. Reprint by
> AMS Press, Inc., 1966, 270 p.*

A. R. Chisholm   (essay date 1934)

[*In the following excerpt, Chisholm elaborates on the conflicts inherent in Leconte de Lisle's metaphysics as exemplified in his poetry.*]

Leconte de Lisle is the first victim of Dionysos in the nineteenth century. By a curious concourse of circumstances and of temperamental disposition he was destined to fall into numerous and in some cases tragic dilemmas, in his life as well as in his thought. Edmond Estève [French critic and author of *Leconte de Lisle, L'homme et l'œuvre* (1922)] tells us how this Republican idealist of 1848 was obliged, by the sheer pressure of poverty, to accept a pension of 300 francs per month from the Imperial exchequer (1864), and that cruel incident might well be taken as a symbol of his career. We know also how his eager participation in the movement for the emancipation of slaves in the French colonies helped to ruin his family in Bourbon, thus adding to his own financial distress; but after all, these are small things in the life of a poet, when we set them up against the deeper and more lasting dilemmas of his intellectual and artistic life.

The greatest and most poignant of these dilemmas has been unwittingly symbolised by L. Raynaud, who tells us that his was 'une âme . . . accessible aux plus hautes préoccupations philosophiques, avec un fonds de violence passionnée aussi', ['a soul . . . open to the highest philosophical concerns, with a fund of passionate violence as well'], for this dilemma takes the form of an unending struggle between his philosophical aspirations towards everlasting peace and oblivion, and the violence of the ever-changing, ever-growing cosmic forces which at times shake him to the depths of his being. Leconte de Lisle's whole intellectual career is an attempt to escape from that all-pervading force of determinism in which the thinkers of his century taught him to recognise the divine force of the universe. This Cosmic Will pursues him as unceasingly as the Hound of Heaven pursued Francis Thompson, as relentlessly as the eye of conscience pursued Hugo's Cain, and we shall see later how it attacked and defeated him in all the philosophical and artistic sanctuaries in which he sought to hide. (pp. 32-3)

It is wrong to suppose that his recognition of the tragic inevitability of the Cosmic Will belongs to that part of his work coming after the *Poèmes antiques.* He tells us himself (much later) that as a youth he felt the inescapable Will of the universe dominating him. . . . (p. 33)

It would be wrong, then, for this and for other reasons, to allocate this dilemma to his later period; but we could more reasonably suppose that he took up (following the track blazed by the savants) the subject of ancient India in order to introduce 'un frisson nouveau' ['a new thrill'] into his *Poèmes antiques,* and having found there a tremendous emphasising of the idea of the Cosmic Will (partly disguised in the form of Mâyâ), was attracted by the complementary idea of Nirvâna as an escape. If that were so, we could say that his actual dilemma started after he had elaborated the theory of *le néant* ['nothingness'] to which, the earlier part of *Poèmes antiques* led him. In any case, after their publication we find the poet torn between a number of philosophical antinomies which undoubtedly added to his natural pessimism and the bitterness engendered by poverty; for we know that a man at war with himself, intellectually, is unhappy, violent, tormented, as Huysmans was when he found himself torn between literature and renunciation. (pp. 33-4)

The poetic sensibility which caused Leconte de Lisle to feel too strongly the everlasting force of the Cosmic Will, led him, instead of accepting it (as the men of science did), to seek an escape: and this desire was no doubt strengthened by his European prejudice against the submerging of the individual in the universal, a prejudice which has found another splendid expression in Rimbaud's *Bateau ivre.* The typical Western mind has always been ready to accept in various forms the idea of a Cosmic Will: but it has put shape into it (through the intellect), logical control (through morality), beauty (through art), and has made even of death not an escape from it but a discipline within it. Thus it has put Will at the service of the individual and of the race. Leconte de Lisle, however, tried to destroy the idea of an Eternal Will by the sheer power of logic, forgetting (or not knowing) Kant's restrictions of the powers of reason, which, caught and bewildered in its own mass of antinomies, can neither prove nor utterly disprove the existence of an eternal *primum mobile.* And there, to sum up, we have the chief of his many dilemmas. He has to recognise the Cosmic Will as the ultimate reality, and yet he tries to postulate a second ultimate reality, *le néant,* as if the two could exist together. This dilemma is well symbolised by two poems of his last volume (*Derniers poèmes*). On the one hand, 'La joie de Siva' shows the indestructible nature of the Cosmic Will, inasmuch as Siva will still exist as a will and an energy when all our world shall have fallen away to nothing . . . while, on the other hand, 'La paix des dieux' shows us all things, even the Gods, passing away finally into the everlasting void. . . . (pp. 34-5)

I have called this dilemma a tragic one. It is not necessarily tragic for all those who become aware of it. Certain passages of Georges Bernanos' book, *L'imposture,* for instance, would lead us to suppose that for the Catholic the idea of an everlasting void is not incompatible with the idea of an everlasting God; but in the case of Leconte de Lisle this, like most of his dilemmas, is a tragic one, because, being a poet, he philosophises not merely with his intellect, but with his whole being; and so his dilemmas go beyond the limits of intellectual detachment, and become an inner torment.

For Leconte de Lisle the Cosmic Will takes the form of a vast energy, which he expresses in the tremendous pantheistic passages of 'Bhagavat' and in many of the Greek pieces in *Poèmes antiques*; in the great animal pictures which constitute one of the best and strongest parts of his work; in the restless striving and moving and clashing of races which fill the pages of *Poèmes barbares.* This energy of nature and the cosmos was as strongly felt by the ancient Hindoo writers as it was by the French poet who sought inspiration in their work, and the hero of Vâlmîki's *Râmâyana* is essentially a man of energy and action, as he is in Leconte de Lisles's 'Arc de Civa'. Vâlmîki loves to dwell on Râma's war-like qualities, or to show him unhurt beneath a shower of arrows like 'an elephant under a shower of rain', and he likes even the tremendous energy of warfare, with its 'overturned chariots, dead elephants, gaping breasts, heads and arms and thighs'. The same energy manifests itself for Leconte de Lisle in the swarming life of the jungle, the incessant movement of both animate and inanimate forms, animals and rivers, flying birds and moving winds, palm-trees swaying in the breeze, and the great sweep of the hot noon across the corn-fields ('Midi'). (pp. 35-6)

The Cosmic Will, as Leconte de Lisle conceives it, is greater than all things, and everlasting. Even if the multitudinous forms of life could be annihilated, if, after the individuals, the human race could be abolished, as he hopes it will in 'L'anathème' (*Poèmes barbares*), some forms of cosmic energy would still persist, such as the flaming eye of the 'Astre rouge' (*Poèmes tragiques*) and the waves over which it broods. . . .

The Cosmic Will is also above the Gods, who, filled with its wild energy, usually take on the most violent and wilful forms, like the Jehovah against whom Cain, 'flagellé de fureur, ivre, sourd, éperdu' ['whipped by fury, drunk, deaf, bewildered'], pits his own wild strength (*Poèmes barbares:* 'Qaïn'); and by virtue of it, man himself can become one of the Gods. Further, it dominates and determines Nature, which is itself above man, as he tells us in 'La fontaine aux lianes' (*Poèmes barbares*). It is the blind yet unerring force which guides the elephants towards their native haunts beyond the desert, so unerringly that they do not even need to watch their path: 'ils cheminent, l'œil clos' ['they trudge on, eyes closed'] (*Poèmes barbares:* 'Les éléphants'). Whatever it is, it is above Nature, for Nature in itself has no real energy. . . . (pp. 37-8)

And that brings us to another aspect of the Cosmic Will. One of its most persistent and most irresistible forms is that of the Everlasting Eros, which dominates even the Greek section of *Poèmes antiques.* There, love is a burning passion, which inflames the very Gods and nymphs with a hot desire for mortals, and makes Helen forget all the traditions of her race. As Eros, the Universal Will drives men to their doom in 'Ekhidna' (*Poèmes barbares*), or impels them onward in an endless torment, like the hot wind which scourges Paolo and Francesca in the fifth canto of the *Inferno.* . . . (p. 39)

Another of the most powerful manifestations of the Cosmic Will takes the form of consuming Hunger and its natural concomitant, Cruelty and lust for Slaughter. In this form, it is the very basis of what is perhaps, after all, his most characteristic and powerful work, **Poèmes tragiques,** while it influences and colours even the Greek section of **Poèmes antiques.** For the Hellenist that he professes to be, this section is not only small, but sombre. . . . [Moreover] it is worthy of notice that in his Greek pieces he has a decided predilection for the *violence* of Greece rather than its ideal of calm. The quiet, impassive beauty of **'Vénus de Milo'** is almost lost amid the tragic violences of **'Hélène', 'Khirôn', 'Niobé'** and **Les Erinnyes** (a play which belongs logically to **Poèmes antiques,** though published at the end of **Poèmes tragiques**).

The most terrible and characteristic example of this manifestation of Will as hunger and cruelty is no doubt **'Sacra fames'** (**Poèmes tragiques**), which should have been placed at the beginning of the volume as an explanatory symbol, just as **'Qaïn'** is placed at the beginning of **Poèmes barbares.** It is this conception of Will as hunger that explains his frequent use of the somewhat paradoxical phrase 'plein de faim' ['full of hunger'] (in **'Qaïn', 'Ekhidna', 'Sacra fames', 'Le jaguar',** etc.): once we realise that hunger is part of the eternal energy of the cosmos, it is easy to understand how it can fill with its active, all-consuming void an empty belly.

Here again, Leconte de Lisle finds in his Indian sources, along with the doctrine of Nirvâna, the quite opposite doctrine of cosmic hunger and cruelty. The two opposites are juxtaposed in the most startling fashion in the *Râmâyana,* for instance: the calm beauty of the incident where Vâlmîki invites his disciple Bharadvâja to admire the 'sacred pool whose peaceful splendour resembles that of a wise man's soul' is followed closely by the long description of a sacrifice of three hundred victims, including the king's finest horse! The author dwells with blood-thirsty delight on the details: the horse is cut up, and three women tied to his red limbs; at dawn the king cuts away the fat from his dead favourite, cooks it, and breathes in its odour to deliver himself from his sins! (pp. 40-1)

Such, then, is Leconte de Lisle's conception of that Cosmic Will which has left so violent a mark on all his work, and to which we have found him bitterly faithful to the end. It is indeed this Cosmic Will that makes the great strength and the chief beauty of his poetry (though it torments the poet). He should have realised that this was inevitable, for his own doctrine, so often repeated (e.g., in **'Bhagavat', 'Vision de Brahma',** etc.), is that Will, and not Mâyâ, is the true creator, Mâyâ being only the illusory appearance of the thing created.

Such is the Cosmic Will from which he sought to escape, and failed. We have next to examine the sanctuaries (Nirvâna and Art) in which he sought refuge from its unending pursuit, and the medium (Mâyâ) through which he sought to utilise it; and we shall see how Will not only follows him into these sanctuaries, but causes them to collapse, altering their shape and structure, as it also frustrates and

transforms two at least of the essential symbols of his art. (pp. 42-3)

Leconte de Lisle's personal conception of Nirvâna is not that of the mystics of India: his *néant* is attained by a violent struggle against the Cosmic Will and not, as in the case of the mystics, by resignation. This is natural enough, for the Indian conception of pantheism in its less vulgar or naturistic forms is quite different from that of the European nineteenth century. The Indian one is surely a pantheism of immanence, a non-dynamic pantheism, and it is in the source of Being that the sage seeks to lose himself. . . . The violent movement of the cosmos is only an illusion, a part of Mâyâ, and consequently there is no need to revolt against it. The European pantheism of the nineteenth century, on the other hand, is a dynamic and historical one, a pantheism of Becoming. . . . [In Indian pantheism, the] individual can become God-like by submission and meditation, by seeking within himself the static divinity which is immanent there. And that is a beginning of Nirvâna (which is, etymologically, a 'blowing out' or 'extinction' of passion, etc.). Leconte de Lisle frequently describes this conception of Nirvâna in the Indian section of **Poèmes antiques**; but there he is only describing objectively: his own idea of the *néant* is not the same. He cannot conceive the void without presupposing the *destruction* of the individual, as in **'Le vent froid de la nuit'** and **'Aux morts'** (**Poèmes barbares**), **'A un poète mort'** (**Poèmes tragiques**) and elsewhere; and, that not being sufficient, the destruction of the race and the world, as in **'Solvet seclum'** (**Poèmes barbares**), this idea of destruction being based, probably, on scientific predictions of a catastrophic ending (see for example **'La dernière vision'** in **Poèmes barbares**). Without this utter suppression of life and consciousness, there can be no complete *néant*. Contemplation of the sources of Being can offer only an adumbration, a symbolic foreshadowing of oblivion. Thus in **'Midi'**, he who has steeped his heart seven times over in 'le néant divin' (and what a hot, dynamic *néant* it is!), nevertheless comes back to 'les cités infimes' ['the petty cities'], that is, to a continuation of life. (pp. 43-5)

But to escape from the Cosmic Will, which is for him, as we have seen, above and in all things, and therefore the ultimate reality, one needs to presuppose a second ultimate reality, into which one may escape. But this cannot be a true ultimate reality *at the same time* as Will, and so it continually breaks down: the *néant* is shattered, either by the irruption of the Cosmic Will itself, or by the force of Mâyâ, its visible representation.

It is only natural that the Cosmic Will itself should break down the hypothetical *néant* of a poet so tremendously dynamic as Leconte de Lisle: and it is not surprising to find him, forgetting for a moment his philosophical accretions, crying out in protest from the depths of his soul against the loss of his own energies. . . . He is far too European to yearn instinctively for Nirvâna, he believes too heartily in the restless, onward striving of the Western races, predestined to inherit the world's hegemony. . . . [He] voices the triumph of Will over resignation.

The *néant* which, finally, is to absorb and destroy humanity is only part of the indestructible energy of the universe after all: this globe of ours will crack and collapse, but it will only go to . . . form part of the Eternal Becoming. Numerous also are the poems where Eros, a form of Will, destroys the idea of the void, both subjectively (i.e., in his own feelings) and objectively (that is, in his personages), as in **'Çunacépa'**, where the ascetic himself is drawn from his meditations to save the lovers from death: this is a curious gesture against oblivion!

Another way in which the Cosmic Will invades the concept of the *néant* consists of introducing into the latter an element of flux which should not be there. For flux, like music, is essentially, as we have seen, part of the Cosmic Will itself. Escape from this Will would therefore naturally have to be an escape into a void of silence and immobility. . . . And yet his *néant* is rarely still. It is either the great undulating heat-masses of **'Midi'** (heat is an energy, not a stillness), or the immense flood of the **'Bhagavat'** apotheosis, or the devouring destiny which, in **'Khirôn'**, is like an 'onde amère' ['bitter wave']; and the void into which the dead poet passes in **'La mort de Valmiki'** is a flux very like the *profonde unité* ['profound unity'] of Baudelaire's 'Correspondances'. . . .All that really perishes is his flesh, devoured by ants. The only boon that this kind of *néant* can offer to a soul yearning for peace is the loss of the individual will, but only with the result of being absorbed into a greater Will, which, as we have seen, is for Leconte de Lisle an evil thing, having for its living symbols Hunger and Hate, Cruelty and Desire, a pitiless Destroying and Becoming. And who can say that this ultimate Will is not self-conscious, torn by its own passions and assailed by self-begotten suffering? He tells us himself that Eros is 'lui-même consumé du mal qu'il fait subir' ['himself consumed by the pain he imposes'] (*Poèmes barbares:* **'Les damnés'**).

It is inevitably in its objectified form, as Mâyâ, or, as Schopenhauer calls it, Representation (Vorstellung), that the Cosmic Will makes its most vigorous onslaught against the *néant* philosophy of this instinctively plastic artist. His Hindoo poet, in **'La mort de Valmiki'**, has somewhat the same dilemma. His desire is to escape 'au-delà des apparences vaines' ['beyond vain appearances'], and yet he spends his life writing an epic which is a glorification of Mâyâ, and in the moment of his death his soul is filled with the resplendent beauties of his own creation. His **'Qaïn'**, too, regrets Eden and its plastic splendours, just as Leconte de Lisle himself so often regrets the lost Eden of his early days in Bourbon, and the whole poem is a magnificent vindication of the life and energy which will persist after Jehovah himself has passed into the void. His **'Chant alterné'** again (*Poèmes antiques*) seems to indicate that the human soul is in perpetual conflict with itself in this respect, the Pagan splendour and voluptuousness of Mâyâ forever waging war on the ideal of renunciation; and all his sympathy is with Hypatia when she defends the Gods, which are her particular Mâyâ, against the assault of oblivion (*Poèmes antiques:* **'Hypatie'**). By a strange irony of chance, this poem (**'Hypatie'**) comes immediately after **'La vision de Brahma'**, with its apotheosis of the void. Moreover, he clearly recognises, on one occasion at least, that Mâyâ is greater than the *néant* itself, the latter being only a part of Mâyâ. . . . And that brings us to the most interesting and possibly the most extraordinary of all his dilemmas: the struggle, manifested within the actual structure of his poetry, between his plastic instincts and the *néant* idea, a struggle in which Mâyâ is always triumphant in the form of his own artistic genius. (pp. 45-9)

In the structure of Leconte de Lisle's poetry we find an attempt to reconcile these two opposites; it is largely an unconscious effort. Even in the poems where he consciously postulates and invokes the infinite void, his plastic genius, working subconsciously, corrects him, transforms his infinite into something finite. **'Midi'**, with its apotheosis of the void and its great plastic lines, is one of the most flagrant cases of this inner contradiction. **'Les éléphants'** (*Poèmes barbares*) give us one of his nearest approaches to a really infinite space. The sand is 'une mer sans limite' ['a sea without limit'], the horizon is vignetted away in its 'vapeurs de cuivre' ['copper steam'], the elephants come in from a *point* on the horizon, and a point does not define; then they pass away again, and the desert reassumes its immobility, its calm immensity. And yet this symbol of the void is reduced and defined: for one thing, the elephants come in from an invisible unknown into a visible space, so that this 'mer sans limite' is not an infinite at all, it is only an enlarged form of our luminous cone, set in a sea of invisibility. And again, even in this outer unknown there is form, definition: there beyond the horizon dwells man ('l'horizon . . . où l'homme habite') ['the horizon . . . where man lives']; a hundred leagues away are sleeping lions, and somewhere out of sight 'la girafe boit dans les fontaines bleues' ['the giraffe drinks in the blue fountains'].

The most unusual method by which Leconte de Lisle's artistic instinct breaks up the infinite void consists of putting it in contact with the finite, thus making it finish, as we have said, along a frontier of visibility. Thus in **'Le sommeil du condor'** (*Poèmes barbares*) the void is to take the form of night, invading and enveloping all things. But we first become aware of this oncoming night along the line where it meets the outlying extremities of a visible, plastic, carefully differentiated world. (pp. 50-1)

[The] visible or finite sometimes stands out in relief against the infinite, thus helping to define it, as in **'Le Runoïa'** (*Poèmes barbares*), where, on an infinite, snow-clad landscape, barring and differentiating it by its own dark mass,

> La tour de Runoïa se dresse toute noire.

> ['The tower of Runoïa stands all black.']

There is a similar contrast in *Le lévrier de Magnus* (*Poèmes tragiques*), where a dark donjon stands out against the unending snow.

Another method by which Leconte de Lisle's plastic instinct defeats his philosophic conviction consists in giving the void itself a shape or in differentiating its details. Thus in *Le désert* (*Poèmes barbares*) the intention of the philosopher is to express the infinite void by the symbol of the flaming silence of the desert under a copper sky. (pp. 51-2)

As an artist, Leconte de Lisle is naturally inclined, when he wishes to utilise the Cosmic Will, to adopt that form of it which is less oppressive, less brutal, the fantasy-world which it creates by its self-objectification, and to which he gives the Sanskrit name of Mâyâ. We need not go into the origins of the Mâyâ doctrine, which may or may not have been the invention of the philosopher Sankara. . . . The main point for us is that Leconte de Lisle defines Mâyâ as the vast illusion of the phenomenal world. . . . (p. 53)

So, then, Mâyâ should be a means of consolation for one

who is seeking to escape the reality of the everlasting Will, for according to this doctrine the forms of life which torment him are only vain appearances, an empty dream. But that is a conviction which Leconte de Lisle fails to maintain permanently. Just as the earth, which, in **'Qaïn'**, is Jehovah's dream, becomes an independent reality, which Jehovah himself cannot destroy, so too Mâyâ is all too often invaded by and identified with the active form of the Cosmic Will, in such a way as to become a living reality. There is no doubting the depths of the poet's regrets, for instance, in **'Le manchy'** (*Poèmes barbares*), where the charm of his 'premiers rêves' ['first dreams'] is part of the undying Eros. So also in **'L'illusion suprême'** (*Poèmes tragiques*), where, in spite of the concluding lines, there is a note of bitterness, which belongs, not to a world of fantasy, but to the eternal energy of life. Here, as in many other poems, we can feel that a good half of Leconte de Lisle's pessimism comes from the shattering of that early love in Bourbon. Love itself is not an illusion: the actual illusion lies in his thinking that he can vanquish love! This becomes even more evident if we remember that in **'L'aurore'** (*Poèmes barbares*) he admits the eternal *reality* of those early days. . . . Moreover, Mâyâ is so closely identified with Will in **'Spectres'** (*Poèmes barbares*), as to become, like Will, an undying energy. . . . And finally, how can a poet, who attributes to the world and its history a purely illusory quality, take this world, even in its past (and therefore, one would think, ultra-illusory) forms, with all the tragic and bitter seriousness of **'Les siècles maudits'**? It is, indeed, the tragic inner conviction of the ultimate *reality* of all these so-called illusions that determines the whole tone and even the title of the *Poèmes tragiques.* (pp. 54-6)

The doctrine of 'l'art pour l'art' ['art for art's sake'] should have given him a very definite means of escape, especially if we remember how supreme his art was, with its impeccable structure, its splendid rimes, its immense rhythmic effects, its occasional but unsurpassed virtuosity. There, surely, he had a means of building up a sanctuary for his soul, a world apart, a world of quiet, classic beauty whose ideal symbol is his **'Vénus de Milo'**. For one thing, however, we have seen how in *Poèmes tragiques* the violence of his reactions against the Cosmic Will carries him far from this ideal of quiet impassive beauty, and how the great animal forms which are a living symbol of this Will haunted his imagination and called for his art. And then again, he recognises himself that art needs the strengthening impulsion of the Cosmic Will. . . . (p. 56)

His doctrine of Art for Art's sake is invaded, then, by the inescapable Will of the Universe; but on the other hand we must recognise how strongly at times he reacts against this invasion. This reaction is the only logical reason which I can find for the inclusion in the *Poèmes tragiques* of several poems which are pure pieces of virtuosity, such as **'Dans le ciel clair'**, **'Les roses d'Ispahan'**, **'Sous l'épais Sycomore'**, **'Le frais matin dorait'** . . . , etc. And yet, inserted in all their beauty amid the gloomy horrors of *Poèmes tragiques,* these pieces have the same effect as those bursts of light and of plastic beauty which Hugo *deliberately* places in the midst of his most sombre pages (the *Massacre de Saint-Barthélemy* in *Quatre-vingt-treize,* the beautiful song in *Eviradnus,* etc.): they enhance and deepen the tragedy. In other words, they serve the Cosmic Will in spite of the poet's apparent intention. And Hugo here

is, if anything, more 'Parnassien' than Leconte de Lisle: these bursts of splendour are deliberately part of his total effect, not a protest against the predominant effect; that is to say, Hugo stands outside his own art, keeps full control of his medium, whereas Leconte de Lisle unwillingly and perhaps unwittingly serves a hated God.

Further, the plastic and impassible beauty of the Hellenic past is invaded on all sides by the philosophy of Will. The **'Hélène'** of *Poèmes antiques* for example is the poignant recital of a struggle between discipline and desire, between calm, happy beauty and the hot masterfulness of Eros, between Parnassian art and the Cosmic Will, in other words; and it is the latter that triumphs. Similarly, **'Niobé'** is largely a tragedy of passion, and I have already drawn attention to the sombreness and violence of most of his Greek pieces.

One of the most subtle and interesting forms of the inescapable influence of the Cosmic Will is its modification of certain of Leconte de Lisle's outstanding essential symbols. One of these inner symbols is that of **'Midi'**, wherein the clear sky, flaming over the hot earth, stands for the idea of Nirvâna, of the 'néant divin'. . . . The complete realisation of the symbol is, however, often frustrated by the intrusion of the Cosmic Will in the form of Mâyâ. . . . [In] **'Midi'** itself the poet's preoccupation with plastic beauty corrects and alters the symbol. So too in **'Phidylé'** (*Poèmes antiques*) we expect an evocation of the *néant;* . . . but Phidylé's sleep becomes, on the contrary, the pretext for a magnificent description of the plastic splendours which form the background of her slumbers: the winding paths, the red poppies in the corn, the birds, the bees; and from these splendours the poet comes back to the divine beauty of her slumbering body itself: and so where Mâyâ finishes, Eros begins! (pp. 57-60)

So much for the frustration of the **'Midi'**-symbol by Mâyâ. It is elsewhere often frustrated by the direct irruption of the Cosmic Will in its strongest forms: Desire, Violence, Cruelty, Eros. . . . Thus in **'Les jungles'** (*Poèmes barbares*) the atmosphere is that of **'Midi'**, but within that slumbrous heat the python's cruel eyes are restless, and the watching panther creeps, and though the tiger 'dort tout un soleil sous l'immensité bleue' ['sleeps the day away under the blue immensity'], he awakens to the gnawing pangs of his everlasting hunger. Precisely the same inner contradiction characterises the **'Panthère noire'** and **'Le rêve du jaguar'** (*Poèmes barbares*). In **'Les éléphants'** (*Poèmes barbares*) the symbol is frustrated by the blind but unerring force of the Cosmic Will which urges the monsters across the sun-drenched desert; while it is flagrantly contradicted in **'Sous l'épais sycomore'** (*Poèmes tragiques*): it is 'l'heure où le soleil blanchit les vastes cieux' ['the hour when the sun whitens the vast skies'], and the virgin sleeps in an innocence which is itself a kind of Nirvâna, but around her move the living symbols of Eros, and an azure butterfly moving towards the warmth of her red lips completes the splendid contradiction. And finally (to cut short an enumeration of cases which could easily be multiplied), in **'Pan'** (*Poèmes antiques*) it is the symbolism of the sleeping Pan himself that contradicts the **'Midi'**-symbol, for Pan is the very personification of the Cosmic Will, and the poet strengthens this idea by showing us an awakening Pan who, when the hot day has passed, is 'enflammé d'amour' ['enflamed with love'] and who 'poursuit la vierge errante à l'ombre des halliers' ['pursues the wandering virgin to the shadow of the thickets']; his heart is certainly not 'trempé sept fois dans le néant divin ['soaked seven times in divine nothingness']!

No careful reader can be unaware of Leconte de Lisle's extraordinarily frequent use of the image of a darted eye. . . . It is impossible that in the case of a virtuoso and a follower of the doctrine of Art for Art's sake this should be a mere cliché, repeated carelessly and *ad nauseam*. We can, therefore, suspect here something in the nature of an essential symbol. The 'œil dardé' is, indeed, the fairly obvious symbol of the Cosmic Will, transmitting its energy in the form of hunger, rapacity, cruelty, lust. . . . [Throughout] **'Les paraboles de Dom Guy'** in the *Poèmes barbares* it tends to become an apocalyptic symbol, distinguished by the passionate imagination which we associate with the Hebrew seërs, so different in this respect from the Indian mystics. But as we should expect, it is in the *Poèmes tragiques* that the symbol is radically transformed by the invasion of the Cosmic Will. The whole of this volume is marked and scored by the symbol of the flaming, active eye which *darts* out upon the world the passion of its cruelty or its hates. The symbol in this form occurs no less than eight times in the opening poem (**'L'apothéose de Mouça-al-Kébyr'**) alone, and we find it again in **'La tête de Kenwarc'h'**, **'L'astre rouge'**, **'Le talion'** (opening lines), **'L'holocauste'** (twice), **'La chasse de l'aigle'**, **'L'incantation du loup'** (twice), **'Hiéronymus'** (where it stands for all the cruelty of religious fanaticism), **'L'Aboma'**, **'Le lévrier de Magnus'** (which simply bristles with this symbol), **'Le calumet du Sachem'**, **'Le romance de Doña Blanca'**, and, of course, in *Les Erinnyes.* And even then, I have mentioned only the most striking cases. (pp. 60-4)

> *A. R. Chisholm, "Leconte de Lisle; or, The Tragedy of the Cosmic Will," in his* Towards Hérodiade: A Literary Genealogy, *1934. Reprint by AMS Press, 1979, pp. 32-67.*

Alison Fairlie   (essay date 1947)

[*In the following excerpt from her study of the* Poèmes barbares, *Fairlie discusses Leconte de Lisle's treatment of historical cultures.*]

Almost always [Leconte de Lisle] had so documented his poems that at first reading at least they appear as impartial narrative, and that even more detailed investigation shows much in the sources to justify his presentation. It is only by tracing the sequence of the different poems and noting the deliberate preference for certain subjects that we begin to see what a large part has been played by his own personality.

First of all, it is obvious that whatever may have been his later views, he did not set out from any purely historical standpoint. During [his early] period he was using the technique of Vigny: the historical and legendary settings were primarily symbols. When he reached the stage of the publication of the *Poèmes antiques*, when, for example, he removed from **'Niobé'** the fourieristic conclusion, he no doubt imagined that he had largely abandoned the old technique. But though **'Niobé'** was now presented as 'une lutte fort ancienne entre les traditions doriques et une théogonie venue de Phrygie' ['a very ancient struggle between the Doric traditions and a theogeny that came from Phrygia'], the original inspiration, the theme of revolt against oppression and the memory of an age of past glory, is so integral a part of the poem that it cannot be done away with. From now on the poems may not voice a direct message, but they still spring from much the same roots in the poet's feelings. Moreover, he does still at times use past beliefs openly as a symbol for emotions of his own experience: as we have seen, **'Le désert'** at its first publication was no mere picture of Arab life, but signified the bitter disappointment which in this arid world greets the human heart in its passionate search for an ideal. If such apparently impartial studies were conceived in a personal spirit, an examination of the themes of the other poems in relation with the poet's own beliefs may reveal something of the same genesis. (pp. 388-89)

[Leconte de Lisle's] assumed impartiality tends to break down as soon as it contemplates the doctrines of catholicism. Scarcely ever is he able to treat it simply as a historical fact. And since he so often turns to subjects which show the struggle between the old pagan beliefs and the faith which succeeded them, his personal prejudice is constantly shining through the apparent impartiality of the form. Among the clearest examples is **'Le Runoïa'**. The passage from the *Kalewala* on which the poem is based did, as presented by Léouzon Leduc, symbolise a struggle between two faiths. But the long speeches of the Christ child, summing up what is to be the effect of his doctrine, have no basis whatever either in the songs of the ancient Finns or in the words of the New Testament. It is the vision of one looking back from the nineteenth century upon the succession of religions and expressing what appears to him to be their essence; a vision which has poetic value in its poignant sincerity and in the vigour of its presentation, but which certainly does not fulfil Leconte de Lisle's own condition that the poet must confine himself to the feelings and ideas of the age which he is representing. It is the same with even a brief legend like *La fille de l'Emyr:* although Leconte de Lisle does not, as Vianey would have it, transform the tale into a direct and bludgeoning attack, but leaves us to draw our own conclusions, yet he does infuse into it something of the melancholy felt by a modern on contemplating this story which in its original form merely celebrated the triumph of mystic faith.

It is important, of course, not to exaggerate in pursuing a kind of gleeful heresy hunt through the various poems. There are times when Leconte de Lisle does plainly attempt to present Christianity fairly, as the charming figure of Saint Patrick in the first half of **'Le barde de Temrah'** bears witness. More frequent are the occasions when if Catholicism appears in an evil light it is because the documents which the poet was using presented it from this very point of view. The torments of Hell which the Church inflicts upon the pagan gods and their believers in **'La vision de Snorr'**, however much Leconte de Lisle's vivid imagination adds to the effectiveness of their ferocity, are by no means more ferocious in intent than those of the *Sôlar liôd* on which the poem is based. Again and again we have to notice that it is rather the choice than the treatment of the subject once chosen which reveals the beliefs and prejudices of the poet. His method is to choose a theme which with little or no rearrangement will fit his own conceptions.

In Catholicism Leconte de Lisle sees the repression of man's legitimate instincts and desires, of his liberty and his virility, and in its later manifestations the aider and abettor of feudal tyranny. Fourierism he may have abandoned in the years immediately preceding and following the 1848 revolution, but throughout his life he never ceases to protest his warmest faith in republican principles and to give expression to it openly in his prose works. Does anything of his political creed appear in the barbarian poems? If we deliberately look for it, certainly yes. **'La vigne de Naboth'** and **'Le talion'** are two of the most eloquent apostrophes ever hurled against the oppression of a tyrannical monarchy; Pedro of Spain is presented as a rapacious and bloodthirsty monster who murders a trusting vassal, a chivalrous brother, and an innocent Queen; Mouça stands undaunted before the cruel and greedy Souleyman, upon whose injustice and cowardice he pours his utmost scorn. Yet here it is once again rather in the choice of subject that Leconte de Lisle's preoccupations appear, than in any very obvious diversion of the material to his own ends. Tyranny has existed from the earliest ages, and from the earliest ages men have rebelled against it. In the Old Testament the tale of Naboth's vineyard was clearly enough intended to show just chastisement inflicted upon the covetous oppressor. Leconte de Lisle has no doubt enriched the invective by selecting much parallel material from other passages of the Bible, but the thought, while it may have its modern application, is proper also to the age in which it is set. The poems on Pedro and **'L'apothéose de Mouça'** do indeed show that Leconte de Lisle is perfectly ready to suppress or alter such facts as do not suit his purpose: to make Pedro by contrast appear the blacker, Fadrique is exculpated from all suspicion of treachery, and it is not mentioned that Abou-Sayd was himself a usurper hated by his subjects; in opposition with the tyrant Souleyman, Mouça's greed and love of excessive pomp are conveniently forgotten. Yet that Pedro and Souleyman were in fact tyrants can scarcely be denied, and, the choice of subject once given, the alterations are as much a matter of subordinating details to one central effect as of consciously or unconsciously presenting a political faith.

With **'Qaïn'** we are on different ground. This is in no sense a reproduction of Hebrew beliefs: it is the most outspoken voicing of the poet's own view of the vast course of human history, and . . . its fundamental thought is probably more political than religious. There could scarcely be a more outstanding example to illustrate the phrase which Leconte de Lisle had applied to the *Légende de siècles:* 'l'écho superbe de sentiments modernes attribués aux hommes des époques passées' ['the proud echo of modern sentiments attributed to men of past epochs']. **'Qaïn'** was never conceived in a spirit of impartial resuscitation: it is the splendid epitome of the poet's sympathy for all who struggle against an overwhelming tyranny, and in it his genius escapes triumphantly beyond the sometimes artificial bonds with which he has sought to bind it.

If political or religious beliefs have played their part in dictating the choice or use of subjects, what of the poet's own personal life? On his political views letters, prose writings and biographies provide external evidence enough for us to form a clear picture with which parallels may be found in the poems, but where Leconte de Lisle's emotional contacts are concerned we still know very little. If the poet who wrote scornfully to his public 'Je ne te vendrai pas mon ivresse et mon mal' ['I will not sell thee my wild joy, nor my wound' (translation by Irving Brown)] did nevertheless place in his narrative poems something of the memories of his own loves, as does here and there seem probable, it is never easy to lay a finger on a direct allusion, for we have not sufficient knowledge of the circumstances. From Flaubert's letters to Louise Colet, in whom Leconte de Lisle had confided in the early 1850s, coupled with veiled references in Calmettes's biography, we can gather at least that he had been deeply in love with a married woman, and that when, after long months of ecstasy, the break occurred, he felt himself bitterly betrayed. There may be allusions to this incident in **'Le jugement de Komor'**. Possibly, too, the fidelity of Christine and the unquenchable passion of Brunhild show what he himself would have wished to find in contrast with what he had experienced: but here the themes exist in the sources, and it can only be said that Leconte de Lisle may have been attracted to them because of his own memories.

Other themes of deeply personal import do, however, thread their way through practically all the barbarian poems, and have fundamentally affected Leconte de Lisle's approach to his subjects. One rises from the ever-vivid memories of his youth in the Île Bourbon, that island paradise which he recalls in such directly personal poems as **'Ultra coelos'**. . . . Freedom, vigour, joy and the beauty of mountain, sun and sea; these are what he remembers of the distant days 'Où je n'avais encor ni souffert ni pleuré' ['when I had not yet suffered nor cried']. Among the barbarians as well as among the Greeks he turns to seek a world like that which he himself remembered or idealised. . . . Again and again, in **'Le Runoïa'**, in **'Le massacre de Mona'**, in **'La légende des Nornes'**, in **'L'apothéose de Mouça'**, in **'Le dernier des Maourys'**, there appears the picture of a past age compounded of liberty, vigour and beauty. These deeply-rooted personal memories and aspirations, coupled with a political faith whose main tenet is the love of freedom, draw him towards a vision of ancient societies often very close to Ménard's conception of Greece. The gods of polytheism, whether it be the polytheism of the Greeks or the Barbarians, are to him the forces of nature, and under their beneficent rule man is left free to develop as his spontaneous and vigorous instincts direct. The Preface to the *Poèmes et poésies* of 1855 sums up the frame of mind in which Leconte de Lisle approaches the study of the old mythologies: 'En général, tout ce qui constitue l'art, la morale, et la science, était mort avec le Polythéisme' ['In general, all that which constitutes art, morality, and science, died with Polytheism'], for polytheism represents 'l'idée de la beauté . . . l'idée du droit' ['the idea of beauty . . . the idea of justice'] and at its base is 'le sentiment de la dignité humaine' ['the feeling of human dignity']. So in the days of the ancient Runoïa the polar stars, the breezes, the birch trees, the waters, the islands, the mists and the sunlight, these 'Forces, grâces, splendeurs du ciel et de la terre' ['forces, graces, splendors of the sky and earth'] were the divinities surrounding the life of man. . . . To all these ages of beauty there succeeds the inevitable destruction, but always the past age is one where force and beauty went hand in hand.

To an expert mythologist this presentation would certainly appear distressingly over-simplified and over-idealised. Yet it must be remembered that even if such an interpretation coincides most conveniently with the ideals, desires and memories of the poet, it was one which in his day appeared sufficiently founded. Ménard had elaborated it with skill and eloquence; Bergmann, after an erudite discussion of the technicalities of mythological explanation, had stated firmly that the old Scandinavian deities represented both natural phenomena and the forces of good in their struggle with evil; Henri Martin stressed again and again the moral content of the Celtic beliefs. No doubt where he confines himself to expounding details of belief from his sources without attempting to interpret their general sense he would find greater favour in the eyes of the mythologist; but as poetry all the incomprehensible subtleties of the Nine Forms, Dylan King of the Sea or Hu-Gadarn Saviour of the Earth have little to capture our imagination, whereas the words of the bard who 'Salua les splendeurs de sa gloire passée' ['saluted the splendors of his past glory'] have a ring of sincerity and a breadth of vision which provoke a response from our own feelings. Closely bound up with his idealisation of the past, and in part responsible for it, is another feeling which was to reach equal intensity. Leconte de Lisle's life was for long years a bitter struggle with material difficulties and extreme penury: always he was to retain the same inflexible dignity and unfaltering firmness of purpose which refused to prostitute his art to the exigencies of popularity or to abandon it for more remunerative pursuits. But the lack of recognition wounded him most deeply, and the popularity of a Béranger or a Du Camp convinced him that true poetry must soon die. . . . He [saw himself] as one of the last defenders of the beauty of the past, holding firmly to the unrivalled splendours of his convictions and his visions, doomed at last to be overwhelmed by processes of decadence and destruction, but indomitable in his unyielding faith. And it is thus above all that his ancient barbarians appear: this same pattern underlies the behaviour of practically all his heroes. The Runoïa, 'dépossédé d'un monde' ['dispossessed of a world'], casting his defiance in the teeth of the power which overwhelms him, and sailing into the sublimity of space, the indomitable Uheldéda and the Celts singing in the face of death, the Bard of Temrah falling upon his sword that he may join his ancestors in Hell rather than submit to a new religion, Skulda crying to her sisters to lament the destruction of the world, Abou-Sayd coldly scornful of the treacherous monarch who has compassed his death, Mouça fiery and untamed before the tyrant Souleyman, the Sachem who alone has survived his tribe and waits in motionless dignity for a violent end, the Maoury in his disdain and hatred for the white invader who has destroyed his race: in all these it is the poet himself who speaks, isolated in his century and turning to the past for consolation and courage. (pp. 389-94)

Always Leconte de Lisle is to identify himself with the oppressed and the vanquished, not indeed in tears, but in strength, courage, force of resistance. As these qualities come to attract him more and more, wishing to represent them at their most intense he turns from the subtleties, the conflicting motives and cramping conventions which in modern life hinder the expression of any passions, to ages and countries where in a less developed civilisation men seem to him simpler and more single-minded in pursuing their desires and holding to their beliefs.

Always it is the virile and vigorous passions which attract him. At first he sees more exclusively what is noble and

beautiful in the ancient societies: gradually, however, force begins to stand out more and more as the focus of interest, of importance in its own right. Sometimes it draws him to the courage which smiles in the face of death; at other times, as in **'Snorr'**, it inspires a shudder of horror; again, particularly in the later poems, the poet comes to rejoice in the intensity of the passions without either idealising or condemning. His task as a writer of 'barbarian' poems is to make us accept and participate in an emotion while all the time realising its extreme strangeness: the emotion must then be one of great intensity, of general purport, but set in circumstances quite alien to the traditions of civilisation, yet solid and convincing. Often he does attain this balance. Elijah's torrent of threats is more fearful than the most dread of the infernal punishments in **'Snorr'**, his appearance perhaps more grotesque than that of any other barbarian, yet he has the authority and dignity of just vengeance descending upon the oppressor. Hervor and Brunhild in a strange Northern setting exult in a terrible revenge, but the unwavering determination with which they execute their desire cannot but stimulate our admiration. In these poems, as in **'Le dernier des Maourys'** where cannibalism is inspired by courage, the method is still the identification of violence from which we should normally shrink with some motive in which we cannot but share. But whereas in the poems of the early 1850s it is the nobility of the barbarian which is stressed, as time passes, Leconte de Lisle becomes more and more willing to represent the ferocity and strangeness of his characters. (p. 395)

It is to this need of Leconte de Lisle's temperament for a vigorous and vital passion that the barbarian as he sees him responds magnificently. There is little that is subtle or complex in any of his characters; there is no conflict within their own souls. If we look over the wide array of mythological or historical figures from the Runoïa, Uheldéda, Murdoc'h, Brunhild, Hialmar, Hervor, to Ruy Diaz, Pedro, Mouça, the Sachem or the Maoury chief, we see that their chief characteristic is their single-mindedness in whatever faith or passion inspires them. His barbarians are certainly stylised; even though he willingly shows the grotesque aspect of their physical appearance they are cast in heroic mould. Almost always he leaves aside such folk-tale elements as do not rise to the heroic plane, and anything verging on the comic is deliberately ignored. . . . His aim is not a complete representation of every aspect of the material on which he draws, but such a choice of authentic detail as may fit into a synthesis of the historical process as he himself feels it to be. Leconte de Lisle has chosen his barbarians from history because of their representative value, but in that choice his personality has played a large part.

So, too, has his sense of art. The more thoroughly we examine the poems the more obvious it becomes that it is the mind of a poet which has governed the ordering of the mass of details. One of the most essential qualities in their conception is the sense of construction: every poem is planned as an architectural whole into which the different parts fit with carefully adjusted balance. Of the spate of fragmentary prophecies which he found in the *Völuspá* Leconte de Lisle has made **'La légende des Nornes'**, a vision in three clear parts, focussed around three speakers representing past, present and future, and with the details in each section so ordered as to correspond or contrast

Frontispiece of the 1858 edition of Poésies de Leconte de Lisle.

century critics had pointed out that these utterly disordered songs and legends as they stood could never appeal to French taste; they were interesting historically, but utterly foreign to the accustomed aesthetic ideal. Leconte de Lisle has broadened this ideal, but he has also to a large extent transformed his material to suit its demands. It was in no sense a direct translation he was attempting: he had himself remarked that verse could not adequately be translated into verse. Those poems, such as **'La genèse Polynésienne'**, where he keeps closest to the original, have shown us most clearly how many were the adaptations which he felt the need to make. His task is a delicate one: in an ordered style and restrained medium he must give an impression of spontaneous inspiration and unleashed force. When he succeeds it is because of a superb capacity for choosing details of scenery, action and image which best suggest to the mind fierce and simple instincts. A close study would reveal how astonishing is the number of images based on physical forces and desires: constantly recurring are metaphors taken from fire, burning sun, wind and torrent, the shedding of blood, devouring hunger. The power of his imagery and the intensity of his vocabulary are well calculated to enhance the atmosphere of primitive passion in settings far removed from all civilised convention. Yet its very variety and vividness is something totally foreign to the authentic material, where brilliant flashes of colour and feeling are often submerged in monotonous repetition or incomprehensible allusion.

The subjects then are chosen often because they coincide with the poet's own temperament and preoccupations: the form is that of a trained artist, deliberately selecting and arranging. Is it precisely in these qualities that the value lies; has Leconte de Lisle then been at his best when he forgot or abandoned his own theories upon history and documentation? Certainly the very finest of his poems, those which will continue to be read and reread, those which show his inspiration at heights of intensity and sincerity which can scarcely be surpassed, are not the historical works: they are the brief and poignantly personal pieces **'Mille ans après'**, **'Le voeu suprême'**, **'Aux morts'**, **'Le dernier souvenir'**, **'Les damnés'**, **'Fiat nox'**, **'In excelsis'**, **'Le vent froid de la nuit'**, **'La dernière vision'**, **'Les rêves morts'**, **'Aux modernes'**, **'L'anathème'**, **'Ultra coelos'**, and many others. For such poems as these there is no need of a deliberate and reasoned appreciation; their roots pierce directly to the very centre of human feeling. The historical poems undoubtedly require more effort, and the modern reader is chary of effort, preferring that poetry should affect him directly, spontaneously, almost imperceptibly. Fully to appreciate much of the matter of Leconte de Lisle's historical works we should require cumbersome annotations, lengthy comparisons with the works on which he drew. Yet sometimes the effort is worth making, for always the more our knowledge of the material, the more we see the undeniable power of the artist arranging and transforming it.

Dangers of course there are in such use of history. The reader may tend to become bewildered by details with which he is insufficiently acquainted, weary of too many strange trappings. Yet in general Leconte de Lisle does use his material skilfully, explaining each allusion by some brief phrase or epithet. Even when we do not altogether follow the significance of Yggdrasill, Fenris, Loki and the rest, the sweeping sense behind **'La légende des Nornes'**

with those of the other two. Similarly in **'Le massacre de Mona'** there is one central action, in which are placed the speeches of priest, bard and prophetess, giving the mythology, history and future tragedy of the Celtic race. In **'La vigne de Naboth'** such care has been given to arrangement that the three divisions, the King's wrath, the Queen's action and the Prophet's denunciation, contain each exactly one hundred lines. Such firmness of structure is entirely of Leconte de Lisle's making: he takes a narrative which in the original winds upon its way through repetitions and digressions, and by arrangement he concentrates the attention upon its salient points. Practically always his poems observe most strictly the classical unities of time and place, yet practically always by skilled construction they transport us over vast spaces of time, for in the mind of one of the heroes is recalled the history of a race, and its future is foreseen by prophet or god. So the reader is led across thousands of past years and made to envisage the successive ages of the future, while he is firmly grounded upon a central theme.

This technique could scarcely be further removed from that of the original poems of such races as the Scandinavians or the Finns. Leconte de Lisle may be representing barbarians, but he is by no means doing it as they themselves would have done. Again and again nineteenth-

is clear enough, the final crashing catastrophe and ringing lamentations are of a majesty which over-rides any obscurity. It is the force of feeling and the skill of form which give the poems their fundamental value. Yet the habit of documentation has served a purpose. It has given the poet the matter for magnificent descriptions, and it has provided him with the basic vision of a historical process which rouses his thought and emotion. The value of his works has little or no relation to their historical accuracy: he may approach an impartial treatment as in the Cid poems and yet write works of little appeal, whereas in **'Qaïn'** he flouts his own theories and produces a masterpiece. Yet undeniably his study has often served him well: each age he represents is strikingly individual, there is always much that is authentic, and vividness of detail and solidity of effect are most frequently the result. His settings do carry conviction and extend our experience into lands of snow or sunlight among characters such as may never have existed but have yet their own compelling life. Quinet, Laprade, Ménard, to mention only these among his predecessors, had had the same vision of the sweep of human history. But it is Leconte de Lisle who can bring the vision alive in all its detail, avoiding the wearisome vagueness of the philosophical epic.

Fundamentally his attitude to the barbarians and to their gods depends on feelings at once intensely personal and very typical of his age. Like his romantic predecessors, he is acutely aware of and tormented by the isolation of the artist in the social struggle. After the events of 1848 he concludes that direct political action is not the poet's task; the Republic he so fervently supported has been stifled, he himself meets with little recognition. More and more his detestation of tyranny, his hatred of the materialistic bourgeois, and his memories of the vigour and freedom of his own youth combine to show him a vision of history in which strength and harmony inevitably fall victim to degeneracy and oppression, yet a faithful few resist staunch to the last. A phrase of his own: 'Le sentiment de la dignité humaine en lutte contre le principe hiératique' ['the feeling of human dignity struggling against hierarchical principle'] sums up the feeling which lies behind the greater part of his historical poems, whether *antiques* or *barbares*. First in Greece, then in the 'barbarian' mythologies, each of which had by countless writers been compared with that of the Greeks to whom he first turned, he chooses subjects which express this theme. The Celts, the Scandinavians, the Polynesians and the rest are of the same pattern as Niobé or Hypatie. They represent the passing of valour or beauty, stoical resistance to tyranny, and in the last analysis the poet himself faced by his own century.

Yet in seeking to solve the problem of the poet's place in society, Leconte de Lisle seeks to justify his existence by giving him a lofty aim: the production of faithful pictures of what is finest in the past to guide, inspire and console; and a far from easy means of attaining this: the discipline of severe study. The barbarians, it is true, symbolise his personal life, his political and religious convictions, his longing to escape from the prosaic, enfeebled, money-bound society of his day. All too obviously such feelings have the deepest affinities with those of the romantics, and it is by study and documentation that Leconte de Lisle seeks to differentiate his works from theirs. Always intransigent in his criticisms of his predecessors, conscious of his lofty position as leader of the *Parnasse,* he would obvi-

ously wish to stand representative of a new and distinct aesthetic. So, as he proceeds from one mythology to another, his barbarians become less obviously ideal. This need to cover their personal significance, coupled with his growing interest in the fierce rather than the harmonious, makes the later barbarians wilder, stranger, less obviously symbolic.

The purely personal poems will undoubtedly remain for many his greatest achievement. The historical poems will be appreciated not as history: they have no absolute 'scientific' value as an impartial picture of the past. At their deepest roots lie the poet's own emotions, his intensely personal reactions to the destiny of humanity. Yet the studies to which he has undoubtedly devoted so much time and care have borne their fruit. Vigny, to whom Leconte de Lisle owes a greater debt than he would have admitted, was conscious that he required a symbol to support and illustrate his thought, and poets in different ages have found many varying symbols to express the emotions of man: it is from his reactions to his reading of legend and history that Leconte de Lisle draws the symbols through which he can convey much of his most fundamental thought and feeling. Sometimes, though more rarely, I think, than is often considered, the poetry may be lost beneath the trappings, yet again and again the poet's reading has first provoked in him a vision of man's destiny, and then served to give colour, solidity and conviction to its expression. In such a poem as **'La paix des dieux'** the two elements have fused and balanced so that towards the close of his life the poet sums up in one of his finest works what was perhaps the most fundamental experience of himself and of the nineteenth century: the agonised search for a faith through the succession of religions, despair at the destruction which has annihilated each in turn, the final knowledge that the gods were but the expression in varying forms of man's struggle with his destiny. It is the content of thought and feeling which is fundamental, but these have been provoked by and expressed through the picture of the gods of the past as they follow each other in a majestic procession of strangeness and splendour.

His vision of man's destiny has its own tragic grandeur: the more mighty the forces of tyranny and destruction, the greater is the human spirit which in his barbarian heroes resists and triumphs in the inflexible courage with which it meets its inevitable fate. We cannot but recall the words of Pascal: 'Quand l'univers l'écraserait, l'homme serait encore plus noble que ce qui le tue' ['If the universe were to crush him, man would still be more noble than that which killed him']. In this vision of mankind, Leconte de Lisle's historical studies form an integral part, of value not for the absolute accuracy of the result, but for the stimulus exerted on the mind of the poet and for the many visions in which his thought and feeling found expression. (pp. 396-401)

> *Alison Fairlie, in her* Leconte de Lisle's Poems on the Barbarian Races, *Cambridge University Press, 1947, 426 p.*

A. Lytton Sells   (essay date 1955)

[*Sells is an English critic, educator, and translator who collaborated with his wife, Iris Lytton Sells, on studies of the lives and works of Oliver Goldsmith and Thomas*

Gray. In the following excerpt, he examines Leconte de Lisle's portrayal of animals in his poetry.]

We know the opportunities that Leconte de Lisle had for observing . . . wild creatures. During his voyages between the Ile Bourbon and Brittany he had watched and studied "le roi de l'espace" ["the king of space"]—the great albatross—and also the shark, that "sinistre rôdeur des steppes de la mer" ["the sinister prowler of the sea steppes"]. It was when he had landed near the Cape of Good Hope, as [critic and biographer Edmond] Estève amusingly recalls, that he had first met the black panther. She was stuffed, to be sure; but crouching in the most realistic attitude in the drawing-room of a wealthy South African. Here also he was much impressed by two young lions, one of whom roared and bounded in a manner that could only be called "sublime." These experiences stuck in his memory; even the homeless dogs he had heard howling on the beach were, much later, made the heroes of a poem; and the black panther was restored to life, removed to the Dutch East Indies, and splendidly baptized as "La reine de Java, la noire chasseresse" ["the queen of Java, the black huntress"].

Later, in Paris, he often went to the Jardin des Plantes, and one cannot help thinking that the young exile from the tropics, alone in the northern city, felt an instinctive sympathy for the great beasts who, pent in their cages, remained as dignified and inscrutable as he. Small wonder that he conceived the idea of picturing them in their native wilderness. He rarely, if ever indeed, depicts the birds and animals of western Europe. And if once, in **"Paysage polaire,"** he portrays the white bears . . . , or, in **"Les larmes de l'ours,"** the brown bear of northern Europe, he is either merely painting a picture or retelling a legend. His own taste is for the great hunting beasts of the jungle and the desert. The lion, the tiger, the jaguar, the black panther, the elephant, and the wolf are real animal-heroes whose lives are independent of man's and who have a place in literature for their own sake. He admires them for their beauty, for their strength, and for their virtues. He admires the elephants (**"Les éléphants,"** 1855) for the stoic endurance and persistence with which they toil on across the desert, guided only by the remembered image—"Des forêts de figuiers où s'abrita leur race" ["of the fig-tree forests where their race took refuge"] . . . He admires the lion who, with his lordly strength and untamed courage, hunts alone, unlike the timid men of Darfur, who herd together for protection. . . . The simple and heroic qualities of these lords of the wilderness, like those of the barbarians—Norsemen, Finns, ancient Celts, among whom the animals figure, probably for this reason—are a silent reproach to the degenerate moderns among whom the poet felt he had the misfortune of being obliged to live.

Once under the influence of the transformist doctrines then current (although *On the Origin of Species* had not yet appeared), Leconte de Lisle imagines a physical kinship with the animals and expresses this fancy in **"Les hurleurs"** (1855). The poem . . . is based on the memory of a few days spent years before, during the time of his happiness and discontent, at the Cape of Good Hope and recollected in the sombre years of loneliness and semistarvation to which the *Poèmes et poésies* (1855) bear a heartbreaking testimony; it is also, like most of these poems, a marvellous work of art that haunts the memory of almost everyone who has read it. He recalls the group of dogs on the beach as though he had seen them only the previous day:

> La queue en cercle sous leurs ventres palpitants,
> L'œil dilaté, tremblant sur leurs pattes fébriles,
> Accroupis çá et là, tous hurlaient, immobiles,
> Et d'un frisson rapide agités par instants.
>
> L'écume de la mer collait sur leurs échines
> De longs poils qui laissaient les vertèbres saillir;
> Et, quand les flots par bonds les venaient assaillir,
> Leurs dents blanches claquaient sur leurs rouges
>   babines. . . .
>
> Devant la lune errante aux livides clartés,
> Quelle angoisse inconnue, au bord des noires ondes,
> Faisait pleurer une âme en vos formes immondes?
> Pourquoi gémissiez-vous, spectres épouvantés?
>
> Je ne sais; mais, ô chiens qui hurliez sur les plages,
> Après tant de soleils qui ne reviendront plus,
> J'entends toujours, du fond de mon passé confus,
> Le cri désespéré de vos douleurs sauvages!

["Between their shivering legs they hid their tails.
Their staring eyes betokened deep distress.
Suddenly quivering, crouching motionless,
They uttered through the darkness mournful wails.

The sea-foam slithered each projecting spine,
Their shaggy hair, and fevered, restless paws.
Their white teeth chattered in their crimsoned
  jaws,
Each time the leaping billows hurled their brine.

Before the changing moon's unearthly light,
What secret anguish, there amid the storms,
Made souls lament within your filthy forms?
Why did you moan, O specters, torn with fright?

Dogs of that gloomy shore, I know not why,
But after all these many vanished years,
There still is dimly ringing in my ears,
The savage grief of your despairing cries!"
           (translation by Irving Brown)]

The "philosophy" of these verses—if such it can be called—impresses us less than it impressed Brunetière when he was delivering his lectures on *L'évolution de la poésie lyrique en France;* it is, rather, to the sincere sympathy they display, to the masked expression of the poet's anguish before the memory of his vanished youth, and to their artistry, that we pay homage.

Perhaps, as Pierre Flottes suggested, it was because Darwin had hinted that the animals might have a religious sense that Leconte de Lisle depicted the grey wolf, "le roi du Harz" ["the king of the Harz"](**"L'incantation du loup,"** 1884), finding his mate and cubs slain by the hunter and sitting on the snowy height to bay the moon. . . . (pp. 259-62)

He was probably better inspired, from the aesthetic standpoint, when he felt pity for the shark, whose cruel rapacity he placed on a level with man's own. . . . Life, he suggests [in **"Sacra fames"** (1884)], is maintained by a system of murder, legitimate and infinitely depressing; it is one of the observations that confirm the poet in his pessimism. One suspects here the influence of Schopenhauer, who enjoyed an exorbitant prestige between about 1860 and 1880.

Yet these pieces are not primarily philosophical and, with

the two exceptions noted, Leconte de Lisle's manner is usually as direct and objective as that of the Greeks. Great attention is paid to the setting, and especially to the appearance of the hero, usually depicted at the outset in a sculptural attitude. Sometimes the poet's vision is mainly plastic, as in **"Les éléphants"**. . . . Sometimes it is rather that of a colorist, as in his picture of the tiger, "le roi rayé" ["the striped king"], in **"Les jungles"** (1855). . . . (pp. 262-63)

Leconte de Lisle had begun with a strong Romantic bent, and this remained with him to the end. At an early age he had striven to discipline and mask it; he had aspired to an art that was to be objective and impersonal, and had met with some success in the poems composed between 1845 and 1851, which were published in 1852 in the **Poèmes antiques.** But the "Romantic" or lyrical tendency broke out in the **Poèmes et poésies** of 1855 and reappeared at intervals later. (p. 263)

Leconte de Lisle, like many of his generation, had imbibed a good deal of Byronism in his youth. It reappeared very strikingly in **"Qaïn"** (1869). . . . **"Le jaguar"** is another manifestation of it which, I believe, may have escaped the notice of the critics. Does it impair the poem's beauty? One hesitates to say so. A poem entirely objective, a poem devoid of human thought or sentiment—an "imitation" which is not an "interpretation" . . .—would have only a limited interest. Much depends, aesthetically speaking, on the total impression. "Souvent un beau désordre est un effet de l'art" ["Often beautiful disorder is an effect of art"], as Despréaux once observed.

There is thus at times, in poems which are for the most part very objective, a reflection or interpretation or even the intrusion of a modern feeling; and therein Leconte de Lisle is doing what most French and English poets have done. Even the Greeks had interpreted, by implication. But Leconte de Lisle is more ambitious in this genre than the Greeks, and equally artistic. Moreover, his animal poems . . . tend to compete successfully with the sculpture and painting of the time. In these respects also—in the simple pleasure the poet feels in portraying physical strength and beauty—they are in the Greek tradition. For the rest, they are so numerous and strongly marked that they almost constitute a new kind of poetry. Although Leconte de Lisle almost certainly found hints for it in such predecessors as Chénier, Burns, and Lamartine (whose *La chute d'un ange* he admired) and although he was taking his place, or rather making a place for himself, in the Greco-Latin tradition of animal poetry, nevertheless he must be reckoned as the greatest practitioner of animal poetry in the nineteenth century.

Leconte de Lisle was an unbeliever, but he was not one of those "ardent missionaries of atheism" of whose negations J. J. Rousseau had once spoken so feelingly. The great poem entitled **"Le Nazaréen"** (1855), in which he addresses our Lord with so much of admiration, and with that nostalgia of the divine which haunts the soul of the thoughtful unbeliever, seems to establish this point. He was, then, an unbeliever; but he foresaw that a godless world would probably not be viable and, in the last resort, not worth living in. This observation arises from such sombre poems as **"L'anathème"** (1855), **"Aux modernes"** (1872), and **"La paix des dieux"** (1888). At the same time he preserved a feeling of wonder and admiration in presence of the magnificent creatures God has created; and in this, he was nearer to Blake and further from the transformists than he probably realized. (pp. 265-66)

He must have been struck by the slaughter of the larger animals which was proceeding during the later nineteenth century and was only arrested, or limited, after about 1895 by the creation of national parks and game sanctuaries. But one judges from **"La forêt vierge"** that he did not think man's "survival value" was very much greater than theirs. . . . (pp. 266-67)

The animal poems reveal something of his reactions to modern biology, but these reactions were personal and not scientific. Unlike Sully Prudhomme, who had had a scientific training, who was a mathematician and a keen and disinterested student of modern astronomy, and who, moreover, understood the significance of modern science and responded to it with an attitude of modified hopefulness—Leconte de Lisle had no true feeling for science, and his response, so far as he responded, was one of despair. Sully Prudhomme could say of himself that "La Science [by which he clearly meant "science" in the English sense of the word] s'était rencontrée avec le Christianisme dans [son] âme" ["agreed with the Christianity in his soul"]. Leconte de Lisle could not have said this. The Christian metaphysics had been driven out of his soul by the lessons of eighteenth-century anticlericalism. Into the vacuum left by the departure of Christian faith—a void which, in the words of Tocqueville, had placed the soul of man "dans une assiette si douloureuse et si contraire à ses habitudes" ["in a situation so painful and so contrary to his customs"] that he has generally been impelled to fill the void by some other belief—into this vacuum Leconte de Lisle had introduced the Brahmanist notion of a world of illusory appearances and the belief that, at death, we are absorbed into, or rather lost in, "the nothingness which is God" ("le néant divin"). This belief, which was fairly comforting, he fortified and rendered positively attractive by his cult of art; because beauty was the one thing that he truly and joyfully believed in. His system of thought (if it deserves the name of "system") was, therefore, a highly personal amalgam of Brahmanism and aestheticism, animated by a loathing for the industrial revolution, a thoroughgoing contempt for modern man, and a cool and even delighted contemplation of the end of the human race and also of this planet, whose "unclean" remnants would "fertilize the furrows of space."

All this is as remote from the spirit of modern science and in particular from the attitude of the biologists, as it is from the Christian attitude, and probably more so. It would appear that during the 1850's he acquired some knowledge of the evolutionary theories of Lamarck and others. It is even possible that, towards 1860, he looked into *The Origin of Species,* or read a review of it; and critics have seen in him a kind of interpreter of Darwinism or at least a partisan of transformism. But the truth is that Leconte de Lisle took from the findings of modern biology only what suited his purpose. He was pleased to learn that the animals were his brothers in the biological sense. Those that were virile and powerful he admired enormously (when he had a chance of shooting a wild boar . . . he was so full of admiration that he forgot to do anything but gaze at it); and the complacency with which he pictured the monarchs of the forest and the plain was a measure of the disdain he felt for a humanity he considered degenerate.

It is not by reference to modern biology that we are able to explain—or rather to put in focus—the animal poems of Leconte de Lisle, but rather, I believe, by reference to the sculpture and painting of nineteenth-century France. The great artistic achievement of medieval France had not been in literature but in church architecture and in the inventing and perfecting of stained glass: in these arts she was original and supreme. The great artistic achievements of nineteenth-century France may prove to have been not so much in literature (if we make an exception for literary criticism and historical writing, in which France *was* supreme) as in landscape painting, animal painting, sculpture, and, perhaps, music. Girardet, Géricault, Ingres, David, Delacroix, Théodore Rousseau, Courbet, Corot, Sisley, Manet, Monet, Cézanne, and, among sculptors, Barye and Rodin (to name only a few in a great galaxy of outstanding artists) will probably be reckoned, in a well-balanced estimate, as having achieved more notable results even than the creative writers of the period. In any event, the relations between literature and the plastic arts were remarkably close; and more than once literature followed in the wake of painting or music.

I have remarked that Leconte de Lisle was the greatest *practitioner* of animal poetry in nineteenth-century France, and it may be asked whether he was, in any approximate sense of the term, its *creator*. It would be hazardous to assert that he drew inspiration for his animal poems from any sculptor or painter; but it is an interesting fact that he was preceded in the art of animal portraiture by the greatest animal sculptor of modern times, namely Antoine-Louis Barye (1795-1875).

Barye's feeling in early years was, like the poet's, Romantic; but he contrived after a time to achieve a somewhat greater impersonality than Leconte de Lisle was to achieve. (pp. 268-70)

Now I do not mean to suggest that Leconte de Lisle was deliberately trying to achieve in poetry what Barye had achieved and was continuing to achieve in sculpture and painting, but that, unconsciously perhaps, this was what in effect he did achieve. He was animated by the same Romanticism, which he strove less successfully to discipline and by the same effort towards an impersonal art. He had the same plastic vision, supplemented by a certain taste for color; the same care for physical and psychological realism; the same admiration and sympathy for great and powerful animals. He treated for the most part the same animals as Barye: bear, lion, tiger, panther, jaguar, wolf, elephant, bull, eagle, giant snake, and a few others, such as the shark and the condor, albatross, and hummingbird. He did not copy Barye, and yet some of his poems read like responses to Barye. The leader of his elephant herd is portrayed in terms which make one think of Barye's bronze statuette; the tiger in **"Les jungles"** is indeed the formidable carnivore whom we see in Barye's statuette of a *Crouching Tiger* and in his water color of a *Tiger Watching an Elephant*. . . . I have not noticed any poem of Leconte de Lisle which appears to be an imitation of Barye; there are, on the other hand, a few in which a different group or "combination" is presented. . . . But the feeling in [Leconte de Lisle's animal] poems appears to me *identical* with the feeling in Barye's statuettes and paintings.

If, as seems certain, Leconte de Lisle was familiar with Barye's works, which during the Second Empire occupied prominent positions in the Louvre, the Tuileries, the Place de la Bastille, and elsewhere, he would take care not to repeat him or imitate him; but if, as I believe, his vision of animals and his attitude towards them was identical with Barye's, he would be unable not to say the same things in a different medium. It is highly to praise Leconte de Lisle to describe him as the Barye of French poetry. (pp. 271-72)

> *A. Lytton Sells, "Leconte de Lisle," in his* Animal Poetry in French & English Literature & the Greek Tradition, *Indiana University Press, 1955, pp. 258-72.*

Irving Putter   (essay date 1961)

[*Putter is an American educator and critic who has written prolifically on the life and works of Leconte de Lisle. In the following excerpt, he elaborates on the sources and significance of pessimism in Leconte de Lisle's poetry.*]

Leconte de Lisle grew up when romanticism was in full flower and lived his mature life in the period of Renan and Darwin. His outlook on life in all its complexity was the fruit of this sequence. For an understanding of the origin and evolution of his pessimism we must probe into the poet's personal nature, while to elucidate the forms of his thought we must constantly refer to his time.

The exterior circumstances of his childhood and youth (1818-1837) do not reveal any clear justification for the growth of despair. Born with a robust constitution into an affectionate family, he spent his crucial early years in an atmosphere of natural beauty. His loosely knit education does not seem to have had any marked effect on his feelings. Nor is there any convincing indication that love played a serious role in his life on Bourbon Island. On the other hand, his poetic temperament was already beginning to distinguish him from those around him. Solitary, serious, and idealistic, he reached out for communion with kindred souls, only to be rebuffed by the practical concerns of his contemporaries.

His six-year sojourn in Brittany (1837-1843) provided fertile soil for the continued development of his character. Cut off from his family, who could not in any case fathom his discontent and melancholy, he felt his incapacity for harmonious social relationships growing rapidly into resistance and revolt. His intransigence emerged along with his pride, sensitivity, and intensified idealism. Nostalgia for his island, which was to become the basis for some of his finest creations, was only one form of his general rejection. More and more obviously he was drawn to spiritual concerns and poetry, but most obvious of all, so far as his view of life was concerned, was his natural tendency to darken all experience by stressing its shortcomings. And little by little he began to generalize his personal dissatisfactions.

The prerevolutionary period brought this process to fruition. Caught up, with no previous preparation, in the ardent socialism of Paris, he had to go through a phase of confused inspiration before he could see clearly the true nature of his beliefs. Increasing admiration for the past and particularly for Hellenic civilization was awkwardly interwoven in his *Phalange* poetry with optimistic flourishes dutifully acknowledging his fidelity to Fourierism. But the sincerity of his attempt to synthesize opposite tendencies could not suppress the inner conflict. Contempt for the mass displayed itself early, as did his feeling that superiority is condemned to suffering. The preponderance of evil weighed more and more heavily on the poet's consciousness as his religious faith crumbled in 1846, and increasingly he dwelt on the anguish of the inaccessible Ideal, in long poems centered on the religious theme. The nature or existence of God, the meaning of life, the implications of death, transcendental doubt, retreat from a restricting society—all became pressing problems before the revolution of 1848. The failure of the reform movement revealed to him his true beliefs, and, when the *Poèmes antiques* appeared in 1852, all the major themes of his pessimism were clearly expressed.

Leconte de Lisle's mature years supplied nourishment for his despair, but only confirm the conclusion that his outlook was the result of his own inner nature. Poverty was acute and prolonged, but was the natural consequence of a conscious choice. There were disappointments in love, but also joys. His literary reputation was not what he would have liked it to be, but there was solid recognition from the best minds of the day. He could not be happy because he was always impelled to dwell on life's deficiencies. Thus, from his youth to his death his work in its broad outlines presents a picture cast in somber hues. Individual themes grow more intense with the years, but the basic outlook never changes.

A romantic and an individualist in his origins, Leconte de Lisle had an intellectual bent which led him to investigate the philosophical currents of his time. In his 1852 preface he proclaimed the necessity for a marriage of art and erudition. Only by combining the discipline of the scholar with the imagination of the artist could works of lasting beauty be created. Leconte de Lisle's own type of thinking made him a logical representative of an emerging tendency in poetry. Such writers as Laprade had helped pave the way ("La passion ne devient poétique en matière d'art que par sa combinaison avec l'intelligence" ["Passion only becomes poetic in matters of art through its combination with intelligence"], preface to *Psyché*), and Leconte de Lisle's friendship with the intellectual Ménard further strengthened his conviction. There can be no doubt that he considered himself a thinker as well as an artist, and in this respect a man of his times. . . . As a consequence he diverged from the romantics, first by adopting the rational activity of his contemporaries to analyze his sorrow, and second by concerning himself with the human condition generally rather than solely with his own disillusionment. For him poetry became "l'histoire sacrée de la pensée humaine" ["the sacred history of human thought"] (*Discours sur Victor Hugo*).

His period is therefore reflected quite clearly in many principal facets of his pessimism. The Christian idealism with which he began, and which so strikingly recalls the work of Lamartine, also characterizes others of his day, from Mme Ackermann to Jean Lahor. But the whole generation's thirst for the absolute was doomed to disappointment by the critical approach to religion and the keen awareness of the instability of all phenomena. The new critical attitude, which came from Germany and deeply influenced thinkers in France and England, was predicated on a sympathetic but objective analysis of the religious myths of all peoples. Leconte de Lisle began a long and desperate pilgrimage through the cosmogonies, theogonies, and creeds of the world. From the Greek to the barbarian and even Christian doctrines he accepted the validity of all religious symbols as fragments of eternal truth, but the endlessly changing spectacle of man's efforts to reach the absolute convinced him only of the relative value and ultimate vanity of each. Compounding his sense of cosmic futility was Leconte de Lisle's abomination of Western man's most immediate spiritual form, Christianity. In essence, he felt, it has departed from the pure ideal of its founder. By its repression of man's natural instincts, by its ethical system based on egoism and inhumanity, by its conception of God, too distant and awesome, Christianity has failed to slake the spiritual thirst of humanity, and its fanaticism has turned history into a blood bath. All of man's higher concerns, including art, have irreparably suffered from its appalling effects. In his belief that Christianity is in its death throes Leconte de Lisle voices the thought of many of his contemporaries. His increasingly violent bias, which not only vitiates his own theories of universal sympathy but injects a type of harshness detrimental to his art, seems to be the poet's reaction to the growing pressure of the Church, represented by the famous Syllabus of 1864. But this violence is unable to disguise his despair about man's cosmic solitude. Neither a materialist nor a philosopher, he is caught between atheism and an unremitting need to believe. Irreligion and pessimism are intimately related in him, as they are in others of his time. . . . Leconte de Lisle, however, differs from others in that he can find no compensating faith aside from his own literary activity. The loss of religion represents for him spiritual impotence, ignorance, and death. This fundamental defeat therefore becomes the overriding aspect of his pessimism.

His view of the elements of life's experience follows a similar pattern. As he longs for unity with the infinite principle, so too he longs for the joys of life and dreads death. As in the metaphysical sphere he can settle for nothing less than the eternal. But wherever he turns he is confronted by death. His constant nostalgia for the youth of the individual and of the world is not only a reaction to the bitterness of the present but a manner of finding a kind of endless duration. Youth, however, is but a fleeting moment, and its freedom, vigor, beauty, and faith only act to intensify the sadness of the poet, whose view of life, like that of so many writers of the time, is that of an aged and weary man. Even love, which Leconte de Lisle never renounces as a consolation, is subject to death. Life itself is a contingency, and the proximity of the abyss became for him and his contemporaries a constant source of agony, as scientists of the day kept before their eyes the end of the world. All is but passing vanity, and, since nothing which passes is essentially real, the entire universe and all its experience is no more than a fraud, an optical illusion. Other writers were voicing the same thoughts, and Leconte de Lisle's "Hindu" aspect expresses certain basic beliefs of subjectivist skepticism. For a poet ardently longing for the real and immutable, illusion becomes an insurmountable obstacle to joy. Life, like religion, does not offer the good. And, like religion, it completes the picture with positive evil. As in Schopenhauer, so in Leconte de Lisle the essence of man's nature is desire which can never be fulfilled and which remains a permanent source of misery. And if suffering is the ineluctable law of the individual, conflict is the law of intercourse between individuals. The whole crushing spectacle amply justifies revolt, and **"Qaïn"** is a lyrical protest not against a nonexistent divinity but against the nature of being. But this masterpiece of Leconte de Lisle does not represent true hope in his general view. His emotional, moral, and even aesthetic tendencies lead him to embrace death as the only solution. Resistance is futile, escape is more natural, hence his fervent invocations to annihilation. Death is the end result of his terrestrial problem, as it is of his metaphysical problem.

The poet's view of his relationship to society does not play the important role which the more universal aspects do, but its effect is plain nonetheless. All about him he saw vulgar materialism and a literature which consented to cater to low spiritual ideals. As a result, he held his age in utter contempt, and by and large he kept it out of his work. However, it is frequently reflected indirectly. The superior individual, as in Vigny, is the victim of society. Here as elsewhere pessimism is necessary, since progress, as society understands it, inevitably conflicts with spiritual nobility. This was a view fully comprehensible to Second Empire writers. The artist and thinker are isolated in society, and must respond, like Flaubert, with scorn. Leconte de Lisle's misanthropy, based doubtless on his concern with principles and masses rather than with individuals, distinguishes him from other pessimists who could combine tenderness with despair. His chief consolations were derived not from men but from nature, which is a relief from life's problems and passions, and particularly from art, which replaces religion, suppresses time, and compensates for society's wrongs. While in the heavens and on earth he could find only sorrow, illusion, and death, in art he found fulfillment and eternity.

If the basic explanation of Leconte de Lisle's pessimism is to be found in the poet himself, the aspects into which it falls reveal the influence of his day. It does not appear that any specific thinkers had a dominant effect on his poetry. There is nothing to indicate, for instance, that he was directly familiar with the work of Schopenhauer, Darwin, or Hume. But that he was well acquainted with the general philosophical currents of his time is beyond doubt. To express his own outlook he selected what he considered the most universal themes, leaving aside what he deemed secondary. The deadening effect of romantic ennui is not part of his pessimism. In 1839 he wrote (***Premières poésies***): "Ce n'est pas l'ennui . . . qui dessèche la vie: . . . c'est le penser sombre" ["It isn't boredom . . . that desiccates life: . . . it is somber thought"]. The "weight of daily toil," which rankled Byron's Cain, is left aside as is the monotonous routine of "la vie pratique" ["the practical life"] which irritated Flaubert. The ravages of sickness, the deformations of the body, its slow destruction by the years, the blight of poverty, the sordidness of the modern city—none of these could find a place in the austere work of this philosophical poet. Little wonder that Leconte de Lisle's pessimism strikes a chord so different from that of Baudelaire or even Flaubert, who could look more directly at their fellow men. Nor did the morbid ever tempt Leconte de Lisle seriously. Life is not a nauseating experience nor a monstrous joke to sneer at, but an overwhelming tragedy. It is the sober dignity of despair which lends

a monolithic character to his work, relating the Hellenic to the Hindu and barbarian cycles, the objective frescoes to the personal pieces, and the elegies to the diatribes.

Yet as we move from the general unity of the work to a closer scrutiny of the elements, contradictions manifest themselves at every turn. . . . Leconte de Lisle is constantly torn between opposing forces. Spontaneously drawn to the joys of life, he simultaneously blackens them at the source. He longs for an instinctive life of unfettered freedom, but envies the reflective man who retires to asceticism. Nostalgia for calm and immobility appears side by side with admiration for intense energy. He strives to assimilate man's aspirations and defeats, but scornfully withdraws to embittered solitude. Suffering is inherent in the nature of being, yet the past seems like a paradise. Desire is a decoy, yet love is a blessing in spite of its sorrows. Cruelty and slaughter are native to man, but heroes display a lofty moral character. Man is dominated by inner and outer laws, but evil is denounced as though man were responsible. Nature consoles, though it is amoral and tortured. All is illusion, but beauty is real. Retreat from suffering is the logical solution, but martyrdom is welcomed. Death is both dreaded and desired. (pp. 385-90)

If by philosopher we mean a rigorously consistent thinker, then Leconte de Lisle is obviously no philosopher; he must be placed in a family with such minds as Renan, Montaigne, and Voltaire, whose antinomies have so often been pointed up and roundly denounced. The situations, attitudes, and expressions in Leconte de Lisle's poetry constantly reveal the conflict within him. Life is a "tourment qui n'est cher" ["uncherished torment"] **("Bhagavat")**, and the poet a "forçat libre enfin, pleurant ses premieres fers" ["convict free at last, weeping over his first chains"] **("La paix des dieux")**, while the young man of **"La fontaine aux lianes"** is enjoined to exhaust his "chères douleurs" ["beloved pains"]. The sage in **"Valmiki"** and Man in **"L'illusion suprême"** turn back from the brink of death to contemplate the glories of the world; even the decaying hermit of **"Çunacépa"** cannot resist the thrill of life which suddenly returns to surge through his veins. The verse in **"Fiat nox"**:

> Toi qui veux être libre et qui baises ta chaîne,

> ["You who wish to be free and who kiss your chain,"]

sums up the poet's dilemma. He cannot pretend, like Leopardi, that he is no longer disturbed by the vanity of life and has accepted all the consequences of despair. His "philosophy" is not a logical system but a group of dominant philsophical attitudes acting more or less in the same direction but constantly being reversed. The vital instinct is perpetually at war with the spirit of negation in his work, giving it intensity and its own peculiar individuality. (pp. 390-91)

The lyrical values he has retained from his romantic youth are thus an implicit denial of total pessimism. His poetry returns in spite of itself to glorify courage, virtue, and freedom. However much he may decry man's bestiality, his heroes hold up an image of which man may be proud. He consciously rejects the numerous pessimistic currents undermining the beauty of love. Nature is not the enemy others profess to see, but an inexhaustible source of peace. Art can grant what God cannot. The power of illusion is irresistible. . . . Leconte de Lisle's poetic temper refuses to allow him to fashion his universe entirely of the desiccating materials of objective thought. He *knows* he is nothing; he does not *feel* himself nothing. The world may be a mechanism controlled by law, but his imagination must create a lyrical world, infusing eternity into his concepts of love, nature, and art. Ennobling idealism remains to resist utter materialism, which degrades. All his consolations make him a poet. . . . (p. 391)

Still, the over-all impression produced by his poetry is one of profound sadness. The legendary and historical pieces, the formal exercises, and the clerical denunciations are today relatively inert. What continues to move us is the part of his work in which personal feeling gives vital form to universal pessimism. Such pieces as **"Dies Irae"** and **"Ultra coelos," "L'illusion suprême," "Le vent froid de la nuit," "Si l'aurore," "Requies," "Fiat nox," "In excelsis," "Le voeu suprême," "A un poète mort," "Mille ans après," "Les rêves morts," "L'anathème"** and **"Aux modernes"** are the fruit of the poet's belief that "la double condition du génie c'est d'être personnel en étant universel" ["the dual condition of genius is to be personal in being universal"]. Here pessimism and lyricism are at one. There is nothing didactic or expository in the philosophy of these laments. Poetic intuition here is an instrument for evoking the deepest resonances of a human sensibility. Symbols of solitude are created; moods of intense lassitude, of age and despondency, permeate the verses; expressions of horror, disgust, and dismay translate the poet's tragic outlook. . . . In these summits of the work, poetry is not placed at the service of philosophy; it is in itself a philosophy, an ordering of the universe according to the exigencies of a temperament and based on its thought, emotion, and imagination. But in the depth of feeling and the sweep of vision the poet's art has fashioned an image reflecting not only his own sorrow but that of the race to which he belongs. (p. 392)

> *Irving Putter, in his* The Pessimism of Leconte de Lisle: The Work and the Time, *University of California Press, 1961, 263 p.*

Geoffrey Brereton   (essay date 1973)

[*Brereton was an English scholar and translator who specialized in French drama and literature. In the following excerpt, he addresses the themes and techniques of Leconte de Lisle's poetry in relation to French literary and intellectual trends of the nineteenth century.*]

It is customary to place after the Romantic heyday a reaction in favour of impersonality known as Parnassianism and roughly contemporaneous with the Second Empire. Revolting against the excessively self-revelatory manner of Musset and his lesser disciples, the Parnassians took up Théophile Gautier's somewhat frigid doctrine of 'art for art's sake', married it to the cult of form prescribed by Théodore de Banville, and produced a type of poetry distinguished by pictorial rather than by emotional or musical qualities. Carefully wrought in detail and definite in outline, this poetry belonged to the same artistic order as Flaubert's prose—particularly in *Salammbô* and the *Trois Contes*—and to the same intellectual climate as the materialistic philosophies of Renan and Taine. In the 1880s it began to be superseded in its turn by Symbolism, with its fluid and twilight intimations of the unconscious. After

Romantic subjectivity, Parnassian objectivity, and after that an integration of the two in such poets as Verlaine and Mallarmé and a number of lesser writers.

So long as this is regarded as a simplified outline, it helps us considerably in following the main currents of French poetry after 1850, as it helped poets of the time to define what they were for and against. Moreover, *parnassien* is a useful critical term which serves to define a recognizable type of verse by no means limited to the contributors to *Le Parnasse contemporain*. But the theory must not be applied too narrowly. For one thing, the greatest poet writing under the Second Empire, Baudelaire, sometimes joins hands with the Parnassians yet can never be confined within their aesthetic. Verlaine and Mallarmé wrote first as Parnassians, and Mallarmé in his own way developed their insistence on formal perfection into the austerest canon of pure Symbolism. No poet of any stature at all remained a pure Parnassian except Heredia, whose poems were not published as a collection until 1893—though it is true that most of them had appeared considerably earlier in reviews. Finally, Parnassianism is better regarded as an extension, or late phase, of Romanticism, rather than as a negation of it.

With these reservations we can approach the work of the man who has gone down to literary history as the leader of the Parnassians, Charles-Marie René Leconte de Lisle. (pp. 166-67)

Leconte de Lisle's poetry was published in the three main divisions of the *Poèmes antiques* (1852, augmented 1872), the *Poèmes barbares* (1862, augmented 1874 and 1878) and the *Poèmes tragiques* (1884), to which the posthumous *Derniers poèmes* (1895) must be added for completeness. But the dates have no great significance as stages of the poet's development. His work can be treated as one body without insistence on its chronological order.

The first impression which this verse would make on a reader coming straight from Musset or Verlaine would be of entering a heavily furnished room of the period. The hangings are of the best velvet, the furniture of ebony and mahogany, the ornaments of massive gilded bronze. An indefinable atmosphere of apprehension broods over this opulent solidity. Absurdly, one hesitates to lift the silver cover of the bacon-dish lest underneath should be the head of the Count with its staring eyes. The tiger-headed rug lies ready to tear at the suddenly writhing legs of the dining-table. Passive, of course, are displayed various exotic trophies: a stuffed eagle, a shark's fin, a four-armed Vishnu. These objects have not been assembled haphazard. As we grow accustomed to the scene we are aware of a powerful harmony uniting its components. Leconte de Lisle is as much in control of his material as Matthew Arnold was of his. Neither was a collector of purposeless bric-à-brac. In the French poet's décor there is unity, there is movement, and there is even something that might be called life if we could find some more familiar form of life to which to relate it. In one of his finest poems, **'Qaïn'**, the seer Thogorma sees in a vision the gigantic children of Cain walking back into their citadel at the end of the day. Clearly this cannot be classed simply as a frieze. . . . (pp. 168-69)

Though 'sculptural', [the verse in **'Qaïn'**] is not static. It has a slow, processional movement in keeping with the whole poem from which it is taken—a long one. Poetry conceived on this scale can afford to be majestic and un-hurried—there can be no quarrel with it on that ground. As for the weakness of some Parnassian poets and some-times of Balzac, Flaubert and Zola in prose—their piling-up of secondary details—Leconte de Lisle avoids this too. His details and his adjectives are carefully selected with a view to the total effect and his description is not so exclu-sively concrete that it fails to convey an atmosphere. (p. 170)

Leconte de Lisle's main concern as a poet—it appears all through his work—was to find the words which most ade-quately conveyed his unusual concepts, without much re-gard for their musical or other aesthetic qualities. Some-times this led him to an exact visual adjective, sometimes to a technical or semi-technical term, and often to an ar-chaic or pedantic spelling of proper names—*Qaïn* for *Caïn*, *Héva* for *Ève*. But it goes further than a preoccupa-tion with the externally picturesque. It reveals a constant effort to preserve the original flavour of the material he was transposing. It is the opposite of the classic search for the *mot juste,* which meant—or was debased to mean—the word which most satisfied the expectation of convention-ally educated people. Leconte de Lisle did not engage in this harmless pastime. (pp. 170-71)

Only a poet-scholar with a complete disregard for salon standards and devoid also of Baudelaire's flair for themes relevant to 'modern life' could have composed towards 1880 **'The Death-Song of a Gaelic Warrior of the Sixth Century'** in which the severed head of the dead chieftain is carried on a spear in the van of the charging Celts. . . . (p. 171)

Here, and in many other poems, Leconte de Lisle seems to have followed up the hint thrown out by Hugo in *Les orientales* and to have carried the Romantic taste for local colour to its furthest limits. But with him it was more than colour; it was form and texture as well. His imagination was so impregnated with the atmosphere of the exotic—apart from the fact that his research into it was much more thorough than Hugo's—that he gives it back as though it were a lived experience. Impersonal as his verse appears (and as he strove to make it), it is thus not anti-Romantic. The generation of 1830, fascinated by the strangeness of the exotic, had tried to express it in French without suffi-ciently assimilating its spirit. Almost inevitably, they failed. Hugo's early work, Gautier's verses on Spain, re-main a painted décor. Leconte de Lisle comes nearer to achieving the impossible. His poems on India are about as Indian, on primitive Scandinavia about as Scandinavian, as *The Three-Cornered Hat,* danced at Covent Garden, is Spanish, or Fitzgerald's *Rubáiyát* is Persian. That, for anyone who is neither a native nor a specialist, is good enough—provided that one looks to poetry for aesthetic pleasure and not for exact instruction or for new light on experience.

The correspondence between Leconte de Lisle's work and Hugo's *Légende des siècles* has often been noticed, but it is hardly close enough for a charge of imitation to be brought against either poet. Hugo conceived a huge epic with the progress of the human spirit as its motif. Leconte de Lisle interpreted history as a descent rather than as an ascent, and his treatment was considerably more fragmen-tary, if more scientific. On the dates, either one could have influenced the other, and since *Poèmes antiques* appeared

seven years before the first volume of *La légende des siè-cles,* it is probable that Hugo borrowed something from Leconte de Lisle's descriptive methods. On the other hand, **'Qaïn'** was first published ten years after Hugo's 'La conscience', which also deals with Cain in his old age and may have suggested the subject to the younger poet, who treated it, however, on a grander scale and in a very differ-ent spirit. In general, it would appear that the two poets glanced occasionally at each other's work before writing from their own strongly held, and different, points of view.

Another ghost walks through Leconte de Lisle's work—the ghost of Vigny. It is difficult to seize, but impossible to lay. Leconte de Lisle could have read nearly all Vigny's work before publishing a line of his own, and it is certain that he did so. Similar themes, verse-forms and even iso-lated lines occur here and there in his pages. But more striking than any resemblances of detail was the deep com-patibility of temperament between the two. The iron world of Vigny was Leconte de Lisle's world—more pro-fusely decorated no doubt, but at least as hard and hostile at the centre. In fact, it was more so, for while Vigny still belonged to the Christian tradition and still thought, in however disillusioned a way, in terms of a moral universe, Leconte de Lisle had taken a further step and believed only in a mechanistic universe. The groundwork of his po-etry was his study of the various gods and religions which, according to the evolutionist explanation, man had de-vised for himself in various historical and geographical circumstances. Brahma, Vishnu and Siva, the Hellenic Pantheon, the Nordic Valhalla, the Egyptian gods had all been valid in their time and place before giving way to Christianity. Christianity in its turn would become out-worn and disappear. . . . (pp. 171-73)

Leconte de Lisle's pessimism, as it is found in such poems as **'Dies Irae', 'Midi', 'Le vent froid de la nuit', 'L'illusion suprême',** is complete. Recoiling in horror from the idea of immortality—'Le long rugissement de la vie éternelle' ['The long roar of eternal life']—he concludes that the only desirable end is the annihilation of the individual personality. . . . (p. 173)

His conception of the 'divine nothingness' into which all life returns derived from Buddhism or Vedaism, which he found the most attractive among the different religions he studied. From the same sources, with a certain admixture of Darwinism, came his conviction that all life, whether human or animal, is fundamentally the same, and that the one common factor in the universe is suffering. This phi-losophy, with its scientific basis, would no doubt have been acceptable to Vigny had he belonged to the same genera-tion and it would have given him a stronger intellectual justification for his personal pessimism. But as it was, Vigny remained a desolate and lonely seeker while Le-conte de Lisle was linked to the advanced thought of his age.

But he too was a poet before he was a philosopher and it seems that his philosophy developed out of his subjects rather than the opposite. He was not led by systematic re-search alone to the Icelandic runes or the war-songs of the Gaelic bards. Temperament drew him to some of the most ferocious episodes in folklore and early literature and par-ticularly to those descriptions of beasts and birds of prey in which he excels. He was more fascinated by the example than by the rule. His Mongolian eagle swoops from the sky to peck out the eyes of the wild stallion; his jaguar, sleeping on a rock in the jungle, dreams that she is tearing at the flanks of plunging buffaloes; his shark and his python slide through their native elements in search of their quarry. The thesis behind this is that nature is amoral—the law is to kill or to be killed and no guilt attaches to the act. Man is as much subject to it as the animals. But in reading these bloodthirsty poems, it is impossible not to remark that the poet's first pleasure was to re-create these beasts by an imaginative attempt to enter into their spirit.

In such a poem as **'L'incantation du loup'**, he takes up a subject which Vigny had used in 'La mort du loup', but instead of narrating the wolf-hunt and ending his poem with a moralizing passage to explain its intention, he simply describes the he-wolf sitting on the snow after the tragedy has occurred. The she-wolf and the cubs have been killed by the hunters and the survivor gazes up at the moon and chews over his hatred of Man. . . . Such poetry may not be the highest art, but at least it is original, and represents as energetic an attempt as that made by the early Romantics to break out of the urban, polished world inhabited by the neoclassics. This casting-back to barbarism and magic is Leconte de Lisle's most durable feature. Sometimes it raises a smile; occasionally it is overdone and smells artificial, but on the whole his world can be accepted. One walks respectfully through it, noting with awe those huge, abandoned constructions of the human mind. One admires his jackal-headed carvings and his monstrous stone flowers and, although all this was created only a century ago, the modern imagination is stirred in much the same way as the poet was stirred by the thought of ancient Egypt or the halls of the Nibelungen. As long as his work communicates this impression, it must be counted as successful. The reservation, which the Symbolists were quick to exploit, and which was presently to be weighted with all the authority of Freud, is that contemporary man cannot be excluded for long from poetry. With his pettiness and his inconsistencies, he forces his way into the foreground and everything that does not converge directly on him is thought of as stage furniture. But is it not possible that a section of the audience should be more fascinated by the décor than by the actors? (pp. 173-75)

> *Geoffrey Brereton, "Leconte de Lisle and He-redia," in his* An Introduction to the French Poets: Villon to the Present Day, *revised edition, Methuen & Co., Ltd., 1973, pp. 166-77.*

Robert T. Denommé   (essay date 1973)

[*Denommé is an American critic and educator who has written extensively on nineteenth-century French literature. In the following excerpt, he focuses on Leconte de Lisle's* Poèmes antiques.]

The preface to the thirty-one poems comprising the original edition of the **Poèmes antiques** in 1852 made it clear that the "exercises" in celebration of past civilizations had scarcely been designed to appeal to readers who considered poetry as little more than sentimental recollections or personalized reveries. As the foremost exponent within the Parnassian movement of a poetic neo-Hellenism, Leconte de Lisle doubtless benefited from Victor de Laprade's versified interpretations of ancient myths in such works as *Psyché* (1841) and *Odes et poèmes* (1844). It should be remembered that de Lisle's growing enthusiasm for Antiquity became further solidified through frequent conversations with the brilliant scholar of Greek civilization, Louis Ménard, who spoke of the possible renascence of a type of evolutionary paganism that could adjust to the requirements of modern civilization. Leconte de Lisle's recourse to the remote past in the **Poèmes antiques,** then, can hardly be described as innovative. Yet, his obsession with Hellenism, for example, in the collection possesses little in common with the more scholarly and practical ideas on the matter of his mentor, Louis Ménard. Rather, it was founded, like the literary antiquarianism of Théophile Gautier, in an interpretation of objectivism which camouflages a decidedly personal reaction to human experience.

As a series of documented studies on Antiquity, the **Poèmes antiques** purported to illustrate the alliance between poetry and science which Leconte de Lisle believed was capable of purifying lyricism of the elements which contaminated it. Richard Chadbourne [see Further Reading] has aptly described what the lyricist of the **Poèmes antiques** understood as science to be the acquisition of a positive historical knowledge and especially that of past religious phenomena. The fact of the matter was that the social and political events of 1848 served as such corroborative justification for his own pessimism that he sought officially to disassociate himself completely from what he considered disdainfully were the dated and pragmatic concerns of nineteenth-century civilization.

If the majority of the poems comprising the **Poèmes antiques** may be considered as the offspring of his own sensitivity, it should be added that de Lisle sought eagerly to objectify his conception of an idealized Antiquity with the external accouterments of a seemingly objective and scientific approach. His notion that the contemporary reader stood to benefit most from the examples of past civilizations which came closest to achieving the human aspiration toward beauty, harmony, and unity stemmed in large measure from his own rejection of all values associated with the society in which he lived. It is no exaggeration to say that the greater number of the **Poèmes antiques** conform more readily to the poet's own dreamworld than to the factual world of Ancient Greece and India. What he felt could no longer be achieved in his own times, Leconte de Lisle sought to achieve through the artful and idealized reconstructions of the remote past. Such an endeavor confers upon the most successful poems of the collection an undeniable lyrical dimension. The charges of impassibility and impersonalism which so many critics are willing to append next to his poetic production attest most eloquently to the fact that Leconte de Lisle's verse still manages to convey to readers that it is essentially lyrical expression which is tempered and authenticated by a serious concern for historical and scientific data.

The definitive edition of the **Poèmes antiques** which appeared in 1874 included some twenty-five additional pieces, most of which were transferred from the **Poèmes et poésies** of 1855 by Leconte de Lisle, who decided to eliminate the latter collection from the work. For the purpose of our analysis of the volume, let us say that the **Poèmes antiques** may be divided into three distinct categories: namely, the Greek poems; the Hindu poems; and the miscellaneous poems. The three cycles of lyrics receive their fundamental unity from the poet's celebration of an idealized beauty which he identifies with past civilizations or with an exotic nature far removed from the immediacies of the nineteenth century.

. . . . .

Such poems as **"Niobé," "Hélène," "La Vénus de Milo," "Khirôn,"** and **"Hypatie,"** most notably, which had appeared previously in the pages of *La phalange* as lyrical symbols of the Fourierist conception of an earthly harmony, are divested in the *Poèmes antiques* of all allusions to any contemporary ideology, and join the other poems as expressions of admiration of the Greek notion of love and beauty. The short epic, **"Khirôn,"** for example, underscores the evolution which had taken place in Leconte de Lisle's attitude from the days of its initial publication in 1847 to its revised appearance in the *Poèmes antiques* of 1852. As a three-part epic poem, **"Khirôn"** recalls the old centaur's visit by Orpheus before whom he begins to sing the praises of the Giants who took up arms against the god, Zeus. Khirôn knows that he has been condemned by "the pale Olympian gods" and awaits calmly and stoically his own murder at the hands of the young Héraklès. To a significant extent, **"Khirôn"** looms largely as the nostalgic recollection or evocation of a primitive time in which the earth had not yet been daunted by the cruelty of capricious gods. De Lisle's centaur, Khirôn, is riddled by doubt and torn by anguish because he is aware that the Olympian gods represent no absolute since they are the fabrications of a people. Orpheus, who holds the torch of poetry, listens in sadness to the centaur, who describes a desire for domination and eternity within him which can neither be squelched nor assuaged:

> And I, as a witness to such prodigious times, while I pitied the vanquished, I applauded the gods, for I was then certain that they were just. Yet, there burned within me a dark secret engulfed as in a flame. As I sat by the flowing waters, I frequently allowed my thoughts, filled with terror and with doubt, to wander. Dreamer! I would say to myself. There is on the snowy crests an eagle who is able to spread his stormy wings and whose eye is constantly fixed upon the sun as he repeatedly attempts to break the stress of the winds in the bewildered space. He knows that his strength is hidden in this eternal struggle, and he derives satisfaction from it. Greedy for light and thirsty for battle—for the earth remains dark and the skies remain low—he soars and ascends into the skies and struggles as his avid claws seize the three-pronged lightning whose fire consumes him.

In the 1847 version which appeared in *La phalange,* both Khirôn and Orpheus recall the destiny of the Romantic poet, a collaborator of the divinity, who leads the people toward progress and instills in them a sense of the ideal. As he appears in the *Poèmes antiques,* Orpheus becomes the intermediary who would attempt to invest the hearts of men with some measure of reassurance. Behind his mythological reconstruction, Leconte de Lisle raises a very personal issue in **"Khirôn"** which will continue to plague and haunt him during his entire career as a poet. To a degree, the poet shares the centaur's predicament since he is also possessed by the same gnawing desire for the absolute which Khirôn is compelled to dismiss as a fatal and logical fabrication of the human mind. In his monumental study of Leconte de Lisle [*The Pessimism of Leconte de Lisle: The Work and the Time*], Irving Putter explains that the poet's pessimism, ostensibly couched in a somewhat erudite or scholarly framework for the most part, stemmed from the religious relativism which issued from the philological and archaelogical discoveries of the scientific age: "It was a principle of pessimism for Leconte de Lisle. He was neither a materialist nor a theoretical philosopher who could be content with faith in some abstract principle." The *Poèmes antiques* as a whole betrays an implicit if not always explicit nostalgia for a past that is no more or for a love and a beauty whose ideal expression is identified with youth or primitivism. The pensive centaur in **"Khirôn"** identifies the happiest years of his existence with youth's initial aspirations: "How beautiful I thought the Earth was while I was young! In those days, the silt of the great waters turned the highest mountain peaks in the Aither region green again." Leconte de Lisle's treatment of mythology in **"Khirôn"** sets the tone for the majority of the poems which constitute the Greek cycle.

One of the most prevalent tendencies among critics and literary historians has been to identify Parnassian poetry with such terms as plasticity, materialism, and verbal description. There can be no denying that such a practitioner of Parnassianism as Leconte de Lisle was moved to evolve a cult of the beautiful in art and literature in reaction to the abusive exploitation of the imagination by some of the leading Romantic poets. To a significant degree, the differences which separated Romanticists from Parnassians proceeded from the manner in which they chose to respond to the riddle of man's enigma. Faced with the dilemma of reconciling the contradiction which existed between the unlimited human aspiration and the narrow limits imposed by reality, the Romanticists elaborated explications more inextricably bound with intuitive feelings than founded in the observation of any external reality. Their language bespeaks an ethereal and vague quality which attempts to translate the metaphysical world rather than the physical one. The leading proponents of Art for Art's Sake and Parnassianism, on the other hand, faced the same dilemma in a more sober and scientific manner. Benefiting from the Positivistic methods introduced during the opening years of the Second Empire, they favored attitudes issuing from the factual observation of the external forms of reality. If Romantic optimism may be described as unfounded in fact, what passes for Parnassian pessimism receives its corroboration from the historical evidence that the riddle of the human enigma remains an insoluble one. Such Parnassian poets as Leconte de Lisle excluded any outright subscription to a spiritual explanation of man's predicament since they adhered officially to an attitude which sought a more factually oriented and materialistic interpretation of the human condition.

In his determination to avoid the cosmogonic and metaphysical interpretations of the Romantic poets, Leconte de Lisle advocated that lyrical expression be made to rest on the more scholarly and objective approaches to art and beauty. The poet, then, shared at least a procedural bond with the scholar and the scientist of the Positivistic age insomuch as he sought to extract his art from the systematic observation of concrete facts and reality. His consequent transpositions of the elements of lasting beauty which he discovered in the material world favored a type of verse

Drawing of Leconte de Lisle in Le monde illustré *in 1894.*

which was far more descriptive than it was suggestive. The cult of beauty in art proceeded from a desire to reconcile the real and the ideal. Such a cult, in fact, prevented his pessimistic views from emerging with any overwhelming or categorical force. If the Parnassian poet disclaimed any possibility of reconciling man's finite nature with any sense of the infinite, the cult of idealized beauty which informed his art permitted him to seek out at least a partial solution to the human dilemma. The very fact that he felt helpless to explain satisfactorily man's persistent aspiration toward permanence frequently induced him to inject an implicit personal ingredient in his descriptions of the beauty which he associated with the concrete world.

On one level, the poem, **"La Vénus de Milo,"** which appeared in 1852, takes on an almost programmatical role as the expression of the Parnassian ideal of enduring beauty and harmony residing in a concrete manifestation of Greek Antiquity. The ten stanzas constitute a visual celebration of the untainted purity and beauty which the sight of the statue of the Vénus de Milo stirs within the contemplative poet. The images which emphasize the statue's perfection endow the poem with its unifying aesthetic coherence. Leconte de Lisle subtly blends the concept of such lasting beauty with the idea of a superior civilization in this poem which may be taken both as a description and an evocation of physical or concrete perfection. Indeed, the images used to convey the sense of permanence which Leconte de Lisle associates with the statue are infused with a nostalgic longing for the Antiquity which encouraged this material yet artistic embodiment of man's notion of eternity. The closing lines of **"La Vénus de Milo"** trans-

late the poet's cult of art and beauty in language that borders on the religious:

> Island, sojourn of the gods! And you, Hellas, my sacred mother! Why could I not have been born also in the holy Archipelago during those glorious centuries when the earth was truly inspired and could see the heavens descend at its first urging! If it is true that my cradle has never been caressed by the flowing waters and the mild crystals of the ancient Thetis, and that I have never prayed to you, Victorious Beauty, at your native altar under the Athenian façades, ignite me, nevertheless, with your sublime spark so that my glory might not be enclosed with me in my anxious tomb. Allow my thoughts to trickle in golden rhythms like a divine metal in an harmonious mould.

Central to any serious claim of objectivity and impassibility in the *Poèmes antiques* is the degree of historical authenticity with which Leconte de Lisle manages to describe and evoke Antiquity. Most scholars and critics agree that the Greece which is conjured up in these poems is actually an idyllic Antiquity which corresponds more to his own psychological needs as an artist than to recorded historical fact. In other words, his Greece is a poeticized Greece which one critic has characterized as an earthly paradise in which the harsh light and the dryness customarily associated with the Mediterranean climate are conspicuously absent. Thus, **"Thyoné"** may be more accurately described as a rearrangement or a personal adaptation of Theocritus' poem. Leconte de Lisle invests his version with a certain languorous quality which makes his shepherd more indolent and given to reverie than the original Greek counterpart. The truth of the matter is that poems such as **"Thyoné"** bespeak a virtual independence from their specific Classical sources. To speak plainly, the Parnassian poet remains above all a poet. The *Poèmes antiques* translates a personal frame of reference, and the Greek context in which de Lisle places his meditations on life and art rescues his lyricism ultimately from precisely the type of effusion he sought to avoid. Examined closely, the poems which comprise the Greek cycle scarcely attempt to mask the poet's personal philosophy or vision of the world. If **"La Vénus de Milo"** and **"Le vase"** may be accurately catalogued as exalted expressions of ideal physical beauty, **"Thyoné"** is a commentary on the frigidity of women, while **"Glaucé"** and **"Klytie,"** for example, may be called portraits of women in love and of desired women, respectively. These are themes which Leconte de Lisle will continue to exploit under different guises in subsequent collections of poems. All of them originate in a personal viewpoint which he will attempt to reconcile with his evolving conception of art and beauty.

There exists perhaps no better single piece of evidence delineating the mental anguish suffered by Leconte de Lisle as a result of the religious relativism which asserted itself in France during the reign of Positivism than the poem, **"Chant alterné,"** which had undergone substantial revision from its first appearance in the June, 1846 edition of *La phalange* for its inclusion in the *Poèmes antiques.* Cast in the form of a dialogue between two interlocutors who are designated merely as roman numerals I and II, **"Chant alterné"** is a celebration of both the Pagan and Christian ideals such as they were manifested in their initial vigor and glory. The mood established through the dialogue is one of nostalgia for the irretrievable past. Led by an irresistible drive for knowledge, modern man recognizes through his spirit of inquiry that the new scientific age has replaced absolute ideals by a religious relativism. In other words, the Positivistic age has put an end to the dogmatic spirit. The final three stanzas, or verbal encounters, of **"Chant alterné"** convey the sense of loss which the poet experiences since, as a poet, he appreciates the value of the Pagan and Christian ideals which have since become devitalized by the modern attitude.

> II. When the wise men began to hesitate, the soul closed its wing, and men bid the heavens a sad and dismal farewell. I had eternal hope germinate in him, and I guided the earth to his God!
>
> I. Oh! sensual delight, the cup of flowing honey from which the earth quenched its thirst! The world was happy then, and it was filled with immortal song. Your beloved daughter, lost and alone, now sees only the grass of neglect and forgetfulness grow upon her altars.
>
> II. Love, unstained love is like an imperishable flame. Man has closed his heart, and the world is now orphaned. Will you ever be born again from the night of your soul? Will there ever be a single dawn that knows no sunset?

The poems, **"Hypatie"** and **"Hypatie et Cyrille,"** which made their way into the definitive edition of the *Poèmes antiques* of 1874, illustrate, once again, how Leconte de Lisle made use of history and legend to convey with seemingly more objectivity a stance or an attitude which remained at least partially rooted in his own subjective response to experience. The historical Hypatia, a scholar of mathematics and astronomy of considerable prestige in Alexandria, had been charged by the bishop Cyril with having instigated and encouraged the persecution of Christians in 415 A.D. A citizenry whose anger had been provoked by the bishop's accusation had Hypatia beaten and burned at the stake. In both poems, Leconte de Lisle has fashioned the historical Hypatia into the symbol of a dying pagan civilization. The poet's sympathy for the pagan martyr stems, in large measure, from his conception of history. He professed the view that religions, like the myths and legends which translate the aspirations of different people in different milieux, do affirm, particularly at their apogees, elements of an eternal human truth and ideal. The sadness projected in both poems emanates from de Lisle's realization that the imminent extinction of Greek Polytheism underscores the irreconcilability of man's limitless aspiration and his limited achievement. The evolution of history attests to the fact that as old myths, legends, and religious beliefs become discarded by societies which have grown more complicated and sophisticated, new myths, legends, and religions emerge in response to the psychological climates created in such societies. The process is thus an endless one.

Leconte de Lisle's emotional identification with Hypatia rests in the fact that, for him, she represents the last though futile expression of faith in an ideal. He associates Hypatia's faithfulness to the gods with an undying allegiance to the cult of beauty. The 1858 poem, **"Hypatie et Cyrille,"** presents the two protagonists as antithetical forces: Hypatia symbolizes a humanity which is endowed with an impulse toward permanence and absolute beauty, while Cyril conveys that attitude which would brutally rob men of their dreams. Hypatia, then, incarnates, through her appreciation of a superior civilization, a nostalgia for an heroic conception of humanity, and Cyril becomes the embodiment of a pragmatic reality which is vile and reprehensible. There can be no mistaking the fact that Leconte de Lisle considers Greek Polytheism a superior expression of religious belief to Christianity. What particularly appealed to him, as a poet, was the intimate bond established in Greek Pantheism between an aspiration toward the divine in the human mind and nature rendered divine through the cult of the beautiful. What de Lisle abhorred in Christianity was its sense of the practical and its apparent indifference to beauty. Hypatia's nurse lashes an indictment against the fanaticism which seeks the destruction of knowledge and art so unremittingly:

> No. I tell you that I have heard only too well their barbaric clamor. I am not in the least mistaken. They all damn you as they invoke your name. Their hearts are furious and their faces are inflamed; my dear daughter, they will tear you to pieces. These monsters are in rags, and like revolting animals, they go about predicting all kinds of evil. Riddled with desire and burning with envy, they blaspheme beauty, light and life itself!

Leconte de Lisle made no attempt whatsoever to squelch his repulsion for Christianity which he held to be an inadequate religion for the requirements of the nineteenth century. From the perspective of his religious relativism, he judged the value of a given religion by the quality of art and poetry it inspired in its adherents. But Christianity, by only increasing human anxiety, fell considerably short of the artistic merits and fulfillment of Classical Greece. Much of the effect or impact of **"Hypatie et Cyrille"** is considerably reduced by the discursive tone of the final section of the poem. Cast in the form of four dramatic scenes, the declamatory tone of the confrontations between protagonist and antagonist divests much of the emotional appeal which such a dramatic meeting of opposites should incite in the reader. Hypatia and Cyril emerge, in the end, as personified allegories of knowledge and fanaticism which engage in a kind of philosophical debate on the cultural worth of Paganism and Christianity. Nonetheless, the final speeches of the third and fourth scenes translate in particularly effective terms the nature of the poet's own stoical attitude with respect to his role and function in society.

> I cannot allow a cowardly silence to induce me to forget that for the sake of my own honor I have a supreme task to accomplish. I must proclaim and confess proudly and openly under the skies the beauty, truth and goodness which the gods have revealed to me. Since two days now, the barefooted monks with their unkempt beards and their dirty hair, looking emaciated because of their fasts, and sunburned, have been leaving the desert and swarming into the city like a vile scum. People say that a sinister and fanatical design brings this hysterical horde into our midst. That may be so. But I know how to die, and I am proud of the choice with which the gods have honored me for a last time. I am, nevertheless, grateful to you [Cyril] for your concern, and only request that I be given a few moments alone.
>
> [Scene IV. (*Hypatia addresses her nurse*)]
>
> "I shall be immortal. Farewell!"

. . . . .

We have seen how Leconte de Lisle, who reacted with disgust to his own times, turned toward the Greek past in whose idealization he sought to replace a philosophical void by a purely aesthetic appreciation of that civilization. The poems on Hindu culture which he included in the *Poèmes antiques* were hardly intended to contribute to the vogue of interest in Eastern philosophies during the 1840's. The fact of the matter was that the metaphysical interpretations of existence expounded in Hinduism and Buddhism fell in nearly perfect accord with his own views and feelings. It is perhaps not an exaggeration to say that Leconte de Lisle sought in Indian impassibility or apathy an explanation and a refuge for his own disillusionment and sadness. His study and observation of human experience—youthful ardor, passionate love, and religious institutions—underlined the inevitable passing of man's most pressing and urgent desires. If aspects of Indian philosophy detectable in Lamartine's *La chute d'un ange* (1838) elicited his curiosity, Eugène Burnouf's *Introduction à l'histoire du Bouddhisme* (1844) and the translations of the sacred Hindu texts proved to be nothing less than a revelation to him. The Buddhist view of human existence as suffering corresponded to his own feeling on the subject which he had been endeavoring to articulate in his poetry up to this time.

Despite the remarkable similarities that exist between Schopenhauerian pessimism and Buddhist doctrine, it remains highly unlikely that Leconte de Lisle had been able to read the German philosopher in any systematic fashion since French translations of the *Aphorisms* appeared only in 1880 and the treatise, *The World as Will and Idea,* from 1888 through 1890. On the other hand, translations of such sacred texts as the *Râmayana* and the *Rig-Veda* were made available in the 1840's and doubtless made a significant contribution to the growing interest in Ancient Indian civilization during that time. Central to Buddhist thought was the concept of *nirvana,* a kind of absorption into nothingness and the supreme deliverance from suffering, the inherent condition of all human existence. Leconte de Lisle's own pessimistic views sprang from the realization that human life was but a desire for eternity and the absolute which was destined to remain unfulfilled. Desire, then, was but a goad for something which man could never really hope to attain. Hence, his suffering. To escape the anguish of such a fate would require a recognition in him that the object of his aspiration is inane. Such an attitude necessarily negates the universe as a positive state in which the gratification of human desire is sought. It was primarily the ideal negation of the personal will and movement in the Buddhist sense of *nirvana* which attracted Leconte de Lisle to Eastern thought and philosophy.

Paradoxically, the state of *nirvana* or absorption into nothingness could only be realized through the practice of virtue and through the vigilant attention of the individual. The final apathy achieved is the result of concentration and meditation. Absolute negation, then, of all subject and object requires an effort of purification within the individual as well as the practice of six transcendental virtues. Leconte de Lisle's interest in Buddhism betrays no evidence that he ever attempted to fulfill any of the requirements which purportedly would have enabled him to achieve the desired final apathy.

In point of fact, the Hindu subjects constitute little more than masks or objective frameworks for the poet's own attitudes in much the same manner that the Greek subject matter enabled him to express his actual reactions to life without resorting to the kind of overbearingness and effusion which marred the verse of so many Romanticists. Like Vigny before him, Leconte de Lisle sought out the philosophical implication of his own experience before he attempted to transpose it into his poetry. In such Hindu poems as **"Sûryâ"** and **"La vision de Brahma,"** for instance, his account of India is more poetic than it is rigorously factual. Scholars and critics are generally agreed that de Lisle often altered elements in Ancient Indian legends, and syncretized aspects of Buddhism and Brahmanism to have his subject matter conform more actively to the requirements of his poetic imagination. Such modifications, to an important extent, harbor Leconte de Lisle's personal revelations. Just as in the Greek poems, the Hindu pieces give the lie to the charge by certain literary historians that de Lisle's verse bears the imprint of impassibility and impersonality.

"Sûryâ," which was written for the original edition of the *Poèmes antiques* in 1852, illustrates Leconte de Lisle's frequent disposition to fuse elements from completely different sources and traditions. Bearing the subtitle, "A Vedic Hymn," **"Sûryâ"** juxtaposes aspects derived from the *Rig-Veda* with other mythologies. Scholars point out that if **"Sûryâ"** were strictly speaking a Vedic hymn, the sea, which underscores an important motif in the poem, appears nowhere in the sacred texts of the *Rig-Veda.* In Vedic mythology, Sûryâ was the sun god who had been abandoned by his mother, the goddess, Aditi. Wandering in the heavens in a chariot drawn by seven yellow horses, Sûryâ sought feverishly to regain his rightful place among the gods. This Indian legend appealed to Leconte de Lisle whose **"Sûryâ"** may best be described as an exalted hymn of praise to the elemental forces of nature. The plight of the sun god, condemned to recover his lost primitive force, incarnated, in many respects, the predicament of the poet who sought to recover a lost spontaneity and power far away from the crass concerns of an utilitarian society. The refrain, repeated no less than four times, evokes the life-giving waters and identifies them with the life-giving power of the mother, Aditi: "Master, your abode is on the shores of the ancient oceans where the great waters come to wash your mystical feet."

"La mort de Valmiki," which was added to the *Poèmes antiques* in 1881, translates with eloquent concision the poet's expression of an absolute faith in the immortality of art. Reworked from an episode in the Hindu epic, *Mahâbhârata,* it recounted the death of an ascetic enveloped in his dreams and spirit of penance. Leconte de Lisle replaces the ascetic, Tchayana, by the father of Sanskrit poetry, Valmiki, whose life was shrouded in legend. A Brahman by birth, the epic poet retreated to a life of meditation in the womb of nature far from the worldly cares of his fellow men. The skeleton of his body was recovered some one thousand years later by Indian wise men. Presumably he had been devoured alive by millions of white ants. Leconte de Lisle's account of the incident in **"La mort de Valmiki"** affords him the splendid opportunity of conveying a quasi-religious affirmation of the endurance of a work of art in a world in which everything is doomed ultimately to be swallowed up in a great void. Contained such as it is within the larger structure of the narrative account of Valmiki's horrible death, the statement on artistic immortality achieves a stunningly antithetical effect with the pervading mood of the poem:

> For the spirit no longer perceives anything about the senses nor about itself.
>
> The long slimy termites, dragging their white bellies, undulate toward their inert prey around whom they gather and circulate, and into whom they sink down and swell like the rising sea foam. They swarm over his feet, his thighs and his breast as they bite into and devour his flesh. They penetrate the cavity of his large head through the eyes, and they become engulfed in his purple mouth which is open. They transform this living body into a stiff skeleton propped up on the Himavat mountain like a god on his altar. That was Valmiki, the immortal poet, whose harmonious soul continues to penetrate and fill the shadows in which we find ourselves. His words will forever remain on the lips of men.

The long narrative poem, **"Bhâgavat,"** traces the itinerary of three wise Brahmans who seek to return to the origin of all life and to lose themselves in the breast of a nature that has mothered all men. If it is true that Leconte de Lisle's account owes more to his own poetic imagination than to any erudite reconstruction of Hindu wisdom, the somewhat rambling aspects of **"Bhâgavat"** enable him to project his complicated assimilation of Ancient Indian philosophy. Conceived as a mixture of evocations of nature and of invocations by Maitreya, Narada, and Angira to the goddess of nature, Ganga, **"Bhâgavat"** unfolds the steps necessary to accomplish their return to the original source. In the opening part of the poem, we encounter the three wise men in the midst of the murmurs and noises of wild birds and animals who simply " . . . were meditating, while they sat in the reeds." The three Brahmans represent, through their respective invocations, three different attitudes to existence. Maitreya is the lover who pursues the dream of an inaccessible ideal, while Narada experiences contentment because he has broken completely with worldly concerns. Angira is the beleaguered metaphysician who remains painfully conscious of the irreconcilability of faith and reason: "I have lived with my eye fixed on the source of all Being, and I have allowed my heart to die in order to know and understand better." The three Brahmans recite an harmonious lament concerning the defective nature of man to Ganga:

> The human lament is the cry of an anguished soul and of a heart that endures torture. Who can hear you without quivering from love and pity? Who can refrain from weeping for you, magnanimous weakness, human spirit which a divine goad excites and wounds, but which ignores you while you cannot hope to attain it. And, now, you shall never be able to limit this unreachable goal during the human night which appears endless to you. Will you be able only to embrace the Infinite in a sublime dream? You are a painful spirit which is carried off into space while you thirst for light and are hungry for beauty. You always fall from the divine altitude where each living soul seeks its origin. And overcome by sadness and terror, you groan; for, who weeps for you, vanquished conqueror?

When the goddess, Ganga, appears, she informs the Brahmans of the power of Nature to absorb men within her bosom. The three wise men begin the ascension to the mountain of Kaîlaça beyond which they hope to find the land of the origin of all life. Various gods appear to them along their journey, and when finally they perceive Bhâgavat, the Brahmans ask but to absorb themselves in him, and escape from the carnal prison which imposes limitation upon man's life. In the end, all remains motionless for in such repose comes deliverance from the inconsequential activities of a world in constant flux. Irving Putter has judiciously pointed out that the inert Brahmans' conscious rejection of life in **"Bhâgavat"** proves to be all the more dramatic and astonishing because everywhere around them in the poetic account, life swarms with an unremitting restlessness. What the Brahmans ultimately experience in this state of indifference to worldly concerns is a feeling of the divine void or *nirvana*. . . . Much of the lyrical effectiveness of **"Bhâgavat"** derives from the poet's adept integration of Hindu mythology and thought with his own reactions to the human predicament.

Like the other verse which comprises the Hindu cycle in the *Poèmes antiques,* **"La vision de Brahma"** achieves considerable success in masking the personal ingredient present in this poetic reaction to man's metaphysical problem. To an extent, Brahma's position with respect to the all-powerful God which he interrogates recalls the position of Christ with respect to God the Father in Vigny's poem, "Le mont des Oliviers." In both cases, the protagonists serve as thin disguises for the poets in question. Moreover the doubt with which Brahma and Christ are invaded translate through clever indirection the uncertainty experienced by Leconte de Lisle and Vigny. Brahma, like Vigny's Christ, is puzzled by the contradiction implicit in the idea of a troubled and imperfect creation emanating from an omnipotent and perfect Creator. He articulates such a question before the God, Hâri, because he hopes somehow that the contradictory elements may be reconciled. Hâri's answer is that the divine void is the only reality which exists, and that such a void is only vaguely conscious of itself in much the same manner in which dreams vaguely allude to reality. The solution to man's anguish rests precisely in the fact that such anguish should be transcended by forgetfulness and self-effacement:

> Brahma! such is the dream in which your spirit is engulfed. Question no longer the august Truth, for, what would you be without my own vanity and the secret doubt of my sublime nothingness? And on the golden summits of the divine mountain of Kaîlaça where white genies swim in pure air, the inexpressible Voice stopped its harmonious flow, and the terrible but holy vision vanished.

Critics reproach Leconte de Lisle for having confused **"La vision de Brahma"** with an indiscriminate combination of Brahmanism and Buddhism which invests the poem with a disquieting element. Buddhist thought precludes any belief in a Supreme Being, and Brahmanism never makes allusion to nothingness. **"La vision de Brahma"** is Leconte de Lisle's own statement on the nature of man's tragic search for the absolute.

. . . . .

The presence of such well-known poems as **"Midi"** and **"Dies Irae,"** grouped under the rubric "Poèmes diverses," underscores the fact that if Leconte de Lisle persisted in projecting his own pessimism into his work, he avoided remarkably well the pitfalls of uniformity and monotony of presentation. Not the least effective verse of de Lisle are the so-called elegiac and descriptive nature poems. However subtly he manages to camouflage his personal feelings, de Lisle remained a poet who could not be content with the mere presentation of scenes and situations. Such poems as **"Midi"** and **"Nox,"** for example, convey the personal conception of a majestic and mysterious nature whose contemplation inspires him with a strange yet undeniable detachment and alienation. For all its power and beauty, nature remains something which is indifferent to the needs of man. This idea had been introduced by Vigny, coincidentally the French Romanticist with whom Leconte de Lisle expressed the greatest affinity. Much like his Romantic counterpart, his observations of nature confirmed the pessimism of his metaphysical attitude. With Vigny also, Leconte de Lisle is predisposed to judgment in his representations of nature. Poems such as **"Midi"** reveal the presence of a powerful imagination behind the plastic descriptions of a minutely observed scene at high noon.

"Midi" emerges as something considerably more than another visual celebration of the sun as a source of life and energy; it also projects a commentary on the relationship between man and nature which conforms to the poet's personal metaphysical views. Whatever emotional balance is achieved in the poem results directly from Leconte de Lisle's ability to describe in such convincing terms a scene which depicts the hot noonday sun beating down relentlessly on a plain and adjacent forest in what presumably must be a French countryside. The opening strophes, through their recurrent reference to images which emphasize a blazing white light which envelops a motionless cornfield, establish the mood for the meditation which terminates the poem. And that meditation proceeds naturally from such notions as heat, immobility, engulfment, and light which are evoked and which penetrate his descriptions: "silver sheets of light fall at noon," "the fields are entirely without shade," "an overwhelming heat," "the earth sleeps in its dress of fire," and "the air burns without the slightest breeze: everything is silent." If the scorching noonday sun invades the surrounding landscape with an oppressive heat, the "white" oxen which lie in the slopes adjacent to the cornfield remain oblivious to all which surrounds them, and appear absorbed in some deep dream. What is particularly felicitous in **"Midi"** is the remarkable way in which the poet conveys an illusion of reality. The oxen, for example, are described in a characteristic pose which is made to coincide ingeniously with the philosophical attitude which is finally spelled out in the closing strophes.

The conspicuous absence of man from the purely descriptive tableau in **"Midi"** invites the poet to address him directly. Such explicitness, however, does not detract from the unity of presentation in the poem, since Leconte de Lisle uses this device primarily as a ploy to infer his message as unobtrusively as possible. There is a lesson for man to infer from the description of a becalmed nature and oxen whose inertness bespeaks numb contentment. The animals respond intuitively to nature unlike man whose instincts have become blunted by his excessive concern with the requirements of a modern society. The last four strophes encourage the prospective onlooker to immerse himself in the tableau of blissful serenity before returning to the lowly cities:

> And close-by, a few white oxen lie on the grass and slowly dribble on their thick dewlaps. Their magnificent, languid eyes appear to be following some inner dream which they never finish. Man, if someday you come upon these radiant fields at high noon with your heart bursting at once with joy and bitterness, then, run away! For nature remains indifferent and the sun consumes everything in sight; there is nothing alive here, nor is there anything that is sad or joyful. But if you are disillusioned in your laughter and in your tears, and if you thirst to forget this troubled world, not knowing anymore how to forgive or how to damn, and you wish to experience one last pleasure in numbness, then, come! The sun will address you in a sublime language. Try to absorb yourself endlessly in its unrelenting ray, and go back slowly toward the lowly and despicable cities with your soul seven times soaked in the divine void.

Despite its classification by Leconte de Lisle as "a miscellaneous poem," **"Midi"** may be joined logically to the cycle of Hindu poems in which aspiration toward nothingness and the divine void is underscored with an unfailing consistency. The nineteenth-century French critic, Sainte-Beuve, singled out the closing strophes of **"Midi"** for the sudden shift in emphasis which complicated the nature of the descriptive tableau. It is precisely such a complication which lends Leconte de Lisle's statement on the indifference of nature to man such a feeling of overriding pessimism in **"Midi."** He went considerably beyond such poets as Vigny and Hugo, who exploited a similar theme in their lyricism. If anything, **"Midi"** asserts the idea that nature is the crucible in which the Darwinian struggle for survival occurs. Unlike his Romantic predecessors, however, who bewailed nature for its apparent indifference to human needs, Leconte de Lisle sees in its impassibility a lesson which can prove to be beneficial to the poet torn by the relativism of the age. If nature does not exactly represent the exteriorization of an inner human aspiration toward permanence, it does contain an appeasing quality which enables the poet to desire an ultimate absorption in it. Too, insofar as it invites man to seek a psychological deliverance from the painful limits imposed by given societies at different moments of history, nature restores to man that peace of mind which the pressing preoccupations of unsatisfactory social organizations have destroyed. The pessimism pervading **"Midi"** issues from the implication that all modern societies fail to respond to the most urgent needs of the individual.

The bitterness with which Leconte de Lisle conveys his pessimism stems precisely from the fact that he entertains nothing but the darkest and most abject notions of modern society. Unlike such thinkers as Renan and Louis Ménard who attenuated considerably their respective conclusions on religious relativism with active concerns for social and intellectual progress, the author of the ***Poèmes antiques*** refused to view human existence except through the idealistic vision of the consummate artist. Nowhere is such an attitude asserted so categorically as in **"Dies Irae,"** the poem which concludes the collection. The title of the poem—Day of Wrath—is borrowed from the thirteenth-century Latin hymn which has since been incorporated into the Catholic liturgy for the dead. Within the ostensible framework of a meditation, **"Dies Irae"** conveys the vision of the total annihilation of mankind. What rescues the poem from disintegrating into an emotional apostrophe is an exemplary balance between a personal and an historical view of the human predicament. Leconte de Lisle evokes the aspiration of youth, the golden age of civilization, and his own bitter disillusionment with remarkable mastery and control. Yet, there can be no mistaking the abject pessimism which the poet's acknowledgment of the displacement of God has engendered in him. Man's only appeasement lies in his dream of a return to his original state of nonbeing:

> Where are the promised Gods, the ideal forms and the great cults clothed in velvet glory? And where is the white ascension of the serene Virtues into the heavens which open their triumphant wings? The Muses, like divine Mendicants, go slowly by the cities as they find themselves the prey of a bitter laughter. After enough blood has trickled from under the headband of thorns, they give out with a sob that is as endless as the Sea. Yet, eternal Evil reigns in full power! The air of the age proves bad for cankered hearts. Forgetfulness of the world and of the multitude, we greet you! Nature, take us back in your sacred bosom.

Formally and thematically, **"Dies Irae"** summarizes superbly the nature of the Parnassian poet's defection from the modern world of relativism. (pp. 44-63)

> *Robert T. Denommé, in his* Leconte de Lisle, *Twayne Publishers, Inc., 1973, 150 p.*

I. D. McFarlane (essay date 1982)

[*McFarlane is an English educator, biographer, and critic specializing in French language and literature. In the following excerpt, he explores Leconte de Lisle's treatment of the pastoral in his poetry.*]

Leconte de Lisle is not the only nineteenth-century poet to have looked back to an idyllic past in which the tensions and disappointments of contemporary life have no part. He has his vision of a paradise lost that took shape under the influence of youthful memories—no doubt with some retrospective falsification—and of various literary models that included epic writers such as Dante and Milton, André Chénier and poets who belonged to the Greek pastoral tradition. However, Leconte de Lisle's version of pastoral has its own special individuality, partly because of the measure of experience he excludes, partly on account of the role allotted to the poet who is naturally capable of evoking that world but must by definition belong to a later stage in human development. Though there is talk of pre-lapsarian innocence, the conditions in which the poet's pastoral world prosper are precarious and the poet is himself often afflicted by a sense of guilt. There is a further consideration: Leconte de Lisle refers to a state of Maya which preceded human existence and will survive it, so that the pastoral world is not a primitive stage, though it acquires virtue by belonging to the past. Occasionally, he suggests that his version of pastoral can approximate to the ideal state of *néant* ['nothingness']—as in **'Le Bernica'** where human consciousness is absorbed

into the surrounding natural objects, but this is not really a characteristic attitude.

Though critics make much of Leconte de Lisle's close observation of nature—and he himself saw merit in this too—it is incontrovertible that his scapes and scenes—especially the pastoral—contain patterns that correspond to deep-seated concerns. Two essential features recur time and again: the woodland and the water, the water of streams, pools and springs. Sometimes there may be discerned in the distance a mountain peak which carries its own symbolism as well. Woods and water are usually to be seen in sunlight that is filtered through the leaves of the trees: the sun, as is well known, plays a major role in Leconte de Lisle's world, as the source of light and life, but in his pastoral scenes the vigour of midday is absent; and the poet has a marked liking for the dawn rising out of the water in rosy hues. Though night, the moon and the stars sometimes enter the picture, their normal symbolism colours poems of a different inspiration. The dominant colours are limited in range—rose, green, blue, yellow—and are often associated with jewels or objects of value (sapphire, emerald, diamond, pearl, honey). Sounds are muted: we are in a world that is certainly not silent, for that would be a feature of the *néant,* but it excludes noise that belongs to a very different, post-lapsarian existence; we seem to experience the silence that follows upon a sound, the soughing of the breeze, the chirping of a bird, certain modulations of the human voice. And there are the flowers, some of which may carry important symbolic value, such as the lotus-flower. The animals that inhabit this idyllic world are not prominent; often they are seen at rest or they embody values that are dear to the poet's heart. That Leconte de Lisle saw this pastoral world as the vehicle of values since lost is confirmed in **'L'aurore'**, to mention only one instance. . . . This world belongs to a past never to be recaptured (except in poetry); in it time, number, space are absent or at least suspended; one of its main characteristics is a form of 'repos' ['repose'], though this may appear a somewhat negative quality. It is a world of harmony—a word that recurs often enough—and of 'innocence'. The poet's mouthpieces often hark back to this primitive state: 'Je revois l'innocence du monde' ['I see again the innocence of the world'], says Qaïn. It is however a world limited in time, in its spatial existence and by the nature of its denizens. We have seen that it was protected from the full force of the sun by a leafy network; it is also sheltered from the stormy sea by the sands that run down to its edge. For Leconte de Lisle the sea has a wide-ranging symbolism: it is consistent with the idyllic life only in its calm and unruffled state, otherwise it carries the threat of danger. It was after all from the sea that Aphrodite arose, and the ocean is more likely to be associated with time, noise, passion, all elements alien to the poet's version of pastoral. Then the dormant animals, so often an embodiment of 'désir' ['desire'], may represent a potential source of disruption. Its geographical position sometimes suggests an intermediate and precarious state: it may be found between the sky from which it seems to draw sustenance and a lower world characterised by sinister torrents, darkness, angular rocks. . . . (pp. 443-45)

Other limits occur at the level of human experience and behaviour. This shows itself particularly in Leconte de Lisle's portrayal of love, love of course being an essential element in pastoral. His attitude to love, neither consistent

Les Roses d'Ispahan

Les roses d'Ispahan dans leur gaine de mousse,
Les jasmins de Mossoul, les fleurs de l'oranger
ont un parfum moins frais, ont une odeur moins douce
Ô blanche Leïlah, que ton souffle léger

Ta lèvre est de corail et ton rire léger
Sonne mieux que l'eau vive et d'une voix plus douce,
Mieux que le vent joyeux qui berce l'oranger,
Mieux que l'oiseau qui chante au bord du nid de mousse.

Mais la subtile odeur des roses dans leur mousse,
Ta brise qui se joue autour de l'oranger
Et l'eau vive qui flue avec sa plainte douce
Ont un charme plus sûr que ton amour léger

Handwritten manuscript of "Les roses d'Ispahan."

nor clear-cut, is a major source of inspiration: on the one hand he considers it as the indispensable experience in human existence, and on the other he sees in it the force that will wreck 'repos' and 'rêve' ['dream'], in other words it threatens the ideal to which Leconte de Lisle constantly claims to aspire. Such fears colour the kind of love that will find its proper place in his pastoral. This world is dominated by feminine figures; usually they are hostile to love which they will either eschew or accept as part of a dream-world never to be realised. . . . It is significant that the nymphs who succumb to passion are sea-nymphs [in **'Glaucé'**]. The wood-nymphs swear allegiance to one or two goddesses whom in any case they tend to resemble: thus Thestylis . . . is likened to Artemis equally renowned for her rejection of man's love. And Cybele is invoked; called Ops by the Romans, she is the equivalent of Mother Nature—and in **'Niobé'** Nature is described as the 'Vierge mère' ['virgin mother']. Cybele is also seen as the embodiment of wisdom, as Leconte de Lisle understands it, and is described as a 'Vierge majestueuse' ['majestic virgin'] who is 'assise au centre immobile du monde' ['seated in the motionless center of the world']. Diana is presented as possessing characteristics of both sexes: on one occasion she is described as a 'Déesse virile' ['virile goddess' in **'Khirôn'**], on another as the 'mâle Chasseresse' ['male huntress', in **'Niobe'**]. Diana and Cybele are both manifestations of virginity, but maternal in their attributes and as it were pansexual in nature, and by their self-contained being they are the incarnation of 'repos'. All these nymph-like creatures are described as 'Vierges' and form part of the 'rêve' and illusory world to which Leconte de Lisle is so attached. They embody furthermore what attracted him in Greek culture, for he saw Greece as 'l'harmonieuse Hellas, vierge aux tresses dorées' ['harmonious Hellas, virgin with the golden tresses'; in **'Dies Irae'**].

Not surprisingly we are in a world of taboos, and there are figures who threaten these nymphs and are all watchers, indeed 'voyeurs' whose eyes invade the privacy of the nymphs' existence and who may pay the penalty for their sacrilege. In **'La source'** a nymph who resembles a feminine Narcissus is sleeping in the water; when she is awakened by a prying Aegipan, she flees—for her virginal quality can only be sullied by the watcher. . . . The figure of Diana reminds one of the legend of Actaeon, killed by his hounds for seeing the goddess bathing. Pentheus fared just as badly, since he was killed by the Bacchae for committing a similar act of sacrilege. . . . The Bacchae are said to be 'ascétiques' ['ascetics'] and their dancing is a sign of their self-sufficiency—Leconte de Lisle here in his discreet way anticipates a late-nineteenth-century interest. Watching and *amour-passion* are thus both instances of an invasion of innocence and virginity and are tainted with guilt. However, there are other, finer, male figures to be found— and not only in the pastoral world—who do not threaten the nymphs and who are in their way self-sufficient; they are solitaries, prizing 'repos' and 'rêve', and do not disrupt harmony. More often than not, they are distinguished (as are some nymphs) by their splendid golden hair, which is a sign of vitality, privileged existence (but not of love); it links them with certain divine figures (e.g. Apollo), or with the Dawn seen as a manifestation of innocence. One such figure, outside the pastoral mode, is Baldur.

In the pastoral existence, the symbolism we mentioned earlier is extended to relate the setting to the figures who live there. The woodland is associated with Cybele and with virginal love; but it is also in sympathy with the Muses. . . . In **'Thyoné'** the shepherd who pursues the nymph in vain (for she is faithful to Artemis) will play his pipes in the woods and so find peace, but in such surroundings passionate love will find no satisfaction. Thyoné herself dissociates the woods from love. . . . and elsewhere they are called 'zones maternelles' ['maternal zones'; in **'La fontaine aux lianes'**]. The associations with woodland water are no less important: more than once the nymphs are seen bathing or sleeping in the water, nor should we forget Diana in this context. The waters symbolise a form of 'repos': Hylas, listening to the 'invisibles *sœurs*' ['invisible *sisters*'] (my italics) of the aquatic regions is drawn below the surface to enter a different form of existence where 'oubli' ['oblivion'] will cover everything. Water and song also come together in Leconte de Lisle's mind. Even outside the strictly pastoral mode, similar connections are to be found: in **'Bhagavat'**, where water also acts as a purifying principle, Maitreya remembers his youth, with a landscape characterised by lakes, swans, woods where there appears the figure of the Virgin, likened to the Dawn and understood as a form of illusion. In the same poem Ganga is described by three sages in terms of song, perfume; golden fluid and dawn; the swan and ivory; she is the 'Vierge aux beaux yeux, reine des saintes Eaux' ['Virgin with beautiful eyes, queen of the holy Waters']. We hardly need to stress the network of maternal concerns which a psychoanalytical approach will throw up; I am interested in the poetic consequences of such preoccupations.

We must now ask how and where does the figure of the poet fit in to this world. Leconte de Lisle's ideal is not in doubt: the poet is mentioned at least twice in the company of heroes and sages, and thus should live in the register of 'rêve'. In a 'Terre maternelle' ['maternal world'], these three categories 'sont assis, parfaits en un rêve éternel' ['are seated, perfect in an eternal dream'], a dream-like state that is at the extremity of human consciousness, between *être* ['being'] and *néant*. The poet's kinship with the Sage stems from the fact that wisdom is the antithesis of passions that destroy the 'rêve'. . . . [His] passion impels him to forsake the peace and safety of the woods, and in this state he has been abandoned by the Muse; he no longer knows the silence and the 'oubli' of the woods faithful to Cybele. In **'Glaucé'**, we hear of the love she bears the shepherd faithful to Pan and Cybele who is symbolised for him by the woods: he realises that Glaucé represents a force for disruption. . . . Significantly when Leconte de Lisle talks of Venus, he describes the statue of Milo, which has no feeling and whose remoteness from the marine Venus or Astarte is affirmed; if anything, she has become a maternal figure 'aux larges flancs' ['of ample bosom'].

Leconte de Lisle has introduced a number of mythic figures who symbolise, with certain important variations, the role of the poet, his status, and an activity that does not seem to be all that 'innocent'. On two points Leconte de Lisle appears not to waver: in the first place, there must be, it would seem, a divorce between art and life, and failure to observe that distinction is a betrayal, as Mallarmé suggested in 'Le pitre châtié'. If, for instance, the poet yields to love, he cannot remain a poet: he leaves the sacred wood and moves nearer the sea. Secondly, and this is just as important, the poet is felt to be different from other beings. There may be an element of elitism in this view—witness Leconte de Lisle's contempt for the crowd—but it is hardly an adequate explanation, since a principle of deprivation is also in play. The poet is likened to Khiron, who was a Centaur and therefore not wholly human; and to the Cyclops, who appears in one poem only but represents that divorce between art and life that is in part the result of the special nature of his being. Since love remains for him an unfulfilled experience, he . . . will sublimate his desire and convert it into art.

But the poet's status is more equivocal than the foregoing remarks might suggest; he seems in fact to be related to both types of male figure that people the pastoral world. Predictably, a measure of guilt has entered Leconte de Lisle's conception of the poet, and this feeling has probably more than one source. There is the more general sense of guilt experienced by all human beings, simply because they have been born into humanity: the theme of the Fall, in various guises, recurs frequently in Leconte de Lisle's poetry, and readers will not have missed the number of times the word 'expiatoire' ['expiatory'] is pressed into service. Then, precisely because the poet is divorced from life, he can only contemplate it as a bystander; but we have seen that voyeurdom was tantamount to sacrilege in the pastoral world of Cybele and Diana/Artemis. At the same time, the poet has to derive, however obliquely, some sustenance from life, but in so doing, he may experience feelings of transgression, a word that carries nuances that 'go beyond' the norm. To the extent that his activity is allegedly the attempted recapture of the past, this feeling of culpability may be tempered, but even here 'innocence' is somehow tainted. To express the guilt (but also the pride)

associated with human endeavour—and especially poetic endeavour—Leconte de Lisle often has recourse to the cluster of myths that surround the Gigantomachia; in this he bears a striking resemblance to Joachim du Bellay. Poetic effort seeks after all to attain divine status by the path of wisdom; the poet, working within time, is none the less striving to transcend time, and wisdom is the search for something that goes beyond earthly being—but such a quest cannot avoid a degree of *hubris*; and Leconte de Lisle is acutely aware of the double-edged nature of poetic activity. Hence the appearance on more than one occasion of the Titan myth, whose importance is further confirmed by ancillary references: for instance, it was Etna that crushed the Titans, but it is also the 'mont cyclopéen' ['cyclopean mountain'] where the Cyclops indulged his 'souffle créateur' ['creative breath', in **'Les épis'**]. Chiron belongs in part to this pattern: his kinship with the Titans is not forgotten. In a sense he is a provisional figure as his poetic significance is flawed: he is the son of time, he regrets the past which maintains an undue hold upon him, he does not represent a perfected state of wisdom. He is rather a sort of John the Baptist—to Orpheus and Achilles—he has however ties with Diana and Cybele which guarantee his passport to the pastoral world. Against this, he has doubted the gods and he awaits the 'jour expiatoire' ['expiatory day', in **'Khirôn'**]. In **'Niobé'** we find Amphion, the apparent model of the ideal poet: he is a solitary figure who dreams and sings; his palace is a work of art where all human elements have been transformed into objects of priceless value ('Dix Nymphes d'or massif' ['Ten nymphs of solid gold'], etc., **'Niobé'**); but this does not prevent his palace from being shattered by the gods, and he commits suicide. He has been supported ardently by Niobé, who praises (and in a sense represents) the Titans' endeavour, but all she can muster in the face of such destruction is a wavering optimism that smacks of defiance rather than of conviction. Other themes and figures are woven into the network: thus Apollo will be seen as the protector of heroes, who are on a footing of parity with the poets. . . . [As] one would expect, his solar symbolism is emphasised, and he is the 'amant des neuf Muses' ['lover of the nine Muses']. Indeed he is as it were a link-figure between the two poles of Leconte de Lisle's attitude: for if his kinship with Diana is recalled, we are also reminded that he is a Titan (**'Parfum de Hélios-Apollon'**). Chiron will be replaced by Orpheus, 'mortel semblable aux Dieux' ['God-like mortal'; in 'Khirôn',], and Achilles with his golden hair is shown to have some of the attributes essential to poetic activity and achievement. . . . [Although Leconte de Lisle] frequently expresses the wish to be reabsorbed into Maya, he does not cease to meditate on the theme that the poet's consciousness is the only thing that can confer value on the Universe: in this he both prolongs a tradition and gives it a twist that will be exploited by others coming in his wake. . . . (pp. 445-51)

I. D. McFarlane, "Pastoral and the Deprived Poet," in Baudelaire, Mallarmé, Valéry: New Essays in Honor of Lloyd Austin, *Malcolm Bowie, Alison Fairlie, Alison Finch, eds., Cambridge University Press, 1982, pp. 443-56.*

FURTHER READING

Bailey, John C. "Leconte de Lisle." In his *The Claims of French Poetry: Nine Studies in the Greater French Poets,* pp. 247-79. London: Archibald Constable and Co., 1907.

Examines the manifestation of pantheism in Leconte de Lisle's works, contrasting his poems with works by Victor Hugo and comparing them with poems by Matthew Arnold.

Behrens, Ralph. "Leconte de Lisle's 'Niobé': Myth into Symbol." *The Classical Journal* 55 (1960): 363-66.

Discusses "Niobé" from *Poèmes antiques* as it exemplifies the process outlined by C. S. Lewis by which ancient myths become symbolic archetypes.

Chadbourne, Richard M. "The Generation of 1848: Four Writers and Their Affinities." *Essays in French Literature,* No. 5 (November 1968): 1-21.

Discusses the works of Leconte de Lisle, Charles Baudelaire, Gustave Flaubert, and Ernest Renan, offering a reassessment of their common achievement.

Charlton, D. G. "Positivism and Leconte de Lisle's Ideas on Poetry." *French Studies* XI, No. 3 (July 1957): 246-59.

Argues that the metaphysical concerns and the pursuit of the ideal in Leconte de Lisle's poetry evidence a divergence from aspects of positivism in his aesthetics.

Denommé, Robert T. "Leconte de Lisle and the Historical Imagination." In his *The French Parnassian Poets,* pp. 76-112. Carbondale: Southern Illinois University Press, 1972.

Elaborates on Leconte de Lisle's "poetic idealization of past civilizations," as well as the form and themes of his poetry.

DiOrio, Dorothy M. *Leconte de Lisle: A Hundred and Twenty Years of Criticism (1850-1970).* University, Miss.: Romance Monographs, 1972, 272 p.

Presents by year over 800 references to international critical works on Leconte de Lisle, with an introduction by DiOrio charting in detail the critical reception of his poetry.

Gilman, Margaret. "Poetry as Art." In her *The Idea of Poetry in France: From Houdar de la Motte to Baudelaire,* pp. 171-98. Cambridge: Harvard University Press, 1958.

Discusses the conflict between form and matter in descriptive poetry by Leconte de Lisle and other major figures in nineteenth-century French verse.

Grant, Elliott M. "Leconte de Lisle (1818-1894)." In *French Poetry of the Nineteenth Century,* second ed., edited by Elliott M. Grant, pp. 271-310. New York: Macmillan, 1960.

Includes a biographical introduction, prefatory notes to selected French-language reprints of works in *Poèmes antiques, Poèmes barbares,* and *Poèmes tragiques,* and questions on the poems designed to assist students.

Grierson, Francis. "Leconte de Lisle." In his *Parisian Portraits,* pp. 131-46. London: John Lane, The Bodley Head, 1913.

Discusses Leconte de Lisle's worldview in the context of nineteenth-century French literary society and offers personal reminiscences of a soirée held at the poet's residence.

Guérard, Albert Leon. "The Poets of Science and Despair:

Leconte de Lisle." In his *French Prophets of Yesterday: A Study of Religious Thought under the Second Empire,* pp. 191-200. New York: D. Appleton and Co., 1913.

Examines pessimism in Leconte de Lisle's poetry in relation to modern verse and thought in France.

Hambly, P. S. "For an Allegorical Reading of Leconte de Lisle's 'Les spectres'." *French Studies Bulletin,* No. 18 (Spring 1986): 7-10.

Analyzes "Les spectres," arguing that in the poem "the three spectres . . . seem to be the dead figures of the Theological Virtues."

Jones, F. "A Pseudonymical Prose Work of Leconte de Lisle: *Histoire du moyen âge,* par 'Pierre Gosset'." *The Modern Language Review* XXXVI, No. 4 (October 1941): 511-14.

Argues Leconte de Lisle's authorship of the prose work attributed to Gosset, asserting that "it gives in more detail than any other work [Leconte de Lisle's] views on history and politics."

Lafleur, Paul T. "Leconte de Lisle." *The Atlantic Monthly* LXXV, No. CCCCLI (May 1895): 694-702.

Describes the subjects, themes, and philosophy of Leconte de Lisle's poetry.

Lattimore, Richmond. "A Note on Leconte de Lisle." *The Hudson Review* IV, No. 2 (Summer 1951): 236-37.

Discusses several poems by Leconte de Lisle translated in the issue, focusing on his depiction of nature and suggesting a lack of subtlety in his works.

Maingard, F. "A 'Source' of Leconte de Lisle's 'Çunacépa'." *The French Quarterly* II, No. 2 (June 1920): 94-7.

Suggests that the farewell scene between Çanta and Çunacépa in Leconte de Lisle's poem is based on an episode in *Chaumière indienne* by French author Bernadin de Saint-Pierre.

Nitze, William A., and Dargan, E. Preston. "The Reaction in Poetry: Baudelaire and the Parnassians." In their *A History of French Literature: From the Earliest Times to the Present,* rev. ed., pp. 602-09. New York: Henry Holt and Co., 1927.

Includes a brief discussion of Leconte de Lisle's poetry.

Putter, Irving. *Leconte de Lisle and His Contemporaries.* Berkeley and Los Angeles: University of California Press, 1951, 107 p.

Treats Leconte de Lisle's "literary reputation in France during his lifetime and attempts to elucidate the nature of the favorable and unfavorable criticisms of his work as well as the general trend of these criticisms."

————. *The Pessimism of Leconte de Lisle: Sources and Evolution.* Berkeley and Los Angeles: University of California Press, 1954, 144 p.

First of a two-volume set comprising the most comprehensive English-language study of Leconte de Lisle. Putter outlines the origins and development of pessimism in Leconte de Lisle's life and literary career. For a discussion of pessimism in the poet's work drawn from the second volume of Putter's study, see the excerpt dated 1961.

————. "Leconte de Lisle's Abortive Ambitions: Unpublished Correspondence." *Modern Language Quarterly* 19, No. 3 (September 1958): 255-61.

Provides excerpts from unpublished letters by and about

Leconte de Lisle in order to reconstruct aspects of his life after 1852.

———. "Lamartine and the Genesis of 'Qaïn'." *Modern Language Quarterly* XXI, No. 4 (December 1960): 356-64.

Asserts the influence of specific passages from works by French poet Alphonse Lamartine on Leconte de Lisle's poem.

———. "Leconte de Lisle and the *Catéchisme populaire républicain*." *The Romanic Review* LVII, No. 2 (April 1966): 99-116.

Regards the optimistic republicanism expressed in Leconte de Lisle's anonymously published pamphlet as an atypical counterpoint to the pessimism expressed in his poetry.

———. "Leconte de Lisle and the French Academy: A Caveat." *Modern Language Quarterly* XXVII, No. 4 (December 1966): 418-30.

Researches historical sources to reassess Leconte de Lisle's relationship with the French academy, "including his various candidatures, and the attitude of Victor Hugo, whom he eventually replaced in the coveted society."

Raitt, A. W. "Leconte de Lisle (1818-94)." In his *Life and Letters in France: The Nineteenth Century,* pp. 101-09. London: Thomas Nelson and Sons, 1965.

Examines the ambiguities in Leconte de Lisle's views on religion, noting the intellectual trends of his era.

Schaffer, Aaron. "Leconte de Lisle and His Disciples." In his *Parnassus in France: Currents and Cross-Currents in Nineteenth-Century French Lyric Poetry,* pp. 72-129. Austin: University of Texas, 1929.

Discusses Leconte de Lisle's life and literary career, focusing on the qualities of his poems that contradict the critical charge that his work is "impassible."

———. *The Genres of Parnassian Poetry: A Study of the Parnassian Minors.* Baltimore: Johns Hopkins Press, 1944, 427 p.

Offers chapters that address Leconte de Lisle's approach to "the descriptive genre," "the philosophic genre," and "classical antiquity and the exotic genre."

Schons, Emily. "Leconte de Lisle's Poems on Peter the Cruel." *Modern Philology* XXXII, No. 1 (August 1934): 67-74.

Scrutinizes possible sources for Leconte de Lisle's portrayal of Peter the Cruel of Castile in "Les inquiétudes de Don Simuel," "Le romance de Don Fadrique," and "Le romance de Doña Blanca," noting in particular Leconte de Lisle's use of the writings of Prosper Mérimée and Alexandre Dumas *père*.

Sells, A. Lytton. "Leconte de Lisle and Sir Walter Scott." *French Studies* I, No. 4 (October 1947): 334-42.

Suggests the intermediary role of Leconte de Lisle's early reading of the novels of Sir Walter Scott on his later interest in folklore and mythology.

Shurr, Georgia Hooks. "Artistic Creativity and Paralysis: Valéry and Leconte de Lisle." *Proceedings: Pacific Northwest Conference on Foreign Languages* XXV, part 1 (19-20 April 1974): 217-21.

Focuses on Leconte de Lisle's poem "Midi" and "Le cimetière marin" by Paul Valéry, asserting that Valéry affirms vitality, whereas Leconte de Lisle stresses death-like nirvana and stasis.

Southwell, Kathleen A. "A Comparative Study of the Works of Leconte de Lisle and César Franck." *The French Quarterly* XIII, No. 1 (June 1931): 1-22.

Compares the temperaments, artistic influences, and techniques of Leconte de Lisle and Belgian-born French composer César Franck.

Stuart, Esmè. "Leconte de Lisle: A Short Study." *The Fortnightly Review* n.s. LVIII, No. CCCXLIII (1 July 1895): 121-31.

Discusses the philosophy of Leconte de Lisle, emphasizing his Western approach to Eastern mysticism.

Swinburne, Algernon Charles. "Memorial Ode on the Death of Leconte de Lisle." *The Saturday Review,* London 78, No. 2040 (1 December 1894): 595-96.

Elegy by the English Decadent poet.

Symons, Arthur. "M. Leconte de Lisle." *The Athenaeum* 2, No. 3482 (21 July 1894): 99.

Obituary tribute in which Symons praises Leconte de Lisle's work and evaluates the successes and limitations of what Symons considers his abstract, intellectual emphasis.

"Leconte de Lisle's Poetry." *Temple Bar* LXXXIX, No. 354 (May 1890): 111-17.

Argues that "in the art of choosing words of charm and colour, and of setting them in jewelled phrases, the greatest of French poets is . . . Leconte de Lisle."

Alessandro Manzoni

1785-1873

(Full name Alessandro Francesco Tommaso Antonio Manzoni) Italian novelist, dramatist, poet, essayist, and critic.

Manzoni is remembered as the author of the first great modern Italian novel, *I promessi sposi* (*The Betrothed*). A complex historical narrative of seventeenth-century Italian life, *The Betrothed* was distinguished by its psychological insight, religious and nationalistic themes, use of common people as protagonists, and introduction of spoken Italian as a medium for literary expression. *The Betrothed* was widely imitated by subsequent Italian novelists, influencing the evolution of both Italian language and literature and contributing to the rise of Italian nationalism in the nineteenth century.

Manzoni was the son of wealthy parents of the Milanese nobility who separated while he was still a child. His early years were spent in religious schools where he studied Catholic theology, philosophy, history, and Latin and Italian classics. During the period of his formal education, which ended when he was sixteen, Manzoni also began to write poetry. After he left school, Manzoni lived with his father for several years in Milan, where his interest in literature, history, and politics was stimulated by the cultural life of the city. In 1805 he joined his mother in Paris. There he continued to write, composing poems that were influenced in form and diction by eighteenth-century Neoclassicism. In Paris, under his mother's auspices, he also met Parisian artists and intellectuals who introduced him to the literary trends of the age, particularly Romanticism. Two years later, Manzoni returned to Italy, and in 1810 he experienced what commentators have called one of the most important events of his life—a strengthening and renewal of his Catholicism. Of great significance to his artistic development, Manzoni's renewed commitment to his religious faith formed the basis for his major works.

Soon after this experience, Manzoni moved to an inherited estate in the country, where he established the sedate and retiring life-style he maintained for the rest of his life. During the next fifteen years, he produced his major works, most notably *Inni sacri* (*The Sacred Hymns*), hymns on religious subjects; *Osservazioni sulla morale cattolica* (*A Vindication of Catholic Morality*), an essay defending the Catholic religion; several poems on nationalistic subjects, including *Il cinque maggio* (*Ode on the Death of Napoleon*); and the historical verse dramas *Il conte di Carmagnola* and *Adelchi*, which display Manzoni's rejection of the Aristotelian unities of time and place in a dramatic work. These works, along with the *Lettre à M. Chauvet* (*A Letter on Dramatic Unities and the Essence of Tragedy*), a formal statement of his disregard for Aristotelian dramatic form, and *Sul romanticismo*, a letter to the Marchese Cesare D'Azeglio in which he rejected the subject matter of classical mythology, comprise Manzoni's chief contribution to the development of Italian Romanticism.

In 1827 Manzoni published *The Betrothed*. Popular and

critical response in Italy was almost unanimously favorable, earning Manzoni a respected position in Italian letters and society. During the next few years, in response to his concern that literary Italian should more closely reflect the language of the common people, Manzoni revised the novel according to the dialect of Tuscany, which he felt was closest to an ideal Italian idiom. This version appeared in installments from 1840 through 1842. Thereafter, Manzoni wrote primarily essays on various subjects, including linguistics, literature, and politics. His life of quiet retirement and study was interrupted in 1860, when, as a result of his revered public status, he was made a member of the Italian senate. Manzoni died in 1873 after a severe fall.

Commentators on Manzoni's work have concentrated their studies on *The Betrothed*. Early critics focused on the relationship of the novel to the historical fiction of Sir Walter Scott and on Manzoni's moral and political concerns, while later critics have emphasized the novel's structure and language. The consensus has been that *The Betrothed*, in its complex interweaving of plot, characterization, theme, and style, is the culmination of Manzoni's literary career. Set in seventeenth-century Spanish-dominated Lombardy during the Thirty Years' War, *The*

Betrothed relates the story of two peasant lovers, Renzo and Lucia, who are separated before their marriage by the machinations of Don Rodrigo, a local nobleman who desires Lucia. Fleeing the city to escape the designs of Don Rodrigo, the couple endure many trials, including the abduction of Lucia and the hardships of famine, war, and plague, before they are finally wed. Throughout this narrative, Manzoni detailed historical events with meticulous accuracy. Particularly noteworthy, scholars point out, are his realistic descriptions of starving, plague-ridden villages and cities and his chronicling of the Thirty Years' War in Italy. Manzoni's characters, both humble and aristocratic, are skillfully portrayed against this background and are often developed through accounts of their past actions. For example, the fate of Gertrude, a nun who takes a lover and commits murder, is only fully understood in light of the revelations of her early home life. The interaction of plot and characterization throughout the arduous travels of Renzo and Lucia effectively reveals Manzoni's major themes: the evil of unbridled passions, the necessity of trust in God and in an afterlife, the corruption of religious and political organizations, and the blight of foreign domination. Scholars note that Manzoni's integration of spoken and literary Italian aptly delineates his characters and conveys his moral, religious, and patriotic themes. While Manzoni later repudiated the form of the historical novel because he believed that it failed to satisfy the aims of either history or fiction, critics consider *The Betrothed* his most important work and a masterpiece of world literature.

PRINCIPAL WORKS

In morte di Carlo Imbonati (poetry) 1806
Urania (poetry) 1809
Inni sacri (poetry) 1815
　　[*The Sacred Hymns* published in "*The Sacred Hymns*" and "*The Napoleonic Ode,*" 1904]
Osservazioni sulla morale cattolica (essay) 1819; revised edition, 1855
　　[*A Vindication of Catholic Morality,* 1836]
Il conte di Carmagnola (verse drama) 1820
Il cinque maggio (poetry) 1821
　　[*Ode on the Death of Napoleon,* 1861; also published as *The Napoleonic Ode,* 1904; and *The Fifth of May,* 1973]
Adelchi (verse drama) 1822
Discorso sopra alcuni punti della storia longobardica in Italia (history) 1822
Lettre à M. Chauvet (criticism) 1823
　　[*A Letter on Dramatic Unities and the Essence of Tragedy* published in *Italian Quarterly,* 1973]
Sul romanticismo (criticism) 1823
I promessi sposi (novel) 1827; revised edition, 1840-42
　　[*The Betrothed Lovers,* 1828; also published as *Lucia, the Betrothed,* 1834; and *The Betrothed,* 1951]
Storia della colonna infame (historical narrative) 1840-42
　　[*The Column of Infamy;* published in *The Betrothed Lovers,* 1845]
Dell'invenzione (dialogue) 1850; published in *Opere varie,* 1845-55
　　[*A Dialogue of the Artist's Idea,* 1899]

Del romanzo storico (essay) 1850; published in *Opere varie,* 1845-55
　　[*On the Historical Novel,* 1984]
Del trionfo della libertà (poetry) 1878
Tutte le opere. 11 vols. (poetry, verse dramas, novel, historical narrative, letters, criticism, and essays) 1957-70

The Monthly Review　(essay date 1826)

[*In the following excerpt, the critic examines Manzoni's tragedies and his prose work* Discorso sopra alcuni punti della storia longobardica in Italia.]

Among Italian writers of our day, he that has taken most firmly his ground as a champion of romanticism, or in other words, of national poetry, is Manzoni, a Milanese by birth, and grandson to the celebrated Beccaria. He has grappled with the question of romanticism in its most tangible shape, that of the drama. In his two tragedies, *Carmagnola* and *Adelchi,* he has taken the facts from national history; he has endeavoured faithfully to invest the characters of his drama with the historical costume, and in both he has discarded the unities, stating at the same time, in temperate, but determined language, his reasons for so doing. Manzoni is also known as a lyric poet of eminence, perhaps the first in Italy, since Monti's poetical career may be said to have now closed. He is also a prose writer of great logical powers, independent in his sentiments, elevated in his conceptions, strict, but impartial in his judgments. In him we see revived a spark of the old Italian spirit, equally distant from morbid sentimentality, courtly insipidity, and outrageous licentiousness. (pp. 482-83)

Manzoni's first tragedy, *Il conte di Carmagnola,* appeared at Milan some years since. The subject is taken from the history of Venice, a chronicle abundant in dark and tragical deeds, and relates to the latter part of the career of that chief of Condottieri, who from the condition of a shepherd, having risen to be the general of Philip Maria Visconti, Duke of Milan, was afterwards persecuted by that ungrateful prince, who owed to him his crown. (p. 483)

In this tragedy, Manzoni happily pourtrays the gallant, but reckless and unbending spirit of that soldier of fortune, and his honest military bluntness, as contrasted with the watchful spider-like policy of the Venetian senate, and their arrogant disregard of justice. The manners of the Condottieri are also displayed; and the condition of Italy during that epoch of civil and inglorious strife, is exhibited in a chorus of great lyric beauty.

The tragedy of Carmagnola was noticed at the time by Italian and foreign critics; and in Germany, where they bestow more attention to Italian literature than in any other country, Goethe, from the novelty of its plan, and the talents of the author, deemed it worth a full dissertation, which he inserted in his periodical on the Arts and Antiquity, (*ueber Kunst und Alterthum,*) published at Stutgard. After speaking highly of the play, he concluded in these flattering terms: "We congratulate Mr. Manzoni, for having so happily freed himself from the ancient rules, and proceeded in his new path with so much steadiness;

his style is simple, vigorous and clear; he is elegant and correct in the details. Let him go on, and disdain the vulgar and weak points of human sensibility, and deal solely with subjects like the present, capable of awakening in us deep and lasting emotions." (pp. 483-84)

Manzoni's second tragedy, *Adelchi,* is, we believe, little known in this country. The subject is the fall of the Longobard kingdom, effected in the year 774, by Charlemagne, who invaded Italy under the pretence of succouring Pope Adrian, then threatened by the Longobards, and who, having taken king Desiderius prisoner, established his power over Italy, and revived the name of the western empire. Adelchi, or Adelgisus, son of Desiderius, opposed for a time the Franks, but betrayed by the Longobard dukes, he was obliged to fly, leaving his father in the hands of the conqueror; he sought refuge in Constantinople, where, several years after, he obtained from the Greek emperor some troops, with which he landed in Italy, gave battle to the Franks and was killed, about the year 788. Manzoni, however, and this is his only deviation from the historical records, supposes Adelchi to have been killed at the time of Charlemagne's invasion, in an encounter under the walls of Verona. The action in this play is rather scanty, the incidents few, and the form of its narrative is sculptural, as Schlegel, we fancy, would call it; this is, however, the case with almost all Italian tragedies, and we doubt whether it is likely ever to be otherwise, even with their historical dramas; for there is, we apprehend, something stately and oratorical in the genius of the language, and also in the taste of the people, which will not always bend to the wishes of the romantic school. However, the beauties of the diction, the numerous poetical and descriptive passages, and the spirit with which the principal characters are drawn in Manzoni's *Adelchi,* amply compensate the reader for the want of greater activity in the plan. It is a great point gained for the Italian drama, its having cast off the heavy fetters of the unities of time and place.

One character in the play, that of Adelchi, not only is not grounded upon history, but what is worse, is altogether improbable. It forms a complete anachronism. Manzoni himself confesses, that 'the designs of Adelchi, his judgments on events, his dispositions, are all pure invention, and that this character has been intruded among the historical personages with an awkwardness, which no reader can more strongly feel than the author.'

Another critique on this drama, censures its dereliction of what is called poetical justice, a sort of abstraction, for which, we confess, we entertain little more respect than for the famed unities. It has been remarked by an Italian writer, that the character of Charlemagne is drawn by Manzoni with severe historical truth; but that his triumph, although unmerited, is yet apt to dazzle the multitude, "and then," thus concludes the critic, "what is there left in such a drama that will console virtue and terrify guilt?" *There is truth,* some one replied for Manzoni; to this it is well that the people should be accustomed. Even the splendour of unjust successes becomes less dazzling to the sight, the more steadily we look at it. It is certainly pleasing to see virtue rewarded, and injustice punished; thus novels generally end; but is it always thus in the real world? And if poetical justice be not consistent with history, then some other moral compensation must be found in its place. This can be done by exciting a feeling of aversion against the

fortunate oppressor. This dislike we feel for Charlemagne, and we derive it from the contrast of his character with those of Adelchi and Ermengardis; from his inglorious conquest, obtained through bribery and shared with traitors; from his own half-stifled remorses, relating to his treatment of his innocent and ill-fated queen; from his cold-hearted hypocrisy, and his cheap magnanimity and admiration for the expiring Adelchi, and for the self-devoted Squire Anfrid. Yet the character of Charlemagne is not destitute of grandeur: his military talents, his political acuteness, the firmness of his resolves, his personal activity, and a certain elegance of tone and manners which distinguish him from all about him; these proclaim him for a man of superior powers, the hero of a half-civilized age.

Manzoni has introduced short lyrical poems which he calls choruses, between the acts of his *Adelchi,* as he had done in his *Carmagnola.* These are different from the Greek choruses, inasmuch as the compositions are independent of the action, and not intended to be recited or sung by any of the dramatis personæ; they are the effusions of the poet's sentiments, and as such belong to the written play, being meant for the reader, to assist him in filling up the historical perspective of the drama. Notwithstanding the indefinite nature of these compositions, and their equivocal position in the tragedy, their poetical beauties have found them favour with several Italian and German critics, who propose that they should be substituted for the common insignificant music of the orchestra between the acts, and form a sort of concert, which would be the echo of the sentiments of the spectators as produced by the play.

We now proceed to Manzoni's prose writings. Next in order to *Adelchi,* and connected with it by the subject we find his *Discourse upon Certain Points of the History of the Longobards.* Two of these points are very important for the general illustration of history: the treatment the Italians met with from the Longobards, during two centuries of occupation from the first conqueror and king of that nation Alboin, who invaded Italy in 568, to the defeat and captivity of Desiderius; the other is the part which the Popes took in the fall of the last named king.

It is not to be wondered at that Italian writers, disgusted with the dismal scene of the wreck of the western empire, and of the calamitous ages of desolation which followed it, should have dwelt with a degree of complacency, upon those among the barbarian conquerors of Italy, who afforded at last some protection and repose to that ill-fated country. The beneficent reign of the Goth Theodoric, is the first of these cheering epochs; and next to it is that of the Longobard kings, by whom a permanent order of things was finally brought about. Their conquests and their authority would have spread over the whole Peninsula, had it not been for the Popes, and it was in consequence of the papal opposition that Pepin, and afterwards Charlemagne, interposed in the affairs of Italy, and overthrew the Longobards.

Our author combats the assertions of Machiavelli, Muratori, and Denina, who pretend that the Longobards and the Italians had so amalgamated as to form but one nation, the individuals of which had all equal rights. He proves from the very laws of the Longobards, which Muratori has collected and illustrated, that they, the conquerors, kept themselves always distinct from the conquered; that they had their separate code of laws, whilst the Italians or Romans, as they were still called at that epoch, were tried and judged according to the Roman law; and it was even decreed that "if a Roman married a Longobard woman, she became Roman, and their children should also be considered as such, and follow the law of the father." Each of the Longobard kings invariably styled himself *Rex gentis Longobardorum;* their mandates are always addressed to their Longobard judges and other officers, whom they call *gentem nostram,* and in their records the name of one single Roman or Italian officer is not to be found. The Popes, in their letters to Pepin and Charlemagne, complain of the Longobard people in terms, which certainly they did not mean to apply to their own countrymen, the Romans or Italians. Stephen IV. calls them *perfida ac fœtentissima Longobardorum gens, quœ in numero gentium nequaquam computatur, etc.* From these and other arguments of a similar purport, our author concludes that the Longobards, during the two centuries of their dominion, remained separate from the original Italians, who were the cultivators of the soil, whilst their conquerors applied themselves chiefly to the profession of arms, and divided among themselves all the offices of government. With regard to their treatment of the subject-population during that period, it was certainly milder than that of their barbarous predecessors, with the exception however of Theodoric; milder than that of the modern Turks towards the Greeks; but yet not so very gentle as Muratori, with his strange predilection for the Longobards, would have it. There is much obscurity in the records of that epoch, and a remarkable silence with regard to the condition of the Italian population, which of itself is an argument of their insignificance; certain facts however have transpired, which serve to throw some light on this point. The Romans or Italians were obliged to pay to the Longobards the third of the produce of the soil, they were bound to lodge and feed the Longobard soldiers, who were distributed over the country, and Paul Warnefrid, a Longobard himself, relates that many of the Roman or Italian patricians had been put to death by the Longobard dukes, for the sake of their property, and the rest divided among them as vassals paying tribute. Another point discussed by Manzoni, and which is of a greater and more general historical importance, is the part which the Popes took in the fall of the Longobards, and in the establishment of Charlemagne's empire.

> In the long struggle between the Popes and the Longobard kings, our author aptly observes, the subjects most dwelt upon are, the ambitious designs of the former. The importance given to these is an effect of that propensity in men to consider the stage of history, as the property of a few persons of rank and influence. But in the struggle before us, the question was not only between churchmen and kings, and their interests and passions; the destiny of millions of men was at stake, therefore, it behoves us to know which of the two belligerent powers was most closely allied to the wishes and to the rights of the great mass of the Italian population, which was best calculated to afford them security and peace, and to administer their affairs with something like justice and humanity. This is the true point on which the question rests.

In the eighth century, the Longobards held long established possession of the North and Eastern parts of Italy, as far as the Duchy of Benevento. Rome, and other central provinces of the Peninsula, still held, nominally, by the Greek emperors, but under the real influence of the Popes, were repeatedly overran, desolated, and threatened with final extermination by the Longobards. The inhabitants had little or no means of defence, the court of Byzantium bestowed no thought or care upon them, even the Exarch of Ravenna, attacked by Luitprand, could devise no better protection, than to entreat Pope Zacharias to intercede with the Longobard king for a cessation of hostilities. The Romans of that day were such as they had been rendered by the pompous cowardice, and the arrogant irresolution of their last emperors; by the frightful succession of barbarian irruptions; by the systematic disarming of the natives effected by the Gothic kings; by the oppression of the Greek governors, whenever they felt strong enough to oppress. This state of things lasted for centuries; centuries of alarm, anxiety, and trepidation; of sufferings without dignity; of slaughter without fight; centuries, in which the Roman name became a stigma, a bye-word, an appellation of contempt; when those who bore this name had to suffer more privations, to endure greater fatigues, to submit to more rigorous discipline, than their great ancestors had imposed upon themselves in order to immortalize it, and to make it feared and reverenced by the whole world. When a people is lowered to such a degree, it has nothing more to hope, not even the compassion of posterity. Subsequent austere writers, seated comfortably by their firesides, far removed from the horrors of those miserable times, condemn the wretches without mercy; and such is their aversion to the sight of their debasement, that they even apologize for, and praise their persecutors, because they discover in the latter a bold and fierce determination of character. And yet the justest feeling of aversion ought to be against determined injustice, bold oppression, and fierce usurpation; and however fallen a people may be, we ought to feel an interest whenever we see a glimmering of hope dawning on them.

The only hope of the Roman or Italian population at that epoch, was centered in their pontiffs. Rome, shorn of every worldly splendour, had yet in its bosom an object of veneration, of religion, and of awe, even for its enemies. This was a Roman, who had in his power to dispense promises or threats of a nature supernatural, solemn, and important. Towards this man, this pontiff, this Roman, were therefore turned all the wishes, all the expectations of his countrymen. We find the Popes, in the calamities of those times, now requesting troops from the Greeks, now imploring mercy from the Longobards, and now assistance from the Franks, according as circumstances required or allowed. But on what occasions did the Popes turn to the Franks for protection? Gregory III. wrote to Charles Martel for aid, when the Longobards were pillaging the territory of Rome. Stephen II. had recourse to Pepin, when Astolphus, after having signed a truce for forty years, marched suddenly against Rome, and demanded that its citizens should acknowledge themselves his tributaries, threatening, otherwise, to put them all to the sword. After Pepin's interference and Astolphus' two successive defeats, and Pepin's famous donation to St. Peter, we find again the Popes appealing to the Franks, to enforce their guarantee, and make the Longobards evacuate the cities of the Exarchate, and the other lands bestowed by Pepin, and this at a time when the Longobards were overrunning the very duchy of Rome. Paul I. was not praying for himself alone, when he implored Pepin's assistance against the Longobards, who, in passing through the cities of Pentapolis, had put every thing to fire and sword; Adrian was not merely looking to his private views, when he complained of the Longobards, who were plundering, killing, and burning in the territories of Sinigaglia and Urbino, who having fallen suddenly on the inhabitants of Blera, while reaping in the fields, killed the primates, carried away a booty of men and cattle, and destroyed the rest. And let it be observed, that this cutting off of the primates, or proprietors of the land, we have seen before in another epoch of the Longobardian occupation; and this might, perhaps, serve to explain, how, among all the barbarian dominations, the Longobardian is that under which the indigenous population is least noticed.

What is the amount, therefore, asks our author, of the charges of Giannone and other writers, Italian and foreign, against the Popes on this particular occasion? That the Popes were endeavouring to prevent the remainder of Italy from falling into the hands of the Longobards, and its inhabitants from being either destroyed or made tributaries to the invaders! But the Popes had also their own private views! This is most likely; for where has a great political object been ever pursued or attained, without a mixture of personal interest or ambition? But in this case, at least, their private views and interests agreed perfectly with those of the Italian population, whom the Popes then saved from utter national annihilation. Central Italy owed to the Popes the preservation of its independence, which afforded the means of reviving afterwards the energies of the remainder of the Peninsula. The sacred fire was kept at Rome; the ambition of the Popes (granting that this was their leading passion), fed it, and through it Italy was rescued both from Greek and Longobard vassalage—its fair name saved from oblivion, and its inhabitants preserved as a distinct people. Charlemagne was the instrument of this: he was himself ambitious, and little scrupulous; his personal conduct towards the house of Desiderius was marked with injustice and cruelty, yet he proved useful to the Italians, by beginning their emancipation. The Franks, whom the Popes called to their assistance, being already masters of a fine country, never thought of colonizing Italy; and the merely nominal authority of Charlemagne's successors paved the way for the restoration of Italian independence, in the republics of Lombardy and of Tuscany; an independence which the Italians defended for five centuries, and which became only extinct, and that but partially, under Charles V. and his Spanish despotism. The glorious era of the Italian republics would probably never have taken place, without the Popes' and Charlemagne's hostility to the Longobards; and Italy, at best, would have run the same monotonous career of feudal oppression and passive obedience, as France under its threefold dynasty. But this is only hypothetical, the reality consists in Italy having been saved at the time from oppressive servitude, and from the rule of strangers.

After stating the subject of the last differences between Adrian and Desiderius; (we speak of Adrian, because the conduct of his predecessor Stephen was not so candid), and after expressing his conviction that the right was on the side of the former, Manzoni disclaims for himself the inference which superficial minds are apt to draw, that the defender of one Pope, in one particular instance, must be the apologist of all that the Popes have done, and of all

that has been done in their name, from the time of Constantine to that of Napoleon; as if in looking to these fourteen centuries of the history of a government like the Roman hierarchy, through a succession of three hundred Popes, of various nations, dispositions and abilities, it were possible to pass one sweeping sentence of approval or reprobation on the conduct of the whole!

Our author next proceeds to examine the facility with which Charlemagne effected the conquest of the Longobard kingdom; and accounts for it by the nature of the federative oligarchy of the Longobards, and their elective monarchy, and still more by the superior character of Charlemagne, who knew how to render the power of his counts subservient to his will. (pp. 484-90)

We have dwelt at some length upon this dissertation, as it will serve to shew the progress of logical reasoning and philosophical investigation in Italy. Another quality which distinguishes Manzoni's writings, is the absence of that querulous tone which too often pervades the pages of Italian writers. Querulousness is the failing of old age, both in men and nations. There is something very undignified in those continual lamentations, in that elegiac style of oratory, which descants with a sort of predilection on the degradation, real or exaggerated, of one's country, and exposes its nakedness to the scorn of strangers. (p. 490)

As for us, we heed not the clamour of parties, whether liberal or ultra, classic or romantic, Cruscan or Anti Cruscan, but we love to see national characters as well as features, and we rejoice when we meet with a mind cast in Italy's best mould, acute, reflecting, somewhat rough and stubborn, but independent and honest, an emanation of that spirit which shone in old Dante and in Michelangelo, which Vico inherited, which gleamed through the wayward feelings of Alfieri, and which we think we can trace now, in two writers of our day, Botta and Manzoni.

We have already mentioned Manzoni's lyrics. He has written several odes or hymns on sacred subjects, which have become deservedly popular in Italy. They breathe the ingenuous expression of pious feeling on the anniversaries of the great events of the Christian revelation, clothed in beautiful language and lofty numbers. We can but give the titles of these compositions:—**"The Nativity"**—**"The Passion"**—**"The Resurrection"**—**"The Pentecost"**—and, **"Il Nome di Maria,"** or the onomastic day of the Virgin. The measure and rhythm vary from joyful to solemn or sad, in happy adaptation to the nature of the subject. (p. 491)

"The Works of Manzoni," in The Monthly Review, *London, Vol. III, No. XV, 1826, pp. 480-93.*

The London Magazine   (essay date 1828)

[*In the following excerpt, the critic discusses* The Betrothed *in relationship to the historical novels of Sir Walter Scott.*]

Count Manzoni, who dared to fling away the trammels of the classic writers on the stage, has also the glory of having given to the world the first *Romanzo in prosa* that can vie with those of England—of England, we say, for there surely is no French or German historic romance that can enter into competition with *I promessi sposi.* And it is not a little extraordinary, that though the labours of the dramatist and the novelist are generally held to be almost incompatiable, an opinion chiefly set afloat by one who strongly feels this incompatibility in his own person, Manzoni has shewn, in our opinion, nearly equal capability for either species of fictitious delineation.

It is said that the romance demands powers of bold, vigorous, minute, and accurate description, of full and animated narration, of grave or gay dialogue, as occasion may demand. Added to this, there must be the power of inventing a natural, well combined series of incidents, gradually and easily leading to a probable conclusion. In the former of these attributes Sir Walter Scott stands pre-eminent; in the last he, and no man, can bear a comparison with Henry Fielding. The drama, on the contrary, demands description in a few brief comprehensive strokes, and brevity and weight must also characterise its dialogue; but it equally requires art in the production and arrangement of incidents. The incompatibility then lies in the difficulty of finding combined in the same writer, the copious style of the romance and the brief nervous diction of the drama. *Halidon Hill* has certainly proved that in one great instance they do not exist in combination.

We would almost venture to say that Manzoni furnishes another instance. We are in the habit of regarding him as a dramatist, because it was in that character we first became acquainted with him; but we will risk the heresy of saying, that the novelist is the character in which he is most likely to excell if he can overcome the fault, common to his drama and his romance, which we shall presently point out. Diffuseness in dialogue is one of the prominent errors of his dramas; and, even in his romance he, like his prototype, not unfrequently runs into this extreme. Of this fault he himself is sufficiently sensible.

The great defect, we fear an incurable one, of Manzoni is the want of the power of properly combining and conducting his narrative. In the *Carmagnola,* each separated scene, taken by itself, is admirable; but they are like pictures arranged in a gallery; they have little relation each to the other. Just so is it in the *Promessi sposi.* Each individual scene and character is admirable, but he is

> Infelix operis summa, quia ponere totum
> Nesciat.

If this fault can be overcome, we see nothing to prevent Count Manzoni from taking his station in the very first rank of historic novelists.

It is a question how far the historic novel is of use. It is said, indeed, that events and characters of real history will, when forcibly and picturesquely displayed by the hand of a great master, make a more lively and firm impression on the mind than those in the dry pages of annalists; and this is true where the history and the romance are of the same age. No one doubts but that the author of *Waverley* makes a more lively impression on our minds than Hume or Robertson; but whether this be an advantage demands a doubt. That it should be so the novelist must be honest; and here Sir Walter has much to answer for. Many a young lady, and many a young gentleman too, we fear, is very firmly persuaded that King Richard returned to England in disguise, and visited hermits' cells; that Lewis XI. was a tolerably worthy personage; and Charles II. a sweet amiable fellow. What, after all, are these high-wrought

melodramatic scenes and characters to the realities of old Froissart? It is not, in truth, on his historical pieces that the better fame of the author of *Waverley* is based; it is on his descriptions of real life and nature, as he has seen them with his own eyes, and not through the spectacles of books,—on his Bradwardines, Dandy Dinmonts, Nicol Jarvies—not on his Leicesters, Charleses, Edwards, Elizabeths, or Marys. In short, no man's description of what he has not seen and known is very valuable; and therefore no novel is very valuable as a picture of manners in which a writer is not describing his own contemporaries or countrymen. Fielding's English squires and peasants will live for ever; so will the Scottish ones of Sir Walter Scott;—and now, for the first time, we witness a true and faithful delineation of the character and manners of the Italian peasantry, by the hand of one intimately acquainted with them.

Count Manzoni wished to portray the state of society in the Milanese, during the early part of the seventeenth century, together with three great events which then occurred; to wit—a famine, a pestilence, and the passage of an army through the country. For each of these he drew his materials from contemporary history and records; and so scrupulously faithful is he, that he even sometimes, contrary to romantic etiquette, quotes his authorities at the bottom of his page. Heinous as this offence may be, in the eyes of novel readers brought up at the feet of the great Gamaliel, he has, by means of it, succeeded in giving a vivid picture of that horrible scourge of man, the plague; with which it would be idle to compare those of Thucydides and Boccaccio; and only rivalled by that of Daniel Defoe, who, like him, felt that truth needs not the meretricious appendage of fiction. With these awful events is interwoven a simple story of two young peasants, the Betrothed, who give name to the tale. (pp. 264-66)

In conclusion, we would observe, that nothing can exceed the truth and nature with which all the characters are drawn; those of the peasantry give us a very advantageous idea of that class in Italy. The descriptions of scenery are faithful and picturesque; the events are probable and unforced. The question of how real history is to be employed in romance, is one at issue between our author and Sir Walter Scott. We candidly confess our leaning is to the side of the Italian, though we fear he is occasionally too historically minute. The language of [*The*] *Betrothed,* perhaps, affords the best model to be met with, of a correct and elegant style of conversational Italian. (p. 266)

> *A review of "I Promessi Sposi," in* The London Magazine, *n.s. Vol. 21, No. II, May, 1828, pp. 264-66.*

Alessandro Manzoni   (essay date 1850)

[*In the following excerpt from Part I of his* Del romanzo storico (On the Historical Novel), *Manzoni examines the elements of history and fiction in the historical novel.*]

The historical novel is subject to two different, in fact, two diametrically opposite criticisms; and since these go to the very essence of the genre rather than mere secondary qualities, it seems that to identify and examine them is a good way, perhaps the best way to come, without preliminaries, to the heart of the matter.

Some complain that in certain historical novels or in certain parts of a historical novel, fact is not clearly distinguished from invention and that, as a result, these works fail to achieve one of their principal purposes, which is to give a faithful representation of history.

In order to show how right these critics may be, I will have to expand upon what they actually say—but without adding anything that isn't already implicit in their own words. And I think if I have them speak this way to the patient, or rather to the author, I will be doing nothing more than developing the logical grounds of their complaint:

"The aim of your work was to put before me, in a new and special form, a richer, more varied, more complete history than that found in works which more commonly go by this name, as if by *antonomasia.* The history we expect from you is not a chronological account of mere political and military events or, occasionally, some other kind of extraordinary happening; but a more general representation of the human condition, in a time and place naturally more circumscribed than that in which works of history, in the more usual sense of the word, ordinarily unfold. In a way, there is the same difference between the usual sort of history and your own as between a geographic map that simply indicates the presence of mountain chains, rivers, cities, towns, and major roads of a vast region and a topographic map, where all of this (and whatever else might be shown in a more restricted area) is presented in greater detail and, indeed, where even minor elevations and less noteworthy particulars—ditches, channels, villages, isolated homes, paths—are clearly marked. Customs, opinions, whether they are generally accepted or peculiar to certain social classes; the private consequences of public events that are more properly called historical, or of the laws or will of the powerful, however these are expressed—in short, all that a given society in a given time could claim as most characteristic of every way of life and of their interactions—this is what you sought to reveal at least as far as you managed, through long hard research, to discover it yourself. And the enjoyment you sought to produce is what naturally comes from acquiring such knowledge, and especially from acquiring it through a representation that I would call living, put into action.

"Granting all this, when has confusing things ever been a means of revealing them? To know is to believe; and for me to believe, when I know what is presented is not all equally true, it is absolutely necessary that I be able to distinguish fact from invention. But how? You want to make real facts known, yet you don't give me the means to recognize them as real? Then why did you want these facts to play an extended, leading role in your work? Why that label "historical" attached to it like a badge and, at the same time, as an attraction? Because you knew very well that there is an interest, as lively and keen as it is singular, in knowing what really happened and how. And after arousing my curiosity and channeling it so, did you think you could satisfy it by presenting me with something that might be reality, but could just as well be a product of your own inventiveness?

"And please don't fail to realize that, in criticizing you this way, I also mean to compliment you: I assume I am speaking to a writer who knows how to choose his subjects well and also how to handle them well. If your novel were te-

dious, filled with ordinary events, possible at any time and therefore not peculiar to any, I would have closed the book without a second thought. But precisely because the event, the character, the circumstances, the means, the consequences that you present attract and hold my attention, a thirst grows in me that is even more keen, insatiable, and, in fact, more reasonable—to know whether I ought to see there a real expression of humanity, nature, Providence, or only a possibility happily found by you. If someone with a reputation for telling tall tales gives you an interesting piece of news, do you say that you "know" that information? Are you left satisfied? Now you (as a novelist, I mean) are like him, like someone who recounts falsehood as readily as truth; and if you do not help me distinguish one from the other, you leave me as dissatisfied as he does.

"Instruction and delight were your two purposes; but they are so bound together that when you fail to achieve one, the other escapes you as well: your reader does not feel delighted, precisely because he does not feel instructed."

Surely these critics could state the case better; but even when they state it this way, one must confess they are right.

However, as I said at the outset, there are other critics who would like just the opposite. They complain instead that in a given historical novel or in given parts of a historical novel, the author does plainly distinguish factual truth from invention; this, they say, destroys the unity that is the vital condition of this or any other work of art. Let us try to see in a bit more detail the basis for this second complaint.

"What," I believe they mean to ask, "is the essential form of the historical novel? The story. And what can one imagine that is more opposed to the unity, to the continuity of the story's effect, to the connection, to the collaboration, to the *coniurat amice* (the friendly league) of each part in producing a total impression, than presenting some of these parts as true and others as the product of invention? The latter, shaped properly, will be just like the former except that they are not true, except that they lack the special ineffable quality of something real. Now, if you point out the quality of truth in those parts that possess it, you deprive your story of its only reason for being, replacing the commonality of its various parts with something that underscores their inconsistency, even their antagonism. By telling me in so many words, or letting me know in some other way, that something is a fact, you force me—whether this was your purpose or not is irrelevant—to think that what preceded it was not fact and that what follows will not be fact either; that the former deserves the credence we lend to positive truth, while the latter deserves only that very different sort of belief that we give to the verisimilar. You naturally lead me to think that the narrative form, though applied to both truth and invention, is really proper and natural only to the former, and merely conventional and factitious for the latter, which amounts to saying that the form is contradictory as a whole.

"And the contradiction could not be more peculiar. You yourself must consider this unity, this homogeneity of the whole extremely important, since you do all you can to achieve it. Choosing from both the real and the possible those elements that harmonize best, you do your utmost to earn the honor that Horace gives to the author of the *Odyssey:*

> And he lies thus, closely mixing the true with the false, so that the middle always refers to the beginning, the beginning to the end.

And for what purpose, if not to lead your readers—seduced, carried away by art—to accept the two parts as a single entity, if you will, just as they are presented? Yet you proceed to undo your own accomplishment, separating on the level of substance that which you have joined together in form! Thus you yourself destroy, in the very course of producing it, the illusion that is art's pursuit and reward, and that is so difficult to create and sustain. Don't you see that joining together bits of copper and bits of tin does not make a bronze statue?"

How to answer these critics? To tell the truth, they are probably right.

A friend of mine, whom I recall with affection and esteem, used to relate a curious scene he had witnessed at the house of a justice of the peace in Milan, many years ago. He had found the judge between two litigants, one of whom was hotly pressing his case; and when he had finished, the judge said to him, "You are right." "But, your honor," the other said quickly, "you must hear me too before deciding." "That is only proper," replied the judge, "speak up and I will listen." The second man then presented his case so effectively, and was so successful, that the judge said to him, "You are right too." At that point, one of the judge's children of seven or eight years who, though

Manzoni at seventeen.

quietly playing at his side with some kind of toy, had been listening to the debate, raised his astonished little face and exclaimed, not without a certain air of authority: "But daddy! It's not possible for both to be right." "Well, you are right too," said the judge. How it all ended, either my friend did not report or I have forgotten, but evidently the judge reconciled all his reactions, by showing Tom as well as Harry that, if he was right in one sense, he was wrong in another. I shall try to do the same with my two sets of critics. And I shall do it in part by using the litigants' own arguments—but drawing from them consequences that neither drew.

My response to the first is: When you demand that the author of a historical novel allow you to distinguish what really happened from what he has invented, you certainly have not considered whether this can be done at all. You prescribe the impossible, nothing less. To convince yourself, simply try to imagine for a moment how reality and invention must be melded in order to form a single story. For instance, in order to detail the historical events to which the author has tied his plot—for surely you would grant that historical events should figure in a historical novel—he will have to combine both real circumstances, drawn from history or other sources (what could better help present those events in their true and, if you will, distinctive form?) and verisimilar circumstances of his own invention. After all, you want him to give you, not just the bare bones of history, but something richer, more complete. In a way, you want him to put the flesh back on the skeleton that is history. For the same reasons, he will have historical characters—and surely you are happy to find historical characters in a historical novel—say and do both what they really said and did as flesh and blood, and what the author has imagined them saying or doing as befits their character and those parts of the plot in which he has given them a role.

Reciprocally, he will tend to include in his invented actions both invented circumstances and circumstances taken from real events of that time and place, for what better way is there to create actions that *could* have occurred in a given time and place? In the same way, he will lend his invented characters both ideal words and actions and also words and actions really said and done in that time and place—quite content to make these ideal figures more lifelike by incorporating in them elements of truth. This should be enough to make you see that the author could not possibly make the distinctions that you ask of him. Or, rather, that he could not try to make them without fracturing his narrative—and I do not mean every now and then, but every moment, many times in one page, often within a single sentence—to say: this is real fact, taken from reliable sources; this is my own invention, but patterned on reality; these words were actually said by the character to whom I attribute them, but on a very different occasion, in circumstances that I have not included in my novel; these other words, which I put in the mouth of an imaginary character, were actually spoken by a real person, or, it was common talk, and so on. Would you call a work like that a "novel"? Would you find it worth any name at all? Could an author even conceive of such a work?

Perhaps you will tell me that you never intended to ask so much. And you may be right. But I am seeking to understand what your words logically imply, as well as directly express. Whether you would want the author to distinguish what is "real" in many cases, or only in a few, or even in one case alone, why would you want him to do so at all? As a whim? No, certainly not. Rather, for a very good reason and one that you yourself have stated; because reality, when it is not presented in a way that makes it recognizable as such, neither enlightens nor satisfies. And does this reason apply only now and then? Hardly; it is by nature a general concern, equally applicable in all cases. And so, if other readers were to complain of similar discomfort elsewhere in the novel, would their complaints not merit the same consideration as yours? Yes, of course, since they are prompted by the same concern: the demand for reality. You see, once you ask the historical novel to identify reality here or there, you are really asking it to identify reality throughout: an impossibility, as I have shown or, rather, led you to see.

Now here is what I say to my other critics: According to you, distinguishing real fact from invention in a historical novel destroys the homogeneity of its effect, the unity of the reader's belief. But tell me, if you would, how you can destroy what does not exist? Don't you see that this inconsistency resides in the basic elements, you might even say in the raw materials, of the work? When, for example, the Homer of the historical novel injects Prince Edward and his landing in Scotland into *Waverley,* he does nothing to alert you that he is dealing with real persons and real facts. The same can be said when he has Mary Stuart flee from the castle of Lochlevan, Louis XI, king of France, sojourn at Plessiz-les Tours, Richard the Lion-Hearted make his expedition to the Holy Land, and so on. It is the characters and the facts themselves that appear this way; it is they that absolutely demand, and inevitably obtain, that unique, exclusive, and ineffable belief that we give to things taken to be fact. This is a belief that I would call historical, to distinguish it from that other unique, exclusive, and ineffable belief that we lend to things known to be merely verisimilar, and that I call poetic. To tell the truth, the damage had already been done before those characters appeared on the scene. For in picking up a "historical novel," the reader knows well enough that he will find there *facta atque infecta*—things that occurred and things that have been invented, two different objects of two different, fully contrary, sorts of belief. How can you accuse the author of such a work of creating disharmony? How can you demand that he maintain throughout his work a unity that its very title has rejected?

You too might say that I exaggerate your claims, that the fact that there are some inevitable difficulties is no reason to add others; that, even if the unified belief we expect from art cannot be had in full, there is no need to diminish it further; that by alerting the reader or by intimating that a given thing is really true, the author creates historical beliefs that perhaps would not otherwise emerge and that are at cross-purposes with art.

Perhaps; but what is the alternative? One of two things, both in my view just as much at cross-purposes with art: deception or doubt.

Perhaps if the reader had not been told that an event in the novel had actually occurred, he would have accepted and enjoyed it as a nice poetic invention. But is this the purpose of art? A fine endeavor, a fine artistic procedure that would consist, not in creating verisimilitude, but in leaving the reader ignorant that what is presented is real! A nice artistic device, one whose effect would depend upon accidental ignorance! For if, while enjoying the apparent poetic invention, the reader were approached and told, "You know, that is an actual fact, taken from a specific document," the poor man would be brought down with a thud from the poetic skies onto the field of history. Art is art to the extent that it produces, not just any effect, but a definitive one. And if this is so, the view that truth alone is beautiful is not only plausible but profound; for the verisimilar (the raw material of art) once offered and accepted as such, becomes a truth that is altogether different from the real, but one that the mind perceives forever, one whose presence is irrevocable. Though it is an object that might come to be forgotten, it can never be destroyed through disillusionment. A beautiful human figure, conceived by a sculptor, never ceases to be a beautiful specimen of the verisimilar; should the sculpture crumble, so would our chance knowledge of that verisimilar; yet its incorruptible essence would survive. But if at a distance in the twilight someone saw a man standing straight and still on a building among some statues and took the man to be a statue himself, would you call that impression a product of art?

It could also happen that a reader, not told by the author that something particularly drawing his attention is a fact, but suspecting that this might be the case because of the nature or, better, the subject matter of the historical novel, might remain doubtful and hesitate, certainly through no fault of his own, quite against his will. To believe, to believe swiftly, readily, fully, is the wish of every reader, except one who reads to criticize. And we take as much pleasure in believing in the purely verisimilar as in real facts, but—you have said it yourself—with a different, even contrary sort of belief. And still, I might add, one condition must always be met: our mind must be able to identify what is before it in order to lend it the appropriate belief. By concealing the reality in what he tells, the author would, as you might wish, keep the reader from lending it a historical belief, but this at the risk of denying him the chance of any belief. Whatever you may say, this effect also runs counter to the purposes of art; for what is less conducive to the unity and homogeneity of the reader's belief than no belief at all?

It is precisely to prevent both the deception I referred to earlier and this uncertainty, precisely to avoid playing a miserable trick on the reader, and, rather, to respond to a probable wish or tacit question of his, that an author can at times be sorely tempted, almost compelled, to point out reality plainly. It is because he senses how much may be lacking in what he writes when it lacks historical support. I am not saying that he is doing the right thing; I don't deny that he does something directly and plainly contrary to the unity of his work: I am saying that to refrain from doing so would not help achieve that unity. He acts like Molière's poor master Jacques who appears first in the cook's jacket, then in the coachman's shirt, because his master, the Miser, wants him to act in both capacities and he has agreed to it.

Summing up all these pros and cons, we can, I think, now conclude that both critics are right: both those who want historical reality always to be represented as such and those who want a narrative to produce in its reader a unified belief. But both are wrong in wanting both effects from the historical novel, when the first effect is incompatible with its form, which is narrative, and the second is incompatible with its materials, which are heterogeneous. Both critics demand things that are reasonable, even indispensable; but they demand them where they cannot be had.

But if this is the case, then I might expect to hear that, in the final analysis, it is the historical novel itself that is completely at fault.

This is precisely my point. I had hoped to show, and I think I have shown, that the historical novel is a work in which the necessary turns out to be impossible, and in which two essential conditions cannot be reconciled, or even one fulfilled. It inevitably calls for a combination that is contrary to its subject matter and a division contrary to its form. Though we know it is a work in which history and fable must figure, we cannot determine or even estimate their proper measure or relation. In short, it is a work impossible to achieve satisfactorily, because its premises are inherently contradictory. Its critics ask too much of it—but too much in what sense? In terms of its potential? Exactly. But here precisely is its critical flaw. Ordinarily, one should be able to ask that factual truth be recognizable as such and that a narrative evoke a homogeneous belief from its reader. But the fact is that in the historical novel the two are at odds, which is unfortunate for the historical novel because the two are precisely meant to go together. And if we needed proof of this, we could readily find it in one of the two modes of writing that the historical novel counterfeits and corrupts, namely, history. For history in fact sets out to tell real facts and so to produce in the reader a unified belief, the credence we lend to positive truth.

But, it may be asked, can we actually get this out of history? Does history really create in its reader a succession of unproblematic and rational beliefs? Or doesn't it often leave the credulous deceived and the more reflective in doubt? Even apart from any will to deceive, has there ever been a history containing nothing but the clear and honest truth?

History, it is true, does not lack its tall tales, even its lies. But these are the historians' fault and are not endemic to the genre. When we say that a historian is embellishing, that he is making a jumble of fact and invention, that we do not know what to believe, we mean to fault him for something he could have avoided. And after all, he did have an alternative, as simple as it was sure. For what could be simpler than refraining from invention? Do you really think the author of a historical novel has this means available to avoid deceiving his reader?

It is just as clear that even the most conscientious, most meticulous historian will not give us, by a long shot, all the truth or as plain a truth as we might wish. But even here it is not the art of history that is to blame; it is its subject matter. For an art to be good and rational, it need not be able to achieve its aim fully and perfectly: no art does. Good and rational art is an art which sets a sensible objective and uses the most suitable means to achieve it, the means that, when applied to the right material, will achieve it as far as the human intellect allows. It is possible

to obtain and convey, if not perfect knowledge, then at least a reasonably accurate impression about certain real facts, about the human condition in a given time and place. This is what history tries to do, assuming it is in good hands. It may not go as far as one might wish, but it does not willfully drag its feet. It does not overcome all the obstacles—far from it—but it refrains from creating any. If it leaves you sometimes in doubt, that is only because it itself is in doubt. History even makes use of doubt (when something is on the right track, everything suits its purpose). It not only openly confesses doubt but, when necessary, promotes it, sustains it, and attempts to substitute it for false convictions. History makes you doubt because it intends to have you doubt, quite unlike the historical novel which encourages you to believe while at the same time removing what is necessary to sustain belief. In the doubt provoked by history, the mind comes to rest—if not quite at its goal, at least at the limit of its possibilities. Here, it draws satisfaction, so to speak, from a relatively final act, from the only achievement of which it was capable.

The doubt provoked by the historical novel, on the other hand, is disquieting. The mind sees in the subject matter before it the possibility of a further act, the desire for which has been supplied, but the means for which has at the same time been taken away. I suspect there is no author of historical novels, or even of a single historical novel, who has not been asked once or twice whether a certain character, fact, or circumstance was true or invented by him. I also suspect that the author must have said to himself: "Traitor! Your innocent question veils a lethal criticism: you are basically complaining that my book has left you, or, rather, caused you to tug at the author's sleeve. I am well aware that a book should make you want to know more than it tells, but that is a different matter. What you want to know are things of which I have already spoken. You ask me, not to add, but to unravel."

It might not be out of place to mention that history sometimes also uses the verisimilar, and can do so harmlessly if it uses it properly and presents it as such, thereby distinguishing it from the real. It can do this without impairing the narrative unity, for the simple reason that the verisimilar does not really try to become part of the narrative. It is merely suggested, advanced, considered, in short, not narrated on the same level or melded with real facts as is the case in the historical novel. There isn't even any danger that this will ruin the unity of the work, for what more natural bond or continuity is there than that between knowledge and inference? When the mind becomes aware of information that arouses its interest but that is fragmentary or lacking crucial details, it tends to invoke the ideal. The ideal must bear a similar general relationship of possibility with what remains of the real, and also the same particular relationship with it—whether of cause, effect, means, manner, or concomitance—as must have had the real circumstances, whose traces are now gone. It is a characteristic of man's impoverished state that he can know only something of what has been, even in his own little world; and it is an aspect of his nobility and his power that he can conjecture beyond what he can actually know. When history turns to the verisimilar, it does nothing other than favor or promote this tendency. It stops narrating momentarily and uses, instead, inductive reasoning, because ordinary narrative is not the best instrument for this, and in adjusting to a different situation, it adopts a new purpose. In fact, all that is needed to clarify the relationship between fact and verisimilar is that the two appear distinct. History acts almost like someone who, when drawing a city map, adds in a distinctive color the streets, plazas, and buildings planned for the future and who, while distinguishing the potential from the actual, lets us see the logic of the whole. History, at such moments, I would say, abandons narrative, but only in order to produce a better narrative. As much when it conjectures as when it narrates, history points to the real; there lies its unity. Where has the unity of the historical novel gone, or, rather, how can it ever develop a unity while it is wandering between opposing goals?

This question permits me to anticipate another objection, even less well founded, but to be expected since it invariably arises in such discussions. We were talking about the historical novel, so the objection goes, and you are comparing it to history, forgetting that they are two types of work with some similar, but also some completely different, purposes.

Quite clearly, such an objection simply begs the question. Certainly, if the historical novel has an equally logical purpose, but one distinct from that of history, it would be odd to compare it with the purpose and methods of history. But the question is precisely whether the historical novel has a logical and therefore attainable purpose of its own and whether, as a consequence, it can have distinct methods to promote it. The purpose of an art reflects its raw material, that is, its subject matter or, rather, its various subject matters. To understand what is peculiar to a material as handled by one art form is to understand what is peculiar to it as handled by any, actual or potential. Since the historical novel finds one of its sources in the peculiarly historical, it should, to this extent, be compared to history. The fact that one can do nothing with historical truth but represent it plainly as such is not a function of the genre in which it appears; it is a function of historical truth itself. Alchemy too had a purpose of its own, distinct from chemistry's, though of course it remained to be achieved. Alchemy also assumed there was a suitable methodology, if only it could be found. Still, there was no better way to learn about alchemy than to compare its experiments and processes of thought with those of chemistry; both, after all, worked with metals. How strange it would have been to hear, "That is all well and good for chemistry, but this is alchemy."

The historical novel does not have a logical purpose of its own; it counterfeits two, as I have shown. Of course, a recital of its purpose—to represent the human condition in a historical era through invented actions—gives an appearance of unity. But for there to be in fact a rational unity (that is, a correspondence between means and ends), something more is necessary, something that has been gratuitously and falsely assumed. The means, indeed the only means, to represent a human condition (or anything else we want to put into words) is to relate our understanding of it as it has emerged from a variety of facts, certain or probable—with whatever limitations and gaps in here in them, or, rather, in our present ability to know them. It is, in sum, to share with others the final victorious words that we utter to ourselves when things become clearest. This, of course, is the way one writes history, and by histo-

ry I refer not merely to a chronological narration of selected human events but to any orderly and systematic account of them. Such is the history to which I propose to compare the historical novel, justifiably, I think, even if a history like this were still only a possibility. In fact, everyone knows that there are many quite good histories of this kind, whose goal is to reveal not so much the political course of a society at a given time as its way of life from any number of points of view.

Perhaps you find that history, particularly of this sort, still falls short of its goal, still fails to exploit what its subject matter, researched and viewed from a broader and more philosophical perspective, has to offer. Perhaps you find that history has neglected certain facts or entire categories of facts whose importance it failed to perceive, or overlooked certain connections or correlations among facts that it had bothered to collect and report, but then left isolated because, at first sight, they seemed to be isolated. Say so then, but say it to history, because history alone can repair the omission. To any writer who sees the chance to deepen our knowledge about this or that historical moment and is willing to take on the task, I say, Bravo! *Macte animo!* (Bless your courage!) Search every document from that period that you can find. Even treat as documents writings whose authors never, in their wildest imaginations, dreamt they were writing in support of history. Select, discard, connect, contrast, deduce, and infer. If you do, rest assured that you will arrive at a far more precise, more definitive, more comprehensive, more accurate understanding of that historical moment than there was before. But even so, what do you end up with but conceptions only more firmly implanted?

But suppose this writer were not to deal with his readers just as he deals with himself, were not simply to convey to them the pure unadorned knowledge that his painstaking research has earned him. Suppose instead he were to set it aside, dismantle it privately, and reconstruct it, along with material of a totally different nature, into something bigger and better? Suppose to make it more vital, he were to make it live two different lives and take as a means what before was strictly an end? But the very nature of these materials does not allow them to be enlisted to serve such alien ends. They tend to do promptly their own bidding, not the bidding of others. The resulting compound hardly produces a more complete representation of a real human condition; it does not even produce the incomplete one that a faithful account of the facts would yield. For positive truth exists for the human mind only to the extent that it is known, and it cannot be known unless it can be distinguished from what it is not. In short, trying to represent positive truth by enlarging it with the verisimilar only serves to diminish it, to efface it in part. I have heard an old story, perhaps even true, about a man who was more frugal than intelligent, who imagined that he could double the oil for burning by adding to it equal parts of water. He knew enough not to simply pour the water on top of the oil, for surely it would sink to the bottom and the oil would float. But he thought he could, by stirring and beating it well, succeed in making it a homogeneous liquid. He beat and beat, and managed to make of it an awful mess that ran together and filled the oil lamp. But now it was worthless. It was no longer oil; indeed, as far as giving off light was concerned, it was less than nothing. This our friend realized as soon as he tried to light the wick.

I have saved for last the most considerable and inexorable objection to my position: the facts. All these ideas, I can hear myself saying, make for lovely theories; but the facts upset them all. To give one example, it would be difficult to name, from among both modern and ancient works, many read more widely and with greater pleasure and esteem than the historical novels of a certain Walter Scott. Try as you may to prove that these novels ought not succeed, the fact is they do.

This objection is weighty in appearance only, however, for its power depends entirely on a confusion, on calling something definitive that is still subject to change. That those novels please the public, and rightly so, is an undeniable fact, but it may be true of those particular novels without being true of the historical novel in general. That this genre will continue to find favor, and therefore be written, is more a question than a fact. In this respect, as in so many others, truth for one era is no guarantee of truth for all time. All too many, and too well known, are the judgments of one age that have been revised by those of another. And if, in citing these revisions of judgments so often and with such contempt, we risk giving new judgments, the reason is that we naturally find our present-day decisions more mature, more authoritative, more definitive than those that came before. And this is hardly surprising, for they are our own. What allows us to scorn judgments of the past is that we are the future; this is no small matter. What allows us to have confidence in our own judgments is that we are the present; and this is no less a matter.

Among the well-known examples to which I alluded, however, let me single out one that is especially analogous to our subject. There has probably been no greater vogue than that of the historical-heroic-erotic novels—I find it hard to settle on a single name—of Mlle Scudéry and of other less famous precursors and successors of hers, in a country and century no less cultivated than the France of Louis XIV. We might cite Boileau's confession, in his introduction to the dialogue deprecating those novels, that, "being young when they were the rage, [he] had read them, as indeed everyone read them, with great admiration, and held them to be masterpieces of the French language."

Of course, it would be even more an eccentricity than an injustice to treat such works as the equals of Walter Scott's. But, for all that separates the authors and the literary genres, there is, as I have suggested, an analogy, even an important point of identity: both are kinds of novels in which history has a role. And let it not be said that those earlier novels only make a pretense of invoking history, almost as a joke, or that no one would possibly think of history in reading those strange sequences of mad and platonic loves or the even stranger speeches and quarrels about them. For how strange it would have seemed to the otherwise quite tolerant readers of *Clélia,* which after all was once very popular and is still even occasionally remembered, had Mlle Scudéry given the name of Virginia to the woman assaulted by Sextus Tarquinius, or made Porsena a king of Macedonia or even of Cisalpine Gaul, or had had Clélia throw herself into the Euphrates or even the Po to swim away from the enemy camp. These earlier readers were not utterly indifferent to the truthfulness of the history that entered into such works; they were only much

more tolerant than present-day readers would be. They did pay attention to history when they read these novels, and why not? After all, if the public accepted and enjoyed works in which history played a vital part and supplied the basics of plot and character as well as time and place, we can only conclude that it wanted history to be there. And the public could scarcely want history to be there without paying attention to it. Still, it must be admitted that readers then paid less attention to it than present-day readers do.

Now, did this change come about suddenly, all at once? It was not at all like that, nor could it have been. The public's tolerance diminished gradually. It demanded ever more history and, with it, ever greater historical detail. This was so not only with the ephemeral and rather silly kind of composition I have been referring to but with all works consisting of history and invention. I am not talking about a steady, continuous process, about a uniform trend; but, beyond the temporary halts and random backward steps that always take place in the development of ideas and events, this was the overall direction, the dominant course. As the tolerance of the public declined—partly as a result of this and partly aside from it, but always because of the same underlying desire for historical truth—writers grew less bold. To an extent, the public (in which professional critics naturally figure prominently) demonstrated, whether by criticism or simple neglect, that it would no longer tolerate extreme alterations of history, thereby forcing writers to include more actual history and greater historical detail. To an extent, the writers themselves, whether by reflecting on their art in the abstract or simply sensing more keenly than ever the critical importance of historical truth in the practice of writing, found new ways to give it prominence in their works. For a while, as always happens with solutions to problems that at the time seem momentous, each of these theoretical or practical responses seemed adequate. But then the demand for historical truth that, for reasons both independent of art and within art itself, continued to grow in the process just described, led to still newer needs and a search for still newer solutions. Each successive solution was a fact, none *the* fact. Each adjustment was progress; none was, or could have been, the destination. For nothing (and we always return to this point) can be the final destination on the path of historical truth but, relatively speaking of course, total and pure historical truth. When parts are alike, improving one strengthens the whole; when they are not alike, improving one destroys it.

With this, I am ready to make explicit what is implied in all I have said up to now, namely, that the historical novel is hardly unique in the inherent contradiction of its premises and in its resulting inability to take on a convincing and stable form. I would not join those who have called it or now call it a false and spurious genre. To me, this view rests upon the entirely erroneous assumption that the way had been found to combine history and invention and that it had worked, but the historical novel came along and ruined it. The fact is the historical novel is not a false genre, but a species of a false genre which includes all compositions that try to mix history and invention, whatever their form. Being the most modern such species, the historical novel is only the most refined and ingenious effort yet to meet the challenge, as if the challenge could ever be met. (pp. 63-81)

Alessandro Manzoni, in his On the Historical Novel, *translated by Sandra Bermann, University of Nebraska Press, 1984, 134 p.*

E. M. Clerke   (essay date 1882)

[*In the following excerpt, Clerke provides an overview of Manzoni's major works, focusing on themes, techniques, and Manzoni's struggle to find an Italian idiom appropriate for literary expression.*]

In each of Manzoni's triad of important works, is a leading idea, referable to a distinct stage of Italian history. *Il conte di Carmagnola* is directed against civil discords, the curse of Italy in the past; *Adelchi* against foreign domination, her existing scourge when it was written; while in *I promessi sposi* looms up more dimly the question of the future, not for Italy alone, but for the world—the aspirations of the masses for enfranchisement and equality. Thus drama is ever with him the vehicle for conveying social speculation. In the two first works the author's protest is spoken by a chorus of the people, while in the third it finds no separate articulate utterance, but is the underlying motive of the plot. In the dramas the sentiment thus conveyed jars with the heroic action of the piece, and conflicts with its main interest, showing a strange duality in the author's sympathy—now identified with his principal personages, now with this collective, impersonal voice of the multitude, expressing feelings hostile to theirs.

Francesco Bussone, the hero of the first piece, is a historical character, who, born at Carmagnola in 1390, in the condition of a shepherd-boy, rose to eminence as a soldier of fortune in the service of Filippo Maria Visconti. This prince, whose power he was mainly instrumental in consolidating, became jealous of him for that very reason, and by a variety of affronts disgusted him with his service, and drove him to enter that of Venice. The tragedy opens with the war in which he is engaged against his former employer, and in which he is at first victorious. His clemency in releasing the prisoners of war, and his slackness in pursuit of the foe, excite suspicions of double dealing on his part, and after a series of intrigues he is inveigled into Venice and executed as a traitor, by orders of the jealous government of the Republic. The drama follows literally the historical facts, save in deciding in favour of its hero the doubtful point of his guilt or innocence. Its subject recalls that of *Wallenstein,* which doubtless suggested it. Despite two fine scenes, in one of which Carmagnola orders the release of the prisoners, in defiance of the Venetian commissioners, and in another takes leave of his wife and daughter on the eve of his execution, the drama is deficient in interest as a whole. It wants the organic vitality resulting from a culminating point of action, and resembles too much a narrative in dialogue. The chorus, interpolated at the end of the second act, and spoken by imaginary spectators of the battle, is an invective against civil bloodshed, and thus traverses the general current of the action, whose central figure is a soldier of fortune. Fine as a lyric, it is dramatically irrelevant, and contrasts in this respect with Max Piccolomini's splendid panegyric on peace in Wallenstein, which, springing from his newborn love for Thekla, is artistically justified as connected with the main action of the piece. The writer of an article on "Italian Tragedy," in the *Quarterly Review,* for December, 1820, though gen-

erally unfavourable to the author, calls this chorus "the most noble piece of Italian lyric poetry which the present day has produced," and subjoins a translation of it *in extenso.*

The subject of *Adelchi* is likewise taken from Italian history, and is furnished by the invasion of Italy and overthrow of the Lombard kingdom by Charlemagne, in 772-4. Adelchi, or Adalgiso, is a Lombard prince, who performs prodigies of valour in defending the kingdom of his father, Desiderio, holding the invaders at bay at Le Chiuse, a line of impregnable fortifications, stretching across the head of the Val di Susa. The Franks are on the point of abandoning the enterprise in despair, when an emissary from the Pope arrives in their camp, by untrodden paths over the mountains, and leads them, by the same route, to the rear of the Lombard position. The feelings of the enslaved Latins, on witnessing the subsequent rout of their oppressors, are described in the chorus, which is thus open to the same criticism as that in *Carmagnola,* of awakening a counter strain of sympathy opposed to that felt for the hero Adelchi. Its effect depends very much on the rhythm, difficult to reproduce in English, but which in the original suggests at once weight and swiftness, like the moving thunder of a galloping horse. (pp. 289-91)

The treachery of the Lombard chiefs, during the sieges of Pavia and Verona, occupy the succeeding acts, the tragedy concluding with the captivity of Desiderio, and the death of Adelchi, who in reality escaped to Constantinople. The fate of his sister Ermengarda, divorced by Charlemagne, and dying of a broken heart, interweaves an element of romance amid the story of battles and sieges, but is almost extraneous to the rest of the action. Her delirious ravings on hearing of her husband's marriage with her rival Ildegarde are finely conceived. . . . But, despite many fine passages, the interest of the drama is marred by want of concentration, the catastrophe being protracted over a battle and two sieges. Manzoni's dramatic power was far inferior to his lyrical gift, but it is his prose that has made him immortal. Here he has perhaps never been surpassed in the graphic power of creating, by a few simple words, pictures which live in the reader's memory for ever, like part of his own actual experience. The pages of *I promessi sposi,* are thus, as it were, strewn with vignettes, a whole scene being suggested by a few touches; now landscapes, like Renzo's overgrown and deserted vineyard, or the village sleeping in the moonlight; now interiors like Don Ferrante's library, or the convent parlour at Monza. Amid these minor gems of genre-painting, great tragic scenes, such as the plague-stricken city, the "Lazzaretto" of Milan, the castle of the "Innominato," stand out in solemn perspective, like the larger features of a landscape, overshadowing the minute details of the foreground.

In his character-drawing Manzoni has a like equality of touch; and the slight sketches of the minor personages of his tale have the same masterly finish relatively to their scale, as the great historical portraits of Cardinal Borromeo and the "Innominato," in right of which he may rank as the Titian of literature. The very supernumeraries of the drama, represented in other works by the merest lay figures, never flit across his pages without leaving some trace of their individuality; and even the garrulous convent porter, who only speaks once as he opens the door for Lucia's mother, has as distinct a personality as the noble figure of Fra Cristoforo himself. Yet Manzoni's detail is never trivial, nor his homeliness vulgar; for we have in him the true artistic discrimination, whose end is always so perfectly attained as to justify its means, however ordinary.

We have seen how he rises to his highest level of eloquence in his tragedies, when interpreting, in lyrical form, the collective feelings of a multitude; and again in his romance, his power is perhaps most fully displayed in the manipulation of masses of men, moving together in obedience to a common impulse, yet formed of incongruous, and often discordant, elements; for he never loses his grasp on the separate units, whilst combining them in single action, putting perfectly before us that multiple personality of a crowd, whose corporate volition is the incalculable sum of many varying individual emotions. The aimless surging of the human tide, moved by contrary currents of opinion, the power of blind caprices, working on many minds in common, the compound instincts of a multitude, have never been so thoroughly realized as in the description of the bread riots in Milan, and the mob-siege of the Forno delle Grucce. We can better illustrate this form of power by a dramatic than by a literary parallel; for we have recently seen on the stage a similar rendering of tumultuous action. The Forum scene in *Julius Cæsar,* as represented by the Saxe Meiningen company of tragedians, when the Roman mob seethes and sways in growing and gathering multitudinous passion under the ferment of Mark Antony's eloquence, resembles Manzoni's description of the riots in Milan, in the way in which the heterogeneous constitution of the crowd, and the individuality of each of its component items, is kept in sight, simultaneously with its homogeneity of general impulse.

The literary parallel that immediately suggests itself for this portion of Manzoni's novel, is the description of the Porteous riot in Edinburgh, one of the best known passages in the *Heart of Midlothian.* But, on analysis of the aims of the authors, we find that no true comparison is possible. What Scott sought to describe was not a miscellaneous chance accumulation of humanity; but a multitude united by a preconcerted purpose, and organized and mustered for its execution like an army. Solid force, dominated by a single impulse too deep and strong to need superficial expression, was the effect here to be produced, requiring the elimination of the ordinary signs of mob-violence. Thus the artistic problem was the reverse of Manzoni's, and had to be solved by opposite means. The following analysis by the latter of the elements of a popular disturbance is a profound study of gregarious humanity.

> In popular tumults there are always a certain number of individuals who, either from the excitement of passion, fanatical conviction, deliberate wickedness, or a diabolical love of disturbance, constitute the force for pushing matters to extremes; proposing and promoting the most violent counsels, blowing the flames when they show signs of subsiding; for such as these nothing is too bad, and they would wish to see neither limit or end to tumult. But, by way of counterpoise, there are always an equal number of others, who work, perhaps, with like ardour and perseverance in an opposite direction; urged, some by friendliness or partiality for those in danger, some without other motive than a pious and spontaneous horror of atrocities and bloodshed. May Heaven reward them! Between the

members of these two parties, conformity of will, even without previous concert, creates an unpremeditated unanimity in acts. What constitutes then the mass, and, as it were, the raw material of the tumult, is a miscellaneous collection of individuals, attached more or less through indefinite gradations to one or other extreme; part excited, part cunning; inclined for a certain measure of justice, as they understand it, or hankering after the sight of some striking act of wickedness; ready for ferocity or mercy, for adoration or execration, according as the occasion offers for experiencing one or other emotion to the uttermost; craving every moment to hear and believe something wonderful, eager to shout, to cheer, or howl for somebody. "Long life!" and "Speedy death!" are the cries they are most ready to utter, and he who succeeds in persuading them that a man does not deserve to be quartered, need not spend much more breath in order to convince them that he is worthy of being chaired; actors, spectators, instruments, obstacles, according to the prevailing current; ready even to be silent if no one gives them the cue to speak; to desist, when instigators are wanting; to disband, when many unanimous voices have said without contradiction, "let us go;" and then to return home, asking one another what it was all about. As this mass, however, disposes of the greatest force, nay, is that force itself, each of the two active parties uses every effort to win it over, to gain possession of it; they are like two contending souls striving to enter into that great body, and direct its movements. They vie with each other as to which shall disseminate the rumours most likely to stimulate passions, to direct impulses, in favour of one or the other purpose; shall get up the cries which excite or allay indignation, beget hopes or fears; shall invent the watchword, that, repeated by voices growing in number and loudness, shall at once, declare, attest, and create the vote of the plurality for one side or the other.

On the tumultuous background of such a crowd as this, Manzoni paints with masterly touches the portrait of the old courtier, Antonio Ferrer, as he shows at his carriage window, "that face of humble, complaisant, obsequious benignity, which he had hitherto reserved for those occasions on which he found himself in presence of his master Don Philip IV., but was now obliged to spend in propitiating the infuriated mob of Milan."

The helpless and uncertain crowd of villagers, roused by the night alarm, the groups in wayside taverns, the gathering knots in the streets of Milan, "like the scattered clouds chasing across the sky after a storm, which make people look up shaking their heads, and say, 'the weather is not settled;' " all such aggregations of human atoms, are described by him with like vivacity and force, while they never impede or confuse the action of the principal characters. We have dwelt principally upon this power of grouping masses of men, because it seems to us Manzoni's typical characteristic among novelists; doubtless derived from that philosophical tendency of his mind which balanced the poetical temperament, and gave him the power of regarding humanity in its social, as well as in its individual aspects.

Goethe, in his preface to an edition of our author's poetical works, published at Jena in 1827, defines lyrical poetry as the highest form of rhetoric, and says he knew no modern poet so qualified to excel in it as Manzoni. Of the lesser pieces which come under this head, *Il cinque maggio,* is incomparably the finest, ranking as it does as the most popular lyric in Italy. (pp. 292-96)

The fame attained by these spirited stanzas astonished no one more than their writer, who declared long afterwards that he was quite unprepared "for the hit made by that ode, full of gallicisms and latinisms." It established him at once in the position of the first lyric poet in Italy, yet was followed by no other effort in the same line.

But Manzoni's influence on Italian literature cannot be measured by the amount of printed matter he produced. The magnitude of his task lay in the fact, that he had to mould the language in which he wrote, by a new creation of Italian prose, in a form adapted to the exigencies of modern literature. For it had been the fate of the idiom of his country to be always written as an artificial coinage, from the fourteenth-century writers, who first forged it as an instrument of culture out of the raw material of the spoken dialect, through all their followers, who aiming at imitating their diction, kept the language in a state of pupilage, cut off from its vital spring in the life of the people. Deprived thus of all power of growth or expansion, it was reduced to a mere literary *argot,* a fit vehicle for the utterances of scholiasts and pedants, but not for the expression of human emotion. The laws by which its bondage was enforced were of a puerility incredible to foreigners, while their violation was punished by literary ostracism. Meantime in Tuscany alone was it spoken in a familiar form, while, through the rest of Italy, varying dialects were the means of oral communication. The literary language was, and is, learned by the cultured classes as matter of education, but remains scarcely less remote from their daily thoughts, than Latin from those of a well-educated Englishman.

Now, down to Manzoni's time, the principal staples of literature, poetry and drama, abstract treatises and historical works, were of a nature to be written with more or less difficulty, out of dictionaries and vocabularies. With a novel, the principal creation of romanticism, the case is different, since dealing with every-day life in its minutest details, it requires the command of familiar expression, such as is learned, in Giusti's phrase, only "from the living dictionary on two legs." How, in Italian, was such a form of utterance to be attained was the problem which occupied Manzoni's thoughts all through his career, and which he sought to solve by grafting the dead branch of literary convention on the growing trunk of the spoken idiom of Tuscany; substituting the *uso fiorentino,* the living custom of Florence, for all the rules of grammars and vocabularies, as the highest standard of philological fitness. This linguistic revolution was the main work of his life. (p. 298)

Now Manzoni's position on entering the field of letters was this. He had no full command of any literary language, writing Italian by a *tour de force,* as one does a foreign tongue or dead language, while the natural expression of his thoughts was in Milanese dialect; and having once published a prefatory treatise on the drama, in what passed as very fair French, he declares that he found it far easier to write that language than Italian. In an appendix to his report on the Unity of the Language, he declares the difficulties attendant on the composition of *I promessi sposi,* were such as "would move to pity," giving a vivid picture of his blind groping in his memory, and in books, for the Italian equivalents for phrases, which presenting themselves in dialect, or in Latin, or in a foreign language, had to be "driven away as temptations."

Written under these difficulties, *I promessi sposi,* particularly in its opening chapters, bears evident traces of poverty of language in its author. The style, indeed, is everywhere forcible from the innate vigour of the ideas expressed; but they seem rather to force the language to fit them than to be naturally or easily clothed by it, and the effect produced is like that of one of Michael Angelo's great unfinished statues, in which the original energy of the conception struggles through the rough hewn block, despite its want of finer shaping. Manzoni himself was so keenly alive to this imperfection in his work that he undertook a laborious course of study to enable him to correct it. . . .

The result of these labours was the revised and Tuscanized edition of *I promessi sposi,* published serially in 1840-42. (p. 300)

It seems not unlikely that in this difficulty of expression we have the clue to the otherwise unexplained mystery of Manzoni's early cessation from literary activity, as well as of the comparative sterility of Italian Romanticism subsequently, down even to the present time. The language is not yet nationalized, seems indeed, almost as far as ever from being so, and literary productiveness during the transition stage is not to be looked for. *I promessi sposi* was written by a herculean effort, such as required, perhaps, the first vigour of the author's mind, and would scarcely be repeated after the initial impulse of his creative genius had spent itself. It thus remains the unapproached masterpiece and monument of a whole epoch of letters. (p. 301)

Perhaps we cannot better sum up the effect produced by Manzoni's writings as a whole than by narrating an anecdote told by Signor Martini, one of his countrymen. When travelling in the neighbourhood of Heidelberg his attention was caught by the sound of his native language, and he came upon two women of the lower class, mother and daughter, engaged in reading aloud and laboriously spelling out *I promessi sposi.* Entering into conversation with them, he asked them if they admired Manzoni, "We love him," was the emphatic reply.

Nowhere, indeed, do we identify the man and the author more completely than in the works of Manzoni, and the impression of a vivid and loveable personality made by them, is one secret of their undying charm. The lover of humanity, he makes himself beloved by it in turn, wins sympathy by sympathy, and makes his way to the intelligence through the affections. A singular combination of intellectual and moral gifts, a mind in complete harmony with itself, a perfect balance of judgment and imagination, of poetic impulse and philosophical self-control, a character disciplined by religion, a heart sound to the core, were no small part of the endowments of the great novelist; giving us as their sum in *I promessi sposi* a perfect work, the fulfilment and expression of a stainless life. (p. 302)

E. M. Clerke, "Alessandro Manzoni and His Works," in The Dublin Review, *Vol. VIII, No. II, fourth quarter, 1882, pp. 273-302.*

Benedetto Croce   (essay date 1924)

[*Croce was an Italian philosopher, historian, editor, and literary critic whose writings span the first half of the twentieth century. He founded and edited the literary and political journal* La critica *(1903-1944), noted for its independence, objectivity, and strong stand against fascism. According to Croce, the only proper form of literary history is the* caratteristica, *or critical characterization, of the poetic personality and work of a single artist; its goal is to demonstrate the unity of the author's intention, its expression in the creative work, and the reader's response. In the following excerpt, Croce asserts that Manzoni's moral vision determines characterization, theme, and form in* The Betrothed.]

Giovita Scalvini, in his essay of 1829 on the *Promessi sposi,* noted that in this romance there is something uniform and insistent, that we do not feel ourselves "wandering freely amid the great variety of the moral world," and are often aware of being "not beneath the great dome of the firmament," which covers "all multiform existences," but beneath that of "the temple which covers the faithful and the altar."

This judgment, although later repeated or renewed by others, who deprived it of its vigour and truth by imparting to it their party passions, was due to an undeniably clear impression by its first author. In my opinion, it deserves to be more profoundly studied and more minutely defined, because it throws open the way to the correct critical interpretation of one of the greatest masterpieces of our literature.

Whence comes this sense of narrowness which one seems sometimes to experience when reading the *Promessi sposi,* but more especially when Manzoni is compared with other poets? We are not made to feel any of what are called the human affections and passions in their full force and in their full development in that romance. The effort towards the truth, the obsession of doubt, the desire for happiness, the ravishment of the infinite, the dream of beauty and dominion, the joys and sorrows of love, the drama of politics and history, the ideals and memorials of peoples and so forth, which supply material for other poets, are not to be found here.

It is not because the author had no experience or knowledge of these things that they are absent; but he has surpassed and subjected them to a superior will, for he has risen above the tumult and has reached calmness and wisdom. And what wisdom! Not the wisdom that feels sympathetically the different human passions, yet remains above them, assigning to each its place and arranging them harmoniously. No, Manzoni's is the wisdom of the moralist, who sees nothing but black and white, on one side justice, on the other injustice; on one side goodness, on the other evil; here innocence, yonder malice; reason on the one side, wickedness and fatuity on the other; approving the one and blaming the other, often with the subtle considerations of the casuist. The world, so various in colour and sound, so closely related in all its parts, so inexhaustible and so profound, becomes simplified, not to say impoverished in his vision. One only of the innumerable strings of the soul vibrates here and the very fact of its being alone gave Scalvini the impression of the uniform and persistent. (pp. 145-46)

The narrowness noted by Scalvini was not due to [Manzoni's] faith, but, on the contrary, to the consequences which Manzoni deduced from it, the rigidly moral point of view to which he believed it right to assign the first place as master of his soul. If it had been possible for Vico, whom he had studied during this first period and whom he had always living and present in his mind, to be at once a pious believer and a great realistic historian, Manzoni might also have been a believer and a poet of passion, as he had already shown himself to be, and as he was capable of becoming ever more completely. Manzoni's was on the whole a romantic soul; he was not merely a moderate literary reformer in the name of certain romantic doctrines.

But we have said: "he might have," as a way of making understood what was then his state of mind. He could not really do this, because all his mental and moral qualities urged him to give a different direction to his imagination. On the one hand, then, he was always bound to chasten his various feelings and passions, to depress, to veil and to leave visible only that part of them consistent of moral effects; on the other, to proceed to free himself from the incubus of history, of history as something serious, as the sole reality or as the reality of which it was necessary to take account. Instead of history, he would have preserved the simple notation of historical facts as resulting from good and evil, and rather from evil than from good, looking upon them rather as mere proofs of human unhappiness, stupidity and folly. This implied that he would have gone more and more in the direction of the transcendental both in sympathy and imagination, he would have inhabited the world beyond as the sole form of the rational life, while regarding the world below as a vale of error and of trial. The end of this passage is represented by the *Promessi sposi,* which is to be described as the work of Manzoni's full maturity, the work in which he attained the completest coherence, but rather from the moral than from the poetical point of view.

This coherence was certainly practical and moral and not logical, representing a sureness and firmness of outlook independent of logic because a critical consideration of Manzoni reveals his manifold rifts. I shall not delay to point them out here, whether because they have already been brought to light by myself and others criticizing Manzoni's theories as to history, art, language, the moral life, and so on, or because a critic of Manzoni's philosophy would easily lose himself in general considerations, such as a criticism of Christianity and of transcendentalism, and more especially of Catholicism and neo-Catholicism. These contradictions would also be discovered in the *Promessi sposi* by anyone who had sufficiently bad taste to treat that work as reality rather than fable and attack it—which would be about the same thing as to attack a Greek god resplendent in his white marble—because there too all is willed and set in motion by the Omnipotent, and nevertheless individuals are conceived as *causæ sui.*

Manzoni's victory over human feelings and affections in the *Promessi sposi,* which he has subordinated to ethical feeling, does not result in these feelings and affections being abolished or cancelled, but by subjecting endows them all with a like impress, or if another image be preferred, clears and colours them, throwing the light of a single torch, the torch of morality, upon the shadows which surround them. Hence his peculiar mode of drawing characters, of setting them in action and of narrating events. When critics have lamented that the characters of the *Promessi sposi* have not the immediacy, the spontaneity and the freedom from restraint of Shakespeare's characters, they have fallen into a misunderstanding, even if they are called Francesco de Sanctis. The personages of the tragedy are Shakespearean, for Adelchi has something of Hamlet and Ermengarda belongs to the family of the Ophelias, Cordelias and Desdemonas. But the personages of the *Promessi sposi* cannot be Shakespearean, the Lucias, the Christophers and the Innominati, owing to the great diversity of sentiment in this work from the tragical cosmic sentiment of Shakespeare. For this reason, in the best of circumstances, such a comparison does not point to a high and a low level of artistic achievement, but to a difference in quality. Everything must be well defined in the *Promessi sposi,* because, whereas in Shakespeare the world is in the power of the forces that form it and transform it, in Manzoni it is supported and corrected by the moral ideal. In the *Promessi sposi,* notwithstanding the marvellous descriptions of countries, of aspects of nature, of journeys (suffice it to recall Renzo's flight to join Adda or his return to his own country and stay at Milan), there are no landscape effects to note, such as are to be found even in the works of minor Italian artists, contemporaries of Manzoni, such as Tommaseo. I am pleased to see that Momigliano, the most recent historian and critic of Manzoni, has understood that "whoever has penetrated into the spiritual organism of Manzoni and therefore sees the whole reflected in the parts, feels the breath of faith even in the page descriptive of the storm, forerunner of the end of the pest." I should not, on the other hand, be prepared to admit that the *Promessi sposi* is a religious poem, as is now quite the fashion to proclaim it, or at any rate not without making the reservation that it is a poem inspired by religious morality, the world perceived by a firmly convinced moralist, which amounts to a more restricted definition of the above saying.

In this respect, Manzoni's method of treating love has especial importance. He clearly shows that he had descended into the abyss to which it may lead and had cast upon it the profound regard of the searcher, as is to be seen in the episode of Ermengarda, but now in the *Promessi sposi,* he has for love a feeling of vigilant suspicion, tinged with disdain. I find it said by him in a posthumous publication that love should not be treated of in such a manner as to lead the reader of the story to indulge himself in that passion: there is more love in the world than is necessary and we should not re-kindle it with our books.

In the *Promessi sposi,* love is either nothing but a natural feeling, which morality surrounds and renders innocuous and purifies by means of the priest's blessing upon the blessed union—in this case it is spoken of with indulgence and compassion and the smile we have for the childishness of children, as in the case of the innocent yet very dangerous loves of Renzo and Lucia; or as in the case of the nun of Monza, where love is a violent passion and is represented as an evil leading to perdition draped in black: "The unfortunate nun replied."

As a fact, love is the irrational-rational, the most direct symbol of life, a mingling of self-love and of self-sacrifice, of voluptuous delirium and of fruitful toil, of weakness and of strength, a fount of purification, or a vortex of im-

purity: in love, man is dominated by nature, yet he affirms himself to be man as he lifts his gaze to heaven. If we look at love from the point of view of passionate love, we shall look at it from the opposite point of view to that of Manzoni and of the moralist, who judge it according to their conscience and moral will. Another poet of the will and of searchings of the conscience, Pierre Corneille, profoundly different from Manzoni both in historical surroundings and in mental qualities, but here resembling the author of the *Promessi sposi,* exhibits a like avoidance of the representation of love.

It is thus plainly understood that the personages of Manzoni's new drama, the *Promessi sposi,* should answer to his new form of inspiration and incorporate the moral activity in its thesis and antithesis. But for this very reason, we are wrong in holding them, as is often done even by De Sanctis, to be "constructed," that is to say, "constructed" according to types and therefore not poetical but intellectualistic. The fact remains that they are not typical, but perfectly individualized, each one with his proper elements of humanity, his own defects, his own faults, his own virtues. Lucia is a good religious soul, but in her eternal search for the right path she sometimes allows herself to be persuaded and disarmed by others without feeling that displeasure which she should feel. She proposes, for instance, to fulfil her vow to the Virgin, but all the same does not succeed in removing Renzo from her heart. Fra Cristoforo turns his fervent blood to good account, though it once led him to commit homicide, and sometimes restrains himself with difficulty. The cardinal Federico Borromeo, strong as he is, yet feels his own weakness and the miserable and terrible condition of mankind, which never altogether succeeds in equating being and the duties of being; wise as he is, he shares in the prejudices of his time.

Don Rodrigo, who represents the other extreme, brings to the persecution of Lucia almost as much punctilio, or misplaced sense of honour, as of brutal caprice. He has the gifts of a perfect gentleman, master of his acts and deeds, and feels remorse in the depths of his soul for the evil which he is led to commit. Similarly, the father of Geltrude, so hard and merciless in his treatment of his daughter, is not a wicked man but a maniac as regards the splendour and beauty of his own house. Where, indeed, is there any trace of the typically good or evil in all these personages? At the utmost, it is possible to detect here and there, but very rarely, in Manzoni's way of presenting them, some slight excess of insistence, an insignificant work, such as is found in every work of art. The truth is that the accusation of typicity or abstractness bestowed upon Manzoni's virtuous or vicious personages is nothing but a new form of the erroneous comparison of his art with some other form of art. Whoever wishes to test the truth of this assertion should place himself at the centre of Manzoni's inspiration and then attempt to think of a way in which his characters could have been better embodied and made to live. He will find that he will never be able to conceive of them as different from Manzoni's conception and realization. Every placing of the accent elsewhere will turn out to be discordant; every heightening of the colour or retouching of the design, a blot. We turn away with horror from the idea of some one who would like to hear the story of the love and crime of the nun of Monza told in the language of a Flaubert or a Zola or to see a little of the sensuality that another Catholic writer (a Catholic of a fantastic kind), Fogazzaro, has poured into his romances, introduced into the *Promessi sposi.*

The critics who tend to diminish to a greater or less degree the value of Manzoni's lofty characters, lofty in good and evil, are really making use of another standard of comparison of an internal nature: that which they draw from another order of characters to be found in the *Promessi sposi,* which they call "medium" and in whom they see the best of his art. Such are the more or less comical personages, or rather those that are comically treated, of whom Don Abbondio is the chief. The number and vivacity of these last are really great, and when we consider them after having considered the series of the others, it would seem as if Manzoni possesses the soul of a La Rochefoucauld, indeed of a Voltaire, who should have become more dexterous and alert in discovering human frailties owing to experience as a confessor and inquisitor and perhaps a tormentor of himself, but who has not by any means lost on that account his gaiety and vigour of comic imagination. And all this on the top of a soul equal to that of a Bossuet or a Bourdaloue as he reveals it in the treatment of his chief personages.

This coupling of contraries finds its explanation in Manzoni's form of spiritual culture, for he was first an encyclopædist and a man of the enlightenment and afterwards a Catholic not without traces of Jansenism. He may thus be said to have harboured a double historical heredity in his singular temperament. This double heredity found a common basis in moral polemics in the name of reason or rationalistic religion and developed logically as though from a single root, because moralism, when it posits an ideal, posits at the same time the images of those that incarnate and of those that oppose it, of those that would wish to incarnate it but do not succeed, or do not incarnate it but pretend to have done so, by means of fictions in relation to others and sophisms in relation to themselves, and so on through an infinite series of instances and degrees; and for this reason we find bracketed on one side the noble or the base, and on the other the comical. But it is difficult, when the mind is fixed upon the one class, to include the other at the same time, or to allow equal merit to both classes.

Manzoni was further always disposed to accomplish the second of the two tasks, and did so gladly, because, as he observes at a certain point in the narrative, "we are all ready to do the things we feel we can do," and having thus quieted his conscience by means of a logical justification, he indulged very freely in satire and irony. We find this especially marked in the character of Don Abbondio, whom he pursues from the beginning to the end of the story, turning him about first on one side and then on the other, never leaving him in peace, and in general in his promptitude everywhere to seize upon tentative attempts, struggles, second thoughts, hidden intentions, the most fugitive and subtle and complicated movements of egoism, of vanity, of fear, and the tortuous complications of passionate reasoning, thrusting them into clear light, which prevents them from concealing or veiling themselves any longer.

Even history is carried away by this comic vein: history which in the first period of Manzoni's art had excited a serious interest in him, as history of the barbaric invasions or of dark Venetian policy or of Napoleon's triumphant warlike course across Europe. But now he proceeds to describe a time which lends itself better to ridicule, the decadent state of Italy when it came under Spanish rule, "both crude and affected." In Manzoni's eyes, that period, which was not without its positive factual value, shows itself, rather than anything else, as a welter of extravagances, follies, blunders and bad reasonings. He treats it, as he had treated Don Abbondio, with the same ferocity of implacable derision, and it is chiefly due to him and to his extreme application of Voltaire's methods that the seventeenth century has assumed a grotesque burlesque aspect in the eyes of readers.

But can we truly say that Manzoni had greater aptitude for the comic than for the serious, the moving and the sublime? Did he succeed in it better? Do the anecdotes and portraits of Don Abbondio and of Don Ferrante, of Donna Prassede and of the avuncular Count, of Perpetua and Friar Galdino and of the worthy tailor with a smattering of letters and the like, succeed in throwing the scene of Fra Cristoforo's pardon or the night of crisis of the Innominato or the lofty colloquies of the cardinal Frederick or the terrible and piteous description of the plague into the shade? Is not the fact rather that the method of the comical and serious parts is intrinsically the same, the pathos of the moral judgment? Is not the preference generally shown for the comic parts of the *Promessi sposi* due to no other motive than the greater facility for laughter in comparison with the concentration of mind required for the contemplation of duty and of suffering?

Not only is the artistic value of the two elements that flow together in the *Promessi sposi* equal, but they are in relation and harmony with one another. And he who arranges them thus harmoniously is the author, too critical not to be autocritical, too acute and too satirical an observer of others not to be diffident towards himself, too full of the sense of ridicule not to avoid with care the ridicule that would result from emphasis, preaching, pious unction, from any sort of exaggeration. Hence the tone of the *Promessi sposi,* so simple yet so measured, able to rise to the sphere of the most sublime emotion, but careful always to place the foot upon firm ground in order to avoid falling from the heights, which should be climbed gradually and gradually descended. The perfection of this book even among the most carefully written and finished works of all literature, the fact of its containing no affectation, nothing mannered or commonplace, nothing unfounded or indeterminate, nothing affixed to it from without, is due to this. It has been said and we have all repeated it without examination, that the historical portions of the romance are too extensive; but here also I am glad to see that Momigliano has contested the traditional opinion. De Sanctis, who likewise shared it, afterwards confessed that those portions seemed to him so beautiful that he would not have dared remove them. It is clear also that if they really were excessive, we should and could always place them at a distance, while continuing to preserve them and to admire their beauty.

The truth of the matter is that the historical portions, here as in every really poetical work, are only historical in appearance, and become dissolved and merged in the two constitutive elements of the romance. Some of them, such as the narratives of the famine, of the plague and of the passage of the marauding soldiery, are one with the serious, sad and troubled portions of the story, and the others, of a satirical and ironical character, go to the formation of Manzoni's vast satire of human follies, which serves as an appendix to the *Praise of Folly* of Erasmus.

It is to be noted that this great book has not obtained the place which it deserves in the literature of the world, though for the Italians of the nineteenth century it possessed the same value as the *Jerusalem Liberated* for those of the eighteenth. This becomes evident when we read the histories of Italian literature written by foreigners. One possible reason for this is the habit of considering abstract forms or kinds as being things in themselves and of primary importance, and of singularizing the novelties and revolutions which take place in them. Regarded from this point of view, the ***Promessi sposi*** appear to be, and are often considered as being, nothing but a romance of Walter Scott, from whom Manzoni borrowed, not only the idea of the historical romance, but also certain devices of composition, such, for instance, as the introduction of comic relief and of characters with a *tic,* such as Don Ferrante and Donna Prassede, who have many similar but far less subtle counterparts in Scott's stories. But the shell is the shell and poetry is the living being that dwells within, and which makes its home there, alters the shell to suit a change of taste and bears the shell with it on its way. Scott put into the shell as a rule his rather slender tale told to amuse the company, but Alessandro Manzoni put into it all human tragedy and comedy, as comprehended by a man of subtle and reserved moral consciousness. (pp. 155-66)

> Benedetto Croce, "Manzoni," in his European Literature in the Nineteenth Century, *translated by Douglas Ainslie, Alfred A. Knopf, 1924, pp. 145-66.*

D. A. Traversi   (essay date 1940)

[*Traversi is an English scholar and literary critic noted for his studies of Shakespeare and T. S. Eliot. In the following essay, he contends that the meaning of* The Betrothed *lies in Manzoni's definition of human freedom as surrender of the will to the laws of Christian morality.*]

In few writers is the correspondence between personal and literary development so close as in Manzoni. His works are few in number—a handful of poems, two experimental tragedies, and one great novel—but they are backed by a considerable body of criticism and a continuous study of the implications of his literary activity. This probing into the nature and conditions of his art derives from historical and personal circumstances. The view of art which he inherited from the eighteenth century and to which, from the first, he devoted himself, was essentially moral in its foundation and civilising in its purpose. Its root was faith in a beneficent social stability based on a generally accepted moral outlook. This faith was substantially that of the great Italian satirist Giuseppe Parini, who had been tutor to Carlo Imbonati, the lover of Manzoni's mother, and whose poetry was greatly admired by that Parisian circle of 'enlightened' Italians in which Manzoni was brought up. Parini's poetry turned upon the necessary relationship between the 'useful' and the 'good.' The nature of 'il buono' had been, for Parini, evident, a certainty shared by

all the worthy elements of society and derived from a consensus of disinterested opinion; the satirist's purpose was to judge humanity in the light of this certainty and to teach that the 'useful' could be attained infallibly only through devotion to the good.

But Manzoni's art, closely related as it is in spirit and aim to eighteenth century enlightenment, was unable to share these assumptions. Parini had assumed an accepted order of society in which every right presupposed a duty and in which the idea of liberty was subordinate to that of devotion to 'il buono.' Manzoni, the formative years of whose life were passed in a Paris that had experienced the French Revolution and in social circles permeated by the sceptical philosophy of the *salons,* was inevitably driven to explore the basis of his ideals. This exploration assumed a double aspect. The foundations of individual morality, which Parini had regarded as self-evident in his conception of 'il buono,' needed to be examined and consciously defined; and the 'social' ideal of 'justice,' by which the relations of society were regulated in accordance with the universally accepted 'good,' had to be related to the new conviction that progress could only be attained by wholesale revolution. Manzoni's work, in short, is an attempt to safeguard his deepest interests and to give full artistic expression to his search for moral coherence in a world of uncertainties.

The uncertainty which underlies the ***Promessi sposi*** is already implicit in the movement of Manzoni's prose. His account of the despair which Gertrude feels when she realizes herself destined against her will to become a nun is not less typical than the sermon in which Cardinal Borromeo expounds the nature and action of Grace to the newly-converted Innominato. The two passages are worth setting side by side because they show how closely related in Manzoni are despair and consolation:

> In tutto il resto di quella giornata, Gertrude non ebbe un minuto di bene. Avrebbe desiderato riposar l'animo da tante commozioni, lasciar, per dir cosi, chiarire i suoi pensieri, render conto a sé stessa di ciò che aveva fatto, di ciò che le rimaneva da fare, sapere ciò che volesse, rallentare un momento quella macchina che, appena avviata, andava così precipitosamente; ma non ci fu verso.
>
> Non ve lo sentite in cuore che v'opprime, che v'agita, che non vi lascia stare, e nello stesso tempo v'attira, vi fa presentire una speranza di quiete, di consolazione, d'una consolazione che sarà piena, immensa, subito che voi lo riconosciate, lo confessiate, l'imploriate.
>
> [For all the rest of that day, Gertrude did not have a single moment of well-being. She would have liked to give her mind rest from so many commotions, to allow her thoughts to be clarified, so to speak, to become conscious of what she had done, of what remained to do, to know what she wanted, to restrain for a moment the machine which, once set in motion, moved so precipitously; but there was no means of doing this.
>
> Do you not feel Him in your heart, constraining, disturbing you, refusing to leave you, and at the same time attracting you, making you feel a hope of peace, of consolation: of a consolation which shall be full, immense, as soon as you recognize it, confess it, implore it.]

The feature common to these two passages, directly opposed as they are in intention, is the *dynamic* nature (so to call it) of their development. The words of which they are formed are not self-sufficient, independent in their effect; each word rather bears, as though implicit within itself, the seed of another which carries the sentiment a step further towards its goal. Gertrude desires no more than a single 'momento di bene,' and this, significantly enough, is the only phrase in the whole passage which is allowed to stand by itself without development or modification. But the logic of the sentence, as it takes form in the multiplication of the verbs, moves irresistibly away from this fixed desire to arrive finally at that picture of the machine relentlessly, 'precipitously' in motion; and the mention of the machine emphasizes both the impersonality and the inevitability of the whole process, before which 'rallentare' serves only to bring out the futility of the victim's efforts to avoid what has now become her destiny. So also with the Cardinal's sermon. The action of God is represented as a vigorous and cumulative force 'che v'opprime, che v'agita, che non vi lascia stare'; and the very 'speranza di quiete' which is presented as the goal of all this activity is reinforced by 'consolazione,' which is then repeated and expanded into 'piena, immensa.'

The implications of this prose are extremely important. Where a 'classical' writer—by which I mean a writer firmly established in an artistic tradition and fully conscious of unquestioned moral standards—seems to stand outside the experience he is describing and to convey something already clearly defined in his own mind, Manzoni is concerned to represent the actual birth of this state and to reproduce the very process of its development. The traditional distinction between the finished thought and its gradual unfolding in the mind is replaced by a new sense of the identity between the process and the completed product; and this revolution is accompanied, in the philosophical sphere with which Manzoni was most deeply concerned, by an even more exclusive insistence upon God's immanence in the process of development. This characteristic has a profound effect upon Manzoni's handling of the novel. His characters are not conceived, so to speak, *from outside* and described with classic detachment, the finished picture preceding and dominating the separate impressions in the mind of the novelist; rather the separate impressions, the actions of the man himself and the details of his environment, come gradually together to form a complete portrait. The timid priest Don Abbondio, for example, is introduced at the very beginning of the book without preliminary description; his character is subtly and, as it were, insensibly built up out of his successive actions. He appears walking 'tranquilly' along a country road, saying his Office, and stopping occasionally to lift his head with a certain air of complacent distraction ('*girati oziosamente gli occhi all'intorno*') [having let his eyes wander lazily] or to kick idly at the pebbles on his path. In this way, Manzoni introduces his character directly into the developing stream of events, and introduces a vast mass of significant detail without standing aside even for a moment from the development of his history. This sense of the absolute continuity between exterior events and the human characters moulded by them, besides striking a distinctively 'modern' note, is a decisive condition of Manzoni's genius.

In this matter Manzoni is the child of his age. What is striking and individual in him is the fact that he felt most acutely the incompatibility between these new developments and the stable, 'classical' basis of his own moral and social instincts. In the *Promessi sposi* we are aware, not only of a world in continual motion, perpetually directed by its own internal logic towards destruction, but also of the desire for something, such as that 'consolation' or that 'moment of well-being,' which will provide a firm basis against the threatened confusion. Manzoni is concerned, throughout his novel, with the threat of anarchy; personal anarchy due to the absence of objective sanctions for his moral instincts, and social anarchy proceeding from the lack of any rational check to destructive self-interest. Manzoni felt that the alternative to a firmly established moral consciousness, guaranteeing the possibility and validity of man's choice between good and evil, was a pitiless determinism—the determinism reflected in the very movement of his prose. Against this threat, he sets the faith in an objective revelation which he had gained from his 'conversion' to Catholicism. The *Promessi sposi* turns upon this relationship between an objective faith and a world threatened by the consequences of irresponsibility leading to meaningless determinism; it is this fact, more than any other, which makes it so much more than simply 'another historical novel.'

Since each of these alternatives—religion and anarchy—remained throughout his life equally real to Manzoni, it is natural that his conversion appears in the novel as something still in the process of development. The actual moment of acceptance, which had taken place many years before, had been rather a recognition of the need for submission than an achievement of personal coherence. It gave him the conviction he later described in a letter to the Contessa Saluzzo: 'It is true that the evidences of the Catholic religion fill and dominate my intellect; I see it at the beginning and end of all moral questions, whenever it is invoked and whenever it is excluded.' In his two plays and in his great novel, Manzoni applies this conviction to the whole field of his experience, seeking to find a place and significance for every part of it in the light of the truth he had discovered; so that the *Promessi sposi* presents a world in continuous and restless motion round a fixed point, which is the Christian revelation. This fixed point is personified by Manzoni in the shape of the only character who is independent of the vicissitudes of the story. The other figures of the book are transformed, in accordance with the conditions imposed by their original dispositions, by the events to which they are exposed; they *develop*, either towards a standard of perfection or away from it. With Cardinal Federigo Borromeo this is not so. The close relationship between the character of Federigo and Manzoni's own problems, as I have stated them, is clear from the first description of him:

> He attended, as I say, to those words and those maxims, took them seriously, tried them out, and found them *true*, he saw, therefore, that there could not be *truth* in other words and other maxims of opposite sense, which are also transmitted from generation to generation, with equal security and sometimes from the same lips; and he proposed to take as standard of his actions and thoughts those which were *true* . . . Persuaded that life is not intended to be a burden for the many and a feast for the few, but rather an obligation for all . . . he

began to consider from childhood how he might render his own life *useful and holy.*

This account of the Cardinal might be a summary of the development of Manzoni's own thought. Like Manzoni, Federigo understood the necessity of ordering his life in accordance with a determined standard of duty. But—and this is the crucial point—the conflicting maxims of the various moral systems propose themselves to man 'with equal security, and sometimes from the same lips,' so that the individual, in the absence of an absolute sanction for his moral instincts, is inevitably exposed to uncertainty and contradiction. The significance of Cardinal Borromeo lay in the fact that he had found a *true* religion ('he found them *true*'—'those which were *true*'—the word is of fundamental importance in all Manzoni's writings) and had adopted it as the norm of his thoughts and actions. Manzoni's approach to ethics is characterized by the very logic which had impelled him towards scepticism. He had already noted in his prose tract on **La morale cattolica** that the defect of all 'natural' systems of morality lay in their inability to avoid 'the shame of giving precepts and advice without being able to propose adequate motives.' The Cardinal had overcome this difficulty by discovering and accepting from the first the correspondence between a true religion and a morality that was 'useful and holy.' In that word 'useful' we may discern a connection, still alive in Manzoni, with the morality sponsored by Parini; and Borromeo, who understood so clearly the necessary relationship between that morality and a supernatural faith, becomes the corner-stone of the **Promessi sposi.**

Manzoni spares no pains to emphasize the distinctive position of his Cardinal. Federigo enters the novel as a man already formed. It is not an accident that he had accepted his vocation 'from childhood' where those around him only reached consciousness of theirs after years of effort; and it is not by chance that his habitual tone is that of the preacher who knows himself to be the mouthpiece of God. He appears for the first time, moreover, at the turning-point of the whole novel, and, having exercised his decisive influence upon the conversion of the Innominato and upon the events immediately arising from it, he does not appear in person again. This does not mean, of course, that Manzoni himself lives in his novel only in the character of Federigo. Manzoni, unlike the Cardinal, had not reached his religious convictions 'from childhood.' On the contrary, the **Promessi sposi** reflects a moral and religious consciousness still in process of development, still occupied with reconciling transcendent truth to the various degrees of human resolution represented by the various characters of his book. The central incident of the whole novel is the encounter between Borromeo and the Innominato, between the upholder of the Catholic certainties and the most arbitrary of feudal tyrants. In relation to that encounter, the various threads of the story fall into place, either as leading up to it or as proceeding logically from it. Renzo and Lucia, the betrothed peasants, fall victims to the whim of Don Rodrigo, in a world where the weak have no protection against the selfish caprice of their supporters; and Don Rodrigo, foiled in his design against Lucia by the foresight of Fra Cristoforo, calls upon the Innominato to help him. The kidnapping of Lucia which follows, and the night passed by her alone in the tyrant's castle, are at once the climax and the turning-point of her misfortunes; they lead up to the conversion of the In-

nominato and his meeting with the Cardinal. At this meeting, the Christian position is explicitly and authoritatively defined; in the second half of the book, which leads through the disaster of the plague to the final marriage of Renzo and Lucia, it is constantly present and serves as a key to the significance of the events described. Within this framework, and always with reference to the certainties proclaimed by Federigo, takes place the drama of the submission of free will to the truth.

The submission of free will to the truth—but the real subject of the **Promessi sposi** is the very possibility of freedom of choice. Manzoni's concern with freedom stands in the closest relation to the spiritual crisis of nineteenth-century Romanticism. There are moments when Manzoni recalls Dostoievsky's analysis of the consequences of absolute egoism. The problem of the will, as it presented itself to him, is briefly this: the corrosive effect of eighteenth-century rationalism upon accepted moral and spiritual traditions gave rise to a conception of the will as not only free, according to the Christian conception of free will, but as *autonomous,* operating independently of all moral or social checks. So we have the murderer in *Crime and Punishment* who killed an old woman because he wanted to have 'the daring,' 'wanted to be a Napoleon,' and later we have the conspirators in *The Possessed* whose activity consisted in the feverish construction of vast plots *in vacancy.* In vacancy: that is the essential point. Never had the act of choice been so insisted upon as the chief indication of the significance of human action: never had there been such an absence of motive for choosing. Without the spiritual sanctions which had served as conditions for the exercise of the human will, the simple capacity to act remained without further significance. The good action and the bad were identical in value, and both ended equally in death, so that Kirillov, in Dostoievsky's story, was led to suicide by his very desire 'to prove my independence and my new terrible freedom.' Manzoni's education and his profoundly moral and civil instincts saved him from this anarchy; but a similar concern with the exercise of the will underlies his submission to a religious philosophy.

Manzoni indicated the nature of this submission in his creation of Lucia. Arguing logically from his insistence on the supreme importance of the act of the will in giving significance to human life, he wrote in 1820 to his spiritual adviser Canon Tosi that the Church 'with her first teaching can raise the simple soul, unaware even of the existence of a moral philosophy, to the highest point . . . of morality itself.' This statement is in no sense sentimental, but a strictly logical deduction from Manzoni's convictions. If the end of the will lies in submission to the *truth,* without which the will itself remains objectless and therefore empty, it follows that any soul which has arrived at this end has fulfilled the condition of its existence: so that Lucia possesses from the first the wisdom which the remaining characters of the **Promessi sposi** have to acquire, if at all, through the laborious conquest of moral insight. The decisive moment in Lucia's career is the night passed by her alone as the prisoner of the Innominato. During that night she gives up all hope of marrying Renzo by vowing her chastity, if she escapes, to the Virgin Mary; and from this central moment, in which Manzoni's idea of submission triumphs, follows the conversion of the Innominato and the final slow resolution of the story.

It cannot be said that Lucia is one of Manzoni's most satisfactory characters. She is essential to the novel, whose scheme demands a representation of the ideal of total submission; but she remains, on the whole, a symbol rather than a person. This 'unreality' corresponds to a certain element of constraint in the whole book. The occasion of the Innominato's conversion—he is decisively affected by Lucia's sanctity—is scarcely convincing, though the process of thought which leads up to it is, as we shall see, profoundly interesting. There is some truth in the judgment that the plot of the *Promessi sposi* is artificial, even 'moralizing'; but it is essential to realize that a deeply individual experience is being compressed, so to speak, into a set mould, whose nature is dictated by Manzoni's determination to submit absolutely to an external standard of truth. That is a condition of Manzoni's genius: not the spontaneous creation of a world, but the setting of a varied experience against a rigid and pre-determined framework to which it must conform. Sometimes the experience overflows the limits of the mould, and issues in that peculiar irony of which Manzoni is a master and of which Don Abbondio is supremely the spokesman. The greatness of the novel lies in this fruitful tension between the rigid form of the plot and the life which circulates within it. The remaining characters of the book have more life than Lucia because we feel in them the gap between ideal and fact. To create a convincing character on the lines of Lucia, Manzoni would have had to identify himself spontaneously with his ideal, much as the biographer of a mediæval saint did so; and, in doing this, he would have ceased to be a modern man.

In Renzo, Lucia's lover, we have the first stage in Manzoni's analysis of the rebellious will. Born, like Lucia, a peasant, and deeply attached to his native soil, Renzo is by disposition one of those who accept the divine law as self-evident, as the basis of a productive and simple life crowned in the Sacrament of marriage. But this desire for natural happiness is not, in Manzoni's view, always enough. When obstructed by the arbitrary designs of Don Rodrigo against Lucia, Renzo determines to take justice into his own hands: 'la farò *io* la giustizia.' At this point, Manzoni's analysis of the individual will merges into his study of the foundations of society. Society must be based on a conception of justice which guarantees the rights of the individual and checks the destructive forces of self-interest; but it is precisely this conception which has most need of a supernatural sanction. Lack of such a sanction in the world of the *Promessi sposi* opened the way to feudal anarchy. Each petty tyrant was concerned only to follow his own will, and the representatives of the law—like the corrupt advocate Azzecca-garbugli to whom Renzo applied for help in his trouble—became parasitic upon the strong in following their own self-interest. The result is expressed in the ironic advice given to Renzo by his cousin— 'seek to avoid justice, as I shall seek to avoid the plague.' But the root cause of this anarchy lies in the individual conscience. Renzo's own 'justice' has no absolute reference, but is simply an affirmation of his own desires and a determination to obtain them by force. In short, Renzo, by following his natural instincts, has placed himself, however excusably, at the level of Don Rodrigo. Short of accepting the standard of perfect justice revealed in the Gospel and actualized in his doctrine of humility, there is for Manzoni no objectively valid (that is, true) conception of justice; there is only the desire, more or less conscious, of the individual to achieve his selfish ends. In the individual, the most natural desires are tainted with self-will and may even lead, as in Renzo, to a willingness to do murder; in society, order and the possibility of progress are sacrificed to anarchy. All this is implied in Fra Cristoforo's retort to Renzo: 'Tu lo sai, tu, quale sia la giustizia'; and again: 'tu, verme della terra, tu vuoi far giustizia.' ['You, indeed, *you* know what justice is'; 'you, worm of the earth, *you* want to do justice.'] Fra Cristoforo, who has himself killed a man in following the impulse of his own pride, knows the consequences of these unchecked affirmations of the self; indeed, he has expiated them in a life-long struggle to achieve humility under the religious habit. Only, therefore, when Renzo has renounced the following of his own will does Fra Cristoforo release Lucia from her vow; and it is important to realize that this dispensation arises from a submission to the ruling of the Church. The way is thus opened to the natural happiness which Renzo desired in his marriage; but the friar's words indicate that even this natural happiness has been transformed in the light of the experience of this book:

> Love one another as fellow-travellers, with the knowledge that you must part, and with the hope of coming together again for ever. Thank God who has brought you into this state, not through a turbulent and transitory happiness, but by hardships and in the midst of misery in order to dispose you to resigned and tranquil joy.

Once more the turbulent experience of life has been brought into submission within the framework of the novel; and once more we must admit, after recognizing the power of Manzoni's control and the essential part it plays in his genius, to a certain sense of loss. There are passages in the *Promessi sposi* which prove the depth of Manzoni's sense of the reality and richness of natural happiness, just as there are passages in which the vivacity and grace of Lucia are fugitively presented. But always there is the sense that experience must be forced into the mould of whose necessity Manzoni is so deeply convinced; and so Lucia becomes less a person than a symbol of consistency, and natural 'joy,' in itself 'turbulent and transitory,' is transformed into something new, 'resigned and tranquil.' But the greatness of the novel consists precisely in the tension between the submission which Manzoni feels to be essential, if the significance and validity of experience is to be maintained, and emotions and ideas whose power and complexity often make it difficult to submit.

Manzoni presents these issues most clearly in two characters who stand a little apart from the main development of his book. The Innominato only enters the story at the summons of the thwarted Don Rodrigo and disappears when his decisive part in it has been played; and the story of Gertrude, the nun of Monza, reads like a romantic incident inserted quite superfluously into the novel. In these two contrasted characters, however, Manzoni's analysis of the problem of free will receives its fullest expression; perhaps their very isolation from the main stream of the book helps to concentrate our attention upon the issues involved. In each case, the human will, conscious of the need for asserting its proper autonomy, is set against the deterministic development of a chain of exterior events which threaten to enslave it. The Innominato, by his conversion, breaks his chain; Gertrude fails to break hers and is lost.

The Innominato appears from the first as something more than a mere tyrant, a mediocrity of the type of Don Rodrigo engaged in the satisfying of his petty desires. This eminence makes him more dangerous than Don Rodrigo, who is, indeed, almost his dependant; but it also makes him, unlike Don Rodrigo, capable of redemption. Tyranny corresponds in the Innominato to an intimate necessity of his nature: the necessity, that is, of exercising a decisive influence upon events, of affirming the power of his own will. 'To do whatever was forbidden by the laws or impeded by any force; to be arbiter and master in the affairs of others, *without other interest than the pleasure of commanding* . . . such had been at all times the principal passions of this man.' 'Without other interest than the pleasure of commanding'—that is the feature which marks off the Innominato from the petty selfishness of Don Rodrigo. It drives him above all to aim at achieving independence from good and evil alike by acting in disregard of all moral checks, which he considers merely as obstacles to the freedom of his action: 'in despite,' as Manzoni says, 'of right and wrong, those two considerations which place so many *obstacles* before the human will, and cause it so frequently to turn back.' The Innominato, in short, reflects Manzoni's interest in the autonomous will which, freed from the obligations of any valid conception of morality, acts only in order to assert its own independence.

Having established in his character this devotion to the pure will, Manzoni proceeds to point out the contradictions which underlie it. The actions of the Innominato are deprived of any significance by their very independence from any moral check and lead logically to a determinism which ends by destroying the very possibility of free will. The crisis which overtakes him when confronted by Lucia is much more than an arbitrary piece of edifying fiction; it is carefully prepared for by a long sequence of developments which lead logically to the recognition of futility. In the moment which precedes this crisis, the Innominato realizes that the whole course of his past life has been void; in the absence of any overruling conception to give significance to his actions, each crime follows its predecessor logically, inevitably, and with the utmost futility. On the one hand, his lawless acts now proceed from mere habit, and have actually become distasteful to him; on the other, he feels himself quite without the strength (in other words, the motive) to arrest what has now become a mechanical development. Having promised Don Rodrigo to carry off Lucia, his thoughts show already a full awareness of his position: 'I have served him because . . . because I have promised and I have promised because . . . it is my destiny.' 'It is my destiny'; the Innominato, caught in his very desire to be not merely free but autonomous, independent of the moral law, has ended by being caught in a determinism so rigid that it implies an abandonment of the very power of choice. 'Time rose up before him, empty of every intention, every occupation, every desire'; the will itself becomes an illusion, and this fact, now clearly realized for the first time, induces in the Innominato the sensation of a 'tremendous solitude'—the solitude of a man who sees no further significance in the exercise of his own power.

At this point, Manzoni brings into play a new consideration—the thought of death. The thought is peculiarly appropriate to the Innominato in his present position. At the end of every course of action, however vast and extravagant, he sees death, before which the simple affirmation of the independence of the will becomes futile, insignificant. The decisive question which now faces him is contained in the thought of his approaching old age: 'To grow old! to die! and then?' The terms in which Manzoni states his problem are traditional, form an integral part of the Catholic outlook; but behind these terms lies his continual preoccupation with the crisis of the independent will. It is noteworthy that the Innominato, like Kirillov in Dostoievsky's *Possessed,* is driven to the thought of suicide.

But the Innominato, like his creator, is too deeply immersed in the Catholic tradition to allow himself to fall into the depths of anarchy. He breaks his chain by his conversion. Looking back, at the decisive moment, over the actions of his fruitless past before the Cardinal he affirms that—'I have one, which I can at once break, undo, repair.' The first verb recalls the chain of determined events which he is breaking by a decisive act of the will. In freeing Lucia, the Innominato submits for the first time to a moral law which henceforth gives significance to his actions by allowing him to choose between good and evil and in the light of which even death becomes a fateful crisis in the spiritual development of the individual. By submitting to the objective content of Christian revelation the Innominato, according to Manzoni, regains his true liberty and frees himself from the empty determinism which had been the logical consequence of his desire for absolute autonomy.

The tragedy of Gertrude, whose fate is precisely the opposite of that of the Innominato, is summed up in Manzoni's brief comment: 'Crime is a rigid and inflexible master, against whom he alone becomes strong who rebels entirely. To this Gertrude *did not wish to resolve herself: and she obeyed.*' Like the Innominato, Gertrude is caught in an inflexible chain of events: only, whereas the chain of the Innominato has been of his own creation, that of the unhappy nun had been imposed upon her by circumstances beyond her control. Desiring for herself from the first the happiness of a wife and a great lady, Gertrude remains throughout unable either to assert her own will against her father or to accept the consolations of the religious state. Manzoni insists that Gertrude, even whilst remaining a nun, could have found happiness by accepting her misfortunes and making them the basis of a responsible life. The Christian religion, he observes, 'is a road so made, that from whatever labyrinth, from whatever precipice a man comes upon it, *and takes a step upon it,* he can from thenceforward walk on with safety and a good will, to arrive happily at a happy end.' In the thought which underlies this passge we feel once more that intimate connection between the individual character and the force of surrounding circumstances which we have seen to be so typical of Manzoni. The behaviour of Gertrude is conditioned, moulded by the logic of past events; the action open to her consists in accepting the complex of circumstances at a given moment and in making it significant by a decisive act of the will. This delicate dovetailing of interior impulse and exterior influence is reminiscent of Machiavelli's statement in the *Principe* of the relationship between man's decisions and the action of impersonal Fortune:

> And I compare her (Fortune) to one of these ruinous rivers which, when they become angry, flood the plains, ruin trees and houses, take land from one part and deposit it on the other: everyone flies before them, everyone yields to their assault, with-

out being able to resist at any point. And yet, although they have this nature, this does not prevent men from making provision with dams and banks when conditions are quiet, so that the floods, when they come, either flow in a channel or make their assault in a manner neither so unlimited nor so harmful.

Manzoni is dealing with the individual conscience and Machiavelli with political expediency, but both are concerned with asserting and defining the prerogatives of the will in relation to a deterministic chain of events. Machiavelli insists that it is the Prince's duty, by his decision, to convert a turbulent and perilous stream into an orderly channel; Manzoni affirms that, to give life significance, it is essential to take one's own step, to *choose* freely, to accept what the logic of past events has made inevitable, in order to give it validity in relation to a religious attitude towards life. It is the kernel of his belief, in fact, that the moral will can insert itself, through its conscious act, at any point into the logical development of a series of events so as to give them meaning and to liberate the personality from the chain of determinism. The story of Gertrude is followed with extraordinary psychological and spiritual insight; but the essential part of it is that Gertrude never made this act of conscious acceptance, so that her life remained a hopeless conflict between helpless desires and the compulsion of external events. Lacking as a girl the courage to oppose her father's will, she yet allowed herself to respond to the advances of a page-boy, so that the discovery of her love merely made her 'guilt' more apparent and her fate more secure. Later, after she has become a nun, she surrenders to her passion for Egidio and commits murder to conceal it. In this way Gertrude, who began as a pathetic victim of circumstances, ends as a criminal. Manzoni's awareness that the circumstances of her childhood, however beyond her control, could only lead unless firmly repudiated to crimes for which she is fully responsible, saves his story from romantic excesses and gives it tragic quality; unlike the Innominato, Gertrude remains throughout the victim of a fate which only a decisive act on her part could have avoided.

The *Promessi sposi* is remarkable, as I have already indicated, for the absolute coherence shown in it between personal and social problems. Manzoni is as much concerned to examine the foundations of the political optimism which he inherited from the eighteenth century as to guarantee the relevance of his own moral instincts. The two problems are, indeed, obviously complementary. If personal morality demands, as we have seen, an objective basis, the conception of social justice, of the necessary relation between rights and duties assumed by Parini and inherited by Manzoni, has equal need of a guarantee; for, in the words of a comment from the *Promessi sposi,* 'Right and wrong are never so clearly divided that either side is possessed only of one or the other.' Without such a guarantee the individual is driven to the simple affirmation of his own will, and society is divided inevitably into the strong, who seek to impose their own desires upon humanity, and the weak, to whom no course is open but resignation. The central fact in Manzoni's meticulous and detailed study of seventeenth-century society is this division between 'i prepotenti' and 'gli umili,' the oppressors and the oppressed. This division becomes, in the absence of the moral law, increasingly and fatally acute: 'You survive to live in an unhappy age: the days we see are evil, but those

Manuscript page from I promessi sposi.

which are maturing will be worse: the sons of the insolent, of the proud, of the violent will be more so than their fathers.' The profound pessimism implied in Manzoni's interpretation of history is simply a logical development from the disintegration of the moral law; the Innominato and Lucia, besides representing contrasted possibilities in the moral crisis of the individual, stand at opposite poles of social development.

But if the unbridled increase of feudal tyranny is a necessary deduction from Manzoni's moral interpretation of events in seventeenth-century Italy, so is the ultimate proof of their vanity. The great plague is the climax of the whole book, the common event in which great and humble are simultaneously involved and from which there is, humanly speaking, no escape. It brings to the 'prepotenti' that sense of helplessness which came to the Innominato with the thought of death; because it is something outside their control, before which every achievement of the will, every affirmation of power, appears irrelevant. Manzoni's account of its birth and development is the supreme example of that dynamic logic which we have isolated as characteristic of his genius and which communicates itself to the movement of his prose. His description of the first appearance of the plague in Milan is typical:

. . . cominciarono, prima nel borgo di Porta Orientale, poi in ogni quartiere della città, a farsi frequenti le malattie, le morti, con accidenti strani di spasimi, di palpitazioni, di letargo, di delirio, con quelle insegne funeste di lividi e di bubboni; morti per lo più celeri, violente, non di rado repentine, senza alcun indizio antecedente di malattia.

[The illnesses and deaths began to increase in frequency, first in the Quarter of Porta Orientale, then in every part of the town, with strange outbreaks of spasms, palpitations, lethargy and delirium, with those dreadful marks of sores and plague-spots; deaths for the most part speedy and violent, not rarely sudden, without any preceding indication of illness.]

The sentence begins quietly with 'cominciarono'; then it pauses, as though to take breath, with an exact description of place, before expanding ominously with 'frequenti.' From this point it flows on with an ever-increasing sense of catastrophe; we have 'malattie,' which give way first to 'morti' and then, with an increase of horror and despair, to 'spasimi,' and the accompanying 'palpitazioni,' 'letargo,' 'delirio,' so that we feel in the very movement of the prose the compelling action of the divine will involving all, humble and exalted alike, in its course. Before this scourge every affirmation of self-will, every act of human power becomes vain, and the individual crisis of the Innominato is repeated throughout society. The only human action which still has value, according to Manzoni, is the willing and humble acceptance of the Christian philosophy which, once accepted, can give significance to these terrible events and value to these sufferings. Upon this acceptance is based, furthermore, the only possibility of true justice; so much is made clear, as we have seen, in the story of Renzo and in the teaching of Fra Cristoforo. In this way, the 'symbolic' significance of Lucia's submission is seen to be capable of extension to the complexities of social life. It is far from Manzoni's purpose or from the spirit of his philosophy to draw misty Utopias, but his relief at having attained personal coherence, at having balanced his moral and his social instincts in the light of Christian teaching, is felt in his wonderful account of the rain-storm which marks the end of the sultriness and horror of the plague and speaks also of a spiritual revival: 'Renzo, instead of worrying, slipped happily into the rain, enjoyed himself in that freshening downpour, in the whispering and murmuring of grass and leaf, all trembling, dripping, bright, and restored to their greenness; he breathed amply, freely, and fully; and in that *resolution* of nature he felt, as it were, more freely and more keenly what had been performed in his destiny.' The ***Promessi sposi,*** written to teach the most uncompromising submission, ends significantly on a note of liberty. (pp. 131-48)

D. A. Traversi, "The Significance of Manzoni's 'Promessi Sposi'," in Scrutiny, *Vol. IX, No. 2, September, 1940, pp. 131-48.*

V. S. Pritchett   (essay date 1951)

[*Pritchett is a highly esteemed English novelist, short story writer, and critic. Considered one of the modern masters of the short story, he is also one of the world's most respected and well-read literary critics. Pritchett writes in the conversational tone of the familiar essay, approaching literature from the viewpoint of a lettered but not over-scholarly reader. In his criticism, Pritchett stresses his own experience, judgment, and sense of literary art, rather than following a codified critical doctrine derived from a school of psychological or philosophical speculation. In the following excerpt, Pritchett provides a general description of theme, characterization, and plot in* The Betrothed.]

I promessi sposi (in English, ***The Betrothed***) is often said to be 'the only Italian novel'. It is certainly the only Italian novel that can be compared with the great European novels of the nineteenth century. It was begun in 1821 when Scott dominated European taste and when Balzac had not emerged from the writing of shockers, and it was revised many times before the final edition of 1840. The last rewriting is said to have taken twelve years and the result is that we have a compendious Romantic work in a state of real digestibility which neither Balzac nor Scott troubled to attain. ***The Betrothed*** was Manzoni's only novel. It contained the fullness of his mind, his sensibility and creative power and (as Mr Colquhoun, a new translator, says in a very informative preface to a new edition [see Further Reading]) seems to represent the culmination of an experience to which life could add no more. In Italy this novel is a kind of Bible; long passages are known by heart; its reflections are quoted in the political debates that have taken place in Italy since the war. But in England, possibly because the chief translation was done over a hundred years ago—and not very well, by a clergyman who disapproved of its theology—the book has been but mildly regarded. The English had already the novels of Scott, with their energetic romance, their bourgeois valuation of life, their alternating choice of the highly coloured and the domestic. Scott was a Tory and, though a generous man, he drew in his horns before the outcome of the Enlightenment, whereas Manzoni had exposed his mind to it in his youth. Our critical ancestors preferred a safer, unreal Italy and, later on, the libertarian, anti-clerical Italy of the Risorgimento. Among the mass of Victorian readers we must remember those who were drawn towards Manzoni by the Oxford movement; but in matters of piety the critics seem to have preferred their own Protestant vigour and sentiment to Manzoni's obedient, passive, Catholic gravity, and it is a good indication of Victorian feeling that the clergyman who translated Manzoni said that he wished the name of Christ could be substituted for that of the Virgin throughout.

Manzoni's reformed Catholicism—that old desire to do without the Jesuits and the temporal power—is a greater obstacle to Protestants, one often suspects, than the ultramontane. Manzoni's religion is, in tendency, liberal and democratic, but it is also melancholy and pessimistic. In ***The Betrothed*** our ancestors would miss what they so much admired in the English novel—the high-minded woodenness of the exemplary characters. The chief victims of tyranny and evil in the story—the two peasant lovers who are forcibly separated by the lawless Don Rodrigo—are passive sufferers who do little to help themselves and are, in fact, finally rescued not by their own efforts but through the aid of a remarkable priest and the sudden conversion of the chief villain. There is no Protestant suggestion of an aggressive worth or a self-reliance that depends on direct access to God; on the contrary there is an ironical recognition of the hapless drama of Fate and of the painful need for selfless love. It is true that the wicked are destroyed by the plague which comes to Milan at the end of the book—this is a magnificent episode—and that the good lovers are quietly rewarded; but the lasting impressions are not of righteous success but of inexplicable luck—the luck in catching the mysterious eye of the Almighty. One is reading a benign, spacious and melancholy fable of the most tender moral sensibility, an epic of understatement; whereas the English novelist of the nineteenth century—and the eighteenth century, too—commonly provided his readers with a number of obvious statues to socially estimable Virtue and the reader admired them because he hoped, if only in his own eyes, to become a statue himself.

Changed times and a translation which is closer to our idiom make *The Betrothed* immediately sympathetic to the contemporary reader, once he allows for old-fashioned methods of narration and apostrophe. We turn with recognition to other times of chaos, as Manzoni himself transposed the upheaval of the French revolution into the material of the religious wars of the seventeenth century. Manzoni is the novelist of those who expose themselves but cannot take sides. They belong, where humanity abides, to the spiritual third force. His personal history was of the kind that makes the psychologist, the man whose thought and feeling are finely meshed; an aristocrat, a Voltairian and militant anti-Catholic, he married a Protestant woman and was reconverted by the Capucines to a profound if ambiguous faith. He writes with the gentleness, the irony, the anxiety and love of one who has passed through a deep personal crisis. His texture is rich, his variety is great; we enter a world of innumerable meanings and contrasts. Beside the account of the plague, which recalls the curious realistic precision of Defoe, must be put very different things, like an abduction to a brigand's castle or a flight to a convent. In contrast again with these, there are comic scenes like the famous one where the peasant lovers try to trick the timid priest into marrying them, which is at the height of Italian buffoonery; the portraits of politicians have the flowering malice of Proust; the historical reflections are wise, subtle and dyed with experience, and in every episode there are psychological perceptions that have the fineness of the French novelists without their often wounding vanity in their own effects. Manzoni was devoid of the intellectual's self-admiration. His grave manner removes the sickliness from piety and restores to it the strength of nature.

I will quote two examples of Manzoni's kind of perception to which the reader of Proust will at once respond.

One is taken from the colloquy between the neurotic and tragic nun and the peasant girl who has found sanctuary with her.

> [The peasant] also tried to avoid replying to Gertrude's inquisitive questions about her story before her engagement. But here the reason was not prudence. It was because to the poor innocent girl this story seemed a thornier and more difficult one to describe than anything which she had heard or thought she was likely to hear from the Signora. Those dealt with tyranny, treachery and suffering—ugly, painful things, yet things which could be expressed but hers was pervaded by a feeling, a word, which she felt she could not possibly pronounce, and for which she would never be able to

find a substitute that would not seem shameless—the word love.

Put this beside a very different situation, an innkeeper putting his drunken guest to bed. He covers the snoring drunk and

> Then, drawn by the kind of attraction that sometimes makes us regard an object of our dislike as attentively as an object of our love, and which is only the desire to know what it is that affects our sensibility so strongly, he paused a moment to gaze at this irksome guest, raising the lamp over his face, and shading it with his hand so that the light fell on him, almost in the attitude in which Psyche was painted as she gazed stealthily at the features of her unknown spouse.

In all the meetings of his characters, in the strong situations and in the neutral, there is this watchful, instinctive, animal awareness of the other person, a seeking of the meaning of their relationship. To compare the innkeeper to a spouse is not grotesque: the drunk man has already involved the innkeeper with the secret police, there is the marriage of two fears. Fear and love are, in fact, Manzoni's subjects.

The story of *The Betrothed* is a strong one. The hired bravoes hold up the cowardly priest. There is murder on the road. There are bread riots in Milan—Manzoni is an excellent narrative writer unencumbered by picturesque baggage—there are flights and pursuits, tremendous confrontations of the tyrannous and the good. The immunity of the priests gives them boldness. There are political intrigue, invasion and looting by foreign armies, the plague. Manzoni is as brilliant as a diplomat in recomplicating the moral issues; the brigand's sudden conversion, for example, frees the girl from her dangers and seems to guarantee her happiness but, perversely and in her terror, she now vows herself to the Virgin! To the obstacle of wickedness is added the obstacle of faith. That delicate tangle of faith and desire and pride has to be undone. The characters are not thrown on in crude, romantic strokes but are put together precisely by a writer who has understood their pattern and the point at which they will behave unexpectedly or feel the insinuations of time, fate and mood. There is not a stock character anywhere; nor can a too gifted author be seen bursting through these figures. The skill in the change of mood or in anticlimax is wonderful.

When Manzoni described how the notion of writing *The Betrothed* came to him—I quote from Mr Colquhoun—he said:

> The memoirs of that period [the Counter Reformation] show a very extraordinary state of society; the most arbitrary government combined with feudal and popular anarchy; legislation that is amazing in the way it exposes a profound, ferocious, pretentious ignorance; classes with opposed interests and maxims; some little-known anecdotes, preserved in trustworthy documents; finally a plague which gives full rein to the most consummate and shameful excesses, to the most absurd prejudices, and to the most touching virtues.

With this stuff he did fill his book. The contemporary reader must reflect that this is exactly the kind of material which has, in our time, become degenerate in the novel. The great, even the extensive subjects, have fallen into inferior hands. They have become the fodder of the middle-brow novelist. Is it really true that this kind of material can no longer attract the best minds in the novel? Has it exhausted itself? Clearly Manzoni, like Scott and Balzac, had the excitement of doing something new and they had the tremendous intellectual and emotional force of the Romantic movement behind them. But they were more than capable inventors, copyists, historians or story-tellers who comfortably relied on a commonly accepted language and values. Indeed, although it is generally said that our lack of these common symbols is the central difficulty for contemporary artists, I wonder whether Manzoni's situation was as different from ours as it seems to be. He is a singular example of the artist, who, finding no common basis for himself and a disjointed society, sets laboriously to make one. His religion was uncharacteristic for a man of advanced ideas; as far as its elusive quality can be discerned, it seems to have connected the ideas of Pascal with those of liberalism and this profound change of spirit led him to seek an equally important change of language. He wished to find a language in which all men communicate with one another and to abandon literary language. Problems of belief raise at once problems of style: in both Manzoni was revolutionary. His case somewhat resembles Tolstoy's though, with Manzoni, conversion was not a mutilation of the artist but his fulfilment. He succeeded (where the English Protestant novelists on the whole failed) in creating characters who were positively good yet his 'message' that love above all, self-sacrifice, courage, long-suffering and charity are the only, and not necessarily successful answers to tyranny and injustice, is not introduced as a sort of pious starch into the narrative, but is native to it. One is undermined rather than incited by this teaching, as in one or two of the Russian writers; and the very pessimism of Manzoni, by which he continually moves the rewards of the righteous just a little beyond their fingertips with a gentle scepticism, is like that of Cervantes. (pp. 298-302)

> *V. S. Pritchett, "Alessandro Manzoni: 'I Promessi Sposi'," in his* A Man of Letters: Selected Essays, *Random House, 1985, pp. 298-302.*

René Wellek (essay date 1955)

[*Wellek's* History of Modern Criticism *(1955-86) is a major, comprehensive study of the literary critics of the last three centuries. Wellek's critical method, as demonstrated in that work and outlined in his* Theory of Literature *(1949), is one of describing, analyzing, and evaluating a work solely in terms of the problems it poses for itself and how the writer solves them. For Wellek, biographical, historical, and psychological information is incidental. Although many of Wellek's critical methods are reflected in the work of the New Critics, he was not a member of that group, and rejected their more formalistic tendencies. In the following excerpt, Wellek outlines Manzoni's Romantic literary theories, highlighting the tension between history and fiction in his works.*]

[Manzoni] became the one great Italian who expressly proclaimed himself a romanticist. Outside of Italy it is not generally realized what position of authority Manzoni eventually assumed in his nation. *I promessi sposi* in Italy is constantly—despite protests such as Croce's—placed beside the *Divine Comedy,* and the weight of Manzoni's austere moralism and poetic fame has given great prominence also to his views on literary criticism.

Manzoni began as a literary critic with a defense, in the **"Preface,"** of his tragedy *Il conte di Carmagnola,* which . . . violated the unities [designated by Aristotle in his *Poetics*] and was based on Italian history. Manzoni [argues] . . . against the unities of time and place [in a dramatic work] and the inconveniences of the French system. He adds a general defense of the stage as an instrument of moral improvement. Manzoni, who by that time had been converted to a strict observance of Catholicism, was deeply impressed by the attacks on the stage made by Nicole, Bossuet, and Rousseau but hoped to refute them by his reform of the drama, which was to adhere very strictly to historical truth and by imaginative reconstruction was to supply the psychological truth implied in the historical events. To bolster his interpretation of the Carmagnola conspiracy Manzoni wrote an elaborate historical commentary and even divided his characters into "historical" and "invented." The **"Preface"** elicited in France a defense of the unities by a little known writer, Victor Chauvet, to which Manzoni replied in a long piece, *Lettre à M. C.—sur l'unité de temps et de lieu dans la tragédie.* This is a very sober, dignified, well-reasoned statement of the case against the unities of time and space. In part Manzoni repeats the arguments known to Johnson and in part adopts Lessing's and Schlegel's argument that French tragedy, by adhering to the unities, violates the very principle of classicism, namely probability. The French sacrifice probability to the rules though the rules were supposedly made to preserve probability. Manzoni comes to a complete rejection of rules by asking, "If the great geniuses violate the rules, what reason is there to presume that they are based on nature and that they are good for anything?" Still, he insists strongly on the unity of action and on the purity of genre, rejecting tragi-comedy as "destroying the unity of impression necessary to the production of emotion and sympathy."

The question of the unities is not, however, Manzoni's central concern. It is merely one instance of his interest in truth. The essence of poetry, he argues, is not invention of fact. All great works of art are based on events of history or on national traditions considered true in their time. Poetry is thus not in the events but only in the sentiments and discourses which the poet creates by entering sympathetically into their minds. Dramatic poetry aims at explaining what men have felt, willed, and suffered because of their actions. The poet is, we might draw the conclusion, a historian who, like Thucydides or Plutarch, invents the appropriate speeches and details for the events supplied by medieval chronicles.

Goethe, who reviewed the *Conte di Carmagnola* with high praise, knew that "for the poet no person is historical" and that all of Manzoni's characters should be and are ideal. In a letter to Goethe Manzoni recognized that the division of characters into historical and ideal is a "mistake caused by his excessive adherence to the historical," and in the next tragedy, *Adelchi,* the division disappeared. But Manzoni could not really have changed his attitude, since he added a long discourse on Langobard history, justifying every detail of the play.

In 1823 he wrote a letter to Marchese Cesare d'Azeglio, another statement in defense of romanticism, which again revolves around the concept of truth. Manzoni there distinguishes negative and positive sides of romanticism. On the negative side his distinction means the rejection of classical mythology (as false and idolatrous), of servile imitation, and of the rules and unities. On the positive side Manzoni admits that romanticism is a vague term, but it is so for an excellent reason. "In proposing that system of abolishing all the norms that are not truly general, permanent, and in every way reasonable, it makes their number much smaller and their selection much harder and slower." Manzoni can think of only one common aim for the romanticists: poetry must propose truth as its object. Truth for Manzoni is, first of all, historical truth, the conquest by literature of a new theme, modern history, and then, though hardly distinguishable to his mind, the truth of Christianity, its ethics, its spirituality. Manzoni rejects as false the idea that romanticism has anything to do with witches, ghosts, and systematic disorder. Poetry was to him history, truthful history, and the novel, at which he was then working, *I promessi sposi* was to be a conscientious re-creation of the past, based on extensive research, in a Christian, Catholic spirit.

But soon after the novel had become the new Italian classic, Manzoni began to feel increasing scruples about the very possibility of a historical novel. *Del romanzo storico* is Manzoni's quiet, closely reasoned argument against the mixture of truth and fiction and thus against his own life work. He presents first the difficulties encountered by the reader who wants only historical truth. The very narrative form makes the demand impossible. But those who want fiction, a continuity of impression and total effect, cannot be satisfied either, because they can never abolish the distinction between the historical "consent" we give to a real figure such as Mary Queen of Scots or Bonnie Prince Charles or King Louis XI of France, and the other, "poetic consent" we give to probable events. History and fiction are irreconcilable. The historical novel is a hybrid which must yield to the light of truth. To show that this is an inevitable process Manzoni seeks support in the history of the other comparable genres, the epic and tragedy. He believes that they were originally based on events considered and felt as true (like those of the Homeric epics or the Greek tragedies), but that late in the process of enlightenment they became increasingly involved in the conflict between fiction and reality and thus have become impossible in modern times. Manzoni's history of the epic and tragedy runs into great difficulties, however, since it is hardly convincing to think even of Homer's listeners as having been interested merely in truth in Manzoni's literal sense; and it is hardly possible to take the appeal to historical sources in medieval romances very seriously. How can Manzoni approve of Virgil, whom he greatly admires, without approving of the modern historical novel? But he makes good analyses of the difficulties of Tasso's *Gerusalemme liberata* and Voltaire's *Henriade* and everywhere finds support for his conclusion that a historical novel cannot be written, since it requires the author to supply the original and the portrait at the same time, both history and its fictional probable imitation.

One can dismiss Manzoni's troubles by means of Goethe's argument against his distinction between historical and fictional figures. All characters in a novel or play are ideal; the view that two kinds of consent are required is false. Even for a historical figure we need only poetic accep-

tance, the "willing suspension of disbelief," in Coleridge's phrase for illusion. At most, one could grant that Manzoni has proved that the historical novel cannot fulfill its professed task of recreating the past truthfully and that historical truth belongs in history and nowhere else. Manzoni clings to an interpretation of Aristotelian "verisimilitude" which, by definition, excludes history, and since he worships only "fact," he must end in rejecting even poetic truth and misunderstanding the very nature of art. Manzoni, quite honestly and logically, ceased to write fiction. But this abandonment of art in favor of truth should not be confused with the naturalism or realism of the 19th century which was then becoming vocal around him. Manzoni's faith in truth and historical fact is religious, as is obvious also from his late dialogue *Dell' invenzione,* which propounds a theory, based on Rosmini's philosophy, that the artist does not create but merely finds the ideas existing eternally in the mind of God. Here Manzoni outlines a new apologetics of art which might have toned down his condemnation of fiction. But what is remembered today is Manzoni's honest grappling with the problem of a dual allegiance to history and fiction, which he could personally resolve only by repudiating art in favor of history. His preference was obvious in his early pronouncements on romantic tragedy, but the dilemma was then still concealed by his artistic instincts. (pp. 261-64)

René Wellek, "The Italian Critics," in his A History of Modern Criticism: 1750-1950, The Romantic Age, *Yale University Press, 1955, pp. 259-78.*

Alberto Moravia [pseudonym of Alberto Pincherle] (essay date 1960)

[*An Italian novelist, short story writer, and critic, Moravia is one of the foremost Italian literary figures of the twentieth century. His depiction of existential themes, based upon mass indifference and the selfish concerns of the bourgeois world, predates the writings of Jean-Paul Sartre and Albert Camus. Deeply informed by the theories of Karl Marx and Sigmund Freud, Moravia's work commonly focuses upon such subjects as politics, sexuality, psychology, phenomenological philosophy, and art. In his exploration of humanity's conceptions of reality, Moravia presents a world of decadence and corruption in which individuals are guided primarily by their senses, and sex serves as a comfort for spiritual barrenness and the inability to love. In the following excerpt, Moravia describes* The Betrothed *as a novel of Catholic propaganda and addresses its strengths and limitations.*]

This is not meant to be a preface to *The Betrothed* so much as a few reflective notes concerning a particular aspect of Manzoni's masterpiece. At the origin of these notes lie the faint uneasiness that some of the characters arouse in us and the novel's actuality at the present moment of Italy's history. The uneasiness and the actuality have an obvious link, for the characters that arouse our uneasiness are the very ones that make Manzoni actual—using the word 'actual' in its practical sense; of course *The Betrothed* will always retain the eternal actuality of poetry whatever contingent situations may arise. To put it better: after the Risorgimento, Italian criticism was in the best possible position for extolling Manzoni's great art while justifying, if not ignoring entirely, the aspect that perplexes us today. Of course in Italy at that time there was no likelihood of a Catholic restoration—quite the reverse. But today things are different, and having been for almost a century one of the great books of our literature, *The Betrothed* is now well on its way to becoming a mirror of contemporary Italy (which would have astounded its author). For it is a fact that Manzoni's novel reflects an Italy which, with a few inessential modifications, could be the Italy of today. The religion of *The Betrothed* has many affinities with the religion of contemporary Italy; the society Manzoni described is not all that different from our own; the vices he condemned and the virtues he highlighted are the very vices that afflict us and the very virtues that are encouraged in us now. Moreover the collapse of the Risorgimento, which was swept away with much else by the disaster of Fascism, brought with it the downfall of many of the differences that could have existed between contemporary Italy and the Italy of *The Betrothed.* So Italians today can hardly be expected to look on Manzoni with a spirit of detachment. It has always been difficult to judge oneself.

Add to all this the debt of gratitude our literature owes to Manzoni who, with Verga, is the founder of the modern Italian novel, and it will be easy to see why the question of Manzoni's art of propaganda has never really been raised. True, in the past there has been talk of the art of oratory in connection with *The Betrothed,* but in a way more or less in line with tradition—that is, distinguishing oratory from poetry and taking it in its old humanistic and didactic sense. As far as we know, no one has ever perceived that Manzoni's art of propaganda, viewed either as to its means or its ends, has nothing whatever to do with the old art of oratory, however generically we understand it, or that it originates in an entirely modern concept, namely the totalitarian one, which is no longer content with traditional oratory (too obvious and limited to be effective), but aims at making propaganda by means of poetry itself, or pure representation and this alone. In other words, Manzoni's art of propaganda in many respects anticipates the ways and means of the art of propaganda as the moderns understand it, that is, the writers of the school of socialist realism. From the outset this school, too, saw the traditional art of oratory as inadequate. It aimed not at the cynicism of fine writing, but at the authenticity and sincerity—however rough—of poetry, as being the only guarantee both of the author's sincerity and of the ideology's infallibility. In a similar way modern totalitarianism, not content with the formal submission that satisfied the older tyrannies, demands real faith or the identification of the writer's conscience with the ideology. Of course Manzoni did not aim at this result, but he achieved it all the same when, though in different circumstances, he found himself facing similar problems. So, a century before socialist realism, we have in *The Betrothed* what, for convenience, we might call an attempt at Catholic realism. And if anyone finds the comparison too bold, we need only recall the common ground of social and political conservatism in which both socialist realism and Catholic realism grew. For socialist realism and Catholic realism are the æsthetic products *par excellence* of conservatism. And if, as we shall show, Manzoni's Catholic realism made—luckily for us—many concessions to decadentism, whereas socialist realism, alas, makes none, this is at least partly due to the fact that the conservatism of a society of recent formation such as the Soviet is bound to be more intransigent than that of a society of long duration such as the Italian. But in both cases conservatism and the art of propaganda justify and uphold one another at the expense of the only really revolutionary force that exists in literature: poetry.

The first observation we should make about *The Betrothed* is that it is the most ambitious and complete book that has been written about real Italian life since *The Divine Comedy.* More than Boccaccio who was not concerned with plumbing the depths of things, more than Machiavelli who was a poet of politics, no more than Dante, perhaps, but no less, Manzoni sought to represent the whole Italian world from top to bottom, from the humble to the powerful, from the simplicity of popular commonsense to the sublimity of religion. Naturally Manzoni's ambition was not overt; indeed his attempt to resolve highly complex and difficult problems and to depict a large variety of happenings suggests rather that it was the spontaneous and inevitable product of a universal mind. And yet we should note here that while the poetic results of Dante's poem exceed his ambition, as it were, and thus nullify it, in *The Betrothed* the results, though remarkable, are less than the ambition, and thus we cannot let ourselves ignore it. When compared with *The Divine Comedy,* which seems wholly inspired and poetic even in its didactic parts, *The Betrothed* presents large areas in which the poetry fails, though it cannot be said that it is replaced by oratory. Manzoni intended these areas to be just as poetic as the others, perhaps even more so, but in fact—in spite of himself and without realising it—he anticipated in them what we have defined as an attempt at Catholic realism.

If we want to distinguish the inspired parts in Manzoni's masterpiece from the propaganda parts, we must ask ourselves the well-worn question: Why did Manzoni write a historical novel? In our view the underlying motive which made Manzoni write a novel about an episode in the seventeenth century rather than an episode in his own time can easily be found if we consider the most obvious aspect of *The Betrothed:* the preponderant, massive, indeed excessive, almost obsessive importance given to religion in the novel. This aspect is especially obvious if seen through Italian eyes, but it is no less so if we compare *The Betrothed* with other nineteenth-century masterpieces that were almost contemporary with Manzoni's novel: *Madame Bovary, La Chartreuse de Parme, War and Peace, The Pickwick Papers, Vanity Fair, Le Père Goriot,* and so on. If we could measure out the dosage of religion, whether Catholic or otherwise, in the contents of the sum total of the above-mentioned novels, it would not come to more than five per cent whereas it would jump to a good ninety-five per cent in *The Betrothed.* Yet the authors of these other novels were involved in the same political and social reality as Manzoni, that of European society after the French Revolution. We repeat: in *The Betrothed* the importance of religion is inordinate and obsessive and in no way corresponds to the real condition of Italian and European society in the nineteenth century and this excessive importance explains why Manzoni had recourse to a historical novel. After all he was not a small-scale romantic realist like Scott but a great moral and social realist like Stendhal, and could easily have chosen as subject an episode in contemporary life. But in fact Manzoni's ambition was not only to represent the whole of Italian reality on a huge scale, but to force this reality—without distorting or amputating it in any unnatural way—into the ideological framework of Catholicism. In other words, as we have already pointed out, over a century before socialist realism was thought of, Manzoni raised, in his own way, the problem of a comparable Catholic realism—that is, of a novel which, with only poetry as means, should achieve a complete identification of the reality represented with the prevailing ideology, or with the ideology he would like to prevail.

Now let us suppose for a moment, however bizarre the supposition may seem, that a Soviet Manzoni took it into his head to tell the story, according to the socialist realist method, of an episode that occurred in the age of the Tsars. Naturally he would avail himself of all the resources of his literary craft to conceal the problems inherent in forcing the reality of the past into the ideology of the present. But our imaginary Soviet Manzoni knows perfectly well that he cannot get out of his difficulties by his literary craft alone, that is with the art of oratory; he knows that much more is expected of him, nothing less than poetry. In other words he knows that he should not apply socialist realism in an extrinsic way but should show that he has found it at the very heart of things, that is, in things that happened decades or even centuries before the revolution. But as he looks at these things more closely he will find they are rebellious, refractory, and extraneous to socialist realism and after a few unsuccessful attempts he will abandon the enterprise and return to the present, that is to say to the familiar circumstances and personalities of five-year plans.

Now just as our Soviet Manzoni is unable, without obvious constraint, to force the reality of the past into the ideological framework of the present, so the real Manzoni was unable, without the same constraint, to force the reality of the present into the ideological framework of the past. We have already pointed out the difference, or rather the abyss, that cuts off *The Betrothed* from the typical nineteenth-century novel. A similar abyss separated Manzoni, as a convinced Catholic, from his own age, inasmuch as his own age, his present, did not permit him to write a novel that was both Catholic and universal. But Manzoni wanted to write a novel in which Catholicism and reality were identical, in which the forces hostile to Catholicism could not claim to be positive either historically or æsthetically, in which propaganda was poetry and poetry was propaganda. So he had to turn his back on his own age and dig into the past for a more propitious moment in history. But which? With a sure instinct he passed over the Middle Ages which had inspired the play *Adelchi,* as they were too far away and different from modern times, and instead chose the seventeenth century when, with the Counter Reformation, Catholicism had attained an appearance of universality for the last time. The seventeenth century was not too far away, at least to some of the more conservative circles of old Milan, as we can see from the poetry of Carlo Porta who had no ambition to make propaganda but confined himself to describing his own age. So to set the novel in the seventeenth century involved no outright invention of characters and situations (as with Scott and other 'historical' novelists), but rather a tracing-back of present characters and situations to their counterparts in the past. So, to sum up: Manzoni chose the past

for the same motives for which modern Soviet writers choose the present, and, in the past, he chose the seventeenth century because then, for the last time, Catholicism informed all Italian life just as today Communism informs Soviet life.

At this point someone may ask why Manzoni was not the writer he could have been had he accepted himself and his own time as they really were and not as the Church would have had them be. A Catholic, yes, but not more Catholic than he was in reality, not more Catholic than Boccaccio, Petrarch, Ariosto, or even Dante, and, anyway, sufficiently sure of his own Catholicism not to feel the need to flaunt it. A writer, in brief, to whom the formulation of Catholic realism, or the art of propaganda, did not appear as a necessity and a duty; a writer content to depict the reality of his own time as it was and not as he would have it be. But whoever asks this is forgetting that Manzoni's Catholic realism, like the socialist realism of the Soviets today, was born, and affirmed itself, in opposition to other ways of feeling and representation that carried every bit as much conviction if not more. Manzoni built up his Catholic realism piece by piece in opposition to the illuminism that lay in himself and all around him. Had there been no enemy against whom Manzoni had to defend himself, had the world around him been Catholic through and through like Dante Alighieri's world, with no cracks and no exceptions, then Catholic realism would never have been born. Manzoni would have been like Dante, simply a writer of his own age. We call Manzoni a Catholic writer, but it would never enter our heads to say the same of Dante. Hence in Manzoni's case the word Catholic implies precisely the artistic, and hence historical, limitation peculiar to all propaganda art. Catholic realism, like socialist realism, is born of an aspiration to universality that reality denies, of a totalitarian impulse that is not confirmed by the facts.

We have spoken of the massive, excessive, obsessive importance of religion in Manzoni's masterpiece. This is apparent not only in the number of characters in *The Betrothed* who belong to the clergy—that is, in the clerical character that Manzoni wanted to give Lombard society in the seventeenth century, one certainly not borne out by reality—but also, if we look at the book from the point of view of style, in the language used by the characters which on every possible and impossible occasion forms a continual refrain of pious invocations, giving the impression that seventeenth-century Italians were like Jews in the bronze age. This plethora of religious references is not due to a systematic exposition of Christian doctrine, as with Dante where it appears as something organic, necessary and inseparable from the events. On the contrary, except for the sermons of Cardinal Borromeo, Father Felice and Father Cristoforo, which are pretty modest in concept, this plethora—examined from the point of view of style, and above all in the dialogue—is entirely exclamatory, totally lacking in dramatic necessity and necessity of characterisation. One gets the feeling that it is due not to the tranquil faith of a Christian who knows he has no need to flaunt his faith, but to the anxiety of a convert fearful of not being able to convince himself and his readers that nothing happens save under the aegis of Providence, as though any event that does not seem linked with Providence in some way contradicts it—which, psychologically, is a characteristically totalitarian preoccupation. So the importance of religion in *The Betrothed* is excessive precisely because it is unsure and betrays an insufficiency rather than a superabundance of inner conviction. Of course Manzoni was religious in spirit (he was religious in an outstandingly genuine way, as we shall see), but probably he was not religious in the manner of Catholic realism, for instance in the manner of Giovanni Papini (to take a well-known example), the manner needed for the art of propaganda. We feel this to be the highest praise possible of Manzoni's religion.

It is, as we know, a delicate point. We shall try to explain our view by a metaphor. Manzoni's masterpiece could be compared to a geological stratification. The first stratum—the one that leaps to the eye and is, in our view, the most superficial—is the art of propaganda fed by a strenuous will to conform and adhere to the Catholic interpretation of life. It is at this level that Catholic realism grows in all its profuse vegetation, like a plant with enormous leaves and tiny roots. The second layer is Manzoni's political and social sensibility which is a phenomenon in its own right and unique in the whole history of Italian literature. To this layer belong all the typical scenes—consistently felicitous with a threat of subtle humour running through them—in which Manzoni illustrates the society of the time; dialogues like the one between the Count Uncle and the Father Provincial, complete scenes like the meal in Don Rodrigo's house, descriptions of ceremonies such as Gertrude's reception or where Cristoforo appears in the presence of the brother of the man he has killed. Finally deep down and further removed is the third layer, that of the genuine, if often obscure, religious and non-religious feelings of the real Manzoni, of the poet Manzoni, of the Manzoni who, besides being a great writer, was also a specific man belonging to a specific society at a specific moment in history. This third layer, speaking broadly and without going into too much detail, can be described by the overall term of Manzoni the decadent, understanding this last word as modern, and giving it a psychological, moral and social significance rather than a literary one. It is to Manzoni's decadentism that we owe the poetry of *The Betrothed*. It will be noted that Manzoni the decadent is the very opposite of Manzoni the Catholic realist—or rather, is the other side of the coin, and it is this that explains and justifies Manzoni's propagandist zeal.

So we find ourselves dealing with a composite novel whose formal perfection is not enough to mask the co-existence of its two parts—the propaganda one, which is never, or only rarely, poetry, and the poetic one which is not propaganda, or is less so than the author would like. If we begin with the first, we will note that the clue to the paucity of inspiration and the purely cerebral procedure is provided by Manzoni's relative inability to fulfil the primary task of Catholic realism—that is, of creating for didactic and propagandist ends absolutely negative and absolutely positive characters, and describing how the former turn into the latter. In other words, and to use Manzoni's terminology, of creating real 'scoundrels' and real 'saints', and describing the transformation, through religious conversion, of scoundrels into saints. This inability, which we shall examine in detail, is very odd in an author like Manzoni who was so obsessed by religion, or holiness, and who was also a convert, that is informed by direct experience in the ways in which the indifferent man and the sinner can be changed into the opposite. Religious conversion, or the transmutation of values, is at the centre of Manzoni's life

and the fairly obvious mainspring of all his work. Now, by a curious contradiction, conversion itself is the weak point of *The Betrothed,* the place at which intimate inspiration gives way to the expediencies of Catholic realism. So that if we wanted to understand what conversion is, and how and why it happens, we would have to look to other books, St Augustine's *Confessions* for example, and look elsewhere, too, for Manzoni's poetry.

As we have said, Catholic realism, like socialist realism, is primarily based on the contrast between negative characters and positive characters, and the conversion of the first into the second. In *The Betrothed* the negative characters, taken in order of importance, are: Don Rodrigo, the Unnamed (up to his conversion), Cristoforo (also up to his conversion), Attilio, Egidio, and finally Griso, Nibbio and the other cut-throats. We do not include Gertrude and Don Abbondio among the negative characters because, as we shall see, they do not belong even indirectly to Catholic realism. The first observation we have to make is that Manzoni's negative characters all belong to the category of those in power, to the ruling class, as we should say today. The second observation is that they are not really wicked (except for Egidio of whom we shall speak later) but are given to stupidity or empty and unjustified violence, and this is not because Manzoni wanted it this way—it was in spite of himself or through inadequate portrayal. Thus the wickedness of Manzoni's negative characters has something abstract about it, it is stated, not portrayed, affirmed, nor proved, and on closer inspection we see that this abstraction derives directly from the conservative prejudices of Catholic realism. For we are left with the impression that if, instead of the criterion of religion, Manzoni had had recourse to some other more modern criterion—such as consideration of the social factor—for defining and judging his wicked characters, these, as if by magic, would have found an inner justification for their behaviour. But Manzoni was unable to transfer judgement from the religious plane to the social plane precisely because of his conservatism, the fact that he himself belonged to the same class as the 'scoundrels' he was accusing. So all he did was to point out the evil, but not its origin. He came very near to doing what our modern conservatives do when faced with the Sicilian Mafia: they punish the agents, but take care not to denounce those who give the orders.

If we look at an artist like Flaubert, who was not at all revolutionary but much freer than Manzoni, we see how the wicked character, Homais, who represents petit-bourgeois philistinism, is really wicked and not, like Don Rodrigo, merely stupid. And this because, in the scale of values of Flaubert's book, bourgeois philistinism is truly and intrinsically evil and poetically felt as such by the author. Anyway, it is not at all difficult to create negative and positive characters—even the authors of thrillers can do that. But to do it properly one has to be armed with a poetically valid moral criterion which is not possible in propaganda art, for it substitutes for real good and evil—as the writer would feel them if he let his own temperament take over—the extrinsic and sermonising good and evil of a given society or belief. With the curious result that characters that seem negative to simple common sense are projected as positive, and vice versa, as, for instance, happens with Soviet socialist realism whose positive characters often become odious owing to their endless good example, whereas the negative ones arouse our sympathy because they seem to escape from the general conformity.

When we take a close look at the negative characters of **The Betrothed** we find that the main reason for their inadequacy is that Manzoni never bothers to explain why and how they are wicked. Don Rodrigo takes a fancy for Lucia, so it seems, owing to that form of lust we could call feudal, in that it comes of idleness and privilege. But about this form of lust, so typical and frequent both in seventeenth-century and eighteenth-century Italian society, Manzoni tells us absolutely nothing. We hear Don Rodrigo talking about Lucia for the first time when he says, 'Let's make a bet on it,' to his cousin Attilio. In other words when Manzoni has already substituted for the obvious motive of the lust that of a Spanish-style point of honour, and has turned this into the pivot of a gigantic machination which, as it lacks any deep justification, ends up out of all proportion with its aim. Now we would not expect a direct and explicit description of Don Rodrigo's passion for Lucia, a thing inappropriate to the atmosphere of **The Betrothed;** we would have been satisfied with an allusion in a few words such as portray the similar passion of Gertrude. As this allusion is lacking, Don Rodrigo does not emerge as a wicked man, nor even as a man with a misplaced sense of honour, but only—to use the affectionate term of his uncle, the Count—as a 'bad boy'. To be sure Manzoni did not share this indulgent estimate, but as he was either unwilling or unable to trace back the wickedness to its true cause, he ends up by endorsing it even against his will. This goes to confirm what we have already said about the inadequacy of religion as a criterion for dealing with characters and situations in the modern world.

We shall never know how and why Don Rodrigo became wicked. Manzoni leaves us equally in the dark as to how or why the Unnamed fell into the depths of iniquity in which we find him when Don Rodrigo turns to him for help. True, as compared with Don Rodrigo's wickedness which is handed to us as a piece of information beyond discussion, the Unnamed's wickedness is allotted a lengthier treatment. But if we compare the two chapters that recount Gertrude's story with the few pages devoted to the Unnamed, we realise that Manzoni had no intention of really telling us about this sinister personality. In the few pages in question there is not a single precise fact or characteristic, much less any unfolding of an inclination or a passion; everything is exceedingly vague and generalised. Manzoni, who elsewhere pursues the analysis of the human heart to extraordinary depths, here hovers on the surface with curious reticence and embarrassment. Even the happy invention of the appellation 'the Unnamed' is more than a stroke of sombre coloration but refers to the near-impossibility of defining the man. Why is he called the Unnamed? Are we to lay the blame on Francesco Rivola and Giuseppe Ripamonti who had good practical reasons for not mentioning the name, or on Manzoni who does not name his character because he has failed to give him recognisable features? Anyway it is symptomatic that quotations from the two above-mentioned chroniclers are repeated by Manzoni without comment either serious or ironical, as also happens with public proclamations or quotations about the 'anointers'—precisely as proof that they can take the place of the detailed and realistic analysis which we had every right to expect given the impor-

tance of the character. We are left with the impression that Manzoni is saying to us, 'He was a wicked man, even his contemporaries said so, so what more can I add?' Whereas it seems obvious that the Unnamed's wickedness, like Don Rodrigo's, is the immediate and typical product of a given society and this is what gave it its form. After rushing through the earlier facts about the Unnamed, Manzoni hurries on to his conversion—an event that would have required deep preparation in view of its enormous significance in the novel's economy.

As for Cristoforo, Manzoni's aim is to make him out to be a man of a violent temper—before his conversion, that is. But alas, we see Cristoforo not as a violent man but as an impulsive one, which is quite another matter: violence is an incorrigible passion of the spirit, impulsiveness is a graduation of action. Cristoforo's real passion, seen in black and white, is really of a social kind that nowadays we should call inferiority complex. But was Manzoni aware that Cristoforo's conversion seems due, not to spiritual travail, but to a kind of haughty inversion of his inferiority complex which initially urges him to assert himself by violence, and then prompts him to do the same by humility? No, Manzoni's intention seems to be to portray a fundamentally good but violent, misled man. From this unresolved relationship between author and character comes our dissatisfaction with the figure of Cristoforo, alike before and after his conversion.

Given these premises and the failure to provide motives for, or reconstruct, the Unnamed's wickedness and Cristoforo's violence, it is hardly surprising that the conversions of these two characters—that is, their metamorphosis from 'scoundrels' into 'saints'—are not at all convincing. Of the two conversions, the one least unacceptable, though only faintly inspired by really religious feelings, seems to be Cristoforo's. Manzoni presents it for us as a social fact rather than a religious one. Its suddenness seems motivated not so much by a sudden illumination as by the practical necessity in which Cristoforo finds himself—that of extricating himself as rapidly as possible from the vicious circle in which he is caught. For all its Counter-Reformation and baroque characteristics, Cristoforo's conversion, then, seems plausible if not admirable. And the scene of Cristoforo's voluntary self-humiliation before the relatives of the man he has killed is a very fine and mannered picture in the style of similar seventeenth-century scenes in the story of the Nun of Monza.

As for the conversion of the Unnamed, from our point of view it is the weakest point of the whole novel, whereas it should have been the strongest—for surely the conversion of a 'scoundrel' into a 'saint' is the biggest test and focal centre of Catholic realism. What is the aim of propaganda art? To convert unbelievers. In what way? By showing them why and how they should be converted. Now, if we read St Augustine's *Confessions*—a book which treats of conversion clearly and simply and within the range of the most uninitiated reader—we feel an almost contagious sense of the irresistibility of conversion whereas the episode of the Unnamed's conversion leaves us at most lukewarm. The Unnamed, once nameless in his wickedness, has become nameless in his goodness. He is a character without a face; he moves over from generalised wickedness to didactic goodness. And the extraordinary thing is that many critics consider the Unnamed's 'night', as it is called, to be among Manzoni's best passages. Any such judgement can only bear witness to a pretty limited experience of the religious act. The truth is that the Unnamed's crisis follows no inner logic proper to him and to him alone, and nor could it, for—as we have said—the psychological situation existing before the crisis was never deeply explored. But the Unnamed's crisis does follow, and point by point, the rules of Catholic realism. Manzoni deliberately turns his back on his own invaluable experience as a convert, which would have served him well in describing a situation in some respects similar, and clings with great logic but little penetration to the portrayal of the ideal conversion of an exemplary 'scoundrel' into an equally exemplary 'saint'. Already before the conversion, the potentially strong scene between the Unnamed and Lucia is in fact surprisingly weak, lacking light and shade and all those contrasts needed to suggest the presence of two psychologies and two distinct and opposing outlooks on life. In this scene the real weakling is the Unnamed, in spite of his angry grimaces straight from a puppet show; he is weak because he is not really wicked, not because wickedness itself is weakness. The really strong character is Lucia, but her strength flounders in a vacuum precisely because the Unnamed's wickedness is not there. Consequently once the Unnamed is by himself, his conversion is coldly and skilfully presented to us, step by step, until he reaches the rock-bottom of his crisis—the temptation to suicide. From this point, starting out with his recollection of Lucia's words, 'God forgives so many things for one work of mercy'—a very precise phrase which indicates not only the cost but the profit of the imminent conversion—the Unnamed begins climbing up the slope again, step by step, until the meeting with Cardinal Borromeo. We have said that his conversion is coldly and skilfully graded; we should now add that it is precisely this shrewd and impersonal gradation that betrays its edifying and didactic character. For it is not the conversion of an individual person—indeed how could it be as the Unnamed himself does not exist?—but a typical conversion, the conversion of everyone and no one, in other words conversion according to Catholic realism. Every bit of it is propaganda, technique, literature, without a single genuine moment—at the very place where Manzoni could most easily have moved us, had he so wished. Yet even here we cannot speak of the art of oratory, for, just like the socialist realist writers, Manzoni intended not to make propaganda but poetry; that is, he intended to give us a poetic reality effectively inspired by Catholicism. He failed; he had to rely on his superb literary technique. Never mind, he is a poet here as elsewhere, even if elsewhere he succeeds in his intention, and here he fails.

It is surely no accident that the absolutely positive character in *The Betrothed*, Cardinal Borromeo, comes up against the absolutely negative one, the Unnamed. It is no accident because the Unnamed, as we have said, is a character created by Catholic realism, so a saint such as the Cardinal, made of the same propagandist material, would obviously be the person to receive him on his conversion. What can we say about the Cardinal? He stands in the centre of the novel like a baroque statue under a gold and marble canopy at the heart of the Counter-Reformation Church; or like a figure by a mannerist painter, all eyes up to heaven, hands joined, halo and ecstasy, upright before a background of stormy clouds and shafts of light. It is a great stylised painting, admirable in its complete and perfect literariness, amusing and interesting if looked on as a sheer product of talent without regard to the meaning Manzoni wants to attribute to it. To be sure the Cardinal expresses himself very well. Even Manzoni grows aware of it and issues his warning at the beginning of Chapter XXVI:

> . . . and to tell the truth, even we, sitting with our manuscript in front of us, and a pen in our hands, even we, I say, feel a certain reluctance to proceed. We find something rather strange in this proposal, with so little effort, of a series of such admirable precepts of heroism and charity, of keen solicitude for others, and of unlimited sacrifice of self. But reflecting that these things were said by one who actually practised them, we will forge bravely ahead.

But while this warning note is a proof of Manzoni's artistic awareness, it cannot—and how could it?—modify the Cardinal's fundamentally propagandist character. And let it here be noted, *à propos* of Manzoni's famous irony that can be glimpsed even in the above quotation, that while it is always deep and beguiling in the truly realist parts of the novel, it seems inadequate, if not positively non-existent, in the Catholic realist parts. The absolutely negative characters such as Don Rodrigo or the Unnamed are taken as seriously as the absolutely positive figures such as Cardinal Borromeo and Father Cristoforo. And this because Manzoni's irony serves always to indicate a complete command of the material; it is inseparable from his poetry. Where it is lacking or inadequate, we guess that Manzoni is operating within fine writing which by its very nature is refractory to irony.

Another of the positive characters of Catholic realism is Cristoforo after his conversion. We have had to divide him into two distinct figures for the purposes of what we are trying to prove. He closely resembles Cardinal Borromeo, the more so as he is shown us in similar situations to the Cardinal's (compare the dialogues between Father Cristoforo and Don Rodrigo, and Cardinal Borromeo and Don Abbondio), and it would be easy to put the friar's sermons into the Cardinal's mouth, and vice versa. But Cristoforo is less of a success artistically than the Cardinal for his action spreads through the whole book and displays the immobility of oratory, whereas the Cardinal is restricted to a short and circumscribed episode. Father Cristoforo is the character with whom Manzoni's Catholic realism has least happy results. The simile with which Chapter VII begins,

> Fra Cristoforo arrived with the air of an able general who has lost an important battle through no fault of his own and goes hurrying off, distressed but not discouraged, worried but not overwhelmed, in haste but not in flight, to reinforce points that are hard pressed, rally his troops, and give out fresh orders . . .

is ugly and almost ridiculous in a way rare in Manzoni, who is possibly second only to Dante for beauty, originality, and apposite imagery. It serves to measure the icy exteriority into which the man who created Don Abbondio or Gertrude falls when he begins applying the rules of Catholic realism. Would Father Cristoforo have been different without Catholic realism? No, he would not have been different, he would simply have disappeared from the novel, for he owes his existence to a kind of subtraction Manzoni made from the character of Renzo in the interests of Catholic realism. In other words Father Cristoforo either preaches sermons, that is, does nothing, or else does the things that Renzo should have done had his character been exploited to the full. It is he who confronts Don Rodrigo instead of Renzo, he makes the Christian reproaches to Renzo that Renzo should have made to himself, he takes on his shoulders part of the persecution in fact destined for Renzo. He is an intermediary in a cowl, superfluous like all intermediaries, who allows Manzoni to leave nothing to the personal initiative of his hero, and to correct his conduct with literary precepts whenever necessary. He is Renzo's conscience, confiscated for the Church's benefit and embodied in a churchman. This is not to deny at all that in seventeenth-century Lombardy such situations could have occurred, of two innocent victims of persecution putting themselves under the protection of a friar. Let us say that the character of Father Cristoforo reveals the smoothness of propaganda rather than the ruggedness of reality.

So far we have been discussing Manzoni's Catholic realism, and seeking to explain the failure of the religious propaganda understood by Manzoni in a thoroughly modern sense—that is to say not as oratory but as poetry, and the only possible poetry. We have said that the clue to the abstract nature of Catholic realism lies in the conversions of Cristoforo and the Unnamed—that is to say in the transformation, by means of religion, of negative characters into positive characters. Now we have to add that when it comes to representing corruption, and corrupt characters, Manzoni excels. What is corruption? It is the exact opposite of conversion. In conversion the character proceeds from bad to good, in corruption from good to bad. It is the transformation of a positive character, or one at least potentially positive, into a negative character. Moreover Manzoni excels when it comes to depicting what we should call public corruption. This consists in society passing from a state of normality to one of abnormality, from a state of order to one of disorder, from a state of prosperity to one of abject poverty. Incidentally, we must note that Manzoni, who expends so much effort on depicting conversion, or the transit from evil to good in the individual, never dealt with the public equivalent to conversion, that is revolution. Or rather he dealt with it in the episode of the hunger riots in which both Renzo and the crowd are inspired by unreservedly revolutionary feelings; but it is typical of Manzoni's conservatism that the whole episode is interpreted in terms of its opposite, in terms of the corruption of a previous state which was positive only because it was the *status quo*.

So when we are dealing with Manzoni's excellence in describing private and public corruption, it is hardly necessary to emphasise the complete success of the character of Don Abbondio, the character of a man slowly and deeply corrupted by fear. Who is Don Abbondio? If Providence is the chief protagonist of **The Betrothed,** then Don Abbondio is her opposite, the one who not only does not perform miracles, but does not even do what he could or should do like other men. In this way, besides being the opponent of Providence, he is—like all those who do not do their duty—its very justification. Don Abbondio refuses to marry Renzo and Lucia because he is afraid; Providence intervenes in the shape of the flea that bites a plague-ridden rat and so transmits the plague to Don Rodrigo. Don Abbondio believes in nothing, not even in

Providence. So great is his unbelief that he will not agree to perform the wedding until it is mathematically certain that the plague, which has already carried away several hundreds of thousands of Milanese, has also made away with Don Rodrigo. For Don Abbondio is not a wicked man but a corrupt man, and his corruption in a corrupt society is looked on with indulgence even by those who are not corrupt. Like the thieves in Butler's *Erewhon,* he is a sick man who deserves compassion rather than hatred.

At the beginning of the novel Don Abbondio is presented to us as a man aware of where good lies and even inclined to perform it. Upright even, an important trait. In other words so far Don Abbondio has done nothing outrageous. Manzoni brings out what could be called the positive side of Don Abbondio in strong relief, so that, later on, the negative effect of Don Rodrigo's injunction will stand out all the more sharply in its corruption. This corruption is a sickness of soul. But Manzoni underlies its diseased nature by the fever that strikes Don Abbondio immediately after his meeting with the cut-throats, a fever that persists throughout the novel and ends only with the death of Don Rodrigo. Thus we have the story of Don Abbondio whereas we do not have the story of Don Rodrigo. But we have it because Don Abbondio is not wicked—though he does evil—but only corrupt, because Manzoni unloads Don Abbondio's guilt onto Don Rodrigo though, as we have seen, telling us nothing whatever as to how Don Rodrigo became the wicked man he is. Thus Don Abbondio's corruption remains rather in mid-air, as it does to Don Abbondio himself, as something that can be forgiven because attributed to remote causes and obscured by a whole number of distant responsibilities. That is to say we find ourselves on the ambiguous soil of corruption, not on the clear unequivocal soil of wickedness.

Don Abbondio's character has been compared to Sancho Panza. But this is not really exact because in **The Betrothed** there is no Don Quixote to act as a foil to Don Abbondio's cowardice and make it comic; Cardinal Borromeo is the opposite of a Don Quixote, and so Don Abbondio's conscience has to do without the salutary stimulus of Don Quixote. True, he seems to be aware of his wrongdoing for a moment during his interview with the Cardinal, but only for a moment. When the plague is over and he meets Renzo again, he is just as cautious as ever— 'You want to ruin yourself, and you want to ruin me.' It is the moment to say that Don Abbondio is the perfect exponent of a particularly Italian kind of corruption, which, for want of a better word, we shall call historical. In Italy one is always coming across men of every class, profession or status, powerful or humble, famous or unknown, intelligent or stupid, old or young, rich or poor, who display a fear of speaking their minds, of offending some authority or other, of taking down their defences, of compromising themselves, of letting themselves go and saying what they think about whatever it may be. At first one is tempted to attribute this to some particular self-interest that might explain, if not excuse, it. But more often than not, no such interest exists. All that exists is fear, fear without any immediate or apparent cause, and coupled with fear, and just as strong, the liking for a quiet life. And as there is no immediate cause we feel almost obliged to delve back to a distant, indirect, ancestral and historical one, so that we think, We must blame the Counter-Reformation, foreign governments, Italian tyrannies, heaven knows what, for this man having water in his veins instead of blood. Don Abbondio's character is living and immortal because he is the very embodiment of a national corruption so ancient that by now it seems second nature.

Don Abbondio is corrupted by the fear instilled in him by Don Rodrigo's cut-throats, whereas Gertrude is corrupted by the suggestion implanted in her by her father and the society to which she belongs. The story of the Nun of Monza has always been praised as one of the finest parts of *The Betrothed,* and with reason. It is not by chance, we might add, that it is the story of a long and tortuous corruption, the transformation of an innocent person into a wicked one, followed step by step with a wonderful, realistic and inventive capacity that we would look for in vain in the descriptions of the conversions, or transformations of wicked characters into good ones. For instance we know nothing of the childhood of the Unnamed; whereas we first meet Gertrude when she is 'still hidden in her mother's womb'. The progressive metamorphosis of the innocent baby into a desperate liar, then a faithless nun, then an adulteress, and finally a criminal, is as strong as anything that has ever been written on the subject of corruption. If we compare the story of Gertrude with the similar one in Diderot's *La Réligieuse,* we feel we are comparing a deep well of black, still water with a swift, clear stream. For whereas Diderot knows the causes of the corruption and points them out for us, Manzoni—as in the case of Don Abbondio—prefers silence. For Diderot the catharsis takes place outside the novel as result of the pending Revolution that the author seems to be forecasting in every line he writes. For Manzoni, the conservative and Catholic, the only possible catharsis is æsthetic, and very remarkable it is, but a catharsis that is only æsthetic is peculiar to decadentism. Even the rottenness in the State of Denmark is purified in a practical way with the blast of trumpets, after the bloody supper, heralding the arrival of Fortinbras. But Gertrude's corruption is a 'fine' corruption, a mysterious, dark corruption, without cause and seemingly without effect; begotten of an ambiguously historical and social destiny, it is lost in the silence and shadow of the Church.

At all events, this decadent Manzoni is at the peak of his powers. In the story of Gertrude (unlike the story of the Unnamed) there is no moment of abstraction, nothing is stated without being shown, or said without being illustrated. This time we have a close series of pictures pressing one after the other—things, objects, situations, characters. Here Manzoni is not content to play the impartial historian, as when he summarised the Unnamed's criminal career in a few pages. From the outset he establishes a strong subjective relationship with the figure of Gertrude, a relationship composed both of sorrowful pity and refined cruelty. So we are utterly astonished to find Benedetto Croce maintaining that the 'method' used in constructing the successful characters in *The Betrothed* is the same as that used in constructing the characters that belong to Catholic realism. For ourselves, we are not going to discuss method, for we have no idea what it means in connection with poetry, but rather the greater or less relationship between the artist and his material. A lively and complex relationship runs between Manzoni and Don Abbondio and Gertrude; whereas between Manzoni and the Unnamed there is little or no relationship, unless we are to use the word relationship about the instrumental relationship between a propaganda writer and his prefabricated and didactic material.

Strange to say the total wickedness that Manzoni was unable to portray in Don Rodrigo (silly rather than wicked) or the Unnamed (quite unreal), he is able to describe in a few lines and with perfect felicity in telling the story of Gertrude's corruption. For here we have Don Egidio, a wicked man, wickeder than Don Rodrigo or the Unnamed because, unlike them, he has motives for his wickedness, and the very modern motives of sadism and sacrilegious lust at that.

> Our manuscript calls him Egidio without mentioning his family name. This fellow had noticed Gertrude from a little window that overlooked a courtyard in the wing of her apartments as she sometimes idly passed or strolled there; and *attracted, rather than alarmed, by the dangers and impiety of the undertaking,* one day ventured to address her. The wretched woman replied.

The provision of a brief, but deeply psychological, motive for Egidio's behaviour is entirely lacking in the case of Don Rodrigo, and we shall never know why or how he took a fancy to Lucia; and this is because Don Rodrigo is a wicked man without roots, in function of Catholic realism, whereas Egidio is a wicked man who is justified, a functionary of the corruption for which, as we have seen, Manzoni had a special feeling. But in the course of the story of Gertrude, Manzoni paints good as well as bad. Here, for instance, we have a few lines that are worth all the edifying eloquence of Cardinal Borromeo:

> One might think that Gertrude would be drawn to other nuns who had not taken part in those intrigues, who liked her as a companion without having wanted her as one, and who showed by their pious, busy and cheerful example how one could not only live, but be happy, there . . . She might have been less against them had she known or guessed that the few black balls found in the box which had decided her acceptance had been put there by them.

Here the goodness is real, deep and mysterious, not the merely preached and mannered goodness of the Cardinal or Father Cristoforo. And as with Egidio's wickedness, we must note that the goodness, too, exists in function of corruption, gets its justification from corruption and is the counterweight to corruption.

To be sure the picture changes when we turn from private to public corruption. There are no more gloomy, narrow, individual destinies, like the episode of the Nun of Monza, nor ruthless caricatures as with Don Abbondio, but collective disasters and tragedies with history as background. Yet if we look closely we see that the procedure is the same. Manzoni begins by showing us the normal, positive, upright condition which is destined to be corrupted: the Duchy of Milan before the war, the city of Milan before the plague. Thereupon, with cruel precision, he notes down the first symptom of corruption, the tiny cloud in the clear sky out of which the storm will develop—the political and military punctilio of the King of Spain that will lead to German troops passing through the Valtellina, and Lovati's entry into Milan—the soldier who introduces the plague. Thereafter, slowly and powerfully and very gradually, he describes the progress of the corruption and its final overflowing. As we have said, the procedure is the one he follows when describing private corruption, and now we should add that what in private corruption is psychological in public corruption becomes physical and material. Gertrude's degradation has its counterpart in the diffusion of the plague in Milan; and it is with the same almost clinical complacency that Manzoni notes both the increasing disintegration of the Nun of Monza and the increasing havoc of the plague. Though unquestionably the episode of Gertrude, for all its strength, stands out less in our minds, and has less importance, than the part devoted to the plague.

It is not difficult to find the reason for the domination of the plague, which, together with the gentle landscapes and certain specific emotions, forms the principal characteristic of Manzoni's singular world. The reason is that a plague is absolute corruption, corruption generalised to cover the particular: with its swellings and fevers and blight of the whole body it is the symbol of all that is unwholesome and disintegrated; and with its mysterious and irresistible way of spreading it is the very image of moral evil against which no defence is possible. So, unique among all writers in all ages for having made a plague one of the principal subjects of his novel, Manzoni (by using the general to cover the particular) is *the* painter of disease or corruption. But there are plagues and plagues; the plague in *The Betrothed,* unlike the plagues in Boccaccio and Defoe, owes its fame to the fact that Manzoni really feels it as a primarily moral phenomenon—rather like the seven plagues of Egypt in the Old Testament. So when he is describing the plague Manzoni feels, so to speak, in his element, in a metaphysical and universal corruption that spares nothing and no one. As in the part devoted to the Nun of Monza, so here in the plague, Manzoni reaches the peak of his art—for instance with the famous incident when the mother hands over her dead child to the *monatti* or corpse-bearers, or the episode of Don Rodrigo. The truth is that corruption inspires the decadent Manzoni every bit as much as conversion weakens and deflates his expressive powers.

The plague, then, as we have said, is corruption *par excellence.* But in *The Betrothed* there are other forms of public corruption, described with the same power, the same slowly mounting drama, the same satisfaction: the episode of the shortages that lead up to the bread riots; that of the war which culminates in the sacking and devastation of the villages invaded by the troops; the one concerning justice, centred round Renzo's arrest, and even earlier in the scene between Renzo and 'Tangle-Weaver', the lawyer. An underlying idea can be seen running like a thread through all these episodes of public corruption. Man can do nothing against evil; evil has to work itself out to the bitter end: then Providence will take charge in its inscrutable manner so as to save those individuals or societies worthy of salvation. Which means we are up against a pessimism of the conservative kind that harmonises well with decadentism, or the delighted and apathetic contemplation of that evil which is judged to be beyond remedy. This explains why, in *The Betrothed,* the descriptions of social unrest have a close resemblance to those of the plague. Manzoni, who is conservative because he is decadent and decadent because he is conservative, has no belief in palingenesis and rebirth. He interprets social unrest in terms of

sterile and disorderly tremors in sick organisms incapable of cure.

Now let us take a further step forward. As we have said, corruption signifies the opposite process to the process of conversion. In conversion you go from evil to good; in corruption you go from good to evil. But in corruption there is also something else; corruption can last indefinitely and become chronic. At times the progress of corruption is so gradual that it passes unobserved. Men, societies, nations, grow corrupt slowly—by stages so imperceptible that they do not observe them. Moreover the corrupt man, the corrupt society, the corrupt nation, do not want—owing to their conservatism—to reform, so they end up by accepting their corruption. Now, for all Manzoni's moralism, it is precisely this that we notice in *The Betrothed.* Corruption, though described with such power, originality and depth, is given no cathartic outlet; it stagnates in the book rather as it stagnates in Italian life, whether yesterday or today. Don Abbondio is corrupted by fear and so he remains to the end; Gertrude is corrupted by lying and cannot escape; Milanese society, for all 'the great broom' of the plague, remained corrupt; and men like Tangle-Weaver and Don Rodrigo and Attilio, who have been carried away by the plague, will be replaced, we feel, by others equally overbearing and dishonest. The point is not that we would like to see these people change their characters, or Milanese society undergo radical reform, it is rather that the make-up of both characters and society excludes any ideal element, that is, any real awareness of corruption. To take a single example: Chichikov, the hero of Gogol's *Dead Souls,* is every bit as corrupt as Don Abbondio, even more so. Yet Chichikov has a semblance of awareness of evil, and it is this that allows him to be a protagonist. Whereas Don Abbondio gets no further than being anything but a huge caricature.

So the stuffy atmosphere of *The Betrothed,* which Tommaso Scalvini attributed to 'a temple that covers the faithful and the altar', is not due to religion (in *The Divine Comedy,* too, we find ourselves in a temple, and yet we can breathe there as deeply as we like), but to Manzoni's conservatism which, like all conservatisms, is decadent and fascinated by corruption, yet incapable of finding a solution on any but the æsthetic plane. *The Betrothed* is a nineteenth-century villa, not a temple, and the air we breathe there is not dogma but social conservatism. This decadent conservatism, or conservative decadence, leads directly, as we have already noted, to Catholic realism, or the attempt to overcome corruption by means of propaganda.

But like all conservatives who are disinterested and in good faith, Manzoni nursed in his heart the dream of a different life, a life incorrupt, pure, simple and outside history—in other words, harmless and in keeping with his conservatism. It is in this dream, as we see it, and not in Catholic realism, that we find the ideal counterbalance to corruption. This dream is expressed in the figures of the two main characters and in the world they represent.

We have kept Renzo and Lucia to the last because they are the finest and most original figures in *The Betrothed,* and also the key to Manzoni's conception of life, society and religion. Unlike Gertrude, these two characters have not been reconstituted from history, in the manner of an essay; we see them through what they do, like Don Rodrigo and the Unnamed. But, unlike Don Rodrigo and the Unnamed, they are alive and real. For the wickedness of Don Rodrigo and the Unnamed are cerebral, whereas Renzo and Lucia have qualities and defects that are intuited by sympathy. What are these qualities and defects? Lucia is gentle, sweet, discreet, bashful and reserved; yet at times affected, obstinate, peasantlike, and inclined to take pleasure in work too much following a kind of stereotyped perfection. Renzo is frank, honest, brave, full of good sense and energy; but also at times stupid, rash and violent. As we can see from the sum of these qualities and defects, Manzoni wanted to portray two peasant figures whom he had probably had the opportunity of observing at length in real life before re-creating them in art—doubtless in the country round Lake Como itself. Manzoni's social sensitiveness, which was so subtle and quick, can be appreciated yet again in these two characters in whom we see all the attributes of a lower social rank yet without that detachment and sense of superiority that often accompany portraits of the kind. Manzoni managed to look on Renzo and Lucia with real affection; the well-known remark at the end of Chapter XV—'that name for which we too feel some affection and reverence'—was not a literary device but the plain and simple truth. Affection of this kind was new and original. In Manzoni's time, as in ours for that matter, to have two working people as the hero and heroine of a novel demanded a not inconsiderable qualitative leap, and a powerful capacity for idealisation. We can judge of the novelty of Manzoni's affection for Renzo and Lucia when we consider that we had to wait for Verga to find another Italian writer who turned a brotherly eye towards the ordinary people.

Manzoni has gathered around Renzo and Lucia, as around two modest but truly venerated idols, all the things he loves in his heart, all the things he contrasts with the society of Gertrude, Don Rodrigo and the Count Uncle. That is to say, with his own society, and in general with society as borne out by history. For to Manzoni history seems nothing but corruption; and Renzo and Lucia are not corrupt precisely because they are outside history. The equation, history=corruption, antihistory=purity, is especially easy to observe in those places where Manzoni puts one of his two main protagonists, who are pure and outside history, face to face with a character who is corrupt because he belongs to history: Renzo and Tangle-Weaver, Renzo and Don Abbondio, Renzo and Ferrer, and, even more, Lucia and Gertrude. In the meeting between these last two we find the fundamental contrast of *The Betrothed* in all its force and significance. On one side there is the country girl who 'blushes and hangs her head', on the other the lustful and criminal young abbess whose portrait is among the finest and the most powerful in the whole novel. At last Gertrude is confronted not by a secondary character but by her opposite. When we compare the brief but real meeting between Lucia and Gertrude with the meeting that is all eloquence and mannerism between Lucia and the Unnamed, we can see that the real contrast between good and evil in *The Betrothed* is not the contrast between the holiness of religion and the impiety of the wicked—along the lines of Catholic realism—but between the natural purity of people and the corruption of history and the classes that make history.

In any case Renzo and Lucia act as catalysts, and everything that Manzoni loved and cherished gathers spontaneously around them. Manzoni described horrors and terrors every bit as much as Poe, if not more, and with a sensibility not all that different. Yet when we use the word 'Manzonian' we imply something very different from the macabre and the terrifying; we imply something gentle, sweet, idyllic, homely, affectionate; something recalling Virgil and Petrarch—that very something which, in the novel, we know as Renzo and Lucia. It is to them that we owe his famous passage of goodbye to the mountains and the flight towards the river Adda; to them we owe his paintings of Lombard landscapes, his loveliest metaphors and images, his poetic passages of family intimacy; to them we owe all that was truly religious in Manzoni—not the religion of Catholic realism along the lines of Father Cristoforo and Cardinal Borromeo, but his own religion, which was, after all, the religion of his hero and heroine. Manzoni's character as creator of Renzo and Lucia—either because it is more positive and lovable than his character as creator of Gertrude and the plague, or else because it corresponds more closely to the Italian sensibility—has finally prevailed over all the alternatives, so much so that it has become almost proverbial and has strengthened Manzoni's public image (incomplete, to say the least) as an educationalist and a faithful and peaceful mirror of the Christian and middle-class virtues of the nineteenth century.

So when we define and explain Renzo and Lucia, we are really defining and explaining Manzoni's ideal world, with the qualities of his decadent sensibility and the rather narrow boundaries of his upper-class conservatism. Who are Renzo and Lucia? They are two working-class people. Their life is extremely simple because they are poor and because they live in a little country village with only a few houses, a mere hamlet. So we have the first ideal: poor, simple country life, not to say primitive and needy country life. Life with no public duties, that is; no civic responsibilities, no political ambitions, no financial cares, in fact none of the headaches of the city-dweller. Life fined down to the bone: work, the family.

But in the little hamlet, the small cluster of houses in which Renzo and Lucia live, there is a church. Renzo and Lucia are religious. Hence, in addition to poor, simple country life, there is also the ideal of a religion that expresses this life directly. It has been said too often that the background of Manzoni's religion was Jansenist; perhaps it was so in his life, but in *The Betrothed* there is nothing to show it. In fact Renzo's and Lucia's religion—which is also the religion of Manzoni, the cultivated and intellectual aristocrat—has much closer links with the parish than the library and is as far removed from learning as is possible. It is the religion of two uneducated people who can neither read nor write; the religion, as we have said, of humble people, and of two such humble people as Renzo and Lucia. It is a religion of the heart rather than of the head, of feeling rather than of reason. A religion, incidentally, that is very modern; the only one, indeed, that is still felt and practised today in a sincere and wholehearted way by the Catholic masses of the world.

In order to become acquainted with the religion of *The Betrothed* we need only compare it with the religion of Dante Alighieri—keeping strictly to its æsthetic results. In *The Divine Comedy* religion penetrates everywhere and is nowhere imposed. There is no line of demarcation between religion and culture, politics, society, *mores*. In *The Betrothed,* on the other hand, religion seems to be the almost exclusive inheritance of humble (that is, uneducated) people; whenever Manzoni turns to describing the ruling (that is, the educated) classes, religion disappears and one gets the impression that it has never existed. Renzo's and Lucia's religion (that is, Manzoni's religion) has for long lost all relationship with learning. The result is that politics (the Thirty Years War, Don Gonsalvo of Corduba, Ambrogio Spinola), learning (the caricature of Don Ferrante) and history as a whole, all fall an easy prey to Manzoni's corrosive irony. With an author of less artistic stature than Manzoni, less reflective, less deep, less complicated, the caricature of Don Ferrante, or the discussion of the Thirty Years War, would have a purely reactionary ring. And this not because Don Ferrante's learning was not a hotch-potch of superstition and mistaken ideas and the politics of the Thirty Years War was not to a great extent absurd, but because Manzoni seems to conclude from this that all learning and all politics are equally misleading and unnecessary. Manzoni makes fun of Don Ferrante because he studied erroneous and misleading books, and does not seem to realise that after all Don Ferrante was a respectable person precisely because he read and studied, even if the books were false and misleading. Similarly, when Manzoni pulls the Thirty Years War to pieces he does not seem to realise that that war was simply a reflection of the war of ideas that was tearing Europe apart at that time and was to end with the rise and establishment of the Reformation countries on the ruins of the Spanish Empire. Assuredly, however, these things could not have the slightest importance as seen through the eyes of two poor little peasants; and especially as seen through the spectacles of their simple religion.

We must remark at this point that the ideal of the poor and simple life, of ignorance, and the religion of the heart, is nevertheless not so extreme and thus revolutionary in Manzoni as, for instance, the fundamentalist and uncompromising evangelism of Tolstoy. Tolstoy, as everyone knows, wanted to live out his ideal to its end, to the point of himself becoming a peasant and working in the fields; whereas Manzoni, as is equally well known, for all his sincere sympathy for humble people, did not himself become humble but spent his life as a shrewd and astute administrator of his property. In reality, as we have said, Manzoni's ideal has narrow limits imposed by his conservatism. It is the ideal of the good master who looks benevolently on the simple people who work for him, treats them with affection and humanity, but never for a moment forgets that he is the master. The ideal, in Manzoni's own words, of the marquis heir of Don Rodrigo who was humble enough to set himself below Renzo and Lucia but not to be on an equality with them. This ideal is made perfectly innocuous as being maintained with great firmness within the limits of a given society—the society Manzoni himself belonged to.

This paternalistic and patronal limitation can be detected in all those places in *The Betrothed* where Renzo and Lucia—or Agnese or the other humble people—are on the scene, by an extremely light, almost imperceptible, yet firm and exact, nuance of upper-class detachment; but above all those passages where Manzoni's affection is tempered with indulgent irony. It is typical of his complicated psychology that after he has made fun of Don Ferrante's

learning, Manzoni makes use of the same learning to make fun gracefully of poor Renzo who is the very opposite of Don Ferrante and has no learning whatsoever. It is Manzoni's way of circumscribing his own ideal and making it harmless; a typically paternalistic way based on the superiority of better education. All the part about Renzo on the road and in the inn after the hunger riots shows a masterly play of this indulgent, yet strongly restrictive, irony of the good master who sees one of his peasants having a drink too many and talking a whole lot of nonsense about things he does not understand and are above his head. Here, and in similar places, the Manzoni who idealises humble people is interrupted by the Manzoni who sees them as they are, naturally in terms of his experience as a master.

Here—to put it frankly—we come to one of Manzoni's most disconcerting sides. And we are all the more perplexed because it is a side closely bound up with Renzo and Lucia, with the two people who are the finest and most original in the book. Critics have often said that the best parts of *The Betrothed* are those that treat of humble characters or Manzoni's feelings of sympathy towards them. And we have already pointed out just how much we agree with this judgement. But there is humility and humility. There is Christian humility which is a universal virtue common to rich and poor alike, and there is servile humility, social, inferior humility which is special to the poor and the outcome of age-long oppression and humiliation. Now we in no wise deny that Manzoni intended to extol that first kind of humility in the characters of Renzo, Lucia, Agnese, and the rest of his plebeian characters, but we only wish that he had not confused it with the second kind of humility which is also present, alas, and in greater quantity than poetic truth would require.

The fact is that we continually find, side by side with expressions of Christian humility in the talk of the characters in *The Betrothed,* phrases that seem to confirm their condition of inferiority, of subjection, of obscurity. Agnese says, 'For us poor people the wool seems more tangled . . . '; Renzo says, 'We poor people can't talk . . . '; and Renzo again, 'With someone who really helps the poor . . . '; Agnese, 'And we poor people can't understand everything'; and again Agnese, 'But you'll forgive me if I speak badly, because we're decent folk'; Lucia, 'We poor women . . . '; Renzo, 'How glad he was to find himself with poor people'; Renzo, 'And sleep like a poor boy . . . '; Renzo, 'The words a poor boy says . . . '; Renzo, 'They want to muddle up a poor boy who hasn't studied'; Renzo, ' . . . Tie down a poor boy'; Lucia, 'The master [that is to say the Unnamed who has kidnapped her] promised it to me. He said, "Tomorrow morning". Where is the master?'; the tailor, 'A gentleman of that sort, like a parish priest'; Agnese, 'You don't need much to make the poor seem rascals' and so on, in many other places. These are the phrases that made Gramsci say that 'the aristocratic character of Manzoni's Catholicism can be detected in amused "pity" towards his working-class figures'. From these phrases it would seem as though Manzoni was at pains to put his humble characters 'in their place' through their own lips; they are indications of the attitude he is always attributing to those characters. What exactly is that attitude? It can easily be summed up: an attitude of resigned subjection, of almost complacent inferiority, of submissiveness beyond discussion. It is the attitude of plebeians totally bereft of pride if not of dignity, literally prostrate before the powerful. Yet what a set of powerful people they are! For one of the most curious and significant of Manzoni's traits is this: that he makes his humble people full of respect for the powerful, while making the powerful totally unworthy of their respect.

Still in connection with Manzoni's attitude to the humble, we could recall the episode of Cardinal Borromeo's visit to the tailor's house where Agnese and Lucia have been taken in. The anecdote is full of grace, a picture typical of a kind at which Manzoni excelled, as giving scope for all his kindly and subtle humour. The Cardinal visits the two women at the tailor's—a good man, according to Manzoni, if rather infatuated, and with the speech he wants to address to the Cardinal firmly in his mind: but when he actually finds himself in the Cardinal's presence he gets all flustered and can only come out with an idiotic 'Just think of it . . . '. As we have said, the incident is very charming and told with great elegance; but when we look at it more closely we cannot fail to note the way in which the humility of the humble man and the power of the powerful man are, so to speak, rubbed in and confirmed. In other words the story underlines the tailor's subjection before the Cardinal and endows him not only with social, but also with moral and intellectual inferiority. Now we are all well aware that it is not very illuminating to compare Manzoni with such a different writer as Boccaccio. But we can hardly resist the temptation to recall, in contrast to the tale of Manzoni's tailor, the story in the *Decameron* which tells of Cisti, the baker, who in a similar situation puts a man of power to shame with a sharp phrase; or the one about King Agilulf's groom who feels so little inferior to the King himself that he manages, by an ingenious trick, to sleep with the Queen. Why make such a comparison? Because while Manzoni seems almost to take pleasure in corroborating that poor people are also inferior, Boccaccio has no fear of showing us the hard core of human equality within the multicoloured shell of social importance. Probably the servitude of the common people was greater in Boccaccio's time than in Manzoni's, five centuries later. But there was more democratic spirit in Boccaccio than Manzoni.

So Catholic realism does not stop at preaching a mannered religion, it also presents us with a social world in its own image and likeness. And it is Catholic realism, speaking through Renzo, that dictates the moral at the end of *The Betrothed:* 'I have learnt not to get involved in riots . . . and not to make speeches in the street.' A moral that is certainly not Christian. Jesus never learnt not to get into riots and not to make speeches in the street. He threw himself into riots, and preached in the streets; and the rest is known. At this point we will be asked why on earth we chose Manzoni so as to speak of Catholic realism, or rather of socialist realism—or the art of propaganda as it is understood today. Our answer is that we chose Manzoni precisely because he is so great an artist. The propaganda art of modern artists is so inferior that there is always a danger of being told that the fault lies not with the propaganda but with the inborn mediocrity of the artists. But with Manzoni we have one of the greatest artists of all time; and yet, for all the resources of his genius—which indeed are infinite when compared with those of socialist realist writers—the art of propaganda as carried out in the modern way, that is to say not with the procedures of eloquence but with poetic portrayal, produces in him the very same effects.

It may be objected that there are no novelists without an ideology, and that thus all novelists in some way practise the art of propaganda in the modern, that is the poetic, way. But we distinguish between the novelists whose ideology is an original creation of their own, lacking an even indirect relationship with political, social and religious situations, and those who, for whatever reason, accept the pre-existing ideology of some institution or party or society or religion. And they accept it not so much because it lies within the reality they are describing (which could partly explain why they accept it) as because they would like it to do so. Stendhal's heroic ideology, Dostoievsky's Christian-decadent ideology—to take two examples—are original creations of those two writers; it would be difficult indeed to imagine a real world governed in practice by either ideology. But Manzoni's Catholic realist ideology, or the socialist realism of the Soviet writers, have nothing original about them, they are the orthodox ideologies of a religion such as the Catholic one, or of a political party such as the Communist one; and alas, it is only too easy to imagine a world governed in practice by either of these. The difference is substantial. Stendhal and Dostoievsky put their ideologies before us in a disinterested way, as they would put a landscape before us; whereas Manzoni and the socialist realist writers try to impose it on us. The obscure uneasiness we spoke of at the beginning thus comes from a suspicion that we are being 'got at'.

So these notes have no other intention than to defend poetry, beginning with Manzoni's poetry. Please do not tell us that poetry does not need defending. It is in fact more threatened today than ever before. For in our time totalitarianism no longer demands decent oratory, it demands poetry. Whereas Manzoni has shown us in his masterpiece (if unknowingly) that anti-historical totalitarianism cannot produce other than propaganda art; and propaganda art, being outside history, is not poetry. (pp. 192-227)

> *Alberto Moravia [pseudonym of Alberto Pincherle], "Alessandro Manzoni, or the Hypothesis of a Catholic Realism," in his* Man as an End, a Defense of Humanism: Literary, Social and Political Essays, *translated by Bernard Wall, Farrar, Straus and Giroux, 1966, pp. 192-227.*

Sergio Pacifici   (essay date 1967)

[*Pacifici is an American educator, translator, and critic, specializing in Italian language and literature. In the following excerpt, he analyzes theme, narrative technique, style, characterization, and setting in* The Betrothed.]

What is *The Betrothed* about? On the surface at least, the question is easily answered, for the novel's plot is possibly one of the most conventional in the history of Western fiction. The German Italianist Karl Vossler once compared the book to a fairytale, since the story has a happy ending and the young man does indeed get his girl at the end of their adventures. Briefly stated, the book revolves around the love of two young silkweavers, Renzo Tramaglino and Lucia Mondella. Their marriage plans are spoiled by a ruthless local bully, Don Rodrigo. Viewed from this angle, the tale has a deceptive simplicity, and exhibits many of the qualities of the romantic, and colorful novels in the Scottian tradition. Nothing could be further from the truth. Not only is Manzoni a writer infinitely more complex than Scott, but he strives to go well beyond a mere blending of facts and fancy. The manifold adventures the two young lovers experience before their goal can be achieved, the long period of trials and tribulations that test their strength, courage, and dimension as human beings are never visualized, and even less described, as fascinating events per se. They are, rather, presented as parts of an intricate design, a pattern ordered by a Supreme Being who governs the universe. Through the events that form the spine of the book, and through the dialogues, monologues, and descriptions that are the very fabric of the novel, the author meant to illustrate the presence of Divine Justice on earth, a Justice that triumphs even when men, overcome by their miseries or about to lose their faith, wonder whether their Father has forsaken them, abandoning them to the forces of evil. The function of each episode in the book not only serves to keep the reader interested in the fictional fate of its heroes, but enables him to extract a lesson, a moral lesson in the highest sense of the term, bound to implicate the reader himself—leading him to a more thorough understanding of the meaning of the human condition.

Viewed from still another angle, it might be said that the vitality of the book is not so much in its ordinary sequence of events that leads us to an inevitably happy resolution of the central crisis, but in the fact that the incidents themselves are skillfully used to paint an absorbing tableau of the events, customs, and manners of a nation during a certain crucial period of its history. Through the book, we see the meaning of a political fragmentation resulting from centuries of internecine wars, petty jealousies, and dependence on foreign intervention or domination to solve internal national affairs. Thus the book becomes an accurate mirror of historical conditions existing long before the wars of the Risorgimento, as well as a telling commentary on the contemporary historical scene. Manzoni's range is so broad, and so acute is his political insight—disagree as we may with his diagnosis of the true reasons for the existence of evil in the world—that precious little escapes his attention, certainly nothing that would add to the interest of the tale he is narrating. A great historical tragedy unfolds before our eyes: a local government literally unable to come to grips with the problems confronting its subjects; a moral degradation that has rendered the ruling class incapable of leading the people or inspiring their confidence; a Church frequently corrupt, or guilty of debasing practices, manipulated by external pressures and torn by internal political schisms; and, last but not least, a vast cast of *popolani* displaying their historical stupidity, often equally incapable of listening to the counsels of reason or the instincts of the heart.

One might argue that in ordinary circumstances the two youths would hardly have had to go through so many hardships just to get married. But the years in which their tale is set, 1628-31, were far from being normal in any sense of the term. In a letter Manzoni wrote to his friend, M. Fauriel, in the summer of 1823, he claimed that he was attempting "to paint sincerely the period and country in which I have placed my story. The materials are rich; everything that shows up the seamy side of man is there in abundance. Assurance in ignorance, pretension in folly, effrontery in corruption are, alas, among many others of the same kind, the most salient characteristics of the period. Happily, there are also men and traits which honour the human race; characters gifted with a strong virtue, remarkable by their attitude to obstacles and difficulties, and by their resistance, and sometimes subservience, to conventional ideas." The pressure and threats of the local tyrant succeed immediately in achieving their goal; for the small town parish priest who is supposed to perform the wedding, Don Abbondio, out of fear for personal safety is easily persuaded to slight his duty. Only by avoiding a direct confrontation with Don Rodrigo's *bravoes* can the priest, hardly a "man born with the heart of a lion," navigate the stormy waters ahead. The wedding is put off with technical, religious reasons Renzo (who does not speak Latin) fails to comprehend. Intuitively persuaded that the priest is acting on orders from above, and subsequently informed by Don Abbondio's servant Perpetua that such is indeed the case, Renzo, on the advice of Lucia's mother, Agnese, takes his case to doctor Azzecca-garbugli (Quibble-Weaver), a well-known lawyer. Through a strange and highly amusing misunderstanding, the lawyer takes Renzo for a *bravo* seeking protection from the law. When Renzo shouts the truth, Quibble-Weaver, himself an admirer and protégé of Don Rodrigo, throws him out in a rage. Now it is the turn of Fra Cristoforo, a wise and honest friar who has befriended the couple, to be summoned for advice. The friar decides to take the matter up directly with the cause of all the trouble, but his attempt is of no avail. At the castle of Don Rodrigo, however, he discovers that the arrogant *signorotto* is planning to kidnap Lucia. Agnese's own plan to have the marriage officially recognized by having the two declare, before two witnesses, that they are man and wife also fails, for the priest goes into a short, but effective, fit and flees. Having exhausted all possibilities, the three decide to part: Renzo goes to Milan, in search of work, while the two women depart for a convent in nearby Monza, where they are placed under the protection of Benedictine nuns.

Calamities follow other calamities. Renzo arrives in Milan during the bread riots and is arrested as an *agent provocateur.* Fortunately, as he is taken to jail, he succeeds in arousing the sympathy of a crowd terribly hostile toward the government, and manages to escape. Lucia, who thought she would be safe in the convent, is betrayed by the very nun who was supposedly protecting her. She is kidnapped by the *bravoes* of another powerful criminal, to whom Don Rodrigo has appealed for help in carrying out his plan. Fortunately, through a miraculous intervention of Divine Providence, Unnamed (*Innominato* being the word Manzoni uses in this case, following the Anonymous Chronicler who is supposedly the original author of the story) repents for a life of crimes, and is converted by Cardinal Federigo Borromeo who is visiting the town. Lucia and her mother are placed under the protection of a family of decent, if misguided, people—Donna Prassede and Don Ferrante. Renzo, informed at last that Lucia is alive, leaves once again for Milan, hoping to find her. This time the city is in the grip of a devastating plague, and Renzo himself is mistaken for one of the *untori* (anointers—people suspected of having spread the deadly virus of the plague) and barely escapes the wrath of the crowd. He finally reaches the *lazzaretto,* the refuge place of all those struck by the plague, and there he falls in with Fra Cristoforo who is spending his last months on earth assisting the sick. In the *lazzaretto* he also finds Lucia who has recovered from the plague and is waiting to return to the village. It is in the *lazzaretto* that we see, for the last time, Fra Cristoforo, who releases Lucia from a vow of virginity made when she was in a cell in the castle of the Unnamed. Now that Don Rodrigo and his not-so-faithful henchman Griso have died, together with many wicked and good people alike, the three can return to their abandoned home by the lake of Lecco. No longer threatened by Don Rodrigo, Don Abbondio can peacefully perform a much-postponed wedding ceremony; and the two lovers settle in a small town near Bergamo, where they have their first child, a girl, whom they promptly name Maria.

Neither a summary of the book, however complete (and mine has merely tried to give the main outline of its plot), nor the author's own attempts to define his aim, succeed in giving an accurate idea of the complexity and extraordinary beauty of *The Betrothed.* "Perhaps," as Mr. Colquhoun has noted, "it is the unfolding impression of hidden layers of meaning that contribute so much to the fascinating humanity of the book." However one reads it, *The Betrothed* is always an absorbing story about people, their simple aspirations and complex greed, their hopes and their frustrations, the power they yield, and the despicable desires that drive them—but also people who are caught in the mysterious workings of history. Not the least remarkable feat of the book is that it shows us the drama of two peasants who are the focal point of the novel simply because, for inexplicable reasons, they become at once makers and protagonists of that immensely fascinating drama we call history.

As a matter of fact, the prominent role historical events play in the novel is the element that has consistently, and inevitably, led to the facile and erroneous categorization of *The Betrothed* as a historical novel. The label, undoubtedly useful for general purposes, is bound to generate some misunderstanding about the nature of Manzoni's work, unless the author's special concept of the genre is taken into account. Indeed, particularly to the student of English literature, the term itself recalls to mind the works of Sir Walter Scott, who, when told that the Italians owed everything to him, is reported to have exclaimed, "In that case [*The Betrothed*] is my best work!" In Manzoni's novel one finds neither the glorification of past history, nor the excesses that typified the historical novel as practiced in other countries. If his work is more palatable than Scott's, this is so largely because it was conceived with totally different and far deeper awareness of the serious obligations Manzoni felt a novelist should have toward the problem of history itself. "It seems to me," he wrote to Cesare D'Azeglio, "that poetry . . . must try in every one of its subjects to discover [both] the historical and moral truth, not only as its goal but as a fuller and more continuous source of the beautiful; since in both orders of things, the false [fiction] can amuse, to be sure, but such delight, such interest, is destroyed by the knowledge of truth and [is] therefore temporary and accidental. . . . The historical and moral truth is more alive and stable as the mind sampling it is more advanced in its perception of truth."

In a lengthy *Letter to M. Chauvet,* Manzoni had clearly outlined his ideas about fiction and poetry, and expressed his opinion that art should not only be intelligible to the common man, but its subject should be drawn from history which, as he stated, would ultimately be illuminated by poetry. His meditations on a question close to his heart led him to the realization that art and truth were anything if not inseparable companions: "Art," he wrote, "should have truth as its objective and the interesting as its means." In his view, imaginative writing could indeed be turned into an excellent instrument to probe reality itself. Manzoni never intended that the poet should take over what is a historian's domain, but insisted that a poet could, by way of his special intuition and sensibility, illuminate the causes and effects of human actions left unexplored by the science of history. The poet, he believed, could not only penetrate history and its secrets; it could make them alive. "To collect the characteristic traits of a period of society and develop them in action," he wrote to Fauriel in January, 1821, apropos Tommaso Grossi's projected epic poem *Longobardi crociati,* "and profit by history, without trying to rival it—that, it seems to me, is something that can still be accorded to poetry, and what alone it can do." Thus, as we can plainly see, Manzoni defined the novelist's goal as twofold: amusement, to be sure, but amusement made meaningful by enlightment and education. He also perceived that in drama—and, by extension, in fiction—the artist should strive to satisfy both the reader's interest in characterization and representation, *and* his natural curiosity in wanting to know "what is really true and to see as much as possible into ourselves and our destiny on earth." It might well be that he chose history as the proper place in which he could locate his fictitious tale simply because it offered experiences and a reality accessible to all, and as such not subject to extensive doubts as to its veracity. He specifically chose the seventeenth century as the time for his tale to unfold partly because of its chonological proximity to his own readers, partly because of the similarities of its socio-political conditions with the nineteenth century's, and perhaps also partly (according to Alberto Moravia) "because then, for the last time, Catholicism informed all Italian life" [see excerpt dated 1960].

It is one of the recognized qualities of the novel that historical and invented events are judiciously mingled and treated with an equal amount of irony which was the product of the author's serenity and detachment. It is, to some extent, thanks to the way the two parts are held together and made into a whole that permits the reader to be less interested in seeing the story resolved than in reading it as an account of how man, not Divine Providence, is to blame for the corrupt and chaotic conditions of his world. A moral vision, firmly founded upon religious principles to which Manzoni adhered without reservations, is thus made concrete through the representation of facts and fancy. This was, as the novel limpidly attests, Manzoni's special formula for putting down on paper, as a poet, what he knew to be historically accurate, and what his religious convictions told him to be true beyond doubt.

Manzoni's readers can hardly miss the significant part religion plays in all of his writings. In a letter to Fauriel, seizing still another opportunity to discuss his important treatise *Osservazioni sulla morale cattolica* (London, 1836; *A Vindication of Catholic Morality or a Refutation of the Charges Brought Against It by Sismondi in His History*) which had just appeared in print, the novelist stated: "Religion only wishes to lead us to wisdom and moderation without unnecessary pain, only to take us by tranquil reflection to that reasonableness which we reach by weariness or by a kind of desparation." Yet, the contradiction between history and religion—or reason and faith—was to leave its indelible mark upon the novel. "Stripped to its essential," comments Mr. Colquhoun, "the dualism of the book is between a religion which reposes all hopes for a just and happy life in the next world, and the rationalism which satirically, acidly hints that the responsibility of a limited class not only aggravates injustices, war, famine and plague, but in essence causes them." Another formidable achievement of *The Betrothed* is its capacity to reconcile and balance Manzoni's genuine respect for history (a respect attested by the numerous readings in history, law, and economics he completed in preparation for the novel) with his religious beliefs. In the end, we perceive that the message of the tale is never allowed to obfuscate or damage the invented parts of the narrative.

History, as we will see, receives a good deal of attention on the part of the author, especially since it serves him to dramatize the great theme of good and evil that is at the center of the story. Indeed, so replete with implications is the conflict, that recent Marxist critics have chosen to interpret it as a brilliant example of class struggle, with the poor, exploited peasants continually at odds with the powerful, rich, and ruthless rulers. Vitally concerned with his theme as Manzoni was, he chose to give it life by examining its roots in human history. The result was an impressive and shocking analysis of the very materials that go into the making of society, and ultimately determine the solidity of the edifice of human relations and feelings. Certainly Manzoni entertained the belief that, fundamentally

Manzoni at the time of the publication of I promessi sposi.

speaking, man is a corruptible but also a decent rational animal. Nonetheless, there is ample evidence pointing to the fact that his idealistic conception of life was tempered by his awareness that the intricate network of laws enacted to uphold peace and order, are frequently manipulated by the ruling class for the sole purpose of aggrandizing its power, or satisfying its otherwise unjustifiable ambitions at the expense of the weak. As Manzoni's chief Italian biographer Alfredo Galletti observes, "the juice of the whole tale is that, in terrestrial affairs, justice is a myth; that laws are made to hurt the naïve to the advantage of the rascals; and that, on the whole, the world is ruled with as much wisdom as can be found in one of Fra Galdino's walnuts. The official representatives of law and society cut no better figure, except for Cardinal Federigo. Lawyers and magistrates, mayors and councillors, police and military, are either servile or corrupt." Living as we are in an era of political, social, and ideological turmoil, of mass demonstrations staged by minority groups desperately fighting to gain the dignity and the rights long denied them, Manzoni's world seems far from being unreal or improbable.

The world, so somberly depicted by Manzoni's imagination as one both cruel and wicked, is partly redeemed by an intense religious feeling informing the novel and allowing the protagonists to live with, and even accept, their condition. If Renzo, Lucia, and Agnese can survive their ordeal, it is because they are assisted by Providence, a mysterious, pervasive force through which God makes His presence felt to His children. Providence, frequently mentioned as though it were a magical force and yet profusely acknowledged by the heroes for enabling them to keep body and soul together, is what gives hope in this life. "Living [in this novel]," Mario Sansone perceptively writes, "consists no longer in wanting to die, but in accepting the law of life, and operating within such a law for the greatest benefit of all . . . God is here—at once the secret and the [very] reason of Life itself." Without the direct intervention of Providence itself, some of the story's most crucial events could neither take place nor be understood in their full significance. Providence sends Fra Cristoforo to help the two betrothed, just as it acts on a treacherous brigand, the Unnamed, moving him first to pity toward Lucia when he hears her imploring words, then to repentance for a life of crimes committed up to that moment, and finally to his conversion to Catholicism. Providence, too, is what brings Fra Cristoforo to his dramatic confrontation with Don Rodrigo, and gives him the strength to utter words whose impact will not be felt until the closing pages of the book. When he realizes that the bully does not wish to listen to the voice of reason and compassion, he shouts,

> I pity this house. A curse hangs over it. You will see if the justice of God can be kept out by a few stones, or frightened off by a pair of sentries. You think God made a creature in His own image in order to give you the pleasure of tormenting her! You think God won't be able to defend her! You've spurned His warning. You are judged for it! Pharaoh's heart was as hard as yours, and God found a way to crush it. Lucia is safe from you: I—a poor friar—I tell you that; and as far as for yourself, listen to what I foretell you. A day will come.

His ominous prediction proves to be accurate, and Don Rodrigo, the chief cause of much anguish and sorrow, dies a horrible death, as does his henchman Griso—both struck by the plague that is another symbolic manifestation of God's ways.

Renzo, returning to his own town from Milan, exhausted by a perilous and long journey, thinks that he is lost. He finds a small shed in the woods, and decides to spend the night there. Before retiring, he kneels down and offers his humble thanks to the Almighty for having guided him to safety. Even Don Abbondio, the cowardly priest, upon learning that Don Rodrigo is finally dead, is ready to acknowledge the beneficial intervention of Providence, in a manner clearly calculated to inject a note of humor into the story while at the same time illuminating still further his character

> Ah! So he's dead, then. He's really gone. . . . Just see, my children, if Providence doesn't get people like that in the end. D'you know, it's a wonderful thing. A great relief for this poor neighborhood. . . . This plague's been a great scourge, my children, but it's also been a great broom: it's swept away certain folk, my children, whom we never thought we'd be rid of any more.

"A high religious feeling," writes Sapegno, "circulates in every part of [Manzoni's] world, penetrates into every event, touches even the most cruel and vile characters. God's intervention in the large and small happenings is always so strong that one can almost touch it with his hand; it is a paternal presence, loving and severe, that palpitates in every thing. . . . In the world [of poor people], sad more than joyful, God's work may be felt above all in the tribulations, in the anxieties, and in those rays of light that open up, suddenly, in the midst of the darkness of anguish and close the door to despair."

One must search the novel, however, to find in capsule form the moral lesson the tale has tried to convey, along with the true meaning of Providence. Renzo and Lucia, reminiscing about their experiences, "came to the conclusion that troubles often come to those who bring them on to themselves, but that not even the most cautious and innocent behavior can ward them off; and that when they come—whether by our fault or not—confidence in God can lighten them and turn them to our improvement. This conclusion, though reached by poor people, has seemed so just to us that we have thought of putting it down here, as the juice of the whole tale." Ever since the book appeared, but more intensely in recent years, many critics have been confounded or irritated by what is obviously meant to be the summation of a complex and long book. By the same token, readers unwilling to suspend their disbelief have remained unpersuaded by the moral of the tale. Yet, lest one is willing to accept the religious and moral foundations on which *The Betrothed* rests, one can hardly begin to understand the book, and even less like it. Ultimately, the major stumbling block that has prevented many readers from seizing the significance of the novel resides in the fact that not many of us believe either in God, or in miracles, or in sudden, mysterious conversions. And Manzoni wrote his work for an audience that firmly believed, because it was living in a pre-Darwinian and pre-Freudian era, that our real life begins the moment we die. Thus, everywhere in *The Betrothed* psychology is subordinated to, or placed after, religion, and reality is forced, in the words of Moravia, "into the ideological framework of

Catholicism." And, because of it, the book betrays its conservative stance, its sympathy toward the *status quo,* its lack of confidence in the ability of man to redeem himself socially, with or without the help of his religion, and fulfill himself as a human being.

Intimately acquainted with the classics of literature of Western Europe as Manzoni was, it is inevitable that echoes of the authors he knew so well and loved so deeply should be found in *The Betrothed.* Indeed, so numerous are his literary debts, ranging from casual borrowing of incidental details to overt reminiscences of episodes and characters, that his major work has frequently lent itself to be studied less for its worth as a poetic expression, than for its sources. Although English was not one of his languages, he was a devoted reader of Shakespeare ("My Shakespeare!" he once said with affection, "Anyone writing poetry must read Shakespeare; how he knows all the feelings!"), and of many English novelists whose works had reached the Italian shores in French translations: Goldsmith, Defoe, Sterne, Walpole, and, of course, Scott. ("Had there not been a Walter Scott," he once confessed to his friend C. Fabris, "the idea of writing a novel would not have occurred to me.") As a faithful student of France, it was natural that he should feel the magnetic attraction of a literature he loved and esteemed so highly. His readings in French were as numerous as they were diversified. They included the chief Renaissance writers, particularly Rabelais and Montaigne; the moralists Bossuet, La Bruyère, Pascal, and La Rochefoucauld; the Encyclopedists Voltaire and Diderot; and the playwrights of the golden age of French theater, Corneille, Racine and Molière. But if *The Betrothed* contains more than a hint of these and numerous other writers, the links one might establish between the classics and our novelist matter little. For he succeeded in fusing his extraordinary readings with his own original and cultured outlook, absorbing the insights of his authors and making them his, coloring them with a special light and refashioning them into something new. Everything he learned, through his studies, observations, and meditation, was carefully filtered through his sensibility and molded, transformed into something that bore the stamp of his personal genius.

The technique Manzoni employed to introduce and narrate his story may serve as a pertinent illustration of the foregoing remarks. There was really nothing novel about his technique, for it has frequently been used before, by Sterne and Walpole among others. But in the hands of the Milanese, it achieves a new, meaningful dimension: it not only gives a special flavor to the book, but becomes an important structural element, giving rise to certain tensions without which the novel would be far less convincing and effective. In his preface Manzoni tells us how he had found "a faded and scratched manuscript," written by an "Anonymous Chronicler." Irked by its awkward, ungrammatical style, he was nevertheless so captivated by the "beautiful story," it contained that he decided to tell it anew. Mr. Colquhoun calls this "a device . . . to bridge the gap between reality and fiction," an assumption that is probably correct. Manzoni, whose views on the role of poetry in the modern world place him in the category of moralists, became singularly aware of the possibilities his method offered him. Indeed, he perceived in the fiction of the finding of the manuscript the element that would enable him to give a ring of authenticity to the story, while at the same time would provide him with a multiple point of view, from which he could narrate *and* invent a compelling story.

The initial pages of the book do much to reveal the nature of the perspectives and roles open to Manzoni. In the first place, his job is to retell a story that is not his own. In a vague sense, his position may be compared to that of a medieval scribe, patiently recopying, in the silence of his cell, an original manuscript. But, as was common with many such copyists, Manzoni immediately takes certain, and admittedly extreme, liberties with his text. As a matter of fact, he edits it in the modern sense of rewriting it *in toto,* for the sake of improving its otherwise unbearably rough style. Not satisfied with recasting the story in his own language, he also adds a number of important passages to the original manuscript. Such sections, judiciously interpolated in the book, are always and clearly identified for what they are—that is, as pages that will illuminate, enrich and clarify the story—written by Manzoni himself. These passages (the most notable of which are to be found in Chapters IX, XXII, XXVIII, XXXI, and XXXII) must be viewed as his personal contribution to the artistic whole, and are meant to supply what might be called historical and biographical information not contained in the manuscript. It goes without saying, that the tone changes with the various perspectives, and rightly so: the story is obviously a work of poetry, while the added chapters or paragraphs are the result of the "editor's" special research in the archives. A subtle irony, a gentle humor and an admirable diligence become the salient qualities of the novel, whose parts have been joined harmoniously by a craftsman who never once permits himself any exaggerations. Manzoni's indulgence and patience toward his readers, especially toward those who might experience some irritation when confronted by what may seem digressions, is so great that he seems to apologize for the necessity of such long biographical-historical sections. In one instance (Chapter XXII), he even advises the reader eager to get on with the story, to "skip straight on to the following chapter," a suggestion that can be taken only at the risk of depriving oneself of one of the memorable vignettes in which the novelist excels.

Not content with employing such apparently naïve devices (naïve only if we forget the fact that the novel has all the appearances of a fairy tale) Manzoni injects still another personal note. Time and again, as he is transcribing the story, he meditates on the events just recounted, and makes what must be considered a distinctly ethical or religious judgment on the key issues posed by the actions or words of the characters. And it makes little difference, in the last analysis, whether Manzoni offers the comment as his own, or the Chronicler's, for the effect is quite similar—all the more since we have learned that there is only a thin line dividing the two.

> We cannot forbear pausing a moment to make a reflection in the midst of all this uproar. Renzo, who had raised all this noise in someone else's house, who had got in by a trick, and was now keeping the master of the house himself besieged in a room, has all the appearance of being the aggressor; and yet, if one thinks it out, he was the injured party. Don Abbondio, surprised, terrified, and put to flight while peacefully attending to his own affairs, might seem the victim; and yet, in reality, it was he who

> was doing the wrong. Such is often the way the world goes . . . I mean, that's the way it went in the seventeenth century.

> Here our anonymous chronicler makes an observation which we repeat for what it is worth. Temperate and honest habits, he says, have this advantage among others, that the more they are settled and rooted in a man, the more sensitive he is to any slight departure from them; so that he remembers it for some time afterwards; and even a folly becomes a useful lesson to him.

It is easy to see, from the two examples taken respectively from Chapters VIII and XIV, how Manzoni, originally committed to transcribing a story he has rewritten in better Italian, frequently betrays the fact that he is also "editing" it, and becomes, by way of his affinity with the moral position of the original narrator, identified with his author. The total effect of a technique that transforms the narrator-commentator into an omniscient seer, is such that it makes us live intimately with the characters, perceiving their aspirations, understanding their frailties as human beings, sympathizing with their plights, and being moved by their situations.

The breadth of vision is matched by an equally astonishing breadth of stylistic virtuosity. Manzoni's sense of language, his exceptional feeling for its possibilities, his inventiveness and versatility are surely among the major achievements of *The Betrothed.* His expressive range is practically limitless: it spans all the way from the lyricism of the passage "Farewell, mountains . . . " (the section being Lucia's adieu to her native ground, at the end of Chapter VIII, a passage regularly committed to memory by all high school students in Italy), to the descriptions of landscapes and feelings, to the incisiveness of his psychological portraits—done with unusual attention to details—to the serene and detached historical passages, whose scholarly seriousness is relieved by touches of light irony. His dialogues and monologues manage to be both vivacious and believable, and their only fault may be a smoothness of diction that may be a bit disconcerting to the reader yearning for a more popular flavor in the characters' speeches. One wishes that Manzoni had made his characters speak in racier, earthier ways, as it befitted their social class. But if the contemporary reader is prone to consider this a disappointing side of the book, he must bear in mind that the author was less preoccupied with rendering his dialogues real in the best sense, than with creating a truly national, literary, and spoken language. In a genuine sense, he was striving for harmony in his style, a harmony that would accompany, or better still translate, his vision of the world.

Harmony is perhaps the one term that helps us understand what must be considered one of the great achievements of the book, certainly insofar as its style was concerned. The concept itself, as descriptive of an ideal goal, must have meant many things to Manzoni: a spare elegance of diction, a moderate and yet thoughtful narrative manner that would enable him to carry his story forward at its just pace. But harmony had also a deeply religious connotation and meaning: for the poet, it signified a complete peace attainable by the spirit of a just man, who accepts the ways of God. Only under such circumstances can harmony, understood as a perfect rhythm, be visualized as beauty: the man at peace with himself and his God can be said to have achieved harmony, a vital prerequisite to human happiness. It is this kind of happiness that is experienced by Lucia or by the Cardinal Borromeo and, at least at times, by Renzo himself. An artist must also strive to experience such harmony, for it paves the way to the perfection—the depth of its whole, the necessity of its parts, the lucidity of the resulting images—to which he aspires.

Everything in *The Betrothed* bespeaks of such harmony, and because of it, it conveys an unusual sense of dignity and of integrity. (pp. 34-50)

We must stand away from the book, and return to it again and again, in order to appreciate fully the complexity of its structure, the richness of its details, the wealth of its anticipatory signals and retrospective illuminations, all these contribute to the diversity and interest of the whole. Few other novelists in modern Italy have so thoroughly mastered Manzoni's exemplary use of the material at his disposal. Fewer still have been able to recreate an era so convincingly as he. Working with an impressive cast of characters, he describes each of them so well—from the protagonists to the lesser figures—that we never find ourselves unable to accept their words or deeds as something not fully consonant with their whole personality. With an Olympian serenity, a tolerant yet penetrating hand, Manzoni delves into the character of his personages without ever forgetting the traits that make them at once strong and weak creatures. His scrutinizing eye by no means confines its gaze to any special social class or to any specific type of individual. Rather, it embraces an extraordinarily broad spectrum of humanity, the rich and the poor, the saintly and the satanic, the educated and the ignorant, the humble and the arrogant, the strong and the weak. A diversified gallery of people—priests, cardinals, monks, soldiers, lackeys, *bravoes,* lawyers, rulers, farmers, administrators, lords, *monatti,* workers, bakers—passes under our eyes: "I've stuffed [my novel]," remarked Manzoni, "with peasants, nobles, magistrates, scholars, war, famine . . . that's to have written a book!" There is room for all of them in the story, to be sure. What is amazing is not so much their number, or their diversity, but the fact that once we have met them, it is difficult to forget them. Many of them have become proverbial in Italian life. (p. 52)

It is ultimately impossible to do justice to Manzoni's novel unless we bear in mind that he occupied a political, religious, and social position that was conservative, if not reactionary, by today's standards. He composed his masterpiece under the influence of his conversion, wishing to dramatize above everything else the truth of his faith. Thus, while the contemporary reader must not object to a novel that is, in every way, a religious work, he may find himself unsympathetic to Manzoni's implicit exhortation to preserve the *status quo.* Such a reader may also resent the view that only the elect will find salvation, just as he will no doubt disagree with a position that indirectly, but unmistakably, equates poverty with social and intellectual inferiority. But what is possibly the book's most disturbing point, is the lesson that it tries to impart to the reader; to him it is presented as the juice of the whole tale. A truly Christian drama is transformed, in the final lines of the book, into an exhortation to conform and keep still, in the face of injustice.

I suppose that it has been such a combination of factors discussed in the preceding pages that have contributed to making Manzoni at once the most classical and limpid novelist of modern Italy as well as the writer who is not always likely to appeal to the interest and curiosity of the contemporary reader. Why is that? The answer, in part, has been suggested by Mr. Wall [see Further Reading]: it is simply too difficult, in the chaotic and uncertain world of today, to be intrigued by a novel where hardly anything happens as the result of what we loosely call pure chance. There is far too much serenity in Manzoni's cosmos or in his manner of recounting his tale, and we live in a historical moment that has taught us to expect, not to say fear, the improbable, erratic gesture that may well doom mankind. There are, in *The Betrothed,* far too many happy resolutions: the good people are invariably rewarded, in this life or beyond it, and the bad people are always punished. No one, I assume, objects to the desirability of such a state of affairs, but most will seriously doubt its probability in human life. Unlike Dante, who was also a great Catholic writer, Manzoni simply stacked the cards against those who were faithless and was unable to create in his novel the tension between the human and the Divine judgment that makes the *Comedy* the intensely dramatic and moving experience that it is.

Having said this, we must acknowledge that *The Betrothed* is a significant novel indeed—not merely because of its admirable moral content, or its limpid style, or its use of humble people as heroes of the story and of a regional setting (two factors that anticipate the innovations of the later *verismo*). Despite the passing of time, it remains a candid portrayal of the virtues and flaws of the Italian temperament, the hopefulness and honesty that characterize the masses of Italy, the arrogance and corruption that typify her ruling elite, and the general level of conformity that has traditionally permeated the entire nation. "It is a fact," notes Alberto Moravia, "that Manzoni's novel reflects an Italy which, with few inessential modifications, could be the Italy of today." "To know Italy," concludes Mr. Wall, "we must appreciate Manzoni, but to appreciate Manzoni, I sometimes feel, we must know Italy." Possibly, this is the largest compliment we can pay a writer; and it is hard to think of anyone else in the history of modern Italy whose work has become one with the spirit of the culture which gave it birth. (pp. 55-6)

Sergio Pacifici, "Alessandro Manzoni: The Historical Novel," in his The Modern Italian Novel: From Manzoni to Svevo, *Southern Illinois University Press, 1967, pp. 26-56.*

Ezio Raimondi   (essay date 1969)

[*Raimondi compares Renzo's travels in* The Betrothed *to a picaresque odyssey, demonstrating how his quest for justice determines theme and structure in the novel.*]

On more than one occasion, Raymond Queneau has observed that the tradition of the Western novel up to Joyce can be traced back to two poles, to two great story types, represented, respectively, by *The Iliad* and *The Odyssey.* What is important in the former, and what also comes to be its definition, is the involvement of the characters in history and the interrelation between them and historical reality. The latter, however, takes its shape from the story of an individual who, through various experiences, acquires a personality, or affirms or rediscovers his own, as does Ulysses. It must also be added that the autobiographical *"récit"* almost always constitutes an odyssey, in the profound sense of an existence which turns back upon itself. If we argue according to these categories, the character of Renzo in *I promessi sposi* makes the novel into a kind of odyssey, not only because he is the "leading man" of the action, with his adventures as "pilgrim," fugitive, and "traveler," but also because the information about him, as will be seen in Chapter 37, is derived from his conversations with, and confessions to, the anonymous storyteller. It is as if, at the origin of the purported seventeenth-century story, there lies, at least to a great extent, the pleasure a reminiscing countryman, a survivor, takes in evoking his past, in telling his story, even imagining it in advance, while it is still in course. And it is actually Renzo who, safe now across the river Adda, murmurs to himself in one of his imaginative monologues: "How pleasant it will be to go strolling, all of us together, along this very road! And go right up to the Adda in a cart, and picnic on the bank, right on the bank, and show the women the place I embarked, the brambles I came down through, the place where I stood looking for a road."

Certainly Renzo's odyssey falls within the pattern of the historical novel and fits perfectly, completed by that of Lucia, into Scott's novel archetype, as described recently, and not without biting irony, by Professor Leslie Fiedler:

> Initially confused about his own ambitions or the true identity and character of those who surround him, often himself maligned and misrepresented, the hero is forced to flee—usually into the midst of some famous historic conflict just then conveniently approaching its climax. The heroine meanwhile has been abducted or is off on some private evasion of her own, for reasons only revealed in the final pages. The two are kept apart as long as possible, but are finally joined by the intervention of either some noble figure out of history or some notorious outlaw fresh from the greenwood (if possible, both). By the same agency, their problems are resolved, their enemies discomfited, all confusions cleared up. The good is revealed as good—and triumphant; the evil as evil—and defeated [*Love and Death in the American Novel*].

But a composite novel like *I promessi sposi,* even while it takes plots and machinery from the narrative tradition, always transfers them into a completely different type of context, which deforms them and modifies them radically in the mischievous light of a subtle polemic against sentimentality and romanticizing, which implies an acute awareness of evil, sin, and the sophistries of the passions and the prejudices in the "abyss of the human heart." (But the "abyss of the human heart" is a formula from the *Osservazioni sulla morale cattolica;* in the novel it will become the "hotchpotch of the human heart.")

Even the theme of the two young people persecuted by the evil man thus takes on a very different coloring, with structural functions that cannot escape the reader who considers the story in its total movement. In fact, if the first eight chapters present the characters as still united in the face of the "misfortune" (or misadventure), as Propp would say, which befalls them and forces them to depart, Chapters 9 and 10 follow Lucia to Monza, into Gertrude's convent; then in Chapter 11, through the link with his antagonist, we return to Renzo, who remains at the center

of the story, whether in or out of Milan, through Chapter 17, after which, for the next two chapters, he turns into a kind of ghost who crops up in the conversation of men of power and finally disappears, along with Fra Cristoforo, leaving the field to Don Rodrigo and the Innominato, the Unnamed. Chapter 20 returns to Lucia, to her misadventures and the encounters that ensue, ending, after the brief parenthesis of Chapter 28 with the domestic picture of Don Abbondio in Chapter 30. At this point, if we interpret Chapters 31 and 32 as a necessary preliminary to what happens immediately afterward, the Renzo theme resumes with him once more in Milan, in the midst of the plague, searching for Lucia; and thus we reach Chapter 36, which marks the reunion of the surviving characters, now nearing the conclusion, the so-called happy ending.

Bound to each other by a common fate and an internal counterpoint of memories echoing sentiments, the two adventures of Renzo and Lucia, from the moment they part company, proceed alternately and determine the double axis along which the story unfolds, so as to become what Burckhardt was later to call a chapter of universal history. However, their linking functions work in two different directions, since on the axis of Lucia we meet Gertrude, the Unnamed, Cardinal Federigo, and even Donna Prassede or Don Ferrante, whereas on that of Renzo (with the exception of the Chancellor, Antonio Ferrer) are arrayed the men of the roads and squares, innkeepers, lawyers, tramps, merchants, sheriffs, honest fellows, artisans, *monatti,* poverty-stricken peasants. Both, as we see, give a stratified, representative picture of Lombard society. But only Renzo actually fulfills an authentic public experience, comes into contact with the machinery of a social system, experiences its absurdities at the lowest level, and makes an attempt to understand something of it. He is the anti-hero of the picaresque tradition, a "poor man" cast into a world of unforeseen snares and forced, in his journey from the country to Milan, into a kind of *Bildungsroman* in which, often without his knowing it, the mystery of existence seems almost to reveal itself. And, to use Propp's paradigms again, it is he who in the end fills the role of the protagonist, both victim and searcher in the face of that complex yet terribly simple reality, justice.

In fact, it is not by chance that he first appears in an indirect way, after the two "bravoes" have uttered the names Renzo Tramaglino and Lucia Mondella, in the portrait which Don Abbondio, head bowed, and muttering to himself, peevishly gives of him: "Oh . . . oh . . . oh . . . he's tough too; as quiet as a lamb while left to himself, but if anyone puts his back up . . . ugh . . . ! And then, and then, his head's quite turned by that girl Lucia, in love like. . . . What silly young fools they are, going and falling in love because they've got nothing better to do, and then wanting to get married, and not thinking about anything else. Little they care what trouble they let a poor honest man in for." Before he has even appeared on the scene, in our eyes he is already involved in the system of violence and disorder which has produced the proclamations, the bravoes, and Don Abbondio, and which is now preparing to assail him with the complicity of another "peaceful and defenseless citizen," accustomed to sticking to "the stronger, but always in the rear guard." The judgment of an "honest man" like Don Abbondio, the "severe critic of those who did not behave as he did," immediately sets up a hierarchy in which the law of the strong is not only confirmed but even extended to another "weak man" according to the logic of time-serving and fear, in a relationship which, from the start, postulates a master-slave dialectic. On the other hand, in spite of all the embarrassments by which he is seized, it is Don Abbondio who has to act as mediator between Renzo and the spirit of the system and to convince a "callow youth," as he calls him while awaiting his arrival, of the need for caution and renunciation; Renzo's journey into the dark universe of absolute power actually begins with him, in a village priest's house.

Now Renzo is confronted with the reality of the plot against him, and learns what it means to be a "poor man" ("It's a bad thing to be born poor, Renzo, my boy") in a world where "it isn't a question of right or wrong" but only "of might," as Don Abbondio, from his long experience, at once explains to him. This remark is terrible, even if the context seems comic, the more so because it is made by a "priest" who, out of weakness, has chosen the path of never opposing power—a priest without love, sadly human and honest, to whom it matters little that "every unjust power, in order to harm men, needs collaborators who will give up obeying the divine law"; "and thus the failure to carry out this law is the most essential condition for such power to be able to act," as the *Osservazioni sulla morale cattolica* teaches us on a page of vital importance. Renzo, of course, is incapable of such moralist's subtleties, for which we must wait until Cardinal Federigo enters the story. As regards the narrator, what interests him as he follows the peasant toward Lucia's house, in the confused impulsiveness of his protest, is to observe that the state of mind of the "oppressed man" is still the responsibility of the "oppressor"; it is almost as if he is suggesting, from another point of view, that the idea of murder, which momentarily comes into Renzo's mind, originates in the very state of society and is the sign of a corruption which contaminates even the thoughts of a man who is "averse to bloodshed."

Although the situation continually postulates it, the word "justice" has not yet occurred, except obliquely in the flat quotation of a proclamation ("the great mischief this kind of person is to public weal, in contempt of justice") or in the officious, agitated words of Don Abbondio ("But you gentlemen are too fair, too reasonable. . . . "). The person who finally utters the word aloud is again Renzo, in the presence of Doctor Quibble-Weaver (Azzecca-garbugli); but it is a grotesque situation of hypocrisy and ambiguity, which serves only to emphasize the solitude of a naïve fellow and to deepen his disappointment. The "Doctor," for whom "no one's guilty, and no one's innocent," introduces Renzo into a cynical, grasping, servile province of law degraded, and of public life reduced to a spectacle of swindling, trickery, and bribery. The visitor's first reaction is exactly like that of a "yokel in the village square [who] is gazing at a conjurer, a sleight of hand performer." Then he begins to understand, and is obliged to talk of "justice," not in the false sense of the lawyer ("if it was a question of deciding between the law and you . . . "), but in the true and painful sense of his very recent experience of oppression. "I haven't threatened anyone; I don't do that kind of thing. I don't; you can ask all round my village, and they'll tell you I've never been up against the law [*"giustizia"* in Italian]. It's I who've

been put upon; and I've come to you to find out how I'm to get redress" (again *"giustizia"* in the Italian text).

As we have said, this is the first time that the term "justice" has appeared in the novel without qualification, in its naked essence as a denial of arbitrary power. But no sooner has it been brought up than the process of distortion begins again, both on the part of Quibble-Weaver, who, on hearing the name Don Rodrigo, immediately opposes the "nonsense, fiddlesticks" of the peasant with his "honest man's" common sense, and, on the part of Renzo, who returns to his women, disconsolate but determined to do something, and this in the name of the justice that he cannot obtain. And while he is conversing with Agnese and Lucia in an atmosphere of general sadness, we hear him declare, at the possibility that the remedy may come from Fra Cristoforo: " . . . in any case I'll get my rights, or have them got for me. There's justice in this world in the long run." The narrator then hastens to add that "a man overwhelmed by grief no longer knows what he is saying," which is by no means a witticism, as it might seem, if it is understood in connection with what has taken shape in Renzo's mind since leaving Don Abbondio and with the "perversion" that can affect the intentions of even an honest man such as he. What he is contemplating, in the last analysis, is murder, revenge; and yet he calls it justice, with the same logic that serves his opponents, thus unsuspectingly contaminating the suffering that he undergoes as an innocent man and his right as an immortal soul.

That this is how the matter stands can be seen at once from the next chapter, where, at a certain point in the flashback to the story of Lodovico-Fra Cristoforo, we read the phrase: "thus hand him over to justice, or rather to the vengeance of his enemies." This connection, however, is not a result of chance, since in the structure of the novel, so symmetrical and so rich in internal echoes, the figure of Fra Cristoforo has a profound link with the situation of Renzo, which often is not sufficiently observed or is interpreted in conventional terms. If there is anyone in whom the friar can almost recognize a part of himself, it is Renzo, who, for a moment, is planning to assault his enemy and is looking forward to a revenge which he considers just; and this explains exactly why his function, in relation to Renzo's spiritual voyage, becomes that of guiding him toward another idea of justice which involves not violence but respect for man. Only to Renzo can he say on meeting him that "the weak gain nothing by showing their claws," and add, from the depths of his own memories, a mysterious "and if . . . ," which is sufficient in itself to convince the listener. In fact, if we wish to clarify this completely, we must go back to the *Osservazioni sulla morale cattolica* . . . , where it is concluded that "the divine law preaches justice to all men, and if in many cases it only proposes patience to those who wish to pursue it, it is proposing the sole means to happiness, since all other means, by rendering them guilty, as a result make them abject and miserable." Don Abbondio, as we have seen, has a very different view of it; and, in fact, his patience follows another route.

Fra Cristoforo's, however, drives him to the mansion of Don Rodrigo "the lair of the wild beast," with the illusion that he will be able to "tame" it, even if all this smacks of the fairy tale. In effect, the good Capuchin obtains nothing, although he invokes justice, charity, innocence, and honor; and, in the end, nothing remains—apart from the biblical appeal to God's justice—but to go back to his "poor creatures" and try to help them in some other manner, and explain to Renzo, who would like at least to know why Don Rodrigo has vetoed his marriage, that the man of power does not even need to give reasons for his whims: "he can insult you and make himself out to be the injured party, jeer at you and pretend he is in right, bully and yet complain." However, Renzo is still far from the "patience" that Fra Cristoforo counsels him and he has by no means abandoned his intention of taking the law into his own hands. He proclaims it once more while Agnese is repeating to him that "justice is always against the poor" and insists, with a mixture of stubbornness and histrionics, until Lucia lets herself be talked into attempting a surprise marriage at the house of Don Abbondio. We return to the level of comedy in a plot with a melodramatic flavor which once again reverses all the situations and all the roles in the game showing us the paradox of the dialectic of power concentrated again on Renzo before the flight from home when Fra Cristoforo takes leave of the fugitives. Even here, however, the experience of the characters passes through the "reflection" of the narrator, who interrupts the story of the night of confusion at the highest point of the force and observes: "We cannot forbear pausing a moment to make a reflection in the midst of all this uproar. Renzo, who had raised all this noise in someone else's house, who had got in by a trick, and was now keeping the master of the house himself besieged in a room, has all the appearance of being the aggressor; and yet, if one thinks it out, he was the injured party. Don Abbondio, surprised, terrified, and put to flight while peacefully attending to his own affairs, might seem the victim; and yet, it was he who was the wrongdoer."

Before Renzo begins, in his turn, to reflect on what has happened to him, we must wait until he enters Milan, until the new events which he witnesses or takes part in drive him time and again into a comparison, into a dialogue with his own memories which is perhaps, on the artistic level, one of Manzoni's greatest discoveries. Now begins his public adventure, his journey as a peasant *déraciné* among the monsters of a city in disorder, in the labyrinth of people and crowds which sweeps him as if into a "whirlpool." Together with the curiosity that arises from his certainty that this is a "day of conquest," what drives him on, without his knowing exactly what he is seeking, is a secret indignation, one might almost say a protest, against the morality of Don Abbondio; and little by little it changes into a hope for justice for himself and for others. In the midst of the turmoil the most generous words, in fact, are his, both when he expresses his "humble opinion" in the "press of people" ("And, as we've seen plainly enough today that we can get our rights by making ourselves heard, we ought to go on like this, until we've set all the other wrongs to rights, and made the world a decent place to live in . . . we would also be there to lend a hand"), and when he confides in the false cutler at the inn of the full moon: "Enough; they ought to put an end to these things! Today, luckily, everything was in plain language and without pen, ink, or paper; and tomorrow, if people know how to set about it, things will be done even better—without touching a hair of anyone's head, though all done legally [*'per via di giustizia'*]."

Yet Renzo's good sense and peasant's wisdom, while it

helps the narrator to obtain extraordinary effects of alienation or estrangement behind his back, does not save him from the snares of the system, which immediately seizes him in its meshes and once more imposes its own rules and roles upon him, in accordance with the Machiavellian logic of public order. Thus Renzo himself undergoes the fate that awaits justice when everyone wants to appropriate it for himself: and so there grows up around his figure no less than around the term "justice" a kind of linguistic perspectivism and gloomy masquerade, in the same style as the Quibble-Weaver scene, but with stranger, more taunting complications. In the words of the crowd, he becomes, from episode to episode, a "rascally peasant," a "Commissioner's man, a spy" (and this only because he opposes brutality: "Shame! Do we want to do the executioner's job? Commit murder? How d'you expect God to give us bread if we go and do atrocities like that?"), and then he is also a "good friend from the country," an "honest fellow," a "stubborn mountaineer," a "good laddie," a "bad character," a "thief caught red-handed." And finally, when he manages to escape after the night of drunkenness and his arrest, reaching the inn at Gorgonzola, the fugitive even finds himself transformed into a mysterious, almost legendary agitator.

> One of them was arrested in some inn. . . . They're not quite sure yet exactly where this man came from, or who had sent him, or what kind of man he was; but he was certainly one of the ringleaders. He'd been raising the devil the day before in the middle of the rioting; and then, not content with that, he had begun to make speeches, and put forward the gallant idea that the whole of the gentry should be murdered. The blackguard! Who'd keep the poor going if the gentry were all murdered? The police had marked him down, and got their clutches on him. They found a bundle of letters on him and were just taking him off to prison. But what d'you think happened then? His confederates, who were patrolling round the inn, came up in large numbers and freed him, the scoundrel.

While Ulysses heard his own story sung by a bard, the traveler of the *Promessi sposi* finds only a merchant, in the midst of a group of curious persons (bystanders), telling the tale of his adventure in Milan, distorting it from the beginning with an exaggerated caution: the caution of Don Abbondio again, more triumphant than ever. Two other speakers immediately echo him, and one confesses: "Knowing how these things go, and that honest folk aren't safe in riots, I wouldn't let myself be carried away by curiosity, and stayed at home." The other makes it clear again, still in contrast with what Renzo had done: "Or I? . . . Why, if by any chance I'd been in Milan, I'd have left my business unfinished and come back home at once. I've a wife and children; and, to tell the truth, I don't like uproars." From the narrative point of view, this game of mirrors under the intent gaze of Renzo is a fine invention, the more so because it prompts him to cross-examine himself, to question his conscience, not straight away of course, because of his fear of being discovered, but soon afterward, when he has left the inn and, alone in the darkness, thinks over the words he has heard, in honest indignation, drawing the moral that it is never worth putting oneself out to "help the gentry," even if they are "fellow creatures."

Meanwhile, in the solitude of the countryside, something more profound ripens in the pilgrim, in a mingling of affections, anxieties, and remorse which gives movement to one of the most memorable chapters of the whole novel, pervaded as it is by an aura of sensations rising in a lucid "crescendo" until the discovery of the river Adda and the sky of Lombardy. As he moves forward once again in a world of simple men and things, gradually, in the inner chronicle of his soul, a feeling of serenity and a ready faith spring up; and the word "Providence" resounds, innocent and joyful, in this poor man's speech. But around him, the landscape again takes on and deepens the gloom that had already accompanied Fra Cristoforo at the beginning of the story: " . . . his eye was saddened every moment by gloomy sights, which made him realize that he would find the same scarcity in the country he was entering as he had left at home. The whole way along, and particularly in the fields and villages, he met beggars at every step—not professional beggars, for they showed their distress more by their faces than by their clothes—peasants, mountaineers, artisans, complete families, from whom came a confused mutter of entreaties, lamentations, and sobs."

At this point, the first phase of his urban odyssey completed, Renzo passes for the time being out of the narrative, even if his image does not in fact altogether disappear, being brought up several times in the conversation of the other characters and distorted, along with that of Fra Cristoforo (a "villager" and an "impudent friar," "a plebeian") among others, in the diplomatic interview between the Father Provincial and the "right-honorable Uncle," as seems to be his fate as long as he is in exile. However, the link always remains indirect, as if following an underground course from which Renzo re-emerges, gathering the principal plot of the story around him only when the plague finally gives him the opportunity to set off again, immunized as he is against the infection, in search of Agnese or his own house. Renzo's role coincides with that of the questioning hero (or hero-searcher) in a world where death holds sway, a world made perilous by corruption and by the great fear of cosmic disorder; at the same time his journey takes on the character of a trial and of an initiation on the level of bare, almost elementary humanity. This begins to come clear as soon as Renzo sets foot in his troubled village and meets Tonio, now no better than the "poor half-wit Gervasio," then Don Abbondio, with his "list of individuals and families" buried, and lastly his friend, whose name we never learn, alone: "sitting on a wooden stool at the door, with his arms crossed and his eyes raised to the sky, like a man overwhelmed by misfortune and grown animal-like through solitude." While it is increasingly affected by horror, his peasant's heart at the same time opens up to the anguished tenderness of his memories, to the solidarity of the affections that survive, to the joy of consoling another man with his own presence, over a little *polenta* and a pail of milk: it is as if he divines that only benevolence can save a man from desperation.

Yet it is clear that his visit to the village is only a preamble, a preparation. The decisive experience is yet to be undergone in Milan, at the heart of the suffering and absurdity. Here the "stranger" with the "knotty stick" to drive him away, who later tells how he ran into an *untore,* an "anointer" with a "meek and humble air," immediately gives Renzo the impression that he has plunged once more into the city of madness, error, and excess. And his "journey," or "itinerary" as it is called several times in the story, with remote symbolic implications, is not slow to re-

veal other contrasts to him in the livid, grim color of death which is now ubiquitous: from the woman on the "balcony" with a "cluster of children," to the "instrument of torture"; from the death carts heaped with "naked corpses," to the "priest" who answers politely; from the "silence" interrupted only by the "lamentations of the poor" or "the shrieks of the delirious," to Cecilia's mother, who commands respect even from a "filthy *monatto,*" or to the "lying witch," who shouts accusations that he is an anointer while Renzo is asking her desperately for news of Lucia. In the reversal of roles that now begins, the "traveler" is forced to protect himself by pretending to be an anointer and to play along with the atrocious *monatti,* who carry him to safety on their cart, joining together in an "infernal chant," almost as if for Renzo too, in keeping with the requirements of the mythical archetype of the journey, a descent into hell is necessary before the right to rediscover the truest part of the self is earned.

Moreover, even the search for Lucia, and this has already been pointed out, is a renewal of the old myth of the *quête.* It is not without reason that in Chapter 33 the sole *filo,* the only thread (Colquhoun translates as "clue") available "for going in search of Lucia," is mentioned, and the whole lazaretto episode is interwoven with ritual gestures and liturgical cadences. But the conversation between Renzo and Fra Cristoforo (for it was necessary to come to him in the end) is something more than a rite or an indispensable purification once it is interpreted in the light of the correspondences that echo throughout the novel. It is here, in fact, that the concept of justice returns to the scene. It has followed us throughout the story, hidden among the rags of the plague like a shadow, a desperate absence. Nor is it surprising, after what we have seen in the early chapters, that it is again Renzo who raises the question, the Renzo who is tormented by the thought that Lucia may be dead, and who is once more set on revenge, as if nothing had happened, as if the plague meant merely a compensation for the oppressed, an equal right to kill for all. Let us observe his words carefully: "if the plague hasn't already done justice. . . . The time's past when a coward with his bravoes around him could drive folk to desperation and get off all free; the time's come when men meet one another face to face; and. . . . I'll do my own justice, I will!"

These words fill Fra Cristoforo with indignation mingled with sadness and dismay. For an instant they represent his defeat by a false, proud justice built upon contempt for man, whereas in Fra Cristoforo's view Renzo must find the road to foregiveness so that the violent destiny which torments the old friar's soul may not repeat itself, not even if it is what Renzo desires in his heart. We mentioned, at the beginning of this essay, the very special relationship which unites Renzo and Fra Cristoforo, as regards the framework of the novel. Now the conversation in the lazaretto throws light on the profound motives for this, since the time has come for the Capuchin to reveal the secret of his existence to Renzo: "I also have hated; I, who have rebuked you for a thought, for a word, I killed the man I hated deeply, whom I had hated for a long time." It is time also to confess to him that the image of that dead man, even if he was a "bully," as Renzo retorts in confusion, continues to haunt his memory in the darkness of a logic which has lost its sense: "D'you think that if there had been a good reason I would not have found it out in thirty years?" It is as if, in the end, Fra Cristoforo wishes to see his own story freed from the obsession with blood which is reflected in the story of Renzo, the story of a man forced to commit an evil deed to learn the justice of God, which is the justice of the free and patient heart. Certainly he is the dramatic "double" of Renzo's Christian conscience and, as such, accompanies him on his mysterious journey as far as the deathbed of Don Rodrigo for a "face to face" meeting, where there is no more room for violence or hatred. And now it will be possible to find Lucia too.

Some readers of *I promessi sposi* have remarked that the story could even end at Chapter 36 and that, in any case, the "idyl" of the epilogue sinks to the level of a minor chronicle, of a domestic comedy which has lost the pace of the novel and the cadence of the great adventure. But perhaps insufficient attention has been paid to the circular construction of the story and to the irony which governs the return of the survivors to everyday life, the irony which is so clear, to say the least, in the disappointment of the curious villagers on seeing the real Lucia, who seems too mediocre in their eyes to be a romantic heroine (who, of course, should be splendid and perfect); the reader of *Ivanhoe* knows perfectly well that Rebecca's admiration of Lady Rowena was unqualified ("long, long will I remember your features, and bless God that I leave my noble deliverer united with"). In other words, the detachment which one notices in the narration after the downpour at the lazaretto and the "sudden turn in Nature" around Renzo, now on his last journey, seems intended to juxtapose a cycle of exceptional occurrences with a world that has become ordinary once more and that has retained little more than a memory, a more or less opaque reflection of them. The great season of dramatic choices is over; the reality of prose, of everyday meetings and conversations in the recaptured warmth of the home and the family, takes over again. And yet the problems that set the story in motion continue to project themselves onto the mirror of their consciences, if only one is capable of detecting the presence of the past in the inner texture of the final conversations. Nor can it be excluded that the irony of the conclusion consists, among other things, in this challenge to the reader.

As to Renzo, it is convenient to turn to Don Abbondio and put him to the test when, his mind at peace, he permits himself to joke with Agnese and the "lady" of the lazaretto in his sly, coarse way. He says: "We've been through some bad times, haven't we, my children, some bad times? Let's hope these few days we've still got in the world will be better. Ah, well! You're lucky in having a bit of time to talk over your past troubles, if no new ones come up; but I, on the other hand, am three-quarters past the eleventh hour, and . . . rascals may die, and one may recover from the plague, but there's no remedy for the years; and, as they say, *senectus ipsa est morbus.*" As ever, Don Abbondio is human, colorful, prodigiously alive; but it is also true that he has learned nothing or, rather, that he has wasted what had moved him at the time of the great adventure, since the phrase "three-quarters past the eleventh hour" is nothing less than a quotation from Cardinal Federigo translated into a comic figure of speech and vulgarized. It was Borromeo who said to him, in his warmer tones: "Let us redeem the time; midnight is near; the bridegroom cannot be far off; let us keep our lamps lighted."

But Renzo, for his part, has learned something of lasting value and declares as much to Don Abbondio himself when the latter, now that he is sure that Don Rodrigo is dead, exalts the plague as the scourge of tyrants and the instrument of Providence. The contrast between the two speeches is striking and by no means accidental. Don Abbondio's overflow in all directions, joyful and unfettered as a *danse macabre.* "Ah! So he's dead, then. He's really gone," exclaimed Don Abbondio.

> Just see, my children, if Providence doesn't get people like that in the end. D'you know, it's a wonderful thing. A great relief for this poor neighborhood. For the man was impossible to live with. This plague's been a great scourge, but it's also been a great broom: it's swept away certain folk, my children, whom we never thought we'd be rid of any more; in their prime and vigor and prosperity, too; and we'd thought the man who'd conduct their funeral was still doing his Latin exercises at the seminary; and then in the twinkle of an eye they've disappeared hundreds at a time. We shan't see him going round any more with that pack of cut-throats behind him, with his show and his haughty airs and his stuck-up way of looking at people as if we were all in the world just by his gracious permission. Anyway, he's not here any more, and we are. He won't send honest folk any more of those messages. He's given us all a great deal of trouble, you see; we can say that now.

Renzo's answer, however, is extremely terse: "I have forgiven him from the bottom of my heart"; but the reader remembers that they are the very words he had pronounced in the presence of Fra Cristoforo in his trial at the lazaretto. Something has remained in his heart ("I realize I had never really forgiven him; I realize that I spoke like a dog and not like a Christian; and now, by God's grace, yes, I forgive him from the bottom of the heart").

If this system of cross-references and allusions has a meaning, and with a writer like Manzoni it seems unlikely not to have one, it is natural to conclude that in the conversation between Renzo and Don Abbondio we see in play once more the great theme of justice in the alternative between fear and love, time-serving and liberty, pride and patience: it is as if for a moment the morality of Fra Cristoforo and the code of Don Abbondio confront each other. But Fra Cristoforo is dead while Don Abbondio continues to live, ready to sit at the table of Don Rodrigo's heir and to share his class prejudices, even on a day of folk festivity, against a newly married peasant couple. In the end the plague has changed nothing: men soon forget and adapt themselves to the rules of the world. Even someone who, like Renzo, remembers and recounts his adventures risks falling back into time-serving and drawing from what has happened the easiest moral lesson of cautious, passive honesty. "I've learnt . . . not to get into riots; I've learnt not to make speeches in the street; I've learnt not to raise my elbow too much; I've learnt not to hold door knockers when there are excited people about; I've learnt not to fasten a bell to my feet before thinking of the consequences. And a hundred other things of the kind." It now seems as if Renzo is admitting that Don Abbondio is right, as if he is accepting his principle, his "favorite phrase," according to which "unpleasant accidents do not happen to the honest man who keeps to himself and minds his own business."

As regards the "hundred other things" which Renzo thinks he has learned, the reader has to guess at what they are, although it is permissible to suspect that the number, with its fairy-tale ring, added to the string of "I've learnt's," conceals a hint of irony against Renzo and his would-be "doctrine." Besides, it is enough for Lucia to intervene with her "smiling" remark that the "troubles" were the ones which came looking for her, for her "moralist's" certainty to be baffled and undermined. In truth, Renzo, as a poor peasant, has to admit that the suffering of the world cannot be explained with reference only to itself, and that "trust in God" remains the sole comfort in man's mysterious journey on the earth. But it is precisely in this that justice consists, the justice for which man may suffer and feel himself brother to all the oppressed, even if he is more familiar with fear than with courage. While there is an impression of having reached a peaceful epilogue, in obedience to renunciation or resignation, the secret discourse of the whole novel starts off again, drawing behind it the anguish of history, the inquietude of contradiction, the feeling of the absurd, as it may reach even the "lowest" on the "world" scale (if we remember the closing of Chapter 27). And the anguish of history is the afflicted stupefaction of their memories as "men lost on the earth" ("as good as lost to the world"), men who have not "even got a landlord." Where Renzo's quest ends, the reader's, perhaps, begins. (pp. 140-52)

> Ezio Raimondi, " 'I promessi sposi': Genesis and Structure of a 'Catholic' Novel," in Interpretation: Theory and Practice, edited by Charles S. Singleton, The Johns Hopkins Press, 1969, pp. 123-52.

S. B. Chandler   (essay date 1974)

[Chandler is a Canadian literary critic and educator. In the following excerpt, he outlines the Christian principles of Manzoni's Osservazioni sulla morale cattolica, emphasizing their relationship to the themes of The Betrothed.]

The **Osservazioni sulla morale cattolica** is a work of fundamental importance for a comprehension of Manzoni's thought and for an appreciation of his subsequent works and, as Giuseppe De Robertis pointed out, the moral world of **I promessi sposi** pre-exists therein in the gradual course of its formation. (p. 36)

Manzoni tells us at the beginning that chapter 127 of Sismondi's *Histoire des Républiques Italiennes du moyen âge* provided the immediate occasion for the work, but Tosi's letter to Lamennais of 13 August 1819 indicates that he encouraged Manzoni to write it. To the Swiss author's claim that corruption in Italy derived in part from the faulty morality preached by the Catholic Church, which distorted the principles of the Gospels, Manzoni replies that this is the only holy and reasoned morality, that any corruption stems from transgression of it, ignorance or wrongful interpretation of it and that no valid argument can be adduced against it. Since Catholic morality is true and certain, no unjust conclusion can be logically drawn from it; Catholic teaching in Italy is the same as elsewhere and thus any shortcomings in Italy would also have to exist elsewhere. Part I of the **Osservazioni** purports to answer nineteen of Sismondi's twenty-two charges, but Manzoni goes beyond them to introduce general considerations which carefully avoid Sismondi's specific criticisms of the Church's attitude in individual historical situations and do not give his view of alleged Italian corruption. The feeling that the Church's performance had sometimes reflected worldly rather than spiritual motives and that she had pursued actions at variance with Christian ethics pervaded Manzoni's anxious investigation of Christianity in history. By confining himself to unexceptionable dogma, he evades the real issue, a circumstance that suggests a persistent uncertainty beneath his apparent resolution. In fact, his reading of history coincides in many respects with Sismondi's. By refraining from detailed consideration of events such as the St Bartholomew Night's massacre, Manzoni avoids imputing responsibility to specific prelates, while issuing a general moral judgment. Yet it is true that the general must precede the particular in his moral contemplation of history. In one of the drafts for the introduction, however, Manzoni points out that French clergy had continued to express their faith despite the hostile atmosphere of the Revolution, while, at the same time, combining liberal principles with opposition to revolutionary excesses. Later, these clergy had not abandoned their liberal principles even though some revolutionaries had recanted; that is, the true concept of justice in the political sphere, like all other moral concepts therein, derives from the immutable morality taught by the Church, a morality opposed to both servility and sedition, even if different interpretations of it may range men on opposite political sides. These passages were omitted from the published version, partly because the proposition that religion could stand on both sides might displease the Austrian censor, since Austria regarded religion as being exclusively on *her* side, and partly because its attribution to both sides implied a doubt whether it stood wholly on the Italian side at this dawn of the Risorgimento.

With a broader background of reading in the New Testament, in Church doctrine, especially as codified in the Council of Trent, in French religious writers of the seventeenth century (Pascal, Bourdaloue, Massillon, Nicole and Bossuet) and in Paolo Segneri, an Italian of the same period, as well as in philosophy, Manzoni formulated the general principles of individual conduct of life which he later embodied in specific characters and situations in *I promessi sposi.* The two processes were not contiguous, for the second required much further thought and a humanizing of the rigorous moral logic of the *Osservazioni:* and the experience of the poem *Il cinque maggio* and the tragedy *Adelchi* lay between them. Manzoni is investigating here the unvarying context of human life in time and its relationship to the eternal. Thus, from his idealist viewpoint, Benedetto Croce was bound to condemn Manzoni's approach to history and his ignoring contemporary speculation on the philosophy of history, since Croce held that truth is not transcendent but is constructed within time and history.

In his refutation Manzoni is unfailingly dispassionate and courteous with his adversary. He scrupulously examines Sismondi's propositions, isolates their logical meaning and contrasts them with the relevant points of Catholic doctrine. His own religious position is founded upon deep logical thought which has demonstrated to him the unity of Church teaching, with all aspects interlocking and leading to total truth. His tranquillity thus derives, not from any innate impartiality or exemption from historical passions, as has been suggested, but from a deliberate avoidance of historical judgments and from a persuasion that a duty to speak on behalf of the truth does not entail a duty to ensure its triumph. In the preface to the reader, Manzoni notes that attacks on religion are more favourably received than defences, which are deemed uninteresting: but the essential question is whether millions of people should abandon the moral code they profess or should study it better and follow it more faithfully. The many who believe that indifference to religion is the fruit of long discussion and an advanced civilization forget that indifference was Christianity's first enemy. Why should we not bear witness in the transient vigour of our youth to that which we shall invoke at the terrible moment of death?

Manzoni begins the work itself by stressing the unity of faith. Truth and its revelation are identical and consequently Church teaching never changes, but the numerous articles of faith are adapted to the discursive nature of the human mind. Acceptance of this unity implies subordination of human reason to the Word of God, but it is logical to accept the revelation of what is clear and unified in the divine mind, that is, of truth. The identity of Catholic principles in all times and places entails identical logical consequences. Any variations derive from non-logical consequences such as differences in methods of application or in historical or national characteristics.

A similar unity underlies Christian moral teaching which alone can demonstrate both the beauty and the advantage of a moral action. Moral philosophy can show only the former of these motives, but, for theology, both meet in God in the eternal unity of the beautiful and the true: the motive for an unpleasant action is truth. Consequently, moral philosophy has a genuine validity but its partial nature produces uncertainty and inconsistencies in its application. Each man is responsible for the moral control of himself because no one can be a sufficient cause of evil to others. Love for one's fellows means a desire for their good, which is that they should serve God. Theology adds the unique quality of grace to assist human will towards the pursuit of the good. This good may mean sometimes the acceptance of death. Whereas in *Il conte di Carmagnola* Manzoni regarded the next life as a tranquil refuge from temporal suffering, he now believes that it completes an order of perfection for which man was created although this order may be begun in this life:

> perchè quando a seguire la giustizia non v'è altra via che la morte, è certo per noi che Dio ci ha segnata quella via per giungere a Lui; perchè il secolo presente non ha il suo compimento in sè; perchè il bisogno che abbiamo di essere approvati non sarà contento che quando vedremo che Dio ci approva.

> (because, when there is no other way than death of following justice, it is certain for us that God has marked out that path for reaching Him; because the present world does not have its completion within itself; because our need of approval will be satisfied only when we see that God approves us.)

Our motive is the ever living idea of order and perfection which we find within us and which guides us to eventual happiness, impossible within the changes and conflicts inseparable from time: the eventual state will be a 'repose', not in the sense of *Il conte di Carmagnola,* but a repose consisting of being absolutely 'in order', of an identification of our will with God's will, of freedom from sorrow because with no inclination to evil and no conflict.

The Church's moral decrees are an extension and application of scriptural teaching, not, as Sismondi had alleged, the mere product of theological schools, nor do these decrees conflict with natural law, which is part of divine law without its moral sanction. The Church, basing itself upon the objective nature of revelation, must intervene to distinguish venial from mortal sins since, for this task, the subjective individual conscience is inadequate; as for mortal sins, they are either condemned as such in the Bible or are manifestly at variance with the human moral purpose.

Manzoni then points out to his adversary that the Church does not engage in, or encourage religious hatred. Condemnation of a sin is compatible with love of a sinner, who must indeed be loved since charity is part of faith and the true state of a man's soul is unknown to others. Thus religious wars are not a logical result of faith; they offend against it; for example, the St Bartholomew's Night massacre stemmed not from faith but from passions. In fact, Christianity has made toleration and virtuous acts normal rather than rare, as in pagan times.

In regard to penitence, an act of faith alone cannot give certainty that a sin is forgiven, for such a certainty is inconsistent with the limitations of the human condition. Human reason accepts the revealed concept that forgiveness depends upon an act of contrition which changes an evil to a good will, but cannot be certain thereof and thus hopes with a mixture of trust and diffidence. Calvin was wrong to suppose that an act of faith suffices for forgiveness: he thereby confused faith and hope and, in fact, eliminated the latter by bestowing on man a certainty he cannot have. The Church's participation in penitence through confession, satisfaction and absolution emphasizes that conversion requires help from a clergy who receive the repentant sinner with love and humility because of the redeeming grace operative in him—the attitude of Cardinal Borromeo towards the Innominato in *I promessi sposi.* The Man-God, in expiation for finite man who had offended against the infinite, had equalled finite with infinite and made redemption possible.

There follows a fundamental chapter on the objection raised by Sismondi that the possibility of conversion at any moment invites delay until the moment of death. While conceding the conformity of this possibility with both the gospels and reason, Manzoni stresses the dangers of delay: the increasing difficulty of repentance as time passes, as sins mount up and vicious habits grow stronger and as God's patience is wearied towards one who has remained deaf to his calls, so that the difficulty is greatest at the moment of death. We cannot count on the ability to make a decision then, for we cannot control the future—and so time itself. Implicit in Manzoni's position is the Pauline view that a sinner's decisions are impeded by the past self he has constructed. The Church warns sinners of the uncertainty of the manner and moment of death and thus a reasonable man will understand that we should be ready, since the Son of Man will come at an hour we do not expect: 'Dunque è ragionevole di vivere in ogni momento in modo che si possa con fiducia presentarsi a Dio; dunque la conversione è necessaria in ogni momento ai peccatori, la perseveranza ai giusti.' (It is reasonable, then, to live at every moment in such a way that you may be able to present yourself to God with confidence; therefore, conversion is necessary at every moment for sinners, perseverance for the righteous.) This doctrine, comments Manzoni, far from concentrating our thoughts on death, is supremely adapted to directing this life, which is a time of trial determining the nature of the next. If a man is in a state of justice at death, he must also be in a state of salvation. Although in a material sense the past is immutable and every man, in reviewing his past, especially his childhood and adolescence, notes many omissions which prevented the attainment of his goals and sadly feels the impossibility of remedying such negligence, religion, at every moment he has recourse to it, consoles him with the knowledge that he is in time to enter on the only way necessary for true and perpetual happiness. The final and irrevocable moral reckoning comes only with death.

If judgment is based on the moment of death, it follows that a man is his complete self at every moment and his position at other moments is irrelevant. It is absurd to complain that one single moment's aberration decides one's eternal fate for, as Bossuet had observed, a sinner is totally committed to sinning endlessly at the moment of transgression; in any case, actions are good or bad according to the eternal law, not to time and earthly life, and, as Manzoni reminded Sismondi, it is not the element of chance in the timing of death which determines an eternal state, because the moral condition at death depends upon a man's will. No question arises of weighing good moments against bad or of compensating for shortcomings by virtuous behaviour. One must employ according to God's law 'ognuno di quei momenti dei quali tutti si darà conto a Dio; che non ve n'ha uno in tutta la vita per il peccato' (each of those moments, of all of which account will be rendered to God; because there is none in the whole of life for sin). An entire life of meritorious actions cannot cover one violent act and the shedding of one man's blood by his brother is too much for all ages and the whole world.

After pointing out that contributions to the subsistence of the clergy cannot buy absolution, for which personal repentance is a prerequisite, and that indulgence granted in the penalty imposed for a sin presupposes a depth of contrition and an intensity of love, Manzoni emphasizes that observance of the Church's precepts represents obedience to Christian moral principles, for the precepts are means to this end. He then proceeds with fine psychological insight to analyse the motives and effects of slanderers. This vice stems from corrupt passion, satisfies the pride of the speaker and affords him a taste of his supposed superiority, enabling him to appear, rather than be, good. Operating secretly from his victim, he has no interest in reforming him and may drive him to violent measures. Justice and charity require open reproval and correction of vices.

In dealing with almsgiving, Manzoni reminds Sismondi that the concept of the performance of a virtuous deed in the hope of eternal reward is fundamental to the Gospel. The reward of goodness and justice is their perfection in heaven, of which an earnest is granted on earth. Love for oneself is a desire for infinite goodness and love for others is a similar desire for them: thus almsgiving represents a wish to help others.

The remaining four chapters of the first part of the *Osser-*

vazioni discuss various topics: Christian humility indicates a recognition of human weakness and the impossibility of goodness without God, and putting oneself under a spiritual director is not subservience but a responsible act.

Although the second part was not finished and has been published only in modern times, it represents Manzoni's thought at that period and needs study here. The first chapter examines the whole relationship between religion and the changing viewpoints of the world: basic Christian teaching is independent of its varied expressions in different ages and of the passions with which it is sometimes advocated. Calm is required in both religious and political affairs, where the Church condemns excessive enthusiasm for schemes of political reform which impose upon their adherents the duty of working for their realization. In both fields, undue enthusiasm may lead to hatred. In every age or generation, few men are capable of subordinating their subjective reason to objective reason and consequently a later age disproves ideas previously considered incontestable. Each generation has a 'spirit', a basic outlook, which is produced by the seminal ideas of a few outstanding thinkers of the previous generation whose opinions are commonly derided or completely disregarded during their lifetimes.

Manzoni then criticizes reactionary clergy: in addition to deriving from the Gospel unauthorized principles which suit their own interests, these men attack some secular tendencies that are really new applications of the Gospel and thus give the impression that Christian ideas are antiquated survivals needing political authority for their preservation. The clergy should welcome new expressions of truth and integrate them into the Christian system.

Religion prescribes the subjection of everything in this world to our purpose in the next: thus the most significant content of each occasion in life lies in its response to divine purpose. Nothing temporal has intrinsic validity and anything that causes us to forget that we are on a journey is vanity and error. Manzoni dismisses any feeling of melancholy at the passage of time by emphasizing the idea of eternal life. No so-called historical necessity excuses opposing injustice to injustice, for the moral obligation is always paramount. Against a celebrated theory of Machiavelli, Manzoni argues that the triumph of evil men results not from the Christian patience of the righteous but from an acceptance of earthly values and goals which permits iniquity on the grounds that it brings advantages and which thus fails to isolate the evil and so bring about their defeat. Christianity has indeed transformed society since the days of pagan violence and cruelty, but its main benefit relates not to temporal life but to bliss hereafter. Its temporal effect has not been directly political, however, but it has predisposed men to more moral conduct in society. It has helped the people, not simply by restraining them and offering them hope, but by checking would-be oppressors; it has shown that, in the deepest sense, all men are equal. In international relations, Christianity has, in a similar way, induced the various peoples to regard each other as brothers in a common eternal mission. The antithesis of the Christian influence on society or on a people would be an individual's identification of a people's purpose with his own and his consequent use of them for private purposes.

The *Osservazioni sulla morale cattolica* mark a notable

step in Manzoni's elaboration of Christian principles and their application, in abstract terms, to individual life, with the accompanying problem of relating the temporal to the eternal. This step formed the starting-point for the dramatization of concrete situations in *I promessi sposi,* but the moral interpretation of historical events, lacking in the *Osservazioni,* continued to offer immense difficulty, especially the place of the righteous individual in the framework of such events. In the *Adelchi,* Manzoni was still seeking a solution within history itself, whereas, in the novel, he resumes the Christian insight of the *Osservazioni* that the completion of individual lives is achieved in an after-life and he rejects the quest for moral patterns in history.

The similarities between passages of the *Osservazioni* and situations and characters in the novel are numerous, and occasional psychological analyses prefigure its characterizations. Giuseppe De Robertis was reminded of the tone and language of Federigo Borromeo, while Ferruccio Ulivi, more convincingly, suggested a point midway between the Cardinal and Manzoni's much admired Massillon. The influence of the French writers of the seventeenth century is obvious in general and in many specific details, but their stern religious teaching is mitigated even if it falls short of the living human terms of Borromeo. The sentiments and language of the *Osservazioni* and the novel are sometimes very close, not simply owing to a common New Testament derivation, but also because Manzoni is passing from exposition to dramatization of the same fundamental points of religion. From time to time, however, the logical reasoning of the *Osservazioni* is permeated by deep emotion, as when Manzoni introduces references to historical persons and acts of justice or injustice: for example, his commendation of the priests who sought to restrain the cruelty of the conquerors of the New World or, more subtly, his ironical comments, which arise from bitterness of feeling. The prose itself, in its lack of ornamentation and avoidance of traditional literary language, reflects the clarity of the author's thought and the humility of his approach; in its vocabulary and syntax it also shows considerable French influence, hardly surprising in view of Manzoni's sources and his wide reading of French works. (pp. 37-45)

> S. B. Chandler, in his Alessandro Manzoni: The Story of a Spiritual Quest, *Edinburgh University Press, 1974, 139 p.*

Gian Piero Barricelli   (essay date 1976)

[*Barricelli is an American educator and literary critic who has published works on such Italian writers as Dante, Boccaccio, Giacomo Leopardi, and Giuseppe Mazzini. In the following excerpt, he identifies elements of Romanticism and realism in* The Betrothed.]

Above the irony and through the humor [of *I promessi sposi*] there dominates a sense of life's seriousness and of its intrinsic and potential beauty. An inner glow of understanding serenity, which not without reason commentators have labeled faith, makes Manzoni communicate with the reader with tacit directness. Despite the "personal" interventions in the play between author and Anonymous Chronicler, Manzoni does not beckon our attention; hence the word "faith," which describes well Manzoni the man,

poet, and essayist, is too concentrated to describe a suffused ethico-religious attitude which warms the novel inwardly but does not point to itself as the work's condition of being. His focus is more on people and how they are than on humans and why they are.

We can speak of both his Romanticism and his Realism. The mixture may be observed in his nature descriptions, however few in number. They stand out in sober style; landscapes are not worded effusively. With the attitude of a Classical realist, Manzoni delights in them not out of sentimentality in the manner of Werther but more in the manner of Keats, out of joy in the contemplation of beauty. Hence his glance was more topographical than ecstatic. Surely the vision of home the exiled protagonists keep experiencing is a topographical vision, like the houses and hills Lucia sees during her "Farewell," or, less poignantly, like the setting Fra Cristoforo observes when he leaves his monastery in Pescarenico to visit Lucia:

> The sky was completely serene. As the sun rose gradually behind the mountain, its rays could be seen descending from the summits of the opposite mountains and spreading rapidly downward over the slopes and into the valleys below. An autumn breeze was shaking the dead leaves from the branches of the mulberry trees, blowing them about, and falling a few feet from the tree. To the right and left, the vineleaves in the vineyards sparkled in varied shades of red on festoons that were still taut; and the freshly turned furrows stood out in vivid brown amid the fields of stubble, white and glistening with dew. The scene was cheerful; but every human figure that appeared in it saddened the eye and the mind.

Someone has said that for the most part his landscapes are implicit in the story rather than described, and where they exist they relate to inner life, but not as Romantic extensions (*à la* René) of the individual character's psyche. The sun rises when Fra Cristoforo moves about, and it is clouded over when the Innominato looks out of his window. But these natural occurrences are not projections of an inner state, as we have seen. They relate aesthetically to the totality of an ethical situation.

Manzoni's "Romanticism" contains eighteenth-century proto-Romantic elements of sensibility, philanthropy, and popularism, but also more immediately Encyclopedic attitudes, such as a "philosophic" critical intellectualism which, as a result of its acuity and his moderate temperament, expressed itself in irony against society and against judicial and religious abuses. His whole manner exhibits that *philosophe* tendency, extended by the Romantics, to educate the masses away from superstitions and errors, and to correct the elite's prejudices and intolerances. It is not the poet Manzoni who exhibits this, but the historian, the political and social critic who wrote an historical novel, one which reflects sadly on man's ability to govern himself. His pessimism vis-à-vis human history, assuaged by his ironic smile, becomes Romantic through the overlay of Christian sentiment imposed upon it by his deeply ethical conscience. Hence his most genuinely Romantic trait, which accords with principles enunciated by one of Italy's first Romantic voices, Giovanni Berchet: the popularization of art, its democratization through choice of subject, use of language, and sense of mission. Arturo Graf properly agrees to the label "Romantic" for Manzoni, and admits that he headed the Italian school, but cautions us with many reservations about the full applicability of the label.

Indeed, if labels are to be sought, that of Realist suits him better. He said it well in talking about plot in a novel:

> As for the course of events and plot, I believe that the best way to do things differently from others is to focus one's attention in reality on the way men behave, and above all on what about it is contrary to the romanesque spirit [*esprit romanesque*]. In all the novels that I have read, I seem to notice an effort to establish interesting and unexpected relationships among different characters, to give them prominence, to find events which simultaneously and in different ways influence the destiny of everybody—in short, an artificial unity which one does not find in real life. I know that this unity pleases the reader; but I think that this is because of an old habit. I know that it is considered a virtue in some works which derive a true benefit of the first order from it; but I am of the opinion that some day it will become an object of criticism, and that one will cite this way of tying events together as an example of the sway which custom exerts on the best and loftiest minds, or of the sacrifice one makes to establish taste.

Manzoni's realism, more particular than Jane Austen's (whose temperament was also largely unsympathetic to the Romantic movement, who wrote more about human than external nature and not about heroic passions but about everyday details of living, and whose subtle wit and worship of calm sense and level-headedness remind us in many ways of Manzoni), comes closer to Gottfried Keller's in that it pays attention to human facts in their natural habitat, as it were. It also reveals an awareness of the shock value of horrific occurrences at certain times in history, such as the macabre spectacle of the "convoy" of the dead being carted away to the *lazzeretto,* an episode whose trenchant realism provides a climax for human stupidity. But at no time can it be said that the author engages the lugubrious, or the gothic, for its own sake. In fact, the gothic repulsed him because it is unrealistic; his classical nature preferred daylight to darkness. Along the same lines, he avoided the presentation of stormy passion and fiery love: a Heathcliff and a Lelia made him turn the other way. In *I promessi sposi,* love is not declared; it does not magnetize attention to itself, and on no page does it tell its story exclusively. But it is interiorized in almost every page, so that it is hard to conceive of any action of Renzo, for example, divorced from its context. There is sentiment in the novel, but no trace of sentimentalism, as there is no dream-world emotionalism. Similarly in the question of language, as we know, Manzoni's aim was not inflation, or, more acceptably, the picturesque enrichment which Romantics in other parts of Europe strove toward, but clarity and realism, words in their educational and pervasively social or national context.

Identification of Manzoni with his characters—possibly with the humble—is possible only on a "religious" level, that is, on the level of their intimate affinity with his own spiritual qualities. If he had not been detached from them (the Marxists would say paternalistic) and had identified with them on the social level as well, *I promessi sposi* would have stood out as a case of Verismo, or Italian Naturalism, long before Verga and Capuana gave it form. But

as it was, Manzoni still opened a window in its direction by intuiting the need to interpret the psychology of the lower class, to scrutinize its motivations, its special logic, its linguistic mechanisms oiled with proverbs and exclamations and interjections, and its confidence in its own perceptions as sources of common sense. An Italian critic writes: "Having known how to strip our literature from humanistic and literary postures, having directed the artist's interest onto the humble classes, having elevated their prestige and human significance in history—this clears the field and opens up our view to this world which is dark but full of a characteristic truth and psychology which the *verist* writer will attempt to reveal by the use of dialectical expressions."

Manzoni's realism embodies a philosophy. More than "Catholic" or "social," as this philosophy has often been classified, it is simply humanitarian, and the humanitarianism is anchored in a realistic view of life. It is not accurate to say that "Manzoni expects the reader to sympathize with his own outlook, a position possible in his age but not in ours" [S. B. Chandler, *Alessandro Manzoni*], though, to be sure, his judgment of men's actions is rendered in the light of eternal Christian morality. If *I promessi sposi* represents his statement of his view of life, the statement is not theological because the morality relates to all human existence and is not bound by dogmatic precepts. That he is an artist who espoused a Christian outlook on the world does not permit us to consider his cult the sole determinant of his art, any more than we should claim that Dante's art is totally dependent on his medieval beliefs. Similarly, Manzoni's compassion for the humble does not permit us to see a kind of socialism as the inspiration of his novel. Ideology and art do not mix when an author proselytizes. This is not the case with Manzoni, whose ideology remains private and contained in an intimate vision which may become a fictional objectification of his personal moral world, but which, for all that, does not force itself upon the reader. It has been observed that the Catholic conscience was being eroded by libertarian thinking in his day, the way Reformation and Counter-Reformation had shaken many tenets of faith in the early seventeenth century, when the novel takes place. However, Manzoni's attempt to blend faith and reality was made without propagandistic overtones, if only because the blending outlined for him the parameters of a realistic moral cosmos.

This point cannot be overemphasized, for many a warped perspective has arisen about Manzoni, whose "juice of the whole tale," as Lucia says in the end, becomes a veritable "message," and as such is not just explained but explicated by a rigid application of what a social and confessional religion maintains. Some have asserted that the novel stems directly from the *Osservazioni.* Others have asserted that Providence directs the course of all action, from falling tiles to plague and from rising dawn to rain, and that even Fra Cristoforo's efforts count little in the outcome of things. This view, subject as it is to entirely religiously based assumptions, emasculates the novel. For *I promessi sposi* is about people, which means about life, and was not written with preordained pedagogical ends of the sermonizing kind. Montano put it well, in reacting to the Crocean stress in the work's "oratory":

> This is a Christian society. The poet believes in the

same values in which it believes; in some way, he is inside it. Men and things are portrayed by one who belongs to that same world, who clearly recognizes the good people and the bad in the same way those living in that world could recognize them. . . . The author has not the slightest interest in altering things and in presenting things in a different light. He knows well that the good and the bad exist in the world; he knows that quite often the bad succeed in the world and that the good succumb. Manzoni . . . is the last person to believe that virtue wins out and is rewarded by God in this world. . . . Manzoni wants to reveal the world as it is; he needs only remain faithful to the Christian view of the society portrayed for which Don Rodrigo is a scoundrel and Fra Cristoforo . . . a generous and fiery man of religion. The poet is like the conscience of the world. The portrait we get is that of a man who believes in the same values. Those are the proportions; there are no prejudices, no distortions. This fact contributes immeasurably to the naturalness, to the realism. The poet undoubtedly has a more elevated conscience; he is in a position to see the superior humanity of Borromeo as well as the cowardice of Don Abbondio or the profound moral beauty of Lucia; but his judgment coincides with the most concrete and objective premises of the society portrayed.

This accounts for the fact that no mysticism enters Manzoni's work. If anything, his interest lies in eternity as actuated by history. Mysticism is tantamount to excess; so is effusive love. And death, as the novel implies, emerges not as the horrid mystery or absurdity of disturbed imaginations, but as a form of terrestrial life, its culminating reality. Like Cardinal Borromeo, to "take things seriously" means to see life realistically as well as with a sense of mission—something ego-bound creatures like Don Abbondio and Sr. Gertrude cannot do. To distinguish abstract moral norms from pragmatic action in our personal conduct amounts to a form of hypocrisy. Yet history reveals how often the hypocrisy is practiced. Injustice and violence characterize the children of Adam and Eve. Hence the pessimism, as the end of *Adelchi* clearly illustrated. Manzoni's finest poetic moments in *I promessi sposi* come when he contemplates universal suffering. He is like Pascal minus the open anguish, and more like Tolstoy; he is "the poet of human misery consoled by divine mercy" [L. Tonelli]. Man wanders astray because he does not see well, and because he hears prejudices echoing all about him; and he wanders in a world which has lost its taste for simplicity and intimacy. *"Vanitas, vanitatum, et omnia vanitas,"* Manzoni too could exclaim toward the end of his life.

But to deduce from this that his portrayal of evil confirms "the insufficiency of the religious criterion before characters and situations of the modern world" [A. Moravia] misinterprets the ethical component of his poetic inspiration, that intimate vision of life. Lay pessimism and spiritual optimism hallmark the philosophy of Manzoni. There is something in this vision of that pomegranate bush he had in his garden in Brusuglio: "I have here in a little garden of mine a young pomegranate which has blossomed richly this Spring, and the flowers have fallen in part, and in part they have held; together, the rankness of all of them and the vigorous health of some announce that this little tree is destined to yield copious and select fruits."

In the fact of poetry, Providence emerges less a faith than a reasonable hope, like the fruit on that tree, less a dogmatic certainty than a universal need, and not a matter of blind, facile belief but of rational desire. Theology emerges simply as moral philosophy, religion as natural morality. Man's heroic measure is taken not in accomplishing great deeds in the mouth of danger but in unassuming strength of character in the midst of human suffering. In this chaotic scenario of life, Manzoni does not turn subserviently to the Gospel's philosophy of suffering but to the conquest of inner man acting freely, and hopefully with the support of his faith. Every chapter of the novel leads to this conquest, and it takes a long time to reach the inner peace of temperance and justice, fortitude, prudence, and charity; it is a long novel, an epic, at the end of which Renzo and Lucia offer us a simple conclusion: " . . . that troubles often come to those who bring them upon themselves, but that not even the most cautious and innocent behavior can ward them off; and that when they come—whether by our own fault or not—confidence in God can lighten them and turn them to our own improvement." This simple conclusion, this "juice" of the tale, discovered by a humble man and woman, is a discovery of God, however defined. It is a conquest far greater than the embattled conquests of powerful rulers and potentates who think they have accomplished great things and who make no discovery. And Manzoni's is a discovery through art, which is a form of moral life, limited, as Galletti says, only by life itself, yet propelled by the aspirations of beauty and purpose, and endlessly struggling against the base instincts of our human nature. (pp. 157-63)

> *Gian Piero Barricelli, in his* Alessandro Manzoni, *Twayne Publishers, 1976, 194 p.*

Alfonso Procaccini   (essay date 1986)

[*In the following essay, Procaccini investigates the relationship between language and theme in* The Betrothed.]

That Manzoni would turn to Shakespeare for an understanding of historical tragedy, and to Sir Walter Scott for an appreciation of the historical novel, is not surprising, for as Lukacs well observes, the classic masters of historical-realistic fiction succeed in narrating and relating past archaic events in contemporary language. By refuting the notion that the use of archaic speech (the language of the time-setting) could bring the past within the grasp of the present, Lukacs points out how the classic writer understands only too well that in order to bring the past to bear upon the present an illusion of that past must be realized. A real sense of the historical is captured only when it is reported, that is, when the writer experiences a personal relationship between past history and his own times. A feeling of continuity must, therefore, be felt toward the past, for without it the past would indeed remain remote, at best only an exotic realm suited for either lyrical documentation or laborious archeology. For Manzoni, both Shakespeare and Scott were committed to secular history; to the world of here and now and to the individuals who live in it.

The use of history for literary purposes means, then, that the past must be brought up to date, that history must be made private and contemporary. To do this, the past must not only be recaptured, but in fact must be resurrected, for we know that the past is by definition dead unless and until it is brought into relation to the present. Its meaning is, therefore, relational and related to the present, such that once the relationship is established the past instead becomes both familiar as well as familial. The relation, of course, is and can only be realized linguistically. The power to resurrect is in itself both the miracle and the mystery of language, for without it the past would forever remain—as Italian grammar aptly terms it, "un passato *remoto.*" Croce's dictum "all history is contemporary history" along with Lacan's theory that the "past" is simply "present speech" point directly to what I wish to suggest here: that one of the reasons why Manzoni was so obsessively interested in the so-called "questione della lingua" and why he devoted so much energy to the re-writing of his *I promessi sposi* may be directly related to the specific debate concerning the nature of the historical novel. We know, of course, that *I promessi sposi* evokes the past in order to criticize as much as to satirize contemporary tyrannies. However, the problem facing Manzoni was preeminently one of dealing with the use of language, namely its function and its style. How could he relate past tyrannies to present ones; and more to the point, how would he make past events dramatically relevant?

In his *Del romanzo storico,* an essay written as an apologia as much as an apology of *I promessi sposi* [see excerpt dated 1850], Manzoni curiously enough reverts back to classical authors to defend the inventive element, the very element which appeared to threaten the very stuff which nurtured the historical novel, namely the historical. In the ever open controversy regarding the relative status of poetry and history, Manzoni not only harks back to Aristotle's classic distinction whereby poetry is taken to be the more philosophical, hence capable of expressing the universal, as opposed to history which tends to express the particular, but more to the point, he traces the roots of the historical novel back to what he called the "primitive or spontaneous epic," i.e., the fable, the genre which fuses and confuses history from story. There is no question that "history" must serve as the backbone of the novel; however it is the poetic or the inventive element which provides the "discourse"—that is, its socio-political message. In other words, by returning to the old distinction and favoring poetry over history, Manzoni was able to implicitly grant to his own novel the same "universal" quality he himself extended to Ariosto's *Furioso* or Virgil's *Aeneid.* This he did by appealing precisely to what he considered significant about Virgil's poetic style:

> Dico quello stile che s'allontana in parte dall'uso comune d'una lingua, per la ragione (bonissima, chi la faccia valer bene), che la poesia vuole esprimere anche dell'idee che l'uso comune non ha bisogno d'esprimere; e che non meritano meno per questo d'essere espresse, quando uno l'abbia trovate. Che, oltre le qualità più essenziali e più manifeste delle cose, e oltre le loro relazioni più immediate e più frequenti, ci sono nelle cose, dico nelle cose di cui tutti parlano, delle qualità e delle relazioni più recondite e meno osservate o non osservate; e queste appunto vuole esprimere il poeta; e per esprimerle, ha bisogno di nove locuzioni. *Parla quasi un cert'altro linguaggio,* perchè ha cert'altre cose da dire. Ed è quando, portato dalla concitazione dell'animo, o dall'intenta contemplazione delle cose, all'orlo, dirò così, d'un concetto, per arrivare al quale il linguaggio comune non gli somministra

> una formola, ne trova una con cui afferrarlo, e renderlo presente, in una forma propria e distinta, alla sua mente (che agli altri può aver pensato prima, e pensarci dopo, ma non ci pensa, certo, in quel momento). E questo non lo fa, o lo fa ben di rado, e ancor più di rado felicemente, con l'inventar vocaboli novi, come fanno, e devono fare, i trovatori di verità scientifiche; ma con accozzi inusitati di vocaboli usitati; appunto perchè il proprio dell'arte sua è, non tanto d'insegnar cose nove, quanto di rivelare aspetti novi di cose note; e il mezzo più naturale a ciò è di mettere in relazioni nove i vocaboli significanti cose note. (*Del romanzo*)

> (By poetic style, I mean the style that distinguishes itself from common usage by its advantage—and a very important one for anyone who exploits it—in expressing ideas that common usage is not called upon to express, but that still deserve to be expressed once they have been conceived. For even quite ordinary things have qualities and relationships that are more arcane and less well known [if they are known at all] than those that are most closely and commonly associated with them. It is precisely these that the poet seeks to convey and that require of him new locutions. *He speaks almost another language,* because he has such different things to say. And just when he is most transported by emotion or inspiration, just at the threshold, so to speak, of an idea for which common usage has no expression, he finds the special language that captures it and renders it clear to the mind's eye. [Whatever ideas he may have had just before or just after, he certainly cannot think of them now.] Rarely does he do this, and even more rarely with much success, by inventing new words as scientists do. Almost invariably, it is by combining usual words in unusual ways, since, after all, the special character of poetry is not so much to teach something new as to reveal new aspects of something already known, and the most natural way to do this is to put words with established meaning into new relationships. [*On the Historical*])

Manzoni's appeal to Virgil's poetry is meant to further reinforce the nature of so-called "realistic" literature: that it should be verisimilar in content, yet unique in expression. It is the use of language, or better, how language is imaginatively used, which gives to realistic fiction its strong grip on life. Fashioning a technique and a style which transform the past into contemporary "news" means that the historical novel can be precisely what the genre claims to be—both historical and novel, both remote and recent. In short, what constitutes the novelty of the historical novel is its ability and power to literally resurrect the past.

Now the theme of resurrection is present at the very opening of *I promessi sposi* on the very first page of the "scratched and faded manuscript" Manzoni claims to have found, wherein he reads: "L'Historia si può veramente deffinire una guerra illustre contro il Tempo, perchè togliendoli di mano gl'anni suoi prigionieri, anzi già fatti cadaueri, li richiama in vita, li passa in rassegna, e li schiera di nuovo in battaglia" (1840). ("Historie may be verilie defined as a mightie war against Time, for snatching from his hands the years emprisoned, nay already slain by him, she calleth them back unto life, passeth them in review, and rangeth them once more in battle array." [The critic

Manzoni at eighty-five.

adds in a footnote: "I am using the Mondadori editions of the novel in **Tutte le opere,** Arnoldo Mondadori Editore, 1954. They will be cited as 1821-1823, 1825-1827, and 1840. Translations of the first two editions are my own; translations of the 1840 edition are from Archibald Colquhoun, trans., **The Betrothed.**"] The passage continues to a point whereupon the narrator abruptly intervenes: "Ma, quando io avrò durata l'eroica fatica di trascriver questa storia da questo dilavato e graffiato autografo, e l'avrò data, come si suol dire, alla luce, si troverà poi chi duri la fatica di leggerla?—" (1840). ("—But when I've carried through the heroic labour of transcribing this story from this faded and scratched manuscript, and I will have brought it to light, as the saying goes, will there be anyone with enough energy to read it?") After some initial doubts as to whether the labour of rewriting the story is of any worth, the narrator reconsiders his project:

> Nell'atto però di chiudere lo scartafaccio, per riporlo, mi sapeva male che una storia così bella dovesse rimanersi tuttavia sconosciuta. . . . Perchè non si potrebbe, pensai, prender la serie de'fatti da questo manoscritto, e rifarne la dicitura?—Non presentato alcuna obiezion ragionevole, il partito fu subito abbracciato. Ed ecco l'origine del presente libro, esposta con un'ingenuità pari all'importanza del libro medesimo. (1840)

> (But just as I was closing up the rubbishy manuscript before putting it away, I felt a pang of regret that so beautiful a story should remain forever unknown; . . . Why—thought I—couldn't the sequence of events be taken from the manuscript and the language recast? No reasonable objection presenting itself, I adopted this course forthwith. And there you have the origin of the present book, stated with a frankness equal to the importance of the book itself.)

Interestingly enough what is here expressed finds its correspondence in Manzoni's own description of his initial interest in writing *I promessi sposi.* He himself tells us of its origin:

> Per togliermi al dispiacere della fallita impresa, . . . sono andato a passare alcuni giorni a Brusuglio, portando meco le storie milanesi del Ripamonti e le opere economico-politiche del Gioia. Già, se non ci fosse stato Walter Scott a me non sarebbe venuto in mente di scrivere un romanzo. Ma trovati nel Ripamonti quegli strani personaggi della Signora di Monza, dell'Innominato, del Cardinal Federigo, e la descrizione della carestia e della rivolta di Milano, del passaggio dei lanzichenecchi e della peste; e viste le gride dei governatori di Milano, riportate nella sua opera dal Gioia, ho pensato: "Non si potrebbe inventare un fatto a cui prendessero parte tutti questi personaggi ed in cui entrassero tutti questi avvenimenti?" E fu la grida che il dottor Azzecca-garbugli fa vedere a Renzo ed in cui si parla della violenza che si facevano per impedire qualche matrimonio, quella che mi spinse ad inventare il fatto dei *Promessi sposi.* (in Ferruccio Ulivi, *Il romanticismo e Alessandro Manzoni*)

> (In order to overcome my sorrow over the defeat of the undertaking, . . . I left to spend a few days in Brusuglio, taking with me Ripamonti's Milanese accounts and Gioia's economic-political works. Indeed, if there hadn't been Walter Scott, it would never have crossed my mind to write a novel. But after reading Ripamonti and discovering those strange characters as the Signora di Monza, the Innominato [Unnamed], Cardinal Federico, and the description of the famine and the uprisings of Milano, the passage of the mercenaries, and the plague; and after reading in Gioia's accounts of the decrees posted by the Milanese officials, I thought: "Couldn't a story be made up wherein all of these characters could partake in all of these events?" And it was the decree that Doctor Azzecca-garbugli shows to Renzo wherein mention is made of the violence done in order to prevent some marriages which moved me to consider writing about *The Betrothed.*)

In another entry Manzoni confesses, "E pensai, questo [il matrimonio contrastato] sarebbe un buon soggetto da farne un romanzo, e per finale grandioso la peste che aggiusta ogni cosa!" (in Ulivi) (I thought that this [the opposed marriage] would be good material for a novel, ending it with the grandiose theme of the plague which settles everything).

But back to the novel! The narrator proceeds and further states that, as it stands, the manuscript "isn't a work fit to present to readers of the present day." Thus, realizing the need to rewrite it, to up-date it, Manzoni concludes: "Ma, rifiutando come intollerabile la dicitura del nostro autore, che dicitura vi abbiam noi sostituita? Qui sta il punto" (1840). ("But having rejected our author's style as intolerable, what kind of style have we substituted for it ourselves? That's the point.") Keeping in mind our earlier reference to Manzoni's remarks about Virgil and his epic, we should likewise ask ourselves what it is that Manzoni is rewriting, and why is it that he wishes to remain faithful to the content, yet alter its style? Stated somewhat differently, why wish to retain the identity of the original when its copy will in effect alter it? If so, then what is the difference between the two manuscripts, and what does it mean to say that the two manuscripts are similar in content yet different in style?

A comparison of the three editions (**Fermo e Lucia**, Prima Composizione del 1821-1823; **I promessi sposi,** Testo critico della prima edizione, 1825-27; **I promessi sposi,** Testo critico della edizione definitiva del 1840) reveals the basic problem Manzoni sought to address in his introductions to each edition. For our purpose, a comparison of the respective introductions themselves reveals Manzoni's distinct yet almost obsessive interest in the problem of style over content, a problem which curiously enough appears to have been already "resolved" in the two introductions Manzoni wrote for the first edition, **Fermo e Lucia:** one written when the novel was begun, the second after it was completed. In the first introduction, following the introduction belonging to the original manuscript, Manzoni the narrator comments:

> Aveva trascritta fino a questo punto una curiosa storia del secolo decimosettimo, colla intenzione di pubblicarla, quando per degni rispetti anch'io stimai che fosse meglio conservare i fatti e rifarla di pianta. Senza fare una lunga enumerazione dei giusti motivi che mi vi determinarono, accennerò soltanto il vero e principale. L'autore di questa storia è andato frammischiando alla narrazione ogni sorta di riflessioni sue proprie; a me rileggendo il manoscritto ne venivano altre e diverse; paragonando imparzialmente le sue e le mie, io veniva sempre a trovare queste ultime molto più sensate, e per amore del vero ho preferito lo scrivere le mie a copiare le altrui; stimando anche che chi ha una occasione per dire il suo parere sopra che che sia non debba lasciarsela sfuggire. (1821-1823)

> (He had up to this point transcribed a curious seventeenth century account, with the intention of publishing it, when with due respect I too reckoned that it would be better to preserve the facts and rewrite it anew. Without getting into all the justifiable reasons which influenced me, I will only offer the true and principal one. The author of this story has intermingled within the narration all sorts of personal reflections; but rereading the manuscript I came up with other reflections and different from his; and while impartially comparing mine with his I would always find mine to be more sensible. Thus for the love of truth I preferred to write down mine rather than his; especially considering the fact that when one has the occasion to express an opinion over whatever may be in question, one shouldn't let the opportunity go by.)

In the second introduction, however, Manzoni in the very first paragraph shifts immediately away from the content to the problem of the style: "Ma copiate le poche righe che abbiam qui poste per saggio, il fastidio che provammo d'una prosa così fatta ci fece avvertire a quello che ne proverebbero i lettori" (1821-1823) (But after having copied down the few lines which we have included here as an

example, we experienced such troubles in reading that prose that we realized what difficulty the readers would experience). Manzoni then closes his remarks and states: "Ci siamo quindi risoluti di rifarla interamente, non pigliando dall'autore che i nudi fatti. Ma, rigettando, come intollerabile, lo stile del nostro autore, che stile vi abbiamo noi sostituito? Qui giace le lepre" (1821-1823) (We resolved, therefore, to rewrite it entirely, taking from its author only the bare facts. But by rejecting our author's style because it was intolerable, what style did we substitute? Here lies the hare! [i.e. That's the question!])

In the two subsequent critical editions (1827 and 1840) the point is even further refined, such that in the final edition Manzoni will write:

> Nell'atto però di chiudere lo scartafaccio, per riporlo, mi sapeva male che una storia così bella dovesse rimanersi tuttavia sconosciuta; perchè, in quanto storia, può essere che al lettore ne paia altrimenti, ma a me era parsa bella, come dico; molto bella.— Perchè non si potrebbe, pensai, prender la serie de' fatti da questo manoscritto, e rifarne la dicitura?— Non essendosi presentato alcuna obiezion ragionevole, il partito fu subito abbracciato. Ed ecco l'origine del presente libro, esposta con un'ingenuità pari all'importanza del libro medesimo. (1840)

> (But just as I was closing up the rubbishy manuscript before putting it away, I felt a pang of regret that so beautiful a story should remain for ever unknown; for as a story (the reader may think differently) it seemed beautiful to me, yes, very beautiful. Why—thought I—couldn't the sequence of events be taken from the manuscript and the language recast? No reasonable objection presenting itself, I adopted this course forthwith. And there you have the origin of the present book, stated with a frankness equal to the importance of the book itself.)

It is most interesting that in the edition of 1827 as well as in the final edition Manzoni changes the word "stile" to "dicitura," itself a poignant indication that the problem of style was of foremost importance to Manzoni: that the form should move from the written, the "writerly," to the oral, the spoken.

Manzoni feels the urge to update the story because, as he states, of its beauty and interest. However, to do so he had to correct its style, for, as it stood, the manuscript was simply a "scarabocchio," a scribble-scrabbled manuscript. He exclaims: "ma come è dozzinale! come è sguaiato! come è scorretto! Idiotismi lombardi a furia, frasi della lingua adoperate a sproposito, grammatica arbitraria, periodi sgan   gherati" (1840) ("Yes that's true; but, then, how commonplace and stiff it is! What a lot of mistakes there are in it! Endless Lombard idioms, current phrases used all wrong, arbitrary grammar, sentences that don't hang together"). In short, the project of deciphering a *scarabocchio* is the job of one who is both a scribe and editor, a job which entails not only arranging and rearranging, but also one of correcting what's there and supplying what's absent. As such, **I promessi sposi** might be said to rest on the metaphor of the book—specifically the manuscript. As a metaphor, the manuscript underscores the double aspect normally associated with it, namely that it is the product of human hands of a different epoch and that most likely it is damaged, or incomplete. Certainly this is the type of manuscript Manzoni claims to be working from.

I promessi sposi is, then, a book constructed out of fragments of other books, hence represents a collection and a revision of scribbled and scattered information. In this sense, it suggests the possibility that the novel stands as a "new testament," to fulfill and bring "to light" the message implicit in the old manuscript. The theological implication in the analogy is not as far-fetched as it might seem, for it is abundantly obvious that Manzoni did wish to supply what was most lacking in the old chronicle, namely a meaning, or what he would call the moral of the story. This is certainly the point made and to be understood in the very closing lines of the novel:

> Dopo un lungo dibattere e cercare insieme, conclusero che i guai vengono bensì spesso, perchè ci si è dato cagione; ma che la condotta più cauta e più innocente non basta a tenerli lontani; e che quando vengono, o per colpa o senza colpa, la fiducia in Dio li raddolcisce, e li rende utili per una vita migliore.

> (After discussing the question and casting around together a long time for a solution, they came to the conclusion that troubles often come to those who bring them on themselves, but that not even the most cautious and innocent behavior can ward them off; and that when they come—whether by our fault or not—confidence in God can lighten them and turn them to our own improvement.)

The narrator then adds: "Questa conclusione, benchè trovata da povera gente, c'è parsa così giusta, che abbiam pensato di metterla qui, come *il sugo di tutta la storia*" (my emphasis) (1840) ("This conclusion, though it was reached by poor people, has seemed so just to us that we have thought of putting it down here, as the juice of the whole tale"). Interestingly enough, in *Fermo e Lucia* Manzoni was even more explicit: "Questa conclusione benchè trovata da una donnicciuola ci è sembrata così opportuna che abbiamo pensato di proporla come il *costrutto morale* di tutti gli avvenimenti che abbiamo narrati, e di terminare con essa la nostra storia" (emphasis mine) (1821-1823) (This conclusion, although reached by a lowly woman, has seemed so suitable that we have thought of setting it up as the moral of all that has happened as well as end our story with it).

For Manzoni's purpose he could very well have kept for his subsequent editions the words "costrutto morale di tutti gli avvenimenti"; for our purpose it is well that he did change it to "il sugo di tutta la storia," for what the latter form suggests is that the original version lacked what his version would include, a plot—the very ingredient which, at least for E. M. Forster or Viktor Shklovsky, distinguishes a mere story from a narrative. In other words Manzoni would, in good Aristotelian terms, supply an organic unity to the story, and thus bring order to the disordered manuscript.

As a new version, then, the fiction of *I promessi sposi* claims to *rewrite* the old version, in the double sense of the word—that it writes it again as well as revises it. Such a fiction is based on a profound belief in the power of man and language to resurrect, or at least to supply meaning. The critique implied goes beyond the mere notion that because characters and events in history are limited or partial, history is by definition inadequate. Fiction or story-

telling supplements history—precisely in Derrida's sense of the "supplement," that is, that it replaces and at the same time adds on. History is to be supplemented because it is essentially lacking—"lacking" perhaps in the same way that Lucia perceives Renzo's account of his adventures. The passage is worth recalling:

> Il bello era a sentirlo raccontare le sue avventure: e finiva sempre col dire le gran cose che ci aveva imparate, per governarsi meglio in avvenire. "Ho imparato," diceva, "a non mettermi ne' tumulti: ho imparato a non predicare in piazza: ho imparato a guardare con chi parlo: ho imparato a non alzar troppo il gomito: ho imparato a non tenere in mano il martello delle porte, quando c'è lì d'intorno gente che ha la testa calda: ho imparato a non attaccarmi un campanello al piede, prima d'aver pensato quel che possa nascere." E cent'altre cose.

> Lucia però, non che trovasse la dottrina falsa in sè, ma non n'era soddisfatta; le pareva, così in confuso, che *ci mancasse qualcosa*. A forza di sentir ripetere la stessa canzone, e di pensarci sopra ogni volta, "e io," disse un giorno al suo moralista, "cosa volete che abbia imparato? Io non sono andata a cercare i guai: son loro che sono venuti a cercar me. Quando non voleste dire," aggiunse, soavemente sorridendo, "che il mio sproposito sia stato quello di volervi bene, e di promettermi a voi." (1840) (emphasis added)

> (The fun was to hear him recount his adventures; and he would always end by enumerating the great things which he had learnt from them to improve his conduct in the future. "I've learnt," he said, "not to get into riots; I've learnt not to make speeches in the street; I've learnt not to raise my elbow too much; I've learnt not to hold door-knockers when there are excited people about; I've learnt not to fasten a bell to my feet before thinking of the consequences." And a hundred other things of the kind.

> Lucia, however, without finding these doctrines false in themselves, was not satisfied with them; it seemed to her, in a confused sort of way, that *something was missing*. By dint of hearing the same refrains repeated again and again, and thinking them over each time: "And I,"—she once found herself asking her moralist—"what d'you think I've learnt? I never went looking for troubles; they came looking for me. Unless you mean to say," she added smiling sweetly, "that my mistake was to love you, and to promise myself to you." (emphasis added)

Manzoni's poetics underscores not only the importance of interpreting history, but more significantly, it emphasizes the importance of reading it through fabulation, or as Manzoni terms it "invention." Poets, Manzoni asserts:

> Se la storia tace, diceva il poeta, tanto meglio: parlerò io. Ora invece sono i poeti che, quando i particolari *mancano* nelle storie propriamente dette, vanno a cercarne in altri documenti, di qualunque genere, affine d'arricchire il soggetto, anzi di formarlo. Ben contenti se riescono a dare, del fatto storico da essi rappresentato, un concetto più compito; più contenti ancora, se riescono a darne un concetto novo, e diverso dall'opinione comune. (**Del romanzo**) (emphasis added)

> (If history is silent, said the poet, so much the better: I will speak. Now, on the contrary, it is the

poets who, when the history books *lack* details, search them out in any available kind of document to amplify or even locate their subject. They are very happy if they manage to produce a more complete idea of the historical fact they are depicting, and even happier if they come up with a new idea, different from the one commonly held. [*On the Historical*]) (emphasis added)

A reading of *I promessi sposi* in terms of the metaphor of the manuscript offers the possibility of re-reading and updating, obviously in lay terms, the medieval metaphor of the *Book of Nature*. Implicit in both metaphors is the assumption that the world can be textualized. However, since *I promessi sposi* represents a corrected version of the original (you will recall that in the introduction the original manuscript was described, among other things, as "scorretto"), it cannot make the same ontological claim that the older theological metaphor would have assumed, namely, that the world can be treated as a text because the world is God's Book, that Nature did provide the text with a privileged origin and reference which guaranteed the mimetic veracity of the fiction. On the contrary, the metaphor of the book sustaining Manzoni's poetics is, to be most exact, "novelistic," for as Edward Said well points out in his *Beginnings,* one of the underlying motives and features of the novel is the author's desire "to create an alternative world, to modify or augment the real world through the act of writing." By claiming to correct the original version then, Manzoni's text supplies the means to keep the original story not only alive but also to provide it with meaning.

Our reading of *I promessi sposi* in terms of the metaphor of the manuscript includes the idea of rewriting ("trascrivere") as well as the notion of revising. But because it is a secular book, any revision is in itself subject to further reviewing. Now I should admit that the manuscript metaphor as I view it is never thematized as the master metaphor that explicitly controls the meaning of the narrative. However, there is a case which suggests this possibility, and that is the character Don Ferrante. Don Ferrante is a bookish personality, one who spends "long hours in his study" ("grand'ore nel suo studio"), one in which he has a "considerable collection of books . . . all choice works, all by the best-reputed authors on various subjects, in each of which he was more or less versed" ("raccolta di libri considerabile, . . . tutta roba scelta, tutte opere delle più riputate, in varie maniere; in ognuno delle quali era più o meno versato" [1840]).

That Manzoni portrays Don Ferrante as an ironic and even satirical character perhaps explains why he is the one to be called upon to speak on the crucial event of the plague. You will recall how the narrator treats him after he produces an overture of rhetorical reasoning in favor of astrological causes to explain the plague:

> *His Fretus,* vale a dire su questi bei fondamenti, non prese nessuna precauzione contro la peste; gli s'attaccò; andò a letto, a morire, come un eroe di Metastasio, prendendosela con le stelle.
>
> E quella sua famosa libreria? È forse ancora dispersa su per i muriccioli. (1840)
>
> (*His Fretus*—that is to say, on these excellent grounds—he took no precaution against the plague, caught it, and went to bed to die, like a hero

of Metastasio, blaming the stars. And that famous library of his? Maybe it is still scattered around the open-air bookstalls.)

The image is somewhat melodramatic, and it applies to Don Ferrante as much as to his books. But in addition to the obvious critique directed toward the use of books to explain human disaster such as the plague, it would be more pertinent to examine the correspondence that exists between the two. The plague, Don Ferrante's library, and, by implication, the anonymous chronicle supposedly rediscovered by Manzoni, are all related in that they all reflect one common feature, that of being composed of heterogeneous and fragmented elements. The implicit yet emblematic characteristic present in all is their disorder. It is for this reason that I don't consider it arbitrary that Manzoni would give Don Ferrante the ultimate word about the plague. Indeed Don Ferrante's misunderstandings of the plague are the very same as those that compel the narrator to investigate and research. The narrator's ironic criticism of Don Ferrante is an indication of the corresponding relation between Don Ferrante's analysis of the plague and Manzoni's own criticism of the manuscript. In fact, the description of the plague parallels and recalls that of the discovered manuscript. In the noted chapter on the plague we read:

> Delle molte relazioni contemporanee, non ce n'è alcuna che basti da sè a darne un'idea un po' distinta e ordinata; come non ce n'è alcuna che non possa aiutare a formarla. In ognuna di queste relazioni, senza eccettuarne quella del Ripamonti, la quale le supera tutte, per la quantità e per la scelta de' fatti, e ancor più per il modo d'osservarli, in ognuna sono omessi fatti essenziali, che son registrati in altre; in ognuna ci sono errori materiali, che si posson riconoscere e rettificare con l'aiuto di qualche altra, o di que' pochi atti della pubblica autorità, editi e inediti, che rimangono; spesso in una si vengono a trovar le cagioni di cui nell'altra s'eran visti, come in aria, gli effetti. In tutte poi regna una strana confusione di tempi e di cose; è un continuo andare e venire, come alla ventura, senza disegno generale, senza disegno ne' particolari: carattere, del resto, de' più comuni e de' più apparenti ne' libri di quel tempo, principalmente in quelli scritti in lingua volgare, almeno in Italia; se anche nel resto d'Europa, i dotti lo sapranno, noi lo sospettiamo. Nessuno scrittore d'epoca posteriore s'è proposto d'esaminare e di confrontare quelle memorie, per ritrarne una serie concatenata degli avvenimenti, una storia di quella peste. (1840)

(Of the many contemporary accounts, there is not one which gives a clear and connected idea of it; as there is not one which cannot help us form one. In each of these accounts, without excepting that of Ripamonti, which surpasses them all, both in quantity and choice of facts and still more in its ways of observing them, essential facts are omitted which are recorded in others; in each of them there are material errors which can be detected and rectified with the aid of one of the others, or of one of the few official acts, published or unpublished, which survive. Often in one can be found the causes of something whose effects can be seen, vaguely, in another. Then in all of them there reigns a strange confusion of times and facts; it is a continual coming and going, as if at random, without any general design, without any design in the details; one of the most common and obvious characteristics, by the way, of the books of that period, particularly of those written in the vernacular, in Italy at least; the learned will know if this was the same in the rest of Europe, as we suspect. No writer of a later period has tried to examine and collate these memoirs with a view to extracting from them a connected series of events, a story of that plague.

The privileged position of the plague both in the novel as well as for Manzoni's interest for writing *I promessi sposi* must certainly be more than an historical curiosity. As a metaphor, the plague, of course, has served literature from its very beginning. We find it present throughout the classical world; in Homer's epic, in Sophocles' tragedy, in Thucydides' histories, in Lucretius' poetic cosmology. In Christian times we see its pervasive influence in many of the arts, most notably in the medieval theme of the *danse macabre,* in Italian Trecento painting, and of course in Boccaccio's *Decameron.* Its range extends from Shakespeare's use of it as a curse in *Romeo and Juliet* to La Fontaine's fable "Les animaux malades de la peste"; from the statistical account of Defoe in his *Journal of the Plague Year,* to Dostoevsky's nightmarish use of it in *Crime and Punishment;* from Camus's spiritual wasteland in *La Peste* to the decadent-decayed existence portrayed by Thomas Mann in his *Death in Venice.* However it is Manzoni who must be credited for the most extensive treatment of the theme—at least in the novel.

The theme of the plague served Manzoni, as it did Boccaccio, to provide a background against which a relatively peaceful—at times even idyllic—existence could be juxtaposed. However, unlike the Black Death which Boccaccio's "lieta compagnia" could and would escape by telling fanciful stories, Manzoni and his modern compatriots would find no other escape but to talk about it. Compared to Manzoni's talk about the plague, Boccaccio's version can only appear, at best, as delightful gossip. But despite any difference there might be in the treatment of the theme, one aspect of the plague is universal; its power to reduce everything down to zero; that is, its power to eradicate all differences. In human terms, the plague represents the impossibility of man's making any difference. All knowledge and judgement concerning mankind is rendered totally invalid. We of the present age know this much more so than Manzoni could have and even better than Dostoevsky did.

Yet the plague is not an apocalyptic holocaust—hence it can be assumed that there still is cause for curing, correcting, rectifying; in short, the reestablishing of differences— or at least those differences which Manzoni would put under the category of faith and good works. As a metaphor, the plague, like the manuscript, then, is a sign indicating disorder. To be more exact, the plague is a metaphor for a mutilated, undifferentiated order which, like the manuscript, calls for assistance and reorganization. This is what Manzoni seems to be hinting at in his description of the two major events which lead up to the plague: the riots and the famine. For example, when he relates the riots of Saint Martin's Day he describes them as "a vast, sweeping, wandering hurricane" (1840); or when he depicts the devastating effects of the famine: "The contrast of rags and luxury, of misery and superfluity, so frequent in ordinary times, had now ceased altogether" (1840). From the long and detailed descriptions of the plague, the most succinct one Manzoni utilizes is the age-old image of the sickle, "[la] falce che pareggia tutte l'erbe del prato" (1840) ("the scythe that levels all the grass in the meadow").

My suggestion is then that the plague assumes a role similar to that of the manuscript in that both function as metaphors for a degenerated and corrupted condition, a condition, however, that also serves as a basis for rebirth and regeneration. It is for this reason, of course, that the location that houses the victims of the plague would be the *lazzaretto*—obviously a symbolic term referring to the figure of Lazarus whom Jesus raised from the dead (John XI:1-44). I take it that it is this double meaning of the plague which Manzoni makes reference to when he writes that his novel should end with a "finale grandioso," that of "la peste che aggiusta tutto." The double meaning, both literal and ironic, of the word "aggiustare" (to settle) in Italian further reinforces the point, for it is precisely the double meaning of the concept which Don Abbondio expresses when he finally agrees to perform the long-awaited marriage: "E poi la peste! la peste! ha dato di bianco a di gran cose la peste!" (1840). It had white-washed, cancelled out everything. Just so, when Renzo and Lucia are finally conjoined, and order and tranquility return to their lives, we hear the narrator poking fun at Renzo's fortune in acquiring a business: "Ma si direbbe la peste avesse preso l'impegno di raccomodar tutte le malefatte di costui" (1840) ("But it seemed that the plague had undertaken to remedy all his mistakes").

To sum up I would like to return for a moment to the final scene of the novel. All is back to normal; all except some thoughtful reminiscing. Renzo looks back and reviews his adventures and what he has learned from them. Lucia, on the other hand, is less certain—she still can't find the missing link; there still is something missing—"che ci mancasse qualcosa." In response to Renzo's somewhat mundane views, hers can only be ironic and paradoxical.

> "[E]io," disse un giorno al suo moralista, "cosa volete che abbia imparato? Io non sono andata a cercare i guai: son loro che sono venuti a cercar me. Quando non voleste dire," aggiunse, soavemente sorridendo, "che il mio sproposito sia stato quello di volervi bene, e di promettermi a voi." (1840)

> ("And I,"—she once found herself asking her moralist—"what d'you think I've learnt? I never went looking for troubles; they came looking for me. Unless you mean to say," she added smiling sweetly, "that my mistake was to love you, and to promise myself to you.")

The "moral" of the story is abundantly clear, as the narrator so unequivocally makes known. For me, however, the final scene might be read as an allegory of the way storytelling—and by extension all of literature—unfolds its discourse. If *I promessi sposi* is a new version of an old manuscript it is so not in the biblico-typological sense, as the New Testament which completes and fulfills the Old Testament; rather it is new in the sense that it functions as a substituting element, a partial remedy. Rather than complete, it supplements its model; thus, like Renzo's discourse, it too is still—in Lucia's words—lacking in something.

In this sense *I promessi sposi* does not differ from the original manuscript it claims to rewrite, for both works can be said to be "open" books; open for the reader to respond critically to the issues therein presented. However, on another level, as I have tried to show, the two books do differ, in that one does enlighten and correct the other. In both cases, however, the important point is *not* whether there is or there isn't a difference, but rather to seek and make a difference. Simply put, *I promessi sposi* acts out the corrective principle, for it promotes the notion that the true function of a text is to teach, that is, to literally "insegnare."

Indeed, Manzoni provides indications of this in the very first paragraph of the novel, wherein we are given the first sign of how man, and by extension his work, *ought* to function:

> Quel ramo del lago di Como, che volge a mezzogiorno, tra due catene non interrotte di monti, tutto a seni e a golfi, a seconda dello sporgere e del rientrare di quelli, vien, quasi a un tratto, a ristringersi, e a prender corso e figura di fiume, tra un promontorio a destra, e un'ampia costiera dall'altra parte; e il ponte, che ivi congiunge le due rive, par che renda ancor più sensibile all'occhio questa trasformazione, e segni il punto in cui il lago cessa, e l'Adda rincomincia, per ripigliar poi nome di lago dove le rive, allontanandosi di nuovo, lascian l'acqua distendersi e rallentarsi in nuovi golfi e in nuovi seni. (1840)

> (That branch of the lake of Como which extends southwards between two unbroken chains of mountains, and is all gulfs and bays as the mountains advance and recede, narrows down at one point, between a promontory on one side and a wide shore on the other, into the form of a river; and the bridge which links the two banks seems to emphasize this transformation even more, and to mark the point at which the lake ends and the Adda begins, only to become a lake once more where the banks draw farther apart again, letting the water broaden out and expand into new creeks and bays.)

Amid the beautiful and serene image of Nature stands one and only one distinct human sign: "il ponte." Notice its function: it unites ("congiunge"), it supplements ("rende *ancor più* sensibile all'occhio,") and acts as an indicator ("e *segna* il punto . . . "). The assumption might be then that as a human instrument *I promessi sposi* stands and likewise functions as a mediating sign; a "bridge" connecting the human with the natural; a means by which man becomes cognizant of his supplemental role; and as an indicator of man's own limitations and dependency on Nature. To be sure, this is how it *ought* to be. However, because such interaction is subject to disruption and corruption, Manzoni feels the call to provide a means or a way for man to cope with what he terms "i guai" (troubles). The "conclusion" reached by Renzo and Lucia after their troubling experience is no doubt Manzoni's own conclusion:

> [I] guai vengono bensì spesso, perchè ci si è data cagione; ma che la condotta più cauta e più innocente non basta a tenerli lontani; e che quando vengono, o per colpa o senza colpa, la fiducia in Dio li raddolcisce, e li rende utili per una vita migliore. (1840)

> ([T]roubles often come to those who bring them on themselves, but that not even the most cautious and innocent behaviour can ward them off; and that when they come—whether by our own fault or not—confidence in God can lighten them and turn them to our own improvement.)

Of course this is the final note with which *I promessi sposi* ends, for like the two young protagonists the narrator likewise feels compelled to apply the *felix culpa* principle as well as provide justification for the calamities that have befallen on all, on both the guilty and the innocent.

The dialogue between Renzo and Lucia in the final pages of the novel is not merely the personal response of the two individuals to their misfortune. On the contrary, it would seem that the two views expressed by the respective protagonists represent the marriage of two minds both of which disclose their limitations as much as their possibilities. *I promessi sposi* is indeed an open-ended novel—open for continual dialogue and resolutions of its themes. In this context might we not entertain the idea that the trials and the eventual rejoining of Renzo and Lucia represent anagogically Man's wish to return to the harmonious existence with Nature hinted at in the very first paragraph of the novel? If such is plausible, it would further strengthen my suggestion that Manzoni would see himself as having a priestly character and function—not unlike that of Don Abbondio—of mediating and rebinding the sacramental tie between Man and Nature. Such appears to be the purpose of Manzoni's book; to aid Man in rejoining Nature, so that together they might in turn be reconjoined to their Creator, as the 24th Psalm would have us remember: "The earth is the LORD's and the fulness thereof; the world, and they that dwell therein."

In conclusion we might say then that *I promessi sposi* is a novel which tempts its reader to make sense of it in thematic terms; then, without repudiating those terms it forces the reader to realize their insufficiency and their ironic applicability for the very novel which suggests them. In short, by claiming to resurrect and correct an original meaning, together with the use of irony to make his reader realize the impossibility of simple or final solutions to problems we all have in common, Manzoni seems in *I promessi sposi* to be demonstrating one particular power of literature, namely its ability to use language as a redemptive instrument. For Manzoni the *Logos* must always be read with both a capital and a small letter.

In this, and if only in this, Manzoni can be surely said to be both a poet and a moralizer, both an epic voice and a Romantic visionary. (pp. 117-33)

> *Alfonso Procaccini, " 'I promessi sposi': 'Ho Imparato',* " *in* The Reasonable Romantic: Essays on Alessandro Manzoni, *edited by Sante Matteo and Larry H. Peer, Peter Lang, 1986, pp. 117-34.*

FURTHER READING

Barricelli, Gian Piero. "Structure and Symbol in Manzoni's *I promessi sposi.*" *Italian Quarterly* 17, No. 67 (Fall-Winter 1973): 79-102.
  Examines the "poetic dimensions" of structure and sym-

bolism in *The Betrothed* to illustrate that the novel "transcends the category of narration in the ordinary sense and enters that of poetry. This 'ascension' serves to liberate the work from the otherwise narrow confines of a strict Christian ethic and confers upon it a broad character of universality."

Beaumont, Jean F. "Manzoni and Goethe." *Italian Studies* II, No. 7 (1939): 129-40.
Focuses on Goethe's literary influence on Manzoni.

Bermann, Sandra L. "Manzoni's Essay 'On the Historical Novel': A Rhetorical Question." *Canadian Review of Comparative Literature* X, No. 1 (March 1983): 40-53.
Demonstrates how Manzoni's essay anticipates modern views of the historical novel and places it "in an ongoing debate within Western literary history—that ancient debate between rhetoric and philosophy."

——. Introduction to *On the Historical Novel*, by Alessandro Manzoni, translated by Sandra Bermann, pp. 1-59. Lincoln: University of Nebraska Press, 1984.
Biographical, critical, and historical essay introducing the first English translation of Manzoni's *On the Historical Novel*.

Bowen, C. M. "Manzoni and Scott." *The Dublin Review* 176, No. 353 (April-May-June 1925): 239-52.
Compares Manzoni's *The Betrothed* to the works of Sir Walter Scott.

Caesar, Michael. "Manzoni's Poetry and the Witnessing of Events." *Comparative Criticism: A Yearbook* 3 (1981): 207-19.
Considers "the tendency towards a rigid division of labour between protagonist and reader . . . as witnesses of the events represented" in Manzoni's poetry.

Caserta, Ernesto G. *Manzoni's Christian Realism.* Florence: Leo S. Olschki Editore, 1977, 257 p.
Study of Manzoni's works, their critical reputation outside of Italy, and the development of Manzoni's Christian principles.

Chandler, S. B. "Point of View in the Descriptions of *I promessi sposi.*" *Italica* XLIII, No. IV (December 1966): 386-401.
Examines the various narrative perspectives Manzoni employed in *The Betrothed,* finding that he "was far too great an artist . . . to adhere rigidly to the attitude of an omniscient author, with the consequent risk of monotony and of weakening the autonomy of his characters: his point of view changes according to the needs of the story's development, and, at the same time, his relationship with the reader must necessarily change. In this way, Manzoni constructs for himself his own special author's personality, thereby differing from Sir Walter Scott, who often maintains so invariable an attitude of omniscience as to lack any real artistic personality."

——. "Passion, Reason, and Evil in the Works of Alessandro Manzoni." *Italica* 50, No. 4 (Winter 1973): 551-65.
An investigation of Manzoni's attitude toward human evil throughout his works.

——. "The Author, the Material, and the Reader in *I promessi sposi.*" *Annali d'Italianistica* 3 (1985): 123-34.
Examines the relationship of the author, narrator, and reader to the device of the fictitious manuscript in *The Betrothed.*

——. "The Concept of Confinement in Manzoni." *Italica* 62, No. 4 (Winter 1985): 285-93.
Discusses Manzoni's view of the link between the temporal and spiritual worlds in his tragic dramas and *The Betrothed.*

Colquhoun, Archibald. "Alessandro Manzoni." In *The Betrothed: A Tale of XVII Century Milan,* by Alessandro Manzoni, translated by Archibald Colquhoun, pp. 606-23. New York: E. P. Dutton & Co., 1951.
Biographical and critical essay.

——. *Manzoni and His Times: A Biography of the Author of "The Betrothed" ("I promessi sposi").* New York: E. P. Dutton & Co., 1954, 281 p.
Definitive English biography of Manzoni chiefly based on his works and correspondence.

Connor, Daniel J., S.T.L. "A Neglected Masterpiece." *The Catholic World* CXVIII, No. 708 (March 1924): 750-56.
Introductory essay on *The Betrothed* emphasizing Manzoni's realism, religious principles, and the similarities between his work and that of Sir Walter Scott.

D'Entrèves, A. P. "Annual Italian Lecture for 1949: Alessandro Manzoni." In *Proceedings of the British Academy, 1950,* Vol. XXXVI, pp. 23-49. London: The British Academy, 1950.
Provides an overview of issues in Manzoni criticism and surveys Manzoni's works, concentrating on *The Betrothed.*

De Simone, Joseph Francis. *Alessandro Manzoni: Esthetics and Literary Criticism.* New York: S. F. Vanni, 1946, 429 p.
Investigates the development of Manzoni's aesthetic theories and surveys his literary criticism.

Dombroski, Robert S. "The Seicento as Strategy: 'Providence' and the 'Bourgeois' in *I promessi sposi.*" *Modern Language Notes* 91, No. 1 (January 1976): 80-100.
Analyzes the principal thematic structures of *The Betrothed* in order "to consider how the element of setting . . . may be raised to a higher degree of historical significance than has been thus far proposed by Manzoni criticism; to show, simply, that rather than being generally symbolic of or antithetical to the reality of Manzoni's times, the Seicento is a concrete means through which this reality is comprehensively known."

Foster, Kenelm. "Alessandro Manzoni (1785-1873)." *Italian Quarterly,* 17, No. 67 (Fall-Winter 1973): 7-23.
General discussion of Manzoni's life and works.

Garnett, Richard. "The Regeneration." In his *A History of Italian Literature,* pp. 327-51. New York: D. Appleton and Co., 1898.
A history of nineteenth-century Italian literature that provides a survey of Manzoni's major works.

Isella, Silvia Brusamolino, and Castellani, Simonetta Usuelli. *Bibliografia manzoniana: 1949-1973.* Milan, Italy: Edizioni il Polifio, 1974, 111 p.
An Italian bibliography of primary and secondary sources in Manzoni studies.

Jeronimidis, Elena D. and Wren, Keith. "A One-Way Ticket to Heaven—History, Politics, and Religion in the Theatre of

Manzoni and Hugo." *Neophilologus* LXVI, No. 1 (January 1982): 66-91.

Examines the nature and purpose of the historical dramas of Manzoni and Victor Hugo, emphasizing their expression of a "religious sense."

Lansing, Richard H. "Stylistic and Structural Duality in Manzoni's *I promessi sposi.*" *Italica* 53, No. 3 (Autumn 1976): 347-61.

Proposes "to show that the stylistic device of pairing words and phrases, from the opening pages of *I promessi sposi*, reflects the author's process of cognition, and reveals, consequently, the way in which he tends habitually to structure experience."

Lanyi, Gabriel. "Plot-Time and Rhythm in Manzoni's *I promessi sposi.*" *Modern Language Notes* 93, No. 1 (January 1978): 36-51.

Observes that in *The Betrothed* "time . . . undergoes a gradual process of loosening, as Manzoni covers longer and longer periods in fewer and fewer pages," concluding that this narrative structure originates in "Manzoni's attempt to maintain the unity of the novel against the asunder historical events around which he chose to weave it."

Lucente, Gregory L. "The Uses and Ends of Discourse in *I promessi sposi:* Manzoni's Narrator, His Characters, and Their Author." *Modern Language Notes* 101, No. 1 (January 1986): 51-77.

Asserts that Manzoni's use of language in *The Betrothed* is central to an understanding of its theme and structure.

Matteo, Sante, and Peer, Larry H., eds. *The Reasonable Romantic: Essays on Alessandro Manzoni.* New York: Peter Lang, 1986, 274 p.

A collection of critical essays marking the bicentennial of Manzoni's birth and treating such important topics in Manzoni criticism as his place in world literature, his relationship to Romanticism, and his use of language and history. Alfonso Procaccini's essay " 'I promessi sposi': 'Ho Imparato' " is excerpted above.

Pallotta, Augustus. "Characterization through Understatement: A Study of Manzoni's Don Rodrigo." *Italica* 58, No. 1 (Spring 1981): 43-55.

A consideration of the character of Don Rodrigo in *The Betrothed* that aims "to shift the focus of analysis from the traditional concern with the moral character of Don Rodrigo's conduct to the inner springs of his personality" in order to discover "a more complex being, one whose individuality, conceived in the light of the Spanish presence in Italy, is intimately tied to the baroque obsession with extrinsic forms of deportment evolving within a fluid interplay between real and ideal perceptions of the self."

Radcliff-Umstead, Douglas. "The Transcendence of Human Space in Manzonian Tragedy." *Studies in Romanticism* 13, No. 1 (Winter 1974): 25-46.

Maintains that the purpose of Manzoni's dramas is to illustrate the futility of human endeavor on earth and the salvation of Christian belief in transcendence.

Reynolds, Barbara. *The Linguistic Writings of Alessandro Manzoni: A Textual and Chronological Reconstruction.* Cambridge, England: W. Heffer & Sons, 1950, 225 p.

Establishes definitive texts of Manzoni's linguistic works and determines the order in which they were written.

Vittorini, Domenico. "The Nineteenth-Century Novel." In his *The Modern Italian Novel,* pp. 8-50. Philadelphia: University of Pennsylvania Press, 1930.

Contains a discussion of Manzoni's life and works which concentrates on *The Betrothed* and its influence on later Italian writers.

Wall, Bernard. *Alessandro Manzoni.* New Haven: Yale University Press, 1954, 64 p.

An overview of Manzoni's life and works that includes chapters on *The Betrothed,* its place in literature, and controversial points in Manzoni criticism.

Herman Melville

1819-1891

American novelist, short story writer, and poet.

The following entry presents criticism of Melville's novel *Billy Budd, Foretopman* (1924), which was completed in 1891 and was also published as *Billy Budd, Sailor: An Inside Narrative* (1962). For criticism of Melville's novel *Moby-Dick; or, The Whale* (1851), see *NCLC*, Volume 12. For discussion of Melville's complete career, see *NCLC*, Volume 3.

Completed in the year of Melville's death, *Billy Budd* is deemed one of his most finely crafted and mature works. Focusing on the execution of a young sailor aboard an English warship, the novel has amassed diverse critical response seeking to determine Melville's final views on such issues as justice, morality, and religion. *Billy Budd* is also consistently praised for its philosophical insight, multifaceted narrative technique, and complex use of symbol and allegory.

Melville began writing *Billy Budd* following a thirty-year period of inactivity as a fiction writer. Having abandoned prose fiction in the mid 1850s, he traveled, lectured, and worked as a customs inspector in New York, during which time he wrote only poetry. Critics generally believe that *Billy Budd* derived from a prose headnote to a poem that was ultimately entitled "Billy in the Darbies," which Melville began in 1886 and intended for his poetry volume *John Marr and Other Sailors* (1888). He removed the work from the collection, however, and by 1888 had expanded the prose section into a short-length version of *Billy Budd*. During that year a popular article appeared in the *American Journal* which renewed public interest in a controversial trial and execution for an alleged mutiny attempt that had occurred in 1842 aboard the *Somers,* an American frigate on which Melville's cousin Guert Gansevoort was an officer. Critics suggest that this incident influenced the creation of the characters and plot of *Billy Budd*. Commentators also observe that Melville, who had undertaken numerous sea voyages in the 1840s, partially derived the events and characters described in the novel from the life and associates of a former shipmate, Jack Chase, who appears as a character in Melville's novel *White-Jacket; or, The World in a Man-of-War* (1850) and to whom *Billy Budd* is dedicated. Following the publication of *John Marr,* Melville rewrote and revised the novel extensively until April 1891. Because he failed to prepare the manuscript for publication before he died, many critics have questioned whether or not Melville fully completed revising the work.

Set in 1797, *Billy Budd* begins with a preface elaborating on the preceding crises of the French Revolution and the mutinies aboard British naval ships at the Nore and Spithead. Billy is introduced as the archetypal "handsome sailor," homeward-bound aboard an English merchant vessel, the *Rights-of-Man,* when he is impressed by an English warship, the *Indomitable* (denoted the *Bellipotent* in the revised transcription). He serves passively as a foretop-

man and is popular with the crew, yet he learns from a shipmate that the master-at-arms, John Claggart, holds a mysterious antagonism towards him. Although Billy refuses an invitation to join in a subversive effort left undefined in the narrative, Claggart later confronts Captain Vere and accuses Billy of fomenting mutiny. Vere is unconvinced, yet brings the two into his cabin and repeats the charge to Billy. Stunned and unable to speak because of a pronounced stutter, Billy fatally strikes Claggart, a superior officer. An impromptu "drumhead court" is held by the captain in which he convinces his officers to hang the foretopman and thus enforce discipline and deter any threat of mutiny. Vere subsequently conducts a private interview with Billy, after which the two appear reconciled. Billy is executed the following dawn, and his only words before he is hanged are "God bless Captain Vere!" The work ends with three reports: an account of Vere's death after a battle against the *Athéiste;* a journalistic rendering of the events surrounding Billy's execution; and a description of the crew's remembrances of Billy, concluding with the ballad "Billy in the Darbies."

Although *Billy Budd* is relatively straightforward in plot, the work's complicated interweaving of historical digression, mythological and biblical allusion, and multiple narrative viewpoints has inspired an abundance of critical commentary. Melville's portrayal of Captain Vere, in particular, has been a focus of ongoing controversy. Early commentators generally found that Melville condoned Vere's actions, recognizing the limitations of society, law, and religion, and expressing what E. L. Grant Watson termed a "testament of acceptance." However, Joseph Schiffman's 1950 interpretation of the work, in which he asserted that Vere is presented as an autocrat whom Melville condemned ironically through an unreliable narrator, inspired numerous critics to explicate the text based on this position. While most subsequent criticism of *Billy Budd* has focused on this debate, other critical approaches have also been applied to the work. Several commentators have examined biblical allusion in the novel and note parallels to the Christian concept of the fall of humanity and the crucifixion of Christ, associating Billy with Adam and Christ, Vere with God, and Claggart with Satan. Other scholars observe a political dimension to the novel in Melville's references to the French and American revolutions, British admiral Horatio Nelson, and to predominating political theories of the eighteenth century. Psychoanalytic criticism of *Billy Budd* generally interprets Vere as a superego repressing the instinctual vitality embodied by Billy, and focuses on the theme of homosexuality in the work, particularly in the interchanges between Billy and Claggart.

Recent criticism has explored the narrative technique of *Billy Budd* and the text's self-reflexive statements on language and art. The status of the novel's original manuscript has also been an object of debate since the publication of a revised transcription by Harrison Hayford and Merton M. Sealts, Jr., in 1962. Attempting to redress earlier transcriptions, the editors identified and amended misreadings of Melville's handwritten words and punctuation marks, excluded corrections they attributed to Melville's wife, and clarified the chronology of the work's composition. Among the significant differences arising from Melville's revisions of *Billy Budd*, the new transcription more clearly displays the author's ambiguous treatment of Captain Vere and has renewed the dispute over his portrayal of the captain. Today, Melville's novel remains highly lauded for its narrative craftsmanship, and its ethical complexity has been compared with classical tragedy and the later dramas of William Shakespeare. The text has been adapted into a celebrated play, an opera, a film, and a television drama. Critics concur that *Billy Budd* represents one of Melville's most significant works, second perhaps only to *Moby-Dick,* and stands as a major accomplishment of nineteenth-century American literature.

(See also *Short Story Criticism,* Vol. 1; *Dictionary of Literary Biography,* Vols. 3 and 74; *Concise Dictionary of American Literary Biography: Colonization to the American Renaissance, 1640-1865;* and *Something about the Author,* Vol. 59.)

John Middleton Murry   (essay date 1924)

[*Murry is recognized as one of the most significant English critics and editors of the twentieth century, noted for his studies of major authors and for his contributions to modern critical theory. Perceiving an integral relationship between literature and religion, Murry believed*

that the literary critic must be concerned with the moral as well as the aesthetic dimensions of a given work. A longtime contributor of literary criticism to the Times Literary Supplement, *he was the last editor of the distinguished review the* Athenaeum *and the founding editor of the* Adelphi. *In the following excerpt from an originally unsigned review, Murry evaluates* Billy Budd *within the context of Melville's literary career.*]

In 1851 Herman Melville published **Moby-Dick;** in the next five years **Pierre,** which was received with cold hostility, **Israel Potter,** and the **Piazza Tales.** Then, to all intents and purposes, there was silence till the end, which did not come till thirty-five years later. The silence of a great writer needs to be listened to. If he has proved his genius, then his silence is an utterance, and one of no less moment than his speech. The silence of a writer who has the vision that Melville proved his own in **Moby-Dick** is not an accident without adequate cause; and that we feel that silence was the appropriate epilogue to Melville's masterpiece is only the form of our instinctive recognition that the adequate cause was there. After **Moby-Dick** there was, in a sense, nothing to be said, just as after *King Lear* there seemed nothing for Shakespeare to say. Shakespeare did find another utterance in *Antony and Cleopatra:* then he too was silent. For, whatever names we may give to the "romantic" plays of his final period, and however high the praises we sincerely heap upon them, they belong to another order and have a significance of another kind than the great tragedies. They are, essentially, the work of a man who has nothing more to *say,* but who is artist and genius enough at last to contrive a method of saying even that.

Herman Melville could not do that, but then nobody save Shakespeare has been able to work that miracle. Probably Melville knew exactly what Shakespeare had achieved in the faint, far reflection of *The Tempest;* for in the [**Battle-Pieces and Aspects of the War**], with which he made scarce so much as a ripple in his own silence in 1866, is this strangely irrelevant verse on Shakespeare:—

> No utter surprise can come to him
>   Who reaches Shakespeare's core;
> That which we seek and shun is there—
>   Man's final lore.

Melville knew where Shakespeare had been: no doubt he also knew where Shakespeare at last arrived; but he could not communicate those mysterious faint echoes of a certitude—that certitude "which we seek and shun"—which are gathered together into *The Tempest.*

Yet Melville was trying to say more during his long silence. How much he struggled with his dumbness we cannot say; perhaps during most of those thirty-five years he acquiesced in it. But something was at the back of his mind, haunting him, and this something he could not utter. If we handle the clues carefully we may reach a point from which we too may catch a glimpse of it; but then, by the nature of things, we shall be unable to utter, what we see. We can only indicate the clues. They are to be found, one at the beginning and one at the end of the silence. *Pierre* is at the beginning. It is, judged by the standards which are traditional in estimating a "work of art," a complete failure. The story is naive, amateurish, melodramatic, wildly improbable, altogether unreal. Let those who are persuaded that a novel is a good story and nothing more avoid *Pierre.* But those who feel that the greatest novels are something quite different from a good story should seek it out: to them it will be strange and fascinating, and they will understand why its outward semblance is clumsy and puerile. Melville is trying to reveal a mystery; he is trying to show that the completely good man is doomed to complete disaster on earth, and he is trying to show at the same time that this must be so, and that it ought to be so. The necessity of that "ought to be so" can be interpreted in two ways: as Melville calls them, horologically or chronometrically. Horologically—that is, estimated by our local and earthly timepieces—the disaster of the good ought to be so, because there is no room for unearthly perfection on earth; chronometrically—that is, estimated by the unvarying recorder of the absolute—it ought to be so, because it is a working out, a manifestation, of the absolute, though hidden, harmony of the ideal and the real. In other words, Melville was trying to reveal anew the central mystery of the Christian religion.

He did not succeed. How could he succeed? Nobody understood *Pierre*; apparently nobody had even a glimmering understanding of it. And the thirty-five years of silence began. At the extreme end of them, moved perhaps by a premonition of coming death, Melville wrote another "story." *Billy Budd* is carefully dated: it was begun on November 16, 1888, the rewriting began on March 2, 1889, and it was finished on April 19, 1891. In the following September Melville was dead. With the mere fact of the long silence in our minds we could not help regarding *Billy Budd* as the last will and spiritual testament of a man of genius. We could not help expecting this, if we have any imaginative understanding. Of course, if we are content to dismiss in our minds, if not in our words, the man of genius as mad, there is no need to trouble. Someone is sure to have told us that *Billy Budd,* like *Pierre,* is a tissue of naivety and extravagance: that will be enough. And, truly, *Billy Budd is* like *Pierre*—startlingly like. Once more Melville is telling the story of the inevitable and utter disaster of the good and trying to convey to us that this must be so and ought to be so—chronometrically and horologically. He is trying, as it were with his final breath, to reveal the knowledge that has been haunting him—that these things must be so and not otherwise.

Billy Budd is a foretopman, pressed out of the merchant service into the King's Navy in the year of the Nore mutiny. He is completely good, not with the sickly goodness of self-conscious morality, but as one born into earthly paradise—strong, young, manly, loyal, brave, unsuspecting, admired by his officers and adored by his shipmates. And he is hated by the master-at-arms, the policeman of the lower deck. Claggart hates him, simply because he is Billy Budd, with the instinctive hatred of the evil for the good. Melville is careful to explain that there is no reason whatever for his hatred; he puts it deliberately before us as naked and elemental—the clash of absolutes. Claggart is subtle and cool, he works quietly, and he is also a man of courage. He involves Billy Budd in the thin semblance of revolutionary mutiny. The master-at-arms deliberately risks his own life in order to destroy his enemy's. He risks it, and loses it, for in the privacy of his own cabin the captain confronts the accuser with his victim, and in a flash of anger Budd strikes the master-at-arms dead. This moment in the story is unearthly. But Billy Budd is doomed:

he has killed his officer in time of war. The captain who understands and loves him presides over the court-martial, and Budd is condemned to be hanged at dawn. Before dawn the crew is piped to quarters.

> Billy stood facing aft. At the penultimate moment, his words, his only ones, words wholly unobstructed in the utterance, were these—"God bless Captain Vere!" Syllables so unanticipated coming from one with the ignominious hemp about his neck—a conventional felon's benediction directed aft towards the quarters of honour; syllables, too, delivered in the clear melody of a singing bird on the point of launching from the twig, had a phenomenal effect, not unenhanced by the rare personal beauty of the young sailor, spiritualized now through late experiences so poignantly profound.

> Without volition, as it were, as if indeed the ship's populace were the vehicles of some vocal current electric, with one voice, from alow and aloft, came a resonant echo—"God bless Captain Vere!" And yet at that instant Billy alone must have been in their hearts, even as he was in their eyes. At the pronounced words and the spontaneous echo that voluminously rebounded them, Captain Vere, either through stoic self-content or a sort of momentary paralysis induced by emotional shock, stood erectly rigid as a musket in the ship-armourer's rack.

> The hull, deliberately recovering from the periodic roll to leeward, was just regaining an even keel, when the last signal, the preconcerted dumb one, was given. At the same moment it chanced that the vapoury fleece hanging low in the east was shot through with a soft glory as of the fleece of the Lamb of God seen in mystical vision, and simultaneously therewith, watched by the wedged mass of upturned faces, Billy ascended; and ascending, took the full rose of the dawn.

> In the pinioned figure, arrived at the yard-end, to the wonder of all, no motion was apparent save that created by the slow roll of the hull, in moderate weather so majestic in a great ship heavy-cannoned.

That is the story, told with a strange combination of naïve and majestic serenity—the revelation of a mystery. It was Melville's final word, worthy of him, indisputably a passing beyond the nihilism of *Moby-Dick* to what may seem to some simple and childish, but will be to others wonderful and divine.

> *John Middleton Murry, "Herman Melville's Silence," in* The Times Literary Supplement, *No. 1173, July 10, 1924, p. 433.*

E. L. Grant Watson   (essay date 1933)

[*Watson was an English novelist and essayist, best remembered for fictional works that reflect the influence of the novels of Joseph Conrad and the psychoanalytic theories of C. G. Jung. In the following essay, he describes the philosophy of* Billy Budd *as Melville's ultimate reconciliation with society and religion.*]

Melville finished the short novel, *Billy Budd,* five months before his death in 1891. It was not published until 1924, when it was included in the Constable edition of 750 copies. No other printing has yet appeared.

The style of this product of Melville's last years is strikingly different from the exuberant and highly-colored prose of that great period of more ardent creation (1850 to 1852) which produced *Mardi, Moby-Dick,* and *Pierre.* Though it lacks that fine extravagance of the earlier books, which laid on the color with prodigality, *Billy Budd* is as rich, or even richer, in Melville's peculiar and elaborate symbolism; and this symbolism becomes all the more effective for being presented in a dry and objective manner. The fine flourishes, the purple patches, which scintillate brilliantly in *Moby-Dick,* and the deep sombre melancholy of *Pierre* are not here. The grandiloquence of youth which tempted Stevenson's very partial appreciation is here transformed into the dignity of an achieved detachment. The story develops simply, always unhurried, yet never lagging. Each character is described with the patience which the complex intention of the theme demands—the color of the eyes, the clothes, the complexion, the color of the skin, of the blood under the skin, the past, the present—these are hints at a deep and solemn purpose, one no less ambitious than to portray those ambiguities of good and evil as the mutually dependant opposites, between which the world of realization finds its being.

The title *Billy Budd* is not without significance, and would strike some readers in its crude simplicity as proof that Melville was lacking in a sense of humor. How could any man, they would argue, write a tragedy and call it *Billy Budd?* But a sense of humor, like almost everything else, is relative. Melville certainly lacked it in the crude form; but he was always conscious of those occasions when he might seem, to a superficial view, to be wanting it. He is particularly conscious of the obvious, but not in the obvious manner; and when he uses such a name as *Billy Budd* to set as the hub round which his own philosophy of life must revolve, he does so consciously, choosing the obvious to carry the transcendental. "I have ever found the plain things, the knottiest of all," he has written; and so he has made the simple man, the every-day Billy, the handsome sailor, the hero of a tragedy. Humor is appreciated most easily when larger things contract suddenly to smaller things—as when a man slips on a piece of orange-peel, thus converting his intention of going about his business to the abrupt act of falling on his back-side. Yet a more imaginative intelligence might, with a sense of humor just as true, see in this fall, the destiny of man, with full chorus of pities and ironic spirits. The easy contraction will seem to the sophisticated too facile to provoke a smile, a larger humor is found in the reverse process, namely in a filling in, in an exaggeration from the particular to the general. With such an added pinch of imagination, the obvious thing becomes the centre of mystery. And so, with a sense of humor which perceived both the obvious and the peculiar quality of the name, Melville deliberately chose "Billy Budd." Moreover, he made the hero of this, his gospel story (as it might well be called), a foundling of uncertain parentage, whose "entire family was practically invested in himself."

It is a mistake for critics to try to tell stories which authors must have told better in their texts. The critic's function is rather to hint at what lies beneath—hidden, sometimes, under the surface. Melville called his story "an inside nar-rative," and though it deals with events stirring and exciting enough in themselves, it is yet more exciting because it deals with the relation of those principles which constitute life itself. A simple-mindedness unaffected by the shadow of doubt, a divine innocence and courage, which might suggest a Christ not yet conscious of His divinity, and a malice which has lost itself in the unconscious depths of mania—the very mystery of iniquity—these opposites here meet, and find their destiny. But Melville's theme is even larger. All the grim setting of the world is in the battleship *Indomitable;* war and threatened mutiny are the conditions of her existence. Injustice and inhumanity are implicit, yet Captain Vere, her commander, is the man who obeys the law, and yet understands the truth of the spirit. It is significant of Melville's development since the writing of *Moby-Dick* and *Pierre,* that he should create this naval captain—wholly pledged to the unnaturalness of the law, but sufficiently touched, at the same time, by the divine difference from ordinary sanity (he goes by the nick-name of "Starry Vere"), as to live the truth *within* the law, and yet, in the cruel process of that very obedience, to redeem an innocent man from the bitterness of death imposed by the same law. A very different ending this from the despairing acts of dissolution which mark the conclusions of the three earlier books: *Mardi, Moby-Dick,* and *Pierre.*

Melville is no longer a rebel. It should be noted that Billy Budd has not, even under the severest provocation, any element of rebellion in him; he is too free a soul to need a quality which is a virtue only in slaves. His nature spontaneously accepts whatever may befall. When impressed from the merchant-ship, the *Rights of Man,* he makes no demur to the visiting lieutenant's order to get ready his things for trans-shipment. The crew of the merchant-ship are surprised and reproachful at his uncomplaining acquiescence. Once aboard the battleship, the young sailor begins to look around for the advantages of chance and adventure. Such simple power to accept gives him the buoyancy to override troubles and irritations which would check inferior natures.

Yet his complete unconsciousness of the attraction, and consequent repulsion, that his youthful beauty and unsophisticated good-fellowship exercise on Claggart, make it only easier for these qualities to turn envy into hatred. His very virtue makes him the target for the shaft of evil, and his quality of acceptance provokes to action its complementary opposite, the sense of frustration that can not bear the consciousness of itself, and so has to find escape in mania. Thus there develops the conflict between unconscious virtue (not even aware of its loss of Eden and unsuspecting of the presence of evil) and the bitter perversion of love which finds its only solace in destruction.

And not only Billy Budd is marked by this supreme quality of acceptance. Captain Vere, also, possesses it, but with full consciousness, and weighted with the responsibility of understanding the natural naturalness of man's volition and the unnatural naturalness of the law. . . . In Captain Vere we find a figure which may interestingly be compared to Pontius Pilate. Like Pilate, he condemns the just man to a shameful death, knowing him to be innocent, but, unlike Pilate, he does not wash his hands, but manfully assumes the full responsibility, and in such a way as to take the half, if not more than the half, of the bitterness of the execution upon himself. We are given to suppose that there is an affinity, a spiritual understanding between Captain Vere and Billy Budd, and it is even suggested that in their partial and separate existences they contribute two essential portions of that larger spirit which is man. Such passages as that quoted lie on the surface of this story, but they indicate the depths beneath. There are darker hints: those deep, far-away things in Vere, those occasional flashings-forth of intuition—short, quick probings to the very axis of reality. Though the book be read many times, the student may still remain baffled by Melville's significant arrangement of images. The story is so solidly filled out as to suggest dimensions in all directions. As soon as the mind fastens upon one subject, others flash into being.

Melville reported in **Pierre** how he fished his line into the deep sea of childhood, and there, as surely as any modern psychoanalyst, discovered all the major complexes that have since received baptism at the hands of Freudians. He peered as deep as any into the origins of sensuality, and in conscious understanding he was the equal of any modern psychologist; in poetic divination he has the advantage of most. No doubt the stresses of his own inner life demanded this exceptional awareness. In this book of his old age, the images which he chose for the presentation of his final wisdom, move between the antinomies of love and hate, of innocence and malice. From behind—from far behind the main pageant of the story—there seem to fall suggestive shadows of primal, sexual simplicities. In so conscious a symbolist as Melville, it would be surprising if there should be no meaning or half-meaning in the spilling of Billy's soup towards the homosexually-disposed Claggart, in the importance of Billy's speech in the presence of his accuser, in his swift and deadly answer, or the likening of Claggart's limp, dead body to that of a snake.

It is possible that such incidents might be taken as indications of some unresolved problem in the writer himself. This may be, but when we remember how far Melville had got in the process of self-analysis in **Pierre,** and when we have glanced at the further analysis that is obvious in the long narrative poem **Clarel,** it seems likely that this final book, written nearly forty years after **Pierre,** should contain a further, deeper wisdom. And as the philosophy in it has grown from that of rebellion to that of acceptance, as the symbolic figures of unconscious forces have become always more concrete and objective, so we may assume that these hints are intentional, and that Melville was particularly conscious of what he was doing.

But let no one suppose that he would ever pin an image to his scale of value, as an entomologist would pin an insect to his board; there is always in his interpretation a wide spaciousness. He lifts some familiar object, holding it to his light, that it may glow and illumine some portion of what must always remain vast and unknown. . . . [In the hanging scene] Melville at his very best, at his deepest, most poetic, and therefore at his most concentrated, most conscious. Every image has its significant implication: the very roll of the heavily-cannoned ship so majestic in moderate weather—the musket in the ship-armourer's rack; and Billy's last words are the triumphant seal of his acceptance, and they are more than that, for in this supreme passage a communion between personality at its purest, most-God-given form, and character, hard-hammered from the imperfect material of life on the bat-

tleship *Indomitable,* is here suggested, and one feels that the souls of Captain Vere and Billy are at that moment strangely one.

In this short history of the impressment and hanging of a handsome sailor-boy, are to be discovered problems almost as profound as those which puzzle us in the pages of the Gospels. **Billy Budd** is a book to be read many times, for at each reading it will light up, as do the greater experiences of life, a beyond leading always into the unknown. (pp. 319-27)

> E. L. Grant Watson, "Melville's Testament of Acceptance," in The New England Quarterly, Vol. VI, No. 2, June, 1933, pp. 319-27.

Charles Roberts Anderson   (essay date 1940)

[*An American critic and educator, Anderson has written extensively on nineteenth-century American literature and the life and works of Melville. In the following excerpt, he discusses Melville's adaptation of historical and biographical sources in the characters and plot of* Billy Budd.]

[At] the time Melville published [**John Marr and Other Sailors**] in 1888 he was exercising the privilege of old age, indulging in fond memories of his own seafaring years of nearly half a century before. And before this year was out, on November 16, 1888, he began the composition of **Billy Budd,** which he dedicated to "Jack Chase/ Englishman/ wherever that great heart may now be/ here on earth or harboured in paradise/ captain of the maintop/ in the year 1843/ in the U. S. frigate/ *United States*"—and John J. Chase had actually been his shipmate as well as the hero of **White-Jacket.** Perhaps the memory of Chase prompted Melville to give his story a setting in British naval history.

The scene is laid in the momentous year of 1797, made memorable by the mutinies at Spithead and the Nore in April and May, which had come near crippling the British fleet at the very outset of the Napoleonic Wars. Some of the much needed reforms had been accomplished by the Great Mutiny, according to Melville, but among the abuses that remained was the traditionally sanctioned practice of impressment. (p. 331)

What can be said of the accuracy of Melville's historical frame? There was no ship in the Royal Navy at this period named the *Indomitable*. But that the novelist was merely casting about for a typical rather than an actual name is indicated by a variant frequently appearing in the manuscript; hence, when he finally made his choice, he may have had in mind the *Irresistible,* the *Invincible,* or the *Indefatigable*—all British ships of war in active service in 1797. Two circumstances seem to point to the last named as the original of Melville's *Indomitable.* For early in 1797, just about the time of Billy Budd's impressment from the *Rights-of-Man,* the *Indefatigable* had fallen in with a ship named *Les droits de l'homme* (though it was a French rather than an English vessel). Again, in October, 1797, a date that coincides with that assigned by Melville to the engagement between Billy Budd's ship and the French ship *L'athéiste,* this same *Indefatigable* fought and captured a French ship (though it was the *Ranger* and not *L'athéiste*) off Tenerife in the Canary Islands—not very far distant, in nautical measure, from Gibraltar. Thus accurately was the *Indomitable* drawn from history.

Likewise, none of the names that Melville gives to his officers appear in the lists of the period, but a model may be suggested for one of them, Captain Edward Fairfax Vere. Since he plays a leading role as Billy Budd's commander and executioner, not only is he fully described but his naval career is detailed. According to Melville, he had seen considerable service, had been in various engagements, and had distinguished himself as a good officer, strict disciplinarian, and intrepid fighter. More specifically: "For his gallantry in the West Indian waters [during the American Revolution] as flag-lieutenant under Rodney in that admiral's crowning victory over De Grasse, he was made a post-captain." The accuracy with which these facts fit the naval career of Sir William George Fairfax seems to be something more than mere coincidence. A contemporary biographical sketch not only assigns the same general traits of character to Fairfax that Melville assigns to Vere, but particularizes a strikingly similar career during the American Revolution. As a lieutenant in command of the cutter *Alert,* Fairfax captured the French lugger *Coureur* in 1778, and was promoted to the rank of post captain, frigate *Tartar,* January 12, 1782, remaining on the West Indian station till the close of the war:

> The complete Defeat given to the French Fleet under the Orders of the Count de Grasse by that of Britian commanded by Lord Rodney, an Action that will ever remain classed among the great and memorable Events in the History of the World, having completely paralysed every attempt, and even hope, of successful Enterprise on the part of the Enemy, no opportunity whatever was afforded to Captain Fairfax, while thus employed, of adding more material and substantial honours to those which he had before so honestly and justly acquired [Anon., "Biographical Memoir of Sir William George Fairfax, Knt.," *Naval Chronicle,* (1801)].

Thus Sir William George Fairfax seems clearly to have been the original of Captain Edward Fairfax Vere, the fictitious surname having probably been added for the sake of the epithet "Starry Vere," which Melville admits was taken from a poem by Andrew Marvell ["Upon Appleton House"].

Even as Billy Budd's frigate and commander were drawn from history, so was the setting for the mutiny itself. It is historically true that even the rigorous manner in which the Great Mutiny had been put down in April and May, 1797, had not entirely cured the disaffection in the Royal Navy, for the evil of impressment, one of the principal complaints, had not been remedied. Consequently, several small mutinies did break out in the Mediterranean fleet in the summer of 1797, in July and again in September, which were promptly put down by the officers, who were apprehensive of a repetition of the Nore and Spithead calamities. And one of the most serious of these, resulting in the execution of three ringleaders, had occurred in the squadron off Cádiz, the locale of Melville's story. Unfortunately, the records of these abortive outbreaks are too meager to afford any check on the details of *Billy Budd.*

One historical clue remains to be investigated. At the conclusion of his story Melville makes reference to what purports to be a contemporary account of the actual mutiny in which his hero was implicated: "Some few weeks after the execution, among other matters under the head of *News from the Mediterranean,* there appeared in a naval chronicle of the time, an authorised weekly publication, an account of the affair." A garbled version of Billy Budd's execution follows, solemnly inclosed in quotation marks. An extensive search for the authority here cited has proved unavailing. There was, in fact, an authorized periodical entitled *The Naval Chronicle* published from 1799 to 1818, though it was a monthly rather than a weekly; but it carried no section headed "News from the Mediterranean," and its twenty volumes shed no further light on the problem of the reality of the events in *Billy Budd.* That this was merely a literary device used by Melville to give an air of authenticity to his tale is indicated by a note in the manuscript at the bottom of the page: "Here ends a story not unwarranted by what happens in this incongruous world of ours."

The modern student should not be surprised at finding Melville's citations of authorities misleading. But, knowing the author's penchant for working from sources, he reexamines the text for less obvious clues. Melville habitually took his setting from one source and the substance of his narrative from another. The framework of *Billy Budd* has been shown to fit reasonably well into British naval history. But what of the story itself? For *Billy Budd* is not merely the account of a threatened mutiny; it is a psychological analysis of characters in which outward event serves the simple purpose of machinery. Claggart, the villain of the piece, is depicted at great length as an innately evil man; whereas the hero, Billy Budd, is sketched in diametrically opposite character as the archetype of "innocent." His very presence on board the ship aroused a spontaneous antipathy in Claggart, so that his sadistic nature could not rest until it played the serpent to this young Adam. As master-at-arms, in charge of the ship's discipline, it was an easy matter for him to lay a trap for the guileless Billy and have him brought up for trial as the leader in a mutinous conspiracy. The final upshot of this villainy was that the Handsome Sailor, though entirely innocent of the mutiny charged against him, suffered an ignominious death by hanging from the yardarm. No materials for such a story can be found in any of the voluminous records of the Great Mutiny of 1797. Yet some actual event must have suggested this theme of the tragic clash of inimical characters, for Melville declares solemnly that *Billy Budd* is "no romance," that it is "a narration essentially having less to do with fable than with fact."

A casual reference in the text itself points to his possible source of inspiration. In deciding the fate of the young foretopman, the drumhead court was instructed by Captain Vere that the exigencies of naval discipline must take precedence over all humanitarian considerations. Discussing their dilemma under these harrowing circumstances, Melville remarks:

> Not unlikely they were brought to something more or less akin to that harassed frame of mind which in the year 1842 actuated the commander of the U.S. brig-of-war *Somers* to resolve, under the so-called Articles of War, Articles modelled upon the English Mutiny Act, to resolve upon the execution at sea of a midshipman and two petty officers as mutineers designing the seizure of the brig. . . . History, and here cited without comment. True,

the circumstances on board the *Somers* were different from those on board the *Indomitable*. But the urgency felt, well warranted or otherwise, was much the same.

What did Melville know of this "mutiny" on the *Somers,* and how much akin were the real and the fictitious stories?

News of this sensational affair had reached the Pacific Squadron a few months before Melville's enlistment in the United States Navy. Gunner W. H. Meyers of the *Cyane* recorded in his journal at Matzatlán, Mexico, March 13, 1843: "Read Bennett's Herald with an account of the 'murder' of Midshipman Spence[r] and 2 men belonging to the Brig of War Somers with an account of the insanity of the Captain." This news Melville certainly heard as soon as he stepped on board the frigate *United States* at Honolulu in August of that year, for such a story would form the staple of ship's gossip for many a month. And from Meyer's words the nature of that gossip can be conjectured: the hanging of Spencer for a mutiny of which he was innocent was equivalent to his "murder," and the commander who brought it about was "insane"—so preposterous seemed the affair to a gunner in Melville's squadron.

Upon his return to America in the fall of 1844, Melville heard the full details of Spencer's execution, for it had caused a national scandal, and the public prints were full of it. The facts in brief were as follows. The United States brig *Somers,* Captain Alexander Slidell Mackenzie, was returning from a transatlantic cruise in November, 1842, when Lieutenant Guert Gansevoort approached the commander and informed him that a conspiracy existed onboard to capture the ship, murder the officers, and convert her into a pirate, and that Midshipman Philip Spencer, a lad of eighteen, was at the head of it. Spencer and two of his fellow seamen were put in irons, and a drumhead court was summoned. For all their investigations the officers could find nothing but circumstantial evidence, beyond that reported by the lieutenant. Two of the prisoners protested their innocence; Spenceer acknowledged all of the charges immediately, but declared the whole affair was a joke, and so to the impartial observer today it obviously was—an innocent though indiscreet boyish prank. The commander, however, fearful of a general disaffection among the crew, instructed the court to find them guilty. As a result, they were hanged from the yardarm. A naval court of inquiry, ashore, justified the action.

The American public, on the other hand, was divided in opinion, some defending Captain Mackenzie, some attacking him. But one feature is common to all the contemporary accounts of the affair: without exception their discussions turned on the analyses of the characters of the accused and the accuser. The most notable of these, and one that Melville surely saw, was a brochure of a hundred pages by Fenimore Cooper [*The Cruise of the "Somers": Illustrative of the Despotism of the Quarter Deck and of the Unmanly Conduct of Commander Mackenzie* (1844)], excoriating the commander for his unmanly conduct and vigorously asserting the innocence of the mid-shipman. Besides his general estimate of the leading characters, there are a number of points in his argument that Melville might have taken note of. Young Spencer, averred Cooper, "all admit was a great favorite of the crew," even as Billy Budd was the idol of his shipmates. Yet the commander's attitude toward him was, without foundation, one of "prejudice which met the young officer, almost as soon as he crossed the gangway of the brig to join her, and which followed him till he crossed it again with the fatal whip around his neck"—an attitude paralleled by the antipathy conceived against Billy Budd from the outset, not by his commander but by the master-at-arms, Claggart. Finally, even this transfer of the role of villain from the captain to the informer and accuser may have been suggested to Melville by Cooper; for the latter, after examining all the evidence against Spencer, dismisses it as inconclusive since it all came from one man, adding: "upon the head of this officious lieutenant, in common with that of the commander, the blood of the executed rests."

Thereby hangs a tale, though its full significance can only be conjectured. For the lieutenant whom Cooper calls "officious" and whose character, merged with that of Commander Mackenzie's, would thus seem to be the original of the villain Claggart, was no less a person than Guert Gansevoort, Herman Melville's first cousin. It has recently been pointed out that this intimate kinsman probably implanted in Melville his first desire to see the watery part of the world. Now it would seem that the part he played in a sea-tragedy in 1842 furnished the germ of his author-cousin's last novel. That Melville was thinking of Lieutenant Gansevoort during the year he began writing *Billy Budd* is evidenced by two references to him in the volume of poems he published in 1888, *John Marr and Other Sailors.* One is merely a reference to his heroism in the Mexican War. The second is much more significant, though here he is disguised under the sobriquet of "Tom Tight":

> Tom was lieutenant in the brig-o'-war famed
> When an officer was hung for an arch-mutineer,
> But a mystery cleaved, and the captain was blamed,
> And a rumpus too raised, though his honour it was clear.
> And Tom he would say, when the mousers would try him,
> And with cup after cup o' Burgundy ply him:
> "Gentlemen, in vain with your wassail you beset,
> For the more I tipple, the tighter do I get,"
> No blabber, no, not even with the can—
> True to himself and loyal to his clan.

Apparently, there was an inside story of the *Somers* mutiny that explained much, and cousin Guert Gansevoort knew all about it. Though he was tight-lipped toward the inquisitive, he may have told Melville enough about the character of Commander Mackenzię to furnish a living model for the sadistic Claggart. But this, unfortunately, has only the validity of reasonable inference.

With such a good story at his disposal, why did Melville wait nearly half a century before putting it to literary use? Quite naturally, the very connection of his cousin with the affair would have been sufficient to make him forego even such tempting material during his lifetime; and at the time of Gansevoort's death in 1868, Melville had given up authorship. When in his old age he returned to the pen, however, there was no such need for reticence. And as he cast about among his naval reminiscences of forty-five years before, there were reasons why Spencer's execution in 1842 came first to his mind. For after long years of decent burial, this old story was revived in June, 1888, by a popular article in the *American Magazine* entitled "The Mutiny on the Somers." In less than six months—on November

16, 1888—Melville had begun the composition of *Billy Budd.*

Certain specific details in this article evidently caught Melville's eye, for they are echoed in his fiction: "Without creating suspicion or in any way changing in his demeanor towards Spencer, the first lieutenant narrowly watched every movement he made"—conduct paralleled by Claggart's snooping on Billy Budd. And again:

> On Saturday, November 26, Lieutenant Gansevoort, executive officer of the "Somers," stepped into the cabin and informed Captain Mackenzie that a conspiracy existed on board, . . . with Midshipman Spencer as chief of the pirate band. Mackenzie was disposed at first to treat the subject lightly. . . . He tried to impress upon his executive the terrible nature of the alleged crime, which might involve the question of life or death. But Gansevoort replied calmly that he fully realized the importance attached to every word he uttered, and at once laid before his superior some astounding information.

This scene, especially in the matter of the attitudes of the commander and the informer, is distinctly reminiscent of the interview in which Claggart, the master-at-arms, first approached Captain Vere with his charges against Billy Budd. Further, the officers assembled for the trial on board the *Somers* consisted of the first lieutenant, the surgeon, the sailing master, and the purser; whereas the drumhead court in *Billy Budd* included exactly the same officers, except that the captain of marines was substituted for the purser. Finally, according to the author of this popular article, Spencer at the time of his execution "begged Mackenzie's forgiveness"; similarly, Billy Budd went to his death with a prayer on his lips, "God bless Captain Vere!"

In general attitude, however, this article was entirely sympathetic with the captain, justifying his conduct and praising him for his prompt discipline:

> Commander Mackenzie was not a man to flinch in the hour of danger or emergency. He had carefully studied the situation, and he adopted what appeared to him the best and most politic course, . . . the safety of the vessel requiring . . . immediate execution.

The writer was determined to redeem a character blackened half a century before when "Fenimore Cooper, with his fertile brain and biting sarcasm, wrote a scathing article and review of the case, handling Mackenzie in an exasperating manner." And so Melville determined to deal with Billy Budd's commander, whose conduct is pictured as blameless of all the villainy attributed to Mackenzie by Cooper, and possibly whispered in Melville's ear by Gansevoort or picked up from ship's gossip on board the frigate *United States* in 1843. This villainy he incorporated in another character, Claggart, in the much more complicated form of a sadism amounting almost to insanity.

While Melville was in the very process of creating his characters, another popular article on the *Somers* mutiny appeared which may have been of considerable help to him. In a fictionized version entitled "The Murder of Philip Spencer," running to three installments in the *Cosmopolitan Magazine* during the summer of 1889, Gail Hamilton entered the controversy with a sensational attack on

Commander Mackenzie and a melodramatic announcement of her purpose:

> In the name of truth, which is eternal; of justice to the dead, which is the highest duty that can devolve upon the living; the verdict of history should be reversed, and everywhere it should be told and known that Philip Spencer and his two companions were illegally and unjustifiably put to death, absolutely innocent of the crimes wherewith they were charged.

Through page after page she re-examined the evidence of guilt and dismissed every bit of it as preposterous, declaring: "All the mutiny that ever was, ever had been, or ever gave sign of being on board the ill-starred ship . . . was the mutiny that came from the mouth of the purser's steward"—Lieutenant Gansevoort's informant. The sentence, she declared, was already decided upon before any trial was held:

> The question of guilt was not agitated, but assumed. The doom of the prisoners was made to turn, not upon the issue of investigation by lawful methods, but upon an outside act which lay wholly in the power of the commander. . . . All their investigations had discovered no mutiny. . . . They had found exactly what they had at the beginning—a yarn of Spencer's, . . . fully and promptly acknowledged, but declared to be a joke.

Yet Captain Mackenzie was in such feverish haste to carry out the execution that he brought all sorts of pressure on his council "to urge expedition" in making the decision which he had practically dictated to them.

No actual charge is made that the commander was insane, but the author described his trepidation as amounting almost to a mania. And many of the epithets applied to him are worthy of note: he used "false and insulting words to Spencer," he was "the father of lies," his character was "brutal" and "sinister," and he was actuated throughout by an "infernally fertile imagination." Perhaps Melville found here the original suggestion for his much more intricate villain Claggart, who, though he passed for a sane and highly respectable man, was nevertheless one of the most dangerous of madmen. Such "lunacy," says Melville, "is not continuous, but occasional; evoked by some special object; it is secretive and self-contained, so that when most active it is to the average mind not distinguished from sanity."

Again, though Spencer is not held up as an entirely blameless lad, he is not only declared to be innocent of the mutiny charged against him, but his innocence is that of a generous, light-hearted youth. And at the climax of the tragedy, when Commander Mackenzie announced to him that he had been condemned to die, the writer in the *Cosmopolitan* rose to rhapsody;

> All that relieves the terrible shadow cast upon human nature by this sad drama, all it contains of manhood or of humanity, dates from this moment; and every glimmer of firmness, courage, unselfishness, greatness of soul, that in any measure lights up the somber stage, shines out from the face of Philip Spencer . . . the true Philip Spencer came forth, the heroic soul he was born to be, glorified already by the light shining upon him through the opening gates of death.

In this character sketch Melville could have found at least a suggestion for his hero Billy Budd, whose youthful good looks, high health, gay spirits, and free heart make of him the archetype of "innocent"—an unsophisticated child-man with the rectitude of an animal, incapable of willing malice or even, in his simplicity, of conceiving its existence.

Thus it would seem to be something more than coincidence that an old story dragged from the oblivion of half a century should appear in two popular articles, treating the "mutiny" on the *Somers* as a drama of inimical characters, in the very years that Melville was composing his farewell story of the sea. It seems more than probable that Melville read these accounts of a sea-tragedy in which his intimate kinsman Guert Gansevoort had played a leading and somewhat ambiguous role, and that he found in them at least the germ of his novelette *Billy Budd.* Moreover, they would have touched off reminiscences of his own sea-faring days, as has been demonstrated, since the news of the *Somers* affair had reached the Pacific Squadron during the period of Melville's enlistment, and since it is known further from the evidence of *John Marr and Other Sailors,* the volume of poems published in 1888, that Melville was already in reminiscent mood this year. Consequently, it is not surprising to find that one of his two leading characters, the master-at-arms to whom he transferred the role of villain, certainly owes something to the actual master-at-arms on the frigate *United States* in 1843-1844.

In *White-Jacket,* in a chapter entitled "A Knave in Office in a Man-of-War," Melville gave a full-length portrait of this character who, in the language of the seaman, was

> the two ends and the middle of the thrice-laid strand of a bloody rascal. . . . It was also asserted that, had Tophet itself been raked with a fine-tooth comb, such another ineffable villain could not by any possibility have been caught.

Exposed as the ringleader of a vicious system of smuggling liquor on board, selling it to the men, and then as chief police officer having them flogged for drunkenness, he was temporarily cashiered. As a messmate, he then came under Melville's closer scrutiny. He was not only "obsequious" and "deferential" toward the officers, but in his bearing toward the men he was a "persuasive, winning, oily . . . Mephistopheles":

> Besides, this Bland, the master-at-arms, was no vulgar, dirty knave. In him . . . vice *seemed,* but only seemed, to lose half its seeming evil by losing all its apparent grossness. He was a neat and gentlemanly villain, and broke his biscuit with a dainty hand. There was a fine polish about his whole person, and a pliant, insinuating style in his conversation, that was, socially, quite irresistible. . . . Nothing but his mouth . . . and his snaky, black eye . . . betokened the accomplished scoundrel within. But in his conversation there was no trace of evil; nothing equivocal; he studiously shunned an indelicacy, never swore, and chiefly abounded in passing puns and witticisms. . . . His intrepidity, coolness, and wonderful self-possession . . . bespoke no ordinary man.

This model Melville must have had in mind when he drew his later portrait of the gentlemanly villain in Claggart, whose "superior capacity" and "ingratiating deference" to officers had gained him his promotion. Rather handsome on the whole, "his hand was too small and shapely to have been accustomed to hard toil" and his "face was a notable one; the features . . . cleanly cut as those on a Greek medallion," all except the chin and the eyes which "could cast a tutoring glance." "But his general aspect and manner were so suggestive of an education and career incongruous with his naval function, that when not actively engaged in it he looked like a man of high quality, social and moral, who for reasons of his own was keeping incognito." To a "more than average intellect, . . . secretive and self-contained," he added an "even temper and discreet bearing." His villainy, cloaked in the "mantle of respectability," was "without vices or small sins," never "sordid or sensual."

More significant than this similarity of outward seeming is the likeness of the two men in their deeper more inward natures. Of his actual shipmate Melville said in *White-Jacket:*

> I, for one, regarded this master-at-arms with mixed feelings of detestation, pity, admiration, and something opposed to enmity. I could not but abominate him when I thought of his conduct; but I pitied the continual gnawing which, under all his deftly donned disguises, I saw lying at the bottom of his soul. . . .
>
> Besides, a studied observation of Bland convinced me that he was an organic and irreclaimable scoundrel, who did wicked deeds as the cattle browse the herbage, because wicked deeds seemed the legitimate operation of his whole infernal organization. Phrenologically, he was without a soul. . . . What, then, thought I, who is to blame in this matter?

This seems, indeed, like the first draft of the more complex villain in *Billy Budd,* whose deeply melancholy expression made Melville pity him one moment as "the man of sorrows . . . [who] could even have loved Billy but for fate and ban" and fear him the next as one whose cool sagacious mind was but the "ambidexter implement for . . . the accomplishment of an aim which in wantonness of malignity would seem to partake of the insane." In short, he was the victim of a "natural depravity" (in the Platonic rather than the Calvinistic sense): "the mania of an evil nature, not engendered by vicious training or corrupting books or licentious living, but born with him and innate." Finally, one is even tempted to surmise that Melville took the name of John Claggart from the actual master-at-arms on board the frigate *United States* in 1843, who appeared on the muster roll as "*John C.* Turner."

No such original for the hero himself, Billy Budd, can be found among Melville's shipmates as recorded in *White-Jacket,* unless it be assumed that the Handsome Sailor was a youthful idealization of Melville's friend Jack Chase, to whom he dedicated his last book. Indeed, there are a number of traits in the characters of the two to warrant this assumption: their common possession of high health and fine looks, their frankness and candor, their free and easy but courteous manners, their good hearts which made them loved by the men, and their excellent seamanship which made them admired by the officers. More specifically, in both cases their masculine beauty was marred by a single defect, Chase by the loss of a finger, Budd by a tendency to stammer; and again, though both were of obscure origin, they were obviously gentlemen and, it is hinted, "by-blows" of some nobleman. Finally, the setting of the story in British naval history would seem to stem from Melville's recollections of Jack Chase, the "true blue Briton."

This change of milieu, however, was at least partly for the sake of dramatic effect. For the story of the mutiny on the *Somers* needed considerable touching up to make it suitable material for the literary artist. It probably furnished nothing more than the germinal idea of *Billy Budd,* which differs from Spencer's tragedy in as many ways as it agrees. A hasty execution based on equivocal evidence through fear of impending mutiny in 1842, a peaceful era in American naval history, could only be charged to hysteria—at best fit subject matter for melodrama, even as Gail Hamilton treated it. But when placed at the outset of the Napoleonic Wars, in the summer after the Great Mutiny of 1797, the clash of humanitarian impulse with disciplinary necessity raises such apprehensiveness to the level of heroic drama. Again, Melville heightens the tragedy by a slight alteration of the high estate from which the innocent hero fell to ignominious death. The hanging on the *Somers* created a national scandal because the young midshipman was the son of the Honorable John C. Spencer, Secretary of War under President Tyler. For such sensational circumstances Melville substituted a quieter, more Greek theme: Billy Budd, the foundling of obviously noble descent, it is intimated, was the natural son of Captain Edward Fairfax Vere, who was thus faced with the historic dilemma of choosing between patriotic duty and paternal love.

At this point Melville made his most effective dramatic invention. Dropping altogether the *Somers* affair, with its purely sentimental story of a naïve youth hanged for mutiny of which he was not guilty, he turned to the more classical device of tragic irony. Convinced of Billy Budd's innocence, Captain Vere ordered the sadistic Claggart to repeat his charges in the presence of the accused, apparently hoping thereby to expose the villainy of the accuser. Dumbfounded by the magnitude of the lie and unable to find words to defend himself, Billy Budd struck the master-at-arms a mortal blow. The case no longer turned on the charge of mutiny, admittedly false. But striking and killing a superior, regardless of how pure the intention or how justified the act, was proscribed in the Articles of War as a capital offense; and with the Nore and Spithead fresh in memory and a French fleet in the offing, discipline could not be relaxed. The execution of the Handsome Sailor transcended anything to be found in the mutiny on the *Somers.*

Thus out of his reading in 1888 and reminiscences of his personal experiences in 1843-1844, heightened through dramatic invention, Melville compounded his last story according to an old formula that had served him throughout his literary career. But he had gone a long way in his technique of composition from the cruder beginnings in *Typee* (1846). In *Billy Budd,* borrowing is reduced to a minimum, and imaginative invention counts for almost everything that makes it, as one critic declares, a masterpiece in miniature. (pp. 332-46)

Charles Roberts Anderson, "The Genesis of 'Billy Budd','" in American Literature, *Vol. 12, No. 3, November, 1940, pp. 329-46.*

F. O. Matthiessen   (essay date 1941)

[*Matthiessen was an American educator and literary critic whose major studies focus on American writers and intellectual movements. As a critic, he believed that the examination of a given work of literature must also consider the social and historical context of that work. Concerning his study of American literature, Matthiessen stated: "I wanted to place our master-works in their cultural setting, but beyond that I wanted to discern what constituted the lasting value of these books as works of art." His works include* American Renaissance *and* Henry James: The Major Phase *(1944). In the following excerpt from the former study, Matthiessen expounds on major themes, characters, and literary techniques in* Billy Budd.]

Judging from the dates on the manuscript [of *Billy Budd*], Melville worked on this final story off and on from the fall of 1888 to the spring of 1891; and even then he did not feel that he had attained 'symmetry of form.' But though many of its pages are still unfinished, it furnishes a comprehensive restatement of the chief themes and symbols with which he had been concerned so long ago. And he had conceived the idea for a purer, more balanced tragedy than he had ever composed before.

He stated explicitly once again that his was a democratic stage, and affirmed the universality of passion in common men as well as in kings. Just as, when dealing with Ahab or with Israel Potter, he had remarked on the outer contrast between his material and Shakespeare's, so now he asserted that 'Passion, and passion in its profoundest, is not a thing demanding a palatial stage whereon to play its part. Down among the groundlings, among the beggars and rakers of the garbage, profound passion is enacted.' He chose for his hero a young sailor, impressed into the King's service in the latter years of the eighteenth century, shortly after the Great Mutiny at the Nore. By turning to such material Melville made clear that his thought was not bounded by a narrow nationalism, that the important thing was the inherent tragic quality, no matter where or when it was found. As he said in one of the prefaces to his verse: 'It is not the purpose of literature to purvey news. For news consult the *Almanac de Gotha.'*

Billy is suggestive of Redburn in his innocence; but he is not so boyish, and not at all helpless in dealing with the other men, among whom he is very popular. He combines strength and beauty, and thereby shares in the quality of Jack Chase himself, as well as in that which Pierre inherited from his grandfather. But no more than Pierre does Billy have any wisdom of experience. Melville's conception of him is Blakean. He has not yet 'been proffered the questionable apple of knowledge.' He is illiterate, and ignorant even of who his father was, since he is a foundling, in whom, nevertheless, 'noble descent' is as evident as 'in a blood horse.' He is unself-conscious about this, as about all else, an instinctively 'upright barbarian,' a handsome image 'of young Adam before the Fall.' How dominantly Melville is thinking in Biblical terms appears when he adds that a character of such unsullied freshness seems as though it had been 'exceptionally transmitted from a period prior to Cain's city and citified man.' He had made a similar contrast between the country and the city in *Pierre;* and he had thought of unspoiled barbarism at every stage of his writing since *Typee.* Here he focuses his meaning more specifically and submits 'that, apparently going to corroborate the doctrine of man's fall, a doctrine now popularly ignored, it is observable that where certain virtues pristine and unadulterate peculiarly characterise anybody in the external uniform of civilization, they will upon scrutiny seem not to be derived from custom or convention, but rather to be out of keeping with these.'

This reflection dovetails in with many passages that struck Melville in Schopenhauer, the newly acquired volumes of whom, along with several in the Mermaid series of Elizabethan dramatists, quickened his interest most in these last years. He was impressed by Schopenhauer's frequent declaration that Christianity presents a significant truth in its claim that human nature is fundamentally corrupt. He also scored in *Studies in Pessimism* (1891): 'Accordingly the sole thing that reconciles me to the Old Testament is the story of the Fall. In my eyes, it is the only metaphysical truth in that book, even though it appears in the form of an allegory.' This preoccupation of Melville's with the Fall can be traced back to some of his markings in *The Marble Faun,* and even further. For he noted in *Henry V* the King's belief that the monstrous ingratitude of Cambridge and Scroop against his trust was like 'another fall of man.' He underlined likewise, in *Richard II,* the Queen's agonized question to the old gardener who had reported the evil news of her Richard's deposition:

> What Eve, what serpent, hath suggested thee
> To make a second fall of cursed man?

Melville also added there that this same thought was 'to be found in Shelley & (through him) in Byron. Also in Dryden.' As far as the last is concerned, Melville might have been thinking of *The State of Innocence, and Fall of Man,* Dryden's theatrical version of *Paradise Lost.* We shall find evidence that he was thinking of Milton directly while envisaging the tragedy of Billy Budd.

One thing to be noted is that whiteness is no longer ambiguous as it was in *Pierre,* or terrifying as in *Moby-Dick.* It has been restored its connotations of purity and innocence, such as it had in *Redburn,* such as were attributed to it more specifically when Melville remarked in *Typee* that 'white appears to be the sacred color among the Marquesans,' and when he caused the narrator of *Mardi* to be mistaken by the natives for the demigod, White Taji. The accretions and variations in Melville's symbolic handling of light and dark could form a separate essay in themselves. How ingrained a part of his imaginative process their contrast became can be judged from a single instance in those self-revelatory notes for the story about Agatha, which he sent to Hawthorne just after finishing *Pierre.* He conceived that this story of a girl who was to be deserted by her sailor husband should open with a shipwreck, and that 'it were well if some faint shadow of the preceding *calm* were thrown forth to lead the whole.' That, incidentally, is the theoretical corroboration of what had been his successful practice in *Moby-Dick,* the intensification of his dramatic effects by making them burst out of just such moments of delusive calm. The contrast between light and shade that he is cultivating here is a peculiarly subtle one, as effective as his symbolical use of the amaranth in *Pierre.* Filled with meditations, the girl reclines along the edge of a cliff, and gazes seaward.

> Suddenly she catches the long shadow of the cliff

cast upon the beach a hundred feet beneath her; and now she notes a shadow moving along the shadow. It is cast by a sheep from the pasture. It has advanced to the very edge of the cliff, and is sending a mild innocent glance far out upon the water. There, in strange and beautiful contrast, we have the innocence of the lamb placidly eyeing the malignity of the sea (All this having poetic reference to Agatha and her sea-lover, who is coming in the storm . . .).

This extraordinary way of presenting good and evil has not really carried us far from *Billy Budd,* where innocence is as inevitably foredoomed by black malice. Billy does not have the spiritual insight of Dostoevsky's Idiot, some share of which came to Pip in his madness [in *Moby-Dick*]. 'With little or no sharpness of faculty or any trace of the wisdom of the serpent, nor yet quite a dove, he possessed that kind and degree of intelligence going along with the unconventional rectitude of a sound human creature.' But his simplicity was completely baffled by anything equivocal; he had no knowledge of the bad, no understanding even of indirection. Honest and open hearted, he concluded everyone else to be likewise. In such an undeveloped nature the only overt flaw was a blemish in his physical perfection, a liability to a severe blockage in his speech under moments of emotional pressure. Melville deliberately recurred in this detail to his memory of 'the beautiful woman in one of Hawthorne's minor tales,' that is to say, to 'The Birthmark,' and thus resumed another element from his past. He found his hero's defect to be 'a striking instance that the arch-interpreter, the envious marplot of Eden still has more or less to do with every human consignment to this planet.'

From the day when Billy was suddenly transferred by impressment from the homeward-bound merchantman *Rights-of-Man* to H.M.S. *Indomitable*—the names of the ships provide an ironic commentary on the act—he came into the sphere of Claggart, the master-at-arms, a type of character whose lineage also goes back to the beginning of Melville's experience. Melville dwells on his striking appearance, on the fact that his features were as finely cut 'as those on a Greek medallion,' except for a strangely heavy chin. His forehead 'was of the sort phrenologically associated with more than average intellect.' His silken black hair made a foil to the pallor of his face, an unnatural complexion for a sailor, and though not actually displeasing, seeming 'to hint of something defective or abnormal in the constitution and blood.' Everything in his manner and education seems incongruous with his present position as a naval chief of police and, though nothing is known of his life on shore, the sailors surmise him to be a gentleman with reasons of his own for going incognito. He is about thirty-five, nearly double Billy's age, and in character his opposite. His skill as master-at-arms is owing to his 'peculiar ferreting genius'; and as Melville probes his cold-blooded superiority, he is led to formulate its essence by way of an allusion to Plato's conception of 'natural depravity':

> A definition which though savoring of Calvinism,
> by no means involves Calvin's dogma as to total
> mankind. Evidently its intent makes it applicable
> but to individuals. Not many are the examples of
> this depravity which the gallows and jail supply. At
> any rate, for notable instances,—since these have
> no vulgar alloy of the brute in them, but invariably

are dominated by intellectuality,—one must go elsewhere. Civilization, especially if of the austerer sort, is auspicious to it. It folds itself in the mantle of respectability. It has its certain negative virtues serving as silent auxiliaries . . . There is a phenomenal pride in it . . .

But the thing which in eminent instances signalises so exceptional a nature is this: though the man's even temper and discreet bearing would seem to intimate a mind peculiarly subject to the law of reason, not the less in his heart he would seem to riot in complete exemption from that law, having apparently little to do with reason further than to employ it as an ambidexter implement for effecting the irrational. That is to say: toward the accomplishment of an aim which in wantonness of malignity would seem to partake of the insane, he will direct a cool judgment sagacious and sound.

Melville's growing interest in this story seems to have lain in such elaboration of the types to which his characters belonged, since nearly all the longer passages of abstract analysis appear to have been added after the first draft. In this formulation Claggart takes on some of the attributes of Ahab's monomania; he possesses also the controlled diabolic nature of a Chillingworth [from Hawthorne's novel *The Scarlet Letter*]. Melville sums up his spiritual dilemma by saying that, 'apprehending the good,' Claggart was 'powerless to be it'; and though Iago [from Shakespeare's drama *Othello*] is not mentioned, the two seem cast in the same mould. Melville had made an earlier sketch of this type in Bland, the subtle and insinuating master-at-arms in **White-Jacket;** but a nearer likeness was Jackson, whose malevolence had so terrified Redburn. The extraordinary domination that this frail tubercular sailor had also managed to exercise over all the rest of the crew was due solely to his fiendish power of will. He was 'a Cain afloat,' with even more of contempt than hatred towards life; and as this quality burned still in his dying eyes, he seemed consumed with its infernal force.

Just as the presence of Redburn's virtue and health had served to stimulate Jackson's bitterest cruelty, so Billy affected Claggart. But Redburn had at least perceived something of what Jackson was, whereas Billy's open good-nature has not even that defense. In a passage that takes us back to a variant of his observations on the power of an Edmund and the helplessness of unaided virtue, Melville reflects that 'simple courage lacking experience and address and without any touch of defensive ugliness, is of little avail'; since such innocence 'in a moral emergency' does not 'always sharpen the faculties or enlighten the will.' In pushing farther than he had in **Redburn** his analysis of how antipathy can be called forth by harmlessness, Melville contrasted Billy's effect on Claggart with what it was on all the others. The Master of the *Rights-of-Man* had hated to lose him, since 'a virtue went out of him, sugaring the sour ones' in its tough crew. He is a natural favorite in any group, a fact that helps condition Claggart's perverse reaction. To characterize what Claggart feels, Melville has recourse to the quotation, 'Pale ire, envy, and despair,' the forces that were working in Milton's Satan as he first approached the Garden of Eden. Melville also jotted down, on the back of his manuscript, some remembered details about Spenser's Envy; and in his depiction of Claggart's inextricable mixture of longing and malice, he would seem to be recurring likewise to the properties

Melville as a young man.

he had noted in Shakespeare's conception of this deadly sin. The necessity of elucidating Claggart's subtlety thus called to Melville's mind the major portrayals of evil that he knew. For all his intellectual superiority, Claggart, like Satan, is incapable of understanding the innocent heart. He cannot conceive of 'an unreciprocated malice'; and therefore coming to believe that Billy must also hate him, he is provoked into bringing about the boy's downfall by reporting him to the captain on a framed-up charge of plotting mutiny.

My account thus far of Melville's antagonists may make this work sound like a metaphysical discourse rather than a created piece of fiction. The abstract elements do break through the surface much more than they did in **Moby-Dick,** yet the characters are not merely stated, but are launched into conflict. A condensed scene brings out the ambiguous mixture of attraction and repulsion that governs Claggart's actions concerning Billy. This is one of the passages where a writer to-day would be fully aware of what may have been only latent for Melville, the sexual element in Claggart's ambivalence. Even if Melville did not have this consciously in mind, it emerges for the reader now with intense psychological accuracy. The scene is where Billy at mess has just chanced, in a sudden lurch of the ship, 'to spill the entire contents of his soup-pan upon the new-scrubbed deck.'

[Claggart], official rattan in hand, happened to be

passing along the battery in a bay of which the mess was lodged, and the greasy liquid streamed just across his path. Stepping over it, he was proceeding on his way without comment, since the matter was nothing to take notice of under the circumstances, when he happened to observe who it was that had done the spilling. His countenance changed. Pausing, he was about to ejaculate something hasty at the sailor, but checked himself, and pointing down to the streaming soup, playfully tapped him from behind with his rattan, saying, in a low musical voice, peculiar to him at times, 'Handsomely done, my lad! And handsome is as handsome did it, too!' and with that passed on. Not noted by Billy as not coming within his view was the involuntary smile, or rather grimace, that accompanied Claggart's equivocal words. Aridly it drew down the thin corners of his shapely mouth.

Everybody laughed as they felt bound to at a humorous remark from a superior, and Billy happily joined in. But entirely out of his observation was the fact that Claggart, as he resumed his way,

> must have momentarily worn some expression less guarded than that of the bitter smile and, usurping the face from the heart, some distorting expression perhaps, for a drummer-boy heedlessly frolicking along from the opposite direction, and chancing to come into light collision with his person, was strangely disconcerted by his aspect. Nor was the impression lessened when the official, impulsively giving him a sharp cut with the rattan, vehemently exclaimed, 'Look where you go!'

Preoccupied as Melville was throughout his career by the opposition between the generous heart and the ingrown self-consuming mind, he never made the merely facile contrast. He had presented the atheistic Jackson as 'branded on his yellow brow with some inscrutable curse; and going about corrupting and searing every heart that beat near him.' Yet he had concluded, through Redburn's own thoughts, that 'there seemed even more woe than wickedness about the man; and his wickedness seemed to spring from his woe; and for all his hideousness there was that in his eye at times that was ineffably pitiable and touching; and though there were moments when I almost hated this Jackson, yet I have pitied no man as I have pitied him.' These feelings were what kept Redburn from becoming an Ishmael. Such compassion for life, matched with the facing of evil in its fullness, makes likewise, as we have seen, the briefest description of the elements that composed Melville's tragic vision.

In Claggart again he does not portray a monster. For when the master-at-arms'

> unobserved glance happened to light on belted Billy rolling along the upper gun-deck in the leisure of the second dog-watch, exchanging passing broadsides of fun with other young promenaders in the crowd, that glance would follow the cheerful sea-Hyperion with a settled meditative and melancholy expression, his eyes strangely suffused with incipient feverish tears. Then would Claggart look like the man of sorrows. Yes, and sometimes the melancholy expression, would have in it a touch of soft yearning, as if Claggart could even have loved Billy but for fate and ban.

Evanescent as that tenderness was, it shows that Claggart is not wholly diabolic, and that the felt recognition of its miserable isolation by even the warped mind partakes in the suffering of the Christ.

Thus Melville's vision tended always to be more complex than the posing of a white innocence against a very black evil. . . . Furthermore, he has added another dimension through the character of Captain Vere, whose experienced and just mind puts him in contrast with both Billy and Claggart. Melville indicates how this captain, though not brilliant, is set apart from his fellow officers by 'a marked leaning toward everything intellectual,' especially for 'writers who, free from cant and convention, like Montaigne, honestly, and in the spirit of common sense, philosophise upon realities.' It reinforces our knowledge of what Melville meant by 'realities' to observe that this last phrase originally read 'upon those greatest of all mysteries, facts.' (pp. 500-08)

[The] struggle between Claggart and Billy is re-enacted on a wholly different plane within the nature of Vere himself. He has the strength of mind and the earnestness of will to dominate his instincts. He believes that in man's government, 'forms, measured forms, are everything.' But his decision to fulfil the letter of his duty is not won without anguish. He holds to it, however, and thereby Billy, who had been defenseless before the evil mind of Claggart, goes to defeat before the just mind as well. It does not occur to him to make any case at his trial. He is incapable of piecing things together, and though certain odd details that other sailors had told him about the master-at-arms now flash back into his mind, his 'erring sense of uninstructed honor' keeps him from acting what he thinks would be the part of an informer against his ship-mates. So he remains silent, and puts himself entirely in his captain's hands.

The final interview between them, in which the captain communicates the death-sentence, is left shrouded by Melville as not having been witnessed by a third party. He conjectures, however, that Vere,

> in the end may have developed the passion sometimes latent under an exterior stoical or indifferent. He was old enough to have been Billy's father. The austere devotee of military duty, letting himself melt back into what remains primeval in our formalized humanity, may in the end have caught Billy to his heart, even as Abraham may have caught young Isaac on the brink of resolutely offering him up in obedience to the exacting behest. But there is no telling the sacrament—seldom if in any case revealed to the gadding world—wherever, under circumstances at all akin to those here attempted to be set forth, two of great Nature's nobler order embrace.

Here the search for a father, if latent in all Melville's Ishmaels, and in all the questings of his homeless spirit for authority, is enacted in an elemental pattern. Following out the Biblical parallels that have been suggested at crucial points throughout this story, if Billy is young Adam before the Fall, and Claggart is almost the Devil incarnate, Vere is the wise Father, terribly severe but righteous. No longer does Melville feel the fear and dislike of Jehovah that were oppressing him through *Moby-Dick* and *Pierre.* He is no longer protesting against the determined laws as being savagely inexorable. He has come to respect necessity.

He can therefore treat a character like Vere's with full sympathy. As the two emerge from the cabin, the captain's face is a startling revelation to the senior lieutenant, since it is transfigured for a moment with 'the agony of the strong.' In contrast Billy appears serene. He had been shocked to the roots of his being by his first experience of the existence of evil; but that tension has been relaxed by the mutual trust that he found in his captain. During his last night, when he is kept under guard on the upper gundeck, his white jumper and duck trousers glimmer obscurely against the cannon surrounding him, 'like a patch of discolored snow in early April lingering at some upland cave's black mouth.' Other images of whiteness rise repeatedly through the final pages, as they alone can express Billy's essence. (pp. 509-10)

At the climax of the story, the 'fervid heart' asserts its transcendent power, in the one passage that takes on the full body of the great passages in *Moby-Dick*. At the scene of his execution,

> Billy stood facing aft. At the penultimate moment, his words, his only ones, words wholly unobstructed in the utterance, were these—'God bless Captain Vere!' Syllables so unanticipated coming from one with the hemp about his neck—a conventional felon's benediction directed aft toward the quarters of honor; syllables, too, delivered in the clear melody of a singing-bird on the point of launching from the twig, had a phenomenal effect, not unenhanced by the rare personal beauty of the young sailor, spiritualized now through late experiences so poignantly profound.
>
> Without volition, as it were, as if indeed the ship's populace were the vehicles of some vocal current-electric, with one voice from alow and aloft, came a resonant sympathetic echo—'God bless Captain Vere!' And yet at that instant Billy alone must have been in their hearts, even as he was in their eyes.
>
> At the pronounced words and the spontaneous echo that voluminously rebounded them, Captain Vere, either through stoic self-control or a sort of momentary paralysis induced by emotional shock, stood erectly rigid as a musket in the ship-armorer's rack.
>
> The hull, deliberately recovering from the periodic roll to leeward, was just regaining an even keel, when the last signal, the preconcerted dumb one, was given. At the same moment it chanced that the vapory fleece hanging low in the East, was shot through with a soft glory as of the fleece of the Lamb of God seen in mystical vision, and simultaneously therewith, watched by the wedged mass of upturned faces, Billy ascended; and ascending, took the full rose of the dawn.

In his steady handling here of his old distinctions between earthly truth and heavenly truth, between horologicals and chronometricals, Melville has gained a balance that was lacking to his angry defiance in *Pierre* and *The Confidence-Man*. Vere obeys the law, yet understands the deeper reality of the spirit. Billy instinctively accepts the captain's duty, and forgives him. Melville affirms the rareness of such forgiveness by means of the double image in which the sudden raising of Billy on the halter becomes also his ascension into heaven, an identification even more complete in an earlier variant of the final clause: 'took the full Shekinah of that grand dawn,' that is to say, received

the divine manifestation by which God's presence is felt by man. How carefully Melville is holding the scales, how conscious he is of the delicacy of the equilibrium he has created, is shown by the fact that the crew, swept in the moment of high tension into echoing Billy's words, reacts in the next with a murmur that implies a sullen revocation of their involuntary blessing, a murmur that is cut short by the command, 'Pipe down the starboard watch, boatswain, and see that they go.'

Appearances were against Billy even after his death. The only report of the event in an official naval chronicle recorded how Claggart, 'in the act of arraigning the man before the captain was vindictively stabbed to the heart by the suddenly drawn sheath-knife of Budd.' Praising the master-at-arms' fidelity to his thankless function, it reflected on 'the enormity of the crime and the extreme depravity of the criminal.' Yet one of Billy's shipmates kept his name alive in some fashion by a doggerel ballad on his tragic end. And Melville added, in a note to his manuscript, 'Here ends a story not unwarranted by what sometimes happens in this incomprehensible world of ours—Innocence and infamy, spiritual depravity and fair repute.' The 'contraries' were still ever present to him, and in the pages dealing with the chaplain he broke again into what had been one of his themes in *White-Jacket*: the incongruity that Christianity should lend the sanction of its presence to a battle cruiser. In his hatred of war he felt that the *Athéiste*, with which the *Indomitable* fell into engagement shortly after Billy's execution, was, 'though not so intended to be, the aptest name . . . ever given to a warship.' In that engagement Captain Vere received a mortal wound, and in his dying hours was heard to murmur the words, 'Billy Budd,' but not in 'accents of remorse.' Melville could now face incongruity; he could accept the existence of both good and evil with a calm impossible to him in *Moby-Dick*. (pp. 510-12)

He showed too what he had meant by calling his age shallow. He knew, as he had known in *The Confidence-Man*, that something more than mere worldly shrewdness was necessary for understanding such characters as those of his villain and hero. We have observed how often in his final story he reinforced himself at critical instances by Biblical allusions. His concern with both Testaments, pervasive throughout his work, now gave rise to his laconic statement that the great masters of legal policy, Coke and Blackstone, 'hardly shed so much light into obscure spiritual places as the Hebrew prophets.' Melville believed that he could probe Claggart's depravity only by means of the illumination gained in meditating on the Scriptural phrase, 'mysteries of iniquity.' And only by profound acceptance of the Gospels was he able to make his warmest affirmation of good through a common sailor's act of holy forgiveness.

At the time of Captain Vere's announcement of Billy's sentence, Melville remarked that it 'was listened to by the throng of standing sailors in a dumbness like that of a seated congregation of believers in Hell listening to their clergyman's announcement of his Calvinistic text.' At that point Melville added in the margin of his manuscript the name of Jonathan Edwards. The rectitude of Vere seems to have recalled to him the inexorable logic, the tremendous force of mind in the greatest of our theologians. Melville might also have reflected that the relentless denial of the claims of ordinary nature on which Edwards based his reasoned declaration of the absolute Sovereignty of God had left its mark on the New England character, on such emotionally starved and one-sided figures as Hawthorne drew, on the nightmare of will which a perverted determinism had become in Ahab. Without minimizing the justice of Vere's stern mind, Melville could feel that the deepest need for rapaciously individualistic America was a radical affirmation of the heart. He knew that his conception of the young sailor's 'essential innocence' was in accord with no orthodoxy; but he found it 'an irruption of heretic thought hard to suppress.' The hardness was increased by his having also learned what Keats had, through his kindred apprehension of the meaning of Shakespeare, that the Heart is the Mind's Bible. Such knowledge was the source of the passionate humanity in Melville's own creation of tragedy.

How important it was to reaffirm the heart in the America in which *Billy Budd* was shaped can be corroborated by the search that was being made for the drift of significance in our eighteen-eighties and nineties by two of our most symptomatic minds. John Jay Chapman was already protesting against the conservative legalistic dryness that characterized our educated class, as fatal to real vitality; while Henry Adams, in assessing his heritage, knew that it tended too much towards the analytic mind, that it lacked juices. Those juices could spring only from the 'depth of tenderness,' the 'boundless sympathy' to which Adams responded in the symbol of the Virgin, but which Melville—for the phrases are his—had found in great tragedy. After all he had suffered Melville could endure to the end in the belief that though good goes to defeat and death, its radiance can redeem life. His career did not fall into what has been too often assumed to be the pattern for the lives of our artists: brilliant beginnings without staying power, truncated and broken by our hostile environment. Melville's endurance is a challenge for a later America. (pp. 513-14)

> *F. O. Matthiessen, "Reassertion of the Heart: 'Billy Budd, Foretopman',"* in his *American Renaissance: Art and Expression in the Age of Emerson and Whitman, 1941. Reprint by Oxford University Press, Inc., 1968, pp. 500-14.*

William Ellery Sedgwick   (essay date 1942)

[*In his* Herman Melville: The Tragedy of Mind, *which was completed at the time of his death in 1942 and published in 1944, Sedgwick outlines a theory of tragedy informing the major works of Melville. The study stresses the conflict between the human mind and heart to present the Melvillean "tragedy of mind," in which "the great man, the fairest possible semblance of humanity, is impelled to achieve a noble and impossible ideal, and in the very effort to achieve this ideal destroys the fairest semblance of humanity." In the following excerpt from that work, Sedgwick suggests that* Billy Budd *presents a balance between idealism and human limitations, comparing the novel with the later dramas of Shakespeare.*]

Melville has accepted the sorrowful mystery of life, "the burthen of the mystery," as Wordsworth called it. He has

accepted it because it is universal. That was the initial step, and taking it Melville was poised to participate in and partake of life more fully. From *Clarel* to *Billy Budd* the transition is far less abrupt than the earlier one from *The Confidence-Man* to *Clarel.* In *Billy Budd* he has simply gone farther along the paths that are beginning to open for him in *Clarel.* In *Billy Budd* there is the same acceptance of the tragedy implicit in human nature. But in still other ways he has, like Lear, taken upon himself the mystery of things as if he were God's spy. That is, his acceptance of life has reached beyond the human lot of suffering and has discovered the mysterious reserves of life which go a long way to mitigate the tragedy which is inseparable from human consciousness.

Melville had poised himself for this in *Clarel.* He had recovered the prerequisite freedom and balance; the freedom and balance which Ahab, transfixed and paralysed by his vindictive hate, had lost and which Ishmael, in spite of the painful drag of his sympathy with Ahab, managed to hold onto: "Doubts of all things earthly, and intuitions of some things heavenly; this combination makes either believer nor infidel, but makes a man who regards them both with equal eye."

It is right and true to call *Billy Budd* Melville's "testament of acceptance"; but we must be careful not to understand either too much or too little by the word acceptance. Melville's "acceptance" was not based on any denial of the tragic facts of life or any ignorance of the inexorable logic of these facts. The world which we are shown in his last book is figuratively—as he had called it long before in *White-Jacket*—and literally, a man-of-war world, and the story of *Billy Budd* is as stark a tragedy as an American writer even to this day has ever penned. (pp. 233-34)

In *Billy Budd* Melville returned to the situation he had represented in *Redburn* between his younger self and the sailor Jackson, and abstracted its essential and universal significance. Of all the ship's company only Captain Vere and Claggart were "intellectually capable of adequately appreciating the moral phenomenon represented in Billy Budd." As for Claggart, as Captain Vere had the insight to discern, in him there was the opposite mystery to Billy's, "the mystery of iniquity." What, Melville asks, "can more partake of the mysterious than the antipathy spontaneous and profound such as is invoked in certain exceptional mortals by the mere aspect of some other mortal, however harmless he be?—if not called forth by that harmlessness itself." Normal human nature affords no explanation of such a one as Claggart, who is at once an object of pity and of the profoundest loathing. He and his kind are free of vulgar vices. He is, says Melville, borrowing a definition attributed to Plato, a case of "Natural Depravity; a depravity according to nature." Melville explains that this is not the same as Calvin's total depravity, because it does not apply to all mankind, but only to certain individuals. This much Melville has to say about the origin of evil. But his interest in his last book is not primarily speculative or metaphysical. It is enough for him that the mysterious facts are confronted—are confronted honestly and honorably.

Melville distinguishes between nature and the world. Primeval nature is good. The world is not under nature's rule. Not nature, not love, but necessity, or fate, rules the world. It is a man-of-war's world and we all fight at command. Idealism which would throw off this yoke of necessity only leads to more misery for man. Of the last decade of the eighteenth century, when the story takes place, Melville wrote,

> The opening proposition made by the Spirit of that Age involved the rectification of the Old World's hereditary wrongs. In France, to some extent, this was bloodily effected. But what then? Straightway the Revolution itself became a wrongdoer, one more oppressive than the kings. Under Napoleon it enthroned upstart kings, and initiated that prolonged agony of continual war whose final throe was Waterloo.

However unintelligible and arbitrary, there is an organic necessity in the world and it cannot be disregarded. A principle of limitation, it is, nevertheless, also a principle of self-preservation. Even where it allows some latitude for choice, men are wise to conform with it by supplementing it with forms and definitions of their own. Captain Vere only repeats Melville's own, now settled conviction, "With mankind . . . forms, measured forms, are everything; and that is the import couched in the story of Orpheus with his lyre spellbinding the wild denizens of the woods." And "this he once applied to the disruption of forms going on across the Channel and the consequences thereof."

This is a far cry from Melville's state of mind in *Pierre,* when in spite of himself he could not bring himself to accept the clamorous moral of his own story; "For it is only the miraculous vanity of man," he wrote in *Pierre,*

> which ever persuades him, that even for the most richly gifted mind, there ever arrives an earthly period, where it can truly say to itself, I have come to the Ultimate of Human Speculative Knowledge; hereafter, at this present point I will abide. Sudden onsets of a new truth will assail him, and overturn him as the Tartars did China: for there is no China wall that man can build in his soul which shall permanently stay the irruptions of those barbarous hordes which Truth ever nourishes in the loins of her frozen, yet teeming North; so that the Empire of Human Knowledge can never be lasting in any dynasty, since Truth still gives new Emperors to the earth.

In *Billy Budd* Melville has completely reversed himself, so that what had been vanity before, to build a Chinese wall in one's soul, is now the part of wisdom. The fruit of Captain Vere's serious reading of books "treating of actual men and events" had been the ripening "of his own more reserved thoughts . . . so that as touching most fundamental topics, there had got to be established in him some positive convictions which he felt would abide in him essentially unmodified so long as his intelligent part remained unimpaired." He was opposed to the revolutionary ideals coming out of France. Unlike so many of his friends and kindred, he opposed them not because they threatened to sweep away the privileges of his class, but because "they seemed to him incapable of embodiment in lasting institutions" and were, he believed, "at war with the world and the peace of mankind." He had established certain fundamental assumptions, and

> in view of the humbled period in which his lot was cast, this was well for him. His settled convictions were as a dyke against those invading waters of

> novel opinion, social, political, and otherwise, which carried away as in a torrent no few minds in those days, minds by nature not inferior to his own.

It is not that Captain Vere (or Melville) has capitulated in the sense of abdicating his speculative mind and his idealism. The conservatism here is not retreat. It is the same as it was in *Clarel,* the expression of Melville's religious consciousness of the organic unity of man. In substituting common sense for the speculative and idealistic view of the situation which confronted him, Captain Vere was implementing this religious consciousness. As he saw here and saw beyond the immediate situation, what is demanded for the ordering of this world is worldly common sense. He obeyed the dictates of common sense not for his own worldly advantage but for the good of all,—for the good of that organic whole which is society.

As an index to Melville's "acceptance," Captain Vere is still more interesting as he faces his own soul. He is obliged by the exigencies of this man-of-war world to disregard all considerations of the absolute good and the ultimate truth. But he does not therefore deny the existence of the absolute good and the ultimate truth. He is the first to recognize Billy's angelic innocence. In the present emergency his innocence cannot excuse the consequences of his act: "We proceed under the law of the Mutiny Act." But he has said, "At the Last Assizes it shall acquit." In his dilemma Captain Vere does not arraign God as a devil-god; nor does he conclude, according to *Pierre,* "that whatever other worlds God may be Lord if he is not the Lord of this." The words occur in the Plinlimmon pamphlet, and in *Pierre* Melville could not bring himself to accept Plinlimmon's relativistic doctrine of virtue in this world. Like his hero, he would have all or nothing and, like his hero, he got nothing; or, because his imagination could not picture nothing, he got worse than nothing: "Now, 'tis merely hell in both worlds."

As Plinlimmon wrote, "What man who carries a heavenly soul in him, has not groaned to perceive, that unless he committed a sort of suicide as to the practical things of this world, he can never hope to regulate his earthly conduct by the same heavenly soul? And yet by an infallible instinct he knows, that that monitor cannot be wrong in itself." So it was with Captain Vere. As for Melville, it can be said that he has accepted the human predicament,—which follows inevitably from the dualism of human nature. Melville began to take account of it, and to chafe under it in *Mardi;* he pressed into it further and wrestled with it in *Moby-Dick.* In *Pierre* he refused to accept it. Now he sees that because a man acts under a worldly necessity he does not therefore debase his humanity: his soul, be it immortal or not, is not soiled thereby. And because a man has accepted the limitations of his nature he is not therefore lacking in human strength and dignity, and is not to be relegated, as we feel that Melville, in the presence of Ahab could not but relegate Starbuck, on the score of "the incompetence of mere unaided virtue or right-mindedness." Further than this he sees that it is possible to be in this world and not of it; that because a man has taken on the burden of human consciousness, with its sad knowledge of good and evil, he is not therefore excommunicated from primal goodness.

Between Billy's instinctive rectitude, that of an upright barbarian, and such as Adam's might have been "ere the urbane Serpent wriggled himself into his company," and Captain Vere's conscious human rectitude there is no estrangement. Far from that, there is a profound reciprocal understanding between the two.

> Fair encounter
> Of two most rare affections! Heavens rain grace
> On that which breeds between them!

It was Captain Vere who, of his own motion, communicated the death sentence to Billy. As to what transpired then, between these two, "each radically sharing in the rarer qualities of one nature," Melville would no more than hint. Captain Vere was old enough to have been Billy's father.

> The austere devotee of military duty, letting himself melt back into what remains primeval in our formalized humanity, may in the end have caught Billy to his heart, even as Abraham may have caught young Isaac on the brink of resolutely offering him up in obedience to the exacting behest. But there is no telling the sacrament . . . wherever under circumstances at all akin to those here attempted to be set forth—two of great Nature's nobler order embrace.

The next morning when Billy stood up for execution before the crew, his last words were "God bless Captain Vere." Not long afterward Captain Vere, dying of a wound received in an engagement with the enemy, was heard to murmur words inexplicable to his attendant, "Billy Budd, Billy Budd."

It is possible to see in these intimations the reflection of a heavenly mystery, in which the idea of divine love, as attributed to Christ, is reconciled with the known facts of the rough justice which overrules the world. There is a suggestion of such a reconciliation in terms of Christianity inasmuch as it is just hinted that Billy Budd, a foundling, was in truth, the son of Captain Vere. (pp. 236-41)

For the rest, in the "testament of acceptance," Melville ascribes a constitutional soundness to humanity. Insofar as it was provoked by wilful idealists, the French Revolution led to worse oppression than before. But taking a long view of it and seeing it as an infection coming to a head in a frame so constitutionally sound as to be able to throw it off, it had a salutary effect which "not the wisest could have foreseen" at the time. In a way "analogous to the operation of the Revolution at large, the Great Mutiny, though by Englishmen naturally deemed monstrous at the time, doubtless gave the first latent prompting to most important reforms in the British navy." Moreover, there is that in the foreground of the story which attests the constitutional soundness of humanity. Between normal human nature and a being like Claggart there is a gap, a "deadly space between." The sailors instinctively distrust him and are repelled by him. Whereas to Billy they respond spontaneously. They are drawn together around him as around a bonfire on a cold day and are stirred to acts of good nature by his cordial influence.

The mind of man is under a tragic necessity to grasp an ideal of life and, concurrently, by following the implications of things as they are, in the interest of truth, to see them as far less fair than they appear and as affording far less security than they appear to offer. That, of course, was what happened to Pierre. Under Isabel's influence he spurned the actual and possible for his ideal of the truthful and virtuous life. At the same time, the world as he had known it, so sure and solid in appearance, seemed to dissolve in fathomless mysteries and terrifying ambiguities. Pierre's experience was Melville's, who reached the conclusion that life is illusory and truth which destroys illusions, also destroys life; in the impulses of human growth the seed of death is planted. It has been affirmed that in identifying himself with his youthful hero, Melville reverted to adolescence. I would not altogether deny that this was so. On the other hand, it cannot be gainsaid that it is implicit in the mature mind to be aware, on one hand, of the discrepancy between the ideal and the actual and, on the other, between the appearance of things and the reality. His realization of these discrepancies was of the substance of Shakespeare's thought in *Hamlet* and *King Lear* and, it would seem certain, throughout the period of his life which produced his greatest tragedies along with such things as *Troilus and Cressida* and *Measure for Measure.* Moreover, wonderful as is Shakespeare's command of objectivity, it is impossible not to feel, in the works which I have just named, the strain on Shakespeare of these realizations. With a little less command, Shakespeare might have turned against life, "the thing itself," just as Melville turned against it in *Pierre.* As it is, Shakespeare betrays a distinct revulsion against no less a principle of life than sexual desire, which is far more than a moral condemnation on his part of sexual promiscuity. Melville did not have at hand, like Shakespeare, an artistic tradition and the artistic contentions for the objective representation of life. Besides, there was that in his inheritance, what I have called his radical Protestantism, which always threatened to turn him (as it did in *Pierre*) against the means as well as the substance of such representation. A cynical generation may identify Melville's radical Protestantism with arrested development. But unless one is prepared to maintain that strong feelings have no place in man's speculations on what it is only human to speculate upon—that a man should think not as a man but as a machine—then one cannot dismiss Melville as an idiosyncrasy of the past, whose intensity is no longer intelligible, or as a case of retarded adolescence. Not at all: "For in all of us lodges the same fuel to light the same fire." Moreover, the sequel to the crisis provoked by Melville's idealism, as we find it in Melville's "acceptance" in *Billy Budd* shows his span of experience to have been typically human. Only the accentuation and timing are peculiar to him—as an individual, conditioned by his inheritance and the time and country in which he lived. In *Billy Budd* we see a mind stabilizing itself on a lower level than that at which it had aimed before, the possible and the actual instead of the impossible ideal.

The character of Melville's prose in *Billy Budd,* expositive rather than declamatory, and matter-of-fact rather than nervously incisive,—as it is in parts of *Pierre,*—is in keeping with the idea of "acceptance." Yet there is, in this last book, an element of present and lyrical experience which the word "acceptance" is inadequate to convey. It stems from the stories written immediately after *Pierre* and is the final and most rare flowering of what lay behind Melville's reserve in these stories. His reserve there, in which we first discern the element of silence in Melville's later writings, wears an expression which we have all seen in human faces, mostly in those of adolescents and old people, from which we barely guessed that they have some primary business of their own which they must be about, of growth and reconciliation, of renunciation and repair, which requires inviolable silence and privacy and, in the side toward themselves, the protection of shadowy recesses of being against the "infinite wakefulness" which threatens in the conscious soul. (pp. 242-45)

Billy Budd is a bloom from the same root as Melville's late flower poems which, in the last year of his life, he dedicated to his wife, reminding her of the flowers which he used to bring her from the meadows above "Arrowhead,"—"that farmhouse, long ago shorn by the urbane barbarian succeeding us in the proprietorship." Now he presents her with "these 'Weeds and Wildings,' thriftless children of quite another and yet later spontaneous aftergrowth." He regards the flowers which he described in these poems, with the same open-mindedness with which he regards his young hero in *Billy Budd.* This perennial growth of earthly loveliness, may it not be the symbol of resurrection into life eternal? These roses of earthly bloom, do they not prefigure Dante's Rose of Paradise? It may be. But in any case, in the patent fact that such loveliness can be at all, there is cause for deep and serene rejoicing. In *Billy Budd* Melville faced the tragic necessities of life. But that life could produce such warmth and radiance as glowed in Billy's heart, which could call forth something of its own warmth and radiance in the most callous and hard-hearted and melt down the barriers between worldly superiority and inferiority; that life has within itself such fuel to light such a glorious flame—this is felt as more than equal compensation for the tragic necessities that human life is under.

Once more the parallel between Melville and Shakespeare comes to the front. For *Billy Budd* stands in the same light to *Moby-Dick* and *Pierre* that Shakespeare's last plays—*Pericles, The Winter's Tale, Cymbeline* and *The Tempest*—stand to the great tragedies. Of Shakespeare in these plays it is often said, as of Melville in *Billy Budd,* that he came to accept life. But if there is any basis for the remark in Shakespeare's case, then, as in Melville's, the word "acceptance" is inadequate. It is too blunt and too passive. In its place I would use the combination of words, recognition, restoration and return. Marina is restored to her father in *Pericles,* Posthumus, in *Cymbeline,* returns from banishment to his native land, and his wife, Imogen, is restored to him as he to her. Perdita's identity is recognized in *The Winter's Tale;* she is restored to her mother, as her mother is restored to her husband, and her husband to his own better nature. In *The Tempest,* Alonzo and Ferdinand, father and son, are returned to one another after each had thought the other drowned. Ariel is restored to freedom and Prospero to his dukedom. There is Miranda's recognition of the nature she shares with, and glorifies in others; "How beauteous mankind is! O brave new world that has such people in't." "In one voyage," says old Gonzalo, summing up, young Ferdinand found a wife—

> Where he himself was lost; Prospero his dukedom
> In a poor isle; and all of us ourselves,
> When no man was his own.

What I have in mind to convey by the words recognition, restoration and return in Shakespeare's last plays is independent of the turns the stories take. It is an element of present and lyrical experience which is of Shakespeare himself. It is felt as constantly moulding the stories to its

own likeness: and it shows otherwise in the quality of Shakespeare's response to life, centering on his heroines the quality of thrilling tenderness—of wonder and surprise intermingled with tenderest recognition. (pp. 245-47)

The final and ever so poignant flowering of Herman Melville, which is the element of present lyrical experience in *Billy Budd,* is the same essentially as Shakespeare's in his last [plays]. The hero was drawn from Melville's friend, Jack Chase, the Jack Chase of *White-Jacket,* but in essence he derives from still earlier and less trammeled sources. In *Omoo,* Melville had described Tahiti. "Such enchantment," he had written, "breathes over the whole, that it seems a fairy world, all fresh and blooming from the hand of the Creator." Almost half a century after Melville had been in the South Seas, writing his last book, he described his hero as like a Tahitian, but as the Tahitians were before civilization had got its dirty paws on them. The story, he remarked, was "not unwarranted by what happens in this incongruous world of ours." What happens in the book apart from the story was warranted by Melville's final insight into the nature of life. In *Billy Budd,* in the person of his hero, of whom he wrote, "the bonfire in his heart made luminous the rose-tan in his cheek," who combined a maidenly grace with great masculine strength, to whom song was more native than speech, in whom there is the same pristine quality, the same immediacy to meadows and gardens and the cycle of the seasons as there is in Shakespeare's last heroines—in *Billy Budd* Melville returned to the contemplation of life as he had painted it in *Typee.* This much is obvious. It is obvious on second sight that there was more to this than wilful or sentimental retrospection. The same enchantment of life which he had thrilled to in his first book, he has returned to by force of insight in his last, and recognized it anew. Now, however, it is not localized; it is not identified as lying afar off,

> Where Eden, isled, empurpled glows
> In old Mendanna's sea.

Such is the force of Melville's final insight that the innocence and loveliness and joy of life is represented on board a man-of-war, Melville's own symbol for the world in its most opposite aspects to life as he had identified it with Typee valley. True, this innocence suffers a shameful death at the hands of this man-of-war world. Yet, in Billy's life there is more promise of salvation for the world than there is of damnation in his death. And Melville has partaken of its salvation. His intellectual passion spent, and illuminated by his insight of a mind which by accepting its limitations has transcended them and has found within itself, at its own mysterious centre, a calm not to be found elsewhere, Melville has been restored to the radiant visage of life, whose shining secret is, it has its salvation in its own keeping. (pp. 248-49)

William Ellery Sedgwick, in his Herman Melville: The Tragedy of Mind, *Cambridge, Mass.: Harvard University Press, 1944, pp. 231-49.*

Richard Chase   (essay date 1949)

[*A distinguished American literary critic, Chase is wide-*

ly recognized for his scholarship in the field of American literature. In his most important work, The American Novel and Its Tradition *(1957), he delineated the romantic characteristics of the American novel, which he believed differentiate it from its more realistic predecessor, the European novel. Chase has also written extensively on the works of Herman Melville, as well as those of Emily Dickinson and Walt Whitman. In the following excerpt, he qualifies the critical view of* Billy Budd *as a tragedy and examines the psychological significance of ritual and Christian allusion in the novel.*]

Melville's last book, a short novel written between 1888 and 1891 and called *Billy Budd, Foretopman,* has generally been praised for qualities it does not possess. It is natural, of course, to wish to see in *Billy Budd* the last ripe word of the aged Melville. And there has been a great temptation, especially on the liberal-religious left, to see in *Billy Budd,* as one writer says, Melville's final "testament of acceptance" [E. L. Grant Watson; see excerpt dated 1933]—his final acceptance of a "tragic" view of life involving an apotheosis of the common man as Christ and an assertion that what is needed in American life is a leavening of individualism and law by the sympathetic passions of the heart. And *Billy Budd* is said to be Melville's definitive moral statement. But this estimate of *Billy Budd* will do our author no service if, as I think, the moral situation in the book is deeply equivocal.

In Melville's writings there are two basic kinds of hero, both akin, in their several variations, to the central figure of Prometheus. The first kind of hero is the false Prometheus, who in one way or another violates the deep-running, natural, and psychic rhythms of life which are necessary for all creative enterprise. The second kind of hero is the Handsome Sailor: the true hero in whom Prometheus tends to put on the full tragic manhood of Oedipus. This second kind of hero is briefly sketched or symbolized as Marnoo, Jack Chase, Bulkington, and Ethan Allen. In each case, he is a full-statured man, great in body, heart, and intellect, a man with great pain of experience behind him, a young man, but still so fully created a man that, in the case of Jack Chase, Ishmael is moved to call him "sire." At the beginning of *Billy Budd,* the Handsome Sailor is again symbolized, in the following manner:

> In the time before steamships, or then more frequently than now, a stroller along the docks of any considerable seaport would occasionally have his attention arrested by a group of bronzed mariners, man-of-war's men or merchant sailors in holiday attire ashore on liberty. In certain instances, they would flank, or, like a bodyguard, quite surround some superior figure of their own class, moving along with them like Aldebaran among the lesser lights of his constellation. That signal object was the "Handsome Sailor" of the less prosaic time, alike of the military and merchant navies. With no perceptible trace of the vain-glorious about him, rather with the off-hand unaffectedness of natural regality, he seemed to accept the spontaneous homage of his shipmates. A somewhat remarkable instance recurs to me. In Liverpool, now half a century ago I saw under the shadow of the great dingy street-wall of Prince's Dock (an obstruction long since removed) a common sailor, so intensely black that he must needs have been a native African of

the unadulterate blood of Ham. A symmetric figure, much above the average height. The two ends of a gay silk handkerchief thrown loose about the neck danced upon the displayed ebony of his chest; in his ears were big hoops of gold, and a Scotch Highland bonnet with a tartan band set off his shapely head.

The emblem of Lucy Tartan enlightens the forehead of the Handsome Sailor as he emerges from the depths of Night into the consciousness of Day. He moves as ponderously, but with as much strength and beauty, as Bulkington in *Moby-Dick,* or as revolutionary America itself, setting forth on the path of civilization.

Still, this magnificent and momentous figure does not appear at full scale in any of Melville's books. But Melville made two attempts to portray him fully: one in *Pierre* and one in *Billy Budd.* Not the least part of the wisdom which Melville had achieved at the end of *Pierre* was his realization that he could not portray this heroic figure, except as a perpetual adolescent whose suicide was entirely justified by the fact that he was no match for the realities of the world. At the end of *Pierre,* civilization was shown to be in the hands of conventional society, military power, and Laodicean liberalism. In *Billy Budd* civilization is shown to be in approximately the same hands. And the hero who opposes these forces is no more capable of doing so than Pierre.

Yet *Billy Budd* is a brilliant piece of writing, nicely constructed and balanced between swift, stark action and moral-philosophical comment. Though it falls sadly short of the pure tragedy Melville apparently wanted to write, it is still a moving drama, if a drama only of pathos. (pp. 258-60)

It is often said that *Billy Budd* shows Melville's final admission of the tragic necessity of law in human society. The fact of the matter is that Melville had admitted this forty years earlier in *White-Jacket* and had reaffirmed it in *Moby-Dick* by showing that the tragic dilemma of Ahab was in part due to his necessary commitment to the external forms of command. He makes no *discovery* of law in *Billy Budd;* he simply deals with the subject more carefully than he had before. Captain Vere's examination and defense of law in a man-of-war world and his decision that a human life must be sacrificed to this law is impeccable, irrefutable, and fully conscious of the pathetic irony of the situation. The flaw in the book is that Melville does not fully conceive of that which, in a genuine tragedy, has to be opposed to law.

Captain Vere and Claggart are perfectly portrayed. The captain's name—Edward Fairfax Vere—perhaps indicates what he is. He is Man (*vir*), but civilized Man. Though personally superior to the laws of "Cain's City," he nevertheless in all practical matters lives according to these laws. He is a superior type of "citified man." Captain Vere is a bachelor of forty-odd years. He is brave without being foolhardy, a disciplinarian but considerate of the interests of his men. He is inclined to be grave and practical; some of his acquaintances call him humorless and observe a streak of pedantry in his character. Yet he is sometimes given to moments of absentmindedness, and when he is seen at the ship's rail gazing meditatively into the blankness of space his nickname, Starry Vere, seems especially to fit him. He has no brilliant qualities but is intellectually superior to his associates. He is a reader of books, preferring authors who deal with actual men and events or who philosophize, like Montaigne, in the spirit of common sense. And though his training has made his mind a "dyke" against the spate of revolutionary ideas coming out of France, his arguments against them are reasoned.

Captain Vere is profoundly moved by the plight of Billy Budd, and Melville tells us that the ordeal of the sentence and the hanging was worse for Vere than it was for Billy. Deciding to communicate the decision of the court to Billy in person, he assumes the relationship we have met so often in Melville's books. He becomes a father to a son. The possibility that Vere may in fact be Billy Budd's father is not contradicted by the author; for Billy was a foundling and, as the author suggests, a by-blow of some English nobleman. In *Billy Budd* the father whom the young hero seeks is shown to be purely mundane; he is "citified man" rather than Zeus or Jehovah. Captain Vere's short interview with Billy Budd, the sacred actualities of which Melville only hints at, is a kind of consummation of a quest he has been making all his life. The whole affair has so shaken him that the ship's surgeon suspects a touch of madness, a question which Melville carefully leaves open. Perhaps the captain's touch of madness is only his own terrible consciousness of having finally fulfilled the destiny of "citified man"—to recognize oneself as Caesar and one's son as Christ.

Melville describes Claggart as being about thirty-five. He is spare and tall, with the clean-cut features, except for a disproportionate heaviness of the chin, of a head on a Greek medallion. His hand is rather too small and there is a sort of intellectual pallor on his forehead. He has a trace of a foreign accent and though nothing is known of his origins, he has affinities, perhaps, with some Mediterranean culture. To say that Claggart is a version of the confidence man—the mysterious impostor from the East—may be surprising, but it is true. Or rather he is the confidence man plus an actively evil nature. The figure in Melville's satire was not the evil man so much as "the moderate man, the inveterate understrapper to the evil man." Claggart is the confidence man invested with a "natural depravity" willed by paranoiac guile and controlled by superior intellect. In his campaign against Billy Budd, he employs all the devices of "confidence." Subtly obsequious, outwardly frank and friendly, he is a "fair-spoken man," speaking in silvery accents with a "confidential" tongue. Conducting himself, as is his wont, with an "uncommon prudence" and speaking with a Pharisaical sense of "retributive righteousness," he sells his case to Captain Vere:

> What he said, conveyed in the language of no uneducated man, was to the effect following if not altogether in these words, namely, that . . . he had seen enough to convince him that at least one sailor aboard was a dangerous character in a ship mustering some who not only had taken a guilty part in the late serious trouble, but others also who, like the man in question, had entered His Majesty's service under another form than enlistment.

Contemptuous of this rhetoric, the captain interrupts with: "Be direct, man; say impressed men." But the sweet voice continues, using the confidence trick of misrepresenting the nature of a man. Billy Budd, says Claggart, is a "deep one"; under the fair exterior there is a "man-

trap." This is an argument the captain cannot ignore; Claggart has merely to enunciate the charge and his case is won. The full character of Claggart emerges *in spite of* Melville's statement that he is "depraved according to nature." Melville states this, perhaps, because he wishes to oppose two "natural" men—Billy Budd, good by nature, and Claggart, depraved by nature—to "citified man," Captain Vere, who is presumably both good and depraved by nature. But to say that one character is good by nature and another depraved can have only a symbolic value. Claggart becomes evil as a civilized man. He becomes evil in the only way which allows us to understand what evil is: by living in Cain's city and making choices of action. It is, indeed, only his being a certain kind of "citified man" which allows his "natural depravity" or his kinship with the torpedo fish a meaningful symbolic value.

So highly "citified" is Claggart's depraved mind that, like the mind of mankind, it generates a compensatory vision of innocence. And this vision is at the root of his ambivalent feeling toward Billy Budd, finding its expression to some extent in a homosexual attraction. Billy Budd's "harmlessness" fills Claggart with both longing and revulsion at the same time that Budd's physical beauty attracts him. Like Milton's Satan, thinking of the Garden, Claggart is capable of looking at Billy Budd and weeping "feverish tears." He weeps at being unable to put off the burden of civilization and be "harmless." But in less regressive moments he can feel the active bitterness of the ambiguous attraction-repulsion which Billy rouses in him. "To be nothing more than innocent!" Such a being is in the deepest sense a mutineer, an apostate from Cain's city. It is very difficult not to agree with Claggart.

The weakness of *Billy Budd* is the central character himself. The trouble is that he is not in any meaningful sense what Claggart says he is: "deep" and a "man-trap." He *ought* to be "deep" and in some inescapable human way a "man-trap." Otherwise he cannot function meaningfully in a tragedy which tries to demonstrate the opposition between human nature and the heart on the one hand and law on the other. Otherwise he cannot possibly be the Handsome Sailor. It is surely significant of uncertainty that Melville, though outwardly identifying Billy Budd as the Handsome Sailor, actually hedges. Melville's dedication of his book to Jack Chase inferentially compares Billy Budd with the Handsome Sailor of *White-Jacket.* After describing the Handsome Sailor and symbolizing him as the giant negro, Melville writes: "Such a cynosure, at least in aspect, and something such too in nature, though with important variations made apparent as the story proceeds, was welkin-eyed Billy Budd, or Baby Budd." Melville is determined apparently to have his cake and eat it too when it comes to the question of what manner of man his hero actually is. After thus presenting Billy Budd as a Handsome Sailor "with important variations," Melville goes on to ignore all possible "variations," referring to his hero throughout the rest of the book as the Handsome Sailor. Obviously Jack Chase and Billy Budd have many things in common, but the abyss between them is prodigious. And Melville could not admit this to himself.

Billy Budd is simple, direct, and kindly. He is a sort of Adam, the Adam as yet untainted by the "urbane serpent." He has the "humane look of reposeful good nature" sometimes shown in statues of Hercules. Lacking powers of reflection, he is a fatalist as animals are fatalists. He is primeval, unspoiled man wandering, as if dazed, in Cain's city. In describing Billy, Melville grows hazily rhetorical: "he possessed that kind and degree of intelligence which goes along with the unconventional rectitude of a sound human creature—one to whom not as yet had been proffered the questionable apple of knowledge." He is a "childman." "He had none of that intuitive knowledge of the bad which in natures not good or incompletely so, foreruns experience, and therefore may pertain, as in some instances it too clearly does pertain, even to youth." One cannot understand the character of Billy Budd except as the final, and almost the first—first *crucial*—self-indulgence of a great intelligence. Looking backward almost fifty years, trying to convince himself that such a man might actually have existed, Melville tries to re-create life on a man-of-war in the image of Eden, insisting that sailors have a particular kind of "innocence" not found in the generality of mankind. And while this may be true in a certain sense—there is no doubt a kind of innocence or at least sexual and mental juvenility in a sailor's life—we must take *White-Jacket* to be Melville's clear account of life on a man-of-war; and in that book he had concluded that man-of-war's men were on the whole less innocent than the rest of mankind. The character of Billy Budd is meaningful only as a moving and revealing comment on Melville's last years.

The author makes an attempt to show that in the course of the story Billy Budd finds the consummation of his destiny. Having been sentenced to die by the man who may possibly be his father, Billy Budd can at last drop the role of Ishmael and become Isaac, the lawful heir of Abraham. When he first begins to be troubled by the evidence of a plot against him, Billy Budd seeks advice from an old sailor described as the mainmastman of the ship. We remember from *White-Jacket* that the patriarchal mainmastman was referred to as an Abraham, and though he is not called that in *Billy Budd,* the parallel is suggestive. It is this old sailor who has given Billy the name of Baby Budd; he refuses or is unable to play the part of Billy's father, as Abraham refuses Ishmael. Later Melville suggests that Billy finds his atonement with Captain Vere: "The austere devotee of military duty, letting himself melt back into what remains primeval in our formalized humanity, may in the end have caught Billy to heart, even as Abraham may have caught young Isaac on the brink of resolutely offering him up in obedience to the exacting behest." This atonement is the logical conclusion to Melville's Ishmael theme, more fully and exactly stated here, in the strict terms of the Ishmael myth, than in *White-Jacket.* In *White-Jacket* the recognition and final meeting of father and son was presented as an act of maturity on the part of the son, a recognition of human depravity, an admission of law, form, and patriarchal majesty, and a consequent liberation of the son's creative energy. In *Billy Budd,* Melville insists on trying to have it both ways: there are suggestions that Billy has experienced a metamorphosis of character through an "agony mainly proceeding from a generous young heart's virgin experience of the diabolical incarnate and effective," and that he is "spiritualized now through late experiences so poignantly profound." The reader accepts this gratefully and with belief. And he reflects that, after all, Melville is going to say that Billy Budd is now the Ishmael who has become Isaac, the harmless Adam who has become the fallen Adam, the foundling of

noble antecedents who has become Oedipus the tragic hero. All this would indicate that Billy Budd's agony has made of him a fully tragic, fully suffering, fully knowing man.

But not so. Billy Budd is hanged after sleeping the night out with the serene happy light of babyhood playing over his features. When a man is hanged, certain mechanical-physical spasms take place in his body; his bowels are emptied, his penis erects, and there is an ejaculation of semen. When Billy Budd is hanged, there is a total "absence of spasmodic movement." The tragedy of Melville's heroes had always been that they were "unmanned" by circumstances or the effect of their own moral decisions. Billy Budd was unmanned by Melville himself. There is a hint that the hanging of Billy Budd was a miraculous euthanasia. We recall that in *The Confidence-Man* an "invalid Titan" had violently quarreled with the peddler of the Samaritan Pain Dissuader for claiming that his balm was "a certain cure for any pain in the world." In portraying Billy Budd, not as Isaac or the fallen Adam or Oedipus, but as the hermaphrodite Christ who ascends serenely to the yardarm of the *Indomitable,* Melville apparently forgot his "invalid Titan."

Billy Budd is a syncretic work of art, and though we must not overemphasize its importance, it is a measure of Melville's final position. It demands to be considered as a "natural" tragedy as the tragedies of Sophocles and Shakespeare are "natural." But it is also a beatific vision, a vision of the hermaphrodite Christ who is mentioned in *Moby-Dick* and who always dimly haunted Melville— that shadowy Christ who, as we have noted, slept restively in Melville's mind after the writing of *Pierre.* If the Rolfe of *Clarel* had appeared in *Billy Budd,* we might have had a fully tragic hero. As it is, we have the Handsome Sailor minus Rolfe, the tragic human core. The residue is something less and more than human, a child or a flower or a radiance. The fall of Simon Magus symbolizes not only the decline of the pagan magic which created *Moby-Dick;* it also symbolizes a reaffirmation of Christianity—more particularly a fresh commitment to the infantile Christ who seeks entrance in *Pierre,* **"Bartleby the Scrivener,"** *Israel Potter, The Confidence-Man,* and *Clarel,* and who is finally admitted in *Billy Budd.* It is surely not true, as some writers, including [American poet and critic] Charles Olson, have alleged, that Melville's weakness for the hermaphrodite Christ is the reason for the disintegration of his art after *Moby-Dick.* For one thing, as I hope I have

The hanging scene as depicted in the film adaptation of Billy Budd.

been able to show, Melville's art did not disintegrate after his best book; it merely changed in various ways, even though these ways were journeys less bracing than the ascent of the magician. Furthermore, in the light of *Billy Budd,* the remarkable thing is that the hermaphrodite Christ appears so little in Melville's other writings; and this is especially remarkable of *Clarel,* the work in which Melville tried most explicitly to deal with moral problems and intellectual positions.

Billy Budd, the "Rose" of Melville's last work, is himself a syncretic conception, the product of nineteenth-century nature worship and the image of the divine child-man. Though of all nineteenth-century writers Melville is the least open to the charge of entertaining a superficial view of nature (indeed his superiority over Wordsworth and Emerson is his *tragic* view of nature), he nevertheless paid something of the romantic homage to the violet by the mossy stone. The frightening insistence with which, after *Pierre,* nature presented itself to him as a stony waste land or a Medean muck, together with his feeling that "Niebuhr & Strauss" had robbed the world of its "bloom," led him to seek for whatever Rose nature in some mysterious or paradoxical way might produce. . . . The idea that nature, dark and hostile as it may be, paradoxically creates the good and the beautiful is restated in *Billy Budd,* where the young hero is said to embody natural goodness and beauty, a flower of nature, which paradoxically also produces a Claggart. As a social symbol Billy Budd has close affinities with the "natural man" or "noble savage," an idea celebrated by the period in which the story takes place.

But if Billy Budd is natural goodness, he is also divine goodness. He is that peculiarly American god, the beatified boy. His career is like that of Christ; he is persecuted by a satanic Claggart and rebuffed and sacrificed by "citified man." With a loose similarity, Wellingborough Redburn had been persecuted by Jackson and rebuffed by Captain Riga. But Redburn is a creature acting in what Rolfe called "Circumstance" and "Time." At the overt levels of human tragedy, Billy Budd is not a definably human being. The moral content of his character is self-contradictory and obscure. Innocence, Mortmain had said in *Clarel,* is the act of the true heart reflecting upon evil. This is, perhaps, the only kind of innocence we want to take seriously or believe in.

Surely we are not more likely to be moved by *Billy Budd* as beatific vision than by *Billy Budd* as natural tragedy. Yet the story is strangely moving. Let us look below the clutter of its overt levels.

At the deep levels of *Billy Budd* there is a massive and terrible image, which, it seems to me, moved the aged Melville so overpoweringly that he was unable to give it direct expression. As Melville says at one point in *Billy Budd,* "every . . . form of life has its secret mines and dubious sides; the side popularly disclaimed." On the night before Billy Budd's execution, the ship, with its decks, is like the story itself. "The night was luminous on the spar-deck, but otherwise in the cavernous ones below—levels so very like the tiered galleries in a coal-mine."

The real theme of *Billy Budd* is castration and cannibalism, the ritual murder and eating of the Host. During his trial Billy proclaims his faithfulness to the king and to Captain Vere by saying, "I have eaten the King's bread, and I am true to the King." When, "without remorse," the dying Captain Vere murmurs, "Billy Budd, Billy Budd," he expresses faithfulness, dependence, and longing. He had eaten of the Host, and he was true to the Host. After forty years Melville had returned to the theme of *Typee.* In that book the young hero had extricated himself from the valley by a sudden exchange of passivity for action. Billy Budd is fatally passive, his acts of violence being unconsciously calculated to ensure his final submission. All of Billy's conscious acts are toward passivity, the first one being his quick acquiescence in his impressment, an act which causes the hero-worshiping sailors to regard him with "surprise" and "silent reproach." In symbolic language, Billy Budd is seeking his own castration—seeking to yield up his vitality to an authoritative but kindly father, whom he finds in Captain Vere. When anyone else stirs the depths of Billy's longing, threatening to bring his unconscious thoughts to consciousness, he flies into a sudden rage. When Red-Whiskers, a sailor who had once been a butcher, maliciously digs Billy in the ribs to show him "just whence a sirloin steak was cut," Billy gives him a "terrible drubbing." And when the minion of Claggart approaches Billy on the moonlit deck and, holding out two shining guineas, says, "See, they are yours, Bill," Billy Budd stammeringly threatens to toss him over the rail. The persistent feminine imagery Melville associates with Billy and his statement that "above all" there was "something in the mobile expression, and every chance attitude and movement suggestive of a mother eminently favored by Love and the Graces," indicate that Billy has identified himself with the mother at a pre-Oedipean level and has adopted the attitude of harmlessness and placation toward the father in order to avoid the hard struggle of the Oedipus conflict. The Oedipus conflict entails, of course, the idea of one's incestuous guilt and one's desire to kill one's father. The psychoanalyst might say that Billy Budd has avoided the Oedipus struggle by forming an attachment to the mother at the prephallic level of "oral eroticism" and has allayed his fears of castration by symbolically castrating himself (by being consciously submissive) and by repressing his rage and hostility against the father in order to placate him. That all Billy's rage and hostility against the father are unconscious is symbolized by the fact that whenever it is aroused it cannot find expression in spoken language. Billy can only stutter and use his fists. This is a mechanism for keeping himself from admitting his own guilt and his own destructiveness. For indeed Billy destroys not only Claggart but himself—and even Captain Vere. For a cloud seems to pass over Vere in his last days, and he dies without achieving the rewards his character had seemed to predestine him to achieve; he dies longing for a "child-man" he had once known.

The food symbolism need not be labored. It recurs frequently, and it is the symbolism which takes us down most swiftly into the coherent lower strata of the story, where there is "a subterranean fire . . . eating its way deeper and deeper." Melville even symbolizes moral qualities by their taste, the innocent character having an "untampered-with flavor like that of berries" as against the guilty character, which has the "questionable smack of a compounded wine." Frequently Billy Budd is compared with animals—a heifer, a horse, a dog, a nightingale, a goldfinch. When he is hanged, he ascends to the yardarm like a "singing-bird," watched from below by a "wedged mass of upturned faces"—as if the sailors were birds expecting to be fed. It is said of Billy Budd (the Lamb of God) that the serpent has never bitten him, but after the accusation Claggart is described as a snake.

The idea of Billy as Host is established early in the story. When the lieutenant of the *Indomitable* goes aboard the *Rights-of-Man* in search of new hands and immediately selects Billy Budd, he drinks some of the captain's grog almost as if conscious of performing a ritual. "Lieutenant," says the captain, "you are going to take my best man from me, the jewel of 'em." " 'Yes, I know,' rejoined the other, immediately drawing back the tumbler preliminary to a replenishing; 'yes, I know. Sorry.' " The captain, referring to the pacifying effect Billy has had on his troublesome sailors, then says, "A virtue went out of him, sugaring the sour ones. They took to him like hornets to treacle." Metaphors such as these evoke the primitive rite of slaughtering the young hero in order to eat his flesh and thus obtain his "virtue," his strength, or his heroic quality.

Later in the story Billy Budd spills his soup at mess, and Claggart, happening to pass by at the moment, is inwardly enraged, though outwardly he is only suavely and ambiguously satirical. Melville seems to feel that the enormous eruption of hostile emotion in Claggart may strike the reader as excessive and hence unbelievable. He therefore prefaces one of his comments on the spilled soup with a paragraph which says in effect that the most ordinary event may be a symbolic act which can arouse momentous passions:

> Passion, and passion in its profoundest, is not a thing demanding a palatial stage whereupon to play its part. Down among the groundlings, among the beggars and rakers of the garbage, profound passion is enacted. And the circumstances that provoke it, however trivial or mean, are no measure of its power.

The palatial stage is surely the conscious mind or the realm of conscious art, and the abode of beggars and rakers of the garbage is the unconscious mind. There are "beggars" in the unconscious mind, calling the ego back among the rakers of garbage, as Billy Budd calls his own ego back. And is not this whole passage intended as a statement that *Billy Budd* does not present the reader with a "palatial stage" where profoundest passions are enacted but that, instead, these passions are being enacted "down among the groundlings"? This comes close to telling us not only what is wrong with the story—simply that its profound passions do not find adequate objective representation—but also what is wrong with Billy Budd as tragic hero—that there is no "palatial stage" in his personality, no conscious structure, no mind whose disintegration we should watch with pity and terror rather than merely with bewilderment and an obscure sense of loss.

When Claggart spies the spilled soup, it seemed to him "the sly escape of a spontaneous feeling on Billy's part more or less answering to the antipathy on his own." He feels that Billy has insulted him. But what is the nature of the insult? Presumably that, in spilling the soup, Billy has symbolically exposed himself to Claggart as the Host, the vessel from which issues "virtue." ("Handsomely done, my lad!" cries Claggart. "And handsome is as handsome did it, too!") The spilled soup has also exposed Claggart's guilt as an eater of the Host and, furthermore, Clag-

gart's fear of his own unconscious desire to be like Billy; for the psychological content of Claggart's desire to share Billy's innocence is his desire to be the passive Host.

Melville tells us that Claggart's jaw is heavy out of proportion with his otherwise delicately shaped face—Claggart's unconscious motives center upon orality. This occurs to us when, for example, he smiles at Billy Budd with an ambiguously "glittering dental satire." One of Claggart's "cunning corporals" is called Squeak, "so nicknamed by the sailors on account of his squeaky voice and sharp visage ferreting about the dark corners of the lower decks after interlopers, satirically suggesting to them the idea of a rat in a cellar." Squeak spies on Billy Budd and in this capacity is described as the "purveyor" who "feeds Claggart's passions."

I am sure that much of the sacramental symbolism in *Billy Budd* is conscious and intended. But some of it may be less conscious. One cannot be sure how much Melville means by pointing out that two other partisans of Claggart in compromising Billy Budd (two of Claggart's "messmates," they are called) are the Armourer and the Captain of the Hold; but it is a haunting idea that the Armourer represents Teeth and the Captain of the Hold represents Belly. Nor can one say what Thyestean implications there may be in the use of parts of the body in referring to Claggart, whose nickname is Jimmy Legs and whose official title is Master-at-Arms.

As the story concludes, the grim symbolism occurs more frequently and with more intensity. In the captain's cabin Claggart's "mesmeric glance," which Melville compares with "the hungry lurch of the torpedo fish," quickly determines Billy's fate. It is the overt threat of castration which always sets off the explosion of Billy's unconscious fears and resentments. There is a terrible upwelling of his passive emotions, as if in a last attempt to control their aggressive counterparts. Briefly Billy has the expression of "a condemned vestal priestess at the moment of her being buried alive, and in the first struggle against suffocation"—images which convey both the desire for, and the fear of, castration. But such emotions as these Billy cannot express consciously. He stutters, and strikes Claggart.

Describing the scene in which Vere informs Billy Budd of the sentence, Melville says, "there is no telling the sacrament." There is no telling; but the sacrament can be symbolized. Lying manacled on the deck during the night, Billy is like "a patch of discolored snow . . . lingering at some upland cave's black mouth." His terrible experiences are of the order that "devour our human tissues." The skeleton begins to show under Billy's cheek for the first time; he lies between two cannon as if "nipped in the vise of fate." After the hanging of this Lamb of God, after the chaplain has knelt down "on his marrow bones" to pray (as the ballad of "Billy in the Darbies" says), after the night has passed and it is full day, "the fleece of lowhanging vapor had vanished, licked up by the sun that late had so glorified it." The very patriarch of the universe feeds on Billy Budd.

The passage Melville calls a "Digression" is difficult and obscure; but I venture the following account. The purser and the surgeon discuss the absence of spasm in Billy's body. (They are at mess during this discussion: we are continually reminded in *Billy Budd* of the verbal kinship of "mess" with the ritual word "mass.") The purser is "a rather ruddy, rotund person, more accurate as an accountant than profound as a philosopher." The surgeon is "spare and tall" (the same words used to describe Claggart): he is caustic, austere, and something of an intellectual. The two men are opposite types. The purser is the unthinking human animal who kills, vicariously, in order to eat. He is the simple cannibal, as is indicated by his placid rotundity (his being like a purse) and by his crude belief that Billy controlled his spasm by "will power." The surgeon is, like Claggart, a lean, emotionally complex and ambivalent sadist: he is more interested in murder than in food, as may be symbolized by his hastily leaving the mess table to get back to a patient in the sick bay. Thus, this very horrifying passage is not really a digression: it is a brief scene which universalizes the theme of the story by presenting two opposite mythical types of man lingering, as it were, over the body.

As the body of Billy Budd, wrapped in canvas and weighted with cannon balls, slides over the rail, the sailors "who had just beheld the prodigy of repose in the form suspended in air" think of the same form "foundering in the deeps"—an image of the act of eating. Over the spot where Billy has sunk, gaunt sea birds wheel and scream; and though the birds are predictably moved by "mere animal greed for prey," the sight has a surprising effect on the sailors. "An uncertain movement began among them, in which some encroachment was made." It is a brief moment of potentially mutinous commotion, which we can understand by noticing that the captain and his officers are symbolically connected with the birds, a connection the sailors unconsciously make. Immediately after the hanging, there had been a similar murmurous impulse to mutiny among the sailors. But the ship's officers had acted quickly. Their authoritative voice was heard in the whistle of the boatswain and his mates, which was "shrill as the shriek of the sea-hawk," which "pierced the low ominous sound" and "dissipated" it, so that in a moment or two "the throng was thinned by one half."

In a man-of-war world, Melville is saying, law feeds on man, being only a translation into social forms of that "horrible vulturism of earth" of which he had spoken in *Moby-Dick.* And with a complex human vulturism Captain Vere feeds on Billy Budd. Notice the sexual-sacramental character of Vere's reaction to Billy's spontaneous "God bless Captain Vere." At these words, "Captain Vere, either through stoic self-control or a sort of momentary paralysis induced by emotional shock, stood erectly rigid as a musket in the ship-armor's rack." The sexual spasm does not occur in Billy Budd because Billy's vitality or "virtue" has been symbolically transferred to Vere. And yet the transference is ambiguous; paralysis and rigidity suggest death just as surely as erection and the potentiality of the musket suggest life. New vitality has been given to Vere as captain and exponent of martial law (Vere as "musket"), but as man and father he has been stricken.

The intimation of Melville's passages about Lord Nelson is that had Nelson been aboard the *Indomitable* instead of Vere (the two are inferentially compared on several occasions), all this might not have happened, or—and perhaps this is the central point—if it had happened, no subsequent cloud would have passed over Nelson, as it does over Vere. Nelson is the invulnerable and fully mature fa-

ther, a mythical hero standing behind Captain Vere, a less majestic figure. Nelson already has the qualities of Billy Budd, so that the ritual transference of vitality need not ruin him with its cruel ambiguities. Nelson has the heroic vitality of Billy Budd and the brilliance and audacity of the "jewel" among sailors; it is Nelson's fatherhood which allows him to make "ornate publication" of the very qualities, in sublimated form, which Billy Budd, in the form of infantile rage and hostility, represses. As Melville presents him, Nelson, the "Great Sailor," is the ultimate heroic possibility of the man-of-war world. But he is not of that order of hero represented by Jack Chase; Jack Chase symbolizes a culture beyond the boundaries of Nelson's world. Nelson would never leave his ship to take part in a republican revolution, as Jack Chase did. He is the mythical father whose very presence on board ship, as Melville says, is enough to forestall an incipient mutiny—the uprising, that is, of the sons against the father.

The imposing structure of personality Melville attributes to Nelson is beyond the reach of Captain Vere because Vere's moral stability is not proof against the uprising of the sons. In Claggart he sees his own hostility toward Billy Budd. (The relation of Vere to Claggart and Billy is the relation of a father to his sons, one of whom assumes the aggressive and hostile role of the father and the other of whom assumes the passive role of the mother.) In Billy Budd, Captain Vere sees his own imperfectly redeemed childhood. Vere, imposing and even heroic as he is, must repeatedly return to his own childhood to feed on it and to murder it. For him there is no other way of supporting, of nourishing, the structure of consciousness, order, authority, and legality which constitutes the man-of-war world. The man-of-war world destroys itself by feeding on its own vitality, as the vulture feeds upon Prometheus.

This is in itself a moving idea; and so is the implied identification of Billy Budd with Christ. But is there not still another source of the massive emotion which rests uneasily beneath the imperfect surface of *Billy Budd?* Consider the connections Melville makes between the captains and literature. Nelson's ship is "poetic"; it has "symmetry" and "grand lines." Of Nelson at Trafalgar, Melville writes:

> If under the presentiment of the most magnificent of all victories, to be crowned by his own glorious death, a sort of priestly motive led him to dress his person in the jewelled vouchers of his own shining deeds; if thus to have adorned himself for the altar and the sacrifice were indeed vainglory, then affection and fustian is each truly heroic line in the great epics and dramas, since in such lines the poet embodies in verse those exaltations of sentiment that a nature like Nelson, the opportunity being given, vitalizes into acts.

Homer is a kind of Nelson. They are the same mythical hero—great captains of the mind, the sea, and the man-of-war world. The author of *Moby-Dick* was such a captain.

Captain Vere "loved books." His name, "Vere," signifies (besides "man") "truth"; he is a speaker of the truth. Both his mien and his interests connect him with different kinds of literature than that associated with Nelson. He likes books "treating of actual men and events, no matter of what era." Such a man of truth is Herman Melville, who writes concerning *Billy Budd:* "The symmetry of form attainable in pure fiction cannot so readily be achieved in a narration essentially having less to do with fable than with fact. Truth uncompromisingly told will always have its ragged edges."

In *Typee,* Melville had already pictured himself as Billy Budd, the youth with the nameless malady who shrank with such inexplicable fear from the tattooing instrument, tipped with a shark's tooth, and who discovered that his elders—the fathers and the warriors of the tribe—were cannibals.

Lord Nelson is not on "the main road"; he is on "a by-path." The central autobiographical figure in *Billy Budd* is Captain Vere. The dark and moving image of the book is Melville as the devourer of his own childhood. An old man with sons of his own, Melville is overwhelmingly moved with pity for the passive, hermaphrodite youth, an image of himself, who must continuously be killed in the rite of the sacrament if books are to be written or the man-of-war world sustained—or indeed if life is to go on at all.

Surely, then—to recall the restrictions on *Billy Budd* which I tried to make in the first sections of this [essay]—I contradict myself. Billy Budd *is* a deep one and a man-trap (but if he is, he cannot be "innocent"!). His personality has extensive moral significance and psychological reality. He is highly effective, since he kills Claggart and even Captain Vere. And Captain Vere, not Billy Budd, is the tragic hero of the story.

It seems to me, however, that how one judges *Billy Budd* depends on what level of the story one is talking about. Potentially the story is one of the great tragedies of Western literature. But the upper level, the conscious structure, the "palatial stage" is far too uncreated, self-contradictory, and noncommittal to articulate the underlying images. At the explicit symbolic and dramatic levels of the story Melville draws back in awe from Billy Budd and can speak of him only by painful acts of will which in the very process of becoming articulate cut themselves off from the deepest sources of emotion and thus remain inexpressive. Billy Budd's stammering is Melville's own. When Billy Budd speaks articulately, he misrepresents his own deepest emotions. So does Melville. (pp. 261-77)

> *Richard Chase, in his* Herman Melville: A Critical Study, *The Macmillan Company, 1949, 305 p.*

Joseph Schiffman   (essay date 1950)

[*Schiffman is an American critic and educator specializing in American studies. In the following excerpt, he opposes earlier critical assertions that* Billy Budd *represents Melville's "testament of acceptance," stressing instead what he considers the ironic viewpoint of the narration.*]

The aged Melville, like the Dansker of *Billy Budd,* "never interferes in aught and never gives advice." Melville wrote *Billy Budd,* his last work, without interjecting moral pronouncements; for this reason the story is usually taken as Melville's "Testament of acceptance" [E. L. Grant Watson; see excerpt dated 1933], or, in the latest and most extended criticism, as Melville's "Recognition of necessity" [see F. Barron Freeman in Further Reading]. Most critics, by mistaking form for content, have missed the main im-

portance of *Billy Budd.* Actually, Melville's latest tale shows no radical change in his thought. Change lies in his style. *Billy Budd* is a tale of irony, penned by a writer who preferred allegory and satire to straight narrative, and who, late in life, turned to irony for his final attack upon evil. (p. 128)

Billy's last words, "God bless Captain Vere," have been taken by almost all critics to be Melville's last words, words of accommodation, resignation, his last whispered "acceptance" of the realities of life. Mumford, for example, says: "At last he [Melville] was reconciled . . . [he found] the ultimate peace of resignation. . . . As Melville's own end approached, he cried out with Billy Budd: God bless Captain Vere!" [See excerpt dated 1929 in *NCLC,* Vol. 3, pp. 340-45.]

The disillusioned of the world toasted Melville as a long-unclaimed member of their heartbroken family. Here indeed was a prize recruit—Melville, the rebel who had questioned "the inalienable right to property, the dogmas of democracy, the righteousness of imperialist wars and Christian missions . . . [who] dared to discuss in a voice louder than a whisper such horrific subjects as cannibalism, venereal disease and polygamy . . . " [Willard Thorpe, Introduction to *Herman Melville: Representative Selections* (1938)] had, in the ripe wisdom of old age, uttered "God bless Captain Vere," thereby accepting authority. A prize catch indeed, if it were really so!

E. L. Grant Watson tips his hat to the Melville of *Billy Budd:*

> Melville [he says] is no longer a rebel. It should be noted that Billy Budd has not, even under the severest provocation, any element of rebellion in him; he is too free a soul [this man with the rope around his neck] *to need a quality which is a virtue only in slaves.* . . . Billy Budd is marked by this *supreme quality of acceptance.* . . . [Melville's] philosophy in it has *grown* from that of rebellion to . . . acceptance. . . .

Watson's bias towards a philosophy of acceptance is clear; he searches in Melville for confirmation of his own dogma. (p. 129)

These critics, it seems to me, commit three basic mistakes in their attempt at divining Melville's final moments of thought in his story. First, they divorce *Billy Budd* from all of Melville's other works in the way that a man might search for roots in treetops. Second, they isolate Melville from the Gilded Age, the time in which Melville produced *Billy Budd.* Third, and most important, they accept at face value the words "God bless Captain Vere," forgetting that Melville is always something other than obvious. It is the purpose of this paper to examine Melville's final work along the lines suggested.

Little is known of Melville's last days, and this should be recognized as a handicap for those who wish to prove the theory of Melville's "acceptance" as well as for those who may hold contrasting views. But the few scraps that do remain of Melville's later life point to an unchanged Melville, the same Melville of *Moby-Dick* and *Pierre.* Mumford reports that in 1871 Melville studied Spinoza, marking a passage which read: " 'Happiness . . . consists in a man's being able to maintain his own being. . . . ' " Mumford goes on to observe significantly: "[This] described [Melville's] own effort. In a more fruitful age, his being would have been maintained in harmony with, not in opposition to, the community; but at all events his vital duty was to maintain it." This is an unchanged Melville. Another scrap of information, from a letter to a British fan, indicates Melville's critical frame of mind in 1885. To James Billson he wrote: "It must have occurred to you, as it has to me, that the further our civilization advances *upon its present lines,* so much the cheaper sort of thing does 'fame' become, especially of the literary sort."

These lines, written just three years before he began *Billy Budd,* sound remarkably like the Melville who more than thirty years before had said of Pierre: "The brightest success, now seemed intolerable to him, since he so plainly saw, that the brightest success could not be the sole offspring of Merit; but of Merit for the one thousandth part, and nine hundred and ninety-nine combining and dovetailing accidents for the rest. . . ."

Matthiessen, in discussing the aging Melville and his *Billy Budd,* significantly speaks of the effects of the Gilded Age on the thinking of American writers. He refers to John Jay Chapman's "protesting against the conservative legalistic dryness that characterized our educated class," and Henry Adams, who "knew that it [the educated class] tended too much towards the analytic mind, that it lacked juices" [see excerpt dated 1941]. Vere answers the description of an educated man characterized by legalistic dryness.

In almost all respects, *Billy Budd* is typically Melvillian. It is a sea story, Melville's favorite genre. It deals with rebellion. It has reference to reforms, in this case impressment. it is rich in historical background, and concerns ordinary seamen. All those features of *Billy Budd* bear the stamp of the youthful Melville.

In one important respect, however, *Billy Budd* is different from almost all of Melville's other stories. It is written with a cool, detached pen, a seemingly impartial pen. This odd development for Melville has had much to do with launching the "acceptance" theory.

In his preface to *Billy Budd,* Melville speaks of the impact of the French Revolution upon the British Navy, and passes both favorable and unfavorable judgment as to its effects. But, in speaking of the sailors and their conditions of life—Melville's strongest interest—he says:

> . . . it was something caught from the Revolutionary Spirit that at Spithead emboldened the man-of-war's men to rise against real abuses. . . . the Great Mutiny [later at Nore], though by Englishmen naturally deemed monstrous at the time, doubtless gave the first latent prompting to most important reforms in the British Navy.

Thus the scene is set, and though Melville uses a cool pen, he is the Melville of old; his heart still beats quickly for the men in the heat and sweat of the hold.

The main character of the piece, Billy Budd, is regarded judiciously by Melville. He is "at least in aspect" the "Handsome Sailor . . . a superior figure of [his] own class [accepting] the spontaneous homage of his shipmates . . . a nautical Murat" perhaps. He could be "Ashore . . . the champion; afloat the spokesman; on every suitable occasion always foremost." Billy Budd *could* be all these things, but he fails actually to become them. Physically he

is well suited for the role, but he is found wanting mentally. Unperceptive, in fear of authority, extremely naïve, suffering the tragic fault of a stammer in moments of stress, Billy Budd cannot qualify as a *spokesman.* Melville lets us know this early in the story, and keeps reminding us that "welkin-eyed" Billy is nicknamed "Baby Budd," and is "young and tender" with a "lingering adolescent expression." He is "a novice in the complexities of factious life," so simple-minded that when asked by an officer about his place of birth, he replies, "Please, Sir, I don't know. . . . But I have heard that I was found in a pretty silk-lined basket hanging one morning from the knocker of a good man's door in Bristol." Melville warns us that Billy Budd "is not presented as a conventional hero."

Melville regards Billy fondly, admiringly in many respects, but critically. He reminds us of Billy's limitations throughout the tale, so when Billy utters those famous words, "God bless Captain Vere," the reader should be qualified to evaluate those words in the mouth of the speaker.

Billy is an ironic figure, as is Captain Vere. Scholarly, retiring, ill at ease with people, "Starry" Vere is in command of a ship at war. Painfully aware of the evil in Claggart, and pronouncing Billy's killing of him the blow of an "angel," Vere nevertheless forces through the death sentence against Billy. A student of philosophy, he ironically rules out all inquiry into the motives for Billy's act and insists that he be tried for striking and killing a petty officer, an approach that can only result in Billy's hanging under the naval code. At heart a kind man, Vere, strange to say, makes possible the depraved Claggart's wish—the destruction of Billy. "God bless Captain Vere!" Is this not piercing irony? As innocent Billy utters these words, does not the reader gag? The injustice of Billy's hanging is heightened by his ironic blessing of the ironic Vere.

Herein lies the literary importance of the tale. The aged Melville had developed a new weapon in his lifelong fight against injustice. Charles R. Anderson put it very well [in his commentary to Schiffman upon reading this essay]:

> The earlier Melville would have railed against the "evil" of such a system [the hanging of Billy], and the "inhumanity" of Vere being willing to serve as a vehicle of it. . . . This is the wonder, the thing that makes *Billy Budd* significant, since Melville discovered so little along this line—that irony is a subtler and finer device for the fiction writer than headlong attack on social abuses.

Billy Budd gives us added proof of Melville's great capacity for growth as a writer. However, his development of a new tool had its ironic counterpart in Melville criticism; many critics mistook Melville's irony for a change in his thinking, rather than a richer development in his craft.

F. Barron Freeman, rejecting the "Testament of acceptance" theory, has substituted the "Recognition of necessity" theory. In an intensive study of the aged Melville's thought, Freeman finds "a calm acceptance of the necessity of earthly imperfection and original sin." In Billy, Freeman sees a "Christian hero" practicing resignation and achieving final, heavenly reward. To Freeman the "importance . . . in the tale of *Billy Budd* lies in the optimistic way in which it suggests an acceptance of Fate."

Thus it becomes clear that Freeman's "Recognition of necessity" theory is not greatly different from the older "Testament of acceptance" theory. In both cases the rebellious Melville ends his days "chastened and subdued." Gone are the mad tossings of the *Pequod,* moored are the homesick soliloquies of Starbuck, in ashes are the beautiful wild fires of the "hot old man," Ahab. The aged Melville became reconciled. . . . In finally approving "the religious concept of earthly imperfection and heavenly goodness" the old sea dog had found his comfortable niche at the ancestral hearth. But Melville's complex tale offers a quite different theme for analysis as well.

Freeman sees in "the calm description of Billy's ascension" Melville's considered judgment of "hope and triumph in death. . . . " Again, style, tone, and form are mistaken for content. For Billy's triumph is not personal; it is social, and so of this world.

As Billy stands on deck with the rope around his neck, "A meek shy light appeared in the East, where stretched a diaphanous fleece of white furrowed vapor. That light slowly waxed. . . . " About to die, Billy, who could not conceive of malice or ill will, offers his humble benediction to Vere. And here the main point of Melville's ironic tale is revealed. The sailors, brought on deck to witness the hanging, echo Billy's words. "Without volition as it were, as if indeed the ship's populace were the vehicles of some vocal current electric, with one voice from alow to aloft, came a resonant sympathetic echo—'God bless Captain Vere.'" But this is not intended for Vere, for: "yet at that instant Billy alone must have been in their hearts, even as he was in their eyes." The men blessed Billy, not Vere, with the words "God bless Captain Vere." Though hanged as a criminal, Billy is lovingly remembered for his martyrdom. The bluejackets keep track of the spar from which Billy was suspended. "Knowledge followed it from ship to dock-yard and again from dock-yard to ship, still pursuing it even when at last reduced to a mere dock-yard boom. To them a chip of it was as a piece of the Cross." Billy dies in helpless defeat only to become ironically reincarnated as a living symbol for all sailors.

And finally Billy is immortalized in a ballad composed by his shipmates. It is a tender ballad, mournful and affectionate, and sings of identification of all sailors with Billy.

> . . . Through the port comes the moon-shine astray!
> . . . But 'twill die in the dawning of Billy's last day.
> A jewel-block they'll make of me to-morrow,
> . . . Like the ear-drop I gave to Bristol Molly—
> . . . Sure, a messmate will reach me the last parting cup;
> . . . Heaven knows who will have the running of me up!
> . . . But Donald he has promised to stand by the plank;
> So I'll shake a friendly hand ere I sink.
> . . . Sentry, are you there?
> Just ease these darbies at the wrist,
> And roll me over fair.
> I am sleepy, and the oozy weeds about me twist.

Thus Billy becomes—under Melville's ironic pen—something he never intended becoming: a symbol to all bluejackets of their hardship and camaraderie. He stammered in life, but spoke clearly in death.

So ends Melville's last book, with the sailors singing "Billie in the Darbies," honoring him as one of their own. In this song Melville sings to bewildered Wellingsborough of *Redburn;* to Jack Chase, the Great Heart of *White-Jacket;* to Steelkilt of *Moby-Dick,* to all the breathing, bleeding characters he ever put on paper.

In *Billy Budd,* Melville presents a picture of depravity subduing virtue, but not silencing it. Billy is sacrificed, but his ballad-singing mates seize upon this as a symbol of their lives. They never accepted natural depravity as victor, and they lived to see the end of impressment.

Melville knew that. He wrote the story of mutinies in the British Navy almost a full century after they took place. He had the tremendous advantage of historical perspective, a fact almost all critics have overlooked. By 1888 one could correctly evaluate the events of 1797. Melville could appreciate the legacy of the impressed Billy Budds and their mates: "the Great Mutiny, though by Englishmen naturally deemed monstrous at the time, doubtless gave the first latent prompting to most important reforms in the British Navy."

Billy Budd, forcibly removed from the ship *Rights-of-Man,* helped bring the rights of man to the seamen of His Majesty's Navy. His shipmates aboard H.M.S. *Indomitable* made this possible, along with the generations of seafaring men who followed. (pp. 130-36)

> *Joseph Schiffman, "Melville's Final Stage, Irony: A Re-Examination of 'Billy Budd' Criticism," in* American Literature, *Vol. 22, No. 2, May, 1950, pp. 128-36.*

Norman Holmes Pearson   (essay date 1951)

[*An American critic and educator, Pearson wrote extensively on nineteenth-century American literature. In the following excerpt, he discusses Melville's use of biblical allegory in* Billy Budd, *paralleling the work's treatment of biblical subjects with that in John Milton's epic poetry.*]

[Just] as behind the history of whaling in *Moby-Dick* were the "linked analogies" of the Old Testament and Shakespeare, so behind the historical data of *Billy Budd* was a similar use of the New Testament and Milton. The effect in both cases was to broaden the implication by calling upon associations. In the *"ego non baptizo te in nomine patris"* of the earlier book, which in terms of the added *"sed in nomine diaboli"* Melville called its secret motto, there was no place for the Son or the Holy Ghost when Ahab renounced the Father for the Devil. In *Billy Budd,* the Son finds his place in the scheme of things for man. In a very recent book, *Milton and Melville* [see Further Reading], Mr. Henry F. Pommer has shown a good deal of the Miltonic influence throughout all of Melville's work. In her book *Melville's Use of the Bible* [see Further Reading], Miss Nathalia Wright has done the same for the influence of the Testaments. But each book is in its way somewhat exclusive. . . . What Melville was doing was to try to give in as universalized a way as possible, not simply a discussion of the mutiny in which his cousin had been so unhappily involved, nor simply a conflict between good and evil in the world, but another redaction of the myth which had concerned Milton himself in the trilogy of his three major works. Though certainly not planned as a trilogy from the start, Milton's chief poems do nevertheless take up complementary questions which only their totality answers in full. It is on these terms that we may look at *Paradise Lost,* concerned with man's fall after a state of innocence, as though it were necessarily followed by a second part in *Paradise Regained,* where we have the pattern of man's redemption through the example of Christ; and in turn, though out of chronological Biblical sequence, by a third, *Samson Agonistes,* in which one man's redemption is at last achieved.

Thus when we read in **Billy Budd** of the relationship between Billy, Claggart, and Vere, we are given a situation analogous to, and dependent upon, Milton's poetry and the Bible which stood behind it. This is Melville's use of the earth as the shadow of Heaven. What must be remembered is that there is only a shadow, and that Melville establishes momentary resemblances rather than complete identities. Thus Billy may without conflict be like prelapsarian Adam; like Christ who took the fallen Adam's place to carry out the obedience Adam denied; and like Isaac in relation to Abraham. But Billy never loses his identity as a sailor. Claggart may be like Satan, the Arch-Enemy who would attempt to rule the earth after his own fall and man's, and yet retain his character as master-at-arms of the *Indomitable.* Vere, too, may bear the same relationship of ultimate command to an Adam-Christ and to a Satan, who was his renegade chevalier, that a captain of a man-of-war does to his men, in an analogy of captaincy to the authority of God which is without the blasphemous assumption of Godhead. These are simply shifting similitudes, which reënforce but do not tie down.

Melville openly contrives the *mystique* of innocence in the person of Billy Budd as pre-lapsarian Adam. Few readers have ignored it. The very name of Budd is by definition an undeveloped shoot or stem, a person or thing not yet mature. In appearance he is "welkin-eyed," as Milton's Adam has an "eye sublime." Billy is, as the captain of the merchantmen says, "my best man," "the jewel of 'em," as Milton's Adam is the "goodliest." Billy and Adam are both paragons of appearance. But Melville is also forthright. "By his original constitution," Melville says, "aided by the coöperating influences of his lot, Billy in many respects, was little more than a sort of upright barbarian, much such perhaps as Adam presumably might have been ere the urbane Serpent wriggled himself into his company." Of his beginning, Billy did not know. He was Adamic and original, seeming to contain his family in himself. His situation is, as Melville puts it, that of "one to whom not as yet had been proffered the questionable apple of knowledge."

But man had eaten the apple long before Billy's time, and Billy was an anomaly. The idea of Adam remained chiefly as an example of what had been lost, and of events which should not have occurred. His place was taken by Christ. . . . "Who was your father?" the young Budd was asked. His ambiguous answer may be read in either of two ways, according to stress: "God *knows,* Sir"; (in mild expletive) or "*God* knows, Sir" (in certification). Though Billy's hands were yellowed by the tar-bucket, as Christ's might have been calloused by carpentry, yet in both was "something suggestive of a mother eminently favored by Love and the Graces; all this strangely indicated a lineage

in direct contradiction to his lot." "Noble descent was as evident in him as in a blood horse." Something has been added to the analogy of Billy Budd to the Jack Chase of **White-Jacket.** In answer to the query of the drumhead court-martial, Billy Budd's answer comes clear: "I have eaten the King's bread and I am true to the King." What sort of loyalty is involved? Above the Prince of Peace stands the King of Kings, as above the sailor who is also a "peacemaker" is the British monarch who rules by divine right. "I have taken communion and remain loyal to God" lurks as a paraphrase of Billy's patriotism. It is as though he recognized in the word "patriotism" the possibilities of the highest connotations of a Fatherland. Through Billy also, as through Christ, is made possible a

> Recover'd Paradise to all mankind,
> By one mans firm obedience fully tri'd
> Through all temptation, and the Tempter foil'd.
> In all his wiles, defeated and repuls't. . . .
> *[Paradise Regained]*

The Tempter for Christ, in *Paradise Regained,* was Satan; and for Billy Budd it was the master-at-arms. In Claggart's character the prototype of Bland was extended to cover the "pale ire, envy and despair" of Satan at the moment when he approached the Garden of Eden for the temptation of man. The occasion of the quotation from Milton which Melville used as epigraph to the description of Claggart was extended to the prolonged temptation of Christ in the wilderness which Milton described in *Paradise Regained.* It was Satan who, among other lures, tempted Christ to join in revolt against the Eternal King by the promise of wealth. Claggart through an intermediary tried Billy with two guineas. "We are not the only impressed ones, Billy," the whisper came. "There's a gang of us.—Couldn't you—help—at a pinch?" Our knowledge of the involvement of **Billy Budd** with Milton supplies the implied answer Billy could not give in stuttering his angry denial. It was Christ's retort to a similar temptation:

> Yet he who reigns within himself, and rules
> Passions, Desires, and Fears, is more a King;
> Which every wise and vertuous man attains:
> And who attains not, ill aspires to rule
> Cities of men, or head-strong Multitudes,
> Subject himself to Anarchy within,
> Or lawless passions in him which he serves. . . .
> Riches are needless then, both for themselves,
> And for thy reason why should they be sought,
> To gain a Scepter, oftest better miss't.
> *[Paradise Regained]*

It was Billy who struck the blow to the head that felled Claggart after the latter's false accusation of conspiracy in mutiny. Here in the accusation we have another of the analogies. When the temptation of the guineas is withstood, Miss Wright points out among her many Biblical parallelisms, "Claggart falsely charges that Billy is disloyal to the king. Only in this way, by treachery, can evil reach good. So Jesus was betrayed by Judas after he had resisted the temptations of Satan in the wilderness, and above him on the cross was hung the same charge, treason." So also is another distinct analogy when Vere exclaims over the dead body of Claggart: "It is the divine judgment of Ananias! . . . Struck dead by an angel of God." But Melville has not forgotten the resemblance to Milton's Satan, in describing Claggart as one, the touch of whose corpse was "like handling a dead snake." This blow at the head, this "capital wound," is the future consequence several times referred to in *Paradise Lost,* and again when Satan spoke in the opening lines of *Paradise Regained* to his cohorts:

> well ye know
> How many Ages, as the years of men,
> This Universe we have possest, and rul'd
> In manner at our will th' affairs of Earth,
> Since Adam and his facil consort Eve
> Lost Paradise deceiv'd by me, though
> Since with dread attending when that fatal wound
> Shall be inflicted by the Seed of Eve
> Upon my head, . . .

But Billy is again like Christ when he will not defend himself before the judges, and is like Christ alone with God in Gethsemane when he has his moment with Vere in the cabin. So at the hanging, which inevitably reminds us of the Crucifixion, it is because of the cumulative analogies that we think beyond Billy Budd and his captain when we hear Billy's clear, unstuttered cry: "God bless Captain Vere." "Father, into thy hands I commend my spirit" is contained in it and echoes from it when "at the same moment it chanced that the vapory fleece hanging low in the East, was shot through with a soft glory as of the fleece of the Lamb of God seen in mystical vision and simultaneously therewith, watched by the wedged mass of upturned faces, Billy ascended; and ascending, took the full rose of the dawn." It is as though . . . the analogy of Abraham and Isaac, and God's pledge to Abraham, had fleetingly returned. We are brought back again, but without the loss of anything, to the realm of man where Billy Budd was a sailor, and Vere his commanding officer, on board a man-of-war whose interwoven cordage showed the H. M. S. *Indomitable* to be in the service of his Britannic Majesty as well as of the King of Kings. (pp. 106-11)

The story of the world which Melville tells in **Billy Budd** is the history of the future of man which Michael outlines to Adam in the final book of *Paradise Lost* and which serves as a kind of gloss to Melville's book. Mutiny as the ubiquitous metaphor in **Billy Budd** follows the archetypal pattern for fallen man established initially by the "rash revolt" of the angels against their King, and repeated by Adam and his consort. For this reason the Mosaic Code had been established, and for the same cause the stringent Articles of War prevailed. As Michael put it:

> therefore was Law given them to evince
> Thir natural pravitie, by stirring up
> Sin against Law to fight; . . .
> So law appears imperfect, and but giv'n
> With purpose to resign them in full time
> Up to a better Cov'nant, disciplin'd
> From shadowie Types to Truth, from Flesh to Spirit,
> From imposition of strict Laws, to free
> Acceptance of large Grace, from servil fear
> To filial, works of Law to works of Faith.
>   [*Paradise Lost*]

The test for the man who would stand upright again, as Billy stood and as Vere was to stand at Billy's execution, was in terms of law and of obedience. There was nothing for Billy to say in the end, but only to act obediently. His was the heroic example of innocence. His rôle was like that of Christ who had taken the fallen Adam's place.

The Honorable Edward Fairfax Vere was man as well as captain. He was *vir* ["man"], as Richard Chase suggests [see excerpt dated 1949], as well as *veritas* ["truth"]. Unlike Billy, the apple of knowledge had been tasted by his lineage. His testing was of a different sort from Billy's, and of a kind closer to our own. Vere knew obedience, and for him reason was what Michael called "right Reason." Against this was the temptation of an allegiance to the heart and to the instincts, as Adam had bitten the fruit for love of Eve. To the original metaphor, Vere gives a new analogy as he reasons with the drumhead court to be firm.

> But the exceptional in the matter moves the heart within you. Even so too is mine moved. But let not warm hearts betray heads that should be cool. Ashore in a criminal case will an upright judge allow himself off the bench to be waylaid by some tender kinswoman of the accused seeking to touch him with her tearful plea? Well the heart sometimes the feminine in man, here is that piteous woman. And hard though it be, she must be ruled out.

This is the temptation which Eve represented, redacted upon the otherwise womanless *Indomitable.* This is the victory which the first Adam had not won. It is Vere alongside Billy. As Vere had paced his cabin before addressing the jury, he was "without knowing it symbolizing thus in his action a mind resolute to surmount difficulties even if against primitive instincts strong as the wind and the sea." It was as though he rejected the pattern of Ahab who had acted only on instinct, and had swept aside our sympathy for a primitivism which could no longer be based on innocence. Vere, as captain, was his majesty's responsible deputy in a world of fallen man.

As such Vere lived, doing with obedience all that should be done. Should he not then, this model of post-lapsarian man, have been rewarded with long years of life and an admiralcy? "On the return passage to the English fleet," Melville wrote,

> from the detached cruise during which occurred the events already recorded, the *Indomitable* fell in with the *Athéiste.* An engagement ensued; during which Captain Vere, in the act of putting his ship alongside the enemy with a view of throwing his boarders across the bulwarks, was hit by a musketball from a port-hole of the enemy's main cabin.

He died, but as he died

> he was heard to murmur words inexplicable to his attendant—"Billy Budd, Billy Budd." That these were not the accents of remorse, would seem clear from what the attendant said to the *Indomitable's* senior officer of marines. . . .

That Melville's third principal character in the story should have died with Billy's name on his lips, is as important to understand as the significance of mutiny or Vere's surmountal of temptation. For on it depends the ultimate tone of the book, without which there could be no final definition. Billy Budd's death may seem to indicate how hard is the path of the beatitudes when followed in life. His story summarized in "an authorized weekly publication" meant nothing but the malformation of episodes which comes with time, and especially for those "whose reading was mainly confined to the journals." For the common sailors the yarn was woven into a popular ballad, and for a time the spar from which he was hanged was divided into chips like pieces of the Cross. "They recalled the fresh young image of the Handsome Sailor, that face never deformed by a sneer or subtler vile freak of the heart within!" The event was within their experience, and they understood it the better for that. Theirs was the final average reaction, as Billy's example drifted into time. The example might help, but actually they would need the "peacemaker" again in the midst, whether on board the merchantman or the man-of-war. Certainly they would still require captaincy like Vere's. (pp. 111-13)

Vere is like a Samson Agonistes, who, having conquered the temptation of the senses and remained true to the will and reason, is redeemed. But unlike Samson, Vere is not given the destruction of the French to serve as substitute for the tumbled temple. Yet Vere, though his ambitions were not satisfied, and the spirit of mutiny would appear again, was not without his consolation. As post-lapsarian man, Vere has learned how to die, in his case by the example of a common sailor who was like a common carpenter. As the true Christian knows how to die in adversity with the peace which the name of Jesus brings to the lips, so "Billy Budd" is to Vere what "God bless Captain Vere" was to Budd. They were "not the words of remorse." Both to Billy Budd, and to Vere by Budd's example, is that joy and success of true captaincy of which Father Mapple [in *Moby-Dick*] had spoken to Ishmael and to us. "Delight— top-gallant delight is to him who acknowledges no law or lord but the Lord his God, and is only a patriot to heaven." Now, though the King of Kings was known chiefly by his rod, is that which Ahab never found through his disobedience and renunciation of true reason for the temptation of the instincts. There was no top-gallant delight for him, as there was for the captain of an *Indomitable* or for a Billy Budd who was in every sense a true foretopgallant-man. (p. 113)

> *Norman Holmes Pearson, "Billy Budd: 'The King's Yarn',' in* American Quarterly, *Vol. III, No. 2, Summer, 1951, pp. 99-114.*

Wendell Glick　(essay date 1953)

[*An American critic and educator, Glick specializes in nineteenth-century American literature, particularly the works of Henry David Thoreau. In the following excerpt, he examines the conflict between social expediency and absolute morality in* Billy Budd, *noting the significance of the narrator's digression on British admiral Horatio Nelson.*]

"Resolve as one may to keep to the main road," Melville wrote in *Billy Budd,* "some bypaths have an enticement not readily to be withstood. Beckoned by the genius of Nelson, knowingly, I am going to err in such a bypath." With these words of caution to the reader who might object to the "literary sin" of digression, the author of *Moby-Dick* launched into a spirited encomium upon the heroism of Lord Nelson, defending the Admiral against any "martial utilitarians" and "Benthamites of war" who might interpret his acts of "bravado" at Trafalgar which had resulted in his death to have been foolhardy and vain. For what reason, the question arises, did Melville feel that the eulogy on Nelson could justifiably be included in *Billy Budd?* What is the meaning of the attack upon Benthamites and utilitarians? This was no pot-boiler which required padding; surely his inclusion of the highly emotion-al defense of Nelson is significant for other reasons than that the chapter makes "more understandable Melville's hearty interest in martial exploits, sayings, and songs" [see Freeman entry in Further Reading].

At the time Melville was writing and revising *Billy Budd* he was in no mood to trifle with peccadilloes. "My vigor sensibly declines," he had written to Archibald MacMechan on 5 December 1889: "What little of it is left I husband for certain matters yet incomplete, and which indeed, may never be completed." He could hardly have been husbanding his strength to communicate his "hearty interest in martial exploits"; his digression away from his narrative in order to praise Nelson must have served in his mind the more serious purpose of clarifying one of the "truths" for which, as he pointed out, *Billy Budd* was but the vehicle. . . . Although it is much more, *Billy Budd* is the cogent fruition of a lifetime of observation and study of the eternal conflict between absolute morality and social expediency; and the digression on Nelson, though it intrudes upon the plot, is central to an understanding of Melville's final resolution of this crucial problem.

In writing *Billy Budd,* Melville made clear at the outset of his novel, he was writing no "romance"; he would not be bound, consequently, in his delineation of the "Handsome Sailor," by any of the conventions usually followed in depicting a romantic hero. Nor would he be bound to refrain from digressing if digression served his purposes. His interest was less in art than in "Truth uncompromisingly told." He was quite willing, he asserted, to sacrifice "the symmetry of form attainable in pure fiction" and to risk "ragged edges" on his final work if by so doing he could tell a story "having less to do with fable than with fact." Thus relieved both from the conventional restrictions usually imposed by art and from the financial exigencies which had dictated the content of some of his early works, he would be free to deal forthrightly and honestly with issues far too serious to be treated cavalierly.

For his *raisonneur* Melville chose Captain "Starry" Vere, a clearheaded realist possessed of sufficient perspective as a result of broad human experience and extensive reading to enable him to weigh the most difficult alternatives and choose rationally between them. No person with lesser qualifications would serve. For the choice which Captain Vere had to make involved more than a simple distinction between blacks and whites; instead it was a choice between two standards of human behavior, to each of which man owed unquestioning loyalty. The Captain's decision, moreover, was to be Melville's as well; and Melville felt no disposition in the waning years of his life to trifle with reality and call the process truth-seeking.

Melville sympathized with Billy Budd as completely as did Captain Vere. He appreciated with the Captain the stark injustice of a situation which finds the individual condemned for adherence to a standard of behavior most men would consider noble and right. But he agreed with the Captain that justice to the individual is not the ultimate loyalty in a complex culture; the stability of the culture has the higher claim, and when the two conflict, justice to the individual must be abrogated to keep the order of society intact. Turning their backs upon one of the most cherished systems of ideas in the American tradition, a system typified by such individualists as Thoreau and Emerson, Melville and Captain Vere brought in the verdict that the claims of civilized society may upon occasion constitute a higher ethic than the claims of "natural law" and personal justice. The ultimate allegiance of the individual, in other words, is not to an absolute moral code, interpreted by his conscience and enlivened by his human sympathies, but to the utilitarian principle of social expediency.

To isolate his problem, to strip it of all irrelevant issues preparatory to making a critical examination of it, Melville chose as his setting a British vessel at sea. The ship-of-the-line *Indomitable,* a smooth-functioning microcosm of society as a whole, was threatened with mutiny. Though the threat was remote, whatever would contribute to the end of knitting together the diverse individuals who made up the crew into a homogeneous unit which would act efficiently in an emergency was fully justified; conversely, that which jeopardized even slightly the clock-like functioning of the crew it was necessary to stamp out ruthlessly. His highest obligation, as Captain Vere conceived it, was the preservation of the tight little society into which the crew had been welded, and the prevention of anything resembling anarchy. The transcendent responsibility of the leaders of the English nation, moreover, was the same as his own, writ large. An intensive study of history had confirmed his "settled convictions" against "novel opinion, social, political, and otherwise, which carried away as in a torrent no few minds in those days"; and he was "incensed at the innovators," not because their theories were inimical to the private interests of the privileged classes of which he was a member, but because such theories "seemed to him incapable of embodiment in lasting institutions," and "at war with the peace of the world and the good of mankind." The world as he viewed it was ruled by "forms"; "with mankind," Melville quotes him as saying, "forms, measured forms, are everything"; that was the import which he saw "in the story of Orpheus, with his lyre, spellbinding the wild denizens of the woods." To preserve the ordered functioning of his crew Captain Vere was willing to sacrifice even the ideal of justice when the absolute necessity arose. What he objected to in Claggart was not that Claggart was remiss in his "duty of perserving order" but that the Master at Arms abridged the ideal of justice unnecessarily, even when the autonomy and general good of the crew were not at stake. Still, the maintenance of order came first, and it was rigorously safeguarded on the *Indomitable* "almost to a degree inconsistent with entire moral volition."

To the idea that order in society should be maintained at all cost Captain Vere adhered "disinterestedly," not because he desired such a regimented society, but because he believed it to be a practical necessity of this world. Like Plotinus Plinlimmon of *Pierre,* he preferred Christian ("Chronometrical") standards of absolute morality to the more mundane, utilitarian standard of expediency; but like Plinlimmon, he had concluded that Christian ideals were unworkable in everyday situations. He was fully aware that a regimented society abridged many private rights, but he realized also that in the absence of such a society a state of anarchy and chaos inevitably arose in which every human right was sacrificed. An ordered society at least guaranteed the preservation of *some* rights; and though this fell short of the ideal of the preservation of *all,* it was far better than the sort of "society" which, in the idealistic attempt to guarantee all rights, degenerated into chaos and so permitted their complete and total destruction. It was not a question of insuring all individual rights or a part of them; the choice was between insuring a part of them or none. The ideal society which abridged no prerogatives and guaranteed all private liberties was, in the considered opinion of Captain Vere, a figment of the imagination.

Recent events, Melville makes abundantly plain, had been responsible for the Captain's position. The Nore Mutiny, though it had been precipitated by the failure of the authorities to redress the legitimate grievances of the seamen, had threatened the military usefulness of the "indispensable fleet" upon which the stability of the entire English nation depended, and consequently had been ruthlessly suppressed. The cataclysmic French Revolution had taught its bitter lesson, both to Captain Vere and to his creator. To the Captain the principle involved in the two events was the same: the English sailors at Nore, in running up "the British colors with the union and cross wiped out," had transmuted "the flag of founded law and freedom defined" into "the red meteor of unbridled and unbounded revolt" of the French. "Reasonable discontent," Melville pointed out, "growing out of practical grievances in the fleet had been ignited into irrational combustion as by live cinders blown across the Channel from France in flames." No price was too great to pay to keep such unhinging forces of anarchy in check; in giving his life to destroy the *Athéiste,* Captain Vere sacrificed himself in defense of the *sine qua non* of civilized existence and in opposition to the false, unworkable doctrines of the French Revolution. The triumph of the *Indomitable* over the *Athéiste* was the triumph of order over chaos.

Yet how staggering was the cost of a stable society! Having decided upon the absolute necessity for maintaining unweakened the strength of the social fabric, Melville shuddered when he contemplated the price exacted in terms of human values; and *Billy Budd* became the balance-sheet upon which he reckoned the price men have to pay for the ordered society which they have to have. The most obvious price was the destruction of "Nature's Nobleman," the superlatively innocent person: every Billy Budd impressed by an *Indomitable* is forced to leave his *Rights-of-Man* behind. To the destruction of innocent persons, moreover, it was necessary to add the mental suffering of the individual forced to make moral judgments. But the total cost is not met even by the sacrifice of Billy Budds and the suffering of Captain Veres; social stability based upon expediency is paid for also with a general, blighting, human mediocrity. The standards of any civilized society are the standards of the great mass of men who make up its bulk; and when maintenance of the stability of society becomes the supreme obligation of every person, the result is a levelling of the superior persons down to the level of the mass. The chief personal virtue becomes "prudence"; the end most worth seeking for becomes "that manufacturable thing known as respectability," so often allied with "moral obliquities," and occasionally, as in the case of Claggart, indistinguishable even from "natural depravity." "Civilization," Melville remarks categorically, "especially of the austerer sort, is auspicious" to natural depravity because natural depravity "folds itself in the mantle of respectability" by avoiding "vices or small sins" and by refraining from all excesses; in short, by exhibiting the prudence which is the only virtue society demands. The natural depravity of Claggart was so insidious because it lacked the trappings in which society expects to see evil garbed, and instead, prudently enfolded itself in "the mantle of respectability." Prudence, while being the mark of the socially adjusted man who rigidly adheres to the utilitarian principle of expediency, may also be the last refuge of scoundrels.

But even when prudence did not take the extreme form of moral obliquity, even when it was not "habitual with the subtler depravity," as it proved to be in the case of Claggart, it left its mark upon the people in the world of Billy Budd. The most "prudent" characters discharged faithfully their "duty" to their king even when to do so clashed with moral scruple, but they fell far short of the personal heroism which inspires others and vitalizes them into acts. Captain Graveling of the *Rights-of-Man* was "the sort of person whom everybody agrees in calling 'a respectable man' "; he was a lover of "peace and quiet" and the possessor of "much prudence" which caused "overmuch disquietude in him," but he was by and large a pedestrian individual who could hardly be depended upon to make any signal contribution to human progress. The old ascetic Dansker had learned from experience a "bitter prudence" which had taught him never to interfere, never to give advice, in other words, to solve the problem of his social responsibility by escaping into a shell of cynicism, and by so doing had disqualified himself for service to society. The *Indomitable's* "prudent surgeon" was singularly unequipped to pass moral judgments and would have "solved" the problem of Billy's murder of Claggart by dropping the whole affair into the lap of the Admiral. Even Captain Vere, who possessed in eminent measure the "two qualities not readily interfusable" demanded of every English sea-commander at the time "prudence and rigor," did not earn Melville's highest accolade as a member of

Portrait of Admiral Horatio Nelson.

"great Nature's nobler order" until he let himself "melt back into what remains primeval in our formalized humanity"; in short, until he forgot temporarily his "military duty," his prudence, and acted in a manner difficult to reconcile with strict social expediency.

To what do these examples of prudence, the highest ethic of utilitarian philosophers, add up? Simply this: in making social expediency an ethic superior to absolute morality, Melville found himself pushed perilously close to a *Weltanschauung* which would admit slight, if any, possibility of personal greatness. Could prudence ever be truly heroic? A society which elevated prudence above all other virtues seemed to be anathema to the sort of moral adventuresomeness which Melville loved, and which for him set the great man off from the mediocre one. Yet such a society seemed to be the only sort which could safeguard men from the perils of "irrational combustion" which followed hard upon an idealism permitted to run its free course unrestrained. Here lay a crucial dilemma: was the race doomed to accept mediocrity as the price of its self-preservation, or was it still possible in a complex society for great private virtues to generate and grow?

Emotionally unequipped to reconcile himself to the bleaker alternative toward which both his experience and his reason had led him, Melville turned to history in the hope of discovering a figure of heroic dimensions whose life would free him from his impasse. Having played the role of champion of man's dignity and greatness for a lifetime, he did not feel that he could relinquish it now; and in the person of Nelson, "the greatest sailor since the world began," he found his answer. Though he recognized that many changes had taken place since Trafalgar, that the "symmetry and grand lines" of Nelson's *Victory* seemed obsolete in a world of "*Monitors* and yet mightier hulls of the European ironsides," he nonetheless insisted that "to anybody who can hold the Present at its worth without being inappreciative of the Past," the "solitary old hulk at Portsmouth" spoke eloquent truth. If he could no longer embrace the simple faith of his youth when he had believed in a law "coeval with mankind, dictated by God himself, superior in obligation to any other," when he had advocated the abolition of flogging on the grounds that "it is not a dollar-and-cent question of expediency; it is a matter of *right and wrong*" [**White-Jacket**]; if the corrosive years had eaten away for him such immutable standards, he could at least salvage somehow a foundation for personal greatness and heroism. Nelson was the man he needed.

He admitted that strict "martial utilitarians," believers in the rigorous application of an inexorable social expediency to every particular situation, would be inclined to take issue with his estimate of Nelson's greatness, even perhaps "to the extent of iconoclasm." For Nelson's exposure of his own person in battle at Trafalgar appeared on the surface to have been militarily inexpedient, even vain and foolhardy; his value to the cause for which he fought was so great that he should have sacrificed his natural desire for personal heroism to the higher principle of preserving a life which was indispensable to the general good. Had his life been preserved and his command of the fleet therefore been retained, the mistakes made by his successor in command might have been avoided; and his sagacity might well have averted the shipwreck with its horrible loss of life which followed the battle. So the "Benthamites of war" argued, and, Melville admitted, with some plausibility; using only the immediate circumstances of the engagement as their criteria they could convict Nelson of behavior out of harmony with the general good, and on these grounds strip him of the glory with which Englishmen had invested him.

But to this sort of iconoclasm Melville would not accede for a moment. "Personal prudence," he countered, "even when dictated by quite other than selfish considerations, is surely no special virtue in a military man; while an excessive love of glory, exercising to the uttermost heartfelt sense of duty, is the first." The Benthamites were wrong; in applying their principle of social expediency to Nelson's deed "of foolhardiness and vanity" they failed to calculate the strength of purpose which such a "challenge to death" injects into the arteries of a nation. Nelson's deed was "expedient" to a degree they lacked the vision to perceive; his name had become a "trumpet to the blood" more stimulating even to the hearts of Englishmen than the name of Wellington; the act which on the surface seemed sheer "bravado" still inspired posterity to deeds of greatness.

Unless, Melville argued, Nelson's "challenge to death" could be considered an act of supreme heroism, conformable to the highest ideals governing human behavior, no deed could be truly heroic; and this possibility he refused to entertain. The vitality of Nelson's example was immortal. In 1891, shortly after he had made his own will, Melville composed this enthusiastic tribute to another great man who had also glimpsed a premonition that death was near:

> At Trafalgar, Nelson, on the brink of opening the fight, sat down and wrote his last brief will and testament. If under the presentiment of the most magnificent of all victories, to be crowned by his own glorious death, a sort of priestly motive led him to dress his person in the jewelled vouchers of his own shining deeds; if thus to have adorned himself for the altar and the sacrifice were indeed vainglory, then affectation and fustian is each truly heroic line in the great epics and dramas, since in such lines the poet but embodies in verse those exaltations of sentiment that a nature like Nelson, the opportunity being given, vitalizes into acts.

The question naturally arises whether Melville intended the digression on Nelson to illuminate the final scene of the novel. Might the answer be that the hanging of Billy Budd is Melville's final commentary upon the theme of the impracticability of absolute standards in a world necessarily ruled by expediency? Billy's noble devotion to absolute justice and right throughout the novel made him a sort of personification of the moral law; his death must have meant for Melville, consequently, that the standard of behavior to which Billy gave his allegiance, though a noble one, is simply unworkable when applied to complex social relationships. There was something unearthly about the death of Billy Budd: he was "an angel of God," returning without fear to his Maker; his pinioned figure at the yardend behaved like that of no mortal man; to the sailors aboard the *Indomitable* the spar from which Billy's body had hung was thought of for some years as a piece of the Cross. The luminous night of the morning when Billy was to be hanged passed away like the prophet Elijah disap-

pearing into heaven in his chariot and dropping his mantle to Elisha. Billy was too good for this world; he properly belonged to another, not to this; and the moral principles from which he acted were appropriate enough for the world to which he belonged. But in a society composed of men, not angels—in a society in which even Claggarts are to be found—an inferior standard, that of expediency, is the only workable one. (pp. 103-10)

> *Wendell Glick, "Expediency and Absolute Morality in 'Billy Budd'," in* PMLA, *Vol. LXVIII, No. 1, March, 1953, pp. 103-10.*

Phil Withim   (essay date 1959)

[*In the following excerpt, Withim expands on Joseph Schiffman's reading of* Billy Budd *as an ironic narrative (see excerpt dated 1950).*]

In 1950 Joseph Schiffman, in an article which reviewed [the major critical interpretations of *Billy Budd*], put forth a suggestion, which he credited to Gay Wilson Allen, "that *Billy Budd* might best be understood as a work of irony." Since this article appeared, a number of other critics have also objected to the "testament of acceptance" theory or have supported an ironic interpretation; sometimes they have done both.

This paper is another step in this same direction. It accepts the point of view that *Billy Budd* was written in a basically ironic style; it will attempt to establish a thesis in harmony with all of the parts of the story and to demonstrate that the "testament of acceptance" theory is essentially self-contradictory.

The body of the story is concerned with the relationships of three men: Billy Budd, John Claggart, and Captain Vere. Whatever arguments may rage concerning other elements of the story, there is general agreement as to the character and significance of Billy Budd and John Claggart. Billy Budd is the Handsome Sailor uniting "strength and beauty," whose moral nature is not "out of keeping with the physical make." Claggart is Billy's reverse. He is pale and unhealthy looking; his visage seems to hint of something defective or abnormal in the constitution and blood. This contrasts with the conjunction in Billy of beauty and goodness. Claggart had an "evil nature, not engendered by vicious training or corrupting books or licentious living, but born with him and innate, in short 'a depravity according to nature.' "

Melville is explicit about his desire to have Billy and Claggart taken as types of good and bad, and this, I think, is the chief argument against those who, like Matthiessen and Freeman, consider homosexualism an aspect of the problem. For if Melville had desired to hint at homosexualism, he would not have denied its possibility; when speaking of Claggart's peculiar nature, he says, "In short the depravity here meant partakes nothing of the sordid or sensual." And speaking of Billy, he says he was "preëminently the Handsome Sailor" who, as Melville has told us in the opening pages of the book, typifies strength united to beauty. In those descriptions of Billy emphasizing his delicate color and the fine detail of his features, the point is to impress us with his purity, his aristocratic heritage, not his femininity. Melville takes care to remind the reader that Billy had thrashed the bully, Red Whiskers.

But it is around the third figure, Captain Vere, that the greatest disagreement has arisen. This suggests that a detailed examination of his character and function is essential to any understanding of the novel. He is described as apparently the best type of British naval man:

> always acquitting himself as an officer mindful of the welfare of his men, but never tolerating an infraction of discipline; thoroughly versed in the science of his profession, and intrepid to the verge of temerity, though never injudiciously so.

He loves to read, particularly those books "treating of actual men and events no matter of what era—history, biography and unconventional writers, who, free from cant and convention, like Montaigne, honestly, and in the spirit of common sense philosophize upon realities." In the reading he found

> confirmation of his own more reserved thoughts— confirmation which he had vainly sought in social converse, so that as touching most fundamental topics, there had got to be established in him some positive convictions which he forefelt would abide in him essentially unmodified so long as his intelligent part remained unimpaired.

This particular sentence creates a question as to Melville's meaning. Does he suggest here that the only result of Vere's reading is that his mind becomes more and more firmly fixed on his earliest opinions, that no author can ever modify them, either because he will not let their ideas penetrate or because he never reads books that do not agree with him; or does Melville imply that Vere's opinions are instinctively right and that all the books in Vere's library, "compact, but of the best" agree with him unfailingly? But it is as yet too early to decide. Melville continues to describe Vere as one whose "settled convictions were as a dyke against those invading waters of novel opinion social political and otherwise" and as one who opposed these novel opinions because they seemed to him not only "incapable of embodiment in lasting institutions, but at war with the peace of the world and the true welfare of mankind." This last phrase sounds suspiciously like cant, like sarcasm. Vere's reasons here are such terribly stock arguments that it is hard to accept them at face value.

The possibility arises that the reader is expected to understand that Vere's reasoning is presented without comment because it is simply and transparently a rationalization of an uninformed and bigoted man who reads only those authors who reinforce his views. But if this possibility is to be accepted as fact, the reader must find other implied criticism of Vere, and, indeed, it does not take much searching. Melville, for example, goes to the trouble of devoting several pages to Nelson, the greatest of English captains, pointing out with approval that Nelson challenged death by his brilliant apparel.

> Personal prudence even when dictated by quite other than selfish consideration is surely no special virtue in a military man; while an excessive love of glory, impassioning a less burning impulse the honest sense of duty, is the first.

[In a footnote, Withim observes, "Wendell Glick, in his article 'Expediency and Absolute Morality in *Billy Budd*' (see excerpt dated 1953), devotes much attention to the Nelson episode, equating Nelson not with Vere but with Billy, and discovers both to be heroic. This may be true, although the differences in station, occasion, and motivation seem to be unsurmountable obstacles to such an interpretation. On the other hand, it seems natural to compare Nelson with Vere: both are captains of ships in time of war, both are asked to deal with mutiny. An additional difficulty with Glick's article lies in the fact that his defense is built on the following unsupported statement: '[Melville] agreed with the Captain that justice to the individual is not the ultimate loyalty in a complex culture; the stability of the culture has the higher claim, and when the two conflict, justice to the individual must be abrogated to keep the order of society intact.' Since this is exactly the point in question, so far as any interpretation of the meaning of *Billy Budd* is concerned, it seems facile to present it as axiomatic."] Nelson, of course, dies a soldier's death, while Vere dies drugged and ashore before ever reaching fame. Nelson is a fighter in direct contact with the enemy; but Vere, in the encounter described in *Billy Budd,* does not have an opportunity to catch the opposing ship. Vere is frequently used for diplomatic missions, the very opposite of a captain's usual job; Vere, says Melville, though a man of "sturdy qualities was without brilliant ones." Nelson is asked to take command of a ship recently involved in the Great Mutiny, for "it was thought that an officer like Nelson was the one, *not indeed to terrorize the crew into base subjection,* but to win them, by force of his mere presence back to an allegiance if not as enthusiastic as his own, yet as true" (italics mine). Vere, in a similar situation, hangs Billy, "thinking perhaps that under existing circumstances in the navy the consequence of violating discipline should be made to speak for itself."

It is clear that this comparison is not favorable to Captain Vere, and if we look back to earlier descriptions, we find that they apparently contain an implied criticism: "ever mindful of the welfare of his men, but never tolerating an infraction of discipline"; "intrepid to the verge of temerity, though never injudiciously so." The second half of each statement could merely qualify the virtue mentioned in the first half, or it could cancel the virtue completely.

After Claggart accuses Billy of projected mutiny, Vere decides to confront the two men with each other in his cabin. There Billy, infuriated by the charge, confused and frustrated by his stammer, strikes Claggart dead. Apparently Vere's purpose in bringing them together is to find out the truth. But how does he expect the interview to accomplish this? Claggart would have accused, and Billy would have denied. There seems to be no relevant reason for Vere's decision. Claggart had suggested that there was substantiating evidence not far away, but Vere had not sent for it, since he wished to keep the affair secret because he was afraid of the crew. In short, Vere's decision is based on the single element of prudence, and he ignores all other elements inherent in the situation. Now Claggart is dead. As Vere looks on, he cries, " 'Struck dead by an angel of God. Yet the Angel must hang.' " Vere must have acute perception, indeed, to see so quickly to the heart of so complex a situation. He realizes instantly that there is no alternative to Billy's death.

Vere calls a court-martial, reserving, however, "to himself as the one on whom the ultimate accountability would rest, the right of maintaining a supervision of it, or formally or informally interposing at need." During the trial the members of the court seem reluctant to hang Billy, and the Captain has to talk them into it. But it is hard to understand why Vere called the court at all. What purpose does it serve? Was it called to guide him to a right decision? But Vere had already made his decision. In any case the court did not guide him; he guided the court. Perhaps he thought the court would overrule him and free the boy. But Vere had reserved for himself the right of supervising and interfering at need. Apparently all Vere wants is to have on record a trial agreeing with his decision.

Vere begins his argument by saying that he would not interfere with their deliberations, but that he sees them at a crisis proceeding " 'from the clashing of military duty with moral scruple.' " He advises them to " 'strive against scruples that may tend to enervate decision.' " When the men look startled, he explains thus:

> "How can we adjudge to summary and shameful death a fellow-creature innocent before God, and whom we feel to be so?—Does that state it aright? You sign sad assent. Well, I too feel that, the full force of that. It is Nature. But do these buttons that we wear attest that our allegiance is to Nature? No, to the King."

This is the main basis of his argument: we do not serve nature but the king.

> "We fight at command. If our judgments approve the war, that is but coincidence. So in other particulars. . . . Would it be so much we ourselves that would condemn as it would be martial law operating through us? For that law and the rigor of it, we are not responsible. Our vowed responsibility is in this: That however pitilessly that law may operate, we nevertheless adhere to it and administer it."

The officer of marines points out that Budd "proposed neither mutiny nor homicide." Vere agrees with him, saying that, after all, " 'At the Last Assizes it shall acquit,' " but not now. " 'War looks but to the frontage, the appearance. And the Mutiny Act, War's child, takes after the father. Budd's intent or non-intent is nothing to the purpose.' "

No one at any time questions his argument. No one suggests that the king's law should be in harmony with nature's law, or that if there is disagreement between them, the allegiance must be to the higher and the more universal law of nature. No one asks Vere to support his peculiar thesis; it is merely slipped in, so to speak, with the analogy of the buttons: because the men wear the king's buttons, they are to violate natural laws. Even though Vere has admitted that the Mutiny Act looks only to frontage, to the appearance, no one suggests that the point of justice is to see through appearance to reality. But the reason that no one questions Vere's arguments is that no one understands them. "Loyal lieges, plain and practical . . . they were without the faculty, hardly had the inclination to gainsay one whom they felt to be an earnest man, one too not less their superior in mind than in naval rank."

Vere, however, soon gives them an argument they can understand, for when the junior lieutenant asks why, if they must convict, they cannot mitigate the sentence, Vere replies that they cannot because the crew " 'will ruminate. You know what sailors are. Will they not revert to the re-

cent outbreak at the Nore. . . . Your clement sentence they would account pusillanimous. They would think that we flinch, that we are afraid of them.' " And this is the only argument the court really understands, for, as Melville says, "it is not improbable that even such of his words as were not without influence over them, less came home to them than his closing appeal to their instincts as sea-officers. . . . " So for all the finely spun thought, the issue is decided by fear. When subtle arguments fail, Vere calls on, not a rational argument, but an emotional one: an appeal to fear.

Another clue to Vere's thinking comes after Billy has been hanged. The men are put to work at various tasks; they are swept into the routine as fast as possible. Melville writes of this:

> "With mankind" he would say "forms, measured forms are everything; and that is the import couched in the story of Orpheus with his lyre spellbinding the wild denizens of the woods." And this [Vere] once applied to the disruption of forms going on across the Channel and the consequences thereof.

Stripped of verbiage, Vere is saying that men cannot think for themselves, that form and habit can control men as if they were no more than beasts. Vere, in an earlier passage, had thought to himself that Billy was a " 'King's bargain,' that is to say, for His Britannic Majesty's navy a capital investment at small outlay or none at all." In this light, Vere, far from being a wise man, balanced in his judgments and fair in his attitudes, is discovered to be narrow, literal, prejudiced, completely circumscribed by the needs of the navy, less compassionate than his officers, and lastly, guilty of that worst of naval sins, over-prudence.

The core of Vere's argument is that we must bow to necessity; " 'For that law and the rigor of it, we are not responsible. Our vowed responsibility is in this: That however pitilessly that law may operate, we nevertheless adhere to it and administer it.' " A logical extension of this argument is that man should abdicate responsibility for unjust law and enforce it mechanically. Man should not try to change that which is wrong, but merely accept injustice and tyranny and lie supinely beneath them; man is to stand by and watch the innocent as indiscriminately ground under the heel of unresisted law as are the evil.

Melville makes his opposition to this view clear by dedicating the book to Jack Chase, his companion years before on the frigate *United States.* It was this voyage that became the story of **White-Jacket,** the novel that cried out so eloquently against impressment, flogging, the captain's tyranny. Jack Chase is here mentioned by name and is referred to as "a stickler for the Rights of Man and the liberties of the world." It would be ironic indeed to dedicate **Billy Budd** to such a man if the novel was devoted to submission. However, the preface helps to make clear the direction of the book. In it, Melville speaks of the French Revolution as an expression of "the Spirit of that Age [which] involved the rectification of the Old World's hereditary wrongs." He points out that, although the revolution had in its turn become an oppressor, the outcome was "a political advance along nearly the whole line for Europeans," and he concludes by saying,

> in a way analogous to the operation of the Revolu-

tion at large the Great Mutiny, though by Englishmen naturally deemed monstrous at the time, doubtless gave the first latent prompting to most important reforms in the British Navy.

In short, tyranny can be successfully resisted.

We can now be sure of the direction of the theme of *Billy Budd.* In local context it suggests that it is wrong to submit to unjust law. Those in power, such as Vere, should do all they can to resist the evil inherent in any institution or government. All men are flawed, but not all men are depraved; and we must not let those institutions designed to control the evil destroy the good. In a larger context, man should not resign himself to the presence of evil but must always strive against it. It is possible to check the validity of this view by making sure that the various incidents, descriptions, and points reinforce it, and that they also contradict the "testament of acceptance" theory.

Observe that Vere dies drugged and on shore before he has "attained to the fullness of fame." In other words, Vere's end is suitable to one who did not deserve such renown as the daring and imprudent Nelson, a man capable, as Vere is not, of inspiring his men to loyalty, of substituting persuasion for coercion.

Observe that Claggart is characterized as civilized and intellectual;

> the man's even temper and discreet bearing would seem to intimate a mind peculiarly subject to the law of reason, not the less in his heart he would seem to riot in complete exemption from that law having apparently little to do with reason further than to employ it as an ambidexter implement for effecting the irrational.

But such men, continues Melville,

> are true madmen, and of the most dangerous sort, for their lunacy is not continuous but occasional evoked by some special object; it is probably secretive which is as much to say it is self contained, so that when moreover, most active it is to the average mind not distinguishable from sanity. . . .

This material comes into sharper focus when considered in relationship to Vere. He, like Claggart, is civilized; he, like Claggart, is intellectual; and he, like Claggart, uses reason to a bad end. Melville had suggested that Claggart was mad, and yet in Chapter 21, the surgeon, after seeing Claggart's body and hearing Vere say that the boy must hang, cannot banish this treasonable thought: "Was Captain Vere suddenly affected in his mind . . . ? Was he unhinged?" The surgeon reports, as instructed by Vere, to the lieutenants and the captain of the marines. "They fully stared at him in surprise and concern. Like him they seemed to think that such a matter should be reported to the Admiral." Melville pushes further; in the next chapter he says,

> Who in the rainbow can draw the line where the violet tint ends and the orange tint begins? . . . So with sanity and insanity. . . . Whether Captain Vere, as the Surgeon professionally and primarily surmised, was really the sudden victim of any degree of aberration, one must determine for himself by such light as this narrative can afford.

Observe that Billy was removed from a ship called the *Rights of Man* by a lieutenant named Ratcliffe.

Observe that, although Vere was "solicitous of his men's welfare," yet the day after Billy was impressed, the captain flogged "a little fellow, young, a novice an afterguardsman absent from his assigned post when the ship was being put about. . . ." It is useful to remember here that, when Melville was a novice, he was almost flogged for the same reason, but was saved by the interference of Jack Chase.

Observe that white is not used to portray innocence, as Matthiessen suggests [see excerpt dated 1941]; on the contrary, it is used as Melville had used it in *Moby-Dick:* to imply terror and possibly evil. For example, Claggart is described as pale in visage; Billy, when accused of treachery, appears "struck as by white leprosy"; the young man who tries to persuade Billy to join a mutiny had "glassy eyes of pale blue, veiled with lashes all but white"; Claggart's voice is silvery and low; the whistles used to pipe the men to witness the punishment of Billy are silver whistles; the moon that shines at midnight as Vere tells the men about Billy's sentence silvers the white spar-deck as, in the ballad also, it silvers the bay where Billy lies shackled, awaiting death. In this light the whiteness of Billy's clothes may not be a sign of his purity but of the evil which is successfully destroying him; and the "circumambient air in the clearness of its serenity . . . like smooth white marble," which surrounds him as he hangs from the yardarm, may be more concerned with all-conquering evil than with submissive purity.

Observe that Vere appears at the court-martial as the sole witness, "and as such temporarily sinking his rank, though singularly maintaining it in a matter apparently trivial, namely, that he testified from the ship's weatherside with that object having caused the court to sit on the lee-side." Vere thus chooses the side which puts him literally and metaphorically above the court and gives him, in the slang meaning of the term, the advantage.

Vere, when preparing to address the court, that is, to persuade it to his opinion, paces the cabin,

> in the returning ascent to windward, climbing the slant deck in the ship's lee roll; without knowing it symbolizing thus in his action a mind resolute to surmount difficulties even if against primitive instincts strong as the wind and the sea.

But Melville has suggested already that the instincts of the untutored barbarian are sounder than the civilized intellect.

Observe that this is corroborated in the very next paragraph. "When speak he did, something both in the substance of what he said and his manner of saying it, showed the influence of unshared studies modifying and tempering the practical training of an active career." But practicality is exactly what is called for. Vere never refers to these qualities, preferring instead to weave a complex skein of thought which none of his court, though thoroughly competent, can follow.

Even the governing circumstance of the entire story, namely, the recent mutinies and the consequent peril hovering over the fleet, does not go unchallenged by Melville. For at the conclusion of Vere's speech, just after his appeal to the fear of a new revolt, Melville describes the court's frame of mind as akin to that

> which in the year 1842 actuated the commander of the U.S. brig-of-war *Somers* to resolve, under the so-called Articles of War, Articles modelled upon the English Mutiny Act, to resolve upon the execution at sea of a midshipman and two petty-officers as mutineers designing the seizure of the brig. Which resolution was carried out though in a time of peace and within not many days sail of home. An act vindicated by a naval court of inquiry subsequently convened ashore. History, and here cited without comment. True, the circumstances on board the *Somers* were different from those on board the *Indomitable*. But the urgency felt, well-warranted or otherwise, was much the same.

Thus, Melville introduces a case whose justice had been considered extremely dubious and which, after forty years, was still being debated in the papers. Melville does not stop here; the last two sentences state that the circumstances are not the same, and that perhaps the need for swift action on the *Indomitable* is urgent and perhaps it is not. Thus even the circumstance responsible for Vere's basic motive is undermined.

It should be pointed out that the adherents of the "testament of acceptance" theory have to deal not only with the unsuitability of Captain Vere as a spokesman for Melville, but they also have to explain away the presence of a number of contradictions which arise in the story solely as a result of their position. For example, if the story concerns the acceptance of necessary evil, then why does Melville continue beyond the death of Billy, where, and only where, an emotional equilibrium favorable to such an acceptance is attained? Vere's untimely death would be a poor reward for so faithful a servant and in the "acceptance" context would be meaningless, for the point is made and the tale ended with Billy's death. Only an ironical reversing of the point would justify continuation of the story.

It is even possible to bring into question the tone of the hanging scene. Joseph Schiffman, B. R. McElderry, and Harry Campbell have each noted contradictions in this scene that arise only if the story is interpreted as an "acceptance" [see McElderry and Campbell entries in Further Reading]. Schiffman points out that, even though the crew echoes Billy's cry, "God bless Captain Vere," they are not thinking of the captain, for, in Melville's words, "yet at that instant Billy alone must have been in their hearts, even as he was in their eyes." (115-24)

If this episode is taken ironically, then it fits the rest of the story as so far interpreted and acquires tremendous power. For Billy is willing to die as Isaac or as Christ was willing; he accepts all the captain's arguments, but it is Billy alone who is noble. The captain suffers and wishes he could avoid this duty, but he has no nobility and above all no trust in man. Yet Billy's very acceptance of his role is the evidence that proves man can be trusted, that man can rise above the need for forms. (p. 124)

Another contradiction inherent in the "acceptance" theory lies in Melville's argument that barbarians with their instincts and warm hearts have sounder values than civilized men with their intricate intellects and their rabied hearts. Would it not be contradictory for Melville to suggest this not once, but twice, and then have Vere, Melville's foremost spokesman, weave a complex intellectual argument? Would it not be contradictory for Melville to have Billy die bravely, crying "God bless Captain Vere," and then have Vere say directly that mankind is a denizen of the forest and must be controlled by form and routine?

Would it not be contradictory, in the "testament of acceptance" framework, for Melville to use for the captain's name a word which at first glance suggests *veritas* "truth," but on second glance can as easily suggest *veritus* "fear," or on third glance, *vir* "man"?

Would it not be contradictory for him to use as symbols of evil flogging, impressment, arbitrary hanging, when these evils had been corrected by the time that he wrote this story, partly through his own writing?

Would it not be contradictory for Melville to use Vere as a symbol of the proper recognition of necessary evil: a man who had opposed the French Revolution and all its new social and political doctrines which since have changed the globe and reduced tyranny, injustice, poverty, and disease? Might it not be argued that, since Vere was wrong in his judgment of these attempts to change existing evils, he might also be wrong about the case in hand?

Would it not be contradictory for Melville to have a captain who is intelligent and widely read in both the ancients and the moderns, who does not apply this breadth of experience, who sees no larger context than the immediate needs of the navy?

Again, would it not be contradictory for Melville to represent Billy as inarticulate, nonthinking, naïve, emotionally adolescent, and morally undeveloped, and then expect the reader to accept his cry, "God bless Captain Vere," as indicative of full understanding, instinctive or otherwise?

And finally, is not the "acceptance" theory contradictory to all that Melville stood for and fought for throughout his entire life? He had been a seaman and had witnessed at first hand the floggings and the tyrannies of the captains. He had never approved of such practices, and in **White-Jacket** he thundered against them from every angle.

> No matter, then, what may be the consequences of its abolition; no matter if we have to dismantle our fleets, and our unprotected commerce should fall a prey to the spoiler, the awful admonitions of justice and humanity demand that abolition without procrastination; in a voice that is not to be mistaken, demand that abolition to-day. It is not a dollar-and-cent question of expediency; it is a matter of *right and wrong*. And if any man can lay his hand on his heart, and solemnly say that this scourging is right, let that man but once feel the lash on his own back, and in his agony you will hear the apostate call the seventh heavens to witness that it is *wrong*. And, in the name of immortal manhood, would to God that every man who upholds this thing were scourged at the gangway till he recanted.

Melville was a fighter, he was stubborn, he never accepted the easy way out. Would it not then be contradictory for him, after a lifetime of resisting practical evil in the world at large and metaphysical evil in his novels, at the very end to discover that he had been wrong all along and that his duty had always been to lie down and accept evil as unavoidable?

It is now possible to review the story swiftly. It begins with a cue from a narrator; a rebellion, like the French Revolution or the Spithead Mutiny, may result in good, although in the beginning it may not seem so. Thus, rebellion is justified in the first pages, the implication being that evil can and perhaps should be resisted. We have seen how the various characteristics of the three main actors are clues to the working out of this theme. Claggart is evil through and through; he possesses the perverted intelligence of a serpent, an intelligence used for irrational purposes. Billy Budd, on the contrary, is pure innocence, acting and judging on instinct alone. When Vere is introduced, his central characteristic is his intellection, by means of which he can justify or rationalize an over-prudence that leads to injustice. The chapter on Nelson reminds us that Vere's kind of caution and Vere's way of preventing possible mutiny are not admirable.

It may be argued that, while both Vere and Claggart possess intelligence, Vere uses his wisely and justly. But this argument collapses when it is perceived that Vere does not do what reason would suggest in so dubious a case, i.e., jail Billy until they reach land. The real point is, of course, that Vere does not act on reason and intelligence at all, but on fear; his intelligence, instead of being a guide, is a perverted instrument. Such scenes as the confusion of the officers and the doubt of the surgeon concerning Vere's sanity make sense only when regarded as putting into issue Vere's stature and ability.

It may also be argued that such episodes are intended to demonstrate that Vere and only Vere has the intelligence and insight to perceive the deeper issues. But this explanation falls to the ground when it is realized that Vere's whole argument is irrational and that his final appeal is to brute force. The ballad at the end becomes particularly rich in this context. Billy is to be sacrificed, but unjustly and unnecessarily so. The ballad, written by one of his comrades who does not understand the issues but who feels obscurely the truth of the matter in spite of a calumnious official report, speaks of Billy as unafraid but sad. Billy, being innocence personified, does not fear death; but as an unjust sacrifice, he is pictured as alone and unhappy. He longs for companionship and affection and thinks wistfully of his friends; in the end he contemplates with a melancholy resignation his death:

> Fathoms down, fathoms down, how I'll dream fast
>   asleep.
> I feel it stealing now. Sentry, are you there?
> Just ease these darbies at the wrist,
> And roll me over fair.
> I am asleep, and the oozy weeds about me twist.

Thus, Billy's cry, "God Bless Captain Vere," is the crowning irony and really the climax of the story, for he was hanged unjustly. Melville says here that a harsh truth of this harsh world is that good folk can be misled, that they can be abused by the evil simply because they are trusting. Thus Melville reminds us that we must keep up the good fight: evil must not remain uncontested. And he does so not by a call to arms but by demonstrating the consequences of unresisting acquiescence. (pp. 125-27)

> *Phil Withim, " 'Billy Budd': Testament of Resistance," in* Modern Language Quarterly, *Vol. 20, No. 2, June, 1959, pp. 115-27.*

G. R. Wilson, Jr.   (essay date 1967)

[*In the following excerpt, Wilson addresses the significance of Melville's use of dramatic technique in* Billy Budd.]

Writing in 1948, Richard Chase made the following assessment of Melville's final work: ". . . *Billy Budd* is a brilliant piece of writing, nicely constructed and balanced between swift, stark action and moral-philosophical comment. Though it falls far short of the pure tragedy Melville apparently wanted to write, it is still a moving drama, if a drama only of pathos" [see Further Reading].

While many critics might argue with Chase's view that *Billy Budd* lacks tragic import, few would dispute his recognition of the inherently dramatic nature of this novella. The head-on confrontation of two apparent absolutes—light and dark, good and evil, angel and fiend—and the dilemma of the man caught between them, the man who must attempt to reconcile the irreconcilable, provide the very essence of drama. Nor have the intrinsic dramatic possibilities of the book been ignored. *Billy Budd* has been produced as an opera (with libretto by E. M. Forster and Eric Crozier, music by Benjamin Britten), as a Broadway play (by Louis O. Coxe and Robert Chapman), and as a motion picture (by Peter Ustinov). All three productions were successful, at least critically.

All three dramatizations elaborate faithfully the story of a merchant seaman of uncommon goodness, Billy Budd, impressed into the Royal Navy during the time immediately following the Admiralty-shaking mutinies of 1797 at Spithead and the Nore. A figure of peaceful innocence, Billy fails to recognize the implacably evil nature of Claggart, the ship's master-at-arms, who has taken an instant dislike to the new crew member. Following an abortive attempt to corrupt Billy, Claggart brings the young seaman before Captain Vere, commanding officer of the man-of-war, and falsely charges him with fomenting a mutiny. Tongue-tied with outrage, unable to answer his accuser, Billy responds with a fatal blow to Claggart's head—a blow that Captain Vere immediately perceives as "the divine judgement on Ananias." And despite his very real comprehension of the human situation, Vere convenes a court martial and persuades its reluctant members that their first and only duty is to the naval service and to its law; Billy must hang. Hang he does, and here the dramatizations conclude. It is only from Melville's version that we learn that, shortly after Billy's execution, Captain Vere is himself mortally wounded in battle and dies uttering, without remorse, the words "Billy Budd, Billy Budd."

With the skeleton of the novella thus dramaturgically bared, it is particularly surprising to turn to Melville's manuscript and find that he has fleshed these bones primarily with exposition, that his presentation is not really a dramatic one. Despite Chase's discovery of a content that balances between "stark action and moral-philosophical comment," Melville has tipped the scales of technique heavily toward the side of narration and away from the side of dramatic development.

This is not to say that no drama exists in *Billy Budd,* but only to suggest that Melville seems, at first glance, not to have recognized the full dramatic potential that he had in hand, a potential that later adapters have had to wring forcibly from his text. He seems to have made errors of both commission and omission—dramatizing fully scenes of minor importance and neglecting, sometimes almost to the vanishing point, others of great importance.

Some examples may be illuminating. The first dramatic scene of the tale concerns Billy's impressment from the merchant ship on which he has been serving; but the characters here developed, the merchant captain and the impressing officer, never reappear to figure in subsequent action. While it is true that the scene gives us our first glimpse of the protagonist, it is a glimpse largely through the eyes of the merchant captain—in effect, only the comments of a second narrator. Subsequently, Melville faithfully reports two dialogues between Billy and an old, Chiron-like mariner apparently only to indicate that Claggart is "down on" Billy and to reveal Billy's naïve refusal to believe that fact. Finally, a detailed conversation between the ship's surgeon and the purser about the execution immediately follows the very brief scene of Billy's hanging. The surgeon plays a relatively minor role in the novella, the purser none at all, and their discourse is suitably ambivalent.

The dramatic omissions seem even more disturbing. None of the three principal characters is ever developed in dramatic terms. Melville never really shows us Billy being good, Claggart being evil, or Vere being—whatever it is we decide he must be to serve our interpretation of the tale. Instead we learn *about* these characters from the anonymous narrator in terms that can only be described as intuitive, the assessment of Claggart, for example, being summed up, at one point, in the biblical phrase "mysteries of iniquity." Prior to the central incident of the story, the killing of the master-at-arms, Melville offers us only one brief interaction between Billy and his antagonist, a scene that occupies less than a page of the text and includes only one spoken remark—Claggart's notoriously equivocal "Handsome is as handsome did it," which critics have described in terms ranging from an expression of homosexuality to the villain's climactic insight into the indomitable nature of his nemesis. But certainly the most incredible omission seems to be that of the final confrontation between Captain Vere and Billy, in which Vere tells the "Handsome Sailor" of the sentence that the Court has passed on him. Not only does Melville refuse to dramatize this critically important encounter for us, but also he even denies us any expository knowledge of its details. And although he permits his narrator some conjectural remarks, the author carefully prefaces them with a matter-of-fact "What took place at this interview was never known."

One critic has cited this evasion on Melville's part as the measure by which the novella is inferior to its Broadway adaptation, in which, of course, this "discovery scene" occurs. Arnold L. Goldsmith contends that the inclusion of the scene in the play permits Billy to go to his death with a full understanding of the complicated interplay of forces that has made it necessary and, thus, with a rational, intellectual acceptance of his doom [see Further Reading]. Unable to find this understanding in the original manuscript, Goldsmith confidently asserts: "Coxe and Chapman have made Billy a kinetic character, whereas Melville's is static."

Even in those scenes that we cannot fault as apparent errors of omission or commission, Melville displays a curious reluctance to set in motion his dramatic machinery.

The central incident, the confrontation of Billy and Claggart in Vere's cabin, for example, begins when the master-at-arms brings his false accusation to the Captain, who is then striding the quarterdeck. Yet, until the penultimate moment, Melville does not report Claggart's speech, choosing rather to let his narrator supply the liar's side of the conversation in indirect discourse while quoting only Vere's curt interjections. The same sort of slippery focus, sliding back and forth between drama and exposition, characterizes other portions of the novella.

We could find a simple, straightforward explanation for these apparently technical anomolies, of course, in the fact that Melville did not live to put *Billy Budd* in final form. At the time of the author's death, as the most recent editors of the story point out, "the manuscript was in a heavily revised, still 'unfinished' state" [see Hayford and Sealts in Further Reading]. Can we then assume that, had Melville lived, he would subsequently have altered materially the dramatic emphasis of the manuscript? I think not.

In producing the first true genetic text of the work and what must surely be the most accurate reading text now available, Hayford and Sealts have identified three main phases of development, each encompassing several stages, through which the story passed in its progress from a very brief prose sketch accompanying the ballad that now concludes the book to the full-blown short novel as we know it. Over the course of five years, as these editors summarize it

> . . .Melville had carried the work through a series of developments intricate in detail but clear in their general lines of growth. In three main phases he had introduced in turn the three main characters: first Billy, then Claggart, and finally Vere. As the focus of his attention shifted from one to another of these three principals, the plot and thematic emphasis of the expanding novel underwent consequent modifications within each main phase. Just where the emphasis finally lay in the not altogether finished story as he left it is, in essence, the issue that has engaged and divided the critics of *Billy Budd.*

An examination of the genetic text that follows this comment reveals that Melville inserted the bulk of the drama into the story early in the second phase. As Melville developed Claggart as an antagonist to Billy, he also framed the dramatic emphasis that he felt necessary to balance the strongly expository type of character examination he was using. Early in the third phase, with Captain Vere increasing in importance, Melville found it necessary to expand one existing dramatization and to add two new ones—the trial scene and the half-expository execution scene. The editors have identified at least four stages through which the manuscript subsequently passed with no substantive change in the balance of drama and exposition. Unless Melville were to enter a fourth phase calling for still another shift in focus, it seems extremely unlikely that he would have discovered any necessity for altering the relationship of technical methods that is reflected in the text as it exists today.

If we can then assume it likely that the limited use of dramatic technique in *Billy Budd* represents the author's chosen plan of development, it seems to me that we can postulate some suggestions concerning the meaning of Melville's final short novel. Save for the recognition of a number of obvious ambiguities, no interpretive consensus of *Billy Budd* exists among critics. Despite the recognized equivocations, every critic seems dedicated to an individual interpretation; each selects his terrain, musters his particular army of quotations, and digs in to defend his position against all attackers. Thus, the number of interpretations is nearly as great as the number of commentators that have attempted an explication of the work. (pp. 105-09)

Many critics recognize *Billy Budd* as a tragedy; others, as my opening quotation from Chase indicates, do not. At least one critic has asserted that it is, in fact, "a parody of tragedy" [see Wagner entry in Further Reading], a critical view that projects Claggart as the hero. I scarcely need add that other readings are more or less equally divided between Billy as hero and Vere as hero.

Billy Budd has been seen as a tight, religious allegory—in which Billy is equated with Christ, Claggart with Satan, and Vere with God—affirming the ultimate triumph of man's spirit. Exactly the same allegorical correspondences have been recognized by other critics who, detecting the presence of irony, assert that the tale resolutely denies the ultimate triumph of man's spirit. Various other allegorical interpretations abound.

Space will not permit a thorough cataloguing of the many additional theories concerning this particular work, but perhaps a listing of some of the many dualities that critics have recognized in the book will be indicative: good and evil, prelapsarian and postlapsarian man, peace and war, justice and law, nature and society, salvation and damnation, order and chaos, and so on—each pair often set forth as necessarily excluding the others.

This wide variety of critical interpretations is not nearly as astonishing as the fact that all of them are defensible with some degree of persuasiveness; and, if we discard the completely topsy-turvy view of those who find only irony and insist that Melville *always* meant exactly the opposite of what he said, the remaining theories can all marshal a convincingly substantial body of evidence for support.

If we consider the existence of this evidence and look back at the way in which Melville developed his story—starting with the rather sophisticated Billy of the ballad, working through the naïve and saintlike Billy of the novella, adding the unrelieved antagonistic evil of Claggart, finally interposing Vere as the man of intelligent good will who is yet not free to act—the conclusion is inescapable that the author was fully aware of his burgeoning meanings. It is impossible to think that he could, as a conscious artist, brood over this last creation for five long years without understanding every nuance of meaning that rippled out in expanding circles from his initial pebble of thought. Melville was preoccupied with portraying a complicated cosmos in which many forces act, react, and interact. Unlike writers who can find the truth about their world in hierarchical levels of meaning, Melville was forced to deal with a world in which the manifold threads of existence were inextricably tangled, in which all meanings were part of the single meaning. It is no wonder, then, that the work as it stands is ambiguous and even inconsistent. But, from a technical point of view, ambiguity and inconsistency are defensible as long as the artist funnels them through a fallible human narrator; they become suspect when expressed in the absolute terms of dramatic action.

And this, of course, brings me back to my primary point. It is my suggestion that Melville could not possibly have further dramatized any important action of the novella without surrendering some portion of the multiple meaning that he had so painstakingly constructed and that he intended to convey in *Billy Budd.* To add drama would demand that one particular meaning be reinforced over another; and this he was unwilling to do, as, I think, the development of the manuscript makes clear. Consider, for a moment, the effect if Melville had tried to include a dramatized "discovery scene" as Goldsmith has suggested he should. If Billy is to be an effective Christ-figure, he must accept the hemp with full knowledge and comprehension, and this must be conveyed in his last earthly meeting with the father-God figure, Captain Vere. Yet, if Billy understands his fate, how is Melville to maintain the important suggestion of virginal innocence required by his projection of Billy as the unknowing, unsullied Adam? How can Billy still function as the passive representative of a beneficent nature cruelly tamed and sacrificed by the demands of an unfeeling society? The answer to both questions, it seems to me, is obvious—he can't. Consequently, Melville's apparently conscious decision not to include such a scene is the only course of action he could have followed without compromising his meaning in some important particular. We can find similar substantiation for the other dramatic "omissions" that might seem, at first reading, to be structural flaws in the book.

Hayford and Sealts, in discussing the perspectives for criticism made possible by their genetic text, pose several questions:

> Would Melville himself, in a "finished" version of *Billy Budd,* perhaps have removed the inconsistencies, if not have resolved the ambiguities . . .? And more fundamentally, would he have undertaken further adjustments of emphasis among his three principals? Only conjectural answers are possible, of course. In our judgement, however, these questions . . . bring critical debate about the work into a new perspective: Was the story as it stood when Melville died . . . complete in all significant respects though "unfinished" in details? Or, on the other hand, was it, because still under revision at a passage crucially affecting its tone and focus (and perhaps for other reasons as well), radically "unfinished"? In short, is *Billy Budd* a unified work of art?

Although the evidence of Melville's dramatic emphasis alone is far from conclusive, it tends, I submit, to support an affirmative answer to that last question. (pp. 109-11)

> *G. R. Wilson, Jr., " 'Billy Budd' and Melville's Use of Dramatic Technique," in* Studies in Short Fiction, *Vol. IV, No. 2, Winter, 1967, pp. 105-11.*

Walter L. Reed   (essay date 1977)

[*Reed is an American critic and educator. In the following excerpt, he examines the conflict between aesthetic and legal forms of order and expression in* Billy Budd.]

The figure of Captain Vere in Melville's **Billy Budd** is a particularly enigmatic one, as generations of critical controversy testify. He proves to be a harsh, even savage disciplinarian but is presented as a man of considerable culture and civilization as well. In one of the last chapters of the story, after Billy's execution, the author reports something of Vere's social philosophy and reflections on the revolution in France; the author credits Vere with a curious application of the myth of Orpheus. " 'With mankind,' he would say, 'forms, measured forms, are everything; and that is the import couched in the story of Orpheus with his lyre spellbinding the wild denizens of the wood.' And this he once applied to the disruption of forms going on across the Channel and the consequences thereof." To the modern reader, this interpretation of the legend is apt to seem highly inappropriate, an irony on Melville's part directed at Captain Vere, showing the distortion of literary values by a military mind. How can Orpheus' "measured forms," traditionally symbolizing the eloquence of the poet, be compared with the punitive measures of the Mutiny Act, which have brought about the death of Billy Budd? Is this not an example of Vere's uncompassionate learning, the pedantic severity indicated by his epithet "Starry Vere"? Indeed, the epithet itself, derived from Marvell's "Upon Appleton House," seems another example of poetic material misappropriated by the military. And in the last two chapters of the book, the military and the poetic are again juxtaposed, the highly inaccurate account of the killing of Claggart from the naval chronicle, followed by the popular ballad "Billy in the Darbies," not exactly an accurate picture of Billy as we have come to know him but a less offensive distortion of the facts.

There is, in fact, quite a pervasive parallelism in **Billy Budd** between the forms of art and the forms of military law. Our initial reaction, that the former are to be preferred to the latter, is certainly reasonable on moral grounds. "Law, as the *creation* of man, needs the imagination and insight of art so that it is not drawn in such a way as to imprison the human spirit. Law and society need the help of the artist, to the end that we do not forget man's natural humanity." This is the conclusion Charles Reich draws in his persuasive interpretation of **Billy Budd** from a legal point of view [see Further Reading]. But on aesthetic grounds this reaction may not be completely satisfactory. By what authority does Vere impose the rigid judgment on Billy, we may ask, and by what authority does the author himself pretend to judge his characters who are purported to have an historically independent existence? In a story so concerned with the problematic nature of the human self, what guarantee is there that the artist's own forms are adequate to represent the mysteries and complexities of Billy's case? Vere may have judged the case preemptorily ("Struck dead by an angel of God! Yet the angel must hang"), but is the author any less prejudiced in the way he presents his hero—"The moral nature was seldom out of keeping with the physical make-up"—or his villain, whose iniquity may be mysterious in origin but is as stereotyped as that of a "Radcliffian romance"?

The question of the adequacy of literary form to the elusive nature of "truth" was one that occupied Melville throughout his literary career, and it is not one which can be easily dismissed, our humanitarian impulses notwithstanding. As his famous remarks on Shakespeare show, Melville regarded the artist as a seeker after absolute knowledge and considered the formal work of art less significant than the visionary insight that lay behind it: "In Shakespeare's tomb lies infinitely more than Shakespeare ever wrote." In **Billy Budd** the "Author"—Melville playing the role of the conventional omniscient author—shows an ambivalence toward the formality of his narrative. "The symmetry of form attainable in pure fiction cannot so readily be achieved in a narration essentially having less to do with fable than with fact. Truth uncompromisingly told will always have its ragged edges; hence the conclusion of such a narration is apt to be less finished than an architectural finial," the Author admonishes soon after Captain Vere's invocation of Orpheus. Again, a critique of formalism, but a critique which is surely disingenuous in a story where good and evil are so schematically divided between two characters, where important scenes like the scene of the judgment in Captain Vere's cabin are so symmetrically conceived and described. In fact, what could be a better "finial" to the story than the last three chapters, giving the three different testimonials to the hero, Captain Vere's enigmatic "Billy Budd, Billy Budd," followed by the military and then the poetic report? Finally, one notices that even in the Author's pronouncement there is an equivocation: "a narration *essentially* having *less* to do with fable than with fact."

Thus we find a parallel drawn between two different kinds of form in **Billy Budd,** and we find that the parallel is not simply a contrast designed to elicit judgment against Captain Vere. The forms of art are clearly better than the forms of military law in many respects, but the difference is not insisted upon—rather the reverse. The thought then arises that Melville may be presenting the parallelism as an equation: the forms of art are no better than the forms of law, there is nothing to choose between them. Kingsley Widmer [see Further Reading] comes close to this conclusion in his analysis of the numerous "myths" of **Billy Budd.** "Melville suggests no alternative to his mocking of mythicizing," he writes, "Myths, heroic, public, or poetic, neither last nor tell the truth. . . . Melville's multiple sequels of cancelling interpretations but confirm the pessimism." Some support for this position can be gained from considering Melville's earlier career as a novelist.

The problem of finding fictional forms to express the "truth," metaphysical and moral, was one which had troubled Melville at least from **Mardi** onward. In **Mardi** his burgeoning visionary ambitions for the most part outstripped his powers of formal organization. A chapter added late in his voluminous revisions refers ironically to a literary masterpiece which "lacks all cohesion; it is wild, unconnected, all episode," to which the only reply is, such is the nature of the world. **Redburn** and **White-Jacket,** like **Typee** and **Omoo,** were much more modest in scope and relied heavily on the realistic framework of the nautical adventure story, but in **Moby-Dick** the metaphysical burden of the Romantic artist was again assumed—much more successfully, as all readers have agreed. There is an exuberant plurality of form in **Moby-Dick,** however—novelistic, dramatic, comic, tragic, forms of realism, of romance, of the tall tale. The encyclopedic diversity of the way the story is told is an index of its epic ambitions. No single mode can capture "the ungraspable phantom of life," as Ishmael calls it, but every conceivable mode is enlisted in this aim. The lack of any symmetry or measured form is a notable feature of the book. (pp. 227-29)

For Melville nature was fluid and formless—and hostile to man. As far as the supernatural realm was concerned, the obvious source of authoritative form was the typology of the Old and New Testaments. But this, too, was finally inaccessible to Melville, who as Hawthorne said, could neither believe nor be happy in his unbelief. Both the forms of Romantic nature and the forms of Biblical revelation are attacked and undermined in *The Confidence-Man,* where the bleak conclusion is that one can only have confidence in confidence itself.

A consideration of the ambiguous formalism of *Billy Budd* in the light of Melville's previous experience as a novelist, and his position as an American author, does suggest that he may be insinuating a reductive equation between the forms of literature and the forms of naval discipline. In *The Confidence-Man,* indeed, he equates the art of fiction, for the most part, with the confidence man's tricks. But *Billy Budd* was written long after Melville had abandoned the writing of prose fiction. His refusal to write novels was much longer than his active career as a novelist, and the gradual process by which this last piece of fiction was composed suggests a careful, or cautious, attempt to reconstitute his art. As Hayford and Sealts have shown in their study of the manuscripts, [see Further Reading], *Billy Budd* grew from a short poem, a dramatic monologue with a prose headnote, through a series of expanding prose versions in which more and more characters and viewpoints were introduced. "All along, Melville's dramatization had the effect, among others, of dissociating the narrator from commitments he had made or positions that Melville might wish to insinuate without endorsing." Working from the poetic kernel, now the concluding "Billy in the Darbies," the final form in which the hero is cast, Melville built up a series of competing and often contradictory structures for comprehending the mystery of such a fate. And he took more time over this relatively short novella than he had over any of his longer novels, including *Moby-Dick.* It would be strange for an author to give so much thought simply to restating a desperate position he had reached some thirty years earlier.

The measuring forms of the Author and the measured forms of Captain Vere may be related in a third way, however. The parallelism may indicate neither strong contrast nor virtual equivalence but instead a symbolic substitution of one type of form for the other. In other words, the military forms adhered to by Captain Vere may be representing—standing in for—the literary forms being advanced by the putative Author of the work. In fact, this last possibility seems to me to be the case. In having to impose the rule of law on Billy Budd's spontaneous nature, Vere is facing problems similar to those Melville had faced in his earlier fiction and that, in the role of the Author of this newly attempted piece, he was facing again, now, because of Vere, at one remove. The burden of formalization is shifted from the Author to Captain Vere, and this shifting is not merely an event in the history of the story's composition but is dramatically enacted in the course of the story as it now exists. As the analysis which follows will show, the Author's attention moves from the relatively simple mystery of Billy's innocence to the deeper mystery of Claggart's villainy to the still more problematic uncertainty over Captain Vere. As his attention shifts the Author becomes increasingly less confident and less explicit in his own representation of the values and motives involved.

Billy is presented first not as an individual but as an example of a type, a stereotype even, "the Handsome Sailor." The type is described at length before the individual is mentioned; the hero's character is thus prejudged by the form through which it is seen. Furthermore, this prejudgment is laid open to question by the apparent difference between the two examples of it that the Author adduces: first, a "common sailor so intensely black that he needs must have been a native African of the unadulterate blood of Ham—a symmetric figure much above the average height," and then the much less imposing figure of Billy Budd. The Author in fact undermines our faith in his typology even as he introduces Billy. He equivocates: "Such a cynosure, at least in aspect, and something such too in nature, though with important variations made apparent as the story proceeds, was welkin-eyed Billy Budd." The symmetric form of the Handsome Sailor is a questionable fit.

Melville's prose style here is reminiscent of the tortured, enigmatic syntax of *The Confidence-Man,* but its qualifications and uncertainties are less aggressively obtrusive. There is a lyricism in the style here as well, for example in the phrase "welkin-eyed" which stands in contrast to the abstract, intellectualized diction which precedes it. One can see here again the conflict between literary and legal form as the language moves back and forth between the archaic diction of poetry and romance and the cautious, convoluted expressions of a legal contract. There is a similar vacillation in the way Claggart, the next character to be considered in depth, is presented. On the one hand, the Author seems candidly unsure of Claggart's inner nature; "His portrait I essay, but shall never hit it" he begins, and later, "But for the adequate comprehending of Claggart by a normal nature these hints are insufficient. To pass from a normal nature to him one must cross 'the deadly space between'." On the one hand he is confident of Claggart's villainy and presents it in the stereotypes of "Radcliffian romance" and the curiously tautological definition of "Natural Depravity: a depravity according to nature," supposedly from Plato. The Author's indecision about Claggart is more pronounced than his indecision about Billy Budd, however. As his attention moves from the character of his hero to the character of his villain, there is an increasing sense of what one critic has called the "omniscient ambiguity" of the story [Edward A. Kearns, "Omniscient Ambiguity: The Narrators of *Moby-Dick* and *Billy Budd,*" *Emerson Society Quarterly,* (1970)].

When we come to Captain Vere and his central role in the trial (he has been introduced earlier), the ambiguity and uncertainty of the Author's judgment are more pronounced still. In an earlier phase of the manuscript the only major characters were Billy and Claggart, and when Melville gave Vere the prominence he now enjoys in the story, he did so in a further declaration of the limits of art's measuring forms. Vere is initially introduced in Chapters 6 and 7, but he only becomes important in the action in Chapter 18, where he is more the agent than the object of inquiry, attempting, like the Author before him, to judge the characters of the seaman and the master-at-arms. The Author, in other words, moves his attention from the principals in the case to the judge of those principals and deals with the problem at one remove. After Vere has made his judgment and Billy has been "formally convicted," Vere's character becomes a problem in its own right. Has he acted with any kind of ethical integrity, or has he merely responded in a mechanical and inhuman way? In Chapter 22 the Author limits his formal knowledge to a remarkable extent, as he recounts, by means of conjecture alone, the scene of Vere's last interview with Billy:

> Captain Vere in end may have developed the passion sometimes latent under an exterior stoical or indifferent. He was old enough to have been Billy's father. The austere devotee of military duty, letting himself melt back into what remains primeval in our formalized humanity, may in end have caught Billy to his heart, even as Abraham may have caught young Isaac on the brink of resolutely offering him up in obedience to the exacting behest.

The passage is paradoxical in the way it evokes an intensity of emotion, but does so indirectly, by surmise. The Author imagines a reconciliation that goes beyond formalism—"letting himself melt back into what remains primeval in our *formalized* humanity"—but is careful not to use the declarative mood. The invocation of Abraham and Isaac, the Biblical type of sacrifice, is a similar case of a form clearly indicated but then held at a distance: "even as Abraham *may* have caught young Isaac on the brink of resolutely offering him up." Fictional uncertainty infiltrates Biblical authority; the phrase "on the brink of resolutely offering" embodies the tension between decisive judgment and holding back.

Thus the terrible formal judgment which Vere imposes on Billy frees the Author from the exegincies of Melville's earlier artistic ambition, the perhaps impossible desire to achieve a formal artistic "representation" of moral and religious "truth." *Billy Budd* is a liberation from the desperate search for a metaphysical mimesis, as Melville dramatizes, in a crude and reduced fashion in Captain Vere, the conflict in his own imagination between a disinterested aesthetic will to form and a committed, ethical and religious will to judgment. One might compare *Billy Budd* in this respect with *Moby-Dick,* where Ahab's ethico-religious commitment emerges out of Ishmael's aesthetic disinterest well along in the narrative, but the differences should be noted as well. Where Ishmael's presence is frequently overwhelmed by Ahab's heroics, virtually disappearing from the last thirty chapters of the book, the Author of *Billy Budd* remains above and in control of Captain Vere. I would also compare *Billy Budd* with Kierkegaard's *Fear and Trembling,* whose extensive use of the Abraham and Isaac story Melville's allusion fleetingly recalls. Both books expose the difference between an author's point of view and a person's act. In *Fear and Trembling* the narrator's aesthetic view must gradually detach itself from the hero's religious passion and does so in a series of widening speculative circles around Abraham's example. But whereas in Kierkegaard the narrative strategy is defensive, the narrator putting his hero at a distance to preserve the mystery of the hero's sacrificial act, in Melville the narrative form is sacrificial itself. We are presented in *Billy Budd* with a double sacrifice: as Vere sacrifices the claims of nature in Billy, the Author sacrifices the claims of art in Vere.

The Author's sacrifice of literary form is tragic and not merely cynical because it acknowledges the value and dignity of that which is lost. The figure of Orpheus has been reduced, but the power of his spell is not denied or ridiculed. This is the sense we are left with as readers, I think: that *Billy Budd* is not simply a tragedy of innocence or justice *per se* but a tragedy of the formality of art, a formality in which content is sacrificed to form, reality to representation, signified to signifier. In his final acceptance of the inevitable fictionality of literature, of its inability to achieve the immanent presence of that which it evokes, Melville looks ahead to more recent critics of Romantic overreaching. "Perhaps all literature lies in this light anaphoric suspension," Roland Barthes writes in another context, "which at one and the same time designates and keeps silent." But like the other great nineteenth-century writers who explored the tragic rift between the aesthetic and the absolute—Kierkegaard, Dostoevsky, Nietzsche—Melville could never be happy in his unbelief. (pp. 231-35)

> *Walter L. Reed, "The Measured Forms of Captain Vere," in* Modern Fiction Studies, *Vol. 23, No. 2, Summer, 1977, pp. 227-35.*

Thomas J. Scorza   (essay date 1979)

[*In the following excerpt from his study* In the Time before Steamships: Billy Budd, the Limits of Politics, and Modernity, *Scorza discusses the novel as a critique of modernity and modern politics.*]

After concluding the execution scene the narrator [of *Billy Budd, Sailor: An Inside Narrative*] makes the observation which [is] the key to understanding the novel as "An Inside Narrative":

> The symmetry of form attainable in pure fiction cannot so readily be achieved in a narration essentially having less to do with fable than with fact. Truth uncompromisingly told will always have its ragged edges; hence the conclusion of such a narration is apt to be less finished than an architectural finial.

The narrator then goes on to relate the story of Vere's death, to reveal the existence of the authorized journal's account of the story, and to reproduce the sailor's ballad, "Billy in the Darbies." In these last three chapters, the narrator thus actually does "finish" his narrative; the chapters reveal conservative Vere's unsettled mind, the obscurantism of mere history, and the sailors' poetic-religious acceptance of Billy's fate. In all, these chapters do in fact complete a picture of the unsettling "uncompromising truth" beyond both history and revelatory religion. This would suggest that the story's "ragged edges" or loose ends do not reveal simply that the narration is substantively "incomplete," but rather that the very substance of the narrative is such that its message is "ragged" or rough. This suggestion especially undermines the reading of the novel which holds that its final attitude is one of Christian "acceptance" because the suggestion hints that the real message of the story is not so easily acceptable.

The method of the narration was appropriately suited to the "raggedness" of its content: the interplay between the straightforward, quasi-historical narrative and the narrator's "conjectures," "bypaths," and dramatizations throws "unequal cross-lights" upon the characters and events of the story and subtly points to the author's own "inside" intentions. The result was that, as in the case of the similarly illumined painting at "The Spouter-Inn" in *Moby-Dick,* "it was only by diligent study and a series of systematic visits to it . . . that you could any way arrive at an understanding of its purpose." Such an understanding, it is argued here, reveals not only that the "Inside Narrative" deliberately supports various interpretations, but also that it does so only in order to distinguish the author's own interpretation from the others, thus ultimately revealing the true picture of political reality. The *purpose* of the narrative is to reveal the truth, and such a purpose would suggest that the message of the story is as "unacceptable" to most readers as is the truth itself. That is, the narrative's "raggedness" also marks Melville's concealed but intentional effort to abrade modern political, religious, and scientific opinions.

Melville placed his story in the setting of the Wars of the French Revolution, in 1797, nearly the end of the century of the Enlightenment. The time was that of *the* political event of the modern age, an event in which the opposing parties each embodied in clearest form the contrary principles of conventional civilization and the natural rights of man. On the one side was Burke's conception of the true rights of men, rights which are real only insofar as they are understood to be impure, that is, woven into the fabric of historically developed social convention. "Men cannot enjoy the rights of an uncivil and of a civil state together," wrote Burke. "That [man] may obtain justice, he gives up his right of determining what it is in points the most essential to him. That he may secure some liberty, he makes a surrender in trust of the whole of it." On the other side, Paine challenged the authority of conventional law and defined freedom according to the pure and abstract natural rights of man, rejecting Burke's notion that rights and liberty need to be "given up" or "surrendered in trust" to others. It was before these rights that convention was to be called in judgment, and it was Paine's prayer that the various national forms of convention would give way to the universal justice of the rights of man. Paine hoped, as he wrote to George Washington, "that the Rights of Man may become as universal as your benevolence can wish, and . . . regenerate the Old [World]." While England had her revolutionaries and France her loyalists, the external opposition of England and France placed these political opinions in higher relief than would be possible in any delineation of internal divisions. The stark juxtaposition of political regimes in *Billy Budd* is thus the crucial background of the events aboard H. M. S. *Bellipotent.*

Whatever may have been the result of the French and British War, the intellectual result of the French Revolution was that "invading waters of novel opinion social, political, and otherwise, . . . carried away as in a torrent no few minds in those days," and this intellectual situation still prevailed in Melville's own time, complicated too by the addition of romanticism as yet another form of "novel opinion." This suggests that the first and most obvious reason why *Billy Budd* might be abrasive to modern readers is that the narrator of the story is so clearly "old-fashioned" and politically conservative. In a modern world in which atheism is fashionable, the narrator speaks favorably of "that lexicon which is based on Holy Writ," and to readers who are imbued with egalitarian notions, the narrator praises the existence of a "virtue aristocratic in kind" in Nelson and in Vere. In all, for the conservative

and old-fashioned narrator, the French Revolution, the ideas behind it, and its aftermath represent an "unbridled and unbounded revolt" against the "constitutionally sound" regime of "founded law and freedom defined." Thus, Melville could not but expect that his use of such a narrator in a world which was in love with "novel opinion" would "little . . . commend [his] pages to many a reader" of his day.

But *Billy Budd* is more abrasive yet because beneath the narrator's Burkean conservatism there lie certain opinions of the author which are similarly opposed to modern opinion, especially also radical atheistic and egalitarian opinion. Melville placed, for instance, "inside" the narrator's description of the "Handsome Sailor" a picture of "natural regality" which asserted the natural legitimacy of human god-kings, and "inside" the description of Nelson, Melville revealed the necessity of the "priestly" and sacrificial in a political milieu which sometimes demands "plenary absolution." And whatever may be the precisely religious or theological implications of these points, the very notions of "regality" and "nobility" involved in Melville's "inside" story placed him in aristocratic opposition to the enlightened egalitarianism of both Anacharsis Cloots and of his own time. While the context of Melville's last novel is the French and British War, it should thus not be surprising that the events of the novel take place totally within one British vessel, totally on the British side. Hence, the suggestion is made that Melville intended to make the unpopular point that the strictly *political* choices to be made in modern times must be made within the horizon of the conservative British regime.

At this point, however, Melville may have been directly abrasive only to the modern liberal's political opinions. But below the author's more profound agreement with some of the narrator's "illiberal" opinions, one saw Melville's critique of both the modern conservative and the romantic alternatives to modern liberalism. Captain Vere, Burke's statesman, not only cannot contain the evil attendant upon political tragedy, but he actually contributes to political tragedy's dimensions by his merely traditionalist principles; and Billy Budd, Rousseau's natural man, is turned into a cannon-like instrument of destruction in the face of unavoidable, inherent, "natural depravity." Burkean prudence is inadequate to the task expected of it, and peaceful, natural innocence is either doomed to destruction or is forced to become, like the *Bellipotent,* tragically "capable of war." In all, thus, *Billy Budd* amounts to an abrasive critique of all of modern politics. Tragedy is endemic to modern politics because attractive romantic innocence is too fragile in a man-of-war world, because modern conservative conventionalism is too limited in vision and scope, and because natural evil is too effective in the complex civilizations of modernity.

This critique of modern politics occurred within a more general critique of the whole of modernity. The composite picture of political virtue which was formed by the "inside" description of the archetypical "Handsome Sailor" and Great Sailor also called into question modern science and its technology, as represented by steamships and ironclads, and modern philosophy, as represented by the enlightened French Assembly and the utilitarian Bentham. Moreover, "natural depravity" was given a more "auspicious" prospect in modern times by modern technology, which replaced "sword or cutlass" with "niter and sulphur" (thereby opening the office of master-at-arms to those who were not virtuously courageous) and by such modern jurisprudential philosophies as those of "Coke and Blackstone," which obscured the spiritual insight necessary to comprehend the "elemental evil" of men like John Claggart. Modernity itself, then, in all its political, scientific, and philosophic dimensions, is the subject of an attack in *Billy Budd.* Put bluntly, modernity induced in Melville a feeling of deep pessimism.

One is entitled at this point to ask precisely what it is about modernity that led Melville to reject and even to attack it. More precisely, one is entitled to ask what Melville regarded as the essential characteristic of modernity; what is its informing theme; or what is the modern characteristic that proved to be so destructive of political virtue and human greatness. And here then one shall see, beneath the narrator's conservatism, beneath the author's hierarchic and aristocratic opinions, and beneath Melville's criticism of the whole of modern politics, the most abrasive of all of the lessons of *Billy Budd.*

The difficulty for the reader is that, at the time of the narrative, the pure "Handsome Sailor" and Great Sailor types are already extinct or on the road to extinction. The reader thus is not shown the effects of modernity upon the unproblematic instances of human and political virtue. Nevertheless, the reader does witness the physical or psychological destruction of the Rousseauean and Burkean variants of these ancient archetypes, and therein perhaps may be seen the true nature of destructive modernity. Since the psychological destruction of Vere is actually ancillary to the physical destruction of Billy Budd, this would mean that the essence of modernity might be revealed in Claggart's hatred for and subsequent attack upon Billy Budd; and it is this hatred and this attack that is most clearly viewed by the reader. Thus, just as Billy's fate as Rousseau's savage man exposed the errors of Rousseau, so too may Billy's fate as a "Handsome Sailor," whom Billy was "something [like] in nature," expose the actual destruction of political virtue by the essence of modernity.

It will be recalled that Billy's similarity in nature to the true "Handsome Sailor" lay in his lack of knowledge and in his essentially prephilosophic character. This facet of

Painting depicting the Indefatigable *in battle with the* Droits-de-l'homme *in 1797. The ships are probable prototypes of the* Indomitable *and the* Rights-of-Man.

Billy's nature was revealed in terms of biblical allusions to "the doctrine of man's Fall." Hence, Billy had no "trace of the wisdom of the serpent"; he had not yet been "proferred the questionable apple of knowledge"; and he was like Adam "ere the urbane Serpent wriggled himself into his company." These biblical allusions occurred within a framework which actually related a secular version of the Fall of man as a result of the "apple of knowledge," that is, a variant of Rousseau's hypothesis that man evolves from a happy, natural savage into a reflecting, reasoning, and therefore "depraved" animal. Nevertheless, the biblical allusions are themselves important, for they point to the ultimate abrasive point of the novel which is being sought. Hence, it is significant that John Claggart is explicitly given the role of the proud and destructive Serpent in *Billy Budd.* Claggart's nature will "recoil upon itself" like Milton's Satan and "like the scorpion for which the Creator alone is responsible"; Claggart ascends "from his cavernous sphere" to accuse Billy of mutiny; his glance into stunned Billy's eyes is "one of serpent fascination"; and moving his corpse is "like handling a dead snake." Thus, Claggart's antipathy toward Billy Budd actually results in the reenactment of the original destruction of the unsophisticated "Handsome Sailor" by the proud purveyor of the apple of wisdom, knowledge, or science.

This satanic Claggart has one trait that distinguishes him from Melville's important earlier villains, Jackson in *Redburn* and Bland in *White-Jacket:* his intellectuality. His "brow was of the sort phrenologically associated with more than average intellect"; he was "dominated by intellectuality"; and he was "intellectually capable of adequately appreciating the moral phenomenon" of Billy Budd. In fact, Claggart's perceptive intellectuality and Billy's simplicity combine to account fully for Claggart's malice towards Billy: "If askance he eyed the good looks, cheery health, and frank enjoyment of young life in Billy Budd, it was because these went along with a nature that, as Claggart magnetically felt, had in its simplicity never willed malice or experienced the reactionary bite of that serpent." Unlike the God-like Dansker, whose knowledge of good, evil, and innocence leaves him yet aloof or transcendent, Claggart's similar knowledge impells him to a "cynic disdain of innocence—to be nothing more than innocent!" Billy Budd is thus destroyed by a person who embodies an uncontrollable hatred for innocence and, by implication, an uncontrolled desire for the advance of prideful knowledge. The destruction of the politically virtuous "Handsome Sailor" by modern science, technology, and philosophy thus points ultimately to the destructiveness of prideful science or philosophy per se.

One may thus conclude that Melville saw the consequences of modernity—atheism, egalitarianism, utilitarianism, scientism, and so forth—as epiphenomena which merely made obvious the moral and political tragedy which was contained in the hubristic birth of philosophy itself. The attack on modern science and philosophy does not lead Melville back to ancient science and philosophy but leads him rather to an attack on philosophy as such. Claggart's intellectually-grounded hatred for simple Billy Budd thus symbolizes the destruction of real human heroism and virtue by the proud love of intellectuality. Moreover, it is impossible not to see Melville's own hand in the revengefulness made apparent in the narrator's exact description of Claggart's murder by Billy Budd; again:

The next instant, quick as the flame from a discharged cannon at night, [Billy's] right arm shot out, and Claggart dropped to the deck. Whether intentionally or but owing to the young athlete's superior height, *the blow had taken effect full upon the forehead, so shapely and intellectual-looking a feature in the master-at-arms;* so that the body fell over lengthwise, like a heavy plank tilted from erectness. A gasp or two, and he lay motionless. [italics added]

Thus one witnesses not only the destruction of John Claggart—who is as pale as the Socrates of Aristophanes' *Clouds,* and who, like the Socrates of the *Symposium,* "never allows wine to get within [his] guard," and who, like the Socrates of the *Meno,* has a numbing effect on speech like a "torpedo fish"—but also another "poetic reproach," this time the reproach of the poet, Herman Melville, to philosophy, the purest source and the clearest manifestation of man's "phenomenal pride."

The above should suggest why it is not adequate to describe Herman Melville, who thus reveals himself as an enemy of Socrates and Socratism, as a "romantic." While Melville certainly shared with the romantics such traits as the longing for the past, the lack of faith in progress through reason, and the advocacy of heart over mind, the past which he advocated and the "state of nature" of which he spoke were, in their hierarchical and politically constraining characteristics, the very antitheses of the Romantics' dreams. More adequate for the comprehension of Melville is to locate him with Aristophanes on the side of the poets in the "old quarrel between philosophy and poetry." Or perhaps, it may be well to understand Melville as he agrees in part with his contemporary, Nietzsche, whose own rejection of modernity led him also to an attack on Socrates. Nietzsche certainly would have agreed with the marginal note of Herman Melville that reads: " 'You are undermining the laws, and are dangerous to the young,' said the judges to Socrates. They said the truth, and from this point of view were just in condemning him."

What final judgment can be made of the author of ***Billy Budd?*** Two lines of thought suggest themselves. As a thinker or "diver" after the truth, Melville may be credited with a very perceptive critique of the modern age. Precisely because this is a major intellectual achievement, it is imperative that Melville not be reduced to the status of a mere advocate of romanticism, or of modern conservatism or radicalism. As a thinker, the Melville of ***Billy Budd*** is far more a disinterested advocate of the truth than a partisan proponent of any modern ideological position.

Secondly, and more importantly, Melville reminds one of the older view of poetry which holds that the great poet's primary task is to teach and therefore to move men. In this older view, the poetic ability to please and delight is understood as the means by which the great poet may present his views of the true nature of good and evil, of justice and injustice, and of nobility and baseness, views upon which he would have his readers or audience direct their own lives. So understood, poetry evidences a claim to knowledge of the nature of things, knowledge which is not the product of reason but of a far more comprehensive process whereby the poet claims to have been inspired by the cosmic dimensions of life. The poet thus faces the philosopher as a rival claimant to wisdom. But while the poet sees the philosopher's exclusive celebration of the power of reason as the quintessential human claim of superiority to nature and its truths, he sees his own openness to the fullness of nature as a celebration of nature itself. Thus poetry, as Aristotle tells us, is an essentially imitative activity.

From this point of view, it is no wonder that Melville, as a poet, would develop a stand against the major representatives of modernity. He saw in the enlightened philosophy of his day an unabashed claim to human superiority to nature. Modern enlightened philosophy was marked by the "gaping flaw" Melville had discerned in the philosopher Emerson, namely, "the insinuation, that had he lived in those days when the world was made, he might have offered some valuable suggestions." Secondly, Burke's conservatism, while opposed to enlightened politics, nevertheless also argued that man, his history and his practical reason, not nature, are the ultimate standards for right and wrong. Thus, Melville presents Burkean Vere as a reader of Montaigne, and he identifies "Montaignism" with the belief, as expressed by Hamlet, that "there is nothing either good or bad, but thinking makes it so." Ironically, while Vere's education was aimed at achieving "a domestic heaven" under the disciplined Puritan rule of a Fairfax, Vere's "settled convictions" actually undermine political rule by severing rank from any ground in nature. And finally, the "return to Nature" advocated by romanticism masks the fact that the romantics' "Nature," following Rousseau, has been stripped of any fixed teleological principle, thus destroying the possibility of fixed natural *standards* for human action. Romanticism's celebration of the child*like* "baby bud," its natural man, results in an inability to distinguish the child*ish* from the manly. Where the romantics expected man's flowering toward perfectibility, Melville saw only an invitation to man's quiescent immaturity.

For Melville, the essential tragedy of modernity is that, in each of its variant forms, modernity denies nature and destroys man's opportunity for true glory. The perennial fact of human life is that nature is the source of both hostility and nobility. Nature's hostility is evidenced in the elemental and martial tempests which threaten man from without and in the intellectualized "natural depravity" which threatens him from within. Nature's nobility is witnessed in its production of natural kings and aristocrats, in whose active fronting of nature's hostility man learns, through the poets, what it means truly to be human. In effect, modern men have tried to turn their backs upon the human condition implied in nature's ambivalence: the enlightened suppose nature's hostility can be overcome, so they live lives of inglorious optimism; the romantic suppose nature is egalitarian and beneficent in the end, so they live lives of ignoble innocence; and the conservative suppose that nature cannot be trusted, so they live in support of authority without being able ultimately to defend any legitimate claim upon the ruled. In these lives lies the tragedy of the modern predicament. Modern man has lived out to its tragic end the hubris implied in the Socratic project; for Melville, modernity presents the full realization of the tragedy inherent in man's attempt to remake his world, an attempt first celebrated in Socrates' "phenomenal pride" in his noetic capacities and first condemned by the biblical "doctrine of man's Fall."

Finally, thus, Melville belongs neither to the modern "left" nor to the modern "right," and neither is his artistic vision of the modern, "protoexistentialist" variety. Rather, he was a poet who imitated nature, and who advanced the "regality" of nature in opposition to modernity's advocacy of the regality of man, an advocacy ultimately derived from the birth of philosophy. Unlike Nietzsche, Melville did not seek to create "measured forms"—he found them and defended them against philosophic destruction. He was a poetic conservative or a pessimist because he believed that the abandonment of modernity would mean, not the achievement of perfection, but a return to an acceptance of the natural limitations of the human condition. He was a poetic radical because he believed that the abandonment of modernity would require man's abandonment of his deepest source of pride, that is, his rejection of the worth of western civilization's celebrated rationalism. In light of these facts, perhaps the most which can be said in incipient criticism of Melville is that **Billy Budd** seems to be the product not of philosophic wisdom, but of a poetic nature, akin to that of a prophet or a giver of oracles, which sees man's glory in heroic deeds, rather than in faith or thought. (pp. 169-80)

> *Thomas J. Scorza, in his* In the Time before Steamships: "Billy Budd," the Limits of Politics, and Modernity, *Northern Illinois University Press, 1979, 210 p.*

Joyce Sparer Adler   (essay date 1981)

[*Adler is an American critic, dramatist, short story writer, and songwriter, with interests in Caribbean literature and the work of Herman Melville. In the following excerpt, she examines Melville's presentation of war in* Billy Budd.]

Billy Budd, Sailor concentrates Melville's philosophy of war and lifts it to its highest point of development. Its themes are recapitulations and extensions of those he had many times developed, and its poetic conceptions are the offspring of earlier ones that had embodied his ideas concerning the "greatest of evils." Even the manuscript record of his revision gives evidence of his need to express as perfectly as possible his thinking about the ill that had been at the center of his imagination for almost half a century and his vision of the "civilized" and "Christian" world in which the essence of war and evil is one. His reluctance to finish is understandable. In his seventies he could not count on another chance to set forth so scrupulously his view of the man-of-war world as a parody of the Christianity it feigns or to awaken other imaginations to "holier" values than those civilized man had lived by.

The view of **Billy Budd** as the final stage in the development of Melville's philosophy of war embraces both the work's abhorrence of war and the war machine (the feeling ignored by those who, in the classical argument about **Billy Budd,** see it as a "testament of acceptance") and its genuinely affirmative, non-ironic, and luminous aspects (the qualities set aside by those who see it in its totality as irony, rejection, or darkness alone). Along with Melville's continued rejection of the world of war there is in **Billy Budd** a new affirmation that within that world's most cruel contradictions lies the potentiality of its metamorphosis. (pp. 160-61)

What happens in **Billy Budd,** with the exception of what takes place within the psyche of the crew, is what Melville had all along demonstrated must necessarily happen—what is, in that sense, fated—in the "present civilisation of the world" [**White-Jacket**]. Impressed from the English merchant ship *Rights-of-Man* to serve the king on the battleship *Bellipotent* in 1797, the year of the Great Mutiny during the Napoleonic wars, Billy is almost literally **White-Jacket**'s sailor "shorn of all rights." Young and of considerable physical and personal beauty, like Melville's typical "Handsome Sailor" in aspect though not like him a "spokesman," called "peacemaker" and "jewel" by the merchantman's captain, and "flower of the flock" and a "beauty" by the lieutenant who carries him off, he is from the first the symbol of the good and beauty "out of keeping" and doomed in the world of war. He is, at the same time, representative of sailors as a class, as the title **Billy Budd, Sailor** conveys. The words of John Marr [in **John Marr and Other Sailors**], describing seamen generally, apply to him: "Taking things as fated merely, / Childlike through the world ye spanned; / Nor holding unto life too dearly, / . . . Barbarians of man's simpler nature,/ Unworldly servers of the world." He is shortly seen to represent also the jewel and flower of youth sacrificed to war, like the soldiers in **Battle-Pieces** "nipped like blossoms," willing children sent through fire as sacrifices to a false god, fated to die because an older generation has failed to rectify wrongs that lead to war. In either aspect—representative or outstanding—he incorporates **White-Jacket**'s conception of a sailor as the "image of his Creator."

Billy accepts his impressment without complaint. Like the crew of the *Pequod* and all but a few sailors on the *Neversink,* he is incapable of saying *no* to anyone in authority, or indeed of speaking at all when he most needs speech to defend himself. His "imperfection" is made concrete in an actual "defect," a tongue-tie, or "more or less of a stutter or even worse." The reverse of this "organic hesitancy"—the ability to speak up to authority—is possessed by no one in **Billy Budd,** but the dedication to Jack Chase, whose outstanding quality in **White-Jacket** had been his willingness to be a spokesman, points up the contrast. There is no one resembling him on the *Bellipotent,* a rereading of the dedication after the novel is read will remind one—no independent spirit to speak up firmly for Billy.

The day after Billy's impressment the *Bellipotent*'s crew must witness an admonitory flogging. The young sailor, now foretopman, vows never to do anything to bring down on himself such a punishment or even a reproof. But while he never does, and while his simple virtue, friendliness, and good looks make him well liked by the crew, these very qualities arouse a "peculiar" hostility in Claggart, the master-at-arms, a functionary "peculiar" to battleships. Billy's goodness calls forth a natural antipathy in Claggart; the devil associated in Melville's imagination with war resides in Claggart as once before in Bland, the master-at-arms in **White-Jacket,** and again is inevitably hostile to all good. What Melville stresses in both masters-at-arms is their function. The diabolical power of each derives from his position, given him by the war machine. Claggart's "place" puts "converging wires of underground influence" under his control. The Navy "charges" him with his police duties so that he can preserve its "order." He lives in "official seclusion" from the light. The words *function* and *functionary* are regularly used in relation to him. Since his qualities are what the navy needs in a master-at-arms, it has advanced him rapidly to his post; and, as with Bland, it defends him—posthumously in his case—even when his evil is exposed. His mystery—something to be probed—is social in its significance and consequences, not something so remote, so emptily abstract and supernatural that one must abandon all attempts to understand it and must accept it as man's fate. The depravity Claggart stands for is encouraged by the values that dominate the world: "Civilization, especially if of the austerer sort, is auspicious to it. It folds itself in the mantle of respectability."

Melville accents the mutually exclusive character of the values of war and peace, for which Claggart and Billy stand, in an unusual spatial way, in terms of "the juxtaposition of dissimilar personalities"; the "mutually confronting visages" of the master-at-arms and the young sailor; and their eventual assignment to "opposite" compartments. Billy is associated with the sunlight; the master-at-arms, with the contrasting space, the shade. They are "essential right and wrong," which in the "jugglery of circumstances" attending war are interchanged. For what is evil for man is war's good; what is good for mankind is that for which war has no place.

An old Danish sailor's thoughts present the question to which the book responds. Seeing in Billy—"Baby," as he calls him—something "in contrast" with the warship's "environment" and "oddly incongruous" with it, he wonders what will befall such a nature in such a world. He warns Billy that Claggart is down on him, but just as Claggart is powerless to contain any good, so Billy is unable to take in the evil of the master-at-arms.

At a moment when the *Bellipotent* is on detached service from the fleet, Claggart seeks an interview with Captain Vere. He accuses Billy of plotting mutiny, a charge well calculated to create fear at that moment, but one Vere cannot credit in the case of the young sailor. Called in to face the accusation, Billy is speechless with horror, his "impotence" noted by the captain. Claggart's eyes as he confronts Billy lose their human expression. His first glance is that of a serpent, his last that of a torpedo fish, Melville again associating the devil, as represented by the serpent, with war, as implied by the torpedo. Unable to use his tongue, Billy can express himself against Claggart only with a blow, which strikes the master-at-arms in the forehead, and the body falls dead.

Vere's instantaneous utterance, "Fated boy," unconsciously pronounces Billy's doom. His response is the result of conditioning so strong that his verdict has the force of an instinct. The moment sets forth dramatically what was put forward as exposition in *White-Jacket* in regard to the power which a man-of-war captain's long-instilled prejudices and training have over his thought. So thoroughly has Vere been dedicated to the ritual of war that to him it seems Fate. He covers and then uncovers his face, the "father in him, manifested towards Billy thus far in the scene . . . replaced by the military disciplinarian." This is a gentler version, but an imaginatively related version, nonetheless, of the two faces of the *Neversink*'s captain, a fatherly one for special occasions and an uncompromising judge's face when he condemns a man to be flogged. The two faces cannot coincide. The face of the military disciplinarian in Vere must take the place of that of the father.

Vere at this point has to make his conscious choice between God's will and that of Mars. He is not in any degree unclear about the nature of that choice; in his mind Claggart has been struck dead by an "angel of God." But neither is he for a moment undecided about his verdict: "Yet the angel must hang." For, as Melville will make increasingly clear, the God whom Vere has been trained to worship is Mars; his religion is war; his thoughts and acts are conditioned by the ritual patterns of warmaking. So he silences that part of himself which recognizes God in Billy; he is, in effect, knowingly striking at God when he decides to sacrifice God's angel. Melville shows him self-alienated to the extreme. Vere does feel sympathy, even deep love for Billy, but "a true military officer is in one particular like a true monk. Not with more of self-abnegation will the latter keep his vows of monastic obedience than the former his allegiance to martial duty." The comparison extrapolates the one in *Clarel* in which an imagined warship is a grim abbey afloat on the ocean, its discipline cenobite and dumb, its deep galleries "cloisters of the god of war." Indeed, as far back as *White-Jacket,* officers had been "priests of Mars" and an English fighting frigate's tall mainmast had terminated, ironically, "like a steepled cathedral, in the bannered cross of the religion of peace." Throughout *Billy Budd* the contrast between the religion of war and "the religion of Peace" is evoked, largely by church images—an altar, a place of sanctuary, confessionals or side chapels, sacraments, covenants, and ceremonial forms—until the *Bellipotent* becomes, in effect, a cathedral dedicated to War. Billy is an offering Vere makes to Mars, an offering not demanded by law or ethics or even military necessity (Melville plainly eliminating these as Vere's felt motivations) but by his own obsession.

Vere's inner compulsion, like Ahab's, drives him so "steadfastly" on that he cannot delay. As he prepares to make his sacrifice, he is so strangely excited that the surgeon who has been called in to attend to the corpse wonders whether he is sane. The question thus raised about Vere's sanity is a symbolic one, the concrete poetic expression of Melville's long conception of war as the "madness" in men. A significant subsidiary question is presented as well: Does Vere's strange behavior indicate a sudden aberration, a "transient excitement" brought about by the unusual circumstances? Vere's devotion to war—his "madness"—is not sudden; it is his constant state of mind. But the peculiar circumstances of Billy's killing of Claggart bring his obsession into sharper focus.

Instead of waiting to submit Billy's case to the admiral when they rejoin the fleet, as the other officers think should be done, Vere sets up the form, though not the substance, of a trial, carefully selecting the members of his court. He conducts the proceedings in extreme secrecy. The naval court-martial that *White-Jacket* condemns as a "Star Chamber indeed!" and compares with the Spanish Inquisition here resembles those palace tragedies that occurred in the capital founded by the czar of Russia, "Peter the Barbarian."

The first part of the trial, which establishes the facts and at which Billy is present, presents in dramatic form ideas set forth in *White-Jacket,* Billy being the representative "plebian topman, without a jury . . . judicially naked at the bar," and Vere the captain clothed with unlimited, arbitrary powers. To Billy, who cannot say *no* to anyone in power, a foundling child who wants to be liked and who fears to call forth even a reproof, Vere, the King's aristocratic "envoy," is someone he could certainly never gainsay. His statement, "I have eaten the King's bread and I am true to the King," recalls the unquestioning obedience exacted in return for food in *Moby-Dick*'s cabin-table scene in which men waiting to be served by Ahab are as little children humble before the captain, whose war they will serve without question, and even Starbuck, the chief mate, receives his meat as though receiving alms. Billy's words, suggesting as they do a sacrament and a covenant, contribute to a contrast between the bargain between men and kings who give them food so that they may feed upon them and the covenant between man and God by which man will live according to the ethical standards represented by God. One realizes at this point why Melville had earlier made Vere refer to Billy as, in "naval parlance," a "King's bargain."

Although Billy symbolizes what is essentially good, he has the weakness of the sailors he represents: his silence gives consent to war's demands. When he grasps what Vere has in mind for him, he acquiesces to the decision as to Fate. His silence—like that of all the others on the *Bellipotent*, including the silence of Vere's humane part—is an accessory of war, partaking of its evil. Thus, an earlier remark about Billy, unexplained at the time, is clarified, namely, that his vocal flaw shows that "the arch interferer, the envious marplot of Eden, still has more or less to do with every human consignment to this planet of Earth."

After Billy is sent back to the compartment opposite the one where Claggart's body is, the second part of the trial, the arrival at a joint verdict, begins. Vere asks the question he knows to be in the officers' minds: "How can we adjudge to summary and shameful death a fellow creature innocent before God, and whom we feel to be so?—Does that state it aright? You sign sad assent. Well, I too feel that, the full force of that. It is Nature." But he urges the court to remember that their allegiance has been sworn to the king, not to Nature. And now, as in his most subtle earlier fiction, Melville speaks through another, saying in part what that character says but in essence and in total intention something far different; it is the technique used with special artistry in the case of Captain Delano in "Benito Cereno" and of Judge Hall in *The Confidence-Man.* Speaking through Vere, Melville espouses the reverse of the religion for which Vere proselytizes. The captain addresses to the court what could stand alone in another context as an eloquent speech against war. He does not intend it so; Melville, however, does, conveying obliquely that war itself is the "Great Mutiny" against God, striking at "essential right." It is Vere, not Melville, who rules out "moral scruple" in favor of that strength in war, that bellipotence, which to him is "paramount." Through Vere's speech to the court Melville reveals the absence of morality in war and shows himself prophetically sensitive to a question whose centrality would not be generally clear until well into the twentieth century, the question of individual conscience and responsibility in time of war. . . . He urges that warm hearts not betray heads that should be cool, that in war the heart, "the feminine in man," must be ruled out. As for conscience, "tell me whether or not, occupying the position we do, private conscience should not yield to that imperial one formulated in the code under which alone we officially proceed."

When one member of the court-martial pleads that Billy intended neither mutiny nor homicide, he replies:

> before a court less arbitrary and more merciful than a martial one, that plea would largely extenuate. At the Last Assizes it shall acquit. But how here? We proceed under the law of the Mutiny Act. In feature no child can resemble his father more than that Act resembles in spirit the thing from which it derives—War.

Yet to the letter of that law Vere works to convert the court; the Mutiny Act is, in the words of *White-Jacket* about the Articles of War, his "gospel."

To guarantee their going along with his "prejudgment," Vere concludes with an appeal to the officers' sense of fear, his argument being that the crew, learning of Billy's deed and seeing him continue alive, will believe the *Bellipotent*'s officers weak and may mutiny against them. This appeal prevails. In any event, Vere's subordinates are, like Billy, "without the faculty, hardly . . . the inclination to gainsay" him. So Billy is sentenced to be hanged at the yardarm at dawn. Vere takes upon himself the burden of telling him privately "the finding of the court," knowing Billy will feel for him.

The narrator gives no account of the interview, only a conjecture that Vere in the end may have developed the passion sometimes "latent" under a stoical exterior: "The austere devotee of military duty, letting himself melt back into what remains primeval in our formalized humanity, may in end have have caught Billy to his heart, even as Abraham may have caught young Isaac on the brink of resolutely offering him up in obedience to the exacting behest." The narrator sees a resemblance between the two situations, the one biblical, the other military, in order that Melville may accent the contrast between the God who created man and the god of war who would destroy him. For God in the story of Isaac and Abraham does not in the end exact the sacrifice. In the history of the ancient Jews, as told by those who composed the Old Testament, the Abraham-Isaac story signifies the first recorded repudiation of the tradition of human sacrifice. It is God's final behest that Isaac should live and that Abraham's seed should multiply through him. But Vere's internal behest condemns Billy, and the tradition of human sacrifice on the alter of war goes on.

Nevertheless Vere does suffer, and intensely; it is one of the most important ideas in the work that all suffer from war. The senior lieutenant sees Vere leave the compartment, and "the face he beheld, for the moment one expressive of the agony of the strong, was to that officer, though a man of fifty, a startling revelation." His is the agony of a martyr to an inhumane religion. By turning from Billy, as Ahab does from Pip, Vere turns from his own humanity, sacrificing to war his capacity for love, for "fatherhood." All that will seem to remain of him from this moment on is his military function. He has adhered to his choice between the values represented by Claggart and by Billy, sacrificing Billy and what he represents and, in effect, upholding what Claggart stands for. And suddenly we know why it was said earlier of Claggart's depravity that civilization, "especially if of the austerer sort" (more denying of its heart), is auspicious to it.

Underlining the reversal of human values in war, Melville

has Claggart prepared for burial "with every funeral honor properly belonging to his naval grade," while Billy lies on the upper deck awaiting an ignominious death. Billy's significance as the good and beauty sacrificed to war is represented as if in a painting. Since all of *Billy Budd* is only some eighty pages, the two-page painting of the young sailor in a bay formed by the regular spacing of the guns must have been of extreme symbolic importance to Melville. [In a footnote Adler observes that "the fact that the passage is in the present tense strengthens the impression of this scene as a picture symbolic of what exists in the world, not just a picture of what Billy looked like at that particular past moment."] Billy lies between two guns "as nipped in the vice of fate." The guns painted black and the heavy hempen breechings tarred the same color seem to wear the livery of undertakers. "In contrast with the funeral hue of these surroundings," Billy lies in his soiled white sailor's apparel, which glimmers in the obscure light. "In effect he is already in his shroud." Worked into the painting is the basic contrast between the ignored values of Christianity and the values actually held sacred in modern civilization. . . . With something of the look of a slumbering child in the cradle, a serene light coming and going on his face as he dreams, Billy is a picture of innocence, beauty, and peace doomed in the world of war.

The chaplain who comes to talk to Billy finds him asleep in a peace that transcends any consolation he has to offer. This chaplain, also an accessory of war, is gentler than the one in *White-Jacket*, but his role, in essence, is the same; indeed it is more fully developed and strongly stated. Melville stresses his function and the contrast between the religion he preaches and the one he serves. (pp. 161-70)

The luminous moonlit night passes away, but "like the prophet in the chariot disappearing in heaven and dropping his mantle to Elisha," it transfers its pale robe "to the breaking day" and a faint light rises slowly in the East. With this association with Elijah and the transfer of his mantle to suggest a progression to a brighter future day, the early phrase, "the mantle of respectability," to signify the cloak which civilization lends to Claggartlike depravity seems to have been meticulously worded to light the difference when this moment would appear. For the transfer of Elijah's mantle to Elisha and the slowly rising light in the East imply an advance to a day when men will no longer worship false gods (the baals from whose designation the name Beelzebub for the devil derives) and will fulfill their latent "God-given" humanity. This prophecy, with the believable reality upon which Melville will base it, is the source of the luminescence that, despite the painful events to come, will irradiate the remainder of the work.

At four in the morning silver whistles summon all hands on deck to witness punishment. The crew's silence, like Billy's, gives consent. Only at the moment of his death does Billy's frozen speech become fluid, touching something deep within the crew. But the greater eloquence is Melville's as he speaks through the young sailor and the scene of his execution. His art makes the spectacle "admonitory" for the reader, as for the crew, in another sense entirely from the one Vere intends. Billy stands facing aft.

> At the penultimate moment, his words, his only ones, words wholly unobstructed in the utterance, were these: "God bless Captain Vere!" Syllables so unanticipated coming from one with the ignominious hemp about his neck—a conventional felon's benediction directed aft towards the quarters of honor; syllables too delivered in the clear melody of a singing bird on the point of launching from the twig—had a phenomenal effect, not unenhanced by the rare personal beauty of the young sailor, spiritualized now through late experiences so poignantly profound.

> Without volition, as it were, as if indeed the ship's populace were but the vehicles of some vocal current electric, with one voice from alow and aloft came a resonant sympathetic echo: "God bless Captain Vere!" And yet at that instant Billy alone must have been in their hearts, even as in their eyes.

> At the pronounced words and the spontaneous echo that voluminously rebounded them, Captain Vere, either through stoic self-control or a sort of momentary paralysis induced by emotional shock, stood rigidly erect as a musket in the shiparmorer's rack.

Imbued with the meaning and suggesting the shape of the whole book, and appearing at the climax of the narrative development, this moment fuses poetic concepts from earlier works and through their union gives birth to something new.

The poetic concepts that carry over involve both imagery and method. The association of Billy with the singing bird about to launch from the twig, confirming him as a symbol of harmony and as a captive in the world of war, has its forerunner in *White-Jacket* when, as the body of Shenly slides into the sea, Jack Chase calls a solitary bird overhead the spirit of the dead man-of-war's man, and all the crew gaze upward and watch it sail into the sky. The use of sound and silence to convey the responses of the crew also has its precedent in *White-Jacket,* as has often been remarked, but here the direction is not from sound to silence but from silence to sound. The creation of a memorable, intensely visualizable scene to pictorialize the form and significance of a social institution is also a tested Melville method, most fully developed in **"Benito Cereno."** Vividly signified in this scene are the war machine's concentration of power, its sacrifice of what is beautiful and good, and its "abrogation of everything but brute Force." It uncovers the ironies and contradictions of the situation: Vere in whom power is centered suffers the most; his humanity is seen to be totally repressed as he stands "erectly rigid as a musket in the ship armorer's rack." At the very moment the humanity in the crew is touched and they react in harmony with Billy, Vere becomes a thing of war whose sole function it is to mete out death, as Ahab at the end is no more than an extension of his weapon. Death-in-life in Vere stands in contrast with Life-in-death in Billy. The benediction, "God bless Captain Vere," gives voice to the feeling shared by Billy and Melville that Vere is the one on the *Bellipotent* most in need of blessing.

The way in which sight and sound are combined in this scene constitutes the new technique Melville's imagination brings forth in this crucial "penultimate moment" on the edge of both death and dawn. What is visual and what is aural join in a strange counterpoint wherein one element is held motionless while the other moves, each working simultaneously both with and against the other, to convey at one and the same moment the seemingly forever fixed picture of the present civilization of the world and movement stirring within it. It is as if in a film action were arrested and the sound continued. The tableau including Billy, the crew, and Vere impresses on the mind a picture that strikingly exhibits the established pattern of the world. It is the picture Vere wishes the admonitory spectacle to impress. But the aural accompaniment flows forward, carrying first Billy's benediction and then the sympathetic, swelling echo from the sailors in whose hearts he is. While what the mind's eye sees is frozen and motionless, the moving sound suggests that the frozen structure may thaw. Something in the heart of the crew, long asleep but intact, has been stirred. The tension between sight and sound, between the apparently immutable form and the growth of feeling within, will continue to the point at which the idea that a seed of change is germinating inside the rigid form will take the ascendancy, giving the work its positive tone. The unusual use of sight and sound in this climactic scene seems to grow out of Melville's desire, newly born in the course of the composition of *Billy Budd,* to explore how the seemingly eternal world of war might begin to be transformed to that fluid, life-giving world of peace so suddenly and startlingly pictured—without any gradual transition to it—in the "Epilogue" to *Moby-Dick.*

As the signal for the hanging is given, a movement in the sky also creates a contrast with the formalized sight below. A cloud of vapor low in the East is "shot through with a soft glory as of the fleece of the Lamb of God seen in a mystical vision, and simultaneously therewith, watched by a wedged mass of upturned faces, Billy ascended; and, ascending, took the full rose of the dawn," his spirit welcomed back into heaven. The climax of the exemplary spectacle the crew has been forced to witness turns out to be one to inspire, one to move the heart and work as a dynamic in the imagination.

The short chapter culminating in the execution closes: "In the pinioned figure arrived at the yard-end, to the wonder of all no motion was apparent, none save that created by the slow roll of the hull in moderate weather, so majestic in a ship ponderously cannoned." The sentence translates into visibility an earlier statement concerning the ordinary sailor: "Accustomed to obey orders without debating them," he lives a life "externally ruled for him." Billy's "impotence," noted earlier by Vere when the young sailor could not speak up against Claggart, is now realized by the lack of any motion originating within his own body, which is externally ruled by the "majestic" motion of His Majesty's Ship *Bellipotent.* His impotence is in sharpest contrast with the omnipotence of the captain who now stands erect as a musket, symbol of civilization's ultimate Force. And yet the world of war, as *White-Jacket* notes near the end, is "full of strange contradictions." Billy does have power. Though impotent to save himself, he has power to invoke the future. His death, illuminating the nature of the world represented by the *Bellipotent,* will quicken the imagination of the crew and in that respect be a good death. But Vere, the king's all-powerful representative, is, in a sense, the impotent victim of the ultimate power concentrated in him. While Billy has the miraculous ability to inspire love for a peaceful way of living, to be in that sense a savior, Vere's potency is only for death. Like Lot's wife, as Melville saw her in *White-Jacket,* he stands "crystallized in the act of looking backward, and forever incapable of looking before." Hence Melville's execution scene is sym-

bolic of both the polarization of power in the world of war and of the contradictions at the heart of such a world, contradictions that must eventually bring a metamorphosis. They have already caused a crack in the rigid mold; the silence, the aural equivalent of the frozen form, has been broken. Eventually music (the ballad) will issue through the fissure in the seemingly unbreakable form.

Moments after the execution the silence is "gradually disturbed by a sound not easily to be verbally rendered." The sound is an omen of a growth of feeling in the crew.

> Whoever has heard *the freshet-wave of a torrent suddenly swelled* by pouring showers in tropical mountains, showers not shared by the plain; whoever has heard the *first muffled murmur of its sloping advance through precipitous woods* may form some conception of the sound now heard. The seeming remoteness of its source was because of its murmurous indistinctness, since it came from close by, even from the men massed on the ship's open deck.

Only seemingly remote, the source is deep within the men. The murmur is indistinct, but there has been some expression, though wordless, of a feeling going back to man's remote origin, and still latent within him. Then, like the "shriek of the sea hawk, the silver whistles of the boatswain and his mates pierced that ominous low sound, dissipating it." The men, yielding to the mechanism of discipline, disperse, and the sound is, for the moment, silenced.

But, again, as the closing "formality" consigns Billy's body to the ocean, "a second strange human murmur" is heard from the sailors as vultures fly screaming to circle the spot. To the crew the action of the vultures, "though dictated by mere animal greed for prey," is "big with no prosaic significance," a phrase that earlier in the growth of the manuscript had read, "big with imaginative import of bale." Though no elaboration follows, the unprosaic significance seems to involve human, as opposed to "mere animal," greed for prey and hints at an awakening of poetic sensibility to the meaning behind the sacrifice of Billy.

An uncertain movement begins among the men, to be counteracted by a drumbeat to quarters not customary at that hour. Vere intends the ensuing ritual to reimpose a strict pattern of conditioned response: "'With mankind,' he would say, 'forms, measured forms, are everything; and that is the import couched in the story of Orpheus with his lyre spellbinding the wild denizens of the wood'." The crew's unresisting participation in the formalities seems to bear out his theory; for "toned by music and religious rites subserving the discipline and purposes of war, the men in their wonted orderly manner dispersed to the places allotted them when not at the guns." But while the day which has followed the rosy dawn brings the firm reimposition of the military forms, "the circumambient air in the clearness of its serenity" is "like smooth white marble in the polished block not yet removed from the marble-dealer's yard"; the uncut marble of future time contains the possibility of being shaped into something different from the static form visible on the deck of the *Bellipotent.*

This introduction of the idea of a freer, more dynamic form is followed at once by a passage about form which bridges the now completed account of "How it fared with the Handsome Sailor during the year of the Great Mutiny" and the three remaining chapters, "in way of sequel," which will embody Melville's creative concept of form and its meaning for him, the writer: "The symmetry of form attainable in pure fiction cannot so readily be achieved in a narration essentially having less to do with fable than with fact. Truth uncompromisingly told will always have its ragged edges; hence the conclusion of such a narration is apt to be less finished than an architectural finial." The counterposition of the two statements about form, Vere's and Melville's, accents the fundamental difference between the thinking of the artist and the man of war. To Vere men are beasts to be tamed, "wild denizens of the wood," who must be bound. Brutishness is their sole potentiality. Melville, whose narrative has just revealed the humanity latent in men, evidenced by the crew's intuitive response to Billy, and has shown the men moved (unbound), has had Vere, the military man, speak of Orpheus, the artist, and find in his music only something akin to that "subserving the discipline and purposes of war." While to Vere war is a sacred, fated form and the *Bellipotent* a place of worship whose architecture is complete, to Melville that architecture is neither holy nor final. Vere would bind man's consciousness; Melville wold awaken it. The conclusion of *Billy Budd* will be "less finished than an architectural finial" because Melville's art strives to be an equation of life, and life to him has no final form—a main theme in *Moby-Dick.* It may seem immutable, but within its set and apparently eternal form there are grains at work. Vere's ideas are to Melville's as long settled, measured, closed, and static form is to the fresh, open, living, growing shape into which the work is about to bloom. The realization of this new shape is a creative act by Melville closely related to his breaking out of the rigid circle of the chase at the end of *Moby-Dick.* The concluding chapters—a "sequel" in the sense of a necessary consequence—burst out of the established pattern of conventional narration and in so doing convey the idea that the rigid form of the world that has been pictured can also be disturbed.

The first of the chapters relates Vere's death. Last seen as a musket, he is himself struck by a musket ball. The incident occurs on the return voyage to rejoin the fleet, when the *Bellipotent* encounters the French battleship, the *Athée* (the *Atheist*), "the aptest name, if one consider it, ever given to a warship." If it is the aptest name ever given a warship, it is the aptest name for the *Bellipotent,* and *bellipotence* and *atheism* become synonymous. Vere's death on the heels of his sacrifice of Billy to Mars is Melville's Judgment upon him for his denial of God. He does not permit Vere to be rewarded even in the way a votary of Mars must desire. . . . (pp. 170-77)

Vere's "Billy Budd, Billy Budd" is his exit line from the drama, and he will not be heard of again. Who "essentially" has he been? The contradictions carefully worked into his characterization—sometimes interpreted as evidence of carelessness or indecision on Melville's part—have been the source of opposite extremes of opinion among critics, all but a few of whom have been impressed by one side of him to the virtual exclusion of the other. But the contradiction within Vere is his very essence; the split in him is as central to his meaning as is the split in Ahab. He is the symbolic figure—not crudely, but finely and fairly, drawn—of civilized man: learned, but not sufficiently imaginative; not devoid of the ability to love, but not allowing this capacity to develop; sensitive to the difference

between the good and evil signified by Billy and Claggart, but the puppet of the god he has been trained to think must rule in this world. His ultimate faith is in Force, not only against the enemy, but in dealing with his own side—utilizing impressment, flogging, and hanging—and in dealing violently with his own heart. Exceptional among the officers on the *Bellipotent,* and even among captains, in his rigidity—there are over a score of references to, or images of, this quality always so appalling to Melville—he is the comprehensive figure of what is dominant in modern civilization. The contradiction within him is the contradiction within it, between war's values and the primeval and enduring needs of human beings. In Vere, as in civilization, there exist two potentials—the one symbolized by the devil of war operating through Claggart and the other signified by Billy as the peace-loving angel of God—God and the devil continuing to be, as elsewhere in Melville's writing, poetic concepts signifying human potentialities and values. It is the tragedy of civilized man, as of Vere—tragic in the sense that creative potentialities are wasted—that he has so far continued to uphold the values symbolized by Claggart and sacrifice those signified by Billy.

As if to underline the idea that the dream of glory in war is doomed, Vere's name is not mentioned in the "authorized" naval account of the *Bellipotent* events quoted in the chapter immediately following his death. The report is Melville's final illustration of how good and evil are interchanged in the world of war and of how "authorized" history may pervert the truth or use it for its own purposes. The article reports Billy's "extreme depravity," while Claggart is said to have been "respectable and discreet," a petty officer

> upon whom, as none know better than the commissioned gentlemen, the efficiency of His Majesty's navy so largely depends. His function was a responsible one, at once onerous and thankless; and his fidelity in it the greater because of his strong patriotic impulse. . . . The criminal paid the penalty of his crime. The promptitude of the punishment has proved salutary. Nothing amiss is now apprehended aboard H.M.S. *Bellipotent.*

But Melville sees everything amiss—except for this, that whereas the report finds that the authorities have nothing "now" to apprehend (in the sense of fear), the crew has begun to apprehend (to be aware of) the fact that something must be amiss, as the concluding chapter opens to view.

With no reason to worship Mars, though they are forced to take part in war's rites, with no illusion that war can satisfy for them "the most secret of all passions, ambition," the crew, inspired by Billy and groping toward some understanding of the mystery surrounding his hanging, has had engraved in its memory the execution scene that Melville has impressed upon the reader's. From ship to ship their "knowledges" follow the spar from which Billy was hanged. "To them a chip of it was as a piece of the Cross." And on the gundecks of the *Bellipotent* their

> general estimate of his nature . . . eventually found rude utterance from another foretopman, one of his own watch, gifted, as some sailors are, with an artless *poetic* temperament. The tarry hand made some lines which, after circulating among the shipboard crews for a while, finally got rudely printed

at Portsmouth as a ballad. The title given to it was the sailor's.

So the inarticulate crew has found its voice. Feelings which had been only a murmur have "found utterance" not only in words but in poetry, however rude. The sailor-poet speaks for the men, unlike the song writer Dibdin described early in the book as "no mean auxiliary to the English government." The sailor's lines are "finally" printed, as the feelings of the crew are "eventually" worded; a slow process is under way. And the ballad, "Billy in the Darbies" goes on to have a life of its own. In this way is Billy resurrected. (pp. 177-79)

"Billy in the Darbies" is extraordinarily subtle and complex. Yet Melville is utterly honest with the reader when he calls the gift of the sailor-poet an artless one. For it is Melville's art—as he speaks indirectly through the sailor's artlessness—which is sophisticated in the extreme. To read the ballad as the sailor's creation is prerequisite to appreciating it as Melville's.

Melville's imagination works through the sailor's; his voice sounds in the overtones with which the narrative has endowed the sailor's simple words. The sailor's descriptive title is Melville's symbolic one: Billy Budd, sailor, lies in the darbies of war, from which he and all other sailors need to be released. (p. 180)

Suggestive plays upon words, as Melville speaks through the language of the sailor, develop main themes of the prose. The "dawning of Billy's last day" will bring also the dawn of consciousness to the crew. "Heaven knows," indeed, who is responsible for the running of Billy up. The sailor's wondering query, "But aren't it all sham?" is Melville's implied question to the reader: "Isn't it all—the whole religion practiced in the *Bellipotent* 'cathedral'—a grotesque perversion of the religion whose music and rites it exploits but whose God in effect it denies?" A "blur" has been in man's eyes, his vision obscured by war and false songs and stories of war. He has been a child "dreaming." (p. 181)

By making the ballad the work of a sailor-poet speaking for the crew whose dormant spirit of harmony Billy has awakened, Melville suggests a coming transfiguration of men and the world. While Billy's body lies bound by the weeds fathoms down, pictorializing the subterranean reality of war as White-Jacket pictures it, as well as the good submerged in man but still capable of resurrection, his memory prompts in the imagination of the crew a subconscious quest for the meaning of his death, an inquiry that may someday ascend to full consciousness. In contrast to Vere who at the trial had spoken of the "mystery of iniquity" but had turned away from probing it, disclaiming moral responsibility, Melville is engaged in fathoming both the mystery of iniquity in the world and the mysterious potency of good. Since good can inspire mankind, even after the death of one epitomizing it, the ballad about Billy's physical end is not an architectural finial, either of the book or of the world it portrays.

The hanging of Billy has been translated into art (both by the sailor-poet and Melville), which in its interaction with life may give rise to a conscious desire by man to change his mode of existence. The *Bellipotent* form is not an inescapable part of the human condition but the result of the failure so far of man's heart and imagination to attempt to understand its mystery and to seek out the transforming possibility within it. Melville's imagination, as it makes itself known in all his works, even the most bitter, does not see civilization's forms as static, complete, devoid of all potentiality for "promoted life." It is incapable of "that unfeeling acceptance of destiny which is promulgated in the name of service or tradition" [William Harris, *Tradition, the Writer and Society* (1967)].

So Melville in *Billy Budd* has shown the world of war, which "fallen" man created and then worshiped, in all its contradictions and potentiality, and his final emphasis has been on the creative in man and on the power of language and art to explore new values and inspire a fresh conception of life. He has written not of original sin but of original good and its continued, though sleeping existence in man, while evil—outstandingly exemplified in war—has been shown as a depravity in man, a fall from his inborn creative potentiality. As far back as the second chapter Melville had introduced this theme, but its deeper meaning for the work had not then been clear:

> it is observable that where certain virtues pristine and unadulterate peculiarly characterize anybody in the external uniform of civilization, they will upon scrutiny seem not to be derived from custom or convention, but . . . transmitted from a period prior to Cain's city and citified man. The character marked by such qualities has to an unvitiated taste an untampered-with flavor like that of berries, while the man thoroughly civilized, even in a fair specimen of the breed, has to the same moral palate a questionable smack as of a compounded wine.

"Human nature" is not under attack here, but what civilization has done to deprave it is. What we have seen in Vere is that his human nature has been so tampered with that he believes he is "not authorized" to determine matters on the "primitive basis" of "essential right and wrong" and that he must fight against his most natural emotions, his "primitive instincts strong as the wind and the sea." On the other hand, primitive good, as symbolized by Billy, has been seen to be too childlike to be able to survive in the present civilization of the world. To transform the institutions of civilization so that good and beauty can thrive in an environment of peace, the members of the crew of man have to develop the desire to probe civilization's nature and articulate their needs and dreams. They must, in terms of the imagery relating to "Baby" Budd, attain manhood *Billy Budd* implies that this may yet be. (pp. 181-83)

Joyce Sparer Adler, " 'Billy Budd' and Melville's Philosophy of War and Peace," in her War in Melville's Imagination, *New York University Press, 1981, pp. 160-85.*

Robert K. Martin   (essay date 1986)

[*Martin is an American-born Canadian critic and the author of* Hero, Captain, and Stranger: Male Friendship, Social Critique, and Literary Form in the Sea Novels of Herman Melville. *In the following excerpt from that work, Martin discusses the depiction of sexuality and political authority in* Billy Budd.]

[A controlling structural pattern through several works of Herman Melville] can be expressed most simply as the encounter of, and conflict among, three fundamental characters: the Hero, the Dark Stranger, and the Captain. It is my contention that this encounter is at the base of works otherwise as different as *Typee, Redburn, White-Jacket, Moby-Dick,* and *Billy Budd.* Although elements of the pattern are also present in other works by Melville, it does not dominate them in the way it does the works already mentioned. . . . (p. 3)

It is perhaps the fact of being at sea that gives many of their particular qualities to these works. The fluidity of the sea itself, and the absence of social norms, serves as a constant reminder of the power of the natural world and of man's very small place in it. At the same time the institution of the sailing ship, whether man-of-war or whaling ship, allows extraordinary authority to the captain, more indeed than would be available to almost any land-based authority in anything but an absolute monarchy. These facts seem to come together in the violent clash of the claims of nature and its ultimate mysteries with those of man, incarnate in the captain, and his attempt to assert authority over the ever-changing. By, for the most part, eliminating the role of women in these novels, Melville can focus on the conflict between two erotic forces: a democratic eros strikingly similar to that of Whitman, finding its highest expression in male friendship and manifested in a masturbatory sexuality reflecting the celebration of a generalized seminal power not directed toward control or production; and a hierarchical eros expressed in social forms of male power as different as whaling, factory-owning, military conquest, and heterosexual marriage as it was largely practiced in the nineteenth century, all of which indicate the transformation of primal, unformed (oceanic) sexuality into a world of pure copulation. (pp. 3-4)

It may be useful, however, to indicate at the outset the fundamental dynamics at work. The Hero, or experiencing self of the novels, is caught between two opposing forces. One of these, represented most often by some form of the Dark Stranger—or, later, the Handsome Sailor—represents a kind of innocence or state of nature. Because of his darkness, he is, either in fact or at least symbolically, outside the world of white European civilization. His push is therefore toward natural law and against social law, a distinction that . . . is crucial for Melville. The opposing force, that of the Captain, or figure of authority, represents the Western world in its search for control—control over space and over other individuals. The Captain is, both formally and symbolically, the representative of legal authority and hence the force of restraint upon the individual. The Hero finds himself caught between these two forces and obliged to choose between them. That choice is a difficult one for all of Melville's heroes, but the novels may be distinguished precisely by the degree to which the Hero is able to make the choice for the Dark Stranger and to accomplish his act of rebellion against the Captain. (pp. 4-5)

Billy Budd is perhaps Melville's ultimate treatment of the encounter between the Dark Stranger (here metamorphosed into the "light" figure of Billy) and the Captain, whose role has been doubled into those of Claggart and Vere. There is no Hero. The absence of a Hero, of an experiencing self, is part of the reason that *Billy Budd* is in many ways Melville's darkest work. . . . [The] Captain executes Billy, but Claggart is dead, Vere himself dies soon after, while Billy lives on in his ballad (a point to which we will return). But the novel gives us no reason to believe that anything will change socially or that any personal change can be effected, since there is no one in the story to respond to the events. It may be that Melville was no longer able to imagine a protagonist as a young sailor; but it also seems likely that he no longer had any illusion that the world might be altered. The Veres will rule, thus allowing the Claggarts their way, and the Billies will die.

Billy Budd is above all a study of repression. All three of the principal characters have transferred energy from one form to another. In Claggart sexual desire for Billy, inexpressible on board ship and on the part of a master-at-arms, is transformed into hatred. For Claggart destruction of Billy is a distorted product of a deep unacknowledgable desire. For Captain Vere an affectionate paternal regard is sacrificed for the sake of a career. A fundamental goodness and desire for order can be expressed only by the suppression of all feeling in the name of authority. Both Claggart and Vere are betrayed by their place in a social order that values control and suppression. The police and the military are devoted to control both internal and external; they require of those under their authority a loss of self and the replacement of personal desire by aggression. They must kill that which threatens their precarious control of self; for that reason murder becomes a kind of suicide. Billy himself also shows the consequences of transferal of energy under repression. His stutter is a physical index of the conflict within himself between speech and silence, the self-enforced suppression of a language of protest. The tongue that should cry out against impressment becomes the arm that strikes the agent of injustice. The sexuality of *Billy Budd* is a sexuality divested of its subversive power: it is the sexual attraction between power and powerlessness, a sado-masochistic drama that contains all its energies and turns them inward. Billy declines to rebel, out of loyalty to a false system, but he dies at the hands of that system in any case. Rebellion is hopeless in this closed world where beauty is simultaneously feared and desired. The destruction of Billy is Claggart's and Vere's attempt to preserve themselves. The intricate *pas de trois* of these doomed characters serves to remind us of the extent to which military action is a perversion of love. In this homosocial world, charged with sexual potential, only strict control of the homosexual within can prevent a mutiny. (pp. 107-08)

Billy's beauty makes him a homosexual icon, not a figure in a realized homosexual relationship. His blankness is a kind of slate on which others inscribe their desires. Lacking his own identity, he becomes that which others desire. He is a sexual object, made over by the perceiver. But he is also the figure of the homosexual as victim. His death indicates Melville's failure of belief in the possibility of change.

One should not, however, exaggerate Billy's flaws. He is presented in a number of positive ways that link him to figures from the earlier novels. His mythic associations are with Hercules and Apollo, images of strength and beauty. But he retains few of the attributes of Apollo, except perhaps, by way of Nietzsche, an opposition to a Dionysian element of celebration. He is associated with the archetype of the Handsome Sailor and hence with phallic power—wayfarers render "tribute" to the "black pagod" or idol like the Assyrian priests before the "grand sculptured Bull." But, as Melville suggests, his relationship to the Handsome Sailor is primarily "in aspect" whereas "in nature" there are "important variations." Billy's appearance is of perfect beauty, the union of masculine and feminine, but his acts show little sign that he has achieved that transcendence of sexual difference. The novel's dedication to Jack Chase, the Handsome Sailor of *White-Jacket* makes Billy's inadequacies clear. Billy is too soft, too weak, and too passive to be considered worthy of the heritage of Jack Chase.

Billy's appeal is pederastic, and he is therefore inadequate as the locus of the erotic energy that Melville felt was necessary to combat tyranny. For pederastic love does nothing to alter the power relationships of heterosexual love; it merely substitutes a powerless boy for a powerless woman. It is not surprising then that both of the authority figures in the novel should be in some sense in love with Billy. He is a tempting figure, but one who does nothing to contradict the order of society. Hence love for him, like the Greek love on which it is modeled, is consistent with a hierarchical society in which slave boys are a perfectly acceptable object of male lust (Billy's link to the African at the beginning of the novella stresses his role as captured slave and renders his love for his master Vere all the more ironic and self-defeating). Melville's task was to make his reader feel the attractiveness of Billy while at the same time recognizing his inadequacies. Melville may himself have felt such an ambivalent response. He seems to have preferred the statue of Antinous in the Villa Albani to all other works of art and even had a cast of Antinous, the beloved of Hadrian, in his room. He clearly fell in love with Hawthorne, although he would later satirize him as a frightened, almost effeminate figure (as Falsgrave in *Pierre,* for instance). But the political context of *Billy Budd* makes it necessary to pass beyond a figure like Billy; and nothing in the story makes that possible. Billy's external beauty is not a sign of spiritual beauty, and so he falsifies both the *Symposium* ideal of ascending love and the Greek aesthetic ideal of a harmony between idea and realization, between content and form. In the archetype of the Handsome Sailor, as established by Melville in the first section, "moral nature" is allied to "physical make." Furthermore, the Handsome Sailor is "intensely black," while Billy has a "rose-tan" complexion. The blue-eyed rosy-cheeked innocent can hardly stand for the values of the Dark Stranger. The introductory passages thus serve to establish an ironic context in which to see Billy, just as the Nelson chapter serves as an ironic context for Vere.

Billy's physical beauty is explicitly linked to that of David, at least in one version of the manuscript: Billy is "goodly to behold" as David is "goodly to look to" (1 Sam. 16:12), just as Claggart's hatred of Billy is a version of Saul's hatred of the David he had once loved ("Saul's visage perturbedly brooding on the comely young David"), an allusion introduced to be denied, since "Claggart's was no vulgar form of the passion." His ability to sing links him to Orpheus—probably as musician and lyrist a variant of the David figure, whose "harp" is often translated as "lyre"— but we recall the fate of that earlier Orpheus, Harry. Even as a figure of Orpheus, Billy seems strangely inadequate. If the quality of his voice is, as Melville says, "expressive of the harmony within," then his stutter seems to bespeak some disharmony. Melville in fact calls the stutter an "or-

ganic hesitancy," a deliberately circumlocutory phrase that calls attention to the role of the stutter as an outward sign of an inner failure of nerve. The degree of innocence that Billy represents simply cannot exist in the world; indeed it becomes a kind of evil, the inability to ever know or judge. . . . Billy's only song is contained in the four words he expresses at the moment of his hanging, "God bless Captain Vere!" For these words there is no stutter, and they are "delivered in the clear melody of a singing bird on the point of launching from the twig." At the moment of death, Billy is in total harmony, in total opposition to the events that have overtaken him. If Billy is to be Orpheus, he must offer us a greater song than this, a mere "conventional felon's benediction." The natural imagery of the bird "launching from the twig" is grotesquely at odds with the actuality of the military execution; it indicates Billy's return to the nature of which he has always really been a part. Orpheus's power comes from his ability to cast a spell upon the violence of nature, from the potential of art to unite nature and a higher intelligence. But Billy's art is mere birdsong, a conventional phrase that has no power to transform nature. His metamorphosis is only his return to his proper element. That Billy represents only nature, a nature without humanity as it were, does not reduce the condemnation of those who destroy him; Vere and Claggart, like Ahab, must bend nature to their purposes and destroy it in order to serve themselves. But it does mean that Billy, however appealing, cannot be the "hero," and that the story of which he is "the main figure is no romance."

Billy is Melville's most reduced version of the Dark Stranger—light instead of dark, weak instead of strong. The shift in this character, along with the absence of the Hero, makes the novel one of political despair. What hope can there be for resistance to unjust authority when there is no alternative? Billy goes to his death without uttering a single word of protest, without harboring a single thought of anger against Vere or his silent shipmates. . . . Billy goes to his death like a lamb to slaughter. Although the light of the dawn may make the fleecy clouds look like "the fleece of the Lamb of God," the comparison does not ennoble Billy or give his death divine significance. It is one last confirmation of his status as a poor dumb animal, killed for human notions he cannot comprehend. At the same time, it is Melville's final assertion of the complicity of the Church in the ways of the state and its consequent abandonment of any message inherent in the story of Christ's sacrifice. From the missionaries of *Typee* to the chaplain of *Billy Budd* the Church is condemned in terms of the very values it claims to represent: brotherly love and peace. If Billy is Christ, he is nonredemptive. His death leads to no new life and asserts merely the Church's inability to respond to a world in which state power has replaced family order. (pp. 108-111)

Claggart, "a sort of chief of police," illustrates the transformation of sexual energy when it is placed at the service of authority. Like a chief of police . . . , Claggart exercises authority that is really in the hands of someone else. His physical discipline (represented here by the rattan) enforces laws he does not make, against crimes he himself commits, or would commit. The police authority, as Melville depicts it, is an arm of the state, prepared to lie and distort in order to preserve its power. The rattan that Claggart carries is thus a perfect figure for the repressive authority that relies upon a transformation of the erotic—it is as if Queequeg's pipe became a tomahawk again. The sexual potential of the rattan is clear in the episode of the spilled soup: Claggart was about to "ejaculate something hasty," but instead "playfully tapped him from behind with his rattan." The playful tap of an instrument of punishment calls attention to this bivalent figure: ejaculate or strike, play or punish, cock or rattan.

Claggart's desire for Billy thus becomes the desire to sodomize Billy (and, in the social context, to sodomize means to exert power). Claggart reconverts dispersed sexual energy (Billy's spilled soup) into directed phallic aggression. As in *White-Jacket,* punishment in *Billy Budd* is the equivalent of physical aggression: whipping is a kind of male rape (including ceremonial undressing) that aims at humiliation as a means to the assertion or maintenance of power. Yet the desires in *Billy Budd* are inverted, so that Claggart's desire for Billy is not only a desire to hurt Billy, but also a desire to *provoke* Billy, so that *he* (Claggart) can be raped by Billy. His false accusation achieves this purpose by finally provoking Billy to raise his arm. At last erect, Billy lacks the means of ejaculation, so verbal force must be replaced by physical, as sexual energy by aggressive. When Billy strikes Claggart, he in some strange way fulfills Claggart's desire: Claggart dies instantly, at last possessed by that which he has sought to possess. He leaves behind, of course, his tongue, the agent of his posthumous victory over Billy. Throughout the novella, speech is the means of power, whether in the insinuating, snake-like hisses of Claggart or the oily subtleties of Vere: Billy of course lacks speech. His stutter is a sign of his powerlessness, an inability at once sexual and verbal. It sprays words without direction, like the soup that Billy spills. Such a generalized *ejaculatio praecox* prevents him from ever employing the power inherent in his beauty, and of course is given form again in the too-quick arm. Billy's sexuality suffuses everything but is too diffuse to make a difference. It is the sexuality that can be employed to divert political energies. Billy has been removed from the *Rights-of-Man;* his fate demonstrates the hopelessness, indeed the destructiveness, of a sexuality removed from politics.

Envy of Billy's physical beauty, desire for that which he cannot have but by his own gestures acknowledges he wants—these forces cumulate in Claggart and are transformed into the hatred that is the opposite side of the coin of love. "But for fate and ban" Claggart "could even have loved Billy." But the moments in which Claggart seems to realize this, in which his expression is one of "soft yearning," are "evanescent," and he quickly returns to his "immitigable look," like a "wrinkled walnut." By his refusal of that yearning, Claggart loses all his own spirit, and what might have been his natural expression of affection becomes instead the venomous kiss of the serpent. Only a few years later Oscar Wilde would write, "Each man kills the thing he loves." So in Melville's darkest mood he recognized the intricate relationship between love and hatred and what seemed like the inevitable destruction of love by a system that needed to make chiefs of police out of its greatest villains. The Claggart/Billy relationship is the only thing that could have altered the bleak outcome of the story or have provided some possibility for the reconciliation of cultural oppositions (Melville located the prototypes of Claggart and Billy near each other in the Capitoline Museum, in the figures of Tiberius and Antinous). Claggart's refusal is not only the rejection of a "banned" love, although it is that, but it is also the larger social process by which all instincts of love are transformed into those of hatred in the name of service to the state and the engines of war. Vere, too, seems a potential lover whose love is repressed. Humorless, undemonstrative, he has made war into a "science" and law into a series of regulations. Although apparently fond of Billy who, he thinks, "in the nude might have posed for a statue of young Adam before the Fall," and even considering him "for promotion to a place that would more frequently bring him under his own observation," he does not allow personal affection (or lust) to overcome a strict adherence to what he claims to be the "forms." Much has been made of Vere's love for Billy as expressed in his stateroom at the time of Billy's sentence, but every action alluded to there is preceded by "may have." Melville is already shifting his tale toward its concern with the means by which history operates to sentimentalize and assimilate by a process of rewriting that becomes explicit at the end of *Billy Budd.* If Vere loves Billy, it is a love that kills in the name of discipline.

If the sexual and psychological drama of the novel is located in the conflict between Billy and Claggart, the political drama is located in the conflict between Billy and Vere. That drama is also partly psychological, since Vere is no mere villain but a portrait of a reasonable man in the service of an unreasoning office. And his service of what he perceives to be his duty in fact exceeds any actual obligations. If Vere were evil in the way Claggart is, we would be faced with a story of primarily psychological import; because Vere is "normal" and yet very much like Claggart, we are faced with a story that deals with a permanent political dilemma: Can the good person serve the state? It is on the issue of Vere that Melville criticism has split most remarkably. The critics who see Ahab as the hero of *Moby-Dick,* in more than a technical sense, are still a small minority. But it appears that a majority of readers have found Vere to be the hero and locus of value in *Billy Budd.* Such a misunderstanding is frightening, not so much for what it says about the ability to deal with the text (and Melville did create problems by writing a text without a hero) as for what it says about the society of which Melville had already so despaired. *Billy Budd* is the first Melville text in which the Captain is given real psychological depth, but his place in a hierarchical structure of power in which mutiny—the revolt of the children against the father—is the greatest danger renders him incapable of realizing whatever potential for love or wisdom he may possess.

Nothing that we know about the role of the Captain from the earlier works would lead us to believe that Melville would create a captain who represents the moral perspective of the author: every Captain in Melville is corrupt, a tyrant, or a madman. But it is of course possible that Melville came to reject everything he had once believed. Let us look then more carefully at Melville's characterization of Vere. He is a snob. With a "leaning" toward "everything intellectual," he always takes to sea a "newly replenished library, compact but of the best." What texts? Those books that "every *serious* mind of *superior* order occupying any *active* post of authority in the world *naturally* inclines" toward (my emphasis). His conservatism is not the product of careful reflection on new ideas, but instead "a dike against those invading waters of novel opinion social, political and otherwise." The pomposity of his character is accurately embodied in the language of these passages, language that is employed as a kind of *style indirect libre,* echoing Vere's conceptions of himself and his stilted, self-satisfied phraseology. He is also a tyrant, exercising total political authority, compared by Melville to Peter the Great and his palace intrigues. His speeches to the court are masterpieces of portrayal, illustrating the false protestations and self-proclaimed honor of the prosecuting attorney. His rhetoric here shifts tone and subject with the ease of *Hamlet*'s Claudius. But at its heart it is the rhetoric of Ahab: "You see then, whither, prompted by duty and the law, I steadfastly drive." The participial clause is enough to assert his honor but hardly enough to disguise the aggressive energy that it seeks to clothe in virtue. (pp. 111-14)

Vere's own language is a parody of judicial argument, marked by the substitution of the abstraction for the concrete. We know that Vere is capable of adopting other rhetorics, but his use of this discourse of law is Melville's depiction of the corruption of the office: in the courtroom one is faced with the temptation to speak, and hence to think, legally and so betray one's humanity: "Quite apart from any conceivable motive *actuating* the master-at-arms, and *irrespective* of the *provocation* to the blow, a martial court must needs *in the present case* confine its attention to *the blow's consequence, which consequence* justly is *to be deemed* not otherwise than as the striker's deed" (I have italicized the most striking examples of legalese). All of these words amount to saying nothing more than that Billy struck Claggart. It is not possible to imagine that Melville would cast as a hero a man who could so abuse the language. But he could imagine that a man of ambition would use such language to assist himself on his way to a glorious career and that such language would be an effective means of concealing, perhaps even from himself, the immorality of what he does. (pp. 115-16)

The society of **Billy Budd** is corrupt, since power creates greed. The weak serve the strong so that they may profit from them. The Church has been turned into an arm of the state and hence becomes a collaborator in murder (the execution of prisoners) and war. Over and over again Melville has called attention to the role of the military chaplain, who by accepting that post betrays the Church to which he claims allegiance. One cannot serve both God and Mammon. The chaplain on the *Bellipotent* is "the minister of Christ though receiving his stipend from Mars"; by accepting such service he "lends the sanction of the religion of the meek to that which practically is the abrogation of everything but brute Force." The Church, which ought to oppose power, abandons its faith so that it can share in power. The "war contractors" have an interest in war, since they have "an anticipated portion of the harvest of death." Having invested their money in preparation for war, and in the production of the instruments of war, their financial motive leads them to encourage war. Peace might bring financial ruin. As the Church collaborates and the capitalists invest, those involved in the hierarchy of the state seek their own advancement. Vere, that double of Claggart, is driven by "the most secret of all passions, ambition." But, as Claggart is never able to profit from his currying of favor with higher au-

thority by denouncing Billy, since he is killed by Billy, so Vere does not live long enough to attain to "the fulness of fame," since he is killed in battle by the French shortly after Billy's execution. The deaths of the two men who might have gained by the death of Billy add a final turn of the ironic screw: all that killing, and not even ambition is served.

Both Vere's defenders and his attackers have pointed to the chapter on Lord Nelson as a model by which to judge Vere. One school argues that Nelson is an example of "supreme heroism"; another claims that although Nelson represents "the ideal version of the governing principle," Vere is "unable to emulate this ideal." But the issue is not whether or not Vere measures up to Nelson: Nelson is a false standard from the beginning. One would be surprised if it were otherwise: a loss of faith in Nelson is one of the most important of Redburn's deceptions in Liverpool. At the base of the statue of Nelson he sees "four naked figures in chains" which he could never look at "without being involuntarily reminded of four African slaves in the market-place." Nelson is thus identified as a hero of the imperial venture, and that venture is one of the enslavement of the nonwhite world. Slavery is at the heart of **Billy Budd.** Billy himself is linked to the "black pagod," and his removal from the *Rights-of-Man* is a synecdochic recreation of the enslavement of the blacks and their loss of rights. They too live under a martial system, virtually deprived of all legal rights, in the name of law (i.e., the protection of property and authority). In his account of Nelson in **Billy Budd,** Melville addresses the issue of Nelson's alleged heroism and sees it as the expression of a desire for glory. Melville pretends to answer the "utilitarians" who claim that Nelson was imprudent in appearing on deck in an "ornate publication of his person." Not so, says Melville, tongue in cheek, "an excessive love of glory" is the first virtue of a military man. It is a defense that condemns by its own absurd terms. . . . Nelson's is the heroism of epic posturing and dramatic self-aggrandizement; it is the historic analogue to the rhetoric of Ahab. **Billy Budd,** is antiheroic in theme and language. In it Melville abandons the language of excess for a plain style appropriate to a heroless world. Society has created the model of Nelson as hero at the price of human liberty; Vere's desire to emulate it can only bring disaster to himself and to others.

Following the execution of Billy, Vere attempts to restore order on the ship and justifies himself with the words, "with mankind forms, measured forms, are everything; and that is the import couched in the story of Orpheus with his lyre spellbinding the wild denizens of the wood." (pp. 117-18)

Many readers make a direct connection between Vere's reference to the "forms" and Melville's allusion in the following chapter to "the symmetry of form in pure fiction," and Hayford and Sealts in their definitive edition even point to Melville's poem **"Greek Architecture,"** with its reference to a respect for inherent "Form." However, the difference between Vere's plural and Melville's singulars must be considered. It is totally misguided to connect Vere's appeal to "measured forms" to a classical concept of "Form." As Melville presents the latter idea in **"Greek Architecture,"** he describes an art that is in harmony with nature, rejecting the "wilfulness" of the individual Romantic artist who imposes his ideas on nature for a response in "reverence for the Archetype." This classical view is consistent with a nineteenth-century concept of organic form, since organic form is derived from nature, the archetype, and not from the human will. Words connected with "form" are never used in this sense in *Billy Budd:* Billy is to be judged "formally" and not by nature; our world is one of "formalized humanity," from which affection is banished. The word "measured" is also used in a negative context: when Claggart accuses Billy he approaches with "measured step." In *Billy Budd,* then, "measured" means calculated, and "forms" are human impositions on nature. This is not the "measure" or the "form" of Greek aesthetics. Nor is Melville's acknowledgment that *Billy Budd* may not achieve "the symmetry of form attainable by pure fiction" a criticism of the work; Melville's aim is the "truth uncompromisingly told" which "will always have its ragged edges." The contrast between "symmetry" and "truth" is one that is important for *Billy Budd,* of course, since it is an aesthetic equivalent of the contrast between the "forms" and justice. Can any reader of *Moby-Dick* really believe that Melville valued symmetry above all else? above truth? Melville's art is always "ragged" because he will not accept the falsification necessary to achieve the illusion of symmetry. Because life is manifold, its representation in art must be flexible enough to capture that diversity.

As . . . in all of Melville's works, his characteristic technique for achieving that representation of diversity is the mixing of genres. That formal solution is employed in *Billy Budd* as well. We have already looked at the chapter on Nelson and seen how this historical interlude functions as a doubly ironic foil for Vere (Vere can never be Nelson, but then Nelson is not worth being anyway) and as a commentary on the Melvillean aesthetics of dissemination. The death of Billy is followed by five such digressions, or five alternate endings. All of them are attempts, as Mary Foley has said, "to apply some law or pattern to the novel's events" in contrast to the "organic form" the novel already possesses ["Digressions on *Billy Budd*" (see Stafford entry in Further Reading)]. All are as false aesthetically as they are false in content. Like the classifications of "cetology," they cannot represent the truth. The first of them is a conversation of the Purser and the Surgeon that echoes the gravediggers' scene in *Hamlet.* Like that scene it shocks by its sharp contrast of vulgarity and beauty, of scientific knowledge and the fact of death. The bawdy humor about the absense of a final ejaculation as Billy was hanged calls attention to the sexual theme and confirms Billy's lack of the seminal power that could at once resist authority and create a new erotic order while at the same time demonstrating the inability of a sexual metaphor to say all there is about Billy: surely he is more than an orgasm, which is in turn more than the discourse of science will allow in its attempt to use language to mystify and to transform the multiple human experience into an analogy that links the body to a malfunctioning engine—in the Surgeon's words it is "a mechanical spasm in the muscular system." Like the discussion of *Hamlet's* gravediggers, their mordant humor reflects on the world around them and on the pretentiousness of science and its inability to deal with human experience. They even deal in a little Greek, discussing *"euthanasia,"* which they apparently take to mean suicide. Just as the gravedigger's false Latin, *se offendendo* for self-defense, turns out to be meaningful (suicide, presumably, is an offense, not a de-

fense), the false Greek is not only a joke at the expense of the pseudo-learned but a hint at Melville's meanings. *Euthanasia* was just acquiring its new sense (as a death inflicted as an act of kindness), and Melville was able to play on the ambiguity inherent in the term.

The second digression is devoted to the response of the men on the *Bellipotent.* Despite their love for Billy, they can offer only a "muffled murmur" for they, like him, are "inarticulate"; their murmur is indeed echoed by that of the birds who fly to the site where Billy's body has fallen into the sea, looking for food. It is one of the book's darkest moments, for the men are nothing more than animals, their highest goal food, whatever impulse they might once have had to resistance having been eroded by years of "martial discipline." They save their own necks, and procure their own meals, by following orders. In that they do no more than Billy had tried to do, and his failure to achieve immunity through following orders is a lesson that never touches them. When he first sees the novice flogged, Billy's response is not anger or revenge but only the resolve never to "make himself liable" to such punishment. Billy is incapable of recognizing that injustice committed against one person is injustice committed against everyone. There is thus a small amount of poetic justice that the crew like him chooses to follow orders rather than rebel. Sauve qui peut ["every man for himself "].

A similar justice of sorts is achieved by Vere in the third digression, in which his death at sea is recounted. One suspects that there is more symmetry in these digressions than Melville had allowed; seeming formlessness turns out to be true form. Claggart, the villain, is given a hero's

Melville's gravestone, Woodlawn Cemetery, Bronx, New York.

death in the newspaper account that forms the fourth digression. Almost every fact in the account is wrong—Billy is said to have stabbed Claggart, who is termed "respectable and discreet," and Billy is thought to be an alien and Claggart a patriot. The account of Claggart's death is a wonderful depiction of the ways in which heroes are manufactured. Perhaps one day there will be a statue to Claggart to match that to Nelson. The final digression, and the final falsehood, is the ballad, "Billy in the Darbies." Several critics have seen the ballad as the novel's most affirmative statement. Ray B. West argues that the ballad "represents Melville's final expression of faith in mankind—faith in the ability of the common man to see beyond the misrepresentations of evil, however disguised" [see Further Reading], and Ray B. Browne sees Billy triumphing through the ballad, in a "resounding affirmation of belief in the ultimate triumph of the Rights of Man and of democracy [see Further Reading]. Despite their Fourth of July rhetoric Melville does nothing of the kind. He concludes with a final poem that is a vivid demonstration of the common man's inability to understand. Melville concludes *Billy Budd* in the belief that tyranny will continue to triumph because no one will ever have the courage to fight back. (pp. 119-21)

The ballad-makers serve the state as much as the war contractors or the chaplains: as Melville wrote of Charles Dibdin in *White-Jacket,* "these songs are pervaded by a true Mohammedan sensualism; a reckless acquiescence in fate, and an implicit, unquestioning, dog-like devotion to whoever may be lord and master. Dibdin was a man of genius; but no wonder Dibdin was a government pensioner at £200 per annum." It is the values inculcated by songs like Dibdin's that create a man like Billy, an innocent prepared to die for the king and bless his executioner. His song, "As for my life, 'tis the King's," cited by Melville in *Billy Budd,* is a perfect motto for the wasted self-sacrifice of Billy. The ballad is the last element (or the first, considering its composition) in the construction of a society ruled by the ambitious, policed by the vicious, and peopled by the mindless. Melville's testament is neither one of acceptance nor one of resistance; it is the testament of despair.

Without a viable model of male friendship, Melville could not envision an alternative to his grim picture of society. Without love could there be change? Melville wanted Billy to prevail. At moments, I believe, he wanted that desperately. He did not want to believe in his own dark vision. Surely a beautiful young man might come along and change everything. But however much Melville's heart yearned for that beautiful young man, he knew he would have no mind to share with Melville, no heart to be a companion to Melville's most intimate self. And he did not really believe that he could ever come again. And so Melville had only memory—and death. The last words of the ballad, with which *Billy Budd* began, represent Eros and Thanatos finally reconciled in the embrace of Death. (p. 122)

Billy Budd concludes with simultaneous absolute closure, in that all three major actors are dead, and literary anticlosure, in that the tale ends with multiple versions of telling, none of them adequate to comprehend the experience itself. In Barbara Johnson's words, the ending of *Billy Budd* "empt[ies] the ending of any privileged control over

sense" [see Further Reading]. As in *Moby-Dick,* Melville is concerned by the inability of art to depict accurately, since it must run the danger of imposing a falsifying order on experience. However, Melville's position, unlike that of some modern deconstructionists, is that there is indeed an experience, no matter how hard it may be to capture. It is for this reason that he places his emphasis not on the futility of art but on the need for a "ragged" art of truth over a "symmetrical" art of falsification. *Billy Budd* enacts the way in which love is repeatedly transformed into death, a process parallel to the transformation of natural right into state order. Slavery, injustice, and repression remained facts of life for Melville, facts that he no longer found the means to combat.

Reading Schopenhauer in his last years, Melville apparently came to believe in the necessity of transfiguring the self. Only in the annihilation of the personal self could human beings find rest. His view thus turned toward death, but a death that was not fully eroticized. There, among the shades, malice might truly be reconciled. Without the elimination of the will, the world was condemned to eternal repetition. The violence of Billy's gesture is a sign of his inability to transcend himself and thus of the dangers inherent in any attempt to confront will with will. Billy dies not as a triumphant Christ, but rather as a self disintegrating into the primal waters of the nonself. Melville still loved Billy, the direct descendant of all his heroes, but his view of society had so altered that Billy was divested of all capacity for change. . . . [The] shift of attention from the Hero to the Captain makes the dilemma one of the employment of power rather than of the resistance to power. Captain Vere indeed engages our sympathy, but only because we know so clearly that he can only save himself by embracing Billy; and that his position as well as his character will never permit him to do. Body and mind thus remain permanently severed, and Billy's effeminacy becomes weakness rather than the triumphant androgyny it once betokened.

The power of the false narratives at the end of *Billy Budd* is the power of assimilation, the ability of a society to make history over agian in its own image. Erotic energy, Melville knew, would be co-opted for public consumption and transformed into defused legends of heroic action. Nonetheless, he left behind a final work that tried once more to tell the truth, to leave behind, if only in the form of defeat, a tale that could bear witness to the power of eros and its conflict with authority. *Billy Budd* confirms Melville's final view that the state, in its benign form of justice (Vere) or its malign form of police power (Claggart), could only perceive love as a threatening force that would ultimately lead to mutiny. Power depends, in *Billy Budd,* on the suppression of eros. Male friendship, once a potent force to counteract the arbitrary authority of the Captain, has now gone underground. Sexuality now exists in the sly innuendo rather than in the bold affirmation of *Moby-Dick.* Feared even as it becomes harmless, sexuality persists only in its inverted form of hatred or its sublimated form of regret. The tale that expresses this vision can only be one that trails off into silence.

Billy Budd appears to be less centrally concerned with sexuality than [Melville's] earlier novels. . . . But in fact it sees sexuality in the broadest possible terms. The novel is filled with an awareness of the ways in which patriarchal structures must control sexuality. The exertion of authority requires the suppression of the erotic. *Billy Budd,* although lacking female characters, is deeply aware of the need of male authority to suppress the female, just as masculine authority suppresses the feminine. Vere's execution of Billy is his final attempt to rid himself of anything that might be soft, gentle, and feminine; like Ahab's refusal of Starbuck's love, it is a final act that leads directly to his destruction, while at the same time creating for the reader a poignant awareness of the degree to which these men have come close to acknowledging a fundamental androgyny by daring to embrace another man. Refusing this gesture of reconciliation, they affirm the perpetual tyranny of man over woman, white over black, society over nature. Billy's homosexual figure of integration is lost, even as the final ballad betrays its memory by transforming him into the heterosexual admirer of "Bristol Molly." So too Melville may have known what history would make of him. (pp. 123-24)

> *Robert K. Martin, in his* Hero, Captain, and Stranger: Male Friendship, Social Critique, and Literary Form in the Sea Novels of Herman Melville, *The University of North Carolina Press, 1986, 144 p.*

William B. Dillingham   (essay date 1986)

[*An American critic and educator, Dillingham specializes in the study of American literature and has written studies on the earlier and the later fiction of Melville. In the following excerpt, he analyzes the characters of Billy, Claggart, and Vere as they reflect the novel's emphasis on the need for individual integrity.*]

A curious but little-noticed fact from Melville's last years furnishes a valuable clue to the theme of *Billy Budd, Sailor.* His granddaughter Eleanor remembered that he composed his final work on "an inclined plane that for lack of more accurate designation one must call 'desk'; for though it had a pebbled green-paper surface, it had no cavity for inkwell, no groove for pen and pencil, no drawer for papers, like the little portable desks that were cherished as heirlooms in the late nineteenth century." It was "open underneath" and rested upon a "paper-piled table" in Melville's room at Twenty-Sixth Street in New York. On one of the inside walls of the inclined plane, he pasted a maxim: "Keep true to the dreams of thy youth." Most biographers and critics overlook or ignore this detail probably because of its seeming triviality\ But Melville was not the kind of person given to pasting wise sayings about his house; so the discovery of this piece of paper attached to his writing desk should have stimulated far more discussion than it has. The maxim—placed for his eyes only—suggests that this was a subject much on his mind during the last years of his life. *Billy Budd* is his final portrayal of a man who failed to know and to be true to himself.

That man is Captain the Honorable Edward Fairfax Vere, a person of pronounced intelligence, unusual depth of feeling, splendid education, impeccable credentials as a naval officer, and unswerving commitment to principles. The context for his life as Melville delineates it is mutiny, a constantly recurring subject in the novel. (pp. 363-66)

This context of mutiny in *Billy Budd* serves as an analogue

to a like challenge within the heart and mind of Captain Vere that comes only a month or two after the rebellion at the Nore. This interval—from May 1797 to the following summer, when the action of the novel takes place—was marked by a sense of unusual alertness among officers of the fleet to the least sign of unrest among the men:

> So it was that for a time, on mor than one quarter-deck, anxiety did exist. At sea, precautionary vigilance was strained against relapse. At short notice an engagement might come on. When it did, the lieutenants assigned to batteries felt it incumbent on them, in some instances, to stand with drawn swords behind the men working the guns.

Captain Vere is thus highly sensitive to the threat of mutiny because of the world situation and, more particularly, the outbreaks at Spithead and the Nore: "For it was close on the heel of the suppressed insurrections, an aftertime very critical to naval authority, demanding from every English sea commander two qualities not readily interfusable—*prudence and rigor*" (italics mine). In one sense, Vere's haste in calling a drumhead court to try Billy, instead of waiting until the ship rejoined the squadron and referring the case to the admiral, is understandable. (pp. 368-69)

Still, Vere's decision appears to his officers as an overreaction, and indeed it is, one brought on not only by his awareness of the general climate of insurrection but also by the long-standing prospect of mutiny *within his own mind.* Through "prudence and rigor," that is to say, rationalization and discipline, he maintains his steady allegiance to king and country. His prudence and rigor—those nemeses of mutiny—are manifested especially in his glorification of what he calls "forms." He is fond of saying: "With mankind . . . forms, measured forms, are everything; and that is the import couched in the story of Orpheus with his lyre spellbinding the wild denizens of the wood." Vere himself has been spellbound by an Orpheus of sorts, and he will not allow anything to break the spell: he is committed to this music wherever it takes him and no matter what it demands of him. It is represented by the martial tunes played immediately after Billy's execution, tones "subserving the discipline and purposes of war." It comes, however, from an Orpheus inimical to his deepest nature and puts him under a spell that he maintains to his death, a spell that makes him into something that by instincts he is not.

Vere's name suggests the two broad areas in which the spell operates, *veritas* and *vir.* He is committed to what, in his enchanted condition, he believes to be truth, to things as they actually are—*veritas.* . . . Under the heading of *veritas,* he has filed away in his intellect certain convictions that act as blinders to keep him on the path that his spell leads him and as filters to keep out any music but that of his false Orpheus. He had "established in him some positive convictions which he forefelt would abide in him essentially unmodified so long as his intelligent part remained unimpaired." By "his intelligent part," Melville means his "prudence," or his ability intellectually to rationalize his actions to match his convictions and thus to achieve thereby a sense of self-justification. Consequently, when stirrings within him threaten mutinously to break the spell and to reform his inner world, his intellect—enchanted as it is—strongly meets the challenge of the insurrection and triumphs like a strong human body over a temporary fever. Just as England meets the mutineers at the Nore head-on and represses them, so does Vere always manage to meet any threat of drastic changes within his own inner realm: "His settled convictions were as a dike against those invading waters of novel opinion social, political, and otherwise, which carried away as in a torrent no few minds in those days, minds by nature not inferior to his own." Melville makes it clear, however, that Vere does not take this position merely because he is a member of the aristocracy. Many of those who, like him, are high-born resisted changes and were "incensed at the innovators mainly because their theories were inimical to the privileged classes." But Vere's commitment is not to material wealth or to maintaining an aristocratic class structure; he is following what he has determined to be the truth, and the reforms espoused by contemporary voices represent to him mutinous threats to "the peace of the world and the true welfare of mankind." He is entirely sincere and high-principled—all the more tragic that he exists under a kind of spell, that what he believes to be strains of noble music issuing from his heart come from another source and are in disharmony with his true inner self.

Vere is also spellbound in his firm commitment to those things represented by *vir*, which connotes in Latin a man of character and courage. In Latin writings the word is frequently used to designate a military man. Whenever his allegiance to all those areas of thought and conduct suggested by *vir* comes in conflict with some deep impulse within his being, he prevents mutiny through the exercise of "rigor." He tells the officers who try Billy: "Our vowed responsibility is in this: That however pitilessly that law may operate in any instances, we nevertheless adhere to it and administer it" so that "private conscience should not yield to that imperial one formulated in the code under which alone we officially proceed." His Orpheus, he is saying, is the "imperial conscience," not his "private conscience." Through rigor he succeeds in stifling the latter in order to preserve his fidelity to "the code," but in doing so he blocks self-understanding and acts contrary to his true self.

Indeed, if he followed his "private conscience," which, Melville implies, should be in control but is not, he would not even be a military officer. Only by violating his essential nature can he remain faithful to the "imperial conscience." By becoming a practitioner of war he has abnegated his real self, and that is the underlying meaning of Melville's comment about a military officer's similarity to a monk: "But a true military officer is in one particular like a true monk. Not with more of *self-abnegation* will the latter keep his vows of monastic obedience than the former his vows of allegiance to martial duty" (italics mine).

The further apart the imperial and the personal consciences, the more is "rigor" required to prevent inner mutiny. Some naval officers do not need to stress sever military discipline to ward off insurrection, either within their actual command or within themselves. There may be so little tension between their imperial and personal consciences that mutiny is not a threat. Melville gives Admiral Nelson as an example of this type and recounts an incident to reveal that he did not need to practice a high degree of rigor. . . . That Nelson does not need to exert se-

vere discipline to keep his men obedient signifies that he does not need to keep constant watch over himself lest he neglect his martial vows. Throughout **Billy Budd**, what happens on the outside is a reflection of what occurs on the inside, and it is in this sense that Melville gave his novel the subtitle *"An Inside Narrative."*

The portrait of Admiral Nelson in **Billy Budd** is somewhat deceptive, for it is not nearly so flattering as it first appears. Though Melville seems to be defending him against the charges of the "Benthamites of war," he depicts the Admiral as a man who has raised the "excessive love of glory" almost to the height of a personal religious conviction. Indeed, words with religious connotations mark his characterization. Nelson had "a sort of priestly motive" and "adorned himself for the altar and the sacrifice." . . . [As Melville states in **White-Jacket**], "the whole matter of war is a thing that smites common sense and Christianity in the face; so every thing connected with it is utterly foolish, unchristian, barbarous, brutal, and savoring of the Feejee Islands, cannibalism, saltpetre, and the devil." His opinion of the "he-man" aspect of a military hero, that which is suggested by the word *vir*, is that it exists in an officer only after loftier traits have been chased away. . . .

To his credit, Vere has to struggle with himself constantly to remain a good military officer whereas Admiral Nelson, to his discredit, appears to have no such problem. The discipline that Vere demands of others suggests the severe rigor that he applies to himself. He never tolerates "an infraction of discipline." He is "resolute." He feels that Billy must be condemned to die or else the crew of the *Bellipotent* would think its captain soft, and that in turn would be "deadly to discipline." He is, in brief, "a martinet as some deemed him." His unusual action in calling a drumhead court, therefore, results from his sensing that a revolution may be imminent within his own being; his true self is stirring and threatening to take over. He thus meets his own personal Great Mutiny and crushes it before reform can take place. It is not a victory to be celebrated.

The surgeon's suspicion that Captain Vere may be "affected in his mind" is well grounded. His actions suggest that he may indeed be "unhinged," and Melville hints that a careful reading of the novel will reveal the nature and source of his form of madness: "Whether Captain Vere, as the surgeon professionally and privately surmised, was really the sudden victim of any degree of aberration, every one must determine for himself by such light as this narrative may afford." The light that the narrative affords shows that the "mental disturbance" which Vere's officers note in him is an intensification of the spell that he has been under all along. Vere has not been Vere. His is "a mind resolute to surmount difficulties even if against primitive instincts strong as the wind and the sea," and that resolution to ward off the challenge of his most basic intuitive urges (his "primitive" self) shows the power of the spell that has him. His spellbound condition is suggested in another way in Melville's description of his dying moments: he is drugged. Though he dies with Billy Budd's name on his lips, "these were not the accents of remorse." He is confident even as he faces death that he has remained true to the "imperial conscience." And he has; the spell retains its control over him to the end.

There is something in Vere, however, that wants to break the spell of the false Orpheus, something that occasionally attempts to usurp the ruling imperial conscience and take its place. It is the genuine Vere, the "King's yarn in a coil of navy rope"; the "Starry" Vere. He is being himself more when he gazes out at the sea in what appears a "certain dreaminess of mood" than when he acts the part of a devotedly patriotic officer leading his men in combat or when he prudently philosophizes "upon realities." Only in rare moments does he seem to allow his instinctive being rather than his spellbound intellect to dominate. Always the music of the false Orpheus breaks in, and Vere shows "more or less irascibility" because he must again become something that he is not. His prudence and rigor immediately control his irascibility, which is actually the outward sign of mutinous stirrings within. If Vere could have prolonged these times of introspection, that "king" within him, his real self, might have gained ascendancy, but it remains captive and buried away.

Since in the novel what happens on the outside parallels what occurs on the inside, the abrupt intrusion of Billy Budd into his captain's life suggests that what I have called the real "king" in Vere is suddenly challenging the imperial conscience, the false king. Consequently, Billy is described in royal, kingly terms. "Noble descent," writes Melville, "was as evident in him as in a blood horse." He has a "natural regality." His bearing is "suggestive of a mother eminently favored by Love and the Graces," and it hints at "a lineage in direct contradiction to his lot" as a common sailor. What Vere is fighting after he witnesses Billy's act of mutiny is the instinctive urge to let this regal young sailor go free. He thinks that he must remain resolute against "primitive instincts strong as the wind and the sea." But what Vere is fighting back—his sympathetic tendency toward Billy—is the attempt of his truest and deepest self to emerge and take control. In addition, Melville suggests that it is not only the true Vere that is being stifled but also the *best* in Vere, his "youth," a pristine force of great power. If Vere had given in to his yearning to free Billy, he would at the same time have freed himself from the spell of the false Orpheus and been able to sense the ineffable wonder and power of the hidden sun within.

Melville thus meant two things by the maxim pasted on his writing desk: "Keep true to the dreams of thy youth." First, he was reminding himself of the necessity to find out what and who you are and of acting and thinking in fidelity to that self-knowledge. Secondly, he was expressing his conviction that once that has been achieved, one is in position to probe this true self through the process of deep diving in order to discover the light and strength within, the primitive, Unfallen Man. (pp. 369-77)

To suggest Billy's role as the projection of man's original human nature, his unfallen nobility, Melville characterizes him with images and references that not only point up kingly qualities, as we have seen, but also his purity and spiritual appeal. . . . The closest we can come to God, Melville seems again to be saying, is through the discovery of our *original* human nature. Consequently, Billy (and the sort of whom he is an example) is associated with such venerated objects as the "grand sculptured Bull" worshipped by the Assyrians and such gods as Apollo, as Lieutenant Ratcliffe of the *Bellipotent* calls him.

Apollo was the Greek god of music as well as of light and prophecy, and, indeed, the appeal of music is an implied metaphor for Billy's magnetism. "He could sing," Mel-

ville writes, "and like the illiterate nightingale was sometimes the composer of his own song." Under usual circumstances, Billy's voice is "singularly musical, as if expressive of the harmony within." His last words, "God bless Captain Vere," are "delivered in the clear melody of a singing bird on the point of launching from the twig." His music stands in opposition to the martial strains to which Vere marches. Billy thus represents the true Orpheus whom the Captain should follow. . . . Orpheus-like [Billy] flings about him a bloom; in fact, his very name, Budd, suggests this function. He is a bud or a flower deriving from the "heavenly seed," a vigorous, life-giving force. Lieutenant Ratcliffe calls him "the flower of his [the King's] flock," and Claggart compares him with a daisy (though not intending a compliment).

The seed-flower imagery used to characterize Billy is part of an extensive system of references that reveals Melville again employing the most fundamental symbols of alchemy to suggest an alchemical-like idea: the sustaining and rejuvenating power of what he calls "the hidden sun." Billy is also associated with the jewel and with gold, two of the most common symbols in alchemy for the aims of the "inward work," the realization through self-knowledge of "an extra-ordinary spiritual state." To Captain Graveling, Billy is "the jewel of 'em," the loss of which will leave his ship lusterless and quarrelsome. The Handsome Sailor of Liverpool wears "big hoops of gold" in his ears, and Billy is compared to "a goldfinch popped into a cage" when he is impressed aboard the *Bellipotent*. He is more frequently referred to, however, in connection with light and the sun. He is tanned by the sun, and his arm is like "lightning." Claggart, on the other hand, remains in "seclusion from the sunlight." If Billy's face was "without the intellectual look of the *pallid* Claggart's, not the less was it lit, like his, *from within*, though from a different source. The bonfire in his heart made luminous the rose-tan in his cheek" (italics mine). He frequently produces a smile that "sunned him." At his death, he seems to merge back into the light that is his source: "The vapory fleece hanging low in the East was shot through with a soft glory. . . . Billy ascended; and, ascending, took the full rose of the dawn." He is reclaimed by that which had sent him: "The fleece of low-hanging vapor had vanished, licked up by the sun that late had so glorified it." That the sun or the light with which Billy is linked at his death is meant to have connotations of divinity is suggested by the fact that "the full rose of the dawn" into which Billy ascended at his death was at one time in the manuscript "the full shekinah of the dawn." Melville had used the term *shekinah* before in his poem **"In the Desert"** to stand for the "fiery standard" of God, and in *Clarel* he employed the word to name the presence of God in nature.

Billy Budd, then, is presented as the Man of Light, not the source of light itself but one who brings the light of nature, which is also the force that to the alchemist was hidden within the self. He is the bringer of the *lumen naturae*. As such, he should be the guide and teacher of those who recognize him for what he is. He is the manifestation of that which can lead to the source of truth, which is within. (pp. 378-81)

The reason that Captain Vere rejects him is that Billy is a mutineer. He brings peace, but before he can be a peacemaker, he must instigate change, sometimes with violence.

A revolution of sorts occurs aboard the *Rights-of-Man* when Billy becomes a member of the crew. Frustrated and quarrelsome sailors undergo a metamorphosis as they allow the Handsome Sailor to, in a sense, rule their lives. What they feel for him brings out the best within them: "a virtue went out of him, sugaring the sour ones." His bitterest foe, the man with the fire-red whiskers, becomes his most devoted follower after Billy strikes him in a fight. (pp. 386-87)

Captain Vere and John Claggart, however, perceive that for them Billy represents a threat to the internal hierarchy they have established. In their radically different ways, they both sense that "a mantrap may be under the ruddy-tipped daisies." In short, Captain Vere is afraid that if he allows him to go free after an act of mutiny, striking and killing a superior officer, Billy will take over his *ship*, not just the *Bellipotent* (where the crew might give Billy their allegiance as the sailors did aboard the *Rights-of-Man*) but also his inner command. He could himself become a subject of Billy Budd, and to do so would mean breaking the spell of his false Orpheus, changing all that he has talked himself into believing, going against his martial vows. In sum, this is the greatest threat that he has ever had to his "settled convictions"; this is the time of his personal Great Mutiny. His prudence and rigor prove to be strong enough to suppress a mutiny that would have brought him peace rather than war.

Billy Budd, then, is a psychological study of how two extraordinary men respond to a phenomenon, a flesh-and-blood version of original human nature (without the corruption of the City of Cain) who is placed suddenly in their midst. He forces them both to the test: either they must align themselves with him or get rid of him. Vere loves him, but the call of his false Orpheus prevails. Claggart *could* love him but his perverted nature prevails. He cannot think or see except in terms of perversion. When Melville writes that he is an example of Plato's concept of innate depravity, he is using *depravity* in its true and original sense of the perversion of truth. Not so much a representative of fallen human nature as a Calvinist would envision it, he is rather an illustration of a phenomenon, a person with an inborn compulsion to distort the truth to himself as well as to others, but he does not understand this about himself any more than Vere understands that his "imperial conscience" is drastically violating his deepest and best instincts and making him play a false role. (pp. 387-88)

Melville is concerned so frequently with madness in his characters that it seems almost to amount to a preoccupation, but it is what brings on madness that is his more essential interest—lack of self-understanding. Madness as Melville conceived it may be defined as a condition marked by the absence of self-knowledge. The greater the difference between what a person is and what he thinks he is, the higher the degree of insanity and, consequently, the more difficult to cure.

Ordinarily Claggart's mind functions without challenges to the systematic perversions it creates. But once in a while "some special object" will appear that causes an inner crisis, one that is not usually manifested in drastic external excitement but "self-contained, so that when, moreover, most active it is to the average mind not distinguishable from sanity." Billy Budd is this "special object." Melville

explains that the reason why Claggart finds the handsome youth such a profound threat is that it is extremely difficult for him to pervert the image of Billy Budd. The master-at-arms tries first to twist Billy's image into some distorted form, to read into him something that would justify his abhorrence of him: "Probably the master-at-arms' clandestine persecution of Billy was started to try the temper of the man; but it had not developed any quality in him that enmity could make official use of or even pervert into plausible self-justification." For this reason, Billy's accident with his soup is a welcome occurrence to Claggart, for he perverts a trifle into a momentous insult and thus gains a motive for pursuing vengeance. Animosity has now become justified "into a sort of retributive righteousness." He thus imagines himself entirely in the right. (pp. 389-90)

[Claggart possesses] the basic traits—superior intellect that searches for answers ("a peculiar ferreting genius"), restless disposition that carries one over the world, a sense of victimization arising from a history of deep troubles, and a prideful, contemptuous, rebellious spirit—of a type of extraordinary person who is likely to formulate for himself a set of convictions that resembles the Gnostic heresy. Though they are vastly different, Ahab and Claggart share the four characteristics listed above, and both adopt Gnostic-like beliefs that tend to justify them in their own minds. Consequently, an examination of these beliefs as they apply to Claggart may get us further within him than critics have been able to go thus far. Indeed, Melville hints at one point that if we were familiar with theological history and beliefs, we might have a better chance to understand a man like Claggart: "If that lexicon which is based on Holy Writ were any longer popular, one might with less difficulty define and denominate certain phenomenal men."

Perverted from birth and preoccupied with a need to justify himself, Claggart has arrived at the basic Gnostic position that the God who created the world is unworthy of his worship. As a victim of the world's hostility, Claggart has to place the blame for what he considers the maliciousness aligned against him. The responsibility for that evil he assigns to the Creator. . . . If there is anything more commonly stated in Gnostic writings than the feeling of the world's foreignness to one of the elect, it is the belief that the Creator—or Demiurge—is blind, arrogant, unfair, and inferior to a higher spirit.

The "phenomenal pride" that Melville attributes to Claggart and those like him is a further suggestion of his Gnostic-like stance. One of the single most important facts about him is that he does not consider himself evil. Melville reports that he is, but that observation must be separated from Claggart's own perverted vision of himself as one who has seen the light—*gnosis,* as the Gnostics called it—and is consequently a very special person, one of the elect. An emerging, destructive pride . . . thus represents a major danger of the Gnostic way of thinking. If one is to get at Claggart it must be understood that he genuinely considers all that he does to destroy Billy Budd, all the scheming and lying, to be eminently right and entirely warranted.

He justifies his plan of persecution by his Gnostic-like view of Billy as an enemy to truth. He intuits that Billy is a kind of logos, a spirit given form; he senses that a manifestation of unfallen human nature has confronted him. (pp. 390-92)

If Claggart had a need to pervert Innocence into something threatening and abhorrent, he could not have found a more convenient justification than the Gnostic position. Seeing Billy for what he is, he must condemn that quality: "And the insight but intensified his passion, which assuming various secret forms within him, at times assumed that of cynic disdain, disdain of innocence—to be nothing more than innocent!"

This gnosticizing of innocence furnishes Claggart with a philosophical basis for rejecting Billy, but it does not equip him with a rationalization for persecuting him. His real reason for wanting him destroyed is that he senses Billy will force him to die in his own vomit of self-revulsion upon being forced to view what he really is, but he must pervert this reason into a more noble and acceptable motivation. He does so by imagining that innocence is not passive but active and that it has consciously insulted him. With the pride of a Gnostic who has come to consider himself a kind of god, he reacts to Billy's accidental spilling of soup across his path with the righteous anger that comes from deeply injurious insult. Now his perversion has supplied him with both the motivation to reject Billy's appeal and to destroy him. Truth *and* Justice, as he now sees them, must be served. That Claggart's rationalization for his conspiracy to destroy Billy is, in a sense, theologically based is suggested by the fact that Melville compares him to Guy Fawkes. Claggart has a Guy Fawkes "prowling in the hid chambers underlying" his nature. Guy Fawkes (1570-1606) joined a conspiracy to destroy the British Parliament building (while King James I and his ministers were meeting) because he convinced himself that this was retributive justice for England's victimization of his own religious sect, the Roman Catholics. Though he confessed under great torture the names of the other conspirators, he remained until his death by hanging sure in his own mind that what he attempted was right. He was a maddened Catholic striking out at what he considered pernicious Protestantism as Claggart is a maddened Gnostic striking out at Christian orthodoxy with its deceptive and enslaving principles. Both men felt themselves eminently justified and were, therefore, so much the madder.

Melville's comment that "Claggart could even have loved Billy but for fate and ban" has led to a fairly widespread interpretation of the master-at-arms as a homosexual. There appears no valid reason to object to this view of Claggart as long as it is kept in perspective. Indeed, Melville's linking of him with Titus Oates strongly supports the theory. The reference to Oates serves foremost, however, to place Claggart in the context of infamous men who acted destructively in the name of a theological ideal. Titus Oates (1649-1705) was the English Protestant clergyman who fabricated the details of the Popish Plot in 1678 in order to stir up animosity and action against Roman Catholics. Incredibly, he charged that an insurrection was being planned whereby Charles II would be assassinated and his Roman Catholic brother James, duke of York, would become king of England, which would be turned over to the Jesuits. Afraid in the extreme of usurpation and rebellion, those from the king on down believed Oates and executed a number of people charged in the supposed scheme. Not until after the death of these innocent people was Oates seen to be a liar. Claggart thus has much in common with Titus Oates beyond the broad, protuberant chin that Melville mentions. He can, like the English clergyman, lie with amazing coolness under pressure. Oates, like Claggart, served in the British navy. Both had severe differences with the world that left them emotionally scarred and periodically cast out. Their pasts cannot stand much looking into. One of the most significant reasons for Melville's associating Claggart with this famous English villian, however, may be the fact that it was widely known that Titus Oates was a homosexual. Though there may be support for the view of Claggart as a homosexual, homosexuality is not the focus of his characterization or a major theme in the novel. It is merely part of a larger, profounder issue. If Melville dropped a suggestion that Claggart is sexually perverted, it was intended to fill out the portrait of this man who is perverted in *every* way. Revealing obliquely that facet of his personality is simply a method of showing the extent to which perversion enters every aspect of John Claggart's being. Essential to an understanding of his characterization is the distinction between his and what might be termed the ordinary form of homosexuality. With the usual homosexual, a different sexual orientation is the reason for one's so-called perversion; with Claggart, it is the result.

Captain Vere has an instinctive abhorrence of Claggart. When the two meet on the quarter-deck, something in the master-at-arms "provokes a vaguely repellent distaste" in his captain. Yet despite the obvious distance between a good man like Vere and a twisted one like Claggart, Melville goes out of his way to create an undercurrent of similarity. Vere is curiously like this man for whom he feels such repugnance. He is just slightly older ("forty or thereabouts" compared to Claggart's thirty-five). The two stand out on board the *Bellipotent* for their obvious superiority of intellect and education. They exhibit an unusual degree of patriotism. (pp. 393-96)

Similarly, Melville links these two disparate characters through their attitudes toward justice and the law. Legal terms abound in descriptions of Claggart and Vere. Claggart's "conscience" is "but the lawyer to his will." He makes "a strong case against Billy" in his mind and decides that justice demands the sailor's death. Vere exclaims that Billy "must hang" even before he is put on trial, revealing that he, like Claggart, has made a "prejudgment." It is "the law," Vere states, that he is "prompted by." Justice and legality are thus easily perverted and become the wrong prompters, as they have for both men, though in different ways and degrees. Both characters are also advocates of fate as the dominant force in our lives, but like patriotism, discipline, and justice, fate has been perverted and has become a scapegoat. Claggart implicates fate as the source of his victimization; it is a collective term that includes for him all the enslaving powers of a hostile universe and pernicious deity. He can blame it for all his woes and resist it. Vere can also blame it and take comfort that it, not he, was in charge of Billy's future from the time when he struck Claggart. "Fated boy," he whispered when Billy struck the master-at-arms. Melville makes both characters blind to what he knew to be the essential truth about fate: "Events are all in thee begun— / By thee, through thee." To a very large extent, a man is his own fate. Thus, the fact that Vere dies with no remorse, blaming Billy's death on fate, constitutes one of the most striking ironies of the novel and undercuts, as elsewhere, one of the most cherished attitudes of his principal character. (p. 397)

Claggart senses, as does Vere, that Billy will force him to face himself squarely. With mutiny as with all the other areas of common interest to Vere and Claggart, Melville begins by explaining Vere's position and making it sound reasonable, then suggesting that Claggart is as much against mutiny—of sorts—as is Vere, and finally implying that because the villain's position is basically the same as that of the man of nobility, the subject should be rethought. And so it should, for Vere needs nothing so much as an inner mutiny where his imperial conscience will be overthrown by those better impulses stirred up in his contract with Billy Budd. That he will not allow such a mutiny brings him into another area of kinship with Claggart. As they share so many other things, they are both perverters and madmen.

The shock value of *Billy Budd,* arising from the recognition of all those ways in which the hero is like the villain, has been scarcely recognized in criticism of the novel, but it leads one with rare force—even for a work by Melville—to the heart of the matter. How dutiful and brave one is, how conscientious and intelligent, how fair and strong, how upright and ethical—none of these things is very important without true knowledge of self and self-fidelity. Indeed, one can possess all of those qualities so admired by the civilized world and still be shockingly similar to the most depraved villain. Keeping true to the dreams of your youth—only that will decisively separate you from other men, even the most corrupt. This it was that Herman Melville reminded himself again and again. The essence of all that he had learned in a long life of probing and suffering was tersely expressed in that scrap of paper pasted on the inside of his desk. It was his struggling to follow that insight that kept him writing and kept him living. (pp. 398-99)

> *William B. Dillingham, in his* Melville's Later Novels, *The University of Georgia Press, 1986, 430 p.*

John Samson   (essay date 1989)

[*In the following excerpt, Samson elaborates on Melville's narrative technique in* Billy Budd.]

Melville gives his last, unfinished work the parenthetical subtitle (*An Inside Narrative*), indicating that *Billy Budd, Sailor* is vitally concerned with what goes on inside the narrative process and that narrative itself is concerned with the attempt to get inside events, here to find the inner truth about the title character. But the relation between title and subtitle is one of contrast, for all the considerable narrative tactics employed by the novel's characters (who are in a sense narrators along with the book's narrator)—the historical analogues, the biographical memories, the Christian patterns, the nautical legends—all fail to get the inside story of Billy. But for that part of the title that describes his work—"Sailor"—Billy remains an enigma, the narrative remains another white lie. The distance between the facts of human experience and the truthful narration of that experience remains unbridgeable. Moreover, as Stanton Garner has convincingly demonstrated, the facts

themselves here are more than questionable, they are wrong; and intentionally so [see Further Reading]. The central issue in *Billy Budd,* that is to say, is the inability of narrative to explain natural phenomena, the inapplicability of past historical patterns to account for present occurrences, and the crucial fictionality of "factual" narrative.

Before the narrative itself Melville places a dedication to Jack Chase that further indicates this problematization. To transfer Jack from *White-Jacket*'s fictional *Neversink* to the historical *United States*—in essence inverting the creative process Melville had followed in his narratives—breaks down the distinction between fact and fiction and may also be a sly joke at the expense of those who have read his novels as autobiographies. And to dedicate *Billy Budd* to that ridiculous spinner of ahistorical and self-serving yarns signals an extraordinary level of irony, directed, I believe, back toward his previous narratives of facts. Like Jack, Melville's narratives of facts have been consistently misread as considerably lighter, more positive than they indeed are, an issue of much concern to critics who see *Billy Budd* as Melville's final "testament of faith." Thus Jack Chase signifies that other J. C. whose historicity—like that of Billy, who is frequently identified as a Christ-figure—is so much at issue in the late nineteenth century, and again crucial to the issue is a contrast between historical or natural fact and the faith or confidence one can have in narratives to represent those facts. In *White-Jacket* Jack Chase's station high in the elitist maintop places him in sharp contrast to Melville's ocean, in which Melville immerses his narrator to little effect and indicates another facet of the facts / narrative opposition. Nature and an understanding of it that is essentially spiritual—albeit dangerous, as Pip's immersion shows—are opposed by a false and essentially politicized faith in narrative. Nature, what is outside man and his institutions, opposes what is inside narrative—its ideology, its tropology, what Hayden White calls *The Content of the Form* [1987]. Melville's presentation of these issues in *Billy Budd,* of concern to Melville throughout his earlier narratives of facts and particularly powerful in *Moby-Dick,* shows this final work to be a metanarrative conclusion to his examination of his culture's white lies.

Each of Melville's narrators, though he sets out to narrate a voyage of exploration, tenaciously resists recognizing any discovery that might threaten to alter his preconceived ideology. Each clings stubbornly to the "facts"—progress and primitivism, religious elitism, genteel capitalism, millennialism, and Revolutionary heroism—gleaned from the narrative chart he has been following. Those narrators of facts whom Melville's narrators follow also cling to these primarily eighteenth-century ideas by echoing the intellectual voyages of those who formulated them: Rousseau, the philosophes, Adam Smith, the millennial Whigs, and Franklin. Melville's narrators try to carry over into the troubled nineteenth century some of the Enlightenment's confidence in racial, cultural, political, and religious superiority. (pp. 211-13)

[*Billy Budd, Sailor*] is composed of a number of short narratives—from several points of view and concerning everyone from Billy to Admiral Nelson—inside the central narrative. Each attempts to get inside Billy's story, yet none, upon close analysis, sheds more than "lateral light" upon the story of Billy. Virtually every detail is qualified with a "might have been" or a "seemed to be"; Melville fills the short text with further qualifications, circumlocutions, and inapplicable historical parallels and allusions. The sheer number of narratives inside *Billy Budd* and the strenuousness with which the various narrators—Claggart, Vere, the narrator himself—attempt to tell their stories expose the power of the desire to secure and narrate the facts.

In this desire the narrators of *Billy Budd* resemble Ishmael; but in projecting their own hopes and beliefs upon the events, they are closer to those earlier narrators of facts. After Billy's death, for example, the sailors "recalled the fresh young image of the Handsome Sailor, that facts never deformed by a sneer or subtler vile freak of the heart within. This impression was doubtless deepened by the fact that he was gone, and in a measure mysteriously gone." The sailors, faced with "the fact" of death and with only a "mysterious" idea of what may be beyond, translate their "image" of Billy into a poetic (if ridiculously hackneyed) narrative. Narrative, here again, is an attempt not just to understand the facts but through that understanding to resurrect what has naturally passed away. Like Ishmael's world of "deadly voids," Billy's contains "the deadly space between" not only Claggart and "a normal nature" but between all people, between the narrator and the facts. In a world where transcendence is at best uncertain, connection between the individual and the nature around him becomes the only way to avoid falling into that "deadly space" at the edge of mortal existence. As the means of asserting that connection, narration—"best done by indirection"—is thus among the strongest, most religious of desires in Melville's world and, as with the sailors, among the most open to politicization.

Billy Budd, seen consistently in religious terms, is himself the "text" of the narrative, the subject each tries to understand and re-present. Billy is Melville's natural man, "a sound human creature," whom Melville's civilized narrator again and again describes as an animal or a barbarian standing "nearer to unadulterate Nature." As a natural man Billy exists in a prenarrative state: from an "organic hesitancy" he tells no stories either of himself or of historical events but, like the Typees, lives completely in the present moment. But when he encounters the afterguardsman he must try, always unsuccessfully, to tell his story. Like a natural child (in both senses of the term), he knows little of his origin, merely born of indefinite parents, and cares little of his end. It is precisely because he is a natural man and does not seek to place himself in history that Billy is such a mystery to those around him. Therefore, the others describe Billy in mythic or legendary terms: he is compared to Apollo, the Handsome Sailor, Christ, and so on.

Claggart, a man of little faith, is the most naive reader of the text of Billy and the most pragmatic of his critics. He reads Billy exclusively from his own viewpoint and egoistically assumes that Billy has the same invidious motives that he himself does. Accordingly, he thinks that Billy will react as he would to himself and his clandestine plans—with malicious irony and avaricious cunning. Claggart seeks not to understand Billy but to confirm in him Claggart's own existence and values. The reading of Billy he presents to Vere, then, is grounded in some factual percep-

tion of the text, but must postulate a warped idea of what lies beneath the surface, a process that destroys the text.

Vere's moral reading of Billy is more sophisticated yet no more successful. In something of a sardonic self-parody, Melville presents Vere as a habitual reader of narratives of facts ("books treating of actual men and events no matter of what era—history, biography and unconventional writers like Montaigne") who "in illustrating of any point touching the stirring personages and events of the time . . . would be as apt to cite some historic character or incident of antiquity as he would be to cite from the moderns." When Vere hears Claggart's narrative, he considers it in the light of the other stories he has heard of Billy as the Handsome Sailor, "and the more he weighed [Claggart's account] the less reliance he felt in the informer's good faith." Narrative "faith" here, as in *Moby-Dick,* is important: Vere's religious preconceptions lead him to consider Billy a prelapsarian Adam, a Christlike "fated boy," and "an angel of God." Yet in reality Vere has no more reason to perceive Billy as Goodness Incarnate than to perceive Claggart as that. He knows nothing of the motivations of either, for neither reveals his inner thoughts. Billy is merely lauded by the crew while Claggart, their superior, is generally disliked. And yet they are quite similar: both have obscure origins, both are exemplary sailors, both have striking appearances. Vere, that is to say, has no good reason to believe either Claggart or Billy, other than their appearance, hearsay, and his own Christian framework of beliefs, which precludes considering them natural men.

When, therefore, Billy's fist intrudes upon Claggart's narration, Vere, like Melville's earlier narrators of facts, has trouble fitting the act into the picture of Billy his faith has generated. In this violent act, Billy shows himself neither an Adam nor a Christ. Vere may call it "the divine judgment on Ananias" and label Billy an angel, but neither of these statements will adequately explain the violence of the attack. Even as he perceives Billy from this Christian perspective, Vere is forced to perceive Billy's actions from a military perspective as well. Thus Vere presents a dichotomy familiar to readers of the earlier narratives of facts: a dubious faith opposed and undermined by an inveterate politics. Vere, as his name might suggest, is a man of the seventeenth century (like Marvell) who can still believe these two spheres compatible, despite living in a century that explodes them. Like Melville's earlier narrators, Vere is caught in this dissociation of sensibility and must act as if "unhinged"; he chooses to place Billy's inner self within the Christian context but his outer within the political. Little wonder the surgeon suspects insanity, for such a schizophrenic determination cannot but warp Vere's perspective, create turmoil for himself, and distance him even further from reality. Indeed, the problem of Billy haunts him until his dying day.

Melville replays these conflicts in his narrator, a contextual critic who amplifies the biases, motivations, and mistakes of Vere. Further testifying to the spiritual desire behind narration, the narrator, like Vere, consistently describes Billy in mythic and Christian terms. And yet, as he tries to approach Billy through the "indirection" and "lateral light" of personal and historical precedents—and incompetently so, as Garner's study indicates—the narrator goes further than Vere. To name a few: he tells of Nelson, the Somers mutiny, the Nore case; he refers to Marvell, the Bible, Thomas Paine; he reminisces about his past and makes the events into a tragedy; he employs inappropriate metaphors, inapplicable allusions, selective detailing, imaginative reconstruction. But all to no avail: he can only "suggest" what Billy "might be like."

Like Vere's, the narrator's biases are exposed by Billy's fist. The facts of the event show Billy not like the Handsome Sailor the narrator remembers, not like a Saint Bernard, not like Christ; nevertheless, the narrator tries all the more strenuously to present Billy as a heroic Christfigure. His motives in doing so are more self-interested than religious; for—like each of the other narrators of facts—he is using the story of Billy to justify his own conservative politics. By stressing the tragic and otherworldly aspects of Billy's story, he diverts it away from revolution and toward an acceptance of the status quo, just as Claggart uses Billy to cement his own position in the ship's hierarchy and in the captain's eyes, just as Vere uses his narrative of the story to keep order on board and to keep order in his perception of the starry system of the universe. These politicizations are no less ridiculous than the final two stories of Billy, one concocted to justify naval policies, the other to satisfy the sailors' romanticism, but both to keep "the people" firmly in their place. Again Melville criticizes the usurpation, for the purposes of political superiority, of the essentially religious desire to understand and narrate the world.

Within the narrator's story Melville places yet another narrative: the surgeon's, as much a comment on the narrator as upon Vere. The surgeon, whose character Melville was developing at the time of his death, is the only person to call into question Vere's judgment by raising the possibility of insanity. He thereby also calls into question the narrator's response to Billy: the surgeon is by no means willing to label Billy either heroic or Christlike. Billy's end, like his whole story, is "phenomenal" only "in the sense that it was an appearance the cause of which is not immediately to be assigned." Unlike Vere, the surgeon is more a man of Melville's late nineteenth century, a scientific naturalist willing only to have faith in facts objectively verifiable. He distrusts terms "imaginative and metaphysical," which would only obscure the facts. Consequently, he refuses his narrative role, refuses to give his version of what goes on inside either Vere (chap. 20) or Billy (chap. 8). Yet the surgeon, like so many of Melville's medicine men, is a rather cold, perhaps heartless scientist who tends to view a person as "a case." In such an attitude are the seeds of an Ahab-like arrogance, the dangers of which Melville noted in a monologue originally titled "The Scientist." He retitled the poem **"The New Zealot to the Sun"** to emphasize his ironic distance from the speaker, who claims that "Science" will ultimately displace religion and "An effluence ampler shall beget, / And power beyond your [the sun's] play." Melville is as skeptical about claims to scientific objectivity—here motivated by a desire for "power" and thus capable of becoming monomaniac—as he is about those claims to cultural superiority voiced in his narratives of facts. Both deny humanity, both threaten the individual.

In Melville's late nineteenth century, more generally, science had to a degree displaced Christianity as the basic nexus of values, the basic story, upon which Western cul-

ture "progressed." In addition to the higher criticism and literary naturalism, Freudian psychology, Marxist social thought, and Darwinian science all attempted to rewrite the white, Western, progressive narrative that Melville's eighteenth- and nineteenth-century sources so strenuously defined and defended. Melville, however strongly opposed to the ideology of these sources, cannot accept in its place a scientific objectivity or a systematic explanation that refuses to recognize the essential indeterminacy and chaos of nature, of the universe, or that prioritizes a collective ideology at the expense of an individual's humanity. (pp. 224-29)

This insistence on the "sovereignty" of the individual led Melville to dismantle the forms and contents of the "Powers" of his day in those uncompromisingly individualistic novels for which he is known in ours.

As in his narratives of facts as a whole, at the end of the one Melville novel perhaps most vitally of our time, Melville "extinguish[ed] this lamp" of Western ideology, but something did follow of Melville's ideological and narrative masquerade: fabulation, metafiction, postmodernism, deconstruction. (p. 230)

> *John Samson, in his* White Lies: Melville's Narratives of Facts, *Cornell University Press, 1989, 246 p.*

FURTHER READING

Bernstein, John. "*Billy Budd*: The Testament of Rebellion." In his *Pacifism and Rebellion in the Writings of Herman Melville,* pp. 202-13. London: Mouton & Co., 1964.
     Analyzes the development of the theme of rebellion in the novel, maintaining that "the ultimate message . . . is a call to rebellion, not only philosophical rebellion but violent revolution if necessary."

Berthoff, Warner. " 'Certain Phenomenal Men': The Example of *Billy Budd*." In his *The Example of Melville,* pp. 183-203. Princeton, N.J.: Princeton University Press, 1962.
     Asserts that Melville sought to delineate exceptional individuals in *Billy Budd,* rather than to allegorically present universal truths.

Boswell, Jeanetta. *Herman Melville and the Critics: A Checklist of Criticism, 1900-1978.* Metuchen, N.J.: Scarecrow Press, 1981, 247 p.
     Offers extensive bibliographic references to critical works on *Billy Budd,* including essays on film, opera, and dramatic adaptations of the novel.

Bowen, Merlin. "Submission: The Way of Weakness." In his *The Long Encounter: Self and Experience in the Writings of Herman Melville,* pp. 198-233. Chicago: University of Chicago Press, 1960.
     Contains discussion of the character of Vere in *Billy Budd,* describing him as "an overcivilized man who has stifled the sound of his own heart and . . . has abdicated his full humanity in the interests of a utilitarian social ethic."

Braswell, William. "Melville's *Billy Budd* as 'An Inside Narrative'." *American Literature* XXIX, No. 2 (May 1957): 133-46.

Suggests that the work can be approached "as an inside narrative about a tragic conflict in Melville's own spiritual life."

Brodtkorb, Paul, Jr. "The Definitive *Billy Budd:* 'But Aren't It All Sham?'" *PMLA* LXXXII, No. 7 (December 1967): 602-12.

Emphasizes the novel's unfinished state at Melville's death, examining in particular the narrator's relation to the events he recounts and the diction of the central characters.

Browne, Ray B. "*Billy Budd:* Gospel of Democracy." *Nineteenth-Century Fiction* 17, No. 4 (March 1963): 321-37.

Addresses the work as a political allegory of the conflict between autocracy and democracy as exemplified by the philosophy of Edmund Burke (1729-1797) and that of Thomas Paine (1737-1809).

Campbell, Harry Modean. "The Hanging Scene in Melville's *Billy Budd, Foretopman.*" *Modern Language Notes* LXVI, No. 6 (June 1951): 378-81.

Asserts that "the overwhelming evidence for the ironical pessimism of Melville in *Billy Budd* lies in the final hanging scene."

Chase, Richard. "Dissent on *Billy Budd.*" *Partisan Review* XV, No. 11 (November 1948): 1212-18.

Criticizes Melville's characterization of Billy, asserting that in the novel "his suffering and death are without moral content."

——. Introduction to *Selected Tales and Poems,* by Herman Melville, edited by Richard Chase, pp. v-xix. New York: Holt, Rinehart and Winston, 1963.

Discusses *Billy Budd* as a tragedy, comparing the novel with Sophocles's drama *Antigone* and Shakespeare's drama *The Winter's Tale.*

Cifelli, Edward M. "*Billy Budd:* Boggy Ground to Build On." *Studies in Short Fiction* XIII, No. 4 (Fall 1976): 463-69.

Discusses Melville's later revisions to the text, noting the increased use of ambiguous language in reference to Captain Vere.

Davis, R. Evan. "An Allegory of America in Melville's *Billy Budd.*" *The Journal of Narrative Technique* 14, No. 3 (Fall 1984): 172-81.

Suggests that Billy symbolizes the United States prior to the advent of industrial society and its institutions.

Dryden, Edgar A. Epilogue to his *Melville's Thematics of Form: The Great Art of Telling the Truth,* pp. 197-216. Baltimore: Johns Hopkins University Press, 1968.

Maintains that the three narratives that follow Billy's death serve to undermine traditional structures of society, politics, and religion.

Eberwein, Robert T. "The Impure Fiction of *Billy Budd.*" *Studies in the Novel* VI, No. 3 (Fall 1974): 318-26.

Focuses on the work's concluding poem, "Billy in the Darbies," as it relates to the narrative tone of *Billy Budd* and to the view of art presented in the novel.

Fite, Olive L. "Billy Budd, Claggart, and Schopenhauer." *Nineteenth-Century Fiction* 23, No. 3 (December 1968): 336-43.

Traces the influence of the concept of human will outlined by German philosopher Arthur Schopenhauer (1788-1860) on Melville's composition of *Billy Budd.*

Fogle, Richard Harter. "*Billy Budd*—Acceptance or Irony." *Tulane Studies in English* VIII (1958): 107-13.

Argues that "*Billy Budd* can like *Moby Dick* be justly described as Melville's nineteenth-century version of classical tragedy."

——. "*Billy Budd:* The Order of the Fall." *Nineteenth-Century Fiction* 15, No. 3 (December 1960): 189-205.

Stresses "the large affirmative elements of *Billy Budd,* which make of it a celebration rather than a condemnation of reality and its mysterious Master."

Franklin, H. Bruce. "From Empire to Empire: *Billy Budd, Sailor.*" In *Herman Melville: Reassessments,* edited by A. Robert Lee, pp. 199-216. London: Vision Press; Tototwa, N.J.: Barnes & Noble Books, 1984.

Criticizes Vere's personal character and actions, and interprets the novel as condemning both British and American political imperialism.

Freeman, F. Barron. "Introduction: Background for *Billy Budd.*" In *Melville's "Billy Budd",* by Herman Melville, edited by F. Barron Freeman, pp. 3-126. Cambridge: Harvard University Press, 1948.

Introduces the first revised transcription of the text. Freeman discusses biographical and historical sources of *Billy Budd,* its textual reconstruction, and the novel's characterizations, themes, and narrative techniques.

Garner, Stanton. "Fraud as Fact in Herman Melville's *Billy Budd.*" *San José Studies* 4, No. 2 (May 1978): 82-105.

Identifies historical inaccuracies in the work, considering them indicative of Melville's use of an unreliable narrator, thereby supporting an ironic reading of the novel.

Goldsmith, Arnold L. "The 'Discovery Scene' in *Billy Budd.*" *Modern Drama* 3, No. 4 (February 1961): 339-42.

Praises the portrayal of Billy in the 1951 dramatic adaptation by Louis O. Coxe and Robert Chapman, particularly lauding the dramatization of the final interview between Billy and Vere.

Haberstroh, Charles J., Jr. "*Pierre* and After." In his *Melville and Male Identity,* pp. 104-36. London: Associated University Presses, 1980.

Examines Melville's presentation of Vere in a biographical context, asserting that the captain represents "the very pattern of dutiful masculine conduct Melville had never been able to conform to himself in any conclusive way."

Hayford, Harrison and Sealts, Merton M., Jr. Introduction to *Billy Budd, Sailor (An Inside Narrative)* by Herman Melville, edited by Harrison Hayford and Merton M. Sealts, Jr., pp. 1-39. Chicago: University of Chicago Press, 1962.

Discusses the composition and publication history of *Billy Budd.*

Higgins, Brian. *Herman Melville: A Reference Guide, 1931-1960.* Boston: G. K. Hall & Co., 1987, 531 p.

Offers numerous references to critical works on *Billy Budd.*

Howard, Leon. "Recollection and Renown." In his *Herman Melville: A Biography*, pp. 319-42. Berkeley and Los Angeles: University of California Press, 1951.

Includes historical and biographical background to the composition of *Billy Budd*.

Ives, C. B. "*Billy Budd* and the Articles of War." *American Literature* XXXIV, No. 1 (March 1962): 31-9.

Evaluates Vere's decision to hang Billy through an examination of the laws and customs associated with the historical Articles of War.

Johnson, Barbara. "Melville's Fist: The Execution of *Billy Budd*." *Studies in Romanticism* 18, No. 4 (Winter 1979): 567-99.

Discusses the work as "a dramatization of the twisted relations between knowing and doing, speaking and killing, reading and judging, which make political understanding and action so problematic."

McElderry, B. R., Jr. "Three Earlier Treatments of the *Billy Budd* Theme." *American Literature* XXVII, No. 2 (May 1955): 251-57.

Parallels the novel's characters and plot with those of popular nineteenth-century works of nautical fiction and drama.

Montale, Eugenio. "An Introduction to *Billy Budd* (1942)." *The Sewanee Review* LXVIII, No. 3 (July-September 1960): 419-22.

Translation of an introduction by the renowned Italian poet.

Noone, John B., Jr. "*Billy Budd:* Two Concepts of Nature." *American Literature* XXIX, No. 3 (November 1957): 249-62.

Discusses the novel as a portrayal of the conflict between the philosophy of Jean-Jacques Rousseau (1712-1778) and that of Thomas Hobbes (1588-1679).

Obuchowski, Peter A. "*Billy Budd* and the Failure of Art." *Studies in Short Fiction* 15, No. 4 (Fall 1978): 445-52.

Elaborates on the view of art presented in the work and concludes that Melville "questions and here rejects finally the efficacy of 'words,' the very art that made the years of brooding over 'the power of blackness' bearable."

Parker, Hershel. "*Billy Budd: Foretopman* and the Dynamics of Canonization." *College Literature* XVII, No. 1 (1990): 21-32.

Traces the critical process by which the novel was established within the canon of English-language literature, noting the significance of variant versions of the text.

Perry, Robert L. "*Billy Budd:* Melville's *Paradise Lost.*" *The Midwest Quarterly* X, No. 2 (January 1969): 173-85.

Expands on Henry F. Pommer's comparison of Claggart with Milton's character of Satan in *Paradise Lost* (see below) and parallels Billy and Milton's Adam.

Pommer, Henry F. "The Influence of Satan." In his *Milton and Melville*, pp. 81-105. Pittsburgh: University of Pittsburgh Press, 1950.

Focuses on the influence of Milton's depiction of Satan in *Paradise Lost* on Melville's portrayal of the antagonists Jackson in *Redburn*, Bland in *White-Jacket*, and Claggart in *Billy Budd*.

Rathbun, John W. "*Billy Budd* and the Limits of Percep-

tion." *Nineteenth-Century Fiction* 20, No. 1 (June 1965): 19-34.

Outlines the manner in which the structure and imagery of *Billy Budd* support the novel's action and themes.

Reich, Charles A. "The Tragedy of Justice in *Billy Budd*." *The Yale Review* LVI, No. 3 (Spring 1967): 368-89.

Explores questions of law, justice, and innocence raised by the work.

Rosenberry, Edward H. "The Problem of *Billy Budd*." *PMLA* LXXX (December 1965): 489-98.

Maintains that the novel's tone and "ethical logic" indicate that "the plainest reading of this disputed book is the only valid reading possible."

Rosenthal, Bernard. "Elegy for Jack Chase." *Studies in Romanticism* 10, No. 3 (Summer 1971): 213-29.

Elaborates on the role of Chase, a former shipmate of Melville's and model for a character in *White-Jacket*, in the creation of the characters and setting of *Billy Budd*.

Sarotte, Georges-Michel. "The Captain and the Soldier." In his *Like a Brother, Like a Lover: Male Homosexuality in the American Novel and Theater from Herman Melville to James Baldwin*, translated by Richard Miller, pp. 70-91. Garden City, N.Y.: Anchor Press / Doubleday, 1978.

Contains a section on *Billy Budd* which applies a psychoanalytic approach to the theme of male homosexuality in the novel.

Sealts, Merton M., Jr. "Innocence and Infamy: *Billy Budd, Sailor*." In *A Companion to Melville Studies*, edited by John Bryant, pp. 407-30. New York: Greenwood Press, 1986.

Offers a plot synopsis, an account of the work's publication history, a survey of critical response, character analyses, issues for additional critical attention, and a substantial bibliography.

Seelye, John. "Final Balance: The Prose Fragments and *Billy Budd*." In his *Melville: The Ironic Diagram*, pp. 152-72. Evanston, Ill.: Northwestern University Press, 1970.

Emphasizes the thematic conflict between human order and nature in *Billy Budd* as represented by martial and natural law.

Springer, Haskell S. *The Merrill Studies in "Billy Budd"*. Columbus, Ohio: Charles E. Merrill Publishing Co., 1970, 142 p.

Presents excerpts from major critical essays through 1967 which were "chosen for their historical importance, representative viewpoints, or creative insights."

Stafford, William T., ed. *Melville's "Billy Budd" and the Critics*. Rev. ed. Belmont, Calif.: Wadsworth Publishing Co., 1968, 272 p.

Includes excerpts of significant critical essays on the novel arranged by topic, a reprint of the 1951 dramatic adaptation by Coxe and Chapman, themes for further study, and a bibliography.

Stern, Milton R. "*Billy Budd*." In his *The Fine Hammered Steel of Herman Melville*, pp. 206-39. Urbana: University of Illinois Press, 1957.

Addresses principal thematic dichotomies in the work, interpreting Billy and Claggart as polarized aspects of Vere's self and discussing Melville's presentation of history, time, and biblical subjects.

————. Introduction to *Billy Budd, Sailor (An Inside Narrative)*, by Herman Melville, edited by Milton R. Stern, pp. vii-xliv. Indianapolis: Bobbs-Merrill Co., 1975.

Outlines biographical and historical influences on the novel, its critical reception, and the political significance of the work.

Sutton, Walter. "Melville and the Great God Budd." *Prairie Schooner* XXXIV, No. 2 (Summer 1960): 128-33.

Suggests that the central concepts of Buddhism, as interpreted by German philosopher Arthur Schopenhauer, influenced the composition of *Billy Budd* and clarify the motivations of Billy and Vere.

Thompson, Lawrance. "Divine Depravity." In his *Melville's Quarrel with God,* pp. 355-414. Princeton, N.J.: Princeton University Press, 1952.

Analyzes themes, allusions, and narrative techniques in *Billy Budd,* considering the novel's viewpoint largely satirical and Melville's attitude toward Christianity pessimistic.

Tindall, William York. "The Ceremony of Innocence (Herman Melville's *Billy Budd*)." In *Great Moral Dilemmas: In Literature, Past and Present,* edited by R. M. MacIver, pp. 73-81. New York: Institute for Religious and Social Studies, 1956.

Examines moral responsibility in *Billy Budd,* referring to the philosophy of Søren Kierkegaard (1813-1855) and arguing that the novel is "moral in the sense of enlarging our awareness of human conditions . . . and of improving our sensitivity."

Vincent, Howard P., ed. *Twentieth Century Interpretations of "Billy Budd".* Englewood Cliffs, N.J.: Prentice-Hall, 1971, 112 p.

Survey of major criticism on the novel through the 1960s.

Wagner, Vern. "Billy Budd as Moby Dick: An Alternate Reading." In *Studies in Honor of John Wilcox,* edited by A. Dayle Wallace and Woodburn O. Ross, pp. 157-74. Detroit: Wayne State University Press, 1958.

Compares Billy with the whale in *Moby-Dick* and interprets the imagery of whiteness associated with Billy and his innocence as representing a frightening inscrutability similar to that of the whiteness of the whale.

Weir, Charles, Jr. "Malice Reconciled; A Note on Melville's *Billy Budd.*" *University of Toronto Quarterly* XIII, No. 3 (April 1944): 276-85.

Emphasizes Melville's characterizations in *Billy Budd* and the work's relationship to his earlier novels.

West, Ray B., Jr. "The Unity of *Billy Budd.*" *The Hudson Review* V, No. 1 (Spring 1952): 120-27.

Deems the novel a thematically and structurally unified work, focusing on Melville's presentation of "'the Crisis of Christendom', with Christendom standing . . . for all of the philosophical, political, and moral concerns of Man."

Widmer, Kingsley. "The Perplexed Myths of Melville: *Billy Budd.*" *Novel* 2, No. 1 (Fall 1968): 23-35.

Asserts that Melville mocks the Christian myths that he presents in *Billy Budd,* and regards the novel's philosophical outlook as largely negative.

Willett, Ralph W. "Nelson and Vere: Hero and Victim in *Billy Budd, Sailor.*" *PMLA* LXXXII, No. 5 (October 1967): 370-76.

Evaluates Vere as a hero, arguing that Melville depicts British admiral Horatio Nelson (1758-1805) "as the rare ideal commander," whereas "Vere is a victim of the historical situation and of his own suppressed emotions."

Wright, Nathalia. *Melville's Use of the Bible.* Durham, N.C.: Duke University Press, 1949, 203 p.

Contains discussion of Christian allusion in *Billy Budd,* focusing on the parallel between Billy and Christ.

Zink, Karl E. "Herman Melville and the Forms—Irony and Social Criticism in *Billy Budd.*" *Accent* XII, No. 3 (Summer 1952): 131-39.

Asserts that in the novel Melville used "heavier symbolism and irony to dramatize his last charge against the artificial 'forms' by which he saw men live blindly and passively."

Lady Morgan

1776?-1859

(Born Sydney Owenson) Irish novelist, travel writer, essayist, biographer, autobiographer, and poet.

One of the first woman writers of Ireland to attain international success, Morgan was among the most popular novelists of the early nineteenth century. Though her novels are not widely read today, their nationalist sympathies and liberal political convictions, along with her dynamic and ambitious personality, make Morgan a noteworthy figure in the history of Irish literature.

The eldest daughter of an Irish actor and his English wife, Morgan was born and raised in Dublin, where her father owned a theater. Spending much of her childhood among actors and entertainers, Morgan acquired a keen understanding of characterization and an adeptness in oral narration, song, and mimicry, abilities which would later facilitate her social advancement and development as a novelist. Following the death of her mother and the failure of her father's theater in 1789, Morgan was sent away to school where she studied French, music, and literature. After graduating from a Dublin finishing school in 1798, she was employed as a governess, but desiring financial independence and fame, Morgan decided to pursue a career as a writer. In 1802, her first novel, an epistolary romance entitled *St. Clair; or, The Heiress of Desmond,* was published, and its favorable reception encouraged Morgan to visit London to contract with a publisher for future projects. Characteristic of her determination and independence, Morgan traveled alone and within days reached an agreement with one of London's most esteemed publishers, from whom she secured payment in advance, an unusual accommodation for the time.

Morgan's popularity was established with her third novel, *The Wild Irish Girl.* After its publication in 1806, Morgan was courted by London society and employed by the Marquis of Abercorn as a live-in companion for his wife. During this time, in which she assisted the Abercorns in their duties as the hosts of social gatherings and entertained them with her conversation, humor, and Irish folk songs, she was introduced to Charles Morgan, a physician, whom she married in 1812. Sir and Lady Morgan, whose titles were arranged for them by the Abercorns, established their residence in Dublin.

For the next thirty years, Morgan traveled and published extensively. While her novels were popular and made her, in her own words, "the pet of the Liberals," critical reaction to her works was at best indifferent and often hostile. Critics regarded Morgan's obtrusive use of foreign phrases and her inflated diction as immature and a detriment to her prose. The Tory journals proclaimed her books subversive for their liberal politics, one reviewer accusing them of "attempting to vitiate mankind under the insidious mask of virtue, sensibility, and truth." In 1816, Morgan and her husband traveled to Paris and collaborated on *France,* a laudatory examination of French culture. The popularity of this volume prompted the Morgans to pub-

lish a companion volume, *Italy;* Lady Morgan's contribution to this volume included severe criticism of the Roman Catholic church and Italy's "oppressive despotism" which led many European countries to ban the book, and in 1824 she herself was banned from the Holy Roman Empire. After 1825, Morgan devoted much of her time to her social life. Her salon, Dublin's first, was attended by famous poets, artists, musicians, and foreign dignitaries. In 1837, she became the first woman to receive a literary pension, an annual stipend granted by the government for her contributions to Irish literature and patriotism. Morgan and her husband resided in Dublin until 1839 when, alarmed by the violent tactics adopted by Irish reformist Daniel O'Connell, they retired to London. During the last ten years of her life, Morgan wrote her *Memoirs.* She died in 1859.

Morgan is best known for her novels, sentimental romances with idealized characters and implausible plots. In addition to entertaining the reading audience of the time, these works were also devoted to addressing common misconceptions about Ireland and to celebrating the Irish and their history. *The Wild Irish Girl,* in depicting the poverty and emotional distress of the Irish people, evoked sympathy and understanding in many English readers; however, the novel was more influential as a fashion guide, creating a demand among women for clothing and coiffures in the style of Glorvina, the novel's heroine. Equally popular was Morgan's 1814 historical romance *O'Donnel,* one of the first novels in English to cast a governess as heroine, which drew praise from Morgan's literary contemporaries Walter Scott and Maria Edgeworth. Within the framework of a simple romantic plot, *O'Donnel* satirized the aristocracy and championed the emancipation of the Irish Catholic church from England's annexation and declaration of Ireland as a "Protestant nation." The focus of Morgan's novel *The O'Briens and the O'Flahertys* was more political than any of her previous "national tales." In this work, Morgan examined the grievances of opposing political and religious factions in Ireland. The continuing relevance of this issue, along with the novel's strong characterization and attention to setting and historical fact, have led many critics to deem *The O'Briens and the O'Flahertys* Morgan's finest work.

During the latter part of her career, Morgan widened the scope of her writing to include a biography of the Italian painter Salvator Rosa, several satiric sketches and essays on the aristocracy, and a sequel to her earlier work on France entitled *France in 1829-1830.* Of her lesser known works, two have been recently examined by critics: *Dramatic Scenes from Real Life* and *Woman and Her Master.* *Dramatic Scenes* consists of dialogue through which Morgan chronicled the sufferings of Irish peasants and condemned the English landowners who exploited Ireland and its people. *Woman and Her Master,* a lengthy history of women, argues for the moral and intellectual superiority of women. Critics have found these works to be almost visionary in their perspectives on Irish political history and the role of women in society.

PRINCIPAL WORKS

Poems (poetry) 1801
St. Clair; or, the Heiress of Desmond (novel) 1802
The Novice of Saint Dominick (novel) 1805
Twelve Original Hibernian Melodies (poetry) 1805
The Wild Irish Girl (novel) 1806
The Lay of an Irish Harp (poetry) 1807
Patriotic Sketches of Ireland, Written in Connaught (essays) 1807
Woman; or, Ida of Athens (novel) 1809
The Missionary (novel) 1811; also published as *Luxima, the Prophetess,* 1859
O'Donnel (novel) 1814
France [with Charles Morgan] (nonfiction) 1817
Florence Macarthy (novel) 1818
Italy [with Charles Morgan] (nonfiction) 1821
The Life and Times of Salvator Rosa (biography) 1824
Absenteeism (essay) 1825
The O'Briens and the O'Flahertys (novel) 1827
The Book of the Boudoir (autobiography) 1829
France in 1829-1830 (travel sketches) 1830
Dramatic Scenes from Real Life (fictional dialogues) 1833
The Princess; or, the Beguine (novel) 1834
Woman and Her Master (history) 1840
The Book Without a Name [with Charles Morgan] (essays) 1841

Passages from My Autobiography (autobiography) 1859
Lady Morgan's Memoirs (autobiography, diaries, and letters) 1862

William Gifford (essay date 1809)

[*In the following excerpt, Gifford reviews* Woman; or, Ida of Athens, *contending that the novel is incoherent and blasphemous.*]

> Bacchantes, animated with Orphean fury, slinging their serpents in the air, striking their cymbals, and utering dithyrambics, appeared to surround him on every side.
>
> That modesty which is of soul, seemed to diffuse itself over a form, whose exquisite symmetry was at once betrayed and concealed by the apparent tissue of woven air, which fell like a vapour round her.
>
> Like Aurora, the extremities of her delicate limbs were rosed with flowing hues, and her little foot, as it pressed its naked beauty on a scarlet cushion, resembled that of a youthful Thetis from its blushing tints, or that of a fugitive Atalanta from its height.

After repeated attempts to comprehend the meaning of these, and a hundred similar conundrums, in the compass of half as many pages, we gave them up in despair; and were carelessly turning the leaves of the volume backward and forward, when the following passage, in a short note 'to the Reader,' caught our eye. 'My little works have been always printed from *illegible* manuscripts in one country, while their author was resident in another.' We have been accustomed to overlook these introductory gossipings: in future, however, we shall be more circumspect; since it is evident that if we had read straight forward from the title page, we should have escaped a very severe head-ache.

The matter seems now sufficiently clear. The printer having to produce four volumes from a manuscript, of which he could not read a word, performed his task to the best of his power; and fabricated the requisite number of lines, by shaking the types out of the boxes at a venture. The work must, therefore, be considered as a kind of overgrown *amphigouri,* a heterogeneous combination of events, which, pretending to no meaning, may be innocently permitted to surprize for a moment, and then dropt for ever.

If, however, which is possible, the author like Caliban (we beg Miss Owenson's pardon) 'cannot endue her purpose with words that make it known;' but by *illegible* means *what may be read,* and is, consequently, in earnest; the case is somewhat altered, and we must endeavour to make out the story. (p. 50)

[The story] may be dismissed as merely foolish: but the sentiments and language must not escape quite so easily. The latter is an inflated jargon, composed of terms picked up in all countries, and wholly irreducible to any ordinary rules of grammar or sense. The former are mischievous in tendency, and profligate in principle; licentious and irreverent in the highest degree. To revelation, Miss Owenson manifests a singular antipathy. It is the subject of many profound diatribes, which want nothing but meaning to be decisive. Yet Miss Owenson is not without an object of worship. She makes no account indeed of the Creator of the universe, unless to swear by his name; but, in return, she manifests a prodigious respect for something that she dignifies with the name of Nature, which, it seems, governs the world, and, as we gather from her creed, is to be honoured by libertinism in the women, disloyalty in the men, and atheism in both.

This young lady, as we conclude from her Introduction, is the *enfant gaté* ["spoiled child"] of a particular circle, who see, in her constitutional sprightliness, marks of genius, and encourage her dangerous propensity to publication. She has evidently written more than she has read, and read more than she has thought. But this is beginning at the wrong end. If we were happy enough to be in her confidence, we should advise the immediate purchase of a spelling book, of which she stands in great need; to this, in due process of time, might be added a pocket dictionary; she might then take a few easy lessons in 'joined-hand,' in order to become *legible:* if, after this, she could be persuaded to exchange her idle raptures for common sense, practise a little self denial, and gather a few precepts of humility, from an old-fashioned book, which, although it does not seem to have lately fallen in her way, may yet, we think, be found in some corner of her study; she might then hope to prove, not indeed a good writer of novels, but a useful friend, a faithful wife, a tender mother, and a respectable and happy mistress of a family. (p. 52)

> *William Gifford, in a review of "Woman; or, Ida of Athens," in* The Quarterly Review, *Vol. I, No. I, February, 1809, pp. 50-2.*

The Belfast Monthly Magazine (essay date 1809)

[*In the following excerpt from a letter to the editor of the* Belfast Monthly, *the correspondent praises Morgan's* The Wild Irish Girl *for its descriptions of Ireland but is disappointed with its depiction of Irish women.*]

My earnest wishes for the character of my countrywomen, induces me to offer some remarks on *The Wild Irish Girl,* which I am confident is not a true delineation of the Irish character, for I have a better opinion of our countrywomen than to suppose their whole attention is occupied in the manner Glorvina's too generally was. The scene in the boudoir is unworthy of a female pen, and I cannot think highly of the refinement of a mind which was capable of imagining such a scene. . . I must say there are some excellent descriptions in *The Wild Irish Girl.* I began to read it with the highest expectations, and was delighted with the half of the first volume, which is excellent. I felt real interest in the story of Murtoch O'Shaughnassey. Miss Owenson seems to have caught some distinguishing traits in the character of the Irish peasantry. Father John is excellent, and she deserves much credit for drawing the character of a benevolent Irish Priest. The description of the castle of Inismore, the Prince, Glorvina, and the old nurse, would be highly interesting to those who are not acquainted with Ireland, or Irish manners, but the tale loses a great deal of its interest when we know that no such castles are now in existence. The furniture of the castle is rather incongruous. If Miss Owenson's motive for writing this book were to reconcile English prejudices, or the prejudices of *some* of the inhabitants of Ireland, against their Catholic neighbours her motive was laudable and praiseworthy; but why in sketching the character of an Irishwoman need she have made Glorvina a flirt and a coquet? (p. 334)

Miss Owenson deserves the highest praise for the patriotism, which is perceivable in all her writings; it is her delineation of the female character to which I object.

Ida is written even in a more affected manner than *The Wild Irish Girl,* but it has been so well reviewed in the Magazine, that I shall only mention as a sample of Ida's coquetry; when Osmyn was standing under the window she heard him, and not wishing to let him know she perceived him, and yet to discover to him that she was in the chamber, she placed the tripod in the middle of the floor, and walked between the lamp and the window, so that her shadow might be seen on the ground where Osmyn was. Is not this *studied finesse?* Miss Owenson's admirers may say I am severe, I trust I am not unjustly so. All have an undoubted right to think for themselves, and I always wish to have an independent judgment. (p. 335)

> *"On the Wild Irish Girl, and Ida of Athens,"*
> *in* The Belfast Monthly Magazine, *Vol. 2, No. 10, May 31, 1809, pp. 334-35.*

Lady Morgan (essay date 1817)

[*In the following excerpt from her preface to* France, *Morgan replies to a review by William Gifford (see excerpt dated 1809).*]

I offer the following work to public notice, with feelings of great intimidation and distrust. To an undertaking, at once arduous and delicate, I have brought none of those advantages most favourable to the *mechanism* of authorship; and in a series of narrated observations, over whose dryness the graces of fiction shed no extraneous charm, I have unavoidably been denied the *time* for leisurely composition. For it was necessary, from the nature of the work (intended to reflect the changeful images of the day, and in their true character and colouring,

> To catch, if I could, the Cynthias of the minute),

to preserve the passing fact in the strength of its original occurrence; to forestall anecdote and anticipate detail, ere the rapid current of public events should force them through the various channels of society, and lessen their value by extending their circulation.

Starting from the post with many abler competitors, my object was, if possible, to distance those by *time,* if I could not rival them in *skill;* and, in my effort to clear the ground, and to arrive *first* at the goal, I fear I have attained my end with more celerity than grace. (pp. v-vi)

[The pages of *France* were] composed between the months of November and March, from the heads of a journal, kept with regularity during my residence in France, in the year 1816; and having bound myself to my publisher to be ready for the press before April, I was obliged to compose *á trait de plume,* to send off the sheets chapter by chapter, without the power of detecting repetitions by comparison, and without the hope of correction from the perusal of proof sheets. Publishing in one country, and residing in another, it was not to be expected that the press would wait upon the chances of wind and tide, for returns either in or out of course.

To the inaccuracies of haste, a fault less excusable has been added; I mean the frequent recurrence of French sentences and dialogues, which break up and disfigure the text; a fault which arose from my anxiety to give impressions with all the warmth and vigour with which I received them; to preserve the *form* with the *spirit;* to repeat the jargon of the court, or the cottage, the well-turned point of the duchess, or the *patois* of the peasant, as I caught and took them down *de vive voix* in my tablets, or retained and recorded them in my journal. While I thus endeavour to account for faults, I cannot excuse; and to solicit the indulgence of *that public* from whom I have never experienced severity, I make no effort to deprecate *professional criticism,* because I indulge no hope from its mercy. There is *one* review, at least, which must necessarily place me under the ban of its condemnation; and to which the sentiments and principles scattered through the following pages (though conceived and expressed in feelings the most remote from those of *local* or *party* policy) will afford an abundant source of accusation, as being foreign to its own narrow doctrines, and opposed to its own exclusive creed. I mean the *Quarterly Review.* It may look like presumption to hope, or even to fear its notice; but *I,* at least, know by experience, that in the omniscience of its judgment it can stoop

> To break a butterfly upon a wheel.

It is now nearly nine years since that review selected me as an example of its unsparing severity; and, deviating from the true object of criticism, made its strictures upon one of the most hastily composed and insignificant of my *early* works a vehicle for an unprovoked and wanton attack upon the personal character and principles of the author. The slander thus hurled against a young and unprotected female, struggling in a path of no ordinary industry and effort, for purposes sanctified by the most sacred feelings of nature, happily fell hurtless. The public of an enlightened age, indulgent to the critical errors of pages composed for its amusement, under circumstances, not of vanity or choice, but of *necessity,* has, by its countenance and favour, acquitted me of those charges under which I was summoned before their awful tribunal, and which tended to banish the accused from society, and her works from circulation: for "licentiousness, profligacy, irreverence, blasphemy, libertinism, disloyalty, and atheism," were no venial errors. Placed by that public in a definite rank among authors, and in no undistinguished circle of society, alike as *woman* and as author, beyond the injury of malignant scurrility, whatever form it may assume, I would point out to those who have yet to struggle through the arduous and painful career that I have ran, the feebleness of unmerited calumny, and encourage those who receive with patience and resignation the awards of dignified and legitimate criticism, to disregard and contemn the anonymous slander with which party spirit arms its strictures, under the veil of literary justice.

In thus recurring to the severe chastisement which my early efforts received from the judgment of the *Quarterly Review,* it would be ungrateful to conceal that it placed

> My bane and antidote at once before me,

and that in accusing me of "licentiousness, profligacy, irreverence, blasphemy, libertinism, disloyalty, and atheism," it presented a *nostrum* of universal efficacy, which was to transform my *vices* into *virtues,* and to render me, in its own words, "not indeed a good writer of novels, but a *useful friend,* a *faithful wife,* a *tender mother,* and a respectable and happy *mistress of a family.* "

To effect this purpose, "so devoutly to be wished," it prescribed a simple remedy: "To purchase immediately a *spelling book,* to which, in process of time, might be added a *pocket dictionary,* and to take a few lessons in joining-hand; which, superadded to a little common sense, in place of idle raptures," were finally to render me that valuable epitome of female excellence, whose price Solomon has declared above rubies.

While I denied the crimes thus administered to, I took the advice for the sake of its results; and like "Coelebs in search of a wife," with his ambulating virtues, I set forth with my Mavor and my Entick in search of that conjugal state, one of the necessary qualifications for my future excellencies. With my dictionary in my pocket, with my spelling book in one hand, and my copper-plate improvements in the other, I entered my probation; and have at last (thanks to the *Quarterly Review*) obtained the reward of my calligraphic and orthographic acquirements. As it foretold, I am become, in spite of the "seven deadly sins" it laid to my charge, "not indeed a good writer of novels," but, I trust, "a respectable," and, I am *sure,* "a happy mistress of a family."

In the fearful prophecy so long made, that I should never write a *good* novel, the *Quarterly Review,* in its benevolence, will at least not be displeased to learn that I have written some that have been *successful;* and that while my Glorvinas, Luximas, and Lolottes, have pleaded my cause at home, like *"very Daniels,"* they have been received abroad with equal favour and indulgence; and that **O'Donnel** has been transmitted to its author in three different languages. Having thus, I hope, settled "my long arrear of GRATITUDE with Alonzo," I am now ready to begin a new score; and await the sentence of my quondam judge, in the spirit of one

> Who neither courts nor fears
> His favour nor his hate.

(pp. vi-xi)

Lady Morgan, in a preface to her France, Vol. I, *Henry Colburn, 1817, pp. v-xii.*

John Croker   (essay date 1817)

[*Croker made extensive contributions to the* Quarterly Review, *the most prominent Tory periodical of the early nineteenth century. While he was a noteworthy critic of literature and historical writings, Croker had a greater role in guiding the political direction of the* Quarterly Review. *First Secretary of the Admiralty and a friend to Tory leaders in government, Croker so effectively channeled the government's views into the* Review *that, from 1830 to 1850, the journal was considered the voice of the old Tory party. In the following excerpt from his review of* France, *Croker pronounces the book morally and politically offensive.*]

France! Lady Morgan appears to have gone to Paris by the high road of Calais and returned by that of Dieppe. In that capital she seems to have resided about four months, and thence to have made one or two short excursions; and with this extent of ocular inspection of that immense country, she returns and boldly affixes to her travelling memoranda diluted into a quarto volume, the title of *France!* One merit, however, the title has—it is appropriate to the volume which it introduces, for to falsehood it adds the other qualities of the work,—vagueness, bombast, and affectation. (p. 260)

Our readers cannot have gone far in this work without being struck with the wonderful similarity of its sentiments and language to those of the *Letters from Paris* [by John Hobhouse] reviewed in a former Number. Both exhibit the same slavish awe when speaking of the usurper, the same impudent familiarity when noticing the lawful monarch; both profess the same admiration of all that was feeble, and treacherous, and bloody in France; the same hatred of all that was firm, and loyal, and virtuous: both evince the same proneness to profanation, the same audacious contempt of every thing savouring of religion and piety. Both mistake the whinings of a few obscure Jacobins for the general voice of the French people; and both,—more insane than the madman in Horace who kept his seat after the curtain had dropped, and heard *miros tragœdos* in an empty theatre,—at a period when every moment brings fresh proof of the return of France to its characteristic loyalty and attachment to its ancient line of kings, can see nothing, can hear of nothing, but plots to overthrow the government, and bring back the golden age of their day-dreams, the reign of rebellion, plunder, and blood.

We shall not, of course, be accused of attributing to Mr. Hobhouse the portentous ignorance and folly of Lady Morgan.—Mr. Hobhouse, unfortunately for himself, is not ignorant, unless of existing circumstances:—but Lady Morgan (and we record it to her praise) possesses one substantial advantage over him. She insults and vilifies the royal family of France, it is true, but she does not outrage humanity so far as to term them 'bone-grubbers,' because they piously sought to give the remains of their sovereign and father, a decent burial. (pp. 285-86)

> *John Croker, in an originally unsigned review of "France," in* The Quarterly Review, *Vol. XVII, No. XXXIII, April, 1817, pp. 260-86.*

Godey's Lady's Book   (essay date 1843)

[*In the following excerpt, the critic, in an otherwise unfavorable review, praises the patriotism displayed in* The Wild Irish Girl.]

As a novel [*The Wild Irish Girl*] certainly cannot be rated very high. The plot shows little inventive talent, and was, moreover, liable to some objection on the score of moral tendency. We allude to the plan of making the Earl of M— and his son both in love with the same lady. The denouement is very awkwardly managed, and we think most readers must have been disgusted, if not shocked by the scene where the unconscious rivals, father and son, meet in the old chapel. There is very little development of char-

acter attempted, each person introduced being expressly designed, as is at once seen, to act a particular part, which is set down in the play.

Nor is the merit of the work in its style, which is both high-flown and puerile. The exaggerated sentiment, so often poured out by the fervid, but uncultivated writer, appears more nonsensical from the pompous phraseology in which it is so often expressed. We wonder how such great words could have been brought together to express such small meanings. This is particularly the case with the descriptive portions of the work. In short, the author, possessing naturally the wildest and warmest phase of Irish temperament, had her head filled and nearly turned by what she calls "the witching sorcery" of Rousseau; and as her taste had been very little cultivated by judicious reading, or her judgment improved by observation, it is not strange that she mistook hyperbole for elegance, and fancied that soft, mellifluous words would convey ideas of super-human beauty. The following description of her heroine, Glorvina, is a fair specimen of this tawdry style.

> Her form was so almost impalpably delicate, that as it floated on the gaze, it seemed like the incarnation of some pure etherial spirit, which a sigh too roughly breathed, might dissolve into its kindred air; yet to this sylphide elegance of spheral beauty was united all that symmetrical *contour* which constitutes the luxury of human loveliness. This scarcely 'mortal mixture of earth's mould,' was vested in a robe of vestal white, which was enfolded beneath the bosom with a narrow girdle embossed with precious stones.

Query, how did the lady look? Can the reader form any clear notion?

Such is the prevailing style of the book, though occasionally, when giving utterance to some strong deep feeling, which usually finds its appropriate language, the author is truly eloquent. How could a novel so written, gain such popularity? Because it had a high aim, a holy purpose. It owed its success entirely to the simple earnestness with which Miss Owenson defended her country. It is all Irish. She seemed to have no thought of self, nothing but patriotism was in her soul, and this feeling redeemed the faults of inflated style, French sentimentalisms, false reasoning, and all the extravagances of her youthful fancy. Ireland was her inspiration and her theme. Its history, language, antiquities and traditions, these she had studied as a zealot does his creed, and with a fervour only inferior in sacredness to that of religion, she poured her whole heart and mind forth in the cause of her own native land. (p. 128)

But though we give Lady Morgan full credit for her patriotism, and willingly allow that she has done her country some service by her writings, yet as her object was chiefly political reform, whenever that is attained, her works must lose most of their interest. She has laboured rather to expose wrongs than to suggest improvements. This rooting up weeds, may be quite as useful in cultivation as planting flowers, but the latter is most pleasant, and as we think, best suited to the hand of a lady. (p. 129)

> *J. K., "Lady Morgan's First and Last Work," in* Godey's Lady's Book, *Vol. XXVII, No. 9, September, 1843, pp. 128-29.*

Horatio Sheafe Krans   (essay date 1903)

[*In the following excerpt, Krans offers an overview of Morgan's novels.*]

Lady Morgan, with her hysterical sentimentality and shrill satirical vehemence, is very different from Miss [Maria] Edgeworth and Mrs. [Anna Maria] Hall, with their English propriety and restraint. Her pure romances, reflections of German romance in their gushing sentimentality and enthusiasm for clouds, waterfalls, and the moral sublime, stand without the scope of Irish fiction as exotic in conception, subject, and coloring. Her Irish stories, ***The Wild Irish Girl, O'Donnel, Florence Macarthy,*** and ***The O'Briens and O'Flahertys*** enjoyed a great vogue in their day, due almost altogether, it would seem, to the fact that she voiced liberal patriotic sentiment at the time of the Emancipation agitation, when Emancipators welcomed a champion, and government journals attacked acrimoniously everything tinged with Emancipation sympathies. Her books became a centre of political controversy. Every one read them. ***The Wild Irish Girl*** went through seven editions in two years. ***The O'Briens and O'Flahertys,*** in its satire and its romance, in its expression of patriotic sentiment, and in its pictures of Irish life, is the best of the national tales. These tales bid for popular favor by an incongruous combination of romantic interest and interest in the portrayal of manners, with an element of social satire and a vein of patriotic sentiment. The romance in Lady Morgan's fiction is a kind of mawkish, sentimental vaporing, that draws on no depth of feeling, and to which the reader of to-day will not patiently submit. The social satire, considering its source, is sharp and harsh in tone, and very bad-tempered. The best spots in Lady Morgan's novels are those in which the customs and characters of the lower Irish are delineated, or, to quote one of the amenities of her *Blackwood* critics, "She is more at home in painting the rude manners in which she was bred than those of the civilized countries into which she has intruded." There seems something contagious in the drolleries of the humble Irish out of which even the weakest of Irish stories can make capital. Lady Morgan caught them well, and presented them in the true Hibernian spirit. Country postilions, the "mine hosts" of the poteen houses, Dublin porters, drivers, and domestics she hit off to the life. Her satire of the gay side of the higher social life of Dublin is also spirited, and readable even to-day. Her patriotic sentiment has the ring of sincerity and enthusiasm, and springs from a zealous hope for a united country where men of all persuasions could stand upon common ground.

In all that concerns literary craftsmanship Lady Morgan fails. There are clumsy, chaotic plots, and actions overburdened with antiquarian dissertations and political discussions. When a critic of the *Quarterly Review* [see excerpt dated 1809], referring to the style of her novels, recommended "the immediate purchase of a spelling-book and a pocket dictionary," he advised well, if not courteously. The style is not merely bad, but positively objectionable in its attempts at fine writing, its endless series of barbarisms and solecisms, and its sprinkling of French and Italian words that serve no better purpose than to display the author's acquaintance with those languages. Lady Morgan was a literary opportunist. Her novels, now only names, owed the vogue they enjoyed in their own day to the fact that they discussed questions of absorbing con-temporary interest, rather than to any intrinsic literary merit. (pp. 278-81)

Horatio Sheafe Krans, "Literary Estimate," in his Irish Life in Irish Fiction, *Columbia University Press*, 1903, pp. 270-325.

Ernest A. Baker   (essay date 1936)

[*In the following excerpt, Baker traces Morgan's development as a novelist.*]

[Lady Morgan's] first two novels, ***St. Clair; or, the Heiress of Desmond*** (1802), and ***The Novice of St Dominick*** (1805), were flimsy sentimental romances strongly tinged with nationalist feeling. In literary quality, ***The Wild Irish Girl*** (1806) was not greatly superior. But it came out at a timely moment, flattering the prejudices of some and exciting curiosity in others. No story in letters was ever put together more clumsily. These glowing epistles are packed with dates and other historical information, including rectified etymologies, and are encumbered with footnotes, for Lady Morgan was always a bit of a blue-stocking. The estranged son of an English earl wandering in Ireland finds himself near the ruinous castle of Inishmore, ancient seat of the princes of that name, who were bloodily defeated and thrust out of their possessions by his own ancestors. The prince to-day is an aged man, poor as a peasant, but too proud to associate with an English nobleman. Glorvina, his daughter, last of her race, far from being an ignorant barbarian, has all the natural graces and the education and high accomplishments of a princess. The incognito falls in love, and Glorvina responds. But she is under some obscure obligation to an unknown benefactor. The lover runs off distracted. Then he hears that Glorvina is to be married. He returns in time to find that the would-be bridegroom is his own father, who like the son has had to suppress his identity in order to win the old prince's consent. Needless to say, the two change places. The sentiment, the gush, the tears—of joy, grief, or simple ecstasy—are worthy of such a fairy-tale.

O'Donnel, a National Tale (1814), is the same story a little better told. [Sir Walter] Scott was pleased with it. She had wished, says the preface, to use Irish history for "purposes of conciliation"; but discovered that to lift the veil was to renew the memory of events that had better be left in oblivion. So she uncovers the evils that are the existing result of bygone wrongs. . . . The sentimentalism is blatant; and, although Lady Morgan makes something of "the amusing spectacle of seeing bon-ton frivolity exhibited in all its idleness and vacuity," her satire of snobbishness is that of an arrant snob. She is irritated most by the opulent idlers who come to Ireland to laugh at the oddities of the peasants, and sneer at the vestiges of ancient grandeur. Irish scenery as well as the splendours of former ages is extolled; like many others by the patriotic, the work is a cross between novel and guide-book, and overburdened with descriptive pages. The Irish consist of poverty-stricken natives and a dispossessed nobility, with a scanty middle class composed chiefly of griping attorneys and other satellites of the usurping lords of the soil. Her droll types, blarneying peasants and sheer buffoons, helped with Lover's and Lever's to establish the stage Irishman, half fool, half mountebank, a myth not utterly destroyed till a century later. Maria Edgeworth had avoided this pitfall;

if she did not see very far into the racial temperament, she did not distort it or rest satisfied with a superficial caricature. Lady Morgan was kind enough to the peasants; but, for her, Irish grievances centred in the disinherited nobility and gentry, Ireland's rightful leaders, whose reinstatement would be the restoration of the age of gold.

Her next political story, *Florence M'Carthy* (1818), has the indispensable love-tale, but is of mediocre interest except for the satire, or rather the invective, hurled at those place-men, "the desk aristocracy," who acted as informers, Government hirelings fomenting sedition, butchering magistrates, and the like, during the years of unrest. John Wilson Croker, who had assailed Lady Morgan with scurrilous abuse in the *Quarterly Review,* is caricatured as one of this pack in Counsellor Con Crawley. She was a privileged spectator of Irish history during the years of her Dublin life, though it was of course her own interpretation that she swore by. *The O'Briens and the O'Flahertys* (1827), the last of her national tales, is more like a series of memoirs reviewing the period 1782-1800, and exhuming solid fragments from the Middle Ages and later times to give further weight to her accusations, than a regular novel; but, though she wrote as a pamphleteer, her record is still one of the liveliest extant of the doings of the volunteers and of the United Irishmen, who were contending for reform and drifting into rebellion. Lord Edward Fitzgerald appears under the alias of Lord Walter Fitzwalter. Her style had improved. Many scenes in this book are as good as anything in Lever, without his persistent farce and horseplay. She makes her hits with mockery, instead of practical joking. But, like most of her compatriots, she overdoes the conversations. They would, if they could, tell the whole story by means of talk, and very discursive talk.

In her *Dramatic Scenes from Real Life* (1833) Lady Morgan actually succeeded in doing this, though she was not aiming at the stage. The contents, *Manor Sackville, The Easter Recess,* and *Temper,* are to be read as novels; they are "a thing that may be read running, or dancing, like a puff on a dead wall, or a sentiment on a French fan," says the preface. The humorous character-sketching and the brisk dialogue in the first show that it is not fair to judge her only by *The Wild Irish Girl.* (pp. 15-18)

> Ernest A. Baker, "The Irish Novelists," in his The History of the English Novel: The Age of Dickens and Thackeray, H. F. & G. Witherby Ltd, 1936, pp. 11-61.

A. Norman Jeffares   (essay date 1971)

[*Jeffares is an Irish educator and essayist. While much of his criticism focuses on the works of W. B. Yeats, his critical studies range in subject from the poetry of Geoffrey Chaucer to twentieth-century literature. In the following excerpt, he discusses* The Wild Irish Girl.]

Sydney Owenson (Lady Morgan) provided Irish, English and European readers with novels which were at first gushingly romantic. But a mixture of antiquarianism and patriotism informed them from the start. . . . She produced *Twelve Original Hibernian Melodies* in 1805; but she had published her first novel *St. Clair: or, the Heiress of Desmond* in 1802, and followed it with *The Novice of*

St. Dominick in 1805. Her fame was firmly established with *The Wild Irish Girl* of 1806.

This novel builds on the earlier experimentation of *St. Clair,* which was addressed to those whose "exquisite native sensibility nurtured by habit, subtilized by the refinements of superior education, united to a tender heart and lively imagination". The young man who narrates the story in letters writes from that part of Connaught where "you find the character, the manner, the language, and the music of the ancient Irish in all their primitive originality; and the names Ossian and Fingal are as well known among these old Milesians as in the Hebrides: to this remote province, whose shores are washed by the 'steep Atlantic', were the native Irish driven by political and religious persecution". The hero hopes to find in Connaught many of the literary traditions which throw light upon the history and character of every country which has preserved them from the wreck of time or the devastation of warfare. He finds much in common with Olivia Desmond, a local heiress who reads, sings Irish songs, plays the harp, and walks. (pp. 293-94)

The story has little action except for its hurried conclusion, and despite its lofty moral purpose it is little more than a fashionable piece of romance and highly strung sensibility. It does catch the intensity, the self-pity, even the abandonment of a youthful love affair—St. Clair's long empty days offer him scope for an introspection encouraged by speculation on his uncertain future. What was new in the novel was the setting. But Lady Morgan did not make so much of the cliffs and the ruins of the West of Ireland, nor of the Irish subject matter as she did in later novels. Sir Patrick liked his cultural history. Olivia liked singing and translating Irish songs, but the novel's intensity was reserved for the development of personal relationships. (pp. 294-95)

[Sydney Owenson's second novel, *The Novice of St. Dominick,*] possesses the pedantry of *St. Clair;* Imogen, the heroine, is lectured mercilessly by De Sorville and elegant literature is discussed within the intervals of gushing descriptions of the heroine's sensibilities. Imogen, however, has much more credibility than Olivia—Sydney herself was growing up. Nature is treated to Mrs. Radcliffe's recipe and a scrapbook kept by Sydney Owenson in 1801 contains the remark that

> . . . at eighteen the passion is but a simple sensation of nature, unmingled, unenriched by those superadded ideas which constitute its purer and more elevated charms. Other sensations mingle with love, as other metals amalgamate with gold—the sympathy of congenial tastes—the blandishments of the imagination—the graces of intellectual perfection—the exaggeration of fancy, glowing with poetic images, and the refinement of taste to apply them to the object beloved—all these heighten and sublimate the passion which has its origin in Nature.

The novel explored the survival of Provençal culture, and while it pleaded for tolerance between races and religions in a France of two centuries earlier, it pointed a moral to its contemporary readers in England and Ireland.

Tensions—and fusions—between different races and religions in Ireland make up a good deal of the history of Anglo-Irish literature. Maria Edgeworth's *Castle Rack-*

rent (1800), for instance, the first regional novel, probably drew much of its strength from the fact that Maria went to Ireland at the age of fifteen—old enough to analyse the differences between the two countries, young enough to have the energy to record the variations in Irish usage of English speech and syntax with affectionate delight. . . . Sydney Owenson had drawn on books for her Provençal parallels; but she had a similar sea change, as she records in the Preface to her *Patriotic Sketches of Ireland* of 1807. For her, however, there was a difference. When she went to England and discovered how little was known there of her own country, it was

> requisite therefore I should leave my native country to learn the turpitude, degradation, ferocity and inconsequence of her offspring; the miseries of her present, and the falsity of the recorded splendours of her ancient state.

She felt as impelled to present her picture of Ireland as Maria Edgeworth had. But whereas Maria Edgeworth undoubtedly mingled some of the *triste utilité* (for which Madame de Staël reproached her) with her delight in story telling, Sydney Owenson found the mere relation of facts unpalatable and moved further into romance in the book which made her famous, *The Wild Irish Girl* of 1806. Published in the same year as Maria Edgeworth's *Ennui,* it shared a similar device, the introduction of an Englishman into the Irish scene.

Maria Edgeworth's *Ennui* suffered from being written with two purposes in mind—it was a moral and didactic attack upon laziness as well as a literary description of Ireland seen through the eyes of Lord Glenthorn, a faded sophisticate who gradually redeemed himself as he shed his boredom, attended to his tenants' interests, defeated a rebel conspiracy and finally resigned his title and estates to his foster brother, the real Lord Glenthorn. *The Wild Irish Girl,* however, has a more concentrated purpose, of informing English readers—through the *persona* of the novel's English hero—about the past civilization of Ireland, surviving mainly in the West, and about the injustices under which the whole country laboured. The device used by both women novelists may have owed something to the prevalence of English travellers' comments on Ireland.

Like St. Clair, the hero of *The Wild Irish Girl,* Horatio M . . . , younger son of the Earl of M . . . , is sent to the shores of the "steep Atlantic"—the amount of repetition of phrases the early Irish novelists permitted themselves from novel to novel is remarkable. His father has sent Horatio to Ireland because instead of reading Coke upon Lyttleton he has been idly presiding "as the high priest of libertinism at the nocturnal orgies of vitiated dissipation". His pursuits have been elegant but unprofitable, and he has a decided prejudice against Ireland which he supposes "semi-barbarous, semi-civilized", having lost the strength of savage life and not acquired the graces of polished society. Yet we realise his destination, when he is disposed in the opening pages of the novel to admire the "compact uniformity" of Dublin, and to impute— liberally—the origin of the many beggars to the supreme police. And Arthur Young is quoted in a footnote as praising the cheerfulness as well as the hospitality of the Irish.

However, this is but a beginning. Horatio M . . . is to set out for the North West of Connaught; and the opening of

St. Clair is used again to describe this as the classic ground of the Irish: he looks forward to beholding the Irish character in all its primeval ferocity; like St. Clair, he makes play in selfpity with his future Kamscathan palace. After the experience of a leaky post-chaise, he tries and approves the stage coach, then walks the last twenty miles. This allows him to adumbrate on the

> bold features of its varying landscape, the stupendous altitude of its "cloud-capt" mountains, the imperious gloom of its deep embosomed glens, the savage desolation of its uncultivated heaths, and boundless bogs, with those rich ruins of a picturesque champagne, thrown at intervals into gay expansion by the hand of nature.

All this awakens the pleasures of tasteful enjoyment in the mind of the poetic or pictorial traveller, and Horatio has very properly equipped himself, as had St. Clair, with sketching materials. He also remarks that

> If the glowing fancy of Claude Lorraine would have dwelt enraptured on the paradisial charms of English landscape, the superior genius of Salvator Rosa would have reposed its eagle wing amidst those scenes of mysterious sublimity with which the wildly magnificent landscape of Ireland abounds.

Lady Morgan's interpretation of the Irish scene derives largely from Salvator Rosa; her "greatest literary pleasure" was in writing his *Life and Times,* published in 1824: but her descriptions of landscape also owe inspiration to Mrs. Radcliffe; with her she indulged in the pleasurable activity of making Nature more terrifying, greater, more significant than ever before. Nature had to conform to a taste in the picturesque: and the "great lakes" and "stupendous heights" crowned with "misnic forests" which Horatio M . . . meets on his walk are later echoed in her descriptions of Sligo in *Patriotic Sketches of Ireland.* The hero's gloom swells through the *Introductory Letters* in antithetical sentences:

> vibrating between an innate propensity to *right* and an habitual adherence to *wrong;* sick of pursuits I was too indolent to relinquish, and linked to vice, yet enamoured of virtue; weary of the useless, joyless inanity of my existence, yet without power to regenerate my worthless being . . .

This uneasy personality makes him fly from himself, his heart chill and unawakened, his "every appetite depraved and pampered into satiety" after his unsuccessful love affair with a depraved Lady C . . . He becomes livelier, when in an area where the clouds incorporate "with the kindling aether of a purer atmosphere". He feels himself the "presiding genius of desolation".

But this solitary state gives way to an exploration *en route* of the cottages of the peasants where women spin, and sing in Irish. He meets an English-speaking peasant who tells him of the hardships in the life of a poor Irish peasant who has had to migrate for seasonal work, his potatoes seized because of his catching a fever and being unable to pay the rent. Horatio has a meal in a cottage, hears Mustock sing the Cualin, and a piper play a jig upon which all join in dancing. There is an air of anthropology about this description of peasant life: Horatio realises he has previously been prejudiced against the peasant character, the courtesy of which is here emphasized.

The next lesson for the reader is a meeting with Lord M . . .'s steward who considers the peasants rebellious, idle, cruel and treacherous: adjectives which could also apply to his own behaviour. Horatio hears more of his exactions from the peasantry, who are afraid to complain to Lord M . . . He shuns the local society of the Os and Macs. His state of mind is Byronic:

> The energy of youthful feeling is subdued, and the vivacity of warm emotion worn out by its own violence. I have lived too fast in a moral as well as a physical sense, and the principles of my intellectual, as well as my natural constitution are, I fear, fast hastening to decay. I live in the tomb of my expiring mind, and preserve only the consciousness of my wretched state, without the power, and almost without the wish to be otherwise than what I am. And yet, God knows, I am nothing less than contented.

After all this introduction and more description of "groves druidically venerable—mountains of Alpine elevation—expansive lakes, and the boldest and most romantic sea coast", Horatio hears of the Prince of Inismore who lives with his daughter Glorvina, his harper and Father John, his chaplain, in a ruined castle which had been battered down by the Cromwellians. (pp. 296-300)

Once in the castle he is attracted by Glorvina though protesting that he is interested in her merely on a philosophical principle: "What had I to expect from the unpolished manners, the confined ideas of this wild Irish girl?" But he longs to study

> the purely national, natural character of an Irishwoman: in fine, I long to behold any woman in such lights and shades of mind, temper, and disposition, as Nature has originally formed her in.

Glorvina's wildness lies in her air and look: she has an "effulgency of countenance": but later, while her looks are *naif,* almost wildly simple, her manner is elegant, though she has been deprived of all those graceful advantages which society confers.

Glorvina soon begins to impart her knowledge to him. She gives him a disquisition on the Irish harp, in which several pages provide but two or three lines of text to the informative footnotes, twenty-two or three lines in small print. Horatio is asked to stay and teach Glorvina drawing: and he forms the idea of reconciling his father and the Prince. The Chaplain and Glorvina begin to teach him Irish, and further instruction upon Irish poetry follows. Glorvina dispenses knowledge with the most unaffected simplicity of look and manner, but with all the precision of a true blue stocking. Her reply to a query as to how the Irish could procure so expensive an article as saffron for dying their clothes illustrates this side of her character:

> "I have heard Father John say" she returned, "that saffron, as an article of importation, would never have been at any time cheap enough for general use. And I believe formerly, as *now,* they communicated this bright yellow tinge with indigenous plants, with which this country abounds.

> "See", she added, springing lightly forward, and culling a plant which grew from the mountain's side—"see this little blossom, which they call here, 'yellow lady's bed straw', and which you, as a botanist, will better recognise as the *galicens borum;* it

communicates a beautiful yellow; as does the *lichen juniperinus,* or "cypress moss' which you brought me yesterday; and I think the *reseda luteola* or 'yellow weed' surpasses them all".

It was small wonder that Mrs. Le Fanu warned Sydney Owenson of the dangers of becoming intellectually admired and revered, but of forfeiting claims on the affection of the heart. She replied that the strongest point of her ambition was to be every inch a woman:

> Delighted with the study of La Voisin [La Voisier?], I dropped the study of chemistry, though urged to it by a favourite friend and preceptor, lest I should be less the *woman.* Seduced by taste, and a thousand arguments, to Greek and Latin, I resisted, lest I should not be a *very woman.* And I have studied music rather as a sentiment than a science, and *drawing* as an amusement rather than an *art,* lest I should have become a musical *pedant,* or a *masculine artist.*

This passage chimes in with her dislike of facts. She is reluctant to overload—by her standards—her heroine with pedantic information, the bulk of which is consigned to informative footnotes: the interest of the romantic reader has to be held. The information is next distributed by the Prince and his chaplain, and Horatio is informed about ancient Irish dress, annals, jewelry, oaths, the true authorship of Ossian, poor scholars, the education of Roman Catholic priests, and other subjects.

He returns to find a letter from his father suggesting a wealthy marriage and he proceeds to Inismore. The romantic side of Glorvina's character is developed. . . . Her taste must be developed. She reads *Heloise* but he presents her with

> such books as Glorvina had *not,* yet *should* read, that she may know herself, and the latent sensibility of her soul. They have of course, all been presented to her, and consist of *La Nouvelle Héloïse,* de Rousseau—the unrivalled *Lettres sur la mythologie* de Monslier—the *Paul et Virginie* of St. Pierre— the *Werter* of Gœthe, the *Dolbrcause* of Lousel, and the *Atala* of Chateaubriand.

The comment made on English novels is that they carry the prize of morality from the romantic fictions of other countries but they rarely seize on the imagination through the medium of the heart, their heroines are most perfect but most stupid beings. Genius and the graces should be added to virtue. Glorvina, then, is a romantic heroine, with genius and the graces being steadily thrown in. She admits Horatio to her boudoir, and there he discovers in her *Bréviaire du Sentiment* several faded snowdrops stained with blood under which she had written some lines translated from the Italian of Lorenzo de Medici and added "culled from the spot where he fell—April the 1st 17—." Yet the boudoir has some mystery about it—how do recent London newspapers arrive there? His father writes to him again, to say that the financially attractive match is arranged and that he will shortly bring the girl and her father on a visit to Ireland.

The third volume opens with Horatio's jealousy of some unknown who is writing to Glorvina. The Prince asks him to accompany Father John on a journey to the North. The rose Glorvina has given him is his charm for the journey— he draws it from his breast where it has lain. The journey offers yet more opportunities of education—the hero sees a funeral, hears a keening, is lectured in history and stays in the house of an independent country gentleman where the food is over plenteous, the ease of the guest being the pleasure of the host. The next information is perhaps the first fictional representation of the Northern Irish character:

> Here the ardor of the Irish constitution seems abated, if not chilled. Here the cead mile failta of Irish cordiality seldom lends its welcome home to the stranger's heart. The bright beams which illumine the gay images of Milesian fancy are extinguished; the convivial pleasures dear to the Milesian heart, scared at the prudential maxims of calculating interest, take flight to the warmer regions of the South; and the endearing of the soul, lost and neglected amid the cold concerns of the country-house and the bleach green, droop and expire in the deficiency of that nutritive warmth on which their tender existence depends.

When Horatio returns he falls into a fever, having seen Glorvina send a letter off to the "first and best of men". The old nurse tells him of the mysterious stranger who had befriended Glorvina, known as the Gentleman, a figure of mystery. He determines to leave, exchanges letters with the prince, but breaks down when Glorvina comes to bid him stay longer. They exchange farewells—for ever.

He goes to Dublin, where his father speaks feelingly of moulding a young girl's character: he too is thinking of marriage. The father leaves for M . . . House where Horatio is to be married.

A lively melodramatic conclusion follows. Horatio's future father-in-law suggests a visit to the West of Ireland to surprise Lord M . . . Horatio goes to the Lodge and finds that the Prince has been jailed for debts. He rushes to the town, discovers a mysterious friend has redeemed the debts and is about to marry Glorvina. A frantic scene ensues in the ruined chapel where it appears that the Earl of M . . . is marrying Glorvina himself. A positively Elizabethan clearing of the stage ensues. The Prince dies, the Earl of M. . . escorts his almost lifeless son out, while the attendants carry Glorvina, also apparently lifeless, to the castle. She makes a temporary recovery: gliding as usual, she reaches the bier and gazes on her father's body, anathematizes those who caused his death, and faints again. However, in four days, her "health and fine constitution were already prevailing over her disorder and acute sensibility". The novel ends with a plea for blending of differences between Catholic and Protestant, English and Irish, in a national unity, symbolised by the ensuing marriage of Glorvina and Horatio. Also the English landowner is to spend eight months out of every twelve in Ireland.

The writing of this romantic, sentimental, pedantic, enthusiastic tale confirmed Sydney Owenson in her desire to write more about Ireland's manners, and about its past history and future possibilities. . . . Her interest in the past led her to write *O'Donnel* (1814), a historical novel; her *Florence Macarthy* (1818) has been compared in its aims to a Faulkner novel of the deep south; and her best novel, *The O'Briens and the O'Flahertys* (1827), was a skilled and sensitive portrayal of the differences between old and new gentry in Connaught, in which she explored the difficulties of deciding between revolutionary and parliamentary methods, analysing what alternatives lay before a young Irishman.

She had developed far from the early novels and her self-delighting exploration of the gay wild Irish girl had given way to a quest for the serious young Irish leader of the nineteenth century—a figure ultimately to emerge, if all too briefly and tragically, after O'Connell's failure, in Charles Stewart Parnell. (pp. 301-05)

> *A. Norman Jeffares, "Early Efforts of the Wild Irish Girl," in* Le Romantisme Anglo-Americain: Mélanges offerts á Louis Bonnerot, *Didier, 1971, pp. 293-305.*

James Newcomer   (essay date 1975)

[*In the following excerpt, Newcomer discusses* Manor Sackville *in the context of Ireland's political struggles.*]

In 1833, Maria Edgeworth wrote apropos of her novel *Helen:* "I should tell you beforehand, that there is no humor in it, and no Irish character. It is impossible to draw Ireland as she now is, in a book of fiction. Realities are too strong, party passions too violent, to bear to see,

---

THE

O'BRIENS

AND

THE O'FLAHERTYS;

A NATIONAL TALE.

BY LADY MORGAN.

IN FOUR VOLUMES.

_____

" A Plague o' both your Houses'!"
                    SHAKSPEARE.

" Je me suis enquis au mielx que j'ai sçeu et pu; et je certifie á touts que ne l'ay fait ny pour or, ny pour argent, ny pour sallaire, ny pour compte á faire qui soit, ny homme ny femme qui vescut: ne voulant ainsi favoriser ny blamer nul á mon pouvoir, fors seulment déclarer les choses advenues."
            Du CLERCQ—*Préface des Chroniques.*

_____

VOL. I.

_____

LONDON:
HENRY COLBURN, NEW BURLINGTON-STREET.
_____
1827.

Facsimile of the title page to the first edition of The O'Briens and the O'Flahertys.

or care to look at, their faces in the looking-glass. The people would only break the glass, and curse the fool who held the mirror up to nature,—distorted nature in a mirror. We are in too perilous a case to laugh. Humor would be out of season, worse than bad taste." That same year Lady Morgan did hold a mirror up to Ireland's distorted nature, though she was no more happy with it than Maria Edgeworth. She wrote about Irish character; she depicted Irish realities; she caught the violence of party passion. "If the soil of Ireland is still bathed in blood, it is not drawn by her enemies, but by her infuriated children"—Lady Morgan has one of her characters say in 1833. And further: "Other virtues, other energies are necessary to lead you to prosperity and happiness. You want not saints, but citizens;—not heroes, but peaceable, industrious, and calculating utilitarians." Like Northern Ireland in 1975, in 1833 Ireland was a perilous case; the lineaments of 140 years ago prefigure the Irish lineaments of today.

Lady Morgan's 1833 work was *Manor Sackville,* published as the first of three drama-like works in *Dramatic Scenes from Real Life.* Hepworth Dixon in 1862, in *Lady Morgan's Memoirs,* calls its manner "very forcible and effective," praises it for its faithful pictures of Ireland, sympathizes with its aims, and speaks of its "vigorous delineation and dialogue. " But it was not successful. It was reviewed unfavorably, and successive commentators up to the near present have deprecated it. Lionel Stevenson in *The Wild Irish Girl: The Life of Sydney Owenson* says only that "the theme of the book, however, was no longer fresh enough to rouse controversy." But now, with the realities of bomb and fire and death searing our eyes daily, those of us who read it may well wonder why *Manor Sackville* has received so little attention. Maria Edgeworth and Lady Morgan saw truly what they saw. After 1833 the one, like the other, could not bear to write again about Ireland as Ireland was.

Ireland's problems were not settled yesterday, are not settled today, and they will not be settled tomorrow by turning our eyes away from the situation as it exists. Lady Morgan, in *Manor Sackville,* requires us to look straight at the picture of unhappy Ireland. In that picture she delineates each element sharply and exactly. In that picture, which has no light except the humor, which flashes like sheet lightning in an ominous sky, she plays the dark shadows of ignorance, cruelty, cupidity, and prejudice against one another.

As regards religion, the characters in *Manor Sackville* are: the English landholders in Ireland, members of the established church; the Irish clergy and lay members of the established church; the Irish members of a Protestant, evangelical sect; and Irish Catholics. Economically the elements are the "haves," all Protestant, and the "have-nots," all Catholic. Socially they are: the aristocracy, employees and hangers-on of the aristocracy, gentlemen, civil servants, servants, and peasants. The *dramatis personae* number well over 40. And in addition to the characters to whom she gives names are "Saints, Sinners, Patriots, Policemen, Whitefeet, Redfeet, and Blackfeet, Conservatives, Destructives, Orangemen, Ribbon-men, Footmen, Groom of the Chambers, 'and others.' "

These themes and characters Lady Morgan places in a wild rural section of northern Ireland, first on the much decayed plantation of a rich Englishman, where about half of the action takes place (three scenes). Scenes four and five take place in and about a tavern in a village that, "from a boggy common, covered with lawless paupers, has become a trim resort of New-Light sectarians. . . . There is too much of the 'painted sepulchre' about its [the tavern's] temporal arrangements. The walls, without, being punctually whitewashed, and flanked with Chinese roses and woodbine; while the interior has added nothing but hypocrisy to the original attributes of idleness, thriftlessness, and misery." Finally, the action moves to the environs and the town of Mogherow, "a genuine Irish town of the third or fourth class, unchanged during the last century [up to 1830]; swarming with pigs, beggars, and children; and richly endowed with shebeen houses, and porter, punch, and spirit stores." "The mountain district, in the vicinity, is of the wildest description, with inhabitants 'to match.' Among the latter, are distributed many unfortunate outlaws, driven there, partly by the sudden rage for large farms and pasture culture, and partly by the labours of an 'active magistracy,' at deadly feud with the religion of the people. In the plain below, there are a few squireens and middlemen, drunk with the insolence of religious supremacy; but from pride and idleness, not much more comfortable in their appearance, than the mass of rack-rented *ci-devant* forty-shilling freeholders, who form the great body of the inhabitants, near the mansions of the resident landlords." All this is in Lady Morgan's "Scene" before the play opens. There is an epilogue in a lovely house in London, to which the protagonist, his life spared, has fled.

The factors of 1975 in Northern Ireland are, only slightly modified, pretty much present in this story of 1833. The English are there. They are there because the union exists and they own property and therefore claim the right to action and influence. Some of them, such as Mr. Sackville in 1830, are good men. They see some things clearly. They recognize that the abuses are deeply rooted. They recognize the evil in "fomenting religious distinctions and nonsensical party feuds, supporting orange-lodges, distributing tracts, and nourishing hatred," in Mr. Sackville's words. They want better government recognizing that "For seven hundred years the history of Ireland has remained the same;—misgovernment, one and indivisible." They feel deeply that good will and reasonable effort and sensible concession will yield helpful results. They feel that "It is in her [Ireland's] interest, now, to forget the past." Lady Morgan's well-intentioned English aristocracy are fools. Were they the wisest of men, they would still fail, for it is not in their power to help Ireland.

Gentry and church both confound the Mr. Sackvilles of the Irish world. Mr. Galbraith, the steward, is a spokesman for the land-holding, office-holding, and power-holding class, when he says that "the finest pisantry in the world, as the agitaytors call them, are just a pack of bloody, murthering papist villains, and care no more for taking the life of a Christian, than if he was a Jew, or a brute beast." When the "pisantry" kill him they only strengthen the will of the forces that oppose them. But those forces are split too.

The local gentry is bigoted, cupidous, and unfeeling. Those of the established church are "The Hon. and Rev. Dr. Polypus—Rector of Newtown Manor Sackville, Vicar of Sally Noggin, and Rural Dean of Mogherow, holding the livings of Shu-beg and Shu-More with an income of four hundred pounds per annum." Probably his income is much greater than this. To get his tithes from the Catholic peasantry he will drive cattle, dispossess tenants, inform, and persecute the poor into desperation and death. The Mr. Galbraiths of the established church, on a lower social level, delude and cheat the aristocracy in their capacities as steward, housekeeper, high sheriff, and surveyor. Blinders on the New-Light Evangelists restrict their vision so narrowly that they serve neither Protestant nor Catholic, rich nor poor, good man nor evil. "The seints," says Mr. Galbraith, "are the ruin of the pleece entirely; and as much agen the raal Christian religion, as by law established, as the Pope himself."

To the two Catholic priests we extend about the same degree of sympathy that we extend to Mr. Sackville—and in the end we expect about the same futility. Father O'Callaghan, who has grown up among the oppressed poor, is moved by the ancient dreams and resentments. "Ireland is the last country," he says, "on the face of creation that should forget the past. It is all she has,—the memory of the time when she was great, glorious, and free." Nor will he surrender, in only one degree, the claim of the Catholic Church to total mastery: "I tell you then, you gentlemen of the Restoration, and you of the New Generation, you must both come back to us. You are in a cleft stick;—faith or reason, Catholicism or Deism. It is the tradition of the true church, alone, that can save you from being split into myriads of sects. . . . You agree in nothing but to hate, calumniate, and persecute us. It is you who have torn the Lord's seamless garment, the emblem of unity and peace." The Catholic priests, aware of wrong, are powerless to do much about it. And then there are the Catholic peasantry, powerless too, deprived, frustrated, desperate, and driven to murder.

Mr. Sackville sums up the religious forces thus: " . . . spiritual pride, and the thirst for spiritual dominion, are among the most powerful causes of Irish misery." The political situation offers no more hope than the religious situation. "False patriots in religion, false patriots in politics, of every shade and colour, inculcate a blind respect for authority; and Catholic and Protestant, orange and green, alike agree in hating and fearing the man who dares to think for himself, and act according to the dictates of an independent conscience," says Mr. Sackville; and again, "Irish politics, indeed, I despair of ever understanding." He means to do good by keeping himself free of politics. But, says Sir Job, high sheriff, "Is it possible that you can expect to keep clear of politics in Ireland. Every thing you say or do here is politics. . . . It is sufficient that you do not join any one faction heartily, to be suspected and hated by all."

It is not a happy picture. No sun shines behind the clouds. There will be no bright tomorrow. No factor or combination of factors presents a solution to Ireland's problems. So it was a century and a half ago. Had solutions been found since 1830, *Manor Sackville* would be perhaps no more than a curiosity, deserving its obscurity. But since solutions have not been found, since the struggle is as lively today as it was then, we can only try to focus our attention sharply on the factors in the hope of forcing from them a new insight and a more pragmatic wisdom.

"Why will the Irish themselves make Ireland uninhabit-

able?" Lady Emily asks in the last scene. "Every day," her husband replies, "will render Ireland more habitable,—that is, if those who share its soil will but do common justice to it; and the day is not I trust far off, when a great change will be effected in its destinies." It is not to Lady Morgan's discredit that Mr. Sackville is wrong in his prognostication. What is the alternative to his hope? Only the acceptance of turmoil and the suffering of despair. Such alternatives thrust upon us once again the necessity of examining the factors. Surely a solution lies somewhere.

One would suppose that solutions would derive from virtue and that virtuous people could be their agents. What social and ethical virtues mark the characters in the drama are distributed between the aristocratic landowners and the impoverished peasants. To the poor, Mr. Sackville attributes noble hearts and lofty spirits. Time will not, after Catholic Emancipation, give them knowledge, liberty, and good government. It is the spokesman of the poor, being carried by the rush of events to his doom, Cornelius Brian, who speaks of Mr. Sackville's "blessed blood" and saves him from the murderous peasants. It is his wife Honor, bereft and doomed too, who says to Mr. Sackville, "Jasus and his holy mother protect you!" Brian extends his generosity even to the informer he has just killed when he says "he was a poor ignorant manial, and a villain born." Both the Sackvilles and the Brians are disinterested, as virtue very likely must be. Mr. Sackville wants to do good to the native Irish. Brian wants nothing beyond justice and enough to eat. If virtue is to save Ireland, the salvation can come only from these two sets of people at opposite social poles—those with money, power, and the desire to help; those who merely want their daily bread.

But virtue does not suffice. In Ireland's "perilous case" the Sackvilles are driven back to England, the curse of the absentee landowner will prevail. Brian and Honor have waded in blood too deeply and must pay with their lives. The hope that the Sackvilles have brought for a few weeks to one little spot in Ireland falls before violent party passions. (pp. 11-17)

Lady Morgan has Mr. Sackville foresee a happy future for Ireland, for education will spread, reason will prevail, peace will come, and prosperity will follow. But Mr. Sackville is oversanguine. Says one of the characters of Mr. Sackville: "Didn't he put his futt in it the other day, by the spache at a great dinner . . . when he bid the people not to be unraisonable". . . . Reasonableness was not Lady Morgan's expectation; it was her vain wish only. She had no reason to suppose, after 1833 until her death in 1859, that reason would prevail in Ireland. *Manor Sackville* externalizes the party passions of Ireland. It illustrates their relations and conflicts. But, beyond the day that it depicted, it predicted a condition for a future Ireland. (p. 17)

James Newcomer, " 'Manor Sackville': Lady Morgan's Study of Ireland's Perilous Case," in Eire-Ireland, *Vol. X, No. 3, Autumn, 1975, pp. 11-17.*

Colin B. Atkinson and Jo Atkinson   (essay date 1980)

[*In the following excerpt, the Atkinsons examine feminist issues in Morgan's* Woman and Her Master.]

Lady Morgan's mind and her work had always been concerned with women. Her heroines dominate the action and become increasingly independent. Romance was never their aim; patriotism informed their hearts more than love, and independence more than marriage. Her interest in women culminated in *Woman and Her Master* (1840), a history of women in the ancient world. She hoped to bring it up to the 19th century, but failing eyesight prevented her from publishing more than the first volume.

She always observed what women did: "I am always studying eminent persons, women above all—eminent no matter for what, de Staël, or Taglioni, *c'est égal.*" She was always inspired to read women's work. While still a governess, she read of the poet Helen Maria Williams (1762-1827), and immediately wrote her an ode. She decided to write a book about Belgium after visiting the atelier of a young Belgian artist, who became the heroine. She read women's work consciously, with "sincerest gratitude for the amusement and instruction they afforded me." In her turn, she would work to instruct and amuse. Not only are her heroines strong women, but she also mentions women writers, painters, patriots, and artists whenever possible. The young Greek heroine of the deliberately titled *Woman; or, Ida of Athens* (1809) tells her young compatriots of their glorious history, and "of those eminent persons, *of either sex,* who had distinguished themselves by their wisdom, their virtues, their talents, their patriotism." When women writers are named, it is not only Sappho and Aspasia, but lesser known poets such as Praxyla and Erinne. In her most obviously feminist novel, *The Princess; or, the Beguine* (1834), the heroine is working on a book "with a view to the illustration of the lives of the able stateswomen to whom Belgium is so deeply indebted." Even a double entendre is twisted into a lesson: the artist heroine speaks of the Flemish masters to the Englishman who would like to seduce her:

> 'And where are we to find . . . the Flemish mistresses?'
>
> 'Which of our female artists?' she asked with naivete. 'We have produced many eminent women in the arts. To begin with Marguerite Van Eyck, the sister of Hubert and John. She cultivated her art with such devotion, that she made a vow to St. Beghe, the patroness of the Beguines, never to marry. And she stuck to it, though she had many offers.'

Surely no woman writer, before or since, has labored so hard to introduce her readers to the history of women.

The wrongs of women are also made clear in her books, though Lady Morgan is more determined to illustrate the good than the evils. But in *Woman and Her Master* she wrote a work which should be placed in the feminist tradition which includes Mary Astell's *A Serious Proposal,* Mary Wollstonecraft's *Vindication,* and John Stuart Mill's and Harriet Taylor's *Subjection of Women.* As with her novels and her nonfiction, however, the book is marred by her weaknesses: her rather turgid style, her lack of a systematic education, but most of all her fierce combativeness in the service of a cause. Nonetheless, *Woman and Her Master* was a pioneering attempt to trace women's agency in history, to demonstrate their power for civilizing that, despite all handicaps, always emerged.

Her analysis begins with the means by which men have subjugated women. In the past and among "savages" it is by greater physical strength, but now other means are used to keep her down, what "*he* calls philosophy and science. . . . " Women are given an education in "the arts which merely please, and which frequently corrupt," and if she tries to do more than she is permitted by social customs, "she is denounced as a thing unsexed. . . . " She cannot make the laws which govern her, has no rights to her own property unless she "is protected by the solitary blessedness of a derided but innocent celibacy, or by an infamous frailty." Matters have not changed over the centuries: "Society, then as now, excluded women from all legitimate sources by which they might provide for their subsistence; and opened its portals only to reward the exercise of their frailties." What was expected of women was the impossible:

> Educating her for the Harem, but calling on her for the practices of the Portico, man expects from his odalesque the firmness of the stoic, and demands from his servant the exercise of those virtues which, placing the elite of his own sex at the head of its muster-roll, giving immortality to the master. He tells her, 'that obscurity is *her* true glory, insignificance her distinction, ignorance her lot, and passive obedience the perfection of her nature.' Yet he expects from her, . . . that conquest over the passions by the strength of reason, that triumph of moral energy over the senses and appetites, and that endurance of personal privations and self-denials, which with him . . . are qualities of rare exception, and practices of most painful acquirements.

Despite this "corrupting influence of oppression," woman's true nature has always manifested itself. She has, even in the most primitive society, been the civilizing and humanizing force, and Lady Morgan called on men to allow "the just development and mutual influence of the two sexes . . . " which alone can effect the further civilizing of humanity.

The knowledge of woman's true nature, her very identity, had almost been lost, Lady Morgan insisted, by the way men wrote history. The wickedness of queens was relished. Women's good qualities were overlooked, if indeed they were mentioned at all by male historians except in "rare instances, and through the eminence of the men with whom they were associated." Those who shone through no reflected male glory left only traces, if that, and the author saw the task of what we could now call a feminist revision to recover the lost history of women. (pp. 85-7)

As might be expected, Lady Morgan's history lacks scholarly objectivity. She had done her research, but her temperament was combative, and she had much to say in what she thought would be her last book. She gave no quarter: where a woman was heroic, it was the result of her own doing; where she was evil, she could not be blamed: "Her faults belonged to the bad men and bad age in which she lived—the worst on record; her virtues and her genius were her own." Men, when cornered, revert to brute force, to tyranny, to the exercise of power. Women, being the embodiment of intelligence and progress, cannot commit the range or magnitude of crime which men can. Woman's position is always insecure for she is always at the mercy of the ruling males. Lady Morgan shocked reviewers by singling out for praise not only the Sarahs and the Deborahs, but also Eve and Jezebel and some of the more blood-thirsty Roman empresses. Where she could not defend, she stated that some women had a more evil effect on history than was allowed by male historians. Though some of her defenses are highly polemical, at best, one at least deserves closer attention. In 1840, one of the main reasons given for women's subordinate position in society, and morally, was Eve's responsibility for the Fall. Lady Morgan defended Eve on the grounds that she was tempted by the promise of knowledge, of God-like intelligence, unlike her lump of a spouse, and to the readers of her time this bordered on blasphemy.

The critical reception of **Woman and Her Master** resembled that given her other books, ranging from a vicious review through judicious criticism to high praise. The attack, as usual, was *ad feminam,* one reviewer castigating her for her great age—she was then in her sixties—and her looks, likening her to an ugly and venomous toad. Her scholarship was slighted, and it was said she praised Jezebel because they resembled each other. The critical reception of **Woman and Her Master** is worthy of closer study for its revelation not only of contemporary attitudes to the "woman question," but also of the hostile atmosphere of literary journalism generally. An aggressive and radical woman was fair game not only as any partisan writer would be to those in other camps, but also doubly vulnerable as an "unsexed creature" and someone outside the "old boys' network." (pp. 88-9)

Sydney Owenson, Lady Morgan, has been called the first professional woman writer, and perhaps she was. As more feminist literary histories are written, the concept of "first" becomes less useful. There is a tradition of literary women stretching back long before Lady Morgan. However, coming when she did, she is an important figure. She maintained her economic independence and expressed her unique self through the profession of letters. She worked at it, researched and planned her works, shrewdly marketed her writing, helped aspiring young writers whenever she could, and was innocently proud of her achievements. But more than that, she was a woman with causes, most notably the celebration of the greatness of Ireland's history and culture, and the greatness of women's. No historian concerned with the history of Ireland in the early 19th century, the feminist literary tradition, or the development of the professional writer can afford to overlook her. Her novels may not be great literature, but they are significant period pieces. Though she is not a Jane Austen or a Charlotte Brontë, Lady Morgan has her honorable place in literary history. (pp. 89-90)

> *Colin B. Atkinson and Jo Atkinson, "Sydney Owenson, Lady Morgan: Irish Patriot and First Professional Woman Writer," in* Eire-Ireland, *Vol. XV, No. 2, Summer, 1980, pp. 60-90.*

FURTHER READING

Review of *France in 1829-1830,* by Lady Morgan. *American Quarterly Review* IX, No. XVII (March 1831): 1-33.

   Satirical account of Lady Morgan's life and career.

Bolster, R. "French Romanticism and the Ireland Myth." *Hermathena,* No. XCIX (Autumn 1964): 42-8.

Discusses nineteenth-century French perceptions of Irish life and literature, including the works of Lady Morgan.

Cahalan, James M. "Changing Times: The Career of Sydney Owenson." In his *The Irish Novel: A Critical History,* pp. 24-30. Boston: Twayne Publishers, 1988.

   Focuses on Morgan's contribution to the development of the Irish novel.

Campbell, Mary. *Lady Morgan.* London: Pandora, 1988, 250 p.

   Biography intended to compensate for longstanding critical neglect of Morgan.

Dean, Dennis R. Introduction to *The Missionary,* by Lady Morgan, p. v. New York: Scholar's Facsimiles & Reprints, 1981.

   Provides historical background to the events of *The Missionary* and discusses the novel's influence on the works of Percy Bysshe Shelley.

Dixon, W. Hepworth, ed. *Lady Morgan's Memoirs: Autobiography, Diaries, and Correspondence.* London: Wm. H. Allen & Co., 1862, 532 p.

   Memoirs, in the prefatory address of which Morgan comments that she has been "the pet of the Liberals of one nation, the bête-noire of the ultra set of another; the poor butt that reviewers, editors, and critics have set up."

Fitzpatrick, W. J. *Lady Morgan: Her Career, Literary and Personal.* London: Charles J. Skeet, 1860, 308 p.
   Biography.

Flanagan, Thomas. "Lady Morgan." In his *The Irish Novelists: 1800-1850,* pp. 109-47. New York: Columbia University Press, 1959.

   Places Morgan's major novels in a historical and political context.

Hazlitt, William. "*The Life and Times of Salvator Rosa,* by Lady Morgan." *The Edinburgh Review* XL, No. LXXX (July 1824): 316-49.

   Examines the strengths and weaknesses of Morgan as an art critic.

Paston, George. "Lady Morgan (Sydney Owenson)." In his *Little Memoirs of the Nineteenth Century,* pp. 95-155. London: Grant Richards, 1902.

   Biographical anecdotes.

Rafroidi, Patrick. "The Romanticism of the Nation's Present." In his *Irish Literature in English: The Romantic Period,* pp. 96-147. Atlantic Highlands, N.J.: Humanities Press, 1980.

   Examines Morgan's contribution to Irish nationalist romanticism in literature.

Stevenson, Lionel. *The Wild Irish Girl: The Life of Sydney Owenson, Lady Morgan.* London: Chapman & Hall, Ltd., 1936, 330 p.
   Critical biography.

Talfourd, T. N. "*The O'Briens and the O'Flahertys,* by Lady Morgan." *Colburn's New Monthly Magazine and Library Journal* XX, No. LXXXIV (1827): 497-505.

Praises the novel for its "succession of rich and various pictures of Irish character, feelings, and manners."

Tracy, Robert. "Maria Edgeworth and Lady Morgan: Legality versus Legitimacy." *Nineteenth-Century Fiction* 40, No. 1 (June 1985): 1-22.
    Examines the influence of Lady Morgan's *The Wild Irish Girl* on Edgeworth's fiction.

Wolff, Robert Lee. Introduction to *O'Donnel,* by Lady Morgan, pp. v-xxvi. New York: Garland Publishing, 1979.
    Critical examination of Morgan's novels.

Nineteenth-Century Literature Criticism

Cumulative Indexes
Volumes 1-29

This Index Includes References to Entries in These Gale Series

Contemporary Literary Criticism

Presents excerpts of criticism on the works of novelists, poets, dramatists, short story writers, scriptwriters, and other creative writers who are now living or who have died since 1960. Cumulative indexes to authors and nationalities are included, as well as an index to titles discussed in the individual volume.

Twentieth-Century Literary Criticism

Contains critical excerpts by the most significant commentators on poets, novelists, short story writers, dramatists, and philosophers who died between 1900 and 1960. Indexes to authors, topics, nationalities, and titles discussed are included.

Nineteenth-Century Literature Criticism

Offers significant criticism on authors who died between 1800 and 1899. Indexes to authors, topics, nationalities, and titles discussed are included.

Literature Criticism from 1400 to 1800

Compiles significant passages from the most noteworthy criticism on authors of the fifteenth through eighteenth centuries. Cumulative indexes to authors, nationalities, and titles discussed are included in each new volume.

Classical and Medieval Literature Criticism

Offers excerpts of criticism on the works of world authors from classical antiquity through the fourteenth century. Cumulative indexes to authors, titles, and critics are included in each volume.

Short Story Criticism

Compiles excerpts of criticism on short fiction by writers of all eras and nationalities. Cumulative indexes to authors, nationalities, and titles discussed are included in each new volume.

Poetry Criticism

Presents excerpts of criticism on the works of poets from all eras, movements, and nationalities.

Children's Literature Review

Includes excerpts from reviews, criticism, and commentary on works of authors and illustrators who create books for children. Cumulative indexes to authors, nationalities, and titles discussed are included in each new volume.

Contemporary Authors Series

Encompasses five related series. *Contemporary Authors* provides biographical and bibliographical information on more than 92,000 writers of fiction, nonfiction, poetry, journalism, drama, motion pictures, and other fields. Each new volume contains sketches on authors not previously covered in the series. *Contemporary Authors New Revision Series* provides completely updated information on active authors covered in previously published volumes of *CA*. Only entries requiring significant change are revised for *CA New Revision Series*. *Contemporary Authors Permanent Series* consists of updated listings for deceased and inactive authors removed from the original volumes 9-36 when these volumes were revised. *Contemporary Authors Autobiography Series* presents specially commissioned autobiographies by leading contemporary writers. *Contemporary Authors Bibliographical Series* contains primary and secondary bibliographies as well as analytical bibliographical essays by authorities on major modern authors.

Dictionary of Literary Biography

Encompasses three related series. *Dictionary of Literary Biography* furnishes illustrated overviews of authors' lives and works, and places them in the larger perspective of literary history. *Dictionary of Literary Biography Documentary Series* illuminates the careers of major figures through a selection of literary documents, including letters, notebook and diary entries, interviews, book reviews, and photographs. *Dictionary of Literary Biography Yearbook* summarizes the past year's literary activity with articles on genres, major prizes, conferences, and other timely subjects and includes updated and new entries on individual authors. A cumulative index to authors and articles is included in each new volume.

Something about the Author Series

Encompasses two related series. *Something about the Author* contains heavily illustrated biographical sketches on juvenile and young adult authors and illustrators from all eras. *Something about the Author Autobiography Series* presents specially commissioned autobiographies by prominent authors and illustrators of books for children and young adults.

Yesterday's Authors of Books for Children

Contains heavily illustrated entries on children's writers who died before 1961. Complete in two volumes.

Literary Criticism Series
Cumulative Author Index

This index lists all author entries in the Gale Literary Criticism Series and includes cross-references to other Gale sources. References in the index are identified as follows:

AAYA: *Authors & Artists for Young Adults,* Volumes 1-3
CAAS: *Contemporary Authors Autobiography Series,* Volumes 1-11
CA: *Contemporary Authors* (original series), Volumes 1-131
CABS: *Contemporary Authors Bibliographical Series,* Volumes 1-3
CANR: *Contemporary Authors New Revision Series,* Volumes 1-29
CAP: *Contemporary Authors Permanent Series,* Volumes 1-2
CA-R: *Contemporary Authors* (revised editions), Volumes 1-44
CDALB: *Concise Dictionary of American Literary Biography,* Volumes 1-6
CLC: *Contemporary Literary Criticism,* Volumes 1-62
CLR: *Children's Literature Review,* Volumes 1-22
CMLC: *Classical and Medieval Literature Criticism,* Volumes 1-5
DC: *Drama Criticism,* Volume 1
DLB: *Dictionary of Literary Biography,* Volumes 1-101
DLB-DS: *Dictionary of Literary Biography Documentary Series,* Volumes 1-7
DLB-Y: *Dictionary of Literary Biography Yearbook,* Volumes 1980-1988
LC: *Literature Criticism from 1400 to 1800,* Volumes 1-14
NCLC: *Nineteenth-Century Literature Criticism,* Volumes 1-29
PC: *Poetry Criticism,* Volume 1
SAAS: *Something about the Author Autobiography Series,* Volumes 1-11
SATA: *Something about the Author,* Volumes 1-62
SSC: *Short Story Criticism,* Volumes 1-6
TCLC: *Twentieth-Century Literary Criticism,* Volumes 1-38
YABC: *Yesterday's Authors of Books for Children,* Volumes 1-2

A. E. 1867-1935 . . . . TCLC 3, 10
See also Russell, George William
See also DLB 19

Abbey, Edward 1927-1989 . . . . . . CLC 36, 59
See also CANR 2; CA 45-48;
obituary CA 128

Abbott, Lee K., Jr. 19??- . . . . CLC 48

Abe, Kobo 1924- . . . . CLC 8, 22, 53
See also CANR 24; CA 65-68

Abell, Kjeld 1901-1961. . . . . CLC 15
See also obituary CA 111

Abish, Walter 1931- . . . . CLC 22
See also CA 101

Abrahams, Peter (Henry) 1919- . . . . . CLC 4
See also CA 57-60

Abrams, M(eyer) H(oward) 1912-. . . CLC 24
See also CANR 13; CA 57-60; DLB 67

Abse, Dannie 1923-. . . . . CLC 7, 29
See also CAAS 1; CANR 4; CA 53-56;
DLB 27

Achebe, (Albert) Chinua(lumogu)
1930- . . . . CLC 1, 3, 5, 7, 11, 26, 51
See also CLR 20; CANR 6, 26; CA 1-4R;
SATA 38, 40

Acker, Kathy 1948- . . . . CLC 45
See also CA 117, 122

Ackroyd, Peter 1949- . . . . CLC 34, 52
See also CA 123, 127

Acorn, Milton 1923-. . . . . CLC 15
See also CA 103; DLB 53

Adamov, Arthur 1908-1970 . . . . . . CLC 4, 25
See also CAP 2; CA 17-18;
obituary CA 25-28R

Adams, Alice (Boyd) 1926- . . . CLC 6, 13, 46
See also CANR 26; CA 81-84; DLB-Y 86

Adams, Douglas (Noel) 1952- . . . CLC 27, 60
See also CA 106; DLB-Y 83

Adams, Henry (Brooks)
1838-1918 . . . . TCLC 4
See also CA 104; DLB 12, 47

Adams, Richard (George)
1920- . . . . CLC 4, 5, 18
See also CLR 20; CANR 3; CA 49-52;
SATA 7

Adamson, Joy(-Friederike Victoria)
1910-1980 . . . . CLC 17
See also CANR 22; CA 69-72;
obituary CA 93-96; SATA 11;
obituary SATA 22

Adcock, (Kareen) Fleur 1934- . . . . . . CLC 41
See also CANR 11; CA 25-28R; DLB 40

Addams, Charles (Samuel)
1912-1988 . . . . CLC 30
See also CANR 12; CA 61-64;
obituary CA 126

Adler, C(arole) S(chwerdtfeger)
1932- . . . . CLC 35
See also CANR 19; CA 89-92; SATA 26

Adler, Renata 1938- . . . . CLC 8, 31
See also CANR 5, 22; CA 49-52

Ady, Endre 1877-1919 . . . . TCLC 11
See also CA 107

Agee, James 1909-1955 . . . . TCLC 1, 19
See also CA 108; DLB 2, 26;
CDALB 1941-1968

Agnon, S(hmuel) Y(osef Halevi)
1888-1970 . . . . CLC 4, 8, 14
See also CAP 2; CA 17-18;
obituary CA 25-28R

Ai 1947-. . . . . CLC 4, 14
See also CA 85-88

Aickman, Robert (Fordyce)
1914-1981 . . . . CLC 57
See also CANR 3; CA 7-8R

Aiken, Conrad (Potter)
    1889-1973 . . . . CLC 1, 3, 5, 10, 52
    See also CANR 4; CA 5-8R;
      obituary CA 45-48; SATA 3, 30; DLB 9,
      45

Aiken, Joan (Delano)   1924- . . . . CLC 35
    See also CLR 1; CANR 4; CA 9-12R;
      SAAS 1; SATA 2, 30

Ainsworth, William Harrison
    1805-1882 . . . . NCLC 13
    See also SATA 24; DLB 21

Ajar, Emile   1914-1980
    See Gary, Romain

Akhmadulina, Bella (Akhatovna)
    1937- . . . . CLC 53
    See also CA 65-68

Akhmatova, Anna   1888-1966 . . . . CLC 11, 25
    See also CAP 1; CA 19-20;
      obituary CA 25-28R

Aksakov, Sergei Timofeyvich
    1791-1859 . . . . NCLC 2

Aksenov, Vassily (Pavlovich)   1932-
    See Aksyonov, Vasily (Pavlovich)

Aksyonov, Vasily (Pavlovich)
    1932- . . . . CLC 22, 37
    See also CANR 12; CA 53-56

Akutagawa Ryunosuke
    1892-1927 . . . . TCLC 16
    See also CA 117

Alain-Fournier   1886-1914 . . . . TCLC 6
    See also Fournier, Henri Alban
    See also DLB 65

Alarcon, Pedro Antonio de
    1833-1891 . . . . NCLC 1

Alas (y Urena), Leopoldo (Enrique Garcia)
    1852-1901 . . . . TCLC 29
    See also CA 113

Albee, Edward (Franklin III)
    1928- . . . CLC 1, 2, 3, 5, 9, 11, 13, 25, 53
    See also CANR 8; CA 5-8R; DLB 7;
      CDALB 1941-1968

Alberti, Rafael   1902- . . . . CLC 7
    See also CA 85-88

Alcott, Amos Bronson   1799-1888 . . NCLC 1
    See also DLB 1

Alcott, Louisa May   1832-1888 . . . . NCLC 6
    See also CLR 1; YABC 1; DLB 1, 42;
      CDALB 1865-1917

Aldanov, Mark   1887-1957 . . . . TCLC 23
    See also CA 118

Aldington, Richard   1892-1962 . . . . . . CLC 49
    See also CA 85-88; DLB 20, 36

Aldiss, Brian W(ilson)
    1925- . . . . CLC 5, 14, 40
    See also CAAS 2; CANR 5; CA 5-8R;
      SATA 34; DLB 14

Alegria, Fernando   1918- . . . . CLC 57
    See also CANR 5; CA 11-12R

Aleixandre, Vicente   1898-1984 . . . CLC 9, 36
    See also CANR 26; CA 85-88;
      obituary CA 114

Alepoudelis, Odysseus   1911-
    See Elytis, Odysseus

Aleshkovsky, Yuz   1929- . . . . CLC 44
    See also CA 121

Alexander, Lloyd (Chudley)   1924- . . CLC 35
    See also CLR 1, 5; CANR 1; CA 1-4R;
      SATA 3, 49; DLB 52

Alger, Horatio, Jr.   1832-1899 . . . . . NCLC 8
    See also SATA 16; DLB 42

Algren, Nelson   1909-1981 . . . . CLC 4, 10, 33
    See also CANR 20; CA 13-16R;
      obituary CA 103; DLB 9; DLB-Y 81, 82;
      CDALB 1941-1968

Alighieri, Dante   1265-1321 . . . . CMLC 3

Allard, Janet   1975- . . . . CLC 59

Allen, Edward   1948- . . . . CLC 59

Allen, Roland   1939-
    See Ayckbourn, Alan

Allen, Woody   1935- . . . . CLC 16, 52
    See also CANR 27; CA 33-36R; DLB 44

Allende, Isabel   1942- . . . . CLC 39, 57
    See also CA 125

Allingham, Margery (Louise)
    1904-1966 . . . . CLC 19
    See also CANR 4; CA 5-8R;
      obituary CA 25-28R

Allingham, William   1824-1889 . . . NCLC 25
    See also DLB 35

Allston, Washington   1779-1843 . . . . NCLC 2
    See also DLB 1

Almedingen, E. M.   1898-1971 . . . . . . CLC 12
    See also Almedingen, Martha Edith von
    See also SATA 3

Almedingen, Martha Edith von   1898-1971
    See Almedingen, E. M.
    See also CANR 1; CA 1-4R

Alonso, Damaso   1898- . . . . CLC 14
    See also CA 110

Alta   1942- . . . . CLC 19
    See also CA 57-60

Alter, Robert B(ernard)   1935- . . . . . . CLC 34
    See also CANR 1; CA 49-52

Alther, Lisa   1944- . . . . CLC 7, 41
    See also CANR 12; CA 65-68

Altman, Robert   1925- . . . . CLC 16
    See also CA 73-76

Alvarez, A(lfred)   1929- . . . . CLC 5, 13
    See also CANR 3; CA 1-4R; DLB 14, 40

Alvarez, Alejandro Rodriguez   1903-1965
    See Casona, Alejandro
    See also obituary CA 93-96

Amado, Jorge   1912- . . . . CLC 13, 40
    See also CA 77-80

Ambler, Eric   1909- . . . . CLC 4, 6, 9
    See also CANR 7; CA 9-12R

Amichai, Yehuda   1924- . . . . . . CLC 9, 22, 57
    See also CA 85-88

Amiel, Henri Frederic   1821-1881 . . NCLC 4

Amis, Kingsley (William)
    1922- . . . . . . CLC 1, 2, 3, 5, 8, 13, 40, 44
    See also CANR 8; CA 9-12R; DLB 15, 27

Amis, Martin   1949- . . . . CLC 4, 9, 38, 62
    See also CANR 8, 28; CA 65-68; DLB 14

Ammons, A(rchie) R(andolph)
    1926- . . . . CLC 2, 3, 5, 8, 9, 25, 57
    See also CANR 6; CA 9-12R; DLB 5

Anand, Mulk Raj   1905- . . . . CLC 23
    See also CA 65-68

Anaya, Rudolfo A(lfonso)   1937- . . . . CLC 23
    See also CAAS 4; CANR 1; CA 45-48

Andersen, Hans Christian
    1805-1875 . . . . NCLC 7; SSC 6
    See also CLR 6; YABC 1, 1

Anderson, Jessica (Margaret Queale)
    19??- . . . . CLC 37
    See also CANR 4; CA 9-12R

Anderson, Jon (Victor)   1940- . . . . CLC 9
    See also CANR 20; CA 25-28R

Anderson, Lindsay   1923- . . . . CLC 20

Anderson, Maxwell   1888-1959 . . . . . TCLC 2
    See also CA 105; DLB 7

Anderson, Poul (William)   1926- . . . . CLC 15
    See also CAAS 2; CANR 2, 15; CA 1-4R;
      SATA 39; DLB 8

Anderson, Robert (Woodruff)
    1917- . . . . CLC 23
    See also CA 21-24R; DLB 7

Anderson, Roberta Joan   1943-
    See Mitchell, Joni

Anderson, Sherwood
    1876-1941 . . . . . . TCLC 1, 10, 24; SSC 1
    See also CAAS 3; CA 104, 121; DLB 4, 9;
      DLB-DS 1

Andrade, Carlos Drummond de
    1902-1987 . . . . CLC 18
    See also CA 123

Andrewes, Lancelot   1555-1626 . . . . . . LC 5

Andrews, Cicily Fairfield   1892-1983
    See West, Rebecca

Andreyev, Leonid (Nikolaevich)
    1871-1919 . . . . TCLC 3
    See also CA 104

Andrezel, Pierre   1885-1962
    See Dinesen, Isak; Blixen, Karen
      (Christentze Dinesen)

Andric, Ivo   1892-1975 . . . . CLC 8
    See also CA 81-84; obituary CA 57-60

Angelique, Pierre   1897-1962
    See Bataille, Georges

Angell, Roger   1920- . . . . CLC 26
    See also CANR 13; CA 57-60

Angelou, Maya   1928- . . . . CLC 12, 35
    See also CANR 19; CA 65-68; SATA 49;
      DLB 38

Annensky, Innokenty   1856-1909 . . . TCLC 14
    See also CA 110

Anouilh, Jean (Marie Lucien Pierre)
    1910-1987 . . . . . . CLC 1, 3, 8, 13, 40, 50
    See also CA 17-20R; obituary CA 123

Anthony, Florence   1947-
    See Ai

Anthony (Jacob), Piers   1934- . . . . . . CLC 35
    See also Jacob, Piers A(nthony)
      D(illingham)
    See also DLB 8

Antoninus, Brother   1912-
    See Everson, William (Oliver)

Antonioni, Michelangelo   1912- . . . . . CLC 20
    See also CA 73-76

Bellow, Saul
  1915- ..... **CLC 1, 2, 3, 6, 8, 10, 13, 15,
  25, 33, 34**
  See also CA 5-8R; CABS 1; DLB 2, 28;
  DLB-Y 82; DLB-DS 3;
  CDALB 1941-1968

Belser, Reimond Karel Maria de   1929-
  See Ruyslinck, Ward

Bely, Andrey   1880-1934 .... **TCLC 7**
  See also CA 104

Benary-Isbert, Margot   1889-1979 ... **CLC 12**
  See also CLR 12; CANR 4; CA 5-8R;
  obituary CA 89-92; SATA 2;
  obituary SATA 21

Benavente (y Martinez), Jacinto
  1866-1954 .... **TCLC 3**
  See also CA 106

Benchley, Peter (Bradford)
  1940- .... **CLC 4, 8**
  See also CANR 12; CA 17-20R; SATA 3

Benchley, Robert   1889-1945 .... **TCLC 1**
  See also CA 105; DLB 11

Benedikt, Michael   1935- .... **CLC 4, 14**
  See also CANR 7; CA 13-16R; DLB 5

Benet, Juan   1927- .... **CLC 28**

Benet, Stephen Vincent
  1898-1943 .... **TCLC 7**
  See also YABC 1; CA 104; DLB 4, 48

Benet, William Rose   1886-1950 ... **TCLC 28**
  See also CA 118; DLB 45

Benford, Gregory (Albert)   1941- .... **CLC 52**
  See also CANR 12, 24; CA 69-72;
  DLB-Y 82

Benn, Gottfried   1886-1956 .... **TCLC 3**
  See also CA 106; DLB 56

Bennett, Alan   1934- .... **CLC 45**
  See also CA 103

Bennett, (Enoch) Arnold
  1867-1931 .... **TCLC 5, 20**
  See also CA 106; DLB 10, 34

Bennett, George Harold   1930-
  See Bennett, Hal
  See also CA 97-100

Bennett, Hal   1930- .... **CLC 5**
  See also Bennett, George Harold
  See also DLB 33

Bennett, Jay   1912- .... **CLC 35**
  See also CANR 11; CA 69-72; SAAS 4;
  SATA 27, 41

Bennett, Louise (Simone)   1919- ..... **CLC 28**
  See also Bennett-Coverly, Louise Simone

Bennett-Coverly, Louise Simone   1919-
  See Bennett, Louise (Simone)
  See also CA 97-100

Benson, E(dward) F(rederic)
  1867-1940 .... **TCLC 27**
  See also CA 114

Benson, Jackson J.   1930- .... **CLC 34**
  See also CA 25-28R

Benson, Sally   1900-1972 .... **CLC 17**
  See also CAP 1; CA 19-20;
  obituary CA 37-40R; SATA 1, 35;
  obituary SATA 27

Benson, Stella   1892-1933 .... **TCLC 17**
  See also CA 117; DLB 36

Bentley, E(dmund) C(lerihew)
  1875-1956 .... **TCLC 12**
  See also CA 108; DLB 70

Bentley, Eric (Russell)   1916- .... **CLC 24**
  See also CANR 6; CA 5-8R

Berger, John (Peter)   1926- ...... **CLC 2, 19**
  See also CA 81-84; DLB 14

Berger, Melvin (H.)   1927- .... **CLC 12**
  See also CANR 4; CA 5-8R; SAAS 2;
  SATA 5

Berger, Thomas (Louis)
  1924- .... **CLC 3, 5, 8, 11, 18, 38**
  See also CANR 5; CA 1-4R; DLB 2;
  DLB-Y 80

Bergman, (Ernst) Ingmar   1918- ..... **CLC 16**
  See also CA 81-84

Bergson, Henri   1859-1941 .... **TCLC 32**

Bergstein, Eleanor   1938- .... **CLC 4**
  See also CANR 5; CA 53-56

Berkoff, Steven   1937- .... **CLC 56**
  See also CA 104

Bermant, Chaim   1929- .... **CLC 40**
  See also CANR 6; CA 57-60

Bernanos, (Paul Louis) Georges
  1888-1948 .... **TCLC 3**
  See also CA 104; DLB 72

Bernard, April   19??- .... **CLC 59**

Bernhard, Thomas
  1931-1989 .... **CLC 3, 32, 61**
  See also CA 85-88,; obituary CA 127;
  DLB 85

Berriault, Gina   1926- .... **CLC 54**
  See also CA 116

Berrigan, Daniel J.   1921- .... **CLC 4**
  See also CAAS 1; CANR 11; CA 33-36R;
  DLB 5

Berrigan, Edmund Joseph Michael, Jr.
  1934-1983
  See Berrigan, Ted
  See also CANR 14; CA 61-64;
  obituary CA 110

Berrigan, Ted   1934-1983 .... **CLC 37**
  See also Berrigan, Edmund Joseph Michael,
  Jr.
  See also DLB 5

Berry, Chuck   1926- .... **CLC 17**

Berry, Wendell (Erdman)
  1934- .... **CLC 4, 6, 8, 27, 46**
  See also CA 73-76; DLB 5, 6

Berryman, John
  1914-1972 ..... **CLC 1, 2, 3, 4, 6, 8, 10,
  13, 25, 62**
  See also CAP 1; CA 15-16;
  obituary CA 33-36R; CABS 2; DLB 48;
  CDALB 1941-1968

Bertolucci, Bernardo   1940- .... **CLC 16**
  See also CA 106

Bertran de Born   c. 1140-1215 ..... **CMLC 5**

Besant, Annie (Wood)   1847-1933 ... **TCLC 9**
  See also CA 105

Bessie, Alvah   1904-1985 .... **CLC 23**
  See also CANR 2; CA 5-8R;
  obituary CA 116; DLB 26

Beti, Mongo   1932- .... **CLC 27**
  See also Beyidi, Alexandre

Betjeman, (Sir) John
  1906-1984 .... **CLC 2, 6, 10, 34, 43**
  See also CA 9-12R; obituary CA 112;
  DLB 20; DLB-Y 84

Betti, Ugo   1892-1953 .... **TCLC 5**
  See also CA 104

Betts, Doris (Waugh)   1932- .... **CLC 3, 6, 28**
  See also CANR 9; CA 13-16R; DLB-Y 82

Bialik, Chaim Nachman
  1873-1934 .... **TCLC 25**

Bidart, Frank   19??- .... **CLC 33**

Bienek, Horst   1930- .... **CLC 7, 11**
  See also CA 73-76; DLB 75

Bierce, Ambrose (Gwinett)
  1842-1914? .... **TCLC 1, 7**
  See also CA 104; DLB 11, 12, 23, 71, 74;
  CDALB 1865-1917

Billington, Rachel   1942- .... **CLC 43**
  See also CA 33-36R

Binyon, T(imothy) J(ohn)   1936- .... **CLC 34**
  See also CA 111

Bioy Casares, Adolfo   1914- .... **CLC 4, 8, 13**
  See also CANR 19; CA 29-32R

Bird, Robert Montgomery
  1806-1854 .... **NCLC 1**

Birdwell, Cleo   1936-
  See DeLillo, Don

Birney (Alfred) Earle
  1904- .... **CLC 1, 4, 6, 11**
  See also CANR 5, 20; CA 1-4R

Bishop, Elizabeth
  1911-1979 ...... **CLC 1, 4, 9, 13, 15, 32**
  See also CANR 26; CA 5-8R;
  obituary CA 89-92; CABS 2;
  obituary SATA 24; DLB 5

Bishop, John   1935- .... **CLC 10**
  See also CA 105

Bissett, Bill   1939- .... **CLC 18**
  See also CANR 15; CA 69-72; DLB 53

Bitov, Andrei (Georgievich)   1937- ... **CLC 57**

Biyidi, Alexandre   1932-
  See Beti, Mongo
  See also CA 114, 124

Bjornson, Bjornstjerne (Martinius)
  1832-1910 .... **TCLC 7, 37**
  See also CA 104

Blackburn, Paul   1926-1971 ...... **CLC 9, 43**
  See also CA 81-84; obituary CA 33-36R;
  DLB 16; DLB-Y 81

Black Elk   1863-1950 .... **TCLC 33**

Blackmore, R(ichard) D(oddridge)
  1825-1900 .... **TCLC 27**
  See also CA 120; DLB 18

Blackmur, R(ichard) P(almer)
  1904-1965 .... **CLC 2, 24**
  See also CAP 1; CA 11-12;
  obituary CA 25-28R; DLB 63

Blackwood, Algernon (Henry)
  1869-1951 .... **TCLC 5**
  See also CA 105

Blackwood, Caroline   1931- .... **CLC 6, 9**
  See also CA 85-88; DLB 14

Buck, Pearl S(ydenstricker)
1892-1973 .... CLC 7, 11, 18
See also CANR 1; CA 1-4R;
obituary CA 41-44R; SATA 1, 25; DLB 9

Buckler, Ernest 1908-1984......... CLC 13
See also CAP 1; CA 11-12;
obituary CA 114; SATA 47

Buckley, Vincent (Thomas)
1925-1988 .... CLC 57
See also CA 101

Buckley, William F(rank), Jr.
1925- .... CLC 7, 18, 37
See also CANR 1, 24; CA 1-4R; DLB-Y 80

Buechner, (Carl) Frederick
1926- .... CLC 2, 4, 6, 9
See also CANR 11; CA 13-16R; DLB-Y 80

Buell, John (Edward) 1927-........ CLC 10
See also CA 1-4R; DLB 53

Buero Vallejo, Antonio 1916- ... CLC 15, 46
See also CANR 24; CA 106

Bukowski, Charles 1920-.... CLC 2, 5, 9, 41
See also CA 17-20R; DLB 5

Bulgakov, Mikhail (Afanas'evich)
1891-1940 ....TCLC 2, 16
See also CA 105

Bullins, Ed 1935- .... CLC 1, 5, 7
See also CANR 24; CA 49-52; DLB 7, 38

Bulwer-Lytton, (Lord) Edward (George Earle
Lytton) 1803-1873 .... NCLC 1
See also Lytton, Edward Bulwer
See also DLB 21

Bunin, Ivan (Alexeyevich)
1870-1953 .... TCLC 6; SSC 5
See also CA 104

Bunting, Basil 1900-1985.... CLC 10, 39, 47
See also CANR 7; CA 53-56;
obituary CA 115; DLB 20

Bunuel, Luis 1900-1983 .... CLC 16
See also CA 101; obituary CA 110

Bunyan, John 1628-1688 .... LC 4
See also DLB 39

Burgess (Wilson, John) Anthony
1917- ..... CLC 1, 2, 4, 5, 8, 10, 13, 15,
22, 40, 62
See also Wilson, John (Anthony) Burgess
See also DLB 14

Burke, Edmund 1729-1797........... LC 7

Burke, Kenneth (Duva) 1897- .... CLC 2, 24
See also CA 5-8R; DLB 45, 63

Burney, Fanny 1752-1840 .... NCLC 12
See also DLB 39

Burns, Robert 1759-1796............ LC 3

Burns, Tex 1908?-
See L'Amour, Louis (Dearborn)

Burnshaw, Stanley 1906-..... CLC 3, 13, 44
See also CA 9-12R; DLB 48

Burr, Anne 1937- .... CLC 6
See also CA 25-28R

Burroughs, Edgar Rice
1875-1950 .... TCLC 2, 32
See also CA 104; SATA 41; DLB 8

Burroughs, William S(eward)
1914- .... CLC 1, 2, 5, 15, 22, 42
See also CANR 20; CA 9-12R; DLB 2, 8,
16; DLB-Y 81

Busch, Frederick 1941- ... CLC 7, 10, 18, 47
See also CAAS 1; CA 33-36R; DLB 6

Bush, Ronald 19??-............... CLC 34

Butler, Octavia E(stelle) 1947- ..... CLC 38
See also CANR 12, 24; CA 73-76; DLB 33

Butler, Samuel 1835-1902 ...... TCLC 1, 33
See also CA 104; DLB 18, 57

Butor, Michel (Marie Francois)
1926- .... CLC 1, 3, 8, 11, 15
See also CA 9-12R

Buzo, Alexander 1944-............ CLC 61
See also CANR 17; CA 97-100

Buzzati, Dino 1906-1972 .... CLC 36
See also obituary CA 33-36R

Byars, Betsy 1928-............... CLC 35
See also CLR 1, 16; CANR 18; CA 33-36R;
SAAS 1; SATA 4, 46; DLB 52

Byatt, A(ntonia) S(usan Drabble)
1936-...................... CLC 19
See also CANR 13; CA 13-16R; DLB 14

Byrne, David 1953?-............... CLC 26

Byrne, John Keyes 1926-
See Leonard, Hugh
See also CA 102

Byron, George Gordon (Noel), Lord Byron
1788-1824 .... NCLC 2, 12

Caballero, Fernan 1796-1877..... NCLC 10

Cabell, James Branch 1879-1958 ... TCLC 6
See also CA 105; DLB 9

Cable, George Washington
1844-1925 .... TCLC 4; SSC 4
See also CA 104; DLB 12, 74

Cabrera Infante, G(uillermo)
1929-.................. CLC 5, 25, 45
See also CA 85-88

Cage, John (Milton, Jr.) 1912- ..... CLC 41
See also CANR 9; CA 13-16R

Cain, G. 1929-
See Cabrera Infante, G(uillermo)

Cain, James M(allahan)
1892-1977 .... CLC 3, 11, 28
See also CANR 8; CA 17-20R;
obituary CA 73-76

Caldwell, Erskine (Preston)
1903-1987 .... CLC 1, 8, 14, 50, 60
See also CAAS 1; CANR 2; CA 1-4R;
obituary CA 121; DLB 9

Caldwell, (Janet Miriam) Taylor (Holland)
1900-1985 .... CLC 2, 28, 39
See also CANR 5; CA 5-8R;
obituary CA 116

Calhoun, John Caldwell
1782-1850 .... NCLC 15
See also DLB 3

Calisher, Hortense 1911-.... CLC 2, 4, 8, 38
See also CANR 1, 22; CA 1-4R; DLB 2

Callaghan, Morley (Edward)
1903-.................. CLC 3, 14, 41
See also CA 9-12R; DLB 68

Calvino, Italo
1923-1985 .... CLC 5, 8, 11, 22, 33, 39;
SSC 3
See also CANR 23; CA 85-88;
obituary CA 116

Cameron, Carey 1952-............ CLC 59

Cameron, Peter 1959-............. CLC 44
See also CA 125

Campana, Dino 1885-1932........ TCLC 20
See also CA 117

Campbell, John W(ood), Jr.
1910-1971 .... CLC 32
See also CAP 2; CA 21-22;
obituary CA 29-32R; DLB 8

Campbell, (John) Ramsey 1946- .... CLC 42
See also CANR 7; CA 57-60

Campbell, (Ignatius) Roy (Dunnachie)
1901-1957 .... TCLC 5
See also CA 104; DLB 20

Campbell, Thomas 1777-1844 .... NCLC 19

Campbell, (William) Wilfred
1861-1918 .... TCLC 9
See also CA 106

Camus, Albert
1913-1960 .... CLC 1, 2, 4, 9, 11, 14, 32
See also CA 89-92; DLB 72

Canby, Vincent 1924-............. CLC 13
See also CA 81-84

Canetti, Elias 1905- .... CLC 3, 14, 25
See also CANR 23; CA 21-24R

Canin, Ethan 1960-............... CLC 55

Cape, Judith 1916-
See Page, P(atricia) K(athleen)

Capek, Karel 1890-1938........ TCLC 6, 37
See also CA 104

Capote, Truman
1924-1984 ..... CLC 1, 3, 8, 13, 19, 34,
38, 58; SSC 2
See also CANR 18; CA 5-8R;
obituary CA 113; DLB 2; DLB-Y 80, 84;
CDALB 1941-1968

Capra, Frank 1897-............... CLC 16
See also CA 61-64

Caputo, Philip 1941-............. CLC 32
See also CA 73-76

Card, Orson Scott 1951- .... CLC 44, 47, 50
See also CA 102

Cardenal, Ernesto 1925-........... CLC 31
See also CANR 2; CA 49-52

Carducci, Giosue 1835-1907...... TCLC 32

Carew, Thomas 1595?-1640 .... LC 13

Carey, Ernestine Gilbreth 1908- .... CLC 17
See also CA 5-8R; SATA 2

Carey, Peter 1943-............ CLC 40, 55
See also CA 123, 127

Carleton, William 1794-1869...... NCLC 3

Carlisle, Henry (Coffin) 1926-...... CLC 33
See also CANR 15; CA 13-16R

Carlson, Ron(ald F.) 1947-........ CLC 54
See also CA 105

Carlyle, Thomas 1795-1881 ...... NCLC 22
See also DLB 55

Carman, (William) Bliss
1861-1929 .... TCLC 7
See also CA 104

Carpenter, Don(ald Richard)
1931- .... CLC 41
See also CANR 1; CA 45-48

Carpentier (y Valmont), Alejo
1904-1980 .... CLC 8, 11, 38
See also CANR 11; CA 65-68;
obituary CA 97-100

Carr, Emily 1871-1945.......... TCLC 32
See also DLB 68

Carr, John Dickson 1906-1977 ...... CLC 3
See also CANR 3; CA 49-52;
obituary CA 69-72

Carr, Virginia Spencer 1929-....... CLC 34
See also CA 61-64

Carrier, Roch 1937- .... CLC 13
See also DLB 53

Carroll, James (P.) 1943-......... CLC 38
See also CA 81-84

Carroll, Jim 1951- .... CLC 35
See also CA 45-48

Carroll, Lewis 1832-1898........ NCLC 2
See also Dodgson, Charles Lutwidge
See also CLR 2; DLB 18

Carroll, Paul Vincent 1900-1968.... CLC 10
See also CA 9-12R; obituary CA 25-28R;
DLB 10

Carruth, Hayden 1921- .... CLC 4, 7, 10, 18
See also CANR 4; CA 9-12R; SATA 47;
DLB 5

Carter, Angela (Olive) 1940-..... CLC 5, 41
See also CANR 12; CA 53-56; DLB 14

Carver, Raymond
1938-1988 .... CLC 22, 36, 53, 55
See also CANR 17; CA 33-36R;
obituary CA 126; DLB-Y 84, 88

Cary, (Arthur) Joyce (Lunel)
1888-1957 .... TCLC 1, 29
See also CA 104; DLB 15

Casanova de Seingalt, Giovanni Jacopo
1725-1798 .... LC 13

Casares, Adolfo Bioy 1914-
See Bioy Casares, Adolfo

Casely-Hayford, J(oseph) E(phraim)
1866-1930 .... TCLC 24
See also CA 123

Casey, John 1880-1964
See O'Casey, Sean

Casey, John 1939- .... CLC 59
See also CANR 23; CA 69-72

Casey, Michael 1947-............. CLC 2
See also CA 65-68; DLB 5

Casey, Warren 1935- .... CLC 12
See also Jacobs, Jim and Casey, Warren
See also CA 101

Casona, Alejandro 1903-1965 ...... CLC 49
See also Alvarez, Alejandro Rodriguez

Cassavetes, John 1929-........... CLC 20
See also CA 85-88

Cassill, R(onald) V(erlin) 1919-... CLC 4, 23
See also CAAS 1; CANR 7; CA 9-12R;
DLB 6

Cassity, (Allen) Turner 1929- .... CLC 6, 42
See also CANR 11; CA 17-20R

Castaneda, Carlos 1935?-.......... CLC 12
See also CA 25-28R

Castelvetro, Lodovico 1505-1571..... LC 12

Castiglione, Baldassare 1478-1529 ... LC 12

Castro, Rosalia de 1837-1885 ..... NCLC 3

Cather, Willa (Sibert)
1873-1947 ...... TCLC 1, 11, 31; SSC 2
See also CA 104; SATA 30; DLB 9, 54;
DLB-DS 1; CDALB 1865-1917

Catton, (Charles) Bruce
1899-1978 .... CLC 35
See also CANR 7; CA 5-8R;
obituary CA 81-84; SATA 2;
obituary SATA 24; DLB 17

Cauldwell, Frank 1923-
See King, Francis (Henry)

Caunitz, William 1935- .... CLC 34

Causley, Charles (Stanley) 1917-..... CLC 7
See also CANR 5; CA 9-12R; SATA 3;
DLB 27

Caute, (John) David 1936-......... CLC 29
See also CAAS 4; CANR 1; CA 1-4R;
DLB 14

Cavafy, C(onstantine) P(eter)
1863-1933 .... TCLC 2, 7
See also CA 104

Cavanna, Betty 1909-............. CLC 12
See also CANR 6; CA 9-12R; SATA 1, 30

Cayrol, Jean 1911-............... CLC 11
See also CA 89-92

Cela, Camilo Jose 1916-...... CLC 4, 13, 59
See also CAAS 10; CANR 21; CA 21-24R

Celan, Paul 1920-1970 ...... CLC 10, 19, 53
See also Antschel, Paul
See also DLB 69

Celine, Louis-Ferdinand
1894-1961 ..... CLC 1, 3, 4, 7, 9, 15, 47
See also Destouches,
Louis-Ferdinand-Auguste
See also DLB 72

Cellini, Benvenuto 1500-1571 .... LC 7

Cendrars, Blaise 1887-1961........ CLC 18
See also Sauser-Hall, Frederic

Cernuda, Luis (y Bidon)
1902-1963 .... CLC 54
See also CA 89-92

Cervantes (Saavedra), Miguel de
1547-1616 .... LC 6

Cesaire, Aime (Fernand) 1913- .. CLC 19, 32
See also CANR 24; CA 65-68

Chabon, Michael 1965?-.......... CLC 55

Chabrol, Claude 1930- .... CLC 16
See also CA 110

Challans, Mary 1905-1983
See Renault, Mary
See also CA 81-84; obituary CA 111;
SATA 23; obituary SATA 36

Chambers, Aidan 1934- .... CLC 35
See also CANR 12; CA 25-28R; SATA 1

Chambers, James 1948-
See Cliff, Jimmy

Chandler, Raymond 1888-1959 ... TCLC 1, 7
See also CA 104

Channing, William Ellery
1780-1842 .... NCLC 17
See also DLB 1, 59

Chaplin, Charles (Spencer)
1889-1977 .... CLC 16
See also CA 81-84; obituary CA 73-76;
DLB 44

Chapman, Graham 1941?- .... CLC 21
See also Monty Python
See also CA 116

Chapman, John Jay 1862-1933 ..... TCLC 7
See also CA 104

Chappell, Fred 1936- .... CLC 40
See also CAAS 4; CANR 8; CA 5-8R;
DLB 6

Char, Rene (Emile)
1907-1988 .... CLC 9, 11, 14, 55
See also CA 13-16R; obituary CA 124

Charles I 1600-1649 .... LC 13

Charyn, Jerome 1937- .... CLC 5, 8, 18
See also CAAS 1; CANR 7; CA 5-8R;
DLB-Y 83

Chase, Mary Ellen 1887-1973 .... CLC 2
See also CAP 1; CA 15-16;
obituary CA 41-44R; SATA 10

Chateaubriand, Francois Rene de
1768-1848 .... NCLC 3

Chatterji, Bankim Chandra
1838-1894 .... NCLC 19

Chatterji, Saratchandra
1876-1938 .... TCLC 13
See also CA 109

Chatterton, Thomas 1752-1770 .... LC 3

Chatwin, (Charles) Bruce
1940-1989 .... CLC 28, 57, 59
See also CA 85-88,; obituary CA 127

Chayefsky, Paddy 1923-1981....... CLC 23
See also CA 9-12R; obituary CA 104;
DLB 7, 44; DLB-Y 81

Chayefsky, Sidney 1923-1981
See Chayefsky, Paddy
See also CANR 18

Chedid, Andree 1920-............. CLC 47

Cheever, John
1912-1982 ..... CLC 3, 7, 8, 11, 15, 25;
SSC 1
See also CANR 5; CA 5-8R;
obituary CA 106; CABS 1; DLB 2;
DLB-Y 80, 82; CDALB 1941-1968

Cheever, Susan 1943-.......... CLC 18, 48
See also CA 103; DLB-Y 82

Chekhov, Anton (Pavlovich)
1860-1904 ...... TCLC 3, 10, 31; SSC 2
See also CA 104, 124

Chernyshevsky, Nikolay Gavrilovich
1828-1889 .... NCLC 1

Cherry, Caroline Janice 1942-
See Cherryh, C. J.

Cherryh, C. J. 1942-............. CLC 35
See also CANR 10; CA 65-68; DLB-Y 80

Dabrowska, Maria (Szumska)
1889-1965 .... **CLC 15**
See also CA 106

Dabydeen, David 1956?-.......... **CLC 34**
See also CA 106

Dacey, Philip 1939- .... **CLC 51**
See also CANR 14; CA 37-40R

Dagerman, Stig (Halvard)
1923-1954 .... **TCLC 17**
See also CA 117

Dahl, Roald 1916-............**CLC 1, 6, 18**
See also CLR 1, 7; CANR 6; CA 1-4R;
SATA 1, 26

Dahlberg, Edward 1900-1977... **CLC 1, 7, 14**
See also CA 9-12R; obituary CA 69-72;
DLB 48

Daly, Elizabeth 1878-1967........ **CLC 52**
See also CAP 2; CA 23-24;
obituary CA 25-28R

Daly, Maureen 1921-............. **CLC 17**
See also McGivern, Maureen Daly
See also SAAS 1; SATA 2

Daniken, Erich von 1935-
See Von Daniken, Erich

Dannay, Frederic 1905-1982
See Queen, Ellery
See also CANR 1; CA 1-4R;
obituary CA 107

D'Annunzio, Gabriele 1863-1938.... **TCLC 6**
See also CA 104

Dante (Alighieri)
See Alighieri, Dante

Danziger, Paula 1944- .... **CLC 21**
See also CLR 20; CA 112, 115; SATA 30, 36

Dario, Ruben 1867-1916 .... **TCLC 4**
See also Sarmiento, Felix Ruben Garcia
See also CA 104

Darley, George 1795-1846........ **NCLC 2**

Daryush, Elizabeth 1887-1977.... **CLC 6, 19**
See also CANR 3; CA 49-52; DLB 20

Daudet, (Louis Marie) Alphonse
1840-1897 .... **NCLC 1**

Daumal, Rene 1908-1944........ **TCLC 14**
See also CA 114

Davenport, Guy (Mattison, Jr.)
1927- .... **CLC 6, 14, 38**
See also CANR 23; CA 33-36R

Davidson, Donald (Grady)
1893-1968 .... **CLC 2, 13, 19**
See also CANR 4; CA 5-8R;
obituary CA 25-28R; DLB 45

Davidson, John 1857-1909....... **TCLC 24**
See also CA 118; DLB 19

Davidson, Sara 1943-............. **CLC 9**
See also CA 81-84

Davie, Donald (Alfred)
1922- ....**CLC 5, 8, 10, 31**
See also CAAS 3; CANR 1; CA 1-4R;
DLB 27

Davies, Ray(mond Douglas) 1944- .. **CLC 21**
See also CA 116

Davies, Rhys 1903-1978........... **CLC 23**
See also CANR 4; CA 9-12R;
obituary CA 81-84

Davies, (William) Robertson
1913- .... **CLC 2, 7, 13, 25, 42**
See also CANR 17; CA 33-36R; DLB 68

Davies, W(illiam) H(enry)
1871-1940 .... **TCLC 5**
See also CA 104; DLB 19

Davis, H(arold) L(enoir)
1896-1960 .... **CLC 49**
See also obituary CA 89-92; DLB 9

Davis, Rebecca (Blaine) Harding
1831-1910 .... **TCLC 6**
See also CA 104; DLB 74

Davis, Richard Harding
1864-1916 .... **TCLC 24**
See also CA 114; DLB 12, 23

Davison, Frank Dalby 1893-1970 ... **CLC 15**
See also obituary CA 116

Davison, Peter 1928- .... **CLC 28**
See also CAAS 4; CANR 3; CA 9-12R;
DLB 5

Davys, Mary 1674-1732............. **LC 1**
See also DLB 39

Dawson, Fielding 1930- .... **CLC 6**
See also CA 85-88

Day, Clarence (Shepard, Jr.)
1874-1935 .... **TCLC 25**
See also CA 108; DLB 11

Day, Thomas 1748-1789............. **LC 1**
See also YABC 1; DLB 39

Day Lewis, C(ecil)
1904-1972 .... **CLC 1, 6, 10**
See also CAP 1; CA 15-16;
obituary CA 33-36R; DLB 15, 20

Dazai Osamu 1909-1948 .... **TCLC 11**
See also Tsushima Shuji

De Crayencour, Marguerite 1903-1987
See Yourcenar, Marguerite

Deer, Sandra 1940-............... **CLC 45**

Defoe, Daniel 1660?-1731 .... **LC 1**
See also SATA 22; DLB 39

De Hartog, Jan 1914-............. **CLC 19**
See also CANR 1; CA 1-4R

Deighton, Len 1929-....... **CLC 4, 7, 22, 46**
See also Deighton, Leonard Cyril

Deighton, Leonard Cyril 1929-
See Deighton, Len
See also CANR 19; CA 9-12R

De la Mare, Walter (John)
1873-1956 .... **TCLC 4**
See also CA 110; SATA 16; DLB 19

Delaney, Shelagh 1939- .... **CLC 29**
See also CA 17-20R; DLB 13

Delany, Mary (Granville Pendarves)
1700-1788 .... **LC 12**

Delany, Samuel R(ay, Jr.)
1942-.................. **CLC 8, 14, 38**
See also CA 81-84; DLB 8, 33

De la Roche, Mazo 1885-1961 ..... **CLC 14**
See also CA 85-88; DLB 68

Delbanco, Nicholas (Franklin)
1942-..................... **CLC 6, 13**
See also CAAS 2; CA 17-20R; DLB 6

del Castillo, Michel 1933-......... **CLC 38**
See also CA 109

Deledda, Grazia 1871-1936 ...... **TCLC 23**
See also CA 123

Delibes (Setien), Miguel 1920- ... **CLC 8, 18**
See also CANR 1; CA 45-48

DeLillo, Don
1936- .... **CLC 8, 10, 13, 27, 39, 54**
See also CANR 21; CA 81-84; DLB 6

De Lisser, H(erbert) G(eorge)
1878-1944 .... **TCLC 12**
See also CA 109

Deloria, Vine (Victor), Jr. 1933-.... **CLC 21**
See also CANR 5, 20; CA 53-56; SATA 21

Del Vecchio, John M(ichael)
1947-..................... **CLC 29**
See also CA 110

de Man, Paul 1919-1983 .... **CLC 55**
See also obituary CA 111; DLB 67

De Marinis, Rick 1934-........... **CLC 54**
See also CANR 9, 25; CA 57-60

Demby, William 1922-............. **CLC 53**
See also CA 81-84; DLB 33

Denby, Edwin (Orr) 1903-1983..... **CLC 48**
See also obituary CA 110

Dennis, John 1657-1734............ **LC 11**

Dennis, Nigel (Forbes) 1912-........ **CLC 8**
See also CA 25-28R; DLB 13, 15

De Palma, Brian 1940-........... **CLC 20**
See also CA 109

De Quincey, Thomas 1785-1859 ... **NCLC 4**

Deren, Eleanora 1908-1961
See Deren, Maya
See also obituary CA 111

Deren, Maya 1908-1961........... **CLC 16**
See also Deren, Eleanora

Derleth, August (William)
1909-1971 .... **CLC 31**
See also CANR 4; CA 1-4R;
obituary CA 29-32R; SATA 5; DLB 9

Derrida, Jacques 1930-........... **CLC 24**
See also CA 124

Desai, Anita 1937- .... **CLC 19, 37**
See also CA 81-84

De Saint-Luc, Jean 1909-1981
See Glassco, John

De Sica, Vittorio 1902-1974 .... **CLC 20**
See also obituary CA 117

Desnos, Robert 1900-1945........ **TCLC 22**
See also CA 121

Destouches, Louis-Ferdinand-Auguste
1894-1961
See Celine, Louis-Ferdinand
See also CA 85-88

Deutsch, Babette 1895-1982 .... **CLC 18**
See also CANR 4; CA 1-4R;
obituary CA 108; SATA 1;
obituary SATA 33; DLB 45

Devenant, William 1606-1649 .... **LC 13**

Devkota, Laxmiprasad
1909-1959 .... TCLC **23**
See also CA 123

DeVoto, Bernard (Augustine)
1897-1955 .... TCLC **29**
See also CA 113; DLB 9

De Vries, Peter
1910- .... CLC **1, 2, 3, 7, 10, 28, 46**
See also CA 17-20R; DLB 6; DLB-Y 82

Dexter, Pete 1943- .... CLC **34, 55**
See also CA 127

Diamond, Neil (Leslie) 1941- .... CLC **30**
See also CA 108

Dick, Philip K(indred)
1928-1982 .... CLC **10, 30**
See also CANR 2, 16; CA 49-52;
obituary CA 106; DLB 8

Dickens, Charles
1812-1870 .... NCLC **3, 8, 18, 26**
See also SATA 15; DLB 21, 55, 70

Dickey, James (Lafayette)
1923- .... CLC **1, 2, 4, 7, 10, 15, 47**
See also CANR 10; CA 9-12R; CABS 2;
DLB 5; DLB-Y 82

Dickey, William 1928- .... CLC **3, 28**
See also CANR 24; CA 9-12R; DLB 5

Dickinson, Charles 1952- .... CLC **49**

Dickinson, Emily (Elizabeth)
1830-1886 .... NCLC **21; PC 1**
See also SATA 29; DLB 1;
CDALB 1865-1917

Dickinson, Peter (Malcolm de Brissac)
1927- .... CLC **12, 35**
See also CA 41-44R; SATA 5

Didion, Joan 1934- ..... CLC **1, 3, 8, 14, 32**
See also CANR 14; CA 5-8R; DLB 2;
DLB-Y 81, 86

Dillard, Annie 1945- .... CLC **9, 60**
See also CANR 3; CA 49-52; SATA 10;
DLB-Y 80

Dillard, R(ichard) H(enry) W(ilde)
1937- .... CLC **5**
See also CAAS 7; CANR 10; CA 21-24R;
DLB 5

Dillon, Eilis 1920- .... CLC **17**
See also CAAS 3; CANR 4; CA 9-12R;
SATA 2

Dinesen, Isak 1885-1962 .... CLC **10, 29**
See also Blixen, Karen (Christentze
Dinesen)
See also CANR 22

Disch, Thomas M(ichael) 1940- ... CLC **7, 36**
See also CAAS 4; CANR 17; CA 21-24R;
DLB 8

Disraeli, Benjamin 1804-1881 ..... NCLC **2**
See also DLB 21, 55

Dixon, Paige 1911-
See Corcoran, Barbara

Dixon, Stephen 1936- .... CLC **52**
See also CANR 17; CA 89-92

Doblin, Alfred 1878-1957........ TCLC **13**
See also Doeblin, Alfred

Dobrolyubov, Nikolai Alexandrovich
1836-1861 .... NCLC **5**

Dobyns, Stephen 1941-........... CLC **37**
See also CANR 2, 18; CA 45-48

Doctorow, E(dgar) L(aurence)
1931- .... CLC **6, 11, 15, 18, 37, 44**
See also CANR 2; CA 45-48; DLB 2, 28;
DLB-Y 80

Dodgson, Charles Lutwidge 1832-1898
See Carroll, Lewis
See also YABC 2

Doeblin, Alfred 1878-1957....... TCLC **13**
See also CA 110; DLB 66

Doerr, Harriet 1910- .... CLC **34**
See also CA 117, 122

Donaldson, Stephen R. 1947-....... CLC **46**
See also CANR 13; CA 89-92

Donleavy, J(ames) P(atrick)
1926- .... CLC **1, 4, 6, 10, 45**
See also CANR 24; CA 9-12R; DLB 6

Donnadieu, Marguerite 1914-
See Duras, Marguerite

Donne, John 1572?-1631 ...... LC **10; PC 1**

Donnell, David 1939?- .... CLC **34**

Donoso, Jose 1924-........ CLC **4, 8, 11, 32**
See also CA 81-84

Donovan, John 1928- .... CLC **35**
See also CLR 3; CA 97-100; SATA 29

Doolittle, Hilda 1886-1961
See H(ilda) D(oolittle)
See also CA 97-100; DLB 4, 45

Dorfman, Ariel 1942-............. CLC **48**
See also CA 124

Dorn, Ed(ward Merton) 1929-... CLC **10, 18**
See also CA 93-96; DLB 5

Dos Passos, John (Roderigo)
1896-1970 ... CLC **1, 4, 8, 11, 15, 25, 34**
See also CANR 3; CA 1-4R;
obituary CA 29-32R; DLB 4, 9;
DLB-DS 1

Dostoevski, Fedor Mikhailovich
1821-1881 .... NCLC **2, 7, 21; SSC 2**

Doughty, Charles (Montagu)
1843-1926 .... TCLC **27**
See also CA 115; DLB 19, 57

Douglas, George 1869-1902....... TCLC **28**

Douglass, Frederick 1817-1895.... NCLC **7**
See also SATA 29; DLB 1, 43, 50;
CDALB 1640-1865

Dourado, (Waldomiro Freitas) Autran
1926- .... CLC **23, 60**
See also CA 25-28R

Dove, Rita 1952-................. CLC **50**
See also CA 109

Dowson, Ernest (Christopher)
1867-1900 .... TCLC **4**
See also CA 105; DLB 19

Doyle, (Sir) Arthur Conan
1859-1930 .... TCLC **7, 26**
See also CA 104, 122; SATA 24; DLB 18,
70

Dr. A 1933-
See Silverstein, Alvin and Virginia B(arbara
Opshelor) Silverstein

Drabble, Margaret
1939- .... CLC **2, 3, 5, 8, 10, 22, 53**
See also CANR 18; CA 13-16R; SATA 48;
DLB 14

Drayton, Michael 1563-1631........ LC **8**

Dreiser, Theodore (Herman Albert)
1871-1945 .... TCLC **10, 18, 35**
See also CA 106; SATA 48; DLB 9, 12;
DLB-DS 1; CDALB 1865-1917

Drexler, Rosalyn 1926- .... CLC **2, 6**
See also CA 81-84

Dreyer, Carl Theodor 1889-1968.... CLC **16**
See also obituary CA 116

Drieu La Rochelle, Pierre
1893-1945 .... TCLC **21**
See also CA 117; DLB 72

Droste-Hulshoff, Annette Freiin von
1797-1848 .... NCLC **3**

Drummond, William Henry
1854-1907 .... TCLC **25**

Drummond de Andrade, Carlos 1902-1987
See Andrade, Carlos Drummond de

Drury, Allen (Stuart) 1918-........ CLC **37**
See also CANR 18; CA 57-60

Dryden, John 1631-1700 .... LC **3**

Duberman, Martin 1930-........... CLC **8**
See also CANR 2; CA 1-4R

Dubie, Norman (Evans, Jr.) 1945- .. CLC **36**
See also CANR 12; CA 69-72

Du Bois, W(illiam) E(dward) B(urghardt)
1868-1963 .... CLC **1, 2, 13**
See also CA 85-88; SATA 42; DLB 47, 50;
CDALB 1865-1917

Dubus, Andre 1936- .... CLC **13, 36**
See also CANR 17; CA 21-24R

Ducasse, Isidore Lucien 1846-1870
See Lautreamont, Comte de

Duclos, Charles Pinot 1704-1772 ..... LC **1**

Dudek, Louis 1918- .... CLC **11, 19**
See also CANR 1; CA 45-48

Dudevant, Amandine Aurore Lucile Dupin
1804-1876
See Sand, George

Duerrenmatt, Friedrich
1921- .... CLC **1, 4, 8, 11, 15, 43**
See also CA 17-20R; DLB 69

Duffy, Bruce 19??- .... CLC **50**

Duffy, Maureen 1933- .... CLC **37**
See also CA 25-28R; DLB 14

Dugan, Alan 1923- .... CLC **2, 6**
See also CA 81-84; DLB 5

Duhamel, Georges 1884-1966 .... CLC **8**
See also CA 81-84; obituary CA 25-28R

Dujardin, Edouard (Emile Louis)
1861-1949 .... TCLC **13**
See also CA 109

Duke, Raoul 1939-
See Thompson, Hunter S(tockton)

Dumas, Alexandre (Davy de la Pailleterie)
(pere) 1802-1870.......... NCLC **11**
See also SATA 18

Dumas, Alexandre (fils)
1824-1895 .... NCLC **9**

Dumas, Henry 1918-1968 .... CLC 62

Dumas, Henry (L.) 1934-1968 ...... CLC 6
See also CA 85-88; DLB 41

Du Maurier, Daphne 1907- ... CLC 6, 11, 59
See also CANR 6; CA 5-8R;
obituary CA 128; SATA 27

Dunbar, Paul Laurence
1872-1906 .... TCLC 2, 12
See also CA 104, 124; SATA 34; DLB 50,
54; CDALB 1865-1917

Duncan (Steinmetz Arquette), Lois
1934- .... CLC 26
See also Arquette, Lois S(teinmetz)
See also CANR 2; CA 1-4R; SAAS 2;
SATA 1, 36

Duncan, Robert (Edward)
1919-1988 .... CLC 1, 2, 4, 7, 15, 41, 55
See also CA 9-12R; obituary CA 124;
DLB 5, 16

Dunlap, William 1766-1839 .... NCLC 2
See also DLB 30, 37, 59

Dunn, Douglas (Eaglesham)
1942- .... CLC 6, 40
See also CANR 2; CA 45-48; DLB 40

Dunn, Elsie 1893-1963
See Scott, Evelyn

Dunn, Stephen 1939- .... CLC 36
See also CANR 12; CA 33-36R

Dunne, Finley Peter 1867-1936 .... TCLC 28
See also CA 108; DLB 11, 23

Dunne, John Gregory 1932-...∴... CLC 28
See also CANR 14; CA 25-28R; DLB-Y 80

Dunsany, Lord (Edward John Moreton Drax
Plunkett) 1878-1957 .... TCLC 2
See also CA 104; DLB 10

Durang, Christopher (Ferdinand)
1949- .... CLC 27, 38
See also CA 105

Duras, Marguerite
1914- .... CLC 3, 6, 11, 20, 34, 40
See also CA 25-28R

Durban, Pam 1947- .... CLC 39
See also CA 123

Durcan, Paul 1944- .... CLC 43

Durrell, Lawrence (George)
1912-1990 .... CLC 1, 4, 6, 8, 13, 27, 41
See also CA 9-12R; DLB 15, 27

Durrenmatt, Friedrich
1921- .... CLC 1, 4, 8, 11, 15, 43
See also Duerrenmatt, Friedrich
See also DLB 69

Dutt, Toru 1856-1877 .... NCLC 29

Dwight, Timothy 1752-1817 ...... NCLC 13
See also DLB 37

Dworkin, Andrea 1946- .... CLC 43
See also CANR 16; CA 77-80

Dylan, Bob 1941- .... CLC 3, 4, 6, 12
See also CA 41-44R; DLB 16

East, Michael 1916-
See West, Morris L.

Eastlake, William (Derry) 1917- ..... CLC 8
See also CAAS 1; CANR 5; CA 5-8R;
DLB 6

Eberhart, Richard 1904-... CLC 3, 11, 19, 56
See also CANR 2; CA 1-4R; DLB 48;
CDALB 1941-1968

Eberstadt, Fernanda 1960- .... CLC 39

Echegaray (y Eizaguirre), Jose (Maria Waldo)
1832-1916 .... TCLC 4
See also CA 104

Echeverria, (Jose) Esteban (Antonino)
1805-1851 .... NCLC 18

Eckert, Allan W. 1931- .... CLC 17
See also CANR 14; CA 13-16R; SATA 27,
29

Eco, Umberto 1932- .... CLC 28, 60
See also CANR 12; CA 77-80

Eddison, E(ric) R(ucker)
1882-1945 .... TCLC 15
See also CA 109

Edel, Leon (Joseph) 1907- ...... CLC 29, 34
See also CANR 1, 22; CA 1-4R

Eden, Emily 1797-1869 .... NCLC 10

Edgar, David 1948- .... CLC 42
See also CANR 12; CA 57-60; DLB 13

Edgerton, Clyde 1944- .... CLC 39
See also CA 118

Edgeworth, Maria 1767-1849 ...... NCLC 1
See also SATA 21

Edmonds, Helen (Woods) 1904-1968
See Kavan, Anna
See also CA 5-8R; obituary CA 25-28R

Edmonds, Walter D(umaux) 1903- .. CLC 35
See also CANR 2; CA 5-8R; SAAS 4;
SATA 1, 27; DLB 9

Edson, Russell 1905- .... CLC 13
See also CA 33-36R

Edwards, G(erald) B(asil)
1899-1976 .... CLC 25
See also obituary CA 110

Edwards, Gus 1939- .... CLC 43
See also CA 108

Edwards, Jonathan 1703-1758 .... LC 7
See also DLB 24

Ehle, John (Marsden, Jr.) 1925- .... CLC 27
See also CA 9-12R

Ehrenburg, Ilya (Grigoryevich)
1891-1967 .... CLC 18, 34, 62
See also CA 102; obituary CA 25-28R

Eich, Guenter 1907-1971
See also CA 111; obituary CA 93-96

Eich, Gunter 1907-1971 .... CLC 15
See also Eich, Guenter
See also DLB 69

Eichendorff, Joseph Freiherr von
1788-1857 .... NCLC 8

Eigner, Larry 1927- .... CLC 9
See also Eigner, Laurence (Joel)
See also DLB 5

Eigner, Laurence (Joel) 1927-
See Eigner, Larry
See also CANR 6; CA 9-12R

Eiseley, Loren (Corey) 1907-1977 .... CLC 7
See also CANR 6; CA 1-4R;
obituary CA 73-76

Eisenstadt, Jill 1963- .... CLC 50

Ekeloef, Gunnar (Bengt) 1907-1968
See Ekelof, Gunnar (Bengt)
See also obituary CA 25-28R

Ekelof, Gunnar (Bengt) 1907-1968 .. CLC 27
See also Ekeloef, Gunnar (Bengt)

Ekwensi, Cyprian (Odiatu Duaka)
1921- .... CLC 4
See also CANR 18; CA 29-32R

Eliade, Mircea 1907-1986 .... CLC 19
See also CA 65-68; obituary CA 119

Eliot, George 1819-1880.... NCLC 4, 13, 23
See also DLB 21, 35, 55

Eliot, John 1604-1690 .... LC 5
See also DLB 24

Eliot, T(homas) S(tearns)
1888-1965 .... CLC 1, 2, 3, 6, 9, 10, 13,
15, 24, 34, 41, 55, 57
See also CA 5-8R; obituary CA 25-28R;
DLB 7, 10, 45, 63; DLB-Y 88

Elkin, Stanley (Lawrence)
1930- .... CLC 4, 6, 9, 14, 27, 51
See also CANR 8; CA 9-12R; DLB 2, 28;
DLB-Y 80

Elledge, Scott 19??- .... CLC 34

Elliott, George P(aul) 1918-1980..... CLC 2
See also CANR 2; CA 1-4R;
obituary CA 97-100

Elliott, Janice 1931- .... CLC 47
See also CANR 8; CA 13-16R; DLB 14

Elliott, Sumner Locke 1917- .... CLC 38
See also CANR 2, 21; CA 5-8R

Ellis, A. E. 19??- .... CLC 7

Ellis, Alice Thomas 19??- .... CLC 40

Ellis, Bret Easton 1964- .... CLC 39
See also CA 118, 123

Ellis, (Henry) Havelock
1859-1939 .... TCLC 14
See also CA 109

Ellis, Trey 1964- .... CLC 55

Ellison, Harlan (Jay) 1934-... CLC 1, 13, 42
See also CANR 5; CA 5-8R; DLB 8

Ellison, Ralph (Waldo)
1914- .... CLC 1, 3, 11, 54
See also CANR 24; CA 9-12R; DLB 2;
CDALB 1941-1968

Ellmann, Lucy 1956- .... CLC 61
See also CA 128

Ellmann, Richard (David)
1918-1987 .... CLC 50
See also CANR 2; CA 1-4R;
obituary CA 122; DLB-Y 87

Elman, Richard 1934- .... CLC 19
See also CAAS 3; CA 17-20R

Eluard, Paul 1895-1952 .... TCLC 7
See also Grindel, Eugene

Elyot, (Sir) James 1490?-1546 ...... LC 11

Elyot, (Sir) Thomas 1490?-1546 ..... LC 11

Elytis, Odysseus 1911- .... CLC 15, 49
See also CA 102

Emecheta, (Florence Onye) Buchi
1944- .... CLC 14, 48
See also CA 81-84

Author Index

Finch, Robert (Duer Claydon)
1900- .... CLC **18**
See also CANR 9, 24; CA 57-60

Findley, Timothy 1930- .... CLC **27**
See also CANR 12; CA 25-28R; DLB 53

Fink, Janis 1951-
See Ian, Janis

Firbank, Louis 1944-
See Reed, Lou
See also CA 117

Firbank, (Arthur Annesley) Ronald
1886-1926 .... TCLC **1**
See also CA 104; DLB 36

Fisher, Roy 1930-............... CLC **25**
See also CANR 16; CA 81-84; DLB 40

Fisher, Rudolph 1897-1934 .... TCLC **11**
See also CA 107; DLB 51

Fisher, Vardis (Alvero) 1895-1968.... CLC **7**
See also CA 5-8R; obituary CA 25-28R;
DLB 9

FitzGerald, Edward 1809-1883 .... NCLC **9**
See also DLB 32

Fitzgerald, F(rancis) Scott (Key)
1896-1940 .... TCLC **1, 6, 14, 28**; SSC **6**
See also CA 110, 123; DLB 4, 9, 86;
DLB-Y 81; DLB-DS 1;
CDALB 1917-1929

Fitzgerald, Penelope 1916-... CLC **19, 51, 61**
See also CAAS 10; CA 85-88,; DLB 14

Fitzgerald, Robert (Stuart)
1910-1985 .... CLC **39**
See also CANR 1; CA 2R;
obituary CA 114; DLB-Y 80

FitzGerald, Robert D(avid) 1902-... CLC **19**
See also CA 17-20R

Flanagan, Thomas (James Bonner)
1923- .... CLC **25, 52**
See also CA 108; DLB-Y 80

Flaubert, Gustave
1821-1880 .... NCLC **2, 10, 19**

Fleming, Ian (Lancaster)
1908-1964 .... CLC **3, 30**
See also CA 5-8R; SATA 9

Fleming, Thomas J(ames) 1927- .... CLC **37**
See also CANR 10; CA 5-8R; SATA 8

Fletcher, John Gould 1886-1950 ... TCLC **35**
See also CA 107; DLB 4, 45

Flieg, Hellmuth
See Heym, Stefan

Flying Officer X 1905-1974
See Bates, H(erbert) E(rnest)

Fo, Dario 1929-.................. CLC **32**
See also CA 116

Follett, Ken(neth Martin) 1949- .... CLC **18**
See also CANR 13; CA 81-84; DLB-Y 81

Fontane, Theodor 1819-1898..... NCLC **26**

Foote, Horton 1916-.............. CLC **51**
See also CA 73-76; DLB 26

Forbes, Esther 1891-1967......... CLC **12**
See also CAP 1; CA 13-14;
obituary CA 25-28R; SATA 2; DLB 22

Forche, Carolyn 1950-............ CLC **25**
See also CA 109, 117; DLB 5

Ford, Ford Madox 1873-1939 ... TCLC **1, 15**
See also CA 104; DLB 34

Ford, John 1895-1973............. CLC **16**
See also obituary CA 45-48

Ford, Richard 1944-............. CLC **46**
See also CANR 11; CA 69-72

Foreman, Richard 1937-........... CLC **50**
See also CA 65-68

Forester, C(ecil) S(cott)
1899-1966 .... CLC **35**
See also CA 73-76; obituary CA 25-28R;
SATA 13

Forman, James D(ouglas) 1932- .... CLC **21**
See also CANR 4, 19; CA 9-12R; SATA 8,
21

Fornes, Maria Irene 1930-...... CLC **39, 61**
See also CANR 28; CA 25-28R; DLB 7

Forrest, Leon 1937-............... CLC **4**
See also CAAS 7; CA 89-92; DLB 33

Forster, E(dward) M(organ)
1879-1970 .... CLC **1, 2, 3, 4, 9, 10, 13,
15, 22, 45**
See also CAP 1; CA 13-14;
obituary CA 25-28R; DLB 34

Forster, John 1812-1876 .... NCLC **11**

Forsyth, Frederick 1938-...... CLC **2, 5, 36**
See also CA 85-88

Forten (Grimke), Charlotte L(ottie)
1837-1914 .... TCLC **16**
See also Grimke, Charlotte L(ottie) Forten
See also DLB 50

Foscolo, Ugo 1778-1827.......... NCLC **8**

Fosse, Bob 1925-1987............. CLC **20**
See also Fosse, Robert Louis

Fosse, Robert Louis 1925-1987
See Bob Fosse
See also CA 110, 123

Foster, Stephen Collins
1826-1864 .... NCLC **26**

Foucault, Michel 1926-1984 .... CLC **31, 34**
See also CANR 23; CA 105;
obituary CA 113

**Fouque, Friedrich (Heinrich Karl) de La
Motte** 1777-1843 .... NCLC **2**

Fournier, Henri Alban 1886-1914
See Alain-Fournier
See also CA 104

Fournier, Pierre 1916-............ CLC **11**
See also Gascar, Pierre
See also CANR 16; CA 89-92

Fowles, John (Robert)
1926-.... CLC **1, 2, 3, 4, 6, 9, 10, 15, 33**
See also CANR 25; CA 5-8R; SATA 22;
DLB 14

Fox, Paula 1923-................. CLC **2, 8**
See also CLR 1; CANR 20; CA 73-76;
SATA 17; DLB 52

Fox, William Price (Jr.) 1926- ..... CLC **22**
See also CANR 11; CA 17-20R; DLB 2;
DLB-Y 81

Foxe, John 1516?-1587............. LC **14**

Frame (Clutha), Janet (Paterson)
1924- ....CLC **2, 3, 6, 22**
See also Clutha, Janet Paterson Frame

France, Anatole 1844-1924 .... TCLC **9**
See also Thibault, Jacques Anatole Francois

Francis, Claude 19??-............. CLC **50**

Francis, Dick 1920- .... CLC **2, 22, 42**
See also CANR 9; CA 5-8R

Francis, Robert (Churchill)
1901-1987 .... CLC **15**
See also CANR 1; CA 1-4R;
obituary CA 123

Frank, Anne 1929-1945 .... TCLC **17**
See also CA 113; SATA 42

Frank, Elizabeth 1945-............ CLC **39**
See also CA 121, 126

Franklin, (Stella Maria Sarah) Miles
1879-1954 .... TCLC **7**
See also CA 104

Fraser, Antonia (Pakenham)
1932- .... CLC **32**
See also CA 85-88; SATA 32

Fraser, George MacDonald 1925-.... CLC **7**
See also CANR 2; CA 45-48

Frayn, Michael 1933-...... CLC **3, 7, 31, 47**
See also CA 5-8R; DLB 13, 14

Fraze, Candida 19??- .... CLC **50**
See also CA 125

Frazer, Sir James George
1854-1941 .... TCLC **32**
See also CA 118

Frazier, Ian 1951-................ CLC **46**

Frederic, Harold 1856-1898...... NCLC **10**
See also DLB 12, 23

Frederick the Great 1712-1786 ...... LC **14**

Fredman, Russell (Bruce) 1929-
See also CLR 20

Fredro, Aleksander 1793-1876..... NCLC **8**

Freeling, Nicolas 1927- .... CLC **38**
See also CANR 1, 17; CA 49-52

Freeman, Douglas Southall
1886-1953 .... TCLC **11**
See also CA 109; DLB 17

Freeman, Judith 1946-............ CLC **55**

Freeman, Mary (Eleanor) Wilkins
1852-1930 .... TCLC **9**; SSC **1**
See also CA 106; DLB 12

Freeman, R(ichard) Austin
1862-1943 .... TCLC **21**
See also CA 113; DLB 70

French, Marilyn 1929-...... CLC **10, 18, 60**
See also CANR 3; CA 69-72

Freneau, Philip Morin 1752-1832 .. NCLC **1**
See also DLB 37, 43

Friedman, B(ernard) H(arper)
1926- .... CLC **7**
See also CANR 3; CA 1-4R

Friedman, Bruce Jay 1930-.... CLC **3, 5, 56**
See also CANR 25; CA 9-12R; DLB 2, 28

Friel, Brian 1929-........... CLC **5, 42, 59**
See also CA 21-24R; DLB 13

Friis-Baastad, Babbis (Ellinor)
1921-1970 .... CLC **12**
See also CA 17-20R; SATA 7

Frisch, Max (Rudolf)
1911- . . . . CLC 3, 9, 14, 18, 32, 44
See also CA 85-88; DLB 69

Fromentin, Eugene (Samuel Auguste)
1820-1876 . . . . NCLC 10

Frost, Robert (Lee)
1874-1963 . . . CLC 1, 3, 4, 9, 10, 13, 15,
26, 34, 44; PC 1
See also CA 89-92; SATA 14; DLB 54;
DLB-DS 7; CDALB 1917-1929

Fry, Christopher 1907- . . . . CLC 2, 10, 14
See also CANR 9; CA 17-20R; DLB 13

Frye, (Herman) Northrop 1912- . . . . CLC 24
See also CANR 8; CA 5-8R

Fuchs, Daniel 1909- . . . . CLC 8, 22
See also CAAS 5; CA 81-84; DLB 9, 26, 28

Fuchs, Daniel 1934- . . . . CLC 34
See also CANR 14; CA 37-40R

Fuentes, Carlos
1928- . . . . . . CLC 3, 8, 10, 13, 22, 41, 60
See also CANR 10; CA 69-72

Fugard, Athol 1932- . . . CLC 5, 9, 14, 25, 40
See also CA 85-88

Fugard, Sheila 1932- . . . . CLC 48
See also CA 125

Fuller, Charles (H., Jr.) 1939- . . . . . . CLC 25
See also CA 108, 112; DLB 38

Fuller, John (Leopold) 1937- . . . . CLC 62
See also CANR 9; CA 21-22R; DLB 40

Fuller, (Sarah) Margaret
1810-1850 . . . . NCLC 5
See also Ossoli, Sarah Margaret (Fuller
marchesa d')
See also DLB 1, 59, 73; CDALB 1640-1865

Fuller, Roy (Broadbent) 1912- . . . . CLC 4, 28
See also CA 5-8R; DLB 15, 20

Fulton, Alice 1952- . . . . CLC 52
See also CA 116

Furphy, Joseph 1843-1912 . . . . TCLC 25

Futrelle, Jacques 1875-1912 . . . . . . TCLC 19
See also CA 113

Gaboriau, Emile 1835-1873 . . . . . . NCLC 14

Gadda, Carlo Emilio 1893-1973 . . . . CLC 11
See also CA 89-92

Gaddis, William
1922- . . . . CLC 1, 3, 6, 8, 10, 19, 43
See also CAAS 4; CANR 21; CA 17-20R;
DLB 2

Gaines, Ernest J. 1933- . . . . . . CLC 3, 11, 18
See also CANR 6, 24; CA 9-12R; DLB 2,
33; DLB-Y 80

Gale, Zona 1874-1938 . . . . TCLC 7
See also CA 105; DLB 9

Gallagher, Tess 1943- . . . . CLC 18
See also CA 106

Gallant, Mavis
1922- . . . . CLC 7, 18, 38; SSC 5
See also CA 69-72; DLB 53

Gallant, Roy A(rthur) 1924- . . . . CLC 17
See also CANR 4; CA 5-8R; SATA 4

Gallico, Paul (William) 1897-1976 . . . CLC 2
See also CA 5-8R; obituary CA 69-72;
SATA 13; DLB 9

Galsworthy, John 1867-1933 . . . . . . TCLC 1
See also CA 104; DLB 10, 34

Galt, John 1779-1839 . . . . NCLC 1

Galvin, James 1951- . . . . CLC 38
See also CANR 26; CA 108

Gamboa, Frederico 1864-1939 . . . . . TCLC 36

Gann, Ernest K(ellogg) 1910- . . . . . . CLC 23
See also CANR 1; CA 1-4R

Garcia Lorca, Federico
1899-1936 . . . . TCLC 1, 7
See also CA 104

Garcia Marquez, Gabriel (Jose)
1928- . . . . CLC 2, 3, 8, 10, 15, 27, 47, 55
See also CANR 10; CA 33-36R

Gardam, Jane 1928- . . . . CLC 43
See also CLR 12; CANR 2, 18; CA 49-52;
SATA 28, 39; DLB 14

Gardner, Herb 1934- . . . . CLC 44

Gardner, John (Champlin, Jr.)
1933-1982 . . . . CLC 2, 3, 5, 7, 8, 10, 18,
28, 34
See also CA 65-68; obituary CA 107;
obituary SATA 31, 40; DLB 2; DLB-Y 82

Gardner, John (Edmund) 1926- . . . . . CLC 30
See also CANR 15; CA 103

Garfield, Leon 1921- . . . . CLC 12
See also CA 17-20R; SATA 1, 32

Garland, (Hannibal) Hamlin
1860-1940 . . . . TCLC 3
See also CA 104; DLB 12, 71

Garneau, Hector (de) Saint Denys
1912-1943 . . . . TCLC 13
See also CA 111

Garner, Alan 1935- . . . . CLC 17
See also CLR 20; CANR 15; CA 73-76;
SATA 18

Garner, Hugh 1913-1979 . . . . CLC 13
See also CA 69-72; DLB 68

Garnett, David 1892-1981 . . . . CLC 3
See also CANR 17; CA 5-8R;
obituary CA 103; DLB 34

Garrett, George (Palmer, Jr.)
1929- . . . . CLC 3, 11, 51
See also CAAS 5; CANR 1; CA 1-4R;
DLB 2, 5; DLB-Y 83

Garrigue, Jean 1914-1972 . . . . CLC 2, 8
See also CANR 20; CA 5-8R;
obituary CA 37-40R

Gary, Romain 1914-1980 . . . . CLC 25
See also Kacew, Romain

Gascar, Pierre 1916- . . . . CLC 11
See also Fournier, Pierre

Gascoyne, David (Emery) 1916- . . . . CLC 45
See also CANR 10; CA 65-68; DLB 20

Gaskell, Elizabeth Cleghorn
1810-1865 . . . . NCLC 5
See also DLB 21

Gass, William H(oward)
1924- . . . . CLC 1, 2, 8, 11, 15, 39
See also CA 17-20R; DLB 2

Gautier, Theophile 1811-1872 . . . . . NCLC 1

Gaye, Marvin (Pentz) 1939-1984 . . . CLC 26
See also obituary CA 112

Gebler, Carlo (Ernest) 1954- . . . . . . CLC 39
See also CA 119

Gee, Maggie 19??- . . . . CLC 57

Gee, Maurice (Gough) 1931- . . . . . . CLC 29
See also CA 97-100; SATA 46

Gelbart, Larry 1923?- . . . . CLC 21, 61
See also CA 73-76

Gelber, Jack 1932- . . . . CLC 1, 6, 14, 60
See also CANR 2; CA 1-4R; DLB 7

Gellhorn, Martha (Ellis) 1908- . . CLC 14, 60
See also CA 77-80; DLB-Y 82

Genet, Jean
1910-1986 . . . CLC 1, 2, 5, 10, 14, 44, 46
See also CANR 18; CA 13-16R; DLB 72;
DLB-Y 86

Gent, Peter 1942- . . . . CLC 29
See also CA 89-92; DLB 72; DLB-Y 82

George, Jean Craighead 1919- . . . . . . CLC 35
See also CLR 1; CA 5-8R; SATA 2;
DLB 52

George, Stefan (Anton)
1868-1933 . . . . TCLC 2, 14
See also CA 104

Gerhardi, William (Alexander) 1895-1977
See Gerhardie, William (Alexander)

Gerhardie, William (Alexander)
1895-1977 . . . . CLC 5
See also CANR 18; CA 25-28R;
obituary CA 73-76; DLB 36

Gertler, T(rudy) 1946?- . . . . CLC 34
See also CA 116

Gessner, Friedrike Victoria 1910-1980
See Adamson, Joy(-Friederike Victoria)

Ghelderode, Michel de
1898-1962 . . . . CLC 6, 11
See also CA 85-88

Ghiselin, Brewster 1903- . . . . CLC 23
See also CANR 13; CA 13-16R

Ghose, Zulfikar 1935- . . . . CLC 42
See also CA 65-68

Ghosh, Amitav 1943- . . . . CLC 44

Giacosa, Giuseppe 1847-1906 . . . . . . TCLC 7
See also CA 104

Gibbon, Lewis Grassic 1901-1935 . . . TCLC 4
See also Mitchell, James Leslie

Gibbons, Kaye 1960- . . . . CLC 50

Gibran, (Gibran) Kahlil
1883-1931 . . . . TCLC 1, 9
See also CA 104

Gibson, William 1914- . . . . CLC 23
See also CANR 9; CA 9-12R; DLB 7

Gibson, William 1948- . . . . CLC 39
See also CA 126

Gide, Andre (Paul Guillaume)
1869-1951 . . . . TCLC 5, 12, 36
See also CA 104, 124; DLB 65

Gifford, Barry (Colby) 1946- . . . . . . CLC 34
See also CANR 9; CA 65-68

Gilbert, (Sir) W(illiam) S(chwenck)
1836-1911 . . . . TCLC 3
See also CA 104; SATA 36

Gilbreth, Ernestine 1908-
See Carey, Ernestine Gilbreth

Hall, Rodney 1935- . . . . CLC 51
See also CA 109

Halpern, Daniel 1945- . . . . CLC 14
See also CA 33-36R

Hamburger, Michael (Peter Leopold)
1924- . . . . CLC 5, 14
See also CAAS 4; CANR 2; CA 5-8R;
DLB 27

Hamill, Pete 1935- . . . . CLC 10
See also CANR 18; CA 25-28R

Hamilton, Edmond 1904-1977 . . . . . . CLC 1
See also CANR 3; CA 1-4R; DLB 8

Hamilton, Gail 1911-
See Corcoran, Barbara

Hamilton, Ian 1938- . . . . CLC 55
See also CA 106; DLB 40

Hamilton, Mollie 1909?-
See Kaye, M(ary) M(argaret)

Hamilton, (Anthony Walter) Patrick
1904-1962 . . . . CLC 51
See also obituary CA 113; DLB 10

Hamilton, Virginia (Esther) 1936-. . . CLC 26
See also CLR 1, 11; CANR 20; CA 25-28R;
SATA 4; DLB 33, 52

Hammett, (Samuel) Dashiell
1894-1961 . . . . CLC 3, 5, 10, 19, 47
See also CA 81-84

Hammon, Jupiter 1711?-1800? . . . . NCLC 5
See also DLB 31, 50

Hamner, Earl (Henry), Jr. 1923- . . . CLC 12
See also CA 73-76; DLB 6

Hampton, Christopher (James)
1946- . . . . CLC 4
See also CA 25-28R; DLB 13

Hamsun, Knut 1859-1952 . . . . . . TCLC 2, 14
See also Pedersen, Knut

Handke, Peter 1942- . . CLC 5, 8, 10, 15, 38
See also CA 77-80

Hanley, James 1901-1985 . . . CLC 3, 5, 8, 13
See also CA 73-76; obituary CA 117

Hannah, Barry 1942- . . . . CLC 23, 38
See also CA 108, 110; DLB 6

Hansberry, Lorraine (Vivian)
1930-1965 . . . . CLC 17, 62
See also CA 109; obituary CA 25-28R;
CABS 3; DLB 7, 38; CDALB 1941-1968

Hansen, Joseph 1923- . . . . CLC 38
See also CANR 16; CA 29-32R

Hansen, Martin 1909-1955 . . . . TCLC 32

Hanson, Kenneth O(stlin) 1922- . . . . CLC 13
See also CANR 7; CA 53-56

Hardenberg, Friedrich (Leopold Freiherr) von
1772-1801
See Novalis

Hardwick, Elizabeth 1916- . . . . CLC 13
See also CANR 3; CA 5-8R; DLB 6

Hardy, Thomas
1840-1928 . . . TCLC 4, 10, 18, 32; SSC 2
See also CA 104, 123; SATA 25; DLB 18,
19

Hare, David 1947- . . . . CLC 29, 58
See also CA 97-100; DLB 13

Harlan, Louis R(udolph) 1922- . . . . . CLC 34
See also CANR 25; CA 21-24R

Harling, Robert 1951?-. . . . . CLC 53

Harmon, William (Ruth) 1938- . . . . . CLC 38
See also CANR 14; CA 33-36R

Harper, Frances Ellen Watkins
1825-1911 . . . . TCLC 14
See also CA 111, 125; DLB 50

Harper, Michael S(teven) 1938- . . CLC 7, 22
See also CANR 24; CA 33-36R; DLB 41

Harris, Christie (Lucy Irwin)
1907- . . . . CLC 12
See also CANR 6; CA 5-8R; SATA 6

Harris, Frank 1856-1931 . . . . TCLC 24
See also CAAS 1; CA 109

Harris, George Washington
1814-1869 . . . . NCLC 23
See also DLB 3, 11

Harris, Joel Chandler 1848-1908 . . . TCLC 2
See also YABC 1; CA 104; DLB 11, 23, 42

Harris, John (Wyndham Parkes Lucas)
Beynon 1903-1969
See Wyndham, John
See also CA 102; obituary CA 89-92

Harris, MacDonald 1921- . . . . CLC 9
See also Heiney, Donald (William)

Harris, Mark 1922- . . . . CLC 19
See also CAAS 3; CANR 2; CA 5-8R;
DLB 2; DLB-Y 80

Harris, (Theodore) Wilson 1921-. . . . CLC 25
See also CANR 11; CA 65-68

Harrison, Harry (Max) 1925- . . . . . . CLC 42
See also CANR 5, 21; CA 1-4R; SATA 4;
DLB 8

Harrison, James (Thomas) 1937-
See Harrison, Jim
See also CANR 8; CA 13-16R

Harrison, Jim 1937- . . . . CLC 6, 14, 33
See also Harrison, James (Thomas)
See also DLB-Y 82

Harrison, Tony 1937- . . . . CLC 43
See also CA 65-68; DLB 40

Harriss, Will(ard Irvin) 1922- . . . . . . CLC 34
See also CA 111

Harte, (Francis) Bret(t)
1836?-1902. . . . . TCLC 1, 25
See also CA 104; SATA 26; DLB 12, 64,
74; CDALB 1865-1917

Hartley, L(eslie) P(oles)
1895-1972 . . . . CLC 2, 22
See also CA 45-48; obituary CA 37-40R;
DLB 15

Hartman, Geoffrey H. 1929-. . . . . . . CLC 27
See also CA 117, 125; DLB 67

Haruf, Kent 19??-. . . . . CLC 34

Harwood, Ronald 1934-. . . . . CLC 32
See also CANR 4; CA 1-4R; DLB 13

Hasek, Jaroslav (Matej Frantisek)
1883-1923 . . . . TCLC 4
See also CA 104

Hass, Robert 1941-. . . . . CLC 18, 39
See also CA 111

Hastings, Selina 19??- . . . . CLC 44

Hauptmann, Gerhart (Johann Robert)
1862-1946 . . . . TCLC 4
See also CA 104; DLB 66

Havel, Vaclav 1936-. . . . . CLC 25, 58
See also CA 104

Haviaras, Stratis 1935- . . . . CLC 33
See also CA 105

Hawkes, John (Clendennin Burne, Jr.)
1925- . . . . . . CLC 1, 2, 3, 4, 7, 9, 14, 15,
27, 49
See also CANR 2; CA 1-4R; DLB 2, 7;
DLB-Y 80

Hawthorne, Julian 1846-1934 . . . . . TCLC 25

Hawthorne, Nathaniel
1804-1864 . . . NCLC 2, 10, 17, 23; SSC 3
See also YABC 2; DLB 1, 74;
CDALB 1640-1865

Hayashi Fumiko 1904-1951 . . . . . . TCLC 27

Haycraft, Anna 19??-
See Ellis, Alice Thomas

Hayden, Robert (Earl)
1913-1980 . . . . CLC 5, 9, 14, 37
See also CANR 24; CA 69-72;
obituary CA 97-100; CABS 2; SATA 19;
obituary SATA 26; DLB 5, 76;
CDALB 1941-1968

Hayman, Ronald 1932-. . . . . CLC 44
See also CANR 18; CA 25-28R

Haywood, Eliza (Fowler) 1693?-1756. . LC 1
See also DLB 39

Hazlitt, William 1778-1830 . . . . . . NCLC 29

Hazzard, Shirley 1931- . . . . CLC 18
See also CANR 4; CA 9-12R; DLB-Y 82

H(ilda) D(oolittle)
1886-1961 . . . . CLC 3, 8, 14, 31, 34
See also Doolittle, Hilda

Head, Bessie 1937-1986. . . . . CLC 25
See also CANR 25; CA 29-32R;
obituary CA 109

Headon, (Nicky) Topper 1956?-
See The Clash

Heaney, Seamus (Justin)
1939- . . . . CLC 5, 7, 14, 25, 37
See also CANR 25; CA 85-88; DLB 40

Hearn, (Patricio) Lafcadio (Tessima Carlos)
1850-1904 . . . . TCLC 9
See also CA 105; DLB 12

Hearne, Vicki 1946-. . . . . CLC 56

Heat Moon, William Least 1939-. . . CLC 29

Hebert, Anne 1916- . . . . CLC 4, 13, 29
See also CA 85-88; DLB 68

Hecht, Anthony (Evan)
1923- . . . . CLC 8, 13, 19
See also CANR 6; CA 9-12R; DLB 5

Hecht, Ben 1894-1964 . . . . CLC 8
See also CA 85-88; DLB 7, 9, 25, 26, 28

Hedayat, Sadeq 1903-1951. . . . . . . TCLC 21
See also CA 120

Heidegger, Martin 1889-1976 . . . . . . CLC 24
See also CA 81-84; obituary CA 65-68

Heidenstam, (Karl Gustaf) Verner von
1859-1940 . . . . TCLC 5
See also CA 104

Heifner, Jack 1946-. . . . . CLC 11
See also CA 105

Heijermans, Herman 1864-1924 . . . TCLC 24
See also CA 123

Hoffmann, Ernst Theodor Amadeus
      1776-1822 .... NCLC 2
      See also SATA 27

Hoffmann, Gert 1932- .... CLC 54

Hofmannsthal, Hugo (Laurenz August
      Hofmann Edler) von
      1874-1929 .... TCLC 11
      See also CA 106

Hogg, James 1770-1835 .... NCLC 4

Holbach, Paul Henri Thiry, Baron d'
      1723-1789 .... LC 14

Holberg, Ludvig 1684-1754 .... LC 6

Holden, Ursula 1921- .... CLC 18
      See also CANR 22; CA 101

Holderlin, (Johann Christian) Friedrich
      1770-1843 .... NCLC 16

Holdstock, Robert (P.) 1948- ...... CLC 39

Holland, Isabelle 1920- .... CLC 21
      See also CANR 10, 25; CA 21-24R;
      SATA 8

Holland, Marcus 1900-1985
      See Caldwell, (Janet Miriam) Taylor
      (Holland)

Hollander, John 1929- ...... CLC 2, 5, 8, 14
      See also CANR 1; CA 1-4R; SATA 13;
      DLB 5

Holleran, Andrew 1943?- .... CLC 38

Hollinghurst, Alan 1954- .... CLC 55
      See also CA 114

Hollis, Jim 1916-
      See Summers, Hollis (Spurgeon, Jr.)

Holmes, John Clellon 1926-1988.... CLC 56
      See also CANR 4; CA 9-10R;
      obituary CA 125; DLB 16

Holmes, Oliver Wendell
      1809-1894 .... NCLC 14
      See also SATA 34; DLB 1;
      CDALB 1640-1865

Holt, Victoria 1906-
      See Hibbert, Eleanor (Burford)

Holub, Miroslav 1923- .... CLC 4
      See also CANR 10; CA 21-24R

Homer c. 8th century B.C.- .... CMLC 1

Honig, Edwin 1919- .... CLC 33
      See also CANR 4; CA 5-8R; DLB 5

Hood, Hugh (John Blagdon)
      1928- .... CLC 15, 28
      See also CANR 1; CA 49-52; DLB 53

Hood, Thomas 1799-1845........ NCLC 16

Hooker, (Peter) Jeremy 1941- ...... CLC 43
      See also CANR 22; CA 77-80; DLB 40

Hope, A(lec) D(erwent) 1907- .... CLC 3, 51
      See also CA 21-24R

Hope, Christopher (David Tully)
      1944- .... CLC 52
      See also CA 106

Hopkins, Gerard Manley
      1844-1889 .... NCLC 17
      See also DLB 35, 57

Hopkins, John (Richard) 1931- ...... CLC 4
      See also CA 85-88

Hopkins, Pauline Elizabeth
      1859-1930 .... TCLC 28
      See also DLB 50

Horgan, Paul 1903- .... CLC 9, 53
      See also CANR 9; CA 13-16R; SATA 13;
      DLB-Y 85

Horovitz, Israel 1939- .... CLC 56
      See also CA 33-36R; DLB 7

Horwitz, Julius 1920-1986......... CLC 14
      See also CANR 12; CA 9-12R;
      obituary CA 119

Hospital, Janette Turner 1942- ..... CLC 42
      See also CA 108

Hostos (y Bonilla), Eugenio Maria de
      1893-1903 .... TCLC 24
      See also CA 123

Hougan, Carolyn 19??- .... CLC 34

Household, Geoffrey (Edward West)
      1900-1988 .... CLC 11
      See also CA 77-80; obituary CA 126;
      SATA 14

Housman, A(lfred) E(dward)
      1859-1936 .... TCLC 1, 10
      See also CA 104, 125; DLB 19

Housman, Laurence 1865-1959 ..... TCLC 7
      See also CA 106; SATA 25; DLB 10

Howard, Elizabeth Jane 1923- ... CLC 7, 29
      See also CANR 8; CA 5-8R

Howard, Maureen 1930- ..... CLC 5, 14, 46
      See also CA 53-56; DLB-Y 83

Howard, Richard 1929- ...... CLC 7, 10, 47
      See also CANR 25; CA 85-88; DLB 5

Howard, Robert E(rvin)
      1906-1936 .... TCLC 8
      See also CA 105

Howe, Fanny 1940- .... CLC 47
      See also CA 117; SATA 52

Howe, Julia Ward 1819-1910 ..... TCLC 21
      See also CA 117; DLB 1

Howe, Tina 1937- .... CLC 48
      See also CA 109

Howell, James 1594?-1666......... LC 13

Howells, William Dean
      1837-1920 .... TCLC 7, 17
      See also CA 104; DLB 12, 64, 74;
      CDALB 1865-1917

Howes, Barbara 1914- .... CLC 15
      See also CAAS 3; CA 9-12R; SATA 5

Hrabal, Bohumil 1914- .... CLC 13
      See also CA 106

Hubbard, L(afayette) Ron(ald)
      1911-1986 .... CLC 43
      See also CANR 22; CA 77-80;
      obituary CA 118

Huch, Ricarda (Octavia)
      1864-1947 .... TCLC 13
      See also CA 111; DLB 66

Huddle, David 1942- .... CLC 49
      See also CA 57-60

Hudson, W(illiam) H(enry)
      1841-1922 .... TCLC 29
      See also CA 115; SATA 35

Hueffer, Ford Madox 1873-1939
      See Ford, Ford Madox

Hughart, Barry 1934-............. CLC 39

Hughes, David (John) 1930- .... CLC 48
      See also CA 116; DLB 14

Hughes, Edward James 1930-
      See Hughes, Ted

Hughes, (James) Langston
      1902-1967 .... CLC 1, 5, 10, 15, 35, 44;
                                  PC 1; SSC 6
      See also CLR 17; CANR 1; CA 1-4R;
      obituary CA 25-28R; SATA 4, 33;
      DLB 4, 7, 48, 51, 86; CDALB 1929-1941

Hughes, Richard (Arthur Warren)
      1900-1976 .... CLC 1, 11
      See also CANR 4; CA 5-8R;
      obituary CA 65-68; SATA 8;
      obituary SATA 25; DLB 15

Hughes, Ted 1930- ..... CLC 2, 4, 9, 14, 37
      See also CLR 3; CANR 1; CA 1-4R;
      SATA 27, 49; DLB 40

Hugo, Richard F(ranklin)
      1923-1982 .... CLC 6, 18, 32
      See also CANR 3; CA 49-52;
      obituary CA 108; DLB 5

Hugo, Victor Marie
      1802-1885 .... NCLC 3, 10, 21
      See also SATA 47

Huidobro, Vicente 1893-1948 ..... TCLC 31

Hulme, Keri 1947- .... CLC 39
      See also CA 123

Hulme, T(homas) E(rnest)
      1883-1917 .... TCLC 21
      See also CA 117; DLB 19

Hume, David 1711-1776............ LC 7

Humphrey, William 1924- .... CLC 45
      See also CA 77-80; DLB 6

Humphreys, Emyr (Owen) 1919-.... CLC 47
      See also CANR 3, 24; CA 5-8R; DLB 15

Humphreys, Josephine 1945-.... CLC 34, 57
      See also CA 121, 127

Hunt, E(verette) Howard (Jr.)
      1918- .... CLC 3
      See also CANR 2; CA 45-48

Hunt, (James Henry) Leigh
      1784-1859 .... NCLC 1

Hunter, Evan 1926- .... CLC 11, 31
      See also CANR 5; CA 5-8R; SATA 25;
      DLB-Y 82

Hunter, Kristin (Eggleston) 1931-... CLC 35
      See also CLR 3; CANR 13; CA 13-16R;
      SATA 12; DLB 33

Hunter, Mollie (Maureen McIlwraith)
      1922- .... CLC 21
      See also McIlwraith, Maureen Mollie
      Hunter

Hunter, Robert ?-1734 .... LC 7

Hurston, Zora Neale
      1891-1960 .... CLC 7, 30, 61; SSC 4
      See also CA 85-88; DLB 51, 86

Huston, John (Marcellus)
      1906-1987 .... CLC 20
      See also CA 73-76; obituary CA 123;
      DLB 26

Huxley, Aldous (Leonard)
      1894-1963 .. CLC 1, 3, 4, 5, 8, 11, 18, 35
      See also CA 85-88; DLB 36

Huysmans, Charles Marie Georges
1848-1907
See Huysmans, Joris-Karl
See also CA 104

Huysmans, Joris-Karl 1848-1907 ... TCLC 7
See also Huysmans, Charles Marie Georges

Hwang, David Henry 1957- .... CLC 55
See also CA 127

Hyde, Anthony 1946?- .... CLC 42

Hyde, Margaret O(ldroyd) 1917- ... CLC 21
See also CANR 1; CA 1-4R; SATA 1, 42

Ian, Janis 1951- .... CLC 21
See also CA 105

Ibarguengoitia, Jorge 1928-1983.... CLC 37
See also obituary CA 113, 124

Ibsen, Henrik (Johan)
1828-1906 .... TCLC 2, 8, 16, 37
See also CA 104

Ibuse, Masuji 1898- .... CLC 22

Ichikawa, Kon 1915- .... CLC 20
See also CA 121

Idle, Eric 1943-
See Monty Python
See also CA 116

Ignatow, David 1914- ...... CLC 4, 7, 14, 40
See also CAAS 3; CA 9-12R; DLB 5

Ihimaera, Witi (Tame) 1944- .... CLC 46
See also CA 77-80

Ilf, Ilya 1897-1937 .... TCLC 21

Immermann, Karl (Lebrecht)
1796-1840 .... NCLC 4

Ingalls, Rachel 19??- .... CLC 42
See also CA 123

Ingamells, Rex 1913-1955 .... TCLC 35

Inge, William (Motter)
1913-1973 .... CLC 1, 8, 19
See also CA 9-12R; DLB 7;
CDALB 1941-1968

Innaurato, Albert 1948- .... CLC 21, 60
See also CA 115, 122

Innes, Michael 1906-
See Stewart, J(ohn) I(nnes) M(ackintosh)

Ionesco, Eugene
1912- .... CLC 1, 4, 6, 9, 11, 15, 41
See also CA 9-12R; SATA 7

Iqbal, Muhammad 1877-1938 ..... TCLC 28

Irving, John (Winslow)
1942- .... CLC 13, 23, 38
See also CA 25-28R; DLB 6; DLB-Y 82

Irving, Washington
1783-1859 .... NCLC 2, 19; SSC 2
See also YABC 2; DLB 3, 11, 30, 59, 73,
74; CDALB 1640-1865

Isaacs, Susan 1943- .... CLC 32
See also CANR 20; CA 89-92

Isherwood, Christopher (William Bradshaw)
1904-1986 .... CLC 1, 9, 11, 14, 44
See also CA 13-16R; obituary CA 117;
DLB 15; DLB-Y 86

Ishiguro, Kazuo 1954- ...... CLC 27, 56, 59
See also CA 120

Ishikawa Takuboku 1885-1912 .... TCLC 15
See also CA 113

Iskander, Fazil (Abdulovich)
1929- .... CLC 47
See also CA 102

Ivanov, Vyacheslav (Ivanovich)
1866-1949 .... TCLC 33
See also CA 122

Ivask, Ivar (Vidrik) 1927- .... CLC 14
See also CANR 24; CA 37-40R

Jackson, Jesse 1908-1983 .... CLC 12
See also CA 25-28R; obituary CA 109;
SATA 2, 29, 48

Jackson, Laura (Riding) 1901-
See Riding, Laura
See also CA 65-68; DLB 48

Jackson, Shirley 1919-1965..... CLC 11, 60
See also CANR 4; CA 1-4R;
obituary CA 25-28R; SATA 2; DLB 6;
CDALB 1941-1968

Jacob, (Cyprien) Max 1876-1944 ... TCLC 6
See also CA 104

Jacob, Piers A(nthony) D(illingham) 1934-
See Anthony (Jacob), Piers
See also CA 21-24R

Jacobs, Jim 1942- and **Casey, Warren**
1942- .... CLC 12

Jacobs, Jim 1942-
See Jacobs, Jim and Casey, Warren
See also CA 97-100

Jacobs, W(illiam) W(ymark)
1863-1943 .... TCLC 22
See also CA 121

Jacobsen, Josephine 1908- .... CLC 48
See also CANR 23; CA 33-36R

Jacobson, Dan 1929- .... CLC 4, 14
See also CANR 2, 25; CA 1-4R; DLB 14

Jagger, Mick 1944- .... CLC 17

Jakes, John (William) 1932- .... CLC 29
See also CANR 10; CA 57-60; DLB-Y 83

James, C(yril) L(ionel) R(obert)
1901-1989 .... CLC 33
See also CA 117, 125

James, Daniel 1911-1988
See Santiago, Danny
See also obituary CA 125

James, Henry (Jr.)
1843-1916 .... TCLC 2, 11, 24
See also CA 104; DLB 12, 71, 74;
CDALB 1865-1917

James, M(ontague) R(hodes)
1862-1936 .... TCLC 6
See also CA 104

James, P(hyllis) D(orothy)
1920- .... CLC 18, 46
See also CANR 17; CA 21-24R

James, William 1842-1910..... TCLC 15, 32
See also CA 109

Jami, Nur al-Din 'Abd al-Rahman
1414-1492 .... LC 9

Jandl, Ernst 1925- .... CLC 34

Janowitz, Tama 1957- .... CLC 43
See also CA 106

Jarrell, Randall
1914-1965 .... CLC 1, 2, 6, 9, 13, 49
See also CLR 6; CANR 6; CA 5-8R;
obituary CA 25-28R; CABS 2; SATA 7;
DLB 48, 52; CDALB 1941-1968

Jarry, Alfred 1873-1907........ TCLC 2, 14
See also CA 104

Jeake, Samuel, Jr. 1889-1973
See Aiken, Conrad

Jean Paul 1763-1825 .... NCLC 7

Jeffers, (John) Robinson
1887-1962 .... CLC 2, 3, 11, 15, 54
See also CA 85-88; DLB 45

Jefferson, Thomas 1743-1826 .... NCLC 11
See also DLB 31; CDALB 1640-1865

Jellicoe, (Patricia) Ann 1927- ...... CLC 27
See also CA 85-88; DLB 13

Jenkins, (John) Robin 1912- .... CLC 52
See also CANR 1; CA 4Rk; DLB 14

Jennings, Elizabeth (Joan)
1926- .... CLC 5, 14
See also CAAS 5; CANR 8; CA 61-64;
DLB 27

Jennings, Waylon 1937-........... CLC 21

Jensen, Laura (Linnea) 1948- ...... CLC 37
See also CA 103

Jerome, Jerome K. 1859-1927..... TCLC 23
See also CA 119; DLB 10, 34

Jerrold, Douglas William
1803-1857 .... NCLC 2

Jewett, (Theodora) Sarah Orne
1849-1909 .... TCLC 1, 22; SSC 6
See also CA 108, 127; SATA 15; DLB 12,
74

Jewsbury, Geraldine (Endsor)
1812-1880 .... NCLC 22
See also DLB 21

Jhabvala, Ruth Prawer
1927- .... CLC 4, 8, 29
See also CANR 2; CA 1-4R

Jiles, Paulette 1943-........... CLC 13, 58
See also CA 101

Jimenez (Mantecon), Juan Ramon
1881-1958 .... TCLC 4
See also CA 104

Joel, Billy 1949-................. CLC 26
See also Joel, William Martin

Joel, William Martin 1949-
See Joel, Billy
See also CA 108

Johnson, B(ryan) S(tanley William)
1933-1973 .... CLC 6, 9
See also CANR 9; CA 9-12R;
obituary CA 53-56; DLB 14, 40

Johnson, Charles (Richard)
1948- .... CLC 7, 51
See also CA 116; DLB 33

Johnson, Denis 1949-............. CLC 52
See also CA 117, 121

Johnson, Diane 1934-........ CLC 5, 13, 48
See also CANR 17; CA 41-44R; DLB-Y 80

Johnson, Eyvind (Olof Verner)
1900-1976 .... CLC 14
See also CA 73-76; obituary CA 69-72

Lazarus, Emma   1849-1887........ NCLC 8

Leacock, Stephen (Butler)
   1869-1944 .... TCLC 2
   See also CA 104

Lear, Edward   1812-1888 .... NCLC 3
   See also CLR 1; SATA 18; DLB 32

Lear, Norman (Milton)   1922- ...... CLC 12
   See also CA 73-76

Leavis, F(rank) R(aymond)
   1895-1978 .... CLC 24
   See also CA 21-24R; obituary CA 77-80

Leavitt, David   1961?-............. CLC 34
   See also CA 116, 122

Lebowitz, Fran(ces Ann)
   1951?- .... CLC 11, 36
   See also CANR 14; CA 81-84

Le Carre, John   1931-... CLC 3, 5, 9, 15, 28
   See also Cornwell, David (John Moore)

Le Clezio, J(ean) M(arie) G(ustave)
   1940- .... CLC 31
   See also CA 116

Leconte de Lisle, Charles-Marie-Rene
   1818-1894 .... NCLC 29

Leduc, Violette   1907-1972........ CLC 22
   See also CAP 1; CA 13-14;
   obituary CA 33-36R

Ledwidge, Francis   1887-1917..... TCLC 23
   See also CA 123; DLB 20

Lee, Andrea   1953- .... CLC 36
   See also CA 125

Lee, Andrew   1917-
   See Auchincloss, Louis (Stanton)

Lee, Don L.   1942-................ CLC 2
   See also Madhubuti, Haki R.
   See also CA 73-76

Lee, George Washington
   1894-1976 .... CLC 52
   See also CA 125; DLB 51

Lee, (Nelle) Harper   1926- ...... CLC 12, 60
   See also CA 13-16R; SATA 11; DLB 6;
   CDALB 1941-1968

Lee, Lawrence   1903- .... CLC 34
   See also CA 25-28R

Lee, Manfred B(ennington)   1905-1971
   See Queen, Ellery
   See also CANR 2; CA 1-4R, 11;
   obituary CA 29-32R

Lee, Stan   1922-.................. CLC 17
   See also CA 108, 111

Lee, Tanith   1947-................ CLC 46
   See also CA 37-40R; SATA 8

Lee, Vernon   1856-1935 .... TCLC 5
   See also Paget, Violet
   See also DLB 57

Lee-Hamilton, Eugene (Jacob)
   1845-1907 .... TCLC 22

Leet, Judith   1935- .... CLC 11

Le Fanu, Joseph Sheridan
   1814-1873 .... NCLC 9
   See also DLB 21, 70

Leffland, Ella   1931- .... CLC 19
   See also CA 29-32R; DLB-Y 84

Leger, (Marie-Rene) Alexis Saint-Leger
   1887-1975
   See Perse, St.-John
   See also CA 13-16R; obituary CA 61-64

Le Guin, Ursula K(roeber)
   1929- .... CLC 8, 13, 22, 45
   See also CLR 3; CANR 9; CA 21-24R;
   SATA 4, 52; DLB 8, 52

Lehmann, Rosamond (Nina)   1901- ... CLC 5
   See also CANR 8; CA 77-80; DLB 15

Leiber, Fritz (Reuter, Jr.)   1910-.... CLC 25
   See also CANR 2; CA 45-48; SATA 45;
   DLB 8

Leino, Eino   1878-1926.......... TCLC 24

Leiris, Michel   1901-............. CLC 61
   See also CA 119, 128

Leithauser, Brad   1953-........... CLC 27
   See also CA 107

Lelchuk, Alan   1938-.............. CLC 5
   See also CANR 1; CA 45-48

Lem, Stanislaw   1921-...... CLC 8, 15, 40
   See also CAAS 1; CA 105

Lemann, Nancy   1956-............. CLC 39
   See also CA 118

Lemonnier, (Antoine Louis) Camille
   1844-1913 .... TCLC 22

Lenau, Nikolaus   1802-1850...... NCLC 16

L'Engle, Madeleine   1918- .... CLC 12
   See also CLR 1, 14; CANR 3, 21; CA 1-4R;
   SATA 1, 27; DLB 52

Lengyel, Jozsef   1896-1975.......... CLC 7
   See also CA 85-88; obituary CA 57-60

Lennon, John (Ono)
   1940-1980 .... CLC 12, 35
   See also CA 102

Lennon, John Winston   1940-1980
   See Lennon, John (Ono)

Lennox, Charlotte Ramsay   1729 or
   1730-1804 .... NCLC 23
   See also DLB 39, 39

Lennox, Charlotte Ramsay
   1729?-1804.................. NCLC 23
   See also DLB 39

Lentricchia, Frank (Jr.)   1940-...... CLC 34
   See also CANR 19; CA 25-28R

Lenz, Siegfried   1926-............. CLC 27
   See also CA 89-92; DLB 75

Leonard, Elmore   1925-........ CLC 28, 34
   See also CANR 12; CA 81-84

Leonard, Hugh   1926-............. CLC 19
   See also Byrne, John Keyes
   See also DLB 13

Leopardi, (Conte) Giacomo (Talegardo
   Francesco di Sales Saverio Pietro)
   1798-1837 .... NCLC 22

Lerman, Eleanor   1952-............ CLC 9
   See also CA 85-88

Lerman, Rhoda   1936-............. CLC 56
   See also CA 49-52

Lermontov, Mikhail Yuryevich
   1814-1841 .... NCLC 5

Leroux, Gaston   1868-1927........ TCLC 25
   See also CA 108

Lesage, Alain-Rene   1668-1747........ LC 2

Leskov, Nikolai (Semyonovich)
   1831-1895 .... NCLC 25

Lessing, Doris (May)
   1919- .... CLC 1, 2, 3, 6, 10, 15, 22, 40;
                                    SSC 6
   See also CA 9-12R; DLB 15; DLB-Y 85

Lessing, Gotthold Ephraim
   1729-1781 .... LC 8

Lester, Richard   1932-............. CLC 20

Lever, Charles (James)
   1806-1872 .... NCLC 23
   See also DLB 21

Leverson, Ada   1865-1936........ TCLC 18
   See also CA 117

Levertov, Denise
   1923- .... CLC 1, 2, 3, 5, 8, 15, 28
   See also CANR 3; CA 1-4R; DLB 5

Levi, Peter (Chad Tiger)   1931- ..... CLC 41
   See also CA 5-8R; DLB 40

Levi, Primo   1919-1987........ CLC 37, 50
   See also CANR 12; CA 13-16R;
   obituary CA 122

Levin, Ira   1929- .... CLC 3, 6
   See also CANR 17; CA 21-24R

Levin, Meyer   1905-1981 .... CLC 7
   See also CANR 15; CA 9-12R;
   obituary CA 104; SATA 21;
   obituary SATA 27; DLB 9, 28; DLB-Y 81

Levine, Norman   1924-............ CLC 54
   See also CANR 14; CA 73-76

Levine, Philip   1928-... CLC 2, 4, 5, 9, 14, 33
   See also CANR 9; CA 9-12R; DLB 5

Levinson, Deirdre   1931-........... CLC 49
   See also CA 73-76

Levi-Strauss, Claude   1908- .... CLC 38
   See also CANR 6; CA 1-4R

Levitin, Sonia   1934-.............. CLC 17
   See also CANR 14; CA 29-32R; SAAS 2;
   SATA 4

Lewes, George Henry
   1817-1878 .... NCLC 25
   See also DLB 55

Lewis, Alun   1915-1944............ TCLC 3
   See also CA 104; DLB 20

Lewis, C(ecil) Day   1904-1972
   See Day Lewis, C(ecil)

Lewis, C(live) S(taples)
   1898-1963 .... CLC 1, 3, 6, 14, 27
   See also CLR 3; CA 81-84; SATA 13;
   DLB 15

Lewis (Winters), Janet   1899-....... CLC 41
   See also Winters, Janet Lewis
   See also DLB-Y 87

Lewis, Matthew Gregory
   1775-1818 .... NCLC 11
   See also DLB 39

Lewis, (Harry) Sinclair
   1885-1951 .... TCLC 4, 13, 23
   See also CA 104; DLB 9; DLB-DS 1

Lewis, (Percy) Wyndham
   1882?-1957................ TCLC 2, 9
   See also CA 104; DLB 15

McGuane, Thomas (Francis III)
  1939- .... CLC 3, 7, 18
  See also CANR 5; CA 49-52; DLB 2;
  DLB-Y 80

McGuckian, Medbh 1950- .... CLC 48
  See also DLB 40

McHale, Tom 1941-1982 .... CLC 3, 5
  See also CA 77-80; obituary CA 106

McIlvanney, William 1936- .... CLC 42
  See also CA 25-28R; DLB 14

McIlwraith, Maureen Mollie Hunter 1922-
  See Hunter, Mollie
  See also CA 29-32R; SATA 2

McInerney, Jay 1955- .... CLC 34
  See also CA 116, 123

McIntyre, Vonda N(eel) 1948- ..... CLC 18
  See also CANR 17; CA 81-84

McKay, Claude 1890-1948 .... TCLC 7
  See also CA 104; DLB 4, 45

McKuen, Rod 1933- .... CLC 1, 3
  See also CA 41-44R

McLuhan, (Herbert) Marshall
  1911-1980 .... CLC 37
  See also CANR 12; CA 9-12R;
  obituary CA 102

McManus, Declan Patrick 1955-
  See Costello, Elvis

McMillan, Terry 1951- .... CLC 50, 61

McMurtry, Larry (Jeff)
  1936- .... CLC 2, 3, 7, 11, 27, 44
  See also CANR 19; CA 5-8R; DLB 2;
  DLB-Y 80, 87

McNally, Terrence 1939- ...... CLC 4, 7, 41
  See also CANR 2; CA 45-48; DLB 7

McPhee, John 1931- .... CLC 36
  See also CANR 20; CA 65-68

McPherson, James Alan 1943- ..... CLC 19
  See also CANR 24; CA 25-28R; DLB 38

McPherson, William 1939- .... CLC 34
  See also CA 57-60

McSweeney, Kerry 19??- .... CLC 34

Mead, Margaret 1901-1978 .... CLC 37
  See also CANR 4; CA 1-4R;
  obituary CA 81-84; SATA 20

Meaker, M. J. 1927-
  See Kerr, M. E.; Meaker, Marijane

Meaker, Marijane 1927-
  See Kerr, M. E.
  See also CA 107; SATA 20

Medoff, Mark (Howard) 1940- ... CLC 6, 23
  See also CANR 5; CA 53-56; DLB 7

Megged, Aharon 1920- .... CLC 9
  See also CANR 1; CA 49-52

Mehta, Ved (Parkash) 1934- .... CLC 37
  See also CANR 2, 23; CA 1-4R

Mellor, John 1953?-
  See The Clash

Meltzer, Milton 1915- .... CLC 26 13
  See also CA 13-16R; SAAS 1; SATA 1, 50;
  DLB 61

Melville, Herman
  1819-1891 ...... NCLC 3, 12, 29; SSC 1
  See also SATA 59; DLB 3, 74;
  CDALB 1640-1865

Membreno, Alejandro 1972- .... CLC 59

Mencken, H(enry) L(ouis)
  1880-1956 .... TCLC 13
  See also CA 105; DLB 11, 29, 63

Mercer, David 1928-1980 .... CLC 5
  See also CA 9-12R; obituary CA 102;
  DLB 13

Meredith, George 1828-1909 ...... TCLC 17
  See also CA 117; DLB 18, 35, 57

Meredith, William (Morris)
  1919- .... CLC 4, 13, 22, 55
  See also CANR 6; CA 9-12R; DLB 5

Merezhkovsky, Dmitri
  1865-1941 .... TCLC 29

Merimee, Prosper 1803-1870 ...... NCLC 6

Merkin, Daphne 1954- .... CLC 44
  See also CANR 123

Merrill, James (Ingram)
  1926- .... CLC 2, 3, 6, 8, 13, 18, 34
  See also CANR 10; CA 13-16R; DLB 5;
  DLB-Y 85

Merton, Thomas (James)
  1915-1968 .... CLC 1, 3, 11, 34
  See also CANR 22; CA 5-8R;
  obituary CA 25-28R; DLB 48; DLB-Y 81

Merwin, W(illiam) S(tanley)
  1927- ...... CLC 1, 2, 3, 5, 8, 13, 18, 45
  See also CANR 15; CA 13-16R; DLB 5

Metcalf, John 1938- .... CLC 37
  See also CA 113; DLB 60

Mew, Charlotte (Mary)
  1870-1928 .... TCLC 8
  See also CA 105; DLB 19

Mewshaw, Michael 1943- .... CLC 9
  See also CANR 7; CA 53-56; DLB-Y 80

Meyer-Meyrink, Gustav 1868-1932
  See Meyrink, Gustav
  See also CA 117

Meyers, Jeffrey 1939- .... CLC 39
  See also CA 73-76

Meynell, Alice (Christiana Gertrude
  Thompson) 1847-1922 .... TCLC 6
  See also CA 104; DLB 19

Meyrink, Gustav 1868-1932 ...... TCLC 21
  See also Meyer-Meyrink, Gustav

Michaels, Leonard 1933- .... CLC 6, 25
  See also CANR 21; CA 61-64

Michaux, Henri 1899-1984 ...... CLC 8, 19
  See also CA 85-88; obituary CA 114

Michelangelo 1475-1564 .... LC 12

Michener, James A(lbert)
  1907- .... CLC 1, 5, 11, 29, 60
  See also CANR 21; CA 5-8R; DLB 6

Mickiewicz, Adam 1798-1855 ..... NCLC 3

Middleton, Christopher 1926- ..... CLC 13
  See also CA 13-16R; DLB 40

Middleton, Stanley 1919- ...... CLC 7, 38
  See also CANR 21; CA 25-28R; DLB 14

Migueis, Jose Rodrigues 1901- ..... CLC 10

Mikszath, Kalman 1847-1910 ..... TCLC 31

Miles, Josephine (Louise)
  1911-1985 .... CLC 1, 2, 14, 34, 39
  See also CANR 2; CA 1-4R;
  obituary CA 116; DLB 48

Mill, John Stuart 1806-1873 ..... NCLC 11

Millar, Kenneth 1915-1983 .... CLC 14
  See also Macdonald, Ross
  See also CANR 16; CA 9-12R;
  obituary CA 110; DLB 2; DLB-Y 83

Millay, Edna St. Vincent
  1892-1950 .... TCLC 4
  See also CA 104; DLB 45

Miller, Arthur
  1915- .... CLC 1, 2, 6, 10, 15, 26, 47
  See also CANR 2; CA 1-4R; DLB 7;
  CDALB 1941-1968

Miller, Henry (Valentine)
  1891-1980 .... CLC 1, 2, 4, 9, 14, 43
  See also CA 9-12R; obituary CA 97-100;
  DLB 4, 9; DLB-Y 80

Miller, Jason 1939?- .... CLC 2
  See also CA 73-76; DLB 7

Miller, Sue 19??- .... CLC 44

Miller, Walter M(ichael), Jr.
  1923- .... CLC 4, 30
  See also CA 85-88; DLB 8

Millhauser, Steven 1943- ...... CLC 21, 54
  See also CA 108, 110, 111; DLB 2

Millin, Sarah Gertrude 1889-1968 .. CLC 49
  See also CA 102; obituary CA 93-96

Milne, A(lan) A(lexander)
  1882-1956 .... TCLC 6
  See also CLR 1; YABC 1; CA 104; DLB 10

Milner, Ron(ald) 1938- .... CLC 56
  See also CANR 24; CA 73-76; DLB 38

Milosz Czeslaw
  1911- .... CLC 5, 11, 22, 31, 56
  See also CANR 23; CA 81-84

Milton, John 1608-1674 .... LC 9

Miner, Valerie (Jane) 1947- .... CLC 40
  See also CA 97-100

Minot, Susan 1956- .... CLC 44

Minus, Ed 1938- .... CLC 39

Miro (Ferrer), Gabriel (Francisco Victor)
  1879-1930 .... TCLC 5
  See also CA 104

Mishima, Yukio
  1925-1970 .... CLC 2, 4, 6, 9, 27; SSC 4
  See also Hiraoka, Kimitake

Mistral, Gabriela 1889-1957 .... TCLC 2
  See also CA 104

Mitchell, James Leslie 1901-1935
  See Gibbon, Lewis Grassic
  See also CA 104; DLB 15

Mitchell, Joni 1943- .... CLC 12
  See also CA 112

Mitchell (Marsh), Margaret (Munnerlyn)
  1900-1949 .... TCLC 11
  See also CA 109; DLB 9

Mitchell, S. Weir 1829-1914 ...... TCLC 36

Mitchell, W(illiam) O(rmond)
  1914- .... CLC 25
  See also CANR 15; CA 77-80

Mitford, Mary Russell 1787-1855 .. NCLC 4

Noyes, Alfred 1880-1958 . . . . TCLC 7
See also CA 104; DLB 20

Nunn, Kem 19??- . . . . CLC 34

Nye, Robert 1939- . . . . CLC 13, 42
See also CA 33-36R; SATA 6; DLB 14

Nyro, Laura 1947- . . . . CLC 17

Oates, Joyce Carol
1938- . . . . . CLC 1, 2, 3, 6, 9, 11, 15, 19,
33, 52; SSC 6
See also CANR 25; CA 5-8R; DLB 2, 5;
DLB-Y 81; CDALB 1968-1987

O'Brien, Darcy 1939- . . . . CLC 11
See also CANR 8; CA 21-24R

O'Brien, Edna 1932- . . . . CLC 3, 5, 8, 13, 36
See also CANR 6; CA 1-4R; DLB 14

O'Brien, Fitz-James 1828?-1862 . . NCLC 21
See also DLB 74

O'Brien, Flann
1911-1966 . . . . CLC 1, 4, 5, 7, 10, 47
See also O Nuallain, Brian

O'Brien, Richard 19??- . . . . CLC 17
See also CA 124

O'Brien, (William) Tim(othy)
1946- . . . . CLC 7, 19, 40
See also CA 85-88; DLB-Y 80

Obstfelder, Sigbjorn 1866-1900 . . . . TCLC 23
See also CA 123

O'Casey, Sean
1880-1964 . . . . CLC 1, 5, 9, 11, 15
See also CA 89-92; DLB 10

Ochs, Phil 1940-1976 . . . . CLC 17
See also obituary CA 65-68

O'Connor, Edwin (Greene)
1918-1968 . . . . CLC 14
See also CA 93-96; obituary CA 25-28R

O'Connor, (Mary) Flannery
1925-1964 . . . CLC 1, 2, 3, 6, 10, 13, 15,
21; SSC 1
See also CANR 3; CA 1-4R; DLB 2;
DLB-Y 80; CDALB 1941-1968

O'Connor, Frank
1903-1966 . . . . CLC 14, 23; SSC 5
See also O'Donovan, Michael (John)
See also CA 93-96

O'Dell, Scott 1903- . . . . CLC 30
See also CLR 1, 16; CANR 12; CA 61-64;
SATA 12; DLB 52

Odets, Clifford 1906-1963 . . . . CLC 2, 28
See also CA 85-88; DLB 7, 26

O'Donovan, Michael (John) 1903-1966
See O'Connor, Frank
See also CA 93-96

Oe, Kenzaburo 1935- . . . . CLC 10, 36
See also CA 97-100

O'Faolain, Julia 1932- . . . . CLC 6, 19, 47
See also CAAS 2; CANR 12; CA 81-84;
DLB 14

O'Faolain, Sean 1900- . . . . . CLC 1, 7, 14, 32
See also CANR 12; CA 61-64; DLB 15

O'Flaherty, Liam
1896-1984 . . . . CLC 5, 34; SSC 6
See also CA 101; obituary CA 113; DLB 36;
DLB-Y 84

O'Grady, Standish (James)
1846-1928 . . . . TCLC 5
See also CA 104

O'Grady, Timothy 1951- . . . . CLC 59

O'Hara, Frank 1926-1966 . . . . . CLC 2, 5, 13
See also CA 9-12R; obituary CA 25-28R;
DLB 5, 16

O'Hara, John (Henry)
1905-1970 . . . . . . CLC 1, 2, 3, 6, 11, 42
See also CA 5-8R; obituary CA 25-28R;
DLB 9; DLB-DS 2

O'Hara Family
See Banim, John and Banim, Michael

O'Hehir, Diana 1922- . . . . CLC 41
See also CA 93-96

Okigbo, Christopher (Ifenayichukwu)
1932-1967 . . . . CLC 25
See also CA 77-80

Olds, Sharon 1942- . . . . CLC 32, 39
See also CANR 18; CA 101

Olesha, Yuri (Karlovich)
1899-1960 . . . . CLC 8
See also CA 85-88

Oliphant, Margaret (Oliphant Wilson)
1828-1897 . . . . NCLC 11
See also DLB 18

Oliver, Mary 1935- . . . . CLC 19, 34
See also CANR 9; CA 21-24R; DLB 5

Olivier, (Baron) Laurence (Kerr)
1907- . . . . CLC 20
See also CA 111

Olsen, Tillie 1913- . . . . CLC 4, 13
See also CANR 1; CA 1-4R; DLB 28;
DLB-Y 80

Olson, Charles (John)
1910-1970 . . . . . CLC 1, 2, 5, 6, 9, 11, 29
See also CAP 1; CA 15-16;
obituary CA 25-28R; CABS 2; DLB 5, 16

Olson, Theodore 1937-
See Olson, Toby

Olson, Toby 1937- . . . . CLC 28
See also CANR 9; CA 65-68

Ondaatje, (Philip) Michael
1943- . . . . CLC 14, 29, 51
See also CA 77-80; DLB 60

Oneal, Elizabeth 1934-
See Oneal, Zibby
See also CA 106; SATA 30

Oneal, Zibby 1934- . . . . CLC 30
See also Oneal, Elizabeth

O'Neill, Eugene (Gladstone)
1888-1953 . . . . TCLC 1, 6, 27
See also CA 110; DLB 7

Onetti, Juan Carlos 1909- . . . . CLC 7, 10
See also CA 85-88

O'Nolan, Brian 1911-1966
See O'Brien, Flann

O Nuallain, Brian 1911-1966
See O'Brien, Flann
See also CAP 2; CA 21-22;
obituary CA 25-28R

Oppen, George 1908-1984 . . . . CLC 7, 13, 34
See also CANR 8; CA 13-16R;
obituary CA 113; DLB 5

Orlovitz, Gil 1918-1973 . . . . CLC 22
See also CA 77-80; obituary CA 45-48;
DLB 2, 5

Ortega y Gasset, Jose 1883-1955 . . . TCLC 9
See also CA 106

Ortiz, Simon J. 1941- . . . . CLC 45

Orton, Joe 1933?-1967 . . . . . . CLC 4, 13, 43
See also Orton, John Kingsley
See also DLB 13

Orton, John Kingsley 1933?-1967
See Orton, Joe
See also CA 85-88

Orwell, George
1903-1950 . . . . TCLC 2, 6, 15, 31
See also Blair, Eric Arthur
See also DLB 15

Osborne, John (James)
1929- . . . . CLC 1, 2, 5, 11, 45
See also CANR 21; CA 13-16R; DLB 13

Osborne, Lawrence 1958- . . . . CLC 50

Osceola 1885-1962
See Dinesen, Isak; Blixen, Karen
(Christentze Dinesen)

Oshima, Nagisa 1932- . . . . CLC 20
See also CA 116

Oskison, John M. 1874-1947 . . . . . . TCLC 35

Ossoli, Sarah Margaret (Fuller marchesa d')
1810-1850
See Fuller, (Sarah) Margaret
See also SATA 25

Otero, Blas de 1916- . . . . CLC 11
See also CA 89-92

Owen, Wilfred (Edward Salter)
1893-1918 . . . . TCLC 5, 27
See also CA 104; DLB 20

Owens, Rochelle 1936- . . . . CLC 8
See also CAAS 2; CA 17-20R

Owl, Sebastian 1939-
See Thompson, Hunter S(tockton)

Oz, Amos 1939- . . . CLC 5, 8, 11, 27, 33, 54
See also CA 53-56

Ozick, Cynthia 1928- . . . . . . CLC 3, 7, 28, 62
See also CANR 28; CA 17-20R; DLB 28;
DLB-Y 82

Ozu, Yasujiro 1903-1963 . . . . CLC 16
See also CA 112

Pa Chin 1904- . . . . CLC 18
See also Li Fei-kan

Pack, Robert 1929- . . . . CLC 13
See also CANR 3; CA 1-4R; DLB 5

Padgett, Lewis 1915-1958
See Kuttner, Henry

Padilla, Heberto 1932- . . . . CLC 38
See also CA 123

Page, Jimmy 1944- . . . . CLC 12

Page, Louise 1955- . . . . CLC 40

Page, P(atricia) K(athleen)
1916- . . . . CLC 7, 18
See also CANR 4, 22; CA 53-56; DLB 68

Paget, Violet 1856-1935
See Lee, Vernon
See also CA 104

Palamas, Kostes 1859-1943 . . . . TCLC 5
See also CA 105

Palazzeschi, Aldo 1885-1974 . . . . . . CLC 11
See also CA 89-92; obituary CA 53-56

Paley, Grace 1922- . . . . CLC 4, 6, 37
See also CANR 13; CA 25-28R; DLB 28

Palin, Michael 1943- . . . . CLC 21
See also Monty Python
See also CA 107

Palma, Ricardo 1833-1919 . . . . TCLC 29
See also CANR 123

Pancake, Breece Dexter 1952-1979
See Pancake, Breece D'J

Pancake, Breece D'J 1952-1979 . . . . CLC 29
See also obituary CA 109

Papadiamantis, Alexandros
1851-1911 . . . . TCLC 29

Papini, Giovanni 1881-1956 . . . . TCLC 22
See also CA 121

Paracelsus 1493-1541 . . . . LC 14

Parini, Jay (Lee) 1948- . . . . CLC 54
See also CA 97-100

Parker, Dorothy (Rothschild)
1893-1967 . . . . CLC 15; SSC 2
See also CAP 2; CA 19-20;
obituary CA 25-28R; DLB 11, 45

Parker, Robert B(rown) 1932- . . . . . . CLC 27
See also CANR 1, 26; CA 49-52

Parkin, Frank 1940- . . . . CLC 43

Parkman, Francis 1823-1893 . . . . . NCLC 12
See also DLB 1, 30

Parks, Gordon (Alexander Buchanan)
1912- . . . . CLC 1, 16
See also CANR 26; CA 41-44R; SATA 8;
DLB 33

Parnell, Thomas 1679-1718 . . . . LC 3

Parra, Nicanor 1914- . . . . CLC 2
See also CA 85-88

Pasolini, Pier Paolo
1922-1975 . . . . CLC 20, 37
See also CA 93-96; obituary CA 61-64

Pastan, Linda (Olenik) 1932- . . . . . . CLC 27
See also CANR 18; CA 61-64; DLB 5

Pasternak, Boris 1890-1960 . . . CLC 7, 10, 18
See also obituary CA 116

Patchen, Kenneth 1911-1972 . . . CLC 1, 2, 18
See also CANR 3; CA 1-4R;
obituary CA 33-36R; DLB 16, 48

Pater, Walter (Horatio)
1839-1894 . . . . NCLC 7
See also DLB 57

Paterson, Andrew Barton
1864-1941 . . . . TCLC 32

Paterson, Katherine (Womeldorf)
1932- . . . . CLC 12, 30
See also CLR 7; CA 21-24R; SATA 13, 53;
DLB 52

Patmore, Coventry Kersey Dighton
1823-1896 . . . . NCLC 9
See also DLB 35

Paton, Alan (Stewart)
1903-1988 . . . . CLC 4, 10, 25, 55
See also CANR 22; CAP 1; CA 15-16;
obituary CA 125; SATA 11

Paulding, James Kirke 1778-1860 . . NCLC 2
See also DLB 3, 59, 74

Paulin, Tom 1949- . . . . CLC 37
See also CA 123; DLB 40

Paustovsky, Konstantin (Georgievich)
1892-1968 . . . . CLC 40
See also CA 93-96; obituary CA 25-28R

Paustowsky, Konstantin (Georgievich)
1892-1968
See Paustovsky, Konstantin (Georgievich)

Pavese, Cesare 1908-1950 . . . . TCLC 3
See also CA 104

Pavic, Milorad 1929- . . . . CLC 60

Payne, Alan 1932-
See Jakes, John (William)

Paz, Octavio
1914- . . . . . CLC 3, 4, 6, 10, 19, 51; PC 1
See also CA 73-76

Peacock, Molly 1947- . . . . CLC 60
See also CA 103

Peacock, Thomas Love
1785-1886 . . . . NCLC 22

Peake, Mervyn 1911-1968 . . . . . . CLC 7, 54
See also CANR 3; CA 5-8R;
obituary CA 25-28R; SATA 23; DLB 15

Pearce, (Ann) Philippa 1920- . . . . . . CLC 21
See also Christie, (Ann) Philippa
See also CLR 9; CA 5-8R; SATA 1

Pearl, Eric 1934-
See Elman, Richard

Pearson, T(homas) R(eid) 1956- . . . . CLC 39
See also CA 120

Peck, John 1941- . . . . CLC 3
See also CANR 3; CA 49-52

Peck, Richard 1934- . . . . CLC 21
See also CLR 15; CANR 19; CA 85-88;
SAAS 2; SATA 18

Peck, Robert Newton 1928- . . . . CLC 17
See also CA 81-84; SAAS 1; SATA 21

Peckinpah, (David) Sam(uel)
1925-1984 . . . . CLC 20
See also CA 109; obituary CA 114

Pedersen, Knut 1859-1952
See Hamsun, Knut
See also CA 104, 109

Peguy, Charles (Pierre)
1873-1914 . . . . TCLC 10
See also CA 107

Pepys, Samuel 1633-1703 . . . . LC 11

Percy, Walker
1916- . . . . CLC 2, 3, 6, 8, 14, 18, 47
See also CANR 1; CA 1-4R; DLB 2;
DLB-Y 80

Perec, Georges 1936-1982 . . . . CLC 56

Pereda, Jose Maria de
1833-1906 . . . . TCLC 16

Perelman, S(idney) J(oseph)
1904-1979 . . . CLC 3, 5, 9, 15, 23, 44, 49
See also CANR 18; CA 73-76;
obituary CA 89-92; DLB 11, 44

Peret, Benjamin 1899-1959 . . . . TCLC 20
See also CA 117

Peretz, Isaac Leib 1852?-1915 . . . . . TCLC 16
See also CA 109

Perez, Galdos Benito 1853-1920 . . . TCLC 27
See also CA 125

Perrault, Charles 1628-1703 . . . . LC 2
See also SATA 25

Perse, St.-John 1887-1975 . . . . CLC 4, 11, 46
See also Leger, (Marie-Rene) Alexis
Saint-Leger

Pesetsky, Bette 1932- . . . . CLC 28

Peshkov, Alexei Maximovich 1868-1936
See Gorky, Maxim
See also CA 105

Pessoa, Fernando (Antonio Nogueira)
1888-1935 . . . . TCLC 27
See also CA 125

Peterkin, Julia (Mood) 1880-1961 . . . CLC 31
See also CA 102; DLB 9

Peters, Joan K. 1945- . . . . CLC 39

Peters, Robert L(ouis) 1924- . . . . CLC 7
See also CA 13-16R

Petofi, Sandor 1823-1849 . . . . NCLC 21

Petrakis, Harry Mark 1923- . . . . CLC 3
See also CANR 4; CA 9-12R

Petrov, Evgeny 1902-1942 . . . . TCLC 21

Petry, Ann (Lane) 1908- . . . . . . CLC 1, 7, 18
See also CLR 12; CAAS 6; CANR 4;
CA 5-8R; SATA 5

Petursson, Halligrimur 1614-1674 . . . . LC 8

Philipson, Morris (H.) 1926- . . . . CLC 53
See also CANR 4; CA 1-4R

Phillips, Jayne Anne 1952- . . . . . CLC 15, 33
See also CANR 24; CA 101; DLB-Y 80

Phillips, Robert (Schaeffer) 1938- . . . CLC 28
See also CANR 8; CA 17-20R

Pica, Peter 1925-
See Aldiss, Brian W(ilson)

Piccolo, Lucio 1901-1969 . . . . CLC 13
See also CA 97-100

Pickthall, Marjorie (Lowry Christie)
1883-1922 . . . . TCLC 21
See also CA 107

Piercy, Marge
1936- . . . . CLC 3, 6, 14, 18, 27, 62
See also CAAS 1; CANR 13; CA 21-24R

Pilnyak, Boris 1894-1937? . . . . TCLC 23

Pincherle, Alberto 1907-
See Moravia, Alberto
See also CA 25-28R

Pineda, Cecile 1942- . . . . CLC 39
See also CA 118

Pinero, Miguel (Gomez)
1946-1988 . . . . CLC 4, 55
See also CA 61-64; obituary CA 125

Pinero, Sir Arthur Wing
1855-1934 . . . . TCLC 32
See also CA 110; DLB 10

Pinget, Robert 1919- . . . . CLC 7, 13, 37
See also CA 85-88

Pink Floyd . . . . CLC 35

Pinkwater, D(aniel) M(anus)
1941- . . . . CLC 35
See also Pinkwater, Manus
See also CLR 4; CANR 12; CA 29-32R;
SAAS 3; SATA 46

Queen, Ellery 1905-1982 . . . . CLC 3, 11
 See also Dannay, Frederic; Lee, Manfred
  B(ennington)

Queneau, Raymond
  1903-1976 . . . . CLC 2, 5, 10, 42
 See also CA 77-80; obituary CA 69-72;
  DLB 72

Quin, Ann (Marie) 1936-1973 . . . . CLC 6
 See also CA 9-12R; obituary CA 45-48;
  DLB 14

Quinn, Simon 1942-
 See Smith, Martin Cruz
 See also CANR 6, 23; CA 85-88

Quiroga, Horacio (Sylvestre)
  1878-1937 . . . . TCLC 20
 See also CA 117

Quoirez, Francoise 1935-
 See Sagan, Francoise
 See also CANR 6; CA 49-52

Rabe, David (William) 1940-... CLC 4, 8, 33
 See also CA 85-88; DLB 7

Rabelais, Francois 1494?-1553 . . . . LC 5

Rabinovitch, Sholem 1859-1916
 See Aleichem, Sholom
 See also CA 104

Rachen, Kurt von 1911-1986
 See Hubbard, L(afayette) Ron(ald)

Radcliffe, Ann (Ward) 1764-1823 . . NCLC 6
 See also DLB 39

Radiguet, Raymond 1903-1923 . . . . TCLC 29

Radnoti, Miklos 1909-1944 . . . . . . TCLC 16
 See also CA 118

Rado, James 1939- . . . . CLC 17
 See also CA 105

Radomski, James 1932-
 See Rado, James

Radvanyi, Netty Reiling 1900-1983
 See Seghers, Anna
 See also CA 85-88; obituary CA 110

Rae, Ben 1935-
 See Griffiths, Trevor

Raeburn, John 1941- . . . . CLC 34
 See also CA 57-60

Ragni, Gerome 1942- . . . . CLC 17
 See also CA 105

Rahv, Philip 1908-1973 . . . . CLC 24
 See also Greenberg, Ivan

Raine, Craig 1944- . . . . CLC 32
 See also CA 108; DLB 40

Raine, Kathleen (Jessie) 1908- . . . CLC 7, 45
 See also CA 85-88; DLB 20

Rainis, Janis 1865-1929 . . . . TCLC 29

Rakosi, Carl 1903- . . . . CLC 47
 See also Rawley, Callman
 See also CAAS 5

Ramos, Graciliano 1892-1953 . . . . . TCLC 32

Rampersad, Arnold 19??- . . . . CLC 44

Ramuz, Charles-Ferdinand
  1878-1947 . . . . TCLC 33

Rand, Ayn 1905-1982 . . . . CLC 3, 30, 44
 See also CA 13-16R; obituary CA 105

Randall, Dudley (Felker) 1914- . . . . . . CLC 1
 See also CANR 23; CA 25-28R; DLB 41

Ransom, John Crowe
  1888-1974 . . . . CLC 2, 4, 5, 11, 24
 See also CANR 6; CA 5-8R;
  obituary CA 49-52; DLB 45, 63

Rao, Raja 1909- . . . . CLC 25, 56
 See also CA 73-76

Raphael, Frederic (Michael)
  1931- . . . . CLC 2, 14
 See also CANR 1; CA 1-4R; DLB 14

Rathbone, Julian 1935- . . . . CLC 41
 See also CA 101

Rattigan, Terence (Mervyn)
  1911-1977 . . . . CLC 7
 See also CA 85-88; obituary CA 73-76;
  DLB 13

Ratushinskaya, Irina 1954- . . . . CLC 54

Raven, Simon (Arthur Noel)
  1927- . . . . CLC 14
 See also CA 81-84

Rawley, Callman 1903-
 See Rakosi, Carl
 See also CANR 12; CA 21-24R

Rawlings, Marjorie Kinnan
  1896-1953 . . . . TCLC 4
 See also YABC 1; CA 104; DLB 9, 22

Ray, Satyajit 1921- . . . . CLC 16
 See also CA 114

Read, Herbert (Edward) 1893-1968 . . CLC 4
 See also CA 85-88; obituary CA 25-28R;
  DLB 20

Read, Piers Paul 1941- . . . . . . CLC 4, 10, 25
 See also CA 21-24R; SATA 21; DLB 14

Reade, Charles 1814-1884 . . . . NCLC 2
 See also DLB 21

Reade, Hamish 1936-
 See Gray, Simon (James Holliday)

Reading, Peter 1946- . . . . CLC 47
 See also CA 103; DLB 40

Reaney, James 1926- . . . . CLC 13
 See also CA 41-44R; SATA 43; DLB 68

Rebreanu, Liviu 1885-1944 . . . . TCLC 28

Rechy, John (Francisco)
  1934- . . . . CLC 1, 7, 14, 18
 See also CAAS 4; CANR 6; CA 5-8R;
  DLB-Y 82

Redcam, Tom 1870-1933 . . . . TCLC 25

Redgrove, Peter (William)
  1932- . . . . CLC 6, 41
 See also CANR 3; CA 1-4R; DLB 40

Redmon (Nightingale), Anne
  1943- . . . . CLC 22
 See also Nightingale, Anne Redmon
 See also DLB-Y 86

Reed, Ishmael
  1938- . . . . CLC 2, 3, 5, 6, 13, 32, 60
 See also CANR 25; CA 21-24R; DLB 2, 5,
  33

Reed, John (Silas) 1887-1920 . . . . . . TCLC 9
 See also CA 106

Reed, Lou 1944- . . . . CLC 21

Reeve, Clara 1729-1807 . . . . NCLC 19
 See also DLB 39

Reid, Christopher 1949- . . . . CLC 33
 See also DLB 40

Reid Banks, Lynne 1929-
 See Banks, Lynne Reid
 See also CANR 6, 22; CA 1-4R; SATA 22

Reiner, Max 1900-
 See Caldwell, (Janet Miriam) Taylor
  (Holland)

Reizenstein, Elmer Leopold 1892-1967
 See Rice, Elmer

Remark, Erich Paul 1898-1970
 See Remarque, Erich Maria

Remarque, Erich Maria
  1898-1970 . . . . CLC 21
 See also CA 77-80; obituary CA 29-32R;
  DLB 56

Remizov, Alexey (Mikhailovich)
  1877-1957 . . . . TCLC 27
 See also CA 125

Renan, Joseph Ernest
  1823-1892 . . . . NCLC 26

Renard, Jules 1864-1910 . . . . TCLC 17
 See also CA 117

Renault, Mary 1905-1983 . . . . CLC 3, 11, 17
 See also Challans, Mary
 See also DLB-Y 83

Rendell, Ruth 1930- . . . . CLC 28, 48
 See also Vine, Barbara
 See also CA 109

Renoir, Jean 1894-1979 . . . . CLC 20
 See also obituary CA 85-88

Resnais, Alain 1922- . . . . CLC 16

Reverdy, Pierre 1899-1960 . . . . CLC 53
 See also CA 97-100; obituary CA 89-92

Rexroth, Kenneth
  1905-1982 . . . . . . CLC 1, 2, 6, 11, 22, 49
 See also CANR 14; CA 5-8R;
  obituary CA 107; DLB 16, 48; DLB-Y 82;
  CDALB 1941-1968

Reyes, Alfonso 1889-1959 . . . . TCLC 33

Reyes y Basoalto, Ricardo Eliecer Neftali
  1904-1973
 See Neruda, Pablo

Reymont, Wladyslaw Stanislaw
  1867-1925 . . . . TCLC 5
 See also CA 104

Reynolds, Jonathan 1942?- . . . . . . CLC 6, 38
 See also CA 65-68

Reynolds, Michael (Shane) 1937-... CLC 44
 See also CANR 9; CA 65-68

Reznikoff, Charles 1894-1976 . . . . CLC 9
 See also CAP 2; CA 33-36;
  obituary CA 61-64; DLB 28, 45

Rezzori, Gregor von 1914- . . . . CLC 25
 See also CA 122

Rhys, Jean
  1890-1979 . . . . . . CLC 2, 4, 6, 14, 19, 51
 See also CA 25-28R; obituary CA 85-88;
  DLB 36

Ribeiro, Darcy 1922- . . . . CLC 34
 See also CA 33-36R

Ribeiro, Joao Ubaldo (Osorio Pimentel)
  1941- . . . . CLC 10
 See also CA 81-84

Ribman, Ronald (Burt) 1932- . . . . CLC 7
 See also CA 21-24R

Rice, Anne 1941- .... CLC 41
See also CANR 12; CA 65-68

Rice, Elmer 1892-1967......... CLC 7, 49
See also CAP 2; CA 21-22;
obituary CA 25-28R; DLB 4, 7

Rice, Tim 1944- .... CLC 21
See also CA 103

Rich, Adrienne (Cecile)
1929- .... CLC 3, 6, 7, 11, 18, 36
See also CANR 20; CA 9-12R; DLB 5, 67

Richard, Keith 1943- .... CLC 17
See also CA 107

Richards, David Adam 1950-....... CLC 59
See also CA 93-96; DLB 53

Richards, I(vor) A(rmstrong)
1893-1979 .... CLC 14, 24
See also CA 41-44R; obituary CA 89-92;
DLB 27

Richards, Keith 1943-
See Richard, Keith
See also CA 107

Richardson, Dorothy (Miller)
1873-1957 .... TCLC 3
See also CA 104; DLB 36

Richardson, Ethel 1870-1946
See Richardson, Henry Handel
See also CA 105

Richardson, Henry Handel
1870-1946 .... TCLC 4
See also Richardson, Ethel

Richardson, Samuel 1689-1761 .... LC 1
See also DLB 39

Richler, Mordecai
1931- .... CLC 3, 5, 9, 13, 18, 46
See also CA 65-68; SATA 27, 44; DLB 53

Richter, Conrad (Michael)
1890-1968 .... CLC 30
See also CA 5-8R; obituary CA 25-28R;
SATA 3; DLB 9

Richter, Johann Paul Friedrich 1763-1825
See Jean Paul

Riding, Laura 1901- .... CLC 3, 7
See also Jackson, Laura (Riding)

Riefenstahl, Berta Helene Amalia
1902- .... CLC 16
See also Riefenstahl, Leni
See also CA 108

Riefenstahl, Leni 1902- .... CLC 16
See also Riefenstahl, Berta Helene Amalia
See also CA 108

Rilke, Rainer Maria
1875-1926 .... TCLC 1, 6, 19
See also CA 104

Rimbaud, (Jean Nicolas) Arthur
1854-1891 .... NCLC 4

Ringwood, Gwen(dolyn Margaret) Pharis
1910-1984 .... CLC 48
See also obituary CA 112

Rio, Michel 19??- .... CLC 43

Ritsos, Yannis 1909-........ CLC 6, 13, 31
See also CA 77-80

Ritter, Erika 1948?-.............. CLC 52

Rivera, Jose Eustasio 1889-1928... TCLC 35

Rivers, Conrad Kent 1933-1968...... CLC 1
See also CA 85-88; DLB 41

Rizal, Jose 1861-1896........... NCLC 27

Roa Bastos, Augusto 1917- .... CLC 45

Robbe-Grillet, Alain
1922- ...... CLC 1, 2, 4, 6, 8, 10, 14, 43
See also CA 9-12R

Robbins, Harold 1916-............. CLC 5
See also CANR 26; CA 73-76

Robbins, Thomas Eugene 1936-
See Robbins, Tom
See also CA 81-84

Robbins, Tom 1936-............. CLC 9, 32
See also Robbins, Thomas Eugene
See also DLB-Y 80

Robbins, Trina 1938-............. CLC 21

Roberts, (Sir) Charles G(eorge) D(ouglas)
1860-1943 .... TCLC 8
See also CA 105; SATA 29

Roberts, Kate 1891-1985.......... CLC 15
See also CA 107; obituary CA 116

Roberts, Keith (John Kingston)
1935-..................... CLC 14
See also CA 25-28R

Roberts, Kenneth 1885-1957 ...... TCLC 23
See also CA 109; DLB 9

Roberts, Michele (B.) 1949-........ CLC 48
See also CA 115

Robinson, Edwin Arlington
1869-1935 .... TCLC 5; PC 1
See also CA 104; DLB 54;
CDALB 1865-1917

Robinson, Henry Crabb
1775-1867 .... NCLC 15

Robinson, Jill 1936-............. CLC 10
See also CA 102

Robinson, Kim Stanley 19??-....... CLC 34
See also CA 126

Robinson, Marilynne 1944-........ CLC 25
See also CA 116

Robinson, Smokey 1940-........... CLC 21

Robinson, William 1940-
See Robinson, Smokey
See also CA 116

Robison, Mary 1949-............. CLC 42
See also CA 113, 116

Roddenberry, Gene 1921-.......... CLC 17
See also CANR 110

Rodgers, Mary 1931-............. CLC 12
See also CLR 20; CANR 8; CA 49-52;
SATA 8

Rodgers, W(illiam) R(obert)
1909-1969 .... CLC 7
See also CA 85-88; DLB 20

Rodriguez, Claudio 1934-......... CLC 10

Roethke, Theodore (Huebner)
1908-1963 ...... CLC 1, 3, 8, 11, 19, 46
See also CA 81-84; CABS 2; SAAS 1;
DLB 5; CDALB 1941-1968

Rogers, Sam 1943-
See Shepard, Sam

Rogers, Thomas (Hunton) 1931-.... CLC 57
See also CA 89-92

Rogers, Will(iam Penn Adair)
1879-1935 .... TCLC 8
See also CA 105; DLB 11

Rogin, Gilbert 1929-............. CLC 18
See also CANR 15; CA 65-68

Rohan, Koda 1867-1947............ TCLC 22
See also CA 121

Rohmer, Eric 1920- .... CLC 16
See also Scherer, Jean-Marie Maurice

Rohmer, Sax 1883-1959.......... TCLC 28
See also Ward, Arthur Henry Sarsfield
See also CA 108; DLB 70

Roiphe, Anne (Richardson)
1935-...................... CLC 3, 9
See also CA 89-92; DLB-Y 80

Rolfe, Frederick (William Serafino Austin
Lewis Mary) 1860-1913...... TCLC 12
See also CA 107; DLB 34

Rolland, Romain 1866-1944....... TCLC 23
See also CA 118

Rolvaag, O(le) E(dvart)
1876-1931 .... TCLC 17
See also CA 117; DLB 9

Romains, Jules 1885-1972.......... CLC 7
See also CA 85-88

Romero, Jose Ruben 1890-1952 ... TCLC 14
See also CA 114

Ronsard, Pierre de 1524-1585........ LC 6

Rooke, Leon 1934-............. CLC 25, 34
See also CANR 23; CA 25-28R

Roper, William 1498-1578.......... LC 10

Rosa, Joao Guimaraes 1908-1967 ... CLC 23
See also obituary CA 89-92

Rosen, Richard (Dean) 1949-....... CLC 39
See also CA 77-80

Rosenberg, Isaac 1890-1918....... TCLC 12
See also CA 107; DLB 20

Rosenblatt, Joe 1933-............. CLC 15
See also Rosenblatt, Joseph

Rosenblatt, Joseph 1933-
See Rosenblatt, Joe
See also CA 89-92

Rosenfeld, Samuel 1896-1963
See Tzara, Tristan
See also obituary CA 89-92

Rosenthal, M(acha) L(ouis) 1917-... CLC 28
See also CAAS 6; CANR 4; CA 1-4R;
DLB 5

Ross, (James) Sinclair 1908-....... CLC 13
See also CA 73-76

Rossetti, Christina Georgina
1830-1894 .... NCLC 2
See also SATA 20; DLB 35

Rossetti, Dante Gabriel
1828-1882 .... NCLC 4
See also DLB 35

Rossetti, Gabriel Charles Dante 1828-1882
See Rossetti, Dante Gabriel

Rossner, Judith (Perelman)
1935-................... CLC 6, 9, 29
See also CANR 18; CA 17-20R; DLB 6

Rostand, Edmond (Eugene Alexis)
1868-1918 .... TCLC 6, 37
See also CA 104, 126

Seton, Ernest (Evan) Thompson
  1860-1946 . . . . TCLC 31
  See also CA 109; SATA 18

Settle, Mary Lee 1918- . . . . CLC 19, 61
  See also CAAS 1; CA 89-92; DLB 6

Sevigne, Marquise de Marie de
  Rabutin-Chantal 1626-1696 . . . . . LC 11

Sexton, Anne (Harvey)
  1928-1974 . . . . CLC 2, 4, 6, 8, 10, 15, 53
  See also CANR 3; CA 1-4R;
  obituary CA 53-56; CABS 2; SATA 10;
  DLB 5; CDALB 1941-1968

Shaara, Michael (Joseph) 1929- . . . . CLC 15
  See also CA 102; obituary CA 125;
  DLB-Y 83

Shackleton, C. C. 1925-
  See Aldiss, Brian W(ilson)

Shacochis, Bob 1951- . . . . CLC 39
  See also CA 119, 124

Shaffer, Anthony 1926- . . . . CLC 19
  See also CA 110, 116; DLB 13

Shaffer, Peter (Levin)
  1926- . . . . CLC 5, 14, 18, 37, 60
  See also CANR 25; CA 25-28R; DLB 13

Shalamov, Varlam (Tikhonovich)
  1907?-1982 . . . . CLC 18
  See also obituary CA 105

Shamlu, Ahmad 1925- . . . . CLC 10

Shammas, Anton 1951- . . . . CLC 55

Shange, Ntozake 1948- . . . . . . CLC 8, 25, 38
  See also CA 85-88; DLB 38

Shapcott, Thomas W(illiam) 1935- . . CLC 38
  See also CA 69-72

Shapiro, Karl (Jay) 1913- . . CLC 4, 8, 15, 53
  See also CAAS 6; CANR 1; CA 1-4R;
  DLB 48

Sharpe, Tom 1928- . . . . CLC 36
  See also CA 114; DLB 14

Shaw, (George) Bernard
  1856-1950 . . . . TCLC 3, 9, 21
  See also CA 104, 109, 119; DLB 10, 57

Shaw, Henry Wheeler
  1818-1885 . . . . NCLC 15
  See also DLB 11

Shaw, Irwin 1913-1984 . . . . . . CLC 7, 23, 34
  See also CANR 21; CA 13-16R;
  obituary CA 112; DLB 6; DLB-Y 84;
  CDALB 1941-1968

Shaw, Robert 1927-1978 . . . . CLC 5
  See also CANR 4; CA 1-4R;
  obituary CA 81-84; DLB 13, 14

Shawn, Wallace 1943- . . . . CLC 41
  See also CA 112

Sheed, Wilfrid (John Joseph)
  1930- . . . . CLC 2, 4, 10, 53
  See also CA 65-68; DLB 6

Sheffey, Asa 1913-1980
  See Hayden, Robert (Earl)

Sheldon, Alice (Hastings) B(radley)
  1915-1987
  See Tiptree, James, Jr.
  See also CA 108; obituary CA 122

Shelley, Mary Wollstonecraft Godwin
  1797-1851 . . . . NCLC 14
  See also SATA 29

Shelley, Percy Bysshe
  1792-1822 . . . . NCLC 18

Shepard, Jim 19??- . . . . CLC 36

Shepard, Lucius 19??- . . . . CLC 34

Shepard, Sam
  1943- . . . . CLC 4, 6, 17, 34, 41, 44
  See also CANR 22; CA 69-72; DLB 7

Shepherd, Michael 1927-
  See Ludlum, Robert

Sherburne, Zoa (Morin) 1912- . . . . . . CLC 30
  See also CANR 3; CA 1-4R; SATA 3

Sheridan, Frances 1724-1766 . . . . LC 7
  See also DLB 39

Sheridan, Richard Brinsley
  1751-1816 . . . . NCLC 5

Sherman, Jonathan Marc 1970?- . . . . CLC 55

Sherman, Martin 19??- . . . . CLC 19
  See also CA 116

Sherwin, Judith Johnson 1936- . . . CLC 7, 15
  See also CA 25-28R

Sherwood, Robert E(mmet)
  1896-1955 . . . . TCLC 3
  See also CA 104; DLB 7, 26

Shiel, M(atthew) P(hipps)
  1865-1947 . . . . TCLC 8
  See also CA 106

Shiga, Naoya 1883-1971 . . . . CLC 33
  See also CA 101; obituary CA 33-36R

Shimazaki, Haruki 1872-1943
  See Shimazaki, Toson
  See also CA 105

Shimazaki, Toson 1872-1943 . . . . . . TCLC 5
  See also Shimazaki, Haruki

Sholokhov, Mikhail (Aleksandrovich)
  1905-1984 . . . . CLC 7, 15
  See also CA 101; obituary CA 112;
  SATA 36

Sholom Aleichem 1859-1916 . . . . TCLC 1, 35
  See also Rabinovitch, Sholem

Shreve, Susan Richards 1939- . . . . . . CLC 23
  See also CAAS 5; CANR 5; CA 49-52;
  SATA 41, 46

Shue, Larry 1946-1985 . . . . CLC 52
  See also obituary CA 117

Shulman, Alix Kates 1932- . . . . . . CLC 2, 10
  See also CA 29-32R; SATA 7

Shuster, Joe 1914- . . . . CLC 21

Shute (Norway), Nevil 1899-1960 . . . CLC 30
  See also Norway, Nevil Shute
  See also CA 102; obituary CA 93-96

Shuttle, Penelope (Diane) 1947- . . . . . CLC 7
  See also CA 93-96; DLB 14, 40

Siegel, Jerome 1914- . . . . CLC 21
  See also CA 116

Sienkiewicz, Henryk (Adam Aleksander Pius)
  1846-1916 . . . . TCLC 3
  See also CA 104

Sigal, Clancy 1926- . . . . CLC 7
  See also CA 1-4R

Sigourney, Lydia (Howard Huntley)
  1791-1865 . . . . NCLC 21
  See also DLB 1, 42, 73

Siguenza y Gongora, Carlos de
  1645-1700 . . . . LC 8

Sigurjonsson, Johann 1880-1919 . . . TCLC 27

Silkin, Jon 1930- . . . . CLC 2, 6, 43
  See also CAAS 5; CA 5-8R; DLB 27

Silko, Leslie Marmon 1948- . . . . CLC 23
  See also CA 115, 122

Sillanpaa, Franz Eemil 1888-1964 . . . CLC 19
  See also obituary CA 93-96

Sillitoe, Alan
  1928- . . . . CLC 1, 3, 6, 10, 19, 57
  See also CAAS 2; CANR 8, 26; CA 9-12R;
  DLB 14

Silone, Ignazio 1900-1978 . . . . CLC 4
  See also CAAS 2; CANR 26; CAP 2;
  CA 25-28, 11-12R,; obituary CA 81-84

Silver, Joan Micklin 1935- . . . . CLC 20
  See also CA 114, 121

Silverberg, Robert 1935- . . . . CLC 7
  See also CAAS 3; CANR 1, 20; CA 1-4R;
  SATA 13; DLB 8

Silverstein, Alvin 1933- . . . . CLC 17
  See also CANR 2; CA 49-52; SATA 8

Silverstein, Virginia B(arbara Opshelor)
  1937- . . . . CLC 17
  See also CANR 2; CA 49-52; SATA 8

Simak, Clifford D(onald)
  1904-1988 . . . . CLC 1, 55
  See also CANR 1; CA 1-4R;
  obituary CA 125; DLB 8

Simenon, Georges (Jacques Christian)
  1903-1989 . . . . CLC 1, 2, 3, 8, 18, 47
  See also CA 85-88; DLB 72

Simenon, Paul 1956?-
  See The Clash

Simic, Charles 1938- . . . . . . CLC 6, 9, 22, 49
  See also CAAS 4; CANR 12; CA 29-32R

Simmons, Charles (Paul) 1924- . . . . . CLC 57
  See also CA 89-92

Simmons, Dan 1948- . . . . CLC 44

Simmons, James (Stewart Alexander)
  1933- . . . . CLC 43
  See also CA 105; DLB 40

Simms, William Gilmore
  1806-1870 . . . . NCLC 3
  See also DLB 3, 30

Simon, Carly 1945- . . . . CLC 26
  See also CA 105

Simon, Claude (Henri Eugene)
  1913- . . . . CLC 4, 9, 15, 39
  See also CA 89-92

Simon, (Marvin) Neil
  1927- . . . . CLC 6, 11, 31, 39
  See also CA 21-24R; DLB 7

Simon, Paul 1941- . . . . CLC 17
  See also CA 116

Simonon, Paul 1956?-
  See The Clash

Tutuola, Amos 1920- .... **CLC 5, 14, 29**
See also CA 9-12R

Twain, Mark
1835-1910 ... **TCLC 6, 12, 19, 36; SSC 6**
See also Clemens, Samuel Langhorne
See also YABC 2; DLB 11, 12, 23, 64, 74

Tyler, Anne
1941- .... **CLC 7, 11, 18, 28, 44, 59**
See also CANR 11; CA 9-12R; SATA 7;
DLB 6; DLB-Y 82

Tyler, Royall 1757-1826......... **NCLC 3**
See also DLB 37

Tynan (Hinkson), Katharine
1861-1931 .... **TCLC 3**
See also CA 104

Tytell, John 1939- .... **CLC 50**
See also CA 29-32R

Tzara, Tristan 1896-1963......... **CLC 47**
See also Rosenfeld, Samuel

Uhry, Alfred 1947?- .... **CLC 55**
See also CA 127

Unamuno (y Jugo), Miguel de
1864-1936 .... **TCLC 2, 9**
See also CA 104

Underwood, Miles 1909-1981
See Glassco, John

Undset, Sigrid 1882-1949......... **TCLC 3**
See also CA 104

Ungaretti, Giuseppe
1888-1970 .... **CLC 7, 11, 15**
See also CAP 2; CA 19-20;
obituary CA 25-28R

Unger, Douglas 1952-............. **CLC 34**

Unger, Eva 1932-
See Figes, Eva

Updike, John (Hoyer)
1932- ...... **CLC 1, 2, 3, 5, 7, 9, 13, 15,
23, 34, 43**
See also CANR 4; CA 1-4R; CABS 2;
DLB 2, 5; DLB-Y 80, 82; DLB-DS 3

Urdang, Constance (Henriette)
1922- .... **CLC 47**
See also CANR 9, 24; CA 21-24R

Uris, Leon (Marcus) 1924-....... **CLC 7, 32**
See also CANR 1; CA 1-4R; SATA 49

Ustinov, Peter (Alexander) 1921- .....**CLC 1**
See also CANR 25; CA 13-16R; DLB 13

Vaculik, Ludvik 1926- .... **CLC 7**
See also CA 53-56

Valenzuela, Luisa 1938-........... **CLC 31**
See also CA 101

Valera (y Acala-Galiano), Juan
1824-1905 .... **TCLC 10**
See also CA 106

Valery, Paul (Ambroise Toussaint Jules)
1871-1945 .... **TCLC 4, 15**
See also CA 104, 122

Valle-Inclan (y Montenegro), Ramon (Maria)
del 1866-1936.............. **TCLC 5**
See also CA 106

Vallejo, Cesar (Abraham)
1892-1938 .... **TCLC 3**
See also CA 105

Van Ash, Cay 1918-............. **CLC 34**

Vance, Jack 1916?-............... **CLC 35**
See also DLB 8

Vance, John Holbrook 1916?-
See Vance, Jack
See also CANR 17; CA 29-32R

**Van Den Bogarde, Derek (Jules Gaspard
Ulric) Niven** 1921-
See Bogarde, Dirk
See also CA 77-80

Vandenburgh, Jane 19??-.......... **CLC 59**

Vanderhaeghe, Guy 1951- .... **CLC 41**
See also CA 113

Van der Post, Laurens (Jan) 1906-... **CLC 5**
See also CA 5-8R

Van de Wetering, Janwillem
1931- .... **CLC 47**
See also CANR 4; CA 49-52

Van Dine, S. S. 1888-1939....... **TCLC 23**

Van Doren, Carl (Clinton)
1885-1950 .... **TCLC 18**
See also CA 111

Van Doren, Mark 1894-1972..... **CLC 6, 10**
See also CANR 3; CA 1-4R;
obituary CA 37-40R; DLB 45

Van Druten, John (William)
1901-1957 .... **TCLC 2**
See also CA 104; DLB 10

Van Duyn, Mona 1921-........... **CLC 3, 7**
See also CANR 7; CA 9-12R; DLB 5

Van Itallie, Jean-Claude 1936- ...... **CLC 3**
See also CAAS 2; CANR 1; CA 45-48;
DLB 7

Van Ostaijen, Paul 1896-1928..... **TCLC 33**

Van Peebles, Melvin 1932- ...... **CLC 2, 20**
See also CA 85-88

Vansittart, Peter 1920-............ **CLC 42**
See also CANR 3; CA 1-4R

Van Vechten, Carl 1880-1964 ...... **CLC 33**
See also obituary CA 89-92; DLB 4, 9, 51

Van Vogt, A(lfred) E(lton) 1912-..... **CLC 1**
See also CA 21-24R; SATA 14; DLB 8

Varda, Agnes 1928- .... **CLC 16**
See also CA 116, 122

Vargas Llosa, (Jorge) Mario (Pedro)
1936- .... **CLC 3, 6, 9, 10, 15, 31, 42**
See also CANR 18; CA 73-76

Vassilikos, Vassilis 1933-......... **CLC 4, 8**
See also CA 81-84

Vaughn, Stephanie 19??- .... **CLC 62**

Vazov, Ivan 1850-1921.......... **TCLC 25**
See also CA 121

Veblen, Thorstein Bunde
1857-1929 .... **TCLC 31**
See also CA 115

Verga, Giovanni 1840-1922 .... **TCLC 3**
See also CA 104, 123

Verhaeren, Emile (Adolphe Gustave)
1855-1916 .... **TCLC 12**
See also CA 109

Verlaine, Paul (Marie) 1844-1896.. **NCLC 2**

Verne, Jules (Gabriel) 1828-1905 ... **TCLC 6**
See also CA 110; SATA 21

Very, Jones 1813-1880.......... **NCLC 9**
See also DLB 1

Vesaas, Tarjei 1897-1970......... **CLC 48**
See also obituary CA 29-32R

Vian, Boris 1920-1959 .... **TCLC 9**
See also CA 106; DLB 72

Viaud, (Louis Marie) Julien 1850-1923
See Loti, Pierre
See also CA 107

Vicker, Angus 1916-
See Felsen, Henry Gregor

Vidal, Eugene Luther, Jr. 1925-
See Vidal, Gore

Vidal, Gore
1925- .... **CLC 2, 4, 6, 8, 10, 22, 33**
See also CANR 13; CA 5-8R; DLB 6

Viereck, Peter (Robert Edwin)
1916- .... **CLC 4**
See also CANR 1; CA 1-4R; DLB 5

Vigny, Alfred (Victor) de
1797-1863 .... **NCLC 7**

Vilakazi, Benedict Wallet
1905-1947 .... **TCLC 37**

**Villiers de l'Isle Adam, Jean Marie Mathias
Philippe Auguste, Comte de,**
1838-1889 .... **NCLC 3**

Vinci, Leonardo da 1452-1519....... **LC 12**

Vine, Barbara 1930-............... **CLC 50**
See also Rendell, Ruth

Vinge, Joan (Carol) D(ennison)
1948-...................... **CLC 30**
See also CA 93-96; SATA 36

Visconti, Luchino 1906-1976....... **CLC 16**
See also CA 81-84; obituary CA 65-68

Vittorini, Elio 1908-1966...... **CLC 6, 9, 14**
See also obituary CA 25-28R

Vizinczey, Stephen 1933-.......... **CLC 40**

Vliet, R(ussell) G(ordon)
1929-1984 .... **CLC 22**
See also CANR 18; CA 37-40R;
obituary CA 112

Voight, Ellen Bryant 1943-........ **CLC 54**
See also CANR 11; CA 69-72

Voigt, Cynthia 1942- .... **CLC 30**
See also CANR 18; CA 106; SATA 33, 48

Voinovich, Vladimir (Nikolaevich)
1932-...................... **CLC 10, 49**
See also CA 81-84

Voltaire 1694-1778 .... **LC 14**

Von Daeniken, Erich 1935-
See Von Daniken, Erich
See also CANR 17; CA 37-40R

Von Daniken, Erich 1935-........ **CLC 30**
See also Von Daeniken, Erich

Vonnegut, Kurt, Jr.
1922- ...... **CLC 1, 2, 3, 4, 5, 8, 12, 22,
40, 60**
See also CANR 1; CA 1-4R; DLB 2, 8;
DLB-Y 80; DLB-DS 3;
CDALB 1968-1987

Vorster, Gordon 1924-............. **CLC 34**

Voznesensky, Andrei 1933- ... **CLC 1, 15, 57**
See also CA 89-92

Waddington, Miriam 1917- .... **CLC 28**
See also CANR 12; CA 21-24R

Wagman, Fredrica 1937- .... **CLC 7**
See also CA 97-100

Wagner, Richard 1813-1883....... **NCLC 9**

Wagner-Martin, Linda 1936-....... **CLC 50**

Wagoner, David (Russell)
1926- .... **CLC 3, 5, 15**
See also CAAS 3; CANR 2; CA 1-4R;
SATA 14; DLB 5

Wah, Fred(erick James) 1939-...... **CLC 44**
See also CA 107; DLB 60

Wahloo, Per 1926-1975 .... **CLC 7**
See also CA 61-64

Wahloo, Peter 1926-1975
See Wahloo, Per

Wain, John (Barrington)
1925- .̈.............. CLC **2, 11, 15, 46**
See also CAAS 4; CANR 23; CA 5-8R;
DLB 15, 27

Wajda, Andrzej 1926-............. **CLC 16**
See also CA 102

Wakefield, Dan 1932-............. **CLC 7**
See also CAAS 7; CA 21-24R

Wakoski, Diane
1937- .... **CLC 2, 4, 7, 9, 11, 40**
See also CAAS 1; CANR 9; CA 13-16R;
DLB 5

Walcott, Derek (Alton)
1930- .... **CLC 2, 4, 9, 14, 25, 42**
See also CANR 26; CA 89-92; DLB-Y 81

Waldman, Anne 1945-............. **CLC 7**
See also CA 37-40R; DLB 16

Waldo, Edward Hamilton 1918-
See Sturgeon, Theodore (Hamilton)

Walker, Alice
1944- ...... **CLC 5, 6, 9, 19, 27, 46, 58;**
SSC 5
See also CANR 9, 27; CA 37-40R;
SATA 31; DLB 6, 33; CDALB 1968-1988

Walker, David Harry 1911-........ **CLC 14**
See also CANR 1; CA 1-4R; SATA 8

Walker, Edward Joseph 1934-
See Walker, Ted
See also CANR 12; CA 21-24R

Walker, George F. 1947-....... **CLC 44, 61**
See also CANR 21; CA 103; DLB 60

Walker, Joseph A. 1935- .... **CLC 19**
See also CANR 26; CA 89-92; DLB 38

Walker, Margaret (Abigail)
1915-.................... **CLC 1, 6**
See also CANR 26; CA 73-76; DLB 76

Walker, Ted 1934- .... **CLC 13**
See also Walker, Edward Joseph
See also DLB 40

Wallace, David Foster 1962-....... **CLC 50**

Wallace, Irving 1916-........... **CLC 7, 13**
See also CAAS 1; CANR 1; CA 1-4R

Wallant, Edward Lewis
1926-1962 .... **CLC 5, 10**
See also CANR 22; CA 1-4R; DLB 2, 28

Walpole, Horace 1717-1797......... **LC 2**
See also DLB 39

Walpole, (Sir) Hugh (Seymour)
1884-1941 .... **TCLC 5**
See also CA 104; DLB 34

Walser, Martin 1927-............. **CLC 27**
See also CANR 8; CA 57-60; DLB 75

Walser, Robert 1878-1956........ **TCLC 18**
See also CA 118; DLB 66

Walsh, Gillian Paton 1939-
See Walsh, Jill Paton
See also CA 37-40R; SATA 4

Walsh, Jill Paton 1939-........... **CLC 35**
See also CLR 2; SAAS 3

Wambaugh, Joseph (Aloysius, Jr.)
1937- .... **CLC 3, 18**
See also CA 33-36R; DLB 6; DLB-Y 83

Ward, Arthur Henry Sarsfield 1883-1959
See Rohmer, Sax
See also CA 108

Ward, Douglas Turner 1930-....... **CLC 19**
See also CA 81-84; DLB 7, 38

Warhol, Andy 1928-1987.......... **CLC 20**
See also CA 89-92; obituary CA 121

Warner, Francis (Robert le Plastrier)
1937- .... **CLC 14**
See also CANR 11; CA 53-56

Warner, Marina 1946-............. **CLC 59**
See also CANR 21; CA 65-68

Warner, Rex (Ernest) 1905-1986.... **CLC 45**
See also CA 89-92; obituary CA 119;
DLB 15

Warner, Sylvia Townsend
1893-1978 .... **CLC 7, 19**
See also CANR 16; CA 61-64;
obituary CA 77-80; DLB 34

Warren, Mercy Otis 1728-1814... **NCLC 13**
See also DLB 31

Warren, Robert Penn
1905-1989 ... **CLC 1, 4, 6, 8, 10, 13, 18,**
39, 53, 59; SSC 4
See also CANR 10; CA 13-16R. 129. 130;
SATA 46; DLB 2, 48; DLB-Y 80;
CDALB 1968-1987

Washington, Booker T(aliaferro)
1856-1915 .... **TCLC 10**
See also CA 114, 125; SATA 28

Wassermann, Jakob 1873-1934..... **TCLC 6**
See also CA 104; DLB 66

Wasserstein, Wendy 1950-...... **CLC 32, 59**
See also CA 121; CABS 3

Waterhouse, Keith (Spencer)
1929- .... **CLC 47**
See also CA 5-8R; DLB 13, 15

Waters, Roger 1944-
See Pink Floyd

Wa Thiong'o, Ngugi
1938-.............. **CLC 3, 7, 13, 36**
See also Ngugi, James (Thiong'o); Ngugi wa
Thiong'o

Watkins, Paul 1964-............. **CLC 55**

Watkins, Vernon (Phillips)
1906-1967 .... **CLC 43**
See also CAP 1; CA 9-10;
obituary CA 25-28R; DLB 20

Waugh, Auberon (Alexander) 1939-... **CLC 7**
See also CANR 6, 22; CA 45-48; DLB 14

Waugh, Evelyn (Arthur St. John)
1903-1966 ... **CLC 1, 3, 8, 13, 19, 27, 44**
See also CANR 22; CA 85-88;
obituary CA 25-28R; DLB 15

Waugh, Harriet 1944- .... **CLC 6**
See also CANR 22; CA 85-88

Webb, Beatrice (Potter)
1858-1943 .... **TCLC 22**
See also CA 117

Webb, Charles (Richard) 1939-..... **CLC 7**
See also CA 25-28R

Webb, James H(enry), Jr. 1946-.... **CLC 22**
See also CA 81-84

Webb, Mary (Gladys Meredith)
1881-1927 .... **TCLC 24**
See also CA 123; DLB 34

Webb, Phyllis 1927-............. **CLC 18**
See also CANR 23; CA 104; DLB 53

Webb, Sidney (James)
1859-1947 .... **TCLC 22**
See also CA 117

Webber, Andrew Lloyd 1948-...... **CLC 21**

Weber, Lenora Mattingly
1895-1971 .... **CLC 12**
See also CAP 1; CA 19-20;
obituary CA 29-32R; SATA 2;
obituary SATA 26

Wedekind, (Benjamin) Frank(lin)
1864-1918 .... **TCLC 7**
See also CA 104

Weidman, Jerome 1913-........... **CLC 7**
See also CANR 1; CA 1-4R; DLB 28

Weil, Simone 1909-1943.......... **TCLC 23**
See also CA 117

Weinstein, Nathan Wallenstein 1903?-1940
See West, Nathanael
See also CA 104

Weir, Peter 1944-................ **CLC 20**
See also CA 113, 123

Weiss, Peter (Ulrich)
1916-1982 .... **CLC 3, 15, 51**
See also CANR 3; CA 45-48;
obituary CA 106; DLB 69

Weiss, Theodore (Russell)
1916- .... **CLC 3, 8, 14**
See also CAAS 2; CA 9-12R; DLB 5

Welch, (Maurice) Denton
1915-1948 .... **TCLC 22**
See also CA 121

Welch, James 1940-........ **CLC 6, 14, 52**
See also CA 85-88

Weldon, Fay
1933- .... **CLC 6, 9, 11, 19, 36, 59**
See also CANR 16; CA 21-24R; DLB 14

Wellek, Rene 1903- .... **CLC 28**
See also CAAS 7; CANR 8; CA 5-8R;
DLB 63

Weller, Michael 1942-......... **CLC 10, 53**
See also CA 85-88

Weller, Paul 1958-.............. **CLC 26**

Wellershoff, Dieter 1925-.......... **CLC 46**
See also CANR 16; CA 89-92

Welles, (George) Orson
   1915-1985 .... CLC 20
   See also CA 93-96; obituary CA 117

Wellman, Manly Wade 1903-1986 .. CLC 49
   See also CANR 6, 16; CA 1-4R;
   obituary CA 118; SATA 6, 47

Wells, Carolyn 1862-1942 .... TCLC 35
   See also CA 113; DLB 11

Wells, H(erbert) G(eorge)
   1866-1946 ...... TCLC 6, 12, 19; SSC 6
   See also CA 110, 121; SATA 20; DLB 34,
   70

Wells, Rosemary 1943-............ CLC 12
   See also CLR 16; CA 85-88; SAAS 1;
   SATA 18

Welty, Eudora (Alice)
   1909- .... CLC 1, 2, 5, 14, 22, 33; SSC 1
   See also CA 9-12R; CABS 1; DLB 2;
   DLB-Y 87; CDALB 1941-1968

Wen I-to 1899-1946 .... TCLC 28

Werfel, Franz (V.) 1890-1945 ...... TCLC 8
   See also CA 104

Wergeland, Henrik Arnold
   1808-1845 .... NCLC 5

Wersba, Barbara 1932-............ CLC 30
   See also CLR 3; CANR 16; CA 29-32R;
   SAAS 2; SATA 1; DLB 52

Wertmuller, Lina 1928- .... CLC 16
   See also CA 97-100

Wescott, Glenway 1901-1987....... CLC 13
   See also CANR 23; CA 13-16R;
   obituary CA 121; DLB 4, 9

Wesker, Arnold 1932- .... CLC 3, 5, 42
   See also CAAS 7; CANR 1; CA 1-4R;
   DLB 13

Wesley, Richard (Errol) 1945-....... CLC 7
   See also CA 57-60; DLB 38

Wessel, Johan Herman 1742-1785 .... LC 7

West, Anthony (Panther)
   1914-1987 .... CLC 50
   See also CANR 3, 19; CA 45-48; DLB 15

West, Jessamyn 1907-1984 ...... CLC 7, 17
   See also CA 9-12R; obituary CA 112;
   obituary SATA 37; DLB 6; DLB-Y 84

West, Morris L(anglo) 1916-..... CLC 6, 33
   See also CA 5-8R; obituary CA 124

West, Nathanael 1903?-1940 .... TCLC 1, 14
   See also Weinstein, Nathan Wallenstein
   See also CA 125; DLB 4, 9, 28

West, Paul 1930- .... CLC 7, 14
   See also CAAS 7; CANR 22; CA 13-16R;
   DLB 14

West, Rebecca 1892-1983 .. CLC 7, 9, 31, 50
   See also CANR 19; CA 5-8R;
   obituary CA 109; DLB 36; DLB-Y 83

Westall, Robert (Atkinson) 1929-... CLC 17
   See also CLR 13; CANR 18; CA 69-72;
   SAAS 2; SATA 23

Westlake, Donald E(dwin)
   1933- .... CLC 7, 33
   See also CANR 16; CA 17-20R

Westmacott, Mary 1890-1976
   See Christie, (Dame) Agatha (Mary
   Clarissa)

Whalen, Philip 1923- .... CLC 6, 29
   See also CANR 5; CA 9-12R; DLB 16

Wharton, Edith (Newbold Jones)
   1862-1937 ...... TCLC 3, 9, 27; SSC 6
   See also CA 104; DLB 4, 9, 12, 78;
   CDALB 1865-1917

Wharton, William 1925-........ CLC 18, 37
   See also CA 93-96; DLB-Y 80

Wheatley (Peters), Phillis
   1753?-1784.................... LC 3
   See also DLB 31, 50; CDALB 1640-1865

Wheelock, John Hall 1886-1978.... CLC 14
   See also CANR 14; CA 13-16R;
   obituary CA 77-80; DLB 45

Whelan, John 1900-
   See O'Faolain, Sean

Whitaker, Rodney 1925-
   See Trevanian

White, E(lwyn) B(rooks)
   1899-1985 .... CLC 10, 34, 39
   See also CLR 1; CANR 16; CA 13-16R;
   obituary CA 116; SATA 2, 29;
   obituary SATA 44; DLB 11, 22

White, Edmund III 1940-......... CLC 27
   See also CANR 3, 19; CA 45-48

White, Patrick (Victor Martindale)
   1912- .... CLC 3, 4, 5, 7, 9, 18
   See also CA 81-84

White, T(erence) H(anbury)
   1906-1964 .... CLC 30
   See also CA 73-76; SATA 12

White, Terence de Vere 1912-...... CLC 49
   See also CANR 3; CA 49-52

White, Walter (Francis)
   1893-1955 .... TCLC 15
   See also CA 115, 124; DLB 51

White, William Hale 1831-1913
   See Rutherford, Mark
   See also CA 121

Whitehead, E(dward) A(nthony)
   1933- .... CLC 5
   See also CA 65-68

Whitemore, Hugh 1936-........... CLC 37

Whitman, Sarah Helen
   1803-1878 .... NCLC 19
   See also DLB 1

Whitman, Walt 1819-1892........ NCLC 4
   See also SATA 20; DLB 3, 64;
   CDALB 1640-1865

Whitney, Phyllis A(yame) 1903-.... CLC 42
   See also CANR 3, 25; CA 1-4R; SATA 1,
   30

Whittemore, (Edward) Reed (Jr.)
   1919- .... CLC 4
   See also CANR 4; CA 9-12R; DLB 5

Whittier, John Greenleaf
   1807-1892 .... NCLC 8
   See also DLB 1; CDALB 1640-1865

Wicker, Thomas Grey 1926-
   See Wicker, Tom
   See also CANR 21; CA 65-68

Wicker, Tom 1926-............... CLC 7
   See also Wicker, Thomas Grey

Wideman, John Edgar
   1941- .... CLC 5, 34, 36
   See also CANR 14; CA 85-88; DLB 33

Wiebe, Rudy (H.) 1934-...... CLC 6, 11, 14
   See also CA 37-40R; DLB 60

Wieland, Christoph Martin
   1733-1813 .... NCLC 17

Wieners, John 1934-.............. CLC 7
   See also CA 13-16R; DLB 16

Wiesel, Elie(zer) 1928-..... CLC 3, 5, 11, 37
   See also CAAS 4; CANR 8; CA 5-8R;
   DLB-Y 87

Wiggins, Marianne 1948-......... CLC 57

Wight, James Alfred 1916-
   See Herriot, James
   See also CA 77-80; SATA 44

Wilbur, Richard (Purdy)
   1921- .... CLC 3, 6, 9, 14, 53
   See also CANR 2; CA 1-4R; CABS 2;
   SATA 9; DLB 5

Wild, Peter 1940-................ CLC 14
   See also CA 37-40R; DLB 5

Wilde, Oscar (Fingal O'Flahertie Wills)
   1854-1900 .... TCLC 1, 8, 23
   See also CA 104; SATA 24; DLB 10, 19,
   34, 57

Wilder, Billy 1906-............... CLC 20
   See also Wilder, Samuel
   See also DLB 26

Wilder, Samuel 1906-
   See Wilder, Billy
   See also CA 89-92

Wilder, Thornton (Niven)
   1897-1975 ...... CLC 1, 5, 6, 10, 15, 35
   See also CA 13-16R; obituary CA 61-64;
   DLB 4, 7, 9

Wiley, Richard 1944-............. CLC 44
   See also CA 121

Wilhelm, Kate 1928-.............. CLC 7
   See also CAAS 5; CANR 17; CA 37-40R;
   DLB 8

Willard, Nancy 1936-........... CLC 7, 37
   See also CLR 5; CANR 10; CA 89-92;
   SATA 30, 37; DLB 5, 52

Williams, C(harles) K(enneth)
   1936- .... CLC 33, 56
   See also CA 37-40R; DLB 5

Williams, Charles (Walter Stansby)
   1886-1945 .... TCLC 1, 11
   See also CA 104

Williams, Ella Gwendolen Rees 1890-1979
   See Rhys, Jean

Williams, (George) Emlyn
   1905-1987 .... CLC 15
   See also CA 104, 123; DLB 10

Williams, Hugo 1942-............ CLC 42
   See also CA 17-20R; DLB 40

Williams, John A(lfred) 1925-.... CLC 5, 13
   See also CAAS 3; CANR 6, 26; CA 53-56;
   DLB 2, 33

Williams, Jonathan (Chamberlain)
   1929- .... CLC 13
   See also CANR 8; CA 9-12R; DLB 5

Williams, Joy 1944-.............. CLC 31
   See also CANR 22; CA 41-44R

Literary Criticism Series
Cumulative Topic Index

This index lists all topic entries in the Gale Literary Criticism Series *Contemporary Literary Criticism,*
Literature Criticism from 1400 to 1800, Nineteenth-Century Literature Criticism, and *Twentieth-Century Literary Criticism.*

NCLC Cumulative Nationality Index

Nationality Index

NCLC Cumulative Title Index

Title Index

Title Index

Title Index

Title Index

Title Index

Title Index

Title Index

Title Index

Title Index

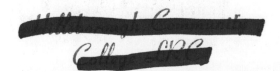